ENCYCLOPEDIA OF THE
DEVELOPING WORLD

ENCYCLOPEDIA OF THE DEVELOPING WORLD

Volume 1
A–E
INDEX

THOMAS M. LEONARD

EDITOR

Routledge
Taylor & Francis Group
New York   London

Published in 2006 by
Routledge
Taylor & Francis Group
270 Madison Avenue
New York, NY 10016

Published in Great Britain by
Routledge
Taylor & Francis Group
2 Park Square
Milton Park, Abingdon
Oxon OX14 4RN

Printed in the United States of America on acid-free paper
10 9 8 7 6 5 4 3 2 1

International Standard Book Number-10: 1-57958-388-1 (set) 0-415-97662-6 (Vol 1) 0-415-97663-4 (Vol 2) 0-415-97664-2 (Vol 3)
International Standard Book Number-13: 978-1-57958-388-0 (set) 978-0-415-97662-6 (Vol 1) 978-0-415-97663-3 (Vol 2) 978-0-415-97664-0 (Vol 3)
Library of Congress Card Number 2005049976

Library of Congress Cataloging-in-Publication Data

Encyclopedia of the developing world / Thomas M. Leonard, editor.
    p. cm.
    Includes bibliographical references and index.
    ISBN 1-57958-388-1 (set : alk. paper) -- ISBN 0-415-97662-6 (v. 1 : alk. paper) -- ISBN 0-415-97663-4 (v. 2 : alk. paper) --
ISBN 0-415-97664-2 (v. 3 : alk. paper)
    1. Developing countries--Encyclopedias. I. Leonard, Thomas M., 1937-

HC59.7.E52 2005
909'.09724'03--dc22

2005049976

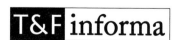

Taylor & Francis Group is the Academic Division of T&F Informa plc.

Visit the Taylor & Francis Web site at
http://www.taylorandfrancis.com

and the Routledge Web site at
http://www.routledge-ny.com

BOARD OF ADVISORS

LIST OF CONTRIBUTORS

Rafis Abazov
Columbia University

Alfia Abazova
Dag Hammarskjöld Library

Janet Adamski
Southwestern University

Ali Ahmed
University of Birmingham

Nadine Akhund
Columbia University

Adam Allouba
McGill University

Samuel K. Andoh
Southern Connecticut State University

Anne Androuais
CNRS/FORUM/University Paris X

Christien van den Anker
University of Birmingham

Gasser Auda
University of Wales

Louis Augustin-Jean
University of Waseda

Rémi Bachand
Université Paris 1 (Panthéon-Sorbonne)

Josiah R. Baker
University of Central Florida

Mina Baliamoune
University of North Florida

Assefaw Bariagaber
Seton Hall University

John H. Barnhill
Yukon, Oklahoma

Graham Barrigan
La Trobe University

Greg Barton
Deakin University

Bob Beatty
Washburn University

Derek A. Bentley
Armstrong Atlantic State University

Mark T. Berger
University of New South Wales

Brian J. L. Berry
University of Texas at Dallas

Charles Boewe
Pittsboro, North Carolina

Valentin Boss
McGill University

Laura E. Boudon
American University

Lawrence Boudon
Library of Congress

Viviane Brachet-Márquez
El Colegio de México

Jillian Brady
Bayswater, Victoria, Australia

Susan Love Brown
Florida Atlantic University

Jürgen Buchenau
University of North Carolina at Charlotte

Ralf Buckley
Griffith University

Melissa Butcher
University of Sydney

Laura M. Calkins
Texas Tech University

David H. Carwell
Eastern Illinois University

James Chalmers
United Nations Development Programme,
Papua New Guinea

Frederick B. Chary
Indiana University Northwest

Dawn Chatty
University of Oxford

Janet M. Chernela
University of Maryland

James Chin
Universiti Malaysia Sarawak

George Cho
University of Canberra

Cristina Cielo
University of California at Berkeley

Katherine Cinq-Mars
McGill University

Andrew F. Clark
University of North Carolina at Wilmington

John F. Clark
Florida International University

Sharon C. Cobb
University of North Florida

Chris Coney
University of Melbourne

Daniele Conversi
London, England

Jose da Cruz
Armstrong Atlantic State University

Cecil B. Currey
Lutz, Florida

Robert L. Curry, Jr.
California State University at Sacramento

Kamran M. Dadkhah
Northeastern University

Kishore C. Dash
Thunderbird, The Garvin School of
International Management

Ansu Datta
Calcutta, India

Kusum Datta
Calcutta, India

Craig Davis
Point of Rocks, Maryland

Alan Dearling
Devon, England

Mahinda Deegalle
Bath Spa University College

Neil Denslow
Poole, Dorset, England

Linus digim'Rina
University of Papua New Guinea

Barbara J. Dilly
Creighton University

Steven C. Dinero
Philadelphia University

Thomas P. Dolan
Columbus State University

Manochehr Dorraj
Texas Christian University

David Dorward
LaTrobe University

Beth K. Dougherty
Beloit College

Emma Dowling
University of Birmingham

Mark A. Drumbl
University of Arkansas, Little Rock

Whitney D. Durham
Oklahoma State University

Mohammad Ehsan
University of Dhaka

Susana A. Eisenchlas
Griffith University

Nilly Kamal El-Amir
Cairo University

Mikhael Elbaz
Laval University

Nader Entessar
Spring Hill College

Jo-Anne Everingham
The University of Queensland

Mark Everingham
University of Wisconsin

Nicholas Farrelly
Australian National University

Mario D. Fenyo
Bowie State University

José Fernandez
University of Central Florida

Volker Frank
University of North Carolina at Asheville

Doris Fuchs
University of Munich

Mobo C. F. Gao
University of Tasmania

Andy Gibson
Griffith University

Brian J. Given
Carleton University

Arthur Goldschmidt, Jr.
The Pennsylvania State University

Michael Goldsmith
University of Waikato

Robert F. Gorman
Southwest Texas State University

Gustavo Adolfo Guerra Vásquez
University of California at Berkeley

Audrey Guichon
University of Birmingham

Juan-Carlos Gumucio Castellon
University of Uppsala

Alexander Gungov
Emory University

Michael M. Gunter
Tennessee Technological University

Michael M. Gunter, Jr.
Rollins College

Baogang Guo
Dalton State College

Michael R. Hall
Armstrong Atlantic State University

Reuel R. Hanks
Oklahoma State University

W. John Hansen
Ann Arbor, Michigan

Syed Hassan
Claflin University

Jonathan Haughton
Beacon Hill Institute for Public Policy

William P. Head
Warner Robins Air Logistics Center

Joseph Held
South Yarmouth, Massachusetts

Sirkku K. Hellsten
University of Birmingham

Anil Hira
Simon Fraser University

Frank J. Hoffman
West Chester University

Ha Thi Thu Huong
TMC Academy

Sylvanus Ikhide
University of Namibia

International Commission on Irrigation and Drainage
New Delhi, India

Muhammad Muinul Islam
University of Dhaka

Serguey Ivanov
American University in Bulgaria

M. R. Izady
New York, New York

B. M. Jain
Rajasthan University

Uzma Jamil
McGill University

Ho-Won Jeong
George Mason University

Helen Johnson
The University of Queensland

Rebecca R. Jones
Widener University

Nantang Jua
University of Buea

Lars v. Karstedt
University of Hamburg

Husain Kassim
University of Central Florida

John Keep
Bern, Switzerland

Kembo-Sure
Moi University

Kenneth Keulman
Harvard University

Arne Kislenko
Ryerson University

Reinhard Klein-Arendt
University of Cologne

Wm. Gary Kline
Georgia Southwestern State University

Yoshie Kobayashi
Gunma Prefectural Women's University

Laszlo Kocsis
Covasna, Romania

Charles C. Kolb
National Endowment for the Humanities

Waldemar Koziol
Warsaw University

Alisa Krasnostein
The University of Western Australia

Wanda C. Krause
University of Exeter

Krum Krumov
Sofia University

Chi-Kong Lai
University of Queensland

George M. Lauderbaugh
Jacksonville State University

Robert Lawless
Wichita State University

David M. Lawrence
J. Sargeant Reynolds Community College

Michael C. Lazich
Buffalo State College

Lavina Lee
University of Sydney

Keith A. Leitich
Seattle, Washington

Hal Levine
Victoria University of Wellington

Jonathan H. L'Hommedieu
University of Turku

Yianna Liatsos
Rutgers University

Tracy L. R. Lightcap
LaGrange College

Natasha J. Lightfoot
New York University

John Lodewijks
University of New South Wales

Staffan Löfving
Stockholm University

Roger D. Long
Eastern Michigan University

P. Eric Louw
University of Queensland

Ludomir Lozny
Hunter College

Ronald Lukens-Bull
University of North Florida

Christopher Lundry
Arizona State University

Carmela Lutmar
New York University

Paul J. Magnarella
Warren Wilson College

Plamen Makariev
Sofia University

Arman Manukyan
Central European University

Richard R. Marcus
University of Alabama in Huntsville

Ross Marlay
Arkansas State University

Daniel M. Masterson
United States Naval Academy

Dee F. Matreyek
Restorative Justice Center of the Inland Empire

Jean F. Mayer
Concordia University

John Mukum Mbaku
Weber State University

Tamba E. M'bayo
Michigan State University

William McBride
Purdue University

Grant McCall
University of New South Wales

Christopher McDowell
Macquarie University

Elisabeth McMahon
Indiana University

Joseph Mensah
York University

Nasser Momayezi
Texas A&M International University

Waltraud Q. Morales
University of Central Florida

Ishmael Irungu Munene
State University of New York at Albany

Ruth Murbach
Université du Québec à Montréal

Norman H. Murdoch
University of Cincinnati

Diego I. Murguía
Universidad de Buenos Aires

Loretta Napoleoni
London, England

Caryn E. Neumann
Ohio State University

Stephan E. Nikolov
Bulgarian Academy of Sciences

LIST OF CONTRIBUTORS

James A. Norris
Texas A&M International University

Milena Novakova
National Assembly of Republic of Bulgaria

P. Godfrey Okoth
Maseno University

Clémentine Olivier
National University of Ireland

Jorge Ortiz Sotelo
Peruvian Institute of Economy and Politics

Lazarus F. O'Sako
Ohio University

Patrick L. Osborne
International Center for Tropical Ecology,
University of Missouri at St. Louis

Tony Osborne
American University in Bulgaria

Úrsula Oswald S.
CRIM-UNAM and Diverse Women for Diversity

Charlene T. Overturf
Armstrong Atlantic State University

Steven Paulson
University of North Florida

Zoran Pavlović
Oklahoma State University

William D. Pederson
Louisiana State University in Shreveport

Carlos Pérez
California State University at Fresno

J. E. Peterson
University of Arizona

María Luisa Pfeiffer
Universidad de Buenos Aires

Aaron Z. Pitluck
University of Konstanz

Vincent Kelly Pollard
University of Hawai'i at Manoa

Nancy J. Pollock
Victoria University

Peter R. Prifti
San Diego, California

Lesley J. Pruitt
Arkansas State University

Ilie Rad
Babes-Bolyai University

Edward A. Riedinger
Ohio State University

Leonora Ritter
Charles Sturt University

Benjamin Rivlin
City University Graduate Center

Paul Rivlin
Tel Aviv University

Bruce D. Roberts
Minnesota State University Moorhead

Magaly Rodríguez García
Vrije Universiteit Brussel

David Romano
McGill University

Horacio N. Roque Ramirez
University of California at Santa Barbara

Stéphanie Rousseau
University of North Carolina at
Chapel Hill

Paul S. Rowe
University of Western Ontario

Werner Ruf
University of Kassel

Tom Ryan
University of Waikato

Arvee S. Salazar
San Fernando, Philippines

Steven S. Sallie
Boise State University

Amandeep Sandhu
University of California at Santa Barbara

L. Natalie Sandomirsky
Southern Connecticut State University

Christopher Saunders
University of Cape Town

Christian P. Scherrer
Ethnic Conflict Research Project

Ulrike Schuerkens
Ecole des Hautes Etudes en Sciences Sociales

Alexander Hugo Schulenburg
Corporation of London

Stephen R. Schwalbe
Air War College

David Schwam-Baird
University of North Florida

James D. Seymour
Columbia University

Rodger Shanahan
University of Sydney

Scott E. Simon
University of Ottawa

Amrita Singh

Udai Bhanu Singh
Institute for Defence Studies

Carl Skutsch
The School of Visual Arts

E. Valerie Smith
Florida Gulf Coast University

Subhash R. Sonnad
Western Michigan University

Radhamany Sooryamoorthy
University of Kwazulu-Natal

Paul Spoonley
Massey University

Jeffrey W. Steagall
University of North Florida

Jason E. Strakes
Claremont Graduate School

Mira Sucharov
Carleton University

Tadeusz Swietochowski
Columbia University

Joseph Takougang
University of Cincinnati

Mary Ann Tétreault
Trinity University

Daniel S. Tevera
University of Zimbabwe

Amos Owen Thomas
Maastricht School of Management

Marius Tita
Bucharest, Romania

Brian Turner
Randolph-Macon College

Ufo Okeke Uzodike
University of KwaZulu-Natal

Cheryl Van Deusen
University of North Florida

John M. VanderLippe
State University of New York at New Paltz

Carlos Velásquez Carrillo
York University

Iain Walker
University of Sydney

John Walsh
Shinawatra International University

Yosay Wangdi
Grand Valley State University

Fredrick O. Wanyama
Maseno University

LIST OF CONTRIBUTORS

Susanne Weigelin-Schwiedrzik
University of Heidelberg

Roland J. Wenzlhuemer
Salzburg University

Bruce M. Wilson
University of Central Florida

James E. Winkates
Air War College, Maxwell Air Force Base

Pamela A. Zeiser
University of North Florida

Eleanor Zelliot
Carleton College

Xinjun Zhang
Tsinghua University

Verónica M. Ziliotto
Universidad de Buenos Aires

Evert van der Zweerde
University of Nijmegen

TABLE OF CONTENTS

LIST OF ENTRIES A–Z

THEMATIC LIST OF ENTRIES

Countries and Regions

Afghanistan
Albania
Algeria
Andean South America: History and Economic Development
Andean South America: International Relations
Angola
Anguilla
Antigua and Barbuda
Argentina
Armenia
Azerbaijan
Bahamas
Bahrain
Bangladesh
Barbados
Belarus
Belize
Benin
Bhutan
Biafra
Bolivia
Bosnia and Herzegovina
Botswana
Brazil
Brunei
Bulgaria
Burkina Faso
Burundi
Cambodia
Cameroon
Caribbean: History and Economic Development
Caribbean: International Relations
Cayman Islands
Central Africa: History and Economic Development
Central Africa: International Relations
Central African Republic
Central America: History and Economic Development
Central America: International Relations

Central and Eastern Europe: History and Economic Development
Central and Eastern Europe: International Relations
Central Asia: History and Economic Development
Central Asia: International Relations
Chad
Chile
China, People's Republic of
Colombia
Commonwealth of Independent States: History and Economic Development
Commonwealth of Independent States: International Relations
Comoros
Congo, Democratic Republic of the
Congo, Republic of the
Costa Rica
Cote d'Ivoire (Republic of the Ivory Coast)
Croatia
Cyprus
Czech Republic
Djibouti
Dominica
Dominican Republic
East Africa: History and Economic Development
East Africa: International Relations
East Asia: History and Economic Development
East Asia: International Relations
East Timor
Ecuador
Egypt
El Salvador
Equatorial Guinea
Eritrea
Estonia
Ethiopia
Fiji
French Guiana
Gabon
Gambia, The
Georgia
Ghana

Grenada
Guadeloupe
Guam
Guatemala
Guinea
Guinea-Bissau
Guyana
Haiti
Honduras
Hong Kong
Hungary
India
Indonesia
Iran
Iraq
Israel
Jamaica
Jordan
Kazakhstan
Kenya
Kiribati
Korea, North
Korea, South
Kurdistan
Kuwait
Kyrgyzstan
Laos
Latvia
Lebanon
Lesotho
Liberia
Libya
Lithuania
Macau/Macao
Macedonia
Madagascar
Malaŵi
Malaysia
Maldives
Mali
Malvinas/Falklands
Marshall Islands, Republic of
Martinique
Mauritania
Mauritius
Mexico: History and Economic Development
Mexico: International Relations
Micronesia, Federated States of
Middle East: History and Economic Development
Middle East: International Relations
Moldova
Mongolia
Montenegro
Montserrat
Morocco

Mozambique
Myanmar
Namibia
Nepal
Netherlands Antilles
Nicaragua
Niger
Nigeria, The Federal Republic of
Niue
North Africa: History and Economic Development
North Africa: International Relations
Northern South America: History and
    Economic Development
Northern South America: International Relations
Oceania: History and Economic Development
Oceania: International Relations
Oman
Pakistan
Palau, Republic of
Palestine
Panama
Papua New Guinea
Paracel and Spratley Islands
Paraguay
Peru
Philippines
Poland
Puerto Rico
Qatar
Romania
Russia
Rwanda
Samoa
Saudi Arabia
Senegal
Serbia
Seychelles
Sierra Leone
Singapore
Slovakia
Slovenia
Solomon Islands
Somalia
South Africa
Southeast Asia: History and Economic
    Development
Southeast Asia: International Relations
Southern Africa: History and Economic
    Development
Southern Africa: International Relations
Southern Cone (Latin America): History and
    Economic Development
Southern Cone (Latin America): International
    Relations
Soviet Bloc

Organizations

Persons

Mao Zedong
Marcos, Ferdinand
Mbeki, Thabo
Meir, Golda
Menchú Túm, Rigoberta
Menem, Carlos
Milošević, Slobodan
Mossaddeq, Muhammed
Mubarak, Hosni
Mugabe, Robert
Mujibar Rahman, Sheikh
Nasser, Gamal Abdel
Ndi, Ni John Fru
Nehru, Jawaharlal
Nkrumah, Kwame
Nyerere, Julius
Okello, John
Pahlavi, Shah Muhammed Reza
Pérez Jiménez, Marcos
Perón, Juan Domingo
Pinochet Ugarte, Augusto
Prebisch, Raúl
Qaddafi, Muammar
Rafsanjani, Ali Akbar
Rahman, Tunku Abdul
Ramos, Fidel
Rhee, Syngman
Sadat, Anwar
Salinas de Gortari, Carlos
Selassie, Emperor Haile
Sénghor, Leopold
Siad Barre, Mohammed
Sihanouk, Norodom
Silva, Luiz Inácio "Lula" da
Somoza DeBayle, Anastasio
Somoza García, Anastasio
Stalin, Joseph
Stroessner, Alfredo
Sukarno
Tito, Josip Broz (Marshall Tito)
Torrijos Herrera, Omar
Touré, Sékou
Trujillo, Rafael Leonidas
Tudjman, Franjo
Tutu, Bishop Desmond
Ulmanis, Guntis
Um-Nyobe, Reuben
Vähi, Tiit
Vargas, Getúlio
Verwoerd, Hendrik
Wałęsa, Lech
Williams, Eric
Wojtyła, Karol (John Paul II)
Wyszyński, Cardinal Stefan
Yahya Khan, Agha Muhammad

Zhou Enlai
Zia ul-Haq, Muhammed

Topics

Acid Precipitation
African Diaspora
Agriculture: Impact of Globalization
Agriculture: Impact of Privatization
Apartheid
Aprismo
Arab Nationalism
Arab–Israeli Wars (1948, 1956, 1967, 1973)
Arms and Armaments, International Transfer of
Arms Industry
Asian "Economic Miracle"
Asian Tigers
Aswan High Dam and Development in Egypt
Authoritarianism
Balfour Declaration
Balkan Wars of the 1990s
Bandung Conference (1955)
Banking
Bantustans
Basic Human Needs
Bedouin
Berbers
Berlin Wall (1961–1989)
Biodiversity Conservation
Black Market/Shadow Economy
Bracero Program
Brain Drain
Buddhism
Bureaucratic Authoritarianism
Camp David Accords (1979)
Capital Flight
Capitalist Economic Model
Caribbean Basin Initiative (CBI)
Cartels
Caste Systems
Children and Development
China: Cultural Revolution
Chinese Revolution
Christianity
Christians in the Middle East
Civic Education
Civil Disobedience
Civil Rights
Civil Society
Collectivism
Colombo Plan
Colonialism: History
Colonialism: Legacies

INTRODUCTION

Historically identified by various terms, the "Developing World" has always existed, but it came into vogue as a concept immediately after the close of World War II in 1945. For the next generation, the "Third World" was the most commonly used term, followed for the next two decades by the "Underdeveloped World." Influenced by trade liberalization, globalization, and the policy agenda known as the Washington Consensus, the term "Developing World" came into prominence in the 1980s. In response, at least one professional organization, the Association of Third World Studies, briefly considered changing its name.

The most commonly asked questions about the "Developing World" focus upon the countries and residents that comprise it, the status of its economy, its political and social characteristics, and its cultural components. At the end of World War II, analysts identified Africa, Asia, and Latin America as the most underdeveloped global regions. Within each were numerous sub-regions, such as South Asia, sub-Saharan Africa, and Latin America's Southern Cone. Over time, the Middle East was added to the mix and the regions were further subdivided. Although the Soviet Union and its East European Bloc often demonstrated advances in scientific achievement, industrial output, or military hardware, it remained an underdeveloped area in terms of the low quality of life for its inhabitants and the lack of civil and human rights, factors that became glaringly apparent with the end of the Cold War in 1991.

Today's conventional wisdom suggests that all but the Group of Seven, or G-7, nations and their periphery fall into the so-called "Developing World." The G-7 is comprised of the world's seven largest industrial nations: United States, Japan, Great Britain, France, Germany, Italy, and Canada, though the industrialized world also includes the other Western European nations, Australia, and New Zealand. By the 1990s Singapore, South Korea, and Taiwan became prosperous nations. The inclusion of the latter three countries suggests that an economic definition of the "Developing World" remains too simplified.

Beyond economic development, analysts came to consider the extent of public participation in the political process. How democratic and representative of its people is any given government? Are human and civil rights secured and protected? What is the availability of basic human services such as education and health care? Are there environmental protections? The assumption is that developed nations are representative democracies where the rights of people are guaranteed, basic human needs are satisfied, and the environment secured from various forms of pollution. Although several of the developed nations fall short in some of these categories, the absence of most is a characteristic of the "Developing World."

The logo map used in the publications of the Association of Third World Studies substantiates the given economic, political, and social definitions of the "Developing World." The G-7 nations and their periphery are absent from that map.

The assistance programs sponsored by the developed world since 1945 reflect the changing definition of the "Developing World." Immediately after World War II, assistance focused upon improvement in infrastructure—roads, ports, electricity, water supplies, and the like—to provide for increased opportunities to export primary products, including raw materials. By the late 1950s and into the early 1960s, assistance programs shifted direction. The end of colonialism, the independence of India and Indonesia, the emergence of new and independent nations in Africa, and Fidel Castro's Revolution in Cuba brought an awareness of the need to focus upon economic opportunities for the general population, improvement in quality of life, and the right of a nation's people to political participation and civil and human rights. These goals remained the objectives of programs sponsored by government and non-government organizations that continued into the 1980s when world politics again shifted. Identified best by the Washington Consensus, a set of suggested reforms set forth for Latin America by the economist John Williamson in 1989, this change in policy by developed nations cut back on their international assistance programs and, instead, called upon the nations of the "Developing World" to remove their protective barriers against foreign investment, provide for the privatization of state owned industries and for increased exports, particularly of so-called niche products. As they invited developing nations to enter the global arena, developed nations increased their pressure on developing nations to democratize the political process, protect civil and human rights, and encourage environmentalism. International agreements since the 1980s often contain provisons for the implementation of plans to address these human needs.

Despite the good intentions, the "Developing World" persists. Poverty, with its concomitant shortcomings in education, health care, housing, and other basic human needs, remains a reality for a disproportionate number of the world's inhabitants. Political democracy and civil and human rights are not universally guaranteed. Environmental pollution continues to go unchecked, taking its most devastating toll upon the "Developing World."

As the twenty-first century dawned, many analysts queried the advisability of imposing the developed world's criteria for modernization upon the "Developing World." The histories of the world's regions varied with their own political experiences, their own ethnic and religious conflicts, and their political, religious, and social traditions that resist and in some cases, outright defy modernization as envisioned by the developed world.

The *Encyclopedia of the Developing World* provides a ready reference work for understanding the issues that affect approximately three quarters of the globe's residents. The *Encyclopedia* is unique because of its focus upon the post 1945 period when the old colonial structures in Africa, Asia, and the Middle East crumbled and elsewhere, as in China, Japan, and Latin America the traditional elite structure has been replaced by something new. During the same time period, the "Developing World" began to demand a greater share of the world's economy and an improvement in quality of life, along with social justice, political participation, and individual liberties.

How to Use This Book

The *Encyclopedia of the Developing World* is composed of almost 800 free-standing entries of 500 to 5000 words in length. They range from factual narratives, such as country descriptions and biographies, to thematic interpretations and analytical discussions of timely topics like global trading patterns, and a combination of all three, such as overview articles on the history and economic development of a particular region. As much as possible, the encyclopedia covers the history, economic development, and politics of the developing world from 1945 to the present, providing the reader with a reliable, up-to-date view of the current state of scholarship on the developing world.

Perhaps the most significant feature of the encyclopedia is the easily accessible **A to Z format**. Cross-referencing in the form of **See Alsos** at the end of most entries refers the reader to other related entries. Each article contains a list of **References and Further Reading**, including sources used by the writer and editor as well as additional items that may be of interest to the reader. Most books or articles cited are easily available through interlibrary loan services in libraries. **Blind Entries** direct readers to essays listed under another title. For example, the blind entry "World Bank" refers the reader to the article entitled with that institution's official name, "International Bank for Reconstruction and Development." A thorough, analytical **index** complements the accessibility of the entries, easing the reader's entry into the wealth of information provided. **A thematic list of entries** is also included to assist readers with research in particular subjects.

Each country has a stand-alone entry, but also is included in larger regional studies. For example, discussion of Chile can be found under the country's entry, but its place in regional matters can be found in "Southern Cone (Latin America): History and Economic Development"; "Southern Cone (Latin America): International Relations"; and "Ethnic Conflicts: Southern Cone (Latin America)." There are stand-alone entries for important individuals, like Jomo Kenyatta, but for context readers should also refer to the country entry on Kenya and the topical entries, such as "Colonialism: History" and "Colonialism: Legacies," to more fully understand Kenyatta's philosophy and objectives. The discussion of "Development History and Theory" is augmented by the entry "Development, Measures of." Both are enhanced by the discussions of the various economic models: capitalist, communist, socialist, and so on. The cross-references will lead readers from stop to stop on such paths throughout the encyclopedia, and the index is another good starting place to find the connected discussions.

A total of 251 authors have contributed the entries to this encyclopedia. They are based around the world, in both developing and developed nations, including Argentina, Australia, Austria, Belgium, Bulgaria, Cameroon, Canada, China, Egypt, France, Germany, Hungary, India, Israel, Japan, Kenya, Malaysia, Mexico, the Netherlands, New Zealand, the Philippines, Poland, Romania, Singapore, South Africa, Sweden, Switzerland, Thailand, the United Arab Emirates, the United Kingdom, the United States, and Zimbabwe. In keeping with the global and interdisciplinary nature of this encyclopedia, contributors represent a variety of fields, among them finance, religion, anthropology, geography, environmental science, and law, with subspecialties such as global business, human rights, ethics, and refugee studies. The expertise of a wide-ranging and diverse group of contributors will provide the reader with a broad-based overview of issues, events, and theories of the developing world.

Acknowledgments

Several people helped to bring this work to its completion. A special thanks goes to Lorraine Murray of Fitzroy Dearborn Publishers, who kindly provided me the opportunity to undertake this project and to Mark L. Georgiev at the Taylor and Francis imprint of Routledge, for directing its completion following Routledge's acquisition of the project from Fitzroy Dearborn. The guidance offered by the Board of Advisors—Ade Adefuye, Akwasi B. Assensoh, Nader Entessar, Stephen Fischer-Galati, Alexander Gungov, Harold Isaacs, Gary Kline, Paul J. Magnarella, John Mukum Mbaku, Alojzy Z. Nowak, Philip Oxhorn, Paul A. Rodell, Houman A. Sadri, Barbara Tenenbaum and Pamela A. Zeiser—ensured the *Encyclopedia's* comprehensiveness. The expertise of each author made possible the accuracy and completeness of the 762 entries. The editorial efforts by Mark O'Malley and particularly Rachel Granfield made this a more readable work. As always, Yvonne offered the encouragement, support, and understanding that only a wife could. This work is dedicated to her.

Thomas M. Leonard

ACID PRECIPITATION

Acid precipitation is caused by rain, sleet, snow, or water vapor in clouds or fog that contain excessively high acid levels. Acid precipitation can be corrosive, damaging both living and nonliving material, and has the potential to destroy ecological systems that have little ability to buffer—or limit—changes in acid levels.

Chemical Background

An acid is typically defined as a substance that increases the concentration of hydrogen ions in an aqueous, or water, solution. Acid levels are measured by pH, which is the negative logarithm of the hydrogen ion concentration in a solution. The pH scale ranges from 0–14. Paradoxically, solutions with a low pH have a greater hydrogen ion concentration than solutions with a high pH. A pH of seven is regarded as neutral. Acidic solutions have a pH lower than seven, whereas alkaline solutions have a pH higher than seven.

Anyone who has taken a chemistry lab course knows that strong acids can be a health hazard. The corrosive effect of strong acids can cause severe, burn-like wounds to the skin and other bodily membranes—the fumes of certain substances, such as nitric acid, can destroy the lungs, and stomach acid can dissolve iron nails swallowed by circus performers (donot try this at home). Acid solutions can affect

chemical reactions in water and soil, thus speeding the loss of nutrients or the buildup of toxic substances in forest soils, for example.

Surprisingly, precipitation is naturally acidic, even when falling from pristine skies. Carbon dioxide in the atmosphere dissolves into water vapor to produce carbonic acid—the same bubbly stuff that, in higher concentrations, makes up seltzer or soda water. Pure rainwater has a pH of about 5.6—the hydrogen ion concentration is about twenty-five times higher than that of water at neutral pH.

Acid precipitation forms when acid-forming substances (other than carbon dioxide) dissolve into atmospheric water vapor. The major types of compounds that form acidic precipitation are nitrogen oxides (the same type of compounds that can form ozone pollution, otherwise known as smog), sulfur dioxide, which forms sulfuric acid, and even hydrochloric acid (the same acid produced by the human stomach).

Natural Sources

Acid precipitation has been falling on the Earth's surface ever since the planet's surface cooled enough to allow liquid water to rain from the sky. Gaseous emissions from volcanoes, for example, have been a major source of acid precipitation for billions of years. Nitrogen oxides are formed by lightning.

A small but significant portion of the sulfuric dioxides that contribute to acid precipitation originates from volcanic activity, but the regions affected by volcanic sources are generally limited to those immediately downwind of volcanic sources. Major eruptions, such as the 1991 eruption of Mt. Pinatubo in the Philippines, may have global effects. Volcanoes also are a major source of hydrochloric acid emissions. Nitric acid formed by lighting is a minor component of acid precipitation today, but it may have been much more important as a source in Earth's early history.

Human-Made Sources

Current acid precipitation problems stem from the dawn of the Industrial Revolution, when coal fueled the development of factories, and environmental regulations were unheard of. Environmental damage from acid precipitation was noticed as early as the seventeenth century, but the term "acid rain" was first used by Robert Angus Smith in his book, *Air and Rain: The Beginnings of a Chemical Climatology*, published in London in 1872. In Smith's time, coal combustion produced significant emissions of nitrogen oxides and sulfur dioxide. Hydrochloric acid pollution from alkali plants was a problem serious enough to warrant legislation by the British Parliament to limit emissions (the Alkali Works Act of 1863).

Coal—used in industry as well as in power generation—is still the major source of sulfur dioxide emissions that lead to acid precipitation. With the rise of the internal combustion engine and the spread of the car culture throughout the world, petroleum has joined coal as a major cause of acid precipitation. Automobile exhaust is the leading source of nitrogen oxide emissions.

Environmental Effects

Acid precipitation has been measured with pH as low as 2.3. At that level, the hydrogen ion concentration is nearly two thousand times that found in unpolluted precipitation and fifty thousand times greater than that of water at neutral pH. Acid precipitation can harm, even destroy, natural environments, particularly those with limited buffering capacity—or limited capacity to limit changes in pH.

The acid harms living systems in a variety of ways. The corrosive effect of the acid physically damages plant and animal tissue. For example, in forests that are frequently exposed to acidic clouds or fog, the acid damages leaf tissue and makes it more difficult for the plant to make nutrients for itself through photosynthesis. Acid precipitation may render soils infertile by mobilizing nutrients that are normally held tightly to soil particles, thus speeding the removal of the nutrients by leaching.

Aquatic animals, especially those that reproduce in water, are particularly sensitive to acid fluctuations. Developing eggs may be damaged. Larval stages may be deformed and fail to develop properly to the adult stage. Sensitive organs in adult animals, such as gills in fish, may be damaged to the point that they cannot function properly and the organism dies. The worst time for many aquatic environments is spring thaw, when lakes, streams, and rivers receive concentrated acidic runoff from the melting snowpack. The thaw often occurs at the time when many aquatic animals are in their egg or larval stages and thus most vulnerable to acid damage.

Human-made structures also are threatened by acid precipitation, because the acids corrode building materials such as limestone, concrete, and iron. Many of the world's greatest archaeological treasures, such as the ruined temples of ancient Greece, are being damaged by acidic precipitation.

Affected Areas

Acid precipitation has evolved from a local problem in the early days of the Industrial Revolution to a global problem today as larger smokestacks, which were intended to ensure that pollutants disperse from the source more efficiently, also ensure that they disperse over wider and wider regions.

Lands downwind of the industrial areas of North America and Europe have been most intensively studied with respect to acid precipitation. But the problem is widespread throughout former Soviet bloc countries where environmental regulation is lax. The problem is spreading throughout the developing world as acceptance of the value of pollution prevention lags behind the drive for increasing industrial development and the diffusion of automobile culture throughout societies where car ownership was once regarded a luxury.

DAVID M. LAWRENCE

See also Deforestation; Environment: Government Policies; Environmentalism; Modernization; Pollution, Agricultural; Urbanization: Impact on Environment; Water Resources and Distribution; World Health Organization (WHO); World Meteorological Organization (WMO)

References and Further Reading

Jacobson, Mark Z. *Atmospheric Pollution: History, Science, and Regulation.* New York: Cambridge University Press.

Karnosky, D. F., K. E. Percy, A. H. Chappelka, C. Simpson, and J. Pikkarainen, eds. *Air Pollution, Global Change, and Forests in the New Millennium.* Boston: Elsevier, 2003.

Pierzynski, Gary M. *Soils and Environmental Quality.* Boca Raton, FL: CRC Press, 2000.

Smol, John P. *Pollution of Lakes and Rivers: A Paleoenvironmental Perspective.* London: Arnold, 2002.

Sullivan, Timothy J. *Aquatic Effects of Acidic Deposition.* Boca Raton, FL: Lewis Publishers.

Underdal, Arild and Kenneth Hanf, eds. *International Environmental Agreements and Domestic Politics: The Case of Acid Rain.* Burlington, VT: Ashgate Publishing, 2000.

White, James C., ed. *Acid Rain: Are the Problems Solved?* Bethesda, MD: American Fisheries Society, 2003.

Wright, John. *Environmental Chemistry.* New York: Routledge, 2003.

AFGHANISTAN

Afghanistan is a landlocked country in Central Asia of over 652,000 square miles in area and a population of about 28 million, including several million refugees in neighboring countries. It is one of the world's most ancient inhabited areas, the site of Stone Age cultures and some of the planet's first civilizations. In the sixth century BC, Afghanistan fell under the influence of the Persian Empire, and Alexander the Great included it in his conquests, but several independent kingdoms managed to emerge in the following centuries. The Afghanis adopted Islam in the seventh century AD. The height of medieval Afghanistan came with the Ghaznavid dynasty: the kingdom stretched from Central Asia to India and was a hub for Islamic culture. Afterward, Afghanistan fell prey to Mongolian and Turkish rulers, such as Tehudjin (the renowned Genghis Khan) and Tamerlane. Afghanistan is a country of highlands and mountains with a semiarid climate. The country' meager economy, which in the 1990s was supplemented by poppy growing and an illegal drug trade, suffered under the influence of Soviet central planning schemes and collapsed in the years of Moscow's invasion, civil war, the Taliban rule, and the subsequent American invasion.

In 1714, the Afghani leader Ahmad Shah Abdali established the country's modern independence, creating the largest Moslem empire of the eighteenth century. Throughout the eighteenth and nineteenth centuries, Afghanis had to deal with constant internal revolts and wars with their neighbors—the Persians and the Sikhs of Kashmir. In the nineteenth century,

Russia and England seized parts of the country. Meanwhile, slow steps toward modernization began under King Habibullah (1901–1919) and his son Amanullah (1919–), called the reform king. In 1918, Afghanistan's first newspaper was started by one of the country's greatest modern intellectuals, Mahmud Tarzi, the leading proponent for modernization and opponent of religious obscurism.

After World War I, Amanullah changed his title to king (Padashah) and continued his program of modernization. In 1929, Habibullah Kalakani overthrew Amanullah, but the tribal leader Nadir Khan replaced and executed him and his supporters, as well as the supporters of ex-king Amanullah. Nadir Khan, in power, seized the property of the wealthy Afghanis and reversed Amanullah's reforms. Mahmud Tarzi fled the country for Kemal Ataturk's Turkey, where he died four years later. A rebellious student assassinated King Nadir in 1933, and his son Zahir assumed the throne, which he held for the next forty years. The young king's uncles served as his prime ministers and advisors. Small-scale industry began and, in 1938, the State Bank of Afghanistan was founded. During World War II, Zahir kept Afghanistan neutral. Amanullah Khan lived in exile until his death in 1960, inspiring a number of revolts in his name.

After the British withdrew from India in 1948, Kabul denounced the 1893 Durand Treaty, which fixed the border with the British colony. Afghani Pashtuns in Pakistan tried, but failed, to declare an independent Pashtunistan, and the Pashtun question remained an inflammatory issue throughout the following years, almost bringing war between Afghanistan and Pakistan. In 1953, Prince Mohammed Daoud, a rival to the king's uncles, became prime minister and asked the United States for arms. On Washington's refusal, Kabul turned to Moscow, cementing close relations between Afghanistan and the Soviet bloc.

Daoud resumed modern reforms, especially those pertaining to the emancipation of women. The *burka* (traditional Moslem female covering) became optional. The University of Kabul became coeducational, and women entered the workforce and government.

In 1964, King Zahir reasserted his power, replaced Daoud with Mohhamad Yusof, and issued a new constitution. The Afghani Communist Party (PDPA) was formed, and one of its leaders, Barbrak Karmal, was elected to parliament. In 1973, while King Zahir was abroad, Daoud, with the aid of the PDPA, overthrew the government and established the Republic of Afghanistan with himself as president. He issued a new constitution that included rights for women. After cracking down on opponents, a communist coup led by Karmal and Noor Mohammad Taraki overthrew his government. Daoud was killed in the coup. A new government took over, with Taraki as president and Karmal as deputy. Taraki carried out bloody reprisals and restored relations with Moscow. The Mujahideen resistance movement was born and the Afghan civil war began.

In the chaos, both the US Ambassador to Afghanistan, Adolph Dubs, and Taraki were killed. The Communist leader Hafizullah Amin became president, but his party rival, Karmal, removed and executed him. On December 31, 1979, the Soviet Union invaded the country and began a long war that debilitated the USSR. As many as fifty thousand Soviet soldiers were killed in the war, which helped bring about the dissolution of the USSR in 1991. Moscow replaced Karmal with a more loyal communist, Najibullah. In 1989, Moscow signed a peace treaty and withdrew from the country. The Mujahideen continued to fight against Najibullah, whom they forced out of power. They had selected Sibhhatulah Mojadidi as the head of an Afghani government in exile, but in power they established an Islamic state, and the people elected Prof. Burhannudin Rabbani president in 1993. The next year, the Islamic fundamentalists formed the Taliban and continued to fight the government. The opposition general, Abdul Rashid Dostum, and the leader of Hezb-e-Islam party, Gulbuddin Hekmatyar, a former Communist, also continued the fight. Furthermore, the country's neighbors, Iran and Pakistan, meddled in its politics. Hekmatyar signed a truce with Rabbani and became prime minister, but the Taliban gradually gained control and began a repressive fundamentalist Islamic government. They executed their enemies, including Najibullah. Women's rights were curtailed as they were forced to resume wearing the *burka* and were forbidden to attend schools or to work outside the home. Men were required to wear beards. The Taliban carried out massive violations of human rights and executions. Furthermore, in these years, Afghanistan suffered several massive earthquakes.

International pressure on the Taliban increased as they planned to destroy historic Buddhist monuments, arrested and executed foreigners, and gave asylum to the Saudi leader of Al-Qaida, Osama bin Laden. After Al-Qaida carried out the bombing of New York's World Trade Center and the Pentagon in Washington, DC, on September 11, 2001, a coalition of forces led by the United States invaded the country and overthrew the Taliban. The attacks against Al-Qaida and the Taliban continued for several years, but a democratic government was restored to Afghanistan under a transitional government led by Hamid Karzai and backed by Washington.

FREDERICK B. CHARY

See also Central Asia: History and Economic Development; Central Asia: International Relations; Mujahedin; Taliban

References and Further Reading

Goodson, Larry P. *Afghanistan's Endless War: State Failure, Regional Politics, and the Rise of the Taliban.* Seattle: University of Washington Press, 2001.
Rasanayagam, Angelo. *Afghanistan: Monarchy, Despotism, or Democracy.* London: I. B. Tauris, 2003.

AFRICAN DEVELOPMENT BANK (ADB)

Established in 1964, the African Development Bank (ADB) is a regional multilateral development bank headquartered in Abidjan, Cote d'Ivoire, with field offices in Cairo, Libreville, Abuja, and Addis Ababa. ADB's shareholders now include fifty-three African countries, or regional member countries (RMCs), and twenty-four non-African countries from Europe, the Americas, and Asia. The African Development Bank (ADB); the African Development Fund (ADF), created in 1972; and the Nigerian Trust Fund (NTF), established in 1976, constitute the ADB group. The ADB's main objectives, as contained in its charter, are to finance investment projects and programs that promote the socioeconomic development of its regional members; to mobilize resources in Africa and outside Africa for this purpose; to provide technical assistance for the preparation, financing, and execution of development projects and programs in Africa; and to cooperate with national, subregional, and regional development institutions in Africa in the fulfillment of these objectives. The ADB itself operates on a nonconcessional basis; the concessional needs of its regional members are addressed through the ADF and the NTF.

The ADB usually commits between $2 billion and $3 billion annually to its development activities, with part of this sum going into joint projects with other donor countries and bilateral and multilateral institutions, including the Bretton Woods Institutions, the Development Bank of South Africa, and the European Union. On a cumulative basis, the ADB had committed no less than $30 billion to various development projects and programs in Africa by 2001. The ADB, whose authorized capital amounts to about $28 billion, derives much of its financial resources from subscribed capital, reserves, funds raised through borrowing, and accumulated net income.

Institutions

The main statutory organs of the ADB, identified in its founding agreement, are the Board of Governors, the Board of Directors, and the Presidency. The Board of Governors, which is the highest policy-making body of the ADB, is made up of one governor for each member country and is charged with the responsibilities of issuing general directives, electing the president, admitting new members, and making amendments to existing agreements. Under Article 32 of the ADB's charter, the Board of Directors is responsible for the conduct of the general operations of the Bank; it approves all loans, guarantees, equity investments, and borrowing, and sets policy guidelines for the ADB. The Board of Directors consists of eighteen Executive Directors, elected for a three-year term, twelve of whom represent regional members, with the rest representing nonregional members. The President, who is the Chief Executive and the legal representative of the Bank, is elected by the Board of Governors for a five-year term, renewable only once. The President is responsible for the management of the Bank in accordance with regulations adopted by the Boards. The President is assisted by five Vice Presidents (as of 2004) for Planning, Policy, and Research; Finance; Corporate Management; Operations in Central and West Africa; and Operations in North, East, and South Africa.

Contribution to Africa's Development

As with most development institutions in Africa, several of the ADB's activities are geared toward poverty reduction through employment creation; infrastructure development; and investments in agriculture, rural development, human resources development, environmental sustainability, and good governance. Given the preeminence of agriculture in African economies, it is hardly surprising that the ADB considers its agricultural and rural development projects as top priorities, complemented with support for agro-based industries, small and medium-sized enterprises, and for micro and rural finance schemes. The bulk of the ADB's projects over the years are for the benefit of local communities, regions, and areas of a particular country. Samples of ADB-financed projects include the Tunisian Railway Infrastructure Modernization Project (2004); the 77.15-million-euro Electricity Distribution Networks Rehabilitation Project in Tunisia (2003); the $10 million Bulk Terminal Project in Djibouti (2003); the 215-million-euro Water Sector Adjustment Program in Morocco (2003); the $500,000 Humanitarian Emergency Grant for Liberia (2003); the $2.35 million grant for the Lakes Edward and Albert Fisheries (LEAF) Pilot Project in the Republic of Congo and Uganda (2003); and the $500,000 grant to help control the spread of Ebola fever in the Republic of Congo (2003).

With due cognizance of the significant role of good governance—broadly defined to include accountability, transparency, and respect for the rule of law and human rights—in development, the ADB has given considerable attention to legal and regulatory reforms, anticorruption mechanisms, and institutional capacity building in member states. In this regard, the ADB encourages its regional members to decentralize their development decision-making process and to give local stakeholders and targeted beneficiaries the means to participate in project planning and implantation.

The ADB, in line with its mandate, has been working closely with various subregional and continental organization and initiatives, such as Economic Community of West African States (ECOWAS); the Southern African Development Community (SADC), African Union (AU), and the New Partnership for Africa's Development (NEPAD), to pursue programs whose impacts extend beyond the borders of individual member countries; such programs include the harmonization of monetary and trade policies, regional integration initiatives, and the fight against HIV/AIDS. Through a Memorandum of Understanding signed on March 14, 2000, the ABD and the World Bank now collaborate on a number of subregional and continental development projects and programs to minimize duplication and to benefit from each other's experience.

Notwithstanding its accomplishment and positive outlook for Africa's future, the ADB is still plagued with problems relating to limited capacity at the national and subregional level for project preparation, implementation, and evaluation; inadequate coordination between the ADB's efforts and those of the numerous regional economic bloc in Africa; and the pervasive poverty, indebtedness, and low savings and investment rates across the continent. These and many other problems—especially those relating to corruption and inefficiency—would have to be addressed, if the bank is to attract concessional financial resources on a sustainable basis from donor countries and multinational financial institutions outside the continent.

JOSEPH MENSAH

See also African Monetary Fund (AfMf); Economic Community of West African States (ECOWAS); Southern African Development Community (SADC)

References and Further Reading

African Development Bank. *Africa and the African Development Bank: 25th Anniversary 1964–1989.* London: Euromoney Publications, in association with the African Development Bank, 1989.

African Development Bank. *Agreement Establishing the African Development Bank.* Abidjan: The Bank, 1967.

Ebong, Ime Ekop. *Development Financing Under Constraints: A Decade of African Development Bank.* Bonn-Bad Godesberg: Verlag Neue Gesellschaft, 1974.

Fordwor, Kwame Donkoh. *The African Development Bank: Problems of International Cooperation.* New York, Oxford, Toronto, Sydney, Paris, and Frankfurt: Pergamon Press, 1981.

Gardiner, Robert K. A. and James Pickett, eds. *The African Development Bank: 1964–1984.* Abidjan: The African Development Bank, 1984.

Mingst, Karen A. *Politics and the African Development Bank.* Lexington, KY: University of Kentucky Press, 1990.

Omar, Kabbaj. *The Challenge of African Development.* Oxford and New York: Oxford University Press, 2003.

White, John. *Regional Development Banks: The Asian, African, and Inter-American Development Banks.* New York: Praeger Publishers, 1972.

AFRICAN DIASPORA

The African Diaspora refers to the dispersion of peoples of African descent beyond their homelands on the continent of Africa to other parts of the world. Since human life began in Africa, in one sense the population of the world represents an ancient diaspora. But the term usually refers to the movement of peoples from the fifteenth century up to the present due to the European slave trade. However, the diaspora also includes those Africans who found their way to the East as the result of slavery, indenture, or voluntary migration. Thus, the African Diaspora encompasses a long history with multiple causes and many populations.

The term "diaspora" was first used in Jewish history to describe the exile of Jews from Judea in 586 BC and Jerusalem in 135 AD and gained frequency after World War II as Jews fought for a homeland in Palestine. The term can be found in the Bible in Deuteronomy 28:25. The term as it was originally used implied an element of force behind the removal of peoples from their homelands. However, in its contemporary usage, it has come to describe any distinct population dispersed from its homeland into the world for any reason. Parallels with Jews as people enslaved and driven into exile has led to many groups referring to their own similar scattered geographical presence as a diaspora.

The term "Black Diaspora" came into use widely beginning in the 1960s, mostly in response to the rising interest in black history in the West and its African roots. When the focus shifted from a racial to an ethnic emphasis, the term "African Diaspora" came into usage. Formal comparative studies of the dispersion of Africans in the West as a result of the slave trade go back well into the nineteenth century and preceded the use of the term. For the most part, studies of the African Diaspora have focused particularly on slavery, emancipation, and its aftermath.

More recently, the African Diaspora refers to people displaced as refugees because of war, political oppression, and economic depression. It also refers to those people who voluntarily left Africa to take advantage of economic opportunities, to join their families abroad, or as victims of human trafficking. Scholars also have begun to include within the concept of the African Diaspora, the movement of peoples within the continent of Africa from one homeland to another for a variety of reasons. Indeed, many scholars have come to speak of African Diasporas in the plural to capture the variation in locales, causes, and characteristics of these diasporic migrations.

Members of a diaspora have beliefs about their origins in common. Cohen (1996:515) has further characterized diasporas by the tendencies of their members to share "a collective memory and myth about the homeland, including its location, history, and achievements" and to engage in "an idealization of the putative ancestral home and a collective commitment to its maintenance, restoration, safety and prosperity, even to its creation."

The creation of the African Diaspora laid the foundation for many of the problems of the developing world during and following slavery, emancipation, and postcolonial independence. Many of these problems persist into the twenty-first century.

Indenture, Slavery, and the African Diaspora

Most scholars agree that one of the main causes of the modern dispersion of Africans is due to both Arab and European slave trades, but most of the scholarship on the African Diaspora has focused on slavery and the forced removal of African peoples from their homelands to Europe and to colonies in the Americas. Slavery was a common institution in both the Near East and Africa. European contact began in 1444 with the Portuguese, who eventually established commerce with African kingdoms, including the slave trade, which increased over time and came to involve many European states, such as Spain, Holland, England, and France. The spread of slavery to the Americas between the fifteenth and eighteenth centuries resulted in the forcible removal of as many as 4 million people from the continent of Africa. Not only did this result in a change of the Americas with the incursion of so many people from abroad, but it also had a devastating effect on African development itself.

Loss of population affected the long-term development of African societies, many of which had had flourishing industries but afterwards found themselves stagnating, economically bereft of a labor population. Some scholars speculate that slavery caused an imbalance between the sexes, because mostly men were enslaved, and may have exacerbated a polygynous way of life and changed the sexual division of labor. Other scholars believe that slavery led to the development of territorial states that confused traditional boundaries, and indigenous religious often succumbed to Christianity.

In the Americas—North, South, Central, and the Caribbean—slavery led to differential conditions due to the variety of environments involved and eventually to formation of many new cultures. For example, besides the variety of forms of agriculture that arose because of the slave trade, rebellions often led to the formation of maroon societies of escaped slaves, many of whom were able to adapt their African customs to the new environments. New languages arose (Creole); new religions (syncretic religions) and racial distinction became a common way of differentiating among people, leading to race-based ideologies and the development of color hierarchies. However, common cultural backgrounds and sheer numbers often allowed for the maintenance or adaptation of African customs. In any case, the common experience of slavery and longing for the homeland created the basic substance of the African Diaspora.

Eventually the slave trade itself fell into disrepute in Europe. Rebellions, moral considerations, and the growth of free trade sentiments eventually undermined slavery and led over a long period to the abolition of the slave trade, and eventually to the abolition of the institution of slavery itself. The Danes were the first modern nation to abolish the slave trade in 1803, although not slavery itself until 1848. Many of the original British colonies in North America eliminated slavery relatively quickly, beginning in 1780 in Pennsylvania. New York began abolishing slavery in 1799 and finished in 1827. However, slavery in the United States as a whole was not abolished until 1865 with the passage of the Thirteenth Amendment to the Constitution of the United States. Slavery ended in Central America in 1824 and in Mexico in 1829, long before it ended in North America.

The first slaves entered the Caribbean in 1502. Haiti eliminated slavery during its revolution and declared its independence from France in 1804, becoming the second republic independent of colonial rule in the Americas (the United States being the first). Slavery ended in British colonies between 1833 and 1838, in French and Danish colonies by 1848, in Dutch colonies by 1863, in Puerto Rico in 1873, and in all Spanish colonies by 1886.

In South America, slavery ended much earlier: in Chile in 1823, in Colombia in 1851, in Ecuador in 1852, in Argentina and Uruguay in 1853, in Peru and Venezuela in 1854, in Bolivia in 1861, and in Paraguay in 1869. Slavery began in the 1580s in Brazil; 1850 brought the end of the slave trade, and slavery ended in 1888.

But even with emancipation, patterns set down in slavery were to have a long-term effect during the long periods of post-emancipation colonialism, and new patterns affecting members of the African Diaspora would develop. Emancipation brought about further migrations of people of African descent, shifting and expanding the nature of the diaspora.

From Colonial Rule to Independence in the African Diaspora

If the nineteenth century can be seen as the century of emancipation from slavery, the twentieth century can be seen as one of colonialism and imperialism that further reshaped the face of Africa, the Middle East, and much of the rest of the world, as well as the century of independence from colonial rule, which affected the many peoples of the diaspora.

After emancipation, black populations of the Africa Diaspora found themselves facing new problems, such as the entrenched power of those who had previously owned them and both formal and informal racial discrimination that reconstituted the boundaries initialized in slavery. Former slave owners/planters, for the most part, retained power over the emancipated populations, who now shifted from slavery into peasantry. Some became farmers in their own right, continuing with and building upon their experience in agriculture and using land made available to them. But others became tenant farmers, engaging in sharecropping. Still others hired out for wage labor, entering into systems in which employers kept them indebted through the payment that could only be used in company stores and by constantly advancing wages.

Throughout much of the African Diaspora, people suffered from economic depressions due to the lack of solid markets. However, with the spread of various industries, the labor force began to shift from a rural, agricultural base with some guarantee of self-sufficiency to an urban, industrialized base with a growing wage labor force. This shift in the early twentieth century led to large pockets of subsistence agriculturalists and large pockets of urban poverty, illiteracy, political patronage systems, political disenfranchisement, and precarious economic conditions culminating in the Great Depression of 1929, which had a worldwide effect.

Once again, huge population shifts caused changes in the distribution of peoples within the diaspora. The Great Migration in the United States took place between 1910 and 1940, when blacks moved in the millions from the South to northern cities such as Chicago. There also was a good deal of movement from the Caribbean to the United States and South and Central America as labor opportunities presented themselves to desperate workers. The crowding of people into cities and its attendant problems created a new consciousness within the African Diaspora itself, emphasizing the common thread of economic and political oppression. Consequently, throughout the early twentieth century, a series of Pan-African congresses were held, and many revitalization movements, such as the formation of new religions, new communities, and even repatriation to Africa movements, arose.

The large, industrialized societies arising in the nineteenth and twentieth centuries had been built largely on the labor of members of the African Diaspora, who did not necessarily share in the emerging wealth and benefits. The rising consciousness of this injustice led to fights for individual rights, human rights, enfranchisement, and political independence across the African Diaspora—struggles that would characterize the second half of the twentieth century.

The end of World War II found a rise in expectations. In the United States, which experienced an unprecedented affluence following the war, this led to the integration of labor unions and the beginning of the modern civil rights movement, which eventually ended legal segregation in the American South and spread to the rest of the country, making people aware of other problems faced by blacks, such as unemployment, lack of housing, denial of access to education, and poverty. In the Caribbean, the collapse of plantation agriculture, the development of agribusiness, and continuing industrialization led to the rise of black nationalism. The 1960s and 1970s saw the independence of many former colonies, such as Jamaica in 1962 and the Bahamas in 1973. In most cases in the Caribbean, black majorities gained political control. However, they still had to contend with the problems left behind when colonial rule ended. In South America, many of these struggles are ongoing.

Transnational Identities and Globalization in the African Diaspora

The continuing migrations of members of the African Diaspora eventually resulted in the what scholars refer to as transnational identities; that is, identities not tied to feelings about membership in a nation-state, but identities tied to others with a common history, who are geographically dispersed. Transnational identities are generated by networks of association that cross political boundaries. These transnational identities often have become the basis for resistance movements, extensive trade networks, the spreading of cultural forms, and further migrations within the diaspora.

The existence of the African Diaspora poses a number of interesting problems for scholars. The meaning of the African Diaspora has changed over time as scholars evaluate its importance in the light of changing sociopolitical conditions around the globe. For one thing, scholars have begun to focus more on the African Diaspora in the East (for example, in those societies located around the Indian Ocean) and the connection of these diasporic populations with populations in Africa.

More recently, some scholars have connected the fate of Africa and its many developmental problems with the similar problems experienced by members of the African Diaspora across the globe. There also is the question of the relationship of diasporic peoples to the original homeland, especially after new generations have passed and experiences have changed. Also, some scholars have begun to look at the connection between African Diaspora studies and African Studies, broadening their concerns not only with the academic connections but with problems on the policy level that seem to affect both Africans in Africa and members of the African Diaspora.

SUSAN LOVE BROWN

See also Pan-Africanism; Third World

References and Further Reading

Adi, Hakim and Marika Sherwood. *Pan-African History: Political Figures from Africa and the Diaspora since 1787.* London and New York: Routledge, 2003.

Bennett, Aubrey W. and G. Llewellyn Watson, eds. *Emerging Perspectives on the African Diaspora.* Lanham, MD: University Press of America, 1989.

Brock, Lisa. "Questioning the Diaspora: Hegemony, Black Intellectuals, and Doing International History from Below." *Issue: A Journal of Opinion* 24(2): 9–12 (1996).

Brodber, Erna. *The Continent of Black Consciousness: On the History of the African Diaspora from Slavery to the Present Day*. London: New Beacon Books, 2003.

Cohen, Robin. "Diasporas and the Nation-State: From Victims to Challengers." *International Affairs* 72(3): 507–520 (July 1996).

Conniff, Michael L. and Thomas J. Davis. *Africans in the Americas: A History of the Black Diaspora*. New York: St. Martin's Press, 1994.

Gordon, Edmund T. and Mark Anderson. "The African Diaspora: Toward an Ethnography of Diasporic Identification." *The Journal of American Folklore* 112(445): 282–296 (Summer 1999).

Green, Charles, ed. *Globalization and Survival in the Black Diaspora: The New Urban Challenge*. Albany, NY: State University of New York Press, 1997.

Hine, Darlene Clark and Jacqueline McLeod, eds. *Crossing Boundaries: Comparative History of Black People in Diaspora*. Bloomington, IN, and Indianapolis: Indiana University Press, 1999.

Jayasuriya, Shihan de Silva and Richard Pankhurst, eds. *The African Diaspora in the Indian Ocean*. Trenton, NJ, and Asmara, Eritrea: Africa World Press, 2003.

Koser, Khalid, ed. *New African Diasporas*. London and New York: Routledge, 2003.

Palmer, Colin A. "Defining and Studying the Modern African Diaspora." *The Journal of Negro History* 85 (1/2): 27–32 (Winter–Spring 2000).

Patterson, Tiffany Ruby and Robin D. G. Kelley. "Unfinished Migrations: Reflections on the African Diaspora and the Making of the Modern World." *African Studies Review* 43(1): 11–45 (April 2000).

Shepherd, Verene A., ed. *Working Slavery, Pricing Freedom: Perspectives from the Caribbean, Africa, and the African Diaspora*. New York: Palgrave, 2002.

Vertovec, S. and Cohen R., eds. *Migration, Diasporas, and Transnationalism*. Cheltenham, England: Edward Elgar, 1999.

AFRICAN MONETARY FUND (AfMF)

Section 19 of the Charter of the African Union that deals with financial institutions provided for the establishment of the African Central Bank, the African Monetary Fund (AfMF), and the African Investment Bank. The "Treaty Establishing the African Economic Community" (the Abuja Treaty) predates this. It called for the establishment of an African monetary union through the harmonization of regional monetary zones. However, not much progress has been made in this direction. The regular meetings of the governors of central banks in Africa under the aegis of the Committee of Central Bank Governors (CCBG) is the closest move in this direction and may be a pointer to the formation of the African Central Bank rather than the African Monetary Fund.

For many years, African countries have advocated for the formation of a regional body similar in function to the International Monetary Fund (IMF) but focused on the growth objectives of Africa. The main complaint against the Bretton Woods Institutions is that, although they had committed to help solve the debt crisis that hit African countries in the late 1970s following the combination of internal and external shocks (sharp fluctuations in commodity prices and high interest rates), many people believe that their stabilization and structural adjustment polices did not work. Additionally, trade liberalization has not been successful in all African countries: many people have suffered fiscal losses because they had hitherto depended on import taxation as their main source of fiscal revenue. Some domestic industries have collapsed due to their inability to withstand competition from subsidized competitors from the industrial countries. These instabilities have resulted in massive capital flight and the creation of weak financial institutions. Privatization has often led to higher prices of goods, especially utilities such as water, telephones, and electricity.

Sub-Saharan Africa (SSA) is the only region in the world where poverty has continued to rise since the early 1980s. The number of people living on less than $1 per day has almost doubled between 1981 and 2001—from 160 million to about 314 million.

Strict conditionalities have been imposed on African countries in exchange for loans and credits. In some cases, this has precluded the ownership of development projects and programs by recipient countries. Many African countries have been neither able nor willing to get financing from the IMF due to their inability to meet conditions set by the institution.

Another argument for an institution like the AfMF could be found in the need to restructure the global financial system to achieve a network of strong regional institutions and their effective linkage to existing international institutions. With the commitment to regional integration, there has been a blossoming of regional trade and regional capital market integration. Also, globalization has enhanced the growth of regional macroeconomic interaction. Other support for the primacy of regional institutions includes the risk-pooling argument, competition in the supply of services to smaller and medium-sized economies, and the sense of ownership that creates a special relationship between financial institutions and member countries. The federalist argument also becomes relevant in this case. Many small countries feel that they stand a chance of being heard only when part of a regional bloc. These arguments have been demonstrated in the effectiveness of such regional arrangements as the European Payments Union, the Arab Monetary Fund, the (ASEAN) Association of Southeast Asian Nations Surveillance Process, and in recent times, the Andean Development Corp.

It is against this background that the idea of creating the AfMF came up with the aim of providing a source of funding for economic development in the continent. The AfMF will be located in the continent and will focus on the continent only, as opposed to the World Bank and IMF, whose resources are available to almost all the countries in the world. In terms of funding, it is envisaged that all African countries will become members through acquisition of shares by making contributions. In addition, countries in the continent with excess reserves can place their reserves as deposits with the Fund. Non-African countries that are sympathetic to Africa's development with excess reserves also could provide funding. The fund also will issue bonds denominated in foreign currency in the Euro or Dollar markets and in the international capital markets.

The AfMF will be the continent's lender of last resort before a country approaches either the World Bank or IMF. The Fund also will provide services to smaller and medium-sized African countries in terms of technical support and advice in development of the banking and financial systems. The main challenge that will be facing the AfMF is that many African countries do not have sufficient resources, and thus countries may not be able to contribute their quota going by the experience with many of the existing regional arrangements.

SYLVANUS IKHIDE

See also African Development Bank (ADB); International Bank for Reconstruction and Development (IBRD) (World Bank); International Monetary Fund (IMF)

References and Further Reading

Ikhide, S. I. "The International Financial System and Aid Delivery." *The World Economy* 27: 2 (February 2004).
Njonjo, Kihuria. "African Monetary Fund: A Viable Option." *East African Standard*. October 12, 2002. (http: www.globalpolicy.org/socecon/develop/africa/2002/1012 afm.htm).

AFRICAN NATIONAL CONGRESS (ANC)

The African National Congress (ANC) was founded by the Zulu lawyer Pixley Ka Izaka Seme. Born in Natal, Seme was raised a Christian, studied at an American missionary school, and attended Columbia University and Oxford University. In 1910, the year Great Britain formed the Union of South Africa, he returned to South Africa to lead the struggle for the emancipation of his people and was admitted to the bar. Here he joined other African lawyers—Alfred Mangena D. Montsioa and R. W. Msimang—working in the interest of the native African population.

Seme originally wanted to uplift the condition of his Zulu nation, but recognizing the humiliation and deprivation of all black Africans, he changed his focus to work on behalf of the entire indigenous population.

Seme with his colleagues called for a meeting of the tribal chiefs and educated Africans in Bloemfontain on January 8, 1912 for "the purpose of creating national unity and defending our rights and privileges." The meeting established the South African Native National Congress to organize the tribes of Africa along national lines. Seme then approached the publishers of the two native Johannesburg newspapers to publish an organ of the Congress. D. S. Letanka, publisher of *Murumiao,* agreed and joined Seme and the queen of Swaziland, Labotsibeni Gwamile Ndluli, to begin the publication of *Abantu-Botho* printed in English, Zulu, and Sotho.

Seme also formed the African Farmer's Association for the purchasing of land in the Transvaal. However, the white farmers reacted, passing the Natives Land Act of 1913 restricting native ownership of farms. Africans then sought work in the mines and elsewhere, often traveling many miles to their jobs. The government then enacted pass laws requiring passports for Africans to move around the country. Initially, in 1919 the ANC supported a demonstration against these laws and a strike of African mine workers in 1920. Nevertheless, in the 1920s the ANC leaders disagreed with the strikes and demonstration and tried to argue with London about the restrictive laws, tactics which brought no results. Other organizations, for example, the newly formed Communist Party, adopted more active policies. The government continued to put in more racist legislation dividing black and white workers. ANC leader J. T. Gunmede, elected in 1927, urged cooperation between the ANC and the Communist Party; but the conservative leadership voted him out of office, leading to the Congress's inactivity in the 1930s.

In the 1940s, under new young leadership exemplified by Nelson Mandela, Walter Sislu, and Oliver Tambo, the ANC adopted a more activist stance. White South Africa in the meantime hardened its stand through its policy of apartheid (segregation) and a more militant Afrikaner (Dutch descendants) nationalism. In 1944 the ANC formed its Youth League. Black Africans began to form their own community and labor organizations. In 1947 the ANC signed agreements with the Indian Congresses, as the apartheid laws segregated not only the native Africans but other races as well. After the Afrikaner Party came to power in 1949, the ANC adopted the Youth League's program of action, starting the Defiance Campaign which included strikes and boycotts.

The Defiance Campaign turned the ANC into a mass organization and spurred the birth of other organizations such as the South African Coloured People's Organization (SACPO) and the Congress of Democrats (COD) which in turn created the Congress Alliance including the South African Congress of Trade Unions (SACTO). The government reacted by arresting or "banning" (a form of limited civil liberties and house arrest) the leaders and prominent supporters—black and white. The Alliance Congress' 1955 Freedom Charter called for equality of rights and opportunity for all races. It also included social welfare demands such as jobs and houses. The government declared the Congress to be a Communist organization planning the violent overthrow of the government, and arrested its leaders.

In the meantime, the women organized protests against the Pass Law as well as boycotts against the government beer halls after they passed a law against traditional beer brewing. The 1950s witnessed many mass demonstrations which were brutally suppressed. The Bantu Authorities Act gave the government the right to replace chiefs, and a number of chiefs cooperated in order to keep their positions. This was a major cause of the great rural Pondoland Revolt of 1960–1961.

There was dissention within the ANC as some, called the Africanists, objected to cooperation with the non-African groups or the Communist Party. In 1959, the Africanists broke off from SNBC and formed the Pan African Congress (PAC). Because of massacres of peaceful demonstrators, the ANC adopted a policy of violence through its underground organization Umkhonto we Sizwe or MK (The Spear of the Nation), but the government cracked down with harsher penalties and in 1963 raided the MK's secret headquarters. The government prosecuted the ANC's leaders, including Nelson Mandela, and sentenced them to long terms at Robin Island. Some leaders like Joe Slovo, a white supporter, and Tambo left the countries to continue the struggle abroad. At Mongoro, Tanzania, in 1969 the ANC decided to continue the struggle through armed revolt and mass political action while opening ANC membership to all races. In the 1970s a new wave of action by workers and students erupted in the country, beginning with the Durban strike of 1973, and culminating in the student demonstration of 1976 against the mandatory use of Afrikaans in the schools instead of English. The massacre of young students by the government led to widespread demonstrations and the death of a thousand at Soweto. Students formed the South African Student Movement (SASM), which the ANC supported. In the 1980s the government offered reforms but continued to bear down on the ANC. The Congress movement was revived with the formation of the United Democratic Front. There were other new mass organizations, for example, the Congress of South African Students and the Congress of South African Trade Unions. A state of virtual civil war developed as the activists attacked black leaders loyal to the government, and the government security forces (often acting on their own initiative) attacked the activists. In 1990, the ANC was unbanned. A new constitution permitted blacks to vote, and in subsequent elections the ANC won and South Africa elected Nelson Mandela president.

FREDERICK B. CHARY

See also Apartheid; Mandela, Nelson; South Africa

References and Further Reading

Holland, Hiedi. *A History of the African National Congress.* New York: G. Braziller, 1990.

Johns, S. and R. Hunt Davis. *Mandela, Tambo, and the African National Congress: The struggle Against Apartheid, 1948–1900: a Documentary Survey.* New York: Oxford, 1991.

AGRICULTURE: IMPACT OF GLOBALIZATION

Globalization is having a vast extent of effects on agriculture from the perspective of developing countries. Due to the impact of globalization, crop selection and agricultural production processes and technologies have changed. Moreover, globalization's impact on agriculture has had a range of social, economic, political, and ecological consequences. The direction and extent of the effects of globalization on agriculture and societies in developing countries differ among and within those countries. Heterogeneity continues to exist at the local level, and local and national cultures and histories retain some importance. However, some general trends have been identified. The majority of scholars argue that developments associated with globalization, such as the liberalization of trade, and capital mobility and concentration, are affecting rich and poor countries in the world very differently. Some claim that we are witnessing a triadization based on the economic, technological, and social integration of North America, (Western) Europe, and, to some extent, Southeast Asia and the increasing exclusion of poorer countries and regions. In developing countries, recent trends in industrialized agriculture and food systems go hand in hand with 840 million people still suffering from chronic hunger and key losses to environments, societies, and people's health arising during and from the "modernization" of agriculture. Scholars perceive a high risk of disruption to agricultural systems and environmental deterioration, social disruption, and dislocation in poorer countries of the world.

In terms of changes in agriculture itself, globalization has affected products as well as production processes and technologies. We witness an increasing specialization of countries on exotic export crops and animal foodstuffs, a shift away from the production of staple foods to new activities demanded by the rich consumers in the North, as well as the agroprocessing industries. New exports such as horticultural products, that is, fresh fruits and vegetables, flowers, poultry, and meat products, are replacing previous export commodities like jute, sugar, or cotton. Within developing countries, furthermore, an increasing specialization of farms, in particular crop and livestock enterprises, and changes in their production structures can be noticed. With rising human population, increasing per capita incomes and the associated rising demand for livestock products in the North, and new technologies becoming available, livestock industries are increasing in number and size, for example.

In general, agricultural production methods are shifting in two directions. On large farms with access to capital and technological inputs, the trend is toward intensive agriculture. Here, the globalization of agriculture is based on high energy inputs and monoculture production systems based on genetically engineered uniformity in organisms manipulated to maximize output. In this area, globalization fosters a homogenization of world agriculture based on a Western monocultural form. At the same time, among the marginalized sectors of society, subsistence agriculture under difficult socioeconomic and ecological conditions prevails. Concurrently, traditional knowledge and more sustainable farming technologies such as complex agroecosystems are facing the threat of extinction.

Social and Environmental Consequences

The social consequences of the impact of globalization on agriculture in developing countries are expected to be particularly severe. Some scholars suggest that globalization will increase income inequalities in the world and progressively exclude poorer societies. Even within developing countries, social gaps are likely to increase. While some sectors of society can be expected to benefit from globalization, the larger share of the population of developing countries is likely to lose, thus leading to larger social cleavages

and conflicts. Groups with market experience and access to information and capital, regional, and global networks and contracts are likely to benefit from increasing globalization. Even some examples of linkages between expanded agricultural product markets and the improved sustainability of small farmer welfare exist.

Yet, the majority of the rural population in developing countries is involved in low-input subsistence agricultural production under social and ecological circumstances made increasingly difficult by globalization. The overall trend is toward a decline in social capital of rural areas, destruction of horizontal networks within communities that are replaced by vertical linkages to distant organization, decreasing opportunities for informal and formal horizontal exchanges, and the erosion of norms and cohesiveness of rural societies. In farming areas unable to compete in global markets, dramatic social changes and land transfer to other uses or abandonment are likely to occur. The new financial power relations along the food chain further induce changes in land ownership in the South, often with negative social implications. Downward pressures on income due to declining real agricultural prices—real agricultural prices had fallen to levels not seen since the 1930s—are likely to lead to further social disruption and dislocation. Scholars have pointed out that the declining commodity prices due to agro-exporting debt-servicing strategies advocated by international organizations have led to prosperity for food traders but falling incomes in the South. In addition, fewer people are likely to be able to derive a stable income from farming, even in successful farming areas. Women in particular are being marginalized with their role becoming that of a laborer rather than a cultivator, a development that is particularly tragic as agriculture employs more than 80% of all economically active women. In general, a distancing of agriculture from the needs and lives of the population in developing countries can be expected.

Changes in agricultural production in developing countries due to globalization also may have extremely negative environmental effects, mainly due to the pollution problems arising from intensive agriculture, ecological vulnerability of monoculture production, and the destruction of habitat. According to some observers, the tendency of globalization to undervalue natural and social capital has fostered the spread of non-sustainable agricultural systems. Such environmental effects interact with the social effects of the globalization of agriculture to the detriment of both. The focus on increasing output with greater use of nonrenewable inputs has the potential to cause losses in natural habitats and wildlife; nutrient losses; soil erosion and site desertification; water pollution with pesticides and fertilizers; contamination of the atmospheric environment with methane, nitrous oxide, and ammonia deriving from livestock, manure, and fertilizers; and associated threats to human health. Innovation in biotechnologies affects crop varieties and characteristics. Crop specialization creates losses in biodiversity, especially in indigenous plants and animals formerly used for food production. In addition, biodiversity-rich forests are destroyed for the creation of large farms.

From a global environmental perspective, however, the globalization of production can allow the relocation of production to environmentally more efficient places, away from greenhouse production, for instance. Furthermore, the expectation that economic globalization and especially trade specialization on the basis of comparative advantage will lead to improved economic conditions leads some scholars to suggest that demand for better environmental quality will increase with increasing incomes in developing countries. Mainstream economists thus tend to view the impact of globalization on international agriculture and the environment very positively and argue that we face a win-win situation. Other scholars, however, point out that there is little evidence for the proposition that globalization will generate positive consequences for global agriculture and environment. Furthermore, one should not forget that globalization also can allow the relocation of production to places with lower environmental standards, which apply less stringent regulations on pesticide use, for example. The overall consequences of globalization and trade liberalization for the conservation of natural environments and the sustainability of different forms of agriculture are likely to be mixed.

Environmental questions may play an even larger role in the future of agriculture. Global climate change regulation creates opportunities for farmers in developing countries while placing some constraints on them at the same time. The agricultural sector is a significant emitter of greenhouse gases. Therefore, climate change policies could affect both agricultural production and trade. Some scholars suggest that future climate change agreements could be tied to international trade agreements. Furthermore, the general need for carbon sequestration is likely to increase in the future. This may present an opportunity for the rural poor to combine food production and carbon sequestration in large-scale agroforestry. At the same time, farmers may face growing incentives to cultivate energy crops rather than food. The consequences of such actions in the form of rising food prices would likely be quite dramatic for the landless poor.

Globalization

A systematic assessment of the impact of globalization on agriculture from the perspective of developing countries depends on a sound conceptualization of the phenomenon of globalization. Unfortunately, definitions of globalization used in academia and in political practice are numerous and range from increasing economic integration and cultural homogenization to the increasing deterritoriality of economic, political, and social relationships and phenomena. The only existing agreement concerns a handful of visible elements associated with globalization: trade liberalization, capital concentration and mobility, shifts in political decision-making authority, and the acceleration of technological innovation and diffusion. In the following, the implications of developments in these four aspects for agriculture in developing countries will be discussed.

Trade Liberalization

Trade liberalization is a pivotal element of globalization. The Uruguay Round Agreement of the General Agreement on Tariffs and Trade (GATT), signed in April 1994 in Marrakesh, included a comprehensive agreement on trade in agricultural products for the first time. This agreement reversed the trend toward protectionism in the area and established a framework for the reduction of trade barriers for agricultural products. At the same time, the Uruguay Round created the World Trade Organization (WTO) as the institution to "house" the GATT, to coordinate and foster international efforts at trade liberalization.

Today, trade liberalization in agricultural products is by no means complete, however. Subsidization and protection and conflicts about them remain, particularly in and between developed countries. Government transfers to the sector remain at very high levels in Japan, the European Union, and the United States. Even the Uruguay Round's conversion of non-tariff barriers to equivalent tariffs fostered little additional market access. Furthermore, we can notice the continuing impact of regional trade blocs on agricultural trade. While these blocs may help to improve resource allocation within a region, they discriminate among members and nonmembers and can have detrimental effects for global resource allocation. Given that the majority of developing countries are not part of the economically powerful trade blocs, they tend to bear the costs of such regional agreements. Some scholars even question whether some actors such as the European Union will ever sufficiently reform its common agricultural policy to comply with the current WTO obligations.

Conflicts do not focus on government subsidies on tariffs only, however. Issues such as food security and the need to protect the environment, which the agreement identifies as non-trade concerns, are highly contentious as well. Such issues are regulated by sanitary and phytosanitary measures, which have been created to protect public health and the environment from pests, diseases, and contaminants in the context of the movement of agricultural products across borders. New definitions of these "non-trade" concerns include rural development, labeling, and consumer concerns over food quality. While most of the contentious issues of the Uruguay Round thus remain, new ones have arisen. In consequence, agriculture was again at the top of the agenda at the WTO meeting in Seattle and a new round of talks on the Agreement on Agriculture began in 2000 despite the Seattle meeting's failure to initiate new comprehensive negotiations. Further trade liberalization in agricultural products is to be expected with new labor entering the market, capital obtaining access to more parts of the globe, production becoming more and more specialized in and among countries, and output being sold in increasingly global markets.

The consequences of the liberalization of agricultural trade for developing countries are controversial. Some scholars adhere to the orthodox economic view that trade liberalization fosters specialization of production based on comparative advantage and thereby provides benefits for all. The majority of experts are skeptical about the distribution of benefits from free trade, however. They argue that agricultural trade liberalization changes the international distribution of income to the benefit of Northern investors and adversely affects income levels and the sustainability of agriculture in the less developed regions of the world. These critical observers agree that trade liberalization provides an incentive for specialization in certain forms of crop production in developing countries. The relatively cheap land with initially high productivity attracts the production of large-scale monocultural crops. Low land prices and the lack of income support structures combined with sometimes favorable growing conditions create an environment in which the production of large quantities of cheap food for mass markets becomes possible. Thus, farming is becoming more concentrated on exports, as developing countries have an incentive to produce and sell more high-value crops and purchase staples in the world market. However, observers fear that the majority of the population in the developing countries does not incur the benefits from these exports, because land ownership by large shares of the population is decreasing, and these people lack access to capital for competitive inputs and to global markets. Furthermore, large-scale, intensive crop production fosters radical changes in existing community structures and institutions—in particular, the growth of "private property" holdings. Besides the often dire social consequences of these changes, they tend to be associated with dislocation and disruption, inequity, unfair and unjust methods of change, and a loss in community environmental stewardship. In particular, the spread of industrialized farms under the ownership of corporations or economic elites has the potential to foster the loss of traditional knowledge and the marginalization of women in developing countries.

Capital Concentration and Mobility

The question of a trade liberalization is closely related to the second emphasis in the globalization perspective: the phenomena of capital concentration and capital mobility. The two factors together are the source of the rise in influence of corporations. In the agricultural sector, accelerated capital mobility and global financial integration have fostered the geographic extension of production-consumption networks with increasingly complex, flexible, and geographically spread sourcing strategies of transnational corporations. They have furthered the concentration of market power in upstream sectors supplying agriculture with technical inputs, as well as in downstream sectors that process, distribute, and sell food. Capital concentration appears to have taken place in most sectors of the food industry, including both farming and non-farming sectors of the agrofood system, with the number of farm businesses steadily diminishing, while the share of total output produced by the largest farm businesses continually increases. Large, multinational corporations have come to dominate the farm sector, the food processing industry, exports, the retail industry, the fast food industry, and marketing and advertising. In particular, food and input traders, manufacturers, and sellers are growing in size in order to be able to compete in a global market. Likewise, food processors have become fewer in number and larger in size. These large companies have benefited from the globalization of capital via credit, finance, aid, and investment. Pursuing the globalization of production, they are looking for ways to decrease production costs and capture greater market shares. This will further strengthen the concentration of trade, which can already be witnessed. Approximately 60–90% of all wheat, maize, and rice, for instance, is now marketed by just six transnational companies. Moreover, even the relationships among the agriculture industry, wholesaling and retailing are increasingly monopolized and have a powerful influence on conditions of supply and demand. The mobility of this capital, the ability to move quickly from one country to another depending on highest returns offered, poses a particular potential threat to the economic and social sustainability in developing countries and can be used by multinational corporations (MNCs) as a bargaining tool with governments.

The consequences of processes of capital concentration in the food sector are multiple. Given the divergence in access to capital and resources between large agri-businesses and small farms, the latter have little opportunity to compete with these large and financially powerful actors. In addition, the dominance of multinational corporations in the food-processing industry leads demand for highly standardized inputs in order to allow the turning out of homogenous food products throughout the world—in particular, new products for affluent markets and the spread of processed food. Furthermore, capital concentration is blamed for declining farm employment, squeezed farm incomes, and increasing capital requirements of farm-based production, as well as the restructuring of economic sectors, labor forces, and nation states in the interest of global investors.

Other important consequences of capital concentration in the food sector apply to the power relationships between the different actors. It appears that the concentration has led to a displacement of production for use by production for the market. With increasing vertically and horizontally integrated production, processing, and distribution, large agro-food companies have gained control over a greater proportion of the food chain. Through the development of credit links and the provision of combined packages of technologies and specialist advisory, input suppliers have obtained more influence over farm businesses as well as over the direction of technological change, especially the promotion of biotechnologies. Here, the role of generic inputs for mass-marketable foodstuffs is particularly noticeable. As pointed out previously, changes in the financial power relations along the food chain also have given rise to changes in land ownership in the South, often with negative social implications.

Capital concentration also is associated with changes in sustainability characteristics of agricultural production. It has been linked to the increasing intensity of cultivation due to heavier uses of fertilizers, pesticides, and heavy machinery, and to a decrease in the organic content of food. MNCs tend to focus on the use of saleable private goods such as tractors, chemical fertilizers, and pesticides rather than less commodified factors such as integrated pest management. Likewise, they bias the economics of agriculture in favor of intensive man-made capital methods. Social and environmental externalities are less important. In the eyes of many observers, therefore, MNCs tend to foster trends inimical to agricultural sustainability.

Some scholars emphasize the need to differentiate between the extent and form of capital concentration in different sectors of the agro-food industry, however. They argue that independent, stand-alone production locations still exist and compete internationally, in contrast to the image of a global, intrafirm division of labor and globally integrated competitive strategies in other economic sectors. At the end of the 1980s, food manufacturers were still much less "globalized" than non-food manufacturers and maintained far weaker trade links with their affiliates.

Shifts in Political Capacity

One of the central foci in the globalization perspective is a shift in political power. Many scholars perceive the power of nation states to be declining vis-à-vis MNCs and International Governmental Organizations (IGOs). In the food industry, global private and public authorities have been gaining leverage over policy and institution building, thereby forcing policy adjustments by governments and threatening state sovereignty. Evaluations of these changes in political decision-making capacity range from the view that the decline of the state is a desirable consequence of international economic integration to the assertion that the rising power of corporations poses a general threat to political authority and legitimacy.

The rise in power of IGOs is associated with the shift towards more international and global forms of regulation. In the context of agriculture, the World Bank, International Monetary Fund (IMF), and WTO are the most relevant actors, although the Food and Agriculture Organization (FAO) and the United Nations Development Program (UNDP) play important roles as well. These international organizations have an increasing influence over the types and characteristics of food exports and imports, and consequently food production. The IMF and World Bank, for instance, have long advocated monocrop agriculture for export in developing countries, although they now may be modifying their position due to persistent criticism of such practices. In addition, structural adjustment programs, with their focus on the elimination of budget deficits and the dismantling of social welfarism, have forced an end to income protection and subsidies for the agricultural sector. In combination with the privatization of common institutions for marketing and distribution of agricultural produce, these attempts to foster international competitiveness often have led to a dramatic deterioration in the social circumstances of small farmers in developing countries. Likewise, GATT negotiations—in particular, the Agreement on Agriculture but also the Trade-Related Intellectual Property Rights (TRIPS) agreement, for instance—and the role of the WTO in reviewing trade policies and overseeing dispute resolution exemplify the strengthening of global regulatory mechanisms in the agricultural sector.

The second important beneficiary, if not cause, of changes in political decision-making capacity associated with globalization are MNCs. Public and private international law are becoming blurred as international economic actors increasingly dominate agenda setting, policy design, and implementation. In fact, some observers perceive a rapid privatization and marketization of all aspects of economic and social life and of the organizing and governing of the world economy. MNCs have gained in political power due to the need of states to compete for investment to create the right environment for ensuring profitability. Governments in developing countries, therefore, increasingly shy away from minimum wage requirements for agricultural labor, policies of small farm support, or the protection of land ownership by the local population. As the "providers" of employment and income, MNCs have entered into a pact with the state, which, in the eyes of observers, effectively confers social and political legitimacy on the enterprises. International law and negotiations are frequently influenced by MNCs as well. International law increasingly relies on nonbonding instruments created and implemented by non-state actors. Likewise, by providing multinational corporations with a prominent role in trade law negotiations and disputes, the GATT/WTO have increased the power of these corporations vis-à-vis nation states.

The changes in the roles of the state, in general, due to globalization are quite controversial among scholars. Some argue that the state is neither being led nor a leader nowadays, acknowledging that the decline of national agricultural markets as strategic economic space relative to the global economic space threatens one of the previous foundations of the nation state. Others, however, point out that the decline of the state is not a uniform development. Although the power of national governments may

have been reduced in some areas, it may have increased in others. Liberalization, in particular, often requires complex "reregulation" under a strong state. Unfortunately, the conditions for states retaining power in these areas are frequently not met in developing countries. If states do not have the financial, human, and political resources to create the solid regulatory framework for liberalization, globalization and the associated ascendancy to power of IGOs and MNCs may lead to a systematic dilution of national sovereignty.

The earlier role of the state in the promotion of agriculture and rural development should not be seen uncritically, of course. Former attempts to improve the situation of small farmers and the landless poor with government intervention frequently did not work. Subsidies led to high land values and capitalization into other fixed assets. This in turn fostered increased farm debt and lower farm incomes. At the same time, price and income supports had led to technological innovations and increased productivity, which in turn meant food surpluses and lower prices.

Finally, the shifts in political power associated with globalization concern the role of the public. Some scholars argue that the public as a critical observer and check on political and economic actors may be losing ground due to the increasing complexity and extension of the global economic and political systems. Others, however, highlight the growing role of civil society and Non-Governmental Organizations (NGOs) in monitoring economic and political developments with respect to agriculture and implementing agricultural programs. In general, evaluations of the potential role of the public depend on assumptions about the availability and transfer of information. For the individual, scholars see a decline in information availability. Based on the "distancing" argument, scholars point out that the spatial and structural separation of food production and consumption decisions leads to a decline in the individual's political, economic, and social decision-making capacity. At the same time, the *relatively* cheap opportunity for information access and diffusion via the Internet may provide individuals with new access to information and global markets. Continuing globalization dynamics may further change the role of the public. To some extent, recent developments appear to restore the initiative to local communities. In fact, current opposition to the global agro-food industry is both locally based and globally coordinated and informed. Thus, what is true with respect to globalization in general also applies to the shifts in political capacity induced by globalization: Globalization is an ongoing process, the final results of which are not yet recognizable.

Technological Innovation and Diffusion

A final but important impact of globalization on agriculture is via technology. Globalization is associated with an acceleration in the speed of technological innovation and diffusion. In principle, this may foster the development of more environmentally friendly technologies, but also that of environmentally problematic ones. In the agricultural sector, technological innovation in the form of biotechnologies predominates. Furthermore, agricultural production is influenced by technological developments in food processing, storage, and transport.

In general, globalization has been fostering the conversion and replacement of natural capital into and by man-made capital. Technological innovation in agriculture currently is focused on the fine-tuning of high-energy input systems for increasing the productivity of a selected few crop species. Innovation focuses on biotechnology to the neglect of knowledge contained in traditional farming methods. Large chemical and pharmaceutical companies control the direction of technological change. The introduction of biotechnology and technological change have transformed what used to be discrete elements of agricultural production processes into an industrial production chain. The industrial production of inputs and processing of farm produce have allowed the increasing appropriation of the value-added proportion of food production by agro-business. In addition, the globalization of agricultural production in combination with the development of new technologies of space and time compression has led to an enormous rise in transport, with food items now on average traveling 50% farther than they did at the end of the 1970s. At the same time, this transport is becoming ever faster, with fresh fruits and vegetables taking less and less time from the field to supermarket shelves.

The benefits of these technological developments accrue to rich farmers or corporations who can afford the costly inputs required and have access to global markets. Thus, the green biotechnology based revolution, and agri-business as its extension, is confined to small sections of the rural population in developing countries. As the majority of small farmers lack access to the necessary inputs, they face marginalization. The differentiated introduction of technological innovations and the changes in land ownership associated with it are causing wide disparities in access to resources and income. Furthermore, these developments lead to a displacement of crop varieties due to more similar global task structures. The encouragement of monocultural production, standardization of produce, and uniformity of agricultural production methods reduces diversity of genetic material. Thus, technological innovation in agriculture associated with globalization runs the risk of eliminating mixed or environmentally balanced types of agricultural systems.

As innovations in biotechnology and high-input agricultural systems are not available for large parts of the population of developing countries, there is renewed interest in traditional systems of agriculture at the local level. Complex agro-ecosystems use crop and associated biodiversity to strengthen the system's stability and resilience. They are based on an understanding of the combined use value of selected crop plants and livestock animals in agricultural production and exist in a great diversity and a various levels of input intensity. These traditional systems tend to be associated with higher levels of sustainability, ecological efficiency, and social justice.

Globalization also has an impact on agricultural research in general. Some scholars suggest that the globalization of agricultural research leads to a privatization of research in developed countries and a few developing countries. In such a scenario, poorer developing countries and their particular agricultural context would be on the losing end both in terms of knowledge creation and in knowledge acquisition. In contrast, explicit regional and local focused research is exactly what would benefit agriculture in developing countries most. Currently, research on agriculture in the context of globalization is coordinated at the Consultative Group for International Agricultural Research (CGIAR) by the International Service for National Agricultural Research (ISNAR).

The Future

As pointed out before, globalization is a process that is by no means complete. Thus, final results of the impact of globalization on agriculture in developing countries cannot be determined at this point. It is unclear, currently, to what extent counter-pressures against globalization and capital concentration in the agricultural and food sectors are likely to develop. Furthermore, substantial heterogeneity remains, for instance, in the characteristics of agriculture, such as farm production practices and production-consumption linkages. Different opinions also exist on fundamental questions of the sustainability of agricultural production in the context of globalization. Some scholars argue that "the limits to growth" have been reached or even passed. Others argue that we will only be able to feed the world if the industrialized countries increase their production as well. Another group of scholars postulates that modernist technologies and increased use of fertilizers and pesticides will help developing countries to sufficiently increase their production. The next group claims that sustainable agriculture is a (if not the only) viable alternative and has the potential to greatly increase productivity on existing lands. The fundamental questions that remain are whether we need new lands, new technologies, or new social solutions.

DORIS FUCHS

See also Agriculture: Impact of Privatization; International Bank for Reconstruction and Development (IBRD) (World Bank) Pollution, Agricultural; Sustainable Development; Technology: Impact on Development; Trade Policies and Development

References and Further Reading

Bonanno, Alessandro, Lawrence Busch, William Friedland, Lourdes Bouveia, and Enzo Mingione, eds. *From Columbus to ConAgra: The Globalization of Agriculture and Food.* Lawrence, KS: University Press of Kansas, 1994.

Dragun, Andrew and Clem Tisdell, eds. *Sustainable Agriculture and Environment: Globalization and the Impact of Trade Liberalization.* Cheltenham, England: Edward Elgar Publishing Ltd., 1999.

Goodman, David. "World-Scale Processes and Agro-Food Systems: Critique and Research Needs." *Review of International Political Economy* 4 (4) (1997).

Lutz, E., ed. *Agriculture and the Environment.* Washington, DC: World Bank, 1998.

Maitra, Priyatosh. "Globalization of Capitalism, Agriculture, and the Negation of Nation States." *International Journal of Social Economics* 24 (1/2/3) (1997).

Michelmann, Hans, James Rude, Jack Stabler, and Gary Storey, eds. *Globalization and Agricultural Trade Policy.* Boulder, CO: Lynne Rienner, 2001.

Solbrig, Otto, Robert Paarlberg, and Francesco Di Castri, eds. *Globalization and the Rural Environment.* Cambridge, MA: Harvard University Press, 2001.

Ward, Neil, and Reidar Almås. "Explaining Change in the International Agro-Food System." *Review of International Political Economy* 4 (4) (1997).

World Trade Organization. *Agreement on Agriculture* (Uruguay Round), Geneva: WTO, 1994.

AGRICULTURE: IMPACT OF PRIVATIZATION

The political and economic transition of communist countries in the 1990s and the similar processes in other developing countries have imposed agricultural privatization as part of the national economic policy. The main arguments for privatization consider it a reliable method for sustained economic growth, prosperity, political stability, and democracy. It is hoped that privatization will increase efficiency, profitability, outputs, and export revenues in agriculture, leading to food self-sufficiency and higher standards of living. Centrally planned economies could not solve the incentive problem for higher yields, due to missing or weak markets, constraining market forces, and lack of wage incentives.

According to the classical Marxist dogma, the industrial proletariat is the driving force of social change. Therefore, the development of agriculture was neglected for the sake of industrialization. At the beginning of the nationalisation/collectivisation of the agriculture, most farmers were peasants performing subsistence farming. They were considered dangerous for the totalitarian regimes, because of their relative independence from state production. As a consequence, after land reforms, their holdings were mainly nationalized, and agriculture was forced into large, state-run farms. Soviet-type large-scale farming was not efficiently run and also placed a heavy burden on the already depleted natural environment, leading to chronic food shortages. Some countries, including Hungary, made numerous and compelled attempts to restructure the agrarian sector, but without much success.

The most important goal of farm restructuring was the creation of efficient and competitive agriculture. Restoring private ownership for land was necessary to make agricultural investment profitable, enabling the sector to function on market principles. Smallholders were considered more profitable and competitive in terms of flexibility and market mobility. They require a lower level of capital investment, and labor costs are low (as it is almost entirely provided by the family who owns the farm). On the other hand, smallholders created by privatization may have lower productivity than do large agricultural enterprises.

The transition of state-directed economies into market economies proved to be a social and economic disaster in the short run for many of them. In Russia, the majority of the ex-Soviet states, and Romania, the privatization process was not transparent, enabling the sale of assets, including land and agricultural infrastructure, at prices well below market. Privatization was seldom carried out under fair competition. Agriculture was again especially hard hit due to early product price liberalization. Import liberalization put smallholders under further price pressures from established large producers. Their export opportunities were reduced drastically, heavily due to the collapse of the intersocialist markets. On the world markets, they faced stiff competition from heavily subsidized western producers.

The attempts of precise restoration and of equitable allocation resulted in *land fragmentation*. Families generally own several small parcels, scattered over a wide area, which inhibits efficient land use. Land reforms aimed at consolidating holdings often ended up in holdings below the minimum subsistence-level size, causing famine in some countries (Ethiopia). The communist land reforms after 1945 expropriated large land holdings, distributing them among landless rural laborers. But in the following decade, the peasantry was forced to establish collective farms, losing their individual ownership rights.

Among the positive effects of privatization, one can mention the lifting of the system of mandatory deliveries to the state reserves and the fact that producers could take entrepreneurial initiatives. The emerging agricultural credit system started to impose financial discipline, but the process was interrupted by the world economic crisis of 1998. Some farms are still relying on subsidies.

The privatization process of land, equipment, and built infrastructure, as well as the restructuring of collective and state farms, was carried out according to the unique sectoral policy mix of each transition country.

The main scheme of privatization was the reinstatement of property rights concerning farmland, most of the built infrastructure, livestock, and machinery—to their former owners or the allocation of such rights to cooperative and state farm members, as well to village residents. Former owners' property rights were restored on the former plot locations, or on equivalent ones. In other cases, the owners were offered ownership coupons or allocation shares in state companies.

The most widespread method of land restitution to the former owners was mainly used in the countries of Central and Eastern Europe and in the former Soviet republics of the Baltic region. Whereas Romania focused on the restoration of land to its former owners, Hungary offered land compensation tickets, too—marketable on the national stock exchange and convertible into other real estate or financial assets.

In Russia, this alternative was rejected due to political reasons and practical impossibility, as most ownership titles had been lost. Restitution was in-kind or in principle and almost free of charge. In-kind restitution was used in Romania, on the original location, if possible, targeting collective farmland. The restoration in Romania, Albania, and Hungary concerned all former owners irrespective of whether they lived in the village or were cooperative members at the time of restoration. In most cases, including Commonwealth of Independent States (CIS) countries, limited ownership rights were granted also to other categories such as rural intelligentsia, war veterans, or young farmer families. Most restoration was in-kind and free of charge, on the original location

or another of equal value. Some countries, such as Lithuania, were granting urban land parcels free of charge if restoration in-kind was impossible.

At the beginning, in the absence of reliable real estate records, the restoring of the plots was a painful and disputed process. The process was complicated also by the fact that at the beginning of forced collectivization, many farmers prosperous enough to be above the subsistence level but not wealthy enough to become large-scale landowners had donated, sold, or simply passed formally their property to poorer neighbors or relatives to avoid being stamped as *kulaks*, the derogatory term for a landlord. Because of this confusion, restoration was difficult due to conflicting claims for the same plot. Even if the identity of the owner(s) was established, the exact location of the land strips could not have been easily determined.

Another problem was that state farms had been established on the best lands. In these cases, ownership was restored in a painstaking manner, conferring at the beginning land-use rights only. In many countries of Central Europe, formal owners were not happy about becoming shareholders of privatized but still state-run farms, perceiving it as a limitation of their ownership rights.

A distinct problem was the successive waves of conflicting legislations that entitled persons without any prior holdings and put them in possession on plots that were later claimed by others. Restoration of common or community ownership, such as communal grazing plots and forests, proved to be even more difficult and led to the forming of managerial associations. In many cases, the majority of the forested areas and arable land are withheld from privatization. Most water resources also remain state property, especially in Russia.

Another privatization scheme was the distribution of compensation securities, or coupons, like those used in Hungary. The coupon's face value was based on the value of the farmland, building, or other asset. This coupon allowed the exchange of land or property into money.

One of the main consequences of the privatization was the dismantling of the *kolhozes* (cooperative farms). Former communist party members were reaping huge profits from the privatization of cooperative and state farms (*kolhozes* and *sovhozes*) by misappropriating, stealing, or buying their assets at undervalued prices. Looting also has accompanied the dissolution of these farms. Though livestock were distributed to the former members, many people had become city dwellers. Thus, cattle stocks plummeted, leading to meat and milk shortages later. Pig stocks also fell, triggering massive imports and subsequent protectionist measures. Huge retail price shocks have accompanied the process, fueling inflation despite a series of IMF-sponsored structural adjustment programs.

The new-old individual owners now had the rightful possession of land, although it sometimes took 10 years for property documents to be issued. The new peasants now had the land but not the proper tools, horsepower, and expertise that their ancestors once had.

The lack of capital, machinery, and technology also took a heavy toll on production outputs. All countries undergoing privatization experienced a serious fall in their gross domestic product during the 1990s, especially Georgia, with an average annual contraction of –16.3%, Moldavia (–14.1%), and Azerbaijan (–10.7%). Although the decrease of industrial production was much greater, compared with agricultural production decline (especially in Lithuania, Romania, and Moldavia), the majority of the countries had not reachieved their pre-reform level of agricultural production a decade later.

Privatization has led generally to the decline of the overall technological level. At least in the short run, tractors were replaced by oxen and carts; manpower was used intensively due to high unemployment and the low cost of labor, a process similar from Romania to Zimbabwe. In more sophisticated privatization schemes, *kolhoz* machinery and equipment was handed over to groups of farmers, under a property-share arrangement.

Due to the lack of funding, the small farms were performing high-cost, small-scale production. The lack of capital made more advanced techniques inaccessible. The use of pesticides and chemicals was virtually aborted, and this nonvoluntary "organic farming" had some positive effects on the environment, including cleaner groundwater and the return of wildlife. Since World War II, agriculture in developed nations has become increasingly intensive, using more capital and fertilizer. This system has spread to developing countries and resulted in producing more abundant, less expensive food—but often with ecological costs as well.

Privatization in the forestry sector led to increased demand on resources, as a source of income, leading to massive deforestation. The developed world has to take initiative with debt for nature swaps. Environmental organizations from developed countries buy portions of the debt much below face value and forgive it in return for environmental preservation efforts in the developing country.

Privatization made the new-old owners more concerned with current survival rather than sustainable development. Lack of alternative energy supplies in rural areas led to using timber as a fuel. Often, when ownership of forest areas was restored, barren

land awaited the owner, because the law didnot specify the state of the forest, only the possession of the land. However, in the cases when forest had survived, a second wave of lumbering has swept across. The deforestation process led to a 10%–30% decrease in the forested area in a decade in certain regions. Brazilian laws have limited lumbering, but enforcement is difficult due its high costs and poorly defined property rights.

Thirteen million hectares of forest are lost to agriculture each year in the developing world, encouraged by development policies like that of Brazil, which offered subsidies in the form of tax breaks for development of forested land for cattle ranching purposes. Other countries, such as Malaysia, encouraged the transformation of jungle areas into oil-palm and rubber tree plantations, in order to develop an export oriented competitive agriculture.

The relative abundance of natural resources and developing countries' dependency on them, has led to low domestic price levels, which discourage conservation. The transition of the developing countries from agrarian societies to industrialized societies results in increased urbanization and subsequently more pollution.

In some developing nations, 90% of the sewage is discharged without treatment. Part of the problem is that water is usually provided below cost, or is subsidized, whereas the costs of the necessary transport infrastructure are high. In Sri Lanka, taxation of the extra use for irrigation purposes was proposed, and governments are pressed by foreign aid donors to stop generous subsidizing for irrigation. Privatization didnot solve, rather made access to clean water more difficult and less affordable, also because water utilities enjoying their natural monopoly status cannot be forced into market competition as prescribed. On the other hand, especially in Africa's arid regions, a growing popular discontent opposes privatization, considering access to clean healthy water a basic human right rather than a commodity.

In some areas and product sectors, however, privatization has led to higher efficiency, but this is still not enough in Russia to have a positive food trade balance, except for sunflower seeds and wheat. The costs of increased productivity are soil degradation, followed by water and wind erosion in the most intensively cultivated southwestern region of European Russia. Soviet practices of using obsolete heavy machinery are causing soil compacting. The soil also is depleted of minerals due to overplanting and overgrazing, insufficient fertilizing. The opposite also happens when overmanuring or runoffs from livestock farms cause pollution. Pesticides such as DDT are still used in developing countries. From the seven thousand crop species available worldwide, 90% of the global food production comes from only thirty of them.

Assessing the overall impact of privatization on the environment is difficult, although sectoral impacts are clearly visible. One problem is that regulations often are lax, and low enforcement limits compliance with them. Lack of reliable information and weaker awareness of ecological problems are paralleled by lack of technology that is capital intensive. However, lack of property rights leads to overexploitation of resources, thus privatization eases this pressure.

In many cases, the free market prevailed after privatization. Most of the farmers were unable to produce for the market because of the small extent of their farm property or lack of any information, experience, or education in this respect. Such people remained at practicing subsistence farming only, which assured survival but no capital accumulation for investment and productivity increase. The more eager ones, mostly former *kolhoz* directors, took on sufficient land to have efficient production. The fluctuation of demand and offer caught the farmers in a countercyclical behavior with respect to market demand: when some products were scarce, everybody rushed to cultivate that crop, which led to a huge increase of the offer in the next few years, causing prices to plummet, and farmers were running in losses or into bankruptcy. The process was fostered by the decreasing purchasing power of the local population, aggravated by inadequate imports of agricultural products.

Many markets of the developed world remained closed, in spite of the trade liberalization. Many developing countries remain totally noncompetitive on world markets and also food dependent in certain respects.

On the positive side, privatization led to an increase of production in many crop sectors where production capacities could have been increased easily, whereas other sectors that needed larger, long-term investment such as horticulture and livestock breeding, experienced limited development. Therefore, there was an increased output from certain products, easy to grow on a large scale, whereas the more labor-intensive products were in shortage, causing huge price fluctuations. Inadequate government response to these market realities had aggravated the situation by imposing protectionism for the sake of a few bigger producers, leaving prices increasing manifold in the short run. State monopoly over fuel and energy prices also led to cost-pushed inflation hitting the consumers, whereas import arrangements and corrupt practices led to market dumping, which destroyed certain producer strata, causing shortage and price surge afterwards in the respective product markets.

Livestock investments are expected to be increasingly economically attractive, more if they are diversified and target not only meat and milk but also other outputs such as traction and manure. As state-owned cattle farms had disappeared, the high demand for milk products involved smallholders in milk production chains. These producers are mainly in remote areas and at the mercy of the milk processor who pays with undervalued prices, but smallholders cannot do anything because they rely almost solely on this regular income. The creation of smallholders associations for the organization of marketing, processing, and distribution is hampered by the lack of mutual trust, due to the experience of forced collectivization, the vanishing social capital, and the lack of both capital and adequate management.

Inadequate monetary policies of the governments lead to overvalued local currencies for the sake of stopping inflation. This, in turn, results in the loss of export potential, also due to the conversion of export earnings at unfavorable official exchange rates that can be equivalent of up to a 100–300% tax on livestock exports, thus this policy favourizes smuggling.

The second variant of privatization was the distribution of land between families, living in rural areas at the moment of the reform. This variant was employed in Albania, Armenia, Iran, China, and Vietnam.

During the 1990–1998 period, Albania's economic performance was especially good in agriculture; its sectoral share has risen to 63% of the gross domestic product, whereas its sectoral employment is the highest in Europe at 59%, which shows a clearly positive impact of privatization. Albania turned from nonexistent private ownership to more than 1.8 million new land properties. Land was firstly assigned free of charge for village residents of that time, whereas local intelligentsia was entitled to land-use rights only. Land was distributed proportionally, based on a per capita allotment, according to the available land in the village and the most recent local census. Privatization produced clearly a land fragmentation, with each family holding an average of four parcels, on average 0.3 hectares, and usually not in a contiguous plot. Some villages, especially in the north of the country, refused to obey the laws, opting instead to the restoration of property to its former owners or their heirs. On former cooperative lands, thus 353,718 families have control over 439,139 hectares, divided into 1.5 million parcels. Former owners are also entitled to compensation of up to fifteen hectares if restoration in-kind is impossible. "Self-help" compensation is also under way, especially in the coastal and tourist areas, where eligible individuals build vacation homes, hindering future tourism development and causing environmental hazard. Many Albanians invested their certificates of property/vouchers with their other savings in privatized former state enterprises that had promised a high rate of return but did not deliver. This had collapsed in 1996, followed by violent civil unrest, and since the state had no available cash to compensate the ex-owners and vouchers became worthless, the only available option was the acceptance of alternative land. Initially, the workers of the state farm enterprises were offered only use rights for the sake of preserving this finest land for foreign investment. This position was abandoned later because of fears of massive layoffs due to accompanying mechanization; thus, this category of persons has received full ownership rights in the end.

The forests are owned by the state, and use rights of between 0.4 and 1.0 hectares per family are given to the permanent residents of the village in order to fulfill their needs for wood and other forest products. Village land associations can hold larger areas of forests and pastures for common use, thus 240,000 hectares of state-owned pastures have been left for common use. These common use rights are not marketable. Similar co-ownership or communal ownership exists also in Romania regarding a lot of pasturelands and forests. The use of such shares can be sold, but nothing can be carved out from the common property.

This variant of privatization also was rejected in Russia, because it inevitably entailed the dismantling of collective and state farms and, subsequently, the destruction of the accompanying agricultural and social service infrastructure (workshops, garages, fuel stations, livestock premises, canteens, schools, medical centers, etc.) created during communism.

Agricultural land privatization, which began in Georgia in 1992, was/is severely limited in size, entitling domestic citizens initially to receive 0.75 hectares of land in ownership, increased to maximum of 1.25 hectares in the lowlands and up to 5 hectares in the highlands, resulting in more than 3 million parcels, and to more than 1 million owners. Although a significant part of agricultural land has been privatized, the majority of it is still owned by the state and is on lease, whereas most of the pastures are not privatized yet.

The third variant was granting land property shares to the peasants. Land was divided into unspecified, conditional landshares distributed for free to the members of collective and state farms. This variant was chosen in Russia, although there was no consensus in the society regarding the concept of agrarian reforms, some arguing for further, deeper impact privatization; others for the socialization of land under strict use control. Similar variants were employed in Moldavia and many ex-Soviet states. The final solution proved to be the free distribution of land and non-land asset shares among employees and pensioners of large-scale farms. It enabled anyone to exchange his land share for a land parcel or to rent its share to an agricultural enterprise, individual farmer, or household. A land plot belonging to lessors of one farm may remain in the joint share ownership of the entity, not subject to the division in kind. These shares are unspecified (conditional), given that a corresponding plot cannot be demarcated on the ground. They also are transferable and can be allotted in case the owner wants to leave the large-scale farm. The reform produced 40 million landowners, including private legal entities, owning 7.6% of the territory, which is still as large as one-third of the actual EU, but the modest results show that main producers are still non–market-oriented units and that the rural population is not capable to adjust to the challenges of the market economy.

The Russian program of land and property privatization was obviously based on the principle of social equity rather than economic efficiency. Thus, pensioners and workers of social infrastructure entities, located on the territories of agricultural enterprises, also received land and property shares, although they were apparently unable to cultivate the land. The size of a property share of each worker or pensioner depended on the length of his tenure and the amount of his salary.

The ideology of farm restructuring was based on the supposition that rural residents would use their rights, rushing to establish private individual farms by the millions and would quit collective and state farms immediately. But unfortunately, this has not happened; only 5% of workers embarked on private initiative, whereas the majority of rural population preferred to stay in the large-scale farms. Many of them (15.2%) preferred to transfer their land and property shares to the agricultural enterprises in order to form their social capital, but most (42.5%) have leased them to large farms.

But the process of privatization of agricultural land in Russia is still far from being complete and can be regarded as failed, as the main producers remain on the large-scale farms. However, with a falling contribution to gross output 30.4%, preserved by the inertia of farm workers wishing to keep their narrow-skill occupation, it was a failed attempt to create a civic society in the countryside. In 1993, experimenting with the introduction of a Western-type farmer creating the "Nizhny Novgorod" model did not give the expected results, because of the shortage of local peasant leaders who could take initiative. The reorganization of most collective and state farms into commercial societies was virtually nominal; people avoided participating in it due to the threat of getting passed shares of their enormous debt burden. Restructuring became imminent as former *kolkhozes* and *sovkhozes* were diminishing in size because of the withdrawal of individual farmers from large-scale farms with their plots, or due to their division. Large-scale private farms are being established, transforming former collective and state farms, but their corporate governance remains weak, causing poor economic performance.

In these managerial-controlled large farms, up to 30% of the marketed output is distributed to the workers, who are also members of the cooperatives, in the form of wages in kind, sales at reduced prices, and collective subsidized consumption. This is obviously advantageous because the bulk of products distributed in such a way are later marketed by households, saving marketing costs for the firm. By shifting these costs to the employees, the overall costs for the cooperative have, in fact, increased due to the low efficiency of such marketing activity. However, many farms also fail, their workforce decreasing drastically as well as their cultivated land area and output. The remaining employees would not be even willing to guard the farm building, as soon as all livestock is gone.

Family farms in Russia are represented by individual private farms and household farms. At the turn of the century, there were more than a quarter of a million individual private farms in Russia; the medium size of such a farm is fifty-one hectares, with three persons working on average. They concentrate on cash crops, offering better lease conditions for the pensioner shareholders and owning their machinery in 95%, but the late starters suffer from the lack of subsidies and cheap loans. Conflicting trends exist in such farm development: while new farms are established, some of the existing farms get liquidated, followed by the transfer of their lands to other farmers and collective enterprises, or the plots are simply returned to the state. A recent trend was a decrease in number from 280,000 to 270,000 and the subsequent increase of their land areas from forty-three to fifty-two hectares.

A part of the liquidated individual private farms is transformed into household farms for tax-avoidance purposes. Small households, although they possess on average five hectares, provide an increasing part of the general gross agricultural output, already exceeding 50%. This process was favored by the households' intent to run their own farms, as many had withdrawn their plots from large-scale farms. However, they often use allotted lands by the agricultural enterprises, as most of the small producers are also the

employees of the firms. They use forages produced by agricultural enterprises received as payment for labor or rent, for livestock breeding, living in a symbiosis with the large-scale farms. The economic instability and the growing unemployment make subsidiary food production attractive to the urban population as well. These households produce mainly for closed-circle consumption as in the Soviet times and supply food for family and relatives in urban areas. Due to the low share of marketed output, their income from this subsidiary production is not significant.

The fourth variant provided for the transfer of agricultural land in the ownership of legal entities (agricultural enterprises), rather than to individuals. This variant of privatization also was used in Moldavia, Ukraine, and other CIS countries except Armenia. The long-lasting debates on whether the land should be transferred free of charge or upon the payment of a fee ended in a compromise: a part of the land was transferred for free, while the rest was sold, mainly through auctions.

Moldavia similarly did not use restitution but distributed state property free of charge in exchange for privatization bonds. Among those entitled to equal, unspecified land shares were former employees, local teachers, medical staff, and professional soldiers. By the end of 2000, 96.53% of the total amount of agricultural land of this highly agricultural county became privately owned—77% by agricultural enterprises (*kolhozes*, *sovhozes*, and consumer unions) and 23% by farmers.

Since privatization began in 1996, in Azerbaijan 24.4% of the land was privatized, resulting in 3.3 million landowners, while the number of collective farms dropped from 2,005 to forty-one. The owners could be only home citizens as in all of the transition countries; their structure included present or former employees and other persons in a similar scheme as those used in Moldavia and Russia.

In Iran, following privatization, almost all of the land is owner-operated, but uncertainties concerning ownership and tenure matters make own-investment uncertain. The country's agricultural policy is based on self-sufficiency; the liberalization of the agricultural markets is not welcomed by either the producers or the consumers. During the first land reform between 1962 and 1972, Iran granted property rights to 1.8 million peasants, working previously in tenure and sharecropping systems on the rather feudal farms, often organized in community-based producer groupings (*bonehs*). Thus, smallholders became the dominant stratum in the agricultural society, 83% the farms having less than ten hectares. Capitalist-type farming units also have developed, but 2 million landless laborers without cultivation rights started to migrate to urban areas. To counteract this, in 1980 the Islamic revolution confiscated the wide latifundia and redistributed them to some 230,000 such farmer families. These farmers were allocated cultivation rather than genuine property rights on holdings varying between one and fifteen hectares. The Islamic principles of social justice, however, counteracted the excessive expropriation of the "*koulak*"-type holdings. The government embarked also on massive collectivization of around one hundred thousand peasant holdings, in order to promote economies of scale and efficient subsidizing channels, creating some thirteen thousand medium-sized cooperatives (*moshaas*), consisting of five to fifteen families each, with an area ranging from twenty to sixty hectares. These farms, however, do not function as their Soviet-type counterparts—in about 80% of them, an effective but informal division of land has actually taken place.

Although privatization in the 1990s in the former Soviet bloc was a widespread policy option, heavily agricultural African countries were reluctant to step into a privatization "roller coaster," fearing widespread famine and chaos. In the former Soviet Union and communist Europe, social justice principles prevailed that inhibited the reestablishment of the old great land possessions, at least for the time being, while in Latin America, privatization favored concentration of land ownership.

When assessing the impact of agricultural privatization on employment, we should bear in mind that most of the developing countries have embarked on forced industrialization, but this has sucked off most of the labor force from the agricultural sector of Central and Eastern Europe. The transition to market economies and subsequent privatization leads to lay-offs and unemployment, as state-owned companies tended to overstaff workers (especially in nontechnical areas), pay higher wages, and provide generous benefits. The effect of privatization on employment was very significant in the industrial sector; agriculture was less affected as the change in ownership structures preserved most of the original workforce of the cooperatives and state farms, attracting also many more redundant industrial laborers as they became landholders. In Russia, large-scale farm employment has shrunk by 45%, while the number of people involved in household production has doubled. Thus, a new type of agricultural employment has emerged: self-employed, individual farmers and their hired workers.

Thus, the impact of privatization was the opposite of the earlier communist nationalization, causing a reflux of workers from urban areas to rural areas, but at a much lower rate than the urban influx by

the starting of industrialization. Thus, privatization mostly increased the level of employment in agriculture, as former communist transition countries lost many industrial jobs, and the former town dwellers returned to their native villages and subsistence farming to compensate for low state pensions. In Kenya, privatization in the 1990s led to an unprecedented concentration of land, which became the most demanded commodity. Prices skyrocketed, and most of the poor were forced to migrate into the shanty-towns, in parallel with losing their (self) employment in the countryside. The establishment of state land allocation programs in Malaysia's jungle areas, by creating a network of young settler villages, has increased employment opportunities in the state-subsidized perennial crop farming. As the economy evolved and offered alternative employment in the services sector, this rural workforce declined, leading to the immigration of cheap foreign labor, whose availability presents no incentives for mechanization and capital-intensive development.

Privatization reduces overstaffing, making companies more efficient, profitable, and attractive by reducing the size of the labor force, replacing political and social objectives with profit maximization, resulting in massive layoffs worldwide. Between 1990 and 2003, up to 80% of the Romanian workforce was laid off in the industrial sector. Most of these workers sought refuge in self-subsistence agriculture, because the services sector could not absorb them fully. Thus, agricultural self-employment rose to 47–53% of the total workforce. Agricultural privatization throughout Central and Eastern Europe has made important shifts in the sectoral employment structure, leading to higher unemployment mainly among professionals as veterinary staff and engineers. Hiring such staff becomes affordable over a certain farm size and revenue only, while the average new holder was a small farmer only. Privatization also has led to some subsectoral shifts; for instance, from grain production to livestock breeding and vice versa to increased competition on the almost perfect domestic markets. However, most of the small producers cannot fight the great trading forces on the liberalized global markets.

LASZLO KOCSIS

See also Agriculture: Impact of Globalization; Capitalist Economic Model; Communist Economic Model; Free Market Economy; Private Property Rights; Privatization; Socialism; Socialist Economic Model; State-Directed Economy

References and Further Reading

Bromley, Daniel W. *Environment and Economy: Property Rights and Public Policy*. Oxford: Basil Blackwell, 1991.

Bromley, Daniel W. and Jean-Paul Chavas. 1989. "On Risk, Transactions, and Economic Development in the Semi-Arid Tropics." *Economic Development and Cultural Change* 37(4): 719–736, (July 1989).

Butler, Stephen. 1996. "Registration of rights to immovable property in the Republic of Reconstruction and Development." London.

Campbell, R. W., ed. *The Postcommunist Economic Transformation: Essays in Honor of Gregory Grossman.* Boulder, CO: Westview Press., 1994.

Csaki, C. (1997). Land Reform in East Central Europe and CIS in the 1990s. *European Review of Agricultural Economics.* 24/3–4.

Fischer, Stanley and Ratna Sahay. 2000. *The Transition Economies After Ten Years.* Washington, DC: International Monetary Fund, IMF Working Paper WP/00/30.

Hashi, Iraj and Lindita Xhillari. "Privatization and Transition in Albania." *Post-Communist Economies* 11 (1) (1999).

Kazlauskiene, Natalija and William H. Meyers. 1996. *Land Policy and Economic Development in Lithuania.* Center for Agricultural and Rural Development, Iowa State University, Ames, IA.

Lerman, Zvi, Csaba Csaki, and Victor Moroz. 1998. *Land Reform and Farm Restructuring in Moldova,* World Bank discussion paper no. 398, Washington, DC.

Nellis, John. 1999. *Time to Rethink Privatization in Transition Economies?* Washington, DC: International Finance Corp., Discussion Paper No. 38.

Prosterman, Roy, Leonard Rolfes, Jr., and Jennifer Duncan. *A Vision for Agricultural Land Reform in Russia,* RDI reports on foreign aid and development nr.100, Seattle, 1999.

Rose, Carol M. *Property and Persuasion: Essays on the History, Theory, and Rhetoric of Private Ownership.* Boulder, CO: Westview Press, 1994.

Serova, E.V. *Agricultural Policies, Markets, and Trade in Transition Economies/Monitoring and Evaluation, 1996.* Paris: OECD, 1996.

Spoor, Max. *Agrarian Transition in former Soviet Central Asia: A Comparative Study of Kazakhstan, Kyrgyzstan and Uzbekistan.* Working papers series, Institute of Social Studies, The Netherlands, No. 298, 1999.

Wegren, Stephen. *Agriculture and the State in Soviet and Post-Soviet Russia.* Pittsburgh: University of Pittsburgh Press, 1998.

AHIDJO, AHMADOU

Born in the Northern Cameroon city of Garoua on August, 24, 1924, Ahmadou Babatoura Ahidjo worked as a radio operator with the Post and Telegraph Services until embarking on a political career in 1946, when he was elected a delegate to the first Cameroon Representative Assembly (ARCAM). In May 1957, he was appointed minister of interior and vice prime minister in Cameroon's first pre-independence government, led by André-Marie Mbida. When Mbida was forced to resign as prime minister in February 1958, he was succeeded by Ahidjo. On October 1, 1961, Ahmadou Ahidjo became Cameroon's first president after reunification between the former French trust territory of Cameroon and the British Southern Cameroons. From the beginning of his administration, the new president faced the twin problem of severe domestic opposition from the radical *Union des Populations du Cameroun* (UPC) and how to maintain national unity and political stability, especially in light of Cameroon's dual colonial heritage. Although Ahidjo had effectively eradicated the UPC threat by the mid-1960s—thanks to French military and diplomatic support—he would spend the rest of his presidency, obsessed with maintaining national unity and political stability, with himself as the ultimate authority in the country. In order to attain both objectives, he pursued a three-pronged approach. First, through the use of an elaborate patronage system, he was able to co-opt many of his political enemies into his administration. Second, he pursued a course that would effectively eliminate all potential challenges to his authority. For instance, on September 1, 1966, Cameroon became a *de facto* one-party state with the creation of the Cameroon National Union (CNU) as the only party in the country. Ahidjo became head of state and chairman of the only party in the country. Later in 1972, in a well-orchestrated move by Ahidjo, the 1961 federal constitution that had created the union between the British Southern Cameroons, and the former French trusteeship in 1961 was abolished in favor of a unitary constitution. That political decision effectively killed the federation and eliminated any chances of secession by the minority English-speaking Cameroon. According to Jean-Francois Bayart, the 1972 unitary constitution was the logical crowning of the twin process of harmonizing the administration of the two federal states and the maximizing of presidential power. Finally, in order to maintain the system that he had created, Ahidjo instituted a vast network of security apparatus that created an atmosphere of constant fear and intimidation among Cameroonians.

Although Ahidjo's greatest legacy was his ability to maintain political stability in Cameroon during a period when many African states were plagued by civil wars and military coup d'états, he also is credited with the careful and prudent management of Cameroon's economy, which culminated in a low rate of inflation and an annual growth rate of 4%. In the area of foreign policy, Ahidjo pursued a policy that ensured peaceful coexistence with Cameroon's neighbors and was in accordance with the objectives of several international and regional organizations of which Cameroon was a member. On November 6, 1982, after more than two decades in office, Ahidjo voluntarily resigned from power and handed over the presidency to Paul Biya, his prime minister and constitutional successor. Shortly thereafter, a rift occurred between the former president and his successor. On July 19, 1983, Ahidjo went on a self-imposed exile to France. He eventually moved to Senegal, where he died on November 30, 1989.

JOSEPH TAKOUGANG

See also Central Africa: History and Economic Development

References and Further Reading

Johnson, R. Willard. *The Cameroon Federation*. Princeton, NJ: Princeton University Press, 1970.

Joseph, Richard, ed. *Gaullist Africa: Cameroon Under Ahmadou Ahidjo*. Enugu, Nigeria: Fourth Dimensions Publishers, 1978.

Kofele-Kale, Ndiva, ed. *An African Experiment in Nation Building: The Bilingual Cameroon Republic Since Reunification*. Boulder, CO: Westview Press, 1980.

LeVine, T. Victor. *The Cameroon Federal Republic*. Ithaca, NY, and London: Cornell University Press, 1971.

Rubin, Neville. *Cameroon: An African Federation*. London: Pall Mall Press, 1971.

ALBANIA

Albania is located in the southeastern region of Europe, known as the Balkan peninsula. A country of 28,748 square kilometers (11,100 square miles), it borders Greece to the southeast, Macedonia to the northeast, and Serbia and Montenegro to the north. To the west and southwest, it borders the Adriatic and Ionnian seas, respectively. Albania is predominantly a rugged mountainous country, except for a narrow strip of coastal lowlands. Its average altitude of 708 meters (2,323 feet) is twice the average altitude of Europe. The climate of the country is Mediterranean overall but varies considerably from one region to another. The western lowlands tend to have hot and dry summers and mild winters, while the northern regions, under the influence of alpine air currents, have greater amounts of rainfall and much colder winters.

Historically, Albania has been the poorest country in Europe over the past century. Prior to World War II, it was overwhelmingly rural (85%), with only a handful of rudimentary industries. The country's pronounced backwardness resulted mostly from five centuries of domination by the Ottoman Turks, plus a legacy of semi-feudal social and cultural conditions. At present, Albania's economy, like those of former East European communist countries, is experiencing a difficult transition. Albania's leaders, profiting from heavy infusions of monetary aid from the international community, are struggling to develop the economy to the point where Albania will no longer be classified as a "third world country."

A New Economic Policy

At the end of World War II, Albania came under the rule of a communist government, headed by Enver Hoxha. The economic policy of the new rulers was straightforward: To transform Albania from a backward agrarian society to an industrial-agrarian one. Industrialization became the end goal, while central planning and state management of the economy were to be the means to that end. The new policy was designed, among other things, to break the economic hold on the country of the former "ruling classes"—in effect, to destroy the landed estate proprietors, the clan chieftains, and the big merchants. The "class struggle" thus became a tangible and permanent component of the blueprint for development.

The government's program for modernization of Albania's economy and society, called for a thoroughgoing transition from private enterprise and a free market system to collectivism and a state-directed economy and social order. Accordingly, the new leadership proceeded to nationalize the wealth and resources of the country, including industry and commerce, natural and mineral resources. In a major step taken in 1945, a year after seizing power, the new regime carried out an extensive agrarian reform, which expropriated the estates of wealthy land owners and distributed them among the peasants. Subsequent steps to mechanize agriculture and make it more productive led finally to its complete collectivization in 1967. As a result, peasant farmers lost control and title to the lands that were given to them earlier. Agricultural holdings now became, in effect, the property of "the state." The peasants resisted in vain the government's program of collectivization.

Nonetheless, the agricultural economy in postwar Albania made progress in some respects. Land reclamation projects converted thousands of acres of malaria-infested swamps into arable land, and mechanization of agriculture led to higher productivity.

Drive for Industrialization

While proceeding with Agrarian Reform measures, socialist Albania took steps to develop the country's meager industry. Beginning in 1951, development was carried out in accordance with Five-Year Plans, a scheme adopted from the Soviet Union. In the course of several decades (1945–1990), Albania managed to change significantly the nature and scope of its industry. With the vast amounts of aid it received, first from the Soviet Union (1948–1960) and later from Communist China (1961–1978), Albania was able to build a fledging industry. Postwar Albania traded political loyalty to the communist giants in return for aid and credits with which to build a viable, self-sufficient economy. Utilizing these external sources of aid, the Stalinist regime of Albania built factories, housing, power plants, and a railroad network; expanded road and communication systems; and achieved a more balanced export–import trade.

Nevertheless, the country did not become economically self-sufficient, primarily on account of the rigidity of its centrally directed economic system. The Hoxha regime was plagued by a bloated bureaucracy, worker absenteeism, and numerous acts of sabotage by disaffected workers and other citizens.

Social and Cultural Initiatives

Despite these problems, the regime made headway in developing various aspects of Albanian society. The drive for the "emancipation of women" made Albanian women equal to men before the law, brought them out of the confines of their homes, and enabled them to participate in all areas of society.

In the realm of social services, the government provided free medical care to the population, as well as free education. Diseases that were widespread before the war, such as malaria, trachoma, and tuberculosis, were eradicated. Likewise, illiteracy, which before the war afflicted 80% of the population, was abolished, except among the older generation.

Socialist Albania succeeded also in transforming the cultural image of the nation. It founded the first university (University of Tirana) in the country and built a substantial network of cultural institutions, including libraries, an Academy of Sciences, museums, a film studio, an opera and ballet theater, and symphonic orchestras.

In sum, the regime laid the foundations of a modern state, but at the price of suppressing the political and human rights of the Albanian people. The endemic weaknesses of the regime led finally to its collapse in 1990.

In the 1990s, Albania moved haltingly toward development under a democratic form of government. A modest number of foreign entrepreneurs began to invest in the country's industry, communication facilities, and the service sector. The introduction of high-tech equipment and products signaled that Albania had entered the era of advanced technology. But the picture of the economy as a whole remained bleak, prompting tens of thousands of people to migrate. On the threshold of the twenty-first century, Albania continued to struggle, as it sought to adapt the free market system to its particular conditions.

PETER R. PRIFTI

See also Balkan Wars of the 1990s; Central and Eastern Europe: History and Economic Development; Central and Eastern Europe: International Relations; Industrialization; Socialism; Socialist Economic Model

References and Further Reading

Biberaj, Elez. *Albania: A Socialist Maverick*, Boulder, CO, San Francisco, and Oxford: Westview Press, 1990.
Jacques, Edwin E. *The Albanians: An Ethnic History from Prehistoric Times to the Present*. Jefferson, NC: McFarland & Co., 1994.
Pano, Nicholas C. *The People's Republic of Albania*. Baltimore, MD: John Hopkins Press, 1968.
Prifti, Peter R. *Socialist Albania Since 1944: Domestic and Foreign Developments*. Cambridge: Massachusetts Institute of Technology Press, 1978.
Skendi, Stavro. *The Albanian National Awakening: 1878–1912*, Princeton, NJ: Princeton University Press, 1967.
Vickers, Miranda, and James Pettifer. *From Anarchy to a Balkan Identity*. London: Hurst and Co., 1997.

ALGERIA

The Democratic and Popular Republic of Algeria is the second largest country in Africa (919,600 square miles), but 90% of its land is barren desert. Most Algerians live in the well-watered northern coastal plains and foothills (the "Tell") where a Mediterranean climate with mild winters prevails. This region includes productive orchards and vineyards, but its cities are subject to violent earthquakes. Two ranges of the Atlas Mountains and an intermountain plateau separate the Tell from the Saharan south, where vast dune fields are broken by mountain massifs. Except for a few oasis towns, the south is populated only by desert nomads. There are rich oil and natural gas fields here, however.

The Algerian population stood at 32.3 million in 2004. The rate of natural increase is low for a Muslim country, reflecting some success for the government's family planning program. An estimated 99% of Algerians are Sunni Muslim, but in the villages, an undercurrent of pre-Islamic mysticism endures. Arabic, the national language, is understood everywhere, but Berber speakers of the Kabylie region struggle for linguistic equality.

Algeria's indigenous Berber tribes absorbed cultural influences from a long list of invaders including Phoenicians, Romans, Vandals, and Byzantine emperors. A more sweeping transformation was brought by Arab invaders who implanted their language and religion. The Berbers became partially Arabized and created their own brilliant dynasties. In the 16th century, when Spain focused its superior maritime power on the North African coast, local Muslims appealed to the Turkish sultan for protection, and Algeria became a self-governing outpost of the Ottoman Empire.

Piracy along the Barbary coast was a constant irritation to western powers. France landed thirty-seven thousand troops in June 1830. French land confiscations sparked resistance—a *jihad* led by Abd al-Qadir was suppressed by 1847, but insurgency in the Kabylie Mountains continued into the 1870s. Algeria was opened to European settlers who were invited to occupy the best farmland, including 1.5 million acres in Kabylia. In time, the settlers came to dominate politics in Algiers.

Some Muslims learned French and worked within the new system, but they could not become French citizens unless they renounced Islamic law. This and other humiliations fed a growing discontent, yet twenty-five thousand Muslims died defending France in World War I. A cautious nationalist movement made little headway between the wars, but British and American troops, who landed in Algeria in 1942, brought with them new opportunities.

Communal violence erupted in Algeria in May 1945. About one hundred Europeans were killed, and perhaps twenty times as many Muslims. Nationalist guerrillas led by Ahmed Ben Bella launched their revolution in November 1954 under the name of the Front de Libération Nationale (FLN). The Algerian war for independence (1954–1962) was extraordinarily brutal. A French army of five hundred thousand men fought the FLN's Armée de Libération Nationale (ALN) in the countryside. Many villages were destroyed under the doctrine of collective punishment, generating a flood of refugees into the cities. Among them were terrorists who knew how to provoke the French into indiscriminate retaliation, which generated more recruits for the revolutionaries.

The European settler community, over a million strong, feared a "sellout" by French President Charles de Gaulle and formed the Organisation Armée Secrète (OAS),which answered terror with terror. De Gaulle concluded that the old order could not be reinstated and negotiated the best settlement he could: the Evian Accords of March 1962 provided independence for Algeria, protection for French settlers, and continued operation of French oil and

natural gas concessions in the Sahara. Approximately seventeen thousand French troops had lost their lives in the war. Estimates of the Algerian death toll range from 150,000 to one million. Almost all remaining French citizens soon left Algeria.

Ahmed Ben Bella was elected the first premier of independent Algeria in September 1962. Ben Bella's vocal support for movements of national liberation everywhere created distrust among the conservative powers, while his pursuit of socialism in Algeria angered elements in his own army who believed socialism to be un-Islamic. Soviet economic advisors recommended that Algeria concentrate on developing heavy industry. However, the results were disappointing, and unemployment grew.

Algeria was founded as a one-party state in which the FLN dominated the executive, legislative, and judicial branches, but suspicion of Ben Bella simmered within the army. On June 19, 1965, Col. Houari Boumédienne overthrew Ben Bella and kept him under house arrest for the next fifteen years. Boumédienne nationalized the French oil industry and reformed landholding patterns. Boumédienne died in office in 1978 and was replaced by Col. Chadli Benjedid, who pardoned Ben Bella. During the 1980s, Algeria's underperforming domestic economy was supplemented by foreign exchange earned by natural gas exports through a new trans-Mediterranean pipeline. As the Soviet Union and China modified their socialist economies, Algeria did so, too.

In 1989, Algeria held multiparty elections for the first time. A new party, the Islamic Salvation Front (Front Islamique du Salut, or FIS), swept local elections in 1990 and legislative elections in 1991. The Algerian army declared a state of siege, canceled elections, and replaced President Benjedid with Mohammed Boudiaf. FIS supporters formed an Islamic Salvation Army (Armée Islamique du Salut, or AIS) and launched a war of merciless nighttime violence. The government jailed more than fifty thousand FIS supporters. Often it was unclear whether the AIS or the army were responsible for cutting the throats of the entire populations of rural villages. An even more radical band, the Group Islamique Armée (GIA), was composed of former Algerian *mujahideen* who had fought in Afghanistan.

In 1999, Abdelaziz Bouteflika was elected president by the usual overwhelming margin. Bouteflika pursued a policy of "Civil Concord" under which FIS fighters lay down their arms in return for amnesty. The GIA fought on, as did the Salafist Group for Call and Combat, which is thought to cooperate with al-Qaeda, but both groups are marginalized.

President Bouteflika was elected to a second term in April 2004 with 85% of the vote. Certain basic political questions remain unanswered, including the balance between civilian and military control and the question of what concessions to make to Berber sub-nationalism. Algeria benefits from high prices for oil and natural gas, which account for more than 90% of Algeria's export earnings, but the agricultural sector lags behind and there is a desperate housing shortage in Algerian cities. Environmental challenges include deforestation, soil erosion, and water pollution from petroleum refining.

In its foreign policy, Algeria pursues a long-running dispute with Morocco over the status of the former Spanish Sahara, but it gives first priority to cooperating with the West in the war against Islamic extremists, who would like someday to overthrow the secular government in Algiers.

Ross Marlay and Lesley J. Pruitt

See also Ben Bella, Ahmed; North Africa: History and Economic Development; North Africa: International Relations

References and Further Reading

Horne, Alistair. *A Savage War of Peace: Algeria, 1954–1962.* London: Macmillan, 1977.
Ruedy, John. *Modern Algeria: The Origins and Development of a Nation.* Bloomington, IN: Indiana University Press, 1992.
Stone, Martin. *The Agony of Algeria.* New York: Columbia University Press, 1997.
Stora, Benjamin. *Algeria, 1830–2000: A Short History.* Ithaca, NY: Cornell University Press, 2001.

ALL-AFRICAN PEOPLE'S CONFERENCE (AAPC)

On December 5–13, 1958, representatives of nationalist movements in twenty-eight African territories met in Accra, Ghana, at the call of Kwame Nkrumah. The All-African People's Conference (AAPC) celebrated past achievements and anticipated future success in wrenching control of Africa from the hands of European imperialists. The urge that sustained the Pan-African movement in the mid-twentieth century had begun with resistance to European conquests in the eighteenth and nineteenth centuries. It evolved from an international struggle led by African Diaspora leaders Marcus Garvey and W. E. B. DuBois in the late nineteenth century. A 1915 rebellion in Nyasaland, led by John Chilembwe, indicated Africa aspirations.

Those attending the AAPC came from Ghana, Liberia, Egypt, Tunisia, Libya, Sudan, Morocco, and Ethiopia. Conveners omitted South Africa, and no other representatives of Southern African colonies

attended. Nkrumah saw only African-ruled nations as independent, but some nationalist leaders in colonial territories were present. The AAPC viewed Africa as a whole, without a Saharan division. Immediately after the meeting, many British, French, and Belgian colonies began to gain independence. Was this due to African leaders, such as the Congo's Patrice Lamumba, meeting to discuss strategy? By 1960, when the AAPC met in Addis Ababa, there were five new members: Algeria, Cameroon, Guinea, Nigeria, and Somalia. Togo and Congo (Leopoldville) were invited but did not come. The AAPC met again in Tunis (1960) and Cairo (1961). After that, the Pan-African idea began to dissipate as new African nations found it difficult to form federations and disagreed with Nkrumah and Senegal's Sékou Touré on whether to become independent of the West and associate as neutrals with communist states. They also disagreed on social reform and centralized economic planning.

In the 1890s, African political associations had begun to form. In 1918, a West African National Congress convened. In the 1930s, French Africans formed political associations, but not until 1947 did four communes in Senegal acquire French citizenship. Nationalist leaders in French colonies included Leopold Senghor and Fodebo Keita. J. B. Danquah led nationalists in the British Gold Coast colony for which he chose the name Ghana. African intellectuals had contact with European and American universities that turned their thinking toward socialism in post-World War I years. An American Negro self-consciousness ideology was growing in the National Association for the Advancement of Colored People, led by W. E. B. DuBois, who called a series of Pan-African conferences. A Manchester Conference in 1945 that included George Padmore, Kwame Nkrumah, and Jomo Kenyatta, began to forge new concepts of the African personality. After World War II, a new day dawned in Africa. The emphasis on freedom in the Atlantic Charter, United Nations, and independence struggles in Asia brought hope to African nationalists. In the late 1940s, Asian nations gained independence from Japanese and then European control. India, Pakistan, Burma, Indonesia, and Indo-China showed Africans how to remove the British, Dutch, and French and form alliances with American or communist nations to support their economic and political aspirations.

The first African move toward independence occurred in the British Gold Coast colony. Africans had fought with British forces in World War II and were profiting from increased trade for tropical goods. But when they failed to produce a better life by 1948, they boycotted European goods and rioted in major towns. In 1947, Danquah and fellow nationalists had come home from England with a radical nationalist, Kwame Nkrumah, and a British commission reported African frustration and proposed a new constitution to replace one they had negotiated in 1946, when Britain granted Africans a majority in the legislative council. The commission recommended rapid moves toward "responsible government." In 1949, the governor appointed an all-African committee to devise a new constitution. Nkrumah would accept nothing less than "self-government now" and was jailed for sedition. Nonetheless, his Convention People's Party overwhelmingly won the first election under the 1951 constitution. Governor Sir Charles Arden-Clarke released him from jail, and his party took major posts in the new government. In 1957, Ghana became the first African state and Britain's first African colony to gain independence. Other West African colonies followed: Nigeria (1960), Sierra Leone (1961), and Gambia (1965).

In French West Africa, under a 1958 initiative by the new Charles DeGaulle regime, all colonies except Senegal voted for autonomy as republics within a "French Community" that would deal with foreign policy, defense, and several other matters. Guinea, under Sékou Touré's Bloc Populaire Senegalais, voted for complete independence and joined in a federation with Mali in 1959. That year, Senegal, Mali, and French Sudan requested independence *within* the French community. In 1960, French colonies in West and Equatorial Africa (Ivory Coast, Niger, Dahomey, and Haute Volta), in spite of their small size and dependency on France, became independent *outside* the French Community. France withdrew administrators from Guinea, as well as economic assistance. The communist bloc in Eastern Europe and Asia became French Africa's new philanthropist.

At the AAPC in 1958, Nkrumah's goal was to form a Pan-African union in the form of a permanent organization to assist nationalists in all colonized territories. Britain and France moved in this direction, but British colonies of Southern Rhodesia and South Africa were ruled by white settler minority regimes. Julius Nyerere led Tanganyika; Britain's first East African colony to gain independence (1961) through interracial cooperation was a new model for a negotiated settlement. Uganda (1962) and Kenya (1963) followed, with hope to form a three-nation federation that might include Malawi and Zambia. But like West Africa, desire to federate went unfulfilled, apart from Zanzibar joining Tanganyika to form Tanzania after the overthrow of the sultan. But independence of Britain's East African colonies provided a base from which Southern African guerilla armies of Robert Mugabe's and Joshua Nkomo's Patriotic Front in Rhodesia could operate in the 1970s, and Nelson Mandela's South African National Party could use in the 1980s to win majority rule in 1994.

Much of this success was due to ties formed between African leaders at the AAPC in 1958. But Nkrumah's yearning for an African federation failed. But not all was lost. Mugabe had spent time in Nkrumah's Ghana as a teacher and had married a Ghanian political activist. Zimbabwe and South Africa independence fighters depended on African nations in the United Nations, on East Africa's frontline nations, and on black civil rights allies in the United States. They also appealed to North and South American and to European sympathizers, the World Council of Churches, and Eastern European communist nations to support their cause. The All-African People's Conference was not so important for decisions it made as for the fact that it brought African leaders together to discuss their dreams of how they would accomplish them.

NORMAN H. MURDOCH

See also Nkrumah, Kwame; Touré, Sékou

References and Further Reading

John Hatch. *A History of Postwar Africa*, 2d ed. New York: Praeger, 1965.
Roland Oliver and J. D. Fage. *A Short History of Africa*. Hammondsworth, England: Penguin, 1966.
Rubin, Leslie and Brian Weinstein. *Introduction to African Politics: A Continental Approach*. New York: Praeger, 1974.
Sanford J. Unger. *Africa: The People and Politics of an Emerging Continent*, 3d ed. New York: Simon & Schuster, 1989.

ALLENDE GOSSENS, SALVADOR

Born June 26, 1908. Before entering a political career, Allende was trained as a medical doctor. He entered the Escuela de Medicina de la Universidad de Chile in 1926, became a leader among the Student Federation, or *Federacion Estudiantes de Chile* (FECH), and experienced first-hand the repression of the Ibañez del Campo dictatorship (1929–1931). Together with Eugenio Matte, Oscar Schnake, and the enigmatic Col. Marmaduke Grove (leader of the thirteen-day Socialist Republic of June 1932), Allende went on to organize a new political party that became one of Chile's most influential and powerful—the Socialist Party of Chile.

Running for the Socialist Party, Allende was elected Representative and entered Congress for the first time in 1937 at the age of twenty-nine. Active as campaign director in what was then the province of Valparaíso, Allende solidified his reputation as a talented and skillful politician, and it is generally considered that his campaign efforts on behalf of the Popular Front—a coalition of the Socialist, Communist, Democratic, and Radical parties, plus the new Confederation of Chilean workers—were crucial in getting Pedro Aguirre Cerda (Radical Party) elected president in 1938. This was a landmark election because it marked the beginning of the Left's ability to participate in, as well as successfully compete in, the political struggle for power. Allende was rewarded the Ministry of Health in the Aguirre Cerda government.

In 1945, Allende was elected senator. During this tenure, Allende became vice president of the Senate, a position he held until 1950. In 1953, Allende was re-elected, representing Antofagasta, a northern province with a strong working-class electorate. In 1969, Allende began his fourth and final term. As senator, Allende authored, or co-authored, a number of laws that led to the creation of important institutions, as well as major welfare benefits, including the Medical College, Family and Pregnancy Assistance, and social security benefits for workers, peasants, widows, and orphans.

In part as result of the Socialist Party's decision to support the 1952 presidential candidate Ibañez del Campo, Allende and others left the party in protest and created the Frente del Pueblo. That year, Allende became the party's presidential candidate. This was the first time Allende ran for president, and he repeated his bid in all subsequent presidential elections (1958 and 1964) until finally, in 1970, he won, representing a united Socialist Party and the Popular Unity coalition, the latter composed primarily of the Socialist and Communist Party. In 1957, Allende was nominated presidential candidate for a second time, supported by the newly created Popular Action Front (FRAP). He lost to Conservative and Liberal Party candidate Jorge Alessandri, son of Arturo Alessandri (president from 1920 to 1924). The candidate of the newly formed Christian Democratic Party was Eduardo Frei. Alessandri's victory was narrow, obtaining only 31.6%, compared with Allende's 28.9% and Frei's 20.7%. In 1964, Allende lost a third time, though he was able to increase his vote to 39%. The Christian Democrat Frei won the election with an absolute majority (56%). The 1970 election was one of the closest ever, and Allende barely won, receiving 36.3%, against Alessandri's 34.9% and the Christian Democrat's candidate Tomic, who received 27.8%. The narrow victory necessitated Congressional confirmation. Allende's (and the Popular Unity's) inability to obtain a solid majority, best exemplified by the strong Center and Right majority opposition in Congress, made it impossible from the beginning to install Socialism via democratic means and continued to be a major stumbling bloc for Allende's "Chilean Road to Socialism."

Allende's dreams of a Socialist Chile were already present in the 1952 presidential race, in which he proposed an agrarian reform, as well as the nationalization of Chile's copper. It is an irony of history that it was not the Socialist Allende but the Christian Democrat Frei who not only started an agrarian reform but also began to give the Chilean state part ownership in the copper companies. This approach to nationalization became known as the "Chileanization." The Left, and particularly Allende and his Socialist Party, were opposed to Frei's "Revolution in Liberty."

Once in power, Allende and the Popular Unity were determined to bring socialism to Chile quickly. Most importantly, copper companies were nationalized, with unanimous Congressional support. In addition, coal and steel companies and many banks were nationalized. Frei's land reform was expanded, and Allende promised land to more peasants. The Allende government froze prices and raised wages. By 1972, it became increasingly obvious that the government's economic policies had run into a crisis. Inflation reached 150%, low copper prices depressed export earnings, foreign exchange reserves ran out by early 1973, and United States-led efforts to block Chile from obtaining international credit added to the economic crisis.

Opposition to the Allende government was fierce, coming from both opposition parties as well as important social sectors such as domestic entrepreneurs whose companies were expropriated. Led by the Christian Democratic Party, Congress often attempted to impeach cabinet ministers or moved to declare Allende's attempts at further socializing the economy unconstitutional. Allende also faced opposition from within the Popular Unity coalition. Particularly the more radical wing of the Socialist Party (for example, Altamirano) or extreme left-wing groups such as the Movement of the Revolutionary Left, of *Movimiento de Itqueierda Revolucionario* (MIR) increasingly pushed Allende to move more quickly towards Socialism. The Communist Party often supported Allende's moderate position, favoring the more difficult Congressional road. Therefore, internal divisions over the pace and scope of Socialism proved to be just as harmful to Allende's Popular Unity government as unyielding congressional opposition. Moreover, workers and unions of the recently nationalized State Ownership Area (APS) were increasingly difficult to control (for example, illegal strikes), and illegal seizures of private property by peasants and workers put Allende on the defensive. The truck owners' strikes in October 1972 and July 1973, and copper workers' strike in April of the same year contributed to the ongoing economic and political crisis. The March 1973 congressional elections added to the confusion, as neither Allende's

Popular Unity nor the opposition landed any clear victory. The Left vote increased slightly—enough to prevent the opposition from obtaining the two-thirds majority required for presidential impeachment, but not enough to give the government a majority in Congress. Through all this, Allende attempted to keep control and maintain governability. He changed his cabinet fifty-six times, and toward the end he brought in military officers. His attempt at amending the Constitution was blocked by Congress in 1972, and the military coup of September 11, 1973, came just days before his call for a national plebiscite over the future course of the country.

Although opinions over Allende's legacy remain deeply divided, the fact remains that his was the first democratically elected Socialist government anywhere in the world. It is not clear whether he committed suicide or whether he was killed by Pinochet's soldiers, who attacked the presidential palace La Moneda on September 11, 1973.

VOLKER FRANK

See also Chile; Pinochet Ugarte, Augusto; Southern Cone (Latin America): History and Economic Development

References and Further Reading

Boorstein, Edward. *Allende's Chile: An Inside View*. International Publishers, New York, 1977.

Falcoff, Mark. *Modern Chile, 1970–1989, A Critical History*. New Brunswick, NJ: Transaction Publishers, 1989.

Francis, Michael J. *The Allende Victory: An Analysis of the 1970 Chilean Presidential Election*. Tucson, AZ: University of Arizona Press, 1973.

Kaufman, Edy. *Crisis in Allende's Chile: New Perspectives*. New York: Praeger, 1988.

Nunn, Frederick M. *The Military in Chilean History: Essays on Civil-Military Relations, 1810–1973*. Albuquerque, NM: University of New Mexico Press, 1976.

O'Brien, Philip, ed. *Allende's Chile*. New York: Praeger, 1976.

Sigmund, Paul E. *The Overthrow of Allende and the Politics of Chile, 1964–1976*. Pittsburgh: University of Pittsburgh Press, 1977.

Stallings, Barbara. *Class Conflict and Economic Development in Chile, 1958–1973*. Stanford, CA: Stanford University Press, 1978.

ALLIANCE FOR PROGRESS

Historical Context

Following World War II, the United States offered many European governments aid to rebuild their economies and to modernize their industrial sectors. This program, known as the Marshall Plan, helped states to ease the social and economic dislocations of the war's devastation and sweeping post-war change. Washington reasoned that ensuring minimum standards of living would keep domestic Communist parties out of government in Europe and ensure that pro-US regimes held on to power. Many Latin American leaders protested that they too deserved such attention from the United States, given their many military and economic contributions to the Allied war effort. However, Europe and Asia monopolized US attentions because of the incipient communist threat that Washington saw there. The Western hemisphere's seeming political stability gave it lower priority than regions that the United States considered threatened by communism (although the United States did open the School of the Americas in Panama, in 1946, to train Latin American military and civilian officers).

Compounding Latin Americans' unhappiness with a lack of economic support, when the United States did act, many saw its tactics as unwarranted interference in the affairs of sovereign states. As well, Latin Americans frequently characterized the United States as indifferent to their interests and solely focused on US political and business concerns. For example, following land appropriations in Guatemala that affected holdings of the US-based United Fruit Company, through the Central Intelligence Agency, Washington encouraged the 1954 ouster of President Jácobo Árbenz Guzmán, that state's democratically elected leader. One demonstration of deteriorating hemispheric relations came in 1958, when an angry mob in Caracas, Venezuela, attacked the car in which Vice President Richard M. Nixon traveled during a goodwill tour of Latin America. Violent anti-US demonstrations in Venezuela, Panama, and elsewhere showed increasing ill will toward the "colossus from the North." Thus, the issue of "what to do about Latin America" became a campaign issue in the 1960 presidential contest between Nixon and his challenger, John F. Kennedy.

Upsetting Washington's assumption that strongman regimes in Latin America would keep it free from communism, in 1959, Fidel Castro and his followers overthrew the dictatorship of Sergeant Fulgencio Batista y Zaldívar in Cuba. After a brief period of support for the new regime, relations between the United States and Castro's government soured. Weeks before President Kennedy took office, the United States broke off diplomatic relations. These events, together with growing violence associated with efforts to return exiled leftist leader Juan Domingo Perón of Argentina to power, forced Washington to turn its attention and resources to the Western hemisphere.

With the Alliance for Progress Kennedy offered a fresh vision, with positive incentives for Latin American states to grow while allocating the benefits widely, through improved literacy, health, education, and productivity, as well as broad redistribution of agricultural holdings. Walt Rostow, head of the State Department's Policy Planning Staff, and other modernization theorists greatly influenced the new president's thinking. Rostow promoted fighting the Cold War by encouraging state-directed economic progress in "underdeveloped" states. Modernization theorists, who dominated the development debate, advanced the notion that building the proper toolkit—certain values and institutional structures—"fixed" states and allowed them to develop. Thus, Kennedy offered help for states to advance and to develop the "correct tools" to encourage progress and to prevent communism from gaining a foothold. He offered a peaceful revolution of economic, social, and political development as an antidote to Castro-style revolution.

The President noted in his introduction of the 1961 Foreign Assistance Act, which restructured the country's foreign aid administration, that current programs were not suited to meeting the needs of the United States or the recipient states. Kennedy underlined the serious—"disastrous"—consequences that economic collapse of affected states would have for US security, and remarked that industrialized states now had a significant opportunity to help less developed states. His Alliance for Progress proposal also served to counterbalance the debacle of the invasion of Cuba at the Bay of Pigs, which, given US planning and funding, severely strained relations in the hemisphere. By making such a visible offer of help to Latin America, Kennedy hoped to reestablish good relations between the United States and its neighbors, while the program also built a middle class sector strong enough to thwart any revolutionary movement.

In August 1961, the Organization of American States' (OAS) Inter-American Economic and Social Council met in Punta del Este (Uruguay). The group drafted a charter for the Alliance for Progress (*Alianza para el Progreso*). The result, the Charter of Punta del Este, brought together President Kennedy's ideas with those articulated by Brazilian President Juscelino Kubitschek in his "Operation Pan America." It sought a plan to bring faster and more evenly distributed economic growth to the states of the Western Hemisphere.

The Program

The United States, together with nineteen Latin American states, signed the original treaty, which made a ten-year commitment. In 1965, they agreed to indefinite extension. By its signature, the United States promised aid and loan guarantees to help to generate additional investment capital for Latin American projects. Other signatory states promised to make reforms, particularly to their tax codes and land-holding regulations, in exchange for an infusion of new funding.

Among the challenges Kennedy sought to meet through the Alliance were moving Latin American states to long-term economic planning and more balanced economic production. Further, through the program, he hoped to encourage greater economic integration in Latin America and to find a solution to the price swings that plagued the commodity markets, especially that of coffee, one of the region's largest exports. Fiscal goals included price stability and prevention of sharp exchange rate fluctuations, to remove the uncertainty that discouraged exports and reduced foreign investment in Latin America.

Quoting the Charter, these factors should translate into "substantial and sustained growth of per capita income" of no less than 2.5 % per year. This, together with "a more equitable distribution of national income" and "comprehensive agrarian reform" to enact an "equitable system of land tenure," would allow states to increase education to allow "as a minimum, access to six years of primary education" for all children. Further, it would allow states to increase availability of low cost housing, and to deliver more services in urban, as well as rural, areas. All of these improvements, then, could help the achievement of another goal: "[t]o increase life expectancy at birth by a minimum of five years." At the urging of public and private officials in the United States, the US administering agency, in 1965, also named population control a "priority area."

Kennedy promised scientific and technical cooperation, emergency food aid, and to help to "rationalize" and reduce military spending by Latin American states (which he considered wasteful, as their forces could not stop any Soviet military challenge.) He also sought greater cultural cooperation; this was the Latin American states' opportunity to send "aid" in the other direction, teaching those in the United States about the rich and varied cultures to the south.

Kennedy pledged $20 billion in assistance, in the form of grants and loans. To initiate the Alliance, he asked Congress for an initial grant of $500 million in May 1961. In addition, he placed responsibility for the program with the newly formed Agency for International Development (USAID). To match the US monetary commitment, Kennedy called on other participants to provide an additional $80 billion investment (for a total of $100 billion in new capital for development.) At the same time, he noted that few Latin American citizens enjoyed full political freedom and thus, that political reforms must advance. As well, Kennedy urged Latin American governments to enact social reforms to set aside outdated tax structures and to put in place new land tenure arrangements. Both reforms would distribute the benefits of economic growth more broadly.

Two years after its announcement, however, the Alliance had not achieved what Kennedy had hoped. Further, it remained a US-led project, rather than a broadly cooperative one. Kennedy considered creating a high-ranking Undersecretary of State for InterAmerican Affairs to signal the program's importance, but his 1963 assassination mooted that change.

Following Kennedy's death, Vice President Lyndon B. Johnson assumed the presidency. Many characterize the Alliance as moving from a more "idealist" to a more "realist" phase with Johnson's inauguration, although others note that Kennedy's failure to react against right-wing coups in the region already had signaled the death (or absence) of his stated ideals. In either case, the reformers Kennedy initially put in power took a backseat to others who focused on growing Communist insurgencies. Thus, they privileged military aid to regimes supportive of US goals of preventing Communism and stopping anti-US activities, over development funding. Further, US backing of regimes that suppressed internal political opposition, often using Alliance resources for training police and military officers, tainted the Alliance for Progress in the eyes of many.

Assessment

From the start, Alliance goals were ambitious and, ultimately, incompatible: moving from monocultural agriculture to diversification of production, land reform that spread ownership, education of populations, particularly in the hard sciences so that all could take advantage of the advances that technology promised, and the spread of democracy and citizen participation. However, the Alliance relied on the same elites who governed, owned land and other means of production, to redistribute wealth and power. Further, while pressing for economic diversification, the United States also wanted protection of its citizens' investments in Latin America. US firms not only owned disproportionate swathes of land but often, they also practiced monocultural cultivation for export. US interests operating in Alliance states, together with Latin American

political and economic elites, often found common cause in thwarting implementation of Alliance reforms. Land redistribution and political opening meant sharing wealth and power, and these resources had to come from those already in control. Thus, the program failed.

The Alliance never reached the lofty goals outlined by Kennedy and others. According to the US State Department web site, only 2% of total Latin America economic growth in the 1960s is attributable to the Alliance. Perhaps more chillingly, the Alliance did not prevent, some argued that it encouraged, the series of military coups that overtook many states of the region. These regimes delayed democratization and brutally suppressed political dissent for the next decade. Finally, the program did little to better relations between the United States and its neighbors in the region.

Clearly, the optimistic plans of modernization theorists—simple application of the proper tools would "fix" underdeveloped states—overreached. Even where the policies worked (for example, greater commodity price stability in the 1960s) increasing population size and continued skewed distribution of gains meant little or no reduction in poverty. Further, as the Cuban "threat" faded, as the US citizenry divided over military involvement in Indochina, and as the US executives became embroiled in scandal, the US government's interest in trying to effect political and economic changes in Latin America waned. Equally, these experiences shook the confidence and optimism of those who thought the country United States could make a difference. Not until President Jimmy Carter's election in 1976 did the United States again commit to effecting positive change in Latin America, rather than simply seek suppression of anti-US groups. By the 1970s, as well, modernization theorists had lost ground to such dependency theorists as Andre Gunder Frank. Many of these theorists were Latin Americanists who argued that international capitalist relations, rather than leading to development, stripped states of resources, leaving them less rather than more developed. Thus, belief that aid for the purposes outlined in the Alliance's charter could help declined in many circles.

In 1973, acknowledging the program's failure, the OAS disbanded the committee that administered it. One part of the Alliance, however, transferred to the private sector, continues today. Partners of the Americas grew out of "people-to-people" exchanges and joint development programs that allowed participation by private actors in Latin America and the United States. In 1970, the USAID moved these hemispheric "partnerships" to the private realm, although USAID, along with other government agencies, continues to fund development projects performed by Partners of the Americas teams.

JANET ADAMSKI

See also Development History and Theory; Modernization; United States Agency for International Development (USAID)

References and Further Reading

Charter of the Punta del Este (www.yale.edu/lawweb/ avalon/intdip/interam/intam16.htm).

Levinson, Jerome, and Juan de Onis. *The Alliance that Lost Its Way: A Critical Report on the Alliance for Progress*. Chicago: Quadrangle Books, 1970.

Lowenthal, Abraham F. *Exporting Democracy*. Baltimore, MD: Johns Hopkins University Press, 1991.

May, Herbert K. *Problems and Prospects of the Alliance for Progress: A Critical Examination*. New York: Praeger, 1968.

Perloff, Harvey S. *Alliance for Progress: A Social Invention in the Making*. Baltimore, MD: Johns Hopkins University Press, 1969.

Rabe, Stephen G. *The Most Dangerous Area in the World*. Chapel Hill, NC: University of North Carolina Press, 1999.

Scherman, L. Ronald, ed. *The Alliance for Progress: A Retrospective*. New York: Praeger, 1988.

ALL-INDIA MUSLIM LEAGUE (AIML)

The All-India Muslim League (AIML) was founded on December 30, 1906, at Dacca, Bengal, India (now Dhaka, Bangladesh), in response to the creation of the All-India National Congress (INC) in 1885, the efforts of Nawab Viqar ul-Mulk (1841–1917), who had been attempting since 1901 to set up a political organization for Muslims, and to the urging of the British Viceroy, Lord Minto (1845–1914), who wanted a moderate Muslim party to counterbalance the increasingly radical Congress. Above all, Muslims wanted to make sure that their views were heard when the British introduced new constitutional reforms. A branch of the League was established in London in 1908.

During the first three decades of its existence, the AIML was mostly a moribund organization, with its members assembling annually at the end of the year wherever the Khilafat Movement or the INC was meeting to debate the issues of the day. Few of its followers bothered to pay annual dues, and most of its members and officials also were members of other political parties. From 1906 until 1910, the party's central office remained at Aligarh. It then moved to Lucknow, and the party was maintained through an annual donation of three thousand rupees by the Raja of Mahmudabad (1879–1931). From 1936 until 1947, the headquarters was in Delhi. The party membership in 1927 was around 1,300 members, and in 1930, fewer than seventy-five people attended the famous session at Allahabad when Muhammad Iqbal (1877–1938) called for the creation of a state for the Muslims of South Asia in the northwest part of India. To encourage membership, the party subscription was reduced from six rupees to one rupee a year, and the admission fee of five rupees was abolished.

With the introduction of a new constitution, the Government of India Act of 1935, the election of candidates for provincial assemblies became crucial as Indians would govern the provinces directly. As a result, the AIML began to be organized as a viable political party. On March 4, 1934, Mohammad Ali Jinnah (1876–1948) became the president of the party, and this heralded a new chapter in its history. Jinnah nominated the Parliamentary Board, which chose party candidates for the general elections in 1936. While party funds mostly came from contributions from three rich supporters, and it was opposed both by the INC and regional Muslim parties, the party began its slow ascent to national importance. This was due to the leadership of Jinnah, and the organizational work of the independently wealthy GeneralSecretary Liaquat Ali Khan (1895–1951), who devoted almost all of his time over the next ten years to the party. The president of the AIML was elected annually, the general secretary for three years. Under the president was the Working Committee of a dozen or so members and then the party members. This organizational structure was also followed in the provinces.

The League was able to establish branch offices in each of the provinces of India in preparation for the general elections of 1936 and contested half of the seats reserved for Muslims. While it obtained some 60% of those seats, it won practically none of the seats in the Muslim majority provinces except for Bengal, where it gained thirty-nine out of 117 seats. These electoral defeats, ironically, were to lead to a complete change in party fortunes as Congress ministries governed in most of the provinces of India in a manner that was viewed as favoring the Hindu community and an attack on Muslim institutions and the Muslim way of life. As a result, there were widespread defections from the INC. In 1939, the League published two widely discussed reports that detailed Congress misgovernment, and this further inflamed Muslim feeling toward the Congress.

In the 1937 annual session held in Lucknow, the League became increasingly militant, with Jinnah declaring that were three entities in India: the Congress, the British, and the League. The All-India Muslim Students Federation was organized, and the League chalked out a Five-Year Plan for the Muslim community. In the 1940 annual meeting held at Lahore, the League, on March 23, 1940, moved the "Pakistan Resolution," whereby the party called for the creation of a separate state for the Muslims of India in the northwest and northeast of India. An estimated one hundred thousand people attended this meeting. Membership of the party had risen to nearly ninety thousand, and it would continue to rise. A party newspaper was created in 1941, the weekly *Dawn,* and it became a daily the following year. In 1943, the League created a planning committee that would plan economic development in the Pakistan areas—a Committee of Action to enforce party discipline among the provincial League parties, and a Committee of Writers to create party pamphlets. The League also actively recruited student workers, especially from Aligarh Muslim University.

All of the organization work of the previous decade led to a tremendous League victory in the 1946 general elections, when it won one-third of the seats in the Punjab, 115 of 250 seats in Bengal, and almost all of the Muslim seats it contested in other parts of India. It buttressed Jinnah's claim that he spoke for the Muslims of India, and the British treated him as such, even in the face of Congress claims, especially those of Mahatma Gandhi (1869–1948), that the INC spoke for all of India. As a result of this electoral victory, an increasing number of Muslim politicians joined the League, whereas those who did not were steamrolled into political oblivion. The League had demonstrated that it was the party of the Muslims of South Asia. When the Interim Government was formed in 1946, Liaquat Ali Khan took one of the most important positions in the government, that of Finance Member.

By early 1947, both the INC and the British agreed that on independence India should be partitioned into the sovereign states of India and Pakistan. With the creation of Pakistan on August 15, 1947, Jinnah became Governor-General, and Liaquat Ali Khan became Prime Minister. The AIML split into two parties, the Pakistan Muslim League and the Indian Muslim League.

ROGER D. LONG

See also India; Islam; Muslim League

References and Further Reading

Ahmad, Muhammad Salim. *The All-India Muslim League: A History of the Growth and Consolidation of Political Organisation.* Bahawalpur: Ilham Publishers, 1989.
Bahadur, Lal. *The Muslim League, Its History, Activities, and Achievements.* Lahore: Book Traders, 1979.
Long, Roger D. "The Muslim League, Islam, and the Mobilisation of Popular Support." *Indo-British Review: A Journal of History,* 15 (1) (1988).
Malik, Ikram Ali. *Muslim League Session 1940 and the Lahore Resolution: Documents.* Islamabad: National Institute of Historical and Cultural research, 1990.
Malik, Nadeem Shafiq, ed. *The All-India Muslim League, 1906–1947.* Islamabad: National Book Foundation, 1997.
Mujahid, Sharif-al. *Muslim League Documents, 1900–1947, Vol. 1.* Karachi: Quaid-i-Azam Academy, 1990.
Ralhan, O. P., ed. *All-India Muslim League, 2 vols.* New Delhi: Anmol Publications, 1997.
Shah, Sayyid Vaqar Ali. *Muslim League in N.W.F.P.* Karachi: Royal Book Co., 1992.

AMIN, IDI

Idi Amin (1923–2003), former leader of Uganda, was one of the most brutal despots ever to rule a country. Born into the Kakwa tribe in the northwest corner of Uganda, sometime between 1923 and 1928 (the exact date remains unknown, as no birth records exist), he attained only a second-grade education.

With minimal education and basic aptitude in five languages, Amin attained the highest rank an African soldier could aspire to in the British colonial army (*effendi*), due primarily to his physical prowess. In 1971, when Milton Obote, Uganda's first prime minister, was attending a Commonwealth Conference in Singapore, Amin staged a coup and became the country's president and liquidated most of the military leaders who opposed his regime. Some estimated that between two hundred thousand and five hundred thousand people were dead from Amin's atrocities by the time he was ousted in 1979.

Socioeconomic Anarchy in Amin's Uganda

Amin started his reign with the promise of a brief military rule to rectify the economic mismanagement and other "sins" of the Obote government, after which multiparty politics were to be reinstituted. Accordingly, Amin quickly released many political prisoners, established an ethnically diverse cabinet, broke the monopoly of state-owned enterprises, and shifted the nation's political ideology toward the West. However, he was not able to engage in thoughtful planning or disciplined spending, relying mostly on his whims, with occasional "guidance" from soothsayers, dreams, and "divine inspiration." Frustrated by the intricacies of ministerial debates, Amin avoided cabinet meetings and once ordered his cabinet to take a nine month vacation.

In 1972, following an alleged dream in which he purportedly received instructions from God, Amin ordered the forty thousand to eighty thousand Asians living in Uganda to leave the country within ninety days. In the same year, he severed diplomatic relations with Israel and, in 1977, with Britain, and turned to the likes of Libya and the Soviet Union for support. With the exodus of the Asians, most of whom were established traders and professionals, Uganda's economy collapsed. Many of the formerly Asian-owned shops that were given to Ugandans were plundered; consumer goods became scarce; unemployment, inflation, and cost of living soared; education, health care, and other social services collapsed; and internal population dislocation, cross-border refugee movements, and commodity smuggling became prevalent.

As Uganda's economy deteriorated and opposition mounted, so did Amin's bloodthirstiness and controversies in international relations: He openly praised the murder of Israeli athletes by Palestine Liberation Organization (PLO) operatives during the 1972 Munich Olympics; he supported the Palestinians who hijacked the Air French flight to Kampala in 1976—which culminated in the famous Entebbe raid by Israel; he nationalized many British enterprises in 1973; and, in 1975, offered himself to be appointed the Head of the Commonwealth. After surviving numerous attempts on his life, Amin invaded Tanzania in 1978, and President Julius Nyerere, who never hid his abhorrence for Amin, mounted a counterattack, forcing Amin into exile in Libya in 1979. Later that year, he settled in the port city of Jeddah in Saudi Arabia. In 1989, he attempted a clandestine return to Uganda to reclaim power but was uncovered at Kinshasa and forced back to Saudi Arabia, where he died in 2003.

JOSEPH MENSAH

See also East Africa: History and Economic Development; East Africa: International Relations; Nyerere, Julius; Organization of African Unity (OAU); Uganda

References and Further Reading

Avirgan, Tony, and Martha Honey. *War in Uganda: The Legacy of Idi Amin*. London: Zed Books; and Westport, CT: Lawrence Hill and Co., 1982.

Grahame, Iain. *Amin and Uganda: Personal Memoir*. London, Toronto, Sydney, and New York: Granada, 1980.

Mamdani, Mohamood. *Imperialism and Fascism in Uganda*. Trenton, NJ: Africa World Press, 1984.

Martin, David. *General Amin*. London: Faber, 1974.

Measures, Bob, and Tony Walker. *Amin's Uganda*. Pasadena, CA: Minerva Press, 1998.

Smith, George Ivan. *Ghosts of Kamala*. London: Weidenfeld and Nicolson, 1980.

AMNESTY INTERNATIONAL

Amnesty International (AI) describes itself as "a worldwide movement of people who campaign for internationally recognized human rights." AI emerged in the 1960s as a reaction against Cold War ideological polarization. It was felt by the founders of AI that a movement of people independent from states and political parties was the most credible way to pursue the defense of human rights as universal ethical norms. The defense of basic freedoms was broadened by AI beyond the defense of political prisoners to include all "prisoners of conscience," a term invented by the organization to describe the situation of being imprisoned for one's ideas or beliefs. Political impartiality and independence, as well as principled action based on the Universal Declaration of Human Rights (1948) and other key human rights instruments, are the founding norms guiding AI's work from its inception until today. AI's founder, Peter Benenson, inspired by his past involvement in Britain's Labour party and by Catholic ideals, was AI's first president from 1964 to 1966. Martin Ennals was appointed secretary general in 1968 and remained in place until 1980. Irene Khan, first woman to become AI's secretary general, was appointed in May 2001.

Originally, Amnesty was conceived as a fixed-term project, a campaign to convince world leaders to adopt a general amnesty for political prisoners. At the beginning, it held the name of the "Appeal for Amnesty 1961" and was publicized by the British newspaper *The Observer*. The campaign coincided with the anniversary of the emancipation of the serfs in Russia and the outbreak of the American Civil War (both in 1861).

The project soon institutionalized itself to pursue and strengthen its activities. In 1963, at Amnesty's second international conference, its Constitution was discussed, and the name "Amnesty International" was born. This conference also produced an International Code of Conduct for political prisoners and calls for greater rights to asylum, a World Human Rights Fund, and an International Human Rights Day on December 10. AI's International Secretariat was established in London. It also was decided that the organization would not accept any funds from governmental sources or political parties to guarantee its independence.

In 1964, AI received consultative status at the United Nations' Economic and Social Council (UN-ECOSOC). From 1963 to 1974, Sean MacBride, an Irish diplomat and jurist, was a member of AI's international executive committee, while he was secretary general of the International Commission of Jurists from 1963 to 1970. MacBride played an important role in AI's advocacy activities at the UN, leading the formation of a coalition of human rights non-governmental organizations (NGOs) for the UN 1968 International Conference on Human Rights in Tehran.

In the 1970s, AI's work started to intensify at the level of the UN. Although the original intent in AI's work was not to lobby the UN as such since the UN was not used to listening to NGOs at that time, it rapidly became clear that an important part of the work of AI would be to advocate for more sophisticated human rights instruments and enforcement bodies within the UN. In 1977, AI's International Secretariat hired its first professional liaison officer dedicated exclusively to this task.

Rapidly, AI developed as a membership-based international NGO through the creation of local committees first in Britain, then Europe, North America, and elsewhere. The organization's own figures today claim more than 1.8 million members. Local Amnesty International committees can be found in more than 150 countries and territories around the world. AI's national sections offices and structures can be found in fifty countries.

One of the central activities characterizing the originality of AI's work is the creation of letter-writing networks to ask authorities for the improvement of the living conditions and the release of prisoners of conscience. Individual cases are " adopted " by local committees that write to state authorities at various levels to bring the cases to their attention. Public attention from abroad on specific prisoners' cases is seen as an effective means through which state authorities can be influenced. One of the principles that was established in AI's first years and remains to this day is the prohibition for local and national AI committees to adopt cases of prisoners from their own countries. This is meant to protect AI activists, and the prisoners they defend, as well as the impartiality of AI's work.

AI's work also has rapidly moved into the field of lobbying and advocating for new international legal norms on human rights protection. Either directly within the UN's official and unofficial negotiations with state officials to draft new treaties and enforcement mechanisms or through mass public campaigns seeking to shape public opinion and create pressure on state officials, AI has developed many new tactics now used extensively by a variety of NGOs throughout the world to influence transnational and international politics.

Another practice of AI that was unheard of in international politics when the organization first started is public criticism of governments for their human rights abuses. The release of detailed reports on human rights violations based on fact-finding missions and other sources has become one of the central activities of the organization. As a result, AI is a key if not the most important information resource on the situation of human rights throughout the world.

Even though AI's work applies to industrialized as well as developing countries, its relevance to the politics of the latter is particularly important. AI has always defended the rights of individuals living under any kind of political regime. At the beginning of AI's work during the Cold War, local committees were asked to adopt a prisoner from each of the three regions of world politics: the East, the West, and the Third World. When the activities of local committees broadened beyond the defense of prisoners of conscience's rights, this rule was relaxed, but AI maintained its impartiality through responding to human rights abuses throughout the world.

In the 1960s, AI's work was predominantly focused on political prisoners, emphasizing political and religious persecution and inhumane prison conditions. In the 1970s, it started to work on torture and disappearances. In the 1980s, its work broadened to include reports on extrajudicial killings. Also in the 1980s, AI started a new campaign for the abolition of the death penalty. In the 1990s, it campaigned for the recognition of "women's rights as human rights" and for the creation of a Permanent International Criminal Court. AI was awarded the Nobel Peace Prize in 1977 for "having contributed to securing the ground for freedom, for justice, and thereby also for peace in the world."

STÉPHANIE ROUSSEAU

See also Human Rights as a Foreign Policy Issue; Human Rights: Definition and Violations; Non-Governmental Organizations (NGOs)

References and Further Reading

Amnesty International's web site: www.amnesty.org

Buchanan, Tom. "The Truth Will Set You Free: The Making of Amnesty International." *Journal of Contemporary History* 37(4): 575–597 (October 2002).

Clark, Ann Marie. *Diplomacy of Conscience: Amnesty International and Changing Human Rights Norms*. Princeton, NJ: Princeton University Press, 2001.

Martens, Kerstin. "An Appraisal of Amnesty International's Work at the United Nations: Established Areas of Activities and Shifting Priorities in the 1990s." *Human Rights Quarterly* 26(4): 1050–1070 (November 2004).

Power, Jonathan. *Like Water on Stone: The Story of Amnesty International*, Boston: Northeastern University Press, 2001.

ANDEAN COMMUNITY

The Andean Community, as the Andean Group has been known since 1997, was initially formed in 1966 within the framework for economic integration laid out in the Latin American Free Trade Association. Under the terms of the Cartagena Accord in 1969,

Bolivia, Chile, Colombia, Ecuador, and Peru formally created the Andean Development Corporation (CAF) and the Andean Pact, which had four objectives:

1. To create a common market,
2. To promote industrialization through specialization in new industries,
3. To gain leverage over transnational corporations and direct foreign investment, and
4. To grant trade and other preferences to less developed members (Ecuador and Bolivia).

The innovative Statute on Foreign Capital imposed restrictions on foreign investment, limiting foreign ownership to 49%. After the military coup in 1973, Chile at first resisted implementation of the statute and then withdrew from the Andean Group in 1976. Venezuela, meanwhile, joined in 1973. In 1979, the Andean Council of Foreign Ministers was created, along with the Andean Parliament and Court of Justice, adding a political dimension to the group.

A renewed effort to strengthen the group came after 1991, although a lingering border dispute between Peru and Ecuador and the Alberto Fujimori coup in 1992 created internal strains. Peru suspended its membership temporarily in 1992, but at the same time, Colombia and Venezuela signed a trade agreement that led, in 1993, to the creation of a Free Trade Zone encompassing Bolivia, Colombia, Ecuador, and Venezuela. The four established a common external tariff in 1995, making the Andean Group a customs union. In 1997, the name was changed to the Andean Community, and its headquarters was established in Lima, Peru, in keeping with an agreement to reincorporate Peru gradually into the free trade zone. In 1998, a framework was signed in Buenos Aires for the eventual establishment of a free trade accord between the Andean Community and the Southern Cone Common Market (MERCOSUR). The current goal is to eliminate internal barriers to services and labor so as to establish a common market by 2005.

As of 2002, the Andean Community encompasses some 115 million people, more than double the figure at its inception. Its collective gross domestic product is $283 billion, and its per capita income is $2,464. Average inflation stands at 11%. Intracommunity trade totals some $5.6 billion, a fifty-fold increase over the level in 1970.

LAWRENCE BOUDON

See also Andean South America: History and Economic Development; Andean South America: International Relations

Further Reading

French-Davis, Ricardo. "The Andean Pact: A Model of Economic Integration for Developing Countries." *World Development* 5 (1–2) 137–153 (January–February 1977).

Grosse, Robert. "Foreign Investment Regulation in the Andean Pact: The First Ten Years." *Inter-American Economic Affairs* 33 (4) 77–94 (Spring 1980).

Morawetz, David. *The Andean Group: A Case Study in Economic Integration Among Developing Countries.* Cambridge: Massachusetts Institute of Technology Press, 1974.

ANDEAN SOUTH AMERICA: HISTORY AND ECONOMIC DEVELOPMENT

The nations comprising Andean South America, Bolivia, Ecuador, and Peru—share a common cultural heritage as well as a lingering colonial legacy that has contributed to their political, social, and economic development since 1945. During the twentieth century, the twin forces of reformism and revolution challenged the neocolonial order that emerged after independence.

Geographically, these nations are located on the Pacific coast, although Bolivia lacks a coast as a consequence of the War of the Pacific (1879–1883). The Andes cut across these nations and separate the coast from the tropical rain forests to the east. Socially, these nations are deeply divided by racial and ethnic cleavages that relegated the Indians to a subservient position within the political, social, and economic structure. Their population can be divided into three general ethnic/racial groups: whites, *mestizos* or *cholos* (racially or culturally mixed peoples), and Indians. In all three nations, the European whites are a numerically small group possessing the wealth and monopolizing political power, a situation challenged by twentieth-century mass political movements.

The export economy contributed to underdevelopment since their primary exports were subject to the fluctuations of world market demand. The Great Depression caused great havoc to the political and economic life of these countries, with new social forces emerging and challenging the traditional elite. The elite responded to this threat through dictatorship and populism. This turbulent period created the political leaders, social forces, and alliances that influenced subsequent events after 1945.

In Bolivia, the early 1940s saw the rise of new reformist and revolutionary political parties, such as the Nationalist Revolutionary Movement (MNR) under the leadership of Victor Paz Estenssoro, which represented a moderate left and middle-class alternative to the traditional parties. In 1946, a brutal populist government that came to power in 1943 was overthrown and a left-right coalition ruled the nation until 1952. With demands for social change increasing, the MNR became important politically in the 1951 presidential elections. The traditional right-wing elites realized that only the military could assure their hold on power. When the exiled Paz Estenssoro won these elections, the military annulled the elections and outlawed the MNR, setting the stage for Bolivia's National Bourgeois Revolution of 1952. On April 9, 1952, the MNR organized a popular armed uprising that led to the fall of the military and the MNR's rise to political power. The MNR implemented a radical social and economic program that transformed Bolivia's socioeconomic structures by nationalizing the tin mines and instituting a major agrarian reform program that formalized the Indian takeover of hacienda lands. Under the revolutionary agitation from 1952 to 1956, the government included labor through its organization, the Bolivian Workers Central (COB). Before the 1956 presidential elections, the MNR had split into a center-right middle-class wing headed by Hernán Siles Zuazo and a left-wing led by the COB. Siles Zuazo's election shifted the direction of the revolution by adopting a state-capitalist model.

In Peru, after 1945, the American Revolutionary Populist Party (APRA), led by Victor Raúl Haya de la Torre, represented the populist challenge against the traditional political and economic system. During the 1945 elections, APRA demonstrated its appeal to the Peruvian masses with the election of José Luis Bustamante y Rivero. In 1946, APRA members sitting in the cabinet, the senate, and the chamber of deputies initiated populist policies that caused a backlash from the economic elite and the military. The military overthrew Bustamante in 1948 and replaced him with General Manuel Odría, who banned APRA and exiled Haya de la Torre.

During Bustamante's administration, the role of the state had increased, and the economy was redirected towards agricultural diversification and industrialization. Under Odría, the status quo ante was restored with the reintroduction of economic policies that favored the traditional exporting elites. In 1950, Odría legitimated his rule by holding elections, which he readily won. From 1950 to 1953, with increasing export demand resulting from the Korean War, Odría actively sought the support of the working masses. Export earnings declined with the end of the war and worker militancy increased. The 1956 elections brought a former president, Manuel Prado Ugarteche, to power. Supported by APRA, Prado defeated Fernando Belaúnde Terry, a politician who later would dominate Peruvian politics. Although Prado continued an export oriented economic policy during

his administration (1956–1962), he also passed legislation favorable to the working masses and legalized APRA and the Peruvian Communist Party.

When an APRA victory proved imminent in the contentious 1962 elections, the military launched a coup and annulled the elections. Under US pressure, new elections were held in 1963, and the military accepted the election results when Belaúnde won. Belaúnde implemented an ambitious developmental program that saw an increased state role favoring the working class, the peasants and the poor. His plans, especially those regarding agrarian reform, were opposed by APRA, Odría's followers, and the traditional landowning elite. The highland peasantry invaded hacienda lands and a guerilla movement emerged. Belaúnde reacted by sending in a reluctant military, which crushed the incipient guerrilla movement and the peasant uprising by 1966. Another major problem that engulfed his government concerned the International Petroleum Corporation (IPC) and negotiations concerning partial nationalization. Under pressure from the United States, the government reached an agreement with the IPC that Peruvian nationalists condemned as a sellout to foreign interests. On October 3, 1968, the military overthrew Belaúnde's government and ushered in a period of major restructuring of Peru's traditional social and economic structures.

In Ecuador, the period of political instability that began in 1931 came to an end with the overthrow of José María Velasco Ibarra in 1947, and the 1948 elections brought a period of presidential stability. During his administration (1948–1952), Galo Plaza, a member of the landowning elite, introduced political, social, and economic reforms. He opened up the political sphere to all contending political parties by incorporating all major political groupings into his cabinet and allowing freedom of the press. He engaged in a vigorous public works project that benefited the banana export sector and provided government credits to this sector, largely financed through loans from the United States and the World Bank. A banana boom contributed to political stability as the Korean War increased demand for other exports. The 1952 elections saw Velasco Ibarra as president for the third time. The uniqueness of this political transition was that for the first time in twenty-eight years power had passed peacefully to the presidential successor. During this presidential administration (1952–1956) government largesse continued with public work project spending and rewards for civilian and military supporters. Velasco Ibarra, who ran as a populist with the support of the Guayaquil-based Concentration of Popular Forces (CFP), had that group's leader exiled once in office and shifted his base of support to the nation's conservative forces. In 1955, problems surfaced with the United States over tuna fishing within the two hundred-mile limit that Ecuador claimed. During the 1956 elections, three political factions ran and another smooth transition followed as Camilo Ponce Enríquez, a rightist candidate supported by Velasco Ibarra, became president and ruled with relative stability from 1956 to 1960. Near the end of his term, the banana boom went bust, resulting in increased unemployment, strikes, and rioting in 1959. The consummate populist politician, Velasco Ibarra, took full advantage of this turmoil by running on a decidedly populist platform, promising far-reaching social and economic reforms. He handily won the 1960 elections and took political power for the fourth time.

The National Bolivian Revolution, under US pressure, shifted right by taking increasingly conservative economic policies. Although the United States did not actively oppose the revolution, it utilized economic pressure to get the government to adopt policies favoring economic stabilization. After 1956, the government compensated the expropriated mine owners, allowed foreign investment, reduced labor participation in the government, and reduced social programs. The military benefited through US training and aid to counter the peasant and worker militias that had emerged during the radical phase of the revolution from 1952 to 1956. The United States lavished aid that financed a developmental program benefiting the Santa Cruz region of eastern Bolivia by promoting agroindustrial enterprises. The Paz Estenssoro Administration (1960–1964) continued these policies but, in 1964, decided to break with the COB and the mineworkers by allying with the military by selecting General René Barrientos as vice president. The United States supported this move as it prevented Juan Lechín, a Trotskyist labor leader, from taking power. Although Paz Estenssoro won the election, his vice president overthrew him in November 1964, and the military dominated the government for the next eighteen years.

The Peruvian military's seizure of power in October 1968 portended a new type of military revolution as General Juan Velasco Alvarado proclaimed a "Revolutionary Government of the Armed Forces," which sought to impose a new economic order that would benefit all Peruvians. The revolutionary government nationalized the IPC, a broadly supported action, implemented a far-reaching agrarian reform program, and nationalized key foreign-owned export industries and enterprises. The 1973–1974 world oil crisis had its ramifications in Peru as prices rose for oil and technological imports, while the price of exports fell, creating a major balance of payment problem. Ill

during this critical period, Velasco saw the end of the revolutionary experiment in 1975 as a struggle within the military emerged. Military conservatives won the struggle and replaced Velasco with General Francisco Morales Bermúdez, who retreated from Velasco's policies and purged the radical leftist elements from government, as well as reformist officers. He instituted an austerity program that deeply affected the working class, ended the agrarian reform, and courted foreign investment. The military experiment with revolution came full circle with the gradual transition to civilian rule, culminating with the 1980 presidential election and the return of Belaúnde Terry.

Velasco Ibarra's 1960 victory in Ecuador did not signify a radical alteration of the living conditions of the urban poor as promised during his campaign. Ever the populist, he denounced the 1942 treaty with Peru and instigated a "Tuna War" with the United States. His campaign rhetoric unleashed unrealistic hopes in the masses that went unfulfilled because the government lacked the necessary revenues as a result of falling exports, increasing unemployment and capital flight. Amid growing protests, the military overthrew him in 1961 and installed Vice-President Carlos Julio Arosemena Monroy. Amid the Cold War atmosphere of the 1960s and the success of the Cuban Revolution, the United States and the military feared that Arosemena was too leftist. In 1963, the military overthrew Arosemena and installed a *junta* that repressed all left-wing opposition while instituting a reformist program influenced by the Alliance for Progress and subsidized by US aid. The *junta* also instituted an agrarian reform program that abolished the feudalistic land tenure system of the *huasipungo* but did little else. With the decline of banana export revenues in 1965, the *junta* increased import duties, which set off a series of strikes. Amid this declining economy, the *junta* stepped down in 1966, and a constituent assembly drafted a new constitution. In 1968, presidential elections were held and Velasco Ibarra, returning from exile, won the elections for the fifth time. Not having a clear political mandate, his political problems were exacerbated by a balance of payment crisis. The Congress and Supreme Court opposed the emergency fiscal measures that he instituted to raise government revenues. In 1970, Velasco Ibarra, with military support, assumed full dictatorial powers and decreed a number of unpopular economic measures that contributed to some fiscal health. Fearing a win by Assad Bucaram in the 1972 presidential elections and the mismanagement of Ecuador's new oil wealth, the military overthrew him. Velasco Ibarra went into his final exile as a military *junta* led by General Guillermo Rodríguez Lara ruled the country from 1972 to 1976.

Rodríguez Lara, declaring that his government was "nationalist and revolutionary," embarked on a state-led developmental program whose goal was the transformation of Ecuador's society and economy by nationalizing industries and creating public enterprises. Oil policy became very important as control of this resource not only provided the necessary revenues for the reforms proposed but also symbolized the regime's nationalist orientation. The *junta* also proposed an agrarian reform, but its effect was limited as a result of landowner opposition. Another balance-of-payments crisis developed as oil earning declined and public expenditures increased. Austerity measures increased protests from the private sector and labor, leading to the overthrow of Rodríguez Lara. A military triumvirate assumed power from 1976 to 1979, which prepared a return to civilian rule, a goal achieved in 1979 with the inauguration of Jaime Roldós.

Although the Bolivian military ruled the country from 1964 to 1982, it did not do so as a unified corporate entity with one definable policy. Implementing policies that ranged from leftist to rightist, it had one overwriting thrust, controlling and repressing the popular social forces that emerged from the revolution. The appearance of Ernesto "Che" Guevara's guerrillas appeared to give credence to the government's repressive aims. The military governments were not able to transcend and unify society's various divisions. These contradictions, along with heavy foreign borrowing and a declining economy, contributed to the slow, torturous transition towards civilian rule, achieved in 1982 with the election of Hernán Siles Zuazo as president.

By the 1980s, all three nations were under civilian rule. They would inherit the problems created by the military governments, as well as a transformed international economic situation that circumscribed their options in terms of economic policies adopted, creating the conditions for new social eruptions. In Peru, Belaúnde's government shifted from the state-led capitalist model of development to neoliberal economic policies, attracting foreign capital and leading to debt renegotiation. For Latin America, the 1980s are known as the "Lost Decade" as a result of declining social and economic indicators. Many Latin American nations were indebted as a result of generous foreign lending based on "petrodollars." From 1981 to 1983, an international debt crisis and a world recession created a severe social and economic crisis for Belaúnde's government, contributing to the rise of the Shining Path (SL) in the highlands. In Lima, a rival revolutionary group, the Túpac Amaru Revolutionary Movement (MRTA), appeared. Belaúnde allowed the military to launch a counterinsurgency

campaign in the highlands, contributing to human rights violations. International border problems re-emerged with Ecuador as the two nations skirmished for five days. Drug trafficking also increased, fueled by the demand for cocaine in the industrialized world, especially the United States. Peru, along with Bolivia, became the largest coca leaf producers as this export replaced the demand for traditional legal exports. Although Belaúnde served out his second presidency (1980–1985), his administration appeared to be a political, social, and economic fiasco.

In 1985, APRA's Alan García Pérez became president, signaling a return to populism and a retreat from neoliberal economic policies. García instituted policies to help the destitute masses that had suffered during the aggressive international economic climate of the 1980s. He shocked world financial markets by defaulting on the foreign debt and limiting interest payments on this debt to 10% of the nation's export earning. The first two years of his administration proved beneficial to the overall health of the economy, but by 1987, his policies were proving detrimental as the trade deficit increased, foreign exchange reserves declined, and private national capital refused to invest. The nation experienced a period of hyperinflation and increased public sector debt as SL and MRTA activity surged and criminal violence increased. Corruption scandals also enveloped García's government. Whilethe private sector and the right organized against the APRA, Alberto Fujimori, a virtual unknown, emerged as an unlikely candidate during the 1990 presidential campaign. Igniting popular passions, his grassroots movement, Cambio 1990, won a majority of the popular vote.

As a result of the oil boom, the Roldós government in Ecuador inherited a relatively healthy economy from the military. Quito benefited the most from economic expansion as government employment increased, contributing to a burgeoning middle class and rising income inequality. Political tempers flared between Roldós and Bucaram, the CFP's populist leader, who challenged the president from Congress. This conflict continued until May 24, 1981, when the president was killed in a plane crash. Vice President Osvaldo Hurtado found the nation in an economic crisis with the end of the oil boom and mounting foreign debt. The right and business community organized against Hurtado's drastic austerity policies. During the 1984 elections, the right and business interests supported León Febres Cordero, a Guayaquil businessman. With a narrow victory, Febres Cordero and his technocrats instituted a neoliberal program that severely affected Ecuador's lower classes. His increasing unpopularity led to the defeat of the right in the 1988 presidential elections as

Rodrigo Borja of the Democratic Left party (ID) won. Saddled with Ecuador's gravest economic crisis in its history, Borja's options were limited, so he continued the austerity policies and accepted International Monetary Fund (IMF) demands. Opposition from the left and the right coupled with rising Indian militancy made governing impossible. The Indians became a new social force in the country's political equation as they demanded agrarian reform and recognition of Ecuador as a multiethnic nation. Borja's party was defeated in 1992 with the election of Sixto Durán-Ballén as president. His government quickly implemented a structural adjustment package that exacerbated the conflict between the government and the labor unions. The Huaorani Indians in the Amazon rain forest also protested government policies favorable to the oil industry, which had devastated their traditional way of life through unregulated pollution and environmental destruction. In 1995, international problems also flared up as the Peruvian boundary dispute over the 1942 Rio Protocol reemerged as a means to deflect the internal political, social, and economic crisis.

Durán-Ballén's vice president, Alberto Dahik, instrumental in fashioning the administration's neoliberal economic policies that were so widely rejected, fled the country in disgrace as a result of a corruption scandal in 1995, which contributed to the rise of a new populist candidate, Abdala Bucaram. Although Bucaram won the presidency in 1996, after six months his administration was brought down amidst charges of corruption and mental incapacity. The Congress deposed him and selected Fabian Alarcón, the congressional president, as the interim president in 1997. A succession crisis ensued as Bacaram's vice president, Rosalía Arteaga, declared herself the legitimate successor. She abruptly resigned after her recognition as president, and Alarcón resumed the presidency until the 1998 elections. Jamil Mahuad Witt, who narrowly won the election, confronted an economic crisis brought on by declining oil prices and high inflation, which was further exacerbated by costly destruction from El Niño. In 2000, large indigenous mobilizations, supported by the military and police forces, forced him from office. Vice President Gustavo Noboa became president and steered the country away from economic chaos by instituting a dollarization policy to stabilize the economy. The next elections brought Lucio Gutierrez, a former army colonel and a military leader of the 2000 mobilizations, to power in 2003. Promising to increase social spending during his campaign, once he took office, he realized that he had to negotiate with the IMF and institute privatization policies. The indigenous peoples who brought him to power felt betrayed. In 2004, higher

oil prices allowed Gutierrez's government to survive the political winds that had befallen his predecessors.

Fujimori in Peru continued the neoliberal experiment that had swept throughout Latin America by instituting a particularly virulent economic shock program, popularly known as the "Fujishock." These measures brought down hyperinflation, but at a huge social cost. The unpopularity of these measures and the continuing guerilla war led Fujimori, with military support, to launch an "autocoup" against his own government by dissolving Congress in 1992, which had wide popular support. In September 1992, the capture of the SL leader led to the decline of the guerilla group. In the war against SL, the military and police had committed numerous human rights violations, especially against the highland Indians. The end of the guerrilla war and Fujimori's neoliberal economic policies brought foreign investment back, which increased his popularity, evident by his overwhelming reelection in 1995. In 1996, Congress passed a law so that Fujimori could run for a third term in 2000. He won the elections against his opponent Alejandro Toledo, an Indian with a Ph.D. in Economics from Stanford University. A corruption scandal soon broke out as Fujimori's intelligence chief was accused of bribing congressmen, participating in the drug trade, and illegal arms shipments to Colombian guerrillas. In November 2000, Fujimori went into exile. In 2001, the nation elected its first Indian president, Toledo, who sought to restore democracy and heal the wounds that had cut deeply through the society during the years from 1980 to 2000. The hopes that Toledo had inspired were soon dashed by the continuing economic crisis. With massive protests against the government's privatization efforts, Toledo declared a state of emergency in 2003. Toledo also came under attack for his private life as his popularity took a steep decline, becoming Latin America's most unpopular president.

Similar problems as those faced by Ecuador and Peru have plagued Bolivia since the election of the leftist candidate Siles Zuazo. Having a popular mandate to implement populist policies, the nation's political and economic crisis circumscribed the options open to the president. Unable to pay the foreign debt and with a huge fiscal deficit, the worsening economic crisis was not only exacerbated by the political, social, and economic demands of the masses but also by the heated debates between the executive and legislative branches over which policies to implement to confront the economic crisis. The political crisis not only reflected the contending social and class forces that had divided the nation after the revolution but also a struggle between two different developmental models. The inability of the government to enact its policies without provoking labor or business led to an impasse that created the most drastic economic crisis in the nation's history. Giving up in frustration after a general strike and an attempted coup, the government decided to hold early elections in 1985. In the hotly contested election, no clear winner emerged, so Congress elected Paz Estenssoro as president for the fourth time.

In 1985, Paz Estenssoro enacted one of the most severe economic stabilization programs in all of Latin America, becoming a test case for a study of neoliberalism. The MNR government shifted its policies away from redistribution to courting private enterprise through reducing state intervention in the economy through its Decree 21060, known as the New Economic Plan, which moved away from the economic nationalist and state-led developmental policies of earlier MNR governments. These policies created a backlash from the popular social forces represented by the COB, which were quickly suffocated by declaring a state of emergency and exiling for the movements' leaders. In order to implement his program, Paz Estenssoro reached an agreement with Banzer and the *Acción Democrática Nacionalista* (ADN). In the 1989 elections, the MNR, ADN, and the *Movimiento de la Izquierda Revolucionaria* (MIR) fielded candidates, but Banzer formed an alliance between the ADN and the MIR, which allowed for the MIR candidate Jaime Paz Zamora's election by Congress. This coalition denied the presidency to Gonzalo Sánchez de Lozada, the MNR candidate who won the popular vote. All three candidates had agreed to continue the neoliberal experiment.

Although representing the left, Paz Zamora continued the patronage system by including many conservative ADN members in his cabinet. In the 1993 elections, Sánchez de Lozada, a US-educated businessman and a major stockholder in the nation's largest private mining company, and the MNR made a comeback with the support of the Movimiento Revolucionario Tupac Katari, an Aymara Indian political organization. To reward this support, Sánchez de Lozada selected Víctor Hugo Cardenas, an Aymara Indian leader, as his vice president, demonstrating the new political role of the Indian and *cholo* masses. Reflecting this broadening indigenous political participation, the 1967 Constitution was reformed in 1994 by declaring that Bolivia was a "multiethnic and pluricultural" nation. His continuation of the neoliberal experiment led to major violent protests against his government. An area of major conflict was in the coca-producing regions of La Paz and the Chapare as coca producers fought against the government's US-supported eradication programs. The Congress decided the 1997 elections by declaring the ADN candidate Banzer the victor, who continued the neoliberal program. Social protests continued and the situation in the Chapare region grew drastic as special police units were sent to eradicate coca production. In Cochabamba, there also were "water wars," popular protests against the attempt to privatize the city's water system. Banzer, diagnosed with cancer, resigned in 2001, and Vice President Jorge Quiroga served out the rest of Banzer' term. In the 2002 elections, the two leading contenders were the MNR candidate Sánchez de Lozada and Evo Morales, a representative of the coca producers and leader of the Movement Toward Socialism (MAS). The Congress once more decided the election by naming Sánchez de Lozada the winner. The social cleavages of Bolivian society created by the neoliberal experiment were made manifest in February 2003, when a major revolt, the *impuestazo*, against the implementation of a personal income tax and spending cuts broke out in La Paz, leading to the death of twenty-seven people and hundreds of injuries. The protests against Sánchez de Lozada's unpopular government continued and in September and October 2003, there were mass mobilizations against a plan to build a pipeline to export natural gas through Chile, leading to numerous deaths and injuries, as well as his resignation. As the Vice President Carlos Mesa, a journalist and historian, assumed power, the opposition gave him ninety days to respond to the political, social, and economic demands of the masses. In July 2004, there was a referendum on the natural gas export plan, which received support from voters but with the understanding that there would be more state participation in the industry and not privatization. President Mesa confronted a stagnant economy, the socioeconomic dislocations caused by neoliberal economic policies, the demands of the coca producers, as well as the political, social, and economic demands of the Indians, working classes, and the poor.

The shift to the left in the leadership of these nations created by the socioeconomic devastation caused by the neoliberal experiment that began in the 1980s portends a pattern that can be discerned in other Latin American nations that have also had disastrous experiences with neoliberalism and globalization, such as Argentina, Brazil, Uruguay, and Venezuela. The Andean nations' indigenous masses have rejected outright neoliberalism and globalization as evidenced by their popular mobilizations against governments antithetical to their political, social, and economic interests. This mass participation in the political process by the Indian masses is another important trend at the dawning of the twenty-first century. Since the colonial period, these nations' Indian peoples have been shunted from full participation in the society. After independence, they were never fully recognized as citizens of the new nations with full political rights. The emergence of indigenous political parties in the three nations signifies that conflict with the traditional conservative *criollo* interests is inevitable in the future. Also, the US "war on drugs," as well as its promotion of neoliberal economic policies through the IMF and the World Bank, promises to exacerbate these conflicts, especially in the heavily Indian rural areas and Amazon region. It will be up to the leadership of these nations to balance the socioeconomic demands of the masses with economic growth based on an equitable distribution of wealth and political power in these multiethnic and multicultural societies.

CARLOS PÉREZ

See also Andean Community; Andean South America: International Relations; Bolivia; Ecuador; Peru

References and Further Reading

Conaghan, Catherine M, and James M. Malloy. *Unsettling Statecraft: Democracy and Neoliberalism in the Central Andes*. Pittsburgh and London: University of Pittsburgh Press, 1994.

Hidrobo Estrada, Jorge. *Power and Industrialization in Ecuador*. Boulder, CO: Westview Press, 1992.

Isaacs, Anita. *Military Rule and Transition in Ecuador, 1972–1992*. Houndmills, Basingstoke, Hampshire, England: Macmillan, in association with St. Antony's College, Oxford, 1993.

Kenney, Charles. *Fujimori's Coup and the Breakdown of Democracy in Latin America*. Notre Dame, IN: University of Notre Dame Press, 2004.

Klein, Herbert S. *A Concise History of Bolivia*. Cambridge: Cambridge University Press, 2003.

Kyle, David. *Transnational Peasants: Migrations, Networks, and Ethnicity in Andean Ecuador*. Baltimore, MD: Johns Hopkins University Press, 2000.

Morales, Waltraud Q. *Bolivia, Land of Struggle*. Boulder, CO: Westview Press, 1992.

Palmer, David Scott, ed. *The Shining Path of Peru*, 2d ed. New York: St. Martin's Press, 1994.

Poole, Deborah and Gerardo Renique. *Peru: Time of Fear*. London: Latin American Bureau, 1992.

Rudolph, James D. *Peru: The Evolution of a Crisis*. Westport, CT: Praeger, 1992.

Sheahan, John. *Searching for a Better Society: The Peruvian Economy from 1950*. University Park, PA: Pennsylvania State University Press, 1999.

Starn, Orin. *Nightwatch: The Politics of Protest in the Andes*. Durham, NC: Duke University Press, 1999.

Stern, Steve J., ed. *Shining and Other Paths: War and Society in Peru, 1980–1995*. Durham, NC, and London: Duke University Press, 1998.

Watters, Raymond F. *Poverty and Peasantry in Peru's Southern Andes, 1963–1990*. Basingstoke, England: Macmillan, 1994.

Wise, Carol. *Reinventing the State: Economic Strategy and Institutional Change in Peru*. Ann Arbor, MI: University of Michigan Press, 2003.

ANDEAN SOUTH AMERICA: INTERNATIONAL RELATIONS

Introduction

The nations discussed in this essay will be those of the Central Andes to include Bolivia, Ecuador, and Peru. They share a common territorial and political heritage as encompassed in the Viceroyalty of Peru until independence in 1824. Thereafter, until the end of World War II, these nations sought through multilateral foreign policies to overcome economic underdevelopment and political instability. Peru and Bolivia's overwhelming defeat by Chile in the War of the Pacific (1879–1883) and a protracted border dispute between Peru and Ecuador that erupted into military conflicts in 1940, 1980, and 1995, continued to shape the conduct of the foreign relations of these Andean nations until the end of the twentieth century. Aside from the narcotics trade, Peru and Ecuador also enforced a two hundred-mile offshore resource zone that primarily applied to fishing rights that led to numerous confrontations with US fishing vessels in the three decades after 1950. On the economic front, the Andean nations continued to work for a viable regional Andean free trade zone, which would give them some economic leverage as the other Latin American nations and the United States continued to integrate their economies. Peru especially sought new economic leverage that would free it from economic trade dominance of the United States. Especially during the government of Alberto Fujimori (1990–2000), Peru aimed to enhance its trade ties with the Pacific Rim nations, especially Japan.

Until 1990, all the aforementioned problems were important to inter-Andean and US-Andean relations, but they remained secondary to the primary concern of Cold War-related issues. Developments particularly influenced by Cold War rivalries were Washington's support for authoritarian military regimes and related arms sales agreements. After 1990, the US-Andean agenda was taken up almost exclusively with counternarcotics and Andean economic integration. Closely related to the drug issue in Peru were the terrorist activities of the revolutionary group *Sendero Luminoso* (Shining Path). Largely funded by narcotics revenues, *Sendero Luminoso* destroyed a sizeable amount of the nation's infrastructure and provoked mass economic disorder in a reign of terror between 1980 and 1992. During these the last two troubled decades of the twentieth century, perhaps as many as fifty thousand Peruvians died and 2 million left the country as a result of the domestic violence and economic turmoil.

The Cold War and the Andean Nations

As a small nation Ecuador has tried to maintain a multilateral approach to foreign affairs since its inception. But in reality, since the end of World War II, Ecuador has remained one of Washington's firmest allies in the region. Ecuador was a signatory of the 1947 regional security treaty that laid the groundwork for the Organization of American States and regional cooperation during the first years of the Cold War. US private investment, the presence of US-dominated multilateral agencies such as the World Bank and the Inter-American Development Bank, as well as a strong Peace Corps contingent since the early 1960s, have maintained a constant US presence in Ecuador in the post–World War II era. Over the years, there has been a growing emigrant stream from Ecuador to the United States that has strengthened the bonds between the two nations. Today, as many as two hundred thousand Ecuadorians live in the United States and fifteen thousand US citizens permanently reside in Ecuador. Additionally, significant US tourism since the 1970s has had a positive impact on the Ecuadorian economy.

Vast reserves of petroleum were discovered in Sucumbíos province in Ecuador's Oriente or eastern jungle region in the late 1960s. Ecuador soon joined OPEC, and its economy has been heavily dependent on petroleum revenues ever since. This has resulted in significant fluctuations in revenues as the world price of oil stayed above $25 through the mid-1980s. This price represented a tenfold increase in the cost of oil at the beginning of the oil boom in 1972. Still, prices leveled off in the late 1980s and early 1990s, placing great strain on the heavily subsidized Ecuadorian economy. In 2001, Ecuador drew on oil revenues to finance 46% of its national budget. Ecuador and OPEC's pricing policies often have been at odds with the priorities of the United States. Still the most controversial issue straining relations between the United States and Ecuador were conflicting interpretations of the limits of territorial waters. As with Chile and Peru, Ecuador claimed a two hundred-mile resource zone and began enforcing this claim during the late 1960s. What resulted were the so-called Tuna Wars. At its height in 1971, this controversy saw Ecuador seize fifty-one US fishing boats. Eventually, by the mid-1980s, the US State Department recognized the inevitable and modified its own resource zone limits to conform to those of the world's leading fishing nations.

Bolivia's 1952 social revolution was one of the first potential challenges to US policies of anticommunism in the hemisphere. Although the dominant ideology of the Revolution was not initially clear, the Eisenhower Administration sought to avoid a potential Marxist revolution in Bolivia by channeling very large amounts of financial aid to the Andean nation. Recognizing that turbulent Bolivia was one of Latin America's poorest nations, in mid-1953, Washington doubled its financial aid and soon after sent five million dollars in food assistance to Bolivia. At the conclusion of the 1950s, Bolivia was the recipient of $100 million in direct aid from the United States. Bolivia ranked first among all Latin American nations in US aid revenues and the leader per capita in world. Without US direct assistance, the Bolivian governments during the 1950s and early 1960s would have suffered significant financial difficulties as the result of the nationalization of the tin industry. Still, when tin revenues declined sharply in the 1970s, Bolivia's economic troubles became quite severe.

Directly related to the Cold War were US bilateral efforts to upgrade and train the Bolivia armed forces in counter-subversion. In significant measure, the substantial military assistance given to Bolivia by the United States in the aftermath of the Cuban Revolution in 1959 paved the way for the establishment of a series of military governments from 1964 to 1982. Much like their counterparts all over South America, with the notable exception of the government of General Juan Velasco Alvarado (1968–1975) in Peru, military dictatorships, operating with the Washington's support effectively quelled leftist urban and rural movements, sometimes at the cost of great suffering. The most "spectacular" success of the Bolivian army ranger units, who were trained in part by the Central Intelligence Agency, was the capture and execution of Ernesto "Che" Guevara in Santa Cruz province in October 1967. Guevara's death effectively spelled the demise of the *foco* theory of rural guerrilla warfare modeled after the Cuba revolution. In Bolivia, the Indian peasantry, which was a central element in the 1952 revolution, was largely marginalized in national affairs during the period of military rule. Bolivia's tin miners met the same fate as declining world prices for tin led to the closure of the nation's biggest mines by the early 1980s. Thereafter, substantial elements of Bolivia's rural population turned to coca production for their livelihoods. The peasantry would not again effectively organize until the 1990s under a markedly different ideology of indigenous mobilization.

Peru and the United States experienced a troubled relationship through most of the Cold War era that seems to be explained only by what could be called "Peruvian exceptionalism" on the part of Washington.

Peru was a very cooperative ally of the United States during World War II. During the early years of the Cold War, the military dictator General Manuel A. Odria (1948–1956) waged a concerted anti-communist campaign jailing hundreds of leftists and exiling hundreds more. During the late 1940s, the US Air Force did provide valuable assistance to Peru with the arduous aerial mapping of its long disputed border with Ecuador. Still, one of the last areas to remain uncharted, the rugged Cordillera del Condor, would become the focal point of hostilities a half century later.

Like Ecuador, Peru confronted US-owned fishing vessels in the tuna-laden Humboldt current in the 1960s, seizing a significant number and imposing heavy fines. Along with Chile, Peru declared a two hundred-mile "resource" zone as early as 1947. This was only one component of an increasingly nationalistic policy that emphasized state ownership of the nation's resource base.

The symbolic focus of this policy was the International Petroleum Company (IPC) and its holdings at Talara, in northern Peru. IPC, a subsidiary of Standard Oil of New Jersey, dominated Peruvian Petroleum production since the 1920s. Efforts to nationalize the company with compensation during the administration of President Fernando Belaunde Terry (1963–1968) failed. The Peruvian armed forces, under the leadership of a leftist populist General Juan Velasco Alvarado, used the IPC issue as an excuse to overthrow Belaunde Terry and establish a nationalist and reformist government in October 1968.

The Velasco regime, after seizing IPC properties, made it clear that it wanted little to do with Washington's policy goals in the region. It quickly reestablished diplomatic ties with Cuba. The Velasco government quickly expropriated IPC holdings and, over the course of the next five years, nationalized almost all of the nation's major industries including US-owned holdings in telecommunications, mining, tourism, and agriculture.

Peru's army leadership was primarily reformist; its Navy was not. This led to serious dispute within the military over policy. Still, the Velasco leadership clique prevailed and from the outset made an emphatic statement of independence from the United States by expelling its military assistance team from Peru in 1969. Anti-US feelings had grown in the Peruvian army and air force when, in 1967, Congress blocked the sale of Northrup F5A Freedom Fighter airplanes to Peru on the grounds that it conflicted with Alliance for Progress goals emphasizing economic development over military spending. This Congressional action came on the heels of the US sale of Skyhawk attack bombers to Argentina and, more importantly,

Hunter attack fighters to Chile in 1967. Congress went even further and blocked the sale of six British Canberra bombers by using a clause in an Anglo-American leasing agreement dating back to the Marshall Plan. The Belaunde regime was thus forced by military pressure to purchase twelve far more expensive Mirage V fighters. This type of episode would be repeated during the government of Alberto Fujimori regarding the purchase of MIG 29 fighters from Belarus after a major border clash with Ecuador. Clearly, the case of Peruvian "exceptionalism" regarding arms sales remained a consistently troubling issue in US-Peruvian relations.

As a result of the enmity created by the F5A cancellation, the Velasco government was not inclined to buy US arms when it set out to rebuild the army's armored division and augment the air forces fight-bomber capability in the early 1970s. Although influential army leaders such as General Jorge Fernandez Maldonado later insisted that arms sales talks were conducted with the United States, France, and Israel in good faith, Peru's military government also solicited offers from the Soviet Union and quickly agreed to a package of arms purchases from Moscow that were by far the largest by any nation besides Cuba in all of Latin America. In a series of purchases between 1973 and 1976, Peru purchased Sukhoi SU 22 fighter bombers, AN-26F Antonov aircraft, T-54 and T-55 medium tanks, 122 and 133 armored personnel carries, Mi-6 and Mi-8 helicopters, and SA-3 and SA-7 surface to air missiles. They soon led to the stationing of as many as one hundred Soviet military advisors in Peru over the course of the 1970s and 1980s. Additionally, significant numbers of Peruvian army and air force personnel were trained in the Soviet Union. Tensions between Peru and Chile rose significantly as many military observers in the United States and Latin America predicted that major military conflict between Chile and Peru would take place as the one hundredth anniversary of the War of the Pacific drew closer in 1979. Washington's policy of Peruvian "exceptionalism" had clearly backfired with regard to broad Cold War objectives. But the ouster of General Velasco in August 1975 and the more moderate policies of his successor General Francisco Morales Bermudez (1976–1980) soon reduced diplomatic tensions except with the lingering problems with Ecuador.

Border Conflict Between Ecuador and Peru

At the end of World War II, Peru had a single border issue: the international frontier demarcation of its border with Ecuador according to the Rio de Janeiro

Protocol of Peace, Friendship, and Limits, signed on January 29, 1942, at Rio de Janeiro, and agreed to by both governments following the retreat of the Peruvian troops from Ecuadorian territories occupied during the war both countries fought in the previous year. The governments of Argentina, Brazil, Chile, and the United Status acted as guarantors of that protocol.

Many Peruvians were disappointed with the outcome of the Rio de Janeiro negotiations, considering it unacceptable that after winning a war their country should return those territories they believed were granted by a Spanish Royal Decree of 1802. On the other side of the border, many Ecuadorians considered that the Rio Protocol sanctioned a significant loss of territories that at some stage had belonged to the Audiencia of Quito, and thus they considered them to be part of Ecuador's patrimony. In reality, the borderline corresponded to human occupation of the zone instead of the legal arguments raised by both countries for more than a century of border disputes. The Rio Protocol validated the effective presence of Ecuadorians in the upper jungle, with agricultural soils, and with large oil fields which will be discovered years later, and of Peruvians in the larger area covered by the lower jungle, with very poor soils.

The process of demarcation had to overcome fifteen differences, and the Brazilian arbiter accepted by both governments resolved ten of them in favor of Ecuador and five in favor of Peru. But eventually, a conflict arose over the true course of the Cenepa River.

In 1951, President Galo Plaza of Ecuador announced that his country could "never accept" a final boundary that did not recognize its rights to a sovereign outlet to the Amazon through the Marañon river. The situation became even more complicated in August 1960, when Ecuadorian President Velasco Ibarra declared the Rio Protocol null and void. The first major conflict since 1941 was fought in January 1981, when Ecuadorian military posts were discovered in the Peruvian part of the Cordillera del Condor. Peruvian President Fernando Belaunde Terry ordered the Peruvian Armed Forces to evict the invaders, and the fighting lasted almost a month, with a number of casualties on both sides. The issue remained unresolved as another similar border incident flared in 1991.

Again, this incident was quieted without resolving the demarcation problem. The Ecuadorian government then proposed the Pope's mediation on the matter in 1992, but the Peruvian government responded instead with the first official visit of a Peruvian President to Ecuador. During his visit, President Fujimori announced that Peru was willing to go ahead with the final solution to the border problem, framed by the Protocol of Rio, intending not only to complete the demarcation process, but also to establish the roads and port facilities necessary for ready access by Ecuadorians to the Amazon River. Fujimori also called for the creation of a Border Integration Zone and the establishment of a public and private plan of investments in that area to compensate for its low level of development. Fujimori's proposal, reinforced by a second visit to Ecuador in August 1992, received no answer, and the situation remained static until January 1995 when a new military conflict erupted in the Alto Cenepa.

This conflict involved almost five thousand men, and both sides suffered significant casualties. Although the fighting was limited to the Alto Cenepa zone, there was a constant danger that it could become a general war all along the Peru–Ecuador border. On February 17, both governments signed a peace declaration at Brasilia, agreeing to initiate conversations in order to find solutions to their differences, whereas the Guarantor countries formed a Military Observation Mission Ecuador/Peru (MOMEP) to avoid further incidents.

After several meetings, in October 1996 the governments of Peru and Ecuador agreed to seek a final solution to their border problems, framed by the Rio Protocol. Accordingly, a new stage of negotiations began, which lasted until January 1998 when four commissions were established to prepare proposals on a Treaty of Trade and Navigation, a Broad Agreement of Border Integration, to define the final border line and to establish some mechanism for mutual trust and security. During the following months, the four commissions met several times in the capitals of the Guarantor countries, being able to conclude their proposals by mid-1998. The most sensitive was the disposition of the final borderline. This was adjudicated with the help of two juridical-technical groups formed by experts of the Guarantor countries. The opinion of these two teams was very difficult to accept by the Ecuadorian public, leading to new border tensions and to a point that in August 1998 it was feared that a general conflict would again erupt between both countries. The situation was finally solved when the Guarantors proposed that the Peruvian government should offer to Ecuador a square kilometer as private property in Tiwinza, an area at the Cenepa valley where the Ecuadorian resistance lasted to the very end of the 1995 conflict. That offer was finally accepted by Ecuador, and on October 26, 1998, a set of treaties were signed at Brasilia that put and end to that centuries-old border dispute. Those agreements opened a new era on Peru–Ecuador relations, and established new hopes for those Peruvians and Ecuadorians living in the border region.

Peru, Chile, and Bolivia

Peruvian relations with Chile and Bolivia were strongly influenced by the outcome of the War of the Pacific (1879–1883). According to the treaty of 1929, between Peru and Chile, the province of Tacna was returned to Peru, whereas the province of Arica remained definitively in Chilean hands. That treaty established the new frontier between both countries and the Chilean obligation to provide a number of facilities for Peruvian use of the port of Arica. Although some attempts were made to fulfill this obligation, with port and rail lines being constructed, the Tacna-Arica, this issue was only finally solved in the year 2000, when both governments agreed that the Chilean obligations acquired seventy years before had already been met.

A protocol signed as a new clause to the 1929 treaty obligated Peru and Chile to refrain from transferring to a third country the territories of Tacna and Arica, without previous consent of the other nation involved. In practical terms, it meant that any Bolivian aspiration to obtain a sovereign seaport through those territories would require Peruvian and Chilean agreement. Due to that, when in 1950, the governments of Bolivia and Chile initiated negotiations about a possible seaport for the former, the Peruvian government showed its opposition to any cession of territories that were previously part of Peru. As part of these negotiations there were some discussions about Bolivian compensation to Chile with water from Lake Titicaca, a possibility that was also rejected by the Peruvian government as co-owner of that lake. To ratify this position, on July 30, 1955, Peru and Bolivia signed a joint declaration that included several topics of integration, as well as a mutual recognition of their sovereignty on the waters of Lake Titicaca, "which only could be used with mutual consent of both states." Two years later, on February 9, 1957, both countries signed an additional convention to develop a plan for the common use of the waters of this lake, agreeing also to build a road between the seaport of Ilo and La Paz. For a number of reasons, these international agreements were only ratified in 1987. With Brazilian funding, the road began to be constructed in 2004.

In 1975, the Bolivian government began new negotiations with Chile aiming to obtain a sovereign littoral, receiving as response an offer of a thin portion of land north of Arica, along the Peruvian border. This territorial cession would be in exchange of territorial compensation elsewhere in Bolivia. Having been consulted, in 1976, the Peruvian government expressed its intention to accept that transaction only

if a special zone was created between the city of Arica and the Peruvian border, under the sovereignty of the three nations. Chile rejected the Peruvian proposal, arguing that such arrangement would change in a substantial way the 1929 treaty. These consultations were conducted at a time when Peru was in a clear process of strengthening and modernizing its military power, mainly with soviet armament, creating a growing concern in Chile on the possibility that Peru could use that power to recover, by force, those territories lost in the War of the Pacific, whose centennial was about to be commemorate in 1979. Even when the presidents of Peru, Bolivia, and Chile met informally in Washington to talk about the Bolivian aspirations, relations between Peru and Chile remained tense and reached a crisis in late 1978, when a Chilean espionage network was discovered in Peru. This led to the expulsion of some Chilean diplomats and the withdrawal of both ambassadors.

This situation lasted until the end of the Military Regime, and in 1980, when both countries appointed new ambassadors, the situation normalized. The administration of presidents Fernando Belaunde Terry and Alan Garcia (1985–1990) sustained the previous position regarding a possible solution for the Bolivian seacoast problem, and Garcia opened negotiations with Chile aiming to reduce tensions along the border by withdrawing military forces from the area and fulfilling the pending issues of the 1929 treaty. Although these negotiations did not achieve their goals, a mutual negotiating process was established by regular meetings of the military representatives of both countries. The Chilean government also built a new rail station at Arica for use of the Peruvian line connecting that port with Tacna. Other details were worked out to ensure the autonomy of the operation of a Peruvian pier constructed in that area. Also ratified was the viability of some Peruvian properties in Arica.

In this context, in February 1987, when Peru and Bolivia finally appointed a binational Authority for Lake Titicaca, according the agreements of 1955 and 1957, President Garcia's government declared that Peru would be ready to accept a Chilean cession to Bolivia a thin strip of land in its former territories, provided Peruvian interests in that zone were not affected.

In the 1990s, under President Fujimori, the Peruvian economy was opened to foreign investment, the majority of which came from Chile. This created unprecedented strong economic links between the two nations. However, bilateral relations were still overshadowed by the pending issues of the 1929 treaty. In May 1993, both governments signed the Lima

Conventions. Both governments agreed to put aside these conventions in 1995 and continue negotiations to reach a final solution to those long-term pending issues. Meanwhile, the Peruvian government signed two other agreements with Bolivia, in 1996 and 1997, aiming to avoid its interference in its negotiations with Chile. Finally, Peru–Chile negotiations ended in November 1999, and early the following year, Peru received the facilities built by Chile in Arica for its use.

Besides the emotional value of the Peruvian presence in Arica, the operation of a pier at that port is part of a larger issue, the long-standing dispute of Peruvian and Chilean ports to control the Bolivian market. In this context, in 1992 Peru and Bolivia signed the agreements of Ilo, which provide the latter with a portion of tax-free land for industrial purpose and another one for a beach for leisure use. In return, the Bolivian government gave similar facilities to Peru at Puerto Suarez on the Paraguay River. The only pending issue with Chile now is the maritime international limit with arbitration recently requested by the International Court of Law at The Hague.

Regional Issues

By the late 1940s, General Odria's regime was attempting to attract foreign investment to help the country with industrialization. Most of the response came from the United States, which reinforced the already strong Peruvian dependence on the North American economy. When Manuel Prado (1956–1962) took office in 1956, he tried to diminish such dependency by fostering economic trade with Europe and other Latin American nations. In this context, Peru took part in efforts to create a free Latin American trade zone, signing an agreement in February 1960, with other six countries, creating the Asociación Latinoamericana de Libre Comercio (ALALC, Latin American Free Trade Association). Despite the free trade of this institution, the process was ineffective. Thus Andean countries began conversations leading to create another mechanism to help their development efforts. As a result of that, in August 1966, the Presidents of Chile, Colombia and Venezuela, as well as the President of Ecuador and the Peruvian Foreign Minister, met and agreed at Bogota, Colombia that they would make their best effort to promote the Latin American economic integration process and to undertake joint steps to accelerate the progress of those countries that were less developed. Three years later, on May 26, 1969, Bolivia, Chile, Colombia, Ecuador, and Peru, followed by Venezuela in 1973,

signed the Cartagena Agreement, establishing the Mercado Comun Andino (Andean Common Market), with headquarters at Lima. The main goal of this new institution was to promote a well-balanced and harmonious development of the country members. In contrast with the European integration process, Andean countries sustained a relatively small commercial exchange and significant political issues, as we have seen, impeded the process of integration.

Although some important measures were taken in the first years of the Grupo Andino, the process has slowed since 1975, mainly because differences about the treatment to foreign investment. Following its "Chicago School" of economic development Chile left the group in 1976. Some other problems arose with the regard to inter-regional trade. This issue was particularly sensitive to Peru because it depended heavily on regional markets to sustain its industry.

That situation lasted until the beginning of the Fujimori government, which made some efforts to reinforce the Peruvian commitment to the Grupo Andino, Fujimori supported the political integration process more than an economic one. According to this new approach to the integration process, in 1991 Peru signed the Caracas Declaration, agreeing with the other Andean countries to establish a free trade zone by January 1992 and a common market by 1995. However, Peruvian relations with other Andean countries suffered a major setback when on April 5, 1992, President Fujimori closed the Congress, thus abrogating the Constitution. This situation, and the Peruvian process to repair its shattered economy as the result of the war with *Sendero Luminoso,* led to the announcement in August 1992 that Peru was temporarily withdrawing from the Grupo Andino in those aspects related to a common import tax, which in fact was crucial to the commercial integration effort. In 1997, after special negotiations, Peru agreed to gradually apply that common import tax.

Another topic of regional cooperation was the defense of the two hundred maritime miles thesis, proposed initially as we have seen, by Chile and Peru (1947), and afterward by Ecuador (1950). The three countries met at Santiago, Chile, in 1952 and agreed to proclaim their sovereignty and exclusive jurisdiction on a minimal distance of two hundred nautical miles from their coast, inorder to preserve resources in that maritime zone and its continental platform. Such a proclamation was strongly opposed by several developed countries, especially the United States and Japan. As part of the effort to defend their maritime resources, in 1952, Chile, Ecuador, and Peru created the Comisión Permanente del Pacífico Sur (Permanent Commission of the Southern Pacific), being joined in 1979 by Colombia. The headquarters of this commission has rotated since then until the year 2000, when it finally permanently established at Guayaquil, Ecuador.

Conclusion

Even with active movements toward globalization in the Andean region, progress against nearly universal problems of poverty, poor health standards, and the establishment of stable ethnic and cultural identities is progressing very slowly. Still, long-standing and potentially volatile issues such as the Peru–Ecuador border dispute and differences among Chile, Bolivia, and Peru are now resolved, allowing these nations to cooperate at an international level never before possible. US–Andean relations are at the moment far too one-dimensional. Focused as they are primarily on the drug trade, funds that could be earmarked for other development issues are generally not available. As long as US interests remain primarily focused upon the Middle East, this situation will remain the same. Meanwhile, the internal politics of the Andean region is rapidly changing. The trend toward greater participatory democracy is continuing, especially among indigenous groups. But indications are that this trend will hardly be synonymous with US policies in the region.

DANIEL M. MASTERSON AND JORGE ORTIZ SOTELO

See also Andean South America: History and Economic Development; Bolivia; Ecuador; Peru; Shining Path/ _Sendero Luminoso_; Territorial Disputes

References and Further Reading

Agüero Colunga, Marisol. _Consideraciones para la Delimitacion Maritima del Peru_. Lima: Fondo Editorial del Congreso del Peru, 2001, 305–308.

Bakula, Juan Miguel. "Las Relaciones del Peru y Chile: Perspective Historica." _Analisis Internacional_ vol. 2 13–14: (April–June 1993).

Clayton, Lawrence. _Peru and the United States: The Condor and the Eagle_. Athens, GA: University of Georgia Press, 1999.

Gerlach, Allen. _Indians, Oil, and Politics: A Recent History of Ecuador_. Wilmington, DE: Scholarly Resources, 2003.

Ivan DeGregori, Carlos. "Chayraq." In _The Peru Reader: History, Culture and Politics_, edited by Orin Starn, Carlos Ivan DeGregori, and Robin Kirk. Durham, NC: Duke University Press, 1995, 460–464.

Klaren, Peter, F. _Peru: Society and Nationhood in the Andes_. Oxford: Oxford University Press, 200

Klein, Herbert S. _Bolivia: The Evolution of a Multi-Ethnic Society_, 2d ed. Oxford: Oxford University Press, 1992.

Luna, Felix Denegri. _Notes for the History of a Frontier_. Lima: Bolsa de Valores, 1996.

Masterson, Daniel M. _Militarism and Politics in Latin America: Peru from Sanchez Cerro to Sendero Luminoso_. Westport, CT: Greenwood Press, 1991.

Morelli Pando, Jorge. "Caducidad de las Convenciones de Lima." _Analisis Internacional_ vol. 12 46–63 (January–April, 1996).

Namihas, Sandra, ed. _El Proceso de Conversaciones para la Solucion Diferendo Peruano-Ecuadoriano, 1995–1998_. Lima: Instituto de Estudios Peruanos, 2000.

Ortiz Sotelo, Jorge. "El Pacifico sudamericano punto de encuentros y desencuentros." Luis Milliones y Jose Villa Rodriquez, eds., _Peru: El Legado de la Historia_. Sevilla: PromPeru, Fundacion El Monte, 2001, 207–219.

Palmer, David Scott. "Peru–Ecuador Border Conflict: Missed Opportunities, Misplaced Nationalism and Multilateral Peacekeeping." _Journal of Inter-American Studies and World Affairs_ 39:3 109–148 (Fall 1997).

St. John, Ronald Bruce. _The Foreign Policy of Peru_. Boulder, CO: Lynn Reinner Publishers, 1992.

Zook, Jr., David H. _Zarumilla-Maranon: The Ecuador-Peru Border Dispute_. New York: Bookman Associates, 1964.

ANGLICAN COMMUNION

The Anglican Communion is the name of the association of Christian churches and leadership that follow the traditions of the Church of England, as contrasted with those of the Roman Catholic Church or other Anglican or Christian sects. While the Anglican and Roman churches both have their roots in the western Christian tradition, the churches of the Anglican Communion follow certain different traditions. The churches of the Anglican Communion are very active in the developing world, due in part to the British colonial roots in many regions. As of early 2005, more than forty separate organizations were members of the Anglican Communion. However, the churches of the Anglican Communion are not limited to former British colonies; the Anglican Communion is active throughout Africa, South America, and parts of Asia that were never under British control. Since the 1950s, this organization has worked to develop independent "provinces" (regional church organizations) that are united by their common beliefs and traditions.

The Anglican Communion differs from the Roman Catholic church in that the Anglican church is based on four "instruments of unity," which are the acceptance of the Archbishop of Canterbury as primate (leader of the church); the Lambeth Conference (which takes place once every ten years); its Primates (archbishops and presiding bishops of the regional churches); and the Anglican Consultative Council, a lower-level association of ordained and nonordained church members. The Primates and the Anglican Consultative Council have meetings of their organizations every two to three years. An ongoing effort of The Anglican Communion is the reconciliation of the various branches of Christianity.

This effort to unify the various branches of Christianity is based on the Anglican Communion's use of the policy of *adiaphora,* the belief that while many practices of different churches may vary from one another, these practices should not divide people from their fundamental beliefs that are derived from scripture. *Adiaphora,* when applied to the many practices that divide Christian (or other religious) denominations, would in theory help to preclude the schisms that fragment the followers of essentially similar beliefs. As of the year 2005, the Anglican Communion faced a crisis of this basis, which resulted from the ordination of a US bishop who was involved in a same-sex union. The more traditional provinces of the Anglican Communion objected to the ordination, feeling that the US diocese had rejected the Anglican Communion's ban on sexual relationships outside of marriage.

The Anglican Communion should not be confused with the Traditional Anglican Communion, a much smaller group that split off from the Episcopal Church in 1977 over doctrinal issues such as the role of women as clergy. Groups such as the Traditional Anglican Communion do not recognize the authority of the Archbishop of Canterbury and are held to be "not in communion" with the Anglican Communion. The confusion between these groups arises over the common use of the word "Anglican."

Many of the groups that have split from the established Episcopal or Anglican churches maintain that they are following the correct doctrinal path, believing that the older organizations have deviated from correct beliefs and procedures. This is very similar to the justification used by King Henry VIII to justify his establishment of the Church of England in the 1530s, that the Roman Catholic Church had strayed from traditions and that Henry's church followed the correct path.

THOMAS P. DOLAN

References and Further Reading

Simcox, Carroll Eugene. *The Historical Road of Anglicanism.* Chicago: H. Regnery, 1968.
The Windsor Report 2004 of The Lambeth Commission on Communion.
Welsby, Paul A. *A History of the Church of England, 1945–1980.* London: Oxford University Press, 1984.

ANGLO-IRANIAN OIL COMPANY (AIOC)

On May 28, 1901, Mozaffaredin Shah Qajar, the shah of Iran, granted William Knox D'Arcy, a British capitalist and speculator, a concession for sixty years to explore for oil in Iran. In return the shah was to receive twenty thousand pounds cash, a similar amount in shares, and 16% of the annual profits. With the help of the British Admiralty, a deal was struck with Burmah Oil, which provided additional capital. On May 26, 1908, a gusher of oil rose about fifty feet above the drilling rig in Masjed Soleiman. The Anglo-Persian Oil Company was formed in 1909.

In August 1914, the British government acquired a 51% interest in the company. In the meantime, the company reached an agreement with the Admiralty to supply it with oil at a discount price.

From the start the Iranian government and the company could not see eye to eye on some issues. Extensive negotiations over royalty payments were conducted between the two sides. These negotiations did not bear fruit, and the British government took the matter to the League of Nations. The outcome was that the two sides were advised to go back to negotiations. Iran, however, did not have many options: Britain was the dominant superpower and Iran needed the oil revenues. Soon a new concession was agreed upon that increased Iran's share of the company's profits, extended the concession period to 1993, and reduced the area under concession by 80%. In 1935, the company was renamed the Anglo-Iranian Oil Co.

During World War II, Iranian oil fields were deemed crucial for the war efforts. One reason for the invasion of Iran by the British and Russian forces in August 1941 was to safeguard the oil fields.

During its years of operation in Iran, the company grew tremendously. The company built a modern refinery, which was the largest in the world, in Abadan on the Persian Gulf. It had subsidiaries around the world.

After the war, nationalism was on the rise, Britain had lost its status as a world power, and US companies had offered fifty-fifty profit sharing deals to Middle Eastern countries. In early 1951, Dr. Mohammad Mosaddeq, the champion of oil nationalization, became the prime minister. He ordered the takeover of oil installations, and British employees of the company left Iran. Over the next two years, a tug of war continued between Iran on one side and the company and the British government on the other. The British government imposed economic sanctions and threatened military action against Iran.

August 19, 1953, witnessed a growing street protest against the government, which was later joined by some military and police units and personnel. By the end of the day, the government was overthrown, and General Fazlollah Zahedi became the prime minister.

After Mosaddeq's downfall, extensive negotiations were held among the United States, Britain, and Iran to find a new arrangement to restart the Iranian oil industry. In October 1954, the Iranian parliament ratified an agreement with a consortium of oil companies to operate the Iranian oil industry. The company had a 40% share in this consortium. The rest of the shares were divided between five US majors (40%), Shell (14%) and Compagnie Française des Pétroles (6%). The company changed its name to British Petroleum (BP) in the same year.

KAMRAN M. DADKHAH

See also Iran; Mossaddeq, Muhammed

References and Further Reading:

Bamberg, James. *The History of the British Petroleum Company: Volume II, The Anglo-Iranian Years, 1928–1954.* Cambridge: Cambridge University Press, 1994.
Bamberg, James. *British Petroleum and Global Oil, 1950–1975: The Challenge of Nationalism.* Cambridge: Cambridge University Press, 2000.
Shwadran, Benjamin. *The Middle East, Oil and the Great Powers,* 3d ed. New York: John Wiley & Sons, 1973.
Yergin, Daniel. *The Prize: The Epic Quest for Oil, Money, and Power.* New York: Simon & Schuster, 1991.

ANGOLA

Located along the southwestern coastal region of Africa, Angola roughly approximates the size and shape of Egypt. The country stretches south of the lower Congo River except for a small enclave, Cabinda, lying north. The population of 11 million is divided into an intricate web of varying ethnic groups. As almost all peoples of Southern Africa, most Angolans speak various dialects or languages of the Bantu family. More than three-fourths of the population resides in the northwest quadrant of the country, concentrating the country's three major ethnic and linguistic groupings.

In the southern third of this quadrant is the largest group, the Ovimbundu, who comprise almost 40% of Angolans. They speak Umbundu, and their territory stretches up from the Atlantic Ocean into the Benguela Plateau, west and south of the Benguela River.

To the north of the Ovimbundu, between the Cuanza and Longa rivers in the south and the Dande River in the north, are the Mbundu, who speak Kimbundu. Representing about one-fourth of Angolans, they are settled from the coast into the Malanje Plateau, below the Benguela. The national capital, Luanda, is located in this region, lying on the coast midway between the Cuanza and Dande rivers. Its population of more than a million contains a mosaic of all the ethnic and linguistic groupings of Angola.

Above the Dande River and descending to the Congo River are the Bakongo. They speak Kikongo and amount to one-sixth of Angolans. To the south and east of these three groups lies the remaining fourth of the population. Varying from portions of 2%–10% of the population, these Bantu-speaking inhabitants are settled in an arc from south to east-northeast that comprises the Herero, Nyaneke-Humbe, Ovambo, Xindonga, Nganguela, and Lunda-Chokwe, respectively.

Two non-Bantu speaking groups inhabit the dry far south. The Click-speaking Khoisan representing 2% of the population, are bush people pushed into this region centuries ago by the advancing Bantu.

Another 2% of the population is *mestiço*, of mixed African and Portuguese colonial breeding. Speaking primarily Portuguese, they are interspersed through the western half of the country and especially in the capital.

Since the end of the fifteenth century, the Portuguese have been a crucial factor in the development, or lack thereof, of Angola. As they made their voyages of discovery during the fifteen century along the coasts of western and eastern Africa, and on to Asia and Brazil, Angola became important as a source of slaves, who were shipped across the Atlantic to the Americas. This trade reached its peak in the eighteenth century and lasted into the middle of the nineteenth century. During the period and with the connivance of local chiefdoms, several million Angolans were shipped across the ocean.

Angola, which holds significant resources of diamonds, iron ore, and petroleum, was one of the last major colonies that Portugal held into the twentieth century. Through the 1930s to the early 1970s, a fascist regime controlled Portugal. After World War II, with independence movements sweeping Africa, the Portuguese authoritarian regime increasingly had to use military force to keep Angola. During the 1960s, three Angolan independence movements arose, concentrated among the Bakongo, Mbundu, and Ovimbundu.

In 1974, the Portuguese overthrew their fascist regime and the following year granted Angola independence. The three independence movements, however, rather than uniting, began a protracted civil war that has devastated the country ever since. These factions comprise the following: the National Front for the Liberation of Angola (FNLA, a Portuguese acronym), the National Union for the Total Independence of Angola (UNITA), and the Popular Movement for the Liberation of Angola (MPLA). Until the early 1990s, each faction received outside aid from countries reflecting the ideologies and strategic interests of the Cold War. Although that war has ended, the Angolan strife has continued into the present century, maintained by the momentum of rivalries and resources of the three factions.

The head of the MPLA, José Eduardo dos Santos, has been president of the country since 1979. With power concentrated around Luanda and among the Mbundu, he received international backing from the Soviet Union and Cuba. He consistently blocked UNITA leader Jonas Savimbi from occupying the presidency. Savimbi's power lay with the Ovimbundu, and his foreign support included the United States and South Africa. The FNLA, with varying leadership, received support from the People's Republic of China, the Chinese thereby countering their Soviet rival.

Decades of warfare have created an economy and society in shambles. The purchasing power of the gross domestic product is little more than eleven billion dollars, no more than a thousand dollars per capita. Life expectancy is just under forty years, and the infant mortality rate is almost two hundred per one thousand live births. More than two-fifths of the population is below age fourteen and over half are between fifteen and sixty-four years of age. Only 3% of the population has survived to age sixty-five or older. Just two-fifths of the population over age fifteen is literate, and the rate of literacy among males is twice that among females. Many people, especially young males, have lost legs and arms due to landmines. More than two-fifths of the population adheres to animist religions; more than one-third is Catholic; and about one-sixth is Protestant.

Angola is a society almost totally fractured along ethnic, linguistic, economic, political, military, and religious fault lines. No conjunction of interests has emerged to form a sustaining national majority. The country has wealth that could serve as a great benefit to its inhabitants. These resources have in practice, however, been a lure resulting in debilitating competition and conflict. An estimated 1.5 million people have died from the combat and violence that have continued since independence.

The death of Jonas Savimbi in 2002 prompted UNITA to initiate a truce with the government, which has so far endured. Most enduring, however, is the wreckage of Angola after decades of warfare.

EDWARD A. RIEDINGER

See also Ethnic Conflicts: Southern Africa; Southern Africa: History and Economic Development; Southern Africa: International Relations

References and Further Reading

Birmingham, David. *Frontline Nationalism in Angola and Mozambique*, Trenton, NJ: Africa World Press, 1992.

Ciment, James. *Angola and Mozambique: Postcolonial Wars in Southern Africa*. New York: Facts on File, 1997.

Guimarães, Fernando Andresen. *The Origins of the Angolan Civil War: Foreign Intervention and Domestic Political Conflict*. New York: St. Martin's, 1998.

Heywood, Linda. *Contested Power in Angola, 1840s to the Present*. Rochester, NY: University of Rochester Press, 2000.

Kaure, Alexactus T. *Angola: From Socialism to Liberal Reforms*. Mt. Pleasant, Harare: SAPES Books, 1999.

Spike, Daniel. *Angola and the Politics of Intervention: From Local Bush War to Chronic Crisis in Southern Africa*. Jefferson, NC: McFarland, 1993.

Tvedita, Inge. *Angola: Struggle for Peace and Reconstruction*. Boulder, CO: Westview Press, 1997.

Walker, Graham. *Angola: The Promise of Riches*. London: Africa File, 1990.

ANGUILLA

Anguilla, the northernmost of the Leeward Islands, is an overseas territory of the United Kingdom. The colony, which lies 240 kilometers east of Puerto Rico and eight kilometers north of St. Martin/St. Marteen, is twenty-six kilometers long and six kilometers wide. There is virtually no arable land on the ninety-one-square-kilometer flat coral island. Two small islands lying off the coast of Anguilla—Scrub Island and Dog Island—account for the remainder of the colony's 102 square kilometers of land. The beautiful beaches along the colony's sixty-one-kilometer coastline, in addition to the virtual lack of crime on the island, make Anguilla an ideal tourist destination. The majority of Anguilla's thirteen thousand inhabitants are descendants of African slaves. About 10% of Anguilla's people live in The Valley, the capital. Most people are devout Anglicans and Methodists. Anguilla is a member of the British Commonwealth of Nations and an associate member of the Organization of Eastern Caribbean States.

Anguilla was first colonized by English settlers from St. Kitts in 1650. In the early nineteenth century, much to the chagrin of the people living on the island, Anguilla was incorporated into a single administrative unit with St. Kitts and Nevis. In 1967, in an island-wide referendum, virtually the entire population voted for secession from St. Kitts and Nevis. Following a secession revolt led by Ronald Webster in 1969, the British military intervened to restore order and stability. In 1980, the British government, in preparation for the independence of St. Kitts and Nevis in 1983, officially made Anguilla a separate British dependency. Most of Anguilla's people do not support total independence. Anguilla is seeking to consolidate its dependence on the colonial power and integrate itself into the global economy.

Although British officials are responsible for defense and foreign relations, local elected officials are responsible for all internal affairs, except security. Anguilla is administered under a constitution that took effect on April 1, 1982. Queen Elizabeth II is represented locally by a governor—Peter Johnstone since 2000—who oversees the Executive Council and the House of Assembly. The governor is appointed by the British government. The House of Assembly consists of 11 members—seven elected members, who are elected by the people of Anguilla every five years; two *ex officio* members, the attorney general and the permanent secretary for finance; and two other members, nominated by the governor after consultation with the chief minister. Although appointed by the governor, the chief minister—Osborne Fleming since 2000—is normally the leader of the majority political party in the House of Assembly. The Executive Council consists of a chief minister and not more than three other ministers appointed by the governor from the elected members of the House of Assembly and the two *ex officio* members.

During the 1980s, the House of Assembly emphasized a policy of revitalizing the island's economy through tourism and foreign investment. Anguilla's economic growth has been a direct result of its improved standing as a tourist attraction, which provided revenue for the private sector through tourist-related services and for the public sector through increased duties. The Caribbean Development Bank (CDB) funded the construction of a new airport terminal to facilitate the flow of tourists. In 1978, fewer than five thousand tourists visited Anguilla. In 1990, the number of tourists approached one hundred thousand. Although tourism has provided lucrative income for the island, the annual threat of hurricanes limits the expansion of the tourism industry. Salt exports to Trinidad and Tobago, offshore banking, and workers' remittances from abroad have contributed to the growth of the economy.

Economic development, however, has led to political and social controversy in Anguilla. The uncontrolled growth of foreign-owned villas on the coast caused real estate prices to soar and threatened to damage the vulnerable ecosystem on the island. In response, the House of Assembly responded with legislation that regulated the height and size of beachfront homes. In addition, restrictions were placed on land sales to foreigners. The attempt by hotel owners to open casinos caused a fiery debate among Anguilla's deeply religious population. Although maintaining their moral and ethical integrity, the people of Anguilla are losing valuable tourist dollars. The expansion of offshore banking, once seen by Anguilla's politicians as the panacea for economic development, has not provided the economic windfall previously envisioned. Rather, the island's banking industry has come under the scrutiny of the US Internal Revenue Service, which suspected money laundering from drug trafficking in the offshore banking facilities.

MICHAEL R. HALL

See also Caribbean Development Bank; Caribbean: History and Economic Development; Caribbean: International Relations; Organization of Eastern Caribbean States (OECS); St. Christopher and Nevis

References and Further Reading

Ferguson, James. *Eastern Caribbean in Focus: A Guide to the People, Politics, and Culture.* Northampton, MA: Interlink Publishing, 1997.
Grossman, Lawrence S. *The Political Ecology of Bananas: Contract Farming, Peasants, and Agrarian Change in the Eastern Caribbean.* Chapel Hill, NC: University of North Carolina Press, 1998.
Petty, Colville, *Anguilla: Where There's a Will There's a Way.* The Valley, Anguilla: C. L. Petty, 1984.
Ramos, Aaron Gamaliel, and Angel Israel Rivera. *Islands at the Crossroads: Politics in the Non-Independent Caribbean.* Kingston, Jamaica: Ian Randle Publishers, 2001.
Showker, Kay. *Caribbean Ports of Call: Eastern and Southern Regions.* Guilford, CT: Globe Pequot, 2004.
Taylor, Jeremy, ed. *The Caribbean Handbook.* St. John's, Antigua, and Barbuda: F. T. Caribbean, 1986.

ANTIGUA AND BARBUDA

The country of Antigua and Barbuda is situated in the Leeward Islands of the eastern Caribbean. Antigua is approximately 108 square miles, whereas its sister isle, Barbuda, is about sixty-two square miles. The nation also encompasses another smaller uninhabited island, Redonda, which is little more than half a square mile and houses a nature preserve. Both Antigua and Barbuda are flat islands bounded on the west by the Caribbean Sea and on the east by the Atlantic Ocean. These islands enjoy a tropical climate but are susceptible to droughts, with annual rainfall averaging about forty-five inches, and hurricanes, with the annual hurricane season lasting from July to October. Coral limestone, swamplands, and mudflats compose Barbuda's topography; it also contains the largest saltwater lagoon in the Caribbean. Antigua has a mix of volcanic hills and plains in the south and west and calcareous limestone soil in the north and east. Antigua's shoreline contains many natural harbors and beaches. Barbuda also has beaches and a large western harbor. Population estimates vary, but generally figures total about seventy thousand people, with 98% of this number residing in Antigua. The population growth rate is approximately 0.6%. The nation's capital is St. John's, located in the northwest section of Antigua.

After a period of Amerindian settlement by Arawaks and Caribs dating back to 3100 BC, Antigua and Barbuda's period of European occupation began with the arrival of Columbus in 1493. After Spanish and French attempts at settlement, the British assumed control of Antigua in 1632 and Barbuda in 1678. The British began production of tobacco in Antigua, but by the 1650s, this crop was abandoned for the more successful sugar cane, which was manufactured regularly for commercial export for more than three centuries afterward. Barbuda's topsoil could not support commercial plantation systems of this kind, and its inhabitants engaged in skilled trades, small-scale farming, livestock raising, or lumber production. The Codringtons, a prominent British sugar-planting family, held Barbuda under a two hundred-year private lease starting in 1685 and used the island's natural resources to supply their Antiguan sugar estates. Antigua was populated by the constant influx of enslaved persons from West Africa that continued until the British government outlawed slavery in 1834. Slave importation into Barbuda generally ended in the mid-1700s, and the population there grew naturally thereafter.

After emancipation, sugar continued to dominate Antigua's economy for more than a century, despite the lag in British West Indian sugar in the world markets from the mid-1800s onward. Like elsewhere in the Caribbean, by the early twentieth century, a trade union movement was borne from workers' dissatisfaction with unpredictable wages and unsavory working conditions in Antigua. Trade unionists also began political organizing from the 1930s onward, commencing the process toward self-government. Mainly through the island's foremost union, the Antigua Trades and Labour Union (ATLU), local leaders spearheaded massive strikes and advocated constitutional reform in the 1940s. The ATLU president, Vere Cornwall Bird, also successfully pushed for full adult suffrage in 1951. By 1967, the constitution was rewritten to grant Antigua full internal self-government, officially becoming an Associated State of Great Britain. Bird was elected as Antigua's first Premier. At the same time, the Antiguan government took control of the collapsing sugar industry and introduced other industries to the island, particularly tourism.

Bird and the Antigua Labour Party (ALP), the political arm of the ATLU, dominated local elections and tolerated little opposition from the 1950s through the 1990s. The Bird government displayed severely authoritarian tendencies, and repeated instances of corruption and scandal overshadowed their contributions to political and economic progress. But in addition to a 1971–1976 term as Premier by George Walter, a former ATLU leader who seceded to form an opposition union and political party, the Progressive Liberation Movement, Antigua remained firmly under ALP control. Bird served as Premier from 1976 onward and became Prime Minister when Britain granted full independence in 1981. He retired in 1994, and his son, Lester Bird, was elected to office. The Bird stronghold ended in 2004, when the current opposition political party, United Progressive Party, won elections and the party leader, Baldwin Spencer, became Prime Minister.

Antigua and Barbuda's economy, formerly dominated by commercial agriculture, became largely dependent on tourism during the late twentieth century. Presently, tourism remains the major focus of the government, but especially after recent global economic downturns and lags in international travel, the government has attempted to diversify the economy by introducing offshore financial services, information technology, and telecommunications services. Smaller industries include construction, manufacturing, and agriculture. Per capita gross domestic product in 2004 was an estimated $11,000, and unemployment is 11%, while poverty is 12%. The country suffers from fiscal imbalances and high levels of external debt, and the government has attempted to address these issues through such measures as taxation restructuring and a reduction in the nation's overpopulated civil service.

Since the early twentieth century, Barbuda has remained grossly underdeveloped relative to Antigua, with various schemes for commercial agriculture having failed and little resources put toward infrastructure, education, or services. Generally, residents must go to Antigua to obtain major goods and services. Barbuda has a small tourism industry, which, along with a limited retail sector and fisheries, produces revenue among its population. Barbudans elect a representative to the Antiguan government, but generally Barbudans consider their political and economic interests to be disregarded by Antiguans. Murmurings about secession from Antigua began in 1968; however, those eventually subsided with the introduction in 1976 of a local governing body, the Barbuda Council, which still exists. A tense but stable association between Antigua and Barbuda continues at present.

Antigua has sufficient infrastructure, with paved roads, a public bus system, and a deep-water harbor in St. John's. St. John's also is home to an airport where major regional and international airlines conduct regular service. Barbuda has a small airstrip that allows for travel to and from Antigua only. Adult literacy in Antigua and Barbuda is estimated at 85%, and the government provides free and compulsory education for primary and secondary schooling. Tertiary educational institutions include the Antigua State College and the University Centre, a continuing education branch of the University of the West Indies.

Infant mortality is seventeen per one thousand live births, and life expectancy is sixty-nine years for men and seventy-three years for women. Health care is available through a Medical Benefits Scheme for all workers and their dependents; the physician-to-population ratio is eleven per ten thousand, and the government provides full immunization coverage for children up to age five. At present, the majority of the population of Antigua and Barbuda is of African descent, with small numbers of other ethnic groups in residence, particularly Portuguese, Lebanese, Syrians, East Indians, and Chinese. Regarding religious beliefs, the country is largely Anglican (about 75%), with Catholicism, other Christian Protestant denominations, Islam, and Rastafarianism also present as well.

NATASHA J. LIGHTFOOT

See also Caribbean: History and Economic Development; Caribbean: International Relations

References and Further Reading:

Berleant-Schiller, Riva, and Susan Lowes, with Milton Benjamin, comps. *Antigua and Barbuda*, World Bibliographical Series, Vol. 182. Oxford: ABC-CLIO Ltd., 1995.

Dyde, Brian. *A History of Antigua: The Unsuspected Isle.* London: Macmillan, 2000.

Hall, Douglas. *Five of the Leewards, 1834–1870: The Major Problems of the Postemancipation Period in Antigua, Barbuda, Montserrat, Nevis, and St. Kitts.* Barbados: Caribbean University Press, 1971.

Henry, Paget. *Peripheral Capitalism and Underdevelopment in Antigua.* New Brunswick, NJ: Transaction Books, 1985.

Lazarus-Black, Mindie. *Legitimate Acts and Illegal Encounters: Law and Society in Antigua and Barbuda.* Smithsonian Series in Ethnographic Enquiry. Washington, DC: Smithsonian Institution Press, 1994.

Lowenthal, David, and Colin G. Clarke. "Slave Breeding in Barbuda: The Past of a Negro Myth." In *Comparative Perspectives on Slavery in New World Plantation Societies,* edited by Vera Rubin and Arthur Tuden. New York: The New York Academy of Sciences, 510–531, 1977.

Smith, Keithlyn B. *No Easy Pushover: A History of the Working People of Antigua and Barbuda, 1836–1994.* Scarborough, Ont.: Edan's Publishers, 1994.

APARTHEID

Apartheid, or racial segregation, emerged in South Africa within a unique context of social, political, economic, and cultural conditions. These conditions led South Africa on a dichotomous course of development in which two realities existed simultaneously. During the official years of apartheid, 1948–1990, the reality of the white South African, either Afrikaner or British, might generally be described as First World, developed, economically secure, educated, and politically powerful. Conversely, the reality of the native African population was a Third World existence, undeveloped, impoverished, undereducated, disenfranchised, and oppressed. Invariably, these two realities between the minority white population and the majority black population could not coexist peacefully. No amount of ideology and religious conviction, gold wealth and economic development, or military and police power could sustain the white minority apartheid regime. The disorder, chaos, and economic decline created by the anti-apartheid liberation struggle, international sanctions, and multinational divestment, and the unabashed iniquity of the racist regime led ultimately to the collapse of apartheid and the creation of a government of national unity with universal and equal rights for all of South Africa's citizens.

Prelude to Apartheid

The Europeans, specifically the Dutch, first settled South Africa in 1652 when the Dutch East India Company arrived in Cape Town to establish a refreshment station for its passing ships headed to the Far East. The British officially arrived in the early 1800s in an effort to colonize and exploit the area's rich resources. For years, the Dutch, British, and Africans coexisted in relative peace, until as the populations and economy grew, as land became scarce, and as the government and individuals became more involved in politics, peaceful coexistence gave way to greater conflicts and bloodshed. In 1835, the deeply religious, Calvinist Afrikaner/Dutch population set out east on a "Great Trek" to find new land away and separate from the ever-present British and African, as well as to establish a community entirely of their own making. The trials and tribulations of the Great Trek, and the subsequent years of conflicts with the native African people and the British, formed a unique Afrikaner identity and civil society that was believed to be ordained by God. This belief eventually provided justification for separate social, political, and economic development between the races.

The century between 1806 (with British occupation of the Cape) and 1909 (the establishment of the Union as part of the British Commonwealth) was considered a "Period of Revelation" in which God made known His will to the Afrikaner people. They were to establish a Christian nation among the heathen natives of Southern Africa.

After the Union of South Africa was established and the equality of the two white races was assured by a constitution, the status of the African population was degraded to the point of being deemed "the colour problem." The Africans and colored who had previously possessed voting rights in the Cape Province were disenfranchised. Nevertheless, the Afrikaner felt inferior to the British during this period of imperialism. English was the language spoken by most (including Afrikaners). Afrikaans was merely a folk language not having yet become fully developed and accepted as an official language. Governmental power, as well as economic power, was in the hands of the British South Africans. The Afrikaners were either traditional farmers or poor urban dwellers. They were, in actuality, second-class citizens.

During the first years of the twentieth century, the Afrikaner *volk* began to reestablish the identity that had been decimated during the Anglo-Boer War years (1899–1902). Their sense of national pride, which was at its height during the years of the Great Trek, began to blossom once again. A renewed pride in their history, language, culture, and religion resulted in an eruption of civic and political organizations in the early part of the century, such as the *Broederbond* (a secret whites-only organization whose aim was to solidify Afrikaner power) and the National Party (NP), which emphasized Afrikanerdom and Christian Nationalism. During this period, the Dutch Reformed Church (DRC), which initially accommodated all sorts of believers—slaves, French Huguenots, German soldiers, and officials—developed into a church identifying itself with one specific population, namely the white Afrikaners. It is at this point that the DRC began to provide legitimacy for the divisive, exclusionary policies of racial and ethnic separation, responding to the political reality of British domination and the pervasiveness of the African.

The early 1900s saw the development of an Afrikaner civil religion based on a belief of their history being ordained by God. This belief permeated every aspect of Afrikaner life. "In the Afrikaner civil religion, God imbues all history with ultimate meaning. He rules sovereign over the world and works His will in the affairs of nations—most visible in Afrikanerdom (Moodie 1975)." This civil religion ultimately developed into the civic, cultural, and political movement of Christian Nationalism.

In response to British domination and the threat posed by the multitude of Africans, a Christian National ideology grounded in the theologies of the Dutch Reformed Church emerged to fulfill the need for a political organization. The Afrikaner National Party was founded in 1914 by the Minister of Justice James Barry Hertzog. In 1934, a faction of the party led by Dr. Malan, broke away and formed the "purified" National Party, which was dedicated to the promotion of Afrikanerdom and unsympathetic to the British. In 1939, after South Africa joined the Second World War on the side of England, the two national parties reunited in an attempt to gain power from the United Party, which supported the British

Empire (the national parties favored Germany). The reconciliation, however, did not last because Hertzog continued to believe in the unity between English and Afrikaner white South Africans and insisted on the principle of equality between them. After Hertzog resigned from politics in 1940, Dr. Malan took over the leadership of this version of the National Party. It was this party, with strong Christian National ideals, that came to power in 1948 and brought with it the policies of apartheid.

The Apartheid System

Almost immediately, after the National Party assumed power in 1948, a multitude of laws were passed further separating the Africans from the whites. These apartheid laws included: the Mixed Marriages Act and the Immorality Act regulating miscegenation; the Population Registration Act, which classified the entire population into various racial and ethnic groups; the Reservation of Separate Amenities Act, which ensured the separation of the races in the "common areas"; and the Groups Areas Act, which classified whole areas of land as suitable for whites or blacks only. *De jure* apartheid was fully entrenched by 1961 when South Africa removed itself from the British Commonwealth and became the Republic of South Africa.

The explosion of apartheid laws in the 1950s created two realities of development within South Africa. One reality was that of the white population—developed, educated, politically and economically powerful, ethnically and culturally "superior," yet besieged by the perceived threat of Communism and the numerically superior African on whose labor they were dependent. The second reality was that of the African population—undeveloped, uneducated, disenfranchised, impoverished, and dependent on and held hostage by the economic and political power of the Afrikaner government.

While all of the apartheid laws were designed to isolate, protect, and keep "pure" the white race (especially the Afrikaner, who distinguished themselves from the British), there were some laws that were especially pernicious and assured that the African could be identified and thus kept out of sight. The Population Registration Act of 1950 designed a system in which every individual was classified according to his or her race. The categories included white, Indian, coloured (people of mixed race), and African. These categories were further subdivided, often depending on nuances of physical characteristics and according to tribal affiliations. Once every individual was classified, the apartheid government passed the Group Areas Act under which each racial group could own land, occupy buildings, and conduct business only in the areas that were designated for that race. This gave an appearance of independent and free development for each of the races. However, in reality, if the whites wanted a piece of property that was occupied by any of the other races, they would declare it a white area and take it. This began years of forced removals and violent relocations of entire African urban communities to lands that were unsuitable and far removed from areas of commerce and employment. In essence, the Group Areas Act instituted geographic apartheid that was furthered by the establishment of the Bantu areas. These Bantu areas or "independent homelands" were designed to allow each of the native African tribal groups to develop according to their free will. In reality, they maintained the status quo where the minority white population owned 87% of the land in South Africa (land that was the most fertile and rich in mineral wealth). The "homelands" were noncontiguous pieces of land, typically the most unproductive and infertile, and geographically remote from the white productive areas. These areas were so underdeveloped and removed from the commerce of the nation that entire populations were forced to leave their homes and families in search of work in the white areas. These apartheid laws assured a huge reservoir of cheap labor to work in the factories, the fields, and the mines.

In an effort to maintain the apartheid system, the government also enacted a number of preservation measures. The Suppression of Communism Act of 1950 established the process by which individuals and organizations could be banned, making them politically impotent. Many prominent anti-apartheid leaders and political parties were subjected to this including Nelson Mandela and the African National Congress (ANC). In addition, the Sabotage Act of 1962 and the Terrorism Act of 1967 gave the government the power to indefinitely detain people without a trial and conduct ambitious investigations and surveillance activities in an effort to root out would-be saboteurs and terrorists. These and other measures created a state that was increasingly militarized and security conscious. Indeed, a paradoxical tension was created between the repressive self-preservation activities of the white government and the growing anti-apartheid liberation struggle. As the liberation movement gained momentum and support, the state inevitably became more repressive.

The Liberation Struggle

During the 1950s, 1960s, and 1970s, the liberation movement grew despite the fact that most of the opposition, anti-apartheid political parties, had been banned. The movement found outlets through churches, labor unions, funeral processions, and other manifestations of civil society. The ANC, before it was banned in 1960, provided a solid foundation in which the liberation movement would function. The Defiance Campaign of 1952 called for the use of boycotts, work stoppages and strikes, and other various forms of civil disobedience to demand changes from the state. More than eight thousand people were arrested and detained during the six-month campaign, and the membership of the ANC grew substantially. The adoption of the Freedom Charter in 1956, endorsing the democratic ideals of equality, universal suffrage and basic individual freedoms resulted in the arrest and trial of more than one hundred of the nation's prominent anti-apartheid leaders. The so-called Treason Trial endured for more than four years and ended with a not guilty verdict for all involved.

The year 1960 saw a turning point in the liberation movement's willingness to employ only peaceful, non-violent means of protest. In Sharpeville, an African township south of Johannesburg, a large crowd gathered peacefully around the police station to protest the Pass Laws (every African was required to carry a pass identifying which ethnic group they belonged to and what tribal area they lived in). The police got nervous and opened fire on the crowd, killing sixty-nine people, including women and children, many shot in the back as they attempted to flee. With this incident, the ANC decided it was time to form a military wing in an effort to engage the repressive state on its own terms.

With Nelson Mandela as the commander in chief, Umkhonto we Sizwe (Spear of the Nation) was formed in 1961. Mandela defended the actions of the ANC at the Rivonia Trial that found him guilty of sabotage and sentenced him to life in prison. He said, "It was only when all else failed, when all channels of peaceful protest had been barred to us, that the decision was made to embark on violent forms of political struggle.... The Government had left us no other choice."

In the mid-1960s, after Mandela and other ANC leaders were sentenced to life in prison, the momentum of the ANC slowed as it was forced to function underground and in neighboring countries where they trained guerilla fighters. The liberation movement continued, however, primarily through labor union activities and strikes and through the rise of the Black Consciousness Movement (BCM). In 1969, the South African Students Association (SASO), an all-black student organization, was founded on the principle of black theology and black consciousness. The beginnings of SASO can be traced to the black caucus that emerged at the national conference of the

University Christian Movement, held the previous year. Many of the leaders of SASO and the BCM were theological students or ordained ministers of the English-speaking churches. The BCM worked within civil society for the economic progress of blacks through cooperative "Buy Black" campaigns and trade union activity. It adopted slogans such as "Black is Beautiful," and "Black man, you are on your own."

The BCM posed a new kind of threat to the apartheid government—the realization that despite all the various methods employed to keep the races separate and distinct, the government could not separate and divide the African's consciousness and desire for freedom from themselves.

In 1976, the students of Soweto, empowered by the ideals of black consciousness, embarked on a protest against the requirement that they learn the Afrikaans language in school (considered to be the language of the oppressor), as opposed to any of the native African languages. The ensuing crackdown of the police and subsequent riots resulted in the deaths of more than five hundred (possibly as many as one thousand) students. The Soweto uprising radicalized the young urban Africans and gave new energy to the anti-apartheid liberation movement. Many young people left the country to be trained as guerillas, while the upcoming generation of youth would refuse to attend school until freedom was won.

The World Community and Apartheid

Meanwhile, during these years of intense anti-apartheid liberation efforts, there was a growing debate within the Afrikaner community regarding the ultimate sustainability of apartheid. A *verligte*, or enlightened, attitude began to emerge among some Afrikaners (as contrasted with the traditional *verkrampte*, or closed attitude), which thought that the Afrikaner should begin to take a more generous and open stance with those who were different at home and abroad. It encompassed the ideas that Afrikaners must adapt to the changing realities in the world, or cease to exist. Even though the *verligte* philosophy was met with staunch resistance, it eventually did lead to changes in the apartheid policies, such as the adoption of a new constitution in 1983 that allowed for new, but separate, parliaments for both the Indians and the coloured. The new constitution, however, was merely window dressing, creating the illusion that freedoms were increasing. The Africans continued to have no rights or representation within the government.

Amid the domestic dynamics of apartheid legislation, increased militarization and repression of the state and the constant struggle for liberation, the South African state was becoming an international pariah. For all intents and purposes, the world politically, culturally, professionally, and athletically shunned and boycotted South Africa because of its apartheid system. Economically, however, South Africa was quite literally a gold mine (producing half the world's supply) and attracted international investment. Despite the continued efforts of the liberation movement to strike, boycott, and conduct work stoppages, the South African economy expanded at one of the fastest rates in the world during the 1960s and 1970s as a result of its gold. When the United States went off the gold standard in 1971, South Africa's earning from gold tripled. When the price of gold plunged in the mid-1970s, the country suffered a recession. Nevertheless, the country continued to be economically viable and developed during the apartheid years, at least for the minority white population.

Because of the exploitable resources in South Africa, multinational corporations were not as quick to shun the country, unlike the world's political, cultural, and athletic communities. Foreign investment into South Africa steadily increased during the 1960s, taking advantage of the economic boom. This investment gave the apartheid regime a degree of legitimacy, at least in their own perception, and served to sustain the system and increase the gap between rich and poor, at least for a time. Because of so many cultural similarities between South Africa and the United States with regards to race relations, US corporations were especially sensitive to follow equal and fair employment practices such as equal pay, desegregation of facilities, and training programs for the African employees. However, this "sensitivity" was not enough to prevent the strikes and boycotts that continued throughout 1960s, 1970s, and 1980s and adversely affected the economy. The downturn in the economy in the 1980s, the continuing pressure from the liberation movement, and international attention and boycotting of multi-national corporations operating in South Africa, led to a mass divestment from the region.

South Africa held a dominant position within the region, economically and politically. Regardless of the fact that most of the so-called "frontline" states (Mozambique, Zimbabwe, Botswana, Namibia, Angola, Swaziland, and Lesotho) have been economically dependent on the South African economy, the South African state engaged in a number of destabilization maneuvers to maintain apartheid and its dominance in the region. The government security forces consistently launched raids into neighboring states during the 1970s and 1980s in an effort to destroy suspected ANC training camps. South Africa became embroiled in the civil war in Angola in an attempt to thwart the rise of communism there. Other countries such as Mozambique, Botswana, Lesotho, and Swaziland were coerced into signing nonaggression pacts with South Africa to stave off the threats of economic strangleholds that South Africa could easily employ to further their political and economic agenda. Indeed, "the regional objective [was] to create and maintain a dependence that will be economically lucrative and politically submissive—and will serve as a bulwark against the imposition of international sanctions (Johnson and Martin 1988)." The role of the South African military grew enormously during the 1970s, in which the defense budget increased nearly 1000%. While the Africans struggled for liberation on the home front, an entire generation of young white men was conscripted into the military and security forces to fight the battle in the frontline states.

Collapse of Apartheid

Apartheid began to implode in the mid-1980s for a number of political and economic reasons. Labor strikes and unrest began to increase. Violence would erupt when the security police would step in, often spreading the clashes between competing African tribal groups. The governments usually did nothing to squelch these intertribal conflicts, and even covertly fostered them, citing as proof that different racial groups could not peacefully coexist. With the violence, the death toll rose. Funerals continued to be one means of political demonstration, often bringing out thousands of people. The government banned this form of expression, which only fueled the growing rage and cycle of violence. The new constitution that was adopted in 1983, granting parliamentary representation to the Indians and coloured, did not alleviate the pressure. This simply highlighted the fact that the apartheid regime continued its oppression and disenfranchisement of the African population. A state of emergency was declared in 1985 in a futile effort to maintain control, but the strikes, boycotts, funeral processions, bombings, and violence continued. The security state responded with arrests, detentions, and torture. Between late 1984 and mid-1986, there were more than 1,600 confirmed deaths and thousands of detentions at the hands of the police.

As anarchy reigned and resistance increased, the government began to place greater restrictions on the media. Indeed, many whites were oblivious to the unrest that was occurring throughout the country. Foreign corporations began to get nervous, some divesting their assets from the country (in part because of the growing international movement against the apartheid regime). The South African economy faced a disastrous downturn as a result of the internal unrest, the need to maintain and increase the security apparatus, and the international community's political and economic sanctions. By the 1980s, the ANC had regained some of its lost status as an anti-apartheid leader. It had declared the 1980s as the Decade of Liberation. The National Party apartheid government began to talk with Nelson Mandela (who had taken on heroic and symbolic dimensions as the martyred leader of the liberation struggle) in 1988.

The final blow to the apartheid system came in 1989 when President Pieter Willem Botha suffered a stroke and resigned first as the head of the National Party and then as president of South Africa. Frederik Willem de Klerk, who back in the 1960s had been the first to coin the descriptive distinction between the *verligte* and *verkrampte* philosophies, succeeded Botha. De Klerk, despite being a National Party loyalist, recognized the need for change and lived up to his inaugural promises to work towards peace. He immediately eased restrictions on protest rallies and marches, and in October 1989 he released a number of political prisoners who were Nelson Mandela's contemporaries and who had been in prison for the past twenty-five years. He also began to systematically dismantle the apartheid structures that had been in place since 1948. He opened South African beaches to all people, irrespective of race, and declared that the Reservation of Separate Amenities Act would soon be repealed. South Africans of all colours would now be free to mingle and socialize at parks, theaters, restaurants, libraries, and on buses for the first time in generations. In addition, he announced that the secret National Security Management System, designed to combat anti-apartheid forces, would be dissolved.

These and other actions were profound changes to occur within the first six months of de Klerk's tenure. The culmination came on February 2, 1990, when he lifted the ban on the ANC and more than thirty other illegal organizations, freed non-violent political prisoners, suspended capital punishment, and lifted restrictions imposed by a state of emergency. Then again, on February 10, 1990, more dramatic events astounded the nation and the world. Nelson Mandela was unconditionally released from prison after serving twenty-seven years of a life sentence. The political reality of apartheid in South Africa changed virtually overnight and without the nation succumbing to an all-out civil war. The hard work of creating a government of national unity was to begin.

Rebuilding a Nation

The process of forming a new government would not be easy. In December 1991, after a year and a half of negotiations and setting of ground rules, the talks on the formation of a new government began. The Convention for a Democratic South Africa (CODESA) continued, intermittingly for over two years with the participation of the National Party, the ANC, and sixteen other delegations representing the gamut of South African political stakeholders. In March 1992, a short time into the first round of CODESA talks, de Klerk announced there would be an all-white referendum on the current political rally. Even though an all-white vote was a vestige of the apartheid system and was opposed on principle by the ANC and other nonwhite groups, it ultimately provided support for the continuation of negotiations. The question was simple: "Do you support the continuation of the reform process which the state president began on February 2, 1990, which is aimed at a new constitution through negotiation?" Sixty-nine percent of the voters supported continuing the unity process. Eventually, the CODESA talks produced an agreement for a government of national unity in which power would be proportionally shared. The first-ever, nationwide, universal, democratic election was scheduled for April 27, 1994. The ANC was elected as the party to head the new transitional government, with Nelson Mandela as South Africa's new president.

On that day, millions of South Africa's citizens, regardless of racial, ethnic, or class background, put an end to the tyranny of apartheid rule. The insidious nature of apartheid affected every aspect of life in South Africa, and consequently, its development process. The entire population, irrespective of race, was manipulated by the system in its effort to sustain itself. The reeducation of the citizenry would be an enormous undertaking. Before the election was held, it was understood by leaders of every ilk—political, economic, and religious—that it would be necessary to begin instilling democratic values into the millions of citizens who had effectively been denied these rights for hundreds of years. These lessons on democracy began with the basics of voting procedures. On a deeper level, it was understood that the adverse consequences of apartheid must be dealt with on numerous levels, not only practically on economic and political levels, but on spiritual and psychological levels as well. The rebuilding and unifying of a broken and divided nation had begun.

DEE F. MATREYEK

See also Botha, P.W.; De Klerk, Frederick W.; Ethnic Conflicts: Southern Africa; Ethnicity: Impact on Politics and Society; Mandela, Nelson; Minorities/Discrimination; South Africa; Southern Africa: History and Economic Development; Verwoerd, Hendrik

References and Further Reading

Adam, Heribert, and Kogila Moodley. *The Opening of the Apartheid Mind.* Berkeley, CA: University of California Press, 1993.

Deegan, Heather. *The Politics of the New South Africa: Apartheid and After.* Harlow, England, and New York: Longman, 2001.

Giliomee, Hermann, and Lawrence Schlemmer. *From Apartheid to Nation-Building.* Cape Town: Oxford University Press, 1990.

Johnson, Phyllis, and David Martin, eds., *Frontline Southern Africa: Destructive Engagement.* New York: Four Wall Eight Windows, 1988.

Leatt, James, Theo Kneifel, and Klaus Nurnberger, eds. *Contending Ideologies in South Africa.* Grand Rapids, MI: William B. Eerdmans, 1986.

Mandela, Nelson. *Long Walk to Freedom.* Great Britain: Little, Brown, and Co., 1994.

Moodie, T. Dunbar. *The Rise of Afrikanerdom.* Berkeley, CA: University of California Press, 1975.

O'Meara, Dan. *Forty Lost Years: The Apartheid State and the Politics of the National Party, 1948–1994.* Athens, OH: Ohio University Press, 1997.

Posel, Deborah. *The Making of Apartheid, 1948–1961: Conflict and Compromise.* Oxford: Clarendon Press, 1997.

Rhoodie, N.J., and H.J. Venter. *Apartheid.* Pretoria: Haum, 1959.

Villa-Vicencia, Charles. *Trapped in Apartheid.* New York: Orbis Books, 1988.

Worden, Nigel. *The Making of Modern South Africa: Conquest, Segregation, and Apartheid.* Oxford and Cambridge, MA: Blackwell, 1994; 2d ed., 1995; 3d ed., 2000.

APRISMO

The Aprista movement, which started in the early 1920s under the leadership of Víctor Raúl Haya de la Torre, initially sought to create bonds between students and workers in Lima, Peru's capital. A "Popular University, created in 1921, it provided a place for students to teach classes to workers. The movement expanded and transformed itself through the formation in 1924 of *Alianza Popular Revolucionaria Americana* (APRA), also called the "Aprista party," a political party that became a key actor in modern Peruvian political life. Haya de la Torre, originally from Trujillo, a northern coastal city of Peru, returned in 1931 from political exile in Mexico, prompted by his involvement in the opposition to the dictatorship of Augusto Leguía.

Aprismo, a Spanish term, is both the ideology and philosophy of the APRA, as well as the activities and role of the APRA in Peruvian society and polity.

Aprista, in turn, is the noun or adjective given to a member or supporter of the APRA.

At the beginning, Haya de la Torre's political program emphasized two levels: one applied to the Latin American continent and calling for the unity of its peoples against US imperialism; the other concerning Peru and seeking to end the oligarchic state in order to foster national integration and more inclusive patterns of development. The transversal theme was the need for indigenous populations to struggle against the historical domination of the elites since the colonial period. While Haya de la Torre was initially close to a key Peruvian leader of Marxist thinking at the time, José Carlos Mariátegui, who contributed to forming the Peruvian Communist party in 1929, APRA's ideology can best be described as reformist, populist, and pragmatic, rather than revolutionary.

The APRA's Role in Politics

The party's creation has been associated with the profound changes or "dislocation" occurring in Peru's coastal economy at the end of the nineteenth and beginning of the twentieth century (Klaren 1973). From a society structured around small farming, the coastal area was transformed by the massive entry of foreign capital and the resulting concentration of land in the hands of a few owners. The farmers then became workers for the most part, while the rate of urbanization was increasing throughout the country with some modest industrialization occurring mostly in Lima. The anti-imperialist discourse of Haya de la Torre found its main constituency within this new proletariat. The support base of the APRA remained predominantly in the urban coastal area throughout the twentieth century, even though the party also reached a national audience early on. Not only workers but also middle classes and some sectors of the peasantry ended up joining in the ranks of the party. This corresponded to Haya de la Torre's vision of reformist political change based on a multiclass alliance led by the middle classes. The party's program was geared towards creating a national state that would carry out redistributive policies and stimulate national development for the benefit of all sectors of society.

In the early part of its history, the APRA condoned or incited its supporters to carry out violent uprisings against the state, which led to confrontations with the military. An example that served as a foundational mythology is the uprising of Trujillo in 1932 when Apristas executed thirty-four army officers, and which ended in the death of around one thousand Apristas. Not surprisingly, the relationship between the military and the APRA was one of sheer distrust, and the tendency of the APRA to be involved in or associated with acts of civil disorder served to justify various forms of repression on the part of security forces until the mid-1950s.

Haya de la Torre lost the presidential elections of 1931 and declared them to be fraudulent. In 1932, after the revolt in Trujillo, the strength of military repression forced APRA's leaders to go in exile again. The party was banned from 1933 to 1945. From 1945 to 1948, and then from 1963 to 1968, the APRA was a key player of democratic politics as an elected party within political institutions, but the social disorder generated by increasing political mobilization of workers and peasants, plus the lack of capacity of the government to undertake genuine reforms, led to military coups at the end of both periods. Between 1948 and 1956, during the dictatorship of Manuel Odría, the APRA was banned yet another time, and its were militants persecuted. The *Confederación de Trabajadores Peruanos*, the first national labor organization created in 1944 by the APRA, was only recognized by the state in 1964. The new left-wing parties created in the 1960s, which grew in strength under the military regime of 1968–1980 partly as a reaction to repression in the late 1970s, displaced the APRA in its ability to act as the voice of the lower classes. The *Confederación General de Trabajadores Peruanos*, a Communist labor organization, was recognized by the state in 1968, ending APRA's predominance in labor representation.

This shift in the political affiliation of the working class was the result of the APRA's move away from a radical discourse toward an inconsistent alliance with the elite, *caudillo*-type regime of Manuel Prado in 1956–1963. All analysts concur in describing that period, which began with the legalization of the party in 1945 and ended with the installation of a reformist military regime in 1968, as one of cooptation of *aprismo*, when compromises were achieved by the party for the purpose of acceding to legal status and political power. The APRA's strategy, in the complex political scenario of that period, was to collaborate with the regime just enough to maintain its political freedom and in the hope that it could benefit from the democratic electoral framework in the future to gain genuine state power.

In programmatic terms, this meant a toned-down, anti-imperialist stance and development proposals relying not on the confiscation of foreign assets but rather in creating new productive conditions for the whole population. It also meant that the APRA was no longer an unconditional ally of the labor movement's demands as it had been before. The legalization of the party launched a new phase of burgeoning mobilization among lower and middle classes, who made increasing demands upon the oligarchic state. The APRA's decision to accept Prado's *Convivencia* pact in 1956 caused a number of defections from the younger ranks of the APRA towards more radical left-wing organizations. The latter were reinforced in their move by the hopes generated by the Cuban revolution shortly after.

After a decade of military rule from 1968 to 1978, during which a number of the reforms advocated by the APRA for years were finally adopted such as the nationalization of petroleum and mining, the APRA found itself without a clear identity. On the one hand, its reformist role had been taken over by the military in the first years of the military regime, and on the other hand, new parties had emerged that were proposing more radical, revolutionary change. Nevertheless, the transition to democracy starting in 1978 and ending with the first universal suffrage elections ever held in Peru in 1980, saw the APRA as a key civilian political force collaborating and negotiating with the military. Partly for this and as a clear rejection of the military, however, Peruvians voted for Fernando Belaúnde Terry, leader of the center-right *Acción Popular* party, as first president of the new democratic regime.

It was only in 1985 that the APRA's dream of governing Peru's destiny materialized. Alan García, a young and charismatic politician, was the first *Aprista* president ever to assume state power. His government, marked by a failed attempt at implementing heterodox adjustment reforms, ended in a period of unprecedented economic crisis and heightened political violence caused by the war between state forces and subversive groups inspired by Maoist (Shining Path–*Sendero Luminoso*) or Guevarist (*Movimiento Revolucionario Tupac Amaru*) ideology. After attempting to nationalize the banking and financial sectors, the García's government alienated the economic elite and lost the 1990 elections at the hands of a new, previously unknown populist leader, Alberto Fujimori. Alan García went in exile for a decade during which the APRA fared poorly in electoral terms. The return of García for the 2001 presidential elections gave a renewed impetus to the party, which is still the most institutionalized of the Peruvian party system.

Aprismo as Populist Politics and Its Influence in Latin America

Aprismo is the incarnation of populism, a dominant pattern of political rule in the Latin American twentieth century. A mass reform party created in reaction to the lack of integration of popular and middle classes in the political process, *aprismo* was based on an organic, corporatist vision of society where the sources of social ills were to be found primarily in foreign economic domination and the submission of the national bourgeoisie—or oligarchy—to foreign-imposed development priorities. Haya de la Torre was a source of inspiration for many other Latin American leaders of nationalistic social change, such as Figueres in Costa Rica, Betancourt in Venezuela, and Perón in Argentina. In Peru, *aprismo* was not the only manifestation of populism. The first populist politician of Peru, Luis Sánchez Cerro, who ran against Haya de la Torre in the 1931 elections, differed from the latter in that he did not attempt to appeal to specific class actors such as unions or professional associations. APRA's support base represented a more diversified class alliance, with membership specifically drawn from organized working classes or middle classes, whereas Sanchez Cerro's mixed ethnic origins made his appeal greater to indigenous peasants, recent migrants, and lower stratum working class.

The structure of the APRA was also typically populist. The charismatic leader Haya de la Torre, who remained in place until his death in 1979, headed the organization through a direct, paternalistic, and personalistic appeal to the masses; the party was vertically organized to mobilize the masses in support of the leader, with the cadres of the party mostly from middle-class background and the majority of the working class militants confined to the party rank-and-file. The figure of the high leader—called *jefe máximo,* meaning highest chief—inspired unconditional loyalty from his followers, with *Apristas* reknowned for the intensity of their emotional attachment to the chief and the party seen as a great family. The charisma of the leader, an essential characteristic of populist politics, derived in part from his constantly referring to his suffering and that of his followers experienced through repression and exile.

Aprismo as a Reformist Program

Aprismo historically emphasized the central role of the state in reforming the economic structure through the redistribution of resources and revenues and breaking with the domination of foreign capital. Its economic policy options favored the Latin American development model of import-substitution industrialization that dominated from the 1940s to the 1970s, but which was only adopted in Peru at of the end of the 1950s. The main causes of the underdevelopment affecting Peru were, according to *Aprismo*, the lack of national integration and the divorce of the state from the rest of society.

Because of its multiclass constituency, the APRA was characterized by its willingness to avoid alienating any class sector. While in broad terms it called for the nationalization of land and industry, in light of the diversity of interests of the peasantry, for example, the APRA never committed to a radical land reform. Moreover, it even supported military repression against peasant land invasions in the 1960s. Haya de la Torre and later, Alan García, adapted the party's discourse to the needs of the day, which inevitably generated different ideological groupings within the Aprista "family." Although the leader was usually capable of mediating these internal differences, the diversity of interests represented within the APRA led to numerous contradictions. One extreme example occurred in the late 1980s when some sectors of the APRA were known for their links with a right-wing paramilitary commando who assassinated suspected members of left-wing subversive groups, while one of these groups, the *Movimiento Revolucionario Tupac Amaru*, had been founded by former APRA militants.

The failure of the first *Aprista* government after more than sixty years of APRA's existence consisted in its weak policy reform capacity and its demise after one term in power. This could be explained by the extremely difficult circumstances in which García took power in the mid-1980s—dominated by economic crisis and political violence. Yet at a more fundamental level, the failure of *Aprismo* is reminiscent of the dilemmas faced by many reformist projects in Latin America. It is connected to the incapacity of the party to create a long-lasting multiclass alliance capable of reconciling a diversity of interests around a reformist project and winning over the entrenched military and oligarchic powers. *Aprismo's* role in the Peruvian and Latin American politics of the twentieth century, however, was fundamental in the transition from closed oligarchic regimes to more inclusionary democratic regimes based on universal suffrage and the recognition of the state's role in fostering national development.

STÉPHANIE ROUSSEAU

See also Haya de la Torre, Víctor Raúl; Peru; Populism

References and Further Reading

Alexander, Robert J. *Aprismo: The Ideas and Doctrines of Victor Raul Haya de la Torre*. Kent State, OH: Kent State University Press, 1973.

Cotler, Julio. "Democracy and National Integration in Peru." In *The Peruvian Experiment Reconsidered*, edited by Abraham Lowenthal and Cynthia McClintock. 3–38, Princeton NJ: Princeton University Press, 1983.

Graham, Carol. *Peru's APRA. Parties, Politics and the Elusive Quest for Democracy*. Boulder, CO: Lynne Rienner Publishers, 1992.

Hilliker, Grant. *The Politics of Reform in Peru*. Baltimore, MD: Johns Hopkins University Press, 1971.

Klaren, Peter F. *Modernization, Dislocation, and Aprismo: The Origins of the Aprista Party, 1870–1932*. Austin, TX: University of Texas Press, 1973.

Stein, Steve. "The Paths to Populism in Peru." In *Populism in Latin America*, edited by Michael Conniff, 97–116. Tuscaloosa, AL, and London: The University of Alabama Press, 1999.

Vega Centeno, Imelda. *Aprismo popular: Mito, Cultura, e Historia*. Lima: Tarea, 1986.

AQUINO, BENIGNO, AND CORAZÓN

Benigno Simeon Aquino, Jr., (1932–1983) was born in Tarlac Province, Philippines. At the University of the Philippines, Aquino was a fraternity brother of his future nemesis Ferdinand E. Marcos. Benigno Aquino worked as a journalist in Korea, Vietnam, and Malaya. In May 1954, he played a role in the capture of Luis Taruc (1913–), a top leader of the left-wing rural *Hukbong Magpapalaya ng Bayan* ("National Liberation Army"). Immediately after the interview with Aquino, Taruc was arrested.

Aquino's future spouse, Maria Corazón Sumulong Cojuangco (1933–), was born into a Chinese Filipino landowning family at Hacienda Luisita, Tarlac Province. She majored in French and minored in mathematics at Mount Saint Vincent College in New York City. In 1954, she interrupted legal studies at Far Eastern University to marry "Ninoy" Aquino. They had five children. "Cory" Aquino also was treasurer of Jose Cojuangco and Sons, Inc.

Entering electoral politics, Benigno Aquino was elected a local mayor and then governor of Tarlac Province. In 1967, he became the youngest person elected to the at-large senate of the Philippines. That year, he also was the opposition Liberal Party's only successful senatorial candidate. As a "fiscalizer" (critic), he attracted national attention. In 1968, Senator Aquino exposed plans by President Marcos to infiltrate and subvert the government of Sabah (North Borneo), Malaysia. Benigno Aquino initially was a typical politician in many respects. Marcos was reelected to a second term in 1969. In the same year, the Communist Party of the Philippines formed its New People's Army. And as poverty and protests by workers and students increased, Aquino grew increasingly popular as a prospective contender in the 1973 presidential elections. When Marcos imposed martial law on September 21, 1972, Senator Aquino was arrested and imprisoned.

Tried in a military court, Benigno Aquino was condemned to death. After more than seven years of imprisonment, "Ninoy" Aquino was allowed to leave the Philippines for heart surgery in Boston. Recovering from his hospitalization, the Aquinos lived together in self-exile in the United States during 1980–1983. And they met with anti-Marcos activists of all political persuasions. Believing that Marcos's illnesses were life-threatening, Benigno Aquino feared that chaos might develop if Marcos died in the absence of a credible opposition figure. A warning from co-dictator Imelda Marcos did not deter him from returning. With Manila International Airport under military control, on August 21, 1983, Aquino was shot to death in broad daylight just after getting off his plane.

Corazón Aquino returned for her assassinated spouse's funeral. His assassination elicited a massive outpouring of sympathy. Drenched by pouring rains, a million or more marched in a somber funeral procession. No one was convicted of masterminding Aquino's murder. As the Filipino elite realized that they were not immune to victimization by Marcos, opposition spread beyond the ranks of radical workers, farmers, and students to bankers and former supporters of the dictatorship. In her new role as widow of a prominent anti-Marcos politician, Corazón Aquino became a symbol of the aggrieved anti-Marcos opposition. And despite the friendship of US President Ronald W. Reagan (1981–1989) for Marcos, a growing faction in the White House began seeing "Cory" Aquino as better prepared to defeat the Communist Party of the Philippines.

Under US pressure, President Marcos announced a "snap" election for February 7, 1986. Ignoring massive fraud and uncounted votes, the *Batasang Pambansa* ("National Assembly") declared Marcos the winner. In reaction to a failed election, boycotts and demonstrations erupted for three weeks. Thus, Corazón Cojuangco Aquino became president in the "People Power Revolution." Terminating the Marcos presidency, a four-day mutiny was led by Deputy Chief of Staff Fidel V. Ramos and Minister of Defense Juan Ponce Enrile. Their desertion was endorsed by Cardinal Jaime Sin, leader of the Roman Catholic church. The rebellious military contingent was protectively surrounded by a massive demonstration by residents of the National Capital Region. And whether freely or under duress, Marcos left the Philippines for the United States.

On February 28, 1986, Corazón Aquino spurned the 1973 Constitution, having herself sworn in under "the power of the people." Seventeen months of rule by decree followed. President Aquino dismissed the *Batasang Pambansa* before it could meet, proclaimed a temporary constitution, and appointed a Constitutional Commission to write a permanent document to be submitted to the voters. Reflecting the politically diverse forces that put Aquino in power, her highly factionalized first cabinet lasted less than a year. But on February 2, 1987, an 80% "Yes" vote on the constitution temporarily quieted most challenges to her legitimacy. In May, elections were held for Congress. The winners were seated at the end of July 1987.

With mixed results, President Aquino engaged in separate peace negotiations with the Moro National Liberation Front (MNLF) in Mindanao and with the National Democratic Front (NDF), which was led by a weakened Communist Party of the Philippines. Human rights violations by police, military, and vigilantes increased during her first two years in office, and she failed to win the Nobel Peace Prize. For editorial writers, "Kamag-anak, Inc." ("Family, Inc.") symbolized political corruption by Aquino's relatives, although she personally did not take public funds for private gain.

Aquino chose not to use her powers of decree to effect sweeping land reform in the highly agricultural Philippines, and no major redistribution of land to farmer laborers occurred. Despite deeper familiarity with US culture and society than any previous President of the Philippines, she could not persuade the Senate to renew the US–Philippines Military Bases Agreement in 1991. Aquino's task was complicated by the unwillingness of the Association of Southeast Asian Nations (ASEAN) to endorse the treaty. On the other hand, she laid the basis for dismantling "crony" megacorporations from the Marcos dictatorship. And having survived two major military coup attempts and several smaller military revolts, she facilitated a peaceful electoral transfer of power to Fidel V. Ramos, minority winner of the 1992 presidential election.

VINCENT KELLY POLLARD

See also Philippines

References and Further Reading

Aquino, Belinda A., ed. *Presidential Leadership and Cory Aquino*. Diliman, Quezon City: University of the Philippines, Center for Integrative and Development Studies, 1990.

Aquino, Benigno S., Jr. *Testament From a Prison Cell*, 2d ed. Makati: Benigno S. Aquino, Jr., Foundation, 2000.

Aquino, Corazon Cojuangco. *The Aquino Administration: Record and Legacy (1986–1992); President Corazon C. Aquino and Her Cabinet*. U.P. Public Lectures on the Aquino Administration and the Post-EDSA Government (1986–1992). Vol. 1. Diliman, Quezon City: University of the Philippines Press, 1992.

Pollard, Vincent Kelly. *Globalization, Democratization, and Asian Leadership: Power Sharing, Foreign Policy, and Society in the Philippines and Japan.* Aldershot, England; Burlington, VT: Ashgate Publishing, Ltd., 2004.

Salonga, Jovito. *The Senate That Said No; A Four-Year Record of the First Post-EDSA Senate.* Quezon City: University of the Philippines Press, 1995.

ARAB ECONOMIC UNITY COUNCIL

The first step toward the Arab Economic Unity Council was the establishment of the League of Arab States (LAS) in 1945, as many Arab countries gained their independence. The League of Arab States consists of three main organs: League Council, Permanent Committees (Arab Specialized Organizations), and General Secretary.

However, because of the extensive duties of these committees they have been replaced by the Arab Specialized Organizations, which cover a wide variety of specialties and support the objectives of the LAS. Eighteen Arab specialized organizations were established. The Arab Economic Unity Council is one of them.

According to the charter of the LAS, political issues were more dominant than economic ones. Only articles two and four deal with the economic issues. Article two defined the aims of establishing the LAS in supporting the economic cooperation between the member states; article four established a number of committees for taking care of this cooperation.

In 1957, the governments of the thirteen member states (membership has since risen to twenty-two states) signed the treaty of the Economic Unity between the Arab League's member states, which was then ratified by the national legislatures of all the member states. Article number three of the treaty established the Arab Economic Unity Council.

The Arab Economic Unity Council has a number of objectives. Primarily, it works to promote and expand cooperation among its members in economics and trade. In 1964, seven years after its founding, the council established the Arab Common Market.

The main purpose for establishing the Arab Economic Unity Council was to determine the best ways to raise the standard of living, upgrade the economics of the member states, and to open the Arab markets for moving industrial and agricultural goods with each other freely. The steps toward these goals include the elimination of all tariffs between member states, to remove all internal tariffs, and to end all restrictions on trade within the member states. Unfortunately, however, the Arab Economic Unity Council's ability to achieve its goals has been limited by disagreements among member states, such as external, political, and economic problems.

NILLY KAMAL EL-AMIR

See also Middle East: History and Economic Development; Middle East: International Relations

References and Further Reading

Mozahem, Ghassan. *The Arab Specialized Organizations at the League of Arab States.* Cairo: Arab Researches and Studies Institute, 1976.

Sarhan, Abdel Aziz. *The Principles of the International Organizations.* Cairo: Dar El-Nahda, 1976.

Shalabi, Ibrahim. *International Organization: The International Regional and Specialized Organization.* Beirut: El-Dar El-Gamia, 1992.

Shehab, Mofid. *League of Arab States, Charter and Accomplishments.* Cairo: Arab Researches and Studies Institute, 1978.

ARAB MAGHREB UNION (AMU)

In February 1989, in Marrakech, Morocco, the leaders of Algeria, Libya, Morocco, Mauritania, and Tunisia signed a treaty setting up the Arab Maghreb Union (AMU).

The AMU was modeled on the European Community (EC) and was formed principally to enable its members to negotiate with the EC, Arab, and African countries from a position of greater strength. In 1995, the free movement of people within the AMU, encouragement for joint investment projects and the creation of a foreign trade bank were proposed, but there was no follow-up. In 1999, a program to reactivate the AMU was put forward, but in 2000, no progress had been made.

The AMU accounts for 40% of the Arab world's area and, in 1998, had a population of about seventy four million. More than million AMU citizens were expatriate workers in Europe. AMU members have not yet established a free trade area, although there are some bilateral projects in operation and under discussion. A number of these involve the European Union, such as a gas pipeline from Algeria to Italy, which passes through Tunisian territory, and gas pipelines from Algeria to Spain and Portugal, which pass through Morocco.

In 1997, about 3% of total AMU external trade was with other members of the AMU. This compared with trade between members of the Association of Southeast Asian Nations (ASEAN) that equaled 22% of its total external trade (in 1998) and intra-EU trade that equaled 61% of total EU external trade.

The barriers to closer economic integration in the AMU are numerous. There are political barriers:

Libya has been subject to a range of international sanctions since 1991; Algeria has been in a state of near civil war for years. There also are structural barriers: the countries in the region have a preference for European goods, and given this cultural bias, it often is hard to sell and/or export locally made goods. Much of the production in the region is competitive rather than complementary, which limits trade at the stage of development prevailing in the region. There are, however, differences in emphasis. Algeria and Libya are energy rich. Morocco is relatively more developed in agriculture, manufacturing, and tourism. Morocco and Mauritania have mining sectors.

Despite the fact that the overall level of development is much lower than in Europe, there are considerable variations in income levels within the region. Gross domectic product per capita in Mauritania is about 10% of that in Libya. The level of integration into the international economy is varied. Morocco and Tunisia are members of the World Trade Organization; they have completed International Monetary Fund–backed structural adjustment programs and have partly convertible currencies, relatively dynamic private sectors, and growing nonpetroleum exports. In contrast, Algeria and Libya are less open to international trade and have smaller and low levels of nonpetroleum exports.

There is significant informal trade in the region based on bartering, smuggling, and other unregistered transactions. Morocco and Tunisia have liberalized their import regions, and registered trade between from them has increased steadily since the mid-1980s.

PAUL RIVLIN

See also North Africa: History and Economic Development; North Africa: International Relations

References and Further Reading

Finaish, Mohamed, and Eric Bell. *The Arab Maghreb Union*, IMF Working Paper, Washington, DC: IMF, 1994.
The Middle East and North Africa. London: Europa, 2001.
Vandewalle Dirk, ed. *North Africa: Development and Reform in a Changing Global Economy*. Basingstoke, England: Macmillan, 1996.

ARAB NATIONALISM

The basis of Arab nationalism is the common culture, history, and language of the Arab peoples. The Arab peoples' geographical realm ranges from the Persian Gulf in the east to the Atlantic Ocean in the West. Arab nationalism, in general, does not entail Islamic ideas. Interestingly enough, many of the early Arab nationalist thinkers were Arab Christians from Syria, Lebanon, and Palestine such as George Antonius and Michel Aflaq. However, Islam is not completely disregarded, even by the Christian thinkers.

On the other hand, the idea of state and regional nationalism has challenged Arab nationalism, especially in the minds of many Lebanese Maronites. Ironically, this challenge has occurred in the Arab states established at the fall of the Ottoman Empire at the end of World War I. Leaders ranging from Gamal Abdel Nasser to Muammar Qaddafi to Saddam Hussein have promoted some type of Arab nationalism at times in their careers. Arab nationalism has been represented in many different ways with many different ideologies, which have occasionally come into conflict with one another.

Early Roots of Arab Nationalism

Arab nationalism gained attention during the First World War with the support of the Allied Powers fighting the Ottoman Turks, but Arab nationalism's roots date from the previous century, the ideas of European nationalism, and even earlier. Previously, much of the Arab world existed under the umbrella of a Muslim community, the Ottoman Empire, rather than ethnic-based self-governance. Over time, European interests began to erode the Ottoman Empire through the establishment of European, mostly French and British, protectorates in North Africa and the Arabian Peninsula. When the Ottoman Empire joined the Central Powers in World War I, it would lose not only the war, but also most of its territory.

Arab nationalism is widely viewed as a European-influenced development dating either from immediately before or during World War I. While there is some truth in this belief, Arab nationalism has native roots from much earlier than the twentieth century and prior to the influence of European ideas, although all early efforts met failure. Several stages exist in the coming of nationalism in the Arab world, as well as in the existence of modern Arab nationalism itself. It may be argued that the earliest idea of Arab nationalism, or at least unity, can be found in the Constitution of Medina in 622 CE. This was perhaps the Prophet Muhammad's way of uniting the Muslim faithful, the *Ummah*, which all happened to be Arabs at this time. Since Islam is a universal religion, accepting regardless of ethnicity, the *Ummah* would later include other groups such as the Persians and Turks. However, internal differences among Arab tribes and within Islam itself kept an enduring unity from developing. Eventually, Arab domination in terms of Islamic rule was lost to the Persians and the Turks.

Arab Nationalism in the 20th Century

The genesis of Arab nationalism in the twentieth century lies with anti-Turkish sentiment. The Young Turk movement, started by a group of young Turkish intellectuals promoting Pan-Turkism and European ideas of secularism in government and society, alienated most Arabs who believed in the unity of the *Ummah*. While the Young Turks did not succeed in deposing the Sultan, they did succeed in removing Arabs from key government positions, including those dealing with religion and administration of Arab provinces, which had been traditionally reserved for Arabs to fill. The Young Turks took these steps fearing the loss of Ottoman territories, which eventually did occur following the Ottoman Empire's collapse and division in its defeat in World War I, thanks in part to the Arab revolts encouraged by the Allies.

The character of Arab nationalism underwent a drastic change leading up to the declaration of Israel as an independent Jewish state in 1948. The Palestinian question united many Arab countries, especially the immediately surrounding ones, in a common cause. A resolution to the Palestinian question, whether violent or peaceful, has been and continues to be a top issue in many official attitudes within, but not limited to, Arab governments. However, the issue of Israel has also been a convenient excuse for many governmental shortfalls within the region. In many instances, a general anti-Israel sentiment has prevailed upon generations of Arab and Muslim youth since the country's independence.

The 1950s and 1960s saw the North African Arab countries gain independence from European imperial powers. The movement against the French in Algeria was particularly bloody, but eventually forced the French hand to relinquish its control and allow that county to seek its own future. This was also part of an overall trend of anti-imperialism spreading throughout Africa. Arab nationalist ideas did not end with independence in North Africa, but the ideology has been as pronounced as in the Arab states farther east. Muammar Qaddafi was a figure to eventually emerge as the leader of Libya and has promoted Arab nationalism, among other ideas, at certain times during his career.

Pan-Arabism

An idea to originate within Arab nationalism is that of Pan-Arabism, which advocates the ideal of a single Arab state. Not all Arab nationalists believe in this ideal. The idea of Pan-Arabism was first espoused by Hashemite Sharif Hussein of Mecca. Hussein was a fervent Arab nationalist who sought to secede from the Ottoman Empire to create an independent Arab state. Through the Hussein–McMahon Correspondence, an agreement was reached between the British and Sharif Hussein for the Arab tribes to rise against the Turks in revolt and to support the Allied effort against the Central Powers in the desert.

However, in 1916, the British and the French reached an agreement of their own about what should happen to the Arab lands after the defeat of the Ottomans. Instead of Arab independence, the Sykes–Picot Agreement outlined the division of the Ottoman lands between Britain and France. The agreement from the Hussein–McMahon Correspondence was negated with France and Britain establishing their mandates. The Balfour Declaration of 1917, which stated that the British looked with favor on the establishment of a Jewish homeland in Palestine, caused more problems for Arab nationalist efforts. The Balfour Declaration would eventually lead to the establishment of Israel on former Palestinian land in 1948. Further damage to Hussein's idea was brought by the conquests of Ibn Saud in the Arabian Peninsula, including the Hijaz, home to Mecca and Medina. In the years after World War I, the Arabs, as a whole, were still not free to choose their own destiny.

The only attempt at a Pan-Arab state is the United Arab Republic (UAR), which combined Egypt and Syria. The idea was the brainchild of Egyptian President Gamal Abdel Nasser. Egypt was the driving force behind the UAR, with the capital in Cairo. This union lasted from 1958 to 1961, when Syria underwent a coup, led by Hafez Assad and the Ba'ath Party, which severed its relationship with Egypt. Near the end of the union, the UAR sought to include Yemen in its governance. The title UAR was used by Egypt until 1970, when President Nasser passed away. Nasser, himself, was a veteran of the 1948 war against Israeli independence. In 1952, Nasser began his bid to lead Egypt by ousting King Farouk I in a military coup. The Muslim Brotherhood made an attempt on Nasser's life during a speech he gave in 1954, and when all the bullets missed, Nasser continued his speech without flinching. This attitude toward his adversity was characteristic of his career. Nasser eventually became president in 1956. That same year, Nasser launched the nationalization of the Suez Canal, much to the chagrin of the British and French. With Israel's support, Britain and France sought to take the canal by force. However, the United States and the Soviet Union, in a rare display of agreement and cooperation, cut this campaign short. The uncompromising nature of Nasser in this situation won him the respect of other Arab countries as a staunch opponent of the European powers and their continued colonial attitudes toward the Arabs. Yet, when Egypt suffered another defeat and the loss of the Sinai Peninsula at the hands of Israel in the Six-Day War in 1967, Nasser publicly pursued resignation of his position, whether for effect or in reality, but was given the endorsement of the Egyptian people to continue his post. In an effort to intimidate Israel, a war of attrition followed with much activity on the Egyptian-held side of the canal. A compromise was reached to end the standoff in 1970, but Nasser was not to continue at helm. He died from a heart attack shortly after the agreement was reached.

Nasser's successor, Anwar Sadat, led Egypt into the Yom Kippur War, in which Egypt suffered yet another defeat. This was an unsuccessful attempt to reconquer the Sinai Peninsula. Egypt, under Sadat, would eventually make peace with Israel, with Israeli Prime Minister Menachem Begin, through the Camp David Accords of 1978. This led to Sadat's assassination by the Muslim Brotherhood in 1981. A vast contrast to Nasser, Sadat was seen as a traitor to the Arab and Palestinian cause.

The Question of Palestine

The events leading up to the declaration of Israel as an independent Jewish state were tumultuous for the Palestinians. At the onset of the Jewish migration, Jewish immigrants bought land in a legitimate bid for a place in the ancestral Jewish homeland in the Levant. Before long, land seizures and acts of intimidation, such as the Jewish riots of 1929, were used against the Arabs to acquire more land and for the Jews to become the dominant ethnic group of the area. The Palestinians engaged in a general strike to protest the deteriorating situation in 1936, but to little avail. The British began formal restriction of Jewish immigration to Palestine in 1939. This measure led some within the growing Jewish community to carry out subversive acts against the British. The end of World War II and the emptying of the Nazi death camps brought an unstoppable influx of Jews from Europe to Palestine. These events led to the movement of Palestinian refugees into neighboring Arab countries.

The surrounding Arab countries prepared for a war in support of the Palestinians in the event the Jews declared an independent state. Indeed, when the British mandate in Palestine was ended on May 14, 1948, an independent Israel was proclaimed. On

the following day began Israel's war for independence when the neighboring Arab states of Egypt, Iraq, Lebanon, Syria, and Jordan invaded. Much to the surprise of the invaders and the rest of the world, Israel emerged victorious. The 1967 Six-Day War led to further land acquisition by Israel and embarrassment on the part of the attacking Arab states. The Gaza Strip and the Sinai Peninsula were captured from Egypt, the West Bank and East Jerusalem from Jordan, and the Golan Heights from Syria. Only the Sinai Peninsula was later returned.

One of the most influential and widely known figures identified with the Palestinian situation is Yasser Arafat. Born in 1929, the young Arafat was inquisitive about the Jewish people that had been arriving in his homeland of Palestine, which was then under the British mandate. At King Fuad University in Cairo, Arafat read Zionist literature and engaged in intellectual discussion with Jews in hopes of better understanding his new neighbors. In short order, Arafat had become a Palestinian nationalist. Though Arafat was never entirely committed to Arab nationalism, he remains a symbol of Arab resistance.

Yasser Arafat attempted to join the fight against the newly declared state of Israel in 1948, but the Egyptians turned him away as being untrained and hastily armed. This was the turning point in which Arafat lost faith in other Arab governments. He felt the Palestinians would triumph only through their own course of action and by winning popular support. Arafat spent much of his time moving throughout the Palestinian diaspora in other Arab countries in attempt to gain support and finances for the Palestinian cause. In Kuwait, he began the groundwork for the *al-Fatah*, or "victory," organization. Initially, monetary support came from wealthy oil industry employees. After some unsuccessful operations against Israel, Arafat became regarded by many Palestinians as a hero for his narrow escapes and resolve to continue, but was branded as a terrorist by Israel. *Fatah* positions became targets for the Israelis during the Six-Day War. Arafat quickly rose to the top of the Palestinian Liberation Organization (PLO) during the late 1960s and early 1970s.

The 1960s were a strenuous time for Arafat and the PLO. By 1970, the large Palestinian presence in neighboring Jordan had become too much for King Hussein to bear, and when three hijacked airliners were exploded at the airfield in Zarqa, King Hussein declared martial law and ordered Palestinian expulsion. This brought Jordan into conflict with Syria, but Jordan was successful in its intentions. It was during this time Arafat had risen to power. Arafat and the PLO relocated to Lebanon, where they established a virtual Palestinian state in the south of the country. Southern Lebanon became a staging ground for Palestinian attacks against Israel.

Though Arafat publicly ordered attacks against Israel to be stopped and denied any role in such attacks, Israel believed him responsible. Another organization known as Black September, rumored to be the terrorist arm of the PLO, emerged and stormed into the world spotlight at the 1972 Olympic Games in Munich, Germany. The games were marred by the kidnapping and murder of eleven Israeli athletes by Black September. Arafat distanced himself from the group but was rumored to have been briefed on the operation.

Lebanon's precarious balance was tipped when the country entered a civil war in 1975. The war would last until 1990, and the PLO is said to have played a major role throughout the war. While based in Lebanon in 1976, the PLO was admitted as a full member to the Arab League. Eventually, Israel intervened in its northern neighbor's chaos by establishing a security zone in the south. Israel went on the offensive shortly thereafter by occupying much of southern Lebanon. September 1982 saw a cease fire brokered and an expulsion of Arafat and the PLO to exile in Tunisia, where he and the organization would remain until 1993. The PLO received financial assistance from Iraq and Saudi Arabia to reconstruct itself.

The first *Intifada* uprising began independently of the PLO in 1987, but Arafat soon took the reigns and encouraged continued resistance from his quarters in Tunis. The 1993 Oslo Accords promoted Palestinian autonomy in the form of the Palestinian Authority (PA) in the West Bank and Gaza and enabled Arafat and the PLO to return to those territories. Arafat was elected president of the PA in 1996. Despite negotiations such as the Wye River Memorandum of 1998 and the Camp David Summit in 2000, Palestinian statehood remains an elusive dream for the Palestinians. Some within the Palestinian community and otherwise feel Arafat demanded too much from the Israelis, and missed an opportunity for an independent Palestine. A second *Intifada* broke out in 2000 in response to the failed negotiations for Palestinian independence.

Arafat's death in late 2004 signaled a new beginning for the process as a power vacuum has been left open for the time being. With both negative and positive contributions to the Palestinian cause, the figure of Arafat in the grand scheme will likely remain an enduring one. The Palestinian cause is an important one for much of the Arab and Islamic world, although Arab governments may only lend superficial and symbolic support.

The Ba'ath Party

The 1940s saw a new wave in Arab nationalism and Pan-Arab thought. Noted nationalist thinker Michel Aflaq, a Syrian Christian, and a circle of other like-minded thinkers founded the Ba'ath Party, which promoted Arab nationalism and Pan-Arabism with an emphasis on socialism incorporating ideas from Italian fascism. Ba'ath ideology accepted all Arabs regardless of religious faith. In this respect, the Ba'ath Party sought to bring secularism to the Arab lands. Pan-Arabism suffered a major blow with the defeat of those Arab states that fought Israel in the Six-Day War. By the 1980s, the idea of Pan-Arabism had been eroded by more Islamic ideas of unity and governance.

Although the Ba'ath Party has promoted Arab unity, there have been problems with the party regarding non-Arab minorities. For example, both Iraq and Syria have infringed upon the rights and freedoms of the Kurdish populations within their territories. Although the Kurds of Iraq under the administration of Saddam Hussein and his Ba'ath Party enjoyed more freedoms than any of the surrounding states with Kurdish minorities, it also provided the most glaring example of violations against its Kurdish population with the *al-Anfal* campaigns of 1988, in which thousands of Kurds suffered and perished in various acts of ethnic cleansing including the use of chemical weapons.

The sole remaining country with active Ba'ath leadership is Syria, under Bashar Assad. Saddam Hussein and the Ba'ath Party were removed from power in Iraq by a US-led coalition in 2003. Although many former Ba'ath Party members are participating in Iraq's new government, they no longer espouse the Ba'ath ideology.

Forums for Arab Expression

Despite the difficulties in Arab unity, several organizations have provided forums for Arab viewpoints to be brought forth, discussed, and acted upon. One organization specifically devoted to Arab unity and discussion is the League of Arab States (Arab League). The Arab League was formed in 1945 by the Arab states of Egypt, Iraq, Transjordan (renamed Jordan in 1946), Lebanon, Saudi Arabia, Syria, and Yemen. According to the Arab League's charter, member countries are prohibited from attacking one another. The stated purpose of the Arab League is to "serve the common good of all Arab countries, ensure better conditions for all Arab countries, guarantee the future of all Arab countries and fulfill the hopes and expectations of all Arab countries."

Although the Arab League is the only organization devoted to Arab views, two other organizations have a large proportion of Arab state members, and their ideas and agendas have been promoted. The Organization of the Petroleum Exporting Countries (OPEC) has been a forum for action by Arab states. Excluding Iran, Nigeria, Indonesia, and Venezuela, OPEC is composed of an Arab majority. This body has manipulated international oil production and prices over the years. The 1973 Yom Kippur War led the OPEC member states to cause an energy crisis by raising oil prices significantly in protest of US support for Israel. OPEC has held substantial leverage in the realm of energy and economics.

The Organization of the Islamic Conference (OIC) has many non-Arab members but has often supported causes of its Arab state members. The organization itself was established in response to vandalism against the *al-Aqsa* Mosque in Jerusalem in 1969. One of the aims of the OIC is to support the Palestinians and their struggle for political recognition and the right to return to their former lands.

The Future of Arab Nationalism

Arab nationalism is by no means a finalized phenomenon. The concept is still in process with many challenges waiting. Arab nationalism has gone through many phases over the course of the last century, and perhaps a new phase of nationalism may arise in the post-Yasser Arafat/post-Saddam Hussein Arab world. Given the current standing of the various Arab states and their relationships, the Pan-Arab idea of a single Arab state seems far off, if not impossible. The best representation of this idea is found in the Arab League. Many obstacles must be overcome for Arab nationalism to realize its goals.

WHITNEY D. DURHAM

See also Arab–Israeli Wars (1948, 1956, 1967, 1973); Ethnic Conflicts: Middle East; Ethnic Conflicts: North Africa; Palestine; Palestinian Diaspora

References and Further Reading

Amin, Samir. *The Arab Nation: Nationalism and Class Struggles*. London: Zed, 1983.
Barnett, Michael. *Dialogues in Arab Politics*. New York: Columbia University Press, 1998.
Choueiri, Youssef. *Arab Nationalism: A History*. Malden, MA: Blackwell Publishers, 2000.
Dawisha, Adeed. *Arab Nationalism in the Twentieth Century: From Triumph to Despair*. Princeton, NJ: Princeton University Press, 2002.
Hourani, Albert. *A History of the Arab Peoples*. New York: MJF Books, 1991.
Huntington, Samuel. "The Clash of Civilizations?" *Foreign Affairs*. 72 (3) (1993): 22–49.
Khalidi, Rashid. *The Origins of Arab Nationalism*. New York: Columbia University Press, 1993.
Khashan, Hilal. *Arabs at the Crossroads: Political Identity and Nationalism*. Gainesville. FL: University Press of Florida, 2000.
Lewis, Bernard. *The Arabs in History*. New York: Harper and Brothers, 1958.
Suleiman, Yasir. *The Arabic Language and National Identity*. Washington, DC: Georgetown University Press, 2003.
Tauber, Eliezer. *The Emergence of the Arab Movements*. London: Frank Cass, 1993.
Tibi, Bassam. *Arab Nationalism: Between Islam and the Nation-State*. New York: St. Martin's Press, 1997.

ARABIAN AMERICAN OIL COMPANY (ARAMCO)

The Arabian American Oil Company (ARAMCO) was originally created in 1936 in Saudi Arabia. It was not officially named ARAMCO until 1944. It was jointly owned by four US oil companies until the 1970s, when the Saudi government began to buy out the company, acquiring a 25% stake in 1973. By 1980, ARAMCO was completely Saudi-owned. However, the name was not changed to the Saudi Arabian Oil Company (Saudi ARAMCO) until 1988.

The company was originally formed out of the partnership between two US oil companies, Standard Oil Company of California (SoCal) and Texaco. SoCal signed a Concession Agreement with the Saudi king in 1933 and obtained concession rights to Saudi oil.

This Agreement formed the mainstay of the partnership between the country and the oil company. According to its terms, the Saudi king, Abdul Aziz bin Saud, received an advance cash payment of fifty thousand British pounds, an annual rental fee of five thousand pounds until oil was discovered in commercial quantities and he was assured of future royalties. In return, the company received exclusive exploration rights for crude petroleum in the eastern province of Saudi Arabia for the next sixty years.

The agreement was amended in 1939 and late 1950, increasing the revenues to the Saudi government and extending concession rights to ARAMCO. Oil revenues provided the foundation of Saudi Arabia's subsequent economic development, allowing the country to embark on an intensive path of industrialization and modernization in the next two decades.

Given the underdeveloped state of the country in the 1940s, ARAMCO had to build much of the infrastructure it needed to transport oil and to provide suitable living conditions for its employees. ARAMCO slowly built residential complexes for its foreign employees and their families in the cities of Dhahran, Abqaiq, and Ras Tanura, in the eastern province. The company constructed highways, roads, ports, airports, railroads, housing, schools, and hospitals. ARAMCO also provided technical, financial, and material assistance to the government, when requested. For example, ARAMCO teams helped find water and develop agricultural projects.

The company has contributed to the country's development in terms of human capital as well. It trained Saudis as doctors, supply experts, machinists, ship pilots, truck drivers, oil drillers, and cooks to meet the needs of the communities it was building. Some of these Saudis later left ARAMCO and started their own businesses, contributing to the local economy. The company also offered scholarships, training programs, loans, subsidies, and other social service benefits to all its employees.

Dependence on foreign labor and expertise has been both a positive and negative factor in Saudi Arabia's development. ARAMCO brought its trained US workers to Saudi Arabia in its initial oil exploration and production phases. Management positions were dominated by US workers until the 1970s and 1980s, when the government put greater pressure on the company to place more Saudis in supervisory positions. In 1984, Ali Naimi became the first Saudi president of ARAMCO. In addition, the company also hired and trained foreign workers, creating a large semi-permanent class of expatriate workers in the country.

UZMA JAMIL

See also Middle East: History and Economic Development; Organization of Arab Petroleum Exporting Countries (OAPEC); Organization of Petroleum Exporting Countries (OPEC); Saudi Arabia

References and Further Reading

Anderson, Irvine H. *ARAMCO, the United States, and Saudi Arabia: A Study of the Dynamics of Foreign Oil Policy 1933–1950*. Princeton, NJ: Princeton University Press, 1981.
Nawwab, Ismail *et al. ARAMCO and Its World: Arabia and the Middle East*. Dhahran, Saudi Arabia: ARAMCO, 1980.
Stocking, George. *Middle East Oil: A Study in Political and Economic Controversy*. Kingsport, TN: Vanderbilt University Press, 1970.

ARAB–ISRAELI WARS (1948, 1956, 1967, 1973)

The Arab–Israeli War of 1948–1949

On April 25, 1920, the San Remo Conference gave Britain the mandate over Palestine; two years later, the Council of the League of Nations confirmed it. On February 18, 1947, as a result of enormous violence and terrorism among Arabs and Jews in Palestine, British Foreign Secretary Bevin announced the decision of his government to submit the Palestine problem to the United Nations. The United Nations Special Committee on Palestine (UNSCOP), composed of representative from eleven nations, was created to examine the issues and to submit proposals for the solution to the problem.

UNSCOP was not able to present a unanimous report. The minority recommended that Palestine become a single federal state, with Jerusalem the capital, and with Jews and Arabs enjoying autonomy in their respective areas. The majority report proposed partition of Palestine into Arab and Jewish states. The Zionists favored partition, while the Arabs rejected it. On November 29, 1947, the UN General Assembly voted to recommend the partition of Palestine by a vote of thirty-three to thirteen, with ten abstentions. Zionists were determined to obtain a decision favoring the majority plan. Prior to the vote, and particularly during the immediately preceding three days, the US Zionists exerted unprecedented pressure on the administration, and both delegations to the United Nations and their governments, to secure the necessary majority. Some correspondence suggests that Truman himself might have intervened at the last minute to ensure success for partition. The State Department acknowledged that the votes of Haiti and the Philippines, at least, had been secured by the unauthorized intervention of US citizens. Soon after, Britain announced that it would terminate the mandate on May 15, 1948, and would evacuate Palestine before August 1.

Almost immediately after the United Nations vote, the armed detachments of Arabs began entering Palestine and attacking Jewish settlements. By February 1, these clashes had resulted in more than 2,500 casualties, and the toll mounted as the days went by. The British troops did not intervene—they were interested mainly in their own orderly withdrawal and in the progressive abandonment of strongholds. The Palestinians were armed by the neighboring Arab states and the Zionists by the United States and

Czechoslovakia. Furthermore, *Hagana*, *Irgun*, and *Stern* groups (Jewish paramilitary organizations) continued raiding British depots for more arms. It is estimated that the Palestinians had about five thousand men with little experience, under the distant direction of the ex-mufti of Jerusalem, who was in exile in Cairo. The Zionists, on the other hand, were better armed and better trained. A large number of their officers and men were veterans of World War II.

On May 14, 1948, the British officially terminated their mandate over Palestine, withdrawing their last forces from the country. On the same day, the new provisional government proclaimed Israel's independence, repealed the British mandatory restrictions on immigration and the sale of land, and converted *Hagana* into the Israel Defense Forces. A few hours later, President Truman extended de facto recognition to this new state on behalf of the United States.

On the morning of May 15, six Arab armies from Syria, Lebanon, Transjordan (now Jordan), Iraq, and Egypt entered Palestine. When one considers that a nation with a population of 650,000 defeated the combined Arab states with a population of forty million, the result seems nothing short of a miracle.

But when actual fighting forces are taken into consideration, a different picture emerges. The combined fighting forces of the six Arab states did not exceed seventy thousand. Of these, only about ten thousand had adequate training. Facing the Arab armies were sixty thousand fighting men of the *Haganah*. In this army, there were three hundred British-trained officers, some twenty thousand veterans of World War II, and three thousand specially trained commandos (*Palmach*). Their morale was high, and the *Haganah* soldiers believed that they were fighting for a common cause. The Arabs, on the other hand, had neither the singleness of purpose nor a unified command. Most of their soldiers did not know what they were fighting for, and their leaders were not without their national and personal vested interests (Armajani and Ricks 1986).

Both armies were ill equipped at the start, but the Israelis were supplied with necessary arms by Zionists in America and Europe, and with airplanes piloted by volunteers from England, the United States, and South Africa. The war lasted from May 15, 1948, until February 24, 1949. Between January and July 1949, a series of armistices were concluded by Israel on the one hand and Egypt, Lebanon, Transjordan, and Syria, on the other hand. By the term of armistice agreements, the contending armies were to hold their positions and were not supposed to be reinforced with additional men or arms. Both sides ignored the second part of the agreement. The Arabs, however, were not able to circumvent the arms embargo on the whole area. However, the Israelis were able to

purchase great quantities of first-class armaments from Czechoslovakia. A large quantity of ammunition also was smuggled from the United States and Britain into Israel.

On May 20, 1948, the Security Council appointed Count Folke Bernadotte, president of the Swedish Red Cross, as UN mediator for Palestine. He arranged a four-week truce starting on June 11. During these weeks, he made proposals of his own for an armistice based on an economic union of both Palestine and Jordan and autonomy for the Jewish state. Bernadotte emphasized that the Arab refugees should have the right to return home. The following day, Bernadotte was murdered in Jerusalem by Jewish terrorists.

By October 31, the Israeli armies with air superiority had pushed the Egyptians out of the Negev and the "Arab Liberation Force" out of northern Galilee. In the meantime, the United Nations debated the Palestine question. Dr. Ralph Bunche, a US citizen, succeeded Bernadotte as mediator. At his headquarters on Rhodes, he gathered Arab and Israeli representatives in separate rooms (the Arabs refused to sit with the Israeli representatives in the same room), working and communicating with both groups until he obtained the first armistice between Israel and Egypt on February 24, 1949. Further agreements were soon signed with Lebanon and Jordan, and finally with Syria. Ralph Bunche received a well-deserved Nobel Peace Prize for his efforts.

Three important problems were left unresolved. The first was the question of boundaries. In all the armistice agreements, the final position of the opposing troops was used to designate temporary boundaries that would presumably be changed at the time of ultimate settlement. The original partition plan of the United Nations was forgotten by everyone except the Palestinians. Israel gained 21% more land than it had under the 1947 partition plan; indeed, it covered almost 80% of the area of the Palestine mandate. Jordan annexed the West Bank of the Jordan River, including Old Jerusalem, which its armies occupied at the time of armistice. Egypt assumed the governance of Gaza Strip.

The second unsettled problem was the question of Jerusalem, Old and New. The city, together with nearby Bethlehem, was envisaged by the United Nations to be under international control. The war changed the status of the city from an international one to a divided one with barbed wires. The Jordanians had control of Old Jerusalem and Bethlehem, where most of the shrines holy to Christianity, Islam, and Judaism are located. The Israelis occupied the greater part of New Jerusalem. Although the United Nations had not abandoned the idea of an international Jerusalem, it allowed the demarcation formula that had been followed in armistice agreements to apply to Jerusalem also. Consequently, the area occupied by Israel and Jordan became separate territories and Jerusalem remained a divided city.

The internationalization of Jerusalem remained on the agenda of the United Nations; every year during the first twenty years of Israel's existence, the delegates passed resolutions concerning the status of Jerusalem, but neither Israel nor Jordan paid any attention to them. As early as 1949, Israel proclaimed Jerusalem as its capital and moved the *Knesset* (parliament) and many of its ministries there. Diplomats assigned to Israel, however, did not recognize this fact and kept their embassies at Tel Aviv.

The third and most vexing problem following the cease-fire agreements between Israel and Arab states was the fate of the Palestinian refugees. In 1949, the legally certified number of Palestinian Arab refugees was almost one million. They mainly went to Gaza, Jordan, Lebanon, Syria, and a smaller number to Iraq and Egypt. There have been conflicting reasons advanced as to why there were so many refugees. It seems that the bulk of the Palestinians, like so many people in countless wars, were in fear for their lives and sought refuge from the war, hoping to return when the shooting was over. At the end of the war, however, the Israeli forces did not allow them to return. Their homes were occupied by tens of thousands of Zionists who poured in from Europe, and their farms and orchards were appropriated by the conquerors without any compensation. Most of the refugees lived in camps and were supported by the United Nations Relief and Work Agency (UNRWA), Friends Service Committee, World Church Service, and other charitable organizations. Egypt confined most of the refugees to the Gaza Strip and discouraged them from swelling their already overpopulated country. In Syria and Lebanon, the refugees were technically aliens, but the educated among them managed to get jobs and gain citizenship. Only Jordan, which had occupied what was left of Palestine, gave the refugees full citizenship. Nevertheless, those who were in camps carried with them an aimless existence; and in the course of years became a saddening aspect of the general mosaic of the Fertile Crescent.

The Suez War of 1956

In an attempt to bring stability to the Middle East and reassure both Israel and Arab States, the West attempted to stabilize the situation in the Middle East with the Tripartite Declaration made by Britain, the United States, and France on May 25, 1950. The three powers pledged to limit arms shipments to the region and to oppose any attempts to alter the existing armistice lines by force. The United States intended to have friendly relations with both Arab States and Israel on a strictly impartial basis. It was in the interest of the United States that the Middle East be strengthened for defense against communist aggression, and that the countries in question obtain their arms from friendly sources.

Meanwhile, the humiliating defeat at the hands of Israel led to the emergence of Arab nationalism and major changes in several Arab governments. Perhaps the most significant change occurred in Egypt. The conduct of the war against Israel convinced the younger officers that their rulers should be replaced. On June 18, 1953, Egypt was proclaimed a republic, and in October 1954, Gamal Abdul Nasser became the president. Egypt under Nasser purchased a sizable amount of modern arms from the Soviet bloc, adding considerably to Israeli and US concern. In an attempt to counter Soviet influence, the Eisenhower administration, in February 1955, promoted the formation of a mutual defense treaty among Britain, Iran, Iraq, Pakistan and Turkey. US officials participated in the defense and anti-subversion committees of what became known as the Baghdad Pact, and the US military and economic aid was granted to members of the group. However, because of several political considerations, the United States decided against becoming a member of the Baghdad Pact.

President Nasser denounced Iraq, the only Arab member of the Pact, for allying itself with the Western powers and asked the Soviets for military equipment. Moscow, angered over the Baghdad Pact, quickly became Egypt's major arms supplier and built a reputation among Arabs as their principal ally in the struggle against Israel. Israel was convinced that the balance of armaments, stipulated by the Tripartite Agreement among the United States, Britain, and France in May 1950, was gravely upset by the Egyptian–Soviet deals. Israel also was disturbed by Nasser's growing ascendancy in the Arab world and his leadership in the Arab unity movement. These developments convinced Israel that it must prepare for a preventive war against Egypt before the military balance shifted in Cairo's favor. After being rejected by the United States, Israel turned to France, which was willing to sell some up-to-date military equipment.

On February 28, 1955, Israel made use of its newly purchased weapons from France to launch a successful raid against an Egyptian position in the Gaza Strip. Ostensibly, the raid was undertaken to demonstrate Israel's military strength and to persuade Arab countries to recognize its permanence. Instead of pressuring Egypt into recognizing Israel, however, the Gaza raid, along with other similar Israeli retaliatory raids into Arab territory, provoked tensions that led to renewed war between Israel and Egypt in November 1956.

Egypt's acceptance of arms from the Soviet Union, its refusal to lift a blockade against Israeli shipping through the Strait of Tiran and Suez Canal, and its recognition of communist China led the United States to withdraw promised financing for the proposed Aswan High dam, the principal symbol of Nasser's ambitious plans for Egypt's agricultural and economic development. Nasser reacted on July 1956 by nationalizing the Suez Canal and refused to guarantee the safety of Israeli shipping, actions directly threatening Israel, Britain, and France. The British government held 44% of all shares in the Suez Canal Company; private French investors held 78% of the remainder. Apart from these direct interests, both nations were frequent users of the canal, which provided the shortest waterway to their oil supplies in the Persian Gulf. The two governments froze Egyptian assets and began planning for joint military action, secretly enlisting Israel's participation in the plan.

In accordance with prearranged secret plans between Israel, Britain, and France, Israel attacked Egyptian positions in the Sinai on October 29. The attack included an Israeli paratroop drop near the Mitla Pass to give the appearance of a threat to the Suez Canal. On the following day, British and French forces attacked Egypt on the pretext of separating the belligerents and to ensure freedom of shipping through the canal. By November 7, British and French forces had secured control of the canal. However, responding to intense international pressure from the United States and the Soviet Union, Britain and France withdrew their forces from Egypt in December 1956. Israel was the last one to withdraw unconditionally from all territories it had occupied during the conflict. The last Israeli troops left Gaza on Match 9, 1957. At the conclusion of the war, Israel failed to achieve its main goal of securing Arab recognition of its legitimacy as an existing state, and it remained technically at war with Egypt as with the rest of the Arab world.

The Six-Day War of 1967

The settlement that ended the Suez–Sinai War of 1956 provided the pretext for the Six-Day War of 1967. Israel agreed to withdraw its forces from the conquered territories largely because of an understanding with Washington that the United Nations Emergency Force (UNEF) would ensure freedom of passage through the Straits of Tiran. Egyptian forces did not reenter the Gaza Strip, and Israel was free from Arab guerilla attacks from that area between March 1957 and May 1967.

During the early months of 1967, there were a series of clashes along the border between Israel and Syria. On April 7, small exchanges escalated into a tank battle and clashes between Israel and the Syrian Air Force. Six Syrian planes were shot down, and victorious Israeli jets swept over the suburbs of Damascus. General Itzhak Rabin stated that the Syrian government needed to be overthrown before Israeli security could be guaranteed. Damascus joined Amman in denouncing Nasser for doing nothing against Israel. During the Independence Day parade in Jerusalem on May 15, Israel gave Nasser the impression that an attack on Syria was imminent. That day, Nasser declared a state of alert in Egypt and sent Egyptian troops into Sinai. On May 16, the UNEF commander was asked to withdraw a limited number of forces so that Egypt could occupy certain positions on the border between Sinai and Israel. Nasser did not ask for the withdrawal of UNEF forces from the Gaza Strip or Sharm el Sheikh. Late on May 16, U Thant, the secretary general of the United Nations, told the Egyptian ambassador that a partial withdrawal of UNEF forces was not possible. Nasser, under pressure from other Arab states, asked for the total withdrawal of UNEF forces on May 18. Nasser sent advanced units to the Sinai border to replace UNEF, but not to Sharm el Sheikh. This hesitation met with scorn from Jordan and some Egyptian officers. Nasser gave in, and on May 21, Egyptian troops occupied Sharm el Sheikh. On May 22, Cairo closed the Gulf of Aqaba to Israeli ships and others sailing to Eilat with strategic cargoes. For Israel, the interference with shipping in the Gulf of Aqaba and the Straits of Tiran constituted a violation of international law and an act of aggression. Suddenly, Nasser was hailed by the Arabs as their savior.

On May 27, Israel's cabinet was discussing the possibility of preemptive military action. On June 2, the new defense minister, Moshe Dayan, argued for an attack without delay. Israeli military strategy, grounded in a perception of the country's geographic vulnerability, placed an emphasis on capturing the initiative by launching a preemptive first strike. There is no evidence to indicate that Nasser ever had a serious intention of waging war on Israel, notwithstanding his concentration of troops in the Sinai Peninsula. Lenczowski argues:

In fact, despite the impressive accumulation of arms of Soviet provenance in Egypt, Nasser with his military instinct and experience would have hesitated to launch an offensive attack and thus risk his own survival. By the same token, there always existed in Israel a school of thought, which might be called territorial-military, that viewed the existing Israeli boundaries as highly inconvenient, insecure, and inviting disaster in case of all-out war with the Arabs. This school was in favor of an enlarged territory for Israel so as to ensure the necessary margin of strategic safety. For this school, therefore assuming that Israel was militarily prepared, a clumsy provocation such as Nasser had conveniently provided by ordering the UNEF out supplied a welcome opportunity for waging a preventive war. (Lenczowski 1980)

Israel launched a well-prepared war on June 5, 1967. In three hours of precise wave attacks, Israeli aircraft struck Egyptian airfields, destroying three hundred of the 431 aircraft in the Egyptian inventory. Then, during the noon hours and early afternoon, similar attacks destroyed the air forces of Jordan and Syria, and Iraqi aircraft deployed at a major airfield in western Iraq. The achievement of immediate Israeli air superiority enabled the outnumbered Israeli ground forces to have the decisive advantage in the land battles that followed. By June 8, Israel controlled the area from Gaza to the Suez Canal and south to Sharm el Sheikh. By June 7, Jordan ceded Arab Jerusalem, Nablus, Jerico, and the rest of the West Bank. Israel pressed into Syria and secured the Golan Heights on June 10. Israel lost around one thousand men; the Arabs around eighteen thousand.

Israel's smashing victory during the Six-Day War stunned the Arabs and left Israel in a position of strength. Arabs, charging the United States for helping Israel, severed their diplomatic relations with the United States. The USSR used this opportunity to increase its role as arms supplier and chief benefactor of the Arabs. The United States moved to replace France as the main supplier of arms to Israel.

On November 22, 1967, the UN Security Council unanimously approved a resolution (Security Council Resolution 242) calling for the withdrawal of Israeli forces from the occupied Arab areas. This resolution remained the basis for all subsequent peace initiatives.

The October (Yom Kippur) War of 1973

Anwar al-Sadat succeeded Nasser after his death in September 1970. Sadat had been among the Free Officers cadre that had overthrown King Farouk in 1952 and had been part of Nasser's leadership council from the beginning. Sadat was painfully aware that diplomacy would not move Israel out of Sinai and other occupied Arab lands. He also doubted that

Russians could effectively help Egypt to get back their lost territories.

In 1972, therefore, Sadat expelled the twenty thousand Russian military advisors and operations personnel serving in Egypt. He hoped that in return the United States would persuade Israel to reach a negotiated settlement. The United States made no attempt to force Israel to compromise; indeed, the United States looked the other way as Israelis began building permanent settlements in occupied territories. The expulsion seemed to diminish the possibilities that Egypt would soon launch a war against Israel. Sadat, meanwhile, knew that with every passing day, the Israeli occupation of Arab lands would come to seem more acceptable, even normal. Soon the world would accept it as a fact. Repeatedly, Sadat warned that war would come if the Israelis did not withdraw. Repeatedly he was ignored.

As early as 1971, he began to prepare for war. Sadat approached Hafez al Asad, the new president of Syria, who eagerly supported the concept of a two-front war. For both Sadat and Asad, receiving sufficient arms from the Soviet Union was the key to their war effort. Because the United States did not take Sadat seriously, he swallowed his pride and turned to Russia for arms.

On October 6, 1973, during the Jewish holiday of Yom Kippur, Egypt and Syria jointly launched an attack against Israel. The Israeli high command, despite sufficient intelligence, was caught by surprise, having misinterpreted the evidence of an impending attack until just hours before it occurred. In accordance with a meticulously planned and methodically executed operation, nearly ninety thousand Egyptian troops, supported by intense artillery barrages and aerial bombardments, crossed the Suez canal, destroyed the much vaunted Bar-Lev defensive line, which Israelis had thought impregnable, then drove several miles deep inside the Sinai. An elaborate air defense system behind the canal effectively neutralized Israeli air strike capabilities against the Egyptian positions. On the Syrian front, Israelis were driven off the Golan Heights.

These stunning victories came as a surprise to everyone except possibly Sadat. "Israel may not have been quite on the verge of extinction, but her national existence was threatened as it had never been before, and her leaders knew that without outside assistance she was doomed. Only the United States could provide the necessary help in the form of new planes, tanks, and missiles (Ambrose and Brinkley 1997). In all, it was estimated that Israel lost five hundred tanks and 120 aircraft and suffered 2,400 killed and as many wounded; the Arabs lost 1,500 tanks and 450 airplanes, while their numbers killed and wounded exceeded Israeli's. Many of these destroyed tanks lie throughout the Sinai still today. The cost to all the combatants was staggering; it has been estimated that Israel spent $7.2 billion.

The Israelis began making frantic demands on Henry Kissinger for supplies, especially after October 10, when the Russians launched a large-scale airlift of supplies to Syria and Egypt, replacing their arms lost in battle. The Russian objective was to support a cease fire after the Arabs had won the maximum advantage from their surprise attack and before Israel had time to mount an effective counteroffensive. On October 13, President Richard Nixon ordered an all-out airlift by US military aircraft direct to Israel. In the end, US deliveries substantially exceeded those of Moscow to the Arabs, proving that America's military capacity in time of crisis was superior to that of the Russians. On October 15, with the US equipment, the Israelis began their counterattack, crossed the Suez at two points, and encircled the Egyptian Third Army while driving the Syrians back from the Golan Heights.

After it became clear that the tide was turning against the Arabs, the United States and the Soviet Union reached an understanding permitting the adoption of UN Resolution 338 which called for a cease-fire on October 22. UN Resolution 338 reiterated that the consenting parties implement Resolution 242 in all its parts. The cease fire did not hold, and on October 24, Soviet leader Leonid Brezhnev proposed to Nixon that they both take action to enforce it. When the United States rejected this, the Soviets seemed as if they would intervene unilaterally, whereupon president Nixon ordered a partial alert of US forces. "The specter of a world war loomed until the passage of UN Resolutions 339 and 340, calling for a cease fire and providing for a United Nations Emergency Force (UNEF), which began to arrive on the lines between the Egyptian and Israeli armies on October 27." (Fisher and Ochsenwald 1990)

Despite the joint US–Soviet role in bringing an end to the 1973 war, Secretary of State Henry Kissinger emerged as the central mediator in postwar negotiations. Flying from Israel to Arab capitals in his specially equipped jet airliner, Kissinger engaged in what came to be known as shuttle diplomacy. Kissinger's efforts gradually produced a series of disengagement agreements. The first agreement, on October 28, 1973, secured Israel's assent for relief of Egypt's encircled Third Army. A subsequent agreement, on November 11, committed both Egypt and Israel to implement Resolution 242 and 338 and to stabilize a cease fire.

In January 1974, Egypt and Israel signed a disengagement agreement. Israel agreed to pull back her troops twenty kilometers east of the canal and allowed limited numbers of Egyptian soldiers to be stationed on the east bank, separated from Israeli forces by UNEF detachments. This agreement significantly reduced the chances of a future surprise attack by either side. Kissinger's assurances that the United States would work for implementation of Resolution 242 and 338 enabled him to secure Asad's acceptance of a Syrian–Israeli Separation of Forces agreement on May 31, 1974. Finally, in 1975, Egypt and Israel signed a Sinai disengagement pact in Geneva.

NASSER MOMAYEZI

See also Ethnic Conflicts: Middle East; Israel; Middle East: International Relations

References and Further Reading

Armajani, Yahya, and Thomas M. Ricks. *Middle East: Past and Present*, Englewood Cliffs, NJ: Prentice-Hall, 1986.
Cleveland, William L. *A History of the Modern Middle East*. Boulder. CO: Westview Press, 1994.
Congressional Quarterly Inc. *The Middle East*, 8th ed. Washington, DC: Congressional Quarterly Press, 1994.
Fisher, Sydney N., and William Ochsenwald. *The Middle East: A History*, 4th ed. New York: McGraw-Hill, 1990.
Goldschmidt, Arthur, Jr. *A Concise History of the Middle East*. Boulder, CO: Westview Press, 1983.
Hamad, Jamil. "Learning from History: The Lessons of Arab-Israeli Errors." *International Relations* (November 1987).
Kerr, Malcolm. "Coming to Terms with Nasser." *International Affairs* (January 1967).
Khouri, Fred J. *The Arab-Israeli Dilemma*, 3d ed. Syracuse, NY: Syracuse University Press, 1985.
Lenczowski, George. *The Middle East in World Affairs*, Ithaca, NY, and London: Cornell University Press, 1980.
Oren, Michael B. "Escalation to Suez: The Egyptian-Israeli Border War." *Journal of Contemporary History* (April 1989).
Quandt, William B. *Decade of Decisions: American Policy Toward the Arab-Israeli Conflict, 1967–1976*. Berkeley, CA: University of California Press, 1977.
Rabinovich, Itamar. "Seven Wars and One Peace Treaty." In *The Arab-Israeli Conflict: Perspectives*, 2d ed., edited by Alvin Z. Rubinstein. New York, NY: Harper Collins Publishers, 1991.
Reich, Bernard. "The State of Israel," in *The Government and Politics of the Middle East and North Africa*. David E. Long and Bernard Reich. Boulder, CO: Westview Press, 1980.
Sachar, Howard M. *History of Israel*. New York: Knopf, 1976.
Shipler, David K. *Arabs and Jew: Wounded Spirits In A Promised Land*. New York: Viking Penguin Inc., 1987.

ARAFAT, YASSER

Yasser Arafat's very name evokes contrasting emotional responses: To some, he was the personification of legitimate Palestinian nationalism. To others, he was a duplicitous scoundrel who told the West he had renounced terrorism while slyly encouraging his "Martyr's Brigades."

Arafat claimed to have been born in Jerusalem, but convincing evidence shows that he was born on August 24, 1929, in Cairo. His father was a merchant, comfortable but not rich. His mother died when he was five years old, and he was sent to live with his maternal uncle in Jerusalem. Estrangement between father and son is indicated by the fact that Yasser did not attend his father's funeral.

Yasser Arafat's life was interwoven with political events in the Middle East. In 1947, Arab states rejected a United Nations plan to partition the Holy Land into Jewish and Palestinian states. Arafat was ready for guerrilla war, but Arab armies invaded the new state of Israel. The cease-fire lines of 1948 created the Israeli borders that most of the world now accepts as legitimate. Arafat returned to Cairo to study civil engineering but immersed himself in Palestinian exile politics and led the Union of Palestinian Students from 1952 to 1956. Arafat was in Cairo to witness the tumultuous events that brought Col. Gamal Abdel Nasser to power, but he always championed Palestinian nationalism over Nasser's wider ideal of Pan-Arabism.

After earning his degree in 1956, Arafat joined the Egyptian Army and fought in the Suez campaign. He moved the next year to Kuwait, where he established a contracting firm while devoting all his spare time to the Palestinian cause. In 1958, Arafat and other Palestinian exiles founded *al-Fatah*, an underground group dedicated to waging guerrilla war against Israel. In May 1964, the Arab League formed the Palestine Liberation Organization (PLO) in East Jerusalem. Arafat opposed the PLO until Fatah could gain control of it. Always in need of a patron but unwilling to cede control of his movement, Arafat allied himself with Syria in 1966 only to find himself imprisoned and threatened with execution by the Syrian Baathist dictator Hafez Assad.

In June 1967, Israeli forces inflicted a swift, humiliating defeat on the combined armies of Egypt, Syria, and Jordan. Now the territories from which Arafat had hoped to liberate his homeland—Sinai, Gaza, the West Bank, East Jerusalem, and the Golan Heights—all fell under Israeli military occupation. This new catastrophe triggered a power struggle within the Palestinian movement. Arafat lacked any coherent ideology but proved a master of media symbolism. His unshaven face, *kaffiyeh*, sunglasses, pistol, and ever-present military uniform were instantly recognizable worldwide.

In 1968, Arafat relocated to Jordan, home to thousands of Palestinian refugees. There, he recruited so many young fighters that he threatened the power of Jordan's King Hussein. The king struck with devastating force in September 1970, killing thousands of Palestinians and driving Arafat into Lebanon. The tenacious guerrilla leader now turned to terrorism yet retained enough legitimacy to be invited to address the UN in 1974. He did so with a pistol strapped to his side.

Civil war erupted in Lebanon in 1975. The next year, Syria sent troops into that country, at least in part to control Arafat. The Palestinian leader's sense of betrayal by other Arab leaders was sharpened when Egyptian leader Anwar Sadat signed a peace treaty with Israel in 1979. The Israeli Army invaded Lebanon in 1982 and drove northward all the way to Beirut. It seemed that Arafat's forced removal to Tunis, so far from his occupied homeland, might signify the end of the PLO. Power struggles erupted inside the organization. However, with funding from sympathetic individuals and governments Yasser Arafat rebuilt the PLO infrastructure to include schools and welfare agencies. He was fully back in control by 1987 when he moved his headquarters to Baghdad. The first *intifada* (spontaneous Palestinian uprising) began in that year. Arafat now found himself struggling to stay ahead of frustrated young militants.

In 1988, Arafat embarked on the pragmatic phase of his long campaign for Palestinian statehood. He boldly declared his recognition of Israel and renounced terrorism (without flatly condemning it when practiced by others). In 1989, the Palestinian National Council elected him president of the hoped-for future Palestinian state. When Saddam Hussein invaded Kuwait in August 1990, Arafat voiced support. This was a strategic blunder, because the Saudis and other Gulf monarchs cut off their subsidies to the PLO, distribution of which had been one of the ways that Arafat maintained control of the movement. Ordinary Palestinians working in the Gulf states paid a price for Arafat's endorsement of the Iraqi invasion, too, as nearly all were summarily fired.

Arafat survived this political debacle and, no less miraculously, walked away from a plane crash in the Sahara Desert in April 1992. In 1993, he signed the Oslo Agreement, which was supposed to usher in Palestinian self-rule in the West Bank and the Gaza Strip over a five-year period. For this achievement, which ultimately came to naught, Arafat, Yitzhak Rabin, and Shimon Peres were jointly awarded the Nobel Peace Prize in 1994. Arafat now was able to enter the Gaza Strip for the first time in twenty-seven years and to begin governing there under the auspices of the Palestinian Authority (PA). In 1996, Palestinians held their first election. Arafat was confirmed as PA leader and his allies gained control of the Palestinian Legislative Council.

From the year 2000 onward, Yasser Arafat's position weakened. He rejected a peace plan urged on him by President Bill Clinton and Israeli Prime Minister Ehud Barak. A second intifada erupted after Ariel Sharon's deliberately provocative visit to the Temple Mount in East Jerusalem. In 2001, Sharon became the Israeli prime minister and George W. Bush entered the White House; both men regarded Arafat as untrustworthy. The US president urged Palestinians to find a better leader and the Israelis laid siege to Arafat's headquarters in Ramallah. In the last years of Arafat's life, the Israeli government relentlessly narrowed his power. He could not even leave his compound in Ramallah until he was on the verge of death, when he was flown to a hospital in Paris. He died there on November 11, 2004, at the age of 75. He was buried in Ramallah, but if the Palestinians achieve a state whose capital is East Jerusalem, he will be reburied there.

Ross Marlay

See also Arab–Israeli Wars (1948, 1956, 1967, 1973); Intifada; Middle East: History and Economic Development; Middle East: International Relations; Palestine; Palestine Liberation Organization (PLO); Palestinian Diaspora

References and Further Reading

Aburish, Said. *Arafat: From Defender to Dictator*. Bloomsbury Publishing, 1999.
Hart, Alan. *Arafat: A Political Biography*. Indiana University Press, 1989.
Karsh, Efraim. *Arafat's War: The Man and his Battle for Israeli Conquest*. Grove Press, 2003.
Rubin, Barry, and Judith C. Rubin. *Yasser Arafat: A Political Biography*. New York: Oxford University Press, 2003.
Walker, Tony and Andrew Gowers. *Arafat: The Biography*. Virgin Publishing, 2003.

ÁRBENZ GUZMÁN, JACOBO

Jacobo Árbenz Guzmán (1913–1971) was born to a Swiss immigrant and a Guatemalan mother in Quetzaltenango, Guatemala on September 14, 1913. In 1932, he began attending the Polytechnic Academy, where he majored in social science and military courses. He graduated at the top of his class as a sublieutenant in 1935 and returned two years later to teach social science and military courses. Shortly after meeting María Cristina Villanova, the rebellious daughter of a wealthy Salvadoran family, they were married in 1939.

Disillusioned with the Ubico and Ponce dictatorships, Árbenz was a protagonist in Guatemala's Revolution of October 20, 1944. Major Francisco Javier Arana, Jorge Torriello Garrido, and Árbenz comprised the revolutionary junta that governed Guatemala after they deposed Federico Ponce Vaides. Shortly afterward, when Juan José Arévalo became president, he appointed Árbenz Defense Minister.

Quetzaltenango's National Integration Party, along with the National Renovation and Revolutionary Action Parties, nominated Árbenz for president during Guatemala's next electoral campaign. On March 15, 1951, after easily winning the presidency, Jacobo Árbenz succeeded Juan Jose Arévalo. His government followed the social, economic, and political reforms brought forth by the 1944 Revolution. His administration proved to be populist and nationalistic, with a political program that included agrarian reform, industrialization, defense of democratic institutions, and Guatemala's sovereignty. Among several major projects, he started the road that connected Guatemala City to the Atlantic Coast—weakening the monopoly that the US-owned International Railways of Central America had on transportation to Guatemala's Atlantic ports. Árbenz's most controversial project was his agrarian reform program after the 1952 passage of "Decree 900."

Unfortunately for the landless and predominantly indigenous majority of Guatemala's inhabitants, Árbenz's confiscation of unused lands from large landholders like the United Fruit Co. generated open hostility to Guatemala's President on the part of the US government. Kinship and collaboration between one of United Fruit Co.'s largest stockholders and the head of the Central Intelligence Agency (CIA) also contributed to increasing tensions with the Eisenhower administration under the guise of the "Red Scare" and McCarthyism. Árbenz's fight against US Imperialism—represented in Guatemala by companies such as Bond and Share and United Fruit Co.—branded him a "communist" and lead to CIA plans for his overthrow.

The CIA's plans to assassinate Árbenz, which were active up until the day he was ousted from office, were not carried out. However, on June 18, 1954, a small army led by Lt. Colonel Castillo Armas—with logistical support from the United States—entered Guatemala from Honduras and took control of the eastern department of Chiquimula. The US-sponsored overthrow of Árbenz's democratically elected government became official on June 27, 1954, when he announced his resignation, after which he and his family took asylum in Guatemala's Mexican embassy. He and his family started their life in exile in Mexico but were forced to move to Switzerland, Czechoslovakia, Moscow, Paris, Uruguay, and Cuba within six years. In 1970, they were finally granted permanent asylum in Mexico, where a demoralized fifty-eight-year-old Árbenz drowned in a bathtub in 1971.

GUSTAVO ADOLFO GUERRA VÁSQUEZ

See also Central America: History and Economic Development; Central America: International Relations; Guatemala

References and Further Reading

Contreras, R., and J. Daniel. *Breve Historia de Guatemala.* Guatemala: Piedra Santa, 2002.

Doyle, Kate, and Peter Kornbluh. "CIA and Assasinations: The Guatemala 1954 Documents." National Security Archive Electronic Briefing Book No. 4, www.gwu.edu/~nsarchiv/NSAEBB/NSAEBB4.

Jiménez, Girón, and Ernesto Bienvenido. *Los Presidentes de Guatemala: Biografías Breves.* Guatemala: Piedra Santa, 2002.

Schlesinger, Stephen and Stephen Kinzer. *Bitter Fruit.* New York: Anchor Press, 1990.

ARGENTINA

Encompassing an area of 1,057,518 square miles, Argentina, in terms of territorial size, is the largest Spanish-speaking nation in the world and the second largest country in Latin America. Argentina, with its 250,000-square-mile Pampas region, has the most fertile soil in Latin America and is one of the world's leading beef and grain exporters. Additionally, Argentina is rich in minerals and is an oil-producing nation, with an estimated three million barrels in reserves.

Argentina's population of 39.1 million inhabitants is not evenly distributed. The Pampas, with 22% of the national territory, is home to 85% of the population. Located in the Pampas, Argentina's capital—Buenos Aires—contains more than one-third of the national population. Largely as a result of a massive European migration during the late nineteenth and twentieth centuries, Argentina has the highest white population in Latin America. Approximately 97% of the population is white—mostly descendants of Spanish and Italian immigrants.

With an impressive educational system, Argentina's population has one of the highest literacy rates in Latin America, and its life expectancy rate of seventy-six years is considerably higher than that of the rest of Latin America. Although Argentina's unemployment rate stands at 16.3%, its gross domestic product purchasing power per capita is among the highest in Latin America at $11,200.

Argentina—land of silver—owes its name to the Spanish *conquistadores*. Argentina, however, was a misnomer, for there was neither gold nor silver. As a result, the Spanish Crowns treated Argentina with benign neglect. In 1776, due to Spanish concerns over possible foreign encroachments on its southern colonies, the Viceroyalty of La Plata was established with its seat in Buenos Aires.

Argentina became no exception as Spanish colonies sought independence in 1810. The Argentines' quest to exercise hegemony over the territories in the Viceroyalty of La Plata led to the creation of the United Provinces of South America. However, provincial animosity and mistrust of Buenos Aires led to the federation's breakup. Argentine independence hero José de San Martín's victory over the Spaniards in Chile in 1818 consolidated independence in the Southern Cone. Independence, on the other hand, opened the way for anarchy as provincial *caudillos* became the real rulers of Argentina. In 1829, Argentina experienced a new era with the rise of Juan Manuel de Rosas. This Argentine *caudillo*, who ruled Argentina until 1852, gave the nation much needed stability at the expense of violating human rights.

During the latter half of the nineteenth century, Argentina experienced further expansion of its frontier, the rise of an effective educational system, and a massive increase in population. European immigration contributed to the rise of the middle class, as well as the creation of the *Unión Cívica Radical*, an anti-oligarchical party. From 1916 until 1930, the *Radicales* were able to curtail the power of the land-owning *estancieros*, the Buenos Aires merchants, and industrialists. However, Radical President Hipólito Irigoyen's ineptitude to deal with the Great Depression led to military intervention in 1930.

After the 1930 coup, Argentina was governed by an ineffective coalition of Socialists, Radicals, and Conservatives known as the *Concordancia*. Besides its corruption, the *Concordancia* is best remembered for the infamous Roca–Runciman Agreement by which Argentina agreed to reduce tariffs on British goods and guaranteed the profits of British-owned public transportation enterprises in exchange for increased British purchases of Argentine beef.

Dissatisfaction with the *Concordancia* administration and the perceived British control of the Argentine economy prompted a group of nationalist Army officers to stage a coup in 1943. Among these officers was Colonel Juan Domingo Perón, who would become the most salient figure in twentieth century Argentine politics.

Entrusted with the post of Minister of Labor, Perón saw Argentine labor as an untapped source of support for his ambitions. Perón organized the workers into the state-sponsored General Confederation of Labor (CGT). Perón granted workers a series of benefits unprecedented in Argentine history.

In 1946, in the fairest presidential election ever conducted in Argentine history, Perón became president. Perón's socioeconomic program during his first presidency from 1946 until 1951 was important for practically every sector of Argentine society. Workers not only obtained benefits, but also received a cumulative 30% higher wages. The military also gained prestige, for 30% of the national budget was earmarked for defense spending. His industrialization program, combined with import-substitution measures, pleased Argentine industrialists who saw in them an opportunity to increase their profits. Perón's nationalization of British railroads and public utilities satisfied nationalists, because it symbolized economic redemption. Civil servants were extremely supportive, as their ranks grew by geometric proportions. Lastly, Perón enjoyed the unequivocal support of the Catholic Church. Not only did the Church view Perón as a bulwark against Communism, but its role in Argentine education was expanded.

The Argentine oligarchy was the one sector of Argentine society opposed to Perón. His populist measures represented a perceived threat to their stability. Perón's antioligarchical rhetoric, however, did very little in changing the power of the *estancieros*. Cognizant of the fact that his socioeconomic program depended on export of Argentine beef and cereals, he did not undertake an agrarian reform program. To do so would have meant a decline in agricultural production and, consequently, a drastic reduction in export revenues.

Although Perón was reelected in 1951, his second term suffered a major blow with the death of his charismatic wife, Evita, in 1952. In addition, the Argentine beef industry with its outdated technology began to face stiff competition from beef-producing nations. Economic woes were exacerbated when Argentine oil production was unable to meet Perón's industrialization program demand. European economic recovery, also contributed to the downward spiral, as European demand for Argentine beef and grain lessened. As a result, the peso declined in value and inflation was rampant.

With the exception of his loyal workers, Perón began to lose the support of all sectors that previously backed him. Finally, in 1955, Perón's quarrel with the Catholic Church over the government's legalization of divorce and prostitution resulted in his excommunication. The Church's action was the *coup de grace* for the Perón regime. On September 16, 1955, the dissatisfied armed forces overthrew him and sent him into exile.

The military regimes of Generals Lonardi and Aramburu (1955–1958) embarked on a de-Peronization campaign, which ultimately failed. From 1958 until 1973, Argentina was beset by political instability. The non-Peronist civilian administrations of Arturo Frondizi, José María Guido, and Arturo Illia (1958–1966) were inept at best, while the military governments that ruled Argentina from 1976 until 1983 never succeeded in de-Peronizing Argentina. Perón, although in exile, was a political genius who knew how to bring out the best in his supporters and the worst out of his enemies, and in 1973, the military had no other choice than to allow Perón's return. After eighteen years in exile, Perón returned to the political arena. With his wife "Isabelita" as running mate, he swept into office with 62% of the vote. A feeble figure, he lasted only ten months in office. On July 1, 1974, Perón died of a heart attack.

Unable to contain a wave of violence between left-wing terrorist groups such as the *Montoneros* and the *Ejército Revolucionario del Pueblo* (ERP) and the right-wing *Alianza Anticomunista Argentina* (The Triple A), Isabel Perón's regime also was beset by inflation, rising oil prices, fallen export revenues, cost of living increases, and a rift between her supporters in the CGT. Finally, on March 24, 1976, the armed forces staged a coup, ending the inept regime.

Military rule in Argentina from 1976 until 1983 was known as the *proceso*. Led by *junta* leader, General Jorge Rafael Videla (1976–1981), the military successfully crushed the *Montoneros*, the ERP, and other terrorist organizations in less than three years. In carrying out this campaign, known as the "Dirty War," close to twenty thousand Argentines suspected of being terrorists were secretly executed. They became known as the *desaparecidos* (the disappeared ones).

Although crushing suspected terrorists was important to the *junta*, economic recovery was just as important. The *junta* appointed a civilian technocrat, José Martínez de Hoz, as Finance Minister. His recipe for economic development, consisting of gradually dismantling the number of state-owned enterprises, bureaucratic reduction, freezing wages, canceling government subsidies, and attracting foreign investments through favorable tax laws and tariff reduction, was well-received by the Argentine elites. It also met no labor opposition, because the *junta* had outlawed the CGT.

Martínez de Hoz's plan yielded positive results. By 1979, Argentina enjoyed a favorable balance of payments and there was a considerable increase in export revenues. The gross domestic product had increased by 7%, and inflation had been reduced from almost 450% to 150%. The Argentine middle class began to enjoy the fruits of Martínez de Hoz's plan, as they went on a shopping spree in Miami and New York City.

In 1981, however, Martínez de Hoz's economic miracle turned into a nightmare. Although his proposed goal of reducing state-owned enterprises was a commendable one, it simply was untenable. Heavy borrowing abroad in order to keep state-owned enterprises afloat, combined with rampant speculation and an overvalued *peso*, were directly responsible for this economic collapse.

In an effort to divert attention from the financial catastrophe, recently appointed *junta* leader, General Leopoldo Galtieri, on April 2, 1982, undertook the recovery of the Falkland/Malvinas Islands, which had been under British occupation since 1823. Although the Argentine Air Force fought bravely, Argentine conscripts were no match for British forces, who successfully expelled the Argentines in June 1981. The Argentine military debacle incurred the people's wrath and the *junta* had no other choice than to return power to the civilians.

In 1983, Raúl Alfonsín of the UCR took office as president. Although he succeeded in restoring civil liberties and constitutional order, his administration was beset by triple-digit inflation, the "Dirty War's" aftermath, and the CGT's bitter opposition to his economic development plan, centering on bureaucratic reduction, and wage controls. Numerous CGT-sponsored labor strikes seriously impacted the Argentine economy. Alfonsín's inability to cope with the economic situation, coupled with his party's fragmentation, resulted in the *Partido Justicialista* (Peronist Party) candidate Carlos Menem's triumph in the 1989 elections.

Upon assuming office, Menem radically departed from Peronist state-controlled economic policies in favor of a development program based on a free-market economy and privatization of government-owned enterprises. Menem's policies, although denounced by the CGT, brought positive results. Inflation was reduced to minimal levels, and the gross domestic product experienced a 10% annual increase. Additionally, Menem's measures were extremely popular with the International Monetary Fund (IMF) and the World Bank, which continued to issue favorable interest loans to Argentina. On the negative side, his program was detrimental to the Argentine poor, as unemployment arose among the poor and less educated.

Riding a wave of popularity, Menem gained the necessary support to change the Constitution to allow immediate presidential reelection, which he won in 1995. Although Menem's second term witnessed continued economic improvement through privatization, it was marred by widespread graft and rampant corruption. In spite of these maladies, *Partido Justicialista* candidate Fernando de la Rúa was elected president in 2001.

De La Rúa's administration experienced recurring economic problems of inflation and an immense foreign debt. Concerns over the country's inability to refinance its debt led to capital flight and a halt by foreign investors. As a result of the financial panic and widespread discontent, De la Ruá left his unfinished term in disgrace.

After a two-year provisional interlude, a presidential primary was held on April 27, 2003. Menem, attempting a comeback, led all candidates, while Néstor Kirchner, another *Justicialista* candidate, finished second. A run-off election was scheduled for May 25, 2003. On the eve of the election, Menem, faced with countless charges of fraud and corruption, withdrew, and Kirchner was declared the winner by default. Although Kirchner's administration faces the difficult task of economic recovery and restoring public confidence, it appears that Argentine democracy has consolidated itself, and Argentines look for a better future.

JOSÉ FERNANDEZ

See also Ethnic Conflicts: Southern Cone (Latin America); Menem, Carlos; Perón, Juan Domingo; Southern Cone Common Market (MERCOSUR); Southern Cone (Latin America): History and Economic Development; Southern Cone (Latin America): International Relations

References and Further Reading

Alexander, Robert J. *Juan Domingo Perón: A History*. Boulder, CO: Westview Press, 1979.

Busey, James L. *Latin American Political Guide*, Manitou Springs, CO: Juniper Editions, 1995.

Ciria, Alberto. *Parties and Power in Modern Argentina*. Translated by Carlos A. Astiz and Mary F. McCarthy. Albany, NY: State University of New York Press, 1974.

McGuire, James W. *Peronism Without Perón: Union Parties and Democracy in Argentina*. Stanford, CA: Stanford University Press, 1997.

Nelson, Joan M. "How Market Reforms and Democratic Consolidation Affect Each Other." In *Intricate Links: Democratization and Market Reforms in Latin America and Eastern Europe*. New Brunswick, NJ: Transaction Books, 1994.

Page, Joseph A. *Perón: A Biography*. New York: Random House, 1983.

Potash, Robert. *The Army and Politics in Argentina, 1945–1962: Perón to Frondizi*. Stanford, CA: Stanford University Press, 1980.

Rock, David. *Politics in Argentina, 1890–1930: The Rise and Fall of Radicalism*. Cambridge: Cambridge University Press, 1975.

———. *Argentina, 1516–1982: From Spanish Colonization to the Falklands War*, Berkeley, CA: University of California Press, 1985.

Smith, William C. "Democracy, Distributional Conflicts and Macroeconomic Policymaking in Argentina, 1983–1989." *Journal of Interamerican Studies and World Affairs* 32 (2) 1–42: (Summer 1990).

———. "State, Market, and Neoliberalism in Post-Transition Argentina: The Menem Experiment." *Journal of Interamerican Studies and World Affairs* 33 (4) 45–82: (Winter 1991).

Wynia, Gary. "Argentina's Economic Reform," *Current History* 90 (553) 57–60: (February 1991).

ARIAS SANCHEZ, OSCAR

Oscar Arias Sanchez (1941–) was born in Heredia, Costa Rica, on September 13, 1941, into a progressive and activist coffee planter's family that believed deeply in Costa Rican independence, democracy and, later, the abolition of the military. Arias did his undergraduate studies at the Colegio Saint Francis and Boston University. He then studied law and economics at the University of Costa Rica, San Jose, before matriculating to the University of Essex in Great Britain. He received his M.A. and Ph.D. from Essex. His dissertation, later published in 1974, was entitled, "Who Rules Costa Rica." The first of many books and articles published by Arias on history and politics, it has won awards and is a well-regarded narrative account of Costa Rican political history.

Throughout his time in school, he was an active member of the social democratic National Liberation Party (NLP). In 1970, he embarked on his political career, becoming a leading supporter of, and loyal assistant to, reformist former President Jose Figures, who was seeking office again. In 1972, Figures was elected President, and Arias was appointed Minister of National Planning and Political Economy.

In 1975, the NLP elected Arias their international secretary and, four years later, general secretary. During the late 1980s, he represented the NLP at many International Socialist Congresses. In 1978, he won a seat in the Legislative Assembly even though the Christian Social Unity Party (CSUP) won the Presidency and a legislative majority.

In 1981, he resigned his seat to work for his party's presidential candidate, Luis Alberto Monge, who won the 1982 election. In 1986, Arias ran for the presidency, outpolling his CSUP rival 52.3% to 45.8%. Even before he became president, he had been a leading voice for peace in Central America. As president, he acted to end the bloodshed in Nicaragua and El Salvador. Although he opposed the communist government in Nicaragua, instead of supporting the US-backed Contras, he engaged the Sandinistas in a peace dialog.

In May 1986, he met with the leaders of Guatemala, Honduras, El Salvador, and Nicaragua to discuss a peaceful solution to the region's conflicts.

Although no concrete plan was approved, Arias was able to get the Central American nations to meet again in early 1987. This time, Arias presented his own peace proposal, one he had originally written on a napkin. This plan became known as the "Arias Plan." It called for the five states to work toward democracy, freedom of the press, and free and open elections for all Central American states. It also pledged these nations to drastically limit the size of their militaries. To this end, Costa Rica reaffirmed the abolition of its military in 1948. The plan, officially known as the "Esquipulas II Accords" or "Procedure to Establish a Firm and Lasting Peace in Central America," was signed by all five leaders on August 7, 1987, in Guatemala. For his efforts, Arias won the 1987 Nobel Peace Prize.

Arias believed in minimal government economic intervention. During his tenure, Costa Rica experienced a 4% annual growth in its gross national product and the lowest unemployment rate in the hemisphere at 5.6%. Costa Rica has, over the past fifteen years, had the most stable economy in Central America and is a model for its neighbors.

Arias was a very visible president. He spent much of his time, without a bodyguard, driving himself through the towns and villages of his country mingling with the citizenry, often over a cup of coffee or a meal in a local restaurant. This pattern has continued since he left office in 1990. Moreover, Arias has become arguably the most famous and respected advocate for peace and disarmament in the world. In 1988, he used the Nobel Prize monetary award to establish the Arias Foundation for Peace and Human Progress. Over the past decade, the Foundation has formed: the Center for Human Progress to promote equal opportunities for women, the Center for Organized Participation to "strengthen the participation and action of civil society in Central America," and the Center for Peace and Reconciliation to work for demilitarization and conflict resolution in the developing world.

From these headquarters, Arias has literally traveled the globe to speak with compelling candor and sincerity about the need for the world to reduce arms and military expenditures, especially in the developing world. He has spoken in dozens of universities and colleges in the United States and Canada, where he is received by enthusiastic and supportive crowds of thousands. He speaks to press associations, business conventions, and academic organizations, such as the Association of Third World Studies' annual international conference held in Costa Rica in November 1999.

One writer dubbed him "Democracy's Guerrilla," another named him the "Warrior for Peace."

However apt, Arias does not just speak of peace in abstract terms. He and his foundations' work force have concrete plans to redirect money away from military organizations in the developing world and toward economic growth, human development, and education. Arias has long argued that the military in Latin America has seldom, if ever, been used to defend national borders. Instead, it has been a tool to support totalitarian governments and for the repression of human rights within their own countries.

Indeed, Costa Rica has been an example to all having nurtured a longstanding belief in demilitarization, firmly established by its abolition of its military following its ruinous civil war of 1948. Arias's reconfirmation of this policy and Costa Rica's relative prosperity have become visible evidence to many developing nations of the validity of Don Oscar's words and deeds. In many ways, Oscar Arias Sanchez has been a product of his nation's democratic and pacifist traditions. However, no one in Costa Rican history and few in world history have spoken so eloquently of the need to work for peace in order to preserve and share the world's dwindling resources, thus, guaranteeing the survival of the planet. Once when chided for his idealism, Arias replied, "politicians have an obligation to be dreamers...to want to change things. No one in Central America can be satisfied with the status quo. There is too much poverty, violence, hunger, and misery."

WILLIAM P. HEAD

References and Further Reading

Arias Sanchez, Oscar. *The Struggle for Peace.* Bloomington, IN: The Indiana Center on Global Change and World Peace, 1990.
Arias Sanchez, Oscar. *Ten Years after Esquipulas: Looking Toward the Future.* Providence, RI: Academic Council on the United Nations System, 1997.
Gudmundson, Lowell. "Costa Rica's Arias at Mid-Term." *Current History*, 417–420, 431–432, (December 1987).
Heubal, Edward J. "Costa Rican Interpretations of Costa Rican Politics." *Latin American Research Review.* 25(2): 217–225, (1990).
Kenworthy, Eldon. *America/Americas: Myth in the Making of US Policy Toward Latin America.* University Park, PA: Pennsylvania State University Press, 1995.
Rolbien, Seth. *Nobel Costa Rica: A Timely Report on Our Peaceful Neighbor.* New York: St. Martin's Press, 1989.

ARISTIDE, JEAN-BERTRAND

Twice-elected president of Haiti, Jean Bertrand Aristide (b. July 15, 1953) is, and likely will remain, a figure of controversy among Haitians, those who characterize US actions in the Caribbean as imperialist, and those engaged in the neoliberal economic policy debate. A leftist and former Roman Catholic priest, Aristide advocated liberation theology, which presses believers to work for political and economic change now in order to help the poor and the disenfranchised. His avocation put him at odds first, with the terror-drenched Duvalier regime, and then, in 1987, with the violent and repressive military rulers who seized power when Jean-Claude Duvalier fled the country. When, in 1990, the Haitians held what many characterize as their first democratic elections ever, Aristide won the presidency with about two-thirds of the vote.

Upon taking office on February 7, 1991, he immediately implemented policies to restore and strengthen the economy, to encourage national economic development that would benefit all Haitians, and to respect human rights. On September 30, 1991, after little more than six months, a military coup d'état unseated him. In exile in the United States, Aristide pressured that government, as well as other Organization of American States and United Nations members, to help to restore Haitian democracy. An economic embargo, followed by a threatened US invasion, led the Haitian military to step down, allowing Aristide to resume his presidency.

Returning to office on October 15, 1994, Aristide brought a contingent of about 20,000, mainly US soldiers. Many characterize his post-coup policies as reflective of the neoliberal economic preferences of Washington, DC, the International Monetary Fund, and the World Bank, including opening Haiti's markets to imported rice, which eventually displaced many domestic farmers. However, Aristide resisted pressures for other neoliberal policies. He also sought to neutralize the military by disbanding it and implementing a civilian police force.

Under the Haitian constitution, Aristide could not succeed himself. Instead, his close associate, Prime Minister René Préval, won the office in 1995. In 2000, Aristide ran and won the presidency with 91.8% of the vote in an election that the major opposition parties boycotted. In response to allegations of irregularities, the United States acted to withhold international loans and aid to the state. Aristide was without vital resources for Haitian development and poverty alleviation. Growing violence, which intensified in January 2004, calls for his ouster, and increasing antigovernment activity marked his last months in office. Soon, significant parts of Haiti were under rebel control. On February 29, 2004, Aristide boarded a plane with his wife and close associates and left Haiti for the Central African Republic.

This remains one of the most contested parts of the Aristide story. Aristide claims that he wrote a conditional letter of resignation, which the United States altered to make effective immediately. Further, he alleges that US forces kidnapped him, threatening bloodshed, and forced him to board the plane leaving Haiti. Aristide contends that he remains the constitutional leader of Haiti and has returned to the region, perhaps with an eye to regaining power. The United States offers a very different story about the Haitian president's exile, arguing that it facilitated his voluntary departure. Haitians remain extremely divided over Aristide and his legacy. The state's grinding poverty, rampant violence, and serious underdevelopment continue, however.

JANET ADAMSKI

See also Caribbean: History and Economic Development; Duvalier, François; Haiti; Liberation Theology; Neoliberalism

References and Further Reading

Chin, Pat *et al.,* eds. *Haiti: A Slave Revolution. 200 Years After 1804.* New York: International Action Center, 2004.

Dupuy, Alex. *Haiti in the New World Order: The Limits of the Democratic Revolution.* Boulder, CO: Westview Press, 1997.

Goodman, Amy, ed. *Getting Haiti Right This Time: The U.S. and the Coup.* Monroe, ME: Common Courage Press, 2004.

Rotberg, Robert I. *Haiti's Turmoil: Politics and Policy Under Aristide and Clinton* (World Peace Foundation Report No. 32). Cambridge, MA: World Peace Foundation, 2003.

ARMED FORCES OF THE PEOPLE

The Armed Forces of the People, or *Forces Armées Populaires* (FAP), was the title given to the national military of Madagascar after the establishment of the regime of Didier Ratsiraka in June 1975. The former National Army of the First Malagasy Republic was rapidly restructured in order to maintain stability and to create an instrument that would facilitate the transition to state socialism. The Charter of the Malagasy Socialist Revolution propagated that same year declared a new role for the military that emphasized indoctrination with the ideological program of the leadership and dedicated subservience to the ruling party. In order to reduce historic interethnic frictions and limit the potential for internal disputes that might threaten the regime, the armed services were separated into several departments: the Air Force and Navy were merged, and the *gendarmerie* (state police) and Intervention Forces were limited in size and as signed with the maintenance of domestic and

presidential security, while the largest number of officers and conscripts were channeled into the Military Development Committee (CMD) and its subordinate People's Army for Development. These forces were occupied with the management of rural agriculture, assistance to the state cooperative farms in the transportation and distribution of foodstuffs, road construction, and ideological work in the countryside. In addition, elements of the army bureaucracy were channeled into the national education system, while officers were assigned to state corporations in charge of agriculture and mining. While the employment of the armed forces in the execution of "revolutionary tasks" was not unique among the Third World socialist states, the extent to which the Malagasy military were relegated to civil and economic functions is significant in its inherent purpose. Despite the stated goals of official doctrine, the involvement of the FAP in development-related activities was intended as a strategy to both curtail popular dissent and contain political ambitions within the officer corps that might foster attempted *coups d'etat.*

As Ratsiraka reoriented Madagascar's foreign relations from the West to the socialist world, the traditional dependence on French training and military aid was replaced with Soviet, Eastern European, and North Korean arms transfers and advisors. Over the next decade, the Ratsiraka government vastly increased recruitment and defense spending, which totaled nearly thirty thousand personnel and one-third of the national budget by the mid-1980s. Despite the expansion of its arsenal due to the influx of foreign assistance, the FAP's role in internal policing and economic activity was reinforced by the overall absence of any significant external threats to Madagascar's national security.

As the leadership's dedication to radical nationalism gradually declined and state-led development models failed to produce economic prosperity, the military reverted to more traditional orientations and sources of aid. When general unrest and nascent democratic opposition movements began to increase by the end of the 1980s, the Ratsiraka regime became increasingly dependent on its elite Presidential Guard units to suppress dissident activity. With the replacement of Ratsiraka in the elections of 1993, the FAP retained its compartmentalized force structure.

JASON E. STRAKES

See also Madagascar

References and Further Reading

Allen, Philip M. *Madagascar: Conflicts of Authority in the Great Island.* Boulder, CO: Westview Press, 1995, 80, 92–94.

Chapin Metz, Helen, ed. *Madagascar: A Country Study*, Federal Research Division, Library of Congress, Washington, DC: Federal Research Division, Library of Congress, 1994.

Covell, Maureen. *Madagascar: Politics, Economics, and Society*. Frances Pinter, 1987, 65–66, 115–119.

Gowm, Bonar A. "Admiral Didier Ratsiraka and the Malagasy Socialist Revolution." *The Journal of Modern African Studies*. 35(3): 409–439 (1997).

ARMENIA

The Republic of Armenia is the smallest state of the former Soviet Union, encompassing some 11,500 square miles of territory. This constitutes only 10% of the ancient territory of the "Greater Armenia." Armenia also is the most ethnically homogeneous state of the former union republics of the USSR. Nearly 93% of the total population of 3.5 million people is Armenian. The rest of the population consists of Russians and Azeris. The proportion of the non-Armenian population of the country has declined since 1991 as a result of the intensification of political and military conflicts in the Caucasus. This is especially true in the case of the Azeri population, whose numbers in Armenia have been decimated because of the ongoing Azeri–Armenian territorial dispute and the out-migration of the Azeris to the neighboring republic of Azerbaijan.

Significant Armenian enclaves exist in several Soviet successor states. According to the 1979 Soviet census, some 560,000 Armenians resided in Azerbaijan Soviet Socialist Republic (SSR), 550,000 in the Georgian SSR, 330,000 in the Russian Republic (RSFSR), and 60,000 others were scattered throughout different parts of the Soviet Union. Although accurate statistics of the number of Armenians in these areas since the disintegration of the Soviet Union are not available, it is safe to assume that sizable numbers have migrated to the Republic of Armenia since the late 1980s and early 1990s. The 1979 Soviet census placed the number of the Armenians residing in the Armenian SSR at 2 million. Since the birth rate in Armenia has declined since 1960, much of the increase in the Armenian population to the current level of 3.5 million is attributed to the emigration of Armenians from other former Soviet Republics, particularly Azerbaijan.

The Armenian plateau is a landlocked mountainous region with an average elevation of 5,500 feet above sea level. Historic or Greater Armenia includes not only the Republic of Armenia but also a small area in northeastern Iran, most of the eastern part of Turkey, and sections of the present republics of Azerbaijan and Georgia. Modern Armenia borders Iran and the Azerbaijan enclave of Nakhichevan to the south, the Republic of Georgia to the north, the Azerbaijan Republic to the east, and Turkey to the west. Although the Armenian region of Turkey was historically referred to as "Turkish Armenia," all references to this term have been removed from modern maps in Turkey, and the names of several Armenian towns and villages have been replaced with Turkish equivalents.

Armenia has a long history dating to the kingdom of Urartu, which was founded in the ninth century BC. Since the Armenian alphabet was not invented until the fifth century AD, sources of early Armenian history are found in documents written in Aramaic, Syriac, Greek, and Middle Persian. Later sources of Armenian history were rendered not only in Armenian but also in Persian, Arabic, Turkish, Latin, Russian, French, and Italian. This has made it difficult to reconstruct an objective and cohesive history of Armenia from ancient times to the present.

During the long centuries of Ottoman control, Armenians prospered. For some four hundred years, the Armenians generally eschewed politics and concentrated on commercial and financial endeavors. Turkish–Armenian relations deteriorated rapidly with the publication of the Armenian National Constitution of 1863, which called for enhanced autonomy for the Armenians under Ottoman rule. The promulgation of this document coincided with the rise of overt nationalistic manifestations among the Armenians. The Ottoman Empire already had been shaken by the increasing nationalistic demands of its subject peoples in the Balkans and elsewhere, and it viewed the rise of Armenian nationalism as a direct challenge to its authority. This resulted in a number of violent episodes between the Ottoman rulers and their Armenian subjects. During World War I, the Armenians' enthusiastic support of the Allied Powers and their welcoming of the invading Russian army infuriated the Young Turks, which impelled them to solve their "Armenian problem" through mass expulsions and massacres. The massacre of 1915 is estimated to have caused the death of more than 1 million Armenians. Turkey's refusal to accept responsibility for this massacre remains a major source of tense relations between Armenia and modern Turkey.

During the period of Soviet control of Armenia, Armenians remained highly nationalistic and resisted Russification attempts. Ethnic secessionism, which became a powerful force in the Baltic region in the winter and spring of 1988, appeared in the Caucasus in January 1988 with the intensification of the Armenian–Azerbaijani conflict over the control of Nagorno-Karabakh, a largely Armenian inhabited area in Azerbaijan. In mid-January 1988, the Armenians in that region, strongly supported by their co-nationalists in the Armenian Soviet Socialist Republic, staged a major revolt in Stepanakert, Nagorno-Karabakh's capital, and demanded that their region be allowed to join Armenia. Azerbaijan refused to accede to this demand. Ethnic tensions between the Azeris and the Armenians reached a dangerously high level by February 1988, where the two sides launched wanton attacks against each others' lives and properties. Many Azeris, forced to leave Stepanakert, moved to other cities in Azerbaijan. With the specter of Azeri and Armenian pogroms looming over the horizon, Moscow suspended Nagorno-Karabakh's local government and imposed direct rule over the area in January 1989. Members of the elite Soviet Interior Ministry troops then occupied the area to maintain order and prevent further inter-ethnic bloodshed in the Caucasus. This measure did not satisfy either side, especially the Azeris, who accused Moscow of aiding the Armenians in Nagorno-Karabakh. Although the Nagorno-Karabakh conflict has now been contained and the area is stabilized, this conflict has had a disastrous impact on Armenia's economy. For example, when the Republic of Azerbaijan accused the Armenian government of providing military support, including troops, to the Nagorno-Karabakh insurgents, it imposed a punishing blockade on Armenia. The blockade of raw materials by Azerbaijan has severely hampered the economic recovery of Armenia as it had denied the country easy access to the energy resources of the region, especially access to Russia's gas and oil supplies. This also has contributed to political turmoil and uncertainty that have hampered Armenia's democratization.

NADER ENTESSAR

See also Commonwealth of Independent States: History and Economic Development; Commonwealth of Independent States: International Relations; Ethnic Conflicts: Commonwealth of Independent States; Soviet Bloc

References and Further Reading

Avakian, Arra S. *Armenia: A Journey Through History.* Fresno, CA: Electric Press, 2000.
Hovannisian, Richard G., ed. *The Armenian People from Ancient to Modern Times,* vol. 2. New York: St. Martin's Press, 1997.

ARMS AND ARMAMENTS, INTERNATIONAL TRANSFER OF

The term "arms transfer" describes the transfer from one country to another of weapon systems, ammunition, and tactical support equipment. Such transfers are typically conducted on a commercial basis, entailing the sale of arms for cash credit, but are sometimes provided gratis through military assistance channels. In addition to these overt, state-sanctioned transfers of arms, there is also a significant black-market trade in weapons to insurgents, separatist groups, and other paramilitary formations. The international arms trade increased about threefold between the beginning of the 1970s and the mid-1980s. By the 1980s, as much as $74 billion worth of defense goods were being transferred internationally each year. In the past two decades, countries in the Middle East, which together contain about 3% of the world's population, have imported more than 30% of all weapons transferred among exporters and importers. After booming in the 1970s and early 1980s, the Middle East arms race slowed in the late 1980s as the Iran-Iraq war drew to a close and the global economic recession cut into the military budgets of regional powers. However, it appears that the arms trade is on the verge of a new expansionary cycle, similar to those of the mid-1970s and the early 1980s. Adding credence to this assessment are a number of disturbing trends: (1) the reinvigoration of the Middle East arms race; (2) the emergence of a major new arms race in the Pacific Rim areas; (3) and the growing intensity of ethnic, tribal, and national conflicts (Klare 1994).

Although the industrialized nations account for a significant portion of global arms imports, the largest share is consumed by the less-developed countries (LDCs). According to the US Arms Control and Disarmament Agency (ACDA), the LDCs were the recipients of approximately 75% of all arms traded on the international market in the 1980s. During the period from 1995 through 1998, the developing Global South countries accounted for 77% of all arms deliveries worldwide, which in 1998 alone were valued at $23.2 billion. There are, however, significant regional variations in arms imports by the LDCs. Not surprisingly, the primary market for arms is to be found in the Middle East, where a potent combination of vast oil wealth and intense regional antagonisms has generated an insatiable demand for modern weaponry. According to the ACDA, Middle Eastern countries jointly imported $203 billion worth of arms in the 1980s, or nearly half of all arms acquired by the developing countries in those years. Large arms markets have also emerged in other conflict-prone areas, including South Asia, East Asia, and Sub-Saharan Africa.

For most of the post-World War II era, arms sales were considered a legitimate form of international trade, or, in the case of the superpowers, as a necessary adjunct to East–West competition in the Third

World. Following the Iraqi invasion of Kuwait, however, the international community became much more concerned about conventional arms trafficking. The fact that Saddam Hussein had been able to accumulate such a massive military arsenal—5,500 tanks, 3,700 heavy artillery pieces, 7,500 armored personnel carriers, seven hundred combat planes, and so on—led many world leaders to regret their earlier failure to control the arms trade. Thus, when the Gulf conflict was over, these leaders pledged to improve constraints on the global arms traffic. Iraq's arsenal, which was made up of weapons and technologies provided mainly by the industrial countries, prompted the Bush administration to reevaluate the wisdom of its past practices. For a time, an international consensus for more effective controls over the diffusion of conventional military technologies appeared to be growing. Nevertheless, even under the succeeding presidents, US nonproliferation policy remained predominantly focused on controlling the diffusion of nuclear, chemical, biological, and missile technologies—not conventional arms.

The international transfer of arms is a composite of a vast number of individual transactions between particular suppliers and recipients. Each of the individual transactions that constitute the weapons trade entails a bilateral arms transfer relationship, involving some manners of exchange in which the supplier provides military equipment to the recipient in return for cash, credit, barter goods, or political/military services (such as participation in military alliances or support for the supplier's positions at the United Nations). Depending on the strength of the motives involved and the extent of the recipient's resources, these relationships can be relatively brief and shallow or can develop into long-lasting associations, involving multiple transfers of major weapons systems.

International System and Arms Transfer

Like all other international relationships, the bilateral linkages that make up the arms trade are to some degree shaped and influenced by developments in the international system as a whole. Developments in the international system affect the directions and magnitudes of the arms transfer. In periods of high international polarization, such as that which prevailed during much of the Cold War era, recipients tend to align with one polar supplier or the other, depending on their geopolitical situation and their ideological preferences. Both superpowers had large numbers of client states that received all or most of their weapons from them or from other North Atlantic Treaty Organization (NATO) or Warsaw Pact suppliers. These patterns were quite predictable. There were few surprises, and much of the arms trade could easily have been correlated with the UN General Assembly votes. Hence, the Eastern European countries procured most of their arms from the Soviet Union during this period, while the Latin American countries procured most of their arms from the United States. Similarly, in times of diminished polarization, such as that which prevails today, recipients tend to be more eclectic in their buying patterns; they seek arms from several major suppliers. The status of global economy also has an impact on the dynamics of the arms flow: periods of prolonged recession tend to produce a decline in arms imports, while periods of growth are usually accompanied by an increase in military orders.

The collapse of the former Soviet Union, and the resulting disappearance of the bipolar system, has produced a significant rearrangement in North-South arms transfer relationships, with many former clients of the USSR turning to suppliers in the West. The political change has removed the competitive ideological dimension from Superpower–Third World relations. It has also reduced the willingness of either the United States or Russia to offer military assistance in the form of grants to arms clients. The resulting difficulty of financing imports of arms is likely to become an increasingly significant restraint in the global arms trade. The end of the Cold War has greatly altered these patterns, presumably in the direction of a more random pattern dictated by the dominance of commercial over the previous mixed ideological and geopolitical considerations. One recent analysis of global arms transfers concluded that "the political factors that dominated the arms trade in the recent past are yielding to market forces. . . . The arms trade is returning to its patterns prior to World War II, when the trade in military equipment was not dramatically different from the trade in many other industrial products" (SIPRI Yearbook, 1988). That would, indeed, represent a return to those policies evidenced earlier, in the 1920s and prior to World War I.

The Persian Gulf War of 1991 has also had a significant impact on the global arms flow, with the United States emerging as the supplier of choice for countries that seek high-tech weapons of the sort used with such devastating effect in Operation Desert Storm. In 1995, the United States accounted for 42% of the total deliveries of major conventional weapons, compared with 28% in 1989. Members of the European Community (EC) accounted for roughly 25% of the deliveries of major conventional weapons recorded in 1995—an increase from the roughly 20% recorded five years earlier. Within the EC, Germany, France, and the United Kingdom accounted for almost 85% of total EC exports of major conventional weapons. In 1995, Russia accounted for 18% of total deliveries, compared with 39% for the former Soviet Union in 1989. The Stockholm International Peace Research Institute (SIPRI) estimated the global value of the trade in major conventional weapons in 1995 at almost $23 billion in 1990. The Middle East accounted for 23% of imports in 1995 and Asia and Europe accounted for 44% and 20%, respectively, in the same year. In regional terms, Asia and Europe replaced the Middle East as the primary market for major conventional weapons in 1988. The primary reason was the end of the Iran–Iraq war and subsequent reductions in imports, particularly by Iraq. Regional governments in the Middle East continue to regard the preparedness of their own armed forces as the most important component of their national security. While this consideration is likely to lead to new orders for military equipment being placed with foreign suppliers, it is unlikely that Middle East sales will return quickly to the levels of the 1970s and 1980s. Much attention is now focusing on Saudi Arabian arms imports. While Saudi Arabia has long been a major arms-importing country, demography places a limit on how much equipment its armed forces can absorb.

The extent of US dominance may be greater than the statistics suggest. Major weapons systems per se are not the central factor in military balance among states. Rather, it is the systems in combination with the required training, logistics, and support. While there are several suppliers of advanced military hardware, by 1992, only the United States was able to deliver the full package, and only that package could give one side a decisive military advantage in an interstate war. Although European countries could achieve such a capability through collaboration, it would take time for the requisite degree of policy coordination to develop, if it did so at all. However, West European companies are not competing successfully with the United States in many markets. The most severe competition for US companies is usually that of other US companies. In recent years, for example, McDonnell Douglas and General Dynamics have contested several fighter aircraft contracts. General Dynamic's F-16 was successful in Japan and South Korea, as was the F/A-18 in Kuwait. This concentration of market share with one supplier reversed the trend of the previous fifteen years, when a growing number of countries became active suppliers.

Recent Trends in Arms Transfers to Developing Nations

The amount of new arms transfer agreements with developing nations has generally declined since 1993. In 1998, developing nations purchased $13.2 billion worth of arms, which was a substantial decline from the value of 1997 deliveries. The decline is partially due to the end of the Cold War. Prior to the Cold War, both the United States and Soviet Union were prepared to subsidize exports of arms transfers and to overlook their political differences with recipients, as those differences were considered to be subordinate to the Cold war competition. The Soviet Union supplied arms to extend its ideology and influences as it competed against the United States for leadership. During the Cold War, both the United States and Soviet Union used arms transfers to promote diplomatic and military ties with emerging powers in the developing world. Between 1975 and 1990 alone, the two superpowers together supplied an estimated $325 billion worth of arms and ammunition to Third World countries.

International arms embargoes are another reason for the decrease in arms transfers to developing nations. Arms embargoes were seldom used during the Cold War, however, such embargoes have been declared in the 1990s against a number of states because of aggression (Iraq), internal wars (Somalia, Liberia, the former Yugoslavia), human rights violations (Haiti, Sudan), and support of terrorism (Libya). It also seems that informal arms export bans, encouraged by the United States but without legal or internationally agreed upon political basis—for instance, on Iran and some other countries— had a restrictive influence on export policies of countries in Western Europe.

Throughout the 1990s, most arms transfers to developing nations were made by two or three major suppliers in any given year. The United States has ranked either first or second among these suppliers every year from 1991 to 1998, with the sole exception of 1997. France has been the most consistent competitor for the lead in arms transfer agreements with developing nations, ranking first in 1992, 1994, and 1997. As competition over shrinking international arms market intensifies, France seems more likely to rank higher in arms deals with developing nations than Russia, a supply nation with seemingly more significant limitations in its prospective arms client base than other major Western suppliers. Major arms suppliers like the United Kingdom and Germany may, from time to time, conclude significant orders with developing countries. Yet it seems that, presently the United States is best positioned to lead in new arms agreement with developing nations. At the same time, it seems likely that very large weapons orders from individual developing nations will be less frequent in the near term.

There are a few reasons for optimism concerning the prospects of initiatives and diplomacy from the more active developed countries on behalf of international restraint in conventional arms transfers. It is conceivable that countries engaged in joint defense programs could be induced to accept a code of conduct restricting a particular type of exports to volatile regions of the world, in return for access to high technology and assured outlets for exports in the developed world. A selective system of restraints on the supply of certain key technologies may prove feasible at this point. Attempting a more comprehensive arms control regiment at this stage could possibly prove elusive and perhaps self-defeating. Any new initiative to regulate international arms trade will increasingly require coordination of both developed and developing states. Those designing new policies will have to confront the primacy of the commercial pressures that are currently driving the quest for arms exports, domestically and internationally. A major impediment to progress internationally continues to be reluctance or inability of the advanced countries to renounce their own dependence on military exports and to move forward with economic restructuring. Even relatively modest control policies will face intense opposition from US industries and European suppliers.

Arms Transfer and Development

According to critics of military spending, arms transfer and procurement is a burden on a nation's economy. Government spending on defense and social programs compete for the same limited government budget and thus must constrain each other. The main argument claims that the opportunity costs associated with arms procurement in general, and arms imports in particular, are too high. Resources used for military purposes compete for resources that otherwise could have been available for socioeconomic development. As military analysts, Saadet Deger and Somnath Sen contended, "the first casualty of enhanced military burden is the reduction of state spending on health, education, and so on, as a share of gross domestic product" (Deger and Sen 1987). In other words, the escalating demand for increasingly sophisticated weapons and the rising price of these imported weapons places pressure on central budgetary expenditures, leaving fewer resources for other purposes. Not only do weapons purchases adversely affect the balance-of-payments position of most Third

World countries and increase their debt burden, but they also crowd out public and private investment, depriving the economy of vital growth opportunities. Generally, these purchases are thought to preclude productive investments in human capital that can greatly assist development.

On the other hand, some scholars point out that it is not procurement that burdens most less industrialized countries, but arms imports, whether paid for fully or by foreign aid, which carry with them hidden costs, such as servicing, training of mechanics, and building infrastructure. Allowing for such factors as maintenance and training personnel, and other support, the actual resources commitment for the import of weaponry could easily double the cost of the equipment's purchase price.

In addition to the potential allocation effect, it is also possible that greater military burdens may have an impact upon human development as a consequence of an increased militarization of society. For instance, the acquisition of arms may increase the influence of the military at the expense of individual liberties. As former Secretary of Defense Robert S. McNamara said in 1992:

> One of the most important effects of military spending, and one that has serious implications for political and economic development, is the degree to which it strengthens the political influence of the armed forces at the expense of civilian groups within society.

For those concerned with the role of the military in society, arms transfers can hinder attempts to serve basic public good and assist in maintaining other nondemocratic elites in power. From this perspective, arms transfers to developing countries are not conducive to social and economic welfare.

However, consensus is lacking as to the harmful effect of militarization on human and economic development of LDCs. The predominant tendency in defense economics regards military spending as the purchase of "defense" or "national security" as public good and, therefore, similar to other public programs. One analyst contends that militarization may instead lead to greater domestic and external stability, providing an environment in which socioeconomic change and pursuit of a better quality of life can take place. The import of arms typically strengthens the military, and in developing countries, the military is often the strongest and most cohesive institution—often more powerful than the government itself. Not only do arms enhance the ability of military to maintain order, but stimulated by arms acquisitions, the organizational development of the military furthers its ability to play a modernizing role in society. It is argued that the military fosters the kind of attitudes necessary for development, both economically and socially (Blanton 1999).

Reginald Bartholomew, former US undersecretary of state for international security affairs, notes that:

> Arms transfer promotes stability in a number of ways, by deterring aggression, by promoting regional cooperation and credible deterrence, by reducing the likelihood that US forces will have to be employed … and by enhancing, indeed our influence among key regional decision makers. (Morrison 1993)

These analysts have been joined in recent years by a growing number of Third World leaders whose policy decisions reflect their tacit agreement with this position. Government officials maintain that arms purchases by developing countries is a way of luring developmental investment, creating competitive trade opportunities, promoting industrialization, improving the country's technological capabilities, creating employment, and promoting technology transfer. For example, only a fraction of the price of weapons purchased is being paid for with cash. The remainder is paid with consumer goods produced in recipient countries.

There is no widespread consensus among those concerned with the possible impact of arms imports on developing countries. For example, Natalie J. Goldring, former deputy director of the Washington- and London-based British American Council, acknowledged that:

> Unfortunately, most arms transfers have immediate benefits, and most arguments against them involve longer-term costs. One of those costs is that arms sales do not always deter aggression. Sometimes they stoke the fires of war. (Morrison 1993)

Obviously, the characterization of arms transfer as unproductive and socially wasteful is subject to some qualifications. Many experts believe that the acquisition of arms has been followed by the outbreak of many civil and interstate wars in those same countries that have followed the realists' dictum that to obtain peace it is necessary to prepare for war. This has renewed concerns about whether the continued dispersion of weapons will increase the probability of future wars.

NASSER MOMAYEZI

See also Arms Industry; Middle East: International Relations; War and Development

References and Further Reading

Blanton, Shannon L. "Examining The Impact of Arms Transfers On Human Development" *Journal of Third World Studies* XVI, 2 (Fall 1999).

Blanton, Shannon L., and Charles W. Kegley, Jr. "Reconciling US Arms Sale with America's Interests and Ideals." *Future Research Quarterly* 13 (Spring 1997).

Deger, S., and S. Sen. "Defense, Entitlement and Development," In *Defense, Security, and Development*, edited by S. Deger and R. West. New York: St. Martin's Press, 1987.

Grimmet, Richard F. *Conventional Arms Transfer to Developing Nations, 1991–1998*. Washington, DC: Congressional Research Service, 1999.

Grimmett, Richar F. *Conventional Arms Transfers to Developing Nations, 1991–1998*. Washington, DC: Congressional Research Service, 1999.

Klare Michael T., and Daniel C. Thomas. *World Security: Challenges for a New Century*, New York: St. Martin's Press, 1994.

Laurance, Edward J. *The International Arms Trade*. New York: Macmillan, 1992.

Limiting Conventional Arms Exports to the Middle East, Congressional Budget Office, September 1992.

McNamara, Robert S. "The Post-Cold War World: Implications for Military Expenditure in the Developing Countries." In *Proceedings of the World Bank Annual Conference on Development Economics 1991*. Washington, DC: International Bank for Reconstruction and Development, World Bank, 1992.

Mosley, Hugh G. *The Arms Race: Economic and Social Consequences*, Lexington, MA, and Washington, DC: Heath and Co., 1985.

Pierre, Andrew J. *Cascade of Arms: Managing Conventional Weapons Proliferation*. Washington, DC: Brookings Institution Press, 1997.

Pierre, Andrew J. *The Global Politics of Arms Sales*. Princeton, NJ: Princeton University Press, 1982.

US Arms Control and Disarmament Agency (ACDA). *World Military Expenditures and Arms Transfers 1995*, Washington, DC: US Government Printing Office, 1997.

World Armaments and Disarmament: SIPRI Year Book 1988, Oxford: Oxford University Press, 1988).

ARMS INDUSTRY

The study of the role of arms industries in the developing world concerns a phenomenon that appeared on the international scene in the 1960s. Several developing countries began to pursue domestic arms production, some with notable success. By the middle of the 1980s, several of these new producers had managed to increase greatly the share of world arms sales by developing countries. However, by the end of the decade, and continuing through the 1990s, the success of some of these producers declined. The claims for what indigenous arms industries could do for their countries' defense, development, political autonomy, or prestige seemed no longer enticing or persuasive.

Arms Industrialization: Motivations and Goals

The motivations for leaders of developing countries to actively pursue arms industrialization fall roughly into four categories. The first occurs in states in a hostile security environment, where reliability of supply of arms of any type is seen as a pressing security need. Second, there are political considerations, such as the desire to lessen dependence on outside suppliers, or the potential use of arms sales as a political tool, or to enhance national prestige. Third, many proponents of arms industrialization touted the promise that such programs could serve as the motor to drive general industrialization, technology acquisition, and economic development. Finally, there often were straightforward economic goals, as the profits from the lucrative world arms markets were expected to be substantial. In practice, the various arguments in favor of establishing arms industries overlapped, and in the experience of the countries under discussion, every imaginable combination of these reasons may have played a role in policy formulation.

International Political Conditions for Arms Industrialization

The great powers, which were also the great arms producers, essentially had control over the provision of those arms to their former colonies. Newly independent states scrambled for whatever supplies and training they could get for their fledgling militaries, whether it was by inviting European officers to help train their officer corps, or by acquiring the latest weapons that the Europeans or Americans deigned to sell them. This situation applied first to Latin American states that had gained their formal independence in the early nineteenth century. The process continued in the same general form as states in the Middle East, then Asia, and then Africa began to gain independence.

In the twentieth century, the major powers controlled the amount and level of sophistication of the arms that the developing countries could receive. In this way, these powers hoped to prevent regional arms races from creating regional crises. With the emergence of the Soviet Union as a major rival to the Western powers, the United States and the USSR began a strategy of using arms to bolster friendly regimes in strategically important regions. This did not always prevent the leaders of developing countries from searching for ways to break away from this particular form of dependency. In fact, the Cold War itself created some of the first opportunities for certain countries to take the first steps in establishing independent domestic arms industries.

For example, the United States had always considered Latin America as its natural sphere of influence, and there was relatively little penetration of Soviet bloc arms exports into the region (except for Cuba and, briefly, Peru). Nevertheless, the rapid professionalization of the Latin American officer corps after World War II, especially in the Southern Cone of South America, created a more sophisticated officer corps that chafed at the arms acquisition restrictions imposed upon them by the United States. When US involvement in the Vietnam War intensified, more and more of US arms production was absorbed by the war effort, so that fewer arms were available to be shipped to Latin American client states. At the same time, the defense industries of Western Europe were coming into their own and technologically advanced weaponry was available in unprecedented quantities on the market. But in order to maintain their production levels, it was necessary for European producers to penetrate the markets that had been controlled by the United States.

The Politics of Arms Acquisition

The Southern Cone countries, especially Brazil, took advantage of this situation. In the mid-1960s, Brazil was ruled by a military regime intent on pursuing an aggressive industrialization policy. The Brazilians wished to bring arms production over from Europe to Brazil, and to eventually own the factories that produced the weapons concerned. The United States could not prevent the Latin Americans from acquiring arms elsewhere, and the Europeans had to sell their weapons or risk serious financial losses that could place their industries at risk. The Brazilians were able to exploit this situation. Any number of advantageous licensing agreements were entered into with European manufacturers of light aircraft, armored vehicles, missiles, ships, and computer systems. The agreements allowed for production runs to be shifted over time from their European base to Latin America, and for Latin American engineers and managers to be involved in all phases of production. The end result was that technological and managerial know-how were transferred from Europe to Latin America. This furnished the foundation for the development of domestic arms industries. The Brazilians arms producing complex grew to include wholly owned state enterprises, mixed public-private ventures, and private corporations.

It should be noted that the Brazilians were not located in a hostile security environment. The last conventional war in which Brazil was engaged on its own borders ended in 1870. Though the Brazilian military regime was concerned with guerrilla insurgencies and internal subversion, pressing security concerns cannot be numbered among the primary motivations for pursuing an arms industrialization policy. In Brazil, the main motivating factors were lessening arms dependence on the United States, and using arms industrialization to induce rapid economic and technological development.

In contrast to Brazil, the cases of Israel, South Korea, and India, among the other successful Third World arms producers, were much more clearly related to their direct security needs. Along with Brazil and China, they became the leading arms manufacturers and exporters outside of the North Atlantic Treaty Organization (NATO) or Warsaw Pact alliances.

As for Israel and South Korea, these were relatively small countries with high security needs. The primary motivating factor for promoting domestic arms industries was defense, followed by a desire to decrease dependence on the United States and gain more political maneuverability. These two countries had military institutions of limited size, and therefore had a limited capacity to absorb the number of weapons that would have to be produced in order to make the industries economically viable. Economies of scale dictated that weapons would have to be produced in large quantities, and therefore an aggressive sales policy also would have to be pursued.

Israel, having arguably the most pressing need, started out manufacturing small arms and refurbishing antiquated arms from World War II stocks. After 1967, as Cold War pressures fueled an arms race between Israel and its Arab neighbors, Israel began to move into higher tech production, relying on its domestic pool of European-educated engineers and scientists. In addition, its frequent military engagements, and its unique situation as fielding a "citizen army" where many of the technicians involved in arms production were also those who used the weapons systems in the field, gave the Israeli industry an unusual advantage for innovative design and testing. The Israelis excelled at small arms and tank manufacture and refurbishing, later moving into aircraft, and finally into areas such as remote-piloted vehicles (RPVs) and electronic surveillance.

South Korea was also in a worrisome security arena, but in terms of defense, the thousands of US troops based in the country functioned as a deterrent force, allowing the Koreans, after the seizure of the government by Park Chung-Hee, to concentrate on rapid civilian industrialization. However, in the late 1960s, as a result of increased hostile activity on the part of North Korea, and the declaration of the "Nixon Doctrine" in 1969, with its subsequent

reduction of US troop strength on the peninsula, South Korean leaders sought to enhance their military capabilities. The country already was geared toward rapid industrialization. Government policies shifted more emphasis into arms production, with packages of investment credits, tax incentives, and guaranteed purchases with generous advances. Major industrial conglomerates (known as Chaebol), which had already adjusted themselves to take advantage of the government's industrialization drive, shifted easily over to defense production, building on advances already made in steel, shipbuilding, and automotive industries.

India also found itself in a unique defensive situation. On the one hand, it had fought several wars with Pakistan, and the threat of more warfare was a constant, especially with the Kashmir dispute. India had also fought a war with the People's Republic of China. Pakistan's role in two military alliances sponsored by the West (CENTO and the Southeast Asia Treaty Organization, or SEATO) made it the recipient of coveted US weapons, especially aircraft. Responding to infusions of these arms into hostile Pakistan, India responded by turning to other arms manufacturers, regardless of bloc. When it appeared that a contract for French Mirage fighter jets would take several years to be completed, the Indians turned to the Soviet Union and entered into licensed production agreements to build MiGs under Soviet supervision in India. While the initial motivation for this move came in response to US weaponry in Pakistan, the agreement also was pursued in the hopes that this would bolster India's efforts to establish a technologically sophisticated weapons industry, and help it to achieve some self-sufficiency.

Market Niches and Restrictions

It was quite clear to those producers who were achieving some success that they would not be able to compete with the arms manufacturers in the NATO and Soviet blocs. Only Israel had a modicum of success in selling to NATO buyers. Most producers made a virtue of necessity, and aimed their products toward those countries and military establishments that could not afford or maintain the extraordinarily high-tech (or so-called baroque) weapons systems available from the advanced industrialized suppliers. Brazil pursued this course most aggressively, with heady success in the 1980s. The material produced by Brazil, tested in its own jungle or desert terrains, was designed to meet the needs of many African and Middle Eastern militaries. Brazil often was able to barter its arms in elaborate deals for petroleum from the Middle East and African countries. Its relative neutrality allowed it, for example, to be a major supplier of Iran and Iraq during their prolonged war in the 1980s. (Israel, for obvious reasons, was not able to sell its arms in the Middle East market, the most lucrative region in the world for arms sales.)

Nevertheless, there were disadvantages for arms exporters in developing countries that were impossible to overcome. To illustrate, in one widely reported incident, Brazil was preparing to close a very lucrative contract to sell a large number of its Osorio tanks to Saudi Arabia in the late 1980s. In tests under desert conditions, the Osorio outperformed other tanks from US and European suppliers. However, in large part because of its political and economic weight, the United States was able to pressure the Saudis to forgo the Osorio and purchase US-made M-1A1 Abrams tanks instead.

This points to one of the frustrating hazards that many of these Third World arms producers faced. Part of the rationale for cultivating domestic arms industries was to make the country less dependent upon the arms suppliers. For many, the relative independence that indigenous arms production promised was traded for either a new form of technological dependence or a new version of political dependence. There also were limits on potential arms sales for these new competitors, because while they may in many cases have been able to provide competitive products, they did not have the political or economic clout to "sweeten" the deal with other offers.

The Israelis and the Koreans often found themselves at a loss when marketing their arms abroad, as the United States had veto power over the arms transfer in so-called Third Country Sales if sensitive technology supplied by the United States or significant parts of US manufacture were used in the production of the weapons system for sale. If the arms manufacturer were negotiating a sale to any country that the United States deemed to be supporting terrorism, engaging in hostile actions, to be involved in a regional arms race, or to be too closely aligned with the Soviets or their clients, such a veto was very likely to be used, often with very dire economic consequences for the producer.

Arms Industrialization and Development

The arguments proffered in favor of arms militarization often included predictions that successful industries, which were always at the cutting edge of technological innovation, could bring much needed technology from the advanced countries to the developing countries. Once local engineers, scientists, and technicians were involved in the research and development and production processes, they, too, would become involved in the dynamic of technological innovation. As the pool of experienced nationals increased, domestic industry would profit from the vaunted "spin-off" effect, bringing new technologies and techniques to other sectors of the economy.

Domestic political controversies raged over whether the vast resources expended on the new industries and related efforts might have been better spent on social programs, education, or indeed, different sorts of economic investment. It also was not always clear that professional officers always favored domestic arms industrialization. For some officers, there was a fear that investment in the domestic production of weapons might take years before coming out with a usable product. Even then those products were all too likely to lag far behind the technological sophistication of weapons available of the market. Some officers would prefer to acquire the best arms on offer, made by experienced manufacturers, in order to be sure that they would not fall behind their rivals in combat readiness.

At the peak years of arms industrialization and exportation for the developing countries, for two countries only did arms exports account for more than 5% of the value of total exports (Israel, 11.2% in 1987; China: 6.3% in 1988). In these peak years, arms accounted for 1.5% of the total value of exports for all developing countries, with a few averaging somewhat more. (Some countries show very high export ratios for arms exports in these years, when in fact those countries, such as Egypt, were serving as conduits for arms destined for the Persian Gulf.) By the 1990s, very few of these countries, again with China and Israel as exceptions, were registering significant levels of arms exports.

Overall, the "spin-off" dividend does not seem to have materialized. In some cases, the organization and technological know-how that allowed for success in the arms industry was already in place, to be exploited by the new arms industries, as in South Korea. In others, local critics alleged that the reverse might have actually taken place, where engineers, managers, and resources were pulled out of other domestic industries and concentrated in arms industries and related research institutions, as in Brazil. In short, very few of the developing countries that were heavily involved in the arms-exporting boom of the 1970s and 1980s have much to show for it in terms of contributions to long-term industrial growth.

The Decline of the World Arms Market

Total world arms exports from all sources peaked in the late 1980s. Not surprisingly, arms from all developed countries together still accounted for the lion's share of exports. But developing countries accounted for more than 10% of all arms exports in their peak year of 1988.

After 1988, however, the formal world arms market declined dramatically. In 1987, world arms exports from all sources were at their highest point, valued at more than $84 trillion. Since then, the value of total arms exports from all sources had fallen to $39.5 trillion by 1994. The value of arms exports from the developing world decreased from $8.5 trillion in 1988 to $1.5 trillion in 1996. The developing world's share of total arms exports decreased from 10.5% in 1988 to 3.4% in 1996. This trend seems to be replicated by almost all of the countries that had actively promoted a vigorous national arms industry in the 1970s and 1980s. The drop in arms exporting activity is remarkably similar in such countries as Argentina, Brazil, Chile, China, Egypt, South Korea, and to a lesser extent, Israel. Though the value of total world arms exports began to rise again in 1998, the participation of arms producers from the developing world is not increasing. The role of the arms industry as such in developing countries seems to be no longer prized.

Exceptions such as North Korea do exist, but that country's *Juche* policy of extreme autarchy makes its arms exporting policy truly exceptional. Such a country can clearly fuel regional arms races, for example, by its sales of missiles to Iran and Pakistan. As for special governmental efforts in developing nuclear technology or chemical and biological weapons by marginalized states such as Iran, North Korea, or possibly Iraq under Saddam Hussein, these fall outside of the experience of those states developing conventionally organized industries. Their "success" also is in doubt.

The confluence of the end of the Iran–Iraq War and the disintegration of the Soviet bloc initiated this rapid decline. The fall of the Soviet Union meant that the Cold War practice whereby the rival powers supported their client states through the sale, leasing,or grant of weapons systems to pursue global strategies essentially ended. While arms still flowed from Russia, much was now being sold to raise hard cash rather than to achieve political ends. Russian arms of all types also began to flood the black market. Many sophisticated arms that flowed into Central Asia during the war against the Soviet occupation of Afghanistan now flowed out onto the black market as well, adding to the worldwide glut of arms.

Another fall-out from the end of the Cold War was the more aggressive pursuit of neoliberal policies by the advanced industrialized democracies, which translated into pressure on developing countries to reduce government expenditure and government involvement in economic enterprises. This pressure to privatize government-owned enterprises extended to many firms involved in defense production. New initiatives in establishing production lines for armaments would be discouraged, and under the new fiscal pressures, would become more difficult than ever before. The idea that military industry led industrialization and technology acquisition was a plausible means for getting developing countries on the high road to successful development was losing ground. In addition, the advances in weaponry in the advanced industrialized countries pushed the technology gap to grow ever more rapidly (as indeed had always been the case). The combination of reduced financial resources and an ever expanding technology gap brought many developing countries back to relying on arms made in the United States and Western Europe, rather than on domestic arms production.

DAVID SCHWAM-BAIRD

See also Arms and Armaments, International Transfer of; Technology: Impact on Development

References and Further Reading

Brauer, Jurgen, and J. Paul Dunne, eds. *Arming the South: the Economics of Military Expenditure, Arms Production, and Arms Trade in Developing Countries*. Basingstoke, England: Palgrave, 2002.

Conca, Ken. *Manufacturing Insecurity: The Rise and Fall of Brazil's Military-Industrial Complex*. Boulder, CO: Lynne Rienner, 1997.

Gupta, Amit. *Building an Arsenal: The Evolution of Regional Force Structures*. Westport, CT: Praeger, 1997.

Inbar, Efraim, and Benzion Zilberfarb, eds. *The Politics and Economics of Defence Industries*. London: Frank Cass, 1998.

Katz, James Everett. *Arms Production in Developing Countries: An Analysis of Decision Making*. Lexington, MA: Lexington Books, 1984.

—— *The Implications of Third World Military Industrialization: Sowing the Serpent's Teeth*. Lexington, MA: Lexington Books, 1986.

Mullins, A.F., Jr. *Born Arming: Development and Military Power in New States*. Stanford, CA: Stanford University Press, 1987.

Stockholm International Peace Research Institute. *SIPRI Yearbook 2003: Armaments, Disarmament and International Security* (http://editors.sipri.org/pubs/yb03/aboutyb.html).

US Arms Control and Development Agency. "World Military Expenditures and Arms Transfers 1997." http://dosfan.lib.uic.edu/acda/wmeat97.

ASEAN FREE TRADE ASSOCIATION

Introduction

The member states of the Association of Southeast Asian Nations, or ASEAN, include Brunei, Cambodia, Indonesia, Laos, Malaysia, Myanmar (Burma), the Philippines, Singapore, Thailand, and Vietnam. The association promotes trade, generates investment and industrial development, resolves disputes among ASEAN-based and external entities, and fosters regional stability and security. Trade promotion is central to the association's aims and objectives. The ASEAN Free Trade Area (AFTA) is the module through which trade is promoted via tariff reduction and eventual elimination on a broad array of products exchanged among member nations. Three concepts explain the impact of reduced or eliminated tariffs: trade creation, diversion in the short run, and long-run trade expansion.

In the short run, lower intraregional tariff rates create trade among member countries when lower cost items produced within member nations gain access to markets of the other ASEAN countries that lower or eliminate their tariff rates on these items. Trade is thereby created within Southeast Asia, replacing a situation where previously only intracountry exchange took place. Trade diversion occurs when lower intraregional tariff rates permit producers within the region to gain access to markets once served by "outside" sources. Since only ASEAN producers receive reduced tariff rates, ASEAN produced items become less expensive than the items produced beyond the region.

In the long run, intraregional trade is expanded due to investment and industrial development that occurs because of the growth in the exports that are triggered by trade creation and trade diversion. ASEAN-based producers take advantage of potential longer run economies of scale by investing in industrial projects that lead to increased levels of production at lower costs. This phenomenon further expands exports.

The Initial ASEAN Effort to Expand Trade

Creating, diverting, and expanding trade requires broad and deep tariff rate cuts. Initially, this failed to occur when the association first took steps aimed at promoting trade among member countries. Its 1977 Preferential Trading Arrangement (PTA) had no more than a minimal impact on export levels, as the rate cuts to which it led were neither broad nor deep. The PTA aimed at lowering tariffs through a mechanism referred to as the "margin of preference (MOP)." The MOP had only limited success for three reasons. First, the "product by product" approach was on a voluntary basis, and countries chose products that were insignificantly traded. Second, a number of voluntarily chosen products faced either minimal or zero tariff rates and therefore the MOP mechanism had little or no effect. Third, the PTA permitted countries to place products on an "exclusion list." Countries often chose to place potentially trade-sensitive products on the list of items that were excluded from MOP treatment.

The member governments that were more enthusiastic about trade expansion were discouraged by the PTA's minimal impact. They tried but failed to introduce measures to add breadth and depth to the scheme, and finally gave up on the PTA idea. In 1992, key member governments persuaded all ASEAN members to create the ASEAN Free Trade Area within which a Common Effective Preferential Tariff (CEPT) mechanism would provide deeper and broader tariff rate cuts.

How AFTA and the CEPT Function

The CEPT scheme functions in ways that add greater depth to tariff rate reductions, as the 1992 agreement put products with existing tariff rates of 20% or less on a fast track toward tariff elimination. The goal was to eliminate tariffs over the period of a decade, or by the year 2003. Tariff rates in 1992 exceeding 20% on protected products were to be reduced in three stages over a fifteen-year period and eliminated by 2008. However, when ASEAN economic ministers met in 1994, they successfully proposed speeding up the time-tables for tariff elimination. Both the fast- and normal-track timetables were shortened in order to meet the progress toward free trade that was made during the Uruguay Round of the General Agreement on Tariffs and Trade (GATT). Tariff rates on items placed on the fast track were to reach zero by 2000 rather than 2003, and those placed on the normal track were to be free of tariffs by 2003 rather than 2008. AFTA has met most of its goals and is on schedule to meet the remaining tariff elimination timetable.

Unlike the PTA, CEPT encompasses all manufactures, processed agricultural products, and capital goods. Discussions continue on issues such as the inclusion of primary agricultural items and services and the elimination of some nontariff barriers to trade. However, there are limits to how quickly the

CEPT can eliminate tariffs: as ASEAN (and therefore AFTA) has gained more members, the association's composition has become progressively more asymmetrical in terms of national per capita income, state of national development, and competitiveness. Brunei and Singapore are higher-income economies, Malaysia and Thailand are strong middle-income economies, the Philippines and Indonesia remain in the lower range of middle-income countries, and the newer members (Laos, Cambodia Myanmar, and Vietnam) continue to be less developed, lower-income, and less competitive economies.

Producers mainly located in the less competitive, lower-income member countries are given more time to meet the amended 1994 timetables in two ways. First, they are given more time to adjust to the occasional negative impact that trade has on domestic employment. Affected products can be put on a temporary exclusion list, but only if a member country proves its case to AFTA. Second, other products are put on a sensitivity list that gives less competitive producers opportunities to expand their productive capacities, particularly in "infant industries" wherein long-run competitiveness can be enhanced. These are industries that require heavy investment and involve long periods before bringing about the industrial expansion that is key to improved competitiveness particularly in situations that have profound effects on countries' macroeconomic performance. However, while affected producers are given longer periods to conform to the principle of tariff elimination, they must eventually conform to AFTA's goal of free trade within Southeast Asia.

ROBERT L. CURRY, JR.

See also ASEAN Mekong Basin Development Cooperation (Mekong Group); Asia-Pacific Economic Cooperation (APEC); Asian Development Bank; Asian "Economic Miracle"; Association of Southeast Asian Nations (ASEAN); Southeast Asia: History and Economic Development; Trade Policies and Development

References and Further Reading

Alburo, Florian A. "AFTA in the Light of New Economic Developments." *Southeast Asian Affairs 1995*. Singapore: Institute of Southeast Asian Studies, 1995.

ASEAN Secretariat, *AFTA Reader: Questions and Answers on the CEPT for AFTA*. Vols. I–V, Jakarta: ASEAN Secretariat, 1995–2000.

ASEAN Secretariat. *ASEAN: Economic Cooperation, Transition, and Transformation*. Singapore: Institute of South Asian Studies, 1997.

Chia, Siow Yue. "Progress and Issues in ASEAN Economic Integration." In *East Asian Economies: Transformation and Challenge*, edited by Kawagoe, T. and Sueo Sekiguchi. Singapore: Institute of Southeast Asian Studies, 1995.

Curry, Robert L., Jr. "AFTA and NAFTA and the Need for Open Regionalism." *Southeast Asian Affairs 1993*. Singapore: Institute of Southeast Asian Studies, 1993.

DeRosa, Dean A. "Regional Trading Arrangements Among Developing Countries: The ASEAN Example," *Research Report No. 103*. Washington, DC: International Food Policy Research Institute, 1995.

Pangestu, M. "AFTA: Going Forward the ASEAN Way." In *ASEAN in a Changed Regional and International Political Economy*, edited by Hadi Soesastro. Jakarta: CSIS, 1995.

Tan, Joseph L. ed. *AFTA in the Changing International Economy*. Singapore: Institute of Southeast Asian Studies, 1996.

ASEAN MEKONG BASIN DEVELOPMENT COOPERATION (MEKONG GROUP)

In 1957, the Mekong Committee was formed by the United Nations, but on a limited scope, focusing only on the Mekong River and the Yunnan Region of the People's Republic of China.

In order to attain high rate growth among the developing countries in Asia and to promote regional economic cooperation, the Asian Development Bank (Manila, Philippines) started some workshops on growth triangles in the early 1990s. The goals of growth triangles are to maintain competitiveness in trade. Among these cross-boundary experiments, the southern China area is considered as an opening for the liberalization of economic policy in the region. In order to reduce transaction and transport costs, geographic proximity was a necessity; infrastructures were an absolute necessity to attain proper functioning of cross-boundary experiments.

In 1992, the Asian Development Bank launched an ambitious program for the ASEAN Mekong Basin Development Cooperation, named the Greater Mekong Sub-region (GMS), with a cost of $10 billion. This region comprises regions like the Yunnan Province of the People's Republic of China, Laos, Vietnam, Cambodia, Thailand, and Myanmar. These participants belong to ASEAN, except Yunnan Province of the People's Republic of China (Than Mya 1996). The GMS region comprises 2.3 million square kilometers and includes more than 260 million inhabitants.

The GMS system prefigures future global region projects. For that purpose, feasibility studies have been undertaken in order to develop vast business opportunities representing this innovative regional cooperation program. The GMS system aims to develop an interrelationship between domestic sectors and regional economic integration and to pump development aid into the region (Abonyi and Pante 1998).

The financial commitments: $2 billion was invested from 1998 to 2003; and for the next ten years, $8 billion will be allocated to infrastructures. The primary objective was to set up regional integration and cooperation, and the second objective was to increase trade and foreign direct investments in the subregion (Asian Development Bank 1997).

The main lines of development undertaken in the framework of GMS are as follows: interregional investment and trade, infrastructure in view of improving regional competitiveness through the transboundary experiment, and capacity building, which means training a supply of labor and managing human resources.

The significant elements were to facilitate transfer of technology and production links and to increase the complementarities between the economies of the subregion, thereby sustaining domestic economic development and leading toward regional integration. In order to achieve these ends, governments have played an active part in coordinating and implementing policies. The dynamism of the governments of the subregion has encouraged the private sector to deregulate foreign direct investment and trade (Abonyi 1997). And to involve the private sector in infrastructure projects, a financing mechanism, called build-operate-transfer (BOT) mechanism, has been developed. With this mechanism, a private company is given the concession to build and operate a project, such as a power plant or a road network. In this way, the government transfers its prerogative to the private sector.

The Global Vision of the Project and Priority Sectors

Because of its greater economic weight in the region, Thailand attracts most of the foreign direct investments. As for public development aid, starting in 2000, the other five countries/provinces have received the greatest share. Thailand, unlike the five other countries/provinces, espoused development and an open economy in the early 1980s. The others have more recently started this double transition, which means changing from a subsistence economy to a diversified economy and from a centralized economy to an economy that is moving toward a market economy (Asian Development Bank 1997).

The rhythm of setting up new projects has been accelerated and the GMS program has initiated study contracts to be used as the basis for these new projects. Eleven priority sectors have been defined as follows: telecommunications; transport; Greater Mekong subregion transport projects and Greater

Mekong subregion cross-border transport agreement; energy (interconnections and energy exchanges); environment; natural resource management; tourism; agriculture; trade facilitation and pilot testing of single-stop customs inspection; investment; and the Greater Mekong subregion business forum.

The estimated cost for the ten-year strategic framework program (January 2003–December 2012) is $12.1 million; this figure does not include all of the projects (Asian Development Bank 2003). This flagship program includes East–West and North–South economic corridors; telecommunications backbone and information and communication technology; regional energy power; human resources and skills; private sector and tourist development competitiveness; environment framework; and cross-border trade and investment (Asian Development Bank 2003).

The telecommunication and information technology backbone comprises five projects, some of which have already been implemented: reform of policies and capacity building in the telecommunications sectors of phase one (Cambodia, Lao PDR, and Vietnam) and phase two (People's Republic of China, Yunnan Province of PRC, Lao PDR, Myanmar, Thailand, and Vietnam). The installation of the telecommunications network that started in 2004 comprises several extensions using fiber-optic technology, which concerned in the first instance Lao PDR and Cambodia and cost $46 million. This is the first phase of the project linking Vientiane to Phnom Penh with the extension toward Vietnam and Thailand. As a part of this technical assistance, the road link Kunning-Haiphong program is under construction and is called the Northern Economic Corridor.

For the production of electric power, Cambodia received a loan of $66 million for the GMS transmission project, which will be used to establish the link between northwest Cambodia and southwest Thailand. The energy independence rate of the Greater Mekong region is 80%, which means it is more than sufficient for its own consumption. Nevertheless, the sale of energy has not yet developed, with the exception of Thailand. Therefore, the GMS will increase the sale of energy, and it is a priority sector for all the GMS countries. With more than eighteen hydraulic power sites, these countries will earn a great deal through the exportation of electric power. Great hydraulic resources have been identified in Yunnan, Myanmar, and Lao PDR. The most industrialized country in the GMS is Thailand, which has an advanced electric power system. For some years now, Thailand has been producing and selling electric power, especially to Cambodia; but after the setup of the regional electric market, Yunnan, Myanmar, and Lao PDR also will become electric power export countries. Nevertheless, rate barriers are preventing the export of electric power. In 2002 in Cambodia, the Inter-Governmental Agreement (IGA) on regional power trade in GMS was signed. This agreement established the Regional Power Trade Coordination Committee.

In the flagship initiative of the GMS, the tourist sector also is considered. The launching of the Mekong Tourism Development Project, which concerns Vietnam, Lao PDR, and Cambodia, represents a total cost of $48 million. For this tourism sector, infrastructures are needed, such as road networks, ports, and airports. These infrastructures are included in the program of northern and southern economic corridors.

The ASEAN Mekong Basin Development Cooperation will change the face of the region, but without the decision of the local people. In the six countries/provinces affected by the program, groups of civilians gather together to protest against the project.

ANNE ANDROUAIS

See also Asian Development Bank; Asia-Pacific Economic Cooperation (APEC); Association of Southeast Asian Nations (ASEAN); Southeast Asia: History and Economic Development

References and Further Reading

Abonyi, George. "Financing the Great Mekong Subregion." *Trends*, Institute of Southeast Asian Studies 77 (January, 1997).

Abonyi, George, and Pante Filologo Jr. "Economic Cooperation in the Greater Mekong Subregion: The Challenges of Resource Mobilization." In *Growth Triangles in Asia: A New Approach to Regional Economic Cooperation*, edited by Myo Thant, Min Tang, and Kakazu Hiroshi. Oxford: Asian Development Bank and Oxford University Press, 1994 and 1998.

Asian Development Bank. "Greater Mekong Subregion, 10-Year Strategic Framework (2003–2012)." Report by GMS Department, Manila, The Asian Development Bank 9(2003):1–19.

Asian Development Bank. "Greater Mekong Subregion: Socioeconomic Review." Manila: The Asian Development Bank: Programs Department (West), 1997.

Asian Development Bank. "Globalization and Regional Integration in Asia." Theme Paper Series, no. 7 (1997).

Krugman, Paul. *Geography and Trade.* Leuven, Belgium: Leuven University Press and Cambridge, MA: Massachusetts Institute of Technology Press, 1991.

Mukdawan, Sakboon. "Putting the People First." *The Nation*, December 18, 2002: p. 8A.

Thant, Myo, Min Tang, and Kakazu Hiroshi. *Growth Triangles in Asia, A New Approach to Regional Economic Cooperation.* Oxford: Oxford University Press and Asian Development Bank, 1994 and 1998.

Than, Mya. "The Golden Quadrangle of Mainland Southeast Asia: a Myanmar Perspective." Institute of Southeast Asian Studies, ISEAS Working Papers, Economics and Finance, no. 5 (1996).

ASIAN DEVELOPMENT BANK (ADB)

The Asian Development Bank (ADB) was established in 1966 with the aim of improving economic development in the Asia-Pacific region. It was one of several regional banks instituted during this period as a response to discontent with the lending policies of existing institutions such as the World Bank and the International Monetary Fund (IMF); a perception of an inadequate supply of funds; and a recognition of the special needs of the regions, in particular the need for more flexibility and local control in the determination of lending policies and the use of resources.

Since its inception, the ADB's membership has grown from thirty-one to sixty-three countries, all of whom are members of the United Nations (UN) or members and associates of the UN's Economic and Social Commission for Asia and the Pacific (UNESCAP). While most of the Asian Development Bank's member states are from the region, stretching the definition to include Central Asia, eighteen members are external, including one of the bank's largest shareholders, the United States. West European countries also are strongly represented.

The ADB's major focus since 1999 has been the elimination of poverty in the region through the promotion of economic growth, social infrastructure, and good governance. The bank meets these objectives by primarily providing loans and investments to developing country members and assistance in planning and managing development projects. It also can provide analyses and recommendations to countries or regional forums. Loans are granted on ordinary or concessional terms to governments and public and private enterprises in diverse sectors including agriculture, infrastructure, transport, communications, energy, natural resources, and finance. In 2003, the bank approved more than $6 billion in loans for sixty-six projects mostly in the public sector. Indonesia, India, China, Pakistan, Bangladesh, and Sri Lanka were some of the largest recipients. The ADB also provides grants and technical assistance, worth some $660 million in 2003. Almost 70% of the bank's lending is from its Ordinary Capital Resources (OCR, www.adb.org/About/fnncemgt.asp), which are sourced from issuing bonds, loan repayments, and contributions from donor countries. The bank's Asian Development Fund (ADF) provides concessional loans that are mostly sourced from donor contributions, with some loan repayments and a portion of resources from the OCR.

The ADB's highest policymaking body is the Board of Governors. Meeting annually, the board comprises one representative from each member country. The president, elected for a five-year period, heads the day-to-day running of operations and policies, assisted by a managing director general, four vice presidents (appointed by the Board of Directors on the president's recommendation and generally representing nonregional countries), and the heads of departments and offices. The president must be from the Asia-Pacific region and has traditionally been a Japanese national. Japan has historically been influential in the establishment and operation of the bank. The Governors elect a twelve-member Board of Directors every two years, eight of whom are elected by Asia-Pacific states and four who are elected by nonregional members.

Despite its original objectives of overcoming the limitations of international funding bodies, the ADB has been subject to many of the same criticisms, including that it is dominated by a few countries (the United States and Japan in particular), and that it favors spending on a particular model of development. While confined by its charter to focus on project lending, the ADB has at times suggested associated policy changes or tied project management and consultancy with loans (Wihtol 1988). Japan and the United States were the largest shareholders in 2004, with almost 16% each of total subscribed capital, and therefore voting power of almost 13%. These two countries have more than a quarter of the total voting power between them. Voting power can fluctuate over time depending on the level of contributions and membership. However, in 2004, twenty-four donor countries were responsible for almost 62% of subscribed capital and had a combined voting power of just more than 57%. This position of strength has led at times to various donor countries delaying or decreasing subscriptions to capital funds to express dissatisfaction with the bank. Therefore, the goal of regional control and flexibility depends to some degree on the cooperation of donor countries.

The most contentious issue has been that of voting rights. ADB voting is weighted toward financial contribution, or shareholdings, and this has generated a fundamental conflict between donors and developing countries. Voting power is determined by the equal distribution of 20% of basic votes plus a proportional vote based on the number of shares of the capital stock in the OCR held by that member. This voting formula was subject to a process of intense negotiation that reflects the inherent tensions between donor and borrowing countries. Initially, Japan had wanted the basic vote to be only 10% but agreed to 20% on the pro visa that the Board of Directors have ten seats only, not the twelve that had been proposed. Developing member countries countered with a claim for greater representation on the board (seven seats as opposed to the six that donor countries suggested).

The final proposal was a board of ten for two years, then an increase in board members to twelve and a ratio of eight developing to four donor country representatives. This meant an actual decrease in developing countries' representation (Wihtol 1988).

The ADB did undergo a reorganization in 2002, moving away from project and sector applications toward a stronger, more holistic countrywide and subregional focus as the key planning strategy. Five regional departments covering East and Central Asia, the Mekong, the Pacific, South Asia, and Southeast Asia have been established, each with a regional management team. This may assist in targeting key areas of need and ties in with a more community-oriented approach to development; however, the larger issues of control of funds and donor country interests still remain to be resolved. Donor and borrowing governments' policies and interests, organizational constraints, and the socioeconomic conditions in the borrowing country will all impact the outcome of any ADB-funded project.

MELISSA BUTCHER

See also International Monetary Fund

References and Further Reading

Alley, R. *The United Nations in South East Asia and the South Pacific*. London: Macmillan Press, 1998.
Bennet, A. L. *International Organisations: Principles and Issues*, 4th ed. Englewood Cliffs, NJ: Prentice Hall, 1988.
Coleman, D. "The Role and Function of International Donor Agencies." In *Aid Management Program Coordination Training Module*. Sydney: Research Institute for Asia and the Pacific, 2002.
Nelson, P. *Anatomy of a Bank Job*. Tanzania: Nelson International, 1995.
Singh, K. *The Globalisation of Finance*. New Delhi: Madhyam Books, 1998.
Wihtol, R. *The Asian Development Bank and Rural Development*. London: Macmillan Press, 1988 (www.adb.org).

ASIAN "ECONOMIC MIRACLE"

East Asia emerged in the 1970s and 1980s as a particularly dynamic region of the wider world economy. By the early 1990s, Japan, along with the newly industrialized countries (NICs) or newly industrialized economies (NIEs) of South Korea, Taiwan, Hong Kong, and Singapore, and the growing economic dynamism of Thailand, Malaysia, and Indonesia, were widely celebrated collectively as the Asian "Economic Miracle." They also were known as the "East Asian Miracle" or the High-Performing Asian Economies (HPAEs) in this period. For some observers, the rise of East Asia also was seen as a serious challenge (or threat) to North America and Western Europe. Both the celebration and the concern dissipated rapidly with the onset of the Asian financial crisis (1997–1998) and the era of the Asian "Economic Miracle" can now be seen as a relatively discrete period in the twentieth century history of the region and the world. The debate over the causes and lessons of the Asian "Economic Miracle" was a highly politicized affair. Some of the most influential explanations for the origin and dynamics of the Asian "Economic Miracle" viewed it as evidence of the efficacy and general applicability of a "free trade" and "free enterprise" model of economic development. A less influential, but still very significant, set of approaches argued that the key to the Asian "Economic Miracle" was the intervention and guidance of the developmental states of the region. At the same time, a growing number of observers inside and outside of East Asia attributed the region's economic success to Confucianism or other cultural/racial characteristics. This approach was encapsulated by the notion of "Asian values" that was held up as both a key to the region's success and a panacea for North America and Western Europe.

Viewing the Asian "Economic Miracle" more broadly, the economic dynamism of a growing number of nation-states in the region can be seen to have been grounded in important ways in the history of the Cold War (particularly the period from the late 1940s to the 1970s), during which the United States led a push to contain communism and secure a capitalist economic order in Asia, combined with the resurgence of Japanese corporate activity in the region to provide the overall framework for the Asian "Economic Miracle." By the time the Marshall Plan (1947) for Western Europe had been promulgated, the United States also had embarked on a major effort to facilitate the industrial rebirth of Japan. This was part of what would become a wider effort to turn as much of East Asia (and then Southeast Asia) as possible into a bulwark against the USSR and then, increasingly, China. With the Chinese Communist Party's victory in October 1949 and the onset of the Korean War (1950–1953), the governmental and military institutions and structures of the US national security state were consolidated as instruments of regional and global power. Meanwhile, the arrangements set down at Bretton Woods in 1944 that had produced the International Monetary Fund (IMF) and the International Bank for Reconstruction and Development (World Bank) contributed to the wider framework for economic recovery and development between the late 1940s and the early 1970s.

At the beginning of the 1950s, the Korean War provided a crucial stimulus to industrial production in Japan as a result of the dramatic increase in the purchase of military equipment and war-related products by the United States. After the Korean War, the sustained US economic and military aid (and capital) that went to South Korea and Taiwan in the 1950s and 1960s played a major role in strengthening the capabilities of these emergent developmental states. Between 1945 and 1979, US military aid to South Korea was $7 billion, while US economic aid from 1945 to 1973 was $5.5 billion. This was more than all the US economic aid to Africa and half the figure for all of Latin America over the same period. In the 1950s, more than 80% of South Korean imports were financed by US economic assistance. The growing power of these states also was linked to the relative weakness of business elites in South Korea and Taiwan and to the weakening of the power of large landowners, as a result of the implementation of land reforms under US auspices. In the 1950s and increasingly in the 1960s, manufacturers based in South Korea and Taiwan (and Japan) also gained privileged access to the North American market, for US geostrategic reasons, at the same time as the United States tolerated protected markets and tight controls on foreign investment in East Asia. Furthermore, the East Asian NICs (South Korea, Taiwan, and Hong Kong), along with Singapore, all entered the world export markets in the 1960s when a consumer boom was under way. Meanwhile, in the 1960s and 1970s, Japanese companies increasingly avoided the rising cost of labor in Japan by relocating operations to the emerging NICs. In this period, Japanese corporations also provided a substantial portion of the machinery and the other components needed for industrialization in Taiwan and South Korea, and they also were an important source of technology licenses.

South Korea emerged as the greatest success story of the wider Asian "Economic Miracle." At the beginning of the 1960s, the country's gross domestic product per capita was comparable to the newly independent former Belgian colony of the Congo Democratic Republic, and many South Koreans viewed the idea of South Korea catching up economically to the Philippines as impossible. By 1996, however, the South Korean economy was the twelfth biggest in the world and the country had become a member of the Organization for Economic Cooperation and Development (OECD). General Park Chung Hee, who ruled South Korea from 1961 until 1979, had been an officer in the Japanese Kwantung Army during the Pacific War, and his approach to economic development was clearly influenced by the Japanese colonial industrial pattern, most importantly the state's close links with the *zaibatsu* (the Japanese conglomerates at the center of Japan's pre-1945 industrialization process). Between the 1960s and the 1980s, state-guided national development in South Korea rested on a close relationship between the South Korean national security state and the country's burgeoning conglomerates (*chaebol*) at the same time as workers and trade unions were controlled via repression and top-down corporatist arrangements. The rapid economic growth and the dramatic social changes of these decades paved the way for the relative decline of the authoritarian developmental state in South Korea during the regime of General Chun Doo Hwan (1980–1988). Although the US reinvigorated the security alliance with Seoul in the Reagan era, Washington also increasingly began to question South Korea's financial and trading practices. These external shifts meshed with domestic pressures for political and economic liberalization and resulted in a transition to democracy by the end of the 1980s. The liberalization of the political system was closely connected to the liberalization of the economy, and Kim Young Sam, the first civilian president of South Korea (1993–1998) in more than three decades, made globalization (*segyehwa*) the centerpiece of his administration.

With the Asian crisis in 1997–1998, the pressure for liberal economic reform in East Asia increased. The IMF loan to South Korea, an unprecedented $58 billion, as well as smaller but still substantial loans to Thailand and Indonesia that came in the wake of the crisis, were conditional on the implementation of a range of austerity measures and economic reforms. IMF officials required the setting up of new regulatory procedures, the shutting down of a range of banks and financial institutions, and the liberalization of capital markets. The IMF also requested that public enterprises be privatized, that cartels be broken up, and that more flexible labor market arrangements be introduced. In South Korea, the IMF found an ally in the government of President Kim Dae Jung (1998–), whose own political and economic goals were strengthened by the early IMF demands. Kim Dae Jung was as committed as his predecessor to globalization, while the combination of the crisis and his assumption of the presidency in early 1998 was seen as an opportunity to undermine key aspects of the collusion between the *chaebol* and the political elite that were central to the developmental state. However, while the crisis has further weakened key elements of the developmental state in South Korea and its variations elsewhere in the region, many of the

arrangements and practices associated with the earlier era of the Asian "Economic Miracle" remain in place. At this juncture, the economic future of East Asia is uncertain. It is clear, however, that China is now emerging as increasingly central to wider economic developments in the region, while the era of the Asian "Economic Miracle" centered on Japan and the NICs of East Asia has clearly passed into history.

MARK T. BERGER

See also ASEAN Free Trade Association; ASEAN Mekong Basin Development Cooperation (Mekong Group); Asian Development Bank; Asian Tigers; Asia-Pacific Economic Cooperation (APEC); Association of Southeast Asian Nations (ASEAN); Export-Oriented Economies; Globalization: Impact on Development; Southeast Asia: History and Economic Development; Southeast Asia: International Relations; Trade Policies and Development

References and Further Reading

Amsden, Alice H. *Asia's Next Giant: South Korea and Late Industrialization*. New York: Oxford University Press, 1989.

Berger, Mark T. "The Triumph of the East? The East Asian Miracle and Post-Cold War Capitalism." In *The Rise of East Asia: Critical Visions of the Pacific Century*, edited by Mark T. Berger and Douglas A. Borer. London: Routledge, 1997.

Campos, Jorge Edgardo and Hilton L. Root. *The Key to the Asian Miracle: Making Shared Growth Credible*. Washington, DC: The Brookings Institution, 1996.

Cumings, Bruce. "The Origins and Development of the Northeast Asian Political Economy: Industrial Sectors, Product Cycles, and Political Consequences." In *The Political Economy of the New Asian Industrialism*, edited by Frederic C. Deyo. Ithaca, NY: Cornell University Press, 1987.

Haggard, Stephan. *Pathways from the Periphery: The Politics of Growth in the Newly Industrializing Countries*. Ithaca, NY: Cornell University Press, 1990.

Stubbs, Richard. "The Political Economy of the Asia-Pacific Region." In *Political Economy and the Changing Global Order*, edited by Richard Stubbs and Geoffrey R. D. Underhill. London: Macmillan, 1994.

Stubbs, Richard. "War and Economic Development: Export-Oriented Industrialization in East and Southeast Asia." *Comparative Politics*. 31 (3) (1999).

Wade, Robert. *Governing the Market: Economic Theory and the Role of Government in East Asian Industrialisation*. Princeton, NJ: Princeton University Press, 1990.

Woo, Jung-En and Meredith Woo-Cumings. *Race to the Swift: State and Finance in Korean Industrialization*. New York: Columbia University Press, 1991.

World Bank. *The East Asian Miracle: Economic Growth and Public Policy*. Oxford: Oxford University Press for the World Bank, 1993.

ASIAN MONETARY FUND

Proposal for the Creation of the Asian Monetary Fund

During the Asian financial crisis that started in July 1997, Japan tried to organize a new financial plan in spite of US opposition. In September 1997, Japan proposed creating the Asian Monetary Fund. This proposal was rejected because it was feared that the AMF would become a rival of the International Monetary Fund (IMF) in the region. So, a few months later, Japan launched a new plan called the Miyazawa New Plan, different from the AMF in style and scope. These changes gained the approval of Western countries. Japanese monetary policy, greatly influenced by the United States up until the Asian crisis, began to break free of US influence, especially concerning East Asian countries, which in turn are changing their attitude toward the Japanese government (Kwan 1998).

The globalization of financial markets can increase in East Asia. Emerging market countries are not yet counting so much in global capital markets but are vulnerable and, in the instance of a financial crisis, need to be supported (Freeman 2003). The IMF has explained that during market turbulence, emerging market countries should be protected. In the event of international capital market failure, domestic markets with their central banks should be equipped with safety nets in order to avoid bankruptcy, and after the 1997 Asian financial crisis, a new international financial architecture was formed (Goldstein 1998).

For the prevention of financial crisis, three actions are needed: (1) strengthen the supervision of creditors and debtors at an international level; (2) increase the liquidity provision of banks; and (3) create an Asian Monetary Fund.

In Asia, a monetary fund could be useful in encouraging the central banks of Asian countries to have sound macroeconomic policies and greater financial market transparency. Such a fund was proposed by the Japanese government in September 1997 at a finance minister meeting in Bangkok to provide financial assistance to countries in crisis (Bergsten 2000). This Asian Monetary Fund proposal was immediately torpedoed by the US government and the IMF. The main reasons advanced were that, on one hand, IMF activities would decrease, and on the other hand, the Chinese government was suspicious of Japanese intentions in the region.

An Arrangement: The Chang Mai Initiative

In 1997 in Manila, a framework group formed by the APEC finance ministers made a proposal to create a common basket peg for exchange rates, as a step toward a single Asian currency (Eichengreen 2002). Three different subjects were considered: (1) the role of currency pegs in Asian countries; (2) the role of the yen/dollar fluctuation; and (3) the tendency for one currency to depreciate and cause the others to do the same (McKinnon 2001).

In March 2000, an ASEAN swap arrangement was proposed at the ASEAN finance ministers meeting. And in May 2000, this arrangement was transformed into Chang Mai Initiative (CMI) (Henning 2002). This initiative encompassed the ten ASEAN countries and also Japan, People's Republic of China, and Republic of Korea. The CMI could include the central bank swap arrangements and IMF arrangements that are subject to conditionality. The IMF would include the same CMI system. This initiative was well-received by Asian policymakers in order to link their regional financial markets to the global market.

Observations were made for the proposal of a system of collective currency pegs the US dollar, to the yen or a basket of Asian and major currencies (Kwan 2001). These three bases were proposed by French and Japanese officials at the Asia-Europe finance minister meeting in 2002 in Japan.

An Option: The Asian Financial Institute

B. Eichengreen (2004) argues in his book, *Financial Options*, that the creation of a zone of financial stability in the region can upgrade the prudential supervision and promote initiatives, done directly by Asian governments and policymakers. One of these initiatives is called the Asian Financial Institute (AFI) and could be established, as the CMI, by the ASEAN ten countries (Brunei, Cambodia, Indonesia, Laos, Malaysia, Myanmar, the Philippines, Singapore, Thailand, and Vietnam), plus Japan, People's Republic of China, and Republic of Korea, which could have the task to set up standards for the Asian financial markets. The creation of the AFI would permit subscriptions and swap lines mentioned in the CMI and define other goals such as financial stability in the region.

However, the question remains concerning the setup of a financial institution for Asian countries and the way to strengthen cooperation among the economies (Yamazawa 1999). The Asian way for financial cooperation is still under consideration.

ANNE ANDROUAIS

See also ASEAN Free Trade Association; ASEAN Mekong Basin Development Cooperation (Mekong Group); Asian "Economic Miracle"; Asia-Pacific Economic Cooperation (APEC)

References and Further Reading

Bergsten, C. Fred. "Toward a Tripartite World." *The Economist* (July 15, 2000).

Eichengreen, Barry. "Hanging Together? On Monetary and Financial Cooperation." In *Global Change and East Asian Policy Initiatives*, edited by Yusuf, S., A. Altaf, and K. Nabeshima. Washington, DC, and Oxford: World Bank and Oxford University Press, 2004.

Eichengreen, Barry. *Financial Crises and What To Do About Them*. Oxford: Oxford University Press, 2002.

Freeman, Nick. J. *Financing Southeast Asia Economic Development*. Singapore: ISEAS, 2003.

Goldstein, Morris. *The Asian Financial Crisis*. Washington, DC: Institute for International Economics, 1998.

Henning, C. Randall. *East Asian Financial Cooperation*. Washington, DC: Institute for International Economics, 2002.

Kwan, C. H. *Yen Bloc: Toward Economic Integration in Asia*. Working Paper. Washington, DC: The Brookings Institution, 2001.

Kwan, C. H. *En to Gen Kara Miru Asia Tsukakiki: Asian Monetary Crisis from the Point of View of Yen and Yuan*. Tokyo: Iwanami Shoten (Iwanami Publisher), 1998.

Yamazawa, Ippei. *Strengthening Co-operation Among Asian Economies in Crisis*. Tokyo: IDE and JETRO, 1999.

ASIAN TIGERS

Introduction

Asian Tigers is a term used to refer to those developing economies in Asia that have been most successful since the 1970s. Of this group, those referred to as the *East Asian Tigers* comprise the most developed countries in the region, including Hong Kong, Singapore, South Korea, and Taiwan. These economies are the most advanced, compared with others in the region. In contrast is the group of countries referred to as the *Southeast Asian Tigers* comprised of countries such as Indonesia, Malaysia, the Philippines, Thailand, and Vietnam. Asian tiger economies (also referred to as newly industrializing countries [NICs] that grew by promoting exports while often stifling domestic competition. As well, the export-oriented industries were built with large infusions of foreign investment capital. The dramatic growth of the Asian tiger economies was based on the export of manufactured goods. As an example in the late 1980s, the four East Asian tigers produced 77% of total manufacturing exports from developing countries. But, as shown by developments in the 1990s, such tactics were unsustainable and other growth engines were being sought. One of these was to deregulate domestic markets in order to stimulate growth.

According to a World Bank Report (1993), the East Asian miracle—achieving high growth with equity—is due to a combination of fundamentally sound development policies, tailored interventions, and an unusually rapid accumulation of physical and human capital. The tiger economies are part of this success and have been referred to as high-performing East Asian economies. Such economies have a record of high and sustained economic growth. In addition, these economies displayed high per capita incomes, along with a much-improved income distribution, compared with most other developing economies. Private domestic investment and rapidly growing human capital were the principal engines of growth. Educational policies were focused on increasing labor skills, and agricultural policies stressed productivity.

Export-Oriented and Import-Substitution Strategies

Outward-oriented export-promotion strategies, as well as import-substitution strategies, in theory, do not discriminate between production for the domestic market and for exports, or between purchase of domestic goods and foreign goods. International development agencies like the World Bank are strongly committed to encouraging developing countries to adopt outward—rather than inward—oriented strategies.

A World Bank study in 1987 of forty-one developing countries covering 1963–1985 has shown that if countries are placed along a continuum of strongly outwardly oriented strategies at one end and strongly inwardly oriented strategies at the other, economic performance, including gross national product growth, tends to decline from outward to inward orientation. The study suggests that strongly inwardly oriented economies fared badly. While the results of the study are highly persuasive, they fail to take into account the relative poverty of the inwardly oriented group of countries, compared with the other group of outwardly oriented countries, a characteristic that is even more important than the lack of economic performance. It may be that poorer countries have greater difficulty than relatively richer countries to progress up the ladder of development.

On another analysis, trade orientation is positively related to levels of per capita income, and outward orientation is more closely associated with a balanced export structure. Where the export structure is dependent on a narrow range of primary products, such economies urgently need to diversify their external trade to remove the threats emanating from the vagaries of international trade.

Export-promotion strategies encourage efficient production where there is no discrimination between the domestic or the export market. The East Asian tigers have successfully generated exceptional growth rates in their economies by using import-substituting and export-oriented strategies.

An indicator of economic development is that, as the country's per capita income and stock of human capital rises, there is a shift from being a net importer of technology and skills to being a net exporter. In this transformation, a transitional stage may occur wherein the economy exports a narrow range of highly specialized technological products while remaining a net importer of technology in aggregate terms. The suggestion is that in the 1990s, some successful developing countries may have reached this phase in their development.

Any one of the East Asian tigers would make an ideal case study for examining issues associated with early stages of technological exports. Such exports comprise the international flow of basic technical know-how management services and other skills. The technology includes the technological components of foreign investment and overseas construction, licensing and technical agreements, consulting services, and other commercial agreements.

The Korean Path

Korea is the classic Asian tiger economy. It had blazed a path to industrial strength based principally on domestic savings. Foreign capital also played an important part in tandem with local financial resources obtained from a rigorous system of taxation and profits derived from the sale of goods to a protected domestic market and to foreign markets. In addition, an institutional framework provided the infrastructure to build a close working relationship between government and private sectors. In the early 1980s, the state-*chaebol* (conglomerate) appeared omnipresent. The deep pockets of the commercial banks together with government wishes provided the entrée for Hyundai, Samsung, LG, and others to carve out market shares in Europe, Asia, and North America.

One pressing issue that impinges on the intermediate economies concerns their spectacular growth and continued impressive performance, compared with other developed economies. The East Asian tigers, for example, have been able to sustain high growth rates, compared with the richer industrial countries over the past 20–25 years. Their per capita incomes have nearly quadrupled, poverty rates have shrunk, and if such growth is sustained, the East Asian region may overtake North America as the world's dominant economic region. How and why this has come about is the subject of contentious debate and divided views.

Sustaining the Growth

Walden Bello (1990) outlined in his book *Dragons in Distress: Asia's Miracle Economies in Crisis* some very telling reasons why tiger economies were in crisis. In 1990, Taiwan recorded its lowest annual rise in gross national product since 1982, and South Korea suffered a $21 billion deficit on its current account after five years of surplus. The crisis of the tiger economy strategy of export-oriented trade and high-speed growth is said to stem from the intersection of three trends:

- The deterioration of the external trade environment because of rising protectionism;
- The loss of export competitiveness as tiger economies continued to depend on labor-intensive production even when labor was no longer cheap; and
- The eruption of long-suppressed environmental, agricultural, and political costs exacted by previous rapid growth.

Many of the tiger economies still remain structured as of the previous pattern of export-led growth at a time when many markets, especially in the United States, Europe, and Japan, were becoming increasingly protected. The markets in Eastern Europe and the Commonwealth of Independent States are hardly significant in either the short or medium terms given their depressed purchasing power and developing economies. Even without trade barriers or appreciation in value of their currencies, tiger economies have lost their competitive edge. Multinational corporations (MNCs) have moved elsewhere in search of cheaper labor, and the product cycle has reached maturity so that goods that were previously profitable and exclusive are now less profitable and are being produced for the mass market. Higher wages have pushed up the cost of living, rural labor reserves have dried up, and as labor has organized itself, it has meant, for example, that many South Korean and Taiwanese manufacturers have relocated their operations elsewhere in Southeast Asia and China.

Free-market economists have long recognized that the close relationships between industry, finance, and politics carried with it the seeds of eventual calamity. In South Korea, the government directed bank loans to favoured *chaebols* in an effort to achieve growth through exports. Interest rates in Korea also were capped, and tough labor rules were imposed on companies, making it illegal, for instance, to fire anyone without union permission.

Thus, it can be observed that the rapid growth rates in the tiger economies have been won at great cost. Notwithstanding the authoritarianism in South Korea and Taiwan and the subsequent eruption in 1987 in South Korea, after two decades of tight control, of new democratic policies that have forced responsibility and accountability, environmental degradation itself is threatening productive capacity.

Previously, Korea with its protected home market allowed the biggest *chaebols* to build huge manufacturing operations without having to develop world-class design and marketing skills. But this has all changed after the economic crisis of the mid-1990s. The government has since passed legislation to encourage competition at home and to give consumers more choice. It has allowed greater foreign ownership of companies, liberalized foreign-exchange transactions, and removed import restrictions.

In Taiwan, the pollution of rivers by upstream industries has devastated the shrimp, oyster, and fish aquaculture industry downstream. Environmental activists in Taiwan have succeeded in delaying the construction of more petrochemical and nuclear power plants—seen as necessities by technocrats to sustain export-oriented growth. Such developments have forced a reevaluation of benefits of past growth in comparison with the value of personal freedom and quality-of-life issues.

Hong Kong, on the other hand, has so far weathered the storm with much less damage than its neighbors. Analysts credit its free-market policies for creating a resilient economy. Companies that made bad investment decisions were simply allowed to go bankrupt without any hint of a government rescue.

Future Prospects

After the economic crisis of 1997, tiger economies are showing tentative signs of recovery, and market-shaping trends that had begun earlier in the decade have begun to accelerate. Fast-moving technology is cutting product cycle time, while oversupply is pushing prices and profits everywhere. These are challenges to tiger economies that previously had prospered by coupling imported technology with cheap labor. The biggest challenge, of course, will be the new and vigorous competition from other emerging markets from around the world. Asian tiger economies now have to grapple with all the implications of market liberalization and try to build growth from the start of the new century of around 8–10%, compared with the former halcyon days of 18–20% of the 1980s.

It may well be that the East Asian tigers are paying a high price for their industrial maturity. The super-competitive economies seem not to be able to avoid the kind of labor confrontations that beset supposedly industrial giants as Britain and countries in the European Union. The main issue seems to be that many of the tiger economies believed that their "Asian values" would help them pull through their travails. But that may be one side of the problem, because there may yet be a close correlation between economic change and political change as well. The economic wonders worked by cheap labor, weak exchange rates, and closed domestic markets may not be sustainable forever. It is ironic that what the Asian Tigers are facing now is the challenge of success. While the Asian Tiger economies have transferred labor from agriculture to industry, invested heavily, and benefited from investment and transfer of technology from abroad, these same economies have to demonstrate their ability to deliver "quality-based growth" rather than growth based on adding ever-increasing quantities of capital and labor.

GEORGE CHO

See also ASEAN Free Trade Association; ASEAN Mekong Basin Development Cooperation (Mekong Group); Asian Development Bank; Asian "Economic Miracle"; Asia-Pacific Economic Cooperation (APEC); Association of Southeast Asian Nations (ASEAN); Export-Oriented Economies; Globalization: Impact on Development; Import Substitution Industrialization; Southeast Asia: History and Economic Development; Southeast Asia: International Relations; Trade Policies and Development

Further Reading

Bello, W. "Korea: Travails of the Classic Tiger Economy." *Focus-on-Trade*, no. 21, December 1997. Assen: Asia House, 1998. (*See also* www.asienhaus.de/asiancrisis/koreancrisis.htm.)

Bello, W. *Dragons in Distress: Asia's Miracle Economies in Crisis*. San Francisco: Food First, 1990.

Goad, G. P. "Look Homeward, Asia." *Far Eastern Economic Review* (June 10, 1999).

Heller, P. S. "Aging in the Asian Tigers: Challenges for Fiscal Policy." International Monetary Fund working paper 97/143, Washington, DC: International Monetary Fund, 1997.

Heller, P. S., and Symansky, S. "Implications for Savings of Aging in the Asian Tigers." International Monetary Fund working Paper 97/136, Washington, DC: IMF, 1997.

Kim, E. M., ed. *The Four Asian Tigers: Economic Development and the Global Political Economy.* San Diego: Academic Press, 1998.

World Bank. *The East Asian Miracle: Economic Growth and Public Policy.* New York: Oxford University Press, 1993.

ASIA-PACIFIC ECONOMIC COOPERATION (APEC)

The Asia-Pacific Economic Cooperation (APEC) forum serves as the primary vehicle for regional economic integration through promoting open trade and competitive market economy in the region. In order to realize long-term goals of free trade, APEC members are committed to completely eliminating regional trade barriers within two decades. Mutual ties are designed to improve access to the region's growing export markets. Increased exports, in turn, are expected to boost the economy and decrease unemployment.

In parallel with the emergence of other regional trading blocs in Europe and North America, APEC has been aiming to stimulate regional economic growth through relaxation of trade barriers and investment liberalization. APEC drew attention with the involvement of all the major economies of the region, some of which are the most dynamic, fastest growing in the world. APEC currently remains a huge trading group accounting for about half of the world's exports and imports.

Origin and Evolution

APEC began as an informal dialogue group with limited membership, in 1989, following the initiatives of the United States, Japan, Canada, South Korea, and the Southeast Asian countries, which wanted to form a regional free-trade pact. Its original aim was to harness economic growth with intertwining economies on both sides of the Pacific Rim. APEC was expanded and more formally institutionalized with the recognition of the significance in economic cooperation among regional political leaders. It was later joined by China, Taiwan, and Hong Kong in 1991, by

Russia in 1998, followed by Mexico in 1993, and such Latin American countries as Peru and Chile in 1994.

The region includes the most wealthy and populous countries in the world. In particular, APEC members constitute the world's biggest exporters in Asia, such as Japan and China, as well as the world's biggest importer, the United States. APEC memberships are further divided into groups of countries reflecting the diverse nature of the region's economic development: advanced economies (United States, Canada, Japan, and Australia), developing countries (Indonesia, Vietnam, Malaysia, Thailand, and the Philippines), rapidly growing but state-dominated economies (China), and transition economies following privatization (Russia).

APEC, reflecting the views of economically advanced countries, in particular, the United States, holds a view that in response to recent economic slowdown, free trade helps build confidence in the markets and guards against protectionism. In particular, APEC gained strength with the support of former US President Bill Clinton, who considered the economic health of the APEC region vital to the continued prosperity of the United States. The US government continues to see a vital economic interest in the development of free trade in the Pacific region given its exports to the region reached a total of $500 billion in 2000.

In developing a road map for the envisioned Free Trade Zone, it was agreed at the 1994 Indonesian meeting that full trade and investment liberalization in the Pacific would be implemented among developed countries by 2010, with extension to developing countries by 2020. As stepping measures, APEC member states elaborated, in 1997, a plan to liberalize trade in chemicals, fish, forest products, and twelve other major sectors with a reduction in import tariffs on $1.5 trillion in goods. Trade and investment flows to be freed across this vast region, which account for more than 50% of the world gross domestic product, will have an impact on the global economy.

The formation of regional trading agreements may well accelerate the process of global economic expansion. Unlike the Word Trade Organization, APEC depends on voluntary cooperation rather than the binding agreements for promoting expanded economic relationships. By serving as an alternative path to trade liberalization, however, APEC can be seen as a galvanizing force for global talks such as the Uruguay Round Table negotiation. In fact, APEC traditionally has pushed for a move to launch a new global trade agreement to build a basis for future economic growth. In the past, its summits strongly endorsed launching new rounds of free trade negotiations.

Annual Meetings and Institutionalization

A series of yearly meetings, culminating in a heads-of-state summit, held each autumn since 1993 have brought top-level attention to regional free trade and investment. These annual forums have reiterated the member countries' commitment to build the world's largest free trade area around the Pacific Rim. As the single most important institution in the Asia-Pacific region, these gatherings serve as ideal venues for the head of states not only to meet regularly as a group but also to discuss current issues on a bilateral basis. Along with top-level meetings designed for both formal and informal discussions about major issues in the region, APEC also provides consultation and negotiation forums among trade and economic ministers.

The exchange of information and views among member economies has been institutionalized through such forums as the Economic Committee transformed from the Ad Hoc Group on Economic Trends and Issues at the Sixth APEC Ministerial Meeting in Jakarta in November 1994. The formal policy committee has been addressing central economic issues that concern member governments and providing the analytical basis useful for advancing agendas.

Agendas

APEC emphasizes economic deregulation and increased competition with reduction in trade barriers. Along with this emphasis, APEC meetings promote increased transparency, openness, and predictability based on the rule of law for the accelerated pace of financial and other market-oriented reforms. Other agendas include higher productivity and innovation with the application of new technology for cost reduction and improved efficiency. Reform of outdated telecommunications regulatory practices is critical for promoting e-commerce. Entrepreneurship development and support for increased competitiveness of small businesses and human capacity building also have been serious agendas for ministerial meetings.

In response to the attacks on the World Trade Center and Pentagon in September 2001, terrorism has also emerged on APEC's new agenda, as it is seen as a major challenge to free, open economies. In a pledge for full cooperation to prevent international terrorism from disrupting market activities, the 2001 APEC summit emphasized close communication and cooperation among financial and economic policy-making authorities. Capacity building and technical cooperation also have been discussed in terms of putting counterterrorism measures into place.

Investment for financial infrastructure and institutions is designed to foster safe and efficient capital markets. As part of enhancing counterterrorism cooperation, APEC members also began to discuss financial measures that can prohibit the flow of funds to terrorists. APEC's Finance Ministers' Working Group on Fighting Financial Crime is looking for strategies to adopt internationally standardized measures such as the use of common accounting rules.

Whereas strengthening financial markets and developing more efficient investment procedures remain key concerns, APEC has been addressing other issues related to trade facilitation through working groups. Modernization of customs procedures and reduction in tariffs are linked to bringing down the ultimate cost to businesses. One of their priorities is to strengthen customs communication networks and enhance a global integrated electronic customs network, by which customs authorities can have a better ability to enforce laws without interrupting the flow of trade. Development of electronic movement records systems focuses on protection of border security, as well as ensuring the smooth movements of goods and investment.

Other areas of economic cooperation include energy security in the region through the mechanism of the APEC Energy Security Initiative. The mechanism looks for various policy tools to respond to challenges for the region's energy supply, as well as short-term supply disruptions. In addition, there has been discussion about the involvement of the public sector in developing electronic commerce and region-wide information technology programs.

APEC also promotes social infrastructure building to take advantage of trade and investment opportunities. Basic education and social services are not adequately provided in underdeveloped parts of the region. In redressing unequal labor productivity, attention also has been directed to improving educational standards and training of skills that are essential for production and trade.

Economic Reform

Because many Asian countries are vulnerable with currency devaluation, financial stability is essential for trade and investment liberalization. Since the structural weaknesses of dynamic economies of Southeast Asia and East Asia were revealed through the Asian financial crisis of 1997–1998, the Pacific Rim leaders consider fiscal and monetary policies to mitigate the adverse effects of a synchronized slowdown of the world economy.

Major Asian economies are called upon to embark on reform of their banking and corporate sectors in order to reverse the slowdown and restore confidence. In alignment with the International Monetary Fund (IMF) and other international financial institutions, APEC supports economic policies that stimulate domestic consumption, promote corporate and corporate restructuring, and attract investment. However, the heavy-handed nature of the IMF rescue packages has not gained economic confidence in the region.

The regional economy has been hit badly by the falling global demand for many of the Asian members' exports (such as electronics). In particular, the recession in the United States is expected to have an impact on the growth in the region due to its heavy dependence on the US market. The prospects for economic growth—especially for China, Mexico, Japan, the Philippines, Taiwan, Malaysia, South Korea, and Singapore—are negatively affected by reduction in their exports to the United States. Instability of member economies (the slowdown in dynamic economic growth in many parts of the region) weakened the impetus for fulfilling a trade liberalization agreement.

Challenges

In spite of the promise of an integrated Pacific trade zone, unity seems to be illusive due to continuing economic and political divide, as Malaysia and other developing countries are opposed to adverse effects of globalization. In addition to the discord between developed and developing countries, the rapid rise in Chinese economic power also is seen as an uncertain factor. Through its expanded role, China wants to challenge Japan as a regional economic leader by offering trade and financial deals to other countries. The Association of Southeast Asian Nations (ASEAN), making up a subregional trade bloc, is wary of the emerging economic power of China while seeking to avoid dependence on Japan. Some countries, such as Mexico, are concerned about the flood of cheap Chinese products in their markets. The tensions over military and political matters between the United States and China, along with US skepticism about China's commitment to free market economy, also can divide APEC in the future.

Gross economic imbalance and wide differences in economic policies provide challenges for further economic expansion of the region. The goal of bringing prosperity to the region through free trade has been hampered by unequal benefit of economic growth and ensuing disparities. As APEC markets are more open today than they were a decade ago, big trading countries with fast-expanding exports can benefit more from participating in regional trade liberalization. Imbalance in trade competitiveness (ascribed to a gap in technology and infrastructures such as transportation and communication) serves as an obstacle to progress towards the regional economic integration.

Despite an emphasis on economic growth, there has been comparatively little focus on social progress. Despite commitments to clean manufacturing and clean energy, there have been few advancements in environmental standards. Economic inequity also remains a problem.

Future Prospects

The free trade pact was forged in the entire region of the Pacific to prevent the imposition of protectionist trade measures. Whereas the main emphasis in APEC still remains the establishment of an open trading and investment system, economic issues are difficult to disentangle from politics. In particular, the incidents of September 11, 2001, put various agendas for economic cooperation in the context of national security and the fight against terrorism.

Strengthening a stable political and social environment for trade, investment, and travel is essential for regional economic growth. As demonstrated by the European Union and the North American Free Trade Agreement (NAFTA), the trend toward further integration and expansion of trade blocs seem to be an irreversible process in an ongoing process toward economic globalization.

Ho-Won Jeong

See also ASEAN Free Trade Association; ASEAN Mekong Basin Development Cooperation (Mekong Group); Asian Development Bank; Asian "Economic Miracle"; Asian Tigers; Association of Southeast Asian Nations (ASEAN); Export-Oriented Economies; Globalization: Impact on Development; Import Substitution Industrialization; Southeast Asia: History and Economic Development; Southeast Asia: International Relations; Trade Policies and Development

References and Further Reading

Aggarwal, Vinod K., and Charles E. Morrison, eds. *Asia-Pacific Crossroads: Regime Creation and the Future of APEC*. New York: St. Martin's Press, 1998.

Bishop, Bernie. *Liberalising Foreign Direct Investment Policies in the APEC Region*. Aldershot: Ashgate, 2001.

Drysdale, Peter and David, Vines, eds. *Europe, East Asia, and APEC: A Shared Global Agenda?* Cambridge, and New York: Cambridge University Press, 1998.

Bergsten, C. Fred. *Whither APEC? The Progress to Date and Agenda for the Future*. Washington, DC: Institute for International Economics, United States, 1997.

Yamazawa, Ippei, ed. *Asia Pacific Economic Cooperation (APEC): Challenges and Tasks for the Twenty-First Century*. London: Routledge, 2000.

ASSOCIATION OF CARIBBEAN STATES (ACS)

The Association of Caribbean States (ACS) was established in Cartagena, Colombia, in 1994 to promote social, political, and economic cooperation among the nations in the Caribbean region. The groundwork for the formation of the ACS had been laid at the Conference of the Heads of Government of the Caribbean Community in Port of Spain, Trinidad and Tobago in October 1992. The creation of the ACS was seen largely as a reaction to the North American Free Trade Agreement between the United States of America, Canada, and Mexico, which went into effect on January 1, 1994. As such, the ASC was a response to the challenges and opportunities presented by the globalization of the international economy and the liberalization of trade relations in the Western Hemisphere. The 25 ACS member states are Antigua and Barbuda, the Bahamas, Barbados, Belize, Colombia, Costa Rica, Cuba, Dominica, the Dominican Republic, El Salvador, Grenada, Guatemala, Guyana, Haiti, Honduras, Jamaica, Mexico, Nicaragua, Panama, St. Kitts and Nevis, St. Lucia, St. Vincent, the Grenadines, Suriname, Trinidad and Tobago, and Venezuela. Three associate member states—Aruba, France (on behalf of French Guiana, Guadeloupe, and Martinique), and the Netherlands Antilles—also are part of the association. The main administrative organs of the association are the ministerial council and the secretariat. Dominican intellectual Rubén Arturo Silié Valdez, the former director of the Latin American Faculty for Social Sciences (FLASCO), has been the secretary general of the association since 2004. The headquarters of the ACS is located in Port of Spain, Trinidad and Tobago.

The ACS is dedicated to strengthening regional cooperation in cultural, economic, political, scientific, social, and technological relations among the member states. As such, the member states hope to build upon their geographic proximity and common historical experiences to create future cultural, economic, and social development for the 250 million people they represent. The ACS strives to facilitate economic development in the region, with the ultimate goal of making member-state economies more competitive in the international market. In addition to economic development, the ACS also strives for the promotion of social development, which includes the fortification of democratic government and respect for human rights. The association also supports the environmental protection of the Caribbean Sea, a body of water that is regarded as the common patrimony of the peoples of the region. The association's four main areas of activity are trade, transportation, tourism, and natural disasters.

The Special Committee on Trade Development and External Economic Relations encourages economic cooperation to expand economic activities, especially trade and investment, in the Greater Caribbean. Special attention has been paid to the efforts of small economies to penetrate the markets of larger trading partners, such as the European Union and the United States. Efforts also have been made by the association to present a common agenda when dealing with agencies such as the World Trade Organization (WTO). The ACS has collected data and statistics about economic performance in the Greater Caribbean. This information, which is available on the Internet, is provided with the goal of increasing and facilitating trade within the Greater Caribbean. In an attempt to increase economic production, foreign loans and grants have been obtained to strengthen the infrastructure of the member nations.

The Special Committee on Transport is charged with increasing the number of flights between the member states, while simultaneously providing greater access to the airlines of member states to the airports of other member states. One advantage of increased air traffic between the member states is the possibility for an increase in regional tourism. The committee also has created a Port and Maritime Information database that includes information on shipping costs. This information should facilitate the expansion of exports and imports in the Greater Caribbean region. In the aftermath of the September 11, 2001 events, the committee has focused on increasing security for air and sea travelers. The committee also cooperates with other organizations in an attempt to limit illegal drug trafficking.

The Special Committee on Sustainable Tourism seeks to promote the expansion of tourism in the Greater Caribbean while simultaneously attempting to ensure the protection of the physical environment. Ecologically and environmentally sound sustainable development policies regarding tourism, one of the largest foreign exchange revenue generators in the region, is essential for the economic development of the Greater Caribbean. Given the importance of the Caribbean Sea to the future growth of tourism in the region, the member states have a vested interest in limiting pollution and monitoring waste disposal. The committee has worked to increase multiple-destination tourism in the region by encouraging more direct air linkages between the member states, organizing language training classes to provide local workers with the skills necessary to handle the increased number of foreign tourists, and developing and expanding local health care programs to deal with such problems as AIDS. The committee also has evaluated the negative impact of the September 11 events on the tourist industry.

The Special Committee on Natural Disasters has encouraged the cooperation of disaster planning and relief agencies in the Greater Caribbean, an area that has been subjected to hurricanes, earthquakes, and volcanic eruptions. The committee is especially concerned with the development of early warning systems that could limit the loss of life during natural disasters.

MICHAEL R. HALL

See also Caribbean Community and Common Market (CARICOM); Caribbean Development Bank; Caribbean Free Trade Association (CARIFTA); Caribbean: History and Economic Development; Caribbean: International Relations; North American Free Trade Agreement (NAFTA); World Health Organization (WHO)

References and Further Reading

International Business Publications. *Association of Caribbean States Business Law Handbook*. Cincinnati, OH: International Business Publications, 2001.

International Business Publications. *Association of Caribbean States Investments and Business Guide*. Cincinnati, OH: International Business Publications, 2001.

Serbin, Andrés. *Sunset Over the Islands: The Caribbean in the Age of Global and Regional Challenges*. Gordonsville, VA: Palgrave MacMillan, 1999.

ASSOCIATION OF SOUTHEAST ASIAN NATIONS (ASEAN)

Historical Background

The formal creation of the Association of Southeast Asian Nations (ASEAN) took place at the First ASEAN Ministerial Meeting held in August 1967 in Bangkok, Thailand. Five Southeast Asian nations (Indonesia, Malaysia, the Philippines, Thailand, and Singapore) signed the ASEAN Declaration. The declaration sought to accomplish three primary objectives. First, the declaration's intent was to accelerate economic growth, social progress, and cultural development in the region through joint endeavors, conducted in the spirit of equality and partnership, in order to strengthen the foundation for the pursuit of a prosperous and peaceful community. Second, it sought to promote regional peace and stability through an abiding respect for justice and the rule of law in the relationship among countries of the region, and to promote adherence to the principles of the United Nations Charter. Third, the declaration committed members to promoting active collaboration and mutual assistance on matters of common interest in the areas of economic, social, cultural, technical, scientific, and administrative affairs.

The declaration made it clear that association membership was open to all Southeast Asian nations provided that they agreed to adhere to the three primary objectives of ASEAN. Upon admission to the association, members must be willing to bind themselves together in friendship and cooperation. According to the declaration's provisions, members must commit themselves to joint efforts aimed at securing for the people of Southeast Asia the blessings of peace, freedom, and prosperity. Prior to being admitted to the association, each member must have signed an Amity Agreement that expresses a willingness to abide by the provisions of the declaration.

Brunei joined the original five in 1985 and during the late 1990s Vietnam, Laos, Myanmar (Burma), and Cambodia became ASEAN members. Throughout its history, the association's primary objectives have been to accelerate economic growth and development among the region's countries and to bring about regional security and stability. The overriding principle underlying the agreement was that all endeavors would be undertaken in a spirit of equality and partnership wherein decisions would be based upon consensus. Peace and prosperity within the community of nations would be built on the cornerstone of nonintervention and respect for national sovereignty. Via signing Amity Agreements and eventually becoming full Association members, the four newcomers brought the association's membership to ten nations.

The Structure of ASEAN

ASEAN's institutional structure evolved into a set of operational modules targeted toward intraregional trade expansion, investment generation and industrial development, dispute settlement, and regional security. Trade expansion is promoted through the ASEAN Free Trade Area (AFTA) and the Common Effective Preferential Tariff (CEPT) system via which tariffs are lowered among member countries. Investment and industrial expansion are promoted through three initiatives: the ASEAN Industrial Project (AIP), the ASEAN Industrial Complementation (AIC), or the ASEAN Industrial Joint Venture (AIJV). The ASEAN Dialogue Partnership System (ADPS) and Post Ministerial Conferences (PMC) are in charge of settling disputes involving an ASEAN member (or members). Regional security is sought through a relatively new module called the ASEAN Regional Forum (ARF).

Six policy arenas are used in order to design, coordinate, and implement the modules that the association uses. The first is the ASEAN summit among the heads of government that meets every three years and in a member country chosen on the basis of rotation. The summit is the highest-level instrument, and it involves the determination of the overall direction of the association. Second is the ASEAN ministerial meeting, the next highest decision-making forum. Held annually, it covers various economic, diplomatic, social, and cultural matters. The third is the PMC that follow the ministerial meeting in which ASEAN foreign ministers meet with their dialogue partner counterparts. The primary function of the PMC is to make certain that both ASEAN members and their global partners avoid serious and unnecessary conflicts. Fourth, a senior officials meeting consisting of officials representing ASEAN foreign affairs ministries is held three or four times a year. Its purpose is to provide consistency in diplomatic, political, and strategic matters among the association's membership. The fifth instrument is an annual meeting of ASEAN economic ministers, wherein an array of economic matters is discussed. Sixth and lastly, senior economic officials meetings are held every three months. This is a working-level group that oversees all aspects of economic cooperation among the association's membership in the fields of trade, tourism, industrial development, mineral and energy, finance and banking, transportation and communications, and agriculture and marine resources.

Intra-ASEAN Trade Promotion

The institutional structure outlined above provides both ASEAN's broad policy aspect and the direct operational framework within which the association undertakes its various activities. Those activities are highlighted by trade promotion. Initially, ASEAN's effort to promote intraregional trade expansion was via a Preferential Trade Agreement (PTA) that proved to be a failure. It provided neither sufficiently deep tariff rate reductions nor sufficiently broad product coverage to yield more than minimal increases in trade among association members. In response to the PTA's unsatisfactory performance, governments of trade-oriented member states called for a full-scale free trade area within the region. The result of their effort was the AFTA/CEPT mechanism that was introduced at the Fourth ASEAN Summit, held in Singapore in 1992.

The aim of free trade proponents was to reduce and ultimately to eliminate tariffs among ASEAN members through the implementation of a two-track, tariff reduction process that added substantially deeper tariff rate cuts and covered a much broader range of products. According to the 1992 agreement, products with an existing tariff rate of 20% or less were put on a fast track toward tariff elimination. The goal of the fast track was to do away with tariffs on affected products in a decade, or by the year 2003. On a normal track, 1992 tariff rates exceeding 20% were to be reduced in three stages over a fifteen-year period culminating in zero tariff rates by the year 2008. The 1992 agreement was modified in 1994 in order to match and conform to the deeper and broader tariff reductions that were negotiated during the Uruguay Round of the General Agreement on Tariffs and Trade (GATT). The GATT tariff reductions were deeper than those called for in ASEAN's 1992 accord. Both the fast- and normal-track timetables were shortened so that items placed on the fast track were to reach zero tariffs by 2000 rather than 2003, and so that those assigned to normal track status were to be eliminated by 2003 rather than 2008.

The 1992 CEPT mechanism provided greater breadth of coverage than the PTA. It encompassed all manufactured items, processed agricultural products, and capital goods. ASEAN officials continue to explore the possibility of extending CEPT coverage to agriculture and services and eliminating nontariff barriers.

As ASEAN grew, it was faced with serious problems that were brought about because of substantial economic and political asymmetry within its membership. In order to deal with the gap in national income levels and market competitiveness, the association provides two exceptions to generalized CEPT coverage. First, the products of noncompetitive industries are put on a temporary exclusion list if such industries need more time to adjust to the microeconomic dislocation that trade can bring about. Second, a member nation can request that certain industries be placed on a sensitivity list in cases where a negative economic impact would be difficult to sustain. The exceptions are important variances to the fast- and normal-track mandates, but they are needed because ASEAN's membership includes higher-income economies such as Brunei and Singapore and middle-income countries such as Malaysia, Thailand, the Philippines, and Indonesia. Membership also included low-income countries including Cambodia, Laos, Myanmar (or Burma), and Vietnam. While lower-income, less competitive, and more sensitive economies need more time to adjust to the micro and macro impact of trade liberalization and openness, ultimately, they must adhere to the general principle of tariff elimination.

Investment Generation and Industrial Development

The generation of investment from both internal and external sources and the industrial development that accompanies it provides the platform from which exports, import substitutes, and nontraded goods are produced throughout Southeast Asia. ASEAN promotes investment and industrialization through three modules: ASEAN Industrial Project (AIP), ASEAN Industrial Complementation (AIC), and ASEAN Industrial Joint Venture.

AIP projects are large-scale enterprises, are located within a single country, are without forward or backward linkages to other project, and have extensive government involvement. There was initial enthusiasm about the AIP module, but it soon waned when it became clear that there were serious implementation problems. One problem had to do with conflicts among member states regarding the location of single-country projects. Additionally, the bureaucratic approval process was cumbersome, and there were conflicts among members over whether certain projects were financially feasible, as many would be large-scale enterprises requiring levels of investment so substantial that they exceeded funding capacities. Consequently, few ventures reached fruition after the 1980 Basic Agreement that created the AIP module. However, during the process of evaluating potential AIP projects, the process identified a number of enterprises that were successfully pursued outside the parameters of the AIP module.

The AIC module was a direct result of the limited success of the AIP approach, where large-scale, government-dominated ventures left little scope for private industry expertise in both project planning and implementation. The Basic Agreement that created

the AIC in 1981 corrected this oversight by involving private-sector personnel who were familiar with market conditions. They collaborated with their public-sector counterparts and became a primary source of ideas. Private-sector leaders helped to put together a system that involved forward and backward linkages among ASEAN producers wherein the stages of production leading to final products were located in different countries. However, the module did not suit all proposed projects because of complications inherent in approval processes and conflicts about where linked projects would be located. More importantly, the AIC did not contain an effort to draw investment capital from outside ASEAN.

ASEAN Industrial Joint Ventures are private sector projects. They operate in more than one country, are neither forward- nor backward-linked to other products, and involve external investment partners. Investors in AIJV projects can locate production facilities anywhere within ASEAN provided that at least two participating member countries are involved. Non-ASEAN financial partners can participate in AIJV projects provided that ASEAN equity participation is 51%.

An ASEAN Industrial Cooperation (AICO) scheme accompanies the three modules, but it differs from them in that firms operating under the scheme are not legal business entities but rather operate under umbrella associations. The AICO requires a minimum of two companies that are domiciled in at least two ASEAN member countries, and there must be at least 30% national equity participation in the business enterprises that operate under the scheme. The AICO provides participant companies opportunities to cooperate and coordinate their business activities, particularly in export promotion.

These modules and schemes are used by ASEAN to generate investments, develop industrial capacities, and expand exports directly. They enable the association to create a regional investment climate that draws other, nonparticipating investors from outside the region, as well encourage capital formation from sources within ASEAN. However, as more trade and investment involving ASEAN-based enterprises and outside entities take place, more opportunities for conflicts arise. Avoiding conflicts and settling disruptive disputes that threaten to deteriorate economic climates have become an important aspect of ASEAN's activities.

Dispute Settlement and Regional Security

The integration of ASEAN into global goods, services, and financial markets brings about an environment within which disputes and conflicts occasionally arise. In response to the threat that unresolved disputes pose to Southeast Asian interests, the association created the ASEAN Dialogue Partnership System (ADPS). The system links the association's membership to key global partners via an ongoing forum that seeks to settle disputes between ASEAN and external entities and, when possible, to prevent disputes from arising. ASEAN launched its dialogue program at its second summit in 1977. Its first linkage was with the United States. The association currently has partnerships with the European Union, Australia, New Zealand, Japan, and other countries important to the region, as well as with international institutions such as the United Nations Development Program (UNDP).

Subministerial dialogue meetings take place every year and a half, with a preparatory meeting prior to the higher-level gathering. The agenda includes both ASEAN's and its partner countries' views on key issues. In addition, some partner countries and ASEAN members have bilateral dispute settlement procedures in the form of joint management committees that oversee the operational details of the procedures. In some cases (such as in the United States and Singapore), bilateral free trade agreements have been negotiated as a direct result of broader ADPS relations.

In 1979, ASEAN initiated a companion feature to the ADPS in the form of a series of post-ministerial conferences (PMCs) that, at the conclusion of ASEAN's annual ministerial conference, bring together high-ranking officials with their ministerial counterparts in partner countries. In this way, at the very highest levels of government, the work of standing committees is supported at a high-level intergovernmental superstructure. The concept of high-level contact was extended to noneconomic issues when the association created the ASEAN Regional Forum (ARF) involving its membership, the countries with which it has ADPS agreements, and other important states, particularly China. The ARF is a nonformal process whereby political, strategic, and security disputes and issues are discussed among the forum's members. It compliments the ADPS and PMC arrangements by extending the scope of high-level discussions beyond economic and financial matters.

Evolving Issues

ASEAN's evolution into a ten-nation country group challenges the association's capacity to secure the three primary objectives contained in the Declaration.

The largest challenge is molding an organization that meets both the founding Declaration's objectives and the specific needs of member countries whose economies range from high income, competitive, and highly developed to very low income, noncompetitive, and persistently underdeveloped. In an effort to alleviate economic asymmetry, the association is working to eradicate poverty. The membership has agreed on principles contained in a recently signed Hanoi Declaration that moves ASEAN in new antipoverty directions, most importantly via concerted efforts to improve human resource bases within the region. In 1999, ASEAN labor ministers acknowledged the importance of improving human resource bases and agreed to exchange information about meeting human needs, providing appropriate intraregional training, offering work-study and on-the-job training opportunities, and discussing individual country experiences. Their aim was to close the development and competitiveness gaps found in Southeast Asia.

ASEAN pursues regional development in a number of other ways, including an attempt to involve the private sector in growth-enhancing economic activities, particularly in lower-income member countries. The association has also created fourteen ASEAN centers throughout the region. Since the Association's membership includes low-income countries, the centers focus on integrating official development assistance with other sources of capital and transfers of technology in order to enhance productivity in agriculture, energy, culture and tourism, and social and institutional development. The association seeks to involve itself in the internal economic development processes of member countries, but it is careful not to intrude into the internal political affairs of member states due to ASEAN's commitment to nonintervention and the protection of national sovereignty.

The growth in the number of member nations taxes the ASEAN commitment to nonintervention. The egregious domestic actions of sovereign states such as Myanmar (Burma) clash profoundly with ideals shared by almost all of the association's other member states and expressed in the Declaration. At present, the association is absolutely committed not to intervene into the internal affairs of any member state even when it conducts oppressive practices. But since a country such as contemporary Myanmar operates outside the framework of the acceptable standards governing human rights, as well as the concept of the civil state, at some time in the future, ASEAN might be compelled to take punitive action against a "rogue" member state. If this happens, ASEAN's actions will challenge the association's avowed commitment to nonintervention.

Other challenging issues face ASEAN. One has to do with finding ways to cope with the cross-border haze pollution stemming from agricultural burning; this may force ASEAN to intervene in members' domestic environmental policies. Another matter is the association's approach to subregional economic integration; currently, two subregions are evolving into "natural economic territories." One is a mature economic growth triangle that involves private sector enterprises in southern Malaysia, Singapore, and several offshore islands of Indonesia. The second is an emerging arrangement in the Mekong Basin subregion where the Mekong Basic Development initiative is attempting to bring about a functional subregion that includes parts of Thailand, Cambodia, Laos, and Vietnam. While governments assist the private sector by financing infrastructure improvements, ASEAN provides technical assistance.

ROBERT L. CURRY, JR.

See also ASEAN Free Trade Association; ASEAN Mekong Basin Development Cooperation (Mekong Group); Asia-Pacific Economic Cooperation (APEC); Asian Development Bank; Asian "Economic Miracle"; Asian Tigers; Southeast Asia: History and Economic Development; Trade Policies and Development

References and Further Reading

ASEAN Secretariat. *ASEAN Economics Co-operation, Transition, and Transformation.* Singapore: Institute of Southeast Asian Studies, 1997.

Chia, Siow Yue and Joseph L. H. Tan, eds. *ASEAN in WTO: Challenges and Responses.* Singapore: Institute of Southeast Asian Studies, 1996.

Cotton, James. "The 'Haze' over Southeast Asia: Challenging the ASEAN Mode of Regional Engagement." *Pacific Affairs* 72(3) (1999).

Curry, Robert L., Jr. "United States-ASEAN Economic Relations." In *United States-Third World Relations in the New World Order*, edited by A. P. Grammas and C. K. Bragg. New York: Nova Science Publishers, 1996.

DeRosa, Dean A. *Regional Trading Arrangements Among Developing Countries: The Asian Example.* Washington, DC: International Food Policy Research Institute, 1995.

Hill, Hal. *Regional Development in Southeast Asia: The Challenges of Sub-National Diversity.* Canberra: Australian National University Press, 1996.

Rao, Bhanoji. *ASEAN Economic Co-operation and the ASEAN Free Trade Area: A Primer.* Singapore: Institute for Policy Research, 1996.

Soesastro, Hadi., "ASEAN and APEC: Do Concentric Circles Work?" *The Pacific Review* 8(3) (1994).

Soesastro, Hadi. "ASEAN During the Crisis." In *Southeast Asia's Economic Crisis: Origins, Lessons, and the Way Forward*, edited by H. W. Arndt and Hal Hill. Singapore: Institute of Southeast Asian Studies, 1999.

Than, Mya, and Carolyn, Gates. *ASEAN Enlargement: Impacts and Implications.* Singapore: Institute of Southeast Asian Studies, 2001.

Than, Mya. *ASEAN Beyond the Regional Crisis: Challenges and Initiatives.* Singapore: Institute of Southeast Asian Studies, 2001.

Tongzon, Jose L. *The Economics of Southeast Asia: The Growth and Development of ASEAN Economies.* Cheltenham and Northampton: Edward Elgar Publishing Co., 1998.

ASWAN HIGH DAM AND DEVELOPMENT IN EGYPT

The Aswan High Dam on the southern Nile River in Egypt is one of the largest engineering projects of the modern era, and it also is a symbol of modernization in a country that was undergoing tremendous social changes in the mid-twentieth century. Construction of the dam involved balancing of complex international politics, as well as nationalist concerns for Egypt and preservation of archaeological sites, and has brought about some degree of control over the seasonal floods brought by the Nile and has made hydroelectric power available to a region that has benefitted from this. However, the damming of the Nile on the scale made possible by the Aswan High Dam has had unforeseen ecological ramifications as well.

Background

The Nile River is one of the longest rivers in the world, originating in Lake Victoria and flowing more than 6,600 km to the Mediterranean Sea. It has long been recognized as the source that allows life to flourish in the Egyptian desert, and the silt that it brought down to Egypt enriched the soil to permit the harvests necessary to support the population there. However, the flooding that brought the silt also ravaged the low-lying areas along the river. In the late nineteenth century, the first attempt was made to control the waters of the Nile with a dam at Aswan, in southern Egypt north of the border with Sudan. This was the first Aswan Dam, for which construction began in 1899 and was completed in 1902 by a British engineering firm. This first dam rose fifty-four meters above the level of the river and was 1,900 meters wide. The dam was originally built for flood control and was increased in size in 1907–1912 and 1929–1934. In 1960, it was upgraded to generate hydroelectric power.

The increasing population of Egypt in the mid-twentieth century, plus a desire to modernize the country after the embarrassment of defeat by the new state of Israel in its 1948 war of independence and a subsequent military coup in Egypt, led the new government to make grand plans that would enable the development of more land and provide electrical power for the growing population. However, the engineering expertise and financial resources for projects of the scale necessary were not available in Egypt, so cooperation with the developed nations would be required. This cooperation was jeopardized when military officers staged a coup and replaced the Egyptian government in the summer of 1952.

Planning for the Aswan High Dam

The Aswan High Dam was just one part of a massive effort to stimulate the Egyptian economy. Plans were made to industrialize the country, to replace the goods that Egypt had needed to import, and to continue producing the things Egypt could export. In addition, the growing population would require more food; instead of importing this, the dam would permit use of more land for farming. Only 3% of Egypt's land was cultivated before construction of the High Dam. For this reason, the dam was considered to be primarily an agricultural investment, not an industrial one, and land reclamation projects constituted a major part of economic planning. However, land reclamation (use of formerly desert areas made useful by irrigation) has proved to be a failure.

Financing of Major Economic Development Projects

In the early years of the Cold War, the United States and the Soviet Union both courted the nonaligned nations, of which Egypt was one. The Soviets had a particular interest in Egypt since it had seaports that could be used by the ships of the Soviet Black Sea fleet, which otherwise would have to return to their bases in the Black Sea and thereby could be kept away from the Mediterranean Sea by a simple blockade.

America's interest in Egypt was in part due to wanting to keep the Soviets from exercising too much influence there, but also to ensure that the Suez Canal stayed open and available for US use. The billions of dollars in aid that the United States had provided to western European nations had kept Soviet influence there at a minimum, and concerns over the nations that were developing made the idea of helping Egypt attractive as well.

To President Nasser of Egypt, the financial assistance proposed by the West brought about concerns of economic exploitation. While the United States and Great Britain had offered to provide a portion of the funding for the dam as a grant, a larger part of the financing was to be in the form of a loan from the World Bank. This would obligate Egypt to pay back the loan, with interest, to an institution that Nasser considered to be a part of the Western world. Additionally, Nasser was concerned that accepting US aid would encourage the US to push for Egyptian acceptance of Israel's existence.

The United States was at first eager to provide financing for the Aswan High Dam project, but when the military government of Egypt made a major purchase of weaponry from Czechoslovakia in 1955, violating a Western arms embargo on that Soviet ally, the United States withdrew its offer of support in July 1956, ostensibly because it did not believe that the Egyptian economy could support payment of the loan. In response, Egypt took control of the Suez Canal Company, a British–French corporation that operated the Suez Canal. Great Britain and France, along with Israel, made plans to attack Egypt to regain control of the canal and destroy the Egyptian military, thereby undermining the Egyptian government. The "Suez Crisis" of October 1956 resulted in the United States criticizing the British–French action, and the event drew attention away from another major military event, the Soviet invasion of Hungary, which occurred at the same time.

The involvement of Great Britain and Israel, two U.S. allies, in the attack on Egypt further alienated Egypt's President Nasser, and he turned to the Soviet Union, which had provided other funds for development in Egypt. Eventually, the Soviets obtained financing for the Aswan High Dam. Other projects financed by the USSR were a major expansion of the port of Alexandria and the construction of the Helwan Iron and Steel Complex near Aswan.

Construction of the Aswan High Dam

The location of the original dam at Aswan was chosen because the channel of the Nile in southern Egypt can be used as a reservoir. Further north, the terrain is flatter and less suitable for placement of a dam. The Aswan High Dam was located further south (but upriver) from the original dam, but its location meant that a portion of the reservoir would actually flood across the border in Sudan. While this did not interfere with the planning of the dam, an agreement was made with Sudan before the dam was actually built.

The placement of large modern dams is dictated by geography, and dams are usually located in areas where natural constrictions of a river can be blocked, thus creating a reservoir behind the dam. Modern dams are usually made of concrete anchored to the natural bedrock. However, the location chosen for the Aswan High Dam does not have solid bedrock, so another technique, the building of a "gravity dam," was used instead.

A gravity dam develops its holding power from the physical mass of the dam instead of through its material. Because bedrock did not exist in the location chosen for the dam, huge amounts of rock rubble were brought to the dam site and deposited on the river bottom. This construction technique is the reason that the dam is so thick (more than 1 km). However, a concrete dam, which could be made thinner, could not have been anchored properly.

The relatively porous nature of the construction material is the reason that approximately one-eighth of the water in the dam is lost to leakage.

Benefits from the Dam

The Aswan High Dam, even during its planning stages, was a symbol of the future of Egypt. Egypt now generates a surplus of electricity, which has permitted greater industrialization. But although electrical generation capability has been tremendously expanded by the dam, the electrical transmission infrastructure was unable to make full use of the power. In addition, seasonal variations in the height of Lake Nasser limit electrical production in the winter.

Cultivation of rice in Egypt has tripled, and annual production is stable because it does not depend directly on the natural flow of the Nile. Irrigation made possible by the steady supply of water has expanded the arable land in Egypt and has permitted farmers to use higher-yield crops such as different strains of corn and to grow rice in the Nile delta, where previously only wheat could be grown.

Negative Aspects of the Awsan High Dam

The planning of the Aswan High Dam generated early criticism over a concern that archaeological sites in the planned reservoir site would be flooded. This had happened with the first Aswan Dam, and in particular, the temples at Abu Simbel were at risk. These temples had been built by actually sculpting them (and their interiors) into the sandstone of the river channel. Between 1964 and 1968, an international effort to move the temples to higher ground disassembled the temples and actually cut away the rock from which they had been sculpted and moved both temples above the level that would be flooded. Other smaller sites were moved as well.

Although the dam was built in part to control the flooding of the northern, lower areas, this flooding provided silt to replenish the cultivated areas there. Once the dam began controlling this flooding, the quality of the soil began to be depleted, and now agriculture requires chemical fertilizer, adding to the cost and chemically polluting the runoff water. This pollution has endangered some aquatic species in the waters where the Nile flows into the Mediterranean Sea.

The silt that would have been carried to the lower reaches of the Nile is instead trapped behind the dam, reducing the capacity of the reservoir.

Economic Development in Egypt

The grand plans for economic development in Egypt that were made by the Nasser government did not lead to the success that had been predicted. Although the Soviet Union did provide financing and expertise for projects such as the improvements to the port at Alexandria, construction of the Aswan High Dam, and for land reclamation projects and land reclamation efforts, were seen as a failure by 1975. Continuing strife in the Middle East over Israel, including the 1967 and 1973 wars, has set back progress in development.

Ironically, the greatest progress for Egypt resulted from a political action, not industrial efforts. President Anwar Sadat's willingness to publicly accept the existence of Israel through the Camp David Accords in 1978 brought Egypt back into comfortable relations with the United States, although it would lead to Sadat's assassination by members of his own military in 1981.

In this century, Egypt's economy has shown little growth, largely because more than half the work force is in the government or service sector and not engaged in manufacturing or agriculture.

Thomas P. Dolan

See also Egypt; Nasser, Gamal Abdel; North Africa: History and Economic Development

References and Further Reading

Abdel-Fadil, Mahmoud. *Development, Income Distribution, and Social Change in Rural Egypt 1952–1970*. Cambridge: Cambridge University Press, 1975.

Burns, William J. *Economic Aid and American Policy toward Egypt 1955–1981*. Albany. NY: State University of New York Press, 1985.

Ikram, Khalid. *Egypt: Economic Management in a Period of Transition*. Baltimore, MD: The Johns Hopkins University Press, 1980.

Waterbury, John. *The Egypt of Nasser and Sadat*. Princeton, NJ: Princeton University Press, 1983.

AUNG SAN SUU KYI

One of the important political leaders of Myanmar/Burma in the modern period, Aung San Suu Kyi (1945–) is a champion of democracy and human rights in a country where the military has held sway for most of its postindependence history.

Aung San Suu Kyi is the daughter of Aung San, the national hero of Burma, who led the struggle for independence from British colonial rule and Japanese occupation and organized the Burmese national army into a fighting force. Suu Kyi was just two years old when Aung San was assassinated on July 19, 1947. Her mother, Daw Khin Kyi, served as Burma's ambassador to India in the 1960s.

Suu Kyi studied at Oxford and married an Englishman, Michael Aris, without ever giving up her Burmese citizenship. After many years in England, she returned to Burma in 1988 to look after her critically ill mother. This coincided with a turbulent period in Burmese politics with the resignation of Gen. Ne Win (in power since 1962 after staging a coup) in 1988. In September 1988, the State Law and Order Restoration Council (SLORC) came into being (rechristened State Peace and Development Council or SPDC in 1997).

Suu Kyi quickly became the center of a wide-based democratic movement, which included students and the general population. She addressed rallies and exhorted the people to unite for a future without a military government. She believed that the army should keep away from politics and that free and fair elections were the only way of deciding Burma's future.

Having cofounded the National League for Democracy, Suu Kyi and her followers pressed the government for early elections. When the elections were held on May 27, 1990, her party won a landslide victory, but SLORC annulled the election results. It claimed that these elections were meant to select some representative to a constitution-drafting body and not for a national assembly.

Suu Kyi was awarded the 1991 Nobel Prize for Peace. Suu Kyi has continued to ask her followers to be nonviolent, although thousands of Burmese have been arrested and many reportedly tortured

and killed. The NLD participated in the National Convention, which was convened in 1993 to draft a new constitution. It walked out when it became clear that the military would continue to play a dominant role in the new government.

The military rulers placed Suu Kyi under house arrest repeatedly (1989–1995, 2000–May 2002, and May 2003–). In late 2004, although many political prisoners were released, Suu Kyi continued to be incarcerated.

UDAI BHANU SINGH

See also Ethnic Conflicts: Southeast Asia; Military and Development; Myanmar; Southeast Asia: History and Economic Development; Southeast Asia: International Relations

References and Further Reading

Azicri, Max. *Cuba: Politics, Economics, and Society*. London: Pinter, 1988.

International Crisis Group. *Burma/Myanmar: How Strong is the Military Regime?* ICG Asia Report No.11, Bangkok/Brussels, December 21, 2000.

Lintner, Bertil. *Outrage: Burma's Struggle for Democracy*. Hong Kong: Review Publishing Co., 1989.

Maung Maung, U. *The 1988 Uprising in Burma*. New Haven, CT: Yale University Southeast Asia Studies, 1999.

Steinberg, David I. *Burma: Prospects for Political and Economic Reconstruction*. Cambridge, MA: World Peace Foundation, 1997.

AUTHORITARIANISM

The Term *Authoritarianism* and Its Historical Roots

The origin of the word *authoritarianism* comes from the Latin word *auctoritas*, meaning influence. In the past, the term was mainly used in a positive sense and was related to individuals with high authority and power. Later, the term was used for labeling the negative aspects of a given individual or the functioning of a given State. Terms like *tyrant* and *despot* were used primarily in ancient Greece. For European regimes, the application of the term *despotism* began during the second half of the eighteenth century and became a focal point of political theory. The application of the terms *Asian despotism* and *Oriental despotism* began later on, during the nineteenth and twentieth centuries. The term *absolutism* also represents the authority of the State, but it is used in a narrower sense and is related primarily to the monarchies. For the first time, the term was used in ancient Rome, but then it was not charged with negative connotation. During the Renaissance, it was used to characterize the untouchable, supreme power. The term absolute is used later on during the sixteenth and seventeenth centuries when discussing the meaning of absolute monarchy.

In the twentieth century, more modern terms like fascism, communism, and totalitarianism are used for indicating authoritative countries. Fascist, communist, or totalitarian are those countries in which authoritarianism is present in all spheres of political, economic, social, and cultural life. The government in such countries imposed total control. The term *dictatorship* originated in ancient Rome but was used in a different meaning. During the twentieth century, the term was actively used to indicate all forms of authoritarian administration lacking democratic values. Even if all the authoritarian and nondemocratic societies can be characterized as dictatorships, not every dictatorship is communist or fascist. There are four aspects of the authoritarianism:

1. Authoritarianism as a quality of the personality (for example, authoritarian personality);
2. Authoritarianism as a type of a leadership of a given group or organization (for example, authoritarian style of leadership);
3. Authoritarianism as a way of governmental administration (for example, authoritarian state); and
4. Authoritarianism as a theoretical concept (for example, the theory of authoritarianism).

Authoritarianism as a Way of Governmental Administration—The Authoritarian State

One of the most important aspects of the term authoritarianism is related to the way of administrating society as a whole—the ruling of a given state. When the way of administrating a given state is authoritarian, it is labeled as authoritarian, and those ruling it are called tyrants, despots, autocrats, dictators, and so on.

It is a well-established fact that from a political, historical, sociological, and philosophical point of view, there are numerous theoretical concepts trying to explain the origin, essence, and peculiarities of an authoritarian state. For example, the entire doctrine of Karl Marx can be presented as a theoretical outlook on how to establish an authoritarian state and how it should function. All authors who describe the

authoritarian leaders and the authoritarian countries, from sixteenth-century Italian political theoretician N. Machiavelli (*The Prince*) to the present critic of the authoritarian Communist State, K. Wittfogel (*Oriental Despotism*), can be regarded as theoreticians of authoritarianism. In literature and in everyday language, people often confuse the terms authoritarian state, totalitarian state, communist state, fascist state, and so on. In order to clear this confusion of terms, it might be useful to apply the thesis that every totalitarian (fascist, communist) state is authoritarian, but not every authoritarian state is totalitarian. For example, Pinochet's military dictatorship in Chile can be classified as authoritarian but not in any case as totalitarian, communist, or fascist. The totalitarian state spreads the authoritarian principle of administration in all spheres in society, that is, everything is under total governmental control—the economy, the financial system, the state administration, the social groups, the individuals, and so on. In authoritarian states, such control is enforced only on some spheres of social life, and in some cases, there might be a combination of both authoritarian and democratic principles of administration. The authoritarian state often is viewed as a state in transition. That means authoritarianism is considered to be a temporary mode of a state's administration. Thus, when we talk about a particular state that we have identified as authoritarian, we keep in mind that its form of administration is transitional. If, in the past, that state was of a fascist or a communist type, considering it at the present moment and defining it as authoritarian, it can sometimes be viewed in a positive light. On the contrary, if in the past a given state was democratic and at the present moment authoritarian tendencies prevail, such a state should be looked at in a negative light.

Varieties of Authoritarianism

Authoritarianism is extremely differentiated and is characterized by many varieties. Some authors view the borders of authoritarianism as diffusive with many varieties to it, so it is very difficult to define where, for example, authoritarianism ends and democracy begins. In literature, there is not a universally accepted classification of the authoritarian way of governmental administration, but there are varying criteria for differentiating types of authoritarianism. For example, depending on the level of control over the masses, authoritarianism can be differentiated as: *hard*, when there is a high level of control, and *soft*, when there is a slight liberalization of the social and political life. If a given state is in transition from authoritarian to democratic form of administration, we talk about *transforming* authoritarianism. Transforming authoritarianism is typical of the situation in Eastern European countries at the end of the twentieth century and the beginning of the twenty-first century. Its opposite is *stable* authoritarianism, evident when authoritarian rule cannot be completely transformed into democracy, and the result is a relatively stable combination between authoritarian and democratic type of government. This type of authoritarianism is typical of some countries in Central America and Africa. In terms of the method of establishment of authoritarianism in a given state, it can be *inherited* or *acquired*. The former variety exists when the rule is inherited, that is, passed from father to son, from one dynasty to another, and so forth. The latter is established under the influence of external or internal factors. Authoritarianism is generally associated with centralized economy, lack of private enterprise, and with a closed economy that in this case can be treated as authoritarianism of a *closed* type. However, there are authoritarian regimes, with established market economy, private initiative, capitalist means of production, and unlike the preceding type, they can be classified as *market* and *open*. Such were the authoritarian regimes in Spain, Chile, and to a certain extent in Greece, Uruguay, Brazil, and others.

Many criteria can be used for distinguishing between the different types of authoritarianism: *with respect to the form of state rule* (monarchy, communist, religious-fundamentalist); *with respect to economic prosperity* (Spain under Franco, Chile under Pinochet); *with respect to the local cultural model*, and so forth.

Authoritarianism, Totalitarianism, and Democracy

When analyzing authoritarianism as a method of state rule, we normally use the classical triad: totalitarianism, authoritarianism, and democracy. J.J. Linz makes the clearest differentiation between the components of this triad on the basis of pluralism, and his thesis has been dominant since 1975. There are three major differences among totalitarianism, authoritarianism, and democracy, namely:

A. *There is always a lack of pluralism in a totalitarian state*, that is, one political party with its own ideology *totally* controls the entire social, political, economic, and cultural life and allows no competition in any sphere. The absence of pluralism is essential for a totalitarian state, not the presence of just one individual (Stalin, Hitler), or a group of individuals (after Hruschov the USSR was temporarily ruled by a party triumvirate), who hold the authority. In a totalitarian state, the absence of pluralism is the foundation for the development of the totalitarian party, which, in turn, creates the "dictator" (an authoritarian individual) who then runs the state. It is the personal qualities of the dictator, however, that determine the stability and solidity of a totalitarian regime (USSR under Stalin), its longevity (China under Mao), its temporary successes (Germany under Hitler), or its collapse (USSR under Gorbachov). When the dictator's power is terminated (death, removal, and so forth), the totalitarian state does not cease to exist, because the totalitarian political party creates a new dictator. The totalitarian state ceases to exist only with the destruction of the single-party political system, that is, with the initiation of pluralism.

B. *There is always an authoritarian personality in the authoritarian regime*, (dictator, despot, tyrant) or a group of personalities with a distinct leader (junta), who takes over the power through elections or military coup. In this case, the dominance of a single party or its ideology is not decisive—in many events, there is political pluralism, free elections, and so on. The personal quality of the authoritarian individual, his/her charisma, and the attractiveness of the party's own ruling doctrine should comply with the basic needs and interests of the social elite and/or of the broad masses.

C. *The presence of pluralism in democracy is obligatory*. The contest between two or more political parties during free elections is the foundation of democracy; owing to this political model, democracy exists. Of course, we are not only discussing political pluralism (the presence of many parties in the political process) but also a pluralism of opinions, ideas, associations, and ownership. In democracy, the presence of a leader with a strong personality or a political party with attractive ideology is not so significant, although a democracy with a distinguished political leader may enjoy greater prosperity. Pre-term elections or the permanent change of parties in power do not show lack of democracy or social regression. If pluralism in a given state is eliminated in some way, it turns from a democratic state into an authoritarian or totalitarian one.

The Transition from Totalitarianism to Democracy

The transformation of authoritarianism into democracy is a complicated and controversial process. In scientific literature, there is no uniform opinion on how long such a process should take, whether the democratic tendencies can be slowed down, whether there will be a reversal of the very process into "hard" authoritarianism, and so forth. Some authors who analyze the transition from authoritarianism to democracy (J.J. Linz, Guillermo O'Donnel, Terry Karl) use different terms such as "immediate death," "hybrid system," "progression to democracy," "delegative democracy," and so on. Based on their beliefs, we can distinguish the following possibilities for the transformation of authoritarianism into democracy:

A. The new democracies may disillusion the people *and may rejuvenate the old authoritarian stereotypes*: In this case, the dream of the "strong hand" may lead an authoritarian person or a group of people to power; that may be followed by the so-called sudden death of democracy. The "sudden death*"* may occur in a peaceful manner or through a coup.

B. If "sudden death" (of democracy) does not occur, the undergoing democratic changes may be accompanied by *permanent disappointment* where democratic changes are only formal and do not comply with the demands of the public. Such a state, in which only a sparkle is needed to return to the authoritarian status quo, is referred to as a "postponed death."

C. *Uncertain transformation from authoritarianism to democracy*: There actually is a permanent tendency of uncertainty in the movement toward democracy that can be described as a permanent swinging of society from its pronounced strive for democracy to a situation of apathy and the will to return to authoritarianism. In such cases, the transformation swings between two extremes: "return to authoritarianism" and "progress toward democracy" (like in Thailand, Haiti, Nigeria, Haiti, and Belarus).

D. *Stable functioning of a hybrid system*: In the hybrid regime resulting from the transition from authoritarianism to democracy, there is a combination of elements of both authoritarianism and democracy. The democratic elements dominate in the economic sphere, while the authoritarian elements prevail in the political one in most cases. Very often the democratic elements are only used to fool the external world and to stabilize authoritarianism. In this event, the democratic tendencies are kept only due to external influence or internal resistance. As an example for semidemocratic, semiauthoritarian hybrid regimes, we can give some states from Central America and Africa.

E. *The establishment of a stable tendency of irreversibility of the democratic processes*: This form of transition from authoritarianism to democracy is characterized by the will and determination of the masses and the ruling elite, be they leftist or rightist, for democratic changes. The pace and cost of reforms do not matter, the direction toward democracy does. As an example, we can give most of the East European countries (Poland, Czech Rep., Hungary, Slovenia, Bulgaria, Romania, among others.)

The Nature of Authoritarianism in Developing Countries

Authoritarian regimes are unique in every country insofar as authoritarian leaders are unique, as are the conditions under which they rule. Regardless of sizable differences, authoritarian regimes in developing countries in the same region share common characteristics and it is for this reason precisely that we speak of Asian authoritarianism, African-type authoritarian rule or Latin American authoritarian rule. By the very nature of power, authoritarian political systems in developing countries can be defined as monarchies, pluralistic, dictatorships, military juntas, to name but a few. The common traits relate to individual aspects of governance. So, for instance, some may employ genocide and political violence to attain power, but others may gain power leverage by legitimate means; some retain their grip on power by sheer eloquence and charisma; others rely on efforts to ensure economic prosperity. Thus, in order to claim domestic legitimacy an unpopular regime may draw overwhelmingly on nationalist ideology. The majority of authoritarian regimes in Asia, Africa, and Latin America justify their existence before the nation by the need for national liberation and revival. At the same time, internationally they explain their unpopular policy actions with the desire to preserve ethnic peace and to prevent civil strife. A number of authoritarian regimes such as those in South Korea, Chile, China, Vietnam, and elsewhere use the economic prosperity of their countries as a tool to legitimize their undemocratic rule.

Authoritarian rule in South America emerged in the complex post-World War II era exemplified by economic surges and declines, political coups, and transitory democratic outbursts. In the 1950s and 1960s, the wave of popular movements contributed to the fall of military dictatorships, including those of Batista in Cuba, Perón in Argentina, Rojas Pinilla in Colombia, Perez Jimenez in Venezuela, and Trujillo in the Dominican Republic. Consequently, authoritarian regimes surfaced in a number of Latin American countries and served as a barrier to the entry of leftist radicals. Later, the 1980s ushered in a period of economic and political stability, and these regimes receded to be replaced by pluralist political systems. This happened in Brazil at the elections in 1982, in Uruguay in 1980 and 1982, and in Chile after 1987, among others. Compared with Asia and Africa, Latin American authoritarianism is very vivid and emotionally colored. It is no coincidence that authoritarianism found its most dramatic personification in Juan Perón, Augusto Pinochet, and Fidel Castro. Perón solidified his authoritarian regime in 1946 and proved himself as a politician of note by creating an ideological faction, institutionalized in a political party and in women's, youth, and professional organizations. The military coup engineered by Pinochet in September 1973 came in response to the threat of his country following in the footsteps of Cuba. The tough military dictatorship he initially established transformed into an authoritarian regime that found legitimacy on the domestic front in significant economic successes. Castro built his mythical image by virtue of his charisma, eloquence, and populist slogans, whereas his authoritarian regime prospered into the early 1990s, thanks to the economic and political propping of the former Soviet Union.

In the early twenty-first century, most of the Latin American countries, such as Chile, Mexico, Argentina, Brazil, and others became prosperous economies, which is a robust guarantee that authoritarian rule has become a thing of the past.

Authoritarian rule flourished in Africa after the collapse of colonialism that began in the early 1950s. In the course of some forty-five years, the African continent was dominated by political chaos exemplified by civil war, clan warfare, military coups, genocide, and ethnic cleansing. In the aftermath of all this, some eighty unconstitutional changes of government were effected. In the 1960s alone, a total of twenty-five presidents and prime ministers fell victim to political violence. The mechanisms employed to impose an authoritarian regime usually fit the same model: a group of military men or armed mercenaries oust the incumbent government in the name of freedom and establish a military regime, after which they found their own political party and establish a partisan dictatorship. African authoritarianism is manifest in a variety of forms: from extreme left extremism to rightist dictatorships. Such, for instance, was the authoritarian regime in Ghana in the early 1960s and Ethiopia in the 1970s and 1980s, all a variety of leftist totalitarianism. Akin to these are the regimes in Mali and Togo, surviving from the late 1960s well into the 1990s, the Cameroon regime that existed in the 1970s and 1980s. African authoritarian leaders usually worship their own person and grant precedence to the party or junta they represent, a case in point being the long-time President of Zaire, Mobutu Sese Seko. Their rule is rooted in administrative centralism and authoritarian power permeated by traditionalism and ethnicity that determine the singular objective pursued by the potentate—personal gain and the enrichment of cronies. In an environment defined by political instability, corruption, absence of popular discontent, and ethnic strife, there were thirty-eight authoritarian political regimes in Tropical Africa in the late 1980s. In the early 1990s, Africa witnessed the beginnings of democratic change, and by the turn of the century, a wealth of multiparty elections had been held in forty-five countries. The end of the Cold War gave a significant boost to this development—it became possible for foreign investors to pressure African governments to liberalize the economy. At the beginning of the twenty-first century, Africa can be most fittingly described by the word "change" associated with two basic notions: abolition of authoritarian single-party systems (including the horrible apartheid system in South Africa) and getting on course to a free market economy.

KRUM KRUMOV

See also Dictatorships; Elections; Totalitarianism

References and Further Reading

Diamond, L., Linz, J. and Lipset, S. M., eds. *Democracy in Developing Countries*. Vol. 4. Boulder, CO: Reinner, 1990.

Eckhardt, W. "Authoritarianism." *Political Psychology* 12, 97–124, (1991).

Han, J., and Ling, L. H. M. "Authoritarianism in the Hypermasculinized State: Hybridity, Patriarchy, and Capitalism in Korea." *International Studies Quarterly* 42(1): 23–53 (March 1998).

Karl, T. L., and Schmitter, P. C. "Modes of Transition in Latin America and Southern and Eastern Europe." *International Social Science Journal* 128, 269–284 (1991).

Kemmelmeier, M., Burnstein, E., Krumov, K., Genkova, P., Kanagawa, C., Hirshberg, M., Erb, H., Wieczorkowska, G., and Noels, K. "Individualism, Collectivism, and

Authoritarianism in Seven societies." *Journal of Cross-Cultural Psychology* 34(7): 304–322 (2003).

Kubicek, P. "Authoritarianism in Central Asia: Curse or Cure?" *Third World Quarterly*, Vol. 19, Issue 1, 15–29 (March 1998).

Linz, J. J. "Totalitarian and Authoritarian Regimes." F. I. Greenstein and N. W. Polsby, eds. In *Handbook of Political Science: Macropolitical Theory*, edited by F. I. Greenstein and N. W. Polsby, 175–411, Vol. 3. Reading, MA: Addison-Wesley, 1975.

Linz, J. J., and Stepan, A. *Problems on Democratic Transition and Consolidation. Southern Europe, Latin America, and Post-Communist Europe*. Baltimore, MD: The John Hopkins University Press, 1996.

McFarland S. G., Ageyev V.S., and Abalakina-Paap, M. A. "Authoritarianism in the Former Soviet Union." *Journal of Personality and Social Psychology* 63(6): 1004–1010 (1992).

O'Donnell, G. "Delegative Democracy." *Journal of Democracy* 5(1): 55–69 (1994).

AWAMI LEAGUE

The Awami League played a leading role in the creation of Bangladesh (formerly East Bengal). It is one of the oldest and most significant political parties in Bangladesh. The origins of the Awami League can be traced to Maulana Adbul Hamid Khan Bhashani, who founded the Awami Muslim League at a convention of workers in Narayanganj, East Bengal, on June 23, 1949. The word "Muslim" was dropped in 1955 to make the party sound more secular. Throughout its long history, the Awami League drew its base of support from the working class of East Bengal—workers, peasants and students.

The rise of the Awami Muslim League is owed to the decline of the Muslim League in East Bengal as frustrated and disenfranchised younger members of the Muslim League sought to break away and establish a democratic state. The Awami Muslim League outmaneuvered the larger Muslim League to become the main opposition party in East Bengal. Building its platform on opposition to Pakistan's intensive policy of cultural assimilation in East Bengal, the Awami Muslim League adopted a wide-ranging platform emphasizing provincial autonomy, recognition of Bangla as a state language of Pakistan, democracy, a parliamentary system of government, and a welfare-oriented economy. The Awami League became the first opposition party in Pakistan in 1954 when it formed a coalition with other opposition parties to unseat the ruling Muslim League.

Starting in the late 1950s, the Awami League was at the forefront of the Bengali autonomy movement. During the rule of General Ayub (1958–1969), the Awami League established its credentials of Bengali interests through its introduction of the Six-Point

Program of the Awami League in 1966. *The Six-Point Program* called for a federal parliamentary system with universal adult franchise, all powers in the federating units except foreign relations and defense, separate currencies for East and West Pakistan, the right of federating units to levy taxes and duties, the right of federating units to negotiate trade and commerce with foreign countries, and the establishment of militia forces for self-defense.

In 1970, the Awami League won 160 out of the 162 allotted territorial seats in East Pakistan's central legislature. They then won 288 out of 300 seats in East Pakistan's Provincial Assembly. As a consequence of their overwhelming victories, the Awami League emerged as the majority party in the Pakistan National Assembly. Instead of allowing the Awami League to form a government, the military intervened—shooting unarmed Bengali protesters in Dhaka and other cities in East Pakistan. The Awami League responded by calling for a noncooperation movement in East Pakistan from March 2, 1971, onward. This led to a short war of liberation. A government-in-exile was formed by leaders of the Awami League until December 16, 1971, when Pakistan ceded Bangladesh's independence.

Following Bangladesh's independence, the Awami League helped frame the Bangladesh constitution in 1992 and then hold Bangladesh's first-ever general elections. Even though the Awami League won a comprehensive victory in the 1973 elections, this did not prevent the abolition of the Awami League in January 1975 through the declaration of a state of emergency and the formation of the Krishak Shamik Awami League (BAKSAL).

KEITH A. LEITICH

See also Bangladesh

References and Further Reading

Chowdhury, Ghulam Akbar. *Politics in Bangladesh and the Role of Awami League*. Calcutta: Ratna Prakashan, 1999.

Miah, M. Maniruzzaman (Mohammad Maniruzzaman). *Five Years of Awami rule*. Dhaka: Gatidhara, 2001.

Mohĭaimena, Moh. ĬAbadula. *Awami League in the Politics of Bangladesh*. Dhaka: Pioneer Publications, 1990.

Nair, M. Bhaskaran. *Politics in Bangladesh: A Study of the Awami League, 1949–1958*, New Dehli: Northern Book Centre, 1990.

AYUB KHAN, MUHAMMAD

Muhammad Ayub Khan (1907–1969), military leader and president (1958–1969) of Pakistan, was born on May 14, 1907, in the Hazara Division village of

Rehana, near Hripur. His father, Mir Dad Khan, was a Risaldar Major in Hodson's Horse. Ayub Khan first joined a school in Sarai Saleh, which was four miles away from Rehana, and later he was transferred to a school in Haripur. In 1922, Ayub passed the matriculation examination and was sent to Alighar University for higher education. In 1926, before taking the B.A. examination, he was selected for the Royal Military College in Sandhurst and sailed for England. Ayub's performance in Sandhust was excellent, earning him several awards and scholarships. He was commissioned in the British Indian army in 1928 and saw active service as a battalion commander, first as a major and then as colonel during World War II.

After the creation of Pakistan on August 14, 1947, Ayub Khan was brigadier, the most senior Muslim officer in British India, and assigned to assist General Pete Rees in the Punjab Boundary Force. In January 1948, Ayub was posted as general commanding officer of the 14th Division in East Bengal (East Pakistan, now called Bangladesh). In 1950, he was posted as adjutant-general in the GHQ at Rawalpindi. In 1951, he was appointed as the first commander in chief of the Pakistan Army, and within a short time, he had created and organized an effective army on professional lines. He was inducted into the federal cabinet led by Muhammad Ali Bogra and served as Defense Minister between 1954 and 1956. As commander-in-chief and defense minister, Ayub Khan played a vital role in joining the United States-sponsored military alliances SEATO and CENTO in 1954–1955. On October 7, 1958, President Iskander Mirza, with the help of Ayub Khan, enforced the first Martial Law in Pakistan and designated Ayub Khan as the chief martial law administrator. However, Ayub Khan snatched away all the powers of Iskander Mirza, imposed martial law on October 27, 1958, and assumed charge as the president of Pakistan, in addition to his role as chief martial law administrator. In 1959, Ayub government signed a bilateral defense agreement of cooperation with the United States, and in this way, Pakistan was regarded as the United States' most allied ally in Asia. Ayub's military coup abrogated the constitution, dismissed the cabinet, banned the political parties, canceled the election scheduled, and usurped the office of president. However, his military takeover was welcomed by most of the people in Pakistan because they were sick and tired of the political instability in the country. He crushed corruption and took steps to overcome several social problems of the country, and all these steps enhanced his popularity among the masses.

In 1961, Ayub Khan appointed a constitutional commission headed by Justice Shahabuddin. The commission presented a report on May 6, 1961.

After examination, it was given the shape of a constitution. On June 8, 1962, the new constitution was introduced. It declared Pakistan as an Islamic republic but with a presidential form of government and basic democratic principles. The president's powers, however, were great and included the ability to override decisions made by parliament. Bengali and Urdu were declared official languages, and the country was divided into two provinces: East Pakistan (now Bangladesh) and West Pakistan (now the entirety of Pakistan).

Ayub Khan remained president under the new setup, and martial law was lifted from Pakistan. Presidential elections were held in 1965, and a combined opposition party nominated Fatima Jinnah (sister of Mohammad Ali Jinnah, the founder of Pakistan) as their candidate in the election, but Ayub Khan managed to sweep the polls. After the election, he inaugurated a system of "basic democracies," tiers of local government councils that also served as electoral colleges.

In 1963, Ayub Khan's government signed the historic Boundary Agreement with China that demarcated the northern border between Pakistan and China. This period was known as the Green Revolution, marked by industrialization and modernization. Pakistan enjoyed about three decades of unprecedented growth, at around 5.6%. Ayub Khan's policies encouraged the private sector, leading to medium- and small-scale industries being established in Pakistan. In his time, Pakistan was a model of development for the emerging nation-states for its rapid economic growth. He launched vigorous reforms such as education, administrative communication, labor, banking, and agricultural and energy reforms. He was the first Pakistani ruler who attempted to bring in land reforms, but the idea was not implemented properly. Ayub Khan also initiated family laws and changed the capital from Karachi to Islamabad in 1962. In 1965, Ayub led the nation in a war with India, and the conflict was ended by the Tashkent Declaration in 1966. The war ended in the rapid decline of the country's economy. All opposition parties criticized Ayub Khan's role during the Tashkent Declaration in 1966 and considered that he had converted a victory on the battlefield to a defeat at the negotiation table.

Ayub's right-hand man, Zulfiqar Ali Bhutto, turned against him and inaugurated a party, the Pakistan People's Party, with the aim of removing him from power. The Awami League under Sheikh Mujeeb-ur-Rahman started challenging his rule as pro-West Pakistan and claimed that his policies had snatched away the rights of Bengalis. The political parties formed an alliance, the Democratic Action

Committee, for removal of Ayub Khan's government. Thus, continuing economic and social inequalities, concentration of power, restriction on press, imposition of a state of emergency, corruption, and ban on civil liberties resulted in chronic political instability in Pakistan, alienated the representative elites, denuded the government institutions of legitimacy, and led to periodic outbreaks of violence to overthrow the government. By the end of 1968, the public resentment against Ayub's regime was at its peak when all classes turned against him, including students, teachers, lawyers, doctors, labor, and engineers. Law and order broke down, and Ayub was left with no other option but to step down. Early in 1969, Ayub Khan announced that he would not seek reelection in 1970, but unrest continued, and on March 25, 1969, he resigned and handed over power to the commander in chief of the Pakistan Army, General Muhammad Yahya Khan, instead of speaker of national assembly.

HUSAIN KASSIM

See also Indian–Pakistani Wars; Pakistan

References and Further Reading

Altaf Gauhar. *Ayub Khan: Pakistan's First Military Ruler.* New York: Oxford University Press, 1996.
Feldman, Herbert. *From Crisis to Crisis: Pakistan 1962–1969.* London: Oxford University Press, 1972.
General Mohammad Musa. *My Version, India-Pakistan War 1965.* Lahore: Wajidalis, 1983.
Hassan, Gardezi, and Jamil Rashid, eds. *Pakistan: The Roots of Dictatorship.* London: Zed Press, 1983.
Mohammad Ayub Khan. *Friends Not Masters: A Political Autobiography.* London: Oxford University Press, 1967.
Ziring, Lawrence. *The Ayub Khan Era: Politics in Pakistan 1958–1969.* New York: Syracuse University Press, 1971.
Ziring, Lawrence. *Pakistan in the Twentieth Century: A Political History.* Karachi: Oxford University Press, 1997.

AZERBAIJAN

Azerbaijan is a part of the geographic region situated on the southern side of the Caucasus Mountains, which stretch from the Black Sea to the Caspian Sea, marking the divide between Europe and Asia. Throughout its history, the country has been the arena of the clashing influences of neighboring empires, Iran and Turkey, and later of Russia, which conquered the South Caucasus in the early nineteenth century. Of the three South Caucasian states of the present day, Azerbaijan is larger than Georgia and Armenia, in population and territory.

The country occupies an area of 86,600 sq. km, roughly equal to the size of Portugal. On the north, Azerbaijan is bordered by the Russian Federation,

while on its northwestern and western borders sit Georgia and Armenia. To the south, Azerbaijan shares a border with Iran. The small autonomous unit of Nakhichevan (approximately 5,500 sq. km) is geographically separated from the rest of Azerbaijan by a strip of Armenian territory, Zangezur. Another autonomous area is Nagorno (Mountainous) Karabagh, covering 4,403 sq. km and populated predominantly by Armenians.

Nearly half of Azerbaijan's territory is covered by mountains. About a fifth of the land is cultivated, and agriculture has always been the largest source of employment. A special feature of Azerbaijan's geographic setting, not shared by either Georgia or Armenia, is the Caspian Sea, the world's largest inland body of water and approximately the size of California. Serving for centuries as the main transportation link between the regions of southern Russia, Iran, and Central Asia, the Caspian Sea stimulated trade along its coastlines. The greatest of the mediaeval trading routes, the Silk Road, linking China with Europe, passed along the southern Caspian coast. This sea provides the habitat to most of the world's sturgeon and is the supplier of black caviar. Above all, the Caspian, off the shores of Azerbaijan and Kazakhstan, is a source of hydrocarbons. The population of Azerbaijan consists, overwhelmingly, of Turkic-speaking Azeris, some 90% of the total of 7.7 million. By religious background, they are predominantly Shi'ite Muslims, with a Sunni minority.

As in many non-European regions of the former USSR, Azerbaijan's population is young, with one-third younger than fourteen years of age. The growth rate has been slowing in the post-Soviet period, falling from 20.2 to 10.1 per 1,000 in 1996. The latter figure reflects not only a declining birth rate but also emigration from the republic. Likewise, life expectancy is down from 70.9 years in 1960 to 63.08 in 1999, a combined effect of the Karabagh conflict and of deteriorating health services. The urban population amounts to 54%. Apart from Baku, with its nearly 2 million inhabitants, other large cities are Ganja (300,000), Sumgait (270,000), Mingachaur (97,000), and Ali Bayramli (70,000).

Of all the changes that came to Azerbaijan under the two centuries of rule by Russia, the most imposing has been the rise of Baku, the largest city of the country, situated on the Apsheron Peninsula. Almost a quarter of Azerbaijan's inhabitants and about half of its urban population live in this metropolitan area. In the second half of the nineteenth century, Baku turned into a quintessential boom city with the highest rate of population growth in the Russian Empire. In 1918, Baku became the capital of the independent republic of Azerbaijan, which lasted until April 28,

1920, when the city was seized by the Red Army. During the Soviet period, the Caspian oil fueled the Soviet Union's five-year plan of the 1930s, as well as the defense effort in World War II. In the postwar years, despite the decline of Azerbaijan's oil industry, Baku maintained the momentum of its urban growth. In the closing years of the Soviet regime, the city was the birthplace of the Peoples Front of Azerbaijan, the focal point of the general strike (September 1989), and the scene of bloody riots against the Armenian residents, the January Days of 1990. The issue of Nagorno-Karabagh became the axis of the political life for Azerbaijan. The reverses suffered by the Azeri forces led to the downfall of the ex-Communist regime of Ayaz Mutalibov in 1992, and his replacement by the first democratically elected president of the republic, Abulfaz Elchibey, who was overthrown the next year by a military coup. The power returned to the former Communist leader Haidar Aliyev. His rule, which lasted until 2003, was marked by a hard-handed internal policy, although it was tolerant of the opposition parties. They could participate in elections that were invariably described as fraudulent. In the economic sphere, the Aliyev regime confirmed the onset of the second oil boom by the conclusion in 1994 of the "Contract of the Century" for exports to Western markets. The crucial problem of transportation would be solved by constructing the pipeline from Baku to Turkey's Mediterranean port of Ceyhan. Baku, the major Caspian region's trade center also is becoming the main hub for the transportation corridor known as the New Silk Road between the Far East and Europe.

The Karabagh fighting was stopped with the cease-fire agreement of 1994, although a peace treaty was never reached. The most painful effect of the conflict, the refugee problem, has remained unsolved. Approximately one in ten of the inhabitants of Azerbaijan is a refugee or a displaced person. They are the poorest group in the country, suffering from an unemployment rate of nearly 80%. Their presence in various areas has created a range of local difficulties, especially with regard to the employment condition, education systems, and health services. The government provides only limited assistance to the refugees, who rely on donations from foreign countries and aid from international organizations. The volume of this assistance has been diminishing, due to what is termed "donor fatigue." Although there is no vision of how to deal with the problem of the refugees, it is generally assumed that their number is too large to be absorbed by the Azerbaijani society. Most of them express the wish to return home as soon as peace is achieved. Typically, for the oil-producing countries, this natural wealth does not create jobs when the abundance of cash leads to the decline of native industries, which are unable to compete with foreign products.

With the new oil boom, Azerbaijan has experienced massive labor migration, consisting largely of refugees and peasants. Most of these migrants moved to Russia, mainly to Moscow, others to Turkey and Iran. The estimates of Azeri immigrants, many of them temporary residents in Russia, reach more than one million, and their remittances exceed the oil income. Thus, despite the pro-Western foreign policy orientation, the links with Russia have grown stronger.

TADEUSZ SWIETOCHOWSKI

See also Commonwealth of Independent States: History and Economic Development; Commonwealth of Independent States: International Relations; Ethnic Conflicts: Commonwealth of Independent States

References and Further Reading

Altstadt, Audrey. *The Azerbaijani Turks: Power and Identity Under Russian Rule*. Azerbaijan: Hoover Institution Press, 1992.

De Waal, Thomas. *Black Garden: Armenia and Azerbaijan through Peace and War*. New York: New York University Press, 2003.

Goltz, Thomas. *Azerbaijan Diary*. Armonk, NY: M.E. Sharpe, 2000.

Guliev, Rasul. *Oil and Politics. New Relationships Among the Oil–Producing States: Azerbaijan, Russia, Kazakhstan, and the West*. New York: Liberty Publishing House, 1999.

Heradstveit, Daniel. *Democracy and Oil: The Case of Azerbaijan*. Wiesbaden: Reichert, 2001.

Iunusov, Arif. "Refugee Factor in Azerbaijan." In *Forum on Early Warning and Early Response*. London: 1999.

Raczka, Witt. "A Sea or a Lake? The Caspian's Long Odyssey." *Central Asian Survey* Vol. 1, 189–218 (2000).

Shaffer, B. *Borders and Brethen: Iran and the Challenge of Azerbaijani Identity*. Cambridge: Massachusetts Institute of Technology Press, 2002.

Swietochowski, Tadeusz. *Russia and Azerbaijan: Borderland in Transition*. New York: Columbia University Press, 1995.

Van der Leew, Ch. *Azerbaijan: A Quest for Identity: A Short History*. New York: St. Martin's Press, 2000.

AZIKIWE, BENJAMIN NNAMDI

First President of the independent Nigeria, proclaimed "Nigerian of the Century" and often compared with such African leaders as his disciple Kwame Nkrumah and Nelson Mandela, Benjamin Nnamdi Azikiwe (1904–1996) was a master politician, unparalleled orator, poet, statesman, and politician.

Benjamin Nnamdi Azikiwe was born on November 16, 1904, in Zunguru, Northern Nigeria, to Onitsha

Ibo parents but later lived with his grandparents in Onitsha. Azikiwe Jr. denied using his anglicized first name after his father was fired by the British administration.

After finishing studies at the Wesleyan Boys High School in Lagos, he attended the Hope Waddell Training Institute in Calabar, where he was captivated by the writings of Marcus Garvey and W. E. B. DuBois, which shaped his vision. In 1925, at the age of twenty-one, Azikiwe enrolled at Storer College, Harpers Ferry, W. Va., where he acquired the largely known nickname "Zik." Struggling with poverty and racial prejudices of earlier twentieth-century America and homesick for Africa, Azikiwe completed his B.A. degree in political science at Lincoln University (1927), later completed his M.A., obtained a certificate in journalism from Columbia University, and finally, in 1934, he earned a M.Sc. with honors in anthropology from the University of Pennsylvania. Invited by Professor Bronislaw Malinowski to start doctoral studies at the University of London, he declined and returned to Africa.

Initially, with a journalistic job in Accra, he ultimately returned back to Nigeria in 1937. In his early thirties, he contributed to the nationalist movement while working in journalism, commerce, and politics. In 1945, he led a general strike and soon after was elected president of the National Council for Nigeria and the Cameroons, a political party reuniting pro-independence groups that emerged during World War II.

After a long period in opposition in the Western House of Assembly, in 1954–1959, Azikiwe became the first prime minister of Eastern Nigeria, one of the then colony's three regions. During his term, adult suffrage, a wide program of economic and social development, and administrative reorganization were introduced. His coalition won the 1959 elections, and, in 1960, he was appointed to the honorary office of governor-general. In 1963, he became the first president of the Republic of Nigeria, serving until deposed by a military coup in 1966. He worked abroad for Biafran secession but advocated reunification when the revolt faded. After returning to Nigeria in 1972, he became chancellor of Lagos University. He ran unsuccessfully for president in 1979 and 1983.

Zik retired back to his home at Nsukka, where he founded the University of Nigeria and lived in peace until his death on May 11, 1996. He was survived by his second wife, Dr. Uche Azikiwe, an esteemed educator.

STEPHAN E. NIKOLOV

See also Biafra: Ethnic Conflicts: West Africa; Nigeria; Pan-Africanism; West Africa: History and Economic Development; West Africa: International Relations

References and Further Reading

Blitz, L. Franklin, ed. *The Politics and Administration of Nigerian Government*. New York: Praeger, 1965.

Coleman, James S. *Nigeria, Background to Nationalism*. Berkeley, CA: University of California Press, 1963.

Ikeotonye, V. C. *Zik of New Africa*. Biography of Dr. Nnamdi Azikiwe. London: Macmillan, 1961.

Jones-Quartey, K. A. B. *A Life of Azikiwe*. Middlesex: Penguin, 1965.

Ojiako, James O. *First Four Years of Nigeria Executive Presidency. Success or Failure*. Apapa: Daily Times. 1983.

B

BA'ATH PARTY

Originally founded in 1942 as the Arab Revival Movement (*Harakat al-Ihyatu al-Arabi*) by two Syrian teachers, Michel Aflaq and Salah Bitar, in 1953, it joined with Akram Hawrani's (Syrian) Socialist Party and became known as the Arab Socialist Ba'ath Party (*Hizb al-Ba'th al-'Arabi al-Ishtiraki*). The Constitution of the party, first articulated in 1947, outlined its ideological foundations: a commitment to a unified Arab nation; a socialist economic system to allow for the state to distribute the national wealth as equitably as possible; sovereignty of the people; and a revolutionary, rather than evolutionary, means of achieving these ends. The party is very much a secular Arab nationalist movement, given the Constitutional references to the sovereignty of the people and the respect for freedom of belief, as well as the fact that Aflaq was himself an Orthodox Christian. The main tenets of the Ba'athist philosophy are summed up in its slogan of "unity, freedom, and socialism" (*wahda, hurriya, wa ishtirakiyya*). Freedom in the Ba'athist context means political and economic freedom from Western colonialism.

The Ba'ath Party's pan-Arab outlook was matched by action in its early years and, by the mid-1950s, the party was established with branches in most Arab states. The basic element of the party structure within each country was the cell (*khalwah*), which contributed members to the regional (*qutri*) congress in each country, which then sent representatives to the pan-Arab (*qawmi*) congress, which, in turn, elected the party's pan-Arab leadership executive. The party emerged in Jordan under the leadership of Abdullah al-Rimawi, and was a strong element of the parliamentary opposition following the 1956 elections. Its influence waned following al-Rimawi's 1959 expulsion from the party and the 1967 Arab defeat. In Lebanon the party was established in 1949. Although it operated openly without government approval until 1958, the pro-Syrian branch of the party has enjoyed a degree of political success since the emergence of Syrian hegemony in Lebanon. North and South Yemeni branches of the party were active from the mid-1950s until their abolition or absorption in the mid-1970s.

It was in both Syria and Iraq, however, that the party was strongest and could entertain notions of governing. In Iraq the party first took power in February 1963, following a crisis brought about after a general students' strike that resulted in the demise of the Qasim government. The Ba'ath-dominated government only lasted nine months, however, before the non-Ba'athist president, 'Abd as-Salam 'Arif, ousted the party in a coup. The Ba'athists regained control by another coup in June 1968. In Syria, the party came to power following the coup of March 1963, in which it participated in a National Council of the Revolutionary Command prior to its members dominating the government. In October 1970, Hafiz Assad overthrew President Salah Jadid in a bloodless coup and was subsequently elected president in a national plebiscite.

The Ba'ath Party's attempts at fulfilling both the pan-Arab and revolutionary socialist elements of its Constitution have been marked by the triumph of rhetoric over any coherent political program to institute its ideology. For much of the party's early existence, Egypt's President Gamal Abdel Nasser, who viewed himself as the leader of Arab nationalism, and Egypt as the vanguard of the Arab nationalist movement, overshadowed the Ba'ath's pan-Arab stance. This was illustrated during the 1958 union between Syria and Egypt that created the United Arab Republic (UAR), which saw the dissolution of all Syrian political parties (including the Ba'ath), although this was reversed upon the dissolution of the UAR in 1961. The high point of Ba'athist pan-Arabism occurred in 1963 when there were talks held regarding the unification of Syria and Iraq, following the Ba'ath's accession to power in Syria in 1963. This was the last time that the Ba'ath Party made any type of move toward formal Arab unification. Indeed, the Ba'ath Party itself has not been able to maintain its own unity, and it has split on a number of occasions, largely over ideological issues. The most significant break came in 1966 when Michel Aflaq took a splinter group of Ba'athists to Lebanon, before moving to Iraq following the Ba'athist coup there in 1968. This split in the party was reflected in relations between the Iraqi and Syrian Ba'athists, each of whom saw themselves as the leaders of the Arab nationalist movement that the Ba'ath Party claimed to represent.

Revolutionary socialism in the economic sphere has also been mixed under Ba'athist rule. There were some attempts at land reform in both Iraq and Syria, although much of the land that was appropriated from the large landowners or belonged to the state has been given to clients of the two regimes. There has been no real move toward the collectivisation of agriculture that the party's 1963 Congress had called for. In Syria, most major industries such as oil, electricity, and banking were controlled by the state, although the retail sector was privately run, and private banks are now allowed to operate. Iraq had for years followed an economic model in line with its Ba'athist socialist ideology, and its oil revenues allowed the government to merely redistribute wealth through subsidisation and government economic activity. Iraq nationalised the Iraq Petroleum Company in 1972. The cost of the Iran–Iraq war, however, forced it to economically modernise, and this began a move toward privatising some industries from the 1980s. Although some land reform was carried out, by the mid-1970s, three percent of the landowners owned a third of the agricultural land, showing the degree to which patronage still influenced landownership. Although the state was still active in the agriculture sector, it was forced to privatise state-owned farms in 1990 because of inefficiencies leading to food shortages.

In both Syria and Iraq, the party's secular outlook and cellular structure encouraged the advancement of people based on political connection or ethnic loyalty. In Syria, for instance, this allowed for the political advancement of the 'Alawi, an offshoot of Shi'a Islam concentrated around the port of Latakia, to dominate the upper echelons of the Syrian military, as well as the Syrian Ba'ath party. In Iraq it was the Sunni Muslims who dominated the Ba'ath and, under the rule of Saddam Hussein, his clan based around Tikrit came to dominate the government. In both countries, membership of the Ba'ath Party came to represent little more than a prerequisite for political advancement and economic gain, rather than a commitment to an Arab socialist ideology.

RODGER SHANAHAN

See also Middle East: History and Economic Development; Middle East: International Relations; Socialism

References and Further Reading

Abu Jaber, Kamel S. *The Arab Ba'th Socialist Party: History, Ideology and Organisation.* Syracuse, NY: Syracuse University Press, 1966.

Rabinovitch, Itamar. *Syria Under the Ba'th.* Jerusalem: Israel Universities Press, 1972.

Roberts, David. *The Ba'th and the Creation of Modern Syria.* London: Croom Helm, 1987.

Tripp, Charles. *A History of Iraq.* New York: Cambridge University Press, 2000.

BAGHDAD PACT

Following World War II, British and American policy makers sought to maintain Western power and diminish Soviet influence in the Middle East, as well as to keep oil reserves from Soviet control. Anglo-American efforts centered on strengthening diplomatic and economic ties to friendly regimes such as Turkey, Iraq, and Saudi Arabia, and using regional resources to support a military presence against the Soviets. At the same time, governments of the Middle East looked to the West for investment, markets, technology, and expertise to develop their own economies, strengthen their militaries, and increase their own regional influence.

In May 1953, Secretary of State John Foster Dulles made an extended visit to the Middle East to assess the possibilities for a "Northern Tier" regional military pact composed of Turkey, Iran, Pakistan, and Iraq. On February 24, 1955, the Prime Ministers of Turkey and Iraq signed the Baghdad Pact, and Iran and Pakistan, along with Britain, joined the Pact in the same year.

In 1958, a revolution in Iraq overthrew the monarchy of Faisal II, and the pro-British Nuri al-Said, and Iraq withdrew from the Pact. The remaining members changed the name to the Central Treaty Organization (CENTO), which then served as the link between NATO and the Southeast Asian Treaty Organization (SEATO), to connect twenty-one states in military alliances against the Soviet Union. In 1964, Iran, Turkey, and Pakistan established an economic wing of CENTO, called the Regional Cooperation for Development, with the purpose of expanding efforts to support industrialization, trade, and investment by expanding economic ties between the three countries. However, while trade with the UK and US expanded about ten-fold for Pakistan and more than twice that for Iran and Turkey, trade between the countries remained limited due largely to the fact that all three were exporters of agricultural commodities, textiles, and raw materials.

From the beginning, American planners conceived of the Baghdad Pact/CENTO as a means to defend against Soviet and communist encroachment, which led to a two-part strategy of military buildup against external threats and domestic economic development against internal threats. Through integrated command structures, coordinated military maneuvers, and training of officers, CENTO worked to update, upgrade, and coordinate the militaries of Turkey, Iran, and Pakistan. Economic aid and cultural programs spread American influence in the Middle East and South Asia. Another function of CENTO, in terms of development, was a series of conferences, held throughout the 1960s and 1970s, which brought together experts from the various member states to present technical findings on topics ranging from management problems in marketing, distribution, and use of fertilizers; to public health and drug addiction; to central banking, monetary policy, and economic development. Through these conferences, scholars, businessmen, state regulators, union officials, engineers, scientists, and others were exposed to American and British managerial and scientific approaches, and had the opportunity to compare experiences with implementing new techniques in their own countries. The conferences lasted through the 1970s.

Following the Iranian Revolution of 1979, the government of the Islamic Republic denounced CENTO as an instrument of Western imperialism. Faced with the withdrawal of Iran, the remaining members decided to dissolve the organization on September 26, 1979.

JOHN M. VANDERLIPPE

References and Further Reading

Cohen, Michael. *Fighting World War Three from the Middle East: Allied Contingency Plans, 1945–1954*. London: Frank Cass, 1997.

Gerges, Fawaz. *The Superpowers and the Middle East: Regional and International Politics, 1955–1967*. Boulder, CO: Westview, 1994.

Persson, Magnus. *Great Britain, the United States, and the Security of the Middle East: The Formation of the Baghdad Pact*. Lund, Sweden: Lund University Press, 1998.

Sanjian, Ara. *Turkey and Her Arab Neighbours, 1953–1958: A Study in the Origins and Failure of the Baghdad Pact*. Slough, United Kingdom: Archive Editions, 2001.

Taylor, Alan. *The Superpowers and the Middle East*. Syracuse, NY: Syracuse University Press, 1991.

BAHAMAS

The Commonwealth of the Bahamas is located to the east and southeast of Florida in the Caribbean Sea. It is an archipelago consisting of hundreds of islands, of which about thirty are inhabited. Originally inhabited by the Arawak Indians who controlled many of the islands in the Caribbean, the Bahamas was the first land found by Christopher Columbus on his 1492 voyage. This "discovery" led to more than 130 years of Spanish rule in the Bahamas and the enslavement and export of the native population, before the islands were formally annexed by Great Britain in 1629.

British rule in the Bahamas during the seventeenth and early eighteenth centuries was undermined by the presence of pirates in the region; however, by the 1720s, the islands were relatively secure. The population by that time was primarily of English and African origin, the latter of whom were slaves. The American Revolution brought about political change in the islands, and they became a Crown Colony in 1783; the revolution had brought about the migration of many Royalists from the US states to the Bahamas. Between 1783 and 1788, the population of the islands tripled as King George III granted settlers free land if they would move there.

The economy of the Bahamas was based primarily on growing and exporting cotton, but the increase in population to islands that could not produce enough food to support the population led to shortages and other problems. These were compounded by crop failures in 1788 and 1789, and cotton production remained low well into the 1800s.

Slavery continued to be practiced in the Bahamas even after Great Britain ended its own slave trade in 1807. Efforts had been made by some abolitionists to either eliminate the practice or moderate slavery; this was of concern to the white minority, which controlled the islands, since they made up only about one-fourth of the population there. By the 1820s it became illegal to separate the members of slave families. The British government worked to emancipate the slaves in its colonies by compensating the owners for their release, and by 1838, all slaves in the Bahamas had been freed.

The Bahamas were used as a base for blockade-running to the southern states in the US Civil War (1860–1865), but the end of that war left the islands with little industry or trade. The thin soil could not support extensive agriculture, and while the climate of the Bahamas is nearly ideal for many crops, the relatively small amount of arable land (and competition from the larger colonies like Jamaica) led to the neglect of the islands. One crop that was profitable in the late 1800s was the hemplike plant called sisal; with the disruption of hemp exports brought about by the Spanish–American War, Bahamian sisal exports were in high demand.

The next phase of economic development in the Bahamas began with World War I in 1914, as the Bahamas were once again seen as a source of the manpower needed to fight the war. More significant was the US decision, in 1919, to prohibit the sale or importation of liquor; Prohibition again made the Bahamas a major source for smuggling into the United States. The revenue collected on liquor destined for the States, plus the profits on that smuggling, brought prosperity to the Bahamas once more. The repeal of Prohibition, combined with the Depression that had already begun in the United States, put the islands back into economic difficulties.

Attempts at developing the tourist trade were interrupted by World War II, but the war brought some economic relief to the islands because Great Britain had agreed to permit the US Navy the use of a portion of Exuma Island under the Lend-Lease Act. While this effectively took land away from Bahamians, the construction of the base there did employ many islanders.

The end of World War II did not bring the economic slump that had happened after the previous war, and instead the tourist industry began to prosper. Particularly since the 1960s, the islands have seen a steady increase in visitors, and port improvements in Nassau and Freeport have facilitated this.

Also in the 1960s, the Commonwealth of the Bahamas started to become more integrated into regional economic issues. In 1968, the Caribbean Free Trade Association (CARIFTA) was established, and although the Bahamas was not a member at that time, it did pursue membership and eventually joined the group, which was renamed the Caribbean Community and Common Market (CARICOM) in 1983. The Bahamas had gained their independence from Great Britain in 1973 and were therefore able to fully control their political and economic policies.

In the early twenty-first century, economic endeavors in the Bahamas are centered around offshore banking and commerce; industrial production is largely intended for domestic use. Some export of seafood products and rum also takes place, but the Bahamas are predominantly a net importer of food and beverages.

The economy of the Bahamas is tied to that of the United States both by geography and by policy. The geographic proximity of the Bahamas to Florida, less than one hundred kilometers away, makes travel by boat, ocean liner, or airplane convenient. The Bahamian dollar is exchanged equally with the US dollar, which means that the Bahamas benefit from policies the United States established to encourage trade. The Bahamas are a center for international banking, and since the government has no personal or corporate tax, many corporations establish their headquarters there. Concerns over illegal money-laundering activities have led to more regulation on financial activities, and this has reduced the amount of investment there.

As has been the case since the days of the American Revolution, the Bahamas continue to be a base for smuggling in the modern world. However, rather than the weapons and supplies brought into the United States in those days or during the US Civil War, or the liquor brought in during the US period of Prohibition, the new commodities are marijuana and cocaine.

THOMAS P. DOLAN

See also Caribbean: History and Economic Development; Caribbean: International Relations; Ethnic Conflicts: Caribbean

References and Further Reading

Alonso, Irma T. *Caribbean Economies in the Twenty-first Century*. Gainesville. FL: University Press of Florida, 2002.

Craton, Michael. *A History of the Bahamas*, rev. ed. London: Collins, 1968.

Payne, Anthony. *The Politics of the Caribbean Community 1961–79: Regional Integration Among New States*. New York: St. Martin's Press, 1980.

Payne, Anthony, and Paul Sutton, eds. *Dependency Under Challenge: The Political Economy of the Commonwealth Caribbean*. Manchester, United Kingdom: Manchester University Press, 1984.

BAHRAIN

Bahrain, meaning "two seas," is one of the smallest countries in the Middle East, with a total land area of

620 square kilometers. Bahrain is an archipelago of about thirty-five islands, six of which are inhabited. Al-Bahrain—the main island and the location of the capital, Manama—is also the country's namesake. Situated in the Persian Gulf, the emirate is fifteen miles between the Saudi Arabian coast and Qatari peninsula. Its total land mass is one-fifth the size of Rhode Island. The main island has a coastline of 161 kilometers and is connected by a twenty-five-kilometer causeway with Saudi Arabia.

Despite its small territory, Bahrain has a great strategic importance. It is eight minutes' flying time from Iran and thirty minutes' flying time from Iraq. Its location near Iran and Iraq, and the main shipping channels to Kuwait and Saudi Arabia, make Bahrain an important player in the collective security efforts in the Persian Gulf. Bahrain's proximity to Iran and Iraq and its vulnerability to air attack and naval infiltration require it to maintain a delicate balancing act in foreign affairs among its larger neighbors. Bahrain and the United States cooperated closely as allies during the first Gulf War, and reached a ten-year bilateral security agreement after the war ended. Today, more than two thousand US military personnel are stationed in Bahrain, and it is the headquarters for the new US 5th Fleet.

Bahrain's climate is hot and humid most of the year, with daytime temperatures regularly topping 100°F. Oil and gas are the country's only natural resources, and they are expected to last only fifteen and fifty years, respectively. Facing declining oil reserves, Bahrain has turned to petroleum processing and refining and has transformed itself into an international banking center. Pearling, which had been a traditional industry, has all but ceased to operate.

All of the approximately 678,000 Bahrainis are Muslims. Bahrain is the only Gulf state where the native population—descendants from the Arabian Peninsula and Iran—outnumbers immigrant residents. The resident aliens, nearly one-third of the people, are mostly non-Arab Asians from India, Iran, and Pakistan. Shi'ite Muslims are thought to slightly outnumber Sunnis in Bahrain, causing much concern for the ruling al-Khalif family who are Sunnis. Although Arabic is the official language, Persian is often spoken among the Iranian-descended Bahrainis. By Gulf standards, Bahrain has a sophisticated population, noted for its intellectual tradition and articulate labor force.

Bahrain's history dates back as far as 2400 BCE, but its modern history begins in the early 1500s with a series of Persian, Portuguese, and Turkish struggles to control the main island that helped make Bahrain a major military and trading center. Between 1507 and 1602, Bahrain was under Portuguese occupation. In 1602, the Portuguese were expelled and Bahrain found itself under the rule of Iran, which lasted until 1783. In that year Arab tribes from the mainland conquered the island, and since 1816 it has been ruled by the Khalif family of the Utub tribe. The Utub tribe had migrated into the region from southern Arabia during the seventeenth century. Before long, however, these Arab rulers fell in the path of Britain, which from 1820 onward established hegemony over the Persian Gulf area. The British extended their domination of Bahrain through a series of treaties. These treaties represented a bilateral arrangement between the British and the sheikhs of Bahrain. Britain acted, however, to keep Bahrain from Turkish and Iranian control, and to secure the approaches to India. New administrative arrangements made Bahrain part of the British Trucial states in 1868, and al-Khalif signed treaties with Britain in 1880 and 1892 that further strengthened this relationship and established a British political resident and agent.

Beginning with World War I, Bahrain began to play an increasingly strategic role in the British hegemony over the Persian Gulf. It served as an assembly point for the British expeditionary force (mostly from India), which was to wage a campaign in Mesopotamia. In 1966, Britain moved to Bahrain the military base that had been headquartered in Aden. On August 14, 1970, Bahrain achieved independence by putting an end to the previous treaty arrangements with Great Britain. On the same day a new treaty of friendship between the two countries was concluded. This date marked the end of a long era of dependent status.

Achievement of independence by Bahrain was preceded by diplomatic moves that involved international complications. The most important of these was the claim of Iran to sovereignty over the island. Iran's claim was based on an historical connection with Bahrain that dated back to Achaemenian times. Moreover, Iran maintained that in reality most of the Bahraini population was of Iranian stock, even if they were linguistically Arabized. In 1970, to resolve what promised to develop into a major international complication, the United Nations undertook a mission to ascertain the wishes of the Bahraini population in regard to their future. Upon completion of its mission, the United Nations declared, in the spring of 1970, that the board consensus in Bahrain was to become independent rather than to be joined with Iran. In May 1970, the Iranian government accepted these findings and abandoned its claim to Bahrain on the condition that an independent Bahrain government would not enter into any alliances, unions, or federation.

Bahrain is officially a constitutional monarchy under the dynastic rule of the al-Khalif family. As of the early 2000s, the al-Khalif family continues to dominate the government, holding all key cabinet positions. The Prime Minister nominates all forty members of the Majlis Al-Shura (Consultative Council), which comments on bills but has no legislative authority. However, in 1999, Crown Prince Sheikh Salman Bin Hamad Bin Isa Al-khalif, who succeeded his father, pushed through economic and political reforms and has worked to improve relations with the Shi'a community. He announced a new national charter, which will see the Majlis Al-Shura replaced by a national assembly elected by universal suffrage. In October 2002, Bahrainis elected members of the lower house of Bahrain's reconstituted bicameral legislature, the National Assembly. Local elections were held for the first time in 2004.

The major challenge for the government of Bahrain is to create employment opportunities for its young population—38.9% of Bahrainis are under fifteen years old. Unemployment has been exacerbated by the rise in the number of expatriates who now make up more than 40% of the population.

NASSER MOMAYEZI

See also Middle East: History and Economic Development; Middle East: International Relations

References and Further Reading

Cordesman, Anthony H. *Bahrain, Oman, Qatar, and the UAE: Challenges of Security*. Boulder, CO: Westview Press, 1997.
Crawford, Harriet. *Dilmun and Its Gulf Neighbours*. New York: Cambridge University Press, 1998.
Khuri, Fuad I. *Tribe and State in Bahrain: The Transformation of Social and Political Authority in an Arab State*. Chicago, and London: The University of Chicago, 1980.
Lenczowski, George. *The Middle East in World Affairs*, 4th ed. Ithaca, NY, and London: Cornell University Press, 1980.
Sick, Gary G., and Lawrence G. Potter, eds. *The Persian Gulf at the Millennium: Essays in Politics, Economy, Security, and Religion*. New York: Palgrave Macmillan, 1997.
Tarr, David R., and Bryan R. Daves, eds. *The Middle East*. Washington, DC: Congressional Quarterly, 1986.

BALFOUR DECLARATION

During World War I the Allies proposed that the post-war world be organized on the basis of nation-states. "Self-determination of nations" was a cardinal notion in US President Woodrow Wilson's fourteen points for the post-war world. Since the great European powers were all either multinational countries or holders of multinational empires, the idea of using the minority nations of one's enemies was adopted as a tool in the conflict. The British and French backed the formation of Czechoslavakia and Yugoslavia out of the Austro-Hungarian Empire. The British stirred up an Arab revolt against the Turks. Germany backed the 1916 Easter Rebellion in Ireland. One aspect of this policy was the British project to support a Jewish homeland in Palestine in order to win over the sympathy of the Jews of the Central Powers for the Allied cause.

The idea of the return of the Jews to Palestine was not new. Napoleon had envisioned the restoration of the Jews to the Holy Land, as had the Russian Decembrist Pavel Pestel. Among the English who advocated the return of Jews to Palestine were Sir Henry Finch in 1621, Lord Lindsay, Lord Shaftesbury, Lord Palmerston, Benjamin Disraeli, Lord Manchester, George Eliot in her novel *Daniel Deronda*, Holman Hunt, Sir Charles Warren, Hall Caine, and others. Lord Shaftesbury, one of the most active spokespersons for a Jewish homeland, called Palestine "a land without a people for a people without a land." Later this became the slogan of Zionism. Moreover, the restoration of the Jews to the Holy Land has been a longstanding concept in British Protestant theology. Some theologians believed that the reestablishment of ancient Israel with the modern Jews was a necessary prerequisite for the Second Coming of Christ.

The idea of a Jewish nation-state in their Biblical homeland was the basic goal of the Zionist movement. However, the plan stirred controversy. Were the Jews a nation or a religion? Since the basis of modern European nationalism was linked primarily to language and religion, most nationalists viewed Jews as aliens in their states. Furthermore, despite the Diaspora of the Jews in Roman times, Palestine had retained a sizeable Jewish population, and the Jewish Passover prayer, "Next year in Jerusalem!" had been passed down from generation to generation through the ages. On the other hand, Palestine had a significant non-Jewish Arab population, both Moslem and Christian, and, furthermore, represented religious values for all three faiths.

The modern Zionist movement crystallized in 1896, when the Viennese Jewish journalist Theodore Herzl, witnessing the anti-Semitism surrounding the Dreyfus affair in France, launched the project to establish a Jewish homeland. Working with wealthy European Jews, Herzl began to purchase land there from the Ottoman government and promote the emigration of Jews from Europe.

The Russian-born Zionist Chaim Weizmann (later the first president of Israel) settled in London in 1904 and began to work for British support of a Jewish homeland in Palestine. In 1906, he met Lord Balfour, who was sympathetic to the idea but urged Weizmann to consider Africa rather than the Middle East (an idea the Zionists had considered earlier but rejected). Weizmann also gained the sympathy of others, including Charles P. Scott, editor of the Manchester Guardian; and Mark Sykes, who later signed the Sykes–Picot agreement with France (see further below). The chemist Weizmann's influence increased during World War I because of the aid he gave to the war effort. Weizmann drafted a plan for a Jewish homeland. There was also a rumor that Germany was considering a similar plan.

During the war the British leaders discussed the idea with prominent English Jews. Julian Amery, an assistant secretary to the British War Cabinet whose mother was a Jew, promoted the plan and also helped create the Jewish legion, Palestinian Jews, who fought with the British in World War I. Lord Arthur Balfour, the British Foreign Secretary, wrote a letter to Lord Rothschild, which stated:

> His Majesty's Government views with favor the establishment in Palestine of a national home for the Jewish people, and will use their best endeavors to facilitate the achievement of this object, it being clearly understood that nothing shall be done which may prejudice the civil and religious rights of existing non-Jewish communities in Palestine or the rights and political status enjoyed by Jews in any other country.

This statement is the Balfour declaration made public on November 2, 1917. At the same time, London and Paris had secretly agreed to divide the Ottoman territories between themselves after the war—the Sykes–Picot agreement. Consequently, the Jewish homeland envisioned was not to be an independent state but rather part of the British Empire. In a 1936 commentary by the Peel Commission investigating Arab–Jewish riots in Palestine, the Commission stated that not only Palestine but also Trans-Jordan was to be part of the Jewish homeland.

After the war, public opinion viewed imperialism and colonization as contrary to the democratic principles that the Allies had said they were fighting for. So the lands designated in the Sykes–Picot agreement were, in fact, given to Britain and France as League of Nations mandates rather than outright possessions as was the case with Alsace-Lorraine, for example. The British mandate also specifically referred to Palestine as the site of a Jewish homeland.

During the peace conference in Paris, Emir Faisal, representing the Arabs of the Ottoman Empire, agreed to a Jewish homeland, along with an Arab independent state existing side by side. However, since no independent Arab state had been created, the Faisal agreement was not valid. Although the United States government did not sign the Paris Peace Treaties, the US Congress,

in 1922, unanimously approved the Balfour declaration with the Lodge–Fish resolution.

Some have argued that the declaration was intended not so much for the Jews of Central Europe but rather for the Jews of Russia and the United States—Britain's allies—so as to gain support for London's policies and war aims. Others believed that the proclamation gave Britain an excuse to renege on promises made to France and the Arabs. The project also bolstered the argument for a British protectorate over the area.

FREDERICK B. CHARY

See also Israel; Palestine; Palestinian Diaspora; Zionism

References and Further Reading

Friedman, Isaiah. *The Question of Palestine: British–Jewish Relations, 1914–1918.* New Brunswick, Canada: Transaction Publishers, 1992.
Reinharz, Jehuda. *Chaim Weizmann: The Making of a Statesman.* New York: Oxford, 1993.

BALKAN WARS OF THE 1990s

After the First World War the victorious Allies created Yugoslavia by adding lands from the defeated Austro-Hungarian Empire to the Kingdom of Serbia. The country suffered through its eighty-year existence amid national tensions derived from an essentially artificial construction. In World War II, the occupying Axis powers divided some of its territory among themselves and created the two puppet states of Croatia and Serbia. After the war Yugoslavia was reassembled under the rule of the Communist leader Josef Broz Tito. In 1949, Tito broke with the Soviet bloc and was able to remain in power as a neutral Communist leader. The force of his leadership and the use of dictatorial powers kept the fractious nationalities together. It was said that Yugoslavia had six republics, five nations, four languages, three religions, two alphabets, but only one Yugoslav—Tito.

In fact, Tito did reorganize the country into a federation of six republics—Croatia, Serbia, Slovenia, Montenegro, Bosnia, and Macedonia. However, the question of nationalities is problematic. Clearly the Croatians, Serbs, Slovenians, and Macedonians are separate nations, as are the Bosniaks (Muslim Bosnians), and the Albanians of Kosovo. However, in addition to the autonomous Albanian region of Kosovo in Serbia, there was also an autonomous Hungarian region in the Banat. Whether the Montenegrins are Serbs or a separate nation is a matter of dispute.

Languages are also disputed. Slovenian and Macedonian are recognized as distinct languages, although for much of the post-war period, Bulgaria refused to recognize Macedonian as anything but a dialect of Bulgarian. Whether Serbo-Croatian is a single language or two languages is another question, and of course there is Albanian and Hungarian for those autonomous regions.

The three major religions are Roman Catholic, Eastern Orthodox, and Islam, but there are both Serbian and Macedonian Orthodox patriarchs and both Shi'te and Sunni Muslims. There are also Protestants and Jews who, although few in number, have had significant political influence.

Throughout the post-war period, tensions among the republics continued to exist, with the wealthier northern republics such as Croatia and Slovenia complaining that they were taxed to support the poorer southern republics of Macedonia, Bosnia, and Montenegro. Less expressed but present in the background there was still national discontent. Most virulent was the conflict between Orthodox Serbs and Roman Catholic Croatians that was based on religious and historical animosity. Croatians have always protested what they perceived as a second-class citizenship in the state since its foundation. Serbs remembered that the fascist Croatian state of World War II committed unbelievable atrocities against the Serb minority in its region. The hostility was exacerbated by the activity of Croatian exile groups abroad.

With the death of Tito in 1979, the national and republican tensions increased and finally erupted. The government tried to solve these problems by establishing a shared executive responsibility balanced by the various republics, including a rotating presidency. Furthermore, since its break with the Soviet bloc in 1948, Yugoslavia had enjoyed more freedoms than other Communist countries. Now political dissent became more open as well. In addition to the Serbian-Croatian conflict, a serious problem developed among the chiefly Muslim Albanians of Kosovo, who began to demand independent instead of autonomous status. Furthermore, fanned by the Muslim fundamentalist and revolutionary movement in the Middle East, Albanian radicals began attacking Serbs living in Kosovo.

The Croatian and Albanian conflicts led to the rise of the Serbian nationalist Slobodan Milosevic in Serbia. Moreover, Yugoslavia was the first of the Communist countries to change its system, and as nationalists won Republican elections in the 1980s, they moved to break away from the Yugoslav federation. In 1990, Croatia elected the nationalist Franjo Tudjman president, and when the federal council rejected the Croatian candidate for president,

Slovenia and Croatia withdrew from the federation on June 25, 1991. Slovenia put up border posts with Yugoslavia, and the federal government in Belgrade sent in the army, but after a few skirmishes they gave up and allowed Slovenia to go its own way.

The more serious break occurred with Croatia. Alija Izbegovic, the president of Bosnia, and Kiro Gligorov, the president of Macedonia, tried to find a way to keep the federation together, as they, along with Montenegro, derived the most benefit from sharing Slovenia's and Croatia's wealth. However, both were prepared to withdraw from the federation if the northern republics could not be persuaded to remain. In the Kraina region of Croatia, the Serbian minority resisted and declared the creation of the Republic of Kraina; the federal government moved in to protect them and add the region to Serbia. In August the Serbs occupied Vukovar.

At the end of May 1991, the European Community had offered Yugoslavia membership if it could resolve its problems peacefully, but fighting between the Serbs and Croatians continued until 1994 despite three cease-fires arranged by the United Nations and the presence of UN peace-keeping forces. As the Serbs got bogged down in Bosnia during the early 1990s, the Croatians drove the Serbs completely out of their republic. The United States, Great Britain, and France hoped that Yugoslavia would remain a single national entity, initially refusing to recognize the new governments. Germany, on the other hand, pressed for recognition of the independence of the republics.

Early in the fighting, Milosevic and Tudjman apparently agreed to divide up parts of Bosnia between them to handle population issues. This prompted the Muslim Izetbegovic to move toward independence for his republic. However, Bosnia had, in addition to its Muslim majority, significant Serbs and Croatians. In March 1992, Izetbegovic arranged for a plebiscite in which the Croatians and Bosniaks voted for independence while the Serbs boycotted the vote. On April 6, war in Bosnia erupted.

The Bosnian Serbs under Dr. Radovan Karadzic and General Ratko Mladic, with the help of Serbs of the federal army, carried out a brutal war of resistance. Atrocities were committed on both sides, but the Serbs proved to be more efficient. Karadovic and Mladic adopted a policy of rape and murder to drive the Bosniaks out of Bosnia. Serbian soldiers herded men and teenage boys into concentration camps and gunned them down. They repeatedly violated Muslim women. The Serbs publicized all this to frighten the Muslims into fleeing the country—a policy called "ethnic cleansing." World opinion made a comparison to the Jewish Holocaust of World War II, and Elie Wiesel, the noted Holocaust survivor, came to

Bosnia to witness and comment on the atrocities. However, while the Nazis murdered the Jews secretly, in an attempt to erase a population, the Serbs committed their atrocities in the open, in an attempt to drive the population away.

Bosniaks retaliated, shelling Serbian villages and neighborhoods. The capital, Sarajevo, was almost completely destroyed by the internecine warfare. Spurred on by Croatian propaganda, most of the world press blamed the Serbs, both those of Bosnia and the remnant Yugoslavia where Macedonia joined the republics that defected. However, the Croatians had a Bosnian area they wished to claim as well, and warfare erupted between them and the Bosniaks in January 1993. Furthermore, Catholics from around the world began pilgrimages to Bosnia during the crisis to visit the shrine of the reputed appearance of the virgin at Medjugorje in 1981.

In April 1994, NATO planes began to enforce a no-fly zone ordered by the United Nations to keep Belgrade's air force from bombing Bosnian sights. Then, in January 1995, Washington, which had earlier negotiated peace between the Bosniaks and the Croatians, arranged a cease-fire between the Bosniaks and the Serbs. However, by spring fighting erupted again in both Bosnia and Croatia. The Bosnian Serbs took more than three hundred UN soldier prisoners, but Belgrade helped bring about their release.

In July 1994, the Bosnians Serbs overran Srebenica and Zepa—supposedly safe enclaves guaranteed by Washington. In August they bombarded a Sarajevo market, killing thirty-seven and wounding eighty-five. The United Nations imposed an arms embargo on the area and economic sanctions against Yugoslavia, both of which had little effect in stopping the war. They also sent humanitarian aid, and Red Cross officials came to Bosnia to arrange for the release of prisoners and monitor the refugee camps. In 1995, NATO and the United Nations intervened further and attacked the Serb positions. By that time 3.5 million refugees had been forced out of Bosnia. A Muslim-Croat force began to take some territories back, and US President Bill Clinton arranged for a cease-fire. Peace talks began in October at the Wright-Patterson air force base near Dayton, Ohio.

While keeping peace on the ground was difficult, diplomacy was able to make some progress. The diplomats worked out a solution based on religion, dividing Bosnia into a bi-state confederation with the Serbs on one hand and a federation of Croats and Bosniaks on the other. None of the areas were contiguous. In November the parties agreed to the peace plan. Tudjman signed for the Croatian and Milosevic for the Serbs as Karadzic and Mladic agreed. Izbegovic signed for the Bosniaks. Many of the refugees returned, but others remained abroad. The International Court of Justice at The Hague declared Karadovic and Mladic war criminals and hunted them down, but they eluded capture. The situation remained unstable and foreign troops mostly from the United States remained on hand to keep the peace. They were still there in 2005.

Without Bosnia as an option Milosevic planned to resettle the Serbs from Kraina in Kosovo. Although Kosovo was now overwhelmingly an Albanian province, it has significant historical meaning for the Serbs. It was here that the Ottoman Empire defeated the Serbs in 1389. Although the battle's significance has been enlarged over the centuries in Serbian historical mythology, it represents a turning point in the nation's history. The traditional date of June 28 was further emblazoned in the country's legends when on that date in 1914 the Bosnian Serb Gavrilo Princip assassinated the Austrian heir to the throne, Grand Duke Franz Ferdinand, in Sarajevo and started the events leading to World War I—the war that eventually led to the formation of Yugoslavia.

In September 1986, Belgrade revealed the conclusions of a year-long study by the Serbian Academy of Sciences (SANU) describing the problems of the Republic of Serbia. Much of the SANU report claimed the Kosovo Albanians were waging a "genocidal" war against the Serbs in the region. It described the events as the worst disaster for Serbia since the 1804 war of liberation against the Ottoman Empire, including the World Wars and Nazi occupation. The document recommended "genuine security and unambiguous equality for all peoples living in Kosovo" and said "Serbia must not be passive and wait and see what the others will say, as it has done so often in the past."

The reaction was fierce. Croatians and Slovenians saw the SANU report as a manifesto for Serbian supremacy in Yugoslavia. The Albanians saw the report as a threat against them. Serbs were divided. Some welcomed it. Others, especially hard-line Communists, denounced the report as anti-Marxist. One Communist who denounced it was Slobodan Milosevic. In 1987 Milosevic, however, made a stirring speech on the anniversary of the 1389 Battle of Kosovo Field that was interpreted as a message of Serbian nationalism—just like the SANU report document. In Kosovo the Communist party head Asem Vlassi opposed Milosevic's pro-Serbian plans. The 1974 constitution, which gave each republic and the two autonomous regions equal authority, put Serbia in the minority. Milosevic continued to press for Serbian nationalism directed against the Albanians of Kosovo and the Croats and Slovenes in their respective republics, and then he moved to incorporate the autonomous regions into the Serbian republic. In November 1988, he arrested Vlassi and dismissed the entire Kosovo Communist leadership. In March 1989 he unilaterally ended the autonomy of the regions, provoking deadly riots. In 1990, he officially incorporated the provinces into Serbia but kept their votes on the executive council, giving Serbia, along with Montenegro, closely associated with it, increased power on the council equal to the other republics.

The change for Kosovo ended its governmental institutions. Belgrade also required employees of state industries, a large percentage of Kosovo enterprises, to take loyalty oaths to Belgrade. Most Albanians refused and the government replaced them with Serbs. More than one hundred thousand Kosovo Albanians lost their jobs. Belgrade also closed the Albanian newspapers and radio and television stations and purged Pristina University. Forty thousand Serbian troops and police moved in to replace the Albanian police force. The province suffered extreme economic hardship and a third of the fathers left the area to work as guest laborers in Germany and elsewhere to support their families. With the Communists gone, the author Ibrahim Rugova, leader of the Democratic League of Kosovo, now became the most important Albanian political leader. Rugova ordered a policy of passive resistance. Albanians did not vote in elections, report for the draft, or pay taxes. Rogova also established alternative institutions to the government—schools and hospitals. He organized an illegal Albanian assembly of Kosovo, which in 1991 ordered a referendum on the demand for republic status. The security forces attempted to prevent the Albanians from voting, but almost the whole population turned out and all but unanimously approved the referendum. In 1992, another referendum elected Rugova president, but Belgrade declared both referenda illegal.

During the war in Bosnia, Kosovo disappeared from the headlines, and its population grew restless. The Dayton Accords did not include the province. Rugova asked for United Nations protection for the province, but received no response. In opposition to Rugova's policy of peaceful resistance, a new organization, the Kosovo Liberation Army (KLA) based in Western Kosovo near Albania (Drenica), appeared and in the spring of 1996 began coordinated attacks on Serbs, both security forces and civilians. The KLA absorbed the Armed Forces of Kosovo, a body directed by an Albanian exile organization in Switzerland under Bujar Bukoshi. The KLA hoped to create a full-scale war and bring about NATO intervention, but NATO and the UN did not wish to get involved in Kosovo after the difficulty of solving the Bosnia problem. Washington denounced the KLA as terrorists, and at one point Rugova even claimed that it was set up by Serbia as an excuse to invade. A multinational commission, the "contact group" (the United States, Russia, England, France, Germany, and Italy), met to monitor Kosovo but could not agree on policy.

In 1997, the situation grew worse. The KLA receiving arms illegally from Albania grew as a guerilla force, while the Yugoslav army aided by a secret militia led by the notorious Zelijko Raznatovic, also known as Arkan, carried out a war of terror against the Kosovo Albanians similar to what had happened in Bosnia. By mid-1998, hundreds had died and hundreds of thousands had fled into neighboring countries—Albania, Macedonia, and Montenegro, whose government, although still part of Yugoslavia, did not approve of the Kosovo campaign. The war threatened the whole Balkan peninsula. NATO, the European Union, and the Organization for Security and Cooperation of Europe (OSCE) now became involved. NATO persuaded the KLA to drop its call for independence, and a group of OSCE peace-keepers moved into Kosovo, but they were not armed and therefore were ineffective. A brokered armistice lasted only two months. In January 1999, Serbian police and militia killed forty-five Kosovars in the village of Racak. Although the Serbs claimed that Racak was the site of a battle between the forces, the international community condemned the incident as a massacre, and began intervention on the side of the Albanians. Initially, most of the Allied intervention employed air forces rather than ground troops. NATO, principally American bombers, began bombarding Kosovo and Belgrade, targeting both Serbian ground troops and installations in Serbia proper. During the air raids on Belgrade, an international scandal occurred when US bombers hit the Chinese embassy. At the same time on the diplomatic front the contact group set forward a non-negotiable program calling for the "status quo plus," which called for the restoration of the autonomous region status of Kosovo and the introduction of an internationally supervised democracy. It also required peace talks to be held near Paris at Chateau Rambouillet. The talks began in February 1999 and lasted five weeks without results, as the Albanians did not want to be part of Serbia, and the Serbs did not want to give Kosovo autonomous status.

Eventually, under the pressure Belgrade stopped its campaign and the Albanians came back, retaliating against the Serbs. The United Nations sent in troops to keep the communities apart. A number of troops from NATO countries also were deployed in Macedonia where the conflict of Albanians and Macedonians also erupted, although it was short of full-scale war.

On April 1, 2001, Slobodan Milosevic was arrested by local authorities in Belgrade and subsequently tried for war crimes at The Hague. He is representing himself in his ongoing case.

In 2002, Yugoslavia officially came to an end as the remaining two republics reorganized themselves as the Federation of Serbia and Montenegro.

FREDERICK B. CHARY

References and Further Reading

Clark, Wesley K. *Waging Modern War: Bosnia, Kosovo, and the Future of Combat*. New York: Public Affairs, 2001.

Cohen, Roger. *Hearts Grown Brutal: Sagas of Sarajevo*. New York: Random House, 1998.

Glenny, Misha. *The Fall of Yugoslavia: The Third Balkan War*, 3d ed. New York: Penguin, 1996.

Holbrooke, Richard C. *To End a War*. New York: Random House, 1998.

Judah, Tim. *Kosovo: War and Revenge*. New Haven, CT: Yale, 2000.

Mertus, Julie, *Kosovo: How Myths and Truths Started a War*. Berkeley, CA: University of California, 1999.

Sell, Louis. *Slobodan Milosevic and the Destruction of Yugoslavia*, Durham, NC: Duke, 2002.

BANDUNG CONFERENCE (1955)

The Bandung Conference, formally known as the Asian-African Conference, was held in the town of Bandung, Indonesia, from April 17 to April 24, 1955. The conference was attended by delegations from twenty-nine, primarily new, nation-states or nationalist movements in Asia and Africa. The meeting in Bandung also included members of the African National Congress, as well as observers from Greek Cypriot and African American organizations. The key figures at the conference included Sukarno, President of Indonesia (1945–1965); Jawaharlal Nehru, Prime Minister of India (1947–1964); Gamal Abdel Nasser, President of Egypt (1954–1970); Kwame Nkrumah, the future Prime Minister of Ghana (1957–1966); Josip Broz Tito, President of Yugoslavia (1953–1980); and Zhou Enlai, the Prime Minister (1949–1976) and Foreign Minister (1949–1958) of the People's Republic of China. The conference was sponsored by Indonesia, along with the governments of Burma (present Myanmar), Ceylon (presently Sri Lanka), India, and Pakistan, and reflected their dissatisfaction with the assertion on the part of US President Dwight D. Eisenhower (1953–1960) that the countries of Asia should not try and remain neutral in the Cold War rivalry between the United States and the Soviet Union. The assembled delegates also emphasized their opposition to colonialism, singling out French colonialism in North Africa for particular criticism. Furthermore, there was a major debate as to whether Soviet domination of Eastern Europe was equivalent to Western European colonialism in Asia and Africa. The final communiqué of the conference condemned all "manifestations" of colonialism and was viewed as an attack on the formal colonialism by the Western European powers, the Soviet occupation of Eastern Europe, and the informal colonialism by the United States. The proceedings ended with a call for increased technical and cultural cooperation between the governments in attendance; the establishment of an economic development fund to be operated by the United Nations; increased support for human rights and the "self-determination of peoples and nations," singling out South Africa and Israel for their failure in this regard; and negotiations to reduce the building and stockpiling of nuclear weapons.

The Bandung Conference was particularly important for its symbolism. It was the first major international conference that sought to bring together the governments of the newly independent nations of Asia and Africa. What was often called the "Bandung Spirit" captured the imagination of an entire generation during the so-called Bandung Era from the 1950s to the 1970s. For example, the Bandung Conference represented a precursor to the formation of the Movement of Non-Aligned Countries. In September 1960, the First Conference of Heads of State or Government of Non-Aligned Countries was held in Belgrade, Yugoslavia. However, rivalry between India and China, culminating in full-scale war in 1962, weakened efforts to unite third-world governments around the anti-colonial and non-aligned agenda symbolized by Bandung. The complicated and conflicting interests of the governments of the new nations in Asia and Africa increasingly worked to undermine the establishment of a coalition of non-aligned governments. For example, the second Asian-African Conference, which had been scheduled to meet in Algeria in June 1965, was cancelled when the machinations of the Sino-Soviet split undermined the planning of the event. Meanwhile, Nehru (a key leader of the Bandung era) died in May 1964. The government of Ahmed Ben Bella (1963–1965) in Algeria was overthrown by the military on June 19, 1965. Then, Sukarno, the host of the 1955 conference, was ousted in September 1965 by a US-backed military dictatorship under General Suharto. Between 1961 and the end of the 1990s, there were a total of twelve non-aligned conferences. As an international organization, it has never played a role of any great significance. By the 1990s, when the Indonesian government under President Suharto took over as chairman, the Non-Aligned Movement was effectively moribund. Another initiative inspired by Bandung was the formation of the Group of 77 (G-77), established at the first United Nations Conference on Trade and Development (UNCTAD) in 1964. The G-77 (which had 133 member governments by the end of the 1990s) focused on economic issues operating as a caucus on development questions within the wider umbrella of the United Nations.

A particularly radical effort to build on the Bandung agenda emerged in the wake of the Tricontinental Conference of Solidarity of the Peoples of Africa, Asia, and Latin America, that was held in Havana in January 1966. While the Bandung Conference had brought together a relatively small number of leaders from mainly recently independent nation-states in Africa and Asia in order to stake out a non-aligned position in the Cold War, the 1966 Tricontinental Conference involved delegates from throughout Latin America, Asia, and Africa and articulated a radical anti-imperialist agenda that located the participants firmly in the socialist camp at the same time as they formally emphasized their independence from the USSR and Maoist China. Regimes that were directly or indirectly linked to the tricontinentalism of the late 1960s and 1970s all attempted to pursue national development in the name of socialism, anti-imperialism, and national liberation. However, by the 1970s, the problems associated with uniting a wide array of governments in a third-world alliance became increasingly apparent. In retrospect, the Bandung Spirit reached its zenith in the 1970s. In this decade, third-world governments increased their numerical influence at the UN as the organization's overall membership rose from fifty-one in 1945 to 156 in 1980, the vast majority of the new member-governments coming from Asia and Africa. In April 1974, the Sixth Special Session of the General Assembly of the United Nations passed the Declaration and Program of Action for the Establishment of a New Economic Order. This formal call for a New International Economic Order (NIEO) sought the restructuring of the world economy in a way that would improve the terms under which the economies of the third world participated in international trade and development. At the end of the 1970s, the UN set up the Independent Commission on International Development (the Brandt Commission), chaired by former West German Chancellor Willy Brandt, to address the North–South conflict. However, with the rise of neoliberalism and the revitalization of the Cold War, under the leadership of US President Ronald Reagan (1981–1988) and British Prime Minister Margaret Thatcher (1979–1990), the various initiatives associated with the Bandung era were increasingly constrained or reversed.

MARK T. BERGER

See also Colonialism: Legacies; Nonaligned Movement; Soviet Bloc

References and Further Reading

Abdulgani, Roeslan. *Bandung Spirit: Moving on the Tide of History.* Djakarta, Indonesia: Prapantja, 1964.

Appadorai, Angadipuram. *The Bandung Conference.* New Delhi: Indian Council of World Affairs, 1955.

Jansen, G. H. *Nonalignment and the Afro-Asian States.* New York: Frederick A. Praeger, 1966.

Kahin, George McTurnan. *The Asian-African Conference, Bandung, Indonesia, April 1955.* Ithaca, NY: Cornell University Press, 1956.

Mortimer, R. A. *The Third World Coalition in World Politics.* Boulder, CO: Westview Press, 1984.

Newsom, David D. *The Imperial Mantle: The United States, Decolonization, and the Third World.* Bloomington, IN: Indiana University Press, 2001.

Romulo, Carlos P. *The Meaning of Bandung.* Chapel Hill, NC: The University of North Carolina Press, 1956.

Young, Robert. *Postcolonialism: An Historical Introduction.* Oxford: Blackwell, 2001.

BANGLADESH

Geography and Population

The People's Republic of Bangladesh, situated in Southern Asia at the Bay of Bengal, comprises 144,000 square kilometres of land. Of its 4,246 kilometres of land boundaries it shares 4,053 kilometres with India and 193 kilometres with Burma. Most of the country's terrain is a flat alluvial plain shaped by three large rivers, the Ganges, Brahmaputra, and Meghna. Flowing down from the Himalayas these rivers join in Bangladesh and—in a vast delta—empty into the Bay of Bengal. Much of the coastline is covered with marshy jungle known as the Sundarbans—the home of the Bengal Tiger. Only the Chittagong Hill Tracts in the southeastern part of the country (with Keokradong as the highest peak at 1,230 metres) and the Sylhet division in the Northeast are hilly. The climate is tropical and features a mild winter (November–February), a hot and humid summer (March–June), and a monsoon rainy season from July to October. The country receives about eighty inches of average annual rainfall with the wettest part in the extreme Northeast with about two hundred inches average annual rainfall. Around 80% of annual rainfall occurs during the monsoon period. Bangladesh is seriously affected by natural calamities such as floods and tropical cyclones almost every year. Due to excessive rainfall and the riverine topography up to a third of the country's landmass gets flooded during the annual monsoon season. The cyclones of 1970 and 1991 and the monsoon flood of 1998 were particularly devastating.

With an estimated population of 141.3 million (July 2004) and a resulting population density of 982 persons per square kilometre, Bangladesh remains one of the most densely populated states in the world. The annual population growth rate is estimated at 2.08%, the birth rate at 30.03 per 1,000 inhabitants, and the death rate at 8.52 per 1,000. The ethnic composition of the population is comparatively homogenous with 98% of the population being Bengalis speaking Bangla (Bengali) in 1998. About 83% of the population are Muslims. Hindus constitute a sizeable minority of 16% (data from 1998).

History

Modern Bangladesh is the eastern part of a greater region formerly known as Bengal. Archaeological evidence suggests that the region has supported a socially and culturally diversified civilisation since at least 700 BC. From the thirteenth century onward, Bengal came under Islamic influence, becoming a part of the Muslim Mughal Empire during the sixteenth century. Most of the population converted to the Islamic faith during the time of Mughal control. With its victory in the Battle of Plassey in 1757, the British East India Company assumed control over Bengal. After the Indian Mutiny of 1857, the British Crown took over the company's possession in India, including Bengal. Late nineteenth century British India saw the gradual emergence of a nationalist movement carried out by local Hindu and Muslim elites. The British government pursued a communalist policy to undermine Hindu–Muslim cooperation, leading to the division of Bengal into two provinces along religious lines during 1905–1912. When the decolonization of British India led to the emergence of two independent states—a Hindu India and a Muslim Pakistan—Bengal was divided again and East Bengal became part of Pakistan in 1947. Although comprising 56% of the total population, East Pakistanis felt underrepresented by the Pakistani government centred in the western part of the country—separated by one thousand miles of Indian territory. Nationalist movements aimed at the adoption of Bangla (Bengali) as a state language (and succeeded in 1952) and advocated greater autonomy. In 1971, tensions peaked when the Pakistani president Yahiya Khan refused to acknowledge the landslide election victory of the Awami League that had won all the East Pakistani seats in the National Assembly. Strikes and tax boycotts finally led to open civil war on March 25, 1971. The Awami League proclaimed the independence of Bangladesh on the following day. Nine months later, on December 16, 1971, the Pakistani army was forced to surrender with Indian military help and Bangladesh became independent. Sheik Mujibur Rahman, the leader of the Awami League, became Prime Minister and tried to stabilise the country's devastated economy. But after a governmental crisis due to heavy inflation and famine, he was assassinated in 1975. After two more coups, Maj. Gen. Zia ur-Rahman assumed power and began a period of military rule. Zia was assassinated in 1981 and his successor was ousted from power by Lt. Gen. Hussain Mohammad Ershad the same year. Ershad was forced to resign in 1990 due to corruption allegations. The general elections of 1991 brought the Bangladesh Nationalist Party (BNP) under Zia's widow Khaleda Zia to power. With strikes and boycotts, the opposition parties drove Khaleda Zia out of office in 1996 and the Awami League under Sheik Mujibur Rahman's daughter Hasina Wazed returned to power. Once again, strikes organised by the opposition paralysed the country's weak economy and ousted Hasina Wazed. Khaleda Zia's BNP re-assumed power from a caretaker government after a landslide election victory in 2001.

Economy

Although stabilisation of its economy has been the chief concern of each of its governments since independence, Bangladesh remains one of the poorest countries in the world. Severe overpopulation, the frequent occurrence of natural disasters, and widespread corruption have hitherto delayed economic development. About two-thirds of the population make a living from agriculture—mostly from rice and jute cultivation—producing only 22% of the Gross Domestic Product (est. GDP 2003: US$258.8 billion; est. GDP 2003 per capita: US$1,900). Tea is grown in the Northeast and the cultivation of sugarcane, tobacco, and wheat is widespread. Fertile soils and ample water supply make Bangladesh the third-largest rice producer in the world. Nevertheless, overpopulation and natural calamities still make the country prone to malnutrition and famine. Bangladesh is the world's largest producer of jute, which remains the most important export commodity of the country. Apart from natural gas, some oil in the Bay of Bengal, and modest coal and uranium deposits, Bangladesh has almost no natural resources. The capital, Dhaka, and the chief port city of Chittagong are the only significant industrial centres. With only 11% and 26% of the labour force working in the industrial and service sectors, the agricultural sector cannot absorb the constantly growing population. Bangladesh is thus a major exporter of labour to the Arabian countries and to Malaysia. Remittances from emigrant labourers remain an important source of foreign income.

ROLAND J. WENZLHUEMER

See also Central Asia: History and Economic Development; Central Asia: International Relations

References and Further Reading

Baxter, Craig. *Bangladesh: From a Nation to a State.* Boulder, CO: Westview Press, 1997.
Glassie, Henry. *Art and Life in Bangladesh.* Bloomington, IN: Indiana University Press, 1997.
Huque, Ahmed. "The Impact of Colonialism: Thoughts on Politics and Governance in Bangladesh." *Asian Affairs* 28: 15–27 (February 1997).
Jahan, Rounaq. *Bangladesh Politics: Problems and Issues.* Dhaka, Bangladesh: University Press Ltd, 1980.
Murshid, Tazeen. "Democracy in Bangladesh: Illusion or Reality." *Contemporary South Asia* 4: 193–214 (July 1995).
Siddiqui, Kamal. *Towards Good Governance in Bangladesh: Fifty Unpleasant Essays.* Dhaka, Bangladesh: University Press Ltd, 1996.
Wood, Geoffrey D. *Bangladesh: Whose Ideas, Whose Interests?* Dhaka, Bangladesh: University Press Ltd, 1994.

BANK FOR INTERNATIONAL SETTLEMENTS (BIS)

The Bank for International Settlements (BIS) has reinvented itself and recreated its mission, sometimes significantly, since its inception. This flexibility allowed the world's oldest international financial institution to survive the uncertain times that marked its initial decades and to transform itself as needed, to maintain and increase its role in the evolving global economy.

The Bank was born amidst the economic troubles marked by the crash of the US stock market in 1929, and the widespread Great Depression. Through the 1930 Hague Agreements, a multinational group of states created the BIS. Founders included Belgium, France, Germany, Italy, Japan, Switzerland, and the United Kingdom, although as part of its post-World War II treaty, Japan renounced all rights as a founder. These governments anticipated United States' membership; however, it refused (discussed below).

As its name reflects, the Hague signatories created the BIS to facilitate multiple settlements from World War I, as defeated Austrians and Germans, as well as

Bulgarians, Hungarians, and Czechs, made reparations and other war-related payments. These went to other states, which had borrowed internationally to fund their war efforts. The Bank served as an agent for reparations and as a trustee for the multilateral Dawes and Young Plan loans that facilitated repayment of these obligations. This original mission helps to explain the BIS's location, in Switzerland—at the heart of Europe, in an historically neutral state.

While the Bank's reparations function ended in 1932, it continued hosting central bankers and national monetary authorities who wished to work cooperatively. The international financial and trade systems had begun failing, strained by the Depression and World War I's aftermath. Many blame the resultant economic downturns suffered by numerous states for contributing to World War II.

During and after this war, Allied planners determined to prevent recurrence of this economic turbulence. Thus, they created the Bretton Woods system to manage international trade and finance. While the Bank predated this system, much of its post-war work supported the Bretton Woods institutions, especially the fixed exchange rate arrangement. The BIS helped to ensure monetary and financial stability as a means of promoting international trade and investment. One way it promoted international financial operations was by acting as a "bank for central banks."

Additionally, as international transactions grew dramatically in the late 1900s, the Bank functioned as a forum for members to discuss and promote rules and standards for international commercial banking and other capital operations. The BIS also served as an educator, offering research, data, and conferences for public and private members of the financial community. Finally, when sovereign debt overwhelmed some states in the 1990s, the BIS played an important role as a coordinator of bridging loans and loan packages.

While BIS founders invited the United States, the world's most powerful economy, to join, and they set aside shares for Washington to purchase, the United States did not become a member, officially, until 1994. US distrust of the BIS, because of suspicions that it assisted the Nazi war effort, overlaid earlier isolationist sentiments, keeping Washington from direct association. BIS activities even led some in the US government to push for liquidating the Bank after the war. While bowing to pressure from the United Kingdom and Bretton Woods institutions, which argued for maintaining the Bank, the United States refused membership. It considered the BIS a potential challenger to the Federal Reserve Bank and Bretton Woods institutions. Further, given the BIS's location, membership, and activities, Washington considered it a regional organization. While Federal Reserve bankers did take part, unofficially, in many BIS meetings, the United States waited more than sixty years to join.

Decision Making

Although the BIS actually is a limited company, owned by shareholders, it enjoys the privileges and immunities granted international organizations under international and national laws. Its members (owners) are sovereign entities; the Bank has no power to force any state to adopt its approved policies, or to punish those that choose not to implement them. Instead, it proposes and promulgates standards, protocols, and best practices that members may then decide to incorporate into national law. Even given this weakness, many BIS policies have been adopted widely, even by non-member states.

Three decision-making bodies run the Bank: the Board of Directors, the Annual General Meeting, and the Management Committee. Five hundred staff, from more than forty countries, support these entities, at the Basel headquarters or Representative Offices in Hong Kong and Mexico City.

A seventeen-person Board of Directors oversees Bank operations. The top central bank or monetary authority official, often the "governor," for Belgium, France, Germany, Italy, the United Kingdom (all founding members), and the United States, serve as ex officio members. Each appoints another national to the Board, for renewable three-year terms. Under BIS statutes, a maximum of nine (currently there are five) additional central bankers from member states may join the Board, by a two-thirds vote of current directors. They also serve three-year renewable terms.

The Board elects a chair from among its members, and appoints a president to head the BIS for a three-year term. Since its second decade, these have been a joint appointment, so the Chair of the Board also serves as President of the Bank. Members meet at least six times annually to direct Bank activities and to receive and address reports from its committees. Board members serve on specialized bodies including the Consultative Committee, the Audit Committee, and the Asian Consultative Committee, which was created after the Asian financial crisis in the late 1990s.

Representing the membership more broadly, the Annual General Meeting (AGM) is the second decision-making entity. The AGM brings together the top officials from all member states' central banks or monetary authorities, more than fifty, plus the head of the European Central Bank. The AGM takes place within four months of the end of the Bank's fiscal year, generally in late June. Perennial agenda topics include dividend and profit distribution, approval of the Bank's annual report and the state of its accounts, and selection of an external auditor. The membership also may meet in extra sessions (called "Extraordinary Meetings"), to amend BIS statutes, to modify its equity capital (number of shares), or to liquidate the Bank. National monetary authorities frequently meet at the Bank to discuss various topics of interest. In general meetings, each member's vote is weighted according to how many BIS shares it owns.

The final decision-making body is the Management Committee, headed by a General Manager. Reporting to the Board, its focus is daily operations and implementation of Board decisions. This committee also oversees the Bank's exposure to risk from capital market transactions. These activities are under the leadership of the Deputy General Manager, who directs a separate risk control unit.

The Bank also hosts the secretariats of a number of separate, but linked organizations. The most prominent of these is the Group of Ten (G10) states, which organized to support International Monetary Fund (IMF) operations in 1962. The BIS hosts the G10 secretariat, providing a physical residence and technical support, as well as funding for staff. The G10 membership—Belgium, Canada, France, Germany, Japan, the Netherlands, Sweden, the United Kingdom, and the United States—exactly mirrors the nationalities of the Bank's directors. Accordingly, ties between the two are quite close.

The G10's divisions include the Basel Committee on Banking Supervision (founded in 1974) and the Committee on Payments and Settlement Services (1990). While these committees are responsible to the G10, they include members from non-G10 states, and often consult with World Bank (WB) and IMF representatives. Many states, including non-G10 and even non-Bank members, have adopted regulations and standards developed by these committees, demonstrating significant international influence. The BIS also provides a home, and some financial support, for secretariats of the Financial Stability Forum, which focuses on increasing exchange rate information and cooperation related to financial supervision and surveillance, and the International Associations of Insurance Supervisors and of Deposit Insurers.

Operations

BIS resources come from sales of shares and its capital transactions. Its members authorized six hundred thousand shares; more than five hundred thousand are outstanding. While its resources are relatively modest among international financial institutions, about six billion dollars, the BIS serves as a depository for national reserves and funds from more than 120 central banks and international organizations. Through this, it controls assets of more than $150 billion, or about seven percent of total international reserves.

In an Extraordinary General Meeting in 2003, the Bank moved from denominating transactions in gold francs, used since 1930, to the IMF-created international unit of account, the Special Drawing Right (SDR). When created, the gold franc exactly reflected the gold exchange rate for Swiss francs (.29 grams of fine gold). By moving to SDRs, the Bank came into line with the IMF, the WB, and a host of other international institutions.

The BIS provides various banking services to depositors. These help national authorities manage and invest capital reserves, both gold and foreign currencies. The Bank provides storage facilities for gold, bilateral account settlement, liquidity advances to central banks, and sale/purchase of gold and foreign exchange. Moreover, it offers customers investment opportunities through a number of highly liquid instruments. With these, banks and organizations can earn returns above those offered on most national bonds and notes, with almost no risk.

Evolution

Over time, the Bank has played a number of different roles within the international system. When its reparations duties ended, the BIS quickly found new missions. These included working with countries and regional groupings, international commercial banking regulation, and research and dissemination of data on topics of interest to the international financial community.

Its operations with states and multinational groups have included coordination of sovereign loans and serving as a central bank or agent to different organizations. These involved lending to support the Austrian and German central banks in the 1930s, as well as lending to Italy, France, and Britain in the 1960s, and helping to coordinate bridge loans to Mexico and Brazil in the 1990s. After World War II, the BIS functioned as a central banker to the states of Western Europe. It acted as the agent for US Marshall Plan funds (1947–1951), facilitated the European Payments Union (1950–1958), and served as the banker for the European Monetary System

(1979–1994). When the fixed exchange rate system collapsed in the early 1970s, in part because of the difficulty in national management of the increasingly international economy, the BIS saw its role in international stabilization grow.

International banking involves additional risks. Banks lend for operations in areas where they may have limited knowledge of markets or actors. Foreign loans may carry risks from currency devaluation, and, occasionally, such political risks as war or expropriation. Yet, in the 1970s, many Western banks expanded into this realm because of its high profit potential. In 1974, two major banks failed—Germany's Bankhaus Herstatt and the United States' Franklin National Bank—because of foreign operations. While officers or associates of both were prosecuted for these failures, the issue of who was liable to creditors remained. The Basel Committee on Banking Supervision was created to consider where responsibility for foreign branch and subsidiary banks lay. The Committee developed the Basel Concordat of 1975, which argued that home and host countries each bore some responsibility for banking operations within their borders.

This was not enough to prevent further problems. The 1982 failure of the Banco Ambrosiano's Luxembourg-based affiliate prompted 1983's Second Basel Concordat. While the Italian central bank took responsibility for Banco Ambrosiano's domestic activities, with no central bank of its own, the Luxembourg bank's creditors had no similar recourse. The Second Basel Concordat promoted supervision of bank assets and liabilities on a consolidated, worldwide basis, giving a bank's home country authority to close inadequately supervised or insolvent foreign subsidiaries and branches. It also clearly placed responsibility for foreign operations with parent banks.

A debt crisis in the 1980s gripped many less developed states and their lenders, and led the US Federal Reserve Bank to push for minimum international standards of capital adequacy and risk measurement for banks making foreign loans. The 1988 Basel Accord on Capital Adequacy raised reserve requirements for banks doing riskier lending. Most states with international banks have implemented it. Following simultaneous closures of Bank for Credit and Commerce International operations in more than sixty countries and the failure of the Continental Illinois Bank, the Committee amended the Basel Accord in 1995 and 1997. This led to the Basel Core Principles for Effective Banking Supervision, which addressed such risks as those stemming from foreign exchange transactions and debt securities. In 2004, the Committee agreed on Basel II, or the New Capital Framework, which further refines supervision of international banking.

Assessment

The Bank has come under scrutiny and criticism for two main reasons (there has long been an undercurrent of suspicion that it conducts nefarious activities, related to the secrecy surrounding its operations). The first issue relates to Bank conduct during World War II, especially the suspicion that its aided Nazi activities by laundering money, facilitating purchase of goods from neutral states, and accepting deposits stolen from the Nazis' victims. Clearly, the Germans used resources held in the BIS to make purchases from third parties, including Spain, Portugal, Turkey, and Romania. Bank officials argued, however, that they were dealing with Germany's anti-Nazi Reichsbank in these transactions. As to stolen and looted gold, the BIS claimed that it could not have known its true origins, as what it accepted was marked with the pre-1939 German stamp. Of course, the Nazis had re-smelted and re-stamped the stolen metal. Immediately after the war, a multilateral agreement approved by the United States and others settled many of these claims.

The second issue relates to the BIS's role in IMF- and WB-organized debt-restructuring packages. Here, the same criticisms that those institutions garner, related to their neoliberal policies, redound to the Bank. In serving as a linchpin of a system that supports the spread of such policies, the BIS, at least indirectly, clashes with those who believe that neoliberalism and current practices hurt the poor. Anti-globalization and other activists have begun to target it, although its relative anonymity prevents the same intense spotlight shone on other international institutions.

The Bank also wins praise from economic and banking experts for facilitating trade and monetary relations. It has developed standards for international banking and risk management. The BIS also worked diligently to minimize Y2K-related banking problems. Further, it is actively promoting greater transparency to prevent money laundering and to encourage banks to act responsibly. It has taken the lead in research and data collection tied to such new financial instruments as derivatives. Its publications, such as its annual report and various quarterly reports, provide research and statistics, free of charge through the Bank's Web site. Overall, the BIS provides highly specialized services to a group of experts. The needs of these actors likely will determine what the Bank's future missions will be.

JANET ADAMSKI

See also Currency Regimes; Debt: Impact on Development; Debt: Relief Efforts; International Bank for Reconstruction and Development (IBRD)(World Bank); International Monetary Fund (IMF)

References and Further Reading

Allen, Linda. *Capital Markets and Institutions: A Global View*. New York: John Wiley and Sons, 1997.
Baker, James C. *The Bank for International Settlements*. Westport, CT: Quorum Books, 2002.
Bank for International Settlements (*www.bis.org*).
Hague Agreements (www.pcacpa.org/ENGLISH/RPC/BIS/1930convention.htm).
Kapstein, Ethan B. *Supervising International Banks*. Princeton, NJ: Princeton University Press, 1991.
Schloss, Henry. *The Bank for International Settlements*. New York: New York University Press, 1970.
Smith, Roy. *Global Banking*. New York: Oxford University Press, 1997.
Ziegler, Jean. *The Swiss, the Gold and the Dead: How Swiss Bankers Helped Finance the Nazi War Machine*. Translated by John Brownjean. New York: Harcourt Brace, 1998.

BANKING

Devoid of all its modern complexities, banking is simply a process that enables individuals with surplus funds or assets (savers) to transfer their surpluses to individuals with shortfalls (borrowers). The intermediary that enables the savers to transfer the funds to the borrowers is the bank. Banking is therefore first and foremost financial intermediation. Since at a very early age in the history of most societies, there was present in one form or the other something called money, which was generally accepted as a medium of exchange and a store of value, the lending and borrowing of surpluses took the form of the transfer of money. Hence, money and banking became inextricably linked. The intermediary, the bank or depository institution, accepted the savings in the form of money from the savers and transferred them to borrowers in the same form.

In theory and practice, if an individual has a surplus, he or she can benefit by lending it to another individual who needs funds to start or complete a project instead of holding the surplus idle. The individual can give the surplus funds directly to a borrower in what is referred to as *direct finance*. Direct finance is fraught with difficulties, especially as societies grow and relationships become impersonal with each person knowing less and less about the other. If a saver seeks to lend directly to a borrower, the lender must be reasonably confident that the borrower is credit worthy, has a viable project, and will not engage in activities that will endanger his or her ability to repay the interest or the principal. The lender will therefore have to collect enough information about the borrower to make a judgment about the probability of repayment based on past behavior. The lender must also possess the expertise to evaluate the worthiness of the project or hire somebody to do so. Finally, the lender must be able to monitor the behavior of the borrower to ensure that no activity is being undertaken that entails a higher level of risk than that contained in the original loan agreement and therefore increases the likelihood of the loan not being repaid according to the original terms. For a one-time direct lending of a small amount, the cost of collecting such information, known as the transactions costs, and the risk for non-payment may be so high as to make the whole venture unprofitable for both the lender and the borrower. The lender will have to charge a very high interest to compensate for the risk he or she is taking and the additional cost associated with collecting information about the borrower. This high cost will discourage borrowers with good projects who now find the project unprofitable as a result of the high cost of borrowing. At the same time, borrowers who had bad projects to begin with and had no intention of repaying, will not be discouraged from borrowing. This is referred to as *adverse selection*. Given the possibility of this risk, lenders might even refuse to lend: good projects and bad projects alike will not be funded and the whole economy will suffer. If there were an entity, with the reputation of always making payments on time, and if such an entity had the expertise to identify creditworthy borrowers and also had the means to monitor their behavior to ensure compliance with the terms of the loan, then savers could simply lend their funds to this entity and the entity would in turn lend the same funds to borrowers. This entity, the intermediary, comes between the saver and the borrower and facilitates the transfer of funds.

This circuitous way of lending, known as *indirect finance*, is what banks do. Banks, as financial intermediaries, reduce transactions cost because of the high volume of transactions they undertake and the resulting economies of scale. They also minimize risk because of the pooling and diversification from lending to a lot of borrowers. Since transactions costs and risk are reduced for both borrowers and lenders alike, more savers are willing to lend (to the intermediary) and more borrowers are able to borrow (from the

intermediary). Banking can therefore be described as the process of channeling funds from savers to borrowers through an intermediary.

Banks as Depository Institutions

Banks are not just financial intermediaries as described previously. They are also depository institutions, a characteristic that makes banking unique among financial institutions and intermediaries. When savers leave their funds with a bank for safekeeping or lend their savings to banks for a return (*interest income*), the bank has acquired a financial asset in the form of cash. At the same time, however, a liability is generated, called deposits. The deposits are liabilities because at any point in time, certain or uncertain, the owner may show up to collect his or her deposits or cause the deposits to be transferred to somebody else. The deposits generally fall into one of three major categories:

1. *Demand or checking account deposits*, which can be redeemed or transferred to another person or entity with no notice using a written order called a *check*. In general, demand deposits do not attract interest income as such, but they do provide convenience of being generally acceptable for payments of goods and services and thus serving as a medium of exchange or money.
2. *Savings deposits*, which unlike demand deposits, cannot be transferred by a written order but may be redeemed with little or no notice. Banks pay owners interest income.
3. *Time deposits*, which have specific maturity dates and specified rates of return and cannot be redeemed before the maturity date, or can be redeemed with a penalty. The interest is higher than that paid on saving deposits because banks can depend on the availability of the deposits for a defined time period.

Since demand/checking account deposits can be transferred from one party to another with a simple instruction to the bank (a check), demand deposits provide a convenient way of making payments in modern societies. In making a payment for a good or service, one may use cash or currency (coins and paper money), or one may transfer his or her demand or checking deposits in the bank. If people do accept currency and checks in payment for goods and services, then the money supply comprises at least the currency and demand deposits in the banks.

Bank Regulation and Central Banking

Whether banks should be free and subject only to the discipline of the marketplace or should be regulated by policy makers is a debate that is ongoing in the economics profession. Some economists use the experience of the US during the "free banking" era of 1837 to 1863 as a good reason to regulate banks. Others look at the same era and see a relatively stable period and argue for no regulation, concluding that the marketplace does a very good job of keeping banks well behaved. Regardless of which side one takes, the mere fact that even prudent banks cannot withstand a *run on the bank*, suggests that if there is a shock, which provokes a crisis of confidence, the most well-run bank will collapse. A run on the bank occurs when, as a result of loss of confidence in the banks ability to repay deposits, customers come in droves to demand repayment. As has already been discussed, banks do not keep a hundred percent reserves to back up deposits. The banks will therefore not survive such runs. Further, banking crises tend to affect the economy in ways that are more pernicious than crises in other sectors of the economy. The collapse of a bank shrinks the stock of money in the economy and with it, the volume of economic activity. A bank may be very well run but may face a sudden excess demand for cash beyond what it may immediately have available. For these and other reasons, modern-day banks are regulated. The agency that has the primary role in regulating banks is the central bank, or the central bank and the treasury, or the finance ministry.

Central banks are described as the bankers' bank and the government's bank, but for the most part the major duty of central banks is to ensure that a country's monetary system operates soundly. As such, over the years, the major responsibility of central banks has been in the conduct of monetary policy. In that role, the central bank seeks to make certain that the stock of money in the economy is just the right amount to ensure that the economy grows at its potential. If the amount of money is too little, it will stifle growth, and if it is too much, it will create inflation. The central bank therefore must walk a tightrope. Whereas commercial banks tend to be private institutions (except in several developing countries where some of the major banks are owned by governments), central banks tend to be government institutions or government and private combined. Whereas commercial banks seek to make a profit for their owners, central banks are by nature non–profit-making institutions. This does not mean that they do not make profits; indeed, central banks do quite well. It simply means that their objective is not to maximize profit.

In the previous discussions, it was indicated that whenever banks make loans, they add to deposits and therefore increase the money supply. It is this money supply that central banks seek to control. To make loans, the banks need cash reserves. The more cash reserves the banks have, the more loans they can make. In one example, FAB had found by experience that it needed 20% of deposits as cash reserves and so it had to keep cash reserves equal to 20% of deposits. Two factors emerge as being responsible for the amount of loans banks can make: (a) the cash reserves available to them and (b) the required cash reserves-to-deposits ratio or reserve deposit ratio, for short. To control the ability to make loans and therefore increase the money supply, these two factors must be controlled. The central bank's power to control the reserves available to depository institutions and set the reserve deposit ratio gives it the ability to control, within some margin, the money supply.

The effects of a change in reserve deposit ratio can be immediate and very powerful. For example, if the central bank changes the reserve deposit ratio from 10% to 20%, it means that for each $100 in deposits that banks have, they must now double the cash reserves they hold. The effect is to force banks to call in loans or refuse to make new ones. The upshot is that deposits will decline and with it the money supply. As the money supply decreases, the cost of borrowing—the interest rate—increases. Conversely, if the central bank seeks to stimulate economic activity, it could do so by reducing the reserve deposit ratio, thus enabling the banks to make more loans with the same cash reserves. Most modern central banks shy away from using the reserve deposit ratio because of its sudden and traumatic effect on the banking system. Indeed, calls for reform of reserve requirements have included demands for its total elimination.

If commercial banks were caught in a situation where they did not have adequate cash to meet withdrawals, they could borrow from the central bank. This facility, referred to as borrowing from the *discount window*, also provides commercial banks with another means to obtain reserves. The commercial banks borrow from the central bank at a rate known as the *discount rate.* In theory, banks borrow from the central bank only when they face a liquidity crunch. Since only a small portion of the banks' assets are in the form of cash, it is possible for a well-run bank to face this liquidity constraint. The central bank as the bankers' bank would then discount some of the notes that the commercial banks have and provide the needed liquidity. This facility ensures that the system as a whole would not cave in as a result of some unforeseen liquidity crisis. Most central banks see the discount window facility as a last resort. Indeed, central banks are often described as the *lenders of last resort* for this very reason. In practice, if the central bank finds a bank utilizing the discount window too often, the central bank could interpret that as a sign that the bank is not being run very well, which might lead to frequent visits by examiners from the central bank—another function the central bank performs. In spite of this, the presence of this facility provides a measure of security to the banking system.

A preferred method of controlling the stock of money in the economy is to indirectly affect the level of reserves available to the banks. In discussing how banks create money, it was mentioned that when customers deposit their cash with banks, it becomes cash reserves, which are then leveraged to create more money. For ease of understanding how the process works, let us define money as currency in circulation (C) plus demand or checking deposits (DD) with banks. Let us assume that the initial total stock of money (the medium of exchange) in the economy is $100. If individuals decide to hold all of the $100 in their pockets, in the form of currency, then the money supply remains at $100. Let us assume that individuals decide to hold only $10 in the form of currency and the remainder, $90, as bank deposits. Let us now define a concept called *monetary base* (MB), consisting of the currency in circulation (C) and the reserves in the banks (R). As can be readily appreciated, the monetary base is equal to $100, all which could be held as currency or as bank deposits. In our example, we have assumed that $10 is held as currency and $90 as bank deposits (cash reserves for the banks). If the reserve deposit ratio is 10%, then with cash reserves of $90, the banks can create total deposits of $900. In this economy, therefore, the money supply could be as much as $990. This potential amount depends on, among other factors, the monetary base. As the monetary base increases, all else remaining the same, the money supply increases; and as the monetary base decreases, all else remaining the same, the money supply decreases.

The factors that determine the stock of money are the following:

1. The reserve deposit ratio
2. The monetary base
3. Individuals preference for currency versus checking deposits
4. Willingness of banks to lend and individuals to borrow

The first two factors are controlled by the central bank, the third and fourth are self-explanatory. We have seen that central banks can alter the reserve deposit ratio and thus alter the banks' ability to create deposits. The central bank controls the monetary base through a process referred to as *open market operations.*

The Central Bank and Open Market Operations

It has already been stated that as the monetary base increases, so does the money supply; the converse is also true. The balance sheet of central banks has as principal assets the securities issued by the government. In the main, these are the assets that back the notes (liabilities) issued by the central bank and that circulate as currency. The banks and the non-bank public also hold some of the same government securities as part of their portfolio. In short, the central bank, the banks, and the non-bank public all hold government securities. If the central bank seeks to increase the money supply, it may choose to do so by buying some of the government securities held by the banks and the non-bank public. If the securities are bought from a bank, the bank gets a credit in the forms of reserves with the central bank. The central bank acquires securities on its assets side, and on its liabilities side, deposits of the bank increase. The increase in the bank's deposits at the central bank is tantamount to an increase in reserves for the bank. With the infusion of these new reserves, the bank can now make loans and create additional deposits, which will increase the money supply. Similarly, if the central bank seeks to decrease the money supply, it can do so by selling some of its stock of government securities to the public. If a member of the public buys some of the securities, he or she pays for it by drawing a check on his or her bank, transferring deposits to the central bank. The effect is to reduce the reserves available to the bank and thus its ability to make loans. The process of buying and selling government securities to increase or decrease the monetary base is what is referred to as open market operations. Table 1 shows the consolidated balance sheet of the Federal Reserve Bank, the central bank of the United States.

As can be seen from the table, more than ninety percent of the assets of the central bank are securities, the bulk of them being government securities or securities of government agencies. On the liabilities side, about an equal percentage is in the form of the notes issued by the central bank. A much smaller percentage—four percent—represents deposits of the depository institutions (the banks), for which the

Table 1

			Amount	Percentage
(a)		Consolidated Balance Sheet of All Federal Reserve Banks (U.S)		
(b)		September 29, 2004 (millions of U.S. dollars)		
(c)		Assets	Amount	Percentage
		Gold certificate account	11,039	1
		Special drawing rights	2,200	–
		Coin	777	–
		Securities	728,368	92
		Cash items in process of collection	5,602	1
		Other assets	39,618	5
(i)		*Total Assets*	*787,605*	
(d)		Liabilities		
		Federal Reserve notes	703,451	89
		Reverse purchase agreements	24,337	3
		Deposits	30,704	3
		Deferred availability cash items	5,938	1
		Other cash liabilities/accrued dividends	2,759	–
		Capital accounts	20,416	3
(i)		*Total Liabilities*	*787,605*	

central bank acts as a banker, and the government or government agencies. With only slight variations, the balance sheets of all central banks have the same structure. It is this structure that enables the central bank to perform the crucial task of controlling the money supply using open market operations.

The balance sheet also shows the other functions the central bank performs. A very small portion (less than 3% in the case of the United States) of the securities consists of loans to the depository institutions under what was discussed as the discount window borrowings. The central bank also acts as a clearing agent for the depository institutions.

Banking Practices in Developing Countries

In many developing countries, by virtue of colonization by Europe, banks and modern banking practices owe their origins to what pertained in Europe or elsewhere in the developed world. For example, in the former British colonies of Africa, Asia, and the Caribbean countries, one runs into such typical British banks as Barclays and Standard Banks. In South America, one sees the presence of the United States in such banks as Goldman Sachs and Citibank. Over the years, local banks have sprung up in several of the developing countries; some of these have become quite large and have mobilized large amounts of capital and deposits from both domestic and foreign sources. In many of the poorer developing countries, however, banks continue to be state owned, and are

plagued by problems that hinder their effectiveness to intermediate. Banking services and their impact on economic development vary widely from one developing country to another. Also, because of the dualistic nature of most of these economies, there are wide variations within countries.

In general, the more advanced the developing countries are, the more sophisticated the banking systems tend to be. Banks in countries such as Indonesia, Thailand, and South Korea have by and large done very well in raising capital for economic development and providing very good banking services with positive impacts on their domestic economies. The same can be said of banks in countries such as Brazil and Argentina in South America. At the other end are the poorer developing countries, mostly in Sub-Saharan Africa and Asia, where banking facilities and services are rare and available to only a very small percentage of the population. It must also be mentioned that even in the more advanced developing economies, access to banking services are not evenly distributed throughout the country; dualism still persists. Some sectors of the same country may have access to banking services and banking facilities while others may be completely without. More often than not, people in the rural areas may not have access to banking services and may depend on moneylenders to raise capital.

A bank's ability to perform the crucial task of financial intermediation depends almost entirely on the amount of deposits and capital it can mobilize. The amount of deposits depends on factors such as inflation, the interest paid to depositors, access to and confidence in the banking system, and the availability of financial instruments such as certificates of deposits. Bank capital, on the other hand, depends on the laws, rules, and regulations in place that determine whether individual citizens and foreigners may own banks; the willingness of domestic residents to keep capital at home or send it abroad; and the ease with which bank stocks can be bought and sold.

In general, sound macroeconomic policies, which lead to low inflation, and positive real interest rates, would encourage bank deposits. Countries such as China, South Korea, and Thailand, which have succeeded in keeping inflation low or have reduced inflation, have seen rapid increases in deposits. In several of the developing countries, however, because of high inflation and sometimes negative real interest rates, deposits are very low. Past incidences of deposit seizures have also contributed to low confidence in the banking system and to low deposits. Laws forbidding foreign participation in certain sectors of the economy have also been used to prevent foreign capital from being utilized in domestic banking sectors. These factors partly account for why banks in developing countries tend to be small and are unable to effectively extend credit.

The aforementioned also explains why, in the 1970s and into the 1980s, some central banks in the developing countries saw themselves as active participants in providing credit for economic development. Credit guarantee schemes, CGS (insurance protection), were introduced to encourage the commercial banks to lend to certain sectors, such as agriculture and housing—sectors that were considered keys to economic growth. The huge losses that resulted led to the suspension of these insurance programs. Essentially, the banks did not undertake the due diligence that would normally accompany credit extensions since they could count on losses being covered by the central bank or the government. When the central banks turned away from direct participation, some of them encouraged access to banking services by setting up rural banks (unit banks). This is a variation on micro-financing, where loans of small amounts are made to individuals or to groups of individuals. Sometimes group members are all collectively responsible for repayment of loans. The idea behind rural banking is that by limiting the range of activities, confining their localities, and fostering a more intimate relationship between banks and customers, bank performance will get better and the rural sector will benefit from the availability of credit, which should promote economic development. For a variety of reasons, chiefly poor supervision of banking activities and corrupt practices, the reality has not been quite what was expected.

A serious, persistent problem in the banking systems in developing countries is the number of bank crises and distresses. Although bank crises can occur in developed countries, such as the savings and loan crises in the United States in the 1980s, in the developing countries they tend to be more frequent, systemic, and more pernicious. Between 1980 and the early 2000s, for example, the developing countries of Latin America and the Caribbean suffered a total of thirty-one *banking crises*—defined as situations where banks have nearly exhausted capital and/or have experienced a run on deposits. In addition, there were fifteen episodes of system distresses and averted crises, where banks had low or negative net worth without a run on deposits. The countries that had these episodes included Argentina and Brazil, which may be considered more advanced developing countries; and Jamaica, Guyana, and Haiti, which are less advanced. Banking crises have not been limited to one continent, however. Episodes have occurred in Southeast Asia, notably Korea and Thailand in the 1990s. Several African countries have also had similar episodes. Since the banks tend to be owned by the state, governments have had to restructure and re-capitalize their banking systems.

The reasons for the crises and distresses are many. The 1980s saw the liberalization of many economies without the necessary institutional constraints on the behavior of the banking system. The result was that credit was extended without proper safeguards. In some cases, especially in state-controlled institutions, lending sometimes did not even follow guidelines established by the banks themselves, let alone international standards. Directives from politicians and state officials sufficed to extend credit to favored sectors of the economy or projects. Also, in some cases, large amounts of credit were extended to state institutions and to the governments. When the state institutions failed, governments were then saddled with the debts or they had to be written off. Compounding the problem is the matter of inadequate and ineffective supervision of the banks. Sometimes, what could have been a minor problem festers as it is concealed or not discovered by bank examiners; when it finally becomes apparent, the results are crises, which then affect the whole economy. These effects linger long after they have occurred, tending to undermine the confidence that citizens have in the banking systems and leading to searches for alternative ways of storing value such as dollarization (the holding of stronger more stable foreign currencies such as the dollar and the euro). In recent times in almost all the developing countries, citizens have resorted to dumping the domestic money in favor of more stable foreign money. Money as such has ceased to perform some of its crucial functions in these countries. From Azerbaijan to Zimbabwe, one sees goods and contracts being priced in dollars instead of in the domestic currencies. Those who are able to do so sometimes hold their deposits abroad, rather than in the domestic banking system, effectively leading to the contraction of domestic credit and economic activity.

The most important lesson that developing countries have to learn, especially from the recent experiences of the countries in Latin America and Asia, is that supervision of banks must be done efficiently and frequently to ensure that problems are dealt with quickly, before they get out of control. This will minimize the crises and their severity when they do occur.

Regional and International Banks

No matter how large banks in the developing countries are, they tend to be small in terms of capital compared with their counterparts in the developed countries. Deposits tend to be from only domestic residents. Further, the concept of syndicated loans, where several banks come together to extend credit to a single borrower, is still not in use in many of the developing countries. Even if it were possible to syndicate loans, very few of the local banks could come up with the large capital required to fund projects that amount, in some cases, to millions of dollars. In response, different developing countries have come together to form regional banks. There are several of these regional banks, and they include Inter-American Development Bank (IDB), founded in 1959, covering the Caribbean and South American regions; the Asian Development Bank (ADB), established in 1966; the African Development Bank Group (The ADB Group); the Islamic Development Bank (IBD), established in 1975; and the West African Development Bank or Banque Ouest Africaine De Developpement (BOAD), established in 1994. Although these banks operate mostly in the regions their names describe, their capital comes from members as well as nonmembers in the developed countries. For example, the United States and Japan have the highest capital subscription to the Asian Development Bank. Japan is a member but the United States is not.

In addition to the regional banks, which help finance large projects, the International Bank for Reconstruction and Development (IBRD), or the World Bank, has also been an active player in the banking scene of the developing countries. It has over the years become one of the most important sources of capital for development.

Traditional Banking Institutions

An essay on banking would not be complete without reference to traditional banking in some of the developing countries. We have defined banking as a process, part of which involves transferring funds from savers to borrowers. In several African and Caribbean countries (and probably in Asian as well), there is a practice known as *susu*, which helps individuals to accumulate funds. Essentially, five or more people (sometimes fewer) decide to contribute to a pool of funds at regular intervals and give it to one person in the group. The group decides the order in which each participant will draw. Each participant stays in the pool until every member has drawn a lot, at which point the process begins all over again or is dissolved. Sometimes there can be several people in the pool and it might take the last person several months to get his or her turn. As inefficient as this might sound, it fulfills its primary purpose of making large sums available to individuals for projects, which cannot be financed with one's own resources. The members of the *susu* depend on each other's integrity to make the system work.

Another form of banking revolves around an individual who goes around collecting small amounts from mostly market women. The individual acts more or less as a collection agent and then saves the collected sums on behalf of the group. He or she makes entries noting each person's contribution. It is not certain whether the collection agent, who must be a trusted person, can then use the contributions to make out loans or not. The scenario, however, is not very far removed from the mythical goldsmith, who acted as a safe haven for individuals to deposit their gold and who then proceeded to lend the deposits, thus becoming the forebearer of modern banking.

Trends in Modern Banking and Implications for the Developing Countries

The trend in modern banking is toward mergers and acquisitions internally and across national boundaries. As of 2002, the five largest banks in the world in terms of total assets were, in order:

Of the fifty biggest banks in the world, eleven are in the United States, nine in Germany, and six each are in Japan and the United Kingdom. China and France each has four of them. The Netherlands has three; Spain and Switzerland each has two. Italy, Canada, and Belgium round it up with one each. Four countries, the United States, Germany, Japan, and

Table 2

Bank (country of inc.)	Assets (in trillions of U.S. dollars)
Mizuho Financial Group (Japan)	1.3 as of 3/2002
Citigroup (United States)	1.1 as of 12/2001
Deutsche Bank (Germany)	.81 as of 3/2002
Sumitomo Mitsui Banking Group (Japan)	.78 as of 3/2002
UBS (Switzerland)	.75 as of 3/2002

the United Kingdom, have more than 64% of the biggest banks. The four countries also control about 65% of the total assets of the biggest banks; accounting for US$14.9 trillion of the $23 trillion. As big as these banks are, the trend is toward more of the same.

As the big bank mergers and branching extend to the developing countries, there are some who argue that it will make the domestic banks stronger and provide more efficient and robust services. There are others who fear that without special provisions, the bigger foreign banks that may have interests at variance with those of the host developing countries will redirect funds away from sectors considered keys to economic development. Regardless of which view one holds, as the world economy gets more and more open, the trend is toward more consolidation through mergers and acquisitions. An appropriate response may be to help local banks to operate more efficiently through proper supervision and training of personnel.

Last Word

The big banks listed above combine what is described as retail banking with investment banking. Retail banking is primarily what has been discussed previously. Investment bankers undertake the task of designing, marketing, and guaranteeing (sometimes not) new securities in what is referred to as the primary market. The primary market is where new securities are bought and sold. An investment banker will therefore work with a customer who needs funds to find savers who are willing to lend to the customer.

In conclusion, banking is about channeling surplus funds to those who need it through an intermediary (retail banking) or by matching savers and borrowers (investment banking). The banks, by reducing costs and minimizing risks, make the terms of borrowing and lending less onerous and thus encourage borrowing and lending and promote economic activity.

SAMUEL K. ANDOH

See also African Development Bank (ADB); Asian Development Bank; Bank for International Settlements (BIS); Caribbean Development Bank; European Bank for Reconstruction and Development; Inter-American Development Bank (IDB); International Bank for Reconstruction and Development (IBRD) (World Bank)

References and Further Reading

Burton, Maureen, and Ray Lombra. *The Financial System & the Economy: Principles of Money and Banking*, 3d ed. Mason, OH: Thompson South-Western, 2003.

Carstens, Agustin, Daniel C. Hardy, and Ceyla Pazarbasioglu. "Avoiding Banking Crises in Latin America." *Finance & Development*, pp. 30–33 (September 2004).

Hanson, James. *Banking in Developing Countries in the 1990s*. World Bank Policy Research Working Paper 3168, November 2003.

McConnell, Campbell R., and Stanley L. Brue. *Macroeconomics: Principles, Problems and Policies*, 15th ed. New York: McGraw-Hill/Irwin, 2002.

Mishkin, Frederic S. *The Economics of Money, Banking and Financial Markets*, 7th ed. New York: Pearson Addison Wesley, 2004.

The Internationalization of Financial Services: Issues and Lessons for Developing Countries. WTO/World Bank Kluwer Law International, The Hague, 2001.

The Web sites of central banks (of which there are many) contain a wealth of information on banking activities. Some of the ones cited in the text are given below.

African Development Bank Group: www.afdb.org
Asian Development Bank: www.adb.org
"Bank of Ghana Statistics." *Bank of Ghana*. www.bog.gov.gh/stats.htm, Tables 4 and 5
Banque Ouest Africaine de Développement (BOAD): www.boad.org
Inter-American Development Bank: www.iadb.org
Islamic Development Bank (IDB) Group: www.isdb.org

Data on global banking can be obtained from the following address on the Internet: www.aaadir.com/world.jsp

BANTUSTANS

Historical Background

The creation of Bantustans, or homelands for Africans, by the nationalist government of South Africa with the 1951 Bantu Authorities Act was nothing but an attempt to carry the existing policy of Native

Reserves, based on the 1913 and 1936 Land Acts, to its logical conclusion. While the Land Acts forbade blacks from owning property outside of specified Native Reserves, the Bantu Authorities Act erected an edifice of separate African ethnic identities, or "Homelands," cloistered within their own boundaries. The South African Government (SAG) evicted thousands of Africans from the industrial and urban centers and barricaded them in one or other of the ten tribal Homelands according to their ethnic/linguistic origin. It planned to prepare these Homelands for "independence" so that all Africans, becoming citizens of one or another of the Bantustans, would cease to be South African citizens. This was expected to counteract the growing African demand for political rights and break the resistance of the African National Congress (ANC) to the apartheid regime.

By the mid-1970s, the SAG had created ten African Homelands (listed with primary ethnic groups and 1976 population): Bophuthatswana (Tswana, 1.1 million), Ciskei and Transkei (Xhosa, 475,000 and 2.4 million, respectively), Gazankulu (Tsonga/Shangaan, 333,000), KaNgwane (Swazi, 209,000), Kwandebele (Southern Ndebele, 150,000), KwaZulu (Zulu, 2.9 million), Lebowa (Northern Sotho, Northern Ndebele, and Pedi, 1.3 million), QwaQwa (Southern Sotho, 91,000), and Venda (Venda, 339,000). The overwhelming majority of their able-bodied adults were away working in South Africa. The Bantustans constituted 13% of the South African land and more than 75% of its people.

The Bantustan scheme was designed to strengthen African tribal identities, to prevent unity between the tribes, and slow the mounting African demand for political rights. But only four Homelands eventually accepted independence. These were Transkei (1976), Bophuthstswana (1977), Venda (1979), and Ciskei (1981). "Independence" was forced upon Ciskei despite 90% of its people having opposed it. Other Bantustans resolutely opposed this nominal independence, as it meant loss of their South African citizenship and complete dependence upon the apartheid regime. Six Homelands acquired self-government. No other country, except South Africa, ever recognized their independence.

Main Features

The Bantustans were only nominally independent as they did not fulfill any criterion of independence. Only two were geographically contiguous, KwaNdebele and QwaQwa. The others included three or more scattered pieces: Ciskei comprised eighteen separate pieces of land and KwaZulu, forty-four. The Homelands were also carved out in such a manner as to cause constant skirmishes between them. Thus, Transkei, the larger Xhosa Homeland, claimed the much smaller Xhosa Homeland, Ciskei, as part of itself and refused to recognize Ciskei's "independence." Border disputes made relations between Lebowa and Gazankulu equally hostile.

Secondly, despite variations in area and population between the larger Bantustans such as Transkei (4.1 million hectar) and the smaller such as QwaQwa (58,000 hectar), all Bantustans were arid, overcrowded, and overworked rural settlements lacking any potential for self-sustenance. KwaNdebele, for example, having little water of its own, relied on tanker-supplied water from South Africa. Ciskei, with a population density of more than four hundred per square kilometer in the 1980s, was constantly in need of more land. With little employment opportunities on their own territory, being economically unimportant, and having poor-quality land that made agriculture nearly impossible, the Bantustans acted as reservoirs of cheap labor for the South African economy. Some of them were simply oversized dormitories for migrant African laborers whose stay in South African industrial centers was dependent upon their remaining in employment.

Consequently, the Bantustans saw little development during their existence of nearly thirty years. Wages of migrant laborers constituted 70% to 75% of the Gross National Product of Lebowa, Transkei, and Venda, and even more for KaNgwane and KwaNdebele. The sole exception was Bophuthatswana, 50% of whose GNP came from its mines, quarries, and the casino complex at Sun City. Unfair competition with white trading houses, such as Frasers, Checkers, and so forth, who had highjacked even the apartheid regime's development schemes for the Bantustans, left African entrepreneurs with bottle store licenses only. These development schemes were meant to foster a class of collaborating petty capitalists in the Homelands, a class that could be used to stem the tide of growing militant nationalism. Later, the failure of these schemes ended up alienating the aspiring Homeland petty bourgeoisie from their rulers.

In addition, the apartheid regime appointed reactionary chiefs who collaborated with the SAG in ruling the Bantustans. These chiefs often brutally repressed the increasing African restiveness and militancy following the emergence of the Black Consciousness Movement and the Soweto uprising of 1976. Secure in their power due to the large number (from 50% in Bophuthatswana to 100% in KwaNdebele and KaNgwane) of legislative assembly seats reserved for them or their nominees, most rulers felt no need to create support for themselves within their constituencies. They openly rigged elections; failing that, they organized coups and countercoups to wrest power from their opponents. The atrocities of the Sebe brothers and Oupa Gqozo in Ciskei, and of the Matanzima brothers in Transkei, created a disjuncture between them and the petty bourgeoisie, and led to their implosion in the early 1990s (Peires 1992).

The apartheid regime itself did not respect the Homelands' independence. It kept them running by making annual administrative grants, aid packages, and "loans" and controlled the Bantustans, including the "independent" ones, by appointing its own men in key ministries of finance, defense, internal security, and so on, primarily to check the growing influence of the ANC. In 1981, the regime unilaterally decided to cede the whole of KaNgwane and a part of KwaZulu to Swaziland and dissolved the protesting KaNgwane legislative assembly.

Shortly before the 1994 democratic elections, Bantustan rulers such as Lucas Mangope in Bophuthatswana, Oupa Gqozo in Ciskei, and the Matanzima brothers in Transkei conspired with the white reactionary parties to preserve their privileged positions. The most ambitious and wily ruler of KwaZulu, Mangosothu Gatsha Buthelezi, conniving with the apartheid regime, unleashed his Inkatha "impies" among the followers of the ANC in Natal and Johannesburg, causing much bloodshed. Buthelezi held out until the last moment before agreeing to be part of a democratic South Africa. It was the impoverished and terrorized peoples of the Bantustans whose support enabled the ANC and other African parties to successfully integrate the Bantustans into a new South Africa in 1994.

KUSUM DATTA

See also Southern Africa: History and Economic Development

References and Further Reading

Bank, Leslie. "Between Traders and Tribalists: Implosion and the Politics of Disjuncture in a South African Homeland." *African Affairs* 93(370): 43–74 (1994).

Davies, Rob, Dan O'Meara, and Sipho Dlamini (compilers). *The Struggle for South Africa: A Reference Guide*, 2 volumes. London, and New Jersey: Zed Books, 1985; new edition, 1988.

Graaf, Johann. "Towards an Understanding of Bantustan Politics." In *The Political Economy of South Africa*, edited by N. Nattrass and E. Ardington. Cape Town, South Africa: Oxford University Press, 1990.

Leeuwenberg, J. *Transkei: A Study in Economic Regression.* London: Africa Publications Trust, 1977.

Mare, G., and G. Hamilton. *An Appetite for Power: Buthelezi's Inkatha and the Politics of Loyal Resistance.* Johannesburg, South Africa: 1987.

Nzimande, B. "Class, National Oppression and the African Petty Bourgeoisie." In *Repression and Resistance: An Insider's Account of Apartheid*, edited by R. Cohen, Y. Muthien, and A. Zegeye. London: Hans Zell, 1990.

Peires, J. B. "The Implosion of Transkei and Ciskei." *African Affairs* 91(364): 365–388 (1992).

Rogers, B. *Divide and Rule: South Africa's Bantustans.* London: International Defence and Aid Fund, 1980.

Southall, Roger. "Buthelezi, Inkatha and the Politics of Compromise." *African Affairs* 80(320): 453–481 (1981).

Southall, Roger. *South Africa's Transkei: The Politics of an 'Independent' Bantustan.* London: Heinemann, 1982.

Streek, B. and R. Wicksteed. *Render Unto Kaiser: A Transkei Dossier.* Johannesburg, South Africa: Ravan Press, 1981.

Two fairly independent South African newspapers, the *Daily Dispatch* and *Weekly Mail*, extensively covered the events in the Homelands between 1990 and 1994. They are useful since very little has been written on the smaller and self-governing Homelands.

BARBADOS

As a developing country, Barbados presents an intriguingly contradictory profile. On the one hand, it possesses characteristics of a well-developed country in terms of an almost universal rate of literacy among the population and ample access to quality public education. On the other hand, it presents characteristics of underdevelopment due to chronic rates of unemployment, varying from 10%–20% at the end of the twentieth century, and underemployment. Much of the population, referred to as "Bajan," emigrates to the United States or other regions for jobs. With a per capita distribution of Gross Domestic Product at about $15,000 per year, Barbados can be classified as a country of middling development.

An examination of Barbadian history provides considerable explanation of the country's development and dilemmas. Although culturally part of the Caribbean, Barbados lies geographically in the Atlantic Ocean, northeast of Venezuela. Midway off the Windward Isles of the Lesser Antilles, it is an outpost in the Atlantic, the farthest east of a Caribbean island. Settled by Arawak, then Carib Indians, the island first received European notice in the early sixteenth century. The Portuguese touched on the island, possibly naming it after the "bearded" appearance of certain trees strung with hanging vegetation.

The English definitively settled the island in the early seventeenth century. They established an initial settlement pattern on the island that consisted of small farms producing subsistence and export crops. Later in the century this pattern was replaced. Sugar, grown on large plantations, became the almost exclusive crop on the island. It was cultivated for export and produced by the labor of slaves. Tens of thousands of Africans were brought to the island, thereby replacing the small, original white population with an African and mixed-race one. The English language and a combination of English with African dialects, Creole, became the languages of the country. The main religion became Anglican (Church of England).

As a result, at the beginning of the twenty-first century, the Bajan population of slightly more than a quarter million people was more than three-fourths of African descent and nearly two-thirds Protestant, primarily Anglican but also Methodist, Pentecostal, and Evangelical. Due to high rates of emigration, native population growth has become virtually stagnant. The area of Barbados is only 430 square kilometers (166 square miles), somewhat larger than the island of Malta in the Mediterranean. Population density is high. More than a third of the land is arable and intensively cultivated. The surface is flat or gently rolling, rising to central highlands. Barbados is not often directly hit by hurricanes.

During the mid-seventeenth century, the free, property-owning minority of the population established a general assembly, organizing one of the first colonial legislatures in the British empire. Moreover, the Anglican Church, the established religion in the empire, assumed a missionary responsibility for basic education, organizing schools. Anglican and other religions concentrated on educational development during the centuries that followed.

However, by the middle of the twentieth century, education was in public hands and available for all at both the primary and secondary levels through government-sponsored technical and vocational training programs. Reducing class and gender biases is a stated objective of educational policy in Barbados so that the full social strength of the country supports national development. Barbados has minorities of Middle Eastern and Asian descent who belong to small Moslem and Hindu communities.

Slavery was abolished at the beginning of the nineteenth century. However, only in the mid-twentieth century did sufficient economic and political reforms occur that would form the basis for independence in 1966. These reforms included increased civil and voting rights for the descendants of slaves, moving toward consolidation of the majority of Bajans into the country's parliamentary democracy.

Spearheading the political and social changes that swept over the country was the Barbados Labour Party (BLP), founded in 1937 by Grantley Adams. A splinter from this party was organized in 1951 as the Democratic Labour Party (DLP), under the leadership of Errol Barrow. These two parties and political figures and others related to them have been the sustaining forces in modern Bajan politics and government. After independence, Barbados became a member of the British Commonwealth of Nations and therefore has the British monarch, as represented in a governor-general, as the head of state.

With independence, not only the political nature of Barbados changed but also its economy. From an agricultural economy based on the export of sugar, it changed in the last decades of the twentieth century to one based on services, primarily tourism. In addition to tourist services, it has developed offshore financial and banking operations. Accompanying services has been development of a light manufacturing sector, especially for construction materials. Manufacturing and agriculture comprise less than a fourth of Bajan economy, which is now overwhelmingly based on services. Barbados has participated in a number of regional Caribbean development organizations, including the West Indies Federation (1958), the Caribbean Free Trade Association (1968), and the Caribbean Community (1973). It hosts a branch of the University of the West Indies.

The cultural development of Barbados reflects its mixed English and African roots. The tiny island has produced some famous players of the British game of cricket (similar to American baseball), most notably Garfield Sobers and Frank Worrell. In addition, it has a music industry based on Calypso or Afro-Caribbean rhythms, a noted Bajan musician being the Mighty Gabby. As an English-speaking country with a presence in popular culture, Barbados reflects the globally integrated tendencies and development of all modern societies.

EDWARD A. RIEDINGER

See also Caribbean Basin Initiative; Caribbean Community and Common Market (CARICOM); Caribbean Free Trade Association (CARIFTA); Caribbean: History and Economic Development; Caribbean: International Relations; North American Free Trade Agreement (NAFTA)

References and Further Reading

"Barbados." *Historical Dictionary of the British Caribbean*, by William Lux. Metuchen, NJ: Scarecrow Press, 1975.

Beckles, Hilary. *A History of Barbados: From Amerindian Settlement to Nation-state.* Cambridge, United Kingdom: Cambridge University Press, 1990.

Carmichael, Trevor. *Barbados: Thirty Years of Independence.* Kingston, Jamaica: Ian Randle, 1996.

Fraser, Henry *et al. A–Z of Barbadian Heritage.* Kingston, Jamaica: Heinemann (Caribbean), 1990.

Potter, Robert B., and Graham Dann. *Barbados*. World Bibliographical Series: 76. Oxford, United Kingdom: Clio Press, 1987.

BASIC HUMAN NEEDS

During the 1970s, development scholars and practitioners were disenchanted with orthodox thinking about third-world development. The lack of sufficient growth and development was leaving behind vast numbers of people, particularly in the world's lower income countries. The disenchantment of the 1970s was not irrationally placed, as much of the third-world was in the midst of a two-decade economic slump. From 1965 through 1986 the average annual real per capita income growth among the world's thirty-nine least-developed countries was only .5%. The group's annual food production per capita fell by 1.5% from 1965 to 1986, a rate barely matching the growth in population. Because of slow growth in production, cereal food aid jumped from 2.6 to 5.8 metric tons annually and overall official development assistance expanded from US$4.8 billion to US$12.9 billion in 1986.

Proponents of a new aid strategy worked to generate an alternative approach that would provide a more successful foundation upon which to construct a more useful approach to development policies aimed at poverty eradication. Their efforts gave rise to the Basic Human Needs (BHN) strategy that resulted from the work of individuals who were associated with the World Bank and the Institute for Development Studies at the University of Sussex. Most prominent among them were Paul Streeten, Shahid Burki, J.C.C. Voorhoeve, and Frances Stewart.

The philosophical commitment of BHN was to raise the sustainable level of living of the masses of poor people as rapidly as feasible and to provide human beings with the opportunities to develop their full human potentials. This commitment focused on (1) meeting the basic needs of the poorest people in the world and (2) establishing a national and international framework for sustainable and self-reliant material progress, particularly among the poorest of the poor. The basic human needs approach provided a comprehensive way to bring global and national resources to bear on overcoming poverty, disease, ignorance, and malnutrition.

The theoretical essence of BHN was threefold: first, to concentrate development efforts on assisting the poorer people in the world's poorest countries to meet their needs on sustainable bases. Second, after identifying the main target group, it was to improve the capacity of the poor to gain access to basic-needs items based upon their productive involvement in producing and distributing basic needs and other items. Third, it aimed at assuring that the income earned by the poor would provide the basis for acquiring (1) adequate levels of nutritious food and (2) sufficient access to potable water and sanitation facilities. It would also permit them to improve (3) opportunities to secure shelter in the form of housing and clothing, (4) gain access to preventive and curative medical services, and (5) participate in formal and informal education and training in order to enhance the workplace attributes of the poor.

BHN's focus on enhancing workplace attributes led to a significant convergence between basic needs and human resource development (HRD), another emerging concept in development theory. Professor Paul Streeten was instrumental in forging the connection by making five key points. First, he pointed out that HRD is both a means and an end because when human development occurs, it leads to increased productivity. Second, he noted that in the longer term, when human development tends to lead to increased productivity it tends to result in declining population growth due to more information and less pressing felt needs for children. Third, he went on to point out that development can improve environmental protection due to increased understandings and appreciation for the importance of sustainable physical environments. Fourth, he noted that human development, when connected to the basic needs concept, would lead to a development program that would facilitate social and political stability, particularly when it is coupled with some form of participatory democracy. And fifth, Streeten concluded that when an approach to development puts people first, as do both the BHN and HRD, human beings are able to enjoy increased productivity, income, and employment opportunities. This leads to a social and economic environments free of artificial barriers (based on ethnicity and gender) that limit opportunities and free market choices.

Implementing BHN meant assuming a daunting task: the poor would have to be located, most likely in rural, agricultural settings in more remote geographical regions of poorer countries. Basic need shortfalls among target populations would have to be determined and the resources needed to eliminate the shortfall would have to be estimated. The prices of the required resources would need to be identified and the total cost of meeting basic needs among the targeted poor would need to be established. Methods of improving worker attributes and generating employment opportunities had to be designed. In addition, methods of providing the basic need items would have to be established, keeping in mind that (a) participation by the poor in the process is critical and (b) effectively integrating the roles of governments and donor agencies is essential.

Skeptics recognized that implementing BHN posed enormous problems. They asserted that the approach was paternalistic because BHN-oriented official development assistance programs would decide what was best for people in poor countries. They contended that the approach was welfare-based and anti-growth and would require an impossible wholesale restructuring of the global economy, and that there would be disproportionate benefits accruing to middle-class entrepreneurs and local officials because the poor would be insufficiently involved in planning processes. Another concern was that modern, capital-intensive production methods in both urban and rural areas would raise expectations but fail to generate income and employment opportunities for the poor, thereby frustrating their pursuit of material improvements to their lives. Proponents countered skeptics' assertions and contentions by arguing that if BHN were implemented properly, all of the concerns expressed by critics would be mitigated.

Critics raised another significant and valid concern that could not be easily dismissed: They observed that many BHN projects that supply potable water, sanitation facilities, health centers, and schools would likely generate insufficient revenues to cover both capital and recurrent costs. The poor, it was argued, needed to be subsidized for a long period until their productive capacities and opportunities permitted them to make cost-covering financial contributions by paying both taxes and the market prices of items needed to meet basic needs. Critics contended that during these long periods, two problems would arise. First, tax efforts by recipient governments in poorer countries could not adequately cover recurrent expenditures associated with maintaining and operating development projects. Second, recurrent expenditures were denominated in local currencies and neither bilateral nor multilateral foreign assistance donors would cover such costs. Their contributions were only denominated in the foreign currencies that would be required to purchase imports to construct capital (investment) projects. The result would be a mosaic of underutilized and undermaintained projects that wasted foreign exchange, imports, and local revenues and that frustrated the hopes and ambitions of target populations.

Proponents argued that recurrent costs could be reduced via taking advantage of economies of scale by linking potable water, sewage, sanitation, and housing projects. Health, nutrition, and education offered further opportunities for cost-effective linkages. BHN proponents acknowledged that the cost of implementing the strategy on a global scale would be extensive because an estimated 0.8 to 2 billion human beings were not able to meet all their basic needs on sustainable bases. Assisting them to do so would give rise to an incremental US$20 billion in capital costs for each of the next twenty years, and since the capital-to-recurrent-cost ratio was an estimated one to two, an additional $40 billion would need to be added to the cost side.

BHN proponents appreciated that a $60 billion increment in official development assistance could create serious "donor fatigue." One strategy to lessen the likelihood of fatigue setting in would be to phase recipient countries into—and donors out of—recurrent cost finance over a reasonable time period. Another alternative would limit the number of projects to ones carefully selected to reach target populations in ways that would speed up income and employment generation and, where possible, to place time limits on donor funding commitments.

Translating basic needs from theory into practice required institutional structures and political support systems, but the early enthusiasm that engulfed BHN ideas eventually dissipated. The initial support system began to take shape within the US Congress where a political effort to bring about a BHN-guided bilateral official assistance program took place. During the late 1970s the support system took the form of a Congressional mandate that would direct Congress to design and implement a bilateral assistance program based upon BHN-oriented concepts. The mandate's stated goal was to increase the income of the poor and to improve their access to public services, thereby enabling people to satisfy their basic needs and to lead decent, dignified, and hope-filled lives. It's goal was also to increase agricultural productivity through small farms and labor-intensive agriculture, lessening illiteracy, reducing infant mortality, improving access to education, lessening population growth rates, and promoting greater equality.

The mandate was not proposed in the form of a legislative bill and putting its contents into practice required formal legislation. This led the late Senator Hubert Humphrey to put forth legislation referred to as the Humphrey Bill that eventually became law. The bill contained two fundamental provisions: (1) it reorganized the government agencies that were collectively responsible for the US aid program; and (2) it directed the agencies responsible for the new governmental structure to pursue basic-needs objectives. Congress and the administration failed to put the law into practice and BHN was largely discarded.

BHN was replaced by significantly different ideas about what the US development assistance program should pursue. Security and military interests became paramount during the Cold War era and the US foreign assistance program became dominated by the Economic Support Fund (ESF). The Fund provided generalized balance of payments and budget support to target recipient countries that were strategically important, regardless of whether or not assistance was directly aimed at poverty eradication. ESF has been most often used to attain political and strategic interests and objectives for the United States and recipient countries, and it has been closely linked to military assistance to recipient countries. Security assistance rose to dominance in the US foreign assistance program, and by 1979, overall aid appropriations were $1.13 billion for development while $1.91 billion was allocated to security supporting assistance via the Fund. The amount designated for development covered both BHN projects and those directed toward infrastructure improvements in air, ground, and water transportation; information and communication networks; energy generation and distribution systems; as well as water and sanitation capital projects.

Over a twenty-five-year period beginning in 1979, BHN has played a progressively less significant role in national planning in recipient countries, as well as in bilateral and multilateral assistance programs. For example, annual US foreign assistance became dominated by security assistance often tied to military aid sent to strategically important but not necessarily poor countries. While basic human needs as a coherent concept slipped into memory, its legacy continued in the form of its link to HRD as an approach to development. Its essence was contained in special programs such as "Women in Development." This program recognized the need to assist women who were attempting to meet the basic needs of children, particularly within the world's thirty-nine poorest countries.

Robert L. Curry, Jr.

See also Children and Development; Development, Measures of; Poverty: Impact on Development; Women: Role in Development

References and Further Reading

Burki, Shahid Javed, and J.J.C. Voorhoeve. "Global Estimates for Meeting Basic Needs." *World Bank Basic Needs Paper No. 1*. Washington, DC: World Bank, 1977.
Curry, Robert L., Jr. "The Basic Needs Strategy, the Congressional Mandate and US Foreign Aid Policy. *Journal of Economic Issues* Vol. XXII (4): 1085–1096 (December 1989).
Curry, Robert L. Jr. "A Review of Contemporary US Foreign Aid Policies." *Journal of Economic Issues* XXIV (3): 813–824 (September 1990).
Leipzinger, Danny, ed. *Basic Needs and Development*. Cambridge, MA: Oelgeschlager, Gunn & Hain, 1981.
Meier, Gerald M., and Dudley Seers. *Pioneers in Development*. New York: Oxford University Press, 1984.
Streeten, Paul, and Shahid Javed Burki. "Basic Human Needs: Some Issues." *World Development (London)* VI (2) (March 1978).
Streeten, Paul. *Thinking About Development*. Cambridge: Cambridge University Press, 1997.
Streeten, Paul with Shahid J. Burki, Mahbub ul Haq, Norman Hicks, and Frances Stewart. *First Things First: Meeting Basic Human Needs in Developing Countries*. New York: Oxford University Press, 1977.

BATISTA Y ZALDÍVAR, FULGENCIO

With the exception of Fidel Castro, no other political figure exercised as much control over twentieth-century Cuba as Fulgencio Batista y Zaldívar. Known as the "arbiter of Cuban politics," he influenced the various sectors of Cuban society from 1933 until 1959.

Born in 1901, the son of a poor sugar worker, Batista joined the Cuban army at age twenty. Following his leadership of the famous "sergeants' revolt" of 1933, he began to rule Cuba through a series of puppet presidents. To his credit, he gave his approval for the promulgation of the Cuban Constitution of 1940. Because of its progressive articles, the document became a model for Latin American democracy.

In 1940, he was democratically elected president. His four-year mandate was characterized by the enactment of populist measures such as collective bargaining, minimum wage, and worker's compensation. In addition, he quickly joined the Allied cause in World War II, which brought prosperity to Cuba.

Once his presidential term was completed, he settled in Daytona Beach, Florida, but returned to Cuba in 1948. A clever opportunist, he took advantage of popular discontent with the administration of President Carlos Prío Socarrás's inability to eradicate racketeering, and he staged a successful military coup on March 10, 1952.

Batista's coup brought about the demise of Cuban democracy. He allowed political parties to continue their activities; however, he himself ran unopposed in the 1954 presidential elections. Even though corruption and graft became the order of the day during his seven-year rule (1952–1959), the Cuban economy made considerable progress. In terms of socioeconomic indicators, Cuba was ranked among the top five Latin American nations, and 59% of the Cuban population had achieved middle-class status. Moreover, there were modest gains in educational and health standards, and Havana experienced a building boom.

In spite of this apparent progress, the Cuban economy was a model of classical subservience as it was critically dependent on sugar exports and intrinsically connected to the United States. Cuba was at the mercy of the United States, which not only granted preferential treatment to Cuban sugar but also fixed its price. Furthermore, approximately three-fourths of Cuban imports were from the United States, and Cuba was the leading importer of US agricultural food products in Latin America. Calls for economic diversification and economic transformation, however, fell on Batista's deaf ears.

Opposition to Batista's rule began to crystallize following the arrival of Fidel Castro in Cuba in 1956. Castro, who had led an ill-fated attack on the Moncada garrison in 1953, began to conduct guerrilla operations in Oriente Province. Unable to neutralize Castro's guerrillas, Batista's corrupt army resorted to repressive tactics. Scores of students, politicians, workers, and peasants were murdered and there were numerous violations of human rights.

As Batista's regime began to collapse, the United States imposed an arms embargo in March 1958. Following the embargo, his days as a leader were numbered, and he fled Cuba on December 31, 1958. After his downfall, he lived in the Dominican Republic, Portugal, and Spain, where he died in 1973.

JOSÉ FERNÁNDEZ

See also Castro, Fidel; Cuban Revolution

References and Further Reading

Fernández Miranda, Roberto. *Mis Relaciones con el general Batista*. Miami: Ediciones Universal, 1999.

Leonard, Thomas M. *Castro and the Cuban Revolution* Westport, CT: Greenwood Press, 1999.

Pérez-Stable, Marifeli. *The Cuban Revolution: Origins, Course, and Legacy*. New York: Oxford University Press, 1993; 2d ed., 1999.

Suchlicki, Jaimie. *Cuba: From Columbus to Castro*. New York: Scribner, 1974; 4th ed., revised and updated, Washington, DC: Brassey, 1997.

BEDOUIN

The term *Bedouin* is the Anglicization of the Arabic term *bedu*. The term is used to differentiate between those peoples whose livelihood is based upon the raising of livestock by mainly natural graze and browse and those who have an agricultural or urban base (*hadar*). Since the opposition of *bedu* to *hadar* is a specifically Arab cultural tradition it is arguable whether non-Arabic-speaking pastoralists in the region should be termed Bedouin. Their origins date back to 6000 BCE on the southern edge of the arid Syrian steppe. By 850 BCE, a complex of oasis settlements and pastoral camps was established by a people known as *a'raab*. These people were the cultural forerunners of the modern-day Arabs. These Semitic speakers were distinguished from their Assyrian neighbours by their Arabic language and their use of domesticated camels for trade and warfare. They carried out a caravan trade by camel between southern Arabia and the large city-states of Syria. By the first century BCE they had moved westward into Jordan and the Sinai peninsula and southwestward along the coast of the Red Sea. The creation of a powerful Islamic state in western Arabia in the middle of the seventh century CE gave a dramatic impetus to Arab expansion. As a result the *bedu/hadar* distinction was reproduced in those Arabized territories where such a regional division of labour was ecologically and geographically practicable.

Today, Bedouin societies are found in the arid steppe regions of Arabia and North Africa and along the margins of rain-fed cultivation. Bedouin living in such areas tend to move camp as dictated by the availability of pasture and sometimes seasonal heavy morning dew (occult precipitation). Often they have access to date gardens or plant grain along their migration routes, which they harvest on their return to winter camping areas. In areas where winter rain falls predictably on mountain plateaux (Morocco), the Bedouin practice transhumance, planting their crops near their permanent homes in the valleys at the onset of rains and then moving their livestock to the highland pastures.

Bedouin societies are always linked to other non-pastoral societies by economic, social, and political relations. In the local context, a Bedouin is a regional specialist in livestock breeding whose closest social and political ties are with his or her pastoral kin. Change and adaptation are key aspects of Bedouin livelihood strategies, and in the current global economy, many Bedouin have sought out multi-resource strategies, seeking wage labour in related activities such as transport and commerce, entering into the unskilled daily wage labour market in construction and agriculture. Some have commercialized aspects of their culture in order to buy into the growing demand for native trinkets in the expanding ecotourism market in the Middle East and North Africa. Others have settled and become less mobile. However, regardless of their multiple occupations and residence patterns, they remain Bedouin culturally as long as they maintain close social ties with pastoral kin and retain the local linguistic and cultural markers that identify them as Bedouin.

The primary economic activity of the Bedouin and the culturally significant marker for self identification is animal husbandry of sheep, goat, and camel. This way of life, sometimes called nomadic pastoralism, is recognized as a specialized off-shoot of agriculture in the evolution of human society. At its core is migration determined by the seasonal variability of pasture and water. Because water and grass can be in short supply in a particular area at the same time that it is abundant elsewhere, survival of herds and herders makes movement from deficit to surplus areas both logical and necessary. Over the past thirty years, trucks and other motor vehicles have come to replace camels as beasts of burden. Today, the truck is often used to bring feed and water to the herds in the desert. Furthermore, the truck has allowed the Bedouin to be more mobile than in the past, permitting some to settle for much of the year in permanent villages (especially for young and the old), while still maintaining access to water, pastures, herds, and places of employment beyond the arid steppe land that is their home.

As with most pastoral societies, the division of labour among Bedouin is determined by the types of animal that are herded. When both large and small domestic animals are kept, the larger animals—camels, and in a few cases cattle—are the responsibility of men. Women are often barred from close contact with these animals. The smaller animals—the goats and sheep—are generally the responsibility of women and older girls. In such communities, women have a very active, independent, and complementary role to play in the society. When only sheep and goats are kept, men tend to be the herders and women help with the feeding and milking of the flock. When such groups settle and come to rely on a multiplicity of income-generating work, women's work tends to become circumscribed and reduced to very narrow domestic activity.

Each Bedouin group seeks to manage a land area that contains sufficient resources to sustain communal life. It seeks to establish a definite zone of control with well-understood, though often variable, limits and certain rights of use denied to other Bedouin groups. Among Bedouin groups these various zones of use-rights or "ownership" are recognized. However, most governments throughout the Middle East and North Africa ceased to recognize Bedouin collective territory and largely consider these arid steppe areas "state-owned" land. In the past, most conflicts were among and between Bedouin tribal groups and generally revolved around the right to use scarce pastures and water resources. Numerous campaigns were once fought to acquire or defend pastures and watering holes. However, since the middle of the twentieth century, modern state governments in the region have largely pacified the Bedouin, and today such conflicts are often settled in government courts relying on the expert advice of respected Bedouin tribal elders.

Most contemporary conflicts between the state and Bedouin society focus on two related areas of concern: degradation of the arid steppe land, and global interests in preserving the world's biodiversity. For decades, governments in the region have encouraged the Bedouin to move off of the arid steppe land and settle. At times this policy is couched in terms of the "damage" that Bedouin do to their environment and derives from theories of land use (equilibrium systems) that are inappropriate to the arid lands of the Middle East and North Africa. Though little, if any, empirical evidence exists to confirm this position, Bedouin tend to be pressured by modern governments to give up a way of life that is regarded as backward, primitive, and out of step with modern, settled society. Conservation or the protection of the world's biodiversity also impinges on Bedouin society as, in many parts of the region, important grazing areas or Bedouin reserves are being taken over by the state to set up nature reserves or to reintroduce endangered mammalian species (for example, oryx and gazelle). The loss of these lands and the failure of many conservation organizations to recognize the traditional knowledge and sustainable practices of the Bedouin are a further blow to their current livelihood strategies.

DAWN CHATTY

See also Middle East: History and Economic Development; North Africa: History and Economic Development

References and Further Reading

Abu-Lughod, Lila. *Veiled Sentiments: Honor and Poetry in a Bedouin Society*, Berkeley, CA: University of California Press, 1986.

Behnke, Roy, Ian Scoones, and Carol Kerven, eds. *Range Ecology at Disequilibrium: New Models of Natural Variability and Pastoral Adaptation in African Savannas*. London: Overseas Development Institute, 1993.

Chatty, Dawn. *From Camel to Truck: The Bedouin in the Modern World*. New York: Vantage Press, 1986.

Chatty, Dawn. *Mobile Pastoralists: Development Planning and Social Change in Oman*. New York: Columbia University Press, 1996.

Cole, Donald. *Nomads of the Nomads: The Al-Murrah of the Empty Quarter*. Chicago: Aldine, 1975.

Cole, Donald, and Soraya Altorki. *Bedouin, Settlers and Holiday-Makers*. Cairo: American University in Cairo Press, 1998.

Fagan, Brian. *Peoples of the Earth: An Introduction to World Prehistory*. Boston: Little, Brown and Co., 1986.

Lancaster, William. *The Rwala Bedouin Today*. Cambridge: Cambridge University Press, 1981.

BEGIN, MENACHEM

Menachem Begin, who was Israel's sixth prime minister, was born in Brisk (now Brest-Litovsk), then part of the Russian empire, on August 16, 1913. He was the youngest of three children born to Zeev Dov and Hassia Begin. The Begin family was uprooted from Brisk by World War I and fled into Russia. When the war ended, the Begin family returned to Brisk and to an independent Poland. Menachem Begin completed his education at a local public high school, and enrolled at Warsaw University in 1931 at the law school, where he finished in 1935.

He was considered a very popular orator among Jewish students in Warsaw, and was full-time active in the Betar Zionist youth movement in Poland after his graduation. He became the head of the Polish branch of Betar in 1939, one of the most influential positions of Jewish leadership in the pre-Holocaust Jewish Europe. When World War II started, Begin encouraged thousands of Polish Jews to emigrate to the Land of Israel, just as the country's gates were being shut by the British mandatory government.

Menachem Begin was arrested in 1940 by the Soviet occupation authorities. He was held in Gulag prison camps, mostly in Siberia, until 1941, when he was freed with other Polish prisoners. He joined the Polish army-in-exile and was assigned to a unit that was dispatched to the Middle East. His parents and older brother remained in Poland and perished in the Holocaust.

He arrived in the Land of Israel in 1942 and was asked soon after to assume command of the Irgun Zva'I Le'umi (known as ETZEL, the Hebrew acronym for National Military Organization). In this capacity he directed ETZEL's operations against British rule. In 1946, under his leadership, ETZEL blew up a wing of the King David Hotel in Jerusalem, where the British Headquarters was located. Some ninety people—Jews, Arabs, as well as British—were killed, despite warnings that there would be a bombing. He wrote about his days as the leader of ETZEL in *The Revolt.* He also wrote another book about his time in a Soviet labor camp, *White Nights: The Story of a Prisoner in Russia.*

When the State of Israel was established in 1948, Menachem Begin, with a few other associates, founded the Herut (Freedom in Hebrew) Party. He headed the party's list in all Knesset elections from the first, in 1949, to the tenth, in 1981, by which time Herut had joined with several other political factions to form the Likud, a party that still exists as of 2005 and that has the highest number of representatives in the current Knesset.

On the eve of the Six-Day War, in May 1967, Menachem Begin was influential in initiating the formation of Israel's first national unity government. He served as a minister without portfolio for all its

duration, from June 1, 1967, to August 1, 1970. He was elected prime minister as a result of the elections of the ninth Knesset on May 17, 1977.

Menachem Begin was the first prime minister to refer to the West Bank as Judea and Samaria, considering them an integral part of the Land of Israel. Soon after being elected he went to visit an Israeli settlement in the West Bank, Elon Moreh, and declared it to be part of "liberated Israel." It was under his tenure that Jews embarked on the wholesale settlement of the territories.

In 1981, Begin ordered the Israeli Air Force to bomb the Osirak nuclear reactor in Iraq. Though at the time Israel was condemned by the international community, it became apparent during the 1991 Gulf War that Israel's action had succeeded in halting Baghdad's drive to acquire nuclear weapons.

Following several visits to the United States and Romania, which was playing as the mediator at the time, Menachem Begin decided to extend an invitation to Egypt's President Anwar Sadat to come to Jerusalem. The Egyptian president accepted the invitation and made his historic visit in November 1977, the first and only Arab leader to do so publicly.

Menachem Begin, as well as many members in the Labor Party, resisted Egypt's initial demands for the return of the entire Sinai and the promise of autonomy to the Palestinians of the West Bank and the Gaza Strip. After twelve days of negotiations at Camp David, Begin presented the peace treaty to the Knesset, and only twenty-nine out of forty-three Likud representatives in the Knesset were among the majority that approved the accords.

Menachem Begin and Anwar Sadat jointly received the Nobel Peace Prize in 1978. When Anwar Sadat was assassinated by Muslim fundamentalists in October 1981, Menachem Begin went to Cairo and walked to the funeral, which was held on a Saturday.

Begin also initiated Project Renewal, in which the Israeli government, in coordination with the Jewish Agency and world Jewry, addressed the problems of Israel's urban neighborhoods and development towns. Numerous improvements in infrastructure, education, social services, and housing were introduced. He also initiated the movement to save Ethiopian Jewry, an effort that led to Operation Moses in 1984 and culminated in Operation Solomon in 1991.

Menachem Begin's name also became synonymous with the Israeli invasion of Lebanon, beginning a war that would cause a sharp political divide in the country. The invasion was staged to uproot Palestinian terrorists in southern Lebanon who had been shelling Israel's north. But it soon escalated to an invasion of Beirut itself, Israel's first incursion into an Arab capital.

In 1983, as the Israeli public was experiencing a deep division over the war, Begin called on Israelis to "show tolerance, rid themselves of hatred and show understanding of each other." He added that "differences of opinion were legitimate and should not lead to physical confrontation." These statements were the closest he came to denouncing violence that led to the killing, by right-wing Jewish demonstrators, of Emil Grinzweig, a Peace Now protester of the Lebanon War.

Begin was deeply troubled by the high death toll of the Lebanon War. He suffered a further devastating blow when his wife, Aliza, died in November 1982.

In September 1983, Menachem Begin stepped down as prime minister, saying he could go on no longer. He spent the final decade of his life living with his daughter in almost total reclusion, and was visited only by a small circle of friends. In those years, the few times that Begin appeared in public, he looked pale and frail. It was in sharp contrast to the image of the great Likud leader who called out at the signing of the peace treaty with Egypt, "No more war. No more bloodshed. No more tears. Peace unto you. Shalom." He died in March 1992 and was buried on the Mount of Olives in Jerusalem.

CARMELA LUTMAR

See also Arab–Israeli Wars (1948, 1956, 1967, 1973); Israel; Zionism

References and Further Reading

Begin, Menachem. *The Revolt*, rev. ed. New York: Nash, 1977.
Begin, Menachem. *White Nights: The Story of a Prisoner in Russia*. New York: Harper and Row, 1979.
Gervassi, Frank. *The Life and Times of Menachem Begin: Rebel to Statesman*. New York: Putnam, 1979.
Haber, Eitan. *Menachem Begin: The Legend and the Man*. New York: Delacorte, 1978.
Quandt, William B. *Camp David: Peacemaking and Politics*. Washington, DC: Brookings Institution, 1986.
Rowland, Robert. *Rhetoric of Menachem Begin: The Myth of Redemption Through Return*. Lanham, MD: University Press of America, 1985.

BELARUS

The Republic of Belarus (by convention called "Belarusia" until 1991) is located in Eastern Europe, bordering with the Russian Federation (Russia) in the east, with Latvia in the north, Lithuania in the northwest, and the Ukraine in the south. The country has a total area of 207,595 square kilometres (80,153 square miles). Its major languages are Belarussian and Russian.

The population of Belarus was estimated at 10,235,000 in July 2000. It is one of the most urbanised countries among the western republics in the Commonwealth of Independent States (CIS) with around seventy percent of the population living in the cities and towns. The country's capital, Minsk, is home for 1,695,700 people (1999), or 16% of the population. Belarus has a population growth rate close to zero due to a low birth rate (9.57 births per 1,000 population [2001, CIA est.]) and sizeable permanent and temporary emigration. It is estimated that its population could slightly decline by 2010.

Belarus is situated on the crossroads from Russia to Western Europe and therefore has experienced turbulent history. Its economy traditionally was based on agricultural production, forestry, and trade. By the eighteenth century most of Belarus's territory had been acquired by the Russian Tsardom. The rise of capitalism in the nineteenth century brought steep social polarisation and poverty, and many Belarusians supported various anti-Tsarist movements or emigrated to the United States and Canada. After the Russian Revolution of 1917, Belarus nationalists declared independence from Russia, but in 1918 the nationalist government was defeated and the Belarusian Soviet Socialist Republic was established, although Poland took a significant part of what had been Belarusian territory. In December 1922, Belarus became a founding member of the USSR; however, it was not until 1939, with recapture of what was known as Western Belarus, that the republic established its present borders. The Belarusian Communist Party (BPT) came to power in the 1920s, to remain the single ruling party for the next seventy years.

The Belarusian development for the next sixty years was largely shaped by the Soviet concept of development. The government nationalised all industries and lands that had previously belonged to nobility and established control over all types of economic activities and central state planning. In the 1930s and 1940s, the government conducted a collectivization campaign, forcing all farmers to join state-controlled cooperatives (*kolkhozy*) and collective farms (*sovkhozy*). The Second World War caused incredible damage to the Belarusian economy, as almost 50% of its industry was destroyed and almost 30% of its population perished during the Nazi occupation of 1941–1944. After the war, Belarus rebuilt its economy with the help of huge investments from the Soviet government, mainly to heavy industry, defence production, consumer good manufacturing (Belarus was among the USSR's top five producers of television sets and radios), nuclear power stations, and others. The government directed huge resources into the social sector, supporting extended free education, medical services to all groups of the population, funding a generous pension system, and installing a comprehensive welfare network. At the same time the government severely limited basic political and religious freedoms, and free entrepreneurship, and thousands of Belarusians, especially former nobility, ended up in labour camps in Russian Siberia or Central Asia.

According to official statistics, the Belarusian industrial production grew thirty-fold between 1940 and 1984. By the end of the 1980s, Belarus had become one of the most industrialised republics in the USSR. The state-led industrialization, however, disregarded environmental issues, and the explosion in the Chernobyl nuclear power station in neighbouring Ukraine polluted almost 20% of the Belarus territory, affecting approximately two million people.

Mikhail Gorbachev initiated the policy of perestroika (glasnost and perestroika), which met strong support, as there was mass anger and dissatisfaction over the political, economic, and environmental situation in the republic fuelled by the effect of the Chernobyl disaster. By 1991, the nationalist movement gained strength in the political arena; this contributed to defeat of the BCP and election of Stanislav Shushkevich, the liberal-minded politician, as the head of the state.

Recent Development

Belarus declared its independence from the USSR on August 25, 1991. President Shushkevich launched the International Monetary Fund, and inspired radical economic reform policy and political liberalisation. However, the radical reforms, also known as the "shock therapy," combined with the sudden withdrawal of the state support of all enterprises, the breakdown of law and order, and collapse of the trade with the former USSR, brought economic chaos and recession. This led to political turbulence and change of leadership in 1994, as Alexander Lukashenko won the presidential election. The new president radically reversed economic policy, returning to the state control of major economic activities and the Soviet-style centralization. President Lukashenko established his iron rule and new policies, which combine extreme forms of authoritarianism with populism and the Soviet-style suppression of opposition. This led to political isolation of Belarus in Eastern Europe. Yet, on September 9, 2001, Mr. Lukashenko won another term in a hotly contested presidential election.

In 1994, the Lukashenko-led government rejected a program of radical economic changes and attempted to reverse the recession and halt the high inflation through re-instituting the state control. The government believed that stimulation of the trade with Russia and the CIS partners would bring economic revival, and it supported greater economic integration with Russia though various integration schemes. It approved a small-scale privatization, limited price liberalization, allowed private entrepreneurship, and opened some sectors of its economy for foreign investments. Belarus introduced its national currency, the ruble, in August 1994, one of the last countries in the former USSR to do so. However, the government was never able to stop the ruble's steep decline, as it plunged from 15,500 rubles per US dollar in 1996 to 730,000 rubles in 1999.

The new currency and attempts at privatization, liberalization, and private entrepreneurship did not have the desired effects. Belarus could not achieve macroeconomic stabilisation and sustainable economic growth, although it avoided economic recession at the level seen in neighbouring Ukraine or Lithuania. According to the World Bank, the Belarus economy declined at an average annual rate of 1.6% between 1990 and 2000. Foreign investors are reluctant to invest in the economy due to red tape among national bureaucracy, and an unfriendly and unreformed business environment.

During the post-Soviet era the Belarus economy experienced considerable structural changes, and agriculture, industries, and services contributed 15.3%, 37.4%, and 47.3%, respectively, to the GDP (World Bank est. 2001). The Belarus exports are based on sales of machinery, domestic appliances, chemicals, and processed foodstuffs in international markets, mainly to Russia (66% of the exports) and to other CIS markets.

The post-Soviet economic changes led to social polarisation in the country and a considerable decline in living standards among some groups of the population, especially in rural areas and small towns, but the state was able to preserve some social benefits in education, the health system, and pensions. Of its population, 23% live below the poverty line (World Bank est. 2001) and average life expectancy is 68 years. In 2001, the United Nations Development Program (UNDP)'s Human Development Index (HDI) put Belarus in 53rd place out of 162, ahead of all the CIS countries.

RAFIS ABAZOV

See also Commonwealth of Independent States: History and Economic Development; Commonwealth

of Independent States: International Relations; Soviet Bloc; State-Directed Economy

References and Further Reading

Belarusian Ministry of Statistics: www.president.gov.by/Minstat/en/main.html

IMF. *Republic of Belarus: Recent Economic Developments and Selected Issues.* Series: Staff Country Report No. 00/153. Washington, DC: author, 2000.

Marples, David. *Belarus: From Soviet Rule to Nuclear Catastrophe.* New York: St. Martin's Press, 1996.

Sherman, Garnett, and Robert Legvold, eds. *Belarus at the Crossroad.* Washington, DC: Carnegie Endowment for International Peace, 2000.

Zaprudnik, Jan. *Belarus: At a Crossroad in History.* Boulder, CO: Westview Press, 1992.

Zaprudnik, Jan. *Historical Dictionary of Belarus.* Lanham, MD: Scarecrow Press, 1998.

BELIZE

Belize, formerly British Honduras, is the newest nation in the Western Hemisphere. Belizean independence from the United Kingdom (UK) occurred in 1981, having been delayed for decades because of a territorial dispute between Guatemala and the UK. Guatemala officially recognized Belize only in 1992, but the border between the nations remains a "line of adjacency" specified in an agreement reached in 2000. However, Guatemala does not recognize the line as the legal border. Belize's northern border is Mexico's Yucatan Peninsula, and the Caribbean Sea lies to the east. Its climate is tropical, and the nation boasts significant terrain diversity, from coastal lowlands to low mountainous regions.

Although geographically situated in Central America, Belize differs from its neighbors in two major respects. First, its legacy as a British colony includes English as an official language, as well as a sound governmental infrastructure. Thus, Belize has allied itself economically with other former British colonies in the Caribbean rather than with its continental neighbors. For example, it has chosen membership in the Caribbean Community and Common Market (CARICOM) rather than affiliation with the Central American Common Market (CACM). Second, Belize remained a haven of peacefulness and stability in Central America during both pre- and post-independence. This reality has led to dramatic ethnographic changes as refugees fled from the serious conflicts in neighboring nations during recent decades, and poses significant challenges for Belizean economic development.

Historical Economic Development

Following the typical pattern of colonies, Belizean economic history derives chiefly from its function as a source of raw materials, particularly raw forest products and agricultural commodities, which were exported to its sovereign. Therefore, from its initial settlement in 1640, Belizean economic activity focused on the exploitation of primary forest products—first logwood, followed by mahogany and chicle. Economic diversification from forestry began only in the 1880s, when the British introduced plantation agriculture (bananas and sugar). However, outbreaks of plant diseases decimated commercial banana production in the 1920s and 1930s. Until that time, Belize's virtually complete specialization in primary products left few opportunities for alternative economic development, except for those establishments that provided the freight-forwarding services, short-term credit, and import/retail functions in direct support of the primary sector. Following the banana crises, Belize began to develop an agro-industry during the 1930s, allowing it to add value to the primary products it produced. These new activities included transforming logs into lumber, sugar cane into sugar and molasses, and citrus products into concentrate.

Economic Development Since 1945

After 1945, sugar, which still accounts for half of Belizean export revenues, and citrus concentrates emerged as Belize's new export staples. Today, agriculture and agro-industry remain the largest sectors of the economy, with the banana industry remaining the nation's largest employer. However, the discriminatory trade policies of developed nations limited export quantities and their prices for these goods, leading some Belizeans to turn to illicit trade. Initially, this meant growing and trafficking in marijuana. In later decades, Belize gained importance as a transshipper of South American cocaine. Among its efforts to combat the development of this illicit sector, the government began in the 1960s to promote diversification into the world's largest and fastest-growing industry—tourism.

Tourism seems perfectly appropriate for Belize, due to its geographic diversity, its stability, its proximity to North America, and its facility with English. In addition, Belize offers the international tourist a wide range of options, including cayes on the world's second-largest barrier reef, tropical jaguar habitats, and a rich cultural heritage that features historical Mayan sites and current Mayan villages. Although traditional tourism in Belize was marine-based, more recent efforts have concentrated on ecotourism and archaeotourism. The government prefers these modes of tourism because they foster long-term viability of the sector, as ecotourists and archaeotourists enjoy the environment without altering it. International tourism in Belize grew rapidly in the 1980s, resulting in a four-fold increase in tourists during that decade. Following the global trend, Belizean tourist revenues have grown more than twice as fast as the gross domestic product (GDP), and more than five times as fast as merchandise trade. Tourism now accounts for ten percent of the Belizean economic activity, up from just four percent in 1984. However, there is significant debate regarding the usefulness of tourism in fostering economic development. However, Belize has clearly staked a significant share of its economic growth potential on tourism.

Changing Ethnic Distribution

Perhaps the most challenging problems in the economic development of Belize derive from its long-standing willingness to accept refugees from its neighbors. Historically, the vast majority of Belize's 250,000 people have been of African descent. Moreover, the Creole population was concentrated in Belize City, which had enjoyed political and economic primacy before independence. At that time Belize's main ethnic groups were Creole (40%), Mestizo (23%), Garinagu (8%), and Maya (10%) (Bolland 1986 Everitt 1986 and Shoman 1994). Recent immigrants have typically been mestizos who had dwelt in rural regions in their former countries, resulting in a dramatic switch in the population distribution by the turn of the twenty-first century to Creole (30%), Mestizo (44%), Garinagu (6%), and Maya (10%).

The Latinization and ruralization of Belize will pose significant problems for Belizean economic development in the twenty-first century. First, the increasing importance of Spanish as the primary language of half the country's population will require significant new resources for primary schooling, either for teaching English or for offering bilingual education. The paucity of resources available for education exacerbates this problem. Moreover, as the global economy becomes increasingly reliant on knowledge, education becomes even more critical. Second, although Belize has had four distinct ethnic populations for decades, they have been geographically separate.

The Hispanic population has tended to concentrate on the Belizean borders with its Spanish-speaking neighbors. In past decades, immigrants have moved into the center of the nation as well, but maintained a separate economic identity through subsistence farming. Recently, however, they have been entering urban areas, generating both more interaction and more competition for resources with the other ethnic groups. The new democracy will be tested severely in its ability to come to grips with the fast-changing nature of its people in the already rapid-paced world of globalization.

JEFFREY W. STEAGALL

See also Caribbean Community and Common Market (CARICOM); Caribbean Free Trade Association (CARIFTA); Caribbean: History and Economic Development; Ecotourism

References and Further Reading

Belizean Studies. Belize City, Belize Institute of Social Research and Action.

Bolland, O. N. *Belize: A New Nation in Central America.* Boulder, CO: Westview Press, 1986.

Everitt, J. C. "The Growth and Development of Belize City." *Belizean Studies* 14 (1986).

Grant, C. H. *The Making of Modern Belize: Politics, Society and British Colonialism in Central America.* London: Cambridge University Press, 1976.

Kelly, Robert C., Debra Ewing, Stanton Doyle, and Denise Youngblood, eds. *Country Review, Belize 1998/1999.* Commercial Data International, Inc., 1998.

Palacio, J. O. "Social and Cultural Implications of Recent Demographic Changes in Belize." *Belizean Studies* 21 (1993).

Perry, Joseph M., Jeffrey W. Steagall, and Louis A. Woods. "Tourism as a Development Tool: The Case of Belize." *Caribbean Geography* 5(1) (1994).

Petch, T. "Dependency, Land and Oranges in Belize." *Third World Quarterly* 8 (1986).

Primack, Richard B., David Bray, and Hugo A. Galletti. *Timber, Tourists, and Temples: Conservation and Development in the Maya Forest of Belize, Guatemala, and Mexico.* Island Press, 1997.

Shoman, Assad. *Thirteen Chapters of a History of Belize.* Belize City: Angelus Press Limited, 1994.

Sutherland, Anne. *The Making of Belize: Globalization in the Margins.* New York: Bergin & Garvey, 1998.

Woods, Louis A., Joseph M. Perry, and Jeffrey W. Steagall. "The Composition and Distribution of Ethnic Groups in Belize: Immigration and Emigration Patterns, 1980–1991." *Latin American Research Review* 32(3) (1997).

BEN BELLA, AHMED

Ahmed Ben Bella, the father of modern Algeria (b. December 25, 1919), was an indefatigable revolutionary leader. He attended school in Tlemcen and emerged more fluent in French than in Arabic. In

World War II, Ben Bella served with distinction in the Free French Army, but when the war ended he returned to Algeria and joined the nationalist Parti Populaire Algérien. In the course of the next three years Ben Bella evolved from an advocate of gradual decolonization into a confirmed revolutionary. He led the Organisation Spéciale, an underground insurrectionist band. In 1950, he robbed the post office in Oran and was captured and imprisoned by French authorities. He escaped in 1952, fled to Cairo, and (with eight others) founded the Revolutionary Committee of Unity and Action to organize the Algerian struggle for independence. Ben Bella received moral and financial support from his hero, Egyptian President Nasser and from Habib Bourguiba, the Tunisian leader.

On November 1, 1954, the Front de Libération Nationale (FLN), led by Ben Bella, began the Algerian revolution. French army troops unintentionally aided the rebels by applying collective punishment to entire villages. This only generated new recruits for the FLN. French agents captured "the Invisible One" (as Ben Bella was called) on October 22, 1956, by hijacking an airplane on which he was a passenger. He spent the next six years in jail, but from captivity he was elected vice-premier of the revolutionary provisional government. By 1960, the French were ready to negotiate and by 1962, they were beaten. The Evian Accords ended the war and confirmed Algerian independence, and the French freed Ben Bella.

After a short period of internal struggle between different branches of the FLN, a socialist faction led by Ben Bella, allied with the revolutionary armed forces (Armée Nationale Populaire) commanded by Col. Houari Boumédienne, seized control of Algiers. Ben Bella was elected prime minister on September 20, 1962, in the first of Algeria's many one-sided elections. One year later, under a new constitution, Ben Bella was elected president for a five-year term. He immediately launched an ambitious program of land reform and education. Post-revolutionary Algeria was in dire straits. At least 250,000 Algerians, and probably many more, had died in the war, and another three million internal refugees crowded the cities. One million French Algerians, including most of the skilled managerial class, left the country. Soviet economic advisors were unable to solve the basic problem of high unemployment.

Ben Bella believed in a neutralist foreign policy that in practice amounted to well-publicized state visits to Egypt, Cuba, and other "emerging nations." He proclaimed support for all wars of national liberation but suppressed a Berber revolt in Kabylia. Ben Bella enjoyed international diplomacy so much that he neglected domestic problems. His administrative style was likewise erratic—the only consistent theme appeared to be elimination of potential rivals. One such, Col. Boumédienne, overthrew Ben Bella on June 19, 1965. Ben Bella spent the next fifteen years in prison, where he was allowed to marry and start a family. The incarcerated socialist now turned to the Koran.

President Boumédienne died in 1978. Ben Bella remained under house arrest until 1980, when he was released and pardoned by the new president, Chadli Benjedid. Ben Bella moved to Switzerland and futilely plotted a return to power. In 1990, Ben Bella returned to Algeria, but his charisma seemed to have faded and his call for Algerian volunteers to defend Saddam Hussein from US aggression seemed irrelevant to most Algerians. In retirement Ben Bella styled himself a progressive Islamist, but his countrymen preferred to remember him as he had been fifty years previously—a passionate patriot.

ROSS MARLAY AND LESLEY J. PRUITT

See also Algeria; North Africa: History and Economic Development; North Africa: International Relations

References and Further Reading

Merle, Robert. *Ahmed Ben Bella*. New York: Walker & Co., 1967.
Ruedy, John. *Modern Algeria: The Origins and Development of a Nation*. Bloomington, IN: Indiana University Press, 1992.

BEN-GURION, DAVID

David Ben-Gurion (1886–1973), Israel's first prime minister and local architect of Israeli statehood, was born David Gruen (Green) on October 16, 1886, in Plonsk, in Russian-occupied Poland. He served as prime minister and defense minister from 1948–1953 and from 1955–1963, presiding over Israel's 1948 War of Independence and the 1956 Sinai Campaign and the accompanying Suez Crisis.

Ben-Gurion came to Zionist thinking from an early age; his father, Victor Gruen, was active in the Hovavei Zion (Lovers of Zion) group in Poland. In 1906, a young Ben-Gurion arrived in Palestine, finding agricultural work in the towns of Petah Tikvah and Rishon LeZion. He soon became active in Zionist circles, writing for the Poalei Zion newspaper *Achdut*, where, in 1910, he Hebracized his name to Ben-Gurion.

In 1912, he left to study Turkish law and government in Istanbul but returned to Palestine at the outbreak of World War I. Because he initially sided with the Ottomans, he was exiled to Egypt in 1915, from where he journeyed to New York. It was there that he met and married Russian-born Paula Munweis, in 1917. These were heady days for political Zionism, and the issuing of the Balfour Declaration by Great Britain in that year, whereby the government declared support for the "establishment of a Jewish national home" in Palestine, led Ben-Gurion to help organize the Jewish Legion for Britain. But by the time he returned to Palestine in 1918, the war had ended.

The war's conclusion enabled Zionist immigrants to focus on establishing a nascent Jewish polity while attempting to secure independence from the British, who then held the Palestine Mandate. Becoming ever-more active in political circles, in 1921 Ben-Gurion assumed the position of General Secretary of the Histadrut (the national labor federation). In 1930, he formed the Mapai Party (precursor to the Labor Party), becoming party leader in 1933. Two years later, he became chairman of the executive committee of the Jewish Agency, effectively becoming head of the Yishuv, the pre-state Jewish community in Palestine.

During World War II, Ben-Gurion attempted to bring European Jewish refugees to Israel; he was also active in the Haganah (the pre-state military) at this time. On May 14, 1948, following the 1947 UN Partition Resolution and the withdrawal of the British Mandate, Ben-Gurion declared independence for the State of Israel. Subsequent parliamentary elections, in January 1949, saw him elected as prime minister.

Ben-Gurion's political reign in Israel was characterized by a policy of *mamlachtiut*, which entailed consolidating independent institutions under over-arching governmental authority. A striking example was the *Altalena* Affair in which, in June 1948, Ben-Gurion ordered the shelling of a ship carrying arms and 900 immigrants and belonging to the rival proto-military *Irgun* faction; the ship sank and sixteen aboard were killed.

Revered by Israelis and known affectionately as the Old Man, Ben-Gurion died December 1, 1973 at Kibbutz Sde Boker in the Negev, where he had retired from politics three years earlier, committed to the pioneering of the Israeli desert region.

MIRA SUCHAROV

See also Balfour Declaration; Israel; Palestine

References and Further Reading

Bar-Zohar, Michael. *Ben-Gurion: A Biography*. New York: Adama Books, 1986.
Heller, Joseph. *The Birth of Israel: Ben-Gurion and His Critics*. Gainesville, FL: University Press of Florida, 2000.
St. John, Robert. *Ben-Gurion: Builder of Israel*. Washington, DC: London Publishing Company, 1998.
Teveth, Shabtai. *Ben-Gurion and the Palestinian Arabs: From Peace to War*. New York: Oxford University Press, 1985.
Zweig, Ronald W., ed. *David Ben-Gurion: Politics and Leadership in Israel*. London: Frank Cass, 1991.

BENIN

The Republic of Benin is situated in West Africa and is bounded to the east by Nigeria, to the north by Niger and Burkina Faso, and to the west by Togo. The total territory is 112,620 square kilometers (110,620 square kilometers land area). Benin stretches 700 kilometers (435 miles) from the Gulf of Guinea to the Niger River. Benin's shoreline of 124 kilometers now includes what used to be known as the Slave Coast, from where captives were shipped across the Atlantic. Next to the coastal area, a plateau zone with wooded savannah extends to the Atakora hills, with elevation ranging from five hundred to eight hundred meters. Atakora is the water reservoir for both Benin and Niger. Climate of Benin is characterized by unusually dry conditions. Rainfall is not as abundant as in the other areas at the same latitude—an anomaly in the tropical conditions known as the Benin variant. The population of Benin is estimated at 6.9 million inhabitants (2004), largely concentrated in the southern coastal region near the major port city of Cotonou (450,000 inhabitants), the chief town of the Atlantic Department seat of government; the capital city of Porto Novo (200,000 inhabitants) in the Ouémé Department; as well as the "Royal City" of Abomey (80,000 inhabitants) in the Central Department of Zou.

Benin and the surrounding area was settled in the thirteenth century by Ewe-speaking people in the south and by Voltaic speakers in the north. Around the fifteenth century, the territory of contemporary Benin was penetrated by the Portuguese, who began the African slave trade. Around 1600, the kingdom of Allada was founded. It broke up into the rival states at Abomey and Porto-Novo in the seventeenth century. Later, Abomey grew into the Kingdom of Dahomey, which dominated the area until the nineteenth century. In 1895, Dahomey became a French territory, included in French West Africa. National liberation uprisings took place in 1915 and 1923. In 1958, Dahomey received autonomy within the frames of the French Community. On August 1, 1960, it achieved independence under the name of the Republic of Dahomey. From 1960 to 1972, Dahomey endured ten cabinet changes and five military coups d'etat. Gen. Christophe Soglo deposed the first president, Hubert Maga, in an army coup in 1963. He dismissed the civilian government in 1965, proclaiming himself chief of state. Then a group of young army officers seized power in December 1967, deposing Soglo. The fifth coup of the decade came in December 1969, with the army again taking power. In May 1970, a three-man presidential commission with a six-year term was created to take over the government. In May 1972, yet another army coup ousted the triumvirate and installed Lt. Col. Mathieu Kérékou as president. Between 1974 and 1989, Dahomey embraced socialism, proclaiming itself a Marxist-Leninist state, and changed its name to the People's Republic of Benin. The name Benin commemorates an African kingdom that flourished from the fifteenth to the seventeenth centuries in what is now southwest Nigeria. Benin renounced Marxist policies by the end of 1989, and in the following year became a multi-party democracy. Prime Minister Nicephere Soglo defeated M. Kérékou to become president in the March 1991 election. However, Kérékou was returned to office in the next election in 1996. Benin has embarked on a path of democracy. Presidential elections in both 1991 and 1996 saw a peaceful transfer of power. Increased freedom of the press and strengthening of civil society institutions reinforced the country's democratic inclination. The continuation of market-oriented economic policies after the 1996 election of President Kérékou has strengthened reforms by demonstrating the broad political consensus around such policies. Benin embraced democracy with particular fervor as a model of reform in Africa. M. Kérékou was re-elected in 2001, though some irregularities were alleged. Benin is considered to be the birthplace of voodoo, now a tourist attraction.

Benin's economy remains dependent on subsistence production of maize, yams, cassava, rice, fruits, and beans; cotton production; and regional trade. The country's main exports are cotton, palm oil products, coffee, crude oil, and cocoa beans. Recent years have seen an increase in exports of cotton and services related to transit trade. Growth in real output has averaged a stable 5% in the past six years, and inflation has subsided, but rapid population rise has thwarted most of this increase. Despite the economic growth over the past few years, Benin remains among the world's poorest countries and the GNI per capita is US$440 (World Bank 2003). The country's productive capacity is further severely compromised by the under-utilization and misuse of existing technical expertise. The BNP, US$6.6 billion (2000), is shared by agriculture 37.9%, industry 13.5%, and services 48.6%.

The economic infrastructure of Benin is poorly developed. There are about eight thousand kilometers of roads, of which one thousand kilometers are asphalted (including ten kilometers of expressways), and an international harbor with modern facilities in Cotonou. The 578 kilometers of railroads are a joint venture with the Republic of Niger. The main airport is near Cotonou and is served by many foreign air companies. The adult literacy rate is 40.9% (males 56.2%, females 26.5%, 2000). Benin's school system is under government control and is free and compulsory. The only university is the National University of Benin. Most of the Benin population, especially within the country, have no access to modern medical care. According to the 1995 data of the World Health Organization (WHO), there have been approximately six physicians and twenty-one nurses for every one-hundred thousand people. Life expectancy for males is slightly more than fifty-one years for males and fifty-two for females. The population growth rate (2.89% annually, 2004 est.), as well as the infant mortality rate (85.88 deaths per 1,000 live births), are among the highest in the region. Benin plans to attract more foreign investment, placing more emphasis on tourism, on new food-processing systems and agricultural products, and the introduction of the new information and communication technologies. The 2001 privatization policy will continue in telecommunications, water, electricity, and agriculture despite initial government reluctance.

STEPHAN E. NIKOLOV

See also Ethnic Conflicts: West Africa; West Africa: History and Economic Development; West Africa: International Relations; West African Monetary Union (WAMU)

References and Further Reading

Argyle, William John. *The Fon of Dahomey: A History and Ethnography of the Old Kingdom.* Oxford: Clarendon Press, 1966.

Akinjogbin, A. *Dahomey and Its Neighbours, 1708–1818.* Cambridge: Cambridge University Press, 1967.

Allen, Chris, and Michael Radu. *Benin and the Congo.* New York: St. Martin's Press, 1992.

Cornevin, R. *La République Populaire du Bénin: Des Origines? Nos Jours.* (People's Republic of Benin: From Its Origins Till Our Days). Paris: Maisonneuve et Larose, 1981.

Decalo, Samuel. *Historical Dictionary of Benin,* 3d ed. Metuchen, NJ: Scarecrow Press, 1992.

Diamond, Stanley. *Dahomey: Transition and Conflict in State Formation.* New York: Bergin & Garvey, 1983.

Manning, Patrick. *Slavery, Colonialism and Economic Growth in Dahomey, 1640–1960.* Cambridge: Cambridge University Press, 1982; new ed., 2004.

BERBERS

Berbers are an indigenous Caucasoid people of North Africa. They live in the area from the Atlantic coast to the Oasis of Siwa in Egypt, from the Mediterranean shore to the oases in mid-Sahara. Berbers make up a clear majority of the population of North Africa in terms of race, and in terms of identity—a substantial part. Racially, Berbers represent up to 80% of the population in Morocco and Algeria, and more than 60% in Tunisia and Libya. Thus, they account for more than fifty million people. Another two million of the nomadic Berbers, the Tuaregs, are scattered over Mali, Burkina Faso, and Niger. In addition, there are about four million Berbers living in Europe, mainly in France. More than half of the people with Berber background are now claiming to be Arabs.

Many theories relate Berbers to the Canaanites, the Phoenicians, the Celts, the Basques, or the Caucasians. Some anthropologists, in light of the Berbers' blond and red hair, as well as green and blue eyes, believe in their European origin. However, they have been in North Africa for more than four thousand years. On the evidence of Egyptian cenotaph paintings, they derive from as early as 2400 BC. The alphabet of the only partly deciphered ancient Libyan inscriptions is close to the script, the Tifinagh, still used by the Tuaregs. Their first state, the second-century BC Numidia in present Algeria, was located west of Carthage. It was conquered by Rome in the Second Punic War and became a province of the Roman Empire.

Until their conquest in the seventh century by Muslim Arabs, most of the Berbers were Christian, and a sizeable minority had accepted Judaism. Many of the early heresies, particularly Donatism, which held that church leaders who had renounced Christianity during Diocletian's persecutions were no longer valid authorities, emerged essentially as a Berber opposition against the Roman rule. "They belong to a powerful, formidable, brave and numerous people; a true people like so many others the world has seen—like the Arabs, the Persians, the Greeks and the Romans. The men who belong to this family of peoples have inhabited the Maghreb since the beginning," wrote the Arab philosopher Ibn Khaldoun in the eighth century. Under the Arabs, the Berbers were Islamized and formed the core of the Arab armies that conquered Spain. In the ninth century they supported the Fatimid dynasty in their conquest of North Africa.

After the Fatimids withdrew to Egypt, they left an anarchy of warring Berber tribes. It ended only with the rise of Berber dynasties, the Almoravids (eleventh–twelfth centuries) and the Almohads (twelfth–thirteenth centuries). Their empire of Mauritania extended over all northwestern Africa and part of Spain. They pushed back Christian kingdoms' advancement south against the fragmented Moors.

When these dynasties faded, the Berbers of the plains were gradually absorbed by the Arabs. Only those inhabiting inaccessible mountain regions, such as the Aurâs, the Kabylia, the Rif, and the Atlas, retained their culture and traditions. When the French and the Spaniards occupied much of North Africa, the Berbers staged the most vehement resistance. At the dawn of colonization, Abd el-Qadir in the Algerian Kabylia halted French occupation until 1847.

The Berber communities are scattered around the North African countries. They often live in independent settlements in remote areas under a loose tribal organization. Of major cities in North Africa, only Marrakech has a population with a Berber identity. Except for the nomadic Tuaregs, who have traditionally been based farther to the southwest (and who have hence become less racially homogenous), the Berbers are small farmers. They have developed local crafts (iron, copper, lead, pottery, weaving, and embroidery). Their conversion to Islam took a long time—up to the sixteenth century. Berbers are Sunni Muslims, but there are numerous traces of former religious practice. The name Berber was derived from "Barbarian" during the Greco-Roman period. The Berbers call themselves Imazighen (Free Men). Their native tongues are of the Hamitic group, but most literate Berbers also speak the language of their religion—Arabic. Berber languages—around three hundred local dialects—are spoken by about twelve million people, not all of whom are considered ethnic Berbers. Berbers use either the Latin or Arabic alphabet to write.

Until very recently, Berbers were considered to be second-class citizens, similar to the Native Americans in the United States, Aborigines in Australia, and the Sámi people (Lapps) in Norway. In such countries as Morocco and Tunisia, Berber is a synonym for being an illiterate peasant dressed in traditional garments. Many of the Berber children drop out of school because they are taught in Arabic. The language barrier often remains a problem throughout adult life, especially when dealing with administration. As with many other indigenous peoples in the world, Berbers are now protesting against the depreciation of their culture and identity, the absence of a written language, and being denied political influence. In the late 1990s in Algeria, confrontation reached dimensions so tense, it invited speculations about the chances of a civil war and a partition of the country. Many Arabs do not support the blossoming of Berber identity in their countries, but so far there has been little aggression between the two groups.

Tuaregs, or Touaregs, are the Berbers of the Sahara, numbering close to two million. They have preserved their ancient alphabet, related to the one used by ancient Libyans. The Tuaregs traditionally maintained a feudal system consisting of a small number of noble families, a large majority of vassals, and a lower class of black non-Tuareg serfs, engaged in agriculture. Tuaregs themselves convoyed caravans and, until subdued by France, were feared as raiders. Strongly independent, they never accepted European hegemony. Though nominally Muslim, they still retain many pre-Islamic rites and customs. A peculiar feature of the Tuaregs is that men go veiled, while the women do not cover their faces. Moreover, women enjoy respect and freedom, and descent and inheritance goes through the female line. The traditional way of life for the Tuaregs (such as raiding neighboring tribes, leading caravans, and demanding taxes from trans-Sahara travelers) has changed. Since the 1970s, droughts and famines have forced many Tuaregs from their desert homes into urban areas. In the 1990s, political tensions caused further relocation. Groups of Tuaregs have fought for autonomy from Niger and Mali, but cease-fires were signed in the mid-1990s.

STEPHAN E. NIKOLOV

See also Algeria; Arab Nationalism; Ethnic Conflicts: North Africa; Islam; Libya, Maghrib Peoples; Mauritania; Minorities/Discrimination; Morocco; North Africa: History and Economic Development; Tunisia

References and Further Reading

Brett, Michael, and Elizabeth Fentress. *The Berbers (The People of Africa)*. Oxford: Blackwell. 1998.
Hiernaux, Jean. *The People of Africa* (*People of the World* series). New York: Charles Scribner's Sons, 1975.
Keohane, Alan. *The Berbers of Morocco*. London: Hamish Hamilton; New York: Penguin Books, 1991.
Montagne, Robert. *The Berbers; Their Social and Political Organisation, with a preface by Ernest Gellner* (English translation of the Vie sociale et la vie politique des Berberes). London: Cass, 1973.
Roberts, Hugh. Perspectives on Berber Politics: On Gellner and Masqueray, or Durkheim's mistake. *Journal of the Royal Anthropological Institute* (March 2002).

BERLIN WALL (1961–1989)

In Europe, as a result of the wartime diplomacy of World War II and the so-called Cold War that followed, a theoretical line, which Winston Churchill called the "Iron Curtain," was drawn between the Eastern Soviet bloc and the Western-European non-Communist countries. While much of the confrontation, perhaps the most important part, was manifested in a *Realpolitik* geo-political stand-off,

both sides emphasized an ideological component that defined the Cold War.

The Western governments formed a new political and economic alliance to end centuries-old warfare among themselves—the Common Market, eventually becoming the European Union, which Washington helped finance through the Marshall Plan. At the same time most of the Western European states joined the United States and Canada in the military alliance NATO (North Atlantic Treaty Organization). For its part the Soviet Union countered with its own economic and military alliances—COMECON and the Warsaw Pact.

East–West differences appeared the sharpest in Germany. The victors of World War II divided Germany into four sections, each occupied by a different victor: the United States, the USSR, Great Britain, and France. By 1949, the Western Allies united their sectors into the Federal Republic of Germany (West) and the USSR established the German Democratic Republic (DDR-East). In a bizarre situation, the capital, Berlin, located well inside the Soviet sector, was also divided into four sectors. Thus, when the two Germanys were formed and the Western sectors united, two Berlins were created—a modern thriving West Berlin and a dilapidated East Berlin, which because of international treaties and economics could not be rebuilt. In 1949, the Soviets tried to force West Berlin to collapse by blocking land access to the city from the West, but the famous Berlin Airlift saved the city.

By treaty, citizens of Berlin could travel throughout the city. Many from the Eastern sector went to the West on the subway or other means of ground transportation. Some stayed there and others even flew to West Germany. The Soviet bloc countries made it difficult—and in some cases impossible—for its citizens to travel to West Germany, particularly the skilled workers and professional class whose training and education could give them higher-paying jobs. By the early 1960s, after the tensions between the blocs were relaxed under Nikita Khrushchev, the number of East Germans fleeing to the west, especially professionals, increased astronomically. About 2.5 million have left since 1949.

This migration presented problems for both East and West. For the East the loss of the educated population and their desire to flee was both an economic and a propaganda nightmare. For the West it meant an economic burden as penniless people moved into their sector. Political tensions increased, and the West Germans feared outbreaks of violence. However, Khrushchev and East Germany solved the problem on August 12, 1961, when they erected a barrier across the city—the Berlin Wall—barring access to the West. Families were divided. Initially composed of barbed wire and cinder blocks, the East German government gradually made the wall more permanent, with facades fifteen feet high and gun towers on top. The wall extended twenty-eight miles inside the city and another seventy miles around it.

More than ten thousand East Germans tried to cross the barrier. Approximately five thousand succeeded, but another five thousand were prevented, and more than 190 were killed in the attempt. Furthermore, the wall became a great propaganda tool for the West Germans as proof of the inferiority of the Communist system; it also aroused a great public outcry. Some wanted NATO forces to tear it down, but the West German authorities saw it as a resolution to many of West Berlin's economic and political issues. Additionally, the propaganda regarding the Wall added to the fear of global war, and the West Germans and their NATO allies did not want to risk a war with the Soviet Bloc.

For the next three decades the Berlin Wall stood as the symbol dividing the two competitors of the Cold War. In the 1970s, Cold War politics became more complicated when relations between China and the Soviet Union worsened and the former's relations with the United States improved. In the late 1980s, a new, more aggressive anti-Communist attitude appeared in Washington and London led by President Ronald Reagan and Prime Minister Margaret Thatcher. Meanwhile in the Soviet Union, stagnation paralyzed the politics and economy led by the aging and unimaginative leadership. Furthermore, Moscow's disastrous and unpopular war in Afghanistan made the need for change even more urgent. In 1985, after the successive deaths of two aged traditional leaders, Mikhail Gorbachev became leader of the Soviets. His initiatives, spurred on by the nuclear disaster at Chernobyl in 1985, led to his policies of *perestroika* and *glasnost*—economic restructuring and openness and discussion. Relations with the West improved. Gorbachev told the Eastern European countries they would have to fend for themselves and one by one the Communist parties there lost power. Citizens found routes to leave and go to the West. On November 9, 1989, as East Germany began to unravel, the Germans dismantled the wall piece by piece.

FREDERICK B. CHARY

See also Soviet Bloc

References and Further Reading

Mur, Cindy. *The Berlin Wall*. San Diego: Greenhaven Press, 2004.

Schweizer, Peter. *The Fall of the Berlin Wall: Reassessing the Causes and the Consequences of the End of the Cold War*. Stanford, CA: Hoover Institution, 2000.

Tusa, Ann. *The Last Division: A History of Berlin, 1945–1989*. Reading, MA: Addison-Wesley, 1997.

BETANCOURT, RÓMULO

Rómulo Betancourt (1908–1981) is often called the father of Venezuelan democracy. President of Venezuela from 1945 to 1948, and then again from 1959 to 1964, Betancourt consistently fought to institutionalize representative democracy in Venezuela. A powerful orator, he wrapped his political agenda in democratic and nationalist rhetoric. His efforts were facilitated by the tremendous revenues generated by Venezuela's petroleum industry, which provided the money needed to co-opt the various pillars of Venezuela's corporatist society. His main vehicle for political control was Acción Democrática (AD), a center-left political party established by Betancourt in 1941. Unlike most Venezuelan leaders who have illegally enriched themselves while in office, Betancourt, a short, chunky pipe smoker, left office with virtually the same amount of money that he entered office with.

Betancourt was born in Guatire, Miranda, not far from the capital, Caracas, on February 22, 1908, the same year that Venezuelan dictator Juan Vicente Gómez seized power. Betancourt's father, a Spanish accountant and poet, had married into a rural, middle-class Venezuelan family. His family had enough money to send Betancourt to the Liceo Caracas for his secondary education. Eventually, he entered the Universidad Central de Venezuela and studied law. He founded and led radical student groups, such as Agrupación de Izquierda (ARDI) and Organización Revolucionaria (ORVE), to protest against the Gómez dictatorship (1908–1935). Because of his protests against the Gómez dictatorship in 1928, he was arrested and jailed. He then went into exile from 1929 to 1936.

His contact with other Caribbean dictators convinced him that it was not enough to simply overthrow Gómez. The system of personalistic authoritarian dictatorships also had to be destroyed. Therefore, in 1931, along with other Venezuelan exiles, Betancourt issued the Plan of Barranquilla, which called for a social revolution in Venezuela. As a young man, Betancourt dabbled with Marxism, joined the Third International, and helped organize the Costa Rican Communist Party during the 1930s. He founded the Marxist-oriented Organización Venezolana (OV) in 1935, which was transformed into AD in 1941. Following his disillusionment with communism, in 1937 communist members were expelled from AD. AD had a strong power base among the labor unions, students, the growing urban middle class, and young military officers. In 1945, AD and a group of young military officers toppled a military government that had succeeded the Gómez dictatorship.

Following the revolution, Betancourt was chosen to lead the civilian/military junta ruling Venezuela until the December 1947 presidential elections that brought AD leader Rómulo Gallegos to power in February 1948. Betancourt initiated universal suffrage, social reforms, and secured half the profits from the foreign oil companies operating in Venezuela. The fifty-fifty petroleum law with the foreign oil companies—Creole (Standard Oil of New Jersey), Gulf, Shell, Texaco, and Mobile—guaranteed the Venezuelan government 50% of all oil company profits in Venezuela. At the same time, Betancourt built a lasting friendship with US industrialist Nelson Rockefeller. Rockefeller's family controlled the Creole Oil Company, the largest US oil firm operating in Venezuela. Rockefeller, who has been described by historian Darlene Rivas as a "missionary capitalist," wanted to make capitalism more socially responsible in Venezuela and supported Betancourt's efforts at social reform.

Numerous elites, generals, businessmen, and large landowners, however, were frightened by AD's populist rhetoric. Marcos Pérez Jiménez overthrew the AD government in 1948. Betancourt went into exile in New York City. He returned to Venezuela after a group of military officers led by Wolfgang Larrazábal ousted Pérez Jiménez in 1958. On October 31, 1958, members of Betancourt's AD, Jóvito Villalba's Democratic Republican Union (URD), and Christian Democrat Rafael Caldera's Independent Political Organizing Committee (COPEI) met at Caldera's home to sign the Pact of Punto Fijo, a civilian plan to avoid inter-party conflicts, strengthen constitutional democracy, and establish a government of national unity to ensure that all political forces (with the notable exception of the communists) were represented in the political system. As such, it was the groundwork for a two-party, power-sharing representative democracy that divided judiciary appointments and leadership positions in Congress. Critics of Betancourt called the Venezuelan government a "pactocracy"—democracy by the consent of those who govern rather than those who are governed.

Betancourt won the December 7, 1959, presidential elections with 49% of the vote. He promulgated a new constitution in 1961 to institutionalize representative democracy, which lasted until the 1999 constitution unveiled by Hugo Chavez. Two important organizations concerning petroleum were created during his administration by Minister of Energy Juan Pablo Pérez Alfonso in 1960. The Corporación Venezolana de Petróleos (CVP), which was designed to oversee the Venezuelan petroleum industry, and the Organization of Petroleum Exporting Countries (OPEC), an international oil cartel established with Saudi Arabia, Iraq, Iran, and Kuwait. Land reform programs distributed undeveloped private property and state lands to increase agricultural production. Oil wealth allowed for compensation to the landowners who had their property confiscated.

Betancourt was faced with threats from both the left and the right. Fidel Castro's government armed members of the Armed Forces for National Liberation (FALN). Betancourt protested Castro's actions before the Organization of American States (OAS) and broke diplomatic relations with Cuba in 1961. Betancourt was also critical of Dominican dictator Rafael Trujillo. Trujillo supported plots by Venezuelan exiles to overthrow Betancourt. Betancourt protested Trujillo's actions before the OAS and broke diplomatic relations with the Dominican Republic in 1960. Trujillo responded by orchestrating an assassination attempt on Betancourt on June 24, 1960. Although Betancourt survived, he was badly burned. Betancourt's foreign policy, known as the Betancourt Doctrine, was based on the premise that Venezuela would deny recognition to any regime, left or right, that came to power through military force.

US President John F. Kennedy viewed Betancourt's government as the best defense against authoritarianism and communism. Betancourt ensured that the 1963 presidential elections in Venezuela were free and honest. For the first time in Venezuelan history, the executive office passed from one constitutionally elected president to another. Awarded a lifetime seat in the Venezuelan Senate in 1973, he died in Doctor's Hospital in New York City on September 28, 1981.

MICHAEL R. HALL

See also Northern South America: History and Economic Development; Northern South America: International Relations; Pérez Jiménez, Marcos; Venezuela

References and Further Reading

Alexander, Robert Jackson. *Rómulo Betancourt and the Transformation of Venezuela*. Somerset, NJ: Transaction Publishers, 1981.

Bergquist, Charles. *Labor in Latin America: Comparative Essays on Chile, Argentina, Venezuela, and Colombia*. Stanford, CA: Stanford University Press, 1986.

Ewell, Judith. *The Indictment of a Dictator: The Extradition and Trial of Marcos Pérez Jiménez*. College Station, TX: Texas A&M University Press, 1981.

Kelly, Janet, and Carlos A. Romero. *United States and Venezuela: Rethinking a Relationship*. New York: Routledge, 2001.

Rivas, Darlene. *Missionary Capitalist: Nelson Rockefeller in Venezuela*. Chapel Hill, NC: University of North Carolina Press, 2002.

Salazar-Carillo, Jorge, and Bernadette West. *Oil and Development in Venezuela during the 20th Century*. New York: Praeger, 2004.

BHUTAN

Bhutan *(Druk Yul)* is located in the eastern Himalayas. It borders on China (Tibet) in the north and on India in the west, east, and south and is approximately 46,500 square kilometers large. Bhutan's southernmost part comprises a narrow strip of land at the fringes of the Ganges-Brahmaputra lowlands and has a subtropical climate. Central Bhutan is characterized by deep valleys cutting through the land in a north–south direction. With an average elevation of approximately 1,650 meters it is of a temperate climate. The northernmost part has a cold climate and an average elevation of four thousand meters. Approximately 70% of the country is forested. Most Bhutanese or *Drukpa* live in the central uplands and the adjacent Himalayan foothills. Total population numbers remain obscure. Estimations range between 600,000 and 2.2 million, hence population numbers, as well as data derived thereof, must be met with great caution. The United Nations Online Network in Public Administration and Finance (UNPAN)—in accordance with official Bhutanese figures—lists a population of 716,000 in 2002. The number of people living in urban areas remains vague as well. The capital, Thimphu, was reported to have fifty thousand inhabitants in 2004. Phuntsholing, close to the southern border, is the only other town with a population over ten thousand.

Although Bhutan is a Buddhist Kingdom and Mahajana-Buddhism enjoys the status of a state religion, approximately twenty-five percent of the population are Hindus who predominantly reside in the south. The official language is Dzongkha, a Sino-Tibetan language. However, since Dzongkha only recently became a written language and is but one of several languages spoken throughout Bhutan, English is extensively used as a lingua franca and for educational purposes. Three major groups comprise the Drukpa, thus reflecting Bhutan's immigration history: Ngalops of Tibetan origin, who have been settling in what became central Bhutan since the ninth century CE; Lhotshampas of Nepalese origin, who immigrated in the nineteenth century CE; and Sharchops, who migrated from what is now Birma and Northeast India to what is now eastern Bhutan in the seventh century CE.

As a political unit, Bhutan was established in the early seventeenth century when Ngawang Namgyal, a Tibetan lama, introduced a dual system of religious and secular government and established administrative districts *(Dzongkhaks)*. This system came to an end when the governor of the district of Trongsa, Ugyen Wangchuck, was elected the first King of Bhutan *(Druk Gyalpo)* in 1907. Since this date Bhutan has been a hereditary kingdom. Due to geographical and political factors combined with cautious diplomacy, Bhutan never came under colonial rule. However, in 1865, Bhutan ceded some borderland to the British empire in exchange for an annual subsidy. In the early twentieth century the British formally took over the country's external representation. With Indian independence in 1947 this function was carried out by India. In a 1949 agreement the territory formerly held by the British was returned and subsidies for Bhutan were granted by India, while at the same time India's responsibility for Bhutan's foreign affairs and its military defense was formalised.

Since the reign of the third king, Jigme Dorji Wangchuck (1952–1972), the country has experienced substantial political and social reforms. In 1953, the national assembly *(Tshogdu)* was established, consisting of 150 members of whom 105 are elected by the public, 10 by the Buddhist clergy, and 35—including the 20 district governors—are nominated by the king. Elections are held every three years. In 1965, the Royal Advisory Council *(Lodoi Tshogde)* was formed. Consisting of nine members—one government representative appointed by the king, six people's representatives elected for a three-year term by the Tshogdu, and two representatives of the clergy—this institution serves as an advisory body to the king and the ministers. During the 1960s a court system with twenty district courts was created, and eventually the High Court was set up in Thimphu in 1968. Ministers were appointed by the king until 1998 when structure was formed consisting of six ministers elected by the Tshogdu and the members of the Lodoi Tshogde, thus forming the Council of Ministers with full executive powers. At the same time the king stepped down as the head of government, at which point this function was passed over to the prime minister, a position annually rotated among the elected ministers. However, the king remains the head of state and maintains responsibility for the army, but the Tshogdu can remove him by a two-thirds vote in favor of the next person in the hereditary line.

Political parties are nonexistent. A number of exile-parties have been founded in relation to the expatriation of Nepalese immigrants in the 1980s. Since then about one hundred thousand persons of

BHUTAN

unclear status live in refugee camps in Nepal with little improvement having been reached on this issue. Other cases of political conflicts were an unsuccessful coup in 1964 involving the assassination of Prime Minister Jigme Dorji, and Indian guerilla groups operating from bases in southern Bhutan in joint operations of Bhutanese and Indian forces in 2003–2004.

Prior to 1961, Bhutan lacked any modern infrastructure. In the first Five-Year-Plan (1961–1966) priority was consequently given to the creation of basic infrastructural facilities such as roads and electrification, whereas the second Five-Year-Plan (1966–1971) centered around development in agriculture, education, and healthcare. The first Five-Year-Plans were exclusively financed by India. Since the 1970s, Bhutan has been continually seeking international contacts. In 1971, the country became a member of the UN, and as of 2004 it had six missions abroad and had joined more than 150 international organisations. India remains Bhutan's most important partner in both economic and political respects, but funding of development projects is not exclusively provided by India anymore.

The Human Development Index (HDI) listed Bhutan at a rank of 136 (of 175) in 2003 while as of 2002 the GDP per capita equaled US$1,969. However, detailed analysis reveals obvious improvements. For example, life expectancy rose from forty-three years in 1970 to sixty-three years in 2002, and infant mortality sunk from 15.6% in 1970 to 7.4% in 2002. With the construction of an airport with a paved runway at Paro and the extension of its hydroelectric capacities, Bhutan has invested in two of its key resources: tourism and hydroelectric power. Besides electricity, major exported goods are calcium-carbide, cement, forestry products, and cardamom; major imports include telecommunications equipment, rice, machinery, and oil. India accounts for approximately 90% of the exports and 75% of the imports. With a literacy rate of 47% in 2002, Bhutan ranks low in worldwide comparison. However, as of 2001, the government was spending 12.9% of its budget on education.

LARS V. KARSTEDT

See also Central Asia: History and Economic Development; Central Asia: International Relations

References and Further Reading

Dogra, Ramesh C. *Bhutan*. Oxford: Clio, 1990.
Galay, Karma. "International Politics of Bhutan." *Journal of Bhutan Studies* 10: 90–107 (2004).
Mathou, Thierry. "Bhutan: Political Reform in a Buddhist Monarchy." *Journal of Bhutan Studies* 1(1): 114–144 (1999).
Rose, Leo E. *The Politics of Bhutan*. Ithaca, NY, and London: Cornell University Press, 1977.
Simoni, Alessandro. "A Language for Rules, Another for Symbols: Linguistic Pluralism and Interpretation of Statutes in the Kingdom of Bhutan." *Journal of Bhutan Studies* 8: 29–53 (2003).
UNDP. "Human Development Reports: Bhutan." (http://hdr.undp.org/statistics/data/cty/cty_f_BTN.html) (2004).
UNPAN. "Key Indicators of Developing Asian and Pacific Countries: Bhutan." (http://unpan1.un.org/intradoc/groups/public/documents/apcity/unpan012567.pdf) (2005).

BHUTTO, BENAZIR

Benazir Bhutto (1953–1996) was born on June 21, 1953, in Karachi (Pakistan). She was the daughter of Zulfikar Ali Bhutto, who was president and later prime minister of Pakistan from 1971–1977. Bhutto was twice prime minister of Pakistan (1988–1990 and 1993–1996), the first woman to be elected to head the government of an Islamic state. She brought new hopes to the people of Pakistan that she would guide her homeland along the path of democracy, freedom, and justice. She was a charismatic politician and symbol of modernity, glory, and independence. Her career took her from the depths of the prisons of dictator Zia ul-Haq to the heights of Pakistan's prime ministership.

Bhutto was tutored by an English governess and enjoyed a pampered, upper-class upbringing. She attended Lady Jennings Nursery School, and the Convent of Jesus and Mary in Karachi. She also studied at Rawalpindi Presentation Convent and was then sent to Jesus and Mary Convent at Murree. She passed O-level examinations from Jesus and Mary Convent, Karachi, at the age of fifteen. In April 1969, she was admitted to Harvard University's Radcliffe College to study politics, philosophy, and economics. In 1973, Bhutto attended Oxford University to study International Law and Diplomacy. She was elected to the standing Committee of the Oxford Union Debating Society and, in 1977, she was elected president of the Oxford Union. Bhutto returned to Pakistan in June 1977 and served as an advisor to her father. In the following decade of political struggle, Bhutto was arrested by the military regime on numerous occasions. In all she spent nearly six years (1977–1983) either in prison or under detention for her dedicated leadership of the then-opposition Pakistan People's Party. Throughout the years in opposition, she pledged to transform Pakistani society by focusing attention on programmes for health, social welfare, and education for the underprivileged. Benazir Bhutto was arrested.

In 1984, she was allowed to leave Pakistan and settled in London.

Bhutto returned to Pakistan in 1986 and married a wealthy businessman, Asif Ali Zardari, on December 17, 1987. Soon after, she led the opposition to military rule. After Zia ul-Haq died in a plane crash in 1988, Bhutto's alliance gained a narrow majority in the parliamentary elections and she became prime minister. As prime minister, Benazir Bhutto emphasised the need to heal past wounds and to put an end to the divisions in Pakistani society—including reducing discrimination between men and women. Bhutto launched a nationwide programme of health and education reform. The Bhutto government, however, was marked by continuous intrigue and able to accomplish little, and was dismissed by President Gulam Ishaq Khan in August 1990. The president accused Bhutto, her husband, and her party of corruption. Zardari was held (1990–1993) on various charges, eventually acquitted, and Bhutto's party lost the late 1990 elections. In 1993, Bhutto again became prime minister and made alliances, including those with the military that enabled her to deal with some of Pakistan's deep-seated problems. In 1996, the Bhutto government was again dismissed by President Farooq Leghari under charges of mismanagement, corruption, and financial embezzlement. Bhutto's husband, Zardari, was the focus of much of the criticism. She had appointed him to the cabinet post of investment minister. Zardari was accused of murdering Bhutto's brother (Mir Murtaza Bhutto), a political rival, as well as of accepting kickbacks and pocketing money from government contracts, and sweeping corruption charges were brought against Bhutto. President Leghari also accused Zardari of "extrajudicial killings" in Karachi, where Bhutto's rivals had been killed by police. In 1999, Bhutto and Zardari were both convicted of corruption; Bhutto appealed the verdict while living in exile with her three children (Bilawal, Bakhtwar, and Aseefa) in the United Arab Emirates and England. In 2001, the Pakistani Supreme Court set aside the corruption charges facing Bhutto and Zardari and ordered a retrial for both of them. On both occasions that Bhutto's government had been dismissed, it was due to the Eighth Amendment that enables the president to remove a prime minister—the amendment had been added to the constitution by a former president, General Zia ul-Haq, to give him leverage to get rid of Prime Minister Mohammed Khan Junejo. Subsequently, President Ghulam Ishaq Khan and Farooq Leghari used it to dismiss Benazir Bhutto's government.

Benazir Bhutto is the author of *Foreign Policy in Perspective* (1978) and an autobiography, *Daughter of the East* (1989). She received the following awards: the Bruno Kreisky Award for Human Rights (1988); the Phi Beta Kappa Award presented by Radcliffe College (1989); the Highest French Award, the Grand-Croix de la Legion D'Honneur (1989); the Noel Foundation Award (UNIFEM) (1990); the Gakushuin Honorary Award, Tokyo (1996); and a Medal of the University of California at Los Angeles UCLA (1995). She has been awarded an Honorary Doctorate of Law, L.L.D, Harvard University (1989); Honorary Doctorate of Law (Honoris Causa), University of Sindh, Pakistan (1994); Honorary Doctorate from Mendanao State University, Philippines (1995); Honorary Doctorate of Law (Honoris Causa), University of Peshawar, Pakistan (1995); Honorary Doctorate of Economics, Gakushuin University, Tokyo (1996); and an Honorary Fellowship by Lady Margaret Hall, University of Oxford (1989). She has addressed an historic US Joint Session of Congress (1989), where she called for the establishment of an Association of New Democratic Nations; the World Economic Forum at Davos, Switzerland (1994); French National Assembly (1994); UN Conference on Population Planning, Cairo (1994); Commission for Human Rights, Geneva (1994); Princeton University, US (1995); School of Advanced International Studies at Johns Hopkins University (1995); and the World Women's Conference in Beijing (1995). She has been called "The world's most popular politician" in the Guinness Book of World Records (1996). The *London Times* (May 4, 1996) included her in its list of the one hundred most powerful women.

HUSAIN KASSIM

See also Central Asia: History and Economic Development; Pakistan

References and Further Reading

Bhutto, Benazir. *Daughter of the East: An Autobiography*. London: Hamish Hamilton, 1988.
Bhutto, Benazir. *Daughter of Destiny*. New York: Simon & Schuster, 1989.
Shaikh, Muhammad Ali. *Benazir Bhutto: A Political Biography*. Lahore: Orient Books, 2000.
Taseer, Sulman. *Bhutto: A Political Biography*. London: Ithaca Press, 1979.
Ziring, Lawrence. "Benazir Bhutto: A Political Portrait," *Asian Affairs* 18(3): 178–189 (Fall 1991).

BIAFRA

The short-lived Republic of Biafra was a secessionist breakaway state from Nigeria, lasting from its declaration in May 1967 to its surrender to the federal state of Nigeria in January 1970. Consisting of the former eastern region of Nigeria, Biafra was bounded by the Gulf of Guinea and Bight of Biafra in the south, by the Niger River and Niger Delta on the west, by the northern regional authority of Nigeria to the north, and by the Nigeria-Cameroon border on the east. The state was created as a homeland for the Ibo, one of the three largest tribal ethnic groups in Nigeria, at its inception encompassing a population of about 15 million. The declaration of the state of Biafra led to an extremely desperate and bloody struggle between the Biafran separatists and the federal government of Nigeria, ending only with the complete surrender of the separatists.

Biafra was the culmination of severe internal turmoil in Nigeria following its independence from British colonial rule in 1960. Nigeria was a state strongly divided among various ethnic groups, most prominently the northern Hausa-Fulani, the western Yoruba, and the eastern Ibo. These ethnic groups were further divided by religion and lifestyle. Northerners were by and large Muslims and the northern economy was generally pastoral and agricultural. In the south, the Yoruba were mixed Christian and Muslim and the Ibos were predominantly Christian. The southern population was widely perceived as a merchant and bureaucratic elite, and southerners were the more significant force in the nationalist movement leading up to 1960.

The creation of a Westminster-style parliamentary government in Nigeria following independence gave the numerically superior north the most powerful role in government. What is more, the party system, which tended directly to represent the significant ethnic cleavages, reinforced the inherent tensions among the major tribal groups. The Nigerian governments elected in 1959 and 1964 favoured the Hausa-Fulani-dominated Northern Peoples' Congress, which was increasingly criticized by southerners for attempting to institutionalize northern dominance in Nigerian politics. A national census taken in 1962 was widely held by southerners to overstate the northern population and sparked further polarization of the electorate. The two major southern parties united to boycott the elections of December 1964, complaining of widespread irregularities in the electoral process, violence, and intimidation. This set the stage for a military coup in which the Nigerian prime minister and several northern prefects were assassinated, and it brought to power General Johnson Aguiyi-Ironsi, an ethnic Ibo, in January 1966.

In the wake of the coup, northern animosity toward ethnic Ibos increased as popular sentiment blamed the Ibo for the overthrow of the government. In May 1966, General Ironsi issued Decree 34, suspending the constitution and declaring an end to the federal system. This sparked widespread riots in the north, in which thousands of Ibos were killed and many thousands more fled as refugees to the south. Instability lasted until the assassination of Ironsi in late July and his replacement by Colonel Yakubu Gowon. Gowon's administration restored the federal system in early September, but the military governor of the eastern region, General Emeka Odumegwu Ojukwu, refused to accept the legitimacy of the new government. Despite an agreement reached between the two in Aburi, Ghana, in January 1967, the Gowon administration refused to accept a system of devolved power proposed by Ojukwu, and the eastern region proceeded quickly toward breaking ties with the central administration. In response to Gowon's announcement of a new federal administration on May 27, the Consultative Assembly of the eastern region requested Ojukwu to declare independence. On May 30, the independent republic of Biafra was declared in the eastern region.

Nigerian federal forces moved quickly to reverse the secession of Biafra. Beginning in July 1967, the federal army moved on several towns in the northern and coastal portions of Biafra with the expectation that the breakaway republic would submit within two weeks. However, a Biafran counterattack launched against the mid-west region of Nigeria in August and September threatened the capital of Lagos until federal forces pushed the separatists back toward the east. From October 1967, the Biafrans were fighting a defensive battle on their own soil against a far superior federal army. After the fall of Port Harcourt to federal forces on June 9, 1968, Biafra remained landlocked and under siege throughout the remainder of the war, supplied only via humanitarian airlift of health supplies and smuggled goods. The former source of supply was curtailed dramatically after Nigerian forces shot down a Swedish Red Cross flight in June 1969.

Throughout 1968 and 1969, famine afflicted the people of Biafra, leading to the deaths of an estimated six thousand to ten thousand people per day. In January 1969, UNICEF reported that approximately two million people had starved to death in Nigeria and Biafra. International support for the Biafran regime was scant. While the federal government continued to receive arms supplies from the United Kingdom and the Soviet Union, Biafra was diplomatically isolated, supplied only by a handful of countries and officially recognized by a small number of African states.

A series of definitive victories on the part of the federal government in late 1969 led to the eventual collapse of Biafran resistance. On January 10, 1970, General Ojukwu fled Biafra, and two days later, Biafran forces surrendered to the federal government. While the government promised to oversee the non-partisan reconciliation of Biafra, it refused to allow most foreign relief efforts in the region following the war, citing their support of Biafra during the conflict.

Many factors contributed to the intensity of the war over Biafra, including the importance of oil extraction in the Niger River Delta and its significance as a trans-shipment point for oil production. Added to this was the ethnic and class basis of divisions between the mostly rural northern majority and the comparatively prosperous and commercially developed southern Ibo. Within Biafra, the war was cast as an independence struggle of African solidarity against the neocolonial dominance of the Nigerian government in league with international commercial interests. While the secessionist movement was conclusively defeated, the Biafran War remains emblematic of the significant internal divisions present in Nigerian politics.

PAUL S. ROWE

See also Ethnic Conflicts: West Africa; Nigeria; West Africa: History and Economic Development; West Africa: International Relations

References and Further Reading

Ekwe-Ekwe, Herbert. *The Biafra War: Nigeria and the Aftermath.* Lewiston, New York: The Edwin Mellen Press, 1990.
Nwankwo, Arthur Agwuncha, and Samuel Udochukwu Ifejika. *The Making of a Nation: Biafra.* London: C. Hurst & Company, 1969.
Schwab, Peter. *Biafra.* New York: Facts on File, 1971.
de St. Jorre, John. *The Nigerian Civil War.* London: Hodder and Stoughton, 1972.
Stremlau, John J. *International Politics of the Nigerian Civil War, 1967–1970.* Princeton, NJ: Princeton University Press, 1977.

BIODIVERSITY CONSERVATION

Biodiversity conservation is one of a handful of environmental issues that highlight the increasingly acrimonious debate about sustainable development in the developing world. The term is of interest globally, but particularly relevant in the Global South as that is where the vast majority of species diversity exists—and that is where development pressures threaten biodiversity most acutely.

In its most basic sense, biodiversity refers to the web of life around us—and, thus, conservation of these resources is tied to the basic human inclination for self-preservation. But as a wealth of literature to date demonstrates, more immediate development interests, perhaps most accurately described as growth pressures, often supercede these environmental issues, which typically require a larger frame of reference. Such short-term approaches create the very conditions they seek to avoid. Yet this is precisely the obstacle that confronts those engaged in biodiversity conservation today.

Before answering this broader question, though, let us define biodiversity. Biodiversity has come, in fact, to incorporate essentially three different levels of analysis. As Harvard entomologist and Pulitzer Prize-winning author Edward O. Wilson notes in his text *Naturalist,* biodiversity "is the total hereditary variation in life forms, across all levels of biological organization, from genes and chromosomes within individual species to the array of species themselves and finally, at the highest level, the living communities of ecosystems such as forests and lakes."

While Wilson's definition is the accepted norm, the most widely distributed analyses focus on the middle level of analysis—the different types of species on our planet. This diversity is found overwhelmingly in the southern hemisphere, in developing states. Even more specifically, this diversity is particularly found in tropical rainforests such as the Amazon. Graphical representations of biodiversity such as those by non-governmental organizations (NGOs) like Conservation International (CI) highlight this phenomenon. Indeed, CI is probably most famous for its hotspots map, which portrays its intensified focus on twenty-five high-priority areas around the world. CI uses its hotspots map to argue that the best strategy in protecting biodiversity is to concentrate upon a relatively small number of areas with high species diversity.

CI pinpoints locations that cover a mere 1.4% of the earth's land surface—but land that is home to more than 60% of the global terrestrial species. Probably the most commonly cited counter-example is the Global 200 program proposed by the World Wildlife Fund (WWF). WWF, known as World Wide Fund for Nature internationally, traditionally identifies two hundred global eco-regions, the most biologically distinct terrestrial, marine, and freshwater regions according to their scientists. Distinctiveness is measured according to total number of species, number of species found nowhere else (referred to as endemism), and presence of unusual evolutionary or ecological phenomena.

In any case, whether one concentrates on the twenty-five hotspots of CI or two hundred eco-regions of WWF, virtually all maps of biodiversity do have one characteristic in common—they all show a decided overlap in diversity across national borders. That means any viable conservation program must be addressed among a number of overlapping states. In some cases, where species such as birds or whales migrate for thousands of miles, these states are not even in close proximity to one another. Thus, there is a need for international, or perhaps more accurately transnational, efforts to truly protect species. Yes local initiatives are necessary, particularly in the developing world where development pressures threaten biodiversity most acutely. Communities and the individuals among them must have a stake in biodiversity conservation. It must be in their interest to protect—to preserve wildlife. Similarly, state-level commitments are necessary. National environmental protection efforts must recognize the ecological base of national economic health. But neither local nor state-level actions are sufficient on their own. Global attention is required as well. This is where the aforementioned NGOs come into the picture. They permeate all three levels. They are uniquely equipped to operate both below and above the state level. They are truly transnational actors.

The last two decades have seen a veritable explosion in the number of environmental NGOs—both large and small, southern and northern hemisphere groups alike. These groups are raising more money than ever before. They are breaking new partnership grounds, both with business and with other NGOs. And they are working both directly with and against states, as well as a select number of international organizations in their conservation protection efforts. This action is most obvious in a handful of international forums. Five international treaties of particular note are the Convention on Biological Diversity (CBD); Convention on International Trade in Endangered Species of Wild Fauna and Flora (CITES); Convention on Wetlands of International Importance, Especially as Waterfowl Habitat (Ramsar); Convention on Preservation of Migratory Species of Wild Animals (CMS); and the Convention Concerning the Protection of the World Cultural and Natural Heritage (WH). A sixth agreement of relevance is the 1989 Basel Convention on the Control for the Conservation of Transboundary Movements of Hazardous Wastes and Their Disposal. Like the CBD, this convention targets assistance of developing countries as a primary objective. Unlike the CBD, though, it fails to address broader issues of diversity protection.

That said, the two most notable here are the CBD and CITES. The Convention on Biological Diversity (CBD) represents the first and only international treaty protecting total species diversity, although the potential of this treaty continues to be stymied by United States' intransigence. While some 187 states plus the European Union are now full-fledged members given their ratified status, the United States is not. A product of the 1992 UN Conference on Environment and Development (UNCED) in Rio de Jainero, Brazil, the Convention entered into force in December 1993 after being ratified in record time. The Earth Summit, as it is popularly known, represented the largest gathering of world leaders in history, with some ten thousand diplomats present. But its progress in terms of conservation has been halting at best. The record of the 1973 Convention on International Trade in Endangered Species (CITES) is more acclaimed. It comes the closest to the CBD in terms of international impact, yet it is by definition limited to known species that are officially recognized as endangered—and only within the context of trade. Still, this convention is useful more generally in that it publishes lists of species in three basic categories. Appendix I is the most protective, prohibiting all international commercial trade in threatened species. Appendix II also provides a degree of protection as it regulates trade in species not currently threatened with extinction but susceptible to such a threat if trade were to be unregulated. Appendix III is simply a list of species that countries stipulate as already protected within their own borders.

The most widely recognized cataloguing of international biodiversity, though, is The World Conservation Union's Red List of Threatened Species. The list is produced by the hybrid non-governmental-international organization known as The World Conservation Union (IUCN). Known globally as the International Union for Conservation of Nature and Natural Resources (IUCN), it is a mammoth federation composed of more than one thousand different members. This includes some eighty states, over one hundred government agencies, and approximately 730 NGOs. IUCN Red Lists were printed in traditional book format until the year 2000, when a switch was made to annual updates in an electronic format on the World Wide Web (see References and Further Reading at the end of this entry).

Despite all these efforts, species numbers throughout the world are dropping at a frightening rate. Some fifty thousand species a year become extinct according to a recent estimate by the Rainforest Action Network. Some of this is due to pollution. Some is due to invasive species, sometimes referred to as non-indigenous or alien species. But by far the primary culprit in this massive die-off is habitat loss due to human development. This includes a litany of activities from logging, mining, and oil drilling to agricultural development and suburban sprawl.

It is unknown exactly how many species there are. While there have been approximately 1.8 million known species catalogued to date, many more are unknown. Estimates range from three million to five million species at the low end, to fifty million to one hundred million species at the high end. This larger number is based on research done by the Smithsonian

Museum of Natural History's Terry Erwin beginning in 1982. An entomologist, Erwin fogged insects in the tree canopies of rainforests in Panama, Brazil, and Peru, trapping the dying insects (especially beetles) on a sticky tarp where he could then study them. From the canopy of a single tree species (*L. seemannii*) Erwin found more than 1,100 species of beetles alone—80% of which were previously unknown to science. From numbers such as these he then drew a series of complicated and controversial extrapolations that some thirty million insects inhabited the Amazon alone.

During the last decade biologists and conservationists have converged to a middle figure of between ten million and thirty million species. But again the range remains a disagreement between three million and one hundred million. Worldwide, more than seven hundred extinctions of vertebrates, invertebrates, and vascular plants have been recorded since 1600. But how many unknown species went extinct? This is a particularly relevant question as this seven hundred number focuses on large, easily observed species; some island species that are relatively easily monitored as well; and the well-studied northern temperate latitudes where most biologists live—but most biodiversity does not.

Some extinction is a natural process. Scientists refer to this as the "background extinction rate" and tell us that the vast majority of species that have ever lived have gone extinct. That is, in fact, what makes the current pattern all the more alarming. The normal background rate is one species every ten thousand years. In 1950, that rate had increased to one every ten years. Today estimates vary widely, ranging from one per day to three per hour. No matter which number you choose, though, it is clear that large numbers of species are dying off—so large a number that this is commonly referred to as the sixth great extinction spasm. The last such extinction spasm was sixty-five million years ago when dinosaurs ruled the planet. Many biodiversity conservation efforts acknowledge not only the inherent worth of species but also the human species' own interests in maintaining as heterogeneous a planet as possible.

The most famous example of the dangers presented by lack of genetic diversity in agricultural crops is the Irish potato famine of 1846. Two others are the 1970 corn blight that wiped out $1 billion in US crops and the 1972 devastation in the Soviet Union wheat industry. The blood of a horseshoe crab helps in the diagnosis of meningitis. Bee venom aids in treating arthritis. More than half the new pharmaceuticals developed today come from species out of the Amazon. Making conservation policy choices only once damage is proven implicitly suggests that either humanity can adequately compensate for those losses incurred—or that the species that are currently being lost are marginal or unnecessary components in the web of life.

MICHAEL M. GUNTER, JR.

See also Deforestation; Environment: Government Policies; Environmentalism; Erosion, Land; Non-Governmental Organizations (NGOs); Rain Forest, Destruction of; Sustainable Development; Wildlife Preservation

References and Further Reading

Bowles, Ian A., and Glenn T. Prickett, eds. *Footprints in the Jungle: Natural Resource Industries, Infrastructure, and Biodiversity Conservation*. New York: Oxford University Press, 2001.

Eldredge, Niles. *Life in the Balance: Humanity and the Biodiversity Crisis*. Princeton, NJ: Princeton University Press, 1998.

Groves, Craig. *Drafting a Conservation Blueprint: A Practitioner's Guide to Planning for Biodiversity*. Washington, DC: Island Press, 2003.

Gunter, Michael M., Jr. *Building the Next Ark: How NGOs Work to Protect Biodiversity*. Hanover, NH: University Press of New England, 2004.

IUCN 2003. *2003 IUCN Red List of Threatened Species* (www.redlist.org).

Leakey, Richard, and Roger Lewin. *The Sixth Extinction: Patterns of Life and the Future of Humankind*. New York: Doubleday, 1995.

Miller, Marian A. L. *The Third World in Global Environmental Politics*. Boulder, CO: Lynne Rienner, 1995.

Rainforest Action Network. "Rainforests Fact Sheets: Species Extinction," www.ran.org/info_center/factsheets/03b.html

Reaka-Kudla, Marjorie L., Don E. Wilson, and Edward O. Wilson, eds. *Biodiversity II: Understanding and Protecting Our Biological Resources*. Washington, DC: Joseph Henry Press, 1997.

Wilson, Edward O. *The Diversity of Life*. New York: W.W. Norton, 1992.

Wilson, Edward O. *Naturalist*. Washington, DC: Island Press, 1994.

Wilson, Edward O. *The Future of Life*. New York: Alfred A. Knopf, 2002.

Wilson, E. O., and F. M. Peter, eds. *Biodiversity*. Washington, DC: National Academy Press, 1988.

World Resources Institute, the World Conservation Union, and the United Nations Environmental Programme. *Global Biodiversity Strategy: Guidelines for Action to Save, Study and Use Earth's Biotic Wealth Sustainably and Equitably*. New York: WRI, 1992.

BISHOP, MAURICE

Maurice Bishop (1944–1983) was the revolutionary prime minister of Grenada from 1979 to 1983. In 1962, he joined with Bernard Coard to form the Grenada Assembly of Youth After Truth. Bishop and Coard led bi-monthly debates in the central market on current events. In 1963, while Coard went to

Brandeis University to study economics, Bishop went to study law at London University's Holborn College. Bishop became chairman of the West Indian Students Society, co-founded a legal aid clinic for the West Indian community in Notting Hill, and was a member of the Campaign Against Racial Discrimination (CARD).

In March 1970, Bishop returned to Grenada where he became active in politics. He was influenced by the writings of Tanzania's Julius Nyerere, especially *Ujamaa: Essays on Socialism* (1968). He founded a political group known as the Movement for Assemblies of the People (MAP), which, in 1973, merged with another political group, Unison Whitman's Joint Endeavor for Welfare, Education, and Liberation (JEWEL), to form the New Jewel Movement (NJM). The NJM was a black-power movement that appealed to many of the island's one hundred thousand inhabitants, most of whom were descendants of African slaves imported during the colonial period. In May 1973, the British government announced that Grenada would receive independence in February 1974. Bishop was concerned that Prime Minister Eric Gairy's Grenada United Labour Party (GULP) would exclude the NJM from the political system. Nevertheless, in 1976, Bishop won a seat in the House of Representatives and became leader of the opposition. In 1977, Bishop visited Fidel Castro in Cuba and established close ties with the communist dictator.

On March 13, 1979, Bishop led a virtually bloodless revolution while Gairy was in New York City speaking at the United Nations about flying saucers and communication with extraterrestrials. Bishop received aid from Cuba and the Soviet Union, began construction of a large airport, and invited Cuban workers to help construct the airport. The United States and several of Bishop's Caribbean neighbors were concerned about Bishop's Marxist ideas and close friendship with Castro. On October 18, 1983, his long-time associate, Minister of Finance Coard, who wanted to pursue a more pro-Soviet policy, overthrew Bishop's government with the support of the army. Bishop was placed under house arrest in his Mt. Wheldale home. On October 19, Bishop marched on Fort George with a large group of his supporters, and was captured and executed. His body was never recovered. In response to the resulting chaos, US President Ronald Reagan sent a joint US–Caribbean military force to Grenada on October 25, 1983, which was welcomed by most Grenadians. Coard and sixteen of his accomplices, the so-called Grenada 17, were sentenced to life in prison.

MICHAEL R. HALL

See also Caribbean: History and Economic Development; Caribbean: International Relations; Grenada; Group of 77; New Jewel Movement; Nyerere, Julius

References and Further Reading

Bishop, Maurice. *In Nobody's Backyard: Maurice Bishop's Speeches, 1979–1983*. London: Zed Books, 1985.

Marcus, Bruce, and Michael Taber. *Maurice Bishop Speaks: The Grenada Revolution and Its Overthrow, 1979–1983*. New York: Pathfinder Press, 1983.

Scoon, Paul. *Survival for Service: My Experiences as Governor General of Grenada*. London: Macmillan Caribbean, 2003.

Steele, Beverley A. *Grenada: A History of Its People*. London: Macmillan Caribbean, 2003.

BLACK MARKET/SHADOW ECONOMY

The black market or "shadow" economy is also known by numerous other names: "underground" economy, "informal" economy, "second" economy, "hidden" economy, "unofficial" economy, "parallel" economy, "alternative" economy, "barter" or "ghetto" economy, and "subterranean" economy. The existence of such a myriad of synonymous descriptions demonstrates the importance of the black market economy in today's world. The shadow economy can be defined as the economy that comprises all economic activities where goods and services are produced but not reported. It therefore includes illicit and criminal activities, as well as all unreported income from the production of legal goods and services, either from monetary or barter transactions. In other words, the shadow economy refers to all economic activities that take place outside the official economy and that would be taxable if reported to the tax authorities.

The shadow economy can be divided into four broadly comparable components: the criminal, irregular, household, and informal sectors. The criminal sector comprises illegally produced goods and services, such as illicit narcotics. In this sector are included all criminal activities carried out by terror organizations in order to fund themselves; examples are credit card fraud and credit card cloning. In fact, all activities of terror groups belong to the black market economy, with the exception of legal activities such as the generation of charitable donations. These latter activities become illegal, that is, they enter the domain of the criminal economy, only when they fund terrorist attacks. The irregular sector includes legally produced goods and services that evade legal reporting requirements, for example, to avoid taxes. The household sector refers to productive activities that take place within private abodes. Something as simple as knitting a cardigan or making a dress and selling it to a friend, without reporting the income, would fall within this category. And, finally, the informal sector can be defined as economic activities that circumvent the costs and are excluded from the benefits of law, such as unregulated micro-enterprise. In this latter category, we might find the plumber who works for a large firm but has private customers on the weekends, or the policeman "moonlighting" as a security guard when off-duty, and both getting paid in cash and not reporting it.

Thus, the underground economy may actually include such innocuous occupations as midwifery, child care, or construction, widening the scope of what is often perceived only as a seedy and corrupt sector of the business world. Following this definition, many entrepreneurs and self-employed persons may find themselves connected to the underground economy in some aspect or another, whether through the employment of people "off the books," or by acting as unlicensed workers themselves, or by exchanging goods without regulation. This aspect of the black market economy should not be undervalued as it represents a considerable section of the shadow economy. In the United States, for example, using this expanded definition, the National Center for Policy Analysis (NCPA) has put at twenty-five million the number of Americans who, in 2000, earned a substantial part of their income underground.

The Size of the Shadow Economy

As a consequence of its very nature, estimating the size of the shadow economy is quite difficult. For a start, people engaged in underground activities do their best to avoid detection, a phenomenon stressed by one of the overall descriptions of this economy, that is, shadow economy. To correctly estimate how big the informal economy is, policy makers and government administrators need information about how many people are active in the black market economy, how often underground activities occur, and how large is the volume of cash generated by these activities. Thus, economists and government statisticians have made a variety of calculations to estimate the size of the shadow economy.

The Economist calculates that the world underground economy is worth $9 trillion, which is about 20% of the world economy. This figure includes unrecorded income, which ranges from legal income, such as that of builders paid in cash, to the proceeds of illicit activities such as drug-dealing and prostitution.

The IMF and the World Bank estimate that the size of the criminal and illegal economy is about $1 trillion. Loretta Napoleoni, an economist specializing in terrorism, estimates that the world's criminal, illegal, and terror economy totals $1.5 trillion. According to all these estimates, the largest component of the black market economy is represented by the irregular, household, and informal sectors.

Friedrich Schneider, professor of economics at the Johannes Kepler University of Linz in Austria, has done extensive work on the growth of the black market economy. He calculates that, in OECD countries, the shadow economy has been steadily growing for the last thirty years—doubling from an average of 10% of the GDP in the 1970s to around 20% in 2000. Growth has also occurred in countries with smaller shadow economies. In the United States, for example, the black market economy is estimated to have jumped from 4% of GDP in 1970 to 9% in 2000.

The fastest growth in shadow economies was in the 1990s when the black market economy of OECD countries rose from an average 13% (1990–1993) to an average 20% at the end of the decade (1999–2000). The dissolution of the Soviet Union and globalization seem to be the key international factors that have boosted this exceptional growth.

Among OECD countries, from 1999–2001, Greece and Italy had the largest shadow economies, equivalent to 30% and 27% of their GDP, respectively. In the middle group one finds the Scandinavian countries, and at the lower end of the spectrum, the United States and Austria, at 10% of their GDP, and Switzerland, at 9%. From 2000 onwards, the shadow economy has continued to grow strongly in most OECD countries.

From 1988 to 2000, the black market economy in transition economies, that is, former communist countries, averaged 23% of the GDP. In 1998–1999, the Republic of Georgia's shadow economy was the largest, at 64% of its GDP; Russia's was 44% of its GDP; and Uzbekistan's was the smallest, at 9%. Among the transition countries of Central and Eastern Europe during the same period, that is, 1999–2000, Bulgaria had the largest shadow economy, at 34% of its GDP, and Slovakia had the smallest, at 11%.

From 1988 to 2000, the shadow economy in developing countries averaged 40% of GDP. In Africa in 1998–1999, Nigeria and Egypt had the largest black market economies, equivalent to 77% and 69% of their GDP, respectively; South Africa, by contrast, had a shadow economy of only 11% of its GDP. In Asia, during the same period, Thailand ranked number one with a shadow economy of 70% of its GDP; Hong Kong and Singapore had the smallest shadow economies, both at 14% of GDP. In Latin America in

1998–1999, the biggest shadow economy was in Bolivia, at 67% of GDP, and the smallest was in Chile, at 19%.

Different policies and factors are at the root of the rate of growth of the black market economy. In OECD countries, increasing taxation, social security contributions, rising state regulatory activities, and the decline of the tax morale are all driving forces behind this growth. In the case of the transition countries, the dissolution of the Soviet economy has left many of these formerly centrally controlled countries with a weak state apparatus, facilitating the blossoming of the informal economy. Finally, in developing countries, the predatory nature of undemocratic regimes and their mismanagement of fiscal revenues represent a strong incentive for the population to join the shadow economy.

The Impact of the Black Market Economy

Shadow economy activities are fast becoming an international problem. The disadvantages and perils of a prosperous shadow economy are apparent everywhere. Of greatest concern is the fact that the activities of the underground economy are unrecorded. Therefore, in countries with considerable informal economies, the statistics on official national income do not accurately represent the true state of a nation's economy. Given that these statistics are employed to generate economic policies, it follows that inaccurate figures often lead to inappropriate policy responses. This phenomenon in turn creates conditions that further stimulate the growth of the black market economy, creating a vicious cycle that is hard to break.

Therefore, the growth of the shadow economy is able to set off a destructive economic cycle. Transactions in the shadow economy escape taxation, thus they keep tax revenues lower than they otherwise would be. The NCPA has estimated that the US federal government loses $195 billion per year due to the failure of people to report income and pay taxes on it. Among individual US states, California has by far the largest underground economy. Because of that, the state government loses between $60 and $140 billion each year in tax revenues. The black market economy, therefore, erodes the tax base and, at the same time, tax compliance. People employed in the formal economy resent the fact that they pay taxes while those in the informal sector do not. Finally, governments may respond to the lower tax revenues by raising tax rates—penalizing those who pay taxes and encouraging a further flight into the shadow

economy that in turn tightens the budget constraints on the public sector.

On the other hand, at least two-thirds of the income earned in the shadow economy is immediately spent in the official economy, resulting in a considerable positive stimulus effect on the official economy. However, it must be added that the informal economy is predominantly cash-based. Thus, a growing shadow economy may provide strong attractions to entice domestic and foreign workers away from the official economy.

A vibrant and flourishing black market economy can also be a symptom of dysfunctional domestic policies. Frequently, the presence of a prosperous underground economy is a consequence of existing economic policies, such as tax or regulatory regimes, that are overly burdensome or oppressive or that just fail to properly address the economic realities. And so the untaxable income generated by the black market economy further reduces potential state revenue. Finally, while some shadow economic activity, such as illicit trade in narcotics, is clearly undesirable, the vast majority of it is for the most part constructive. It may provide basic needs to consumers in developing countries at a lower cost than "legitimate" substitutes; and to the producers or providers it may generate income when there are no viable alternatives.

The underground economy is clearly far more complex than media stereotypes or common knowledge might suggest. Many people are not even aware of their involvement in it. Activities in this sector can run the gamut from laundering money to underreporting tips, and may involve everyone from drug kingpins to rural farmhands. Its moral terrain is complicated and frequently contradictory. For example, although some government officials have argued against employing illegal immigrants—for the protection of the employee—on the grounds that they can easily be exploited, the government itself may refuse citizenship to these same people, forcing them to seek employment "underground" in the first place. In another example, permitting employees to receive tips in cash, which may go unreported or underreported, may benefit workers in the short term; however, it may also be used by employers to justify the paying of lower wages and not providing other benefits to these same employees. Many of the entrepreneurs and individual workers who participate in this economy may not be proud to do so, but in some cases they feel they have few alternatives—or at least few sanctioned alternatives—to build up their businesses or generate income. Taking all these factors into account, it is likely that, despite its dangers, drawbacks, and risks, the underground economy will continue to thrive and remain an important—and probably growing—component of the larger economy.

See also Money Laundering; Terrorism

References and Further Reading

American Public Media (Producer). "Diary of an Upscale Drug Runner." *Underground Economy* [a Marketplace Special Series] (November 12, 2001). (http://market place.publicradio.org/features/underground/)

Ledeneva, Alena V. *Russia's Economy of Favors: Blat, Networking, and Informal Exchange.* Cambridge: Cambridge University Press, 1998.

Napoleoni, Loretta. *Terror Inc.* London: Penguin, 2004.

Naylor, R. T. *Wages of Crime: Black Markets, Illegal Finance, and the Underworld Economy.* Montréal: McGill-Queen's University Press, 2002.

Roemer, Michael, and Christine Jones, eds. *Markets in Developing Countries: Parallel, Fragmented, and Black.* San Francisco: ICS Press, 1991.

Schneider, F., and D. Enste. *Hiding in the Shadows: The Growth of the Underground Economy.* International Monetary Fund, 2002. http://www.imf.org/external/pubs/ft/issues/issues30/ (c20042475)

Schneider, F., and D. Enste. *The Shadow Economy. An International Survey.* Cambridge: Cambridge University Press, 2003.

BLACK SEA ECONOMIC COOPERATION ORGANIZATION (BSEC)

Following the end of the Cold War and the breakup of the Soviet Union, the foreign ministers of eleven countries—Albania, Adzherbaizhan, Armenia, Bulgaria, Georgia, Greece, Moldova, Romania, Russia, Turkey, and Ukraine—met in Istanbul in June 1992 on the invitation of Turkey to deal with mutual economic questions regarding the Black Sea nations. The meeting led to the signing of the "Summit Declaration on Black Sea Economic Cooperation" by the presidents of the states—the Bosphorus declaration. The organization based its formation on previous multinational conferences on European cooperation, such as the Helsinki Final Act (1975), Conference on Security and Cooperation in Europe (CSCE) (1972), and most of all the Paris Charter for the New Europe (1990). The organizers stated that the goals of the organization were compliant with the United Nations Charter and sought to promote democracy, human rights, fundamental freedoms, economic literacy, social justice, and mutual security. They believed that the organization could be a model for future European cooperation. It stressed their belief that they would bring to the Black Sea region peace, prosperity,

stability, and security while promoting neighborly relations among the states. In 2003, Macedonia and the Federation of Serbia and Montenegro were invited to join.

The Black Sea Economic Cooperation Organization (BSEC) was one of several such regional organizations created in the wake of the fall of the Soviet Union dealing with economic, political, cultural, and social issues. Both littoral and nearby countries are members. The countries in the BSEC comprise a population of three hundred and fifty million, and represented one-fifth of the world's trade. In addition, there are a number of other countries with observer status. These include Austria, Egypt, France, Germany, Italy, Israel, Kazakhstan, Poland, Slovakia, and Tunisia. Representatives from the United States, the United Nations, The United Nations Economic Commission for Europe, and the European Commission (EC) have attended meetings as well. The International Black Sea Club, an association of cities on the Black Sea with representation by the mayors, also has observer status. The members also stressed that the new organization would not interfere with the relations the countries had with other nations or international bodies such as the European Union.

The structure of the organization consists of a general secretary and a rotating presidency. The highest forum is the group of the member states' presidents. The regular decision-making body is the council of foreign ministers. The BSEC also has parliamentary (PABSEC) and business groups (BSEC BC). The PABSEC has three committees—the economic, commercial, technological, and environmental affairs; legal and political affairs; and cultural, educational, and social affairs. Other associated bodies are the Black Sea Universities Network (BSUN) and the Union of Road Transport Associations (BSEC-URTA). The organization has committees or working groups dealing with agriculture, crime and terrorism, transport, energy, health and pharmaceuticals, the environment, emergency assistance, tourism, telecommunications, science and technology, statistics and economic information, and trade and economic development. Official languages are English and Russian, but French translations are provided at meetings. The governments are attempting to create a business-friendly environment in the region and promote the training of young specialists in business management and technology. One of the main goals is foreign investment. The organization has arranged visa simplification for entrepreneurs, truck drivers, and others of its member countries and looked into the issue of double taxation of businesspersons. The business sector has established BSBIN, an Internet-based network for promoting interest in the member states' investment opportunities. The motto of the BSEC is, "More concrete projects, more support and encouragement for enterprises, companies, and firms!"

In September 1998, the Black Sea Studies center (ICBSS) opened in Athens under the auspices of the organization with the goal of sharing research and technology by the scholarly communities of the member states. In January 1999, a BSEC Black Sea Trade and Development Bank (BSTDB) opened in Thessaloniki, Greece, to fund the organization. In 2001, they established an earthquake protection agency stationed in Thessaloniki. The bank is the engine of the organization. The BSEC relies on the private sector to meet its goals.

Some of the member countries were reluctant or unable to support the BSEC project fund. Contributions were based on a scale suitable to the wealth of the countries, but only four members, led by Greece, had contributed. The members have stressed the need for more active participation of the member states and the need to develop practical contacts with other international organizations. Turkish Deputy Prime Minister Absullatif Sener believes funds from other institutions such as the World Bank would be possible if the members supported the projects.

The organization has pushed for further development of cooperation between the BSEC and the European Union. They want a relationship similar to that which other regional organizations such as MERCOSUR and ASEAN have with the EU. They have worked with international associations dealing with railroads and ships, such as the Black Sea International Ship Owners Association (BINSA) and the Black Sea Region Association Shipbuilders and Ship Repairers (BRASS). The BSEC cooperates with Black Sea organizations such as the TRACECA, the Transport Corridor Europe–Caucasus–Asia organization and the Black Sea Pan-European Transport Area (Black Sea PETra) group. The Black Sea Naval Cooperation Task Group (Blackseafor) formed in 2001 is a spin-off of BSEC consisting of six littoral states—Turkey Bulgaria, Romania, Russia, Ukraine, and Georgia.

The United Nations General Assembly passed a resolution for the cooperation of the body and all its agencies with BSEC. The BSEC has worked with the UN's Food and Agricultural organization (FAO).

FREDERICK B. CHARY

References and Further Reading

Aybak, Tunç. *Politics of the Black Sea: Dynamics of Cooperation and Conflict.* London: I. B. Tauris, 2001.

Cottey, Andrew. *Subregional Cooperation in the New Europe: Building Security, Prosperity, and Solidarity from the Barents to the Black Sea.* New York: St. Martin's Press, 1999.

Developing Entrepreneurship and a Sustainable SME sector in BSEC countries. New York: United Nations, 2002.

BOLIVIA

Bolivia is a diverse and multiethnic nation in the geographical center of the South American continent. It is one of the poorest developing countries in Latin America, consistently ranking low on the United Nations Human Development Index (a composite of education, GDP per capita, life expectancy, and income distribution). Seventy percent of its territory lies in the Amazon Basin, and more than a third of its 8.5 million people are primarily of European and mixed racial and ethnic origin (mestizos). Indigenous groups, primarily of Aymaran (20%–25%) and Quechuan (35%–40%) ancestry in the highlands and of Guaranian descent in the lowlands, comprise some 62% of the country's population. Especially after constitutional changes in 1994 formalized Bolivia's legal status as a "pluriethnic" nation, grassroots indigenous movements in the highlands and lowlands increased in intensity and political clout. Modern-day governments have been forced to compromise with powerful (and often intransigent) indigenous leaders.

Bolivia has been landlocked since Chile defeated it in the War of the Pacific in 1879, and subsequent Bolivian governments have never given up the goal of the return of some portion of the "lost" coastal territory of the Atacama. Historically, Bolivia's Pacific coast and lowlands have been underpopulated and physically isolated from the main political and commercial centers. These former territories, however, were rich in natural resources: guano, saltpeter, and silver mines along the Pacific coast, and rubber in the Amazonian region bordering Brazil, which was lost in the Acre War at the turn of the twentieth century. More national territory was lost in the Chaco War with Paraguay (1932–1936). Fortunately, Bolivia managed to retain the lands rich in oil and natural gas along its border with Argentina. These resources have helped mitigate some of the country's extreme indebtedness and chronic poverty. Since 2004, a dispute known as the "gas war" has been taking place in Bolivia, where various sides are in disagreement as to whether natural gas should be developed by a multinational consortium and sold to California markets.

The land mass of today's Bolivia traverses three distinct topographical regions: the high Andean plateau or Altiplano; the rich sub-Andean valleys; and the subtropical and tropical forests of the eastern lowlands. The majority of Bolivia's population settled on the Altiplano and nearby valleys. Bolivia's population has primarily been agricultural. However, less than 40% are rural today. Since the 1970s, Bolivians have migrated in greater numbers to lowland departments and cities. Regional forces have not only greatly influenced the country's history and overall socioeconomic development, but some believe they may also threaten Bolivia's future governability. The cultural divisions between the peoples who claim the Andean identity of the *kolla* and those who identify with the lowlander cultural and ethnic heritage of the *camba* have been exacerbated by the dispute over plans to export natural gas. The Camba nation is increasingly restive and intolerant of the ethnic tensions, political instability, and poverty of highland Bolivia.

Bolivia has had more than two hundred palace revolts and minor revolutions since its independence in 1952. As the second Latin American social revolution of the twentieth century, the Bolivian National Revolution of April 1952, like the earlier Mexican Revolution that served as its model, initiated widespread political and socioeconomic change. Among the Bolivian revolution's major reforms were universal suffrage, land distribution, nationalization of the tin mines, and the expansion of public education. Although not Marxist, the revolution was radical; it overthrew a conservative and repressive oligarchy, and its nationalist economic agenda heightened tensions with the United States, especially during its first decade.

At the head of this revolution was Bolivia's first revolutionary president, Víctor Paz Estenssoro, his presidential successor, Hernán Sile Zuazo, and Juan Lechín Oquendo, the fiery Trotskyite head of the leftist mine workers' union; as well as the political party the three had founded a decade earlier, the National Revolutionary Movement (*Movimiento Nacionalista Revolucionario*, or MNR). The MNR represented a wide coalition of classes that included intellectuals, students, miners, workers, and peasants. This multi-class alliance proved to be the recipe for revolutionary success. The party itself reflected this class and ideological diversity with the majority of members espousing a vague program of national dignity and economic development and self-determination, and only its labor left wing favoring a revolutionary and socialist agenda.

By 1964, the conflicting tendencies and agendas within the MNR brought Bolivia's "development-oriented revolution," in the words of James M. Malloy, to an abrupt end. The counterrevolution, ironically headed by the "new" military, reorganized after the revolution into a "modernizing" and productive force for national development, initiated eighteen years of military dictatorship. Ernesto "Che" Guevara attempted, but failed, to provoke his continental revolution against imperialism from Bolivia in 1967.

Several attempts to reestablish constitutional civilian rule were frustrated in the thwarted elections of 1978, 1979, and 1980. That year the so-called "cocaine coup" of General Luis García Meza and his "cocaine mafia" turned Bolivia into a pariah nation internationally. In 1982, the country finally returned to democracy with the election of Hernán Siles Zuazo. The transition to democracy, however, was rocky and did not solve the almost insoluble problems of underdevelopment, poverty, corruption, and instability. Hyperinflation and the global crash of tin prices in 1985 and massive mine closings in 1986 plunged the country into economic recession and further political unrest.

Armies of unemployed miners swarmed into the lowlands to grow coca leaf, the primary input for cocaine production and the drug trade. Subsequent democratic governments confronted a crisis of democratic populism and opposition to the neoliberal or free market economic policies adopted in 1985, and to the militarization of the so-called "drug war" after 1986. Privatization of state enterprises by the technocrats of the first Gonzalo Sánchez de Lozada government (1993–1997) and the forcible "zero coca" eradication policy of President Hugo Banzer Suárez (1997–2001) increased armed resistance by unions and coca leaf growers' federations. Many Bolivians felt that the resulting government repression and violations of human rights threatened further democratization. Nevertheless, by 2001 the Bolivian government claimed the complete eradication of illegal coca leaf in the Chapare region of the country.

Bolivia's eradication success—at best only a temporary reduction of 90% of coca production—bought billions of dollars in foreign aid and debt forgiveness by the United States, the International Monetary Fund, and the World Bank. In its wake, however, loomed a more pronounced crisis of governability. Since 1985 every administration has been forced to govern through an unwieldy "mega-coalition" of political parties and to survive the almost constant political protest. In October 2003, demonstrations and peasant roadblocks nationwide precipitously cut short Gonzalo Sánchez de Lozada's second term in office.

Constitutional and democratic rule was preserved this time when Vice President Carlos Mesa Gisbert assumed the reigns of government. However, Bolivia's people and leaders continue to face the difficult challenges of development and democratization, as well as the new and still-emerging challenge of globalization. Bolivian leaders hope a foreign policy of multilateralism and regional cooperation and integration will help them promote democracy and economic prosperity at home.

WALTRAUD Q. MORALES

See also Andean South America: History and Economic Development; Andean South America: International Relations

References and Further Reading

Grindle, Merilee S., and Pilar Domingo. *Proclaiming Revolution: Bolivia in Comparative Perspective.* Cambridge, MA: Harvard University Press, 2003.

Hylton, Forrest. *We Alone Will Rule: Native Andean Politics in the Age of Insurgency.* Madison, WI: University of Wisconsin, 2003.

Klein, Herbert S. *A Concise History of Bolivia.* Cambridge: Cambridge University Press, 2003.

Lehman, Kenneth D. *Bolivia and the United States: A Limited Partnership.* Athens, GA: University of Georgia Press, 1999.

Léons, Madeline Barbara, and Harry Sanabria, eds. *Coca, Cocaine, and the Bolivian Reality.* Albany, NY: State University of New York, 1997.

Malloy, James M., and Eduardo Gamarra. *Revolution and Reaction: Bolivia, 1964–1985.* New Brunswick, NJ: Transaction Publishers, 1988.

Morales, Waltraud Q. *A Brief History of Bolivia.* New York: Facts on File 2004.

Morales, Waltraud Q. *Bolivia: Land of Struggle.* Boulder, CO: Westview Press, 1992.

BOSCH, JUAN

Juan Bosch is regarded as the greatest prose writer in Dominican literature and one of the most salient figures in Dominican political history. The Dominican masses' plight was his favorite theme, both as a writer and politician.

In 1937, following his condemnation of dictator Rafael Leonidas Trujillo's massacre of fifteen thousand Haitian migrants, Bosch sought refuge in Cuba. While in Cuba, Bosch founded the Partido Revolucionario Dominicano (PRD), a left-of-center group committed to the elimination of the Trujillo regime and bringing democracy to the Dominican Republic.

After Trujillo's assassination, on May 30, 1961, Bosch returned to the Dominican Republic. Committed to bringing social justice and change through reforms rather than class struggle, Bosch became a presidential candidate in 1962. Campaigning on promises for jobs, better, housing conditions, and liberty and justice for all, he built a formidable power base among the poor masses living in the capital's slums and the countryside's landless peasants.

On February 27, 1963, Juan Bosch became the first freely elected president of the Dominican Republic in thirty-eight years. His government's landmark event was the Constitution of 1963. Proclaimed on April 29, the constitution resembled the Cuban Constitution of 1940 with its provision for civil and political rights, land reform, collective bargaining, and free compulsory education.

Bosch's liberal democratic recipe for development consisting of a mixed economy, an agrarian reform through the distribution of idle Trujillo estates to the peasants, establishment of government-sponsored grassroots organizations, and industrialization through the nationalization of Trujillo enterprises, ran into opposition from different segments of Dominican society. His granting of political rights to communists and his support for peasants' cooperatives angered the Dominican elite who accused him of being surrounded by communist agents. His war on corruption and inefficiency gained him the enmity of a firmly entrenched bureaucracy. His much publicized land reform program, as well as his industrialization efforts, were met by his opponents' legal maneuvers, for the constitution also guaranteed the right to private property. Finally, Bosch's strict interpretation of the constitution's separation of church and state earned him the Catholic Church's visceral enmity.

Caught between his detractors who criticized him for moving too fast, and his supporters who chastised him for being too cautious, Bosch, at times, was vague and indecisive. Citing him as another red menace, the military hierarchy toppled Bosch on September 25, 1963.

In 1965, young army officers, demanding his return from exile, ousted the ruling civilian junta. The uprising, however, was short-lived because US President Johnson, fearing another Cuba, sent US forces to the Dominican Republic.

Bosch returned to the Dominican Republic and ran for president in 1966, losing to Joaquín Balaguer. By the 1970s, Bosch's radical views on development that could only be realized through a populist dictatorship could not coexist with the moderates on the PRD. As a result, he left the party and founded the Partido de la Liberación Dominicana (PLD) in 1973. Committed to strengthening the state's role in the nation's life and bringing about radical socioeconomic change, the PLD's Marxist orientation never set well with the Dominican electorate, for Bosch unsuccessfully ran for the presidency in 1978, 1982, 1986, 1990, and 1994. In spite of his losses at the polls, Bosch was a still a most respected figure by friends and foes alike. His followers admired his sincerity and honesty, while his detractors recognized his zeal and charismatic appeal. He died at the age of ninety-two on November 1, 2001.

JOSÉ B. FERNÁNDEZ

See also Caribbean: History and Economic Development; Dominican Republic

References and Further Reading

Black, Jan Knippers. *The Dominican Republic: Politics and Development in an Unsovereign State*. Boston: Allen & Unwin, 1986.

Guerrero, Miguel. *El golpe de estado: Historia del derrocamineto de Juan Bosch*. Santo Domingo, Chile: Editora Corripio, 1993.

Hartlyn, Jonathan. *The Struggle for Democratic Politics in the Dominican Republic*. Chapel Hill, NC: The University of North Carolina Press, 1998.

Moya Pons, Frank. *The Dominican Republic: A National History*. New Rochelle, NY: Hispaniola Books, 1995.

Wiarda, Howard, and Michael Kryzanek. *The Dominican Republic: A Caribbean Crucible*. Boulder, CO: Westview Press, 1982.

BOSNIA AND HERZEGOVINA

Bosnia and Herzegovina, one of the youngest European countries, is a product of the 1990s breakup of the former Yugoslavia. Located in Southeastern Europe (colloquially known as the Balkan Peninsula), this country is almost entirely surrounded by Croatia, Serbia, and Montenegro, leaving only a small window on the Adriatic Sea in the southwestern town of Neum. The Dinaric Alps and hilly countryside contribute to a generally rugged landscape. The country's interior has a predominantly continental climate, with hot summers and cold winters. The southwestern region enjoys a pleasant Mediterranean climate. Alluvial plains of the Sava and Bosna rivers form the country's leading region of agricultural production and are among the few lowlands in a complex topography of high elevations and narrow passages carved by rivers. The capital, Sarajevo (population 602,000; 2004), is centrally located in a medieval core area from which the contemporary nation gradually evolved.

Bosnia and Herzegovina's population of just four million is sharply divided by ethnicity and religion, even though 99% of the population is of South Slavic origin. Of the three leading ethnic groups, Bosniaks (43%) practice Islam, Serbs (31%) are Eastern Orthodox Christians, while Croats (15%) are Roman Catholics. Bosniaks, previously known as Muslims, are generally Croats and Serbs who converted to Islam during the time of Ottoman Empire rule in the region. Throughout recent history such differences contributed to frequent open antagonisms in the multinational country and they remain a major obstacle to cooperation and national cohesion.

Initially, the area was home to a small and short-lived medieval kingdom known as Bosnia, which experienced a zenith in the fourteenth century under King Tvrtko Kotromanić (1338–1391), and its southern province Herzegovina. The region was soon overrun by advancing Ottoman Turks who, in 1463, introduced Islam to the local population. Until 1878, it was an integral part of the Ottoman Empire. During this period, the economy was developing slowly and resources were drained by the Turks, rather than being used to develop local infrastructure. By 1878, as a result of the Berlin Congress, the Habsburg Monarchy achieved control over Bosnia and Herzegovina. At the time, this region was one of the least developed in Europe. The Habsburgs implemented a better economic policy that revitalized the region's economy. This was particularly true in terms of infrastructure development in an attempt to better integrate the region into their empire. New roads and railroads were constructed connecting previously isolated areas. Finally, in 1908 the Habsburg Monarchy annexed Bosnia and Herzegovina, triggering a serious political standoff with neighboring Serbia. Ultimately, the resulting tensions led to the beginning of World War I (1914–1918), after Serb nationalist Gavrilo Princip assassinated the heir to the Habsburg throne, Archduke Franz Ferdinand, in Sarajevo. In the aftermath of World War I, Bosnia and Herzegovina found itself in the kingdom of Serbs, Croats, and Slovenes, which in 1929 became known as Yugoslavia. In 1945, Yugoslavia's kingdom was replaced by a communist regime, led by Josip Broz Tito. Under his leadership, the country was organized into six autonomous republics, including Bosnia and Herzegovina, each of which was provided with the Soviet-modeled rights for eventual potential independence.

Even though after World War II the economic production and gross domestic product increased multifold, the republic still lacked an industrial infrastructure comparable to that of the more economically developed Yugoslav republics, Slovenia and Croatia. Communism did not allow an entirely free market economy, though compensation trade between republics was encouraged. Bosnia and Herzegovina, rich in various mineral resources, was perceived as being a leading provider of raw materials, resulting in a lack of development in the secondary and tertiary sectors of the economy. Such policies severely limited economic diversification. Additionally, the political leadership rejected economic reforms in fear of undermining the communist ideology, leaving many citizens unemployed and well below the average national scale of living. During the 1960s and 1970s, significant numbers of the republic's residents left in pursuit of better-paying jobs in other Yugoslav republics, or in Western European countries, primarily Germany.

Through the 1970s and 1980s, Bosnia and Herzegovina experienced difficulties common to the developing world in that era. High borrowing from international creditors, trade deficits, and insufficient control over corruption all contributed to a further rise in unemployment, external debt, and inflation. Following the death of President Tito and his iron-fist rule, Yugoslavia was governed by a body of representatives from the six republics and two autonomous provinces. It was unable, however, to prevent various separatist tendencies, which led to the country's break-up in 1991. Bosnia and Herzegovina found itself on a path toward independence. Not long after the independence referendum passed, the political situation worsened dramatically. Serbs feared being disenfranchised and cut off from Serbia, while Croats and Muslims pushed for political independence. These differences ultimately resulted in armed conflict that lasted from 1992 to 1995. The signing of a peace accord in Dayton, Ohio, resulted in the formation of the Republic of Srpska and the Croat–Muslim Federation as two internal political units of Bosnia and Herzegovina. Both entities have the benefit of internal autonomies and at the same time provide representatives to a national government to conduct foreign and economic policies.

Atrocities in the 1990s left the country completely ravaged. The result was some 250,000 people dead or missing, more than one million persons displaced, and the economy all but shut down. The country's infrastructure was almost entirely severely damaged or destroyed. After the war, few factories reopened, and many of those that did were obsolete. Most of those that were revitalized underwent privatization. Post-war environmental issues include widespread clear-cutting of forests and millions of landmines scattered throughout the countryside. Although the annual GDP is slowly improving, it will take years if not decades to reduce the existing negative trade balance and lower imports that are running three times higher than exports. Unofficial unemployment rates run close to 40%. The country hopes to gain membership in the European Union during the next decade.

ZORAN PAVLOVIĆ

See also Balkan Wars of the 1990s; Central and Eastern Europe: History and Economic Development; Central and Eastern Europe: International Relations; Ethnic Conflicts: Central and Eastern Europe

References and Further Reading

Country Watch Incorporated. *Bosnia and Herzegovina Country Review*. Houston, TX: 2004.
Ding, Wei et al. *Bosnia and Herzegovina: From Recovery to Sustainable Growth, A World Bank Country Study*. Washington, DC: World Bank, 1997.
Malcolm, Noel. *Bosnia: A Short History*. New York: New York University Press, 1996.
Silber, Laura, and Allan Little. *Yugoslavia: Death of a Nation*. New York: Penguin, 1997.

BOTHA, P. W.

Pieter Willem Botha was born in 1916 at Paul Roux, Free State province, South Africa. An Afrikaner nationalist political activist as a teenager, he moved to the Cape province in 1938 to become a full-time organiser for D. F. Malan's National Party (NP) and spent his entire working life as a party political functionary within the Cape NP. He represented the George constituency in Parliament for thirty-six years (1948–1984). Botha was deputy-minister for the interior from 1958 to 1960. He joined the Cabinet in 1961 when he became the minister for coloured affairs. As minister of defence from 1966 to 1980, Botha was instrumental in building a powerful security infrastructure and military-industrial complex. The latter was instrumental in speeding up South Africa's industrialization/urbanization. Botha, having inherited a small military and security infrastructure, advocated "militarization" so that white South Africans could defend themselves against what he regarded as a "communist onslaught." Military capacity was increased through compulsory military conscription of whites and the recruitment of an enlarged permanent defence force of professional soldiers (which included significant numbers of black South Africans, Namibians, and Angolans). Militarization also involved building a South African armaments industry (to overcome sanctions), an oil-from-coal industry and a nuclear industry. Under Botha, South Africa became an exporter of armaments and (via the Armaments Corporation/Armscor) built assault rifles, aircraft, helicopters, field guns, missiles, missile guidance and communication systems, tanks, and armoured personnel carriers. Botha built a reputation as a highly competent manager while overseeing this militarization process. Militarization created a powerful "securocrat" (security-bureaucrats) support base for Botha as ever-higher percentages of South Africans became involved in the military-industrial complex. This military-industrial complex came to be driven by securocrats (see following paragraph).

Botha became prime minister in 1978, in the wake of the "Information Scandal" (the discovery that taxpayers' money had been used to fund the establishment of a pro-NP newspaper). The scandal unseated the government of John Vorster and precipitated a struggle over who would lead the NP, and in what direction. The NP verkramptes (conservatives) advocated retaining Verwoerd's apartheid model; the verligtes (progressives) advocated rapid change to end apartheid; the centrists, under P. W. Botha, advocated abandoning Verwoerd's model through a process of reform to end apartheid. P. W. Botha became the first NP prime minister without a northern power base since 1954. This precipitated a sea change within the NP as power shifted from the Transvaal to the Cape NP. The latter leaned toward laissez faire economics, while the Transvaal NP traditionally favoured state interventionism, segregation, and race-based job-reservation (to promote the interests of working and lower middle-class Afrikaners). As prime minister (from 1978 to 1983), Botha advocated ending apartheid by "reform" from a position of (white) strength. He called upon whites to "adapt or die." For Botha the conundrum was how to end white rule and facilitate black political participation without imperilling white interests, and how to remain in control of the state while ending white rule. Botha adopted a dual policy—on the one hand, heightened internal security measures; a tough foreign policy; military destabilization of neighbouring governments who were seen to be supporting "terrorism" against South Africa; and "hot pursuit" actions against ANC and SWAPO guerrilla bases in neighbouring states. On the other hand, he advocated internal reform and a new constitution that would give "coloureds" and Indians representation in Parliament. The latter triggered a verkrampte revolt leading to a split in the NP—in 1982, large sections of the Transvaal NP left to form the Conservative Party (which opposed Botha's reforms and advocated a return to Verwoerd's apartheid model).

Botha's reforms involved trying to build a "consociational" democracy of the sort advocated by Lijphart. *Consociationalism* proposed separate government structures for each ethnic group (because, it was argued, conventional liberal democracy could not be made to function in an ethnically divided society). The elected leaders of each of these ethnic governments would then come together to jointly rule South Africa as a confederation. Consociationalism proposed that the leaders—who would serve within a rotating presidency—would be forced to work together collaboratively by the model. But simultaneously, consociationalism allowed each ethnic government to veto any confederal policy it believed threatened its interests.

As a first step to establishing consociational governance, the Tricameral Parliament was launched in 1984, which created three Parliamentary chambers (for whites, coloureds, and Indians), plus a multiracial President's Council. Botha became state-president in 1984. He intended to follow this up by creating a fourth chamber for urban blacks, and then link this four-chamber parliament to the black homelands within a (confederal) Constellation of States. However, the Tricameral reforms were not seen as going far enough, and initiated a period of intense political turmoil (1985–1990) borne of a struggle between Botha's state and the United Democratic Front/UDF. Botha's response was to centralize power in the Office of the State President and the State Security Council (SSC). Executive power grew at the expense of the legislature and judiciary and governance became highly managerialised. The SSC became a parallel Cabinet and virtually "governed" the country through an extensive securocrat managerial system called the National Security Management System (NSMS). Securocrats were military, police, and intelligence officers (functioning within the SSC/NSMS) who supported the notion of reforming "from a position of strength." Growing SSC intrusiveness in governance upset most Cabinet ministers and their (civilian) public service department heads as securocrats usurped state power under Botha's patronage, but fear of Botha (who was called "the big crocodile") kept the securocrats in control. Under Botha, South Africans were told the country faced a "total onslaught" (from "communist terrorists"), which had to be countered by a "total strategy." This legitimised SSC "co-ordination" of politics, society, and economy in the interests of winning the war, and set in motion growing secrecy, self-censorship, state terrorism, and a decline in public accountability. From 1985–1989, Botha's securocrats fought wars in Namibia, Angola, and Mozambique, as well as fighting against anti-apartheid forces (ANC and UDF) inside South Africa. The Namibian war was fought against SWAPO (who wanted Namibian independence). The wars in Mozambique and Angola were fought to destabilize governments providing logistical support for ANC and SWAPO insurgents. Botha saw these Mozambiquean and Angolan wars as necessary to counter "communist terrorism." The war in Angola became especially intense once Cuban, Soviet, and East German forces were deployed to save the Angolan government, and by 1988, the Angolan war had escalated into an intense conventional war with the South Africans fighting a force of more than fifty thousand Angolans/Cubans/Soviets. Under foreign pressure, Botha negotiated peace with Mozambique (in terms of the Komati Accord of 1984); negotiated an end to the war against Angolan/Cuban/Soviet forces in Angola in 1988; and negotiated independence for Namibia (which became effective in 1990). But inside South Africa it was apparent he was unable to push the internal reform agenda far enough or fast enough. Botha suffered a mild stroke in 1989. The anti-securocrat group inside the NP (led by F. W. De Klerk) seized the opportunity to dismantle the SSC (securocrat) network. Botha was forced to resign in 1989 and De Klerk became leader of the NP and state president. After coming to power, the ANC government tried to force Botha to testify to the Truth & Reconciliation Commission and to apologise for apartheid. He refused, saying he had nothing to apologise for. The industrial-military complex created by Botha remains an important feature of South Africa's post-apartheid economic structure.

P. ERIC LOUW

See also Apartheid; Mandela, Nelson; South Africa

References and Further Reading

Botha, P. W. *My Vision for Southern Africa*. Johannesburg: Southern African Editorial Services, 1983.

Bridgland, F. *The War for Africa*. Johannesburg: Ashanti Publishing, 1990.

Frankel, P. H. *Pretoria's Praetorians*. Cambridge: Cambridge University Press, 1984.

Lijphart, A. *Democracy in Plural Societies*. New Haven, CT: Yale University Press, 1977.

Louw, P. E. *The Rise, Fall and Legacy of Apartheid*. Westport, CT: Praeger, 2004.

Prinsloo, Daan. *Stem uit die Wilderness. 'n Biografie oor oud-pres PW Botha*. Mossel Bay, South Africa: Vaandel Publishers, 1997.

Seekings, J. *The UDF*. Athens, OH: Ohio University Press, 2000.

Worden, N. *The Making of Modern South Africa*. Oxford: Blackwell. 2000.

BOTSWANA

The Republic of Botswana is located in southern Africa, bordering on South Africa in the south, Zimbabwe in the east, and Namibia in the west and north. In the northeast, divided by the Zambezi River, Botswana also shares a short stretch of border with Zambia. The country covers an area of 600,372 square kilometers at an elevation of approximately one thousand meters. The southwest is dominated by the Kalahari Desert. In the north the inland delta of the Okavango River comprises one of the last large wildlife resorts in Africa. The climate is semiarid with hot summers and warm winters; however, due to the high elevation, temperatures show considerable annual and day–night variation. In the south temperatures below zero are not uncommon. Throughout the country various types of savanna—scattered trees in the north, grass in the south—are the predominant vegetation. As of 2002 about 70% of the approximately 1.6 million *Batswana*—a term customarily used to refer to citizens of Botswana—lived along the eastern border where natural conditions allow for the best access to water. Towns with fifty thousand or more inhabitants are the capital, Gaborone; Francistown; Molepolole; and Selebi-Phikwe, all located in the eastern part of the country.

Botswana's population is made up of several ethnic groups speaking up to twenty-six different languages of which twelve are spoken by four thousand or fewer speakers. The largest group is the Tswana, speaking a language belonging to the Bantu family, and numbering more than one million speakers. The Tswana, living in what is now Botswana since about 1800 CE, have been the most influential of Botswana's autochthonous groups for more than a century now. Tswana and English are the country's two official languages. The groups living in the area for the longest time are the speakers of various Khoisan languages who are generally and simplistically referred to as *Bushmen*.

Prior to 1885 the area settled by Tswana was not a political entity in a narrow sense. However, the Tswana were politically organized in local kingdoms/chiefdoms. In 1876, Tswana chiefs unsuccessfully requested British protection against the Boers in neighboring Transvaal. Germany's colonization of South-West Africa (Namibia) in 1884, however, initiated a change of mind. Eager now to counter German influence, in 1885 the British established British Bechuanaland, which was incorporated into the Cape Colony and later became part of South Africa in 1910; and the Bechuanaland Protectorate, which became the Republic of Botswana in 1966. In 1948, the National Party came to power in South Africa, putting into action the apartheid regime, which ended any plan to incorporate Bechuanaland Protectorate into South Africa. Instead the demand for independence from British rule increased steadily. With the acceptance of a limited democratic self-government in 1964, the British cleared the way for a constitution effective in 1965, which subsequently led to the first general elections. At the same time the seat of the government was moved from South African Mafikeng to newly established Gaborone. The elections were won by the Botswana Democratic Party (BDP), led by Seretse Khama, who was elected the first president when independence was formally obtained on September 30, 1966. Since that time Botswana has been a parliamentary republic. The president, being chief of the state, head of the government, and commander in chief of the armed forces in a personal union, is elected by the members of the National Assembly. Elections for the National Assembly are usually held every five years. The House of Chiefs, comprising the heads of the Tswana chiefdoms, serves as an advisory body without legislative or executive powers. The national election in 2004 yielded forty-four seats for the BDP, twelve for the Botswana National Party (BNP), and one for the Botswana Congress Party (BCP). Subsequently Festus Mogae was re-elected president. The BDP has continuously been in power at the national level; however, the BNP has its share of power by governing several town and regions. The armed forces were established in 1977 but appeared to be powerless when South Africa attacked alleged guerrilla camps on Botswana's territory in 1985 and 1986.

Having adopted a laissez-faire attitude toward economic development, the British left a highly underdeveloped country. A large number of Batswana earned an income as migrant laborers in South Africa. Money transfers from these workers comprised a considerable contribution to Botswana's economy. However, with independence the government initiated mining operations, which was soon to become the country's most important industry. As of 2002, Botswana's diamond production amounted to 28,397 million carats, accounting for approximately 50% of the GDP, and making the country the world's third-largest producer of diamonds. In addition, copper, nickel, coal, and other mineral resources are extracted. The other major economic factor besides mining is the raising and processing of cattle. Since independence Botswana has had the fastest growing economy in Africa, and compared to the 1971 census, population numbers had almost tripled in 2002. With a per capita GDP corresponding to $8,170 PPP in 2002, Botswana qualifies as a middle-income country. Prior to independence no public facilities for post-primary education or technical training were provided. Therefore, the new government placed early priority upon rapid expansion of secondary and tertiary education. Youth literacy has been constantly on the rise with 89.1% of youths between fifteen and twenty-four years of age being literate in 2002. In the school year 2001–2002 the secondary enrollment ratio was 55%. Among the major infrastructure projects were the construction of the road to Zambia (1973–1976); the completion of the railway between South Africa and Rhodesia, running over Botswana's territory, in 1974; and the International Airport in Gaborone, opened in 1984. Economic growth was supported by a series of years with favorable conditions for agriculture and the discovery of diamonds at Orapa in 1967. However, despite these lucky coincidences, the benefits of these developments would have been much less had it not been for the government's careful planning, economic management, and diplomacy.

In spite of remarkable economic success, social inequality is extreme and unemployment rates are high. The greatest challenge is the exorbitant number of citizens with HIV/AIDS. As of 2003, almost 40% of the population between fifteen and forty-nine years of age are infected. The decrease of life expectancy from 56.1 years in the early 1970s to 39.7 years in 2004–2005 clearly reflects the impact of the disease. The government—in some cases in cooperation with large corporations—takes efforts to control the disease by a combined program of free medical treatment and public education about risks and prevention of infection.

LARS V. KARSTEDT

See also Ethnic Conflicts: Southern Africa; Khama, Sir Seretse; Southern Africa: History and Economic Development; Southern Africa: International Relations

References and Further Reading

Colclough, Christopher, and Stephen McCarthy. *The Political Economy of Botswana. A Study in Growth and Distribution.* Oxford: Oxford University Press, 1980.
Dale, Richard. *Botswana's Search for Autonomy in Southern Africa.* Westport, CT, and London: Greenwood, 1995.
Picard, Louis A., ed. *The Evolution of Modern Botswana.* London, and Lincoln, NE: Rex Collings and University of Nebraska Press, 1985.
Samatar, Abdi Ismael. *An African Miracle. State and Clan Leadership and Colonial Legacy in Botswana Development.* Portsmouth, NH: Heinemann, 1999.
Toit, Pierre du. *State Building and Democracy in Southern Africa. Botswana, Zimbabwe, and South Africa.* Washington, DC: United States Institute of Peace Press, 1995.
UNDP. *"Human Development Report 2004"* (http://hdr.undp.org/reports/global/2004/).

BOUMÉDIÈNNE, HOUARI

The longest-serving Algerian head of state remained largely as an enigmatic personality both for the Algerian people and the outside world. Houari Boumédiènne (1932–1978) preserved a strictly secluded personal life and avoided public appearances. Very little is known about his personal life.

Born as Muhammad Ibrahim Bukharruba in a rustic family, even the year of his birth is contested. Most sources state 1932 and Heliopolis as the date and place of his birth, but others say he was born in Guelma on August 23, 1927, or Clauzel near Guelma on August 23, 1927, or August 16, 1925. He got his education at the Islamic Institute in Constantine, later in Tunis, and the al-Azhar University, Cairo, Egypt. There he joined other North African nationalists, entered the Parti Populaire Algerien, and received military training from the Egyptian army. After secretly reentering Algeria (1955), he joined the forces of the Algerian liberation movement, later known as the Front de Libération Nationale (FLN). There he accepted his pseudonym under which he is largely known and became guerrilla commander. Following the internal strife within the Armée de Libération Nationale, Boumédiènne opposed the FLN leadership of Ben Youssef Ben Khedda and helped replace him with Ahmed Ben Bella. He was the youngest to be given the rank of colonel, the highest rank in the FLN in 1957. From 1960, he was the chief of staff of the army outside Algeria. Boumédiènne supported Ben Bella, the first president of Algeria, and was appointed deputy prime minister, minister of defense, and chief of staff. On June 19, 1965, he led a bloodless coup d'état he called the "Revolutionary Resurgence," aiming to prevent deepening internal divisions and abuses of power. Boumédiènne assumed the positions of head of state and the government and chairman of the Revolutionary Council. The authoritarian Revolutionary Council consisted of twenty-six military commanders and key officials closely associated with Boumédiènne. Until a new constitution was adopted, this predominantly military body had to foster cooperation among various factions in the army and the party. Ben Bella was put under house arrest, where he spent the next fourteen years in complete isolation from the outside world. Most leaders of the opposition were exiled abroad or deeply within the country. Boumédiènne disclosed himself as an ardent nationalist, deeply influenced by Islamic values, and he was noted to be among the few prominent Algerian leaders to speak better Arabic than French. He seized control of the country not to initiate military rule, but to protect the interests of the army, which he felt were threatened by Ben Bella. Because of the lack of a power base outside the military, Boumédiènne's position was initially contested. FLN radicals criticized Boumédiènne for neglecting the policy of "self-management" and betraying "rigorous socialism." Some military officers were unsettled by what they saw as a drift away from collegial leadership. Coup attempts and at least one failed assassination attempt followed in 1967–1968, after which opponents were exiled or imprisoned and Boumédiènne's power consolidated. On January 4, 1967, M. Khidder was murdered in Madrid, and on October 18, 1970, another prominent opponent, Krim Belkacem, was also killed.

Boumédiènne was the unchallenged leader of Algeria until his death. Unlike many dictators, Boumédiènne never permitted his portraits to be spread around, and disliked delivering speeches at massive political meetings. Firmly led by him, the Revolutionary Council exercised collegial responsibility for overseeing the activities of the government. The largely civilian Council of Ministers, or Cabinet, appointed by Boumédiènne, conducted the policies. The Council included an Islamic leader, technical experts, and FLN regulars, as well as others, providing representation of a broad range of Algerian political and institutional life.

Under Boumédiènne, Algeria, rich in oil and gas, entered a period of steady economic growth. Agricultural production failed to meet the country's food needs. The so-called "agricultural revolution" that Boumédiènne launched in 1971 called for the seizure of additional property and the redistribution of the newly acquired public lands to cooperative farms. A national charter was adopted in 1976, starting an extensive land reform, with the provision of extended utilities and services to previously underserved Algerians. With the adoption, after much public debate, of a new constitution in 1976, he was elected president without competition by 95% of the votes for a six-year term.

Fervently anti-imperialist, the government under Boumédiènne upheld the third-world liberation movements and especially the Polisario warfare of the Western Sahara against Morocco. He was able to avoid ideological confrontations and maintained good relations both with the communist bloc and Western countries, as well as regional international prestige among liberated African nations and the Non-Aligned Movement. From August 5, 1973, until August 16, 1976, Boumédiènne chaired the Non-Aligned Movement. In this context he addressed the UN General Assembly in 1974, and avowed "war to the West." Boumédiènne succeeded in mediating between Iran and Iraq, which had fought a bloody border war between 1971 and 1974, and obtained a cease-fire. He even persuaded the Shah and Saddam Hussein to meet in Algiers to sign a memorandum of understanding that would open the way of negotiations for a final settlement of the border dispute.

Toward the end of his rule and life, Boumédiènne initiated reinvigoration of the FLN as a political party. He intended to transfer power to this party in order to establish a viable political system instead of the departed public institutions, but these arrangements were hindered by a severe rare blood disease that caused his death on December 27, 1978. The day he came to power, June 19, is still an official holiday, Readjustment Day, and the airport of Algiers, Technical University, and other sites are named after him. The appointed president after Boumédiènne, his close associate Col. Chadli Benjedid released Ben Bella into voluntary exile, but did not continue his predecessor's policies.

STEPHAN E. NIKOLOV

See also Algeria; Arab Nationalism; Ben Bella, Ahmed; Berbers; Ethnic Conflicts: North Africa; Maghrib

Peoples; Nonaligned Movement; North Africa: History and Economic Development; North Africa: International Relations

References and Further Reading

Ahmedouamar, Mohamed Tahar. *Algeria, State Building: Through the Period of Instability, July 1962–December 1969*. Washington, DC: Compasspoints, 1976.

Entelis, John P. *Algeria: The Revolution Institutionalized*. Boulder, CO: Westview Press, 1986.

Humbaraci, Arslan. *Algeria: A Revolution That Failed. A Political History Since 1954*. New York: Praeger, 1966.

Jackson, Henry. *The F.L.N. in Algeria: Party Development in a Revolutionary Society*. Westport, CT: Greenwood Press, 1977.

Ottaway, David B., and Marina Ottaway. *Algeria: The Politics of a Socialist Revolution*. Berkeley, CA: University of California Press, 1970.

Quandt, William B. *Revolution and Political Leadership: Algeria, 1954–1968*. Cambridge, MA: MIT Press, 1969.

Zartman, I. William. "The Algerian Army in Politics." In *Soldier and State in Africa*, edited by Claude E. Welch, Jr., 224–249. Evanston, IL: Northwestern University Press, 1970.

BOURGUIBA, HABIB

Habib Bourguiba was born on August 3, 1903, in the Tunisian coastal town of Monastir. He had a bilingual education (French and Arabic). From 1924–1927 he studied law and political science in Paris (*licence de droit, diplôme de sciences politiques*). There he had close contacts with members of French socialist parties. Upon his return to Tunis he worked as a lawyer.

Since 1922, he was a member of the Tunisian nationalist party *dustur* (Arabic: Constitution; refers to the liberal constitution promulgated by the Bey of Tunis as early as 1861, twenty years before Tunisia became a French protectorate). Soon he came to oppose the conservative positions of the *dustur* party's leadership. Together with mostly younger intellectuals he founded, in 1934, the Neo-Destour party, which was more socially oriented and openly claimed political rights for Tunisians; they edited a nationalist daily newspaper, *l'action tunisienne*. Subsequently, he was jailed several times and deported by the French colonial authorities. In August 1942 (still in prison), he urged his party to support the Western Allies during World War II while public sympathy in Tunisia was strongly for the German–Italian axis. In 1945 he fled to Cairo where he formed close contacts with British and American diplomats. In 1952, he called for violent resistance against colonialism, including armed attacks against French settlers and police. In

order to calm political unrest and violence, the French colonial authorities eventually granted Tunisia internal autonomy in June 1955; on March 20, 1956, Tunisia became independent. However, French troops continued to be deployed in the country. In April 1956 the Bey, still officially ruling the country, nominated Bourguiba prime minister, who then supported French repression against dissidents of his own party. In July 1957 he deposed the Bey, proclaimed Tunisia a republic, and established an authoritarian one-party system, eventually making himself president of the republic for life.

The most crucial problem for the precariously independent state was the Algerian Liberation War (1954–1962): While French troops were still in the country, the Algerian liberation army used Tunisia as a sanctuary. Striking against them, the French air force bombed the Tunisian town of Sakiet Sidi Yucef in 1958, killing more than one hundred persons, mostly children. Under pressure from the United States and the UN, France stopped military interventions on Tunisian territory and finally withdrew parts of its troops, except for the naval basis of Bizerta. The attempt to "free" this last stronghold of the French army led, in 1961, to a warlike conflict around that city. Fighting stopped because Bourguiba could always count on the support of the UN and the United States in its demand for the respect of the Tunisian sovereignty. After the Camp David accords between Egypt and Israel (1978) and the exclusion of Egypt from the Arab League, Tunis became the residence of this organization. When Israel invaded Lebanon in 1982, the PLO transferred its headquarters to Tunis.

Bourguiba always stood for pro-Western (that is, pro-US) positions, kept a clear distance from the Soviet Union, but never made any compromise over Tunisian sovereignty. On Nov. 7, 1987, he was deposed by his prime minister and former minister of interior Zine el-Abdin Bin Ali (in a "medical coup d'Etat"), who declared Bourguiba senile. Held under house arrest, he died in his palace in Monastir on April 6, 2000.

WERNER RUF

See also North Africa: History and Economic Development; Tunisia

References and Further Reading

Camau, Michel, and Vincent Geisser, eds. *Habib Bourguiba—La trace et l'héritage*. Paris: Karthala, 2004.

Moore, Clement Henry. *Tunisia Since Independence*. Berkeley, CA: University of California Press, 1965.

Ruf, Werner. Tunisia: Contemporary Politics. In *North Africa*, edited by Richard I. Lawless and Allan F. Findlay, 101–119. Beckenham, Kent, United Kingdom: Croom Helm, 1984.

BRACERO PROGRAM

As the United States began World War II efforts in 1942, it experienced a labor shortage that drew many women into wage labor. It also pulled in foreign workers. The need for agricultural harvesters was especially acute. Drawing on an earlier program, Washington developed an agreement with Mexico City to bring laborers temporarily to the United States. In exchange, the Mexican government negotiated worker protections. This arrangement, the Bracero or "Helping Arms" Program, covered more than four million people. Braceros received permits allowing US employment for between four weeks and six months, renewable to eighteen months. They worked mainly in US border states, doing agricultural labor—picking cotton; vegetables; fruit, especially citrus; and thinning sugar beet crops; as well as doing railroad maintenance. It began winding down in 1947, but the Korean War, starting in 1950, renewed US labor needs.

The two countries periodically renegotiated the program. For example, 1942's Bracero agreement made the US government, through the War Food Administration, the contractor of Mexican labor, with farmers and others as "sub"-employers. Dropped in the agreement of 1947, 1951's Public Law 78 reinstated this requirement, which Mexico pressed for so the US government would be responsible for workers' treatment.

The US government, as the contractor, paid some or all of the workers' transportation costs to and from recruitment centers, generally on the border, as well as living expenses during their travel. The contracts guaranteed Braceros a minimum wage and required payment of a subsistence wage if workers were idle (and unpaid) more than 25% of working hours. To participate, employers certified they could not find resident labor for their needs. They were required to pay Mexicans at least the local "prevailing wage" to protect domestic workers. Further, subcontractors promised to provide housing at no charge, adequate meals at low cost, and medical care.

At Mexico's insistence, the agreements included anti-discrimination provisions. That is, they prevented hiring of Braceros into communities that discriminated against Mexicans. Mexico City interpreted this as giving it a right to withdraw workers from localities found to discriminate. While many still suffered unfavorable treatment, this provision did have some enforcement. Thus, no Braceros went to Texas for the first five years of the program.

The Braceros' work was difficult and, at times, brutal. Lee Williams, the US Labor Department official in charge of the program, called it "legalized slavery." Work commonly required using the short handle (generally under two-foot) hoe or *cortito*. Farmers favored it because workers were less likely to inadvertently damage crops. Often, however, users had to stoop or even to crawl along planted rows. If workers complained about conditions, or refused to work for the wages offered, they could be deported. Thus, while in theory Braceros could complain to a Mexican consulate who would notify the US Department of Labor, this rarely happened. Frequently, contracts were English only, violating the Bracero agreements. Thus, some workers signed without knowing to what they had agreed, leaving them vulnerable to exploitation.

The Bracero Program ended in 1964. Edward R. Murrow's documentary, *Harvest of Shame,* contributed to its demise. The film graphically acquainted US citizens with the poor living and working conditions, and even outright abuse, that many Braceros suffered.

The program suffered from two major and related flaws. In addition to the failure of growers and the US government to enforce Braceros' rights fully, the growth of alternative labor flows undercut Braceros' bargaining power. Even working together, the two countries could not prevent non-Bracero workers from entering the United States, offering farmers an alternative, albeit illegal, to more-expensive Braceros. And, the United States and Mexico did not always agree. For example, while cooperating with the Immigration and Naturalization Service's "Operation Wetback," in 1954, the Mexican government refused Washington's request to use police forces to prevent non-Bracero immigration.

The United States, in responding to the problem of non-Braceros, initially excluded from the program any employer caught with unauthorized workers. However, as this almost guaranteed future use of unauthorized workers, the state soon ended this prohibition. Washington also offered an amnesty that regularized workers' status by bringing them into the program. However, this created a disincentive for hiring Braceros to begin with, as employers had to contribute to transportation costs. As well, the US government began flying non-Bracero workers to central Mexico, far from the border, as a means of preventing their return except as Braceros.

Currently, many in the two countries call for expansion of the H2-A visa temporary worker program that allows Mexican agricultural laborers into the United States, or even for a new guest worker program. While Mexican governments have favored this, in the United States, deep divisions remain.

Mexico City opposed ending the Bracero Program and subsequent administrations generally supported new programs to allow temporary immigration for employment. For example, Mexico currently has such an agreement with Canada. However, most would resist any program extending such prerogatives to non-Mexican workers. Including laborers from Central American and Caribbean states would reduce employment of Mexicans. Further, any new program would have to address the legacy of mistreatment of Braceros and put in place real protections. The costs involved might dissuade some US employers.

Some in the United States who oppose such programs dispute any need, claiming an ample supply of native labor. They argue an increase in the supply of workers would lower wages and benefits for current employees. Others see it as an effort to undercut farm workers' attempts to organize, because temporary laborers have different concerns and less interest in unionization than do permanent workers.

Some against temporary-worker programs point to the growth in Mexican immigration attributed to the Bracero Program. By escalating workers' contacts with employers, and exposing them to opportunities in the north, the program aided immigration of non-legal workers. Some calculate that for each Bracero, one unauthorized worker came. Many workers brought family members, and not all returned to Mexico when permits expired. Thus, some argue that any new program would heighten unauthorized immigration.

Those favoring such programs generally make two, often-related arguments. First, many contend the country *does* need Mexican workers to overcome a labor shortfall. They note that a new arrangement could bring workers already in the country into compliance with US laws. Second, this, in turn, would increase security by giving the government better information about who is in the country and why. Increased control over immigration would thus enhance national defense.

This issue, with its historic legacy, likely will remain on the political agendas of both nations.

JANET ADAMSKI

See also Labor; Mexico: History and Economic Development; Mexico: International Relations; Migration

References and Further Reading

Centro de los Trabajadores Agrícolas Fronterizos: www.farmworkers.org/bracerop.html

Craig, Richard B. *The Bracero Program: Interest Groups and Foreign Policy.* Austin, TX: University of Texas Press, 1971.

Davis, Marilyn. *Mexican Voices, American Dreams: An Oral History of Mexican Immigration to the United States.* New York: Henry Holt & Co., 1990.

Galarza, Ernesto. *Merchants of Labor: The Mexican Bracero Story.* Santa Barbara, CA: McNally and Loftin, 1964.

García y Griego, Manuel. "Mexico and US Guest Worker Proposals in 2000." (www.iejournal.com/01spring/01-S2.PDF).

Kiser, George C., and Martha Woody Kiser, eds. *Mexican Workers in the United States: Historical and Political Perspectives.* Albuquerque, NM: University of New Mexico Press, 1979.

Rasmussen, Wayne D. A History of the Emergency Farm Labor Supply Program, 1943–47. *Agricultural Monograph 13.* Washington, DC: US Department of Agriculture, September 1951.

Suárez-Orozco, Marcel, ed. *Crossings: Mexican Immigration in Interdisciplinary Perspectives.* Cambridge, MA: Harvard University Press, 1998.

BRAIN DRAIN

Brain drain is the movement of highly skilled professionals from poor developing countries to work and take up residence in the rich industrialized nations. Historically, the migration of highly skilled labor has always been in existence. Brain drain, however, emerged as significant policy issue in the 1970s due to the migration of a large number of highly skilled research scientists, educators, technologists, and health-related personnel from developed countries to the developed world. The current development challenges faced by third-world countries have drawn further attention to brain drain among economists, scholars, governments, and population experts (Grubel 1994; Pizarro 1993).

The United States followed by Britain are the most popular destinations for professionals from the third world (Taylor 1999). The actual process of estimating the scope of brain drain has been hampered by the absence of uniform statistics on the number and characteristics of international migrants. However, using the 1990 US census data, Carrington and Detragiache (1999) estimate that approximately 1.5 million highly educated professionals settled in the country from Asia and the Pacific. The largest groups came from the Philippines (730,000), then China (400,000), and in the third place were both India and Korea with more than 300,000 immigrants each. Approximately 95,000 of the 128,000 African immigrants were highly educated professionals. Brain drain from Central America and the Caribbean is substantial. For those with college-level education, immigration rates are above 10%. In Guyana more than 70% of individuals with tertiary education have migrated.

Causes of Brain Drain

Broadly conceived, the causes of brain drain can be analyzed along two contrasting models, the person-centered and the nation-centered models (Zahlan 1981). In the person-centered model, the concern is with the number of immigrants, their professional qualifications, and the push and pull factors that stimulate the movement. The "preference differential" (Pizarro 1993), as manifested in stronger and more developed economies that lead to higher wages, better conditions for professional advancement, more social recognition, less restrictive living conditions, and greater political stability, act as a potent pull factor for third-world professionals. The absence of these favorable conditions constitutes the push factor in the developing countries. In this model, emphasis is placed on the migrant and the host country, while the country of origin plays a passive role.

The nation-centered model, on the other hand, considers brain drain as a factor of cultural, scientific, and developmental policies. In this model, efficiency in the utilization of highly skilled people is of utmost importance since, in the long run, it contributes to the development of society. Highly skilled individuals migrate to developed countries where they can be efficiently utilized. Thus, the movement of highly skilled professionals from developing countries to developed ones is a process in efficient allocation of human resources. In this model, the individual is of less importance as the totality of societal development is of prime significance.

Causes of brain drain can also be categorized according to three characteristics, each based on a pair of opposing factors: push–pull, objective–subjective and general–special (Vas-Zoltan 1976). Whereas push factors propel people to leave their home country, pull factors attract people to the countries to settle down. The push–pull factors can be delineated further into objective causes if they are beyond the competence of a country, such as the lack of scientific traditions or subjective causes, if they can be influenced by decisions of the state, as in the lack of realistic manpower policies. Push–pull factors, whether subjective or objective, are regarded as general if they are independent of the will or decision of the individual, for instance, the prestige of foreign training or low or high standard of living. The factors are special if they depend on the will of the individual such as desire for direct contact with scientific colleagues abroad.

Brain Drain and Underdevelopment

At a conceptual level, brain drain represents a political, economic, and social problem (Vas-Zoltan 1976). When the best professionals emigrate and settle in more advanced countries, it is a significant political phenomenon. Brain drain expresses the internal difficulties of the country left behind, as well as the mercilessness of international competition, a struggle waged by unequal forces (Vas-Zoltan 1976). It is also an economic problem in that the more underdeveloped a country, the more it loses from brain drain, whereas only the developed countries profit from it. In social terms, brain drain is a problem since it involves a change of domicile from the underdeveloped countries to the developed ones. The greatest numbers of migrants are from engineering, medicine, science (natural), nursing, and a number of the social sciences.

In what ways has brain drain negatively affected development in third-world countries? The "drain effect," as the impact is often known, manifests itself in various forms. The most immediate impact is economic adjustment costs. Economic efficiency calls for an optimum mix of human capital with physical capital and unskilled labor. Replacement of the skilled labor cannot be sourced from other sectors but must be done through time-consuming education. The national economy, as a result, may experience a sustained period of inefficiency in production. A corollary outcome is the decline in national economic output. Human capital is an essential ingredient in national economic development, and where its loss due to emigration exceeds the original overall capital per worker, the total output per capital in the country declines. Furthermore, economic productivity is a function of the optimum capital–labor ratio. Brain drain leads to a smaller ratio resulting in lower labor productivity and reduced income per capita.

Brain drain also results in the loss of national economic investment. In most third-world countries, higher education is financed through taxes in anticipation of returns to the society in the form of increased productivity, a greater tax base leading to more revenues for further development, and the advancement of the country in science and technology. Brain drain, therefore, represents a loss in national investment since it is the most gifted and dynamic who are sources of leadership in various fields who usually emigrate.

The decline in economic investment in the source country further exacerbates the inequalities prevailing between developing and first developed countries (Grubel 1994). Citizens from developing countries lower their incomes to finance education, the benefits of which now accrue to emigrants who reside in comfort in their new abode in the rich industrial countries. The emigrants also add to the already healthy tax base and development efforts of the people whose incomes are far greater than those who financed their education in their countries of origin. Development projects, medical services, and technological innovations suffer in the source country due to the absence of skilled labor, while the same skilled labor supports the expansion of medical and technical projects in the already affluent nations. The overall impact is the inequitable transfer of resources from poor to rich nations.

Brain drain is responsible for the decline in labor income in the source country. The emigration of persons with above-average human capital decreases the capital–labor ratio in the losing country. As a consequence, labor incomes, especially for unskilled labor, fall relative to income from the capital (Grubel 1994). Compounding this problem is the unequal access to higher rewards occasioned by emigration. Brain drain does not permit those in lower income brackets to obtain the unequal and higher rewards opened by emigration. These are received by those with higher education—predominantly those from higher socio-economic groups (Bhagwati 1976).

Through the emulation effect (Bhagwati 1976), brain drain leads to an increase in professional salary levels in developing countries. Reduction in massive wage differentials between various groups has been one of the key objectives in social and economic planning in these countries. The perpetuation of these salary differentials flies in the face of development efforts geared to maintaining desired salary structures.

Inequalities are prevalent where remittances sent by emigrants begin to play a critical role in the economic life of those left behind. While in some cases remittances may narrow income inequalities, in other instances they tend to accentuate them. Households receiving remittances have suddenly found themselves in a higher socioeconomic level than their counterparts in a region that hitherto had been comparatively homogenous in income. This kind of inequality, according to Taylor (1999), has lead to some households feeling "relatively deprived" within their reference group, which in turn creates new incentives for migration. Through this process, brain drain becomes a self-perpetuating process in migrant-sending areas.

Family welfare is a frequent casualty of brain drain. Education of children in most third-world countries is a social investment that yields returns when the educated take care of their parents in old age. Where the state finances education, the taxes derived from employed graduates contribute toward pensions, medical care, and similar programs for the elderly. Thus, emigration entails reneging on a moral obligation toward the older population, especially where emigrants do not transfer money from abroad for care and maintenance of their parents. Emigration

of the highly skilled population lowers the welfare of those left behind who have to confront a high tax burden to care for the elderly.

National Development and Brain Drain

Countries with large highly educated labor reap the most immediate benefits of brain drain. Nations such as India have large populations of highly educated scientists, engineers, and doctors, some of whom are unemployed. For such countries, emigration of highly skilled professions has small or zero negative impact but rather generates employment or full employment for individuals who would otherwise have remained jobless or underutilized. In this way brain drain contributes to the nagging problem of unemployment of highly educated professionals.

One of the most beneficial aspects of brain drain relates to the role of remittances—earnings sent back by emigrants. Mexico ($3.7 billion) and Philippines ($440 million) are the leading third-world countries in remittance receipt; other significant countries include Egypt, Brazil, and Pakistan (Taylor 1999). Besides contributing to foreign exchange reserves, remittances have a multiplier effect on incomes, employment, and production in migrant-sending areas. Remittances directly contribute to income in such areas and, as long as the remittances exceed the value of production lost due to brain drain, they do reverse lost-labor-and-capital effects of migration (Djajic 1986).

Remittances have played a critical role in providing finance for public projects such as parks, churches, schools, electrification, road construction, and sewers. In the Philippines, Dominican Republic, and Mexico, they have contributed toward the equalization of incomes among various socioeconomic groups. Since they favor poor and middle-income rural and urban families, remittances raise the income of small farmers, and rural-worker, as well as urban-worker households (Aschi 1994). In Mexico, they have been at the core of capitalization of migrant-owned businesses, underscoring the impact of brain drain on enterprise growth where remittances are an important consequence of emigration (Massey et al. 1987).

Brain drain provides impetus for skill formation in poor economies with insufficient growth potential. In these economies, returns from human capital tend to be low and thus are limited incentives to acquire higher education—a stimulant to economic growth. The emigration of the highly educated to a higher-wage country raises the returns to education, which leads to an increase in human capital formation (Beine et al. 2001; Mountford 1997). Granted that only a proportion of the educated population migrates, in the long term the average level of the educated population segment in society would increase.

Highly educated people in a poor country have been known, occasionally, to be a political liability. In a number of African countries academics, especially the academic proletariat of underemployed intellectuals, has provided leadership for unrest and revolutions. Such political activities have often proved to be detrimental to the development of the countries. Allowing the emigration of such highly skilled potential revolutionaries has had positive externalities for the home country.

In conclusion, it is germane to note that brain drain continues to impact developing countries in multifarious ways. The nature of its impact, nevertheless, depends on the local socioeconomic conditions, the level of educational and scientific development, as well as the prevailing political climate.

ISHMAEL IRUNGU MUNENE

References and Further Reading

Aschi, Beth. *Emigration and Its Effects on the Sending Country*. Santa Monica, CA: The Rand Corporation, 1994.

Beine, Michele et al. "Brain Drain and Economic Growth: Theory and Evidence." *Journal of Developing Economics* 64 (2001).

Bhagwati, Jagdish. "The Brain Drain." *International Social Science Journal* XXVIII(4) (1976).

Carrington, William, and Enrica Detragiache. "How Extensive is Brain Drain?" *Finance and Development* (June 1999).

Djajic, Slobodan. "International Migration, Remittances and Welfare in a Dependent Economy." *Journal of Development Economics* 21 (1986).

Grubel, Scott. "Brain Drain, Economics of." In *The International Encyclopedia of Education*, edited by Torsten Husen and Neville Postlethwaite. New York: Elsevier Science, 1994.

Massey, Douglas et al. *Return to Aztlan: The Social Process of International Migration from Western Mexico*. Berkeley, CA, and Los Angeles: University of California Press, 1987.

Mountford, Andrew. "Can a Brain Drain Be Good for Growth in the Source Country?" *Journal of Development Economics* 53 (1997).

Pizarro, Jorge. "Intraregional Migration of Skilled Manpower." *CEPAL Review* 50, (1993).

Taylor, Edward. "The New Economics of Labor Migration and the Role of Remittances in The Migration Process." In *Migration and Development*, edited by Reginald Appleyard. New York: United Nations and IOM, 1999.

Vas-Zoltan, Peter. *The Brain Drain: An Anomaly of International Relations*. Budapest: Akademiai Kiado, 1976.

Zahlan, A.B. *The Arab Brain Drain*. London: Ithaca Press, 1981.

BRAZIL

Brazil is the largest country in Latin America. It covers almost half of the South American continent, dominating the Atlantic coast with an area of approximately 3.3 million square miles. Brazil's 2002 population exceeded 175 million. Estimates of the ethnic and racial composition of the population vary. Just over half are of European origin, especially Portuguese, Italians, and Germans. More than 40% are of African or mixed African-European descent. There are also significant communities of Japanese origin, and endangered indigenous Amerindian communities. The official language is Portuguese. The national capital is Brasilia. In 2003, Brazil's GDP was $1.38 trillion; its GDP per capita was $7,600.

Government

Brazil's current constitution was adopted in 1988. The Federal Republic of Brazil consists of twenty-six states and the Federal District. The president is head of government and head of state. The president is elected to a four-year term by direct election. In 1997, the constitution was amended to allow a president to serve two consecutive terms. The Brazilian Congress includes the Chamber of Deputies and the Senate. The Chamber has 513 deputies, who are elected by proportional representation from each state. The least populous states are guaranteed eight seats in the Chamber, while no state may have more than seventy deputies. Three senators are elected from each state (and the Federal District) to the Senate, for a total of eighty-one seats.

In 2002, eighteen parties were represented in the Chamber and eight in the Senate. No party had a majority. The largest party in the Chamber or Senate need not be the president's party. Though enjoying strong independent powers, the president must create coalitions in order to pass the executive's legislation. States are powerful in the federal system. In addition, influential state political machines often control their states' deputies and senators at the federal level.

From Colony to Independence

The Portuguese explorer Pedro Cabral landed in easternmost South America in 1500. The territory was originally called Santa Cruz, then Vera Cruz. Most traders knew the territory because of its most sought-after export, brazilwood (used to make red dyes), which gave the country its eventual name: Brazil.

Colonists attempted to enslave the indigenous population, but this proved futile, as the land was much too sparsely populated. Many Amerindians who were enslaved died, or else escaped into the hinterlands where European settlers were loath to chase them. As an alternative source of labor, millions of African slaves were imported between the sixteenth and the nineteenth century. There were periodic slave revolts, during which slaves escaped to the hinterland and often established settlements, called *quilombos*.

The Nineteenth Century

Unlike the Spanish and British colonies of mainland North and South America, Brazil did not achieve independence through warfare. The exile of João VI of Portugal to Brazil during the Napoleonic Wars raised the status of Brazil within the Empire, but ultimately led to its break with Portugal in 1822. João's son Pedro became Emperor of Brazil upon independence, leaving Brazil as the only newly independent state in the Americas that was not a republic.

Pedro proved an incompetent and unpopular leader, and abdicated in 1831, leaving Brazil in the hands of a regency until his son, Pedro II, could be crowned emperor. Pedro II revealed himself to be a more astute ruler than his father. Key events during his reign included the War of the Triple Alliance (1865–1870), pitting Brazil, Argentina, and Uruguay against Paraguay. Brazil moved toward the full abolition of slavery, crystallizing divisions among the elites. Those groups ordinarily supportive of the monarchy were increasingly alienated by Pedro II's actions. The Church hierarchy resented Dom Pedro's liberal views toward religion. On the other hand, republican, abolitionist, and positivist values became deeply rooted among the commercial and professional groups, including the military. Slavery was abolished altogether by 1888, making Brazil the last state in the Americas to end this institution. This act also brought tensions between elites to a head; in November 1889, the military forced Pedro II's abdication, and a republic was established. A sign of the depth of positivist influence on Brazil is the republic's flag, which carries the positivist slogan, *Ordem e Progresso* ("Order and Progress").

A pattern of machine politics soon developed in the republic, with the northeast and east, and other remote areas, developing a system known as *coronelismo* (similar to the *caudillismo* of Spanish America). The political machines of the five leading states, São Paulo, Rio de Janeiro, Minas Gerais, Bahia, and Rio Grande de Sul, dominated national politics well into the twentieth century.

The Twentieth Century

In the early twentieth century, various radical movements began to spread among workers, especially European immigrants in the major cities of the southeast. Younger army officers were angry about the slow pace of modernization, and about the indifference and corruption of leading politicians. A number of revolts broke out among lower officers and cadets (referred to popularly as *tenentes*, or lieutenants). In 1924, *tenentes* in São Paulo and Rio de Janeiro revolted. The rebellion was put down, but a number of *tenentes* refused to surrender and began a three-year trek through the backlands of Brazil, hounded by army and militias. This group, led by Luis Carlos Prestes (hence the popular name, "The Prestes Column"), experienced firsthand the severe poverty and backwardness of Brazil. They eventually reached Bolivia. They had earned a reputation as Brazilian Robin Hoods, which enabled them to negotiate their way back to Brazil. Some even resumed their army careers. Prestes become the leader of Brazil's Communist Party. Other *tenentes* were more impressed by radical revolutionaries of the right, such as Mussolini.

In 1930, an understanding between state political machines colluding to elect the president broke down. The resulting confusion created a political opening for an anti-machine political grouping called the Liberal Alliance, which ran a politician from the south, Getulio Vargas, as their presidential candidate. Though representing anti-machine voters, Vargas still operated according to the rules of machine politics. He secretly negotiated a congenial post-election settlement with the São Paulo machine. When the São Paulo leadership reneged on this, Vargas cried foul, and public indignation, as well as army impatience, led to a military intervention placing Vargas in the presidency. Vargas called for a constitutional assembly to draw up a new constitution in 1934. Vargas could "legally" be a candidate for the presidency again, and was elected by the Congress. By 1937, Vargas was ensconced in power, enabling him to suspend the 1934 Constitution and establish an authoritarian dictatorship called the *Estado Novo* (New State). The *Estado Novo*, though not fascist, had a highly corporatist structure, but had no official party or coherent ideology. The new regime outlawed the Communist Party. The Brazilian fascists, called *Integralistas*, hoped that Vargas would prove to be one of them. But within a year, Vargas outlawed the *Integralistas* as well.

Brazil was officially neutral at the outbreak of World War II. Though military officers favored the Axis, Vargas felt that Brazil's interests lay with the United States. Striking a deal that gained for Brazil advanced US technology and weaponry, Vargas committed Brazilian troops to fight alongside the Allies in Italy. This had the effect of turning influential military leaders toward a pro-Allied stance, but also toward an anti-dictatorship stance. By the end of the war, the Brazilian officers pressured Vargas to relinquish power. This he did, in 1945, with a fair amount of grace, and cunning. He established two political parties before returning to civilian life, which would back him in his successful campaign for president in 1950. His final term as an elected president was tumultuous, and in a final stand-off with the army in 1954, he committed suicide rather than be removed from power by force.

The next decade saw impressive advances for the economy, including the establishment of Brazil's automobile industry. Brazil's capital moved from Rio de Janeiro to the futuristic-looking new city of Brasilia. But rapid economic expansion also created bottlenecks, and by the 1960s, populist politicians, including Presidents Quadros and Goulart, ran afoul of conservative forces and the military. Tensions ran especially high during Goulart's term, which ended with a military takeover in 1964.

The Military Regime

The Brazilian military regime was the first of the so-called "bureaucratic authoritarian" regimes in South America. Argentina, Chile, and Uruguay would follow. The regime brought technocrats into the government and established a network of government and public–private industries in what were considered areas vital to the country's security. At first, Brazil met with impressive successes, and the period from 1967 to 1974 was called the "economic miracle." But with the worldwide oil crisis starting in 1974, Brazil's industrial growth slowed, and Brazil fell deeply into debt. By the 1980s, Brazil was the leading debtor nation in the world with an external debt of $95 billion.

With the economy in serious decline, the regime's legitimacy eroded. Though not nearly as bloody as its sister regimes in Chile and Argentina, the Brazilian regime was nevertheless very repressive, withholding basic civil rights and sponsoring "death-squads" that attacked regime opponents considered "subversive."

By the 1970s, groups that had either supported the regime or had been quiescent began to agitate for a return to democracy. By the early 1980s, fissures were opening up within military ranks as well, and military unity was threatened.

The New Republic

By 1985, the military returned the government to civilian hands. The election of the first civilian president in twenty-one years took place with Congress acting as an electoral college, despite massive protests for direct elections. A longstanding opponent of the military regime, Tancredo Neves, was elected president. A last-minute switch by the politician José Sarney from the pro-military party to the anti-military coalition allowed Sarney to be chosen as vice president. Neves, already ill when elected, died before the inauguration. Sarney became the first civilian president. Thereafter, presidents have been chosen through popular vote.

Fernando Collor de Mello, who became president in 1989, was the first popularly elected president since 1964. Though elected on an anti-corruption platform, Collor was himself accused of corruption, leading to his impeachment in 1992. Despite many fears, the impeachment crisis did not undermine the new democracy. Following the Constitution, Vice President Itamar Franco assumed the office.

Serious economic instability, accompanied by extremely high inflation, dogged successive governments. President Franco's finance minister, F. H. Cardoso, introduced a new currency (the fifth since 1986) and tighter monetary controls. This finally brought inflation under control. It also propelled Cardoso into the limelight, enabling him to capture the presidency in the 1994 elections. Once in office Cardoso was able to amend the Constitution to allow him to run for a second term. He served as president until 2002.

In 1991, Brazil, Argentina, Paraguay, and Uruguay signed the Treaty of Asunción, creating the Common Market of the South, or MERCOSUL (*MERSOCUR* in Spanish). This act reflected the trend toward liberalized economic policies in the Southern Cone. It was also part of a worldwide movement to facilitate regional integration and free trade. In this post-Cold War period the influence of international financial and trade organizations such as the International Monetary Fund and the World Trade Organization (WTO) was increasing. The United States was organizing the North American Free Trade Agreement, and in 1994 called for a hemispheric summit in Miami to lay the groundwork for a Free Trade Area of the Americas (FTAA). The Cardoso administration was committed to economic liberalization and free trade, but there were growing doubts as to whether Brazil or any other Latin American country would be able to deal with the United States on an equal footing when it came to negotiating terms in the FTAA. MERCO-SUL began to assume greater political importance as a means of increasing political leverage, as well as reducing Brazil's vulnerability to international economic crises.

In 2002, Lula da Silva of the Workers Party won the presidential election. At first international investors and financial institutions were nervous about the victory of an openly socialist candidate, helped to power by growing public dissatisfaction with liberalization's failures to help large segments of Brazil's electorate. Lula's domestic budgetary discipline surprised observers and reassured investors. However, on the international scene Brazil took an aggressive high-profile stand in negotiations in the WTO and the FTAA. In the former case Brazil formed a bloc with India and South Africa to force Europe and the United States to renegotiate agricultural trade policies. In the latter, Brazil aligned with Argentina to resist what they saw as Washington's vision for the FTAA as an extension of NAFTA.

The economy was still subject to periodic crises under Presidents Cardoso and Lula da Silva. Other issues of continuing importance include the persistence of extreme poverty in the north and northeast of the country. *Favelas,* or shantytowns, surrounding many of Brazil's major cities continue to grow as thousands of poor migrate from the countryside. Periodic tensions between police and drug gangs based in the *favelas* continue to flare up. The 1990s also saw the emergence of groups such as the *Sem Terras,* or Landless Workers Movement (MST), which aggressively presses for land reforms promised in the 1988 Constitution. There are also concerns over human rights violations, especially against street children in major cities, against the indigenous peoples in the Amazon region, and against peasants and labor organizers, especially in remote areas. There is also the problem of profound environmental degradation in the Amazon region and the coastal forests in the north due to extensive prospecting, logging, and increased industrial farming for growing export markets.

DAVID SCHWAM-BAIRD

References and Further Reading

Bethell, Leslie, ed. *Colonial Brazil.* New York: Cambridge University Press, 1987.

Bradford, Burns E. *A History of Brazil,* 3d ed. New York: Columbia University Press, 1993.

Da Costa, Emilia Viotti. *Da monarquia à república: momentos decisivos,* São Paulo: Editorial Grijalbo, 1977, as *The Brazilian Empire: Myths & Histories,* Chapel Hill, NC: University of North Carolina Press, 2000.

Dimenstein, Gilberto. *Democracia em Pedaços: Direitos Humanos no Brasil,* São Paulo: Companhia das Letras, 1996.

Dulles, John W. *Vargas of Brazil: A Political Biography.* Austin, TX: University of Texas Press, 1967.

Freyre, Gilberto. *Sobrados E Mucambos*: decadencia do patriarchado rural no Brasil, São Paulo: Companhia Editora Nacional, 1936, as *The Mansions and the Shanties: The Making of Modern Brazil,* translated by Harriet De Onís. Berkeley, CA: University of California Press, 1986.

Holanda, Sérgio Buarque de. *Raízes do Brasil,* 8th ed. Rio de Janeiro: J. Olympio, 1975.

Hunter, Wendy. *Eroding Military Influence in Brazil: Politicians Against Soldiers.* Chapel Hill, NC: University of North Carolina Press, 1997.

Mainwaring, Scott P. *Rethinking Party Systems in the Third Wave of Democratization: The Case of Brazil.* Stanford, CA: Stanford University Press, 1999.

Sader, Emir, and Ken Silverstein. *Without Fear of Being Happy: Lula, the Workers Party and Brazil.* New York: Verso, 1991.

Skidmore, Thomas. *Politics in Brazil, 1930–1964: An Experiment in Democracy.* New York: Oxford University Press, 1986.

Skidmore, Thomas. *The Politics of Military Rule in Brazil, 1964–1985.* New York: Oxford University Press, 1988.

BRUNEI

Brunei (also known by its official name Negara Brunei Darussalam) is located on the Island of Borneo in Southeast Asia; encircled by the territory of Malaysia in the east, south, and west; and bounded on the north by the South China Sea. The country has a land area of 5,765 square kilometers (2,226 square miles), its territory slightly smaller than the state of Delaware—the second smallest state in the United States.

The population of Brunei was 365,251 in 2004 (CIA est.). The country's capital city, Bandar Seri Begawan, is home to about seventy thousand people (2004 est.) or 20% of the population. Brunei has a population growth rate of 1.9%, and it is estimated that its population could double by 2050. Malay is the official language; English and Chinese are also spoken. Islam is the official religion and also the largest, with 67% of the population; 13% are Buddhist; 10% are Christian; and another 10% practice indigenous or other religions.

The Bruneians, who have close cultural and linguistic links to Malays of Sabah and Sarawak, have been known as sailors, fishermen, farmers, and soldiers. In the fifteenth and sixteenth centuries the

Brunei Sultanate controlled most of northern Borneo and the southern Philippines. During the modern era, relations between Bruneians and their neighbors have often been driven by the British colonial policies. The British authorities undermined the power of the sultanate and gradually it lost most of its territorial possessions to its competitors. In the mid-nineteenth century the territory of what is now the Malaysian state of Sarawak was lost to "White Raja" James Brooke, the former officer of the British East India Company. Brunei became a British protectorate in 1888.

The major economic and social changes were brought to Brunei with the discovery of huge oil reserves in 1929. The economic development in Brunei during the twentieth century relied on state planning and control. Since the 1930s, the country has received large revenues from the oil and later gas explorations and became one of the richest countries in the world. For many decades nearly 50% of the Brunei's GDP and nearly seventy percent of its revenue derived mainly from its oil and gas sectors. The government invested heavily in development of its transportation and communication infrastructure, industries, agriculture, tourism, and other services. Yet, agricultural and manufacturing sectors remained underdeveloped and the tourism sector attracted many fewer tourists than neighboring Malaysia or Singapore. In the post-World War II era the government also introduced a free education and comprehensive welfare system at all levels to all its citizens, and eradicated mass illiteracy by the 1960s.

The United States, United Kingdom, and East Asian countries remained Brunei's main trading partners, and the chief markets for its products. According to official statistics, the Brunei's international trade grew rapidly throughout the post-World War II era. The crude oil, liquefied gas, and garments remained the chief export products, while foodstuff, machinery, and manufactured goods remained the chief import products.

In 1959, the monarch of Brunei introduced the Constitution that gave the country internal self-ruling under the British Protectorate. Yet, the government was slow to introduce political changes. Only in 1984 did Brunei declare its full independence from Britain. The elections to the Legislative Council were held in 1962, but were canceled soon after. The Parti Rakyat Brunei (Brunei's People Party) that won the elections attempted to seize the political power by force, but was defeated. This party, along with some other political groups, was banned from entering the political arena ever since the uprising. For five decades the absolute power has remained in the hands of a monarch (Sultan Hassanal Bolkiah since 1967), who has

held concurrently the positions of prime minister, minister of defense, minister of finance, and chief of police. He appointed a legislative council in 1970 and regularly consults with five counseling bodies: the Council of Ministers, Privy Council, Council of Religious Authorities, Legislative Council, and the Council of Succession.

Ever since declaring independence from the United Kingdom in 1984, the Sultan of Brunei emphasized the importance of Islamic values and political and economic stability even at the cost of liberalization of the political and economic systems. However, since the 1990s, he showed interest in political and economic changes. In 2003, the consultative councils were introduced at the kampung (village) and mukim (district) levels and in 2004 the Sultan promised to introduce the Legislative Council at the national level sometime in future.

In the economic area, Brunei experienced some difficulties in the aftermath of the Asian and Russian financial crises of 1997–1998, as there was steep decline in demand and in world prices for commodities. There was also a growth in unemployment in the country. The national currency—Ringgit, the Brunei dollar—also experienced a turbulent time, fluctuating quite considerably due to the instability in the regional financial and currency markets. The government acknowledged existing problems and promised to diversify its economy, to privatize some enterprises, and to invest in the creation of knowledge-intensive sectors of the economy.

There is also the issue of social instability. For many years the dominant Bruneian majority preferred employment in the public sector or well-paid managerial positions in the private and state-owned enterprises. All labor-intensive and lower-paid jobs in agriculture, construction, manufacturing, and service sectors were often considered to be non-prestigious, and they were left to the ethnic minorities or expatriates from the Philippines and the Indian subcontinent. However, during the last decade there were very few new jobs in the public sector and consequently there was a rise in unemployment rate and growing social discontent among the people. The government must create many more jobs, as about 29% of its population (CIA est. 2004) are young people under fifteen years old who would enter the job market within the next five to six years.

Brunei's exports are narrowly based on sales of oil and gas in international markets, accounting for almost 90% of total export earnings (CIA est. 2004). The country depends heavily on imports of machinery, industrial consumer goods, and food products.

Despite some economic difficulties, however, the country's economy experienced a strong recovery due to the sharp rise in world prices for oil and gas in 2003–2005. Brunei managed to reverse some decline in living standards among the population and remained one of the richest countries in Southeast Asia in terms of per capita income. In 2004, the UNDP's Human Development Index (HDI) put Brunei in 33rd place out of 177, well ahead of such countries as Argentina, Bahrain, or Kuwait.

RAFIS ABAZOV

See also Ethnic Conflicts: Southeast Asia; Southeast Asia: History and Economic Development; Southeast Asia: International Relations

References and Further Reading

International Monetary Fund. *Brunei Darussalam: Recent Economic Development*. Washington, DC: author, 1999.

Saunders, Graham. *History of Brunei*, 2d ed. London: Routledge/Curzon, 2002.

Singh, Ranjit. *Brunei, 1839–1983: The Problems of Political Survival*. Singapore: Oxford University Press, 1984.

Singh, Ranjit, and Jatswan S. Sidhu. *Historical Dictionary of Brunei*. Lanham, MD, and London: Rowman and Littlefield, 1997.

BUDDHISM

Buddhism is a way of living harmlessly and mindfully on the earth. The practice of Buddhism is an ancient method of mental purification. This practice consists in mindfulness of breathing and other techniques of meditation based on yoga. Application of Buddhist meditation techniques ideally results in skillful actions that are conducive to enlightenment and beneficial to all beings. "Buddha" means "one who is awake." A prime example of one who is awake or enlightened is the particular Buddha called "Siddhartha" who lived in the Magadha region of north India in the fifth century BCE.

Some of the Buddha's main teachings are the causal interconnectedness of everything; harmlessness to all beings; eradication of caste as a criterion for worthiness; balancing likes and dislikes to see things as they really are; eliminating all obsessions; and cleaning the mind of possessive, acquisitive, dualistic, and egoistic thinking.

Buddhism began in India and spread throughout South and Southeast Asia, as well as throughout Central and East Asia. As empirical data from Prebish and Baumann shows (2002), Buddhism is practiced worldwide. Census taking may not measure the full extent of Buddhist practice, since one can be a Buddhist simply by "taking refuge" (in the Buddha, Dharma, and Sangha), and there are even those who practice Buddhism without calling themselves Buddhist.

In the developing world of South and Southeast Asia, B. R. Ambedkar in India, A. T. Ariyaratne in Sri Lanka, Chatsumarn Kabilsingh in Thailand, and Hari Bansh Jha in Nepal are among those with influential, socially engaged interpretations of Buddhism.

Buddhists in the developing world have often construed "suffering" or "unsatisfactoriness" (*dukkha* in Pali) in such a way that suffering can be eliminated in some significant part by improving the material conditions of life. Hari Bansh Jha suggests interpreting the elimination of suffering in a utopian sense, such that one can bring about the elimination of suffering by social and economic change. In Buddhism, one difference from Marxist theory is that material change should be based on a purification of the mind free of egoism, and not simply on development of class-consciousness; equal distribution of goods; and proletarian control of the means of production, consumption, and distribution.

What the dedicated aspirant on the Buddhist path seeks is enlightenment—to become "awake" to patterns of self-deception, self-centeredness, and greed. The practice is seen as being awake and working for social liberation in this very life. Being awake in this sense would have outcomes toward inclusive thinking, especially in the economic sphere. Economically successful Buddhists do not think that their wealth is at all proof of personal goodness. Ariyaratne, for example, quotes with evident approval the economics of Schumaker as it appears in *Small Is Beautiful*. As explained by A. T. Ariyaratne and others, *sarvodaya* means the welfare of all. At the level of state policy, a government according to *sarvodaya* would be one that implements social and economic policies with zero tolerance for poverty.

Among some Buddhists in the developing world, such as followers of B. R. Ambedkar, there is little or no interest in traditional ideas of karma and rebirth as these appear in Pali Buddhist texts. In India, B. R. Ambedkar (1891–1956) wrote on Buddhism, established Siddharth College, and reinterpreted Buddhism to help the oppressed classes. He took self-ordination as a Buddhist monk in 1956. In movements like this one, the Buddhist doctrine of suffering and its elimination is interpreted as relating to social change, inclusion for *dalits* ("untouchables"). To paraphrase Ariyaratne, the fundamental difference between modern economics and Buddhist economics is that modern economics emphasizes maximizing consumption by increasing production to satisfy continually created needs, whereas Buddhist economics tries to maximize human satisfaction by choosing the best pattern of consumption in relation to basic human needs. Use of local resources is emphasized, in contrast to participating in a global pattern of proliferation of desires in consumer behavior. A post-colonial, neo-Gandhian influence is present here that could not have been present at the time when traditional textual Buddhism emerged.

One form that Buddhism takes in the developing world is proactive in wishing to abolish poverty and work against forces that would have it otherwise. It is helpful to compare Western Buddhism, wherein one can distinguish (a) Western "socially engaged Buddhism" from (b) Western Buddhism that emphasizes the practice of meditation without social action. Comparing these, Buddhism in the developing world is more like (a) in the hearing the call to action, yet is also like (b) in moving away from traditional, literal views of rebirth realms.

An emphasis on self-reliance is a characteristic emphasis of Buddhism. Being Buddhist in the developing world means having an inclusive attitude of spiritual uplift and self-reliance. Everyone must be self-reliant on the Buddhist path. This self-reliance is emphasized in the early tradition of Theravada Buddhism and contrasts with the reliance on other power in some parts of the Mahayana tradition. Yet although one must be self-reliant and show vigor, no person is isolated from another. We are all linked in an inescapable network of mutuality. According to Ariyaratne, Sarvodaya takes a view of development according to which development is a process of awakening. This process has the human being at the center, with the objective of the personality awakening. The goal is not to create rich persons or rich communities, but to create a no-poverty society. Sarvodaya is dedicated to discovery and fulfillment of the Basic Human Needs (BHN) so that there is no poverty. BHN includes simply: clean environment, water, clothing, food, house, healthcare, communication facilities, energy requirements, education, and cultural and spiritual needs. There may also be as many as fifteen to twenty "subneeds" under each BHN category.

Knowing and seeing for oneself is consistently emphasized in the Buddhist tradition. When Buddhism occurs in the developing world, metaphysical concerns are generally completely absent or downplayed. The focus is on the here and now, and in eliminating suffering (construed to include ameliorating the condition of workers). This is seen, for instance, in the fact that Jha's *Buddhist Economics and the Modern World* is, in his words, "Dedicated to Lord Buddha the father of socialism."

The heart of Buddhist compassion is nonviolence. The message of the Buddha, like that of Gandhi (whose work Dr. Martin Luther King studied), is to overcome all opposition and duality through the message of love. This does not mean that socially engaged Buddhists must acquiesce in the face of social and economic exploitation. Theirs is a way of constructive engagement, attempting to make a friend of the other.

Thinking of the future of Buddhism in the developing world, one main emphasis of Buddha's teaching is the Middle Way. Traditional textual Buddhism has distinct senses of the middle way: (a) soteriologically, a middle between Brahmanical soul substance eternalism and Carvaka materialist annihilationism; (b) ethically, a middle between the sensualism of the princely palace prior to renunciation and the asceticism of the Jaina teachers with whom Buddha studied before enlightenment. Although these distinctions are prominent in traditional textual Buddhism, in the developing world, a new sense of the term "middle way" seems emergent: (c) politically, a middle way between communism and capitalism.

FRANK J. HOFFMAN

See also Nepal; Sri Lanka; Tibet

References and Further Reading

Ambedkar, B. R. *The Essential Writings of B. R. Ambedkar*, edited by Valerian Rodrigues. New Delhi; New York: Oxford University Press, 2002.

Chalam, K. S. *The Relevance of Ambedkarism in India.* Jaipur: Rawat Publications, 1993.

Jha, Hari Bansh. *Buddhist Economics and the Modern World.* Kathmandu: Dharmakirti Baudha Adhyayan Gosthi, 1979.

Kabilsingh, Chatsumarn. *Thai Women in Buddhism.* Berkeley, CA: Parallax 1991.

Kadam, K. N. *The Meaning of the Ambedkarite Conversion to Buddhism and Other Essays.* Mumbai: Popular Prakashan, 1997.

Kenadi, L. *Revival of Buddhism in Modern India: The Role of B. R. Ambedkar and the Dalai Lama XIV.* New Delhi: Ashish Publishing House, 1995.

Macy, Joanna. *Dharma and Development Religion as Resource in the Sarvodaya Self-Help Movement.* West Hartford, CT: Kumarian Press, 1983.

Prebish, Charles and Martin Baumann, eds. *Westward Dharma.* Berkeley, CA: University of California Press, 2002.

Rahula, Walpola. *The Heritage of the Bhikkhu.* New York: Grove Press, 1974.

Schumacher, E. F. *Small Is Beautiful.* New York: Harper & Row, 1973.

BULGARIA

Location

The Republic of Bulgaria lies in southeastern Europe in the eastern part of the Balkan Peninsula. Located along key land routes and historical migration roads between Europe, the Middle East, and Asia, it occupies a strategic position particularly because of its proximity to the Turkish Straits of Dardanelles and Bosphorus.

With a land area of 110,912 square kilometers, Bulgaria is bordered by Romania along the Danube River (north), Turkey (southeast), Greece (south), and Macedonia-FYROM and Serbia-Montenegro (west). The population of 7,973,890 (2002 est.) comprises Bulgarians (83.9%), Turks (9.4%), and Roma (4.7%). The capital, Sofia, has a population of 1,088,700 (2003 est.).

Land and Climate

The topography is varied: in the north, the Danubian plateau is the most fertile farmland. In the center, the Balkan Mountains (Stara Planina) traverse the country from east to west. In the southwest, the Rhodope and Pirin Mountains culminate with the Musala Peak (2,925 meters), the highest point on the Balkan Peninsula. In the west, the Black Sea coastline is a popular Eastern European tourist area. Between the Black Sea and the Rhodope lies the Thracian plain. Forests cover more than one-third of the territory. The climate is continental temperate, with cold, snowy winters and hot, dry summers. The Danube, the Iskur, the Maritsa, and the Struma are the principal rivers.

History Until 1945

Human settlement in the region dates to prehistoric times. The Thracians established the first civilization in 3500 BC. Later the country was successively integrated into the Roman and the Byzantine Empires. During the seventh century AD the Bulgars, nomadic tribes from central Asia, took control of the country. They adopted Christianity in 865. Two Bulgarian kingdoms flourished during the Middle Ages. In 1393, following the fall of Tirnovo, Bulgaria was integrated into the Ottoman Empire until 1878. The Ottoman rule was direct and controlling because of the proximity of the center of the Empire, Constantinople-Istanbul.

Following the Russian–Turkish war of 1877–1878 and the treaty of Berlin (July 1878), Bulgaria became an autonomous principality. In 1908, following the Young Turk revolution, the prince of Bulgaria, Ferdinand of Saxe-Cobourg-Gotha, proclaimed independence.

One of the main issues from the nineteenth century until 1945 was the expansion of the Bulgarian territory: In 1885, Eastern Roumelia was successfully incorporated into Bulgaria, but the government failed to integrate Macedonia in 1912–1913. The claim toward the Macedonian territories partly explained Bulgaria's choice to side with Germany during WWI and WWII. After 1918, Alexander Stamboliski and the Agrarians ran Bulgaria until 1923. Political turmoil marked the interwar period. In 1935, King Boris III established his personal dictatorship.

In 1945, Bulgaria became a People's Republic and fell within the Soviet sphere of influence. It became a member of the Soviet-led military alliance, the Warsaw Pact (1955), and the communist economic organization, COMECON (1949).

Current Economy

Bulgaria is traditionally an agricultural country (20% of the GDP). The principal crops are wheat, oilseeds, vegetables, fruits, and tobacco. Roses are also grown in the Valley of Roses, an area well known for manufacturing perfume. Bulgaria's natural resources include bauxite, copper, lead, zinc, coal, oil, and natural gas. There are also many mineral springs. The major industries are machine building; metalworking; food processing; engineering; and the production of chemicals, textiles and electronics.

After a difficult economic transition between 1989 and 1997, recovery has been slow and partial. The recent economic situation is characterized by a positive GDP, 4.8% in 2002 and 4.3% in 2003; the inflation rate was 5.6% in 2003. Unemployment is moderate for the region with 14.3% (2003). Bulgaria remains sensitive to international fluctuations as more than 45% of her exports consist of raw materials. The importance of services has increased from 29.5% of GVA (Gross Value Added) in 1989 to 58.8% in 2002. The Bulgarian economy moved toward a service-oriented model as the industry's share went down from 59.4% of GVA in 1989 to 28.7% in 2002. Tourism and communications have shown a robust growth. The private sector's share of GVA reached 72.2% in 2002. However, like most of the ex-communist states in the region, Bulgaria suffers from corruption and a substantial "gray economy," which ranged from 20% to 30% of GDP in 2002–2003.

Bulgaria's Developments After 1945

From 1945 to 1989, Bulgaria was a strong totalitarian regime, and one of the closest of the East European countries allied to the Soviet Union. Under the leadership of Todor Zhivkov (1962–1989), an almost complete political immobility prevailed. However, the communist regime deeply transformed the Bulgarian society. Through education and the development of the industrial sector, a consistent urban middle class emerged from a traditionally agricultural society. By the late 1980s only one-fifth of the population was still directly involved in farming.

In the late 1970s, Zhivkov's daughter, Ludmilla Zhivkova, who was the head of the commission for Arts and Culture, brought a new wind. Emphasizing Bulgarian nationalism, history, and culture, she tried to distance her country from Soviet ideology. A few years later a timid civil society started to emerge as demonstrations took place on the streets because of concern for the ecology, as well as unions meeting in Sofia (1987–1989).

Zhivkov resigned on November 10, 1989, one day after the fall of the Berlin wall, signaling a "quiet transition." Since then, Bulgaria has acquired a reputation as an "island of stability" in the Balkans, as the country escaped the bloody transition of Yugoslavia. However, in spite of the establishment of a new set of institutions, a parliamentary democratic republic, the adoption of a new constitution (1991), and the staging of regular elections, no political party has been able to establish a long-term government and major economic reforms have proved difficult to enact.

The development of Bulgaria has been challenged by three major issues: First, Bulgaria's transition toward a free market economy proved to be a slow, painful process that is far from being accomplished. In the early 1990s the standard of living fell by about 40%. Then, the UN sanctions against Yugoslavia and Iraq hurt the already damaged economy. In 1996, the economy collapsed, and social turmoil threatened the new democracy as a severe political crisis occurred. The resignation of socialist Prime Minister Videnov resulted in a general election, which was won by the Union of the Democratic Forces (UDF). Since then a slow recovery and political stability prevail. The government has been moving to introduce structural reforms, such as privatization, liquidation of state-owned enterprises, liberation of agricultural policies, and the reform of the country's social insurance programs. In July 2001, following a general election, an unexpected coalition government was formed. Simeon of Saxe-Cobourg-Gotha, the son of Boris III, became prime minister and the socialist candidate, Georgi Parvanov, became president of Bulgaria.

Second, the status of the Turkish minority was successfully modified. Under the communist regime, the Turks had been forced to assimilate into Bulgarian language and culture. A brutal and strong policy was introduced in 1984–1985 when the authorities forced the Turks to adopt Bulgarian names. Later, during the summer of 1989, about 320,000 left the country for Turkey. The army was deployed. After 1990, the new government successfully implemented a radical change of policy to fully integrate the Turks politically and now they have representatives in the government and parliament. Since 1991, Turks have enjoyed equal rights with Bulgarians.

Third, Bulgaria opted for a new foreign policy driven by three objectives: Sofia establishes cooperation with Washington; Bulgarian soldiers participate in the military operations conducted in Bosnia-Herzegovina, in Afghanistan, and in Iraq; and Bulgarian military bases are open to US forces. In March 2004, Bulgaria became a member of NATO. Because of its historical ties to Russia, Bulgaria still retains some links with that country, although after 1989, Bulgaria tried to distance itself from what was still the Soviet Union, a communist country. More recently, with the election of President Putin, the relationship between the two countries has improved. Sofia still imports 85% of its energy resources from Russia (gas, oil, nuclear energy), and more than 80% of Bulgaria's trade is with former Soviet-bloc countries. Finally, in 1995, the EU accepted Bulgaria's candidacy.

NADINE AKHUND

See also Central and Eastern Europe: History and Economic Development; Ethnic Conflicts: Central and Eastern Europe

References and Further Reading

A Concise History of Bulgaria, Cambridge, MA: Cambridge University Press, 1997.

Banac, Ivo, ed. *The Diary of Georgi Dimitrov 1933–1949*. New Haven, CT: Yale University Press, 2003.

Bell, John D. *The Bulgarian Communist Party from Blagoev to Zhivkov*. Hoover Institute Press, Stanford University, 1986.

Crampton, Richard J. *The Balkans Since the Second World War*. New York: Longman, 2002.

Hupchik, Dennis P. *The Bulgarians in the Seventeenth Century: Slavic Orthodox Society and Culture Under Ottoman Rule*. Jefferson, NC: McFarland, 1993.

Jelavich, Barbara. *History of the Balkans*. Cambridge, MA: Cambridge University Press, 1983.

Lampe, John, and Mark Mazower, eds. *Ideologies and National Identities: The Case of Twentieth-Century Southeastern Europe*. Budapest: Central University Press, 2003.

Roudometoff, Victor. *Collective Memory, National Identity and Ethnic Conflict. Greece, Bulgaria and the Macedonian Question*. London: Praeger, 2002.

Simsir, Bilâl N. *The Turks of Bulgaria (1878–1985)*. London: K. Rustem & Brother, 1988.

BUNCHE, RALPH

Dr. Ralph Johnson Bunche was a scholar/activist in the fields of civil rights, human rights, decolonization, and peacekeeping. He was born in Detroit, Michigan, August 7, 1903, and became the first African American, and person of color of any origin, to be awarded the Nobel Prize for Peace. He received this international honor in 1950 for his success as United Nations mediator in bringing about the 1949 armistices between Israel and its Arab adversaries, Egypt, Jordan, Lebanon, and Syria. Son of an itinerant barber and raised by his maternal grandmother, Bunche fashioned several path-breaking careers, in academia, as a civil rights leader, and as a civil servant in both the United States government and the United Nations.

Bunche, the scholar, earned his PhD at Harvard and was an early student of Africa and the problems of race. He became professor and first chair of the new political science department at Howard University in 1929 and was elected president of the American Political Science Association in 1953. He was in the forefront of the struggle for civil rights in the United States in the 1930s and 1940s. From 1923 to 1941, he was primarily a scholar; from 1941 to his death in 1971, he was primarily a practitioner and activist.

Bunche's focus on the conditions and experiences of indigenous peoples and cultures subject to colonialism paralleled and was linked to his interest in the condition and experience of black people in his own US society. To Bunche, the condition of African Americans and that of the blacks in Africa, as well as that of colonial peoples throughout the world, was part and parcel of the same problem—that of racism and economic deprivation. He was an early leader in the development of US understanding of Africa. Because of his expertise on Africa and colonial problems, he was recruited into the World War II Office of Strategic Services, where he headed the Africa Section of the Research and Analysis Branch. In 1944, he moved to the State Department where in the post-war planning unit he was involved in the creation of the United Nations and played a particularly central role in the evolving process of decolonization. He helped create the United Nations at San Francisco in 1945 and had a central role in the adoption of three chapters of the UN Charter that dealt with post-war colonialism. For two decades, as under-secretary-general—the highest post held by an American in the UN—he played a leading role in the conception and conduct of the UN's peacekeeping

function. In the last decades of his life, Bunche was one of the most widely known figures on the international scene. He died in New York City on December 9, 1971.

Benjamin Rivlin

See also Arab–Israeli Wars (1948, 1956, 1967, 1973)

References and Further Reading

Bunche, Ralph J. *Ralph J. Bunche: Selected Speeches and Writings*, edited by Charles P. Henry. Ann Arbor, MI: University of Michigan Press, 1995.

Henry, Charles P. *Ralph Bunche: Model Negro or American Other*. New York: New York University Press, 1998.

Rivlin, Benjamin. *Ralph Bunche: The Man and His Times*. New York: Homes & Meier, 1990.

Urquhart, Brian. *Ralph Bunche: An American Life*. New York: W.W. Norton, 1993.

BUREAUCRATIC AUTHORITARIANISM

Bureaucratic authoritarianism (BA), a term coined in 1973 by Guillermo O'Donnell, is a member of the very extended family of authoritarian regimes, generically characterized by "limited, not responsible, political pluralism, without elaborate and guiding ideology, but with distinctive mentalities, without extensive, nor intensive political mobilization, except at some points in their development, and in which a leader, or occasionally a small group, exercises power within ill-defined limits but actually quite predictable ones" (Linz 1964). By this path-breaking definition, authoritarianism has been clearly distinguished from totalitarianism, a regime in which the state's total monopoly over power, as framed within an all-encompassing ideology, sets forth a program of radical transformation of society that mobilizes the whole population, yet excludes (or exterminates) all those suspected of incompatibility with, or enmity toward, the said program.

Although authoritarianism had been widespread in Europe and elsewhere early in the twentieth century, its study began in earnest in the 1960s with Franco's Spain as its first study subject, a country that was difficult to place squarely in the totalitarian camp, despite its initial alliance with Nazi Germany. The term acquired its full significance in the following decade, with the widespread emergence of a new kind of undemocratic rule in Latin America, which abruptly ended the era of proto-democratic populist mobilizations in Argentina, Uruguay, and Brazil, and that of democratic socialism in Chile.

By merging the general concept of authoritarianism with the debate on dependent capitalism and professionalization of the military (Stepan 1971, 1973), Guillermo O'Donnell (1973) identified bureaucratic authoritarianism (BA) as a new variety of authoritarianism, typically exemplified in Argentina's 1976–1983 military dictatorship. The "bureaucratic" qualifier added the element of rational management of the state and the economy, coupled with the rejection of the corporatist and populist past, hence the exclusion of the organizations (unions, parties, and so on) and interest groups that had partaken in the populist alliances. In other words, with BA's modern rational state organization and its disregard for the maintenance of legitimacy toward key groups in society and the popular masses, authoritarianism took one step in the direction of totalitarianism, yet stopped short of putting forth a total ideology or mobilizing the masses.

The concept was immediately heralded as a major turning point, providing, as it seemed, just the key to the puzzle over the repeated emergence of military regimes in Latin America from 1964 to 1976. To all accounts, BA aptly portrayed the regime that had taken power in Argentina from 1976 to 1983, and prided itself on having reestablished law, order, and economic growth on sound managerial and technocratic (as opposed to ideological) grounding, while eliminating the communist peril. But it also aimed at including other cases, such as Brazil, Uruguay, and Chile, also taken over by the military from 1964 to 1985, 1973 to 1985, and 1973 to 1989, respectively. With time, however, the initial enthusiasm over this formula began to dim, not only in view of the human rights atrocities they perpetrated, but also for their failure to reestablish economic growth (excepting Chile in the mid-1980s), their fiscal and borrowing recklessness, and their propensity to adopt corporatist self-serving welfare provisions that excluded the rest of the population. Even among their erstwhile allies (such as business and the middle classes), these regimes were eventually discovered to be seriously lacking in the virtues by which they had defined themselves, and not sufficiently similar to one another to justify the use of a single type. Thus it was argued, for example, that rather than a pure BA, the Argentine military from 1976 to 1983 represented a mixture of extremely exclusionary authoritarianism and totalitarianism (the latter in view of the enclaves in charge of the repression, torture, and disappearance of "subversives"), while Brazil's military was seen as more inclusionary, due to the maintenance of elections, parliament, and unions (albeit under the control of the military). Chile, by contrast, changed over time from an extremely stark to a more negotiable authoritarian rule. Lastly, in their relentless witch hunts of the Tupamaro guerillas, the military in Uruguay proved the most repressive of the four countries, despite the country's long tradition of democratic rule.

When these regimes returned to civilian rule, they also did so in remarkably different ways: virtual expulsion of the military in Argentina after the Malvinas military fiasco; their total discredit in Uruguay as expressed in a plebiscite; a transition planned by the military themselves in Brazil; and initially the retention of considerable political and military power by the dictator in Chile under the constitution of 1980.

Despite their limitations, shared by most typifications, Linz's and O'Donnell's work on authoritarianism, and that of others following them (Malloy 1977; Collier 1979) mark an important watershed in political theory signifying the demise of the then-dominant ideas on political modernization, which had predicted imminent democratization for Latin America's relatively advanced industrialized countries. Together with the ongoing debate on dependent capitalism, these works thereby opened an extremely rich and fruitful debate that radically changed the research questions debated within the academic community.

The conceptual birth of authoritarianism and its BA variant also had important policy repercussions, insofar as in the building of strategic alliances against potential Soviet/Cuban expansionism, US policy makers found authoritarian governments to be politically more acceptable allies than other undemocratic rulers. This in no small part contributed to the legitimation and consolidation of these regimes and the consequent unchecked spreading of human rights abuses. With the change of policy in the Carter administration, however, and the generally dismal economic performance of these regimes, external support began to falter, thereby preparing the grounds for the third wave of democratization, beginning with Argentina in 1983.

At first glance, little discrepancy between Linz's and O'Donnell's ideas on authoritarianism is apparent if we focus on regime structures only. In contrast to Linz, however, O'Donnell gives primary importance to the social base of regimes: BA regimes are said to rest on a coalition of high-level military and business technocrats working in close association with foreign capital. They exclude subordinate classes (outlawing any kind of political organization thereof, and pursuing labor, peasant, or urban popular leaders with Dirty War techniques), and are therefore "emphatically antidemocratic" (Collier 1979). The "limited pluralism" included in Linz's definition is hereby given an important corrective: since BA regimes include only a very small elite, their politics can be called factional rather than "plural." Equally absent from O'Donnell's BA is the notion of "mentality," a somewhat vague concept in Linz's definition.

The most important difference between the two authors is that Linz aimed at typifying the structural characteristics of a wide variety of authoritarianisms, regardless of origin or policies, whereas O'Donnell was theorizing on an historical sequence of regimes ending up with the birth of BAs in Latin America. At Stage One, oligarchic democracies, which had ruled from the nineteenth century to the Great Depression, were supported by economic elites (landed, and mining) whose power was based on the export of primary products to industrialized countries. At Stage Two, these oligarchies whose wealth was destroyed by the Great Depression, were overthrown by populist leaders (as Perón in Argentina, Kubichek in Brazil, Battle in Uruguay), based on multi-class coalitions of urban elites and popular sectors, and sustained by import substitution industrialization (ISI). Finally, at Stage Three, the rise of BA regimes was said to have coincided with the end of the easy phase of import substitution, leading to domination by military-technocratic elites and the exclusion of popular sectors from the benefits of new capital-intensive industrial growth.

O'Donnell's economic explanation of the rise of authoritarianism had a mixed reception, with calls for a more actor- and ideology-mediated view of the transition from populist economic policy (ISI, currency overvaluation, inflation, and debt) to more orthodox market-oriented policies (Hirshman 1979). His hypothesis of the "deepening" and "exhaustion" of import substitution, alleged to have led to authoritarian rule, was also questioned, based on available evidence that these difficulties had arisen before the breakdown of democracies, and had in part been solved before the military coups that ushered in BA.

A second kind of critique concerned the overextended use of the BA concept, which came to describe almost any Latin American or Southern European non-democratic regime in the 1970s, whether populist and inclusionary, as post-revolutionary Mexico, or elitist and exclusionary, as Chile under Pinochet (1973–1989) or Argentina under the military junta (1976–1983). In the case of Mexico, the term was initially held to be applicable, despite three fundamental differences between Mexico and typical BA regimes: the inclusion of the popular sectors (via state corporatist mechanisms); the presence until the 1980s of a governing elite that was more populist than technocratic; and the preservation, well into the 1980s and even into the 1990s, of ISI and tailored welfare programs. Additionally, Mexico's military was nowhere on the political map at any time since 1910, which may have contributed to the uncanny stability of the post-revolutionary regime.

When all was said and done, however, O'Donnell's concern for the alliances and coalitions backing up Latin America's BA regimes has been crucial to understanding the logic and evolution of these regimes, and has easily translated into today's concern for the social composition of political forces supporting or weakening the newly reestablished democracies. In fact, it was argued that we owe the demise of these dictatorships in large part to the dissolution of the alliances between *blandos* (softliners) and *duros* (hardliners) within the military, and between the military and business.

The debate on authoritarianism was soon to be interrupted *sine die* when the Argentinian military returned to civilian rule in 1983, shortly followed by Uruguay, Brazil, and Chile. Despite the suddenness of the change, however, the potentially enduring overlap between authoritarianism and democracy initially received relatively little attention. Excepting the role of the Catholic Church (mostly seen as mitigating authoritarianism), and important (yet relatively marginalized) work on social movement mobilizations during the four military dictatorships, the tendency to think of these regimes as indivisible units had left little room for the study of their weaknesses, and the forces at work preparing for re-democratization. As a result, subsequent democratization was overwhelmingly attributed to top-down elite negotiations and deliberate "crafting" from above. Likewise, the authoritarian ways of governing displayed by some of the new democracies (as the Menem administration in Argentina) or fighting Parliament with plebiscitarian techniques (as Fujimori's administration in Peru) were given short shrift.

Since the return to civilian rule in Southern Europe in the 1970s and in Latin America in the 1980s, the debate on BA has become a relatively neglected subject. The concept was perhaps so specifically descriptive of Latin America at a certain historical juncture (especially of Argentina, as some critics of O'Donnell have argued), that it was bound to fall into disuse after re-democratization. Yet authoritarianism, the more general term, and one not necessarily referring to military rule, has remained alive and well. The reason is the persistence in new and old democracies of authoritarian traits and institutional niches, and the tolerance of authoritarian practices.

Rather than continue along the line of typifying regimes as indivisible wholes, as in the past, the research task confronting analysts in the twenty-first century is to unravel the patchwork nature of political regimes and discover the relations of interdependence linking their different component parts. As such, the study of authoritarianism and some of its bureaucratic aspects is bound to remain fruitful, independently of the disappearance from the scene of specific kinds of authoritarian regimes that led to coining the term.

VIVIANE BRACHET-MÁRQUEZ

See also Argentina; Authoritarianism; Brazil; Chile; Uruguay

References and Further Reading

Brachet-Márquez, Viviane. "Undemocratic Politics in the Twentieth Century and Beyond." In *A Handbook of Political Sociology*, edited by Thomas Janoski, Robert Alford, Alexander Hicks, and Mildred Schwartz. Cambridge, MA: Cambridge University Press, 2005.

Collier, David, ed. *The New Authoritarianism in Latin America*. Princeton, NJ: Princeton University Press, 1979.

Hirschman, Albert O. "The Turn to Authoritarianism in Latin America and the Search for its Economic Determinants." In *The New Authoritarianism in Latin America*, edited by David Collier, 61–98. Princeton, NJ: Princeton University Press, 1979.

Linz, Juan J. "An Authoritarian Regime: The Case of Spain." In *Mass Politics, Studies in Political Sociology*, edited by Erik Allard and Stein Rokkan. New York: Free Press, 1970.

Linz, Juan J. *Totalitarian and Authoritarian Regimes*. Boulder, CO, and London: Lynne Rienner, 2000.

Malloy, James, ed. *Authoritarianism and Corporatism in Latin America*. Pittsburgh: Pittsburgh University Press, 1977.

O'Donnell, Guillermo. *Modernization and Bureaucratic Authoritarianism: Studies in South American Politics*. Berkeley, CA: Institute of International Studies, 1973.

Rouquié, Alain. *The Military and the State in Latin America*. Berkeley, CA: University of California Press, 1987.

Stepan, Alfred. *The Military in Politics. Changing Patterns in Brazil*. Princeton, NJ: Princeton University Press, 1971.

Stepan, A. "The New Professionalism of Internal Welfare and Military Role Expansion." In *Authoritarian Brazil Origins, Policies and Future*, edited by A. Stepan. New Haven, CT: Yale University Press, 1973.

Stepan, Alfred. *The State and Society. Peru in a Comparative Perspective*. Princeton, NJ: Princeton University Press, 1978.

BURKINA FASO

Burkina Faso, formerly known as Upper Volta, is a small, landlocked country in the West African region. It is located North of Ghana and shares its other borders with Benin, Niger, Mali, Côte d'Ivoire, and Togo. Its total area of 274,200 square kilometers is mostly flat with some hills in the west and southeast of the country; 50% of the country's land is forest and woodlands. Burkina Faso's climate is tropical overall; the winters are warm and dry while the summers are hot and wet. However, the country has experienced a number of recurring droughts, which have severely affected agricultural activities. The majority of the twelve million Burkinabés are farmers; they either cultivate cash crops such as cotton, peanuts, and sesame, or food crops such as millet, rice, and vegetables. The Mossi are the largest ethnic group in the country with 40% of the country's population. Other represented ethnic groups include: the Senufo, the Gurunsi, the Lobi, the Bobo, the Mande, and the Fulani. To date, there has been no conflict among the country's ethnic groups. The country is among the poorest of the poor countries of the world, ranking 171 out of 174 countries in the United Nations Development Program Human Development Index.

Burkina Faso's short history has been quite turbulent. Even as a French colony, it oscillated between having its own colonial status and being part of other colonial territories such as the French Sudan or Côte d'Ivoire. It finally became its own, more stable, colonial territory in 1947 and gained its political independence on August 5, 1960. During the first twenty years of its existence, Burkina Faso relied heavily on French economic assistance and experienced a number of military coups. Blaise Compaoré, the country's president as of this writing, has been slowly and successfully moving the country toward political and economic liberalization.

After difficult attempts by Upper Volta's first president, Maurice Yaméogo, to create a national identify among the ethnic groups that make up Burkina Faso, the country lived through four military coups involving different leaders and factions. General Sangoulé Lamizana was the first to stage a military coup. He assumed the presidency in 1966 and alternatively restricted and allowed national political activity while in office until 1980. He was overthrown by Colonel Saye Zerbo, one of his own officers, and the latter was deposed by another Mossi officer, Jean-Baptiste Ouédraogo, in 1982. This last coup was met with public indifference, even though it was the first to result in civilian or military deaths. During this time, the country did not change much economically. It was particularly dependent on French aid because of a number of economic and military cooperation agreements signed between France and Upper Volta prior to independence. French assistance between 1960 and 1972, for instance, equaled five times the Burkinabé government's budget for 1972, $2 billion.

On August 4, 1983, Thomas Sankara, previously prime minister under Ouédraogo, was freed from prison by 250 Burkinabé soldiers and took charge of the country. In favor of complete autarky, this Marxist revolutionary sought to rid his home country of French exploitation and bring home the thousands of Burkinabé laborers continuously working in Côte d'Ivoire. He created the National Council of the

Revolution (NCR) at the national level and the Committees for the Defense of the Revolution at the local level to revolutionize life in Burkina Faso and restructure its social space. The state was working to organize segments of the country's civil society. Sankara also changed the name of the country from Upper Volta to Burkina Faso, or "The Land of Men of Integrity," in August 1984. His positions and policies were not popular with most Burkinabè citizens, regardless of social class, and alienated Westerners and the international financial institutions. On October 15, 1987, following months of economic unease and social tension, Thomas Sankara was assassinated and Blaise Compaoré took over as the country's leader.

Compaoré immediately wanted to "rectify" the revolution begun by Sankara. He allowed the formation of several political opposition groups (although none based on ethnic or religious identity), as well as the creation of new, more independent media. He created the Popular Front to replace the NCR and serve as a forum for all major political entities. He led the creation of a new, more democratic constitution in 1991. This new governing document called for the separation of power between the executive, legislative, and judicial branches of government and created a second legislative body, the Chamber of Representatives, to be a consultative body. It also made it illegal for military personnel to hold political office. Although change continued to be slow and Compaoré is still in power (as of this writing), his reforms have definitely created a more open society. A number of increasingly democratic multi-party elections have been held since 1987, among them two presidential, one municipal, and two parliamentary voting opportunities.

Compaoré also accepted capitalism as the economic system of choice for development in Burkina Faso. He thus regained assistance from the International Monetary Fund and the World Bank starting in 1991, with the signature of a structural adjustment plan and loans totaling $31 million. Compaoré launched serious economic reforms of the public, banking, and fiscal sectors of the economy while liberalizing agricultural trade. Despite the severe devaluation of the CFA franc in 1994, the 1990s were a comparatively a good decade for the country as it moved toward the production of more expensive agricultural products such as sun-dried tomatoes and green beans for export. Since 1999, its overall annual GDP has been more than 5%. In July 2000, as an indication of its economic and social progress, Burkina Faso was approved for $400 million in debt relief under the World Bank's Heavily Indebted Poor Countries Initiative. According to IMF and World Bank standards, the country has done well economically and reduced poverty since then, despite the continuing crisis in neighboring Cote d'Ivoire. Burkina Faso continues to receive much assistance from the international financial institutions.

LAURA E. BOUDON

References and Further Reading

Boudon, Laura E. "Burkina Faso: The Rectification of the Revolution." In *Political Reform in Francophone Africa*, edited by John F. Clark and David E. Gardinier. Boulder, CO: Westview Press, 1997.

Decalo, Samuel. *Burkina Faso: A Bibliography*. Santa Barbara, CA: Clio Press, 1994.

Deschamps, Alain. *Burkina Faso, 1987–1992: Le pays des hommes integrés*. Paris: L'Harmattan, 2001.

Englebert, Pierre. *Burkina Faso: Unsteady Statehood in West Africa*. Boulder, CO: Westview Press, 1996.

McFarland, Daniel Miles. *Historical Dictionary of Burkina Faso*. Lanham, MD: Scarecrow Press, 1998.

Otayek, René. "Burkina Faso: Between Feeble State and Total State, The Swing Continues." In *Contemporary West African States*, edited by J. Dunn, D. B. Cruise O'Brien, and R. Rathbone. Cambridge, MA: Cambridge University Press, 1989.

Zagré, Pascal. *Les politiques économiques du Burkina Faso: une tradition d'ajustement structurel*. Paris: Khartala, 1994.

BURMA

See Myanmar

BURUNDI

Burundi is a small but densely populated country of 27,834 square kilometers with a population of 7.7 million (2004). The country is bordered by Rwanda to the north, the Democratic Republic of Congo to the west, and Tanzania to the south and east. Lake Tanganyika and the Ruzizi River separate Burundi and the DR Congo. The capital is Bujumbura.

Burundi's religions are dominantly colonial; about 60% are Christians, mostly Roman Catholic; Swahili Muslims comprise 5%; and others are mainly followers of traditional religions. The main language is Kirundi; French and Kiswahili are also spoken. There are seven major ethnic groups: Hutu, Tutsi, Ganwa (royal clans), Hima (also seen as a clan of Tutsi), Swahili Muslims, pygmoid indigenous Twa, and Mbo.

The European colonization reached Burundi in the 1880s. In 1918, Burundi and Rwanda were given to Belgium as a mandate of the League of Nations and later the UN until 1962. The Belgians were in need of Hutu and Tutsi as laborers in the mines and plantations. The Tutsis were told by the colonizers that they were "born to rule" while Hutus were "born to serve." The devastating effects of such racism continue to be felt today in both Rwanda and Burundi.

By instigating and militarily supporting the Hutu revolt in Rwanda in 1959, the colonialists created the dictatorship of the majority, but the Ganwa-Tutsi constitutional monarchy in Burundi remained in place, though it waned in power and influence. In 1959, the pan-Africanist Ganwa prince Louis Rwagasore drew huge crowds at mass rallies demanding immediate independence. Rwagasore became the head of Uprona, the Tutsi-dominated Union for National Progress.

Between 1959 and 1966, tens of thousands of Tutsi in Rwanda were murdered and tens of thousands fled to Burundi and other nearby countries. In the following decades, mutual cycles of extreme violence ravaged Central Africa. Burundi's descent into violence began in 1965 with a Hutu military coup, which was quelled. Afterwards, the first massacres took place.

In 1972, a state-organized, selective genocide was carried out by the army against tens of thousands of Hutus and against the political opposition among Tutsi-Banyaruguru. Educated Hutu and Tutsi dissidents were rounded up by the army and murdered. Up to a hundred thousand people are estimated to have died.

Burundi's young democracy disintegrated and Uprona became a tool of the military, leading to the institution of military rule dominated by Tutsi-Hima. The Ganwa nobility was finally ousted from power by Captain Michel Micombero, the head of the new military power elite, who remained in power from 1966 to 1976. In the fall of 1976, Colonel Jean Baptiste Bagaza, a Tutsi-Hima and a relative of Micombero, staged a bloodless coup.

Under the eleven-year Bagaza regime, there were no further massacres; but there was no power sharing either. All provincial governors and most civil servants were Tutsis. Uprona was made into a single "unity" party. Bagaza introduced limited reforms and attracted Western aid. Human rights violations were simply "overlooked." Aid and coffee export financed the first glimpse of modernity: the electrification of urban centers and bitumen roads.

Bagaza fell in a coup in 1987 by Major Pierre Buyoya, who reintroduced power-sharing, giving an equal share of posts to Hutu and Tutsi. In 1990, France—followed by other donors—made aid conditional to multi-party democratization. A new constitution was accepted by referendum, but the transition to democracy was full of uncertainties.

The second free and fair elections (after those in 1961) took place on June 1, 1993. Uprona was challenged by the Hutu-dominated Frodebu, the Front for Democracy in Burundi (Front pour la Démocratie au Burundi). Frodebu candidate Melchior Ndadaye (a Hutu moderate) was the clear winner. Ndadaye had been in office one hundred days when he was murdered during a failed military coup on October 20, 1993. His assassination triggered a series of organized massacres against the Tutsi minority.

Within weeks, fifty thousand Tutsi farmers and thousands of Hutu Upronists were slaughtered by Hutu Frodebists. From October 1993 to spring 1998, Burundi was engulfed in "ethnic" slaughter that claimed the lives of tens of thousands of unarmed civilians and caused the displacement of hundreds of thousands more. After almost three years of mixed regimes under Hutu leadership, Pierre Buyoya seized power again in a bloodless coup in June 1996. Neighboring governments imposed an economic embargo on the land-locked country to force it to reintroduce democratic rule.

Still, the conflict raged on, fuelled by a seemingly unstoppable flow of arms. Tanzania and Zaire allowed Hutu rebels to use their territory. The fallout from the genocide and civil wars in Rwanda and Burundi caused instability in the neighboring states: rebels from both countries continued to hide out in the Democratic Republic of the Congo.

The political turnaround in Burundi came in June 1998 with the "partnership" between government and parliament, based on a joint political platform, and the transitional constitution of June 6, 1998. Traditional forms of reestablishing social harmony, such as the old institution of arbitration known as abashingantahe, similar to a Truth and Reconciliation Commission, were adopted at a national level.

Direct talks between the military foes culminated in the Arusha Peace Accords of August 2000. All parties—except the armed groups—signed the accords, which became the base for a three-year transitional period, starting in 2001 and slated to end with elections. For the first eighteen months, Pierre Buyoya (Uprona) remained president; Domitien Ndayizeye (Frodebu) then took over, and remained in office as of 2005. The period was extended because the Constitutional Court failed to validate a draft constitution in time. One rebel group still refuses to sign the accords, and hence the elections could not be held by October 31, 2004, when the transitional period should have ended; they have been postponed repeatedly.

Leadership quarrels had led to several splits within both rebel groups. The armed wing of Palipehutu, the FNL, is active in the northern provinces bordering Congo and sometimes in the Bujumbura area. The FNL has an inherently tribalist agenda. By 2005, most FDD factions joined the government camp, with only the FLN continuing strikes against "soft targets," mainly Tutsi civilians, Hutu "traitors" (Upronists) and even refugees from the Congo.

The key issues underlying the conflict are those of the control of state power and state resources. Main features of the intrastate conflict are fictitious ethnicity, minority governance, regional divide, and spillover effects of the Congo crisis. A regional effort to end conflict was agreed to by eleven regional heads of state on November 22, 2004, in Dar es Salaam.

CHRISTIAN P. SCHERRER

See also East Africa: History and Economic Development; East Africa: International Relations; Ethnic Conflicts: East Africa

References and Further Reading

Amnesty International (AI). *Burundi: Between Hope and Fear*. London: Author, 2001.
Association pour la Lutte Contre le Génocide. *Burundi: The October–November 1993 Tutsi and Moderate Hutu Genocide*. Bujumbura: A. C. Génocide–Cirimoso, 1997.
Chrétien, Jean-Pierre. *The Great Lakes of Africa. Two Thousand Years of History*. New York: Zone Books, 2003.
Gahama, Joseph. *Le Burundi sous l'administration belge*. Paris: Karthala, 1983.
Kay, Reginald. *Burundi since the Genocide*. London (MRG–Report 20), 1987.
Lemarchand, René. *Burundi: Ethnic Conflict and Genocide*. Washington, DC: Woodrow Wilson Center Press, 1994.
République du Burundi. *Accord sur la plate-forme politique du régime de transition. Acte constitutionnel de transition*. June 6, 1998.
Scherrer, Christian P. *Genocide and Crisis in Central Africa: Conflict Roots, Mass Violence, and Regional War*. Westport, CT, and London: Præger, 2001.
United Nations International Commission of Inquiry for Burundi (CEINUB). Report on the Violence in Burundi 1993, Pursuant to S/RES 1996/1012. New York: UN, 1996.

BUTHELEZI, MANGOSUTHU GATSHA

Buthelezi was born in 1928 at Mahlabathini, KwaZulu-Natal province, South Africa. Buthelezi, who traces his ancestry to the Zulu King Dingane, was appointed a hereditary chief in 1957.

KwaZulu was the homeland created for Zulu people. Because Zulus are South Africa's largest ethnic group, Buthelezi exercised considerable influence. In 1970, Buthelezi became Chief Executive Officer of Zulu Territorial Authority (ZTA). The ZTA evolved into the KwaZulu Legislative Assembly (KLA), which was dominated by Buthelezi's Inkatha Freedom Party (IFP). The IFP (formed in 1975 as a National Cultural Liberation Movement) had more than two million

members. The IFP advocated Zulu self-determination, a "Zulu renaissance," a Zulu-monarchy, the promotion of traditional-African culture, and black liberation from white control. Buthelezi supported apartheid because he believed apartheid's homeland system allowed Zulus political autonomy.

Buthelezi established the KwaZulu homeland capital at Ulundi, site of the final Zulu defeat at the hands of the British. This was deemed symbolic of the re-emergence of the Zulu kingdom and the end of colonial subjugation. During the 1980s and 1990s, the IFP came to support capitalism and consociationalism. The IFP strongly opposed the ANC's armed struggle against apartheid and rejected the African National Congress (ANC)'s advocacy of socialism, sanctions, and majoritarian-democracy within a unified South African state. The IFP engaged in a violent struggle against the United Democratic Front (internal wing of the ANC) during the 1980s and 1990s. Despite this, Buthelezi repeatedly called for Nelson Mandela's release from prison.

Under Buthelezi, the IFP stood for a multi-racial capitalism; non-violent resistance to the apartheid state; and the politics of negotiating with white South Africans. Buthelezi also built an alliance with local white capitalists during the apartheid era. Buthelezi's vision of development insisted on leaving an autonomous space for adherents to traditional African culture who did not wish to be "developed"/Westernized. Buthelezi opposed the socialist model of development, preferring to encourage the growth of an indigenous business class and then relying on "trickle-down" economics to deliver benefits to the wider population. Although Buthelezi worked within the apartheid system as KwaZulu's chief minister (from 1972–1994), in 1976 he rejected the idea that KwaZulu would become fully independent of South Africa. This challenged the central tenet of apartheid that each of South Africa's ten "black nations" would be given independence (which would have left South Africa without any black citizens).

During the negotiations to end apartheid (1991–1994) Buthelezi became a powerful focus of conservative opposition to the deal being hammered out between the ANC and the National Party. Buthelezi wanted a federal system, allowing for Zulu autonomy, while the ANC wanted a unitary (integrationist) state. A violent struggle ensued between Inkatha and ANC supporters. Buthelezi's refusal to participate in the first one-person-one-vote elections (1994) nearly plunged South Africa into a civil war. The IFP entered the elections at the last minute and won control of the KwaZulu-Natal province. A rapprochement (albeit tense) eventually took place between the IFP and the ANC. Buthelezi was South Africa's minister of the interior from 1994 to 2003, and on occasion even served as South Africa's acting president.

P. ERIC LOUW

See also African National Congress; Apartheid; Mandela, Nelson; South Africa

References and Further Reading

Buthelezi, Mangosuthu. "Independence for the Zulus." In *South African Dialogue: Contrasts in South African Thinking on Basic Race Issues*, edited by Nic Rhoodie. Johannesburg: McGraw-Hill, 1972.

Buthelezi, Mangosuthu. *Power Is Ours*. New York: Books in Focus, 1979.

Louw, P. E. *The Rise, Fall and Legacy of Apartheid*. Westport, CT: Praeger, 2004.

Mare, Gerhard, and Georgina Hamilton. *An Appetite for Power. Buthelezi's Inkatha and the Politics of 'Loyal Resistance.'* Johannesburg: Ravan, 1987.

Mzala. *Gatsha Buthelezi: Chief with a Double Agenda*. London: Zed, 1988.

C

CABRAL, AMILCAR

Founder and secretary-general of the *Partido Africano da Independência da Guineé Cabo Verde* (PAIGC), Amilcar Cabral (1925–1973) led what many think was the most successful African revolutionary movement. The revolution Cabral led in Guinea-Bissau resulted in independence in 1974 and was the direct cause of the revolution in Portugal, which ended the last surviving fascist regime in Europe. Though Cabral was noted in his lifetime as a revolutionary theorist and strategist of guerrilla war, most continuing interest in Cabral centers around two major areas: his analyses of the role of national culture in liberation movements and the dangers of the postrevolutionary period in the Third World.

Cabral's analysis of the role of national culture in liberation movements is based on his definition of imperialism as an attempt to destroy and supplant the history of colonized peoples. In his view, the reorientation of production in colonized areas to suit imperial goals could not succeed if it was aimed at only economic relationships. Colonial governments also had to subvert the political, religious, social, and artistic culture of indigenous peoples to prepare them for "assimilation" into the metropole's value systems. Cabral thought that national liberation was only feasible if this process was reversed by recapturing national culture. Thus, liberation movements should nurture the reassertion of culture, promoting attitudes conducive to self-determination and assertions of national worth. This would undermine the ability of imperial governments to assert control over colonized peoples during the liberation struggle and enable liberation movements to form new national cultures that could resist attempts to undermine independence (Bienen 1977).

Cabral's analysis of the dangers of the postrevolutionary period is tied to these ideas. He saw that successful liberation movements must be based on political organizations that conduct an empirical analysis of actual social relationships and form strategies accordingly. This task falls to the urban "petty bourgeoisie" of bureaucrats, teachers, lawyers, and small businessmen because they are the only people with the skills necessary. They, however, are the ones most closely tied to the imperial relationships and values that must be overcome. Liberation movements are caught in a dilemma. The class that has to lead them is the one most likely to stop short of a restoration of national economic and cultural integrity. Cabral warned that only those members of the petty bourgeoisie who cut their ties with imperial institutions by joining liberation organizations should be trusted. His call for a class suicide by the petty bourgeoisie as a prerequisite for successful liberation still has relevance, albeit little hope for success (Cabral 1969; Meisenheider 1993).

Cabral's insistence on the political reformation of national cultural values to fit changed circumstances, not to restore a mythological past, in today's climate of religious and ethnic movements.

TRACY L. R. LIGHTCAP

References and Further Reading

Bienen, Henry. "State and Revolution: The Work of Amilcar Cabral." *Journal of Modern African Studies* 15, no. 4 (1977).

Davidson, Basil. *No Fist Is Big Enough To Hide the Sky: The Liberation of Guinea and Cape Verde.* London: Zed, 1981.

Chabal, Patrick. *Amilcar Cabral: Revolutionary Leadership and People's War.* New York: Cambridge University, 1983.

Meisenheider, Tom. "Amilcar Cabral's Theory of Class Suicide and Revolutionary Socialism." *Monthly Review* (November 1993).

CAMBODIA

Cambodia, situated on the southern part of the Indochina peninsula in Southeast Asia, covers an area of about 69,898 square miles. It extends 280 miles north to south and 360 miles west to east. It shares land borders with three countries: Thailand to its west and north, Laos to its north, and Vietnam to its east. The mountains, the plains, and the highlands constitute its three major geographical units. Cambodia is bounded by mountain ranges such as the Dangrek Mountains on the Thai border. The highlands of the northeast in the area bordering Laos and Vietnam provide fertile volcanic soil suitable for cultivation of plantation crops like rubber and coffee. But it is the Tonle Sap ("great lake") in the heart of the country that works as a natural flood regulator by drawing the excess water of the Mekong River during the monsoon. A fertile plain extends from the Dangrek Mountains in the northwest to the Vietnam border in the southeast enriched by the river system. The Mekong River traverses more than three hundred miles, flowing north to south through Cambodia before entering Vietnam. It has a long coastline along the Gulf of Thailand. The seasons (dry and rainy) are governed by the northeast and southwest monsoons. The climate is tropical, with the monsoon season lasting from May to early November, followed by a dry season from December to April. The population is estimated at approximately 13.3 million, with an estimated growth rate of 1.8% annually (2004). The capital, Phnom Penh, has a population of about 1.5 million people.

Cambodia was under the Hindu kingdom of Funan for the first six centuries CE until it was overthrown by the Chen-la Khmers in the sixth century CE. The Angkor kingdom dominated from the ninth to the fourteenth centuries during which the Khmer genius created such architectural wonders as the temple complex of Angkor Wat. The Thai armies sacked and captured Angkor by 1431. The extensive Cambodian state authority gradually dwindled as it gave in to Thai and Annamite onslaughts. It began its modern phase in 1863 when it became a French protectorate. Attempts at revolt were nipped in the bud while the institution of the Cambodian monarchy was retained as a shield against popular upsurge. King Norodom signed the treaty of 1884, which effectively placed the entire internal administration of Cambodia in the hands of France. In 1887, Cambodia became part of the wider Indochinese Union. During World War II, the French Vichy regime retained hold of Cambodia, followed briefly by an "independent" government with Son Ngoc Thanh as prime minister. The French reestablished their colonial rule with the end of Japanese occupation. As an anticolonial struggle ensued, King Norodom Sihanouk took the lead in negotiating independence that was announced on November 9, 1953, and reaffirmed by the Geneva Agreement of 1954. As Cambodia got entangled in the US war in Vietnam, the Right (alarmed at what they saw as pro-Communist, pro-Vietnamese foreign policy) organized the *coup d'état* led by General Lon Nol in March 1970. Lon Nol in turn was overthrown by Pol Pot's Khmer Rouge in April 1975. The genocidal policy of Khmer Rouge provoked Vietnamese intervention on December 25, 1978, and the People's Republic of Kampuchea (PRK) led by Heng Samrin was formed. It was renamed State of Cambodia (SOC) in April 1989. Vietnam began its withdrawal in September 1989. Meanwhile, Pol Pot's rebel Government of Democratic Kampuchea renamed itself the Coalition Government of Democratic Kampuchea (CGDK) in 1982, bringing together various factions (including the Khmer Rouge, Funcinpec, and Khmer People's National Liberation Front).

A transitional period under United Nations Transitional Authority in Cambodia (UNTAC) following the Paris Accord of October 23, 1991, culminated in national elections in May 1993. Norodom Sihanouk was reinstated as monarch in September 1993. He helped arrange a power-sharing agreement between Norodom Ranariddh of Funcinpec and Hun Sen of the Cambodian People's Party (CPP). This arrangement, however, unraveled when the latter overthrew Ranariddh in July 1997. Following the second national elections in July 1998, a coalition government was formed in November with Hun Sen of CPP again as prime minister. In the July 2003 general elections, the CPP won but failed to win a clear majority. This delayed coalition with Funcinpec by one year (July 2004) when Hun Sen became prime minister again. Following Norodom Sihanouk's abdication, Norodom Sihamoni, his son, became king in October 2004.

During the colonial period, Cambodia emerged as a supplier of primary products (including rice and rubber). It had poor social and physical infrastructure. Education and health were neglected. The initial plans sought to remedy this. The economy remained primarily agricultural (more than 70%). Cambodia initially received foreign aid from the United States (1955 until 1964, when it refused US assistance), and then the country started receiving aid from Vietnam and the Soviet bloc in the 1980s and aid from the United Nations in the 1990s. The Khmer Rouge period (1975–1979) left about 1 million dead and devastated the economy by destroying existing economic institutions. After 1979, the centrally planned economy faced the ill effects of an international embargo. In 1988, it began introducing economic reforms. When a new constitution was introduced in 1993, the right to private property was restored, and market forces were allowed to operate. A new investment law and reforms in the taxation system and the banking system were introduced. The arrival of UNTAC accelerated the economy. Investments registered a fall due to the 1997 Asian economic crisis. In terms of the human development index, Cambodia's gross domestic product (GDP) growth (percentage change) fell from 6.9% in 1999 to 4.5% in 2002 but was slated to rise to 5.5% according to ADB projections. Cambodia ranks 130th in UNDP's list of 177 nations. Life expectancy at birth is about 57 years. Industrial growth has been led by growth in garment manufacturing. Trade relies on export of light manufacturing and natural resources and the import of petroleum products, transport vehicles, machinery, and consumer durables. Tourism is an important foreign exchange earner, and it got a boost when the open skies policy was initiated. Cambodia's growth prospects brightened when it became a member of the Association of Southeast Asian Nations in 1999 and a member of the World Trade Organization in 2003. But real growth would depend on improvement of infrastructure and greater investment in health and education.

UDAI BHANU SINGH

See also Association of Southeast Asian Nations (ASEAN); Drug Trade; Drug Use; Khmer Rouge; Southeast Asia: History and Economic Development; Southeast Asia: International Relations

References and Further Reading

Albritton, R. B. "Cambodia in 2003: On the Road to Democratic Consolidation." *Asian Survey* 44, no. 1 (2004).
Bruce St. John, Ronald. "The Political Economy of the Royal Government of Cambodia." *Contemporary Southeast Asia* 17, no.3 (1995).
Martin, Marie Alexandrine. *Cambodia: A Shattered Society.* Translated by Mark W. McLeod. Berkeley, CA: University of California Press, 1989.
Kevin, Tony. "Cambodia and Southeast Asia." *Australian Journal of International Affairs* 54, no.1 (2000).
Osborne, Milton. *Sihanouk: Prince of Light, Prince of Darkness.* New South Wales, Australia: Allen & Unwin, 1994.
Ott, Marvin C. "Cambodia: Between Hope and Despair." *Current History* 96, no. 614 (1997).
Vickery, Michael. *Kampuchea: Politics, Economics, and Society.* Boulder, CO: Lynne Rienner, 1986.

CAMEROON

Shaped like a slightly distorted triangle, Cameroon is located in the transitional zone between West and Central Africa. It is bordered on the west by Nigeria, Lake Chad to the north, Chad and the Central African Republic to the east, the People's Republic of the Congo to the south and southeast, Gabon and Equatorial Guinea to the south, and the Atlantic Ocean to the southwest. The Cameroon Mountain, which reaches a height of 13,350 feet/4,069 meters at its peak near the coast, is the highest mountain in West Africa and the most dominant physical feature in the country. Temperatures in Cameroon range from an average of 68 degrees Fahrenheit/20 degrees Celsius around the lower slopes of the Cameroon Mountain to more than 90 degrees Fahrenheit/32 degrees Celsius in the extreme North. Rainfall exhibits a similar disparity, with an average annual rainfall of 400 inches/1,016 centimeters around the coastal areas to less than 62 inches/157.5 centimeters near the northern town of Maroua. The vegetation follows a similar pattern to both the temperature and rainfall, ranging from a dense forested region in the South to the dry Sahel region near Lake Chad.

During the European colonization of Africa, Cameroon became a German colony. However, German rule in Cameroon was short-lived. At the end of World War I, the former German colony was partitioned between France and Britain, to be administered as League of Nations Mandates and later as United Nations Trusteeships. France got four-fifths of the territory, while Britain got the rest, consisting of two noncontiguous territories along Nigeria's eastern border. On October 1, 1961, the former French trusteeship, which had gained its independence on January 1, 1960, reunited with the southern section of the British territory known as the British Southern Cameroons to form the Federal Republic of Cameroon with Ahmadou Ahidjo as its first president. Under the new federal constitution, the former French territory became East Cameroon, while the British Southern Cameroons were renamed West Cameroon. On September 1, 1966, Cameroon became a one-party state when Ahidjo seized control of the country. This development was followed on May 20,

1972, with the dissolution of the federation in favor of a unitary state called the United Republic of Cameroon. The creation of a unitary state was the culmination of Ahidjo's objective of creating a strong centralized state with him as the ultimate authority.

Ahidjo remained Cameroon's only head of state until his voluntary retirement in November 1982. Paul Biya, the prime minister, became Ahidjo's constitutional successor. Although President Biya initially promised to introduce political reforms in Cameroon, not much changed. In fact, apart from the symbolic change of the single party's name from the (CNU) to the Cameroon People's Democratic Movement (CPDM), Biya adopted the same repressive policies and constitutional arrangements that had allowed his predecessor to stay in power for more than two decades. Because of domestic unrest and external pressures from Western industrialized nations following the end of the Cold War and the collapse of the Soviet Union in the early 1990s, Biya was forced to institute political reforms, including the legalization of a multiparty system. Even so, Biya has managed to remain in power, with the CPDM as the dominant party in parliament. In fact, support for many of the opposition parties, including the Social Democratic Front (SDF), the Cameroon Democratic Union (UDC), and the *Unions des Populations du Cameroun* (UPC), all of which were critical in forcing Biya to institute reform, has fizzled as many opposition leaders have been co-opted by the regime. Nevertheless, the liberalization of political space has created opportunity for greater political discourse, including the emergence of various Anglophone groups that are highly critical of the way the English-speaking minority has been ignored and marginalized by the majority French-speaking Cameroonians since reunification in 1961.

For more than two decades after independence, Cameroon was seen as the model state for positive economic growth in Africa. President Ahidjo and his successor pursued the policy of planned liberalism (renamed communal liberalism under Biya), which advocated significant government control over resource allocation as the most effective way to deal with poverty and achieve rapid economic development. The country has a varied and rich base of natural resources, and, accordingly, agriculture remains the most important sector of the economy, employing more than two-thirds of the labor force. After agriculture comes the services sector, which employs about 20% of the country's labor resources. The overwhelming majority of farm workers in Cameroon are women, most of whom produce the bulk of the food crops consumed locally and exported to neighboring countries. Most men who work in

agriculture are engaged in the production of cash crops (cocoa, cotton, coffee, palm kernels, and bananas). Since petroleum became an important export commodity in the mid-1980s, the rate of urbanization has accelerated as many rural inhabitants have abandoned their jobs in the rural areas in search of opportunities for economic advancement in the urban sectors.

Cameroon's real gross domestic product (GDP), measured at average 1995 prices, was $6,319 million US dollars in 1980, but by 2000, it had increased to $10,044 million. Although real GDP grew at a healthy rate of 8.5% between 1975 and 1984, it registered at a rate of –0.1% during the period 1985–1989. Since then, there has been some recovery resulting primarily from contributions of the petroleum subsector.

Cameroon's industrial sector, which includes mining, manufacturing, construction, and power, employed about 9% of the labor force in 1990. In the late 1990s, this sector was accounting for as much as 18.6% of the country's GDP. Mining, although it employs only 0.05% of Cameroon's labor resources, has become the most important source of income for the central government in Yaoundé. Cameroon also has large reserves of natural gas, bauxite, iron ore, uranium, and tin. These resources, however, remain largely undeveloped.

Manufacturing, which employs about 7% of the labor force and accounts for as much as 10% of the GDP, is concerned primarily with the processing of both domestically produced commodities (petroleum refining and processing of agricultural products) and imported raw materials (notably alumina imported from Guinea and processed at the aluminum smelter plant at Edea). This sector (based on value of output) is dominated by food products (16.2%); beverages (13.1%); petroleum and coal products (13.0%); and wood products (12.6%).

Trade is very important to the Cameroon economy. Within the country, trade flows from south to north, and vice versa, and from rural to urban areas. Cattle, beans, groundnuts (peanuts), and several cereals move from the north to the south; kolanuts, cassava, yams, and plantains move from the south to the north; and maize (corn), several varieties of yams, chickens, and other food products move from the middle-belt to other parts of the country.

Cameroon's most important import trade partners are France, Nigeria, Germany, and the United States. Most of the country's export trade is carried out with Italy, France, Spain, and the Netherlands. Major exports include petroleum and petroleum products, timber and timber products, cocoa beans, and coffee.

Cameroon is a member of the Franc Zone, which includes most of France's former colonies in Africa.

Before the euro became the common currency for the European Union (EU), metropolitan France and its many overseas territories belonged to the Franc Zone. The (CFA) franc is the currency of the African Franc Zone countries, which include Cameroon, and is issued by the *Banque Centrale des États de l'Afrique de L'ouest* (BCEAO) in the West African monetary area and the *Banque des États de l'Afrique Centrale* (BEAC) for the Central African monetary area. After the EU achieved monetary union and national currencies (including the French franc) were withdrawn, the CFA franc became officially pegged to the euro at a fixed exchange rate.

Cameroon has yet to provide itself with a transport system that can effectively meet its requirements for moving goods and people—food crops and other commodities from the rural agricultural areas to the urban areas, as well as labor resources to where they are needed most. At reunification in 1961, the government made improving road, rail, port, and air infrastructures a major goal of national policy. By the mid-1980s, however, the country only had about sixty-two thousand kilometers of road, only 2,500 kilometers of which are paved. Poor road conditions make it difficult for farmers to transport their commodities to markets in the urban centers.

Cameroon has been served quite well in the past by air links, although Cameroon Airlines (CAMAIR), the national airline, has encountered a lot of management and financial problems in the last several years. Several international carriers, however, continue to provide air transport services to Cameroonians traveling out of the country. International airports can be found at Douala, Yaoundé, Garoua, and Bafoussam.

Douala remains the country's oldest and most important seaport and is responsible for more than 95% of traffic. It is the primary port of exit for goods originating in several countries in central Africa. Smaller ports deal in more specialized cargo: Limbe (petroleum); Kribi (timber and cocoa); and Garoua (cotton).

The government dominates telephone, television, radio, and telegraph services. Cameroonians, however, have access to foreign broadcasts, including the BBC, VOA, Radio France, and several other services from around the world. Television, which was first broadcast in 1985, now reaches virtually all parts of the country. Although the government has been making an effort to provide viewers with locally produced programs, foreign programs remain very popular.

In general, economic growth and development have not been as rapid as most Cameroonians had expected at reunification in 1961. Many problems remain, even in 2005, and particularly vexing to many Cameroonians is the relatively high level of poverty that exists in the country, especially among women, youth, and rural inhabitants. Many Anglophones remain quite frustrated about their economic and social conditions and blame the highly centralized administrative system for making it very difficult for them to improve their welfare. Despite these difficulties, many Cameroonians remain optimistic and believe that the deepening and institutionalization of democracy would provide them with the wherewithal to deal with poverty and improve their living conditions. Hence, many of them, including those in the Diaspora, are working very hard to improve governance and public accountability through the deepening and institutionalization of democracy.

JOSEPH TAKOUGANG

References and Further Reading

Ahidjo, Ahmadou. *The Political Philosophy of Ahmadou Ahidjo.* Monaco: Paul Bory Publishers, 1968.
Biya, Paul. *Communal Liberalism.* London and Reading: Macmillan Publishers, 1987.
DeLancey, Mark W. *Cameroon: Dependence and Independence.* Boulder, CO, and San Francisco: Westview Press, 1989.
Fonge, Fuabeh P. *Modernization Without Development in Africa.* Trenton, NJ: Africa World Press, 1997.
Johnson, Willard R. *The Cameroon Federation,* Princeton, NJ: Princeton University Press, 1970.
Joseph, Richard A., ed. *Gaullist Africa: Cameroon Under Ahmadou Ahidjo.* Enugu, Nigeria: Fourth Dimensions Publishers, 1978.
Kofele-Kale, Ndiva, ed. *An African Experiment in Nation Building: The Bilingual Cameroon Republic Since Reunification.* Boulder, CO: Westview Press, 1980.
LeVine, Victor T. *The Cameroon Federal Republic.* Ithaca, NY and London: Cornell University Press, 1971.
———. *The Cameroons: From Mandate to Independence.* Berkeley, CA, and Los Angeles: University of California Press, 1964.
Mbaku, J. M., and J. Takougang, eds. *The Leadership Challenge in Africa: Cameroon under Paul Biya.* Trenton, NJ: Africa World Press, 2004.
Takougang, Joseph, and Milton Krieger. *African State and Society in the 1990s: Cameroon's Political Crossroads.* Boulder, CO: Westview Press, 1998.

CAMP DAVID ACCORDS (1979)

For thirty years, Israel remained isolated from and at war with its Arab neighbors. Besides the 1948 war of independence, three other wars were fought between Israel and various Arab states. In 1956, the Egyptian President Gamal Abdel Nasser, who hoped to become the major leader of the Arab world, nationalized the Suez Canal. Israel joined England and France to invade Egypt and retake the canal. In 1967, the Six

Day War erupted when Egypt and Jordan blockaded the Red Sea port of Elat. Israel found itself at war with Egypt, Lebanon, Syria, Jordan, and Iraq and rapidly defeated all opponents. From its neighbors, Israel then seized territory, including Jerusalem that Israel declared to be its capital. From Egypt, Israel took the whole Sinai Peninsula. In these confrontations, the Soviet Union backed the Arab states, and Israel found its allies in the West, particularly the United States. Thus, the Middle East question became linked to the Cold War. In 1970, Nasser died, and Anwar Sadat, a more conservative leader, replaced him. In 1972, Sadat ordered troops to attack Israel once more on the most holy Jewish holiday—*Yom Kippur*, the Day of Atonement.

With the surprise attack, Egypt made initial gains, but in the end the borders stayed about the same—Israel still kept the Sinai. Both sides had significant casualties, and Sadat's brother, a pilot, died in the war. Furthermore, Sadat was dissatisfied with Moscow's aid and ceased military relations with the Soviets. Sadat was now ready to make peace with Israel. In a dramatic speech in 1977, he announced to the Egyptian parliament that he would go anywhere to make peace, even to Jerusalem. Other Arab leaders condemned Sadat, but Israel was ready to welcome him, the first of any Arab leader to visit. The two countries had been at war since 1948. Israel's leaders and people enthusiastically greeted Sadat when he arrived in November 1977. The prime minister of Israel, Menachem Begin, made a return trip to Ismaila, Egypt.

Begin, leader of the right-wing Likud coalition, always maintained a hard line when dealing with Palestinian issues. However, Israel public opinion forced him to deal with Sadat, but succeeding negotiations reached a deadlock. American president James Carter, anxious that this opportunity for peace not be lost, offered his services as an "honest broker." He invited both Begin and Sadat to the presidential retreat at Camp David, Maryland, to work out their differences.

Meetings began on September 5, 1978, and twelve days of difficult negotiations followed. Sadat wanted the Sinai returned, and Begin wanted to break Israel's isolation, but each wanted more. Sadat's position in the Arab world demanded that he work on the Palestinian question as well, although some Arab extremists would allow absolutely no dealing with Israel. Begin needed recognition of Israeli security with all Arab capitals and retention of land captured in its 1967 Six-Day War. Two agreements were hammered out. The first was a draft peace treaty between Cairo and Jerusalem; the second was a wider proposal for a general peace between Israel and the Arab nations of the entire regions. In the end, only the basic issues were resolved. Israel left the Sinai and Cairo, and Jerusalem exchanged ambassadors.

The preamble to the treaties stated that United Nations Security Council Resolutions 242 and 338 served as the basis for resolution; the preamble also noted among other factors that the Middle East was the "birthplace of the great religions," that it had faced four wars in thirty years, and that the people of the region "yearn for peace" as was evidenced by the enthusiastic reception the people of Israel and Egypt gave Sadat and Begin on their visits to those countries. The "opportunity for peace . . . must not be lost," the preamble added.

The document also stated that a comprehensive peace required the guarantee of sovereignty territorial integrity and independence of the countries of the region and their right to live in peace as well as have secure and recognized borders without threats of force. Cooperation of the nations of the region in promoting economic development and security would lead to regional stability; measures such as demilitarized zones, international peacekeepers, and monitoring could be used to ensure peace in the region.

According to the Egyptian–Israeli agreement, Israeli forces were to gradually leave the Sinai desert over a period of three years after the treaty and return the entire area to Cairo. Israeli ships would be able to use the Suez Canal. The second treaty, which was more vague, stated that Israel would recognize a Palestinian state on the West bank of the Jordan River and the Gaza strip, areas that Israel occupied since the Six Day War. Jerusalem would also partially withdraw it troops from those areas over a three-year period in preparation for final peace talks. The two parties signed the peace treaty on March 26, 1979, and Israel withdrew from the Sinai and honored the first treaty. However, the country did not act on the second.

The accords, however, were a remarkable breakthrough. Begin and Sadat jointly received the Nobel Peace Prize for 1978. Moslem and Arab extremists regarded Sadat as a traitor and on October 6, 1981, members of Egyptian Islamic *Jihad*, a Muslim extremist group, assassinated him while he was presiding over a military ceremony commemorating the *Yom Kippur* War. However, despite difficulties and disagreements, diplomatic relations between Israel and Egypt continued. In 1994, Jordan became the second Arab state to recognize Israel. Sadat was one of a long line of statesmen and spiritual leaders—Henry IV of France (1910), Mohandas Gandhi (1948), and Yizhak Rabin (1995)—who were assassinated by religious fanatics because they tried to accomplish the difficult task of bringing peace and toleration between different religious groups that shared the same territory.

FREDERICK B. CHARY

See also Arab–Israeli Wars (1948, 1956, 1967, 1973); Israel; Middle East: International Relations; Palestine

References and Further Reading

Friedlander, Melvin A. *Sadat and Begin: The Domestic Politics of Peacemaking.* Boulder, CO: Westview, 1983.

Hurst, David. *Sadat.* London: Faber and Faber, 1981.

Kamil, Muhammad Ibrahim. *The Camp David Accords: A Testimony.* London: Routledge & Kegan, Paul, 1986.

Silver, Eric. *Begin: The Haunted Prophet.* New York: Random House, 1984.

Smith, Charles D. *Palestine and the Arab-Israeli Conflict*, 3d ed. New York: St. Martin's, 1996.

Telhami, Shibley. *Power and Leadership in International Bargaining: The Path to the Camp David Accords.* New York: Columbia, 1990.

CANADIAN INTERNATIONAL DEVELOPMENT AGENCY (CIDA)

The Canadian International Development Agency (CIDA) is the federal agency charged with planning and implementing most of Canada's international development programs. Similar in scope and agenda to the US Agency for International Development (USAID), CIDA strives to reduce poverty in the Third World to form a more secure, equitable, and prosperous world. After World War II, most Canadian aid to the developing world, channeled through the Department of External Affairs, took the form of contributions to the United Nations and its agencies. In 1959, the Department of Trade and Commerce, cognizant of the growing need for foreign aid in the developing world, established the Economic and Technical Assistance Bureau to coordinate Canada's efforts to stimulate Third World development. In 1960, the Economic and Technical Assistance Bureau was transferred to the Department of External Affairs and renamed the External Aid Office. Given the rapid expansion of foreign aid by the Canadian government during the 1960s, coupled with the increasing number of underdeveloped African nations gaining their independence from Europe at the same time, the Canadian government created CIDA in 1968 to replace the External Aid Office. Currently, CIDA administers 80% of the Canadian foreign aid budget, while the rest of the foreign aid budget is administered by the Department of Finance and the Department of Foreign Affairs, which had previously been known as the Department of External Affairs.

CIDA, which supports projects in more than 150 countries, works in partnership with developing countries; Canadian organizations, institutions, and businesses; and international organizations and agencies. Like many development agencies around the world, CIDA is working in cooperation with other aid agencies to foster development in the Third World. CIDA's development agenda follows the guidelines established by world leaders at the September 2000 UN-sponsored Millennium Summit, which called for eradicating extreme poverty and hunger; achieving universal primary education; promoting gender equality and empowering women; reducing child mortality; improving maternal health; combating the human immunodeficiency virus (HIV)/acquired immunodeficiency syndrome (AIDS), malaria, and other diseases; promoting sustainable environmental policies; and working in greater cooperation with international aid agencies to foster development in the Third World.

CIDA programs and projects have benefited thousands of people in many developing countries. In Tanzania, CIDA has helped a nongovernmental organization establish and operate nine clinics. Since 2000, almost five hundred thousand people have visited the CIDA-supported facilities. In Senegal, a CIDA-supported program has supported a network of savings and loans institutions that have facilitated the availability of credit available to the rural poor. The financial institutions are self-sustaining and have benefited more than eighty thousand people.

Through the International Youth Internship Program, CIDA has sent thousands of recent college graduates, between the ages of nineteen and thirty, to developing countries to gain work experience in their field of study while simultaneously assisting in international development programs. In 2004, the Canadian government unveiled the Canada Corps to increase Canadian development efforts in the Third World. The first Canada Corps mission was a team of five hundred volunteers who observed elections in the Ukraine. In addition, CIDA's Industrial Cooperation Program provides financial support to Canadian companies interested in investing in the developing world.

MICHAEL R. HALL

See also Poverty: Impact on Development; United Nations Development Program (UNDP); United States Agency for International Development (USAID)

References and Further Reading

Braatz, Susan M. *The Role of Development Assistance in Forestry: The Forestry Policies and Programs of the*

World Bank, the US Agency for International Development, and the Canadian International Development Agency. London: International Institute for Environment and Development, 1985.

Canadian International Development Agency. *A Developing World.* Ottawa, Canada: Canadian International Development Agency, 1987.

Gillies, David William. *Commerce Over Conscience?: Aid-Trade Links in Canada's Foreign Aid Programme.* Montreal, Canada: McGill University, 1987.

Kanbur, S. M. Ravi, Todd Sandler, Kevin M. Morrison, and Ravi Kanbur. *The Future of Development Assistance: Common Pools and International Public Goods.* Washington, DC: Overseas Development Council, 1999.

van Belle, Douglas, Jean-Sebastien Rioux, and David M. Potter. *Media, Bureaucracies, and Foreign Aid: A Comparative Analysis of the United States, the United Kingdom, Canada, France, and Japan.* Gordonville, VA: Palgrave MacMillan, 2004.

CAPITAL FLIGHT

Strictly speaking, "capital flight" means the rapid outflow of capital from a country or region after investors lose confidence in the country's economic prospects. In an aggravated situation, domestic residents will anticipate the devaluation of the home currency and therefore will convert their savings into foreign assets. Their expectations will be self-fulfilling because this causes the exchange rate of the abandoned domestic currency to plummet. Since the debt crisis of the 1980s in the developing world, the term "flight" came to be applied more broadly to capital outflows from residents of developing countries.

Capital flight occurs when domestic investors fear their government would give precedence to its foreign capital rather than its domestic debt obligations. Other causes include the loss of confidence in adequate foreign debt management and domestic economic policies or the increased country-specific risks of legal and political instability. The situation contrasts with the nationalization period, during which foreign direct investments are at risk, but domestically owned assets are considered safe from expropriation.

Governments usually try to stop capital flight by devaluating the domestic currency. If this succeeds, the fleeing "hot money" returns shortly. If not, it will remain abroad until conditions improve—in this respect, it is a kind of classical financial speculation. Another way to tackle this symptom—though this has sometimes caused financial crises on its own—is the installation of currency boards. Countries commit to converting domestic currency at fixed exchange rates, but to make this commitment credible, the currency board should hold a backup of gold and foreign reserves of at least 100% of the domestic

currency issued. If capital flight occurs, the supply of domestic currency shrinks, causing interest rates to rise automatically.

A currency board can also put pressure on the financial institutions if interest rates rise sharply. If local inflation remains higher than that of the country to which the currency is pegged, the domestic currency may become overvalued and uncompetitive. Because of the fragility of banking systems in the emerging market, the currency may not withstand this regulation, and furthermore, these boards cannot act as a central bank, being a lender of last resort to stop bank panic. Argentina's decision during its crisis in 2002 to devalue the peso in spite of adopting a currency board a decade earlier showed the vulnerability of such solution, which did not prove to be a panacea.

Capital flight does not necessarily mean that money is leaving the country. It also occurs if investors, both foreign and domestic, suddenly lower their valuation of all domestic assets. The extraction and expatriation of profits by foreign firms are other forms of capital flight. For instance, 10% of Nigeria's petroleum revenue is paid to the foreign oil companies as royalties, and the companies reinvest their profit in Europe. The driving force behind these outflows is generally a perceived decline in the return or an increase in the risk of the long-term assets held in Nigeria. This flight capital is held offshore until conditions improve, such as in the case of Mexico in the 1990s.

Capital flight is among the risks the globalized financial markets pose. Foreigners make portfolio investments whose flows are easily reversible. If these investors panic, they can sell their assets in to avoid capital losses. Due to the increased international mobility of capital, the portfolio investment of foreign investors is much more dangerous than foreign direct investment; foreigners are much more likely to try to get rid of their shares at the first sign of falling profits. Mere suspicion is enough to make the "growing bubble" of high investment expectations burst, as seen in the East Asian financial crisis that started in 1997. Thus, the vicious circle of capital flight and currency instability destabilizes the economy.

The spreading of such investor pessimism to other countries' markets, called "contagion effects," is another negative implication of excessive capital mobility. Neoliberal financial reform increases the vulnerability of the countries because it abolishes many of the economic boundaries that separate national economies. Increasing the linkages among national economies also increases the possibility that one country will fall victim to financial and macroeconomic instability that originates elsewhere.

Because investors tend to view developing countries in an undifferentiated fashion, they will often pull out of every country in a market if they perceive problems in one. This "guilt by association" contributed to serious difficulties in Brazil following Mexico's financial crisis. The Asian crisis was itself a case of contagion from Thailand to the Philippines, Malaysia, South Korea, and Indonesia. Events in Asia in 1997 exemplify the way that a vicious cycle of capital flight and currency depreciation can culminate in national financial crises.

The potential for capital flight, made possible by the removal of controls on capital movements, often prevents governments from promoting progressive economic and social policy. If foreign investment is undertaken for the sole purpose of tax evasion, it leads to capital and tax revenue shortage in the source country as well. Most of such capital flight comes from corrupt financial transactions linked to criminal activity, such as drug trafficking, racketeering, and extortion. Moreover, tax authorities in developing countries seldom filter these transfers for money laundering. Great capital flights often emerge from corrupt county leaders, dictators, and military rulers like Mobutu Sese, Haile Selassie, Nicolae Ceausescu, and the Marcos family. Another cause of flight can be the threat of nationalization, sudden regime changes, or antiminority violence and ethnic tensions as in Russia, Indonesia, and Zimbabwe.

In larger terms, capital flight refers not only to financial but also to physical or human capital. Human capital is the economic potential contained in a person, some endowed at birth and the rest received from the product of training, education, and experience. In broader terms, capital flight is the stock of manpower available for an enterprise or economy. Human capital consists also of intellectual capital; thus, its flight could mean the "flight of intellectuals" to the wealthier nations. This is known also as "brain drain." Although significant outflows of human capital will likely have a negative effect on economic growth, feedback effects of returning money may actually stimulate economic growth. For instance, the money sent home from the United States by Latin American immigrants could be bigger than the total FDI going to this region. In addition, the "flight of intellectual capital" causes the outflow of intellectual materials, such as information, technology, experience, and intellectual property, that might otherwise be used for development. One example is the Western ownership of copyrights to music from developing countries.

Ironically, developing country leaders court foreign investors to provide the necessary financial capital, but they do not try to court the expertise or retain human capital that will develop and manage the investments and resources within the region. "Brain drain" also leads to technological gaps, forcing developing nations to export raw materials and also their workforce. For instance, Africa, with a population of 800 million, was always a producer and exporter of muscle power and a consumer of technology by the import of refined materials. The payment of profits to overseas shareholders is a kind of capital flight leading to an increase in the level of poverty and thus political instability. This, in turn, creates a market for the importation of arms, wherein the remaining capital goes to arms-exporting developed nations.

Foreign direct investment coming from countries like South Korea, Mexico, Taiwan, and Malaysia as domestic manufacturers invest in export-substituting or strategic plans in the European Union and the United States, or shifting of domestic assets by local inventors for the sake of portfolio diversification into more liquid and better foreign markets, may not be considered capital flight. Liberalization and development of domestic capital markets can reverse the flow.

Methods of Capital Flight

There are several ways in which investors and corporations can circumvent official controls and transfer funds abroad illicitly. The most common method involves "misinvoicing" based on trade either by underinvoicing exports or overinvoicing imports. Other ways are the overseas transfers of unexisting or overstated franchises, loans, and license payments to associated companies abroad—frequently, these are virtual companies in tax havens in such areas as Cyprus and the Cayman islands. Bank transfers can also be used to avoid official recording systems, particularly by making use of increasingly complex financial derivatives in offshore financial centers to avoid capital controls.

Transfer Volumes

The International Monetary Fund (IMF) estimates that citizens of developing countries amassed about $250 billion worth of foreign assets between 1975 and 1985 (compared to a total foreign debt of $800 billion). Although Mexico had the largest holding ($40 billion to $50 billion), Venezuela's and Argentina's holdings were a larger proportion of national income, nearly equaling their foreign debt. A similar situation was in Indonesia, Nigeria, the Philippines, and even South Korea. Although it is difficult to estimate the volume of capital flight, the IMF and World Bank have stated that the stock of Sub-Saharan flight capital in 1990 was equivalent to 39% of the region's total real private wealth. The most heavily indebted nations, Nigeria and Sudan, send out more than 100% of their gross national product (GNP). The ratios were 10% for Latin America, 3% for South Asia, 6% for East Asia, and 39% for the Middle East, of which capital could have meant a serious investment if kept at home. The Overseas Development Institute found higher rates for 1994. The outflow of flight capital as a proportion of annual export earnings was 78% in Argentina, 9% in Brazil, 16% in China, 59% in Ghana, 41% in Indonesia, and 9% in Malaysia. The size of these outflows in relation to export earnings is clearly a source of concern.

Methods of Overcoming the Causes of Capital Flight

The best treatment targets capital flight's causes rather than its symptoms and effects. This involves improving domestic economic and financial conditions, implementing sound macroeconomic policies, maintaining low levels of debt and possibly high levels of growth, and creating functional and broad capital markets, as well as solid institutions. Smaller steps include the establishment of independent Central Banks to stop extraordinary access of government officials to public funds, thus reducing corruption and embezzlement. Capital flight can be stemmed and reversed through enhancing cooperation between developed and developing nations and between the commercial and tax authorities of the source and destination countries. Some suggest imposing international sanctions on depository safe-haven countries like Switzerland, but this would hit the Swiss economy and its lending capacity because one-third of the capital flights would end up there.

On an international scale, new tax treaties or tax harmonization by encouraging sales taxes and relying less on taxes on interest and profits, as well as exchange of data on income paid to foreigners, would help close the loopholes in the international taxation system that facilitate capital flight and other illicit funds transfers. Yet another option is to reduce the tax benefits of capital flight offered by rich countries. This would require greater economic stability and institutional certainty in the source countries and more rigorous tax enforcement and cooperation in

the destination states, but offshore tax havens and international competition for capital make new tax treaties unlikely.

To counteract capital flight, governments impose restrictions on capital mobility abroad through capital controls that limit the transfer of foreign investors' profit or the domestic residents' investments abroad. Capital control, as well as flight, is not characteristic only of developing countries. Many developed counties imposed them until the early 1990s, when most of them liberalized almost completely their capital markets.

The pattern was more mixed in developing countries. Latin American countries imposed capital controls during the debt crisis of the 1980s and then scrapped most of them afterward. Asian countries began to loosen their widespread capital controls in the 1980s, a process accelerated during the 1990s. Capital controls encouraged black markets for foreign currency and ultimately failed to keep money at home. They had also unwanted side effects of deterring foreign investment. The Asian capital flight of the late 1990s revived interest in this method. There was also discussion of the introduction of a "Tobin tax" on short-term capital movements.

Governments can also limit capital flight by keeping domestic currency undervalued relative to other currencies or by keeping local interest rates high. Developing countries in particular can promote the development of domestic financial markets that offer investors a "safe" alternative to foreign assets.

Small countries with limited domestic financial markets and currencies that are more vulnerable to external shocks can hold a portfolio of foreign assets and try to diversify their exports over the longer term. Many groups, such as the so-called Asian Tigers, have been successful at this, and have promoted export-oriented growth combined with technological development that make them preferable targets for capital inflows.

In the end, the most practical strategy for reducing capital flight is for governments to pursue sound fiscal and monetary debt relief and commercial policies guaranteed by international financial organizations that minimize the need for large changes in exchange rates and that restore confidence.

LASZLO KOCSIS

References and Further Reading

Cardoso, Eliana, and Rudiger Dornbusch. "Foreign Private Capital Flows." In *Handbook of Development Economics*, edited by T. N. Srinivasan and Hollis Chenery. 1989.
Eaton, Jonathan. "Public Debt Guarantees and Private Capital Flight." *World Bank Economic Review* 1 (1987).

Kahn, Moshin S., and Nadeem Ul Haque. "Capital Flight from Developing Countries." *Finance and Development* 24 (March 1987).

Kindleberger, Charles P. Manias. *Panics and Crashes: A History of Financial Crisis.* 1989.

Lessard, Donald L., and John Williamson eds. *Capital Flight and Third World Debt.* 1987.

CAPITALIST ECONOMIC MODEL

The capitalist economic model is the foundation for the modern global economy. Alternative economic models, including communism and socialism, have been proposed and tested throughout history. However, the capitalist model has survived all others. The Union of Soviet Socialist Republics disbanded into its constituent nation-states, which promptly reverted to the capitalist economic models that had made their former enemies so prosperous. Even the Socialist bastion of the People's Republic of China has recognized the need to allow capitalist activity in large regions of the country to provide the financial resources that could help the party remain in power. Capitalism now reigns in all but a few nations, although its form varies substantially across countries. The US model is among the purest forms of capitalism, relegating economic decisions to the marketplace in the vast majority of cases. Western European nations, believing that the unfettered capitalist model is too harsh to the poor and the unfortunate, have adopted a more "caring" version of capitalism, in which market forces are tempered with government policies that foster the redistribution of wealth and blunt capitalism's sharper edges. The Japanese model provides a more pervasive role for government, owing to social factors that tend to rank the group above the individual. Developing nations feature other forms of capitalism. In such models, the political and economic elite tends to hold sway over economic policies, with the effect of exaggerating the natural inequities inherent in the free market.

Tenets of Capitalism

The capitalist economic model is based on the free market. Individuals are assumed to make decisions according to their own set of incentives. If individuals may make decisions freely, then each economic transaction implies that both parties must be better off having executed it than they had been before making the trade. So long as this economic activity does not generate significant side effects on others in the economy and as long as significant competition exists, it is also the case that when individuals act in their own self-interest, they simultaneously maximize the economic well-being of the society.

Historical Roots

Free market economics predates capitalism, which properly developed from the events accompanying the industrial revolution. Before that period, the main factors of production were land, labor, and know-how. With the industrial revolution, however, capital became a critical resource for efficient production. Traditionally, "capital" referred to physical capital—the buildings and machinery that enhanced productivity. However, the financial sector adopted the term in the twentieth century to designate the financial resources that were necessary for modern economic activity.

The original capitalists were wealthy individuals who were able to transform their financial assets into the physical capital necessary for production. It became difficult for individuals without capital to compete with factory owners. Because capital was so concentrated in the hands of a relatively small group of people, capitalists had much more market power than any individual worker; this advantage allowed the capitalists to exploit workers at extremely low wages, while simultaneously reaping large returns on their capital investments. Social reactions to this unequal distribution of economic power varied across nations and time periods. One school of thought, which encompasses socialism and communism, rejected the capitalists and the market mechanism that made them rich, preferring to place trust in the hands of a benevolent government. A second reaction was the formation of labor unions to counteract the monopoly power of employers. Later, governments became involved in the regulation of labor markets and workplace environments to provide further protection for individuals.

Modern Capitalists

No longer are huge sums of personal wealth required for a person to become a capitalist. Nearly two centuries of prosperity generated by the capitalist global economy have generated a new breed of capitalist. Rather than investing their personal fortunes in a single economic entity, middle class investors become capitalists through their stock market investment. Stock markets allow firms to raise *financial capital* by issuing shares of the company. Investors purchase those shares, thereby laying claim to a portion of any profits generated by the firm. In developed countries, even those with a small amount of savings can participate in the market this way. Even in developing countries, most pensions are financed through stock market investments, making the club of capitalists large and truly global. Financial capital is one key component of the modern economy.

The second important type of capital is the *physical capital* necessary for production of both goods and services. Both developed and developing nations rely on foreign sources of physical capital to supplement that supplied domestically. Such foreign infusions are known as foreign direct investment (FDI). FDI was originally invested by colonial powers to their territories abroad. However, during the twentieth century, the majority of FDI was invested by developed countries in the economies of other developed nations. With improved technology, communications, and transportation infrastructure, however, the FDI pattern has recently begun to return to its developed-to-developing country origins, with the People's Republic of China having replaced the United States as the top destination for FDI every year since 2002.

The availability of financial and physical capital is a necessary condition for economic growth under capitalism. Increasingly, however, critical inputs into business are managerial know-how and the entrepreneurial spirit. These intangible inputs to the production process are often overlooked by commentators on capitalism, many of whom focus exclusively on the role of capital. Managerial know-how has evolved from Frederick Taylor's simple analysis of worker efficiency in the early twentieth century to become a complex discipline. Managers must be concerned with the opposing goals, such as maximizing both long-term market share and short-term profit, minimizing costs, and keeping workers happy and motivated. The lack of management know-how explains why many promising developing-country enterprises are unable to compete in international markets.

Entrepreneurial spirit, while often confused with management know-how, is actually a completely different concept. By nature, entrepreneurs are risk takers who forego steady paychecks for the opportunity to create freely and the chance to make millions. They have played key roles in the development of the capitalist economy, having provided the initiative that began global corporations and continues to generate the fresh ideas that push the technological frontier. Although it is common to believe that the role of the entrepreneur in developed countries has been diminished, owing to the economic domination of large multinational corporations (MNC) during the latter half of the twentieth century, this view is incorrect.

The aforementioned technological and communications enhancements that have shrunk the world have resulted in significant downsizing of MNCs in developed countries in recent years, with global capital mobility allowing traditional manufacturing jobs to exit high-wage developed countries and enter low- and middle-income countries near the turn of the millennium. The creativity and flexibility of the entrepreneur offer the best hope of job creation in such nations. Indeed, entrepreneurs in developed countries typically generate over 80% of new jobs.

Capitalism's Shortcomings

Despite the indisputable benefits that capitalism brings in terms of economic growth and the enhanced quality of life that accompanies higher average incomes, the capitalist economic model has critical deficiencies. In the early years, capitalists often took advantage of their workers, offering deplorable working conditions and requiring long hours, even for child labor. As the model produced economic growth, however, workers began to take some power back by forming labor unions. When capitalists tried to bust the unions, politicians took note of the number of voters being hurt and passed legislation ensuring a more equal balance of power between labor and capitalists. At one extreme, contract negotiations for large industries in Germany have three participants—management, labor, and the government. Certainly in developed countries, some excesses of early capitalism are merely historical phenomena. Several Western European countries, for instance, now mandate a workweek of fewer than forty hours.

Capitalism has been less successful in bringing prosperity to developing countries. These countries often fail to enforce their child labor or occupational health and safety regulations. While the lack of management training and limited access to capital provide part of the explanation, several other factors are important. Undoubtedly, the most important of these causes is corruption. Certainly, the financial scandals (such as Enron, WorldCom) of the early twenty-first century make it plain that even the most developed nations have not conquered corruption. On a national level, corruption is endemic in most developing countries. On the macroeconomic level, the political decision makers are often also those capitalists who own a nation's major industries. Certainly, the economic self-interest of these individuals makes it unlikely that the economic rules will change to allow substantial economic gains to become widespread, initiating a vicious cycle that prevents economic growth. Disillusioned workers become less productive, squeezing the capitalists' profits and leading them to hold more tightly to the wealth they already possess. Strikes originally intended to apply pressure on owners have become ingrained into the social fabric in countries like Brazil, whose strikes often have no particular rationale except to prove to management that labor can strike.

On a microeconomic level, red tape and the resultant bribery hinder economic progress. In some developing nations, starting a new business can take months of paperwork or might generate outrageously high start-up fees. For instance, in the first few years of the Czech Republic's post-Soviet experience, starting a new firm officially generated fees that exceeded the average annual income in the country, cutting off the main source of job creation—the small business sector.

Corruption also occurs on the international scale. As in the domestic case, differential power provides the opportunity for abuse. Although international economic institutions such as the World Bank and the International Monetary Fund (IMF) were founded after World War II to help low- and middle-income countries develop, their agendas are clearly influenced by the geopolitical and domestic special interests of the developed nations that provide the bulk of their funding. Even the World Trade Organization (WTO), which has certainly benefited rich as well as poor nations, has a poor record of balanced treatment of developing countries. For instance, the outcomes of the Uruguay Round of trade-barrier reductions strongly favored developed countries, particularly the United States and Western Europe. Although other forces played important roles, this imbalance partially explained the violent breakdown of the so-called Millennium Round of negotiations in Seattle, Washington. When the round restarted in Doha, Qatar, developing countries took a proactive approach. Originally led by India and later joined by China, developing nations for the first time committed to negotiating together to balance the power of the developed world.

The behavior of capitalists in developed countries has also been blamed for devastating financial crises. Beginning with the crash of the Mexican peso in December 1994, developing countries have seen a rash of currency crises (such as in Southeast Asia, 1997; Russia, 1998; Brazil, 1999; and Argentina, 2001). To be sure, much of the blame rests with the affected countries themselves. Poor financial sector oversight, unrealistically pegged exchange rates, and inappropriate monetary and fiscal policies abounded. However, developing countries point to the financial capital provided by developed-country investors as a major problem because it is too mobile. Investors have long argued that to ensure the safety of their investments abroad, countries had to allow them to withdraw their financial capital immediately if economic fundamentals warranted. However, such free outflow of capital, known as capital flight, could easily cause a panic. If investors believe that the currency of the host nation was about to depreciate or be devalued, the economic incentive is to withdraw the investment. Unfortunately, once investors begin to suspect that the currency could fall in value, there is a self-fulfilling prophecy. When they withdraw their investment, the demand for the host country's currency falls dramatically, decreasing its value. Developing nations have alleged that international currency speculators even have the incentive to start or exacerbate a currency crisis in order to profit. As a result, some countries now place strict controls on the exit of financial capital, requiring a waiting period between the investor's announced intention to withdraw capital and the withdrawal itself.

Other problems associated with capitalism include environmental degradation, overfishing, and inability to access medical treatments (such as AIDS drugs). Despite its problems, however, capitalism is unchallenged as an engine of economic growth.

JEFFREY W. STEAGALL

See also Capital Flight; Collectivism; Communist Economic Model; Development History and Theory; Free Market Economy; Marxism; Mixed Economy; Socialist Economic Model

Further Reading

Bauer, Sir Peter T. "The Vicious Circle of Poverty." *Weltwirtschftliches Archiv* 95, no. 2, (1965).

Galbraith, John Kenneth. *The New Industrial State*, 3d ed. New York: New American Library, 1978.

McCraw, Thomas K. *Creating Modern Capitalism.* Cambridge, London: Harvard University Press, 1997.

Rand, Ayn. *Capitalism: The Unknown Ideal.* New York: New American Library, 1967.

Scully, Gerald W. "Rights, Equity, and Economic Efficiency." *Public Choice* 68, nos. 1–3, (1991).

Schumpeter, Joseph A. *History of Economic Analysis.* New York: Oxford University Press, 1954.

Von Mises, Ludwig. *The Anti-Capitalistic Mentality.* New York: Van Nostrand, 1956.

CARDOSO, FERNANDO HENRIQUE

Fernando Henrique Cardoso was born in his grandmother's house in Rio de Janeiro on July 18, 1931, and grew up in São Paulo, Brazil. Cardoso served two terms as Brazil's president, from January 1, 1995, to

January 1, 2003, winning both elections with an absolute majority. Cardoso received his Ph.D. from the University of São Paulo in sociology, and during the 1960s, he emerged as an influential intellectual in the analysis of social changes, especially in Latin America, and of international development, dependency, democracy, and state reform. With the publication of his seminal work *Dependency and Development in Latin America* (1969), Cardoso established his reputation as a world-class sociologist. During the 1960s, Cardoso also became an outspoken critic of Brazil's bureaucratic authoritarian regime, which came to power after ousting the government João Goulart in 1964 and remained in power until 1985, when Brazil had its first democratic election after twenty-one years of military dictatorship. It is interesting to point out that Cardoso is the son and grandson of Brazilian generals; however, he did not opt to follow his grandfather or father's footsteps and enter Brazil's famous military academy (*Escola Military da Agulha Negra*). In the late 1960s, Cardoso was arrested and interrogated by military security forces, in addition to having his research institute bombed. To escape this persecution, Cardoso spent the 1970s and early 1980s living and teaching in the United States, France, and Chile, before returning to Brazil.

Upon returning to Brazil, Cardoso founded the Brazilian Social Democratic Party (PSDB) and, overcoming his past reputation as a leftist intellectual, was elected senator in 1982. As a member of the Brazilian senate, Cardoso became a key drafter of the 1988 constitution. In September 1992, the Brazilian Chamber of Deputies overwhelmingly voted for the impeachment of Fernando Collor de Mello, the young and previously unknown former governor of the poor northeastern state of Alagoas, following allegations of corruption. Rather than facing a full impeachment and the possibility of losing all of his political rights, Collor de Mello resigned, and his vice-president, Itamar Franco, assumed the presidency.

Franco, the former senator from the state of Minas Gerais, lacked any political base and political direction in the aftermath of Collor de Mello's resignation. During the Franco administration, inflation soared to an annual unprecedented rate of 2490% in 1993. Brazil's economic perspectives were the worst in the history of the republic. Franco tapped Cardoso to become, in 1994, his finance minister. Prior to becoming finance minister, however, Cardoso had served as Brazil's minister of foreign relations for six months, from 1992–1993. During the short period as minister of foreign relations, Cardoso, the multicultural intellectual sociologist, was able to bring Brazil to the international spotlight. One of his greatest accomplishments as foreign minister was the formation of the Southern Cone Common Market (MERCOSUR).

The MERCOSUR or MERCOSUL, a four-partner association between Brazil, Argentina, Paraguay and Uruguay, was established in 1991 with the signing of the *Treaty of Assuncion*. The scheme envisioned the creation of a free trade zone that would eventually evolve into a full-fledged "common market" along the lines of the European Union. Under the MERCOSUL treaty, Brazil's archenemy in Latin America, Argentina, was no longer a threat to Brazil's national security. Instead, in this new international system of the twenty-first century, Argentina is an essential piece of Brazil's foreign policy to create a stronger Latin America vis-à-vis the United States and the rest of the world. In October 2003, Argentina and Brazil signed what has been referred to as the *Buenos Aires Consensus*. This important document signed between Presidents da Silva and Néstor Kirchner reflects their common aspiration for economic growth with social justice and manifests their determination to transform the MERCOSUL trading block into a catalyst for building a shared future. The consensus, according to Greider and Rapoza, is a "proposed alternative to the much-despised Washington Consensus, which has straitjacketed developing economies with its harsh economic rules."

Upon assuming the position of minister of finance, Cardoso's first goal was to bring Brazil's rate of inflation under control. Cardoso launched the Real Plan, an anti-inflation program, which within two years brought Brazil's rampant rate of inflation under control. Riding on the coattail of his Real Plan success by taming Brazil's hyperinflation, Cardoso launched his presidential candidacy and was elected president in 1994 in a landslide victory against his opponent Luis Inacio "Lula" da Silva, Brazil's 2005 president. Cardoso received 34,350,217 votes (54.28%) to "Lula" da Silva's 17,112,255 (27.04%). During his first term in office, Cardoso was able to maintain Brazil's inflation under control, and Brazil's new currency introduced by Cardoso, called the *real*, remained stable. Cardoso also introduced a privatization program and economic modernization, both of which have been criticized for their unexpected manifestations of social exclusion. As William C. Smith and Nizar Messari have pointed out, the Cardoso administration was caught in an inescapable dilemma of contemporary Brazilian politics: how to reconcile the exigencies of the market and globalization with the equally compelling needs to promote democracy while combating poverty, violence, and social exclusion.

JOSE DA CRUZ

See also Brazil; Southern Cone Common Market (MERCOSUR); Southern Cone (Latin America): History and Economic Development; Southern Cone (Latin America): International Relations

References and Further Reading

Font, Mauricio A., ed. *Charting A New Course: The Politics of Globalization and Social Transformation: Fernando Henrique Cardoso.* New York: Rowman & Littlefield Publishers, 2001.

Goertzel, Ted G. *Fernando Henrique Cardoso e a Reconstru-ção da Democracia no Brasil* [*Fernando Henrique Cardoso and the Reconstruction of Democracy in Brazil*]. São Paulo, Brazil: Editora Saraiva.

Smith, William C., and Nizar Messari. "Democracy and Reform in Cardoso's Brazil: Caught Between Cliente-lism and Global Markets?" *The North-South Agenda. Papers* 33 (September 1998).

Skidmore, Thomas E., and Peter H. Smith. *Modern Latin America.* 6th ed. New York: Oxford University Press, 2005.

CARE

The Cooperative for Assistance and Relief Everywhere (CARE) is one of the world's largest nonprofit voluntary agencies involved in the provision of humanitarian relief and development assistance. Founded in the United States after World War II to provide relief packages to displaced persons in Europe, CARE has evolved into a global confederation of eleven national nongovernmental organizations (NGOs) with an international secretariat headquartered in Brussels, Belgium. CARE activities, initially directed only at humanitarian food aid, have expanded to include a range of development assistance reaching tens of millions people annually throughout Africa, Asia, the Caribbean, Europe, Latin America, and the Middle East. Forms of assistance include agricultural aid, small business credit programs, emergency food aid, food security and delivery, education and training programs, primary health care, reforestation programs, road building, and water purification and sanitation programs. These programs are focused at the family and community level. CARE attempts to involve beneficiary populations in the project development process while seeking to promote social justice and respect for the dignity of persons.

The mission of CARE is to provide relief and development aid to individuals, families, and communities in the poorest countries of the world. The chief goals of this CARE assistance are to promote self-reliance and self-help among aid beneficiaries, to increase economic opportunities, to deliver emergency aid, to serve as an advocate in policy making by governmental institutions, and to promote policies of nondiscrimination.

Historical Development

In 1945, CARE, an acronym that initially stood for Cooperative for American Remittances to Europe, was established by twenty-two American private agencies to coordinate the delivery of aid packages to millions of displaced persons in Europe. The CARE packages initially consisted of American Army surplus food parcels, each of which provided enough food for ten people to have a meal. To personalize the process, Americans who had relatives in Europe could obtain and send the packages to their families in war-devastated Europe, until governments there could promote economic recovery. CARE began to assemble its own packages with contributions from American businesses, eventually sending more than 100 million CARE packages to the needy in Europe. The packages contained various meats, margarine and lard, fruit preserves, honey, raisins, egg and milk powder, and coffee. In 1948, CARE began to tailor the packages to the food preferences of people from various cultures, as well as started to provide blankets and basic tools, medicine, and school supplies. As CARE activities began to expand beyond Europe in the late 1940s and early 1950s to reach needy people in Asia and other parts of the world, the acronym CARE was revised to stand for Cooperative for Assistance and Relief Everywhere, reflecting the more global scope of CARE relief activities.

By the 1950s, Europe had largely recovered from the terrible damage of World War II, and CARE began to send its aid packages to newly emerging countries. In 1954, with the emergency needs waning and with the formation of a new Food for Peace aid initiative by the US government, CARE began shifting its emphasis from emergency aid to longer term developing programming and food distribution. It also served as a major conduit through which the US government provided surplus grains to countries experiencing food shortages. CARE has continued to serve as one of the US government's largest implementing partners in the field of humanitarian aid.

In the 1960s, CARE began to branch out from food aid to provision of health care; in the 1970s, in the wake of major droughts and famines in Africa, CARE began to specialize in agro-forestry, clean water programs, and other development-related activities. In the early 1980s, CARE also specialized in providing secure transportation of food assistance into conflict zones and disaster-stricken areas where food diversion was problematical, such as in Somalia. In many emergency situations, food warehouses and shipments tend to be diverted by local employees and then sold on local markets, thus diverting sometimes fairly large percentages of food aid intended for refugees, displaced persons, and other communities in distress. To reduce this problem of food diversion, CARE trained specialists in food logistics and transportation and offered these services to governments and relief agencies of the United Nations, thus providing greater security for food shipments from the ports to the delivery points where food was then rationed to those for whom the aid was intended. In addition, CARE also became involved in construction of roads to enhance assistance delivery and to promote greater farm-to-market access for local farmers. Like many NGOs, CARE evolved into a dual-purpose agency, providing both emergency humanitarian aid and long-term development assistance, especially as the decolonization process of the 1960s led to the independence of more than a hundred countries, many from the developing world that had vast needs for economic development assistance.

Initially an American relief initiative, CARE eventually expanded in the 1980s, as several national chapters of CARE were formed in other countries, including Australia, Austria, Canada, Denmark, France, Germany, Japan, the Netherlands, Norway, and the United Kingdom. With this internationalization of CARE, an international secretariat was established in Brussels to coordinate the work of the various national CARE members.

CARE Programs for Development

While humanitarian relief aid remains a major part of CARE's portfolio of assistance programs, a large portion of its activity increasingly focuses on development assistance. CARE International, which coordinates the work of ten national members, is involved in more than six hundred projects in about sixty countries throughout the world. As a seasoned nongovernmental organization, CARE develops projects in consultation with local staff in the countries of assistance and with the line ministries of the countries in which the projects are located. Such an approach increases the likelihood that the project benefits will be sustained beyond the time that CARE ceases to fund a project.

As is true for most NGOs that got their start focusing primarily on humanitarian assistance and

emergency aid in the aftermath of World War II, one can trace a certain evolutionary process by which CARE and other humanitarian bodies gradually looked beyond emergency assistance to longer term development aid. Thus, as developing countries emerged onto the international stage in the 1960s and 1970s, CARE initiated programs to meet basic human needs. International assistance bodies, such of the World Bank, had begun to emphasize this approach in the 1970s. The basic human needs approach to development emphasized provision of the fundamental forms of aid to promote agricultural development so that food self-sufficiency might be achieved. Programs emphasizing access to medicine and health care, sanitation, and education were common elements of a basic human needs approach. Sensitivity of aid programs to the environment began to surface during the 1970s and 1980s. Efforts to cope with deforestation and desertification emerged in CARE and other NGOs.

During the 1980s, the emphasis began to shift somewhat as a reflection of the more conservative governments in the United States and Europe. Programs promoting privatization, credit schemes, support for small business, and the like became more popular ways of promoting economic growth and development. In targeting refugee aid in Africa and Central America, the international aid community and the UN system took note of the developmental impact of refugees and returnees on the economic and social infrastructure of countries receiving them. This notion was consistent with CARE's aid philosophy to take into account refugee-related impacts on development; to promote relief programs that helped to strengthen host country capacities in cooperation with local organizations; and, through enhancement of local capacities, to enable implementation of sustainable outcomes. In a similar spirit, CARE undertook programs to advance the education of girls and the advancement of women. Because many of the countries of assistance had experienced civil wars and thus were littered with mines, CARE undertook programs of land mine safety. Lasting peace in such cases depended on the development of conflict resolution capacities in post-civil war situations.

In the 1980s and 1990s, with a welter of civil war situations being resolved and numerous new situations emerging, CARE and other NGOs organized assistance for the promotion of civil society. With the demise of global communism and the governments that promoted Socialist alternatives to Western development aid, many governments in the developing world realized that significant reforms of their governmental structure would be necessary. In many cases, fragile and new governmental structures emerged from the ashes of civil war, and efforts to ensure democratization and accountability on the part of new governments were undertaken. NGOs assisted in this process by targeting aid on community development programming that encouraged healing of wartime wounds, promoted interethnic cooperation, and encouraged development of civic institutions.

Today, CARE programs run the gamut of the many different emphases in development assistance programming. CARE is still very much in the humanitarian aid business. It continues to provide food aid in the form of emergency assistance and in more development-oriented contexts, such as food-for-work programs. Health care for women and children is another major focus of CARE programs, touching on both humanitarian and development-related projects. More than 3 million people in thirty-one countries benefit from CARE's water and sanitation programs, while more than 1 million have benefited from CARE education and training programs. One of the major areas of CARE development assistance takes the form of training programs for farmers in the agricultural sector. CARE also supports reforestation programs. In the year 2000, CARE supported the planting of 13 million trees. CARE's basic infrastructure aid includes the building and repairing of roads through food-for-work or cash-for-work programs. CARE has also sponsored credit and marketing support for the development of businesses and enterprises. Much of this aid is targeted at women to provide them with previously unavailable opportunities to participate in business enterprises. The range of CARE development programming is, then, comprehensive.

CARE has also over the years developed an advocacy focus by which it attempts to influence policy making of governments at both the national and local levels. The goals are to enhance the empowerment of the poor, to promote the enlistment of the energy and talents of impoverished people in the quest for sustainable prosperity, and to advance human rights and humanitarian goals.

Conclusion

CARE is one of the world's largest and most highly regarded NGOs. Starting as an entirely American operation with a focus on relief to war-torn Europe, it now has eleven national members and undertakes humanitarian and development aid activities throughout the world. Spending only 9% of its revenues on overhead and administrative expenses, it is one of the most cost-efficient NGOs in the world. Governments,

the European Union, and UN agencies trust CARE with the implementation of large relief programs, contributions of commodities, and considerable multilateral funds. In the year 2003, CARE's programming budget was about $446 million. CARE International's assistance reaches about 30 million people in more than seventy countries. CARE complements its relief activities with the promotion of grass roots and community-oriented development programming. In pursuit of this twofold agenda of humanitarian and development assistance, CARE hires local staff whenever possible to implement its programs. This development assistance philosophy aims at promoting an attitude of local ownership of the programs, thus increasing the likelihood that they can be sustained.

CARE is an influential player in the international humanitarian and development assistance community, serving on the front lines of some of the world's most complicated and visible humanitarian relief situations, such as in Somalia during its refugee crisis of the early 1980s and its civil war in the early 1990s. But much of CARE's work is less noticeable, being undertaken in far-flung regions of the globe—quiet battles are waged by its staff in solidarity with local communities to overcome the harsh realities of grinding poverty that affect so much of the developing world.

ROBERT F. GORMAN

See also Basic Human Needs; Disaster Relief; Humanitarian Relief Projects; Non-Governmental Organizations (NGOs)

References and Further Reading

Campbell, Wallace. *The History of CARE: A Personal Account.* New York: Praeger, 1990.
Johnston, Philip. *Somalia Diary: The President of CARE Tells One Country's Story of Hope.* Atlanta, GA: Longstreet Press, 1994.
Linden, Eugene. *The Alms Race: The Impact of American Voluntary Aid Abroad.* New York: Random House, 1976.

CARIBBEAN BASIN INITIATIVE (CBI)

The Caribbean Basin Initiative (CBI) originally referred to the Caribbean Basin Economic Recovery Act of 1983 (CBERA). It has since become a general term used to refer collectively to the Caribbean Basin Economic Recovery Expansion Act of 1990 (CBERA Expansion Act) and the US Caribbean Basin Trade Partnership Act (CBTA) of 2000. Future US economic legislation concerning the Caribbean basin will likely also be included under this label.

The CBI legislation was passed following the United States and Organisation of Eastern Caribbean States (OECS) invasion of Grenada in 1983. Its purpose was to provide economic growth in the Caribbean basin, on the assumption that such growth would help create democratic stability in the region, which would then benefit the United States economically in particular and socially in general. The original CBI legislation included such provisions as expanding the number and amount of products that could enter the United States duty-free, encouraging direct investment from US corporations in the region through tax incentives (which allowed for products such as textiles to have preferential access to US markets), and increasing direct US aid significantly. The perceived benefits of the legislation would increase opportunities for US exports and business investment while at the same time reducing illegal immigration to the United States and lessening the attractiveness of the illegal drug trade by providing economic alternatives locally. The CBI's intent was to promote economic development and diversification through private sector investment. It was seen as a program that could further US foreign policy goals in the Caribbean basin by creating economic opportunity and could do so without the infusion of large amounts of direct government aid.

Currently, twenty-four countries benefit from CBI legislation: Antigua, Aruba, The Bahamas, Barbados, Belize, British Virgin Islands, Costa Rica, Dominica, Dominican Republic, El Salvador, Grenada, Guatemala, Guyana, Haiti, Honduras, Jamaica, Montserrat, the Netherlands Antilles, Nicaragua, Panama, St. Kitts and Nevis, St. Lucia, St. Vincent and the Grenadines, and Trinidad and Tobago. Further countries may be included at future dates if the US president designates them as beneficiary countries. Such designation must take into account various factors, such as if the designated beneficiary country provides for internationally recognized workers' rights, has met US counternarcotics certification, provides transparency and non-discrimination in government procurement, and protects intellectual property rights and the like. Most, although not all, criteria tie the designated country to obligations that have been reached by the World Trade Organization. The US president may also withdraw, suspend, or limit benefits if it is determined that a country is no longer meeting criteria for designation.

The benefits for designated countries under the CBI are various. The primary benefit, and the one that has the most prominence, has been to allow for duty-free imports into the United States in perpetuity for a wide range of products manufactured in CBI countries. Coupled with duty-free access to US markets for Caribbean manufacturers, the CBI also provides government assistance to programs that purport to benefit private sector development. Given the US domestic political agenda when the CBI was first created, CBI's emphasis on the private sector is hardly surprising. The program would, its supporters argue, allow economic development in the region at a minimal long-term cost to US taxpayers. Expanded local economies would alleviate a demand for continued direct US aid. Among the benefits that the CBI provides is direct US economic aid to programs within designated countries that aid private sector development. These include creating skills training programs and local Chambers of Commerce, financing essential imports, initiating business development missions, and continuing general efforts to improve local business environments and encouraging local investors. It has been argued that the larger, more economically developed and diversified states in the region, such as Jamaica and Trinidad and Tobago, have benefited the most from CBI to date.

Expansion of benefits to designated states in recent legislation indicates that this concentration on private sector development will continue barring a drastic change in US economic aid policy. Goods from other countries that are assembled in CBI-designated states have had to undergo substantial transformation and have at least a 35% value added to be allowed into US markets under the duty-free provision. This requirement can be waived if the components are of 100% US manufacture.

The CBI is perhaps one of the earliest examples of the "trade not aid" US foreign policy programs that began to arise during the Reagan administration and has continued through both Democratic and Republican administrations since. Interestingly, the credit for the CBI does not lay with the Reagan administration but rather with then-Prime Minister Edward Seaga of Jamaica. Seaga had suggested a comprehensive plan to promote economic development and democracy in the Caribbean. Seaga's conservative political credentials, coupled with the spectre of increased political instability in the region following the assassination of Maurice Bishop in Grenada, brought his plan to the forefront of the Reagan administration. While the CBI was not nearly as generous or encompassing as Seaga's plan, it did serve as the basis of the US policy.

Regardless of Seaga's initial role, there is little doubt that the CBI was formulated with US domestic policy in mind. Following the Grenada incursion of 1983, the Caribbean region did take on a foreign policy role for the United States that it had not seen since the Cuban missile crisis of the early 1960s.

The Sandinista government in Nicaragua, a Soviet "combat brigade" in Cuba, civil war in El Salvador, and Marxist insurgents in Colombia all brought attention to perceived political instability in the region. This did not negate the domestic political reality that foreign aid, with few exceptions, is rarely viewed favorably by US voters. The CBI allowed policy makers to have it both ways—giving economic assistance to allies in the region while arguing that the true beneficiary of such programs would be not just US foreign policy objectives, but US business interests as well.

The overall success of the CBI is mixed. There has been growth in industry in the Caribbean region, which arguably would not have occurred without the various tax and duty-free treatments the CBI provides. "Nontraditional" exports from the region, such as electronics, have increased. At the same time, economic growth has not approached the level that both US and Caribbean policy makers predicted at CBI's initial passage. It has been argued that the granting of duty-free status to manufactured goods, for example, has not offset economic losses due to quotas on agricultural imports, especially sugar, to the United States. Textiles exports to the states have continued to decline even with the benefits the industry receives under CBI legislation.

One obvious benefit of the CBI has been to create a legislative "hook" through which the Caribbean region has been able to remain visible in further US trade negotiations and subsequent policy. As was seen with the passage of the Caribbean Basin Economic Recovery Expansion Act of 1990, the creation of the US–Caribbean Free Trade Partnership Act of 2000, discussions to include the Caribbean basin in NAFTA, and even the addition of the Caribbean region to important economic articles in the 2001 Africa Growth and Opportunity Act, the existence of the CBI creates an environment that makes it far easier for US policymakers to direct resources to the Caribbean region. Without an existing framework in place, as other regions of the world have discovered, it is usually difficult to convince policy makers in the United States to concentrate on the concerns of their region.

DAVID H. CARWELL

See also Caribbean: History and Economic Development; Caribbean: International Relations

References and Further Reading

Barry, Tom, Beth Wood, and Deb Preusch. *The Other Side of Paradise: Foreign Control in the Caribbean.* New York: Grove Press, 1984.

Deere, Carmen Diana, coord. *In the Shadow of the Sun: Caribbean Development Alternatives and US Policy.* Boulder, CO: Westview Press, 1990.

Johnson, Peter. "Caribbean Basin Initiative: A Positive Departure." *Foreign Policy* 47 (summer 1982).

Knight, Franklin W., and Colin A. Palmer, eds. *The Modern Caribbean.* Chapel Hill, NC: University of North Carolina Press, 1989.

Lowenthal, Abraham F. "The Caribbean Basin Initiative: Misplaced Emphasis." *Foreign Policy* 47 (summer 1982).

Pastor, Robert. *Whirlpool: US Foreign Policy Toward Latin America and the Caribbean.* Princeton, NJ: Princeton University Press, 1992.

Winetraub, Sidney. "The Caribbean Initiative: A Flawed Model." *Foreign Policy* 47 (summer 1982).

CARIBBEAN COMMUNITY AND COMMON MARKET (CARICOM)

The Caribbean Community and Common Market (CARICOM) was established by the Treaty of Chaguaramas signed by the prime ministers of Barbados, Guyana, Jamaica, and Trinidad and Tobago in Chaguaramas, Trinidad, on July 4, 1973. It went into effect on August 1, 1973. In 1974, Antigua, Belize, Dominica, Grenada, St. Lucia, St. Kitts and Nevis, St. Vincent and the Grenadines, and Montserrat also signed the treaty. In 2004, the Bahamas, Suriname, and Haiti joined as full members, with Anguilla, Bermuda, British Virgin Islands, Cayman Islands, and the Turks and Caicos accepted as provisional members. From its inception, CARICOM has had three primary areas of concern: the promotion and integration of the economies of the member states; cooperation in certain noneconomic areas (that is, education and health), which member states perceive cooperative endeavors as beneficial; and coordination of foreign policy concerns of its members both within and outside of the Caribbean region.

The Conference of Heads of Government is currently the highest decision-making body in the organization. Consisting of the heads of government of the member states, the conference is responsible for the general policy direction for CARICOM, as well as final decisions on treaties and relationships between CARICOM and non-member states and international organizations. Each member of CARICOM has one vote, and a unanimous vote is required to create binding decisions. Under the conference, the Community Council of Ministers is the second-highest body in CARICOM. The Community Council of Ministers consists of one ministerial representative from each member, and all major decisions must also be made by a unanimous vote. The council is responsible for financial arrangements within CARICOM, as well as coordinating the various lower councils and developing overall strategic plans to recommend to the conference. The council is also responsible for coordinating CARICOM's actions with non-member states and international organizations.

Four specialized councils exist under the direction of the Community Council of Ministers, each with responsibility for a specific policy area. The Council for Trade and Economic Development is primarily concerned with trade and economic development and oversees CARICOM's single-market policies; the Council for Foreign and Community Relations coordinates relations between CARICOM and non-member states and international organizations; the Council for Finance and Planning coordinates economic policies of the member states in areas of financial and monetary integration; and the Council for Human and Social Development promotes human and social development.

The Caribbean Community Secretariat in Guyana is the primary administrative office. The secretariat has no official decision-making power, although it is generally accepted that it has played a role in decision making through the exercise of its bureaucratic powers—studies, reports, project evaluations, policy projections, and the like. The official role of the secretary is to serve the region as a whole, rather than any individual or group of states.

Nine lesser Standing Committees of Ministers are responsible for specific sectoral aspects of regional integration—health, industry, education, labor, foreign affairs and defense, finance, agriculture, transport, and mining. Various institutions, while independent, are officially associated with CARICOM. These include such entities as the Caribbean Development Bank, the University of the West Indies, the Caribbean Marketing Enterprise, and Caribbean Meteorological Council.

CARICOM was created following the example of the European Economic Community and seeks to achieve economic integration through voluntary free market methods. By removing barriers to the flow of goods, services, and capital, it is hoped the region can somewhat mitigate the problems of economies of scale, external dependence, and economic fragmentation. Regional integration through CARICOM, it was hoped, would lead to sustained growth by encouraging market expansion, economic cooperation, and investment in this newly expanded economic environment. The result, according to the EEC model, would eventually lead to lower unemployment, higher standards of living, and balanced growth.

The specific mechanisms that CARICOM has adopted to achieve these broad goals have been trying to remove duties, quotas, and any other identifiable tariff and non-tariff barriers to trade as well as adopting common external tariffs (CET) and common protective policies (CPP). CET will stimulate internal industrial production by imposing low barriers to capital goods and raw materials while imposing higher barriers to finished products. CPP protect specific regional industries. It was expected that these two programs would lead to increase in trade and investment among the members.

The success of CARICOM has been mixed. In areas of defense and foreign policy, there is little doubt that CARICOM has lead to greater solidarity among the members. Regional security and territorial integrity are a shared concern of all members, and agreement on these matters has given CARICOM a strengthened bargaining position when dealing with regional and extraregional actors and when dealing with multinational negotiations. In other areas of functional integration outside of economic concerns, CARICOM has also shown success. Cooperation in regional transportation, education, and health initiatives has been and continues to be successful.

However, in what is usually seen as the most important aspects of CARICOM, economic cooperation and development, the outcomes have been more mixed. CARICOM has been successful in easing restrictions on movement of persons between member states for economic reasons through the Free Movement of Skills initiative.

Economic cooperation has improved during the last thirty years among CARICOM members, yet the hoped-for economic benefits have remained largely unrealized. Domestic political concerns coupled with a wariness to limit sovereignty by allowing regional organizations control economic policies continue to limit the possible effectiveness of CARICOM. A major stumbling point has been a failure to create a common policy concerning foreign investment. The hoped-for reduction of external dependency and greater regional self-reliance has not matched expectations. Even with CARICOM, individual member states are faced with their own domestic political realities when faced with economic decisions. Something as seemingly valuable as cross-listing stocks on the various regional stock exchanges has been problematic at best because different states have viewed the costs and benefits of doing so differently. As is the case in most countries, parochial interests will usually overshadow regional integration in economic matters. A clear example of this has been the continued failure to develop a monetary union. This has been a goal of CARICOM since its inception, yet it appears to be as distant now as it was then. Relinquishing absolute control of a state's currency, even if economic benefits can be clearly argued, remains politically difficult.

DAVID H. CARWELL

See also Caribbean Free Trade Association (CARIF-TA); Caribbean: History and Economic Development; Caribbean: International Relations

References and Further Reading

Berry, Tom, Beth Wood, and Deb Preusch. *The Other Side of Paradise: Foreign Control in the Caribbean.* New York: Grove Press, 1984.
CARICOM. *Report to the Secretary General of CARICOM.* Georgetown, Guyana: CARICOM, yearly since 1974.
Deere, Diana Carmen, coord. *In The Shadow of the Sun: Caribbean Development Alternatives and US Policy.* Boulder, CO: Westview Press, 1990.
Knight, Franklin, and Colin A. Palmer. *The Modern Caribbean.* Chapel Hill, NC: University of North Carolina Press, 1989.
Payne, Anthony, and Paul Sutton. *Dependency Under Challenge.*
Powell, David. *Problems of Economic Development in the Caribbean.* London: Alfred H. Cooper and Sons, 1973.
Young, Ruth C. "Political Autonomy and Economic Development in the Caribbean Islands." *Caribbean Studies* 16, no. 1 (March 1973).

CARIBBEAN DEVELOPMENT BANK (CDB)

The Caribbean Development Bank (CDB) was established at a conference of plenipotentiaries of eighteen countries and territories by an agreement that was signed in Kingston, Jamaica, on October 18, 1969, and went into effect on January 26, 1970. On January 31, 1970, the Inaugural Meeting of the Board of Governors was held in Nassau, Bahamas. The permanent headquarters of the institution is located in Wildey, St. Michael, Barbados. Its purpose is to foster the economic growth and development of its member countries in the Caribbean and to promote economic cooperation and integration among them. The first article of the charter establishing the CDB requires that the institution give special regard to less developed member countries of the region.

Membership in the CDB is open to regional states and territories, as well as to nonregional states that are members of the United Nations, any of its subsidiary agencies, or the International Atomic Energy Agency. Members are classified as either regional or nonregional and borrowing or nonborrowing. There are currently twenty-five members of the CDB. Of these, twenty are regional and five are nonregional. Regional countries include Anguilla, Antigua and Barbuda, Bahamas, Barbados, Belize, British Virgin Islands, Colombia, Cayman Islands, Dominica, Grenada, Guyana, Jamaica, Mexico, Montserrat, St. Kitts and Nevis, St. Lucia, St. Vincent and the Grenadines, Trinidad and Tobago, Turks and Caicos,

and Venezuela. Nonregional countries are Canada, China, Germany, Italy, and the United Kingdom. Although the CDB is committed to broadening its membership base with borrowing and nonborrowing as well as regional and nonregional members, borrowing members hold a permanent majority of the voting power in the CDB, and regional members represent a permanent majority in the Board of Directors. Suriname (1997) and Haiti (2003) have been admitted as borrowing members, although all of the formalities for their entrance have not yet been completed.

The CDB is administered by a board of governors, a board of directors, a president, two vice presidents, as well as other officers and staff. The highest policy-making body of the CDB is the board of governors, in which all of the bank's powers are vested. With the exception of matters concerning the admission of new members, a change in capital stock, amendment of the charter, election of directors and the president, and the termination of bank operations, the board of governors may delegate its powers to the board of directors. The board of directors oversees the general policy and direction of the CDB. It also exercises all powers delegated to it by the board of governors and is responsible for making decisions regarding concerns such as loans, borrowing programs, and the bank's administrative budget. As chairman of the board of directors, the president is responsible for appointing staff and for the organization and operation of the CDB. Below him are two vice presidents: a vice president of finance and a vice president of operations. In the absence of the president, the ranking vice president performs the duties and exercises the authority of the president. The CDB has an additional staff of ninety-nine professionals from eleven different countries and ninety-eight support staff, primarily from Barbados.

The CDB aims to be the leading financial institution for Caribbean development. In close collaboration with its borrowing member countries, the bank encourages social and economic development and works toward the systematic reduction of poverty in the region. To promote development and reduce poverty, the CDB assists its regional members in the coordination of their development programs. This allows members to better use their resources and harmonize their economies, which makes them more complementary, and promotes the orderly expansion of their international, particularly intraregional, trade.

Also recognized as an associate institution of the Caribbean Community and Common Market (CARICOM), and therefore as an institution pursuing the same broad purposes as that association, the CDB promotes projects that include aspects of regional economic integration. In the agricultural sector, it has been involved in the rationalization of the Windward Islands banana industry and the rehabilitation of the sugar industry of the more developed member countries, as well as in promoting agricultural diversification in the Organization of Eastern Caribbean States (OECS). It has also financed projects directly and through regional institutions such as the Caribbean Food Corporation. In industry, the CDB is actively involved in supporting projects that aim to reduce regional competition and thus make industrial development in member countries more complementary. In addition to providing capital loans and technical assistance to regional projects in shipping and air transport, the CDB has actively facilitated the development of intraregional transport facilities.

Recognizing that community involvement is essential for sustained and inclusive development in rural areas, the CDB has also been active in poverty-reduction initiatives for the rural poor. Established in 1979, the CDB's Basic Needs Trust Fund (BNTF) program provides resources for the improvement of conditions in poverty-stricken rural communities. This program facilitates the delivery of basic public services to poor communities. Projects include the provision of schools, health services, water systems, roads, drains, and day care centers. Since its inception, the BNTF Program has positively affected 1.6 million of the region's poor inhabitants, with two-thirds living in rural areas. The Canadian International Development Agency (CIDA) and the United States Agency for International Development (USAID) have contributed additional resources to the fund.

Because borrowing member countries of the CDB are particularly vulnerable to natural disasters—and because they are forced to respond to disasters while coping with social and economic problems associated with economic diversification, debt management, inflation, and poverty—the bank has also introduced means to help its members mitigate and recover from disasters. Prior to the implementation of its National Disaster Management Strategy in 1998, the CDB's disaster relief policy focused on restoration and rehabilitation in the aftermath of a disaster. The strategy implemented in 1998, however, places greater emphasis on reducing the risks and vulnerability of borrowing members to disasters by raising preparedness and improving the scope of collaborative efforts among developmental institutions working with disasters in the region. Recently, the CDB's Disaster Mitigation Facility for the Caribbean (DMFC), with the support of USAID, has been involved in projects designed to strengthen a region's ability to cope with disasters and to decrease its vulnerability to disasters. The DMFC is also active in the

provision of financial assistance to borrowing members to be used for the purpose of implementing functional disaster mitigation practices and increasing the capacity of the CDB to address disaster management issues. The CDB's current disaster management strategy strives to incorporate disaster mitigation into all of its policies, programs, and projects.

The CDB also mobilizes additional financial resources for the development of its regional members. Such finances come from within as well as outside a region. The CDB has thus far raised loans from the European Investment Bank (EIB), the World Bank, and the International Development Bank (IDB), as well as on the capital markets of Trinidad and Tobago, the United States, and Japan. By providing aid to financial institutions in a region and supporting the establishment of consortia, the institution further encourages public and private investments in development projects. The bank may also finance directly any projects contributing to the development of a region or any of its regional members.

In appraising and preparing prospective projects, the CDB considers its costs and potential impact on local and regional development and on poverty and vulnerability. Project appraisals assess factors such as legal, technical, commercial, organizational, and environmental validity; the project's contribution to the removal of economic bottlenecks; and the ability of the borrowing country to service additional external debt. Prior to the commencement of a project, the CDB provides its regional members with the appropriate technical assistance. Technical assistance (TA) operations are meant to complement project operations by assisting in the transfer of techniques as well as facilitating the development of expertise and the identification and promotion of opportunities for investment in the borrowing members of the CDB. Technical assistance often involves, but is not restricted to, undertaking or commissioning preinvestment surveys and identifying and preparing project proposals. In addition to providing financial and technical assistance and helping regional members better coordinate their economies, the CDB is also active in the promotion of regionally and locally controlled financial institutions and of a regional market for credit and savings. The charter of the CDB further stipulates that the institution may undertake or promote such other endeavors as they may advance its purpose.

The financial resources of the CDB consist of ordinary capital resources (OCR), mostly comprising subscribed capital and borrowings and special funds resources (SFR). Its lending activities are divided into two broad categories: *ordinary operations* and *special operations*. Ordinary operations are financed from the bank's OCR, and special operations are financed from its SFR, although a project may require that some aspects be financed as ordinary operations and others be funded as special operations. While ordinary operations of the CDB embrace all of its borrowing members, the bulk of its special operations are in less developed member countries. Excluding instances in which the territory or member country objects to the CDB's financing of an undertaking, the bank may participate in or make direct loans to the governments of its regional member countries, to public as well as private entities operating within such countries, and to international or regional entities concerned with the development of a region's economy.

Whether forming part of a national, subregional, or regional development program, the CDB provides principally for the financing of specific projects. Projects financed either directly or indirectly by the CDB since it commenced operations in 1970 cover a broad spectrum of developmental activities dealing with ports, livestock, fisheries, export services, agriculture, roads and bridges, industrial estates, water, power, electricity, infrastructure, waste management, sea and air transport equipment, airports and runways, tourist facilities, education, residential mortgages, and human resource development. The focus of such projects is on promoting social equity and protecting the environment.

DEREK A. BENTLEY

See also Caribbean Basin Initiative; Caribbean Community and Common Market (CARICOM); Caribbean: History and Economic Development; International Bank for Reconstruction and Development (IBRD) (World Bank); Organization of Eastern Caribbean States (OECS); United States Agency for International Development (USAID)

Resources and Further Reading

Apostolopoulos, Yorghos, and Dennis J. Gayle, eds. *Island Tourism and Sustainable Development: Caribbean, Pacific, and Mediterranean Experiences.* Westport, CT: Greenwood, 2002.
Baker, Judy L. *Poverty Reduction and Human Development in the Caribbean.* New York: World Bank Publications, 1997.
Burki, Shahid Javed, Sebastian Edwards, and Sri-Ram Aiyer. *Annual World Bank Conference on Development in Latin America and the Caribbean 1995: Proceedings of a Conference Held in Rio de Janeiro.* New York: World Bank Publications, 1997.
Caribbean Development Bank: *Twenty-Fifth Anniversary: Whiter the CARICOM Region, Whither CDB in its Support?* Wildey, Barbados: Caribbean Development Bank, 1996.
Ferguson, James. *Far from Paradise: An Introduction to Caribbean Development.* New York: Monthly Review Press, 1990.
Hall, Kenneth O. *Reinventing CARICOM: The Road to a New Integration.* Kingston, Jamaica: Ian Randle Publishers, 2003.
Hall, Kenneth O., and Duke Pollard, eds. *The CARICOM System: Basic Instruments.* Kingston, Jamaica: Ian Randle Publishers, 2003.
Hardy, Chandra. *The Caribbean Development Bank.* Miami, FL: North-South Institute, 1995.
Knight, Franklin W. *The Caribbean: The Genesis of a Fragmented Nationalism.* New York: Oxford University Press, 1990.
Martin, John, and Jose Antonio Ocampo. *Globalization and Development: A Latin American and Caribbean Perspective.* Stanford, CA: Stanford University Press, 2003.
Reid, George. *Shocks and Strategies: Jamaica and the Caribbean Development Bank.* Miami, FL: North-South Institute, 1985.

CARIBBEAN FREE TRADE ASSOCIATION (CARIFTA)

When independence became generally accepted as the future of the British colonies in the Caribbean following World War II, the problem arose concerning what form independence would take. Initially, Great Britain believed that its former colonies would form a federation, leading to a single political entity spread over the several island states. As a prelude to full independence, the British West Indies Federation was created in 1958 comprising ten member states, including Jamaica (as well as the Cayman Islands and the Turks and Caicos), Trinidad and Tobago, Barbados, Antigua, Montserrat, St. Kitts and Nevis, Grenada, St. Vincent and the Grenadines, St. Lucia, and Dominica. A Customs Union was part of this federation; however, in its four years of existence, political concerns in trying to create a single political entity from ten separate states overshadowed economic concerns. Because the British colonies had relatively small populations who historically had provided agricultural and some industrial raw materials to the home country, very little trade had existed between the islands. Although the West Indies Federation came to an end in 1962, it is rightly considered the beginning of attempts at greater regional integration among Caribbean states.

When Trinidad and Tobago announced its decision to leave the Federation in 1961, Prime Minister Williams proposed the creation of a Caribbean community, consisting not just of the former members of the federation but of all Caribbean island states and the Guianas. To discuss this new attempt at regional integration, the first Heads of Government

Conference was held in Trinidad in July 1963. This lead to a series of Conferences concerning the creation of a Free Trade Area that culminated in the Agreement of Dickenson Bay, Antigua, in December 1965. The Dickenson Bay Agreement created the Caribbean Free Trade Association (CARIFTA).

The initial members of CARIFTA—Antigua, Barbados, and British Guiana (Guyana)—deliberately delayed the official beginning of CARIFTA to allow time for other states in the region to join. CARIFTA came into force on May 1, 1968, with eleven states as members. In recognition of the differences in levels of development, countries were divided into two classes: most developed countries (MDCs) were Trinidad and Tobago, Jamaica, Barbados and Guyana; the less developed countries (LDCs) were Antigua, Dominica, Grenada, Montserrat, St. Kitts and Nevis, St. Lucia, St. Vincent, and the Grenadines. In recognition of their differing levels of development, the LDCs were given some preferential treatment in lifting some trade barriers.

CARIFTA was intended as a true free-trade area, with all members pledging to eliminate tariffs and quota systems on each member's products. It was modeled on the European Economic Community, albeit much less ambitious. Indeed, Great Britain's attempts to join the EEC in some ways motivated the governments in the Caribbean to form CARIFTA. It was feared that Great Britain's successful entry into the EEC would deny its former colonies preferential access to British markets with exports such as sugar and bananas. This would deny the Commonwealth Caribbean its primary market for exports. Their own regional trade union was seen as a possible means of alleviating some of their economic disadvantages.

CARIFTA was not an overly ambitious attempt at integration. Coming after the failed West Indian Federation, this was most probably inevitable. It concentrated on removing barriers to intraregional trade. CARIFTA gave very little attention to renegotiating the relationships its members had with states outside the region and relied on consensus for what policies it did develop. CARIFTA was a first step into realistic integration among the Commonwealth Caribbean states. When complete political federation failed, it was necessary to find a basis for the level of cooperation that would be politically viable to the states in the region, and CARIFTA provided that. In 1973, the eighth Heads of Government Conference of CARIFTA voted to transform CARIFTA into a true common market and transform CARIFTA into the Caribbean Community and Common Market (CARICOM). CARICOM would continue to promote economic integration, but it would also expand the areas of cooperation beyond purely economic concerns.

DAVID H. CARWELL

See also Caribbean Community and Common Market (CARICOM); Caribbean: History and Economic Development; Caribbean: International Relations

References and Further Reading

Grugel, Jean. *Politics and Development in the Caribbean Basin: Central America and the Caribbean in the New World Order.* Bloomington, IN: Indiana University Press, 1995.

Parry, J. H., Philip Sherlock, and Anthony Maingot. *A Short History of the West Indies.* New York: St. Martin's Press, 1987.

Payne, Anthony. *Change in the Commonwealth Caribbean.* London: Chatham House Papers, the Royal Institute of International Affairs, 1981.

Webb, Steven Benjamin. *Prospects and Challenges for the Caribbean.* Washington, DC: World Bank, 1997.

CARIBBEAN: HISTORY AND ECONOMIC DEVELOPMENT

The history of the Caribbean, or even its economic history, cannot be summarized in a few paragraphs. Few generalizations can be made, and there is little agreement among scholars on some aspects of the region. Even the geographic delimitation of the region represents a problem. It is customary to include, in this region, all the islands lying between North and South America, along an arc of about 4,500 kilometers, from the western tip of Cuba to the southern coast of Trinidad.

The Archipelago

If we disregard the mainland of the Caribbean—as the nomenclature below does—the following terms can be used more or less interchangeably to describe the archipelago: "islands of the Caribbean," "the West Indies" (albeit this term often refers exclusively to the Anglophone islands), or "the Antilles" (often a French term), which are sometimes divided into "the Greater" and "the Lesser" Antilles. The Greater Antilles comprise Cuba, Hispaniola (shared by the Dominican Republic and Haiti), Jamaica, and Puerto Rico.

Economically and administratively speaking, the archipelago can be broken down as follows: (i) the Eastern Caribbean (Antigua and Barbuda, Barbados, Dominica, Grenada, St. Kitts (also St. Christopher) and Nevis, St. Lucia, St. Vincent, and the Grenadines): (ii) the British dependencies (Anguilla, British Virgin Islands, Cayman Islands, Montserrat, Turks, and Caicos); (iii) the French Caribbean (Guadeloupe, Martinique and satellite islands, and half of St. Martin); (iv) the United States's possessions (Navassa Island, Puerto Rico, and the US Virgin Islands); (v) the Netherlands Antilles (half of St. Martin, Aruba, Bonaire, and Curacao); (vi) and the larger islands (Cuba, Hispaniola—Dominican Republic and Haiti—Trinidad and Tobago) that constitute the focus of this discussion. The Bahamas and Guyana can be added to the picture, although these are technically beyond the Caribbean Sea.

Territory, Population, Climate, and Language

The size of the territory of the island-nations ranges all the way from Cuba, with about 111,000 square kilometers, to St. Kitts and Nevis, with 261 square kilometers. As for the population, Cuba boasts of more than 11 million people, and St. Kitts and Nevis is the smallest independent country, with a population estimated at less than thirty-nine thousand. The agriculturally productive lands of Montserrat, a British dependency, were reduced by about two-thirds because of recent volcanic activities, with the eruption of the Soufriere in 1995; much of the population fled the island to the United Kingdom and other countries. Many of the islands lie within a seismic zone; the most notable eruption in modern times was that of Mont Pelée in Martinique in 1902.

In regards to the climate, the Caribbean archipelago is well-known for its tropical weather (only the Bahamas lie north of the tropical zone as well as beyond the Caribbean Sea), mitigated by the ocean breeze. In fact, the sea and the climate may be the islands' main common assets. Variations in temperature between daytime and nighttime and between summer and winter are more pronounced in the northern islands and at higher altitudes. Although the natives may disagree, even wintertime is beach weather; in fact, the winter is the high point of the tourist season.

Another reason why the Caribbean is more popular with the tourists in the winter is the hurricanes that are prevalent during other seasons. Practically all the islands of the Caribbean can and have been affected, at one time or another, by hurricane-force winds in the summer and fall, between June and November, especially in September. Whether it is hurricane season or not, the winds almost invariably blow from the East.

All of these islands have been colonized, starting around the sixteenth century and continuing well past the middle of the twentieth century and in a few cases to the present; the lone exception is Haiti, more exactly the Haitian side of Hispaniola, which achieved independence (and emancipation) by 1804. Consequently, the population of the Caribbean can be divided by language into Anglophone and Francophone, hispanophone, and speakers of Dutch, reflecting the former presence of the respective European imperial powers. In some cases, local or indigenous languages, including Papiamento in the Dutch islands, are spoken; various creole languages, the most recognized being the Creole of Haiti, are added to the mix; and pidgin languages or pidginized versions of European languages are also present. Further mixtures exist to complicate matters, such as the "Spanglish" spoken by many Puerto Ricans.

Political Background and Balkanization

Politically speaking, as a result of the Corollary to the Monroe Doctrine enunciated by Theodore Roosevelt at the beginning of the twentieth century, "flag independence" and some form of parliamentary government, along with a greater or lesser degree of a free-market economy, prevail in most of the region. Revolutionary Cuba is the obvious exception. Other nations, such as Grenada (1979–1983) or Guyana, or even Jamaica and the Dominican Republic, which have attempted to establish closer ties with Cuba, have experienced direct or indirect American intervention. The *cooperative socialism* advocated by Forbes Burnham in Guyana was an attempt to find a third way in social and economic policies (but was also a reaction against the previous regime, Cheddi Jaggan's Marxist approach), as was the *democratic socialism* advocated by Michael Manley in Jamaica; Burnham's line failed because of internal, including ethnic, contradictions, while Manley's attempt encountered opposition from the Cold War policies of the United States.

Some islands or groups of islands have yet to achieve any sort of independence, most notably Puerto Rico and the Virgin Islands, which are possessions of the United States. The British Virgin Islands and Montserrat are still part of the British empire, and Martinique and Guadeloupe are considered departments or administrative units of "metropolitan" France. Unlike the French or Dutch islands, Puerto Rico enjoys some autonomy. In fact, it is officially described as a "commonwealth," but, for practical purposes, its status is somewhere in limbo between statehood as a state of the United States and full independence. The dependent political status of these island territories would render their economic integration difficult, if not impossible.

There is no region in the world more balkanized than the island-nations of the Caribbean since decolonization; indeed, several countries have less than one hundred thousand inhabitants (St. Kitts and Nevis has a population of about thirty-nine thousand, Dominica around seventy-three thousand), whereas Cuba has 11.2 million, the Dominican Republic has 8.4 million, and Haiti has almost 7.6 million (these figures are estimates for the year 2003).

The balkanization of the region is a handicap in more ways than one; since each island-nation, however small, has its own government, with a more or less elaborate civil service and diplomatic corps, the export earnings of the country, which are the revenues from taxes and tariffs, are siphoned off to pay the salaries and benefits of elite government officials. The process of balkanization did not end with decolonization. While there are centripetal tendencies (discussed in the following paragraphs), the centrifugal tendencies remain strong. For instance, Anguilla split from St. Kitts and Nevis to remain British, there is a movement in Nevis for independence from St. Kitts, and many Tobagonians (residents of Tobago) are keen on obtaining greater autonomy if not complete independence from Trinidad.

Ethnicity and Culture

Ethnically speaking, the population of most islands is predominantly Afro-Caribbean, that is, Caribbean of African ancestry. According to some censuses and informal surveys, however, there are White majorities in Puerto Rico and the Dominican Republic, although these claims have been challenged by social scientists and others concerned with matters of "race" who argue that the social pressures in both lands favor White or Spanish ascendancy and the denial or rejection of African blood. Moreover, almost half the population of Trinidad and of Guyana is of East Indian origin. There is also a Chinese minority on many islands.

Culturally speaking, the situation is even more complicated. Varieties of Western civilization (such as British, French, and Spanish) have assimilated elements from the original Arawak and Carib Native American cultures, even though the Native American population died out or was killed off within 150 years of the arrival of the Europeans (except for a small contingent on the island of Dominica and in Belize).

The influence of various cultures of West Africa can be clearly observed in Haiti, Cuba, and some of the smaller island-nations. In the twentieth century and at present, the political, economic, and cultural influence of the United States has often become dominant, not only in Puerto Rico and the Virgin Islands, but also throughout the region.

The term "African Diaspora" is often used in the context of demography and culture to refer to the dispersal, involuntary or voluntary, of the African population throughout much of the world; but there is also a Diaspora within the Diaspora, that is, the dispersal of several million people from the Caribbean, settling in some European countries, notably England and France, in the United States, and Canada (in the case of the Anglophone West Indies, the Caribbean Diaspora amounts to about 40% of the population that remains).

Economic History and Industrialization

Perhaps the least diverse and controversial aspect of the Caribbean is its economic history. To oversimplify, this history has been dominated by the plantation economy, more specifically the cultivation of the sugarcane. Sugar became queen of the Caribbean and, indeed, of the Atlantic world trade, for three hundred years, from early in the sixteenth century until the beginning of the nineteenth century. Sugar continued to dominate the economies of most islands in the nineteenth century and in the first third of the twentieth century, although it had long lost its status as the most profitable item in world trade.

Since the first third of the twentieth century, the region as a whole has undergone modernization—as advocated by the St. Lucian economist W. Arthur Lewis in 1950 and 1951—along institutional and economic lines, while remaining or becoming underdeveloped at the same time. Modernization is evident in various ways: the growing importance of the service sector and, in some cases, of the manufacturing sector, accompanied by neglect of agricultural production, apart from the production and export of sugar in Cuba and of bananas, especially in the lesser Antilles.

The benefits of an increasing demand for bananas in Europe has been mitigated by a drop in world prices and by competition, both from South America and from United States-owned transnational corporations (Chiquita, Dole, and Del Monte brands) in South and Central America; in fact, this competition has led to international tension between the United States and the European Union, which came to a head in the late 1990s. Nevertheless, bananas account for roughly half of all "export" earnings in the case of Guadeloupe and Martinique but are also significant, in absolute figures, for St. Lucia (almost 60% of export earnings), Jamaica, St. Vincent, and Dominica (almost 70% of export earnings).

Few of the island-nations are self-sufficient with regard to food supply, even with regard to their staple food. The paradox has reached extremes: although rice is a staple food in Puerto Rico, none of it is locally grown. While there still are orange groves and coffee plantations in Puerto Rico (gone wild), the oranges and coffee consumed by Puerto Ricans come exclusively from abroad. Although some of the island-nations still specialize in the production of certain cash crops, the population of the entire region has become dependent, to a greater or lesser extent, on food imports and on loans from the World Bank and the International Monetary Fund to help pay for those imports. Indeed, loans from the World Bank and other foreign sources have reached $2.5 billion in the case of Trinidad and Tobago, $3.9 billion for Jamaica, and $4.6 billion for the Dominican Republic. These amount to extremely high per capita debts; they also explain, in part, the relatively high growth rates in gross domestic product (GDP).

Perhaps the common trait in the contemporary economy of the entire region is the reliance on the tourist trade and, to a lesser extent, on remittances from abroad. The Caribbean Diaspora not only contributes financially but also technologically by introducing skills acquired abroad. On some of the islands, the tourist trade has become the number one contributor to the economy, far exceeding revenues from agricultural exports and manufacturing, in some cases accounting for up to 80% of the export earnings. But the reliance on income from tourism has its drawbacks: the repatriation of profits to the foreign owners of hotels and hotel chains, the lack of linkages to other sectors of the local economy (the installations and even the food are mostly imported), and the low level of skills required from the workforce and, consequently, the relatively low salaries. Among the intangibles, the negative impact on pride, identity, and self-respect may be deplored.

Moreover, apart from the very marginal benefits provided by visits from cruise ships—limited to a few spots favored by the liners—the income from the tourist trade has been declining in the case of several island-nations over the past few years. Development and modernization may themselves prove a mixed blessing, for they negatively affect the tourist trade, which has been either the main or an important source of revenue for most island-nations (including Cuba). The more modern the island, the less likely it is to remain a tourist spot; this general rule also explains why Cuba has become the number one destination for tourists. Although only 1.2 million tourists visited Cuba in 1997, the projection, as confirmed by sources from outside Cuba, are for between 4 and 5 million visitors by 2007, outdoing the Mexican "Riviera."

Industrialization programs have been launched in the region; perhaps the best known of these are the Puerto Rican programs created during the New Deal and World War II and organized by the Puerto Rican Reconstruction Administration. These programs were popularly known as Operation Bootstrap. An industrial park was also set up at Point Lisas in Trinidad under Prime Minister Eric Williams, taking advantage of the windfall profits resulting from the oil boom. Although some industrialization did result, neither of these programs was successful enough to catapult the country or the island from the ranks of the underdeveloped. The political conditions in Cuba were more favorable for central planning of development, but, here too, internal and external factors combined to defeat the effort. Thus, Cuba remains a country largely dependent on the monoculture of sugar, whereas Trinidad and Tobago continues to depend on its exports of crude and refined oil and gas. The manufacturing sector of the latter contributes less than 10% to the country's GDP; the balance of payments, favorable until 1982, has been unfavorable since that time. Indeed, since the island-nations are small, so are the domestic markets; hence, nearly all consumer goods have to be imported.

Economic, Social, and Political Progress

No generalizations can be made about economic or social achievements in the region; if anything, the contrasts are stark. While the per capita gross national income is $7,530 (as of 1995) in Puerto Rico—far lower than in any state of the United States—and $4,750 in Trinidad and Tobago (as of 1999) and growing, the corresponding figure for Haiti is only $1,400, and at least three quarters of the population has no share in production. Life expectancy in Cuba is age 76.3 and is almost as high in Dominica, Puerto Rico, and Jamaica; it is less than age 52 in Haiti. Infant mortality rate in Cuba is below seven per thousand, lower than in the United States and most industrialized nations. It is thirty-nine per thousand in the Dominican Republic and seventy-six per thousand in Haiti. The growth in the GDP has been around 5% during the past three years in Grenada (2002–2005), around 6% in Trinidad and Tobago, and more than 8% in the Dominican Republic. The growth has been even higher in some of the small island-nations of the Eastern Caribbean, whereas it is negative in Haiti.

All of this information seems to confirm the notion that Haiti is the poorest country not only in the Caribbean but in the entire Western Hemisphere. Using a combination of socioeconomic indices, some of the island-nations are ranked in the upper third among all the countries of the developing world. Cuba is doing well as far as social indices go, but the data regarding economic achievements are simply not available (at least not to the World Bank).

Decolonization has proved a mixed blessing. Most of the Anglophone Caribbean enjoys political independence, with Jamaica and Trinidad and Tobago achieving independence in 1962. Those two influential nations led the path to independence, followed by Barbados and Guyana in 1966, the Bahamas in 1973, Grenada in 1974, Dominica in 1978, St. Lucia and St. Vincent and the Grenadines in 1979, and Antigua and Barbuda in 1981.

The island-nations have adopted some kind of parliamentary system along with civil rights and regular elections. In a few cases, authoritarian regimes have taken over until dislodged or overthrown. The most obvious example of such a regime is Cuba, where the regime led by Fidel Castro has replaced, in the name of socialism, earlier authoritarian systems. Haiti and the Dominican Republican have had more than their share of dictators, although in both cases there have been elections that were relatively free according to most observers. In Haiti, we have the anomaly of the same democratically elected president displaced twice by inside forces or outside intervention. Other examples of *coups d'état* include the New Jewel movement led by Maurice Bishop in Grenada, which itself became the victim of a counter-*coup d'état*, leading to Bishop's assassination and a few days later to outside intervention by the United States.

The government of Guyana has also been the victim of outside intervention (notably by the United Kingdom and the United States), although lack of stability there is due in large part to ethnic dissension. Although ethnic divisions have plagued the government of Trinidad and Tobago as well, there the parliamentary system has weathered all the crises rather successfully. In Barbados, the passing of power from one regime to the next has been peaceful. In Jamaica, even though there is no ethnic strife, the passing of power from one party to the next has been more troublesome, with plenty of violence incidental to polling. All in all, however, there is hope for the establishment of solid, lasting civil societies throughout most of the region.

Even politically and diplomatically, with the possible exception of Cuba, most of the island-nations may be considered part of the American sphere of influence, enjoying less than full independence. Economically, independence entailed disintegration rather than integration. Some islands and some nations are doing better than others. Puerto Rico and the Virgin Islands have benefited economically from their ties with the United States, enabling their residents to travel to-and-fro between island and mainland, even though the impact of the colonial system may have been deleterious on the morale and the morals. A few of the island-nations stand a chance of escaping the vicious circle of underdevelopment by virtue of profits from oil (in the case of Trinidad) or from bauxite (in Jamaica and Guyana).

Economic integration began with the establishment of a British West Indies Federation in 1958, but that federation was short-lived. This balkanization has prompted attempts at reintegration, such as the failed West Indies Federation, between 1958 and 1962. Among relevant international organizations, there is the relatively successful Caribbean Community and Common Market (CARICOM), the successor to the Caribbean Free Trade Association set up in 1968, entailing economic cooperation among the Anglophone West Indies; for instance, it has adopted a Common External Tariff in 1992.

CARICOM was established by the Treaty of Chaguaramas (in Trinidad) in 1973. While the Treaty was originally signed by Barbados, Jamaica, Guyana, and Trinidad and Tobago, it was eventually expanded to include at least fifteen states and spread geographically and culturally beyond the Anglophone West Indies to include Haiti and Suriname. Concrete steps have been taken by this organization to integrate the economies of at least some of the island-nations and to establish a common market and a free-trade association. CARICOM has also taken steps to coordinate foreign policy and intervene in combating regional problems, such as the spread of AIDS. Moreover, it has repeatedly adopted resolutions to reinforce civil society in the islands, including civil rights, the parliamentary system, free press, and the fight against corruption.

Other manifestations of cooperation among the islands include the campuses of the University of West Indies (UWI), founded in 1948; it now has campuses on Jamaica, Trinidad and Tobago, Barbados, and Guyana. The Caribbean Group for Cooperation in Economic Development (CGCED) was established in 1977 by some Anglophone countries (including Belize in Central America); it has expanded beyond the Anglophone Caribbean to include Haiti, the Dominican Republic, and Suriname. These are certainly positive signs indicative of potential economic, political, and social progress; indeed, such progress is not likely to take place anywhere in the Caribbean without effective cooperation.

MARIO D. FENYO

References and Further Reading

Kempe, Ronald Hope. *Economic Development in the Caribbean.* New York: Praeger, 1986.

Mandle, Jay R. *Persistent Underdevelopment; Change and Economic Modernization in the West Indies.* Amsterdam: Gordon and Breach, 1996.

Payne, Anthony, and Paul Sutton. *Charting Caribbean Development.* Gainesville, FL: University Press of Florida, 2001.

Ramsaran, Ramesh, ed. *Caribbean Survival and the Global Challenge.* Kingston, Jamaica: Ian Randle, 2002.

Shepherd, Verene, and Hilary M. Beckles, eds. *Caribbean Freedom: Economy and Society from Emancipation to the Present.* Markus Wiener, 1996.

Watts, David. *The West Indies: Patterns of Development, Culture and Environmental Change Since 1492.* Cambridge: Cambridge University Press, 1987.

CARIBBEAN: INTERNATIONAL RELATIONS

Although the entire Western Hemisphere experienced European colonialism, the Caribbean islands were subjected to the most pervasive, diverse, and lengthy European colonial experience. Since the initial arrival of Christopher Columbus in the region in 1492, the European nations and the United States after 1898, for a plethora of economic and strategic reasons, vied with each other to establish colonies. In 1945, the entire Caribbean region—with the exception of Haiti, the Dominican Republic, and Cuba—was still controlled by the United States, the United Kingdom, France, and the Netherlands. As such, foreign policy was conducted by the colonial powers. Notwithstanding the independence of Haiti, the Dominican Republic, and Cuba, these nations conducted their foreign policy in the shadow of US diplomatic imperatives. Haiti, the Dominican Republic, and Cuba—all of which had been militarily occupied by the United States for prolonged periods during the first half of the twentieth century—were cognizant of the fact that their foreign policy initiatives were conditioned by the vagaries of US foreign policy.

In the post-World War II period, Antigua and Barbuda, the Bahamas, Barbados, Dominica, Grenada, Jamaica, St. Kitts and Nevis, St. Lucia, St. Vincent and the Grenadines, and Trinidad and Tobago achieved their independence. Meanwhile, Anguilla, the British Virgin Islands, the Cayman Islands, Guadeloupe, Martinique, Montserrat, the Netherlands Antilles, Puerto Rico, the Turks and Caicos Islands, and the US Virgin Islands remained European and US colonies. The exigencies of the Cold War, especially as manifested in the 1959 Cuban Revolution, brought a new prominence to Caribbean international relations. Notwithstanding sporadic, and frequently unsuccessful, attempts by some of the independent Caribbean nations to assert a foreign policy independent of that of the United States, most Caribbean nations have pursued a pro-US foreign policy aimed at strengthening their economic infrastructure. John F. Kennedy's Alliance for Progress provided funds to strengthen the economic and military infrastructures of pro-US governments in Latin America and the Caribbean.

The three most significant regional organizations in the Caribbean region are the Association of Caribbean States (ACS), which facilitates consultation, cooperation, and concerted action among member states concerning issues such as economic development; the Caribbean Community and Common Market (CARICOM), which supports economic cooperation through the Caribbean Common Market; and the Organization of Eastern Caribbean States (OECS), which promotes extensive cooperation among the English-speaking member states in the Eastern Caribbean.

Haiti

Following a violent slave revolt that lasted for thirteen years, Haiti, which occupies the western third of the island of Hispaniola, became the Western Hemisphere's second independent nation in 1804. As such, Haiti became the world's first independent black republic. During the first half of the nineteenth century, slaveholding nations, such as the United States, intimidated by the only successful slave revolt in the Western Hemisphere, refused to grant Haiti diplomatic recognition. The onset of the US Civil War, however, allowed President Abraham Lincoln to grant Haiti diplomatic recognition. During the twentieth century, the economic and political influence of the United States in Haiti was more influential than that of any other country. The United States was Haiti's most important trading partner and the most important source of foreign economic and military assistance. From 1915 until 1934, the United States, primarily concerned with protecting access routes to the Panama Canal, militarily occupied Haiti and controlled the nation's foreign policy.

During the Duvalier dictatorship (1957–1986), successive US presidential administrations overlooked the authoritarian nature of the Haitian government. François and Jean-Claude Duvalier exploited US fears of communism in the Caribbean following Fidel Castro's successful 1959 revolution in Cuba. US policy makers viewed Haiti as a bastion of anti-communism in the Caribbean. As such, the US government provided the Haitian dictatorship with generous amounts of economic and military aid. In 1987, after the Duvalier regime had been overthrown, the United States briefly suspended all aid to Haiti. In 1989, the US resumed economic aid to Haiti on the condition that the Haitian government continue to make progress toward holding democratic elections and cooperate in US efforts to control the international drug trade.

In 1991, Jean-Bertrand Aristide, a defrocked Roman Catholic priest, became the nation's first democratically elected president. The Haitian military, however, overthrew Aristide nine months later. A US-led United Nations peacekeeping force intervened in 1994 and restored Aristide to power. Regardless, political and economic instability, notwithstanding large infusions of economic aid, continued. As such, a virtually endless flow of refugees has sought asylum in the United States. Aristide, who returned to power in questionable elections in 2000, became increasingly authoritarian and lost the support of US policy makers. An armed revolt in early 2004, coupled with US pressure for his removal, resulted in Aristide's exile in February 2004. A US-led force attempted to restore order and stability, while the international community pledged more than $1 billion in economic aid.

Haiti's relations with the Dominican Republic have been tumultuous. Haiti militarily occupied the Dominican Republic from 1822 until 1844. Haitian occupation, and subsequent attempts to reconquer the eastern two-thirds of the island of Hispaniola, seriously strained diplomatic relations between the two nations during the nineteenth and twentieth centuries. Notwithstanding the almost constant flow of Haitians crossing the border in search of employment in the Dominican sugarcane fields, border conflicts have frequently erupted into violent conflict. In 1937, Dominican dictator Rafael Trujillo orchestrated the massacre of twelve thousand Haitians in the Dominican Republic. Nevertheless, during the Duvalier regime, the Haitian government facilitated the procurement of Haitian cane cutters for the annual Dominican sugarcane harvest. By 2000, the presence of more than 1 million people of Haitian origin in the Dominican Republic, many of whom were illegally present, caused an additional strain in Dominican–Haitian relations.

Because of Haiti's unique cultural and historical legacy in the Caribbean, ties with other Caribbean nations have been limited. During the colonial period, the United Kingdom and France, fearful that the Haitian experience would encourage economic and political instability in their colonies, discouraged contact between their Caribbean colonies and Haiti. This lack of contact continued into the postindependence era. Haiti remains the least developed nation in the Western Hemisphere.

Dominican Republic

The Dominican Republic achieved its independence in 1844 after being militarily occupied by Haiti for twenty-two years. After a brief period of economic and political pandemonium, the Dominican government voluntarily petitioned to return to Spanish colonial status in 1861. Realizing that Spanish colonial status was not the panacea for their economic and political woes, Dominican elites proclaimed independence in 1865. Although the Dominican Republic—pursuing a liberal, export-led economy based on exports of raw materials to Europe and the United States—experienced a brief period of economic and political stability during the last two decades of the nineteenth century, political and economic chaos had returned to the nation by 1900. Ongoing economic and political chaos, the threat of European intervention, and the desire to protect the access routes to the Panama Canal, convinced the United States to militarily occupy the Dominican Republic from 1916 to 1924.

During the Trujillo dictatorship (1930–1961), successive US presidential administrations overlooked the authoritarian nature of the Dominican government. Rafael Trujillo exploited US fears of Nazism during the 1930s and communism during the Cold War to garner US economic and military aid. Trujillo proclaimed himself the most ardent anti-Communist in the Western Hemisphere and closely aligned his foreign policy with that of the United States. His voting record in the United Nations (UN) was parallel to that of the United States. Following Fidel Castro's successful 1959 revolution in Cuba, US policy makers were concerned that Trujillo's authoritarian excesses might lead to the establishment of a second Communist regime in the Caribbean. In 1960, the Organization of American States (OAS) imposed diplomatic sanctions against the Dominican Republic as a result of Trujillo's participation in the attempted assassination of

Venezuelan President Rómulo Betancourt. The United States, therefore, supported the overthrow and assassination of Trujillo in 1961. President John F. Kennedy's attempt to make the Dominican Republic a showcase for democracy resulted in the election of Juan Bosch to the presidency of the Dominican Republic in 1963. Conservative elements in Dominican society, however, overthrew Bosch, who had been pursuing a leftist-oriented foreign and domestic policy, in September 1963.

In 1965, a counterrevolution designed to restore the deposed Bosch to power resulted in a civil war. President Lyndon B. Johnson, under the pretense of forestalling the establishment of a second Communist state in the Western Hemisphere, sent twenty-three thousand US troops to restore order and stability. The unilateral US military intervention was quickly transformed into a multinational OAS-sponsored intervention. US-supervised elections in 1966 were won by Joaquín Balaguer, who closely aligned the Dominican Republic politically and economically with the United States. In return for his pro-US foreign policy, Balaguer was rewarded with generous sugar quotas and increased economic aid. Subsequent Dominican governments have pursued a foreign policy closely tied to that of the United States. The United States is the nation's most important trading partner, and remittances from Dominicans living in the United States contribute substantially to the Dominican economy. The Dominican government has also cooperated with US officials on issues such as reducing illegal immigration, the return of stolen cars to the United States, and the extradition of fugitives. In addition, the Dominican Republic sent troops to Iraq in support of the fight against terrorism.

Historically, relations with Haiti have oscillated between sporadic to tense. Lingering Dominican animosity against Haitians, dating back to the 1822–1844 military occupation, has fomented distrust of the Haitian government. In addition, Dominicans, who view themselves as Hispanic and European, tend to view Haitians as black, uncivilized, and African. Frequently, in an attempt to keep the civil unrest in Haiti from spreading to the Dominican Republic, the Dominican government has closed the Dominican–Haitian border. During the 1990s, however, the Dominican government supported the attempted democratization process in Haiti. A point of contention between the two nations is the presence of more than 1 million Haitians in the Dominican Republic, many of who are there illegally.

Although the Dominican Republic's most important diplomatic relations are with the United States, the nation maintains accredited diplomatic missions in most Latin American nations and the major European nations. The Dominican Republic's relations with Cuba increased during the 1980s. Although the Dominican government is cognizant of US hostility toward Fidel Castro's regime, the Dominicans and Cubans implemented sports and cultural exchanges during the 1980s. The Dominican Republic also maintains close diplomatic relations with Venezuela, the supplier of the majority of the Dominican Republic's petroleum needs. The Republic of China (Taiwan) has extensive cultural and economic relations with the Dominican Republic. The Dominican Republic is one of the few nations in Latin America to recognize the Taiwanese government as the legitimate Chinese government.

Cuba

Unlike the rest of Spanish-speaking Latin America, which achieved independence at the beginning of the nineteenth century, Cuba—the largest island in the Caribbean—did not attain independence until 1902. Given Cuba's geographic position, the Spanish government was able to isolate Cuba from the revolutionary movements seeking independence on the mainland between 1814 and 1824. In 1895, scholar José Marti launched an independence movement that contributed to the demise of Spanish colonial rule. Citing humanitarian, economic, and national security concerns, the US intervened in the Cuban struggle for independence. The so-called Spanish-American War of 1898 resulted in Spain relinquishing control of Cuba and Puerto Rico to the United States. Prior to appropriating funds to fight the war, the US Congress passed the Teller Amendment, which stated that the US had no intention of annexing Cuba. Thus, at the conclusion of the war, the US government made plans for Cuba's independence. Puerto Rico, however, which was not covered by the Teller Amendment, was made a US colony.

The 1901 Platt Amendment was a precondition for Cuban independence. It provided for an extensive degree of US control over Cuban affairs, made Cuba a virtual protectorate of the United States, and set the stage for the symbiotic alliance between Cuban elites and US policy makers and businessmen that lasted until 1958. Thus, in 1902, Cuba was granted independence. Cuba's foreign policy, however, was closely regulated by the United States. Although the Platt Amendment was abrogated in 1934, the United States continued to dominate

Cuban internal and external affairs. In addition, it also continued to control the vast naval base at Guantanamo Bay. Fulgencio Batista y Zaldívar, who directly or indirectly ruled Cuba from 1934 until 1958, received generous economic and military aid packaged from the United States. Just like Trujillo, Batista was an ardent anti-Communist. Batista's corrupt and brutal authoritarian regime, however, fueled a revolution led by Fidel Castro during the 1950s. On January 1, 1959, Castro's revolutionary forces entered Havana as Batista departed into exile.

Castro's nationalist rhetoric was infused with a certain degree of anti-Americanism. Castro was determined to break the symbiotic alliance between Cuban elites and US businessmen and politicians. The Cuban leader rounded up more than five hundred of Batista's closest supporters and executed them after a brief trial. More than one-tenth of Cuba's population, more than five hundred thousand people, fled to the United States. Castro used the derogatory term *gusanitos* (little worms) to refer to these exiles. By 1961, Castro had nationalized, without compensation, all US investment in Cuba. The US severed diplomatic relations with Cuba on January 3, 1961. Newly elected President John F. Kennedy supported a CIA-directed invasion of Cuban exiles in April 1961. The goal of the invasion was to overthrow Castro—who was viewed by most US policy makers as a Communist—and restore a pro-US government to power in Havana. The Bay of Pigs invasion, however, was a fiasco. Within a matter of days, the entire Cuban exile force had been killed or captured. Castro, who feared subsequent invasions, pursued a closer alliance with the Soviet Union. The Cubans had replaced dependency on the United States with dependency on the Soviet Union. Cuban sugar exports, which had primarily gone to the United States, were now sent to the Soviet Union.

In October 1962, the Soviet Union attempted to install medium-range nuclear missiles in Cuba, which provoked the Cuban Missile Crisis. The Soviets claimed that the warheads were defensive in nature, while the United States claimed that the warheads were offensive in nature. The crisis proved to be one of the most tense moments in the Cold War. After a series of messages between Kennedy and Soviet leader Nikita Khruschev, the Soviets agreed to dismantle the missile sites in Cuba. In return, the United States promised that it would not invade Cuba. In addition, the United States promised, albeit secretly, to remove nuclear warheads from Turkey. To appease the Cubans, the Soviet Union promised to provide Castro's regime with extensive military and economic aid. Castro used this aid to develop a cradle-to-grave

social welfare state. This program was relatively successful until communism collapsed in Eastern Europe in 1991.

The cornerstone of Castro's foreign policy was the attempt to spread Communist revolutions around the world. Castro spent millions of dollars and deployed thousands of troops in Africa and Latin America, which inhibited diplomatic relations with many nations. During the 1980s, Castro sent fifty thousand troops to Angola and twenty-four thousand troops to Ethiopia. Castro's foreign adventures, however, were curtailed during the 1990s after Soviet funding was terminated. Cuba has abandoned, for the most part, its financial support of revolutionary movements in Latin America and Africa. Nevertheless, the Cuban government continues to maintain relations with several revolutionary groups throughout Latin America and Africa.

The cessation of massive infusions of Soviet aid also produced a severe economic crisis in Cuba. Castro gradually opened up the economy to limited private enterprise and encouraged foreign investment. Nevertheless, the United States continued to enforce the economic embargo that had been in place since the 1960s. In 1996, the Helms-Burton Act tightened the economic embargo. Although Castro remains a totalitarian pariah in the Western Hemisphere, he has attempted to portray his regime as a moderate Socialist state. In anticipation of Pope John Paul II's 1998 visit, which was a huge public relations event for the aging dictator, Castro declared Christmas an official holiday in 1997. In 2000, Cuba signed a barter agreement with Venezuela that provided for the exchange of Venezuelan petroleum for Cuban goods and services. Cuba's arrangement with Venezuela has kept the Cuban economy afloat.

Jamaica

After three centuries of colonial rule, the British government granted Jamaica internal autonomy in 1953. The United Kingdom, however, continued to control defense and foreign relations. In 1958, Jamaica joined the West Indies Federation (WIF). Nationalist labor leader Alexander Bustamante, however, opposed Jamaican participation in the WIF and convinced Jamaican voters to opt out of the association in 1961. Jamaica became independent on August 6, 1962, with Bustamante serving as the nation's first prime minister. Jamaica is a member of the British Commonwealth.

On the day after independence, Bustamante described Jamaica as a pro-US, anti-Communist

CARIBBEAN: INTERNATIONAL RELATIONS

nation. During the 1960s, Jamaica frequently sided with the United States when voting on Cold War issues in the United Nations. In the early 1970s, however, Prime Minister Michael Manley decided that Jamaica had to reorient its foreign policy away from that of the United Kingdom and the United States. In 1972, Manley's government granted diplomatic recognition to Fidel Castro's regime in Cuba. Relations between Jamaica and the United States deteriorated when Manley supported Cuban interventionism in Africa. Relations with the United States, however, improved greatly when Edward Seaga became prime minister in 1980. Seaga worked closely with the Ronald Reagan administration. Reagan made Jamaica the centerpiece of his Caribbean Basin Initiative (CBI). Reagan and Seaga established a close working relationship. Seaga was the first foreign leader to visit Reagan after his inauguration in January 1981, and in 1982 Reagan was the first US president to visit Jamaica. Seaga supported the US intervention in Grenada in 1983, as well as the continuation of US economic sanctions against Cuba.

Although relations with the United Kingdom remain close, economic relations with the United States are predominant. The United States is Jamaica's most important trading partner, and almost 1 million US tourists visit Jamaica annually. The Jamaican government actively seeks to increase US foreign investment in Jamaica. In addition, the US government provides millions of dollars per year for development projects. Since Jamaica is the Caribbean's largest producer of marijuana and an important transshipment point for cocaine, US government officials have worked with Jamaican officials to limit the flow of illegal drugs to the United States. Since 1997, US officials have had the permission to enter Jamaica's territorial waters and search ships in an effort to fight drug trafficking. Since 2000, Jamaican authorities have seized several tons of marijuana annually and have actively prosecuted thousands of drug smugglers.

Trinidad and Tobago

The British, who acquired Trinidad in 1797 and Tobago in 1814, incorporated the two islands into a single colony in 1888. Trinidad and Tobago joined the West Indies Federation (WIF) in 1958. In 1962, following the example set by Jamaica, Trinidad and Tobago withdrew from the WIF, which effectively ended the association. Trinidad and Tobago became an independent nation on August 31, 1962, and joined the Commonwealth of Nations.

Eric Williams was prime minister from 1962 until his death in 1981. Williams supported greater economic integration in the Caribbean. In 1967, Trinidad and Tobago became the first Commonwealth nation to join the Organization of American States (OAS). Although the nation has maintained an independent voting record in the United Nations, Trinidad and Tobago has maintained a friendly relationship with the United States. Significantly, Trinidad and Tobago insisted on maintaining diplomatic relations with Communist nations, especially Cuba. In 1972, Trinidad and Tobago, along with Jamaica, Barbados, and Guyana, established diplomatic relations with Cuba. Although Williams desired relations with Cuba, he consistently pointed out the superiority of the capitalist system over the Socialist system. Trinidad and Tobago opposed the US-led invasion of Grenada in 1983. In 1994, Trinidad and Tobago supported US peacekeeping efforts in Haiti.

As the most industrialized country in the English-speaking Caribbean, Trinidad and Tobago has a commanding presence in the Caribbean Community and Common Market (CARICOM). Trinidad and Tobago is committed to free-market economic policies and encourages foreign investment. By 2000, virtually all state-owned industries and corporations had been privatized. US investors have more than $1 billion invested in Trinidad and Tobago. Trinidad and Tobago supplies the majority of the liquefied natural gas imported by the United States. In addition, the nation has cooperated with the United States in the war on drug trafficking.

Barbados

Barbados achieved independence on November 30, 1966, and joined the Commonwealth of Nations. Before independence, Barbados was a member of the West Indies Federation. In 1973, Barbados was one of the founding members of CARICOM. Since independence, Barbados has transformed itself from an economy dependent on the sugar industry to an economy based on tourism. More than 1 million tourists, mainly from the United Kingdom and the United States, visit Barbados each year. Barbados receives extensive economic and military aid packages from the United States. Barbados has also cooperated with US authorities in the war on drug trafficking.

Prior to 1982, Barbados's foreign policy was primarily driven by economic issues. Although Barbados established relations with Cuba in 1972, those relations were distant. In 1982, Prime Minister

Tom Adams began to focus on national and regional security concerns. Adams was concerned about the Marxist government of Maurice Bishop in neighboring Grenada. In 1983, Adams was the biggest supporter of the US-led invasion of Grenada. In 1994, Barbados supported the US initiative to promote democracy in Haiti.

Bahamas

Although the United Kingdom continued to control defense and foreign affairs, the Bahamas were granted internal self-government in 1964. Independence was achieved on July 10, 1973, and the Bahamas became a member of the Commonwealth of Nations. The economy is almost entirely dependent on tourism. More than 4 million tourists—mostly from the United States—visit the Bahamas annually. Virtually all food and manufactured imports come from the United States. The Bahamas maintain a strong international relationship with the United States. Although the Bahamas has diplomatic relations with Cuba, the two nations do not have resident ambassadors. The largest threat to internal security is the massive infusion of illegal Haitian immigrants. The Bahamas has cooperated with the United States in the war on drug trafficking.

Grenada

Grenada achieved independence from the United Kingdom on February 7, 1974, and joined the Commonwealth of Nations. Grenada's first prime minister, Eric Gairy, was overthrown in a bloodless *coup d'état* by the New Jewel Movement (NJM), which established a Marxist government with ties to Cuba, the Soviet Union, and other Communist nations. The People's Revolutionary Government (PRG) turned Grenada into a Soviet–Cuban client state. The stockpiling of vast quantities of Soviet-supplied weapons was a matter of great concern to Grenada's neighbors. In October 1983, an internal power struggle resulted in the death of Prime Minister Maurice Bishop. Following a period of pandemonium, a US–Caribbean force landed on the island to restore order and stability. Since 1984, US–Grenada relations have been friendly and the United States has provided significant amounts of economic aid. The United States, Venezuela, and Taiwan have embassies in Grenada. Grenada has embassies in the United Kingdom, the United States, Venezuela, and Canada. Grenada

strongly supported US efforts to restore democracy to Haiti in 1994.

Dominica

Dominica was granted independence on November 3, 1978, and joined the Commonwealth of Nations. The main priority in foreign relations is economic development. Prime Minister Eugenia Charles was a strong supporter of the Organization of Eastern Caribbean States (OECS). Charles also defended President Ronald Reagan's October 1983 invasion of Grenada at the Commonwealth Summit in India in November 1983. The government of Dominica supported the US initiative to restore democracy in Haiti in 1994. The United States has funded multimillion-dollar development projects in Dominica.

St. Lucia

St. Lucia achieved independence on February 22, 1979, and joined the Commonwealth of Nations. The main priority in foreign relations is economic development. St. Lucia seeks to conduct its foreign policy primarily through its membership in the OECS. St. Lucia participated in the 1983 invasion of Grenada and maintains a cooperative relationship with the United States.

St. Vincent and the Grenadines

St. Vincent and the Grenadines achieved independence on October 27, 1979, and joined the Commonwealth of Nations. The main priority in foreign relations is economic development. St. Vincent and the Grenadines seeks to conduct its foreign policy primarily through its membership in the OECS. St. Vincent and the Grenadines supports US efforts to eradicate drug trafficking in the Caribbean.

Antigua and Barbuda

Antigua and Barbuda achieved independence on November 1, 1981, and joined the Commonwealth of Nations. The main priority in foreign relations is economic development. During the Cold War,

Antigua and Barbuda's government was vehemently anti-Communist. Antigua and Barbuda supported the US peacekeeping initiative in Haiti in 1994. In addition, Antigua and Barbuda has cooperated with US agents in the war on drug trafficking.

St. Kitts and Nevis

St. Kitts and Nevis achieved independence on September 19, 1983, and joined the Commonwealth of Nations. The main priority in foreign relations is economic development. Relations with the United States have been friendly, and the United States has supplied the nation with generous economic aid packages. St. Kitts and Nevis sent a contingent of police to participate in the US invasion of Grenada in 1983.

MICHAEL R. HALL

See also Alliance for Progress; Anguilla; Antigua and Barbuda; Aristide, Jean-Bertrand; Bahamas; Barbados; Batista y Zaldívar, Fulgencio; Betancourt, Rómulo; Bishop, Maurice; Bosch, Juan; Caribbean Basin Initiative; Caribbean Community and Common Market (CARICOM); Caribbean Development Bank; Caribbean Free Trade Association (CARIFTA); Caribbean: History and Economic Development; Castro, Fidel; Cayman Islands; Commonwealth (British); Cuban Revolution; Dominica; Dominican Republic; Drug Trade; Duvalier, François; Grenada; Guadeloupe; Haiti; Jamaica; Martinique; Netherlands Antilles; New Jewel Movement; Puerto Rico; St. Christopher and Nevis; St. Lucia; St. Vincent and the Grenadines; Trinidad and Tobago; Trujillo, Rafael Leonidas; Virgin Islands (British); Virgin Islands (United States); Williams, Eric

References and Further Reading

Abbott, Elizabeth. *Haiti: The Duvaliers and Their Legacy.* New York: McGraw-Hill, 1988.
Atkins, G. Pope, and Larman C. Wilson. *The Dominican Republic and the United States: From Imperialism to Transnationalism.* Athens, GA: University of Georgia Press, 1998.
Braveboy-Wagner, Jacqueline Anne. *Caribbean in World Affairs: The Foreign Policies of the English-Speaking States.* Boulder, CO: Westview Press, 1989.
Cockcroft, James D. *Latin America: History, Politics, and US Policy.* Chicago: Nelson Hall Publishers, 1996.
Dupuy, Alex. *Haiti in the New World Order: The Limits of the Democratic Revolution.* Boulder, CO: Westview Press, 1997.
Galvez, William. *Che in Africa: Che Guevara's Congo Diary.* Melbourne, Australia: Ocean Press, 1999.
Gleijeses, Piero. *Conflicting Missions: Havana, Washington, and Africa, 1959–1976.* Chapel Hill, NC: University of North Carolina Press, 2002.
Joseph, Gilbert M., Catherine C. LeGrand, and Richard D. Salvatore, eds. *Close Encounters of Empire: Writing the Cultural History of US–Latin American Relations.* Durham, NC: Duke University Press, 1998.
Langley, Lester. *America and the Americas: The United States in the Western Hemisphere.* Athens, GA: University of Georgia Press, 1989.
Lowenthal, Abraham F. *Research in Latin America and the Caribbean on International Relations and Foreign Policy: Some Impressions.* Washington, DC: The Wilson Center, 1982.
Nash, Philip. *The Other Missiles of October: Eisenhower, Kennedy, and the Jupiters, 1957–1963.* Chapel Hill, NC: University of North Carolina Press, 1997.
Palmer, Bruce. *Intervention in the Caribbean: The Dominican Crisis of 1965.* Lexington, KY: University Press of Kentucky, 1989.

CARTELS

Cartels Defined

A "cartel" is an arrangement among some or all suppliers that is designed to restrict output, raise prices, and increase the profits of members. Within most developed countries, cartels are illegal, but this was not always the case, and they were common in the United States prior to the antitrust Sherman Act (1890), in Germany prior to 1945, and in the United Kingdom until 1956.

Less-developed countries (LDCs) are affected by cartels in two main ways—as members of international producer cartels, such as the Organization of Petroleum Exporting Countries (OPEC), and as importers and consumers of goods produced by private, international "hard-core" cartels, such as those recently prosecuted in lysine and carbon electrodes.

International Producer Cartels

The centerpiece of the New International Economic Order, which was widely discussed in the 1970s and sought to usher in a new relationship between developed and developing countries, was supposed to be the development of International Commodity Agreements.

Ostensibly, the main purpose of the agreements was to stabilize prices. The main instrument for achieving price stability was the establishment of buffer stocks, which are features of the tin, rubber, and cocoa agreements.

In practice, however, most LDC producers hoped and perhaps expected that the commodity agreements would increase the prices they received over the long term. Buffer stocks could not achieve this, but export controls might, and such controls were features of the sugar, coffee, and tin agreements. In these cases, it is meaningful to refer to them as cartels.

Table 1 summarizes the features of eight of the most important producer agreements; with the possible exceptions of rubber and cocoa, all have been referred to as cartels at some point. But with the exception of the diamond cartel, and perhaps OPEC (which is considered consider in more detail in upcoming paragraphs), none of the other commodity agreements is currently effective at raising the longterm producer price; Gilbert (1996) captures the idea well in an article entitled "International Commodity Agreements: An Obituary Notice."

To get a better sense of the dynamics of producer cartels, consider the three cases of tin, coffee, and diamonds:

- *Tin:* Although tin producers had cooperated on and off since 1921, the first International Tin Agreement was concluded in 1954 and came into operation in 1956. The International Tin Council (ITC) established and maintained a buffer stock, using it to stabilize prices. In this, it had some success; between 1957 and 1977, the price fell below the (admittedly low) price floor just once and then only briefly. Prices were high in the 1970s as Malaysia's oncedominant production fell, and the minimum price was raised; consumers switched to aluminum, and Brazil entered the market. By the early 1980s, the ITC had an unsustainably large buffer stock, and when the tin market collapsed in November 1985, the ITC owed £900 million, most of it inadequately backed by collateral in the form of tin that had halved in value.

- *Coffee:* The first international coffee agreement was established in 1962, when Brazil was clearly the dominant oligopolist and was in a position to punish noncooperation (by releasing stocks of coffee). During the following decade, coffee prices were higher and more volatile than in the previous decade. The coffee agreements ended in 1989, when the United States refused to participate; by then, new producers had eroded Brazil's position, and Brazil itself was increasingly ambivalent about the desirability of trying to boost the price of coffee; it is the second largest coffee market in the world. Pasour (1990) argues that commodity agreements "tend to freeze the pattern of production, protect high-cost producers, and restrict the growth of lower-cost supplies." This applies well to coffee.

- *Diamonds:* De Beers sought to establish a diamond cartel in 1934 in response to a depressionera drop in diamond prices. The firm has a stake in half of the world's twenty-three operating diamond mines and uses the technique of *single channel marketing*, whereby it buys diamonds from suppliers and then sells them through the Central Selling Organization. The market for rough diamonds is worth $6 billion annually and is an important source of revenue for several developing countries, including Botswana, Namibia, South Africa, Tanzania, Sierra Leone, the Democratic Republic of Congo, and Angola. Other major producers are Australia, Canada, and Russia. Executives of De Beers never travel to the United States, where they risk prosecution for their anticompetitive practices.

Table 1: The major cartel-like international commodity agreements

	Diamonds	Oil	Tin	Coffee	Rubber	Cocoa	Bauxite	Sugar
Year of first agreement	1934	1960	1954	1962	1980	1972	1974	1954
End of cartel-like agreement	2000	...	1985	1989	1999	1988	1994	1983
Were export controls used?	Yes	From 1983	Yes	Yes	No	No	Yes	Yes
Was a buffer stock used?	Yes	No	Yes	No	Yes	Yes	No	No
Approximate share of market (%)	78–90	31–56	72–86	90–95	80	?	73–80	?
Organization	De Beers	OPEC	ITC	ICO	INRO	ICCO	IBA	ISA

Sources: Gilbert (1996); Alhajji and Huettner (2000).

Note: Other international commodity agreements, with limited cartel features, include copper, iron ore, bananas, olive oil, and wheat.

Is OPEC a Cartel?

At least 250 economics textbooks use OPEC as a classic example of a cartel. Formed in 1960, OPEC is typically seen as the prime mover behind the four-fold rise in the price of oil in 1973, its subsequent doubling in 1979, and the maintenance of high oil prices in the early 1980s.

This view is controversial, and several observers argue that it is misleading to view OPEC as a cartel (or at least as an effective cartel). They point out that OPEC did not set production quotas until 1983; did not monitor quotas (that is, try to identify cheaters) until 1985; has never, as an organization, moved to punish quota violations; and faces elastic demand because its share of the world market is comparatively modest. In addition, they note that there are alternative and better explanations for oil price movements. The rise in price in 1973 was associated with the Arab–Israeli war, high world demand, and a drop in new discoveries; the jump in 1979 was due to the Iran–Iraq war; the high prices of the early 1980s were sustained because Saudi Arabia, the dominant exporter, reduced output sharply; and the low prices of the late 1980s occurred despite OPEC quotas and were due to the ending of Saudi Arabia's unsustainable program of output reductions.

The ineffectiveness of OPEC as a cartel may be contrasted with the effectiveness of the major oil companies (the *Seven Sisters*: BP, Esso, Gulf, Mobil, Shell, Socal, and Texaco) that formed a cartel in 1928 after a secret meeting in Achnacarry, Scotland. The companies agreed to divide the market and were highly profitable during the subsequent four decades.

Private International "Hard-Core" Cartels

In July 1995, the US Department of Justice announced an investigation into a private international cartel that sought to control the market for lysine, an additive to animal feed. This was the first of a number of successful investigations into international "hard-core" cartels; since then, the United States and European Union (EU) authorities have pursued 167 cartels (Carlton and Perloff 2005), levying fines over this period of more than $4 billion. Most developing countries have weak laws governing cartels; Brazil and Mexico are exceptions, but only the latter has levied a fine on a hard-core cartel. The victim was ADL, a ringleader in the lysine cartel, and a senior executive famously declared that "our competitors are our friends; our customers are the enemy."

As theory would predict, most of the cartels were formed in industries with relatively homogeneous products where the lead time for investments was long and the top four sellers accounted for at least four-fifths of the market. The reasons for the surge in cartels—most were formed during 1988 through 1992—are not entirely clear, but may have reflected lax enforcement in the United States and a change in managerial compensation practices that put a premium on boosting profits.

Although many of the cartels operated only in the EU or NAFTA countries, more than half of the cartelized sales were global and affected developing countries to at least some extent. Connor (2003) estimates that these forty-two global cartels on average involved 4.9 companies, had combined sales over about the period 1990–2002 of about $111 billion (see Table 2), and on average overcharged by 27%.

Table 2: Summary of available information on known international cartels, 1990–2002*

	No. of cartels	No. of companies per cartel	Total sales affected, $ billion	Overcharge rate, %
Total	98	5.9**	211	25
Of which:				
Global	42	4.9	111	27
EU or NAFTA only	55	8.3**	102	34
Memo:				
In food and feed ingredients	42	3.8	86	26
In organic chemicals	50	4.9	102	27
In cement [EU]	1	42	61	25
In graphite, carbon products	7	4.7	6	n.a.
In other industries	33	11.8	11	n.a.

Source: Connor (2003).

Notes: *Approximate time period. Sales refer to entire period.

** Excludes Eurozone bank cartel.

n.a., not applicable.

Table 3: Imports from known cartels by country category, 1997

	Low income	Low-middle income	Upper-middle income	All developing countries
Value of imports from cartels, $ billion	12.0	23.4	45.7	81.1
Cartelized imports as % of total imports	8.8	5.3	7.3	6.7
Cartelized imports as % of gross domestic product (GDP)	1.1	0.9	1.5	1.2

Source: Levenstein and Suslow (2001).
Note: Classification of countries follows the World Bank, *World Development Report 2000/2001.*

At the time that they were first identified, the typical global cartel had been in existence for at least six years.

International (global) cartels would impose costs on consumers in developing countries. The effects on LDC producers are less clear; on the one hand, they may benefit from the higher prices created by the cartel, but there is also some evidence that cartelized firms made access to technology more difficult and took active steps, such as predatory pricing or filing antidumping suits, to keep LDC production at bay. There are growing calls to ban hard-core cartels under a World Trade Organization competition agreement.

Based on information of thirty-seven international cartels prosecuted by the United States or EU in the 1990s, coupled with moderately detailed information on trade, Levenstein and Suslow (2001) estimate that cartelized products represented approximately 2.9% of LDC imports in 1997 (see Table 3). Under the reasonable assumption that these goods were overpriced by a fifth, then private international hardcore cartels overcharged LDCs by $16 billion in 1997, an amount equivalent to one-third of official development assistance in that year.

JONATHAN HAUGHTON

See also New International Economic Order (NIEO); Organization of Arab Petroleum Exporting Countries (OAPEC)

References and Further Reading

Alhajji, A. F., and David Huettner. "OPEC and Other Commodity Cartels: A Comparison." *Energy Policy* 28 1151–1164 (2000).

Carlton, Dennis W., and Jeffrey M. Perloff. "Cartels." In *Modern Industrial Organization*, 4th ed. Pearson/Addison Wesley, 2005.

Connor, John M. "Private International Cartels: Effectiveness, Welfare, and Anticartel Enforcement." West Lafayette, IN: Purdue University, 2003.

Eckbo, Paul L. *The Future of World Oil.* Cambridge, MA: Ballinger, 1976.

European Commission. "International Hard Core Cartels and Cooperation Under a WTO Framework Agreement on Competition." Submitted to World Trade Organization, 2002.

Gilbert, Christopher L. "International Commodity Agreements: An Obituary Notice." *World Development* 24, no. 1 1–19 (1996).

Levenstein, Margaret, and Valerie Suslow. "Private International Cartels and Their Effect on Developing Countries," Background Paper for the World Bank's *World Development Report 2001.* Washington, DC, 2001.

OECD. *Hard Core Cartels: Recent Progress and Challenges Ahead.* Paris: OECD, 2003.

Pasour, E. C. "The International Political Economy of Coffee." *The Review of Austrian Economics* 4 241–248 (1990).

Pepall, Lynne, Daniel J. Richards, and George Norman. "Collusion and Cartels." In *Industrial Organization: Contemporary Theory and Practice*, 2d ed. Mason, OH: South-Western, 2002.

CASTE SYSTEMS

Caste is an age-old institution, evolved through several centuries. As a system of stratification, it has existed in many parts of the world and is being practiced today in some countries. But the caste system of closed endogamous descent groups as prevalent and practiced in India is not found elsewhere (Bayly 2000; Kolenda 1984). Caste is a well-entrenched phenomenon in countries like India.

"Caste" comes from the Portuguese word *casta* meaning species, breed, race, or lineage. The Portuguese first used this word to refer to various segmental groups found in the Indian society. By definition, caste is a form of social stratification involving a system of hierarchically arranged, closed, endogamous strata, the membership of which is ascribed and between which contact is restricted and mobility is impossible (Jary and Jary 2000). In other words, caste is characterized chiefly by hierarchical arrangement, endogamous nature, and membership by birth.

Caste groups have their own distinctive culture manifested in their behaviour, mannerisms, dress, speech, habitat, rituals, superstitions, beliefs, and religious practices, as well as in every other socio-economic, political aspects of their life. Under this system, the social position of individuals is determined not by their wealth but by their ascriptive membership. Each caste is a large-scale descent group and forms an interdependent cooperative but inegalitarian segment consisting of a set of occupational groups, ordered by purity and pollution customs (Kolenda 1984). Pollution separates castes as distinctive entities.

Due to the differences in the ideologies of hierarchy and inequality, the caste system cannot be compared to other systems of racial stratification. Society is divided into permanent groups that are specialized, hierarchically arranged, and separated in matters of consumption, marriage, sex, and ceremonies related to social life such as birth, marriage, and death (Dumont 1970).

The term "caste" was used to refer to tribes and castes in India until the nineteenth century (Kolenda 1984). Caste groups with varying degrees of respectability and circles of social intercourse are a pan-Indian scheme (Srinivas 1952). According to the census count, in 1901 there were 2,378 castes in India; it is estimated that there are about three thousand caste groups presently found in India, formed of mixed unions between different *varnas* or between the *varna* and the offspring of mixed unions.

The caste system is a complex one composed of several Hindu ideas, namely, pollution, purity, and social units of *jatis*, *varnas*, and *dharmas* (religious duties). The system is, however not typical to Hindus alone but is common among Muslims, Christians, and Jews with relative variations. Muslim caste, for instance, differs from the Hindu caste wherein no ethico-religious ideas of hierarchy or regulation of intercaste relations are found. In addition, no *varna* categories are spotted among the Muslims (Srinivas 1965).

The essence of caste is *varna*. *Varna* denotes the division of Hindu society into four orders of Brahmana (Brahmin priest and scholar), Kshatriya (ruler and soldiers), Vaishya (merchant), and Sudra (peasant, labourer, and servant). The Brahmana, Kshatriya, and Vaishya are the "twice-born" castes, while the Sudras are not. There are also the untouchables who are not part of the *varna* system but fall outside the four *varnas*. Although the caste system is found in various forms in different parts of the world, including Asia and Africa, India is known for both its origin and its rigorous practice.

Origin

The expressions of caste are evident in the sacred writings of the *Vedas*, compiled between 1500 and 1000 BCE in India. Several factors, both individual and collective in nature, have contributed to the emergence of caste system. Conquest, race differences, religion, and economic development are prominent among the factors (Kroeber 1930). According to the Hindu tradition, the caste system is originated from four *varnas*. Brahmins sprang from the mouth of the deity, the Kshatriyas from his arms, the Vaishyas from the thigh, and the Sudra from the feet. Brahmins are assigned divinity and are allowed to perform the duties of studying, teaching, sacrificing, assisting others to do sacrifice, giving alms, and receiving gifts. Designated as the source of strength, Kshatriyas are allowed to perform the duties of studying, sacrificing, giving alms, using weapons, and protecting treasure and life. For the Vaishyas, work is important. They are supposed to study, do sacrifice, give alms, cultivate, and engage in trade, while Sudras serve all the three higher *varnas* (Hutton 1946).

Occupational theorists hold that occupation is the sole basis of caste distinction, and the caste system is a process of evolution of occupations (Nesfield 1885). Some believe that the origin of the system should be observed in the peculiar circumstances of a complex system of a society with a cross-division of guilds, which is largely a matter of colour. There are also scholars who argue that rituals are responsible for the birth of the caste system. Hutton finds reason in the geographical isolation of the Indian peninsula for the origin of the system. Apart from this, for him, there are other valid reasons, such as the primitive idea that food transmits qualities as well as the ideas of totemism, taboo, pollution, ablution, ritual sacrifice, ancestor worship, and sacraments. Beliefs in reincarnation, the doctrine of *karma*, hereditary occupation, and trade and craft secrets are added to his list. Not less important is the exploitation by a highly intelligent hierarchy that evolved a religious philosophy in this regard (Hutton 1946).

Features

The caste system operates within a limited locality, say in a village or in a few neighbouring villages (Kolenda 1984). Characteristically it has several identifying features. The following paragraphs describe the prominent ones.

First, the system divides the society into segments, and therefore, a caste-based society is not a homogenous one. Castes are the groups with a well-developed life of their own. The membership in a caste group is determined by birth. Second, it is based on hierarchy. Caste groups are ranked in the order of social precedence. In India, for instance, Brahmins are at the top, while the Kshatriyas, Vaishyas, and Sudras follow them in a descending order of hierarchy. The castes that come under each of these four *varnas* are again hierarchically positioned. Nonetheless, there is ambiguity in the matter of the order among the castes, particularly between the middle rungs (Srinivas 1991b). Caste groups have their own rights, duties, and privileges. The higher castes enjoy the power and privileges that are customarily denied to the lower castes. Lower castes are expected to provide services to the upper castes at times of special social occasions, such as birth, marriage, and death.

Third, the caste system has its features of restrictions on feeding and social intercourse. Restrictions imposed on giving and accepting food and drinks from other castes are for retaining the purity of castes. The castes from whom individuals could accept cooked food and drinking water are either equal or superior, whereas the castes from whom they do not accept food and water are inferior. Fourth, caste groups have civil and religious disabilities and privileges. Caste groups live in separate quarters, and the lower groups will stay away in isolation, usually away from the high castes. Castes who are at a lower level are not allowed to use public amenities including wells, roads, and schools in the village. The shared belief is that wells get polluted if a low caste person draws water from them. Entry to public places including places of worship is decided by the principles of pollution and purity. Lower castes are not only prohibited from wearing dress and ornaments similar to that of the higher castes but also not allowed to follow the customs of the higher castes. On occasions of birth, marriage, and death, they perform extra duties to the higher castes for which they are paid money or given gifts. This practice is known as *jajmani, bara balute, mirasi,* or *adade.* The relationship between a *jajman* and the lower caste is unequal, but stable, sustained on mutuality and is inherited (Srinivas 1965).

Fifth, caste groups are allowed to have only restricted choice of occupation. No caste groups have been given the freedom to change their occupation but to follow their hereditary one. *Hali* system (*hali* means plough), for instance, prohibits the twice-born from ploughing the earth (Ghurye 1979; Kolenda 1984). Finally, caste systems have restrictions on marriage. Caste groups are divided into subgroups, and the members of the subgroups are not permitted to marry those from other groups. Endogamy is strictly adhered to.

Caste groups have their own separate governing bodies called caste *Panchayats.* Authorized to deal with all aspects of the customs and practices of caste groups, *Panchayats* act as a council for each caste group. The council can also decide on matters such as eating, drinking, adultery, fornication, or any other caste affair. Members are liable for punishment if they do not observe the caste prescriptions. Punishments are rendered in the form of outcasting, giving fines, offering feasts to the offender's castes, and assigning corporal and religions expiation (Ghurye 1979). The caste system, in other words, is characterised by unique features like hierarchy; endogamy; hypergamy; occupational association; restrictions on food, drink, and smoking; caste organisation; and privileges and disabilities.

A caste group may be labelled as "dominant" when it preponderates numerically over other caste groups in a given area and when it wields overriding economic and political powers. When a caste group is able to enjoy one form of dominance over the other castes, it can frequently acquire other forms of dominance as well. Numerical strength and wealth can take a caste to the upper levels of the ritual hierarchy. In other words, when a particular caste group changes its rituals and ways of life along the lines of the higher castes, it will be able to move up in the social ladder. In some cases, the dominance of a caste group becomes decisive with all the powers, including the maintenance of law and order. It can punish those individuals who breach the caste customs and practices and ensure the observance of caste codes to the members (Srinivas 1991a).

Caste Systems in the World

The caste system, albeit not in the way it is practised in India, is observed in several countries but in variant forms. The Spartan division of the society into citizens, helots, and slaves shows the signs of a caste system. In the Roman Empire, there were patricians, plebeians, and slaves. These classifications, however, were on the basis of land holding and wealth, not on the criteria of the Indian caste system (Kroeber 1930). Some, like Lloyd Warner, describe the blacks and whites in the United States as caste groups rather than races because they are socially and not biologically defined categories (Beteile 1992). Bourdieu referred to the racial divide between whites and Muslims in colonial Algeria as a caste system.

Caste-like groupings also exist in China and Madagascar (Bayly 2000). In both South Africa and the southern United States, caste has been used to explain the systems of racial stratification (Jalali 1992). In Fiji, there are chieftains associated with their own clans who have a specific function to perform. These castes are graded according to their functions.

Burma under the Burmese monarchy had seven distinct classes of outcastes: Pagoda slaves, professional beggars, executioners, lepers, deformed and mutilated persons, and coffinmakers. Each of them had specific functions (occupations) and positions in the society. People from these outcaste classes could not enter a monarchy or become Buddhist monks (Hutton 1946). Japan is often referred to as "a land of caste" though a clear hereditary or occupational distinction is not made out (Kroeber 1930). Japan's *bushido* code defines a hierarchy consisting of warriors (*samurai*), commoners, merchants, and untouchables; this hierarchy more or less resembles the *Varna* system of India. But this hierarchy is not associated with the proliferation of smaller caste groups (Bayly 2000). The *Eta* in Japan constitutes a community of outcastes, who reside on the fringes of the Japanese society. They are considered subhuman, wear distinctive clothing, and have no social activities with other classes. Though the Japanese government had abolished all such feudal discrimination way back in 1871, the position of *Eta* in the society has not improved. They are still being discriminated against at school, at places of employment, and in trade and marriage (Hutton 1946).

In Africa, among the Masai, there is a tribe of hunters called *Wandorobo*. Resemblances to a typical caste system are found in the modern Africa, too. Among the Somali of the East Horn, there are certain outcaste classes of *Tomal, Yebir*, and *Midgan*. Pollution and taboo are common among them. The case is no different in East Africa either. In the Rwanda and Burundi regions, there are three racially and economically distinct groups, namely the *Tussi, Hutu*, and *Twa*. With the *Twa*, no *Hutu* or *Tussi* will enter into marriage. The *Tussi* look down on the *Hutu* for eating mutton and goat-fish. In the Ibo society, a group of people called *Osu* offer similarities to a caste group. The *Osu* became a class apart and live in segregated areas. Calling anyone an *Osu* is an insult.

Among the Jews and Gypsies, the system is in vogue. In Egypt, the fighting men were divided into two categories. They were, for generations, not allowed to learn and practice any other craft or trade. The swineherds in Egypt were not granted permission to enter temples. Being a priest was also a hereditary occupation. Herodotus mentions seven "clans" of priests, as well as fighting men, herdsmen, swineherds, tradesmen, interpreters, and navigators in Egypt. There are also classes of craftsmen, farmers, and artificers in Egypt that were hereditary and compulsory.

As it is clear, caste is being practiced in several parts of the world in varying forms. However, the most rigorous form of its practice is observed in southern Asia, specifically in India.

Caste Today

In the wake of modernisation, changes in caste systems are evident in societies where the system is strictly followed. India is no exception. The system in India has been a hindrance to the development of the society. However, the significance of the caste system on the lives of Indians is on the decline, particularly in the urban and suburban areas and among the educated and professionals. Because the society is under the influence of Western ways of life, values, and outlook, the caste system ceases to exert a great influence on individuals (Srinivas 1965). Caste becomes less and less a criterion that decides social interaction, prestige, and social position. Hypergamy is now not strictly followed in many parts of India. Rules relating to pollution and purity are no more rigidly observed.

The link between the caste and occupation is breaking. Occupations are no more associated with particular castes. The resultant occupational mobility has weakened the importance of the caste system in the modern society. Since independence in 1947, India has passed several constitutional provisions to provide for reservations in education and employment affecting acceptance and mobility to the lower castes. Attempts by the lower castes to liberate themselves from the bonds of the caste system and from the clutches of the domination of higher castes have paid-off well. Sanskritization, as Srinivas called it, helped the lower castes to improve their social standing. "Sanskritization" is a process by which the lower castes emulate the Brahmin style of life, adopt the Sanskrit rituals, and hire the services of Brahmin priests to purify their customs. As part of this process of Sanskritization, a lower caste may adopt vegetarianism and even give up drinking liquor.

Caste as a system of social stratification, however, maintains its hold over the prevailing social structure and is manifest, both covertly and overtly, in a number of realms of social intercourse. Endogamy is not that stringently followed now as is the case with the practices of purity and pollution (Beteile 2002). But there are forbidden areas of interaction between castes, preventing their intensive association and assimilation. Despite this, the impact of the caste on the social structure and political and economic spheres has not been negligible. Caste is still a potent source of social identity and political mobilisation. Specifically, caste has evolved its importance in manifold directions: employing as a means of promoting political ambitions, relating to labour force recruitment, and involving with religious beliefs and customs (Thorner 2002). Organized endeavours of caste groups have brought them political and economic advantages in the form of increased share in job reservations and in the development projects and programmes designed by the government. Political organisation along caste lines has resulted in improving the presence of caste groups in various political decision-making bodies of the country. Constitutional provisions, combined with the enactment of new legislations, and the timely constitution of commissions to look into the position of castes have changed the lot of particularly backward castes in India. All these changes have had a cumulative effect on the economic well-being of the castes, who started suffering from disabilities before 1947. If the trends in India are any indication, the caste system will lose its vigour to the class system in the new era of liberalisation and globalisation.

RADHAMANY SOORYAMOORTHY

See also India

References and Further Reading

Bayly, Susan. *Caste, Society, and Politics in India.* New Delhi: Cambridge University Press, 2000.
Beteile, Andre. *Society and Politics in India: Essays in Comparative Perspective.* New Delhi: Oxford University Press, 1992.
Dumont, Louis. *Homo Hierarchicus: The Caste System and Its Implications.* London: Vikas Publications, 1970.
Fuller, C. J., ed. *Caste Today.* New Delhi: Oxford University Press, 1997.
Jalali, Rita. "Caste and Class." *Encyclopaedia of Sociology.* New York: Macmillan Publishing Company, 1992.
Jary, David, and Julia Jary. *Sociology,* 3d ed. Glasgow: HarperCollins Publishers, 2000.
Kolenda, Pauline. *Caste in Contemporary India: Beyond Organic Solidarity.* Jaipur, India: Rawat Publications, 1984.
Kroeber, A. L. "Caste." *Encyclopaedia of the Social Sciences.* New York: The Macmillan Company, 1930.
Nesfield, John C. *Brief View of the Caste System of the North-Western Provinces and Oudh.* Allahabad, India: North-Western Provinces and Oudh Education Department, 1885.
Srinivas, M. N. *Religion and Society Among the Coorgs of South India.* London: Oxford University Press, 1952.
———. "Social Structure." *The Gazetteer of India: Indian Union.* New Delhi: Ministry of Information and Broadcasting, Government of India, 1965.
———. "Varna and Caste." In *Social Stratification,* edited by Dipankar Gupta. New Delhi: Oxford University Press, 1991a.
———. "Dominant Caste in Rampura." *Social Stratification,* edited by Dipankar Gupta. New Delhi: Oxford University Press, 1991b.
Thorner, Alice. "Caste and History." *The Hindu.* 4 April 2002.

CASTRO, FIDEL

Fidel Castro Ruiz was born into a prosperous sugar-planting family in rural eastern Cuba, probably on August 13, 1926. He attended the country's best Jesuit schools, graduating from Colegio Belen in Havana in 1945 and going on to earn a doctorate in law at the University of Havana. He practiced law for two years before becoming a left-wing revolutionary. His first act was an unsuccessful attack on the military government of Fulgencio Batista y Zaldívar on July 26, 1953, when he attacked the Cuban army's Moncada barracks. He spent fifteen months in prison but was released as part of a general amnesty, after which he went into exile in the United States and Mexico. He returned to Cuba in December 1956 with a guerrilla force. Fighting began in the Sierra Mountains, and Castro seized power on January 1, 1959, becoming prime minister after Batista fled the country. He then abolished the office of prime minister to become first Head of State, then Council of State President, and finally, Council of Ministers president in 1976. Castro gradually imposed a Communist-style regime over the following years, including land reform, widespread nationalisation, and, eventually, central planning. Such reforms caused a hostile reaction in the United States that culminated in a total trade embargo being imposed in 1960. The Soviet Union thus increased the aid it was giving to Cuba, and this became vital to the Cuban economy. It allowed Castro to introduce important domestic initiatives, especially improvements in literacy and health care, along with an activist and reasonably independent foreign policy. Castro became a leading figure among less-developed countries, and Cuba had an influential role in Latin America and Africa. It became an important nation in the Group of 77, chaired the nonaligned movement (1979–1983), and was elected onto the United Nations Security Council in October 1989.

Castro gained this leadership role through an active policy of aiding poorer nations, particularly those in Africa. Cuba's military interventions, especially in Angola (1975 and 1987) and Ethiopia (1977), gained most attention in the West as the arrival of thousands of troops proved decisive in these wars. These Cuban interventions, along with support for revolutionaries in Latin America, continually irked the United States and prevented any attempts at reconciliation. In Africa, however, Cuba was generally supported as it was fighting colonialism in Angola and opposing a military attempt to change postimperial borders in Ethiopia. This was an important issue among the Organization of African Unity (OAU), which Cuba had helped to form.

Cuba was also one of the largest providers of civilian aid during the Cold War; Castro sent a huge number of aid workers to Africa, including many doctors. By the mid-1980s, there was one Cuban aid worker in Africa for every 625 Cubans; the equivalent figure for the United States was one for every thirty-four thousand. The first doctors were sent in 1963 when many professionals were leaving Cuba because of the revolution. Despite this, however, Castro did not charge for his aid until 1978, when he began to ask for a relatively modest fee and then only from oil-producing nations. These Cuban doctors were therefore cheaper than those being offered by Western powers. A large number of teachers, especially primary school ones, have also gone to Africa and other less-developed countries with up to twenty-two thousand students going the other way each year because of Cuban scholarships allowing them to study at a high school or university.

In domestic policy, education has been Castro's most impressive achievement. Since the revolution, primary school education has become nearly universal, and literacy rates have improved immensely. Secondary and higher education remains limited, however, and subject to political interference. Health care has also been cited as a Cuban success, but Castro was able to build upon a good if insufficient pre-Revolutionary infrastructure. However, he has closed the gap in access between rural and urban areas, as well as replaced the large number of doctors who fled in the early 1960s.

Castro has also greatly influenced the Cuban economy that has suffered from his changing beliefs. In the early 1960s, the government nationalised all businesses in Cuba except for the smallest farms and abolished the market and wage differentials. This led to widespread inefficiency and underemployment. The centralised system called for extensive planning, but the technicians needed for this had either fled or been fired. Thus, the economy failed to grow, and rationing was introduced in 1962. In 1964, Castro abandoned the limited attempts made to diversify the Cuban economy and instead concentrated on its traditional staple crop: sugar. A long-term trading deal was signed with the USSR, and this relationship became the foundation of Cuba's economy until the 1980s. The Soviet Union, and later its Eastern European allies, overpaid for huge amounts of Cuban sugar and provided other subsidies as well.

The Cuban economy recovered in the 1970s as the sugar price rocketed and Castro introduced limited market reforms. However, a drop in the sugar price in the second half of the decade led to an economic downturn. More serious were the collapse of the Soviet Union and the fall of communism in 1989. Cuba was heavily reliant on aid from these countries by then; Soviet aid alone equalled 10% of Cuba's gross domestic product (GDP), and the ending of this cash flow led to a drop in Cuban living standards. Castro, however, refused to follow the Eastern Europeans into introducing democratic reforms and instead asserted his power. He overhauled the leadership of the government that had been remarkably stable since the mid-1960s and introduced a widespread clamp-down on corruption.

Castro survived the collapse of the Soviet Union, but he has been reduced on the world stage. Cuban troops were withdrawn from Angola, Ethiopia, and Nicaragua, and the regime stopped backing rebels in El Salvador and Chile (where General Augusto Pinochet Ugarte had left power). In part, this reflected the ending of Soviet aid, but it also showed the success of Cuba's army, as the side they had backed won in every instance. Subsequently, Cuba has focused upon improving relations with foreign governments, especially in Europe, Latin America, and Canada. Relations with the United States remain fraught, however, despite some successful agreements such as the 1988 deal to end the Angolan war and bilateral migration deals in the 1980s and 1990s. The United States still imposes the trade embargo that was tightened further during the Clinton presidency to include sanctions against companies from Third World countries.

NEIL DENSLOW

See also Angola; Batista y Zaldívar, Fulgencio; Caribbean: History of Economic Development; Caribbean: International Relations; Chile; Cuban Revolution; Education; El Salvador; Ethiopia; Group of 77; Health Care; Migration; Nicaragua; Organization of African Unity (OAU); Pinochet Ugarte, Augusto

References and Further Reading

Domínguez, Jorge. *To Make A World Safe for Revolution: Cuba's Foreign Policy.* London, Cambridge: Harvard University Press, 1989.

Geyer, Georgie Anne. *Guerrilla Prince: The Untold Story of Fidel Castro,* 3d ed. Kansas City, MO: Andrews McMeel, 2001.

Gonzalez, Edward. *Cuba Under Castro: The Limits of Charisma.* London and Boston: Houghton Mifflin, 1974.

Paterson, Thomas G. *Contesting Castro: The United States and the Triumph of the Cuban Revolution*, Oxford, and New York: Oxford University Press, 1994.

Quirk, Robert E. *Fidel Castro*. New York: Norton, 1993.

Szulc, Tad. *Fidel: A Critical Portrait*. New York: Morrow, 1986.

CAYMAN ISLANDS

The Cayman Islands are located west-northwest of Jamaica in the Caribbean Sea, roughly halfway between Cuba and Honduras. This location has been the key to the significance of these otherwise small islands. Originally part of the British colony of Jamaica, the Cayman Islands became a crown colony when Jamaica became independent in 1962. As a crown colony, the Caymans hold the British monarch as head of state, while locally a governor, legislative assembly, and executive council provide for the administration of the islands. All defense needs are provided by Great Britain.

This arrangement is common in British Overseas Territories located at great distances from London.

Prior to the 1800s, no permanent settlements existed in the Caymans, and their chief significance was as an occasional base for pirates in the region. As a part of the British colony of Jamaica, the islands were not large enough to have much political power, and it was after they were separated from Jamaica that the Cayman Islands developed increased importance as a tax haven for Americans and Europeans. The tourism industry also began to develop in the 1960s and is the major industry for the islands today.

The tourist industry has given the Cayman Islands one of the lowest unemployment rates in the Caribbean. The service sector (which includes tourism) makes up more than 95% of the economy of the islands. The Cayman Islands has one of the highest rates of female employment in the region as well. Overall, the Cayman Islands are nearly unique in the Caribbean in that poverty is nonexistent; only the Netherlands Antilles, the Bahamas, and Cuba have their entire populations above the poverty level.

Because the Cayman Islands have no direct taxation, the administrative location of businesses to the islands makes them attractive; along with the Bahamas, the Caymans have become a major center for offshore banking. However, the ease of transfer of funds and bank secrecy rules made offshore financial centers like these centers of money laundering as well. The US General Accounting Office rates the Cayman Islands as one the top two countries in which the transfer of profits from illegal activities takes place. However, since 1984, the government of the Cayman Islands has become more cooperative in combating money-laundering activities and has forced banks to be more accountable in identifying their customers. The Cayman Islands have also joined with the United States in a treaty to fight the trafficking of narcotics.

Another category of business attracted by the low tax burden of the Caymans is that of multinational corporations, also known as International Business Companies (IBCs). Ivelaw Griffith estimates that more than twenty-six thousand such corporations were registered in the Caymans in 1994, a tremendous number considering that the total population of the islands was less than thirty-three thousand at that time. That number of businesses nearly doubled by 2004. Along with this activity is the practice of merchant shipping companies registering their vessels in countries that have low standards of inspection and low taxes; nearly all the large merchant vessels registered to the Cayman Islands are foreign-owned.

An unusual source of revenue to the government of the Cayman Islands is the production of postage stamps. Rather than simply accommodating the needs of residents of the islands and of tourists, stamps are produced for the purpose of collection. The hobby of philately (stamp collecting) values stamps inversely to the size of the country that produces them; with the Caymans having only 262 square kilometers of territory on all three islands, stamps (both used and unused) are in high demand.

The popularity of the Cayman Islands for tourists, which has provided the basis for the largest segment of the nation's economy, places further demands on the islands themselves. The largest of the islands, Grand Cayman, is the most developed, with an airport and shipping ports as well as the country's largest city, George Town. Each of the other islands, Little Cayman and Cayman Brac, has an airfield, and plans are being developed to accommodate greater numbers of tourists on those islands. Because physical space is limited and large numbers of people will put pressure on the still-unspoiled land and beaches, however, the issue of how to undertake economic development without destroying the attraction of the islands is still being debated. Because the Cayman Islands have no natural resources, any degradation of the islands' appeal to tourists would increase the need to rely on the islands' role as an offshore financial center and would greatly change the level of employment and, subsequently, the standard of living for the people of the Cayman Islands.

THOMAS P. DOLAN

See also Caribbean: History and Economic Development; Caribbean: International Relations; Ethnic Conflicts: Caribbean; Money Laundering

References and Further Reading

Bryden, John M. *Tourism and Development: A Case Study of the Commonwealth Caribbean.* Cambridge: Cambridge University Press, 1973.

Griffith, Ivelaw L. *The Political Economy of Drugs in the Caribbean.* Eastbourne, United Kingdom: Anthony Rowe, 2000.

Knight, Franklin W. *The Caribbean: The Genesis of a Fragmented Nationalism*, 2d ed. New York: Oxford University Press, 1990.

Mitchell, Sir Harold. *Caribbean Patterns: A Political and Economic Study of the Contemporary Caribbean*, 2d ed. New York: John Wiley & Sons, 1972.

CEAUSESCU, NICOLAE

Romanian Communist dictator Nicolae Ceausescu liked to be called the "Genius of the Carpathians," but the failed development schemes of his regime of twenty-four years left permanent scars on his country.

Nicolae Ceausescu was born on January 26, 1918, the third of ten children. His childhood was marked by resentment of his alcoholic father. At age fifteen, he was arrested for street fighting. He was attracted to communism as a teenager and is said to have vowed to become "Romania's Stalin." He was arrested again at age eighteen for distributing Communist pamphlets. Romania sided with Hitler in World War II, and Ceausescu spent most of the war years in prison. This furthered his political education because he had ample time to talk politics with his cellmate, Gheorghe Gheorghiu-Dej, who became his Communist mentor and patron. Ceausescu escaped from prison in August 1944, as Soviet troops were approaching Bucharest.

Ceausescu ran for office in 1946 before the Communists had consolidated their grip on Romania. On election day, he shot to death a bank manager who had refused to make a campaign contribution. By 1947, the Romanian Communists had eliminated all rivals. Ceausescu served as minister of agriculture from 1948 to 1950 and as deputy minister of the armed forces from 1950 to 1954. Gheorghiu-Dej emerged as an undisputed Communist boss. Ceausescu became a full member of the Politburo in 1955, and for the next ten years maneuvered to eliminate rivals. When Gheorghiu-Dej died of cancer in 1965, Ceausescu became general secretary of the Communist Party.

Ceausescu refused to follow Moscow's foreign policy line. He condemned the 1968 invasion of Czechoslovakia and refused to allow Soviet bases on Romanian soil. For this, he was praised by Presidents Nixon and Ford and was toasted in Washington by President Carter. But his megalomania expanded, and his paranoia deepened. He appointed his wife, Elena Petrescu, as first deputy prime minister. A 1971 visit by the couple to North Korea and China seemed to fertilize their imaginations regarding the perquisites of unlimited personal power. Ceausescu claimed that "a man like me comes along only once every five hundred years." Bookstores displayed a thirty-volume set of his speeches. Elena, a high school dropout, now boasted a doctorate in engineering and presided over the Romanian Academy of Sciences. All photographs of Ceausescu had to be edited so that no one could appear taller than he. The tyrant worried that the American CIA might try to kill him by dusting his clothing with poison, so he put on brand new clothes every morning. His secret police force swelled to include 180 thousand agents. A network of underground tunnels and bunkers radiated outward from his People's Palace in Bucharest, a building 466 feet high with 3,875,000 square feet of floor space. There were forty other presidential palaces around Romania, some of which the leader never visited. Life became much harder for the average Romanian. Because Ceausescu wanted a young population, the government banned contraception and denied medical care to old people. Thousands of unwanted children ended up in orphanages.

The Ceausescus' downfall came in 1989 when anti-Communist revolutions swept Eastern Europe. Romanian troops fired on demonstrators in Timisoara on December 17, but the overconfident couple flew off to visit Iran the next day. When demonstrations spread to Bucharest they hurried home. Addressing a huge crowd from the balcony of his palace, Ceausescu froze with fear when his people booed him. He and Elena fled by helicopter but were hunted down by the army, which defected to the rebels. On December 25, 1989, Nicolae and Elena Ceausescu were summarily tried and condemned. Three hundred people volunteered for the three-man firing squad.

ROSS MARLAY

See also Central and Eastern Europe: History and Economic Development; Central and Eastern Europe: International Relations; Ethnic Conflicts: Central and Eastern Europe; Romania

References and Further Reading

Behr, Edward. *Kiss the Hand You Cannot Bite: The Rise and Fall of the Ceausescus.* New York: Villard, 1991.

Ceausescu, Nicolae. *Nicolae Ceausescu: The Man, His Ideas, and His Socialist Achievements.* Bertrand Russell Peace Foundation, 1972.

Deletant, Dennis. *Ceausescu and the Securitate: Coercion and Dissent in Romania, 1965–1989.* ME Sharpe, 1996.

Fischer, Mary Ellen. *Nicolae Ceausescu: A Study in Political Leadership.* Boulder, CO: Lynne Rienner, 1989.

Pacepa, Ion M. *Red Horizons: The True Story of Nicolae and Elena Ceausescu's Crimes, Lifestyle, and Corruption.* Regnery, 1990.

CENTRAL AFRICA: HISTORY AND ECONOMIC DEVELOPMENT

Joseph Conrad, in his novel *Heart of Darkness*, painted a picture of Central Africa as a home to a horrific legacy of environmental degradation, exploitation, and violence. Conrad's book, written during the heyday of the colonial era, pointed out some of the horrors wrought by colonial-era disruption of native societies. Despite the wave of independence that swept the region in the years since World War II, the damage caused by this disruption, and by later events that augmented it, has still not been repaired.

Central Africa is difficult to define—for the purposes of this discussion, the region includes Cameroon, the Central African Republic, Chad, the Democratic Republic of the Congo (formerly Zaire), the Republic of the Congo, Equatorial Guinea, Gabon, and the island nation of São Tomé and Príncipe. The region is even more difficult to characterize physically and culturally.

The Physical Setting

The region spans more than thirty-five degrees of latitude, from the northern tip of Chad at the Tropic of Cancer (230° 26′ N) to the southern tip of the Democratic Republic of the Congo (approximately 130° 27′ S). Longitudinally, the region stretches almost twenty-five degrees, from the Gulf of Guinea and South Atlantic Ocean east to the Great Rift Valley.

Except for those portions of the region along the Guinea and Atlantic coasts or in the depths of the Great Rift Valley, Central Africa occupies a massive plateau in the center of the continent. Much of the southern portion of the region lies within the Congo Basin, a broad, relatively low-lying region (about one thousand feet above sea level), drained by the Congo River. The northern portion is drained by two river systems—the Sanaga (Cameroon) and the Niger (Central African Republic and southern Chad)—or else is internally drained (northern Chad).

Aside from the Congo Basin and coastal plains, the area is ringed with upland areas in the southern portion of the Democratic Republic of the Congo, bordering the Great Rift Valley, through the heart of Cameroon and the Central African Republic and in the Tibesti Massif of northern Chad. Volcanoes are associated with many of the upland areas in the region. Active volcanoes can be found along the Great Rift Valley in the eastern part of the Democratic Republic of the Congo, as well as in Cameroon and São Tomé and Príncipe. The volcanoes of the Tibesti Massif are young but have been mostly inactive for several thousand years.

Climate, Flora, and Fauna

With such a wide latitudinal range, it should be no surprise that the region encompasses a diverse array of climates. The core of the region—much of Cameroon, the Democratic Republic of the Congo, the Republic of the Congo, Equatorial Guinea, and Gabon—is a tropical wet climate characterized by high temperatures and high precipitation with no dry season. The year-round growing season with adequate rainfall supports an extensive equatorial rainforest, second in extent only to that of the Amazon and Orinoco basins of South America.

The rainforest is a complex environment. Despite the well-developed forest cover that typically features a tree canopy consisting of three layers—scattered emergents that tower above the main canopy, the canopy itself in which the crowns the of trees form a more or less closed layer, and an understory of trees that survive in the shade of the canopy—the soils are often poor because the high temperatures favor rapid decomposition of plant and animal material, and the high precipitation quickly leaches the nutrients from the soil. The rainforest supports a diverse array of animals, including forest elephants, great apes (gorillas, chimpanzees, and bonobos), hippopotami, lions, leopards, crocodiles, a host of monkeys, parrots and other birds, pythons, and many others.

To the north and south of the tropical wet climate zone lie tropical savanna climate belts, characterized by high temperatures but that have strongly seasonal rainfall. The savanna consists of grassland with scattered trees. The frequency of trees decreases with increasing distance from the tropical wet climate zone. Fire is an important component of these ecosystems, helping maintain the grass cover. The savannas are home to many of Africa's characteristic animals, including elephants, rhinoceroses, giraffes, zebras, wildebeest, various antelopes, lions, cheetahs, and baboons.

North of the northern savanna belt is the semiarid grassland—or steppe—of the Sahel. The climate of the Sahel is characterized by high temperatures but also with seasonal rainfall characterized by periodic droughts. Because many of the residents of the region depend on subsistence farming, the droughts, especially when combined with chronic overgrazing, can be devastating as the fragile vegetation cover is destroyed. In such cases, desert often replaces steppe in a process called *desertification*. In fact, the sands of the Sahara Desert to the north have been spilling into the Sahel, thus permanently moving the boundary between the two regions farther and farther south.

The northern two-thirds of Chad fall within the Sahara, the greatest desert region in the world. The desert climate features clear skies, high temperatures, and little or no rain. The landscape of the Sahara is a mosaic of rocky plains, arid peaks (such as in the Tibesti Massif), and massive sand seas (called ergs) with the huge, ever-moving dunes that the name Sahara conjures up. Plant and animal life in the region is quite sparse.

Economy

Geological and Hydrological Resources

The nations of Central Africa control a wealth of natural resources. One of the most important exports from the region is petroleum and petroleum products. The petroleum industry, including in some cases refining as well as oil production, has flourished for years in Cameroon, Democratic Republic of the Congo, Republic of the Congo, Equatorial Guinea, and Gabon. The Central African Republic and Chad both possess potentially important oil reserves. Chad joined the ranks of oil-producing nations in 2003. The Democratic Republic of the Congo possesses important reserves of another fossil fuel, coal, while the Republic of the Congo and Equatorial Guinea possess reserves of another fossil fuel, natural gas.

Other important geological resources include bauxite (aluminum ore; Cameroon, Democratic Republic of the Congo), cadmium (Democratic Republic of the Congo), cobalt (Democratic Republic of the Congo), copper (Democratic Republic of the Congo, Republic of the Congo), diamonds (Central African Republic, Democratic Republic of the Congo, Republic of the Congo), germanium (Democratic Republic of the Congo), gold (Central African Republic, Chad, Democratic Republic of the Congo, Equatorial Guinea, Gabon), iron ore (Cameroon, Democratic Republic of the Congo, Equatorial Guinea, Gabon), kaolin (Chad), lead (Republic of the Congo), manganese (Democratic Republic of the Congo, Equatorial Guinea, Gabon), natron (sodium carbonate; Chad), phosphates (Congo Republic),

potash (Republic of the Congo), radium (Democratic Republic of the Congo), silver (Democratic Republic of the Congo), tin (Democratic Republic of the Congo), titanium (Equatorial Guinea), uranium (Central African Republic, Democratic Republic of the Congo, Republic of the Congo, Equatorial Guinea, Gabon), and zinc (Democratic Republic of the Congo, Republic of the Congo).

In addition to mineral resources, Cameroon, Central African Republic, Democratic Republic of the Congo, Republic of the Congo, Gabon, and São Tomé and Príncipe have significant hydropower resources.

Biological Resources

Many of the nations in the region (Cameroon, Central African Republic, Democratic Republic of the Congo, Republic of the Congo, Equatorial Guinea, Gabon, São Tomé and Príncipe) possess large tracts of tropical forest; thus, it is no surprise that timber and wood products are important to their economies. Some of the major tree-based products include coconuts (São Tomé and Príncipe), copra (São Tomé and Príncipe), palm kernels (São Tomé and Príncipe), palm oil (Democratic Republic of the Congo, Republic of the Congo, Gabon), rubber (Cameroon, Democratic Republic of the Congo, Equatorial Guinea, Gabon), and quinine (Democratic Republic of the Congo).

Agriculture is important throughout the region. Important crops include bananas (Cameroon, Central African Republic, Democratic Republic of the Congo, Equatorial Guinea, São Tomé and Príncipe), beans (São Tomé and Príncipe), cassava or manioc (tapioca; Central African Republic, Chad, Democratic Republic of the Congo, Republic of the Congo, Equatorial Guinea), cinnamon (São Tomé and Príncipe), cocoa (Cameroon, Republic of the Congo, Equatorial Guinea, Gabon, São Tomé and Príncipe), coffee (Cameroon, Central African Republic, Democratic Republic of the Congo, Republic of the Congo, Equatorial Guinea, Gabon, São Tomé and Príncipe), corn (Central African Republic, Democratic Republic of the Congo, Republic of the Congo), cotton (Cameroon, Central African Republic, Chad), grains (Cameroon), gum Arabic (Chad), millet (Central African Republic, Chad), oilseed (Cameroon), papaya (São Tomé and Príncipe), pepper (São Tomé and Príncipe), peanuts (Chad, Republic of the Congo), potatoes (Chad), rice (Chad, Republic of the Congo, Equatorial Guinea), sorghum (Chad), sugar (Democratic Republic of the Congo, Republic of the Congo, Gabon), tea (Democratic

Republic of the Congo), tobacco (Central African Republic), and yams (Central African Republic, Equatorial Guinea).

Central Africa features a number of animal-based industries. Livestock (primarily cattle but that may also include camels, goats, and sheep) are economically important in Cameroon, Chad, Equatorial Guinea, and Gabon, while the poultry industry is a vital part of São Tomé and Príncipe's small economy. The fishing and fish-processing industries are obviously important to the coastal nations (Cameroon, Equatorial Guinea, Gabon, São Tomé and Príncipe), but they are also important in landlocked Chad, which borders on part of Lake Chad, the largest lake in the Sahel. (Chad shares the lake with Cameroon, Niger, and Nigeria.)

Other Industries

The economy of Central Africa has moved beyond extraction. Additional industries based on the region's natural resources include brewing (Central African Republic, Chad, Republic of the Congo, São Tomé and Príncipe), cigarette making (Chad, Democratic Republic of the Congo, Republic of the Congo), meatpacking (Chad), soap making (Chad, Republic of the Congo, São Tomé and Príncipe), and textile manufacturing (Cameroon, Central African Republic, Chad, Democratic Republic of the Congo, Gabon, São Tomé and Príncipe).

Other industries include assembly and manufacturing (Cameroon, Central African Republic, Democratic Republic of the Congo), chemicals production (Equatorial Guinea, Gabon), and ship repair (Gabon).

Colonial Legacy

Despite the region's vast natural wealth, few of the nations have been able to capitalize on their resources to build stable economies and societies. Part of the reason for this failure lies in the colonial history of the region because the colonial powers did not promote independence and economic self-sufficiency among the vassal states.

Most of the central region, like almost the rest of Africa, was gobbled up by European powers in the scramble for Africa in the late nineteenth and early twentieth centuries, although two of the countries, Equatorial Guinea and São Tomé and Príncipe, had been colonies for far longer. Equatorial Guinea, first claimed by Portugal in 1474, was traded to Spain in 1778. São Tomé and Príncipe was colonized by the Portuguese in 1485.

The Portuguese, who pioneered the trade route around the Horn of Africa to Asia, had explored much of the territories along Africa's West Coast. However, they did not claim all of the territories they visited, thus opening the door for other colonial powers. Germany beat the British to establish a colony in what is now Cameroon, in 1884, although the Germans lost the colony in the aftermath of World War I, with France being awarded 80% of Cameroon's present-day territory and Great Britain being awarded the remaining 20%.

France did not wait for World War I to begin claiming colonies in Africa, however. The French acquired much of the region that now makes up the Republic of the Congo (called Middle Congo at the time) between 1882 and 1891. They occupied what is now Gabon in 1885, the Central African Republic between 1885 and 1887, and Chad between 1891 and 1900. The territories were consolidated into French Equatorial Africa in 1910.

Belgium's King Leopold II took over what is now the Democratic Republic of the Congo in what was essentially a private colony, called the Congo Free State, between 1877 and 1885. In setting up the colony, Leopold proclaimed a humanitarian interest in the welfare of the native residents. However, the violence of his regime is now notorious, and most of the region's residents were subjected to forced labor. Anything not already owned by Europeans became Leopold's private property, and with the labor of the enslaved population, ivory and rubber were extracted.

Leopold began a war against Tippu Tip—the most powerful Arab slave trader in the world at the time—who competed with Leopold for ivory. The war, carried out primarily by tribal proxies, featured brutal torture of prisoners, including cannibalism, on both sides of the conflict.

As demand for rubber soared in the 1890s, the Belgians used terror as a weapon to scare the populace into increasing production. The Force Publique—led by European officers but with primarily native troops—killed, tortured, raped, and mutilated uncooperative villagers. Mutilation typically involved chopping off the right hands of victims, who more often than not died since they received no medical attention afterward. An accurate estimate of the casualties will never be known, but millions died as a result of Leopold's atrocities.

Joseph Conrad's novel *Heart of Darkness*, published in 1902, helped call attention to Leopold's regime. Two years later, Sir Roger Casement, the British Consul, published a damning eyewitness report. The Belgian Parliament, in its own report, confirmed Casement's findings in 1905. Belgium annexed Leopold's domain in 1908, but by then, the rubber boom that drove his brutal profit-taking measures was dead, as were untold numbers of victims.

Independence: Steps Forward and Back

Belgium, Britain, and France were all but spent in the aftermath of World War II. Britain and France began preparing for some degree of autonomy among their colonial holdings. Britain had planned for outright independence but also planned to bide its time until rioting in Accra, the Gold Coast (now Ghana), encouraging the British to accelerate the process. (The Gold Coast was granted independence in 1957.) France was also encouraged to let go of its colonies sooner than it had hoped following its debacle in French Indochina (1950–1954) and the bloody Algerian war of independence (1954–1962).

The Belgian Congo (as the Congo Free State had been renamed) survived World War II unscathed and boasted of a profitable economy. The Belgians blindly thought that a good economy and improved quality of life, in areas such as education and health care, would keep the natives happily in the imperial fold. But the Congolese, noticing the nationalistic tide elsewhere on the continent and not overly impressed with Belgian reform proposals, grew restless as well. Days before a Belgian-only commission was to announce plans for local elections leading eventually to the formation of a national assembly, a riot broke out in Léopoldville (now Kinshasa) on January 4, 1959. The Force Publique violently restored order, but the die was cast. Belgium's King Baudouin soon announced that the colony would be granted full independence—and it was, the following year after only a six-month warning. The new nation was soon called the Democratic Republic of the Congo.

The remnants of French Equatorial Africa were subdivided into the Central African Republic, Chad, Middle Congo (renamed Central African Republic), and Gabon in 1958. The four nations were admitted as semiautonomous members of the French Community the same year, but they were granted independence in 1960. The French Cameroon gained independence in 1960, and in the next year, the primarily Christian southern portion of British Cameroon voted to join the new republic.

Spain and Portugal, which had remained neutral in World War II, took more time to release their colonies. Spain, in response to pressure from nationalists in Equatorial Guinea, as well as in the United Nations, granted the colony independence in 1968.

The islands São Tomé and Príncipe had been uninhabited at the time the Portuguese arrived in the fifteenth century. Nevertheless, the residents of the colony desired self-rule in the twentieth century. A Portuguese regime committed to dissolution of Portugal's overseas empire seized power in 1974, and São Tomé and Príncipe, among others, was granted independence the following year.

Failures of Democracy

Most of these nations were ill prepared for independence. In probably the most extreme example of economic devastation in the wake of abandonment by a colonial power, most of the Portuguese professionals fled São Tomé and Príncipe, leaving few skilled workers—only one doctor on the two islands; many abandoned businesses and plantations, and the remaining populace had a 90% illiteracy rate. Manuel Pinto da Costa, secretary general of the leading independence group—the Movement for the Liberation of São Tomé and Príncipe (MLSTP)—was named the nation's first president. Da Costa established a Socialist, single-party (MLSTP) state.

The fledgling Democratic Republic of the Congo, when it was set free, was not much better off. The nation possessed vast natural wealth. But Belgian officials fled the country, leaving the new nation with few trained administrators. The educational system was in its infancy— the first Congolese university graduate finished his degree only four years before, in 1956. Tribal leaders held more power than the central government, and the central government was itself divided philosophically. The first prime minister, Patrice Lumumba, was a Marxist, while the first president, Joseph Kasavubu, favored the West.

Within months, a military *coup d'état* broke out in the capital. Katanga, the southernmost and richest province, seceded, and an anti-Communist, Moise Tshombe, was declared its president. The United Nations (UN) sent peacekeepers into the country. Lumumba turned to Soviet Premier Nikita Khrushchev for assistance, setting up a Cold War conflict. The United States, via the Central Intelligence Agency, funneled arms, money, and personnel to the country. With such assistance, Kasavubu and his loyal Colonel Joseph Mobutu overthrew the Lumumba government. Lumumba was later assassinated. UN forces helped the government regain control of Katanga. Mobutu, in 1965, deposed Kasavubu, declared himself leader, and renamed the country Zaire.

The other nations in the region also formed single-party states typically led by strongmen such as

Mobutu: Ahmadou Ahidjo in Cameroon, David Dacko in the Central African Republic, François Tombalbaye in Chad, Fulbert Youlou in the Republic of the Congo, Francisco Macías Nguema in Equatorial Guinea, and Léon M'Ba in Gabon.

Unending Conflict

Cameroon

Single-party rule did little to bring peace and stability to the region. In some cases, armed conflicts began before independence. For example, the Union of Cameroonian Peoples (UPC) started a rebellion in the French Cameroon in 1955. The movement kept struggling even after the French Cameroon achieved independence in 1960. Ahidjo outlawed all opposition political parties in 1966. Government forces captured the last major UPC leader in 1970. Ahidjo resigned and constitutionally transferred power to Prime Minister Paul Biyo in 1982, but he launched a failed *coup d'état* against Biyo in 1984 and subsequently went into exile. Biyo has stayed in power despite questionable multiparty elections in 1992, 1997, and 2004.

Central African Republic

Instability seems endemic to the region. In the Central African Republic, Dacko was deposed in a *coup d'état* by a relative, Colonel Jean-Bédel Bokassa, in 1966. Bokassa proclaimed himself emperor of the Central African Empire in 1976. Atrocities by the Bokassa government stirred unrest, and in 1982, Dacko—backed by French forces—returned the favor and deposed Bokassa in 1982, but he was again deposed in 1981 by General André Kolingba. Kolingba initiated the transition to civilian rule, and the Central African Republic remained a democratic state despite several mutinies by military officers from minority tribal groups. The civilian government was finally deposed in a 2003 *coup d'état* by General François Bozizé, who acted with broad popular support. Bozizé won a disputed election for president in March 2005.

Chad

In 1965, Chad erupted in civil war between the Muslim north and east against the Tombalbaye's southern-led government. By 1975, Tombalbaye's erratic and brutal leadership led to a *coup d'état* in which he was ousted by forces led by General Félix Malloum, but the Malloum government disintegrated in yet another civil war in 1979 in which eleven factions (to some extent defined by tribal origin) struggled for supremacy. The Organization of African Unity (OAU) stepped in, persuading the factions to form a transitional national unity government (GUNT). The coalition, which featured President Goukouni Oueddei and Minister of Defense Hissène Habré (the former prime minister), began to fall apart almost as quickly as it had been thrown together. Libya exploited the rift, sending in its own troops, and France and Zaire sent in troops in response (while an OAU peacekeeping force remained neutral).

While France and Zaire withdrew their forces following a pact with Libya in 1984, the Libyans stayed, but the Libyans were driven back inside their own borders between a defeat by Habré's forces and an unfavorable World Court decision. Habré had been brutal in his suppression of dissent, however, and this brutality led to a breach with one of his own generals, Idriss Déby, who attacked from the Darfur region of the Sudan. Déby's troops, assisted by the Libyans and unopposed by the French, marched into the capital city of N'Djamena unopposed on December 2, 1990. Despite unrelenting challenges—including armed uprisings, such as one by a rebel group in the Tibesti region of northern Chad—Déby has remained in power. He has nudged the country toward democracy, although his 2001 presidential election was marred by allegations of fraud.

The Democratic Republic of the Congo

After seizing power, Mobutu implemented a program of Africanization and, in keeping with the policy, changed his name from Joseph Mobutu to Mobutu Sese Seko Koko Ngbendu Wa Za Banga. He concentrated all power in his hands, and, for two decades, was successful in suppressing dissent. As the Cold War came to a close at the end of the 1980s, Mobutu's hand weakened, and the government, undermined by corruption—including Mobutu's massive embezzlement of government funds—began to fall apart. Mobutu managed to remain as head of state as a result of power sharing between rivals. Mobutu's downfall came from the East. As the ethnic strife in Rwanda and Burundi spilled westward across Zaire's borders, Mobutu persecuted one of the groups involved, the Tutsis. As the Tutsis fought back, Zairean dissident groups joined them. The coalition, which became known as the Alliance des Forces Démocratiques pour la Libération du Congo-Zaïre (AFDL), was led by Laurent-Desire Kabila, who repeatedly defeated Mobutu's forces. Peace talks between the government and the AFDL failed in early 1997, and Mobutu fled, allowing Kabila to seize the capital unopposed. He renamed the country the Democratic Republic of the Congo.

Unfortunately, Kabila failed to prove as able a political leader as he was a military leader; the civil war, with the involvement of troops from five other nations, resumed shortly after he assumed power. Despite efforts to broker a peace deal, the fighting between government and rebel troops continued. Kabila was assassinated in January 2001. His son, Joseph, succeeded him. Joseph Kabila managed to broker brief peace deals, but ethnic clashes, coupled with government incompetence, reignited fighting in the northern and eastern part of the country. Ugandan-backed forces control a strip of territory in the North, while Rwandan-backed forces control a strip of territory in the East. Some believe the reason for the continued Ugandan and Rwandan involvement in the Congolese conflicts is to provide cover for looting the nation's abundant resources—including diamonds—in the region.

Republic of the Congo

Youlou's reign in the Republic of the Congo was marred by ethnic and political strife, and he was deposed in a military *coup d'état* in 1963. The military installed a provisional civilian government led by Alphonse Massamba-Débat—who was elected president—but Débat was himself ousted in 1968 in a *coup d'état* led by Captain Marien Ngouabi. Ngouabi declared himself president, renamed his National Revolutionary Movement the Congolese Labor Party (PCT), and led the nation until his assassination on March 16, 1977. The PCT tapped Colonel (later General) Joachim Yhombi-Opango as president. Yhombi-Opango was himself removed in 1979 and replaced by Defense Minister (and Colonel) Denis Sassou-Nguesso.

With the demise of the Soviet Union, the Marxist-leaning government of the PCT began to crumble, and democratic reforms were implemented, leading to multiparty elections in 1992. The fledgling democracy staggered into another civil war in 1997 that brought Sassou-Nguesso back to power. Throughout six years of continued bloodshed, Sassou-Nguesso's government managed to sign peace accords with all of the nation's rebel groups, the latest pact being signed in March 2003.

Equatorial Guinea

While the people elected Francisco Macías Nguema the first president of Equatorial Guinea, during his first term he systematically dismantled the nation's constitution and awarded himself the title of President for Life in 1972. Macias and his henchmen provided only one government service—internal security, accomplished by terror of the citizenry—and began dismantling the nation's civil society as effectively as they had earlier shredded the constitution. Macias's nephew, Teodoro Obiang Nguema Mbasogo, ousted his uncle, who was arrested, tried, and executed. Obiang assumed the presidency in 1979 and tried to repair the damage done by the Macias regime. A new constitution was drafted with the assistance of the UN and put into effect in 1982. Obiang was reelected president in 1991, 1996, and in 2002, although those elections are widely regarded as flawed. While the country's coffers are now full as a result of oil revenue, living standards for much of the populace do not reflect the government's wealth.

Gabon

Gabon's first president, M'Ba, died in 1967 and was succeeded by El Hadj Omar Bongo, who has remained head of state since. Bongo initiated reforms leading to a nominal multiparty democracy in 1990. The new constitution, adopted in March 1991, included a Western-style bill of rights. Bongo was reelected in the first multiparty presidential elections in 1993, but the results were disputed. He was reelected again in 1998. Months before the next scheduled presidential election (in December 2005), there were no real challengers to Bongo's leadership and no signs that he planned to pass the reins of government to a new generation.

An Exception

São Tomé and Príncipe

São Tomé and Príncipe embraced the ideals of democratic reform in 1990, changing its constitution and allowing opposition political parties. The first multiparty elections were held in 1991 and—in a pattern not characteristic of the region—the elections were free, transparent, and without violence. Miguel Trovoada, a former prime minister who had been sent into exile in 1986, was elected as an independent candidate. He was reelected in 1996. Democracy has reigned except for one week in 2003 when the army, complaining of corruption and of concerns over the fair distribution of oil revenues from discoveries in the Gulf of Guinea, seized power. President Fradique de Menezes, elected in 2001, was quickly restored to office.

Looming Disaster

If the political and ethnic conflicts have not been enough to retard progress in Central Africa, an emerging disease discovered in the early 1980s has the power to set back development in the region for generations. That disease is acquired immune deficiency syndrome (AIDS).

The first signs of AIDS were noticed in the late 1970s among gay men from Sweden and the United States and among heterosexual men in Haiti and Tanzania. The syndrome was first described in 1981 and the virus that causes it, human immunodeficiency virus (HIV), was identified in 1983. The virus attacks the immune system, destroying the body's ability to fight off other infections. As patients' defenses get overwhelmed, they succumb to a host of other diseases, such as Kaposi's sarcoma, a formerly rare type of skin cancer, and pneumonia caused by *Pneumocystis carinii*.

While HIV can be spread by sharing of needles contaminated with HIV-infected blood, or by use of contaminated blood products, it is primarily transmitted by sexual contact. Promiscuous sexual activity, whether between homosexuals or heterosexuals, promotes spread of the disease.

HIV probably originated in the Congo, possibly as a related virus jumped from apes or monkeys to humans as the animals were butchered for food. The first victim of AIDS (diagnosed retrospectively) died in a hospital in Kinshasa in 1959. Nearly 30 million people in Sub-Saharan Africa are infected with HIV; while Central Africa is the likely source of the virus, the hardest hit areas are in Southern and East Africa, where HIV infection rates in some cases exceed 25%. Infection rates in Central Africa range from a high of 13.5% in the Central African Republic to a low of 3.4% in Equatorial Guinea. (No data are available for São Tomé and Príncipe.)

Adults aged fifteen through forty-nine, the age group most responsible for running civil society as well as for rearing families, are hit hardest by HIV infection. As a result, HIV/AIDS threatens social stability in nations where infectious rates are highest. AIDS orphans, those children whose parents have died of AIDS, are a growing problem in Sub-Saharan

Africa. There are at least 12 million AIDS orphans in Sub-Saharan Africa—the Democratic Republic of the Congo has more than nine hundred thousand— and the number is expected to grow. The effects on the orphaned generation may have long-lasting, potential disastrous effects on Central Africa's development.

DAVID M. LAWRENCE

See also Ahidjo, Ahmadou; Algeria; Authoritarianism; Cameroon; Central Africa: International Relations; Central African Republic; Chad; Children and Development; Civil Rights; Colonialism: History; Colonialism: Legacies; Congo, Democratic Republic of the; Congo, Republic of the; Corruption, Governmental; *Coup d'État*; Deforestation; Democratization; Desertification; Dictatorships; Economic Community of Central African States (ECCAS); Elections; Energy: Impact on Development; Environment: Government Policies; Equatorial Guinea; Ethnic Conflicts: Central Africa; Gabon; Globalization: Impact on Development; HIV/AIDS; Human Rights as a Foreign Policy Issue; Human Rights: Definition and Violations; Infectious Diseases; Lake Chad Basin Commission; Libya; Lumumba, Patrice; Marxism; Military and Civilian Control; Military and Development; Military and Human Rights; Minorities/Discrimination; Natural Disasters; Organization of African Unity (OAU); Organization of Petroleum Exporting Countries (OPEC); Peacekeeping Operations, Regional and International; Population Growth: Impact on Development; Poverty: Impact on Development; Public Health; Rain Forest, Destruction of; Refugees; Rwanda; Self-Determination; Single-Party States; Socialism; Sudan; Uganda; Urbanization: Impact on Development; War and Development; White Community in Africa; Wildlife Preservation

References and Further Reading

Barnett, Tony, and Alan Whiteside. *AIDS in the Twenty-First Century: Disease and Globalization*, 2d ed. New York: Palgrave Macmillan, 2003.

Birmingham, David, and Phyllis M. Martin, eds. *History of Central Africa: The Contemporary Years Since 1960*. New York: Addison-Wesley Longman, 1998.

Conrad, Joseph. *Heart of Darkness: An Authoritative Text, Backgrounds and Sources, Criticism*. New York: W.W. Norton, 1987.

Edgerton, Robert B. *The Troubled Heart of Africa: A History of the Congo*. New York: St. Martin's Press, 2002.

French, Howard W. *A Continent for the Taking: The Tragedy and Hope of Africa*. New York: Alfred A. Knopf, 2004.

Ghosh, Jayati, Ezekiel Kalipeni, Susan Craddock, and Joseph R. Oppong, eds. *HIV & AIDS in Africa: Beyond Epidemiology*. Malden, MA: Blackwell Publishing, 2004.

Guest, Robert. *The Shackled Continent: Power, Corruption, and African Lives.* Washington, DC: Smithsonian Books, 2004.

Hochschild, Adam. *King Leopold's Ghost: A Story of Greed, Terror, and Heroism in Colonial Africa.* Boston: Houghton Mifflin, 1998.

Hunter, Susan. *Black Death: AIDS in Africa.* New York: Palgrave Macmillan, 2003.

Packenham, Thomas. *The Scramble for Africa: White Man's Conquest of the Dark Continent from 1876 to 1912.* New York: Avon Books, 1991.

Reader, John. *Africa: A Biography of the Continent.* New York: Alfred A. Knopf, 1998.

CENTRAL AFRICA: INTERNATIONAL RELATIONS

Defining Central Africa

The central part of the African Continent, usually known as Central Africa, is a region that has been defined in many ways, but on this occasion the definition will include the following countries: the Central African Republic (CAR), Chad, Gabon, the Democratic Republic of the Congo (DRC), Cameroon, and the Republic of the Congo.

All these countries share the characteristic of having French-speaking populations. With the exception of the Democratic Republic of the Congo, which formerly was a Belgian colony, the other countries were included among the French colonial territories. As a matter of fact, France was closely related to its territories after achieving independence and still plays a role in some of the countries; for instance, Chad, Gabon, and the CAR host French troops in their territories. This is an ethnically diverse region with large followings of Islam and Catholicism developed, together with other religions. Most of these countries have a diversified agricultural production, and these products are part of their exports.

Economic Development and Global Integration

In their first decades of independence, most African countries opposed the neocolonialism trends. During the 1990s, however, African countries abandoned their exclusive bilateral policies with the superpowers or colonial metropolis and began functioning as a bloc in the world scenario. Despite hopes that this change would make them stronger, the formation of these blocs made them more vulnerable as they began to depend more and more on their linkages with the Western world.

At the time the Central African countries gained more freedom, they opened their economies to the world, with consequent markets and investments diversification. Regional organizations were also formed, including the Central African Peace and Security Council (COPAX), the Central Bank of Central African States (BEAC), and the Economic Community of Central African States (ECCAS) created in 1983 with the mission of promoting cooperation among state-members, encouraging self-sustained development, and improving inhabitants' lives. This latter agreement includes a progressive plan toward the elimination of custom taxes among state-members and the establishment of a common external tariff for all state-members. In addition, the plan takes into account improvements in the industry sector, transports and telecommunications, and the free traffic of goods and services all in a twelve-year period. Besides the countries of the region, Burundi, Equatorial Guinea, Rwanda, and São Tomé and Príncipe are also included in this agreement. Angola is categorized as an observer.

The programs and politics of structural adjustment set by the International Monetary Fund (IMF) have a ruling presence in the region. In the 1980s, the IMF played a leading role in the economic policies adopted by the DRC. In exchange, the country's external debt was reconsidered, and the IMF was awarded a considerable loan, which was followed by a monetary devaluation and other austerity measures. These were later abandoned in 1986, but in 1989, the DRC was forced to establish a new economic reform due to the economic instability it was suffering.

During the 1990s, the economic instability in Gabon encouraged the IMF to introduce a plan to stabilize the economy and the World Bank to promote a structural adjustment. In a similar way, Chad is also largely dependent on foreign assistance and capital for most public and private sector investment projects.

More recently, Cameroon has also embarked on various IMF and World Bank programs designed to spur business investment, increase efficiency in agriculture, improve trade, and recapitalize the nation's banks. In 2000, the country completed an IMF-sponsored, structural adjustment program; however this institution is pressing for more reforms, including poverty reduction programs.

On the whole, the adjustments have improved the macroeconomic conditions in some countries, but the population's living standards have worsened.

The accelerated external opening has made the continent more vulnerable, and the foreign investments have not helped the general population. Foreign companies' investments, most of the time done in alliance with corrupt governments, leave almost no revenues for the common people. The *spill-over effect*, supposed to happen after the promising investments took place, does not seem to have done much to improve African's living conditions.

These countries are mainly raw-material exporters, with slight activity in industrial development and a diminishing participation in world trade. In the case of Gabon, it has begun a process of industrialization highly dependent on foreign capitals. This fact has worsened social problems by accelerating the exodus of peasants to the cities, creating in this way cheap working labour for the multinational companies and destroying at the same time the possibility of an alimentary self-sufficiency. As a consequence, the region is constantly vulnerable to the uncertain and ever-changing fluctuations in the prices of raw materials, the oscillations of international trade, the external debt payments, the internal conflicts, and the decrease of international aid.

Conflicts and Development in the Postindependence Period

In addition to facing the challenges of AIDS, poverty, food shortages, chronic undernourishment problems, high external debts, and economic crises, Central Africa also faces other conflicts that cause great instability in the region.

According to a United Nations (UN) report by the Central Africa Consultive Committee in charge of security issues, the causes of *internal conflicts* and the insecurity in this area are closely linked with the rivalries between ethnic groups, the lack of democracy of political powers, the fragility of state institutions, the deficient public sector policies, poverty and underdevelopment, failure in the transitions toward democracy, the proliferation of paramilitary groups, as well as the unrestricted circulation of weapons, vital space troubles, economic difficulties, and other such factors.

One of the reasons that accounts for these conflicts lies within the history of these countries. The borders of many states were not originally established as borders between independent states but as territorial divisions among the superpowers by the end of the nineteenth century in the times of imperialism. Boundaries were created artificially and in an arbitrary way, without regarding the different ethnicities or people's religions. Therefore, almost all the African territory is characterized by incomplete borderlines, a fact that usually arises territorial, ethnic, tribal, and religious disputes. Ethnic identity and religious fanaticism are often exploited by political and military elites who want to monopolize the access to power and resources by excluding the members of other ethnicities or religions.

Most of the time, different attempts to explain wars in Africa make the mistake of considering the *ethnic factor* as the decisive one. Although this is an important factor, it is important to emphasize the existence of areas of potential natural resources conflicts. These areas often coincide with areas that are chronically unstable; while conflicts are often characterized as the result of ethnic or political wars, the real reason for conflicts may lie in interests concerning *natural resources,* such as oil or diamonds.

Two other factors tend to increase the internal climate of constant conflicts. On the one hand, the socioeconomic crisis is a consequence of the wars, and on the other hand, the sale of weapons helps to maintain the existing conflicts or to create new ones in other countries. These conflicts are not only the result of internal causes but also a consequence of the interaction between internal dynamics and external influences, which many times tend to worsen internal factors.

External influences are continental as well as extra-continental. International organizations and Western powers like the United States, Great Britain, France, and Belgium are involved and exert pressure on the African conflicts by supporting the allied groups and by offering political, financial, and military support to defend their own economic, political, or strategic interests.

As in other regions of the continent, these disputes have a plurality of causes and factors with similar effects: an increase in refugees and displaced people, a deterioration of the economy, a rise in food shortages, and a spread of diseases.

Most African disputes have their origin in the years of African independence, mainly during the second half of the twentieth century. The distribution of the continent's territory among the colonial powers occurred during the twentieth century. As a consequence, during the 1960s, a large amount of new states emerged whose main characteristic, besides having little experience in the exercise of their sovereignty, was a clear political instability.

After World War II, with the objective of linking its African colonies in a significant association, France started making them independent. The territories that in 1910 had become part of the French Equatorial Africa gained their independence in 1960, creating the present states of the Central African Republic, Chad, and the Republic of the Congo.

The DRC, formerly known as Zaire, was part of the Belgium colonies. In 1959, as an answer to the increasing demands for complete independence by the main nationalistic parties, the DRC's government announced the forthcoming elections with the aims of establishing an autonomous government. In 1960, the DRC proclaimed its independency.

After World War I, Cameroon's territory, which had formerly been annexed by Germany, was divided among the British who kept the area near Nigeria and the French who kept the rest of the country. After Word War II and within an expanding decolonization process, these territories also gained their independence in 1960. The British part of Cameroon became a part of Nigeria.

Brief History of Recent Country Conflicts

The postindependence period is distinguished by constant instability. Since their beginnings, the Central African governments have been characterized for being authoritarian and very corrupt. In the case of the CAR, after its independence, an authoritarian government was established after which three tumultuous decades of misrule were finally deposed, and civilian rule was established in 1993.

Two autocratic presidents have ruled Gabon since independence from France. President Bongo has dominated Gabon's political scene for almost four decades.

Chad endured three decades of ethnic warfare as well as invasions by Libya before a semblance of peace was finally restored in 1990. During this period, the repression forced citizens to find refuge in the Central African Republic.

In Cameroon, President Ahmadou Ahidjo faced a revolt fostered by a pro-Communist party. He held his position until 1982 when he resigned. In 1984, former prime minister Paul Biya took his place, faced successfully an attempt of *coup d'état*, and is still in charge of the government.

In the DRC, after independence, ethnic disputes and military revolts have provoked violent disorders, all of which intensified when the prime minister of the province of Katanga proclaimed his independence from the country and asked Belgium for military help. To solve this conflict, the United Nations Security Council authorized the disembarkation of military troops to restore the order in Cameroon and avoid a civil war.

However, this UN intervention was not an easy one because the active UN general secretariat died in mysterious circumstances when he was trying to obtain a cease-fire between UN troops and Katanga's forces. In 1977, the DRC was invaded from Angola by former residents of Kananga. The invasion was rejected with the military aid of Belgium, France, Morocco, and other states.

The Republic of the Congo has also seen great disturbances after its independence. This period has been characterized by *coups d'état*, instability, and radical administrations that ended in a brief and violent civil war. During the Cold War, this country signed a cooperation and friendship treaty with the former Union of Soviet Socialist Republics (USSR) and maintained good relations with Communist states all over the world.

The fall of the bipolar system in 1991 destroyed the East–West alignments. Although the African continent seemed to lose strategic importance for the superpowers, tensions did not decrease, some conflicts remained, and new ones appeared. In addition, many countries in their surroundings acted as partners but also as rivals.

The northern part of Chad is still an unstable area, where revolts occur against the government. Besides, Chad still has strong tensions with its neighbour, the CAR. In March 1996, the conflict between Cameroon and its neighbour Nigeria arose again because of the border territory of Bakassi. In July 2003, due to an International Court of Justice verdict, Nigeria agreed to return the Bakassi peninsula together with other thirty-three border towns to Cameroon.

The CAR has suffered a large amount of uprisings and *coups d'état*. The 1995 and 1996 revolts gave birth to a French intervention to support President Patassé, who would be later reelected. After the 2003 *coup d'état*, transition institutions have been established, and an electoral calendar has been set for March 2005. However, the situation remains fragile and changeable.

Gabon is not free from internal political instability, but a small population, abundant resources, and considerable foreign support have helped make Gabon one of the most prosperous and stable African countries. As for its external role, Gabon played a relevant one in the Chad–Libya conflict in the 1980s.

The DRC was involved between 1994 and 1996 in the Rwanda conflict, hosting large quantities of refugees in its border territory. In 1997, this situation caused trouble when the presence of Hutus refugees, several of whom were responsible for the killings in Rwanda, provoked the Tutsis revolt. This rebellion, supported by the United States, Rwanda, Uganda, Burundi, and Angola, spread over the DRC territory and weakened the Mobutu's regime that was supported by France. This all ended when Kabila came into power. Once there, Kabila reestablished relations with Cuba, China, and North Korea and criticized the contracts with multinational firms that had been signed by Mobutu. In 1998, Kabila's government was subsequently challenged by Rwanda, and Uganda backed the rebellion. Troops from Zimbabwe, Angola, Namibia, Chad, and Sudan intervened to support Kabila. Finally, a cease-fire was signed in 1999, but Kabila was assassinated in 2001. The next year, his daughter signed a peace agreement with Rwanda.

Some neighbouring Central African countries even encouraged this unstable situation and took advantage of it. According to a 2002 UN report, Rwanda and Uganda were involved in the benefits obtained in the DRC war. Both countries were exporting diamonds and coltan, minerals imported from the DRC (these two countries do not have such resources within their territories).The situation in the Republic of the Congo is similar to that of DRC because this country is also a victim of its richness in minerals. After a long Marxist–Communist period, the Congo returned to democracy in the 1990s. Between 1993 and 1994, the Republic of the Congo was submerged in regional and ethnic tensions that provoked violence outbreaks. In 1997, a violent and armed battle burst in the country's capital city. The former President Sassou-Nguesso deposed the governor Lissouba with the help of Angola. He suspended the constitution and announced that democracy would come back after three years of transition. In the 2002 elections, which were considered dishonest by the opposition, Nguesso was the winner. A peace treaty was finally signed in March 2003.

The civil war that provoked so many damages to this country is closely linked with the petroleum reserves. The Republic of the Congo is Africa's fourth largest petroleum producer with significant potential for offshore development. As an example, Lissouba had negotiated an agreement with the American company Occidental Petroleum (Oxy); however, the Elf company, very powerful in the Republic of the Congo as well as in Gabon, supported Nguesso to withdraw Lissouba from government. This situation was published in the papers and generated a mass media scandal.

Oil Extraction and a New Strategic Position of Africa in the Global Scenario

By the time the Cold War ended, a new strategic geography appeared: the conflicts that used to have an ideological-political bias were becoming more focused on the control of natural resources. Therefore, many African countries that previously were of no interest whatsoever for Western powers have begun to occupy a most important place in the political planning of them. The natural resources allow the intervention of several multinationals, many times taking advantage of the conflicts in the area, like in the Republic of the Congo incident mentioned previously.

In spite of the fact that Latin American and the Persian Gulf are the largest zones where the United States obtains oil, the United States imports more petroleum from Africa than from Saudi Arabia and obtains more from Angola than from Kuwait. According to the US Department of Energy, the African states produce 11% of the oil world production, and they are expected to produce around 13% in 2025. This number confirms that the United States has increased its interest in the African oil resources as an alternative to the Middle East. The Central African region mainly occupies an important place: Gabon, where the main international firms operate, exported 140 thousand oil barrels a day to the United States in 2001. The oil, however, does not only go to the United States; for instance, the Republic of the Congo exports most of its production to France.

Chad is another country of great oil importance. Therefore, Exxon Mobil, ChevronTexaco, and Inter-American Development Bank (IADB) have financed the construction of an oil pipeline 1,070 kilometers in length, which goes through Cameroon to the sea to be transported by ship. In addition, there has been a lot of oil prospecting in the Republic of the Congo, Gabon, and Cameroon. This area's petroleum is not only abundant and of excellent quality, but also the proximity of these platforms to the US coasts make the oil easier and cheaper to transport.

But not only the United States is interested in the countries of the African region: the previously mentioned French petrol company Elf is also interested. This firm has experienced several scandals regarding corruption in alliance with the local governments and the strategic interests of France.

The zone where the oil is extracted, however, is characterized by instability, disorder, and internal conflict, all of which are injurious factors for its production. Owing to this chronic unsteadiness, the United States has focused on mutual economic and political cooperation relations with some countries of this region and also offers military support consisting of training and equipment. The main aim of this foreign policy is to help these petrol states to recover stability. The foremost benefited state is Nigeria, being also the main oil supplier in Africa, but the United States also exerts some military influence in

Chad, Gabon, and the Republic of the Congo, other oil-exporting countries.

On the other hand, this further military involvement of the United States provokes consequences in Muslim countries like Chad, where the opposition force has allied with extremist groups such as Al Qaeda.

This involvement of the United States is carried out from a military and geostrategic point of view. The countries of the Central African region are important as long as the superpowers continue to import oil and minerals from the area. Their foreign policy is specifically linked with the countries' resources, while the major and most urgent problems such as HIV, tuberculosis, and malaria are not a priority, and many times, remain ignored.

Natural Resources and Development

The discovery of huge amounts of oil and mining resources in African countries has not brought the stability and prosperity that the market value of these resources might suggest. Profit is generated but largely for the governments and the multinational companies. These facts show that the richness of a country does not depend on how many natural resources reserves it has but on how the income generated from those reserves is distributed. In the way, this situation has occurred in Central Africa during the late twentieth and early twenty-first centuries—the existence of large amounts of reserves does not seem to have improved people's living standards but, on the contrary, has worsened them.

Central Africa is a fine example of how the struggle for the control of diamonds or oil has contributed to encourage regional and civil wars, as well as authoritarian and corrupt governments. In addition, the region does not receive all the necessary aid that it should from the international community, and the help received does not reach all countries. For instance, the United States has a selective mechanism of aid. First, from the United States's $10 billion destined to international aid, only $1 billion is destined to the Sub-Saharan African countries, among which are the Central African ones. Second, those countries that qualify for aid must meet a certain criteria of eligibility. In 2000, the Bush administration approved the African Growth and Opportunity Act as a tool for the growth and integration of Africa to the global economy. Such act is centered in the promotion of a free market and the expansion of commerce and investments, offering preferential taxes and other economic benefits for those countries that undertake economic reforms.

Although this program promotes economic growth for the African continent, the benefits of this act are centered in the oil and mining sectors; only a few countries have been selected among the beneficiary ones, and all of these selected countries, such as Angola, are strategically linked with the United States. As with the political economy, the attempts of developed nations to promote security, peace, democracy, and human rights have not been, for the most part, successful.

DIEGO I. MURGUÍA AND VERÓNICA M. ZILIOTTO

See also Cameroon; Central Africa: History and Economic Development; Central African Republic; Chad; Colonialism: History; Colonialism: Legacies; Congo, Democratic Republic of the; Congo, Republic of the; Corruption, Governmental; Ethnic Conflicts: Central Africa; Gabon; Neo-Colonialism

References and Further Reading

Clark, John F., ed. *The African Stakes of the Congo War*, New York: Palgrave, 2002.

Birmingham, David, and Phyllis M. Martin, eds. *History of Central Africa*. New York: Longman, 1983.

Gann, Lewis H. *Central Africa: The Former British States*. Englewood Cliffs, NJ: Prentice Hall, 1971.

Kennedy, Paul M. *Preparing for the Twenty-First Century*. New York: Random House, 1993.

———. *The Rise and Fall of the Great Powers*. New York: Random House, 1988.

Klare, Michael T. *Resource Wars: The New Landscape of Global Conflict*. New York: Henry Holt, 2001.

Klare, Michael T. "The New Geography of Conflict." *Foreign Affairs* (May/June 2001).

Rotberg, R. I., ed. *Imperialism, Colonialism, and Hunger: East and Central Africa*. Lexington: Heath, 1983.

Scanlon, Paul A., ed. *Stories from Central & Southern Africa*. Heinemann, 1983.

Scherrer, Christian P. *Genocide and Crisis in Central Africa: Conflict Roots, Mass Violence, and Regional War*. Westport, CT: Praeger, 2002.

United Nations Development Program (UNDP). *Human Development Report 2004. Cultural Liberty in Today's Diverse World*. UNDP, 2004 (http://hdr.undp.org).

CENTRAL AFRICAN REPUBLIC

As its name suggests, the Central African Republic is situated in Central Africa. It is landlocked, surrounded by Cameroon on the west, Chad in the north, Sudan in the east, and Democratic Republic of the Congo and Republic of the Congo in the south. The largest part of the country is occupied by the vast Azande plateau. The highest point is Mont Ngaoui at 4,658 feet (1,420 meters), and the lowest point is the

Oubangui River at 1,099 feet (335 meters). The climate is subequatorial/tropical, with hot and dry winters and a mild to hot rainy season from April to October. The average monthly temperature is 72 to 85 degrees Fahrenheit (21 to –31 degrees Celsius), precipitation is about 50 to 55 inches (1,270 to 1,397 mm yearly. Main rivers are in Oubangui, which forms the border with Congo (Kinshasa) and Sangha. Most of the vegetation is tropical high grass savanna grassland, but there are dense and moist rain forests in the southwest and dry savanna grasslands in the extreme northeast. The 2004 population was estimated at 3.75 million, with a growth rate of 1.56% annually. Large areas in the East remain virtually uninhabited, and most of the population is concentrated in the western half of the country. The capital, Bangui, is located on Oubangui River, is the largest city, and has a population of about seven hundred thousand.

From the sixteenth to nineteenth centuries, the people of the present-day Central African Republic were devastated by slave traders. The French penetrated the region between Ubangi-Shary in 1889 and occupied it in 1894. Known as the colony of Ubangi-Shari, the area that is now the Central African Republic was united with Chad in 1905. Five years later, it was joined with Gabon and the Middle Congo to become French Equatorial Africa. A rebellion in 1946 led by B. Boganda forced the French to grant self-government. In 1958, the territory voted to become an autonomous republic in the French Community, and on August 13, 1960, President David Dacko proclaimed the republic's independence from France. Dacko moved the country into Maoist (Mao Zedong) China's orbit but was overthrown in a *coup d'état* on December 31, 1965, by the army chief of staff Colonel Jean-Bédel Bokassa. On December 4, 1976, he proclaimed the Central African Empire, and Bokassa professed himself the emperor. His regime was epitomized by brutality and excessive abuse. He was overthrown in another *coup d'état* on September 20, 1979. Former President Dacko returned to power and restored the country's original name.

An army *coup d'état* on September 1, 1981, deposed President Dacko again. A military government came to power, led by André Kolingba. He established, in 1987, a single ruling party, the Central African Democratic Assembly. In 1991 through 1992, President Kolingba, under pressure, announced a move toward parliamentary democracy. In elections held in August 1993, Prime Minister Ange-Félix Patassé defeated Kolingba, promising to pay salaries due of the military and civil servants. In 1995, the country adopted a new constitution. However, Patassé was unable to keep his promises to the

miltary, which staged a revolt in 1996. At Patassé's request, French troops suppressed the uprising. In 1998, the United Nations sent an all-African peace-keeping force to the country. In elections held in September 1999, amid widespread charges of massive fraud, Patassé easily defeated Kolingba. Patassé survived a *coup d'état* attempt in May 2001, but two years later, in March 2003, he was overthrown by General François Bozizé. In the last two years, thousands of people fled the country's turmoil, creating a humanitarian crisis in neighboring Chad. In December 2004, a new constitution was adopted by a referendum. It gives a presidential term of five years, renewable only once, and entrusts the prime minister with extensive powers. The constitution also mandates a 105-member national assembly. Elections for the president and the national assembly were held March 13, 2005, the first since the Bozizé *coup d'état* and the two subsequent years of military rule.

Economic development is hampered by the landlocked location, shaky political situation, generally unskilled work force, and inherited abandoned and mishandled macroeconomic projects. The Central African Republic is one of Africa's poorest and most isolated nations. About 60% of the population is employed in agriculture, including cotton, coffee, tobacco, manioc (tapioca), yams, millet, corn, rice, bananas, and timber. Cattle breeding and fishery are scantily developed. Industries include diamond mining, logging, brewing, manufacturing textiles, making footwear, and assembling bicycles and motorcycles. Per capita gross domestic product (GDP) was $1,100 in 2003 and is expected to shrink. Internal political instabilities overlap with conflicts in Chad, leaving refugees and rebel groups in both countries. Sudan has pledged to work with CAR to stem violent skirmishes over water and grazing rights along the border.

Transportation infrastructure is poorly developed. There are no railways, and roads total 14,795 miles (23,810 kilometers) (only about 400 miles, 643 kilometers, are paved). There are fifty-two airports but only three with paved runways. Waterways total 1,740 miles (2,800 kilometers), primarily resulting fromthe Oubangui and Sangha rivers. The GDP is expected to shrink in 2004. Income distribution is oddly disparate. International aid—mainly from France—can hardly meet essential humanitarian needs, particularly for preventing the spread of AIDS.

In 2003, the adult literacy rate was approximately 51% (63.3% for males and 39.9% for females). Although eight years of schooling for children 6 to 14 years old is officially compulsory, less than 60% of school-age children attend school. There is a university in Bangui, founded in 1966, and a National

School of Arts. No modern health care system exists outside Bangui, which itself has only one major hospital. A number of hospitals and clinics staffed and operated by missionaries provide relatively good care to those who can reach them. For the majority of Central Africans, however, little is offered by the poorly equipped facilities. There are approximately 3.5 physicians and 20 nurses for every 100,000 people. In 2004, the estimated life expectancy was determined to be 39.7 years for males and 43.1 for females. According to the same 2004 estimates, the population growth rate is 1.56% annually, and infant mortality is 92.15 per 1,000 live births. Overall, the country has a poorly educated population and a long history of poor economic policies.

STEPHAN E. NIKOLOV

See also Central Africa: History and Economic Development; Central Africa: International Relations; Ethnic Conflicts: Central Africa

References and Further Reading

Kalck, Pierre. *Central African Republic*. Santa Barbara, CA: Clio Press, 1993.
Kirk-Greene, Anthony, and Daniel Bach, eds. *State and Society in Francophone Africa since Independence*. New York: Palgrave Macmillan, 1995.
Needham, D. E. *From Iron Age to Independence*. Longman, 1974.
O'Toole, Thomas. *Central African Republic in Pictures*. Lerner Publishing Group, 1985.

CENTRAL AMERICA: HISTORY AND ECONOMIC DEVELOPMENT

Geographers consider the area of Central America to stretch from the south of Mexico to the tip of Panama in the Southwest. Historians, economists, and political scientists, on the other hand, generally consider the Central American region to consist of Guatemala, Honduras, El Salvador, Nicaragua, and Costa Rica. These five countries, it is argued, experienced similar colonial governance and have maintained close economic and political ties over the centuries. Social scientists generally do not consider Belize as part of Central America because it was a British, not a Spanish, colony and it became an independent, sovereign state only in 1981, more than 150 years later than the rest of the region. Economically and politically, Belize is more closely identified with the former British colonies in the Caribbean than its neighboring Central American republics. Similarly, Panama is also generally not regarded as an integral part of Central America. Panama has a rather unique history. It is a relatively young country; it was formally a part of the South American country of Colombia until 1903. The creation of Panama was significantly aided by the United States, which had been interested in the area to build what became known as the Panama Canal. The country was effectively split in half by the interoceanic canal and its land buffer, which was sovereign United States territory. Because of the similar colonial histories of Guatemala, Honduras, El Salvador, Nicaragua, and Costa Rica, the fact that they were governed as a single entity in the Central American confederation until the mid-1830s, and their continued interconnectivity, this discussion will examine those countries alone while excluding Panama and Belize.

Although Central American countries are linked by several similarities, there are also major differences in their economies and their application of economic and social policy, which became particularly apparent after World War II. Today, there is considerable variance in the levels of wealth across Central American countries. At the end of World War II, gross domestic product per capita (GDP/c) in the five major Central American states lay within a narrow band of $90. Costa Rica enjoyed the highest GDP/c at $282, while Nicaragua suffered from the lowest at $191. In the subsequent forty years, Costa Rica's GDP/c increased to $806 (in constant 1970 US dollars), but that of Guatemala, the next highest, grew only to $440. Honduras, the poorest country in the region, showed little economic development with just $273 per capita, which is lower in real terms than Costa Rica's GDP/c in 1945. In the post-World War II period, the extent of economic development varied greatly across the region. The increasing economic and social gaps between the countries in the post-World War II period have become still more pronounced through the present time.

Historical Origins of Economic and Social Development

The colonial period laid the foundations for future trade and economic development in the region. For most of Central America, the economic system established by the Spaniards, the *Encomienda* system, underpinned the region's economic development. The *Encomiendas* were land grants that forced indigenous peoples to work in a serf-type relationship. This system permitted the creation of large *haciendas* (a large plantation estate) throughout the region. In the postindependence period and especially after the 1870s, coffee and bananas dominated the countries' economies. There were, though, significant differences between these two dominant sectors and across the countries.

In the case of coffee, the production and export remained in the hands of Central Americans, but banana production and exports were controlled by foreign companies with few economic links to the local economies. While coffee production was domestic and encouraged by targeted government policies, the rise of the banana industry was an unplanned outgrowth of the Central American political elites' attempt to develop their countries' infrastructure and help the coffee sector. To aid in the construction of the railroads, Central American governments granted US railroad-building companies large areas of land where the railroads were to be built. These companies used their land grants to plant and cultivate bananas as they constructed the railroads. These companies also developed high levels of vertical integration; the bananas were transported on the companies' railroads to their own ports and then shipped on their own ships to the US markets. The banana companies became economically and politically successful within their economic enclaves. In the case of Honduras, for example, the companies eventually controlled more than two-thirds of the country's territory, and they tended to interfere in Honduran politics to advance their economic interests.

By the start of the twentieth century, the agrarian basis of Central America's economy was firmly established. The economies were based on the exportation of two primary products, coffee and bananas. A third sector involved peasant farmers producing basic foods for their own consumption or the local market. The two export sectors relied on a labor market based on debt peonage that was encouraged and fostered by national vagrancy laws. This type of labor relationship did not develop in Costa Rica due to the paucity of indigenous peoples, which resulted in the creation and maintenance of small farms. The banana companies tended to import labor from the Caribbean to overcome the lack of a labor force living in the coastal areas of Costa Rica near plantations.

The export-based economic development strategy, which served the region well, took a severe hit in the 1930 when the Great Depression struck the US economy and spread to other countries. This world depression severely reduced demand for Central American exports, which in turn significantly reduced the tax revenue for governments across the region. The economic turmoil led, in part, to a reconsideration of the economic development model.

The post-World War II period in Central America marked a major transformation of their economies and the adoption of an Important Substitution Industrialization (ISI) strategy. The goal of this strategy was to erect protective tariff barriers against goods produced outside of the region and to encourage domestic producers to make replacement goods without having to compete with more efficient international producers. It was thought that the tariff barriers would be a short-term strategy that would protect the Central American infant industries only until they could compete with the internationally produced imports.

Key to the success of this strategy was the creation of the Central American Common Market (CACM). All five Central American countries agreed to join the CACM, although Costa Rica was a little reluctant at first and did not formally join until 1963, two years after the other four countries.

The years from the 1960s until the late 1970s were an economically prosperous time for the region. For example, in the period of 1960 to 1968, the GDP (in constant terms increased) was 5.9% per year and 4.7% in the following five-year period (1968–1975). This impressive growth record was driven by the secondary sectors (manufacturing, construction, transportation) and tertiary sectors (commerce, banking, and other services). The traditional agricultural and mining (primary) sector, although still important, was slowly eclipsed by the other two more rapidly expanding sectors (Acuña-Alfaro 1999:7). Thus, the period of economic expansion of the 1960s and 1970s also resulted in a reorientation of the region's economies away from primary production and toward secondary and tertiary sector activities. The late 1970s, though, saw another major depression for Central America's economies spurred by a series of unfortunate events. Prices for Central American exports generally declined, which was problematic because these were the countries' major earners of international currency. At the same time, the prices of imports rose rapidly, especially for oil. As the countries' import bills exceeded their exports, the governments needed to borrow money on the international market, and this was exacerbated by the second major oil price hike in the late 1970s. By the end of the 1980s, the region's international debt reached $7.7 billion. The continuing economic crisis caused international borrowing to balloon to more than $14 billion three years later. But when Costa Rica became the hemisphere's first country to default on its international debt, this particular avenue for dealing with the economic downturn was effectively closed.

Furthermore, the increasingly violent internecine wars in El Salvador, Guatemala, and Nicaragua were destructive in human and economic terms and eventually led to the virtual cessation of the CACM.

The wars killed hundreds of thousands of people and forced millions more to seek refuge in neighboring countries, as well as increased government expenditures on expanding military capabilities. With the exception of Costa Rica, which had and has no standing army, the 1980s saw major increases in military expenditures across the region, especially in Nicaragua, at a time of declining government revenues.

The 1980s and 1990s

The 1980s are generally regarded as a "lost decade" for Central America. A major economic crisis was sparked by a number of factors: the international recession, the debt crisis, political violence, falling export prices, rising oil prices, and internecine wars in three of the region's countries. The wars also effectively cut off trade routes throughout Central America. According to Victor Bulmer-Thomas (1991), real GDP per capita was lower in 1990 than it had been in 1980. Although the economic decline affected all Central American countries, for some the economic collapse was significantly more pronounced. In Costa Rica, for example, the cumulative decline in GDP/c from 1980 to 1990 was 4.7%. At the other extreme, Nicaragua's cumulative decline was almost 43% for the same period. The other countries ranged between 19% (El Salvador) and 14% (Honduras). The middle point (1985) was the nadir of this collapse of GDP growth; although some countries began a slow economic recovery (Costa Rica, Guatemala, and Honduras), GDP per capita in El Salvador remained flat and in Nicaragua it continued its decline.

The decline in per capita GDP was compounded by the rapid increase in population growth rates. For example, the population of the entire region in 1950 was slightly less than 10 million people, but by 2003 it was more than 35 million. In addition to the increase in population, there was a marked change in where people lived, which reflected the relative decline of traditional agriculture. In 1965, for example, 38% of Costa Rica's population lived in urban areas, but by the start of the 1998, 47% were classified as urban dwellers. Corresponding numbers for the rest of the region are even more pronounced with the exception of Guatemala; for two countries, Honduras and Nicaragua, the majority of their populations now reside in urban areas. In Honduras, the urban population increased from 23% to 51%, and the Nicaraguan numbers increased from 43% to 55%. El Salvador also saw major growth in its urban population during this period from 39% to 46%. Guatemala,

though, remained the most rural population in the region with only a slight increase from 34% in 1965 to 39% in 1998 (World Bank 2000, World Development Indicators; Unesco n.d.).

These events and the ensuing economic depression set in motion a series of economic policy reforms across the region. These reforms, widely known as neoliberal or Washington Consensus reforms, were encouraged by international financial institutions such as the World Bank and the United States Agency for International Development (USAID) as conditional loans. A major part of these reforms was an emphasis on reducing the role of the state in the economy and the insertion of Central American goods and services into the world economy as well as the introduction of new nontraditional export products. In all countries of Central America, the export of agricultural goods declined as a percentage of total exports. For example, comparing the period before the major economic depression (1979) with the period of economic growth (2001), the percentage of total exports for agricultural products decreased from slightly more than 70% to 30%. The most striking decline is in the case of El Salvador, which declined from approximately 65% to about 15% in 2001 (*Proyecto Estado de la Región* 2003:138).

The collapse of traditional agro-exports is reflected in the coffee sector's contraction across the region as a percentage of all exports. With the exception of Nicaragua, where coffee has increased its share of that country's exports, all other countries have been harmed by the world's overproduction of coffee and the consequent collapse of world coffee prices. In Costa Rica, for example, coffee declined from 18% of the country's total exports to less than 5%. The most pronounced decline is the case of El Salvador, where coffee declined from almost 38% of all exports to approximately 10%.

The Contemporary Period

How should economic success be measured? As already stated, the commonly used indicator of economic development is gross domestic product per capita (GDP/c), which measures total market value of goods and services produced in a country divided by the total population. Thus, if the economy is growing more rapidly than the population, then the GDP/c will increase, and the country will be labeled as increasing its economic well-being. But if the country experiences slow economic growth or rapid population growth, then the GDP/c will decline. This measure, although widely used, is a very crude and incomplete measure. For example, it fails to include how the country's income is actually distributed or to take into account the population's living conditions.

One good indicator of economic development is average life expectancy. Big differences can be noted across the region: life expectancy in Costa Rica is seventy-eight years, which is nine years more than neighboring Nicaragua and thirteen years more than Guatemala. Life expectancy in Honduras and El Salvador is seventy-one years. The level of poverty is another indicator of how profoundly economic development has affected the population. The Human Poverty Index (percentage of the population living in poverty) for 2000 was 4% in Costa Rica compared with 23.5% for Guatemala, 24.4% for Nicaragua, 20.5% for Honduras, and 18% for El Salvador. An indirect measure of a population's well-being comes from the region's literacy rates. All the countries have experienced substantial improvements in the literacy levels in the postwar period. For example, in Honduras the literacy rate in 1950 was 35%; in 2003, it was 80%. Similar improvements have been seen across the region including in Guatemala, which had the lowest level in 1950 (29%) and high level of 70% in 2003. But there remain major differences across the countries; Costa Rica's literacy rate is almost 96%, while Nicaragua and Guatemala still have rates in the low- to mid-70% range.

In response to the shortcomings of the GDP/c measurement instrument, the United Nations Development Programme (UNDP) devised a measurement technique to capture the results of economic growth on the actual population. This measure, the Human Development Index (HDI), is a composite measure of development that takes into account life expectancy, health, education, and standards of living. Using the HDI measurement also reveals the stark contrast among the region's countries. Costa Rica's HDI ranks the country 45th in the world (above some "developed" countries). The next highest Central American country's HDI is El Salvador at 103rd, while the region's other countries are ranked between 115th (Honduras) through the 121st (Guatemala).

These figures are not unrelated to the level of social expenditure per capita undertaken by the various countries in the region. Costa Rica spends more than six times as much on social programs per capita than the next highest country, Guatemala. Costa Rica spends $622 (in 1997 US dollars) compared to $107 in Guatemala, $82 in El Salvador, and $57 in both Nicaragua and Honduras (*Proyecto Estado de la Región* 2003:31). These policy priorities reflect decisions made by political leaders and are, in part at least, a reflection of the regime type of each country.

In the case of Nicaragua, for example, the Somoza family dominated the political and economic scene before the Sandinistas took over in 1979 and then diverted much of the government's expenditures to fight the US-backed counterrevolution. Social expenditure was in the first instant not a priority, and in the second period, it was severely restricted by war expenditures.

Natural Setbacks to Economic Recovery

Apart from international interventions and political policy decisions that have hampered economic and social development, the Central American region's economic well-being is, periodically, affected by severe natural disasters. For example, the Nicaraguan earthquake in 1972 devastated Managua, leaving much of the city in ruins and killing more than ten thousand people. Apart from earthquakes, hurricanes are also common events. In the period from 1972 through 2001, there were six major hurricanes that pummeled the region. Hurricane Mitch slammed into Central America in 1998 at a time when many of the preconditions for economic growth were being put into place; according to the InterAmerican Development Bank, political reforms, the end of the civil wars, and economic reforms were all in place as the hurricane hit. More than 11,000 people died, and 15,300 were missing; 438 bridges and 164,000 homes were destroyed. The total estimated economic cost of the hurricane was set at $6.5 billion, with the majority of that destruction concentrated in Honduras and Nicaragua.

CAFTA

The Central American Free Trade Agreement (CAFTA) was signed by the five Central American countries in May 2004. The Dominican Republic joined in December 2004. It remains to be ratified by the US Congress before it can take effect. According to the joint statement by the Central American Presidents in December 2002, for the Central American states, the goal of the agreement is to open up the US markets to Central American products; attract US investment to the region; strengthen the region's democracy, rule of law; and to foster economic and social development. This agreement will be an extension of the neoliberal economic policies advocated as solutions to Central America's economic problems of the 1980s and 1990s.

As with earlier economic development in Central America, this new economic development strategy tying the region to international trade, particularly with the United States, reflects the continued link between regional economic development and internal politics and international politics. Most remarkable is the divergence in economic and social development across the region in spite of a common history and proximity of the countries.

BRUCE M. WILSON

See also Central America: International Relations; Central American Common Market (CACM); Costa Rica; El Salvador; Ethnic Conflicts: Mexico and Central America; Guatemala; Honduras; Nicaragua

References and Further Reading

Acuña-Alfaro, Jairo. 2000. *The Political Economy of Development in Central America.* Master's thesis in political economy. University of Essex (www.geocities.com/jaacun).
Bethel, Leslie, ed. *Central America Since Independence.* Cambridge: Cambridge University Press, 1991.
Bulmer-Thomas, Victor. "A Long Run Model of Development for Central America." *Research Paper #27.* London: ILAS, 1991.
Hall, Carolyn, and Héctor Pérez Brignoli. John V. Cotter, Cartographer. *Historical Atlas of Central America.* University of Oklahoma Press, 2003.
Perez-Brignoli, Hector. *A Brief History of Central America.* Berkeley, CA: California University Press, 1989.
Proyecto Estado de la Región. Segundo Informe sobre Desarrllo Humano en Centroamérica y Panamá. San José, Costa Rica: UNDP, 2003.United Nations Development Programme. *Human Development Report 2004* (http://hdr.undp.org/).
Valladares, Licia, and Magda Prates Coelho. "Urban Research in Latin America: Towards a Research Agenda." *UNESCO*, n.d. (http://www.unesco.org/most/valleng.htm).
World Bank. "World Development Indicators." World Bank, n.d. (http://worldbank.org/data/wdi2004/index.htm).
Zuvekas, Clarence. 2000. *The Dynamics of Sectoral Growth in Central America: Recent Trends and Prospects for 2020.* Institut fuer Iberoamerika-Kunde, CA2020. (http://ca2020.fiu.edu/Themes/Clarence_Zuvekas/Zuvekas.pdf).

CENTRAL AMERICA: INTERNATIONAL RELATIONS

Problems of Definition

Defining the region of Central America is not as easy as it might seem. On the one hand, Central America is often narrowly defined as the five contiguous states of Guatemala, Honduras, El Salvador, Nicaragua, and Costa Rica. These five countries all have Spanish as their official language, are former Spanish colonies, and share similar historical trajectories and a dominant cultural heritage. These historical, political, and cultural factors rather than geographical proximity are the reason that these five countries are generally viewed together as a region. On the other hand, two other states, Belize in the northeast and Panama in the southeast, are geographically part of Central America but are generally not regarded as part of Central America. Belize, an English-speaking, former British colony, did not achieve independence until 1981, more than 150 years after the rest of the region. Belize is also politically and economically more closely tied to Britain's other former Caribbean colonies than the core states of Central America. Politics in Belize have also been at variance from much of the rest of Central America as it has enjoyed parliamentary democracy rather authoritarian rule and civil wars.

Panama, for its part, is generally not included in studies of Central America because of its unusual history including its much later creation in 1904 with the United States acting as midwife. The presence of US troops and US control over the Panama Canal, which physically splits the county in two, further separates Panama from the rest of the region. Since the 1980s, though, both of these countries have become increasingly involved in the political and economic life of the isthmus. This discussion examines primarily the international relations of five of the Central American countries: the republics of Guatemala, Honduras, El Salvador, Nicaragua, and Costa Rica.

Central American International Relations from Independence Through World War II

Central America's high level of cultural homogeneity prior to the Spanish conquest was maintained during the colonial period. When the region became independent of Spain, the individual provinces (countries) quickly joined the short-lived Mexican Empire.

With the fall of the Mexican Empire, the five states of Central America formed the *Provincias Unidas del Centro de América* (United Provinces of Central America), which itself collapsed in 1839, after years of internecine violence between competing military strongmen. The notion of Central America as a single state did not die with the collapse of the United Provinces; it has been an ongoing concept through the present day.

The United States has been a major (if not *the* major) player in the internal politics and economic lives of Central America since its independence from Spain. First, the Monroe Doctrine declaration clearly placed Central America in the United State's "backyard." Second, as the United States continued to claim territory further westward, the need for a quick route to cross from the East Coast of the United States to the West became more pressing. With it came a renewed interest in Central America as a possible transcontinental route, which also attracted the attention of US filibusters such as William Walker, who invaded and took control of Nicaragua in the 1850s. Later, the United States intervened in Central American civil wars; in 1912, the United States, for the first time, sent troops into Nicaragua to support one side of a civil war to try and stabilize the region. US troops remained in Nicaragua until the 1930s when US foreign policy changed under the presidency of Franklin Delano Roosevelt.

US governments, though, did not have a monopoly interfering in Central America's internal politics. Other countries, particularly the United Kingdom, took control of what was originally known as British Honduras and eventually Belize. The United Kingdom also engaged in gunboat diplomacy in Central America, including the bombing of the Nicaraguan town of Grenada. It was also the British Navy that captured the US filibuster William Walker and handed him over to the Honduran military, which eventually executed him. US companies (primarily banana companies) also flexed economic and political muscle in the region and became dominant political actors in some Central American countries.

Relations between the United States and Central America improved during the Roosevelt administration's (1933–1945) Good Neighbor Policy. President Roosevelt, an early advocate of unilateral US intervention and annexation in Latin America, rejected the corollary to the Monroe Doctrine and became the first sitting US president to visit Latin America and the Panama Canal Zone. These overtures to Latin America in general and Central America in particular paid a dividend in improving international relations with Central America. For example, after the Japanese attacked Pearl Harbor, the Central American countries showed their support for the United States by joining World War II against the axis powers. Henry Raymont (2005) argues Roosevelt's policy toward Latin America led to an improved and consolidated inter-American system (including the creation of the Organization of American States) and an end to Latin American mistrust of the United States.

Post-War International Relations

With the conclusion of World War II, the United States shifted its attention to rebuilding Europe's economies through the Marshall Plan and left the Central American countries to address their own substantial economic problems with little economic aid. The end of the Roosevelt era was accompanied by the start of the Cold War, which in turn reoriented United States–Central American relations and set the stage for regional international relations through the end of the 1980s.

The new era of preventing communism from taking hold in Central America began in the early 1950s when President Eisenhower employed the CIA (acting with the support of dictators in Nicaragua and Honduras) to undermine and eventually overthrow Guatemala's democratically elected government, headed by President Jacobo Árbenz. This intervention effectively ended Guatemala's first experiment with democracy and ushered in years of dictatorship, civil war, and state terrorism.

The *coup d'etat*, which took place at the height of the Cold War, removed a democratically elected president whom the United States viewed as a Communist and whom US banana companies operating in Guatemala saw as a threat to their economic position. As part of the growing anti-Communist movement in the United States, overthrowing Árbenz successfully pushed the Organization of American States to support a US resolution stating communism was a threat to the region and was "incompatible" with the OAS charter. This declaration gave a new judicial rationale for US intervention in the internal affairs of its neighboring republics as well as demanding collective action from the other Latin American states to stem the perceived tide of communism in the Western Hemisphere. According to Henry Raymont (2005), the success of the US policy in removing Árbenz established a model for US interventions in other Central American countries, particularly Nicaragua and Panama in the 1980s.

Another major shift in US policy toward Central America came in response to the Cuban revolution in 1959 and the election of John F. Kennedy and lasted through the early 1990s. Although President Kennedy paid more attention to Latin America than any president since Franklin Roosevelt, the Alliance for Progress, Kennedy's policy initiative that was designed to encourage economic development and democratic governance, ultimately became another tool in the United States's anti-Communist policy. In the case of Central America, though, the economic development and democratic reform goals eventually took second place to internal security goals. With the death of Kennedy and the assumption of President Johnson to office, the emphasis of the alliance changed; emphasis on democratic governance was no longer a precondition for Central American countries to receive US aid and diplomatic recognition. Instead, Kennedy's policy of ostracizing newly created military dictatorship was replaced by willingness to deal with any government that was friendly to the United States and sufficiently anti-Communist.

As the Central American economic situation worsened in the 1960s and 1970s, successive US administrations tolerated the rise of dictators and the abuse of human rights as the only solution to eradicating nascent insurgencies and rebellions. Even the administration of Jimmy Carter, who had made human rights a central part of his international relations agenda, was caught in the contradiction of a perceived need to fight communism in Central America and the promotion of democratic governance and respect for human rights. El Salvador, for example, witnessed years of dictatorial oligarchic rule and increasing levels of brutality and democratic fraud. The Carter administration's attempt to rein in the government's political violence by ending military aid to the country was thwarted by the Salvadorian *junta*'s decision to refuse the aid in advance. Again, even with the murders of two US land reform workers, the Archbishop of San Salvador, and nine thousand other Salvadorians, the United States did little to end the bloodshed. In the case of Nicaragua, Carter's actions with respect to the Somoza dictatorships were poorly implemented and had serious consequences of bolstering the dictatorship, which was eventually toppled by domestic insurgents, the FSLN (Sandinistas). The Ronald Reagan presidency marked a new direction in United States–Central American relations. Reagan saw the Sandinista regime in Nicaragua as a Communist regime that was attempting to export its revolution to Guatemala, Honduras, and El Salvador.

According to Reagan and his appointees, Central American political violence was caused by the influence of international communism rather than by domestic ills such as economic crises, dictatorship, brutal repression, and corruption within the region. Alexander Haig, Reagan's secretary of state, signaled the administration's new direction for its relations with Central America when he noted that "International terrorism will take the place of Human Rights in our concern" (Raymont 2005:236).

While the United States saw its relations with Central America through a Cold War lens that showed Soviet and Cuban Communists sponsoring the rebellions in Guatemala and El Salvador and supporting the Sandinista government in Nicaragua with subsidized oil and major flows of armaments, other countries (including the European Union) did not view the Soviets and Cubans as the root of the region's problems.

It was clear that the Soviets and the Cubans were at least tangentially involved. Fidel Castro, for example, visited Managua, Nicaragua, in 1980 on the first anniversary of the Sandinista Revolution and promised military support if the country were invaded by the United States. President Daniel Ortega added to the perception of Soviet involvement when he visited Moscow in the early 1980s and signed economic agreements with his Soviet hosts.

The Reagan administration increased the stakes in its international relations with Central America; it began a proxy war against Nicaragua and increased military aid to dictatorial governments in Honduras, El Salvador, and Guatemala. The *quid pro quo* for Honduras's aid was that it allowed Nicaraguan counterrevolutionary insurgents to attack Nicaraguan territory from Honduras. The US strong-arm tactics were also used on Costa Rica, which has a constitutional ban on the existence of a standing army. Costa Rica was cajoled to support the US position against the Sandinista government of Nicaragua. On one hand, this should have been relatively easy for the Costa Ricans, who are noted for their general hostilities toward Nicaraguans (stemming back to Costa Rica's civil war and subsequent two invasions of Costa Rican territory by Nicaragua in the late 1940s and early 1950s). But when Oscar Arias assumed the presidency in 1986, he found that Costa Rican territory had been routinely used to harbor Nicaraguan contras and used to stage attacks on Nicaragua. Arias moved to end this situation and tried to close down many of the clandestine runways that were used by the United States and the contras. The US response was to cut US aid to Costa Rica. In 1983, for example, US aid to Costa Rica was more than $200 million, but this collapsed to about $100 million in 1990 at the end of Arias's term in office (Wilson 1998).

A major turning point in Central America's international relations came with the intervention of a group of Latin American countries (Mexico, Panama, Venezuela, and Colombia), known as the Contadora group, which attempted to create a negotiated settlement to the ongoing Central American crisis. While Contadora's mid-1980s efforts produced a number of agreements to end the conflicts in the region, it was not until the agreements between the presidents of the Central American countries were signed in the late 1980s that real progress was made.

In 1987, President Oscar Arias Sanchez of Costa Rica received the Nobel Peace Prize for his leadership in the creation of a negotiated peace process that helped foster a negotiated settlement to the civil wars in El Salvador, Guatemala, and Nicaragua. The Costa Rican's initiative and its international validation through the Peace Prize rankled the United States, which had opposed a negotiated settlement to the crises.

The Escapulas II agreements that helped end the years of internecine fighting in Guatemala, El Salvador, and Nicaragua also laid the framework for increased levels of regional cooperation and integration. This agreement also created the System of Central American Integration (*Sistema de Itegración Centoamericano*, SICA) and the Alliance for Sustainable Development (*Alianza para el Desarrollo Sostenible*, ALIDES), which were the institutional tools to increased levels of regional integration.

Another political innovation was the creation of the Central American Parliament (commonly referred to as PARLCEN). This body has representatives from all Central American countries with the exception of Costa Rica. It is ironic that while the process of regional integration has been broadened to include Belize, Panama, and the Dominican Republic as associate members of the Central American Parliament, Costa Rica has consistently refused to join this political body. This is especially interesting as PARLCEN was, in large part, the brainchild of former President Oscar Arias of Costa Rica.

With the end of the civil wars and the return to democratic politics across the region in the late 1990s, relations between the Central American republics have improved. This is reflected in the increased number of high-level meetings of Central American presidents to discuss and thrash out treaties and agreements of a variety of development related issues. Between 1998 through 2002, for example, there were twelve such meetings involving Central American presidents. These meetings are in response to a region-wide desire to increase economic trade and political ties within the region.

Central America's national parliaments have ratified many international treaties concerning human rights, but there is considerable variation in the number of treaties signed by each country as well as in terms of the effectiveness of the enforcement of the treaties. The keenest signatory to major international human rights treaties has consistently been Costa Rica. This is perhaps in part due to the country's history as a consolidated democratic state for more than fifty years. Between 1950 and 1998, Costa Rica has signed seventeen international human rights treaties and has regularly lived by the constrictions

of the agreements, especially since the creation of its Constitutional Court (Sala Consitucional) in 1989. During the same period, Nicaragua has ratified only five, which includes the genocide treaty of the early 1950s that all countries of Central America have signed. Honduras similarly signed only five treaties. El Salvador and Guatemala have tended to sign more treaties since the early 1980s.

The most significant recent development in Central American international relations was the move to reinvigorate the moribund Central American Common Market (CACM), which was created in the 1960s and effectively collapsed during the 1980s due to disruptions in trade because of the various civil wars. In the postwar period, as part of the movement toward reducing the role of the state in economic activities and the increasing level of globalization, the Central American states collectively negotiated a free trade agreement with the United States (CAFTA, Central American Free Trade Agreement). Although this agreement has been written, it is only slowly being ratified by the various national assemblies in Central America. Once again, though, the US Congress appears to be less than willing to ratify the treaty, which means that it cannot take effect and leaves the Central America countries outside of a major trading block.

BRUCE M. WILSON

See also Alliance for Progress; Árbenz Guzmán, Jacobo; Arias Sanchez, Oscar; Belize; Central America: History and Economic Development; Central American Common Market (CACM); Contras; Costa Rica; El Salvador; Ethnic Conflicts: Mexico and Central America; Guatemala; Honduras; Human Rights as a Foreign Policy Issue; Human Rights: Definition and Violations; Nicaragua; Organization of American States (OAS); Panama; Panama Canal Treaties, 1977; Sandinista National Liberation Front (FSLN); United States–Dominican Republic–Central American Free Trade Agreement

References and Further Reading

Armony, Ariel C. *Argentina, the United States, and the Anti-Communist Crusade in Central America, 1977–1984*. Athens, OH: Ohio University Center for International Studies, 1996, c1997.
Bethel, Leslie, ed. *Central America Since Independence*. Cambridge: Cambridge University Press, 1991.
Booth, John A. *Understanding Central America*. Boulder, CO: Westview Press, 1999.
Foster, Lynn V. *A Brief History of Central America*. New York: Facts on File, 2000.
Hall, Carolyn, and Héctor Pérez Brignoli. John V. Cotter, Cartographer. *Historical Atlas of Central America*. University of Oklahoma Press, 2003.

LaFeber, Walter. *Inevitable Revolutions: The United States in Central America*, 2d ed. New York: W.W. Norton, 1993.

Mahoney, James. *The Legacies of Liberalism: Path Dependence and Political Regimes in Central America*. Baltimore, MD: Johns Hopkins University Press, 2001.

Perez Brignoli, Hector. *A Brief History of Central America*. Berkeley, CA: California University Press, 1989.

Raymont, Henry. *Troubled Neighbors: The Story of US-Latin American Relations from FDR to the Present*. Boulder, CO: Westview Press, 2005.

Weinberg, Bill. *War on the Land: Ecology and Politics in Central America*. New York: Zed Books, 1991.

Wekesser, Carol, ed. *Central America: Opposing Viewpoints*. San Diego: Greenhaven Press, 1990.

Wilson, Bruce M. *Costa Rica: Politics, Economics, and Democracy*, Boulder, CO: Lynne Rienner Publishers, 1998.

CENTRAL AMERICAN COMMON MARKET (CACM)

The Central American Common Market (CACM), or the Mercado Común CentroAmericano (MCC), was the first Latin American attempt at economic integration in the twentieth century. The idea came out of Resolution Number 9 in the Fourth Period of the Sessions of the United Nations' Economic Commission for Latin America (ECLA), on June 16, 1951. It is important to note that while historically there have been several attempts to return to a politically integrated Central America, the CACM represented an outside entity's economic vision for the region.

In 1951, El Salvador initiated the trend proposed by ECLA, signing trade treaties with Guatemala and Nicaragua. The following year, the ministers of economy from all Central American nations (Panama was not included) came together to create the Committee for Economic Cooperation for Central America (CCE). For the rest of the decade of the 1950s, El Salvador, Guatemala, Honduras, Costa Rica, and Nicaragua continued with several of these bilateral agreements, lasting only between one and four years. But it was not until June 10, 1958, in Tegucigalpa, Honduras, at the fifth meeting of the CCE that Central American representatives subscribed to a Multilateral Treaty of Free Trade and Economic Integration, becoming effective on June 2, 1959. A General Treaty of Central American Economic Integration became the key policy instrument; all five countries had ratified the treaty by September 1963.

The post-World War II conditions for a vibrant, integrated industrial region in Central America presented formidable challenges. Made up of geographically and demographically small nations, Central America possessed a small internal market, with national markets even less significant in the Latin American context, much less in the global one. With roughly 8 million inhabitants in 1950, and a gross annual product of only $1.4 million, per capita income was a mere $175 (US) for the entire region. The vast majority of Salvadorans and Guatemalans earned considerably less, an average of $95 for the former and $80 for the latter. These poverty rates were further concentrated in the rural sector, where two-thirds of Central America's population made their home. The regional infrastructure for industrialization was equally poor, with roads and railways favoring foreign-owned export industries, such as those of the powerful United Fruit. With high illiteracy rates and poor health condition and nutrition rates, the workforce certainly could not have been expected to reach high standards of industrial production in the new period of transition.

Yet, despite these challenges, the impetus for growth and development spurred by the ideals of the CACM made for political and economic changes. The general goals of the CACM included the liberalization of intraregional trade, the establishment of a free trade area involving an increasing number of manufactured goods, and a customs union. The General Treaty also provided for a Central American Bank for Economic Integration (CABEI). From the 1950s through the 1970s, the economic gains spurred under the treaty were impressive by most standards. Overall, gross internal product in the region grew at a rate of 5.2% between 1950 and 1978. Similarly, trade within the region increased in the two decades between 1960 and 1980, from US dollars of $33 million to $1,129 million. Intraregional exports that amounted to $31 million in 1960 grew to $285.2 million by 1970. Based on export rate indicators, Guatemala and El Salvador particularly benefited from the increase in intraregional trade. Guatemala sold 32.3% of its exports to the regional market in 1970, while El Salvador compared favorably at 35.3%. Intraregional purchases were also very favorable in 1970, with Honduras, El Salvador, and Nicaragua purchasing 25% of their imports from the CACM. With the exception of Nicaragua, intraregional exports continued to grow steadily in the 1970s. By the 1980s, with growing political unrest and revolutionary struggles in the region, trade declined, and the CACM collapsed. A global recession in 1982 only compounded an already depressed regional situation. From 1980 to 1985, intraregional exports that had steadily climbed in Central America since the 1950s suffered drastic declines: from $260.1 to $137.6 million for Costa Rica; from $295.8 to $157.2 million for El Salvador; from $440.8 to

$205.0 million for Guatemala; from $91.4 to $19.9 million for Honduras; and from $75.4 to $24.1 million for Nicaragua.

Increasing foreign debts accompanied these falls in exports. At the beginning of the 1970s, the region's foreign debt was not altogether unmanageable, amounting to $1.35 billion. But this debt grew steadily in the decade, an average of 23% annually, reaching $1.93 billion in 1973 and $6.875 billion by 1979. For El Salvador and Honduras, the debt overwhelmed them even more at this time, growing an average of 33% annually. The extreme rise in petroleum products stemming from the first oil crisis in 1973 and the second in 1978 made Central America and the CACM even more vulnerable, raising the cost for industrialization.

The lofty goals for economic integration through the CACM met several challenges. Ideological difference between governments stymied multilateral accords from the beginning. In January 1960, for example, Honduras, El Salvador, and Guatemala formed a separate economic association, hoping to have a common market within five years. Under the sponsorship of the US government, El Salvador and Honduras initiated a bilateral treaty for economic unity, incorporating Guatemala as soon as this third country found out about the initial goals. The three-country treaty went further than all previous and future accords in establishing the free flow of goods, people, and capital. Costa Rica and Honduras in particular reacted angrily to this trilateral move; the latter's complaints eventually led to a December 1960 General Treaty for Central American Economic Integration signed by Guatemala, El Salvador, Honduras, and Nicaragua; Costa Rica signed on in July 1962.

The liberalization of trade relations as stipulated by the CACM benefited those with an already strong industrial base in the region, largely foreign, mostly US-owned corporations. In the 1960s, for example, under the climate of free trade, foreign companies trading in fruit, such as Castle & Cook and United Fruit (later becoming United Brands), diversified their products into food processing. Along with the underpaid employment that came with their growth, the development of regional, national industries was further frustrated. The so-called soccer war between El Salvador and Honduras in 1969 also disrupted the CACM significantly. Their breaking of official relations that year brought disarray to the commercial flow of goods. Located literally at the center of Central America and bridging the regional integration by land, Honduras played an important role in facilitating a smooth road for the mobility of goods across land.

Such economic relations with the United States have usually been part of the equation in the CACM's goals for the economic integration and for its failures. When the CACM was first ratified in the early 1960s, US corporations vying for the new regional market expanded their direct investments, doubling between 1950 and 1970. While CABEI's purpose was to promote regional industrialization, the Central American Bank instead supported US investments. The fact that the United States provided most of the fund's capital facilitated the favoritism given to US companies in the region. Thus, while the CACM expanded regional markets, it did not protect these new, relatively weak markets from the overwhelming competition coming from the United States. The retardation of the region's industrial economy and its close association with US markets were plainly clear by the early 1980s. By 1981, the CACM had thirteen items for which it provided 10% or more to US markets, with bananas easily topping that list. The fact that twenty years after the establishment of the CACM it was bananas and not an industrial product that topped the exports list made a more diversified, regionally controlled Central American economic integration quite a dream.

Logistical challenges became more pronounced in the 1970s and 1980s, with changes brought upon by the fall of the Somoza dictatorship and rise of the Sandinista government in Nicaragua and with the armed revolutionary challenges in Guatemala and El Salvador. Mired in these social, economic, and political shifts, the region continued to experience an increase in the annual deficit of balance of payments. Limited internal supplies and overseas markets' protective measures also presented critical roadblocks to the efforts of the CACM. Increasing debts within the region and especially to outside lenders prevented member nations from investing larger portions of their funds to develop a stronger industrial infrastructure. Not positioned competitively as an industrial player, Central America under the CACM never achieved the desired goals, despite producing measurable growth up to the end of the 1970s.

While the failures the CACM suffered were largely economic, political, and social dilemmas frustrated whatever gains had been achieved in the 1950s and 1960s. Between 1945 and 1973, capital flow and the exporting output were positive. Yet, little new employment was generated in the process. Everyday conditions in the rural sector, easily the least developed and most poverty-stricken segment, remained virtually unchanged, despite signs of modernization in the larger urban centers. The modernization of agriculture actually disempowered a vast majority of rural workers, turning them into an underpaid and more easily exploitable wage labor force with little-to-no land ownership for basic subsistence. Overall, the vast majority of Central Americans did not benefit directly or indirectly from the new flows of monies. The gains from limited Central American economic integration went to the elite, a post-World War II pattern that reached its peak in the 1970s. At this time, the average income of those belonging to the top 5% of the wealthy class exceeded more than thirty times the average earnings of those making up the lowest 20% of the poor class. Such drastic income polarization proved that growth without a more equitable social well-being could not bring about overall regional development. Health, housing, and educational standards improved, but not to the levels expected from that of "developed" nations. The stagnant social conditions for the majority of Central Americans that remained a pattern since after World War II, and especially in the rural sectors, were in part the fuel behind the armed struggles in Guatemala, Nicaragua, and El Salvador.

With a more politically stable region following peace accords in El Salvador and Guatemala, the 1990s saw a renewed interest in the CACM. Yet, its immediate, gigantic competitor, the 1994 North American Free Trade Agreement (NAFTA), made a new and improved CACM less attractive. With a desire to become part of the more powerful economic North American block, Central American nations have placed less interest in their own regional integration. Costa Rica, for one, with declared interest to join NAFTA, entered into a free trade agreement with Mexico in 1994. The earlier goal for economic integration shifted to export-led growth, reducing external tariffs to increase trade liberalization, a usual requirement from international lending agencies such as the International Monetary Fund (IMF) for procuring further loans.

The transnational dimensions for all of the CACM members, but especially for El Salvador, Nicaragua, and Guatemala, have meant that remittances from citizens working abroad have kept their respective economy afloat, regardless of the success of economic development. For El Salvador, for example, the trade deficit has been offset by remittances (an estimated $1.6 billion in 2000) from the hundreds of thousands of Salvadorans living abroad. Coupled with external aid, these remittances have kept a national and regional economy afloat, with inflation falling to single-digit levels. The fact that as of January 1, 2001, the US dollar was made legal tender alongside the colón suggests that this country's economic integration too is linked more to North America than to its Central American neighbors.

In the 1990s, natural and infrastructural disasters such as those brought on by Hurricane Mitch in 1998 proved the CACM to be of little long-lasting effect in the face of large catastrophes. In 2001, border disputes between Guatemala and Belize and between Honduras and Nicaragua undermined attempts to integrate the management and conservation of one of the region's growingly scarce resources: water. While seemingly paradoxical, growth, relative development, and great poverty all came at once with the CACM. Industrialization rose, but so did the polarization of resources between social classes.

HORACIO N. ROQUE RAMÍREZ

See also Central America: History and Economic Development; Costa Rica; El Salvador; Guatemala; Honduras; International Monetary Fund (IMF); Mexico: History and Economic Development; Nicaragua; North American Free Trade Agreement (NAFTA); Panama; Sandinista National Liberation Front (FSLN); United Nations Economic Commission for Latin America and the Caribbean (ECLAC)

References and Further Reading

Barry, Tom, and Deb Preusch. *The Central American Fact Book*. New York: Grove Press, 1986.

Bulmer-Thomas, Victor. "The Central American Common Market: From Closed to Open Regionalism." *World Development* 26, no. 2 (1998).

CEPAL. *La Industrialización en Centroamérica: 1960–1980*. Santiago de Chile: CEPAL, 1983.

Dunkerley, James. *Power in the Isthmus: A Political History of Modern Central America*. London: Verso, 1988.

Guerra-Borges, Alfredo. *Desarrollo e Integración en Centroamérica: Del Pasado a las Perspectivas*. Mexico City: Instituto de Investigaciones Económicas de la Universidad de México y Coordinadora Regional de Investigaciones Económicas y Sociales, 1988.

———. *La Integración Centroamericana Ante el Reto de la Globalización*. Managua: CRIES (Coordinadora Regional de Investigaciones Económicas y Sociales), 1996.

Irvin, George, and Stuart Holland, eds. *Centroamérica: El Futuro de la Integración Económica*. San Jose, Costa Rica: Editorial Dei, 1990.

Pérez Brignoli, Héctor. *A Brief History of Central America*. Translated by Ricardo B. Sawrey A. and Susana Stettri de Sawrey. Berkeley, CA: University of California Press, 1989.

———. *Historia General de Centroamérica: De la Posguerra a la Crisis*. Vol. V. Madrid, Spain: European Communities, Sociedad Estatal Quinto Centenario, and FLACSO, 1993.

Rosenthal, Gert. "Principales Rasgos de la Evolución de las Economías Centroamericanas desde la Posguerra." *Centroamérica: Crisis y Política Internacional*. Mexico City: Siglo XXI Editores, 1982.

Torres-Rivas, Edelberto. *History and Society in Central America*. Translated by Douglass Sullivan-González. Austin, TX: University of Texas Press, 1993.

CENTRAL AND EASTERN EUROPE: HISTORY AND ECONOMIC DEVELOPMENT

Lying outside the borders of the ancient Roman Empire, Central and Eastern Europe's inhabitants—the Germans and Slavs—were among the peoples that brought an end to that empire. In the Middle Ages, the countries of the modern region were born. Almost all of them at one time or another in the past controlled great nations.

During the early Middle Ages, the people of Central and Eastern Europe converted to Christianity, a major catalyst in the differentiation of the nations. In addition to Germans, West Slavs separated into Poles, Czechs, and Slovaks; East Slavs into Russians, Ukrainians, and Belo Russians; and South Slavs into Bulgarians, Croats, Serbs, Montenegrins, Macedonians, and Slovenes—all of which eventually formed nation-states. In addition, in other nations appeared the Romanians, descendants of the Roman and indigenous peoples; the Balts—Lithuanians and Letts; and non-Indo-European speakers—Hungarians (Magyars), Estonians, and Finns.

By 1715, the great power system arose to dominate European affairs, and the great powers of Eastern Europe—Austria, Russia, and Prussia—effectively gained control of the northern portion of the regions, while the Turkish Ottoman Empire held sway over the Balkans.

The economy of the lands of Central and Eastern Europe in the Middle Ages was chiefly agricultural with some mining of iron, silver, copper, other minerals, and later, coal. The land was owned by the nobility and gentry classes and worked by peasants who remained in a condition of serfdom until the nineteenth century. Casmir the Great (1333–1370) of Poland invited Jews expelled from Western Europe to his kingdom, and many others found their way to other cities of Central and Eastern Europe where they worked as merchants and artisans. The economy of the Ottoman lands in Europe was similar to those of the North—agriculture and mining. Lands were managed for the sultan by Moslem knights and worked by Moslem and Christian peasants. Here also the sultan invited Jews as artisans, chiefly Sephardim from Spain in contrast to the Ashkenazim north of the Danube.

After the era of the French Revolution, the great powers reorganized the continent hoping to keep the *status quo*, but national revolutions had already began to erupt in Europe. Serbia began its revolt in 1804. Greece followed next. The major forces of revolt were the rise of nationalism and classical liberalism carried by the growing middle classes and the younger generation. Furthermore, the spread of the industrial revolution eastward into continental Europe brought about the growth of Socialist and anarchist ideologies. Another powerful national movement existed among the aristocracy and intellectuals of Poland, whose country had been gobbled up by Russia, Prussia, and Austria at the end of the eighteenth century. Now the Poles wanted their independence once more.

The ruling aristocracy kept these movements in check more or less for thirty years until serious revolutions broke out in 1848. In France and Germany, the focus of nationalism, liberalism, and socialism came to the fore. For Austria it was the worst. There, Italian, Czech, Romanian, and especially Hungarian rebels demanded independence. The efforts failed, but the Austrian government had to fight a war against a Hungarian republic declared by Laos Koussuth (1802–1894) and only with the unwanted help of Russia was able to defeat it. The revolutions finally ended serfdom in Prussia and Austria. Russia ended it in 1863.

The Revolutions of 1848 acted as a catalyst on the national movements of Eastern Europe. Within a little more than two decades, Germany and Italy were unified. As for the national minorities of Eastern Europe in the Russian, Austrian, and Ottoman Empires, the desire for independence increased. German Austria came to terms with the Hungarians, creating the unique Austro-Hungarian Empire to find a balance versus the various Slavic minorities. Austria and Hungary were completely independent in all domestic policies united only in foreign policy and the military. The emperor was at the same time king of Hungary.

The two states treated their national minorities differently. In Austria, the government followed a policy of cultural autonomy. Most of the Catholic minorities—the Slovaks, Slovenians, and Croatians—were satisfied with this solution. Only among the Czechs was there a strong movement looking for dissolution of the Empire and even possibly a pan-Slavic state led by Russia.

In Hungary, the government followed a policy of "magyarization"—forcing minorities to become Hungarians by assimilating into society principally by adopting the Hungarian language. This policy can be compared to the United States's "melting pot" practice of the early twentieth century, but some national minorities, including Slovaks, Romanians, and Croatians, objected.

Poland, with its territory and population divided among Germany, Russia, and Austria, continued its activity for a resurrection of independence. The Catholic Poles preferred Catholic Austria of the three.

Meanwhile in Russia, national movements blossomed among the more than one hundred non-Russian nationalities. St. Petersburg's policy, like that of Hungary, was "Russification." However, unlike Hungary, being Russian meant being Russian Orthodox. This only exacerbated the nationalist movements as the minorities joined the variety of anti-Tsarist and antigovernment political movements that arose, and terrorist national groups began violent activity.

The Ottoman Empire followed Austria's multicultural policy at least for non-Moslems, but the European nations still aimed for complete independence. After the Crimean War (1854–1856), when a coalition including England, France, and Turkey defeated Russia, the protector of the Romanian provinces, Romania was able to unite as an autonomous state in Turkey. Serbia and Montenegro enjoyed the same status. In the 1870s, uprisings by Serbs in Turkish Bosnia and Bulgarians led to the Russo-Turkish war in 1877–1878, which was resolved by the 1878 Congress of Berlin. Serbia, Montenegro, and Romania gained *de jure* independence, and northern Bulgaria gained *de facto* status while remaining under Turkish legal control. Southern Bulgaria was in a similar but less independent status, and Macedonia, which had been conquered by Russia, was returned to Turkey. Bosnia remained a part of Turkey but administered by Austria.

Bulgaria was dissatisfied with its allotment and wanted to achieve the boundaries outlined in the Treaty of San Stefano, which Turkey and Russia had signed in March 1878 before the Congress of Berlin modified it. In 1885, they managed through a *coup d'état* and a short victorious war against Serbia to add southern Bulgaria. In 1908, Sofia's Prince Ferdinand (1993–1918) declared his *de jure* independence from Turkey in conjunction with Austria's outright annexation of Bosnia to the chagrin of the Serbs. In the meantime, terrorists operated in Macedonia (the Internal Macedonian Revolutionary Organization—IMRO). Both Macedonians and Bulgarians claimed the organization as their own, and by the 1920s, when Macedonia was mainly under Greece and Yugoslavia control, the IMRO split into Bulgarian and Macedonian wings. Greek rebel groups were also operating in the region.

In 1912, Bulgaria, Serbia, Greece, and Montenegro went to war against Turkey and drove it from Europe except for Istanbul (First Balkan War, 1912–1913). However, Austria and Italy prevented the Serbs from adding Albania, which had declared its independence during the war and whose land had been designated to Belgrade by its treaty with Sofia. The Serbs then announced their intention to keep Western Macedonia, which had been assigned to Bulgaria.

Furthermore, the Greeks, who had made no territorial agreements, moved in and occupied southern Macedonia. In June 1913, Bulgaria attacked Serbia and Greece (Second Balkan War, 1913) and lost even more territory, including Edirne, to Turkey.

The Serbs coveted Austrian Bosnia; when Gavrilo Princip of the Serbian irredentist group Young Bosnia assassinated Archduke Franz Ferdinand, the Austrian heir to the throne, on June 28, 1914, World War I erupted five weeks later. All major powers and Balkan countries were drawn into the conflict—Russia, England, France, Italy Montenegro, Serbia, Romania, and Greece on one side; Germany, Austria-Hungary, Turkey, and Bulgaria on the other.

When the war ended, the map of Europe was redrawn. The Russian Revolutions in 1917 brought the Communist Party to power and Russia out of the war in March 1918 before the final armistice. Thus, Soviet Russia, along with the Central Powers, became the pariahs of the post-World War I world. New countries were carved out of the multinational empires—Yugoslavia, Czechoslovakia, Lithuania, Estonia, Latvia, and Finland. Poland was reconstituted. Romania increased at the expense of its neighbors. Montenegro disappeared.

The interwar period lasted less than twenty years—from 1918 to 1939—during which time the countries of Central and Eastern Europe fought each other to grab their neighbors' territory. By 1922, Soviet Russia was able to regain Ukraine and Belarus and establish them as union republics in the newly formed Union of Soviet Socialist Republics (USSR). The other countries of Central and Eastern Europe in the 1920s established constitutional parliamentary republics, but during the great depression of the 1930s, they one by one (except for Czechoslovakia) turned to authoritarianism and fascist-type governments.

Most of the countries were agrarian with relatively little industry. This brought conflict between communities in cities and in the countryside, as well as the rise of strong peasant parties; while peasant parties had great success at the polls, they were sometimes overthrown by force as in Bulgaria and Poland or gerrymandered out of power as in Romania.

Leaders of almost all the countries tried to adjust to economic crises by hoping to restore their large medieval empires at the expense of their neighbors. Economic development remained at a standstill. Foreign investors moved in and exploited the countries for their rich natural resources. This was the case for France in Yugoslavia and Italy in Albania. During the depression, Germany set up trade agreements in the countries largely based on credit, which bound the nations to Berlin. Within the nation-states, another method of economic exploitation placed minorities, particularly the Jews, at a disadvantage to the ruling nation. Examples of this were the exploitation of Croats at the expense of Serbia in Yugoslavia; Slovaks at the expense of Czechs in Czechoslovakia; and Germans, Jews, Ukrainians, and Belo Russians at the expense of Poles in Poland.

With World War II, the countries fell once again under the influence of the great powers—at the start of the war, Germany was in power; at the end of the war, the Soviet Union held power over the countries, with a few exceptions such as Greece and Turkey. The USSR maintained its control by establishing the Cominform as a network of Communist parties, Comecon as an economic network, and, in response to the Western military alliance of the North Atlantic Treaty Organization (NATO) and the Soviet military alliance, the Warsaw Pact. Under Soviet domination, the Eastern European countries were ruled by coalitions led by Communist parties. Moscow oversaw the purge of independent Communists from the leadership. Because of the history of invasion patterns into Russia, control over the northern tier states—Poland, Hungary, Czechoslovakia, and East Germany—was more vital to the Kremlin than the Balkans, and the Red Army remained in the North. In the South, the Soviets relied more on political accommodation.

In Poland, the Communist Party lacked support because of its ties to Moscow. After being dissolved in the 1930s, it grew during the war under the name the Polish Workers Party (PWP) and was a major force against Nazi occupation. Afterward, Moscow backed its loyal "Lublin Committee," but Wladyslaw Gomulka (1905–1982), who had some independence from the Soviets, emerged as the Communists' most popular figure. With the help of Moscow, the PWP formed a government with the Social Democrats and Peasant Party and maintained its power by bullying its opponents with unwarranted arrests and even executions. Supporters of the anti-Communist leadership, which had spent the war years in England, engaged the Communists in armed conflict in 1945 but lost to them, enabling the government to more thoroughly maintain its control. The government also quickly nationalized the country's economy.

The Polish peasant leader Stanislaw Mikolajczyk (1901–1966), the most popular politician, left the government coalition and formed his own party. However, by controlling the elections of 1947, the PWP overwhelmingly defeated him. Mikolajczyk left the country. After expelling Gomulka in 1948, the party leadership had disappeared. In 1951, the constitution was amended, and the Communists loyal to Moscow gained complete control of the country.

In Czechoslovakia, which the Germans had occupied since 1939, the prewar leaders Eduard Benes

(1884–1948) and Jan Masaryk (1886–1948), who also had been in exile in England, signed agreements with Moscow to reestablish the state including aspects similar to the Soviet Union. As elsewhere, the Communists gained control by joining a coalition with other parties. The Communists also had strong support in the country and did not need to use strongarm tactics in the first postwar elections. However, in the summer of 1947, the tide turned against them when Moscow prohibited Prague from participating in the Marshall Plan and when some of the parties in the governing coalition ruled against the Communists. The Communists then used their control of various organizations and local police stations to destroy their rivals by armed force and political maneuvers. They forced Benes from office and most likely murdered Masaryk. By May 1948, the Communists were in complete control of the government. In fact, the fall of Prague to Moscow was a major turning point in European politics, ending for good the Grand Alliance of World War II and beginning the Cold War.

Unlike Poland and Czechoslovakia, Hungary, Romania, and Bulgaria were not occupied by but allied to Germany. In those countries, the Red Army drove out the Germans and, by agreement with the West, had the major occupation role. As the Red Army advanced into Hungary, the Communists followed the usual pattern and established provisional governments based on coalitions with other antifascist parties. Since the Western countries retained some voice in the country through the Allied Control Commission and Moscow was concentrating on Poland, there was less interference in Hungarian elections in 1945 and 1946. The popular Smallholders Party (SHP) therefore gained the majority of votes. However, by agreement, the coalition continued. The Communists in control of the ministry of interior were able to turn the police forces into their own army. They also had important sympathizers in the other parties of the coalition excepting the SHP. To attack the latter, they began a press campaign accusing the SHP of reactionary and anti-Russian politics, and the Communists also used divisions with the SHP to weaken it. In 1947, after the peace treaty between Hungary and the Allies was signed, the Communists took their final steps. They arrested leaders of the SHP and the anti-Communist Catholic church, including Cardinal Jozsef Mindszenty (1892–1975), and they forced the SHP prime minister Ferenc Nagy (1903–1979) to go into exile by threatening his family. In 1949, Budapest adopted a new constitution based on that of the Soviet Union.

As the Red Army approached Romania in August 1944, young King Michael arrested the pro-German dictator Ion Antonescu and put in a government friendly to the Allies, including a Communist. The Romanian Communist Party was extremely weak and remained part of a coalition while building its strength through various front organizations with other parties. Furthermore, since the Allies allowed Moscow major influence in Romania, the Soviets interfered in the country's internal politics, creating a rapid change of prime ministers. Communists took over the government bureaucracy, and Moscow also was able to gain control of the country's economy through the Allied treaties. By manipulating the elections of 1946, the Communist-controlled coalition gained the government. King Michael abdicated in 1947, and Romania became a republic under Communist control.

After rapidly marching through Romania, the Red Army then entered into Bulgaria in early September 1944. Sofia had established an antifascist pro-Western government, but Moscow would not agree to an armistice unless the Fatherland Front—a coalition including Communists—took over. The Bulgarian Communist Party was one of the strongest in Eastern Europe, but the Agrarian Union, another member of the Front, was more popular. Both the Communists and the Agrarians had engaged in violent political wars with the governments of the other parties since the 1920s. Now the Front took its revenge through war crime trials, eliminating any opposition. In the next step, George Dimitrov, the hero of the 1933 Reichstag Fire trial and former leader of the Comintern, returned to Bulgaria and assumed the position of prime minister. The young King Simeon (1937–) (who would, in 2001, return to Bulgaria as prime minister) went with his family into exile, and the Fatherland Front declared Bulgaria a republic. The Communists then turned on their opponents within the Front and gained complete control by 1948.

When Josef Broz-Tito (1892–1980) fought the attempts of Moscow to rein in his independent policies, Soviet leader Josef Stalin (1879–1953) expelled him from the Cominform and the Communist community. Tito went on to turn Yugoslavia into a one-party independent and neutral Communist state with more if still restricted freedoms than the Soviet bloc countries. Instead of the central planning that ruled the economies in the Soviet bloc, he introduced a measure of real workers' control in the factories and made trade agreements with the West. Tito also became a leader along with Jawaharlal Nehru of India (1889–1964), Sukarno (1901–1970) of Indonesia, Kwame Nkrumah of Ghana (1909–1972), and Gamal Abdel Nasser of Egypt (1918–1970) of the Unaligned Movement. Yugoslav citizens had more freedom of movement than other citizens of Eastern European

countries and traveled to Germany as *gastarbeitern* (guest workers). Josip Broz Tito reformed Yugoslavia into six constituent republics—Serbia, Croatia, Montenegro, Slovenia, Macedonia, and Bosnia—and two autonomous regions—Kosovo for Albanians and the Banat for Hungarians. Thus, he followed Stalin's model in the USSR and, just like Stalin, set the pattern for future republics. King Alexander (1921–1934), when he established his royal dictatorship in 1929, had reorganized the country on a geographical basis to attempt to deal with national rivalries. It did not work. Tito, of mixed Croatian–Slovenian parentage, gave the republics autonomy, but the hatred remained and proved fatal for the future.

Because of wartime agreements and strategical issues, Stalin gave only lukewarm support to the strong Greek Communists and their attempts to take control of the country where the West supported the unpopular monarchy. As a result, with US aid under the Truman doctrine, the Monarchists and Conservatives won the Greek Civil War (1944–1949) and kept the country out of Communist hands. Greece and Turkey, its rival, joined NATO.

Romania, also because of its southern tier position, was able to maintain a more autonomous position in the Soviet bloc. After the war, "native" Communists led by Gheorghe Gheorghiu-Dej (1901–1965) were able to win a power struggle against the "Muscovite" group led by Ana Pauker (1894–1960) and Vasile Luka (1898–1960). They convinced Stalin to let them rule. In 1965, Gheorghiu-Dej's leadership fell to the weak and corrupt Nicolae Ceausescu (1918–1989), who used the Soviet southern tier system to carve out a niche between East and West, defying Moscow on some issues. These issues included maintaining relations with Israel after the 1967 Six-Day War when the other bloc countries severed them or participating in the 1984 Los Angeles Olympics despite a USSR boycott. However, Ceausescu assured Moscow of his loyalty. Yet when social and economic conditions eased in the 1980s elsewhere in Eastern Europe, he instituted an even harsher dictatorship. In the Russian Revolutions of 1989, he was the only Eastern European leader executed by his people.

Albania under Enver Hoxha (1908–1985) followed its own path. Hoxha had sided with Stalin against Tito, whom he suspected of trying to incorporate Albania in his plans for an expanded Yugoslavia. With the "destalinization" campaign of Nikita Khrushchev, Hoxha broke relations Moscow. The country, unlike Yugoslavia, remained relatively isolated by refusing relations either with the USSR or United States, although it did continue relations with China after Moscow's break with Peking, and relations with other Western and Soviet bloc countries continued. Economically, Albania tried, not always successfully, to rely on its own resources with limited trade.

With all the southern tier countries following unique paths, Bulgaria chose loyally to follow the Soviet Union. In the wake of the break with Tito, Todor Zhivkov (1911–1998) emerged as the leader of the Bulgarian Communist Party in 1954, at first with others, then alone. He remained as such with only a few unsuccessful attempts to remove him until 1989.

In the northern tier states, Moscow maintained a much stricter control. The Soviets relinquished Finland and Austria, although they retained the territory gained in World War II and a little extra to make sure it bordered Norway and Sweden. In the other countries—Poland, Hungary, Czechoslovakia, and East Germany—Moscow maintained the Red Army presence and, through the Tito-area purges, saw to it that the Communist parties with leaders loyal to Moscow held supreme power, although the parties ruled through token coalitions with remnants of other left-wing parties. Moscow retained the Polish territory it had taken in 1939 according to the infamous Soviet–Nazi Pact, but Poland extended westward to the Oder-Niesse border with Germany regaining the medieval Polish kingdom of Silesia. The Soviets also arranged that the eastern borders of the Eastern European states be adjusted so that the USSR had contingent boundaries with Poland, Hungary, Czechoslovakia, and Romania. After the death of Stalin, there were a number of uprisings that invariably brought about Soviet responses ranging from pressure to make changes within the party to armed intervention. The first serious revolt was in East Germany immediately after Stalin's death. In 1956, uprisings in Poland brought Gomulka back to power. However, the Polish revolts inspired the more severe Hungarian uprising led by Imre Nagy (1896–1958), who had left the Communist Party. Nikita Khrushchev responded by sending in Soviet troops and executing Nagy.

Khrushchev, however, allowed Gomulka and the new Hungarian leader Janos Kadar (1912–1989) to practice polycentrism, a more moderate form of communism, in their countries. In 1968, after Leonid Brezhnev replaced Khrushchev as supreme leader of the Soviet Union, the chief of the party of Czechoslovakia, Alexander Dubcek, pushed the policy to the limit in the "Prague Spring," permitting even more freedoms. Just as in 1956, Soviet troops intervened in Hungary, although Dubcek, unlike Nagy, survived.

Resistance and uprisings, however, continued. In 1970 in Poland, a series of strikes and demonstrations brought down Gomulka, and Eduard Gierek (1913–2001) replaced him. One aspect of polycentrism in Poland was the semiautonomy of the Catholic Church, which became a beacon for dissidence. This dissidence increased with the election of Karol Wojtyla (1920–) to the papacy as Pope John Paul II in 1978. A dissident intellectual group, the Workers' Defense League (KOR), fought for the liberation of Poland, but the real crisis occurred with strikes in the Lenin shipyards at Gdansk led by the electrician Lech Walesa (1943–) in 1980. Walesa and his coworkers formed the Solidarity (*Solidarnosc*) Union, which did not bring in Soviet troops but forced the imposition of marshal law and the replacement of Giereck with Marshall Wojciech Jaruzelski (1923–). It also helped to bring the end of the Communist monopoly in Eastern Europe when Mikhail Gorbachev (1931–) brought in his sweeping changes in the Soviet Union.

Soviet politics dominated postwar Eastern Europe economics as well. Under Stalin, this meant essentially bilateral trade agreements for the benefit for Moscow. Comecon, the Soviet economic union, assigned special tasks to each of the countries; for example, it assigned Bulgaria agricultural produce, while Czechoslovakia and East Germany received more industrial assignments. Furthermore, according to treaties with the United States and England, Moscow was allowed to confiscate factories and other economic goods from Germany. Moscow designated Eastern European countries people's democracies because, unlike the Soviet Union, they had not yet achieved the stage of socialism. However, Marxist theory demanded that each of the countries have an industrial capacity to hasten the growth of proletariat and lessen the percentage of the peasantry. This led to inappropriate use of resources, such as in the unproductive *Kremikovtsi* steel mill in Bulgaria. Furthermore, the Stalinist application of "central planning" and five-year plans continued and would remain a factor in the economies until the fall of communism. The planners emphasized quantity at the expense of quality and especially the environment, which greatly suffered under the system. Yugoslavia, as indicated previously, went its own way. The United States broached the countries in 1948 about joining the Marshall Plan, but Stalin refused to accept the offer.

Khrushchev's policy of polycentrism allowed more flexibility in the economies of Eastern Europe. The countries diversified and also made their own trade agreements with non-bloc countries. There was a greater emphasis on consumer goods, and they also accepted deficit balances of trade. As time went by, more freedom of travel and contact with relatives in the West allowed hard currency to come in, and some citizens were able to purchase goods in the "dollar shops" present in all the countries. The Soviet Union under Brezhnev in 1965 introduced a more consumer-oriented and management incentive policy called *Libermanism* after the economist Evsei Liberman (1897–1983). The Soviets had tried modified market economies in the past—during the 1920s with the New Economic Policy of Vladimir Lenin (1870–1924) and attempted it again in more serious vein in the 1980s under Gorbachev's *Perestroika* restructuring. Gorbachev's concurrent policy of *Glasnost,* openness or freedom of expression, soon led to the frank discussion that the whole system of centralized planning and collective agriculture was at fault and helped bring down the Communist system in the USSR and Eastern Europe. In some of the countries, small private enterprises such as restaurants and taxi services were permitted. Capitalist firms began to operate in Eastern Europe—hotel chains like Japanese Otani, French Novotel, and the American Sheraton. In the 1980s, there was even a McDonalds in Budapest. Hungary most successfully introduced Western-style market economy on a consistent basis, but even Bulgaria attempted it. In other places, the experiment only lasted a short time. Poles had even been allowed to go as guest laborers to the West, but the Polish economy collapsed over the solidarity crisis. In Romania, the system failed because of Ceausescu's mismanagement; in Czechoslovakia, it failed because of the Prague Spring.

Much of the economy was in the form of illegal black markets, especially when citizens could get goods from foreign visitors or Western relatives as well as from travel abroad (if permitted). There was also a gray market barter economy characterized by citizens exchanging goods and services either within a country or between citizens of one country with another (since travel within the Socialist bloc was easier than travel outside the bloc; Polish glass for Czech linen is an example of this trade). The non-Communist countries integrated into the European market systems seeking trading alliances with the various European economic associations, such as the Common Market, The European Free Trade Association, and the European Union (EU).

Because of its government's inability to solve the economic crises, Poland negotiated an agreement with the Independent Self-Governing Trade Union Solidarity by which elections for a new parliament were held in February 1989. The Communists were guaranteed one-third of the lower house. The other parties in the PWP had another third, but the remaining third and the upper house were for open contests. Solidarity overwhelmingly won those seats. Although the Communists were also guaranteed the government, they failed to form one and turned the reins over to Solidarity, which began the process of introducing a free market economy. Throughout the 1990s, Solidarity controlled the government. Walesa was the first freely elected president since World War II. However, little progress was made to reforming the economy, and with dozens of new parties, political turmoil reigned. As the new millennium began, the Social Democrats (the former Communists) made a comeback when working with other left and center parties.

In 1988, Imre Pozsgay in Hungary spearheaded reforms, including freedom of the press and independent labor unions through the Communist Party politburo; the following year, the government changed the electoral laws leading to contested elections. At the same time, Moscow and Budapest signed an agreement calling for the withdrawal of Soviet troops from the country. Ceremonies in 1989 honoring Imre Nagy and those killed in the 1956 uprising marked the end of Communist rule in Hungary. In the first elections of 1990, center and right-of-center parties defeated the Communists (renamed the Hungarian Social Democratic Party), and the new government rapidly converted to a democracy and a market economy. In the elections of 2002, however, the Social Democrats in coalition with the Free Democrats narrowly won.

Although the Communist government in Prague gave lip service to Gorbachev's reforms, they were reluctant to make changes. In 1988, demonstrations occurred throughout the country in reaction to the reforms elsewhere in the Soviet bloc. Then, in November 1989, student demonstrations in Bratislava and Prague led to massive demonstrations of up to a half million protesters. By the end of the month, the Communist Party gave up power, and Alexander Dubcek, the hero of the Prague Spring, came back as speaker of the national assembly. Vaclav Havel (1936–), the writer and leading dissident, was elected president. This smooth changeover has been dubbed the Velvet Revolution; two years later, the country peacefully divided into the Czech Republic and Slovakia, ending seventy-five years of stormy history.

In Romania, the attempted arrest of Pastor Laszlo Tokes occurred in December 1989 (and brought about a mass rally against the government in Timisoara). Even though Tokes was a Hungarian, the city's Romanian population still supported him. Demonstrations in Bucharest followed, forcing the Ceausescus to flee. However, they were arrested, tried, and executed. The new government outlawed the Communist Party, but ex-Communists remained in control. New demonstrations followed in 1990, and the government brutally suppressed them. A new constitution was written, and gradual democratic and economic market reforms were introduced.

In Bulgaria, Zhivkov began losing support in 1988 when he refused to accept the advice of party and technical leaders for improving the economy. In elections for leadership in the professional associations in the spring of 1989, the party slates were voted down. Later in the year, after the fall of the Berlin Wall, a huge demonstration of protesters against Zhivkov's mismanagement, especially in the wake of environmental disasters, led to a *coup d'état* against him by members of the party. As elsewhere, reforms of the new government introduced political democracy and a market economy. The Communist Party, renamed the Bulgarian Social Democratic Party, still maintained some support, but it had to share power with the Union of Democratic forces over the next decade and a half.

The collapse of communism established a new era in Central and Eastern Europe. Politically, it led to the breakup of the artificial post-World War I federations. In 1994, Czechs and Slovaks mutually agreed to dissolve their state into the Czech Republic and Slovakia. Yugoslavia broke into its constituent republics—Slovenia, Croatia, Bosnia, Macedonia, and the Federation of Serbia and Montenegro. However, the dissolution was accompanied by a decade of bitter war involving foreign interventions. The Soviet Union broke up into its fifteen constituent republics, accompanied by war in some of the new states. Thus Lithuania, Estonia, and Latvia reappeared as independent countries once more, and Belarus, Moldova, and Ukraine joined the states of Central and Eastern Europe. The boundaries of the countries, however, remained the same. In these countries of Central and Eastern Europe, multiparty parliamentary democratic republics became the standard. The Communist parties, calling themselves Socialists or Social Democrats, participated and still had strength; for the most part, however, they remained as opposition forces and not in power. In perhaps the strangest situation, the leader of the Socialists (Communist Party) was elected president in Bulgaria, and the pretender to the throne, Simeon Saxe-Coburg-Gotha, was elected prime minister. In addition to the wars in some areas, the new states suffered from crime, corruption, assassinations, and conflicts with minorities—all problems that had existed in the interwar period. However, unlike that period, there was a genuine commitment to fit into modern democratic Europe. The countries applied and generally won affiliation with the North American Treaty Organization (NATO) and the EU. By 2004, Bulgaria, the Czech Republic, Estonia, Hungary, Latvia, Lithuania, Poland, Romania, Slovakia, and Slovenia were in NATO; Austria, the Czech Republic, Estonia, Finland, Hungary, Latvia, Lithuania, Poland, Slovakia, and Slovenia were in the EU.

Market economies and foreign investment also became the standard for all of the countries with various degrees of success. The countries formed regional associations, such as the Black Sea Economic Cooperation Group and the Visegrád group, to promote private enterprise and government and private cooperation in the economy. Throughout the regions' agriculture, forestry and mining has remained important, but industry has remained behind Western standards.

FREDERICK B. CHARY

See also Central and Eastern Europe: International Relations; Ethnic Conflicts: Central and Eastern Europe

References and Further Reading

Biezen, Ingid van. *Political Parties in New Democracies: Party Organization in Southern and East-Central Europe*, New York: Palgrave Macmillan, 2003.

Cox, Terry. *Social and Economic Transformation in East-Central Europe: Institution, Property Relations, and Social Interests.* Cheltenham, United Kingdom: E. Elgar, 1999.

Crampton, R. J. *Eastern Europe in the Twentieth Century.* London: Routledge, 1997.

Frucht, Richard. *Encyclopedia of Eastern Europe: From the Congress of Vienna to the Fall of Communism.* New York: Garland, 2000.

CENTRAL AND EASTERN EUROPE: INTERNATIONAL RELATIONS

Eastern Central Europe or Central Europe is the descriptive title generally given to those states that lie between Germany and Russia. These states can be broken into three fairly distinct regions. The Baltic States include Estonia, Latvia, and Lithuania. The Balkans include Albania and the states of the former Yugoslavia: Bosnia-Herzegovina, Croatia, Macedonia, Serbia, and Slovenia. The Central European states are Bulgaria, Czech Republic, Hungary, Poland, Romania, and Slovakia. This discussion will refer to the whole region as "Central Europe." Throughout their history, the domestic politics of the states and the region as a whole have affected international relations. Pressured by external enemies and often rent by internal conflicts, which left them vulnerable to military advances, the states in Central Europe have frequently played a strategic role in the history of Europe and, in the twentieth century, the world.

The idea of Central Europe or *Mitteleuropa* has long been more cultural and political than geographical; it has often been noted that Prague, in the Czech Republic—a Central European state—lies to the west of Vienna, yet Austria is considered to be a Western European state. Historically, these three regions have been pawns in competing games between empires. The end of World War II saw the imposition of yet another empire on the countries of Central Europe. In the years immediately following the end of World War II, the Soviet Union under Stalin moved to consolidate its hold on those states lying immediately to its west. The extension of Soviet influence and control from the Balkans north to the Baltic States brought those states into a new form of empire. At post-World War II conferences in Yalta and Potsdam among the Allied leaders, Stalin cited Russia's security concerns as the basis for maintaining a Soviet military presence in those states. Given the role of the Soviet Union in defeating Germany, the Western powers were inclined to acquiesce.

1945–1989

While their political autonomy has at times been in question, the states of Central Europe have played a significant role in international relations. In the period between 1945 and 1989, these states acted as an introduction of the "Socialist community" into Europe for the Soviet Union and as a staging ground for the Soviet army. Stalin cited the same security concerns with regard to the Balkans as he had with Eastern Europe; however, those reasons did not sit as well in that area. The movement of the Soviet Union through the Balkans follows a long-running pattern of Russian expansion toward the straits of the Dardanelles.

In response to the creation of the North Atlantic Treaty Organization (NATO), Stalin formed the Warsaw Pact between the Soviet Union and its satellite states. As members of the Warsaw Pact, the central European states played a more dangerous role between NATO forces and Russia. The Warsaw Pact was also utilized as an internal control mechanism designed to keep the satellite states in line with Soviet policies.

The imposition of Communist rule varied among the Central European states. The Baltic States of Estonia, Latvia, and Lithuania were forcefully absorbed by the Soviet Union and recreated as republics within the Union of Soviet Socialist Republics (USSR). The Baltics have always maintained that the Soviet takeover was illegal. Thus, their presence on the international stage between 1945 and 1989 was limited to their strategic role as staging areas for the Soviet military. The Balkan states were initially considered to be Soviet satellite states, yet by the end of the 1960s, Russia had very little influence in that area; Albania had found a new ally in Mao Zedong's China and formally left the Warsaw Pact, while Tito had broken with Stalin and also pulled Yugoslavia out of the Warsaw Pact.

The Central European states became Soviet satellite states with Communist governments playing a subsidiary role to the Soviet government in Moscow. The decade immediately following World War II saw the economic development of Central Europe closely follow that of the Soviet Union. It is true that under the Soviet system, the states of Central Europe experienced almost half a century of political stability, which was unusual for the area. However, political stability under Soviet communism did not mean a peaceful evolution into developed, industrialized nations. The societies of Central Europe were more sophisticated and economically developed than Russia under Stalin. This contrast meant that participation in the industrialization program instituted by Stalin actually undermined any economic gains made by Central Europe before World War II.

Following the Communist takeover, the Soviet Union nationalized industrial production and began a program to collectivize the agricultural sector. The economies of Central Europe were exploited to speed up the recovery of the Soviet economy. Stalin viewed his acquisition of the economic structures of the Central European states as war reparations. In addition, all foreign trade in the satellite states was to be directed to Moscow. The Council for Mutual Economic Assistance (CMEA or Comecon) was established in January 1949 to speed the economic integration of the region with the Soviet Union. Under Comecon, the satellite states were obliged to purchase Soviet raw material exports at highly inflated prices and sell the finished products to Russia cheaply. Industrial output doubled in Czechoslovakia between 1948 and 1955, and in the less industrialized satellite states, particularly Bulgaria and Romania, output rose 12%–14% per year between 1950 and 1955.

After Stalin's death in 1953, there was some loosening of economic controls from Moscow, and for a while a new course was adopted that included raising wages, cutting prices and taxes, boosting agricultural production, and reducing investment in heavy industry. However, in 1955, the policy of economic integration was pursued even more strongly, and Central Europe became even more dependent on the Soviet Union for raw materials for the industrialization programs. The rapid industrialization in the 1950s began to have a negative impact on the socioeconomic development of the region by the late 1950s and early 1960s.

In addition to economic changes, the death of Stalin brought about significant cultural changes for Central Europe. After 1955, cultural relations with the West were renewed in all states except for Bulgaria and Romania. While maintaining the appearance of fidelity to Soviet ideology, there was a general reorientation toward the West coupled with a renewal of national themes. In Poland, in particular, the Catholic Church was given more freedom to operate. The economic and social consequences of Stalinism had bred increasingly higher levels of tension throughout Central Europe. The loosening of controls allowed people to begin talking about the shortcomings of Communist regimes and brought about a slight lessening of tensions.

Revolution and Rebellion

Despite the excesses and terror of the Stalin years, many people remained supportive of the national Communist parties and adhered to the Communist Party line in the Central European states. However, the loosening of controls after Stalin's death had unquestionable ramifications for Central European governments and citizens. October 1956 has been termed "Polish October" for the actions that preceded and followed the Eighth Party Plenum held in Warsaw that year. Polish party leader Wladyslaw Gomulka managed to convince Soviet leaders that Poland would remain loyal to Moscow and continue to support Soviet foreign and defense policy. He managed to prevent Soviet military intervention in Poland. Hungary was not so fortunate.

In 1956, revolution in Hungary was the first and most fundamental challenge to Soviet domination in the region. There was no mass support for the Communist Party in Hungary. The Soviet Army had imposed Communist Party rule in Hungary, and the party barely clung to power. Soviet economic policies had resulted in a considerable lowering of standards of living and disaffection of the great majority of the population. Prior to 1955, there had been no active opposition to the Soviet regime, but with the death of Stalin and the lessening of the terror, the hostility to the regime began to surface. The revelation of crimes committed during the Stalin era caused the previous Hungarian leadership to be discredited, and the minor, halfhearted attempts by the new regime to enact reforms only increased the activities of the opposition. Inspired by Poland, Hungary moved its events much faster and further than Poland had. The demand for the withdrawal of Soviet troops, release from the Warsaw Pact, and the recognition of Hungary's neutral status brought in the Soviet tanks on November 4, 1956. Outside of Western Europe, the invasion of Hungary did not have much impact. The United States and other NATO states did not want to risk a direct US–USSR conflict through Western intervention in Hungary. The bloody suppression of the Hungarian uprising and the reluctance of the United States and European states to become directly involved underlined the uncertain status of Central Europe as a player on the international stage.

Further splits in the Communist world brought Central Europe once more to the world's attention. The 1960 split between China and the Soviet Union publicly introduced the idea that multiple interpretations of communism were possible. The creation of a Communist world with multiple centers of Communist ideology and policy gave rise to speculation in Central Europe that those states could also create their own brand of communism without Soviet influence or interference. This idea of "polycentrism" took hold in Central Europe and spread rapidly.

Albania, the smallest of the Central European states, was the first to break away from Moscow. Albania had based its Communist government on two fairly important factors: its leaders were fanatically loyal to Moscow and even more Stalinist than Stalin; second, much of Albania's loyalty had been based on a strong rivalry, bordering on hatred, with Yugoslavia. When Moscow began making overtures to Tito in an effort to win back Yugoslavia, Albania decided to look elsewhere for inspiration and protection. In 1961, Albania formally left the Warsaw Pact and found a willing ally and protector in Mao Zedong, who was happy to get a foothold in Europe. There was no real political, economic, or military value in the alliance, but it did allow for a Chinese presence in Europe. Its relationship with China has continued to severely hamper Albanian economic and social development. It remains one of the poorest and least developed nations in southeastern Europe.

Romania soon followed Albania and began to dissociate itself from the Soviet Union. The desire for a more independent policy clashed with Moscow's attempt to increase the centralization of the Soviet system. The break between Romania and the Soviet Union was initially economic in character; Romania opposed Comecon and its initiative to more closely coordinate economic policies between the Soviet Union and Central Europe. It was argued that such close integration would impede Romanian industrialization and economic development. Romania succeeded in this undertaking and at the same time managed to improve and expand diplomatic and economic relations with the West. This independent Romanian course was limited to foreign policy; the national Communist Party retained firm control of domestic economic and social policies.

Czechoslovakia was not immune to the changes moving through Central Europe. In early 1968, Alexander Dubček was installed as the new leader of Czechoslovakia. He began to promote economic reforms much more vigorously than had been done in the past. Dubček's intention was to keep Socialist principles in industry and agriculture but at the same time expand trade links with the West. He maintained that he had no intention of leaving Comecon or the Warsaw Pact, but the changes in Czechoslovakia caused a great deal of unease in Moscow. Czechoslovakia shares a border with Austria and thus the West. The permeability of this border was not lost on Moscow, and the threat perception increased accordingly. Romania did not share any borders with Western states. On August 21, 1968, having failed to stop what became known as the "Prague Spring" through other forms of pressure, the Soviet Union along with other Warsaw Pact members (except Romania) invaded Czechoslovakia.

The "normalization" of Czechoslovakia in the wake of the invasion marked the beginning of a period of economic and social stagnation throughout the region. The invasion of Prague quelled the hopes for gradual change in Central Europe. By the end of the 1960s, the "Sovietization" of Central Europe appeared to be complete. The various rebellions had been put down, and the process appeared to be irreversible. Control over Central Europe by the Soviet Union was codified in the Brezhnev Doctrine, which maintained that the Soviet Union would not give up any of the territory it had gained at the end of World War II. The socioeconomic system that was taking shape under Soviet influence was not very successful, but it did appear to be more or less permanent. Leadership was less repressive than it had been under Stalin, and intellectuals in most states were allowed a limited degree of freedom; however, economic growth rates began decreasing in the late 1970s and never really recovered. It bears remembering, though, production figures in the Soviet-controlled economies were often vastly overstated, so there was no way to really know the true state of the economy.

The primary grounds for maintaining the ties between Central Europe and the Soviet Union were the strategic military considerations of the Soviet Union. As mentioned, the Central European states were used as a buffer zone between the Soviet Union and the West. As relations with the West and Central Europe gradually improved, the argument that defense against the West was a necessity became harder to make, and it became more difficult to make those states adhere closely to Soviet policies. The exception to this rule was Czechoslovakia. Under the "normalization"

imposed after the Prague Spring, Czechoslovak opposition and the economy subsided into stagnation and did not reappear until the late 1980s.

Yugoslavia also proved to be an exception to Moscow's control over the governments of Central Europe. Yugoslavia was expelled from Comintern (the Communist international party) as early as 1948, yet it managed to maintain its independence and avoid a Soviet invasion. Tito broke with Moscow over the implementation of Communist policies and was able to preserve Yugoslav independence from Moscow following Stalin's death. Under Tito, Yugoslavia played an important role in world affairs as the leader of the nonaligned movement. Along with Nasser in Egypt and Nehru in India, Tito symbolized the transformation of smaller states into nonaligned status within the politics of Cold War bipolarity.

1989 and Beyond

The year 1989 has been called *annus mirabilis*, the miraculous year. Political scientists, analysts, diplomats, and politicians had been unable to predict the end of communism in Central Europe. The fall of the Berlin wall and the subsequent breakdown of the Communist systems that had directly and indirectly supported its existence were seen as a miracle. The collapse of Soviet power and Communist control caused a mass movement toward democratic forms of government in the entire region. The nature of the regime change and the nature of the previous Communist system have shaped the political systems that subsequently arose in Central Europe. It is now important to briefly examine some particulars for each area in the Central European region and then move to a more general discussion of international relations for the entire region from 1989 to the present.

The Baltic States

The Baltic States spent the time between 1945 and 1991 as republics within the Soviet Union. The changes in Central Europe brought about sweeping changes in the Baltic States as well. Almost immediately they began agitating for independence from a slowly imploding Soviet Union. In 1991, taking matters into their own hands, Estonia, followed by Lithuania and Latvia, declared their independence from the Soviet Union and their reestablishment as sovereign states. All three Baltic States had long maintained that the Soviet takeover was an illegal annexation and therefore they were not subject to Soviet control. The fear was that the Soviet Army would move out to reestablish control over the breakaway republics, and, in fact, there was an abortive attempt by the Soviet Union to do just that. The Soviet Union feared that if the Baltics were allowed to leave, then other republics would do the same.

Reestablishing themselves as independent states, the Baltics have resumed their former relationships with the Scandinavian states, and all three applied for membership in NATO and the EU. NATO formally invited the Baltic States along with Bulgaria, Romania, Slovakia, and Slovenia into the alliance at its Prague Summit in November 2002. EU membership for the Baltic States was finalized in May 2004. Membership in both organizations has provided the Baltics with their long sought-after reunification with Europe. Russian reaction to these developments has been much more subdued than originally feared. In fact, Russia has signed several agreements with NATO and is officially a junior partner with the alliance. It is clear that the Baltics will continue to play an important role in European–Russian relations.

Central Europe

Political change in Central Europe after November 1989 was rapid and profound. The general atmosphere in Central Europe was one of independence and renewed economic development, and by January 1990, elections had been held in most of the states with former opposition leaders taking on the role of newly elected post-Communist leaders. Intense political and economic change followed quickly. In Poland, Lech Walesa, leader of the trade union turned political party, Solidarity, was elected president. In Czechoslovakia, playwright Vaclav Havel was elected to that country's presidency three months after being released from jail, in a transition so uneventful it has been nicknamed the "Velvet Revolution." Romanian opposition forces captured Nicolae Ceausescu and his wife and executed them by firing squad on Christmas Day 1989. Events were moving so quickly that academics and politicians alike had a difficult time following along.

In 1992, the "Velvet Divorce" of the Czech and Slovak republics followed the Velvet Revolution in Czechoslovakia. This move resulted in an economic loss for Slovakia. A recipient of a large part of the Soviet industrialization program, Slovakia was unprepared for the rigors of a free market economy. Compounding the problem was the general economic

downturn that permeated Central Europe. Poland brought in Jeffrey Sachs of Harvard University to assist in its economic reform. After experiencing a rapid and severe economic downturn, Poland began recovering at about the time that the other states were beginning what would turn out to be a multiyear decline in economic growth. All of the post-Communist economies were experiencing severe economic declines that included increasingly higher inflation and unemployment rates coupled with a devaluation of currencies. The overall economic slump had a political impact as well. Democratic politics became increasingly unstable, encouraging a reaction against Western-style economic reforms and promoting nostalgia for the former regimes.

In 1999, Poland, Hungary, and the Czech Republic were formally admitted to NATO as full members of that alliance. Once again, questions with regard to Russian reaction surfaced. In early 2000, some of those fears were put to rest; Russia announced it had "forgiven" Hungary and the others for joining NATO and would continue to maintain relations with those states. As with the Baltic States, the Central European states all applied for membership in the EU as soon as that option became available. Along with the Baltics, Poland, Hungary, the Czech Republic, Slovenia, Slovakia, Cyprus, and Malta became full members of the EU in May 2004.

Bulgaria and Romania have active applications with the EU and are expected to be admitted in 2007. Membership in the EU has brought a new set of problems and promises for the post-Communist states of Central Europe. Their acceptance as full members indicates that the EU believes that these states can satisfactorily meet the necessary obligations that come with forming the eastern border of that organization. The challenge now becomes maintaining achieved levels of economic growth and political development.

The Balkans

The Balkan states, Albania, Bosnia-Herzegovina, Croatia, Macedonia, Serbia, and Slovenia experienced perhaps the roughest transition in Central Europe. Albania, after breaking with the Soviet Union in 1961, subsequently broke with China in 1978. It spent most of the twentieth century being largely ignored by the rest of the world. Isolated and backward, Albania has never been considered a state with much to contribute to the world. Early in the post-Communist period, the Albanian economy fell victim to a pyramid scheme that collapsed the entire economy. Italy, its neighbor across the Adriatic Sea, has become more involved in Albanian domestic affairs due to the long-standing relationship, as well as for reasons of proximity. A mounting refugee crisis has strained Italian police and immigration forces. The collapse of Yugoslavia and the resultant warfare have only added to Albania's problems.

The disintegration of Yugoslavia was perhaps the single most important factor in bringing the Balkans to the attention of the world. The dissolution of the Soviet Union encouraged the Yugoslav states to take a similar path. Serbia and Montenegro have formed a two-state federation, while Slovenia and Croatia, bordering Austria and Hungary, respectively, moved rapidly to establish relations with those states and with Europe in general and to distance themselves from the former Yugoslavia. This move has contributed greatly to their continued economic growth and ability to maintain some distance from the troubles of the other states. As already mentioned, Slovenia became a member of the EU and NATO, and Croatia is working to fulfill its EU application obligations.

For most of the 1990s, Serbia and Albania have been engaged in ongoing wars that have required the presence of United Nation (UN) peacekeepers to maintain any semblance of order. Serbian aggression in Bosnia-Herzegovina and then into Kosovo has resulted in the creation of a UN war crimes tribunal to deal with accusations of genocide on both sides of the situation. In addition, a growing refugee crisis has strained the already limited resources of Albania and required an increased and ongoing UN presence in the area. Since late 2000, with the ouster of Milosevic and his supporters in the government, Serbia has been working to become more integrated and involved with the international community. The cessation of hostilities has, obviously, greatly contributed to economic growth and political development in the area.

Returning to Europe

Perhaps the most dramatic demonstration of the end of the Cold War was the immediate shift in focus from East to West in the foreign policies of the Central European states. Almost without delay, these states announced their intentions to "return to Europe." A "return to Europe" included full integration into the political, economic, and security structures of the West. These goals have been accomplished for most of these states; the admission of these states into NATO and the EU has supported and even accelerated the reform process throughout Central Europe. The former Communist states have not only undergone radical changes in their domestic structures (political transitions from authoritarian systems to democratic systems and centralized, planned economies replaced with free market capitalist systems), but they have also dramatically changed their outlook and policies with regard to the countries of the West.

The initial euphoria brought about by the fall of the Berlin Wall and the subsequent collapse of the Communist regimes was soon dispelled by the harsh realities of radical structural change. The "shock therapy" approach to economic restructuring exacerbated the general economic depression being felt throughout Europe; social inequalities became more pronounced, and the reemergence of racism, anti-Semitism, and aggressive nationalism contributed to a sense of futility with regard to the future prospects of the region.

With the collapse of communism, historian Francis Fukuyama declared the "end of history." However, it appeared that what was happening in Central Europe was not the end of history but the renewal of historical conflicts. Regional cooperation has never been a hallmark of East Central European relations. The control imposed over the region by Moscow had simply masked old problems rather than putting an end to them. Central Europe was and is facing many of the same problems of state-building, developing economically, combating ethnic conflicts, and reintegrating with the rest of Europe. Yet it must be noted that these recurring problems are taking place in a very different world than that which existed the last time Central Europe stood on its own on the world stage.

Globalization and its concurrent increase in economic competition and interdependence, transnational interactions, and formal and informal integration have fundamentally changed international relations at all levels. Supranational organizations, such as the EU, and broad international treaties are slowly replacing the state as the central actor in the global arena. Central Europeans now find themselves emerging from their relative isolation and forced regional semi-integration into a world of voluntary and, some might argue, necessary political and economic integration, as well as increased competition. In short, the world is a very different place than it was fifty years ago.

Adrian Hyde-Price has suggested that there are seven major factors that have changed the context of regional relations in Central Europe. To begin with, the end of the Cold War has initiated an external environment that is generally supportive of political and economic reforms in the former Communist states. The growth of complex interdependence has altered the relationships between European states and the rest of the world. In addition, the end of the Cold War has meant the end of hostilities between the two superpowers whose moves dominated the international stage for so long. The second factor is a reflection of this change. Central Europe no longer sits between two hostile powers that used the region as a military staging area. Third, the creation of multilateral frameworks for consultation and cooperation, such as the Organization for Security and Cooperation in Europe (OSCE) and the Council of Europe, has provided an institutionalized basis for resolving conflicts and imposing sanctions on those states that fail to adhere to the new norms of democracy, human rights, and democratic values.

The fourth factor impacting the context of regional relations is the fact that despite old arguments regarding the "true" borders of some states, there have been no serious attempts to alter the currently internationally recognized borders that were laid down at the end of World War II. Fifth, in conjunction with the acceptance of current international borders, with a few notable exceptions, there has not been the violent response to ethnic minorities living within state borders. The problems, while they do definitely exist (see Ethnic Conflicts: Central and Eastern Europe), have been less intense than during the period between World Wars I and II.

The sixth factor is the ongoing existence of democratic political systems in the majority of the states. Albania and, until recently, some of the former Yugoslav republics are the notable exceptions to this general rule. However, despite its apparent fragility, democracy continues to develop in the region. Finally, the last factor is the change in the international environment itself. As mentioned earlier, the growing economic integration in Europe and the rest of the world has helped the overall economic condition of the international arena.

Conclusion

Poor bilateral relations between the states of Central Europe have long played a role in that region's inability to maintain a united front against common enemies or present a regional response or interest with regard to other international issues. With the dissolution of the Soviet empire, several regional organizations within Europe reached out to include various states in Central Europe. The success of these organizations and the positive impact on Central European economies has led to the growth of intraregional organizations as well as increased interest in extraregional and supranational organizations.

One of the first steps taken by the Central European states after 1989 was to declare their withdrawal from the Warsaw Pact and begin negotiations to join NATO and the EU. The requirements for admission to both of these organizations provided support to governments trying to sell economic and political reforms to an otherwise reluctant and economically hard-hit populace. Membership in NATO in particular was supported as a means to insure against any possibility that Russia might decide to reassert control over the region. In particular, the Baltic States were eager to join to be assured of preserving their long-desired independence. Memberships in NATO and the EU are viewed as necessary steps to the dual goals of returning to Europe and increasing the pace of economic development to match that of the West.

Memberships in NATO and the EU also were viewed as essential to security and reform efforts by the Central European states. With a few notable exceptions, almost every former Central European Warsaw Pact state is now a member of NATO. The expected admission of Bulgaria and Romania to the EU in 2007 will complete the overall goal of those states for returning to Europe. Both the application processes and membership in those two organizations have increased the pace of reforms and kept those governments on track to continuing political and economic reforms.

If a person accepts the argument that the extent to which international organizations can affect the behavior of states is determined by the nature of the international organizations themselves, then NATO and the EU, due to their nature of economic and military integration and the democratic values underlying the policies of those organizations, have profoundly impacted domestic policies and infrastructures in the Central European states. Implementation of the reforms necessary to meet the requirements of those two organizations has required a great deal of change on the part of the Central European states. In addition, in their attempts to meet those requirements, the Central European states found themselves working in close contact with many different international organizations. The collapse of communism has greatly expanded the international horizons of the Central European states.

REBECCA R. JONES

See also Central and Eastern Europe: History and Economic Development; Ethnic Conflicts: Central and Eastern Europe

References and Further Reading

Brown, J. F. *Hopes and Shadows: Eastern Europe after Communism.* Durham, NC: Duke University Press, 1994.

Derleth, J. William. *The Transition in Central and Eastern European Politics.* Upper Saddle River, NJ: Prentice Hall, 2000.

European Union. 2005. Home Page: www.europa.eu.int

Hyde-Price, Adrian. *The International Politics of East Central Europe.* Manchester, England: Manchester University Press, 1996.

Laqueur, Walter. *Europe in Our Time: A History 1945–1992.* New York: Viking, 1992.

Lewis, Paul G. *Central Europe since 1945.* New York: Longman Publishing, 1994.

NATO. 2005. Official Home Page: www.nato.int

Pridham, Geoffrey, and Tatu Vanhanen, eds. *Democratization in Eastern Europe: Domestic and International Perspectives.* London: Routledge, 1994.

Przeworski, Adam. *Democracy and the Market: Political and Economic Reforms in Eastern Europe and Latin America.* Cambridge: Cambridge University Press, 1991.

Schopflin, George. *Politics in Eastern Europe, 1945–1992.* Oxford: Blackwell Publishers, 1993.

Skidelsky, Robert. *The Road from Serfdom: The Economic and Political Consequences of the End of Communism.* New York: Allen Lane, The Penguin Press, 1995.

Smith, Graham. *The Post-Soviet States: Mapping the Politics of Transition.* London: Arnold Publishers, 1999.

White, Stephen, Judy Batt, and Paul G. Lewis, eds. *Developments in East European Politics.* Durham, NC: Duke University Press, 1993.

CENTRAL ASIA: HISTORY AND ECONOMIC DEVELOPMENT

Historical Overview

Central Asia lies at the concurrence of three influential world areas: Asia, Europe, and the Middle East. Traditionally, the geographical boundaries of the Central Asian region run from the Caspian Sea in the west to Xinjiang in the east and reach as far southward as the Hindu Kush mountains. The discussion here will focus on the heart of this vast territory, or *Transoxiana* as the Greeks called it, the land beyond the Oxus River, the modern Amu Darya. This centralized location resulted in the region serving as a cultural interface, absorbing a multitude of ideas, practices, and technologies from virtually every corner of the Eurasian landmass, and on occasion generating its own unique contributions. Humans have lived in this part of the world since prehistoric times, as numerous caches of petroglyphs attest— some at Saimaly Tash in central Kyrgyzstan date to 3000 BC. One of the earliest organized societies to occupy the broad, sweeping plains the Russians many centuries later would call the *steppe* were the Saka people, more commonly called the Scythians. These aggressive, nomadic warriors were craftsmen of exquisite works in gold and left the landscape dotted with *kurgans*, or burial mounds of their chieftains. A kurgan unearthed in southern Kazakhstan in the 1960s revealed a magnificent costume composed of hundreds of individual gold pieces.

While many of the ancient peoples of Central Asia were nomadic, the cities, typically sited along the streams draining the mountains to the south and east, would spur both economic and cultural connections to the rest of the world. These settlements were strung across the region from Xinjiang in the east, through the Fergana Valley on the western slopes of the Tien Shan, and continued westward along the Amu Darya and its tributaries, finally culminating in the fertile Khorezm oasis lying just east of the Caspian Sea. This was the heart of the famed Silk Road, an artery that joined the East and West almost continually for two millennia. Under the influence of the Sogdians, an Indo-European people related to the Persians, many of these trading centers would amass considerable wealth and power. Among the oldest and most influential was the fabled city of Samarkand, which attracted the attention of Alexander the Great, who made a conquest of both the city and one of its most beautiful residents, Roxana, in 328 BC.

Around 700 AD Muslim armies gradually pushed into Transoxiana from eastern Persia, displacing the local religions of Zoroastrianism, Buddhism, and others with the ascendant faith of Islam. The defeat of a Tang Dynasty army on the banks of the Talas River in 751 AD would ensure that Central Asia would belong not to China but to the *Dar ul Islam*, or realm of Islam, for the next 1,300 years. The Muslim conquest resulted in the transformation of Central Asian culture almost immediately in the urban areas and more gradually among the loosely knit nomadic communities along the margins of oasis civilization. Within three centuries, Central Asian cities would emerge as vital sources of Islamic scholarship and produce great advancements in science, philosophy, art, literature, and architecture. This era of relative stability and tranquility was shattered in the mid-thirteenth century with the arrival of the Mongols, under the leadership of Genghis Khan. Initially, the Mongol conquest was destructive and disruptive, as many of the region's cities were razed and the inhabitants put to the sword. But Mongol domination also eventually increased trade with other parts of the vast Mongol empire, and the conquerors themselves in some cases converted to Islam and adopted local customs, spurring a recovery of the region's culture.

By the mid-1300s, Mongol power was collapsing in Central Asia, as the empire disintegrated and the heirs of the Great Khan struggled for control. The void would be filled by a fierce conqueror nearly the equal of Genghis Khan himself, who, like the Mongol ruler, rose from humble origins to control a vast empire. Amir Timur, or as he is known in the West, Tamerlane, was born at Kesh (modern Shakhrisabz, near Samarkand). Eventually, his empire would stretch from northern India in the south, to Baghdad in the west, and to Moscow in the north, covering most of western Asia, while Samarkand would become one of the most important cities in the world. Marching against China in the winter of 1405, Amir Timur died of a fever and was interred in a magnificent mausoleum in Samarkand. Like the Mongol empire, the Timurid state crumbled as most of those following Amir Timur showed to be less capable at managing an empire. Central Asia's economy and culture stagnated, as its great distance from the world's oceans hindered both social and technological exchange. Simultaneously, a new power was awakening to the north. The Russians, once vassals of the Mongols, were building an empire of their own, and it was only a matter of time before their push toward the south would bring them to Central Asia.

Russian interest in the resources and strategic position of Central Asia dates to at least the time of Tsar Peter the Great, if not earlier. Peter's efforts to court the local rulers met with quite limited results, but within a century and a half his successors were establishing a string of forts across the northern steppe lands of Kazakhstan, garrisoned by Cossacks. Russian absorption of the steppe nomads, primarily the three Kazakh "hordes" and their cousins the Kyrgyz, was a slow, inexorable process that took most of the nineteenth century. The Tsar's incursions deeper into Central Asia were in part a response to British expansion into Afghanistan at the same time, the strategic contest known as the "Great Game." A seminal event in the conquest of Central Asia by the Russian empire was the capture of Tashkent from the Khanate of Kokand in 1865. The loss of Tashkent opened the way for absorption of the Khanate's territory, and by the end of the nineteenth century the Khanate had been eliminated, and Russia was administering the bulk of the region as "Turkestan." Immigration of Slavic settlers to Central Asia in the last decades of the century skyrocketed, and tensions between the newcomers and the indigenous peoples were rooted mostly in economic issues, especially land ownership, but cultural differences also contributed to friction between the groups. Periodic revolts and violence rocked the region through the last half of the nineteenth century.

A "soviet," or council, was established in Tashkent several weeks before the Bolsheviks took power in the Russian capital in 1917. The Russian Civil War (1918–1921) was as destructive and chaotic in Central Asia as it was elsewhere, and it was only after the Red Army of General Mikhail Frunze took over the Bolshevik forces that the region was secured for the Communists. By 1922, the new regime was in control, although an insurgency, the "Basmachi," continued to harass Soviet forces for another decade. The advent of Josef Stalin in the late 1920s ushered in a disastrous era for Central Asia. Stalin intensified the antireligious campaign until World War II, when circumstances forced him to adopt a more conciliatory stance toward Islam and other faiths. Stalin's program to collectivize agricultural holdings had catastrophic consequences for the region's nomadic populations, specifically the Kazakhs and Kyrgyz. Both groups suffered severe declines in their numbers, and rather than turn their livestock over to the state, they slaughtered millions of head of cattle and sheep, leaving the animals in the fields to rot. On the positive side, Stalin's rule also witnessed widespread industrialization, a tremendous rise in literacy among Central Asians, and the modernization of transportation and communication facilities, especially in urban areas.

Stalin's successors during the Soviet period generally followed the policies he had set in place in Central Asia although certainly not with the same ruthlessness. Nikita Khrushchev initially relaxed the harsh restrictions on religion from the Stalin era, only to reverse course in the late 1950s, urging a new antireligious campaign. Khrushchev also was responsible for the famous "Virgin Lands" program, which was designed to increase agricultural production in the Kazakh Soviet Socialist Republic (SSR) by bringing millions of acres of previously uncultivated land into production. The new acreage was worked mostly by Russian and Ukrainian volunteers, many of whom stayed after the campaign had run its course. This influx of settlers helped to increase the percentage of Slavs there, making them the largest group in the northern regions of the republic. By the late 1950s, the Kazakh SSR had taken on new strategic importance for several reasons. First, the launch site for the Soviet space program, Baikonur, was located in the southern Kazakh SSR. Kazakhstan also acquired the dubious distinction of serving as the USSR's main testing ground for nuclear weapons, a role that led to severe environmental problems in eastern Kazakhstan.

Central Asia had long been a producer of cotton, but by the early 1960s, the Soviet administration was devoting increasing amounts of investment to this crop. Cotton was known as "white gold," a reference to the valuable hard currency the fiber earned for the USSR on the world market. Between 1960 and the mid-1980s, vast stretches of new lands, never before cultivated in Central Asia, were put into cotton production, and yields skyrocketed. But this bonanza came at a high cost. All the new land was irrigated, and the water for irrigation was drawn from the region's two main streams, the Amu Darya and Syr Darya. These rivers had fed the Aral Sea for thousands of years and were its only source of recharge. In the 1980s, it had become clear that the Aral was collapsing because the rivers were delivering miniscule amounts of water to the Aral Sea, and the surrounding region had become an ecological wasteland. Today, the sea continues to shrink, and the commercial fishing industry, which once produced a sizable portion of the USSR's caviar and other fish products, is gone. The health of millions of people in western Uzbekistan and Kazakhstan has been severely damaged, and the countries affected still struggle to adequately address this tragic remnant of their Soviet legacy.

By the mid-1980s, most of the Central Asian Soviet Socialists republics had been under the control of leaders who had been in place for decades, the majority of them appointed by Khrushchev in the early 1960s. While this had led to considerable stability in the Communist Party structure in Soviet Central Asia, it also had generated massive levels of corruption, nepotism, and abuse of authority. The arrival of Mikhail Gorbachev at the helm of the Soviet Union in March 1985 signaled a change, and over the next several years, Gorbachev systematically replaced the old guard leadership in Central Asia. It was in Central Asia, in fact, that Gorbachev was given his first lesson in the importance of ethnic politics in his crumbling empire. When he removed the long-time First Party Secretary Dinmukhamed Kunaev from the Kazakh SSR in December 1986, putting in his place an ethnic Russian from outside the republic, violent protests rocked the Kazakh capital of Alma-Ata (Almaty) for several days. Unfortunately, this would not be the last instance of ethnic animosity bursting forth in Central Asia. In 1989, in the Uzbek SSR, violence erupted between the majority Uzbeks and a minority group, the Meskhetian Turks, that resulted in dozens of deaths; however, a far worse episode occurred near the city of Osh in the southern Kyrgyz SSR the following year, in which Kyrgyz and Uzbeks battled each other for days, resulting in several hundred deaths. On the eve of Soviet collapse, Central Asia appeared to be a cauldron of environmental and ethnic turmoil.

The attempted *coup d'état* against Mikhail Gorbachev in August 1991 caught the leadership in Central Asia off-guard, and few in Central Asia seemed prepared for the abrupt collapse of the Soviet Union within four months and the countries' sudden emergence as independent states. The five new Central Asian states have struggled in their efforts to shift to capitalistic economies and establish the framework of civil society. While none of these countries could be labeled democracies in the Western sense, Kazakhstan, Kyrgyzstan, and Tajikistan have made some progress toward creating pluralistic political systems. Uzbekistan has remained authoritarian, while the leader of Turkmenistan, Saparmyrat Niyazov, has crafted a cult of personality that Stalin himself would likely envy. Most of the presidents are former Communist Party leaders, and most have retained their positions for almost fifteen years due to rigged elections and repression of opposition figures and parties. Economic progress has been uneven and sporadic. While the variety and general quality of goods has improved, living standards have either remained stagnant or actually declined relative to costs. Potential economic development varies across the region, as some countries are well-endowed with valuable resources, but others, particularly Kyrgyzstan and Tajikistan, are more poorly endowed.

One aspect of Central Asian culture that has certainly changed from the Soviet era is the advent of Islam. In the early 1990s, thousands of new mosques and medressehs were constructed in the region, and many people became interested in learning more about their Muslim heritage after being separated from the greater Islamic realm for almost seventy years. In Tajikistan, the Islamic Renaissance Party became a major political force in the country and played a central role in the country's civil war in the 1990s. By the late 1990s, some leaders in the region were warning of the radicalization of Islam, a concern underlined by the rise of the Taliban in neighboring Afghanistan. Uzbekistan cracked down on Islamic believers in 1998, passing harsh antireligious legislation, but in February of the next year, Tashkent was shaken by a series of car bombs. Subsequently, small groups of armed insurgents of the Islamic Movement of Uzbekistan (IMU), supported by the Taliban and possibly Osama bin Laden, infiltrated Kyrgyzstan from bases in Afghanistan and Tajikistan in the summers of 1999 and 2000. These raids accomplished little in a strategic sense, but they highlighted the instability of the region, a concern for the West but also for Russia and China, each of which possesses restive Muslim populations. In addition, by the late 1990s, Central Asia had acquired a new geopolitical dimension, as significant deposits of petroleum and natural gas had been discovered in the Caspian basin, and Western oil companies were deeply invested in exploiting and delivering these resources to the global market.

After the terrorist attacks on September 11, 2001, on the United States's East Coast, including New York's World Trade Center in the Twin Towers, and the Pentagon Building in Washington, Central Asia's significance became magnified for the United States due to its proximity to Afghanistan. Within weeks of the attacks on the United States, American officials had negotiated agreements with Uzbekistan, Kyrgyzstan, and Tajikistan for the use of air bases in those countries, and many of the raids conducted against the Taliban regime were carried out from these facilities. After the ouster of the Taliban from power in Afghanistan, the United States has continued to maintain a military presence in the region, generating unease in both Russia and China that both resent the American presence in Central Asia. The geopolitical significance of Central Asia, viewed as a frontline region in the "war on terror," has become obvious to US policy makers. Some argue that these new nations remain vulnerable to the threat of Islamic militancy, while others suggest that the most reliable method of stabilizing Central Asia is to advance civil society, promote democracy, and encourage economic development, thereby undermining the attraction of extremist doctrines. What seems certain is that the Central Asian region is just as vital and strategic today as in the days of Alexander.

Economic Development

For at least two millennia, Central Asia's economic development balanced on two pillars: agriculture and trade. Production of crops was concentrated in the oases that spread along the streams that drained the great peaks lying to the south, providing precious water that the arid climate did not. Soils in the river valleys were extremely fertile, once sufficient water was brought to them, so over time complex and extensive networks of irrigation works appeared. The fields and orchards of the region produced a surplus in most years, allowing for a division of labor and the rise of cities. Some urban places in Central Asia, such as Samarkand, may have been established several thousand years ago. The settlements clustered along the streams, inadvertently occupying the most accessible passages through the heart of the region and sitting adjacent to the only reliable sources of water in the dry, sometimes parched, heart of Asia. This geography would turn out to be fortuitous when trade began to flourish between Europe and Asia.

Precisely when caravan business developed along the famed Silk Road is impossible to determine because the process was undoubtedly gradual and inconsistent initially. Certainly, by the first or second century after the time of Christ, there was an active and regular exchange of goods between China and the Roman Empire, with silk being the most prized and valuable commodity traded. The Central Asian oasis cities, situated directly between these two vast states, were ideally located to benefit from the commercial transactions of these two giants. There was much more than silk exchanged, of course—gold, spices, slaves, gemstones, and many other goods were in demand. Central Asian merchants, acting as middlemen, acquired substantial wealth as a result. Although trade was often interrupted by war, pestilence, or famine, the Silk Road functioned for at least 1,500 years, funneling great wealth through the heart of Asia.

The Russian conquest of Central Asia brought changes in the region's fundamental economic structure. In the oases, the Russian administration greatly increased the amount of productive land by enlarging the irrigation system or rebuilding what the indigenous population had allowed to degenerate. Much of the new land was used to grow cotton, especially after the introduction of American varieties that were more productive. In the steppe region, large numbers of Slavic settlers were brought in who occupied land formerly used by the Kazakhs and Kyrgyz nomads for grazing, gradually turning the northern steppe into a zone of grain production. Many of the nomads abandoned their lifestyle for agrarianism as well. The primary economic activity for these peoples slowly shifted from animal husbandry to agriculture, with the bulk of production in wheat. By the turn of the twentieth century, Central Asia had become a major source of cotton and grain for the Russian empire.

Before the arrival of the Russians, there was virtually no industrial development even in the urban centers, but the Tsarist administration initiated some efforts to industrialize the Central Asian economy. In the northern steppe, the discovery of coal and other mineral resources led to the emergence of limited industrial production, based mostly on extraction and smelting or ores. In the south, little effort to industrialize was made to avoid competition with the textile industries in European Russia. Some small-scale development was allowed in the textile and food processing industries, primarily for local consumption, but virtually all manufactured goods were imported from Russia. Infrastructure, especially railroads, was significantly expanded at the same time, mostly with the goal of increasing the flow of Central Asia's mineral and agriculture wealth to the industrial centers of northwestern Russia. In essence, the Russian empire exploited Central Asia in a classic colonial mercantile relationship, leading to stunted economic development.

After the disruption of the civil war, the Soviet government attempted to expand industrial production in Central Asia. This effort did not show significant results until the late 1920s, but with wide-scale electrification, which became a major goal of the new regime, economic development proceeded apace. In the North, huge coal deposits in Kazakhstan led to rapid and massive industrialization in Karaganda, Semipalatinsk, Petropavlovsk, and other cities, with a focus on iron and steel and petrochemicals. In the South, much emphasis was placed on Tashkent, which became an industrial center producing a great variety of goods. During World War II, entire factories and enterprises were relocated to Central Asia from regions of the USSR threatened by the Germans, and this strategic repositioning enhanced the industrial capacity of the entire region. However, much of the cotton produced in Central Asia continued to be refined in other parts of the Soviet Union, and many of the industries there emitted dangerous levels of pollution.

In the agriculture sector, the Soviet regime completely transformed the production system by collectivizing nearly all agricultural holdings. Two types of enterprises resulted: on the "collective farms," farmers were assigned production quotas and shared any surplus; on the "state farms," those working the land were paid cash wages like factory workers. The Soviets continued to expand production of cotton due to the large sums of foreign currency its sale on the international market brought in for government coffers. These earnings were vital for purchasing goods and equipment that the USSR could not produce itself. From 1960 to the mid-1980s, the acreage in Uzbekistan and Turkmenistan increased exponentially, boosting cotton production but also resulting in increased demand for water. Ultimately, this "monoculture" of cotton would cause imbalances in economic development and one of the greatest environmental disasters of all time, the collapse of the Aral Sea, as noted previously.

On the positive side, although the Soviet regime exploited Central Asia for its resources and invested relatively little in developing local industry, except in the case of northern Kazakhstan, the Soviet administration greatly increased levels of literacy and education, constructed significant infrastructure, and

developed the resource base of the region. But the benefits of the Soviet legacy are quite unevenly encountered across Central Asia. Kazakhstan inherited a well-developed industrial base and an extensive transportation and communications system, while tiny Tajikistan, the poorest republic in the USSR, received relatively little investment from the center, except in the areas of hydroelectric power generation and a few related industries.

Since the Central Asian republics achieved independence in 1991, all states have been struggling to shift their economies from a command economy to a system based on market mechanisms, with varying degrees of success. The legacy of the Soviet system has proved difficult to overcome because many of the linkages from that period have collapsed, and new economic relationships must be cultivated. The lack of democratic institutions has hurt the economic transition, and corruption is pervasive in all the countries at every level. Investment capital is badly needed, as the transportation and communications systems need upgrading and expansion, and many of the industrial facilities left from the Soviet period are outmoded. The quality of education has declined in most of the Central Asian states because funding has been reduced due to poor economic performance. Substantial foreign investment has flowed mostly into extracting the region's resources, but in other sectors, foreign investors for the most part have avoided the region. In some countries, notably Uzbekistan and Tajikistan, demographic growth remains high, stressing local resources and services. Unemployment and inflation were serious problems in the 1990s and remain worrisome, although both have dropped in recent years.

Yet there are some reasons to expect economic progress in the region. Tourism remains underdeveloped in all five countries, and its increased presence could stimulate job creation and investment, if the necessary infrastructure can be developed. Kazakhstan and Turkmenistan, both endowed with a wealth of hydrocarbon resources, have a significant potential for economic growth and improving living standards, if their oil and gas can reach the world market efficiently. Uzbekistan's agricultural wealth and industrial development also present advantages, but the government there has moved quite slowly in reforming the economy since the collapse of the USSR. The two smallest countries, Kyrgyzstan and Tajikistan, are poor and remote but control what may soon be the region's most vital resource: water. If additional investment can be found, and if greater cooperation and coordination of goals and strategies might be achieved among the new states of Central Asia, then the region stands a good chance of successfully overcoming its historical and geographic disadvantages and fully integrating into the global economy.

REUEL R. HANKS

See also Afghanistan; Bangladesh; Bhutan; Central Asia: International Relations; Ethnic Conflicts: Central Asia; India; Iran; Maldives; Nepal; Pakistan; Sri Lanka

References and Further Reading

Allworth, Edward, ed. *Central Asia: 120 Years of Russian Rule*. Durham, NC: Duke University Press, 1989.

Grousset, Rene. *The Empire of the Steppes: A History of Central Asia*. New Brunswick, NJ: Rutgers University Press, 1970.

Manz, Beatrice, ed. *Central Asia in Historical Perspective*. Boulder, CO: Westview Press, 1994.

Melvin, Neil. *Uzbekistan: Transition to Authoritarianism on the Silk Road*. Amsterdam: Harwood Academic Publishers, 2000.

Olcott, Martha. *Kazakhstan: Unfulfilled Promise*. Washington, DC: Carnegie Endowment for International Peace, 2002.

Rumer, Boris, and Stanislav Zhukov, eds. *Central Asia: The Challenges of Independence*. Armonk, NY: M.E. Sharpe, 1998.

Soucek, Svat. *A History of Inner Asia*. Cambridge, England: Cambridge University Press, 2000.

CENTRAL ASIA: INTERNATIONAL RELATIONS

The collapse of the Soviet Union ended three centuries of direct Russian control of Central Asia. Some analysts thought that the disintegration of the Soviet Union would lead to a new "Great Game" in the region involving Russia, Iran, and Turkey. The region's geostrategic location, its socioeconomic and political ties with Russia, and its historic and cultural ties to Iran and Turkey provided natural attractions for Moscow, Tehran, and Ankara to exert influence in the region. The Central Asian states, by virtue of their membership in the Commonwealth of Independent States (CIS) and the ties of their *nomenklatura* (officialdom) to Russia's power hierarchy, maintained their foreign policy orientation toward Moscow. Civil strife in the postindependence Central Asia allowed Russia to maintain its influence in the region through direct or indirect military intervention to stabilize its porous borders and guard its southern flank.

Russia's involvement in Tajikistan's civil war is a good case in point. Beginning in February 1990, a series of events spurred periodic upheavals and antigovernment revolts in that country. In February, riots erupted in the capital city of Dushanbe, ostensibly over preferential housing allocations issued to Armenian refugees from Nagorno Karabakh. In March, he elected Tajik Supreme Council (parliament) and named Kahar Mahkamov as president. On August 24, 1990, Tajikistan issued a "declaration of sovereignty," paving the way for eventual independence from the Soviet Union. Mahkamov, however, was never popular with Tajik nationalists who viewed him as more pro-Soviet than pro-Tajik. Furthermore, Mahkamov had a Tartar wife, and his children had married non-Tajiks. The president's "authenticity" remained suspect during his tenure.

Mahkamov committed a major political blunder by supporting the August 1991 conservative military *coup d'etat* in the Soviet Union. After the failure of the *coup*, anti-Communist demonstrators demanded Mahkamov's ouster, and he was forced to resign on September 9, 1991. The same day, Tajikistan declared its independence. Parliamentary chairman Kadreddin Aslonov replaced Mahkamov. Aslonov immediately banned the Communist Party and froze its assets. In parliament, the Communist Party retaliated by forcing Aslonov's resignation and replaced him with Rahman Nabiev as acting president and parliamentary chairman. Nabiev had been first secretary of the Communist Party but had lost his position in 1985 during Mikhail Gorbachev's anticorruption campaign. Nabiev replaced the Communist Party ban and restored the privileges of the old party operatives. Fearing a return to the old guard, the opposition organized massive demonstrations against the new government, eventually forcing Nabiev to agree to conduct free presidential elections.

The opposition to Nabiev, based on a broad sector, was led by the Democratic Party of Tajikistan, the Islamic Renaissance Party (IRP), the nationalist Rastokhiz Party, and the Pamir-based Lali Badakhshan Party. In April 1992, this unusual coalition organized massive demonstrations demanding the resignation of parliamentary chairman Safarali Kenjaev. Although the government initially agreed to consider Kenjaev's ouster, it reneged on its promise, leading to the storming of the parliamentary building by the opposition. After this episode, Kenjaev resigned his post. However, he still had supporters, particularly in the district of Kulab. This prompted Nabiev to restore Kenjaev to his post on May 3, 1992, which precipitated another major crisis with the opposition. Fierce fighting ensued between the forces loyal to Nabiev and those of the opposition, leading to a bloody civil war, which not only threatened the foundation and territorial integrity of Tajikistan but also challenged the emerging political order in Central Asia.

Continuing gridlock and instability eventually led to a bloody civil war in Tajikistan, which spilled over to the neighboring states. The civil war in the 1990s cost the lives of more than twenty thousand people and caused the displacement of 10% of the country's population. Human rights violations, such as torture and physical annihilation, or real or imaginary opponents of the regime, were extensive and documented by such international human rights organizations as Amnesty International and Human Rights Watch.

In the West, the civil war in Tajikistan was generally portrayed as a struggle between secularists and Islamic Fundamentalists or between Democrats and the Communists. In fact, the main cause of the civil war stemmed in local and regional loyalties. These relations were exacerbated by the involvement of the Russian army and the Uzbek government. One side of the civil war was represented by those whose political bases were in Khojand and Kulab. As members of the "old guard," they represented an order that was more palatable to the interests of the Russian Federation and the government of Uzbekistan. Their opponents in the civil war, the Islamic-Democratic opposition, represented new political forces based in such areas as Kurgan Teppe, Garm Valley, the Pamir region, and the district around Dushanbe.

Russia's military involvement in Afghanistan enabled the deployment of the 201st Motorized Division and border guards, who had been directly involved on the side of the old guard apparatchiks since the beginning of the civil war. Supporters of the old guard used Russian and Uzbek army equipment, including tanks, during the course of the civil war. Uzbekistan provided direct military assistance, particularly in Khojand and Dushanbe, to the government forces. Since Tajikistan had no air force, Uzbek airplanes bombed strategic rebel positions on behalf of the Tajik government. New security organizations were formed in Tajikistan through Uzbek and Russian involvement in Tajikistan's internal affairs. Moreover, the CIS-Tajik collective security treaty allowed the permanent stationing of some twenty-five thousand multinational soldiers on Tajik soil.

In regional terms, Russia's continuing involvement in Tajikistan poses a number of questions. Tajikistan shares no common border with Russia, and the once significant Russian population in Tajikistan has been reduced to a negligible size through emigration since the early 1990s. Furthermore, Russia has minimal commercial stake in Tajikistan. Yet, contemporary Tajikistan remains Russia's last foothold in Central Asia. For many Russians decision makers, it is psychologically satisfying to maintain Moscow's presence in Tajikistan as long as possible. All other former Soviet republics in Central Asia and the Caucasus have drifted away from Moscow except Tajikistan. President Rahmonov is the only Central Asian leader who has not challenged Moscow's policies, either in Central Asia or in international affairs.

In addition to Russia, the other two regional actors whose policies have implications for stability and peace in Tajikistan are Uzbekistan and Iran. Uzbekistan has long been leery of the growth of political Islam in Central Asia, especially in neighboring Tajikistan. Under President Islam Karimov, virtually all opposition to the government of Uzbekistan has been eliminated, and no independent press operates in the country. Karimov has managed to develop a strong cult of personality by strengthening his own personal power over the most significant governing institutions in Uzbekistan. For example, he occupies the presidency and heads the Council of Ministers simultaneously. Karimov has succeeded in gaining the support of the United States under the guise of "fighting terrorism" and has intensified the government's brutal crackdown on all types of dissent in his country. The same pattern has been replicated in Turkmenistan under Separmurad Niyazev, the country's authoritarian president.

Uzbekistan's domestic politics and its geopolitical location have largely been responsible for Karimov's heavy-handed policies toward political developments in neighboring Tajikistan. When the Tajik civil war started, Uzbekistan adopted a similar policy to that of Russia. Fearing both the spillover effect of the revival of political Islam in Tajikistan and the stirring of nationalist sentiments among its own large Tajik population, the Uzbek government joined the Russian forces to support the Tajik government against its Islamic-Democratic opponents. However, the position of Uzbekistan with respect to developments in Tajikistan began to change in mid-1994. One reason for this shift of policy is that President Karimov no longer fears Tajik nationalism, and the threat of the spread of political Islam from Tajikistan has subsided considerably.

Although Tajikistan no longer poses any significant security challenge for Uzbekistan, uncertainties about future developments in Tajikistan will continue to allow Uzbekistan to act as a political hegemon in that country. In this role, Russia remains Uzbekistan's only regional rival. From Dushanbe's perspective, Uzbekistan's dreams of becoming a regional heavyweight and serving as a godfather for Tajikistan may redound to the detriment of Tajikistan's political development. For example, on November 3, 1998, the rebel Colonel Mahmud Khudoyberdyev and his supporters invaded Tajikistan from their bases in Uzbekistan. Although the government forces suppressed this rebellion five days later, Tajikistan found itself at the brink of another war. President Rahmonov blamed Uzbekistan for this uprising, and Tajikistan claimed that Uzbekistan gave sanctuary to Khudoyberdyev and his fleeing fighters. This episode clearly demonstrates the uneasy Tajik-Uzbek relations and the unpredictability of regional conflicts in Central Asia.

Iran has also been a regional player in the recent political developments in Tajikistan. Iran's interest in Tajikistan is more cultural and historical than political. Iran has no common borders with Tajikistan, and in view of Tajikistan's weak economy and poverty, the country has minimal economic attraction for Iran. However, because of a common linguistic lineage, Iran has sought to develop sociocultural links with Tajikistan and the Tajik people. It has done so by inviting Tajik cultural figures to Iran on a regular basis. Iran has allocated scholarships to Tajik students and has actively promoted the exchange of literary and artistic groups, as well as tourism, between the two countries. Since Tajikistan's independence and throughout the Tajik civil war and beyond, Iran has been careful to maintain contact with all sides and remain neutral in Tajikistan's political imbroglio. In this vein, Iran has been in the forefront of numerous mediation efforts between secular and Islamic forces in Tajikistan and has been instrumental in bridging the once insurmountable gap between the Tajik government and opposition forces. In general, Iran shares with Russia some common security interests in Tajikistan. But Tehran can hardly match Russia's influence and assets in Tajikistan and cannot counterbalance Uzbekistan's more ambitious goals in the region.

Another major issue affecting Central Asia's international relations was the status of the Soviet-era nuclear weapons. After the collapse of the Soviet Union, Kazakhstan, Central Asia's largest republic, was the only country in the region that possessed nuclear weapons. However, the Kazakh government agreed to transfer the control of these weapons to the Soviet Union and later declared itself to be a nonnuclear state. The five Central Asian republics of Kazakhstan, Kyrgyzstan, Tajikistan, Turkmenistan, and Uzbekistan also began negotiating amongst themselves to create a nuclear-weapon-free-zone (NWFZ) in the region. On September 27, 2002, after almost five years of negotiation, the Central Asian republics signed a NWFZ treaty in Samarkand, Uzbekistan. This agreement was hailed by Jayantha Dhanapala, United Nations Undersecretary General for Disarmament Affairs, as a great step forward for nuclear nonproliferation and nuclear disarmament. Disagreement amongst the Central Asian states almost derailed the signing of the Samarkand agreement. For example, Kazakhstan, Kyrgyzstan, and Tajikistan had already signed a collective security treaty with Russia in 1992. As a result, they wanted to preserve Russia's prerogative to deploy nuclear weapons on their territories should they find it advantageous to their security interests. However, this would have weakened the NWFZ treaty. The final language of the treaty committed the Central Asian states to establish a complete NWFZ in the region while recognizing that each state would not jeopardize the existing security arrangements with Russia.

On the economic front, the Central Asian states are members of the Economic Cooperation Organization (ECO), which links them with the broader southwest and southern regions in Asia. The genesis of the ECO dates back to 1964, when Iran, Pakistan, and Turkey established the Regional Cooperation for Development (RCD). After the Iranian revolution of 1979, the RCD became a *de facto* moribund organization. Under Iran's initiative, the RCD was revived under its new name. After the disintegration of the Soviet Union, Iran encouraged the Muslim republics of the Soviet Union to join the ECO to create an Islamic common market. Azerbaijan, Turkmenistan, and Uzbekistan were the first former Soviet republics to apply for ECO membership, followed by Kyrgyzstan, Tajikistan, and Kazakhstan. It is interesting to note that Romania also reportedly asked to join the ECO, and Turkey sought to include northern Cyprus in this grouping. Iran successfully lobbied against the inclusion of both states, and no formal action was taken in this regard.

The ECO member states' dream of establishing a thriving market stretching from the Caspian region to the Indian Ocean may not be realizable in the near future. It is true that the ECO has established a number of institutions, such as a shipping line and an investment and development bank, to facilitate communication, trade, and transportation among its members. Indeed, meetings of various organs of the ECO occur regularly, and protocols and memoranda of understanding are signed among the participants. However, daunting obstacles remain in the ECO's path.

First, most of the members of the ECO have vulnerable economies characterized by poor performance. Even the oil- or gas-rich members of the ECO suffer from economic mismanagement, corruption, cronyism, and a relatively low level of industrialization. Second, it is now clear that political and ideological divisions will continue to hamper meaningful cooperation among some member states. Third, uneven burden sharing in the organization will ultimately redound to the detriment of the founding states, like Turkey and Iran, as they seek to keep the weaker Central Asian members "happy" in their organization. Last, but not least, territorial disputes among member states, such as those between Tajikistan and Uzbekistan, do not help foster political unity in the organization.

Another important factor affecting Central Asia's international relations is the continuing uncertainty about the legal status of the Caspian Sea. Before the creation of the independent states of Central Asia, the Soviet–Iranian agreements of 1921 and 1940 served as the basis for the legal status of the Caspian Sea. According to Iran, the Caspian water body is a closed lake and not a sea, and the aforementioned Iranian–Soviet agreements did not specify any division of the Caspian Sea; rather, they solidified the Caspian's legal status as a body of water under the joint control of Iran and the Soviet Union. In the absence of any new agreements governing the Caspian's legal status, Iran has insisted any further developments/claims must be based on either the distribution of the outer seabed and Caspian subsoil into sectors divided equally among the five riparian states, or the resources should be shared commonly by all five states. Furthermore, any agreement on the legal status of the Caspian must be unanimous, and no single littoral state should be granted the right to veto the decisions of the other states or undertake unilateral measures in violation of the agreed principles. Last, Iran has insisted on declaring the Caspian as a demilitarized zone and that, due to the fragile nature of the Caspian's ecosystem, all economic activity undertaken in the region must take into account the Caspian Sea's environment.

Iran's position has been largely at odds with those of the other Caspian states in Central Asia. Russia, whose own position on the legal status of the Caspian Sea paralleled those of Iran, has now moved away from Tehran. In early 1998, Azerbaijan announced that Moscow and Baku had agreed to divvy up the Caspian seabed. This was followed by an agreement between Russia and Kazakhstan to divide their international waters in the northern part of the Caspian Sea. When Turkmenistan gave its endorsement to the Russian–Azerbaijan and Russian–Kazakh proposals, Iran was left isolated. However, both Russia and Turkmenistan have modified their positions, and territorial disputes between Azerbaijan and Turkmenistan have muddied the water further.

For its part, Iran has taken measures that, in effect, have challenged its own official position on the legal status of the Caspian. For example, in late 1997, Iran announced its intention to open its sectors of the Caspian Sea for development by international oil companies. In early December 1998, Iran announced that the Anglo-Dutch Shell and Britain's Lasmo had signed a major deal with Tehran to undertake oil and gas exploration in Iran's sector of the Caspian Sea. After the deal was made public, Azerbaijan issued a strong statement claiming that unilateral actions should not be undertaken by Iran in areas that may fall within Azerbaijan's seabed and territorial waters. Iran, which has consistently condemned unilateral energy agreements between Azerbaijan and foreign oil companies, now found itself on the other side of the controversy. In response to Baku's objections, Tehran reminded Azerbaijan of the need to devise a new Caspian legal regime that is acceptable to all parties to avoid further conflicts over sovereignty issues. Iran's foreign ministry also, once again, reminded Azerbaijan of the terms of the 1921 and 1940 Soviet–Iranian agreements regarding the Caspian Sea.

What is important to note is that neither the 1920 treaty nor the 1940 agreement provides a clear framework for determining the legal status of the Caspian Sea. In fact, the 1921 treaty did not directly address Iranian or Soviet territorial sovereignty in the Caspian. Rather, it only implicitly gave Iran the right to deploy its navy in the Caspian Sea, but it also gave the Soviet Union the primary responsibility for the security of this body of water. The 1940 agreement did reserve a ten-mile wide area off the coast of each country for exclusive fishing zones, but it made no reference to either country's sovereign rights in the Caspian Sea.

There are two specific documents that do address the issue of Russian and Iranian sovereign rights in the Caspian Sea. These agreements are the 1723 Russo–Iranian Alliance Treaty and the Iran–Soviet Memorandum (known as the Aram–Pegov Agreement) signed in August 1962 between the Iranian Foreign Minister Abbas Aram and Nikolai Pegov, Russia's Ambassador to Iran. The treaty grants Russia sovereignty over the length of the Caspian Sea, while the memorandum recognizes Iran's sovereignty in an eighty-mile wide area below the line from Absheron to Hassan Kiadeh in the southern Caspian. Perhaps because Iran still hopes to gain support for its position on the equal distribution of the Caspian Sea among the five riparian states, it has failed to register the Aram–Pegov Memorandum with the United Nations. This would give a degree of international legitimacy to Iran's legal rights in the Caspian and would strengthen its position vis-à-vis the position of the Central Asian states and Russia. The Iranian parliament also needs to approve the area delineated by the Aram–Peg line as internal Iranian waters, hence subject to its exclusive sovereignty.

These measures will allow all Central Asian riparian states plus Russia and Iran to initiate pragmatic discussions with each other to draft a blueprint of a Caspian legal regime whose principles are acceptable and beneficial to all.

Kazakhstan and Turkmenistan are the two Central Asian states whose energy resources have placed them in a unique position to enhance their international stature and have allowed them to play a greater regional role than the energy-poor countries in Central Asia. Kazakhstan has signed several major agreements with Western oil companies, while Turkmenistan's natural gas resources are attractive to the outside world. In addition to signing agreements with Western oil companies, Kazakhstan has sought to engage in oil swap deals as a means of earning immediate financial gain from its oil production. For example, in January 1997, Kazakhstan shipped five hundred thousand barrels of oil to northern Iran in exchange for an equal volume of Iranian oil to be shipped from the Persian Gulf on Kazakhstan's behalf. However, oil swap deals have become less regular and unpredictable.

Turkmenistan has been a key country in various pipeline schemes to get Central Asia's energy resources to the outside world. In December 1997, Iran's President Mohammad Khatami made his first trip abroad as president to Turkmenistan to inaugurate a gas pipeline linking Turkmenistan and Iran. The pipeline runs 270 miles from the Turkmen field of Korpeje across the Iranian border of Kord-Kuy, where it links with the existing network of East-West gas pipelines. Turkey has also joined this pipeline project. In 1996, Turkey and Iran signed a $20-billion agreement for the purchase of natural gas from Iran, and Turkey completed a 188-mile pipeline between the Iranian border and the Turkish city of Erzerum.

The United States has consistently favored the so-called Eurasian transportation corridor, which would include bypassing Iran and the Persian Gulf routes, in favor of pipeline routes from Turkmenistan to Turkey via Georgia. The US attempts to exclude Iran from the various pipeline proposals in Central Asia and the Caspian region may redound to the detriment of the long-term stability of the region and damage the fragile economies of the littoral states. All of the Caspian pipeline routes carry political and economic risks. The western route, which has vigorously been promoted by the United States, Turkey, Azerbaijan, and Georgia, bypasses both Russian and Iranian territory. Essentially, two major pipelines encompass the western route. The most expensive of all pipeline schemes is the Baku–Ceyhan pipeline, which will directly link Baku's oil fields to the Turkish Mediterranean port of Ceyhan. Although major oil companies initially balked at the prospect of building a pipeline whose cost may exceed $4 billion, they eventually succumbed to Washington's political demands. While this pipeline may become operational as early as 2006, the governments of Turkmenistan and Kazakhstan have expressed reservations about the wisdom of the Baku–Ceyhan route.

A second, and less expensive, western pipeline links the Caspian to the Georgian port of Supsa on the Black Sea. There are several drawbacks to this scheme. First, oil will have to be shipped by tankers from Supsa to the Bosphorus, the strategic waterway that divides Europe from Asia. However, Turkey has announced its intentions to limit tanker crossings and traffic through the Bosphorus to protect the ecological system of the area. In addition, political instability in Georgia, including secessionist movements by the South Ossetians and Abkhazians, makes this route a hazardous one. In addition to the western route and the economically advantageous southern route, which has long been opposed by the United States on political grounds, there is also an eastern route to get Central Asia's energy resources to the outside world. This route basically involves Chinese and Kazak energy deals and does not affect the overall energy picture in the region.

For several years, the United States has also pushed the southeastern route. As initially envisioned, this proposed pipeline would link Turkmenistan with the Pakistani port of Gwadar through western Afghanistan. The American oil company Unocal and Delta-Nimir of Saudi Arabia were the staunchest proponents of the southeastern pipeline. The total cost of the project was estimated to reach $2 billion. It was in this context that the United States, through its Saudi and Pakistani allies, began to support the ultra-Fundamentalist and reactionary Taliban movement in Afghanistan with the hope of bringing much needed political stability to that war-torn country. Without political stability in Afghanistan, the proposed pipeline would not have been politically and economically feasible. Both Unocal and Delta-Nimir played a significant role in providing the necessary funding to pay off various Taliban officials. Unocal's Vice President Chris Taggart even described Taliban's control of Afghanistan as a "positive development." Of course, the terrorist attacks of September 11, 2001, in the United States derailed the southeastern pipeline proposal after the US war against the Taliban regime and its al-Qaida supporters in Afghanistan.

The US war in Afghanistan catapulted Kazakhstan, Kyrgyzstan, Tajikistan, Turkmenistan, and Uzbekistan to the forefront of the "war on terrorism." Not only were these countries recruited to provide logistical support to the US war efforts, but they became tempting areas for establishing US military bases in what had been considered as Russia's "backyard." One of the least known by-products of the "war on terrorism" has been the deployment of US forces in various Central Asian countries. A number of former Soviet bases have now been refurbished and turned into US forward bases for military operations in the Middle East and Eurasia. In the words of former US Secretary of State Colin Powell, the US interest and presence in Central Asia would be of a kind that could not have been dreamed of before the 9/11 tragedy. The United States may indeed become the preeminent outside power in the region whose influence may drastically change Central Asia's international relations in the twenty-first century.

NADER ENTESSAR

See also Afghanistan; Bangladesh; Bhutan; Central Asia: History and Economic Development; Commonwealth of Independent States: International Relations; Ethnic Conflicts: Central Asia; Ethnic Conflicts: Commonwealth of Independent States; India; Iran; Iran–Iraq War, 1980—1988; Kashmir Dispute; Maldives; Nepal; Pakistan; Sri Lanka; Tajikistan; Taliban; Uzbekistan

References and Further Reading

Allworth, Edward, ed. *Central Asia, 130 Years of Russian Dominance: A Historical Overview*. Durham, NC: Duke University Press, 1994.

Amin, Shahid M. *Pakistan's Foreign Policy: A Reappraisal*. New York: Oxford University Press, 2000.

Bill, James A. *The Eagle and the Lion: The Tragedy of American-Iranian Relations*. New Haven, CT: Yale University Press, 1988.

Cartlidge, Cherese. *The Central Asian States*. San Diego, CA: Lucent Books, 2001.

Chadda, Maya. Building Democracy in South Asia: India, Nepal, Pakistan. Boulder, CO: Lynne Rienner Publishers, c2000.

Cohen, Stephen P. *India: Emerging Power*. Washington, DC: Brookings Institution Press, 2001.

Ganguly, Sumit. *Conflict Unending: India-Pakistan Tensions Since 1947*. New York: Woodrow Wilson Center Press; Columbia University Press, c2001.

Hagerty, Devin T. *The Consequences of Nuclear Proliferation: Lessons from South Asia*. Boston, MA: MIT Press, 1998.

Margolis, Eric S. *War at the Top of The World : The Struggle for Afghanistan, Kashmir, and Tibet*. New York: Routledge, 2000

Olson, Robert W. *Turkey-Iran Relations, 1979–2004: Revolution, Ideology, War, Coups, and Geopolitics*. Costa Mesa, CA: Mazda Publishers, 2003, 2004.

Pollack, Kenneth M. *The Persian Puzzle: The Conflict Between Iran and America*. New York: Random House, 2004.

Rotter, Andrew Jon. *Comrades at Odds: The United States and India, 1947–1964*. Ithaca, NY: Cornell University Press, 2000.

Saikal, Amin, and William Maley, eds. *The Soviet Withdrawal from Afghanistan*. Cambridge: Cambridge University Press, 1989

Sicker, Martin. *The Bear and the Lion: Soviet Imperialism and Iran*. New York: Praeger, 1988.

Talbott, Strobe. *Engaging India: Diplomacy, Democracy, and the Bomb*. Washington, DC: Brookings Institution Press, 2004.

CENTRAL INTELLIGENCE AGENCY (CIA)

Prior Intelligence Organizations

In 1941, President Franklin D. Roosevelt established the Office of Coordinator of Information (COI) and appointed General William "Wild Bill" Donovan as its head. In 1942, the COI became the covert Office of Strategic Services (OSS). Eventually, sixteen thousand wartime OSS agents provided espionage for and assistance to the European resistance movements.

The end of World War II saw the demise of the OSS. There were no covert agencies between then and the establishment of the Central Intelligence Agency (CIA) in 1947; during those years, legal intelligence capabilities consisted of information gathering and analysis.

President Harry Truman established the CIA, modeled on the OSS, under the National Security Act of 1947. Accountable to the president through the National Security Council, the CIA's functions were analysis and coordination of intelligence activities of other government departments. In 1948, it established a covert action component.

The first threats were in postwar Europe. The CIA backed right-wing generals in Greece against the Communists in 1947. In 1948, when Italian Communists threatened to win elections, the CIA bought votes, infiltrated and disrupted broadcast propaganda, and engaged in threats. The Communists lost.

In 1949, under Operation Mockingbird, the CIA recruited American news organizations and journalists to spy and spread its propaganda. Coopted were the *Washington Post*, *Time*, *Newsweek*, and the networks, as well as AP, UPI, Reuters, and more. The CIA claimed its stable included twenty-five organizations and four hundred journalists.

The CIA's Radio Free Europe, established in 1949, encouraged the 1956 Hungarian uprising by broadcasting Nikita Khrushchev's denunciation of Stalin and by implying that America would help the Hungarians. During the failed rising, seven thousand Russians and thirty thousand Hungarians died.

CIA in the Developing World: The 1950s

The CIA's activities in the developing world, as in Eastern Europe, centered on battling communism, which frequently meant undermining popularly elected reformers. The removal from power of unfriendly foreign leaders was known as "executive action." Frequently, the CIA backed the right-wing opposition, often the military. One example was the CIA support in the 1953 overthrow of Iran's democratically elected leader, Mohammed Mossadegh. Many critics believe this was due to his threats to nationalize British oil assets. When Jacobo Árbenz nationalized the National Fruit Company and began land reforms in Guatemala in 1954, the United States classified him as a Communist and thus an enemy. The CIA provided bribes, disinformation, propaganda, financing, logistics, and other support to a *coup d'état* that ousted Árbenz in 1954. Other executive action assassination victims included Patrice Lumumba of the Congo, Rafael Trujillo of the Dominican Republic, and General Abd al-Karim Kassem of Iraq. In Laos between 1957 and 1973, the CIA averaged almost one *coup d'état* per year. Haiti was the target in 1959, when the US military helped "Papa Doc" Duvalier take over.

Once in place after a *coup d'état* the right-wing dictator often received CIA assistance in training his security forces. The CIA has trained Latin American military leaders at the School of the Americas (SOA), first in Panama, then at Fort Benning, Georgia. During the 1980s and 1990s, criticism arose over the large number of SOA graduates who went on to prominent places in dictatorial regimes. (One out of seven members of DINA, the Chilean intelligence agency under Augusto Pinochet, were SOA graduates.) In 2001, SOA was renamed the Western Hemisphere Institute for Security Cooperation (WHINSEC); however, it remains at Fort Benning.

Cuba

The CIA's major failure was the effort to unseat Fidel Castro of Cuba. After Castro ousted General Fulgencio Batista in January 1959, the United States accepted Castro until he cut the rents of low-wage earners by up to 50%, confiscated the seized property of former governing officials, nationalized the telephone company and halved the rates, and redistributed land owned by American companies. The United States stopped providing Cuba with technology and technicians needed to keep its economy afloat. Then the United States cut back on its purchase of Cuban sugar. Castro refused to back off, nationalized $850 million in US property in 1960, sold his sugar to the USSR and Eastern Europe, and got weapons and technicians and machinery from the USSR. In March 1960, the CIA got the green light from Eisenhower for a $13-million project to train guerrillas for action within Cuba. Operation Mongoose involved four hundred CIA officers.

The CIA's Technical Services Division assigned Sidney Gottlieb to find ways to undercut Castro with the people. Gottlieb came up with a plan to spray a hallucinogenic drug in a television studio where Castro was to appear. Another idea was to contaminate Castro's shoes with thallium so his beard would fall out. Deputy Director of Plans Richard Bissell rejected these ideas and decided to have Castro assassinated. In September 1960, the CIA opened discussions with Johnny Rosellina and Sam Giancana of the Mafia, eventually offering $150,000 for the assassination.

When John F. Kennedy came into the presidency, he learned of the CIA's plans for an invasion force. His advisors convinced him that Castro was unpopular, and the people would rise at the first opportunity, and Kennedy feared being seen as soft on communism. On April 14, 1961, US B-26 airplanes began bombing Cuban airfields, leaving Castro with eight planes and seven pilots. On April 16, fourteen hundred exiles landed at the Bay of Pigs. The invasion lasted seventy-two hours, with all the invaders killed, wounded, or captured. A CIA shakeup ensued, and the agency focused on covert attacks on Cuba's economy.

The 1960s

In Ecuador, the CIA-backed military ousted the elected Juan Bosch, replaced him with a friendlier vice president, and let the CIA fill the vice presidency.

The CIA's involvement in Ecuador spanned 1960 through 1963. In the Congo (Zaire), the CIA assassinated Patrice Lumumba in 1961, but the people resisted efforts to impose a leader friendlier to the United States. Four years of unrest ensued. The CIA was active in Brazil in 1964 and, in 1965, was active in Indonesia, Greece, Congo (Zaire), and the Dominican Republic. The CIA intervened in Greece again in 1967 and helped capture Che Guevara in Bolivia. In Vietnam, Operation Phoenix in South Vietnam began—eventually twenty thousand Viet Cong and bystanders would die.

In 1969, Dan Mitrione, officially a police advisor, arrived in Uruguay, where he instructed the government in torture techniques. In 1970, the leftists captured and killed him. Cambodia's Prince Sahounek, popular for keeping his country out of the Vietnam War, was overthrown in 1970. His replacement, Lon Nol, entered Cambodia into the war, energizing the opposition Khmer Rouge, which took power in 1975 and killed millions.

Another CIA effort took place in Chile, where Salvadore Allende and his Socialist Workers' Party seemed headed for victory in 1970. International Telephone and Telegraph and other international companies feared the worst. Richard Helms of the CIA took the corporation's money and transferred it to conservative Chilean parties. Allende won anyway, and President Richard Nixon ordered Helms to assist a Chilean army *coup d'état* against Allende. Allende died fighting the *coup d'état* of September 11, 1970, and the more amenable Augosto Pinochet took power.

The Attempts to Rein in the CIA in the 1970s

Congress enacted the Case-Zablocki Act in 1972 in an attempt to make the CIA accountable. Congressional termination of CIA funds for the secret war in Cambodia came in 1972. Then investigation of the Watergate break-in revealed that seven of the perpetrators had CIA histories. The reformist William Colby, Deputy Director for Operations, began an internal cleanup of the CIA, which he continued after he became director when Helms was fired by Nixon.

Exposés such as *The CIA and the Cult of Intelligence* (1974) by Victor Marchetti and John Marks and *Inside the Company* (1975) by Philip Agee generated public outrage, and Frank Church headed a Senate Investigation intended to reform CIA's accountability. In 1974, Seymour Hersh exposed long-standing CIA domestic surveillance under Operation Chaos, and Congressional hearings led to the firing of James Jesus Angleton, who ran the programs that opened mail and surveilled antiwar protesters.

When the Senate Foreign Relations Committee investigated the CIA in 1975, Helms denied passing money to the plotters or otherwise assisting in the overthrow of Allende. The Senate and the CIA inspector general found that Helms lied to the committee, engaged in illegal domestic surveillance, and had a role in the murders of Lumumba, Kassem, and Diem. Helms received a two-year suspended sentence in 1977 for lying to Congress.

More Interventions: The 1970s and 1980s

Even as the Congress worked to get control of the CIA in the 1970s, in Angola the CIA backed Jonas Savimbi of UNITAS, driving his opponents into the clutches of the Soviet Union and Cuba. In 1979, the CIA lost the Shah of Iran, backed the anti-Soviet forces in Afghanistan, and continued in El Salvador and Nicaragua; it targeted Honduras in 1983.

Although the Congress stopped funding CIA efforts in Nicaragua in 1976, the CIA continued off-book funding until 1984, when it got funding again. In 1984, after aid to the Nicaraguan Contras was fully outlawed, Lieutenant Colonel Oliver North, US Marine Corps, used the CIA's networks to continue financing the Contras.

JOHN H. BARNHILL

See also Castro, Fidel; Contras; Counterinsurgency; Coup d'État; Guevara, Ernesto "Che"; Sandinista National Liberation Front (FSLN)

References and Further Reading

Agee, Philip. *Inside the Company: CIA Diary*. New York: Farrar Straus & Giroux, 1975.
Blum, William. *Killing Hope: US Military and CIA Interventions since World War II*. Monroe, ME: Common Courage Press, 1995.
Goodman, Melvin A. "CIA: The Need for Reform." Center for International Policy Policy Report (February 2001): www.fpif.org/papers/cia/index_body.html
Kumar, Satish. *CIA and the Third World: A Study in Crypto-Diplomacy*. London: Zed, 1981.
Marchetti, Victor, and John Marks. *The CIA and the Cult of Intelligence*. New York: Dell, 1974.
Vankin, Jonathan, and John Whalen. *The 60 Greatest Conspiracies of All Time*. Secaucus, NJ: Citadel Press, 1997.

CENTRAL TREATY ORGANIZATION (CENTO)

The Central Treaty Organization (CENTO), originally known as the Baghdad Pact, was a mutual defense and cooperation alliance in the Middle East from 1955 through 1979. In the early 1950s, the United States wanted to establish a Middle East Defense Organization to contain the spread of Soviet communism. The Eisenhower administration saw Egypt as the linchpin of such an arrangement, but Egyptian leader Gamal Abdel Nasser rejected the proposal. The United States then began to pursue the possibility of an alliance among the "northern tier" countries—Iran, Turkey, and Pakistan—that it believed recognized the danger of the Soviet threat as Nasser did not.

With urging from the United States, Turkey and Pakistan signed a treaty of friendship, cooperation, and mutual defense on April 2, 1954; the United States already had such a commitment with Turkey because of Turkey's membership in NATO and had signed a mutual defense pact with Pakistan in May. Despite Nasser's calls for Arab states to refuse membership in Western-sponsored pacts, Iraq signed the Baghdad Pact with Turkey on February 24, 1955. Based on Article 51, the self-defense clause of the United Nations Charter, the treaty provided for security and defense cooperation, noninterference in one another's domestic affairs, and accession by any state in the region concerned with peace and security. It was to remain in force for five years and could be renewed for additional five-year periods. Britain acceded in April 1955, followed by Pakistan in September and Iran in November. Although the United States did not officially accede to the treaty, it belonged in all but name. The organization was headquartered in Baghdad.

Nasser vociferously attacked the Baghdad Pact, largely through radio broadcasts on Voice of the Arabs. He opposed Western-sponsored defense pacts on several grounds: they were a method for dividing the Arab world; they were neoimperial because they permitted the stationing of foreign military missions on Arab soil; they were directed against the wrong enemy, the Soviet Union and not Israel; and they ultimately served only Western interests. In September 1955, Nasser's popularity in the Arab world soared when he announced Egypt had signed an arms deal with Czechoslovakia, thus successfully defying the West by "leapfrogging" over the Baghdad Pact. The United States, viewing this as the first serious evidence of Soviet penetration of the Middle East, offered to supply Egypt with arms if Nasser would cancel his deal with the Soviet bloc, but he refused.

The confrontation between Nasser and the West over the Baghdad Pact reached a climax in late 1955. Despite an agreement with Nasser to refrain from attempts to draw other Arab states into the pact, Britain continued to pressure Jordan to join. Massive popular demonstrations and rioting in Jordan against the British and the Americans caused three governments to fall in rapid succession. Order was restored only after Jordan announced it would not join the Baghdad Pact.

Popular sentiment in Iraq also mounted against the pact and the government's pro-British policies. Nasser's radio campaign helped spur increasing opposition to the government, especially in the army. Following the ill-fated Suez invasion by Britain, France, and Israel in July 1956, Nasser's stature and influence in the Arab world reached new heights. This increased pressure on Iraq's isolated, pro-Western government. On July 14, 1958, Arab nationalist army officers overthrew the Iraqi monarchy; the intra-Arab struggles surrounding the Baghdad Pact were a significant factor in triggering the Iraqi revolution. The new Iraqi government withdrew from the Baghdad Pact in March 1959.

In August 1959, the Baghdad Pact was renamed the Central Treaty Organization, and its headquarters were moved to Ankara, Turkey. The United States officially remained outside of CENTO, but after the Iraqi Revolution, it had signed identical mutual defense agreements with Iran, Pakistan, and Turkey; these were very similar to the commitments the United States would have assumed as a member of CENTO. CENTO's main military task was to coordinate the security arrangements of its members. It held yearly joint maneuvers, including air and naval exercises. American and British military aid was largely delivered through bilateral agreements, but the formal existence of this organization had increased the levels of assistance that they provided to members.

For its northern tier participants, CENTO functioned more effectively as a vehicle of socioeconomic development than as a security arrangement. Improving communications links between the three countries was a top priority. Rail links were developed between Iran and Turkey as well as Iran and Pakistan, and an all-weather highway was constructed between Iran and Turkey. Turkish ports at Trabzon and Iskenderun were modernized, as were telephone, telegraph, and teletype communications links. The members wanted to encourage and expand free trade among themselves. A multilateral technical cooperation fund was established to underwrite the exchange of experts, information, and ideas related to economic development. Agriculture, education, and culture also received attention. Their growing closeness in economic matters led Iran, Pakistan, and Turkey to establish the Regional Cooperation for Development in 1964.

By the mid-1960s, enthusiasm for CENTO was waning. Iran's relations with the Soviet Union warmed up, dimming its fears about Soviet aggression. Pakistan called on the organization to assist it in its 1965 and 1971 wars with India, but CENTO declined in both cases. The United States even suspended military assistance to Pakistan as a result of the 1965 conflict, which it viewed Pakistan as having precipitated. Turkey's invasion of Cyprus in 1974 caused the British to withdraw the troops they had stationed in Turkey, leaving CENTO moribund. CENTO officially ceased to exist after the Iranian Revolution in 1979, when Iran withdrew.

As a security arrangement aimed at preventing the spread of Soviet influence into the wider Middle East, CENTO was unsuccessful. Several Arab states, notably Egypt, Syria, and eventually Iraq, signed treaties of friendship and cooperation with the Soviet Union. Moreover, it merely duplicated existing Western commitments to Turkey through the North Atlantic Treaty Organization and to Pakistan through the Southeast Asia Treaty Organization. Its main accomplishments came as a result of heightened social and economic cooperation among the northern tier countries, particularly in the modernization of transportation and communication links.

BETH K. DOUGHERTY

See also Baghdad Pact; Middle East: International Relations; Nasser, Gamal Abdel

References and Further Reading

Duffy, A. E. P. "The Present Viability of NATO, SEATO, and CENTO." *Annals of the American Academy of Political and Social Science* 372 (1967).

Howard, Harry N. "The Regional Pacts and the Eisenhower Doctrine." *Annals of the American Academy of Political and Social Science* 401 (1972).

MacClosky, Monro. *Pacts for Peace: UN, NATO, SEATO, CENTO, and OAS.* New York: Richards Posen Press, 1967.

Ramazani, R. K. *The Northern Tier: Afghanistan, Iran, and Turkey.* Princeton, NJ: D. Van Nostrand Company, 1966.

CHAD

The Republic of Chad is a land-locked country situated in north central Africa measuring 496,000 square miles. Chad's topography is generally flat except for a range of hills along the eastern border and relatively high, barren mountains in the far northwest. The climate is hot and arid in the northern desert regions as it averages less than eight inches of rainfall annually. In the south, the climate is wet and tropical, and this zone receives thirty-nine inches of rain. The population is estimated at 9.5 million, with an annual growth rate of 3.2%. The capital city, N'djamena, known as Fort Lamy until 1973, lies at the confluence of Chad's main rivers: the Logone and the Chari. It has an estimated population over seven hundred thousand.

The better climatic conditions in the southern region make it possible for population to settle and become farmers. Most people live in the South, where the major cities are located: N'djamena, Moundou, Sarh, and Abeche. However, Chad's population is mainly rural, as the urban population rate is around 25%. Classical African religions, Islam, and Christianity are Chad's religions. French, Arabic, and Sara are the official languages, with more than 120 dialects.

Chad, already a French colony since 1897, and three other colonies were administered together as the French Equatorial Africa (AEF). Significant advances were made with the French Constitution approved in 1946 that granted Chad and other African colonies the right to elect a territorial assembly with limited powers. In November 1958, the AEF was officially terminated. Chad gained its independence on August 11, 1960. That same year, Francois Tombalbaye, leader of the *Parti Progressiste Tchadien* (PPT), became the first president of the Republic of Chad. Since 1960, Tombalbaye's government faced several conflicts due to many local and external displeased groups; in 1969, the Muslim guerrilla provoked a great attack on the government, and Tombalbaye had to ask the French for help. In 1975, Tombalbaye was assassinated, and Colonel Felix Malloum gained control. During Malloum's military government, Chad entered into a war with Libya, accusing the latter of boundary violations. In 1979, Malloum abandoned his position, and with the mediation of Sudan, a cease-fire was obtained. Goukouni Ouddei became president. The war continued, and in 1987 the Libyan occupants were expelled, allowing Chadian troops to conquer the northern zone of Aouzou. In 1988, Chad and Libya reached an agreement over that zone. In 1990, Idriss Deby became president, and a temporary state of peace was achieved. In 1998, a rebellion broke out in northern Chad, which sporadically flared up despite two peace agreements signed in 2002 and 2003 between the government and the rebels. Deby has been president since 1990.

Chad's economic development suffers from its geographic remoteness, drought, lack of infrastructure, and political instability. In 2004, Chad's nominal gross domestic product (GDP) was estimated at $10.6 billion with per capita income at approximately $1.2, which makes the country one of the poorest in Africa, even poorer than Rwanda. Traditionally, Chad's economic performance has been very dependent on fluctuations in rainfall and in prices of its principal export commodities, especially cotton, the major export product (40% of total exports in 1999). Cattle and gum (Arabic) are also exported. More than 80% of the workforce is involved in agriculture (subsistence farming, herding, and fishing, especially in Lake Chad).

Recently, oil fields have been discovered in the South. The Doba Basin oil project will pump oil from reserves in Chad through an underground pipeline to coastal Cameroon. This is supposed to stimulate major investments into Chad, and it is expected to double government tax revenues.

Chad has been highly dependent on foreign assistance, being one of the most indebted poor countries in the world. In 2002, 65% of the GDP were imports, while exports only reached 12%. This unbalance has traditionally been financed through more debts.

Infrastructure, education, and health systems were not consistently developed during the last fifty years due to the long and devastating civil war and also due to the lack of economic resources.

As for Chad's infrastructure, it is largely undeveloped in the country. There are no railroads and no ports. Its telecommunications system, as well as its water, electricity, and gas providing facilities, are almost nonexistent. All this affects the population, whose living conditions are not good. The population living under the poverty line in 2001 was estimated at 80%. The general life expectancy at birth did, however, improve in the last thirty years, passing from an alarming thirty-nine years in 1970 to forty-four years in 2002 (UNDP 2004), but this number is still very low. In the United Nations Human Development Index (HDI) (2004), Chad was listed among the last countries of the list. The infant mortality rate was estimated at ninety-four per one thousand live births, a high number, which is the result of poor health care.

Since independence in the 1960s, the Chad government has tried to extend the health care system. With foreign aid, new medical facilities have been built, and many health care professionals have been trained. The public system had improved, but since the 1995 liberal reforms, a system of payment for treatment and medicine has been introduced that benefits only those who can afford it. This has resulted in a higher standard of health care for private people but not for the poor. Besides, the government's public health expenditure is only 2% of the gross domestic income (GDI), which makes it even harder to improve the

conditions. As a result, infectious and parasitic diseases are a constant problem, tuberculosis is common, and AIDS is on the increase; outbreaks of cholera and meningitis have occurred, and the guinea worm and malaria are also a constant problem.

The education system was largely damaged during the war, with the results of a present adult literacy rate of only 45% and more than 60% of women illiterate. The primary enrollment ratio was 58% in 2001, but the secondary enrollment ratio was only 8% in that same year. Most girls do not attend school.

DIEGO I. MURGUÍA

See also Central Africa: History and Economic Development; Central Africa: International Relations; Ethnic Conflicts: Central Africa

References and Further Reading

Azevedo, Mario J. *Roots of Violence: A History of War in Chad.* Amsterdam: Gordon and Breach, 1998.

Azevedo, Mario J., and Emmanuel U. Nnadozie. *Chad: A Nation in Search of Its Future.* Boulder, CO: Westview Press, 1998.

Burr, J. Millard, and Robert O. Collins. *Africa's Thirty Years' War: Libya, Chad, and the Sudan, 1963–1993.* Boulder, CO: Westview Press, 1999.

Colello, Thomas. *Chad. A Country Study.* Washington, DC: US Government Office, 1990.

Foltz, William J. *Chad's Third Republic: Strengths, Problems, and Prospects.* (CSIS Africa Notes, No. 77). Washington, DC: Center for Strategic and International Studies, 1987.

Kelley, Michael P. *A State in Disarray: Conditions of Chad's Survival.* Boulder, CO: Westview Press, 1986.

Nolutshungu, Sam C. *Limits of Anarchy: Intervention and State Formation in Chad.* Charlottesville, VA: University Press of Virginia, 1996.

United Nations Development Program (UNDP). *Human Development Report 2004. Cultural Liberty in Today's Diverse World.* New York: Hoechstetter Printing, 2004: http://hdr.undp.org

CHÁVEZ, HUGO

Hugo Rafael Chávez Frías, born July 28, 1954, became president of Venezuela in 1998. Chávez became widely known in 1992, when, as a former paratrooper and graduate in military sciences, he headed a failed military attempt to topple the government of President Carlos Andrés Pérez. After two years of imprisonment, Chávez emerged as the leader of a new political party, the Movement for the Fifth Republic. Breaking the stranglehold of a discredited party system that had dominated Venezuelan politics since 1958, Chávez ran for the presidency in 1998 and won by the largest percentage of voters (56.2%) in four decades. He pledged to eradicate corruption, reform the public sector, and expand opportunities for the poor.

Upon taking office in early 1999, Chávez embarked upon what he referred to as his "Bolivarian Revolution," named after Venezuela's hero of independence, Simon Bólivar. Without legislative consultation, Chávez suspended Congress and authorized the rewriting of the Venezuelan Constitution. The new constitution contained far-reaching reforms, extending to all Venezuelan citizens the rights of health, welfare, and political expression. At the same time, it increased the power of the president and extended the presidential term of office.

In a show of widespread support from Venezuela's impoverished majority, Chávez supporters won roughly 60% of the seats in the 2000 local assembly elections. In the same year, Chávez consolidated all Venezuelan labor unions into a single, state-controlled Bolivarian Labor Force.

Chávez's policies were met with increasing hostility from many in the middle and upper classes. Controversial economic measures that he instituted in 2001 gave rise to mass protests and strikes. An alliance of opponents from the military, business, and media sectors brought about a *coup d'état* on April 12, 2002. Within forty-eight hours, Chávez was reinstated after the post-*coup* government collapsed in the face of rebellion by loyalist troops and massive protests. The event generated widespread uprisings both in support of, and in opposition to, Chávez. Social chaos and violence were repressed by the metropolitan police. The overthrow was condemned by the leaders of Latin American states and international organizations.

Pressure intensified in 2002 and 2003. After a prolonged general strike led by the management of Venezuela's oil company, PDVSA, Chávez replaced the managers and consolidated control of the state company. Having secured the state oil enterprise, Chávez shifted oil revenues toward welfare programs. These actions provoked criticism against Chávez from domestic as well as international sources.

Chávez's government has aroused as much dissent as it has loyal support. His strongest backing comes from the impoverished rural and urban workers who make up Venezuela's majority (an estimated 80%). The privileged upper-middle and upper classes regard his government policies as Socialist and authoritarian. This last group, less numerous but more affluent and powerful, organized a four-day petitioning drive to bring about a recall referendum. The referendum, which was supervised by an international oversight committee, took place on August 15, 2004. Chávez was the undisputed victor.

JANET M. CHERNELA

See also Venezuela

References and Further Reading

Blanco, Carlos. *Revolución y Desilusión: La Venezuela de Hugo Chavez.* Caracas, Venezuela: Los Libros de la Catarata, 2002.
Wilpert, Gregory. *The Rise and Fall of Hugo Chavez: The Revolution and Counter-Revolution in Venezuela.* Zed Books, 2004.

CHIANG CHING-KUO

Chiang Ching-kuo, Chiang Kai-shek's son, is often credited for the "Taiwan miracle" of the 1970s, when Taiwan achieved a 13% growth rate, $4,600 per capita income, and the world's second largest foreign currency reserves.

Born in Zhejiang Province, China, on March 18, 1910, Chiang Ching-kuo went to Moscow in 1925 to study the Soviet social and economic system. He was sent to Siberia after his father adopted anti-Communist stances in the Nationalist Party (KMT) but was eventually allowed by Stalin to return to China with his Russian wife in 1937. From 1938–1941, he held various high-level political posts in the Jiangxi Province, where he implemented public works and development projects. Chiang fought in World War II and the subsequent civil war with the Communists, making several important military decisions, before following his father to Taiwan in 1949.

Chiang held a series of important posts in Taiwan. He was director of secret police from 1950 to 1965, minister of defense from 1965 to 1969, vice premier from 1969 to 1972, and premier from 1972 to 1978. In 1978, he succeeded his father as president, a post he held until his death in 1988. He was involved in the economic development of Taiwan throughout his career. From 1955 to 1960, he worked on planning and construction of the Central Cross-Island Highway. He chaired the Council for International Economic Cooperation and Development (CIECD) from 1967 to 1973. As president, he strongly supported the work of economic ministries and agencies, including CIECD's successor, the Council for Economic Planning and Development (CEPD), and the Chinese External Trade Development Council. The fiscal policies of his economic technocracy, as well as the institutions they created, contributed to Taiwan's export-oriented development.

Chiang was the driving force behind the Ten Major Construction Projects and Twelve New Development Projects of the 1970s, many of which were extensions of Japanese infrastructure projects of the 1930s. The ten projects were seven infrastructure projects, including the Chiang Kai-shek International

Airport, a freeway, two railways, and a nuclear power plant as well as three heavy industrial projects of an integrated steel mill, a petrochemical complex, and a large shipyard. The twelve projects included infrastructure projects and expansion of the steel mill. By 1983, government ownership of industry had increased to 19%. In Chiang's second term as president from 1984 to 1988, he also completed the Fourteen Major Construction Projects. These projects provided the upstream materials and infrastructure needed for the expansion of the many small and medium enterprises that dotted the Taiwanese countryside, contributing to a legacy of growth with equity.

In contrast to his more autocratic father, Chiang Ching-kuo was somewhat of a populist, often emphasizing his close friendship with Taiwanese people. Throughout the last years of his life, he oversaw important changes in Taiwan's political environment. In 1987, he permitted people from Taiwan to travel to China, eventually making it possible for Taiwanese private investment there. In the same year, he also lifted martial law, lightened restrictions on newspapers, and permitted the creation of opposition political parties, albeit only after strong pressure from human rights activists. Some people in Taiwan thus remember him for laying the foundation of Taiwan's later democratization. When he died in 1988, he was succeeded by Lee Teng-hui, the first native Taiwanese president of the Republic of China.

SCOTT E. SIMON

See also Chiang Kai-shek; China, People's Republic of; Taiwan

References and Further Reading

Leng, Shao Chuan. *Chiang Ching-kuo's Leadership in the Development of the Republic of China on Taiwan*. Lanham, MD: University Press of America, 1993.
Rubenstein, Murray A., ed. *Taiwan: A New History*. Armonk, NY: M.E. Sharpe, 1999.
Taylor, Jay. *The Generalissimo's Son: Chiang Ching-kuo and the Revolutions in China and Taiwan*. Cambridge, MA: Harvard University Press, 2000.
Wade, Robert. *Governing the Market: Economic Theory and the Role of Government in East Asian Industrialization*. Princeton, NJ: Princeton University Press, 1990.

CHIANG KAI-SHEK

Chiang Kai-shek was a central figure in the history of China and Taiwan. Born in the Zhejiang Province on October 31, 1887, he studied at the National Military Academy in China and then the Military Staff College in Tokyo, where he met Sun Yat-sen and joined his United Revolutionary League, forerunner of the Chinese Nationalist Party (KMT). In 1923 and 1924, he traveled in the Soviet Union to study the political and economic system and to seek its aid. After Sun's death in 1925, Chiang assumed the three leadership positions of the Republic of China (ROC): president of the republic, KMT party chairman (which he purged of Communists), and commander of the armed forces. In 1926 through 1927, he led the Northern Expedition against recalcitrant warlords and unified China. In 1927, he married Soong Mei-ling, whose powerful banking family provided skills and resources important to economic development.

The ideological underpinnings of economic development in the ROC were based on Sun Yat-sen's Three Principles of the People: democracy, nationalism, and peoples' livelihood. From 1927 to 1937, the KMT implemented an economic development program in the Yangtze Valley, mostly concentrating on technical improvement rather than structural changes in land ownership. Although Sun had called for land-to-the-tiller land reform, Chiang was unable to implement such a policy due to landlord resistance. After the 1937 Japanese invasion and battles with Mao Zedong's Communist forces, he had to concentrate on defense. Chiang eventually lost China, partly because he relied on landlord support for his rule and was resented among the peasantry.

At the end of World War II, the Allies gave Japan's colony of Taiwan to the ROC. When the Communist Party took China in 1949, Chiang was forced to move to Taiwan, which became the only territory under his control. In Taiwan, he inherited a strong base for economic development. Under Japanese administration from 1895 to 1945, Taiwan had developed an infrastructure of ports, highways, and railroads as well as universal education. Modern agricultural development had already made Taiwan into a major producer of sugar, rice, tea, and other foodstuffs.

As the leader of a one-party state, Chiang ruled Taiwan with an iron fist. Fiercely opposed to both Communism and Taiwanese self-determination, he used the military to violently suppress Taiwanese protests in 1947 and began a period of martial law that would last forty years. Cowered by state violence, Taiwanese landlords had no choice but to comply with a "land-to-the-tiller" Land Reform of 1953. That reform laid the base for widespread rural industrialization and relatively equitable income distribution.

With the United States's support, Chiang promoted industrial development, giving technocrats control of the economy. After the outbreak of the Korean War, the United States began a massive program of economic and military aid to Taiwan, including monetary support, provision of development advisors, and preferred market access for Taiwanese products. In the 1960s, Taiwan began export-oriented industrialization, focusing initially on textiles, chemicals, machinery, and consumer goods. In 1965, Asia's first export-processing zone (EPZ) was established in Kaohsiung. This and subsequent EPZ developments secured Taiwan's place as an important subcontractor in an international division of labor. By the early 1970s, Taiwan was exporting capital goods and foreign aid to Southeast Asia. Chiang remained president of the Republic of China in Taiwan until his death of a heart attack in Taipei on April 5, 1975, and the reins of power passed to his son Chiang Ching-kuo.

SCOTT E. SIMON

See also Chiang Ching-kuo; China, People's Republic of; Chinese Revolution; Taiwan

References and Further Reading

Crozier, Brian. *The Man Who Lost China: The First Full Biography of Chiang Kai-shek*. New York: Scribner, 1976.
Fenby, Jonathan. *Chiang Kai-shek: China's Generalissimo and the Nation He Lost*. New York: Carroll and Graf, 2004.
Payne, Robert. *Chiang Kai-shek*. New York: Weybright and Talley, 1969.
Rubenstein, Murray A., ed. *Taiwan: A New History*. Armonk, NY: M.E. Sharpe, 1999.

CHILDREN AND DEVELOPMENT

The construction of modern ideas about the child began in Euro-American ways of thinking about childhood during the Enlightenment period in the nineteenth and twentieth centuries. The new view of the child as an efficient, autonomous, and flexible being became institutionalised in professional arenas dedicated to caring for children, such as child welfare, schooling and education, social policy, social work, child psychiatry, as well as an array of public institutions. Although contemporary and powerful Euro-American ideas about the child are now dispersed globally in formal education, and by means of discourses and images transmitted by the international media, many cross-cultural researchers are noting that their impact is restricted by indigenous customs and local ways of being, a number of which also provide counter-narratives to Western ideas about the child.

In Euro-American societies, images of the child display the psychological and social effort that is required to maintain the clear distinction between adult and child that is important to Western societies. The clear distinction works to separate childhood from the social ideals and behaviours that constitute being adult. Dual and opposing categories of child and adult are established and maintained in a conceptual dichotomy that, many social scientists argue, does not take into account most children's actual continuity of growth and development. As a consequence, the notion of childhood as a pure and uncontaminated socially constructed category is inadequate to encompass and understand children's work, child sex work, and child soldiers at war, activities in which many children perform resolutely unchildlike actions.

Images that constitute notions of the child and childhood also become significant when linked to conceptualising, designing, and planning development projects. Images of impoverished children are used to encourage relatively wealthy Euro-American donors to contribute to development agencies' work in war zones or with profoundly impoverished peoples. But all three notions of child, childhood, and development have been severely critiqued when applied across cultures. Changes in global social and political frameworks since the 1980s have dramatically reshaped the daily lives of women, men, and children in the developing world. As active agents, they have become increasingly integrated into global production and consumption processes, the social and cultural effects of which have been multiple, contradictory, inclusive, and exclusive. When the implications of globalisation across cultures and at the grass roots in developing countries are examined, the very specific effects of increased global integration on children in developing countries become apparent. Therefore, many cross-cultural researchers now maintain that the ways in which children in developing countries negotiate complex and rapid changes in diverse and contrasting circumstances must be examined and theorised.

Despite the OECD's (2003:27) claim that the impact of globalisation is not significant, many social scientists argue that it must be considered. Globalisation is not a new phenomenon because children have always been impacted by conquest, slavery, and emigration. However, in the twenty-first century, due to the variety of encounters between different societies, many definitions of globalisation now exist. A useful working definition, according to Kaufman *et al.* (2001), is that globalisation is a process that opens nation states to many influences that originate beyond their borders. In applying this definition, an examination of the ways in which globalisation as a process impacts upon children's lived experiences and how children may be encouraged to be participants in a globalised world is made available. For example, the increased level of global consensus on children's rights, as reflected in the Convention on the Rights of the Child (CRC), has great potential for supporting the work of child advocates, including children and youth themselves. Since the mid-1980s, the United Nations International Children's Emergency Fund (UNICEF) has given more attention to child protection as an element of children's rights concomitant with its key interests in child survival, health, and well-being. The Commonwealth Secretariat is focusing on human rights for women and female children, concentrating on the human immunodeficiency virus (HIV) and acquired immune deficiency syndrome (AIDS) issues, violence against women and female children, and the promotion of human rights through the Commonwealth Secretariat judiciary.

An examination of the wide-ranging impacts of globalisation and the ways that local peoples negotiate and constitute its processes suggest that a precise definition of development is problematic. In Euro-American discourse, "development" initially implied notions of positive change or progress and, following World War II, became associated with ideas of resource extraction and institutionalizing and improving national economic growth. Hence, development was measured by indicators such as the gross domestic product (GDP) or health care access figures and was perceived as synonymous with planned social change. In the 1990s, however, development was subject to ideas that incorporated notions of processualisation, transmogrified into the developing world, and was attributed different and disputed meanings.

Earlier concepts of development were characterized by ideologies associated with evolution and were strongly linked to processes of colonization. Citizens of developed nations often believed in the inherent superiority of their economies, societies, and technologies compared to those deemed to be enduring rudimentary or low-level technology. The sociopolitical ideals of Euro-American nation-states were to help Asian, African, and South American peoples to model their societies on the industrialized nations. As a consequence, economists were initially and, to some extent, still retain their power as principal theorists of development.

Development projects, however, have often failed because the Euro-American discourse of progress is a powerful and globally institutionalized ideology that, many political theorists argue, is immune from criticism. They also maintain that in globalising world markets, technology and knowledge are commodities that must be sold. More significantly, they contend, development has often proved counterproductive and has worsened people's lived experiences in remote and grass-root communities because the multiple interests of stakeholders concerning development projects have not been acknowledged. As mutual understanding between developer and local people was rarely a goal, indigenous and local people's knowledge was frequently dismissed or ignored in favour of more powerful Western scientific discourses and practices. Political theorists also contend that powerful social and economic elites in developing countries willingly rejected the knowledge of socially and politically disadvantaged peoples, and, where and if local knowledge was recognized, it was incorporated only in situations where Western science could profit by its use. Because project designers did not always recognize that people in indigenous and local communities were capable of active human agency, they were often unaware of their different needs and goals or that people in indigenous and local communities may engage with the ideas of development and then reject development as unsuitable. Given such lack of understanding among powerful adults about the needs and priorities of indigenous and local adults across cultures, theorists argue, the many and varied needs of children situated in development ideologies, project designs, and implementation have generally been of little concern.

Child Labour and Development

Social scientists and cross-cultural researchers contend that a key dimension to any analysis of the link between children and development is that of child labour. While the dominant mood of much research into child labour is marked by indignation and feelings of compassion, quality studies portray how it is a complex phenomenon that varies considerably within and across countries. Most international authorities, such as UNICEF and the International Labour Organisation (ILO), define a "child" as a person below the age of sixteen; for certain types of hazardous or socially undesirable work, a minimum age of eighteen is stipulated. The concept of child labour is debated, with some researchers arguing that work undertaken by children below the specified age is exploitative and others arguing that labour is a right as long as performance does not harm the child's basic needs of nutrition, health, education, and recreation. UNICEF and the ILO propose child labour be tolerated during a transitional period of economic growth until eradication can be achieved.

Most studies of child labour link to children's schooling and focus on gender and urban/rural dimensions. Some studies are specific to a country. Those on Vietnam, for example, focus on the several and varied impacts of French colonization, regional differences, land reform, historical processes, institutional arrangements, and attitudinal differences to show how child labour is more accepted in northern Vietnam than in the southern part of the country and to aid the formulation of development policies. Other studies based in Europe subvert Euro-American perceptions of Europe (as a developed group of nations) in their examination of issues such as the Albanian economic crisis and its effects on children, particularly the rise in child labour, the loss of later-year schooling, and the assaults on prepubescent children by older armed teenage gangs.

Although most researchers contend that the majority of child labour in the developing world is found within family activity in rural areas, many authors provide details of other kinds of child labour, such as that of urban or street children. The parking boys of Kenya who clean and guard a driver's vehicle while the driver is absent are an example; other examples include the informal sector street vendors of peanuts, cigarettes, and pens in many African and Southeast Asian countries and those in most developing economies, who wash dishes in informal eating establishments such as kiosks and street or beach cafés.

Laws are often in place to severely restrict the labour of children, but researchers have noted that social and governmental attitudes, employers, parents, and children themselves contribute to its continuance. Connections between poverty and child labour exist, with children from the poorest areas and families tending to work at early ages, but it has also been argued that child labour may be a cause of poverty as well as a consequence. Child labour has been recognized as key to policy formation issues, but researchers allege that governments are reticent to recognize the problem, the public is insensitive to it, and many child labourers are socially and politically invisible. Nonetheless, while the expansion of world trade has raised many developing countries' GDP, and the absolute number of children living below the poverty line is decreasing, there is growing income inequality within and between many countries. And, while local cultures are adapting to and transforming global trends in local ways, local action on its own may not be sufficient to improve conditions when they are determined not just by a factory owner but also regional and international trade treaties and conventions. Although the relationship between income inequality and child labour at the macroeconomic level has been stressed, authors have recently argued that children are the prime actors who determine how they respond to rapid changes. They contend that the active agency of children also requires recognition because children frequently adapt more readily than parents and elders in their communities.

Nieuwenhuys (1994) clarifies how impoverished children engage in a range of activities that are seldom remunerated but are necessary to family livelihood. But work undertaken within a family context is rarely acknowledged as socially or economically meaningful, despite being the dominant form of labour in peasant and industrialized societies. Social and economic theorists have described how children are excluded from conceptualizations and analyses of the division of labour in Western industrialized countries. Rather, children are positioned ideologically and practically as serving their childhood in schools. Childhood has thus been scholarised in the industrialized West, and the proper relationships of children to adults are constituted as structurally and economically dependent. Furthermore, contemporary economic theorists argue that classical economic theory ignores children's unremunerated work within the family, as it is conceived as creating use value rather than the exchange value necessary to source profit and capital growth. In addition, analyses of children's unremunerated work encounter hostility from political and economic elites when scholars characterize it as exploitation. For these reasons, many researchers argue that child labour is too malleable because the term enables employers to use children without acknowledging their work. Some suggest the more inclusive children's work, as it encompasses any activity done by children that contributes to production, gives adults free time, the more their work facilitates the work of others, or substitutes for the employment of others. As many working activities have negative consequences for the children performing them, it then becomes essential to understand household decision-making processes, to devise multidimensional policy approaches, and to acknowledge the prime role of private responses, such as the potential for corporate social responsibility (OECD 2003).

Child Sex Work

The tourism and entertainment sector is considered to be a soft area of development, so it is not often analysed by economic or political theorists. However, in the latter decades of the twentieth century, the issue of child sex work became a key focus of research for cross-cultural and feminist researchers. They noted that much of the labour in accommodation and food provision occurs in the informal economy, is of diverse character, and involves multifarious minor transactions that are difficult to capture via research projects of limited duration or standard accounting procedures. Working conditions often involve lengthy tours of duty, job insecurity, low or no wages, minimal opportunity for collective or enterprise bargaining, and negligible or no occupational health and safety conditions. Low pay is exacerbated by apprentice or trainee positions, and payment of tips or commissions on food or beverages occurs only when sold. Labour conditions tend to favour children as their attractiveness and allure become important qualifications for work in hospitality and entertainment, and their economic vulnerability provides an easy pathway to the provision of commercialized sex. In addition, rapid urbanization, labour migration, and growing male unemployment have placed strain on customary patterns of family structure and female dependence and have driven unskilled girls into formal and informal sector work as maids, domestic servants, market and street vendors, bar girls, and waitresses. Female children often work in commercialized versions of socially acceptable domestic or marital roles such as cleaning, food preparation, care of younger children, and doing laundry. Nonetheless, a significant impact of their work is exposure to sexual opportunity, either through casual contact with customers or as a structured aspect of hospitality and entertainment duties.

Montgomery (2001) confronts the challenges presented by Western discourses of children's rights that presume such rights are universal in her analysis of child sex work in a slum community in northern Thailand. The limited life choices and survivalist pragmatism that inscribe young people's decisions in an environment inhibited by severe poverty are portrayed. While recognizing children's vulnerability, the discourse of children's rights is critiqued, as it is seen as rarely recognizing children as proud human agents who garner self-esteem, express love and filial duty, and struggle to make informed choices via practices designed to financially support their families. Other researchers similarly note that among rescued child sex workers under fourteen years of age in Thailand, the majority was uneducated and came from low-income families. Their working hours ranged from six hours to a full day, and they served three to fifteen customers daily. In rehabilitation centers, they were offered social and medical services and skills training for one year, but also endured severe discipline and social humiliation. As a consequence, many chose to return to the relative freedom and dignity of the streets.

Researchers of child sex work portray communities' perceptions that sex work is not harmful and that life is difficult for everyone. They note the importance of children's ties with their family and kin, describing how regular customers are incorporated into kin networks where they are perceived to fulfill kinship roles of reciprocity. Children also create status within their fragment of often profoundly hierarchical broader societies by indebting younger children through pimping activities, constructing rank via traditionally hierarchical relationships based on age, and, through the acquisition of money, wielding direct and indirect power in materialist microcultures where money and power are indistinguishable.

Data about children's work anchored in field research suggests that childhood be rethought in terms of the ways it functions as a permanent social category that contributes to the maintenance and advancement of particular global and local social orders that are patriarchal and hierarchal in nature. Governments in Sweden, Germany, and Australia have taken action to control the activities of nationals who engage in pedophilic activities in their home territory or abroad. Researchers note that countries such as Thailand and the Philippines, driven by the difficulties produced by rising HIV infection rates, have reviewed their legislation, taken steps toward law enforcement on behalf of sexually exploited children, and altered their Labour Code. Nonetheless, it is argued, without solving basic social and economic difficulties manifest in poverty, it is difficult to effectively translate laws into practical action.

Gender Differences

For the reasons just described, health issues for children in developing countries are significant. Apart from violence upon their person during their work activities, and malnutrition, key risk factors for child sex workers are contracting a sexually transmitted disease, including HIV; drug use to dull hunger and block the psychological and physical difficulties of street life; and for girls, pregnancy. Pregnancy is but one consideration of gender difference that is essential to any analysis of how children manage the impact of development. The social status of a child's male and female relatives and caregivers can vary dramatically so that issues of violence, gender roles, and discrimination are directly relevant to children's well-being. Although female children in developing countries are gaining educationally, they are less likely than boys to be enrolled in school, to be literate, or to attain a high level of education. UNICEF (1991) and AusAid note that discrimination against girl children is extensive, particularly in South Asia, and that forms of bonded labour and extensive trafficking in children exist throughout Southeast Asia.

Education is seen as an important factor for all children in developing countries but particularly for women and girls. For example, studies in India show that children of educated women are more likely to go to school, and the more schooling women receive, the more probable it is that their children will also benefit from education. Skills that female children acquire at school not only result in improved health outcomes for themselves and their children but also, eventually, for their grandchildren. Education also leads to more equitable development, stronger families, better services, and better child health; women who have been to school are less likely to die during childbirth. The costs and consequences of depriving girls of education are great as girls become particularly vulnerable to poverty and hunger and are at greater risk than boys of becoming infected with HIV/AIDS, of being sexually exploited, and being drawn into child trafficking.

The last decade of the twentieth century saw the narrowing of the gender gap in primary school enrollment globally. The ratio of girls' gross enrollment rate to the boys' rate in developing countries increased from 0.86 to 0.92. Girls' enrollment in nearly two-thirds of developing countries increased over the decade, with the biggest improvement seen in Benin, Chad, the Gambia, Guinea, Mali, Mauritania, Morocco, Nepal, Pakistan, and Sudan. In Morocco, the proportion of enrollment of girls in rural areas increased from 44.6% in 1997–1998 to 82.2% in 2002–2003. Yet, the primary school completion rate for girls lags way behind that of boys, at 76% compared with 85%. UNICEF (2004) reported that 83% of all girls out of school in the world live in Sub-Saharan Africa, South Asia, and East Asia and the Pacific.

Analyses of the social impact on female children of the Taliban regime in Afghanistan, from 1996 to 2001, note the Fundamentalist Islamic group made minimal investment in the country's welfare and development during its period of rule. Education was severely hindered, and girls were especially neglected and oppressed. Nonetheless, a 2001 report based on a survey of more than one thousand Afghan men and women living in Afghanistan and nearby refugee camps noted that more than 90% of respondents indicated strong support for the rights of Afghan women and overwhelmingly endorsed equal access for girls to education, freedom of expression, and legal protections for the rights of women and participation of women in government; this response suggests potential for improvement in the lived experiences of female children.

Current Emphases in Research

Current emphases in research on children and development are working to bridge the gap between knowledge about children's worlds and modes of being and those deemed to be part of adulthood. Many researchers now critically assess both boys' and girls' daily work within familial contexts and question why their work appears as morally neutral within an analytical framework of class, kinship, gender and household organisation, state ideologies, and education. Research is showing how children confront the challenges of combining education with home life and ongoing contributions to household income, how they balance the demands of adults, and how they live as children and contribute to global social interaction through local action.

Feminist groups are particularly critical of the phenomenon of female infanticide that, they argue, has accounted for millions of gender-selective deaths throughout history. They contend that it remains a critical concern in a number of developing countries, notably China and India, and that its continuance reflects the low status accorded to women generally and to female children in particular in many developed and developing countries. Infanticide is seen as closely linked to the phenomena of sex-selective abortion, which targets female fetuses almost exclusively and the overall neglect of girls.

Research is moving forward concerning children and development by moving beyond the conventional perspective of working to understand children's impoverishment solely at a particular point in time. Bradbury et al. (2001) are arguing for an examination of children's movements into and out of poverty, in addition to conventional modes of analysis. The adverse impact on an individual child's living standards of being poor depends on past poverty; that is, those who have been poor for an extensive period are likely to be more deeply impoverished than those who are newly poor, as families' financial and skill capacities are depleted over time. A child's accumulated poverty history also advises whether impoverishment is concentrated among a small group of children or is widely shared, and length of time in poverty has effects on adulthood via development and future life chances.

Another innovation in research about children and development suggests including children and childhood within sociological and development thinking to ensure children are recognized and accepted as participant agents in social relations and that childhood is understood in terms of its relation to adulthood. Proposals that scholars can learn from children about the gaps and lack of fit between their experiences and their positioning in the social order, often taken for granted by adults, are offered, as are suggestions that children's social status must be raised and an arena for consideration of their rights and responsibilities be provided because children are embedded in societies and therefore in economies, governments, and cultures. A clear critique has been mounted of the concept of child labour as inadequate to analyse much of the work performed by children in rural societies because it assumes an immature human being exposed to a certain type of undesirable activity rather than an exploration of the activities undertaken by children, as well as their variety and their valuation. A further critique of research on children's work in rural societies exists, with arguments that such work has seriously suffered from the use of *a priori* judgments about which activities are suitable for children and that judgments are made on the basis of moral considerations introduced by colonial powers and initially reflected in their child labour legislation. Researchers and development planners are urged therefore to value the everyday work activities performed by children in their varied rural and urban settings and to incorporate children's needs and concerns into development planning.

HELEN JOHNSON

See also Basic Human Needs; Globalization: Impact on Development; Labor; Women: Role in Development; Sex Trade/Trafficking

References and Further Reading

Black, Maggie. *In the Twilight Zone: Child Workers in the Hotel, Tourism, and Catering Industry*. Geneva: International Labour Office, 1995.
———. *Combating Child Labour: A Review of Policies*. Paris: OECD, 2003.
Bradbury, Bruce, Stephen Jenkins, and John Micklewright. *The Dynamics of Child Poverty in Industrialised Countries*. UNICEF and Cambridge: University of Cambridge Press, 2001.
Deolalikar, Anil. *Poverty, Growth, and Inequality in Thailand*. Manila, Philippines: Asian Development Bank, 2002.
Escobar, Arturo. *Encountering Development: The Making and Unmaking of the Third World*. Princeton, NJ: Princeton University Press, 1995.
Gardner, Katy, and David Lewis. *Anthropology, Development, and the Postmodern Challenge*. Chicago: Pluto Press, 1996.
Hobart, Mark, ed. "Introduction: The Growth of Ignorance?" *An Anthropological Critique of Development: The Growth of Ignorance*. London: Routledge, 1993.
Kaufman, Natalie, and Irene Rizzini, eds. *Globalisation and Children: Exploring Potentials for Enhancing Opportunities in the Lives of Children and Youth*. New York: Kluwer Academic/Plenum Publishers, 2002.
Kloep, Marion. "When Parents Discuss the Price of Bread: Albanian Children and the Economic Crisis." In *Troubling Children: Studies of Children and Social Problems*, J. Best ed. New York: Aldine de Gruyter, 1994.
Mayall, Berry. *Towards a Sociology for Childhood: Thinking from Children's Lives*. Buckingham, Philadelphia, PA: Open University Press, 2002.
Montgomery, Heather. *Modern Babylon?: Prostituting Children in Thailand*. New York, Berghahn Books, 2001.
Nieuwenhuys, Olga. *Children's Lifeworlds: Gender, Welfare, and Labour in the Developing World*. London and New York: Routledge, 1994.
Pottier, Johan, Alan Bicker, and Paul Sillitoe, eds. *Negotiating Local Knowledge*. London: Pluto Press, 2003.
Seabrook, Jeremy. *Travels in the Skin Trade: Tourism and the Sex Industry*, 2d ed. London: Pluto Press, 2001.
UNICEF. *The State of the World's Children 2004: Girls, Education, and Development*. Section for Development Programmes for Women, Programme Division. New York: UNICEF, 2004.

CHILE

Geography and Population

The Republic of Chile lies on the western coast of South America and stretches approximately 2,600 miles north to south and 90 miles east to west. At 292,258 square miles, it is nearly twice the size of California. The desert in the north of the country, bordering Peru and Bolivia, contains great mineral wealth (copper, nitrates, timber, iron ore), while the fertile central area is rich in terms of population and agricultural resources. Forests, grazing lands, volcanoes, lakes, canals, peninsulas, and islands dominate southern Chile. Its Andean mountains border with Argentina on the east.

In 2004, Chile's population numbered 15.8 million, 85% of which live in urban centers, primarily (40%) in the country's capital, Santiago. Most of the population has Spanish ancestry, but there are also a significant number of Irish, English, and German descendants of the colonial and postcolonial period. About eight hundred thousand Mapuche Indians, who were ruthlessly repressed by the Chilean governments of the nineteenth century, live in the south-central area.

Approximately 6 million Chileans form the active population, out of which 5.5 million are employed (2003) in services (63%), industry (23%), and agriculture (14%). Unemployment (9.4% in May–July 2004) still poses a serious problem for modern Chile.

Education is compulsory until the age of twelve, and the adult literacy rate is 96%. The majority of Chileans (89%) are Roman Catholic. The Catholic Church, as well as freemasonry, has played an important role in the political, social, and cultural life of Chile.

Historical Overview

From the mid-1500s until 1810, Chile was under the rule of the Spanish crown. The revolt that led to Chile's independence brought little social change. The War of the Pacific with Peru and Bolivia (1879–1883) enabled the young republic to expand its territory northward and to acquire valuable nitrate deposits that, together with other mineral and agricultural exports, led to significant economic growth. This era of national affluence and the establishment of a parliamentary-style democracy in the late nineteenth century served principally the interests of the ruling oligarchy, who were represented by the conservative and liberal parties.

The interwar period witnessed the rise of the middle and working classes. Marxist parties and a middle-class centrist party, the *Partido Radical*, were founded with strong popular support. The Radicals, in a coalition with the Socialists and Communists, dominated Chilean politics from the mid-1930s until 1952. This was a period of increased state intervention in the economy, increased industrial production, and overall economic growth but also of inflation and economic dependence on the United States. American copper companies were able to manipulate Chilean copper production and prices while resisting tax increases. As a result, the Chilean leftist parties became highly critical of the policy pursued by their coalition partners of the *Partido Radical*. The disillusion with the economic policy of the Radicals, who seemed incapable of establishing sound noninflationary economic growth and of transferring the benefits of the industrial and economic growth to larger segments of the Chilean population, led to the end of the Radical era in 1952.

The succeeding government, however, led by the old dictator Carlos Ibañez until 1958, did not restore the power of the traditional political elite. On the contrary, the reforms of the electoral system during his presidency extended the franchise to a larger segment of the Chilean adult population and made voting both secret and compulsory. It also dictated stronger penalties for electoral fraud or bribery; weakened the power of the oligarchy; and enabled Marxists, Christian Democrats (from the *Partido Demócrata Cristiano*, formally established in 1957), Radicals, and other parties to gain popularity in various regions of the country. Furthermore, Ibañez allowed the Communists—who had been outlawed in 1948—to return to national politics and facilitate the organization of workers. At the same time, this permitted them to form, together with the Socialist party, a new leftist coalition called *Frente de Acción Popular*.

From 1958 until 1973, rightist and leftist political parties alternated in Chilean official institutions. None of them were able, however, to tackle the fundamental economic problems of Chile. Throughout the 1930s and 1950s, the Chilean governments pursued a policy of state intervention to create import substitution industries, but they failed to reform the regressive tax system, making them, consequently, heavily reliant on deficit financing and foreign borrowing.

As elsewhere in the world, the 1960s were a period during which radical and revolutionary ideas flourished. For Chile, this was also a period of growing polarization among the Chilean population. In 1964, the Christian Democrat Eduardo Frei won the popular vote for the presidency with his campaign "Revolution in Liberty." Frei embarked on far-reaching social and economic reforms, without, however, endangering the capitalist economic system. In light of Castroite fear following the Cuban Revolution of 1959, the Frei administration was viewed by many observers abroad as the best alternative to a Marxist-dominated Chile. By 1967, however, Frei encountered increasing opposition from the parties of the Chilean Left and radical elements within his own Christian Democratic party. They considered Frei's reforms inadequate. Society in Chile was divided between those urging for deeper changes and those wanting to prevent radical transformations.

The end of the 1960s witnessed a further radicalization of the Chilean Left. Salvador Allende, a member of the Socialist party and leader of the *Unidad Popular*—a coalition of Socialists, Communists, Radicals, and dissident Christian Democrats—won the presidential election of 1970. Allende wanted to build a Socialist society by legal means. His program included structural reforms such as nationalization of private industries and banks, agrarian reforms to destroy the *hacienda* system, and strengthening of the political and economic power of workers. But Allende's "Road to Socialism" was soon confronted with the United States's CIA-backed opposition of political parties on the Chilean Right, private enterprises, a large segment within the army and the US government led by Richard Nixon, who were all mistrustful of the Chilean authorities. The economic recession of the 1960s continued into the 1970s (with the exception of the first year of Allende's government) and contributed to the growing opposition to the *Unidad Popular* government.

The social unrest in the early 1970s brought the Chilean military into the political arena. In September 1973, a military *coup d'état* led by General Augusto Pinochet overthrew Allende, and in December 1974, Pinochet declared himself President of Chile. The militaries had neither a clear political nor economic policy. Their only clear political program was the "depoliticization" of Chilean society, which meant the repression of supporters of Allende's Socialist project and the military control of virtually all important national institutions, to guarantee stability and economic growth. Massive human rights abuses were justified by the doctrine of "national security." The national committees set up by the civil governments in the 1990s to examine human rights violations committed by the military regime reported approximately three thousand killings or disappearances and many more victims of torture, persecution, prison, and exile.

After 1973, trade unions and political parties of the Left were severely oppressed by the militaries, but resistance to the Pinochet regime never died out entirely. The economic collapse of 1982–1983 led to the rise of open opposition to the regime. General Augusto Pinochet remained in power until 1988, after being denied a second term of presidency by a plebiscite (provided by the 1980 Constitution in which the Chileans expressed their desire to organize presidential elections). The Christian Democrats Patricio Aylwin and Eduardo Frei Ruiz, leading a seventeen-party coalition, the *Concertación de los Partidos por la Democracia*, governed the country from 1990 until 1999. The elections of January 2000 brought Ricardo Lagos, of the Socialist party and leader of the *Concertación*, to the presidency of Chile for a six-year term.

Socioeconomic Development of the Last Decades

Following the rough economic postwar period, the 1973–1990 military government pursued for the first time in the history of Chile a rigid free market economic model, drawn by the so-called Chicago Boys, a group of economists trained at the *Universidad Católica* in Santiago and the University of Chicago. This neo-liberal model contained three main objectives: (i) economic liberalization to increase the role of markets; (ii) reversion of the state-interventionist trend (prevailing in Chile since the interwar period) and privatization of state-owned companies; and (iii) stabilization of inflation. Chile committed itself to free trade, welcomed large amounts of foreign investment, and limited the government's role in the economy to regulation.

Market-oriented economic policies were continued and strengthened by post-Pinochet governments. In contrast to other Latin American countries, the Chilean economy grew at an impressive rate in the period between 1987 and 1997, reaching a 7% growth in real gross domestic product (GDP). This impressive economic growth declined in 1998 because of tight monetary policies (implemented to keep the current account deficit in check), lower export earnings (a product of global financial crisis), and a severe drought that reduced crop yields and caused hydroelectric shortfalls and electricity rationing. By 2003, exports and economic activity showed clear signs of recovery, and growth rebounded to 3.3% in real GDP. Experts expect a GDP growth of around 5% in 2004 and 2005, as copper prices, exports earnings, and foreign investment increase.

The World Economic Forum's 2004 Competitiveness Rankings shows that Chile has not only improved its position (ranked twenty-second, compared to twenty-eighth in 2003), but it continues to be the most competitive economy in Latin America. Foreign investors are also attracted to Chile because of its high quality of life: low-cost, high-standard housing; well-known international private schools; and relatively low criminality rates compared to other Latin American countries.

Chile is traditionally an export economy, particularly dependent on its copper exports. The state-owned firm CODELCO is the world's largest copper-producing company. Other important non-mineral exports are wood products, fruit, processed food, fish, paper products, and wine. In 2003, Chile's largest export markets were Asia (30.8%), Europe (24.4%), and North America (23.7%). It also imported consumer goods, chemicals, motor vehicles, fuels, electrical machinery, and heavy industrial machinery from its major suppliers in 2003: Argentina (20.3%), the European Union (17%), United States (13.6%), Brazil (10.1%), and China (6.9%).

Successive Chilean governments concluded free trade agreements with commercial partners in the Western Hemisphere, the European Union, Japan, and South Korea, among others, to promote export-led growth. In June 2003, Chile and the United States signed an ambitious trade agreement that will lead to completely duty free bilateral trade within twelve years. Chile has also been a leading proponent of the Free Trade Area of the Americas (FTAA).

According to the United Nations Development Programme, Chile has been highly successful in reducing poverty since the end of the Pinochet regime. The share of Chileans with incomes below the poverty line—defined as twice the cost of satisfying a person's minimal nutritional needs—fell from 45% in 1987 to 18.8% in 2003, while the rate of indigents (those living in extreme poverty, not being able to cover the minimal nutritional needs) fell from 17.4% to 5.7% in the same period. Unemployment—which rose from 4.4% in 1970 to 1973 to 30.4% in 1983—has declined steadily from the mid-1980s (6.2% in 1997). During the last decades, the Chilean governments have also increased subsidies for education and housing and have made considerable achievements in key social indicators such as infant mortality, life expectancy, and women's labor market participation. However, some analysts criticize the highly "economicist" approach in the studies of Chile and Latin America, in general, as well as the official statistical methods used to measure poverty. The Chilean economy has made strong economic gains since the mid-1980s, but not all Chileans have taken part in this boom. The unemployment rate rose in the late 1990s and remains stubbornly high in the first years of the new millennium (9.4% in May–July 2004). A World Bank study on inequality (2004) reported that Latin America and the Caribbean show higher rates of socioeconomic disparity than other regions in the world. If Chile differs from other Latin American countries when it comes to economic growth and competitiveness, it does not when it comes to income distribution. Social inequality in Chile remains high by international standards. The Gini index—a statistical measure of inequality in which zero expresses complete equality and one hundred total inequality—for Chile increased from fifty-four in the 1990s to fifty-seven in 2004. Especially, Chileans of indigenous origin represent a group of concern. Indigenous people are 56% more likely to live in poverty, receive half the income of nonindigenous people, and have 2.2 years less schooling. World Bank reports on education also highlight that—despite the higher social spending and despite the fact that a vast majority of Chileans has access to public education—the lingering gap between the performance of private and public schools and schools in urban and rural areas still calls for a solution.

MAGALY RODRÍGUEZ GARCÍA

See also Allende Gossens, Salvador; Pinochet Ugarte, Augusto; Southern Cone Common Market (MERCOSUR); Southern Cone (Latin America): History and Economic Development; Southern Cone (Latin America): International Relations

References and Further Reading

Bethell, Leslie, ed. *Chile Since Independence*. New York: Cambridge University Press, 1993.

Collier, Simon, and William F. Sater. *A History of Chile, 1808–2002*. New York: Cambridge University Press, 2004.

De Ferranti, David, Perry Guillermo, H. G. Ferreira Francisco, and Michael Walton. *Inequality in Latin America and the Caribbean: Breaking with History?* Washington, D.C.: The World Bank, 2004 (http://lnweb18.worldbank.org/LAC/LAC.nsf/ECADocByUnid/4112F1114F594B4B85256DB3005DB262?Opendocument).

Ensalco, Mark. *Chile Under Pinochet. Recovering the Truth*. Philadelphia, PA: University of Pennsylvania Press, 2000.

French-Davis, Ricardo. *Economic Reforms in Chile. From Dictatorship to Democracy*. Ann Arbor, MI: University of Michigan Press, 2002.

Garretón, Manuel Antonio. *Incomplete Democracy. Political Democratization in Chile and Latin America*. Chapel Hill, NC: University of North Carolina Press, 2003.

Hickman, John. *News from the End of the Earth. A Portrait of Chile*. New York: St. Martin's Press, 1998

Loveman, Brian. *Chile. The Legacy of Hispanic Capitalism*. New York: Oxford University Press, 2001.

Oppenheim, Lois Hecht. *Politics in Chile. Democracy, Authoritarianism, and the Search for Development*. Boulder, CO: Westview Press, 1993.

Sigmund, Paul E. *The United States and Democracy in Chile*. Baltimore, MD: Johns Hopkins University Press, 1993.

CHINA: CULTURAL REVOLUTION

During the early 1960s, the leadership of China fell to Deng Xiaoping and Liu Shaoqi, both of whom were longtime and important members of the Chinese Communist Party (CCP). Both favored a more pragmatic and bureaucratic approach to social and economic development and moved quickly to restore order in China through a centralized network of administration under CCP control. Under the leadership of Liu and Deng, Chinese industry and agriculture achieved a range of new successes in increased productivity and improved stability. But the CCP and the centralized agencies that directed this expansion of the Chinese economy grew rapidly and created a new bureaucratic elite that increasingly assumed the lifestyle and mannerisms of a privileged class.

Mao Zedong's great displeasure with the "right opportunist line" of the CCP under the leadership of Deng and Liu prompted him to initiate what he called the Great Proletarian Cultural Revolution in 1966. Mao's call for "continuing revolution" was supported by Lin Biao, the commander of the People's Liberation Army (PLA), and a group of leftists centered on Mao's wife, Jiang Qing. Among these were the so-called Gang of Four, which included Jiang and three young politicians from Shanghai: Zhang Chunqiao, Wang Hongwen, and Yao Wenyuan. In general, Mao was supported by many of China's young people, who were frustrated by the current state of Chinese society. Organizing themselves as the Red Guard, these youth became the vanguard of his campaign against "capitalist roaders" within the ranks of the Communist Party.

Mao's charisma and prestige enabled him to win the support he needed to accomplish the initial objectives of the Cultural Revolution. Deng Xiaoping was driven from power and exiled from the capital, and Liu Shaoqi died while under house arrest in 1969. Mao's goal was to do away with the "four olds": old customs, old habits, old culture, and old thinking. This included not only the old ways of the CCP but of China itself, including historical artifacts. In addition, many teachers, government workers, and other educated professionals were subjected to severe persecution.

During the summer of 1967, however, key units of the PLA revolted, forcing Mao to call for a restoration of order. While the Cultural Revolution would formally continue until Mao's death in 1976, it lost strength after the PLA mutiny. In 1971, Lin Biao attempted to overthrow Mao; the *coup d'état* failed, but Mao's leadership was nevertheless discredited in the eyes of many Chinese. In 1972, China had even opened negotiations with the United States and hosted a visit by President Richard Nixon in an effort to readjust the country's international strategic position.

Reform Under Deng Xiaoping

Following the death of Mao in September 1976, and the subsequent arrest of the Gang of Four, the Cultural Revolution was brought to a close. Throughout 1977 and 1978, China's leaders moved on several fronts to acquire new technology and establish a broader economic basis for future growth. This included such measures as the construction of a major port facility at Shanhaiguan in the Hebei Province and the negotiation of a lucrative industrial development package with Japan.

The leading proponent of this shift toward openness and modernization was Deng Xiaoping. After his banishment, Deng resided in Jangxi Province until February 1973, when a series of shifts in Cultural Revolution politics led Mao to recommend his political rehabilitation. Deng's return to the central leadership did not last long, however, and in April 1976 he once again was condemned by Mao for his rightist tendencies and was forced from his position. But following the death of Mao and the arrest of the Gang of Four, Deng was again allowed into the ranks of the central leadership.

Following the Third Plenum of the Eleventh Central Committee of the CCP in December 1978, Deng emerged as the most powerful leader in the Communist hierarchy and moved quickly to bring reform-minded supporters such as Hu Yaobang and Zhao Ziyang into the ruling Politburo. Adopting the slogan "practice is the sole criterion of truth,"

Deng condemned the Cultural Revolution and vigorously promoted the Four Modernizations in the areas of agriculture, industry, national defense, and science and technology. Universities, with strictly merit-based admission, were established to train scientists and technicians. In the countryside, peasants were permitted to engage in formerly forbidden "side occupations," which included a wide range of private initiatives in growing, processing, and marketing agricultural commodities. The managers of state industries were also allowed greater flexibility in rewarding individual productivity among their workers and determining output on the basis of market considerations. In general, China moved closer toward a mixed rather than a strictly planned economy.

Attention was also directed toward political reform, and major efforts were undertaken to combine "centralism" with "people's democracy," thus broadening the base of decision making within the ranks of the CCP. Measures were also taken to ensure judicial organizations greater independence and to reinforce the principle of equality before the law. These political reforms and new legal protections did not, however, extend as far as many had hoped. Deng's harsh suppression of the Democracy Wall movement in early 1979 following publicly posted appeals for a Fifth Modernization, or democracy, clearly demonstrated the limits of political change. While new freedoms would be allowed in the sphere of economic development, the CCP would tolerate no challenge to its political supremacy.

Throughout the 1980s, Deng's policy of *gaige kaifang,* or "reform and openness," was expanded, at least economically, as new programs were implemented to stimulate growth in agriculture and modern industry. To promote foreign investment and develop China's export industries, four "special economic zones" were created near major coastal cities. These zones served as the incubation quarters for a variety of new joint enterprises and manufacturing ventures with foreign corporations. Improved political relations with Japan and the United States at this time opened the markets of these countries to Chinese goods, creating a favorable balance of trade and encouraging a greater flow of capital into China.

Unfortunately, the phenomenal economic growth of China in the 1980s also generated some negative consequences, such as inflation, unemployment, and increased corruption among government officials. The hardships and uncertainty of the new economy, combined with a lack of democratic reform by the Communist government, led university students to take to the streets in protest, culminating in the Tiananmen Square massacre of the summer of 1989. Deng's suppression of the demonstrations at

Tiananmen squashed political dissent and reasserted the authority of the CCP, despite or perhaps in reaction to concurrent collapse of the Communist governments of the Soviet Union and Eastern Europe.

Until his death in February 1997, Deng continued to promote modernization and economic expansion in China while handing the reins of political power over to a new generation of technocratic leadership.

Continuing Reform Under Jiang Zemin and Zhu Rongji

After Deng's death, the presidency of China was conferred upon one of his chief political protégés, Jiang Zemin, a trained engineer and former Shanghai Party boss who had been brought to the capital in 1989 to help pacify the country in the aftermath of the Tiananmen disaster. The following year, the key position of Premier of the State Council was transferred from the conservative Li Peng, who had played a predominant role in the suppression of the Tiananmen protests, to Zhu Rongji, who had directed much of China's economic growth in the mid-1990s. Under Jiang and Zhu, economic reform was expanded as the country continued its rapid integration into the international economy.

See also China, People's Republic of; Chinese Communist Party; Chinese Revolution; Communist Economic Model; Deng Xiaoping; East Asia: History and Economic Development; Jiang Zemin; State-Directed Economy; Taiwan

References and Further Reading

Baum, Richard. *Burying Mao: Chinese Politics in the Age of Deng Xiaoping.* Princeton, NJ: Princeton University Press, 1994.
Evans, Richard. *Deng Xiaoping and the Making of Modern China.* New York: Viking, 1994.
Gilley, Bruce. *Tiger on the Brink: Jiang Zemin and China's New Elite.* Berkeley, CA: University of California Press, 1998.
Goldman, Merle, and Roderick MacFarquhar, eds. *The Paradox of China's Post-Mao Reforms.* Cambridge, MA: Harvard University Press, 1999.
Hsu, Immanuel C. *The Rise of Modern China,* 6th ed. New York/Oxford: Oxford University Press, 2000.
Miller, H. Lyman. *Science and Dissent in Post-Mao China: The Politics of Knowledge.* Seattle: University of Washington Press, 1996.
Salisbury, Harrison. *The New Emperors: China in the Eras of Mao and Deng.* Boston: Little, Brown & Co., 1992.
Shirk, Susan. *The Political Logic of Economic Reform in China.* Berkeley, CA: University of California Press, 1993.
Spence, Jonathan D. *The Search for Modern China.* New York: W. W. Norton & Company, 1999.

CHINA, PEOPLE'S REPUBLIC OF

Located at the eastern end of the Eurasian continent, the People's Republic of China occupies a land area of approximately 3.7 million square miles: an area larger than all fifty states of the United States of America. The country encompasses a wide variety of regional climates and topographies, stretching from the Amur River adjacent to Russian Siberia in the north to the tropical jungles of mainland Southeast Asia in the south. The arid Tarim basin and the high Tibetan plateau dominate the western and southwestern portions of the country. While vast in area, China lacks an abundance of land suitable for agriculture and is forced to feed its 1.3 billion people—nearly 25% of the world's total population—on only 7% of the world's arable land. Agricultural self-sufficiency and economic development have thus proved to be especially challenging goals for the leaders of modern China.

Historical Background

Throughout most of China's four thousand-year recorded history, the country has been ruled by a succession of imperial dynasties that rose to power and later declined in a historical pattern known as the "dynastic cycle." Among the most noteworthy and long-lived of these dynasties were the Zhou (1045 BCE–256 BCE), the Han (207 BCE–220 CE), the Tang (618 CE–907 CE), the Ming (1368 CE–1644 CE), and the non-Chinese (Manchu) Qing (1644 CE–1911 CE). During the course of this long traditional era, Chinese civilization progressively expanded outward from its birthplace in the Yellow River valley as it extended its political and cultural hegemony over neighboring peoples and regions. The state was governed through an elaborate system of bureaucratic administration centered on the emperor, or the Son of Heaven as he was referred to in classical historical accounts. The ancient Chinese regarded their country as the virtual center of human civilization, a concept reflected in its traditional designation as the Middle Kingdom.

With the arrival of increasing numbers of Western traders and missionaries in the early and mid-nineteenth century, China's traditional system of political administration and interstate relations came under intense pressure. Following the country's humiliating defeat by the British in the Opium War (1839–1842), China's rulers were forced to open the country more widely to Western penetration and implement a wide range of economic and political reforms to meet the challenge of Western wealth and power. The reforms undertaken by the Qing dynasty rulers were insufficient, however, to satisfy the nationalist aspirations of a new generation of enlightened Chinese, and under the leadership of Sun Yat-sen and his Revolutionary Alliance, the dynasty was overthrown in the Nationalist Revolution of 1911–1912.

But the new republican-style government established by Sun Yat-sen was unable to consolidate its hold over China, and by 1916, the country descended into a decade-long period of political fragmentation during which most of the country fell under the control of regional warlords. Throughout this time, young Chinese intellectuals vigorously promoted social and political reform in the New Culture and May Fourth movements, while Sun Yat-sen worked for political reunification and modernization through his Nationalist Party Guomindang. In 1921, the Chinese Communist Party (CCP) was also established with the assistance of the Moscow-based Comintern (Communist International), thus providing the Chinese with a Marxist alternative to their country's political future.

An alliance ("united front") between the CCP and the Guomindang succeeded in reuniting the country in the Northern Expedition of 1926–1928. But with the death of Sun Yat-sen in 1925, leadership of the Guomindang fell to Chiang Kai-shek, a staunch anti-Communist who shortly after achieving his military objectives in the Northern Expedition embarked on a violent campaign to exterminate his former CCP allies. Fleeing to the countryside, Communists under Mao Zedong temporarily established a rural base in Jiangxi Province, but in October 1934, they were forced on their heroic six thousand-mile Long March flight from Guomindang forces, finally establishing a new base near the village of Yan'an in remote Shaanxi Province. By late 1936, Japanese incursions in northern China forced Chiang to accept a second united front with the Communists that would last for the duration of World War II.

Soon after the surrender of the Japanese to Allied forces in August 1945, President Truman dispatched General George Marshall to China to attempt to mediate a peaceful resolution to the political conflict between the Guomindang and the CCP; but the bitter legacy of the prewar period and the irreconcilability of their political agendas proved insurmountable. In the summer of 1946, Chiang Kai-shek moved quickly to take advantage of the military advantages he enjoyed by attempting to dislodge the Communists from their base in Manchuria, thus sparking civil war. Chiang failed, however, to win popular support for his corrupt and inefficient regime, and by 1949, his Nationalist forces were defeated by the People's Liberation Army and forced to flee to the island of Taiwan.

People's Republic of China

With the establishment of the People's Republic of China in October 1949, a new chapter in the history of modern China began. Under the leadership of Mao Zedong, who was regarded with cult-like devotion by his political supporters, the new Communist-led government embarked on a concerted campaign to remove the last vestiges of foreign imperialism and build a new China. The first step in this process was a massive effort to redistribute land to the peasant masses by expropriating the holdings of the rural gentry and wealthier peasants. This campaign was occasionally marked by extreme violence and persecution as the Communist leadership sought retribution against their alleged class enemies. The government also moved vigorously to suppress prostitution, opium, and other criminal activities that had flourished during the prerevolutionary period.

In 1950, the government passed a series of laws that provided the legal framework for a thoroughgoing reform of Chinese society. A new marriage and divorce law, for example, greatly improved the lives of women by granting them new marital and property rights. The Chinese government also undertook a series of mass campaigns in the early 1950s to consolidate its control over China's urban population and "rectify," through intensive indoctrination and intimidation, any potential political opposition. These campaigns were prompted in large part by fears of American aggression at the time of the Korean War, during which large numbers of Chinese troops were allied with the North Koreans.

Throughout the mid-1950s, China's industrial economy was developed on the basis of the Soviet model, with the assistance of hundreds of Russian technical advisors and large quantities of Soviet equipment. A Central Planning Commission was established, and in 1953, the first Five Year Plan was launched, scoring impressive achievements in the development of heavy industry. During this period, most large businesses and financial institutions were nationalized and brought under the control of new government ministries assigned to manage the various segments of the expanding Socialist economy.

Great Leap Forward

Although the Communist government had attained considerable success in restoring key sectors of the industrial economy during its first years in power, agricultural production continued to lag. By the mid-1950s, therefore, the Chinese government began to push more vigorously for agricultural collectivization. Mao Zedong was the primary force behind this effort, for he was eager to socialize the agricultural economy and believed that China was uniquely positioned to make a revolutionary stride toward the classless utopian society he envisioned as the highest goal of Marxism. The Great Leap Forward, as Mao's ambitious initiative of 1958 became known, was an attempt to radically restructure Chinese society and decentralize the Chinese economy by reorganizing the population into huge collectives, or people's communes. These people's communes were intended to become the centers of both agricultural and industrial production, in which the collective will of the masses would inspire "more, better, faster, and cheaper" modes of production.

In the end, the Great Leap Forward proved to be an unmitigated disaster. The decentralization of industry, exemplified by experimental enterprises such as "backyard furnaces," proved horribly inefficient, and agricultural production declined precipitously as overzealous officials misallocated resources and manpower. Furthermore, many peasants resisted the communal living arrangements imposed upon them and failed to manifest any genuine dedication to the larger Socialist aspirations of their leaders. The consequences of Mao's failed experiment were "three bitter years" of catastrophic famine (1959–1961) during which as many as 20 million Chinese are believed to have lost their lives.

The tragedy of the Great Leap Forward not only caused untold hardship for the Chinese people but also badly damaged relations between China and the Soviet Union. The "Sino-Soviet split" of 1960, in which the two countries completely severed political relations, was caused largely by Mao's pretentious criticism of the Soviet Union's "revisionist" domestic and foreign policies. But as the failure of the Great Leap Forward became apparent, Mao's own policies came under criticism by the top leadership of the CCP, and following a meeting of the Central Committee in December 1958, he was obliged to "retire from the front line" and to allow other prominent party officials to set administrative policy.

Cultural Revolution

During the early 1960s, the leadership of China fell to Liu Shaoqi and Deng Xiaoping, both of whom were highly esteemed for their long and distinguished careers of service to the Communist cause. Both men favored a more rational approach to social and economic development and moved quickly to restore prosperity to China through a centralized system of planning and administration. Under the leadership of Liu and Deng, Chinese industry and agriculture recovered quickly from the Great Leap Forward and achieved steady progress in improved productivity and economic stability. But the growing power of the agencies and institutions that directed this renewed expansion of the Chinese economy gave rise to a new bureaucratic elite that increasingly assumed the lifestyle and mannerisms of a privileged class.

Mao's great displeasure with the "right opportunist line" of the CCP leadership and the new elite that it had engendered prompted him to initiate the Great Proletarian Cultural Revolution in 1966. Mao's call for "continuing revolution" was supported by Lin Biao, the commander of the People's Liberation Army (PLA), and a core of leftist radicals led by Mao's wife, Jiang Qing. Mao was also supported by many of China's young people, whose frustration and resentment over some of the inequities they endured under the current system could easily be channeled toward overthrowing the established order. Organizing themselves as the Red Guard, these youth were impassioned with a cult-like devotion to Mao and became the vanguard of his campaign against "capitalist roaders" within the ranks of the party.

The power of Mao's charisma and prestige enabled him to win the support he needed to accomplish the initial objectives of the Cultural Revolution. The first victims of his campaign were those leaders of the CCP who had long resisted his radical agenda, including Deng Xiaoping, who was driven from power and then exiled from the capital, and Liu Shaoqi, who, after cruel mistreatment by the Red Guards, died while under house arrest. But as the Cultural Revolution progressed, the targets of attack were broadened to include anything or anyone associated with the "four olds": old customs, old habits, old culture, and old thinking. During this most violent and disruptive phase of the Cultural Revolution, many precious artifacts from China's past were defaced or destroyed, and millions of teachers, government workers, and other educated professionals were killed or subjected to severe persecution.

By the summer of 1967, chaos arising from the violent factionalism of the various Red Guards forced even Mao himself to condemn the "ultra-Left tendencies" of the movement and call for a restoration of order. The Cultural Revolution lost even more of its ideological impetus following Lin Biao's failed attempt to overthrow Mao in 1971, an event which greatly discredited Mao in the eyes of many Chinese.

Thus, while the Cultural Revolution would formally continue until the mid-1970s, it would not be as radical or destructive as it had been during its initial phase. Indeed, in 1972, China even opened negotiations with the United States and hosted a visit by President Richard Nixon, ending years of bitter confrontation and opening the pathway to the eventual normalization of relations in 1979. And in 1973, Deng Xiaoping and some other former members of the CCP persecuted during the early phase of the Cultural Revolution were "rehabilitated" and allowed back into the leading ranks of the government.

Reform Under Deng Xiaoping

Following the death of Mao in September 1976, and the subsequent arrest of Jiang Qing's Gang of Four, the Cultural Revolution was finally brought to a close. By this time, most Chinese had grown weary of the economic stagnation and political extremism of the Cultural Revolution and had begun to yearn for a more pragmatic approach to social and economic development. Thus, throughout 1977 and 1978, China's leaders moved on several fronts to acquire new technology and establish a broader economic base for future growth. This included such measures as the construction of a major port facility at Shanhaiguan in the Hebei Province and the negotiation of a lucrative industrial development package with Japan. At the Third Plenum of the Eleventh Central Committee of the CCP in December 1978, Deng Xiaoping emerged as the most powerful leader in the Communist hierarchy and moved quickly to bring reform-minded supporters into the ruling Politburo. Adopting the slogan "practice is the sole criterion of truth," Deng condemned the leftist radicalism of the Cultural Revolution and vigorously promoted the Four Modernizations in the areas of agriculture, industry, national defense, and science and technology.

One of the early measures taken by the Chinese government to promote the Four Modernizations was the establishment of key universities to train a new generation of scientists and technicians. Admission to these new schools would be based on academic merit and not on one's class background or ideological zeal, as it had during the Cultural Revolution. In the countryside, peasants were permitted to engage in formerly forbidden "side occupations," which included a wide range of private initiatives in growing, processing, and marketing agricultural commodities. The managers of state industries were also allowed greater flexibility in rewarding individual productivity among their workers and determining output on the basis of market considerations. In general, throughout China, private incentives and market forces were allowed to function more freely as a stimulus to social and economic development.

Deng and his supporters also directed their attention to political reform, and major efforts were undertaken to combine "centralism" with "people's democracy," thus broadening the base of decision making within the ranks of the CCP. Measures were also enacted to ensure that judicial organizations would have greater independence, and a greater effort was made to reinforce the principle of equality before the law. These political reforms and new legal protections did not, however, extend as far as many had hoped. Deng's harsh suppression of the Democracy Wall movement in Beijing in early 1979 following publicly posted appeals for democratic reform, or the Fifth Modernization, clearly demonstrated the limits of political change. While vast new freedoms and incentives were promoted in the economic life of the country, the CCP would not tolerate challenge to its political supremacy.

Throughout the 1980s, Deng's policy of *gaige kaifang*, or "reform and openness," was progressively expanded as new programs were implemented to stimulate growth in agriculture and modern industry. To promote foreign investment and develop China's export industries, four "special economic zones" were created near major coastal cities. These zones served as the incubation quarters for a variety of new joint enterprises and manufacturing ventures with foreign corporations. Improved political relations with Japan and the United States at this time opened the markets of these countries to Chinese goods, creating a favorable balance of trade and encouraging a greater flow of capital into China.

But the miraculous economic growth of China in the 1980s also generated some negative consequences, such as severe inflation, high unemployment, and rampant government corruption. These factors, combined with the anxiety growing out of the hardships and uncertainty of the new economy, led university students to take to the streets of Beijing in protest in April 1989, culminating eventually in the tragic Tiananmen Square massacre of June, during which several hundred demonstrators were killed by PLA troops. In the end, Deng's ruthless suppression of the Tiananmen protests effectively squashed political dissent and reasserted the authority of the CCP at a time when the Communist governments of the Soviet Union and Eastern Europe were rapidly collapsing under similar forms of popular opposition.

Continuing Reform Under New Technocratic Leadership

Until his death in February 1997, Deng continued to promote modernization and economic expansion in China while handing the reins of political power to a new generation of technocratic leadership. In 1993, the presidency of China was conferred upon his chief political protégé, Jiang Zemin, a trained engineer and former Shanghai Party boss who had been brought to the capital in 1989 to help pacify the country in the aftermath of the Tiananmen disaster. Jiang successfully perpetuated Deng's strategy of promoting liberal economic reform while maintaining the CCP's authoritarian grasp on political power. In 1997, the country enjoyed an important foreign policy success with the British return of Hong Kong to PRC control under the "one country-two systems" policy that protected the democratic rights of the city's residents under the new Hong Kong Special Administrative Region (HKSAR).

In 1998, the key position of Premier of the State Council was transferred from the conservative Li Peng, who had played a predominant role in the brutal suppression of the Tiananmen protests, to Zhu Rongji, another engineer by training who had directed much of China's economic growth in the mid-1990s. Under the technocratic leadership of Jiang and Zhu, the country focused on rapidly integrating itself into the international economy. China's admission to the World Trade Organization in 2001 marked the culmination of this process while providing a new framework for future social and economic development. China was also granted the privilege of hosting the 2008 Summer Olympics in Beijing, yet another sign of the approval and admiration of the international community.

The ability of the CCP to smoothly transfer political leadership to a new generation was demonstrated in March 2003 by the peaceful retirement of Jiang Zemin and the orderly designation of Hu Jintao as the new president of the People's Republic of China. At the same time, Zhu Rongji willingly acceded his post of Premier of the State Council to Wen Jiabao. Hu and Wen were also trained originally as engineers and seem determined to continue the pragmatic approach to social and economic development pioneered by Deng Xiaoping and his successors.

If China's leaders are able to navigate a peaceful resolution to the simmering dispute over the return of Taiwan and begin moving the country in the direction of democratic reform, the remaining obstacles to improved relations with the international community will have been lifted. But China's new leaders also face the formidable challenge of completing the country's transformation to "market socialism." The growing disparities in wealth arising from China's rapid economic development have generated serious social tensions and exacerbated crime and government corruption. The new generation of leadership must therefore move quickly to regulate and reform the political system and strive to distribute the benefits of economic expansion to a much broader segment of its vast population. If this can be done successfully and the current pattern of development continues, China appears destined in the twenty-first century to become an economic and political superpower of preeminent importance to the future of the international community.

MICHAEL C. LAZICH

See also Chiang Kai-shek; Chinese Communist Party; Chinese Revolution; Communist Economic Model; Deng Xiaoping; Mao Zedong; Zhou Enlai

References and Further Reading:

Baum, Richard. *Burying Mao: Chinese Politics in the Age of Deng Xiaoping.* Princeton, NJ: Princeton University Press, 1994.

Evans, Richard. *Deng Xiaoping and the Making of Modern China.* New York: Viking, 1994.

Gilley, Bruce. *Tiger on the Brink: Jiang Zemin and China's New Elite.* Berkeley, CA: University of California Press, 1998.

Goldman, Merle, and Roderick MacFarquhar, eds. *The Paradox of China's Post-Mao Reforms.* Cambridge, MA: Harvard University Press, 1999.

Hsü, Immanuel C. *The Rise of Modern China.* 6th ed. New York and Oxford: Oxford University Press, 2000.

Miller, H. Lyman. *Science and Dissent in Post-Mao China: The Politics of Knowledge.* Seattle: University of Washington Press, 1996.

Salisbury, Harrison. *The New Emperors: China in the Eras of Mao and Deng.* Boston, MA: Little, Brown & Co., 1992.

Shirk, Susan. *The Political Logic of Economic Reform in China.* Berkeley, CA: University of California Press, 1993.

Spence, Jonathan D. *The Search for Modern China.* New York: W. W. Norton & Company, 1999.

Walder, Andrew. *Communist Neo-Traditionalism: Work and Authority in Chinese Industry.* New York: Columbia University Press, 1986.

CHINESE COMMUNIST PARTY (CCP)

The Chinese Communist Party (CCP) was founded in 1921 as part of the Communist International's (Comintern) strategy to support the construction of socialism in Russia by having Communist parties assume leadership over nationalist movements against imperialist expansion in Asia. The mission of the party was to regain territorial integrity, sovereignty, and unity for China by supporting the bourgeoisie in its modernization effort and in its fight for national independence. The strategy was to join the bourgeoisie and its party, in this case the Nationalist Party Guomindang, in a united front to help the country move on to capitalism. This strategy was also aimed at hindering the bourgeoisie to make full use of its power by limiting its ability to exploit workers at its own wish.

A first attempt to put this theory into practice ended with a disaster. Even before the Guomindang took over power in 1927, it tried to destroy its former ally. As a result, the CCP retreated to the countryside and went through years of internal debate trying to define a strategy independent of the Comintern and that would be successful because it was rooted in Chinese society. The focus of the party shifted from the cities to the countryside, from political issues to military means of mobilization and participation, and from close cooperation with the Comintern to independence. This shift was propagated among party members during the 1942–1945 Yan'an Rectification campaign, which prepared the party organizationally for the Communist takeover while the Anti-Japanese War laid a military and political basis for the later victory. Mao Zedong, who was elected leader of the CCP on its Seventh Party Congress in 1945, is said to have been the inventor of this victorious strategy. Until today, Mao-Zedong-Thought stands for the successful sinification of Marxism-Leninism in China and is heralded as the guiding principle of the CCP.

After the Communist takeover in 1949, the CCP entered a period of intensive cooperation with the Soviet Union, but the majority of its leadership soon felt uneasy with this renewed partnership. For Mao Zedong, the Soviet Union had become a negative example, after Stalin's death, of a Socialist country degenerating to revisionism and later on to Socialist imperialism. Many leading members of the party supported his idea that China should neither submit to Russian chauvinism nor should it internally go through the same degeneration process as to be observed in Russia. Consequently, the CCP started to focus on class struggle and not on economic issues. Even though the Great Leap Forward had already shown at the end of the 1950s many of the problems resulting from the continuation of the revolution under conditions of postrevolutionary construction, it was only after the Cultural Revolution (1966–1976) and Mao Zedong's death that the CCP leadership departed from Mao's line.

After a period of reorientation under Hua Guofeng, the CCP leadership under Deng Xiaoping introduced a set of policies focused on economic development. In December 1978, the Party's Eleventh Central Committee decided on its Third Plenary Session to allow for a gradual introduction of market economy and the opening of the country to foreign investors. This set of policies, without which China's unprecedented economic growth could not have taken place, is now attributed to Deng Xiaoping and said to be his personal contribution to the development of Mao-Zedong-Thought. In the twenty-first century, the CCP has redefined its role as a party of people as a whole acting as a modernization agent on behalf of the Chinese nation longing to catch up with the most advanced nations of the world. During its Sixteenth Party Congress, the CCP publicly acknowledged its new role by integrating this idea into its statutes and linking them to its leader Jiang Zemin. On the same occasion, the CCP elected its present leadership under Hu Jintao.

Since its fundamental change of policies in 1978, the CCP has shifted its focus from class struggle to economic development; at the same time, it has held the notion that economic development is more important than political change. Its legitimacy is therefore solely based on economic growth and efficiency. While this strategy has so far been quite successful, it has not prevented major frictions to arise. The 1989 student movement in Beijing and other parts of the country showed the party leadership that economic growth without political reform could easily lead to a legitimacy crisis and to major splits inside the CCP, the victim of which turned out to be the then-party leader Zhao Ziyang. Since then, the CCP has been able to accommodate most of those taking part in the 1989 protest movement but is now confronted with social unrest in the countryside and among workers in the cities.

SUSANNE WEIGELIN-SCHWIEDRZIK

See also China, People's Republic of; Chinese Revolution; Deng Xiaoping; Mao Zedong; Marxism; Zhou Enlai

References and Further Reading

Cheek, Timothy, and Tony Saich, eds. *New Perspectives on State Socialism in China.* Armonk, NY, and London: Sharpe, 1999.

Fewsmith, Joseph. *Dilemmas of Reform in China. Political Conflict and Economic Debate.* Armonk, NY, and London: Sharpe, 1994.

MacFarquhar, Roderick, ed. *The Politics of China, 1949–1989.* Cambridge: Cambridge University Press, 1993.

Saich, Tony. *The Rise of the Chinese Communist Party.* Armonk, NY, and London: Sharpe, 1996.

Saich, Tony, and Hans van de Veen, eds. *New Perspectives on the Chinese Communist Revolution.* Armonk, NY, and London: Sharpe, 1995.

CHINESE REVOLUTION

The Chinese Revolution, in the narrow sense of the word, was a protest movement under the leadership of the Chinese Communist Party (CCP), which was founded in 1921 under the influence of the international Communist movement and came to power in 1949. The protest movement was directed against the growing influence of foreign powers on Chinese territory and inequality of income and land distribution in the countryside, as well as against poverty among the urban working class population. Its main aims were to restore sovereignty of the Chinese state over Chinese territory, to distribute land to the tillers so as to overcome inequality among poor peasants, and to strengthen the state's influence on the process of industrialization to accelerate industrial growth and limit the exploitation of the workers. The Communist Revolution in this sense is part of the international Communist movement under the leadership of the Communist International, although the CCP had realized in the 1940s that its only chance to rise to power would be to define itself as a genuinely Chinese political force independent of any foreign influence whatsoever.

During the first phase of the revolution, the focus of the protest movement was located in major Chinese cities, and the forms of protest imitated the model of Communist movements in Western industrialized countries. Starting from 1924, the CCP followed the advice given by the Communist International and built a united front with the Nationalist Party Guomindang. Convinced that the Communist movement in China had to help the bourgeois democratic revolution to succeed, the CCP agreed to join the GMD in an effort to put an end to regionalization in China and reestablish a powerful central state that had been lacking since the fall of the last dynasty in 1912. When the united front split in 1927, it was the Guomindang, however, that formed the central government and forced the CCP to retreat to the countryside, where it had to develop a survival strategy. Using the fragmentization of village life and the weakness of the state for their own purposes, the Communist Party saw the possibility to develop its influence in the villages and surround the cities by the countryside, attacking its enemies where they were weak and strengthening its own ranks by recruiting peasants from newly "liberated" areas for locally organized militias. Because the cities were unable to survive if cut off from the surrounding countryside, the cities had to give in after a certain time. Step by step, the territory under Communist control grew to become a major threat for the central government. Only after several large-scale military attacks by government troops was the army, under Communist leadership, compelled to leave its territory and embark, in October 1934, on the legendary Long March. The end of the march came in October 1935, resulting in a diminished party with its new center at Yan'an. The CCP was now ready to establish a second united front against Japanese aggression with the national government of the Guomindang.

During the Sino-Japanese War (1937–1945), the Communist army used guerrilla tactics to fight the enemy behind the lines and develop its own strength by bringing peasants willing to fight against the Japanese aggressor under its influence. Simultaneously, the party started reorganizing itself by launching a rectification campaign, in the course of which Mao Zedong was elected supreme leader of the party and Mao-Zedong-Thought its guiding principle. The experience of the Chinese revolution as summarized in Mao-Zedong-Thought was defined to consist of three elements: the Communist Party as the driving force of the revolution, the Communist army supporting the claim for political power by military means, and the united front as an instrument to unite with large parts of the population. By the end of the war, the party and its leadership were just as well prepared to continue their march to power as the army was ready to take over the Chinese territory starting in the far north of the country and fighting its way down south. The last phase of the Chinese Revolution was a fierce civil war between Communist troops and the army of the central government in which the question of political power was resolved on the battlefield with military means. In the course of this civil war, the central government was forced to retreat to the island of Taiwan, leaving the whole of mainland of China within the boundaries of the last dynasty except for Hong Kong to the Communist Party.

The Chinese Revolution, in a broader sense of the word, starts with the Xinhai Revolution of 1911 and the fall of the dynasty in the spring of 1912. It continues through the whole of the twentieth century and will not end before China will have found a stable political system that allows for the economy to grow fast enough for the Chinese population to live in relative prosperity. In this context, the efforts of the Communist Party to build socialism in China since 1949 are included as are .the attempts of the local gentry to overthrow dynastic rule and establish a republican order after 1911. The aim of the Chinese Revolution in this sense is to find a new political order capable of uniting the country within the boundaries of the Qing state and to establish China internationally as one among the leading nations of the world. As both ends have not yet been achieved, the Chinese revolution has not reached its aims and is therefore still going on. The CCP has time and again reiterated the two aims described in the beginning of this paragraph; however, since the death of Mao Zedong in 1976, the party has refrained from referring to the necessity of continuing the revolution. To the contrary, during the last years of the twentieth century, the Communist Party shifted its focus from political change to stability and order as a precondition for economic growth, while at the same time making efforts to unite the country by reintegrating Hong Kong and Macao and resisting all kinds of independence movements within its boundaries.

SUSANNE WEIGELIN-SCHWIEDRZIK

See also Chiang Kai-shek; China, People's Republic of; Chinese Communist Party; Mao Zedong; Marxism; Soviet Bloc; Zhou Enlai

References and Further Reading

Bianco, Lucien. *The Origins of the Chinese Revolution (1915–1949)*. Stanford, CA: Stanford University Press, 1971.

Fairbank, John King, and Albert Feuerwerker. *The Cambridge History of China: Republican China, 1912–1949*. Vol. 13, Part 2. Cambridge: Cambridge University Press, 1986

Saich, Tony. *The Rise of the Chinese Communist Party.* Armonk, NY, and London: Sharpe, 1996.

Saich, Tony, and Hans van de Ven, eds. *New Perspectives on the Chinese Communist Revolution.* Armonk, NY, and London: Sharpe, 1995.

CHRISTIANITY

From the nineteenth century to the mid-twentieth century, just after World War II in 1945, most of the developing world was controlled, directly or indirectly, by European nations or the United States. This meant subservience of Third World political, economic, and cultural entities to imperial powers that mandated a congenial environment to their interests. A major element of this regime was Christian missions that followed the flags of their respective imperial states into Asia, Africa, and Latin America. The governments, those of European countries and corporations, provided stipends and land to missions that were willing to dominate the natives' religious and educational systems and thus redefine their indigenous culture.

The Euro-American states asked missionaries to establish schools, clinics, and churches in cities and villages and supplied oversight, funding, and an administrative apparatus. Where economic sectors, such as the East India Company, were more dominant

than the political sectors, companies offered missions the same incentives as did imperial governments to establish these cultural institutions.

The mission schools, churches, and clinics made the missionary the advocate for a European form of Christian culture. To accomplish this enculturation of the natives to British, French, German, Spanish, Dutch, or Portuguese dress, language, and customs, including their form of the Christian religion, the missions managed local village life by providing a pastor, teachers, and physicians. To the degree that natives adopted European customs, they were deemed to be "civilized" and no longer "heathens" or "pagans," and the "darkness" of their land was said to be lifting. So the imperial states and economic enterprises turned to Roman Catholic or Protestant missions for this "civilizing" task of turning Asian, African, or Latin American lands into miniature versions of the homeland: "Little Europes."

Europeans and Americans deemed virtually everything "native" as "heathen," and all of the products of Western civilization were deemed "Christian" and "civilized." As a result, there was a ban on native religious rites, such as communicating with ancestors through spirit mediums, performing native dances, making native drinks, praying to gods, and performing rituals. Christian missions replaced these with rites they saw as progressive and moral and an improvement over "demonic" practices. They also "rechristened" landscapes that had a native religious tradition to honor European saints, conquerors, or missionaries. Even if there was a form of native monotheism, the missionary changed the deity's name to a Christian equivalent. Not until Africans, Asians, and Latin Americans acquired control over the Christian churches and schools did they begin to incorporate native names and rituals into their Christian theologies, but this did not occur in most countries until the end of the colonial era, when missionaries from Europe, North America, and New Zealand began to withdraw in the 1950s.

In the process of taking control of the indigenous cultures, economies, and political structures, the Christian missions joined the European state and mining company governments in expropriating native land. A near universal pattern was for the Europeans to force natives to move to designated areas of the least arable lands. In those Native Reserves, they set up a civil service of Native Commissioners and Native Police to collect hut taxes and other revenues and to enforce labor regimes that capitalized on cheap and often forced labor. These Native Reserves were akin to what the United States called Indian Reservations under the control of the Bureau of Indian Affairs. The methods and functions of the Christian missions in the developing world were very similar to those for aborigines who were also under missionary influence in Australia and New Zealand. The imperial rulers allowed Christian denominations to work in these reserves and to divide up the country into denominational domains where they assumed responsibility for providing schools, churches, and clinics to educate, proselytize, and heal the natives, respectively. The Christian minister, whether European or native, was the teacher, the pastor, and often the person who replaced the native healer with European medicine. All of this was done in close collaboration with the government.

Churches recruited missionaries from Europe, North America, and Australasia. The nineteenth century marked the greatest missionary successes since the apostles' treks across the Roman Empire in the first five centuries of the common era, the conversion of Ireland and Europe from the sixth through the eleventh centuries, and the missionary work in the regions of South, Central, and North America in the fifteenth through the eighteenth centuries. With the exception of North America and Australasia, Europeans normally did not exceed 15% of the total population that they ruled.

In the nineteenth century, the enormous success of Christian missions caused the Christians of Europe, North America, and Australasia to hope that Christ's second coming would likely be brought about by human effort as they worked to win the world for Christ. This was the postmillennial theological dogma that Christ's thousand-year reign on earth would likely commence in their own time. This euphoric mood gradually changed in the late nineteenth and early twentieth centuries as problems of controlling an empire increased and as native resistance grew. Military and civil service expenses often outran profits from trade in areas where there were limited mineral or other lucrative natural resources.

Africans or Asians had not ceded their lands and cultures to Euro-American empire builders without a fight. Bloody battles pitted the European machine gun against African and Asian spears, knives, and arrows. In Latin America, revolutions expelled Spanish and Portuguese rulers by the early nineteenth century but retained the Catholic Church alongside indigenous Indian and African religious practices. European intruders could never assume that "natives" did not resent their political, economic, and cultural exploitation. "Exploitation" was not the word missionaries chose for what they saw as humanitarian work and for accepting native lands for the work done at their mission stations. But there were always a few who agreed that Christian missions were co-conspirators with political and economic interests in abetting the exploitation of the native population.

A few missionaries raised their voices against forced labor, unfair taxes, and the lack of a majority voice or majority rule in the government of the state and the church. In the 1930s, the dissenters increased. Anthropology pointed to connections between the cultural elements of religion, language, and custom, as well as to political and economic spheres. Some missionaries witnessed how the detachment of people from their traditions and lands had disrupted their lives and cultures. Some missionaries saw their involvement in this cause as a violation of the essential message of the Christian Gospel, Jesus teaching of love and hope, particularly in relation to the priority of helping the poor as opposed to enriching people of higher class.

This restlessness reached a climax during and after World War II. From 1939 to the end of the twentieth century, Africans and Asians organized to rid their lands of European and North American imperialism that had failed to recognize the principles of democracy (majority rule) that President Woodrow Wilson's Fourteen Points of 1918 had declared essential to self-government. This program called for decolonization of empires. While European withdrawal from colonies did not take place in 1918, and while many Europeans did not see self-determination as a right of native peoples of Africa or Asia, the colonized people began to adopt the principles of self-government from their European colonizers. When they spoke of liberation and human rights, they were often echoing what they had learned in Christian mission schools and universities. It was becoming impossible for Christians to ignore economically ambitious multinational corporations that took wealth from Third World colonies or to ignore the churches that abetted political, economic, and cultural domination of their people.

In August 1941, US President Franklin Roosevelt and British Prime Minister Winston Churchill had reiterated Wilson's call for self-determination, although they did not tie the democratic principle directly to the developing world. But leaders of independence movements in colonized nations made the connection, as did missionaries who tied themselves to the well-being of the people they served. They were becoming aware of cravings for self-government, economic equity, and a revival of their cultural traditions.

By the 1960s, the preachers of a Liberation Theology were making it the equivalent of the political revolutions that were emancipating African, Asian, and Latin American Christians of the developing world from Euro-American domination in their political, economic, and cultural lives. That this was not accepted by political leaders after World War II any more than it was after World War I did not cause the liberators to be less zealous. Opponents of decolonization resisted the burgeoning Third World political revolutionaries, which they accounted for as a result of Communist infiltration and doctrine.

Liberation theology was, as its European opponents saw it, essentially a class-based theology of atheist upheaval against Western Christian civilization. But priests and ministers who embraced it saw it as assisting the poor in their strivings for hope and faith. Phillip Berryman, a priest in a barrio in Panama in 1965–1973, embraced the new theology in a period when missionary and native Catholic clergy in Latin America were enunciating a liberation movement among their congregations. El Salvador's archbishop Oscar Romero saw the new theology as liberating the poor in their communities. Many conservative church leaders and lay Christians saw liberation theology only as atheistic Marxist dogma.

Many independence leaders of the 1950s to the 1990s were educated in Christian mission schools and universities. Christians of Africa, Latin America, and Asia may well have seen a "liberation theology" as a match for their political and economic aspirations. And if capitalist nations in the West did not agree to their revolutionary goals, the former colonies were ready to turn to Eastern Europe, North Korea, and China to find a political structure that fit their aim of removing colonial domination. So in the case of Zimbabwe, the Patriotic Front's dependence on Eastern Europe and North Korea for weapons turned Robert Mugabe and Joshua Nkomo to support a Communist political philosophy rather than their Roman Catholic mission training.

Out of a mid-2004 global population of 6,364,317,000, 32.9% were Christian. Of these, 382,816,000 were African; 323,936,000 were Asian; and 497,949,000 were Latin American. This added up to a total of 1,204,701,000 Christians in areas where most developing nations are located. In Europe, North America, and Oceania (lands of central and south Pacific), there were 799,862,000 Christians. Therefore, the balance of membership in Christian denominations is shifting to the developing world. The shift is having an effect on Christian churches and on the international conciliar movement. Third World Christians are sending missionaries to urban areas of the West. This is particularly true of Latin American, Korean, and West African missionaries from traditional denominations as well as indigenous churches, particularly Pentecostals. If present trends continue, this domination of Christianity by the developing world will make this a reverse missionary movement, aimed primarily at Asian, Latino, and African migrants.

NORMAN H. MURDOCH

See also Liberation Theology

References and Further Reading

Barrett, David B., and Todd M. Johnson. "Annual Statistical Table on Global Mission: 2004." *International Bulletin of Missionary Research* 28, no. 1 (January 2004): 24–25.

Berryman, Phillip. *Liberation Theology: The Essential Facts about the Revolutionary Movement in Latin America and Beyond.* London: T. B. Lauris, 1987.

Cory, Catherine A., and David T. Landry, eds. *The Christian Theological Tradition.* Needham Heights, MA, 1996.

Moynahan, Brian. *The Faith: A History of Christianity.* New York: Doubleday, 2002.

Shenk, Wilbert R., ed. *Enlarging the Story: Perspectives on Writing World Christian History.* Maryknoll, NY: Orbis Books, 2002.

Walls, Andrew F. "Converts or Proselytes? The Crisis over Conversion in the Early Church." *International Bulletin of Missionary Research* 28, no. 1 (January 2004): 2–6.

CHRISTIANS IN THE MIDDLE EAST

Christianity began as a Jewish sect in the Middle East and has maintained a presence in the region since its foundation. It rapidly expanded despite persecution during the first three centuries of the common era, such that indigenous churches were founded on every corner of the Roman Empire of the day. The growth of Christianity was accelerated by the conversion of Constantine and the edict of toleration in 313, ushering in a period during which Christianity became the dominant religion of Asia Minor, the Levant, Egypt, and North Africa.

Major divisions arose among the Middle Eastern Churches as a result of dissenting opinions in the following centuries, each of which had a significant impact on the divisions of Middle Eastern Christianity. The first of these came as a result of the Ecumenical Councils of Ephesus in 431 and Chalcedon in 451, when the Nestorian and non-Chalcedonian Churches separated from the mainline Roman church in disagreement over the nature of Christ. The second came with the Great Schism that divided the Eastern Orthodox from the authority of the Roman Catholic Church in 1054. These divisions created a patchwork of different Christian churches throughout the region, including many national and autocephalus groups, such as the Coptic, the Syrian Orthodox, the Greek, the Assyrian, and Armenian Churches as well as the Roman Catholic (or Latin) Church. During the later Middle Ages and into the early colonial period, the Roman Catholic Church succeeded in reconciling some of the ancient churches back to papal authority. This spawned the creation of eastern-rite Roman Catholic groups known as Uniate Churches. These include the Maronite, Greek Catholic, and Chaldaean Churches.

Today, Christians in the Middle East fall generally into four families based on these divisions: the Oriental Orthodox Churches; the Eastern (Greek) Orthodox Churches; the Roman Catholic and Uniate Churches; and the Protestant Evangelical Churches founded by Western missionaries since the Reformation.

With the ascendance of Islam as a political force beginning in the seventh century, Christianity in the Middle East fell into a long period of decline. What had been the dominant religion became an ever-dwindling minority. The imposition of a special poll tax (*jizya*) and behavioural restrictions placed on Christians by the Muslim conquerors impelled many to seek conversion over the centuries. Official toleration of Christians was subject to the vicissitudes of imperial policy. In 1009, the Fatimid Caliph al-Hakim ordered the destruction of the Church of the Holy Sepulcher in Jerusalem, ushering in fears among Christians about persecution at the hands of Muslims and leading to the declaration of the first Crusade. However, given their foreign extraction and devotion to eastern sects of Christianity, Eastern Christians tended to fare as badly at the hands of the Crusaders as did Muslims.

During the later Ottoman period, intervention by the European powers brought Christians under foreign sway. Various colonial powers sought to bring certain Christian populations under their protection as a means of establishing claims on the crumbling Ottoman state. During the same period, the Europeans came to a series of agreements, known as "capitulations," that enshrined the rights of non-Muslim subjects within the empire. The capitulations gradually came to apply to indigenous Christians, who were emancipated from most of the limitations on their participation in public life as a result of the Noble Rescripts of 1839 and 1854. As a result, Christians began to be employed in the bureaucracies and militaries of Middle Eastern states. At the same time, the Ottoman administration agreed to maintain the existing position of the various Christian sects with regard to holy places within the empire, a concession that came to be known as the Status Quo agreements. The Status Quo continues to be cited as the authority for the division of responsibilities among Christian sects with regard to custodianship of the holy places.

In the period of Ottoman decline, Christians came to take an important role in the early secular nationalist movements and achieved an unprecedented measure of influence in Middle Eastern societies. In Egypt, Coptic Christians assumed places in the upper levels of the nationalist administrations, and one Copt, Boutros Ghali, became Prime Minister from 1908 to 1910. In Lebanon, the increasing population and wealth of Christians improved their relative standing, and European support of nationalist tendencies emboldened them to demand greater power in the area of Mount Lebanon and the coastal cities. This eventually led to the creation of "greater Lebanon" under the French protectorate after 1920 and the declaration of the modern state of Lebanon in 1943 as a state dominated by a Christian majority.

Elsewhere, Christians became central figures in pan-Arab movements. Michel Aflaq, an Eastern Orthodox adherent of Syrian descent, was a founder of the Ba'athist movement in 1947, and Christians have continued to play an important role in the Syrian and Iraqi Ba'ath parties. Christians also played a prominent role in the early Palestinian liberation movement, including George Habash, who founded the Marxist-oriented Popular Front for the Liberation of Palestine (PFLP) in 1967, and Naif Hawatmeh, leader of the Democratic Front for the Liberation of Palestine founded in 1969.

With the creation of independent republican states in the Middle East, the central role that Christians played in the nationalist movements began to fade. In Egypt, many were targeted by the nationalizing reforms brought about by Gamal abd al-Nasser's Free Officers' revolt. Elsewhere, the growth of Islamist nationalism endangered the secular definition of Arab identity and threatened to alienate Christians from their societies. This process intensified after the defeat of the Arab nations and Israeli occupation of the West Bank and Gaza Strip in the Middle East war, which brought about a sea-change in Arab politics beginning in 1967.

Following 1967, Christians were typically forced into a defensive position, finding that the waning of secular nationalist movements eroded their economic and political clout. In Lebanon, the massive influx of Palestinian refugees and internal demographic shifts favouring the Shi'ite population brought a challenge to Christian dominance. Muslim sects supported a more aggressive policy toward Israel coupled with constitutional reform to recognize the decline of the relative proportion of the Christian population. Christians by and large viewed the Palestinians as interlopers and felt that Lebanon should refrain from supporting their cause. The revolutionary changes occurring in Lebanese society increasingly polarized the indigenous sects and led to civil war beginning in 1976. While there remained internal divisions among the Christian Lebanese over the direction of foreign policy, the leadership of the Lebanese Phalange, notably Bashir Gemayel, managed to unite many of the Christian-dominated groups in opposition to the Palestinian presence. From 1980, the united Lebanese Forces militia sought to defend a Christian enclave in east Beirut and Mount Lebanon, and in 1982, it supported an Israeli incursion designed to rout Palestinian militants. However, Syrian intervention and the rise of Shi'a militancy in the South dealt a strategic blow to the Lebanese Forces, which were weakened and eventually acquiesced to constitutional changes under the Taif Agreement of 1989.

In Egypt, the increasing popularity of Islamist elements critical of the state's *infitah* policies and the conclusion of a peace treaty with Israel led the regime of Anwar Sadat to placate the opposition by assenting to a certain number of their demands. While Sadat deliberately adopted Islamist slogans and rhetoric, the most significant policy change involved a drive to include the Islamic Shari'a as the source of Egyptian law. This drew widespread opposition from the usually quiescent Coptic Christian clergy, who staged demonstrations and made statements critical of the regime. In the autumn of 1981, a widespread crackdown against critics of the regime included the decertification of the Coptic pope and his placement in internal exile. With the assassination of Sadat, open criticism of the regime began to fade, and the pope was reinstated in 1985.

Among the Palestinians, regional Christian organizations responded to the plight of refugees. While Christians maintained an active presence in the Palestinian resistance, many in the diaspora emigrated to new countries of origin or were naturalized to their host countries. A large number remained within the state of Israel, where they remain in large numbers among the cities of Galilee and the northern coast, such as Nazareth, Haifa, and Acre. Elsewhere, they remained numerous in Jerusalem and the surrounding cities and villages. Many of the leading families became involved in local politics in the occupied territories. During the period of the first *indifada,* starting in late 1987, these were involved in organizing local committees of resistance.

In Syria and Iraq, strong nominalism nurtured nonecclesial forms of Christian political activity even as associations with other religious minorities helped to reinforce secular pan-Arabism. In Jordan, Christians maintained a quiet support for the monarchy and participated openly in public life. In other regions of the Arab world and in Iran and Turkey, Christians remained a tiny minority, subject to occasional public interest but given little importance in public life and policy, although they have been granted a set number of seats in the Iranian parliament since the revolution of 1979.

Today, Christians number between 12 million and 14 million in the Arab countries of the Middle East, although the exact population remains obscure given its politicization. They remain concentrated by and large in the Arab nations of the eastern Mediterranean. Christians in Egypt, mostly adherents of the Coptic Orthodox Church, compose somewhere around 10% of the population of 76 million. A mixture of Maronite and Greek Uniate Churches and the Eastern Orthodox dominate the Christian population of Lebanon, which now comprises somewhere around 30% of a population of 3.5 million. In neighbouring Syria, Christians number somewhere around 10% of the population and form about 5% of the population of Iraq and Jordan and among the Palestinians.

The number of Christians in the Middle East is in significant decline, in both absolute and relative terms. This is due to a low birth rate and a high rate of emigration. Certainly the growth of Islamism as a popular ideology and the concomitant erosion of secular nationalist principles have had a role in motivating Christians to leave the region. In addition, Christians find it relatively easy to network and connect to Western societies. As a result, Middle Eastern Christians have formed an increasingly large diaspora in countries such as the United States, Canada, and Australia. The spread of Arab Christians to Western societies has prompted the creation of many external groups interested in supporting coreligionists who have remained in the region, especially among Egyptian Copts, Lebanese Maronites, and Iraqi Assyrians. Within the region, the growth of evangelical groups and a small but growing number of Christians from a Jewish background in Israel (known as "Messianic" Jews) have begun to change the complexion of Middle Eastern Christianity.

Both formal and informal international networks of Christians have become publicly active in the past few decades. The Vatican has retained an active role given its responsibilities in sharing custody of many of the holy sites and its leadership among a great number of Middle Eastern Christians. An official pilgrimage by Pope John Paul II in 2000 increased the visibility of Christian groups and promised to improve relations between Christian sects and between Christianity and Islam. The ecumenical movement now encompasses each of the four families of churches under the banner of the Middle East Council of Churches. Mission activity and *ad hoc* networks of Christians has brought the Christian message in contact with the majority Muslim population, in particular through the development of interreligious dialogue efforts, the media, and the involvement of Christian development agencies. Partnerships between local Christians and Western Christian organizations remain low-key, however, in view of the widespread suspicion among Arabs that Christian groups might have a neocolonial agenda. One factor contributing to this view is the association of conservative Western Christian groups with the pro-Israel Christian Zionist movement. Several Middle Eastern Christian groups have taken an active role in seeking to counteract such alliances, applying liberation theology as an alternative viewpoint.

PAUL S. ROWE

See also Ethnic Conflicts: Middle East; Middle East: History and Economic Development

References and Further Reading

Atiyah, Aziz S. *A History of Eastern Christianity*. London: Methuen, 1968.
Bailey, Betty Jane, and J. Martin Bailey. *Who are the Christians in the Middle East?* Grand Rapids, MI: William B. Eerdmans, 2003.
Betts, Robert Brenton. *Christians in the Arab East: A Political Study*. Atlanta, GA: John Knox Press, 1978.
Cragg, Kenneth. *The Arab Christian: A History in the Middle East*. London: Mowbray, 1992.
Dalrymple, William. *From the Holy Mountain: A Journey among the Christians of the Middle East*. New York: Henry Holt, 1997.
Haddad, Robert M. *Syrian Christians in Muslim Society*. Princeton, NJ: Princeton University Press, 1970.
Prior, Michael, and William Taylor, eds. *Christians in the Holy Land*. London: World of Islam Festival Trust, 1994.
Ye'or, Bat. *The Decline of Eastern Christianity under Islam*. Translated by Miriam Kochan and David Littman. London: Associated University Presses, 1996.

CHUAN LEEKPAI

As a long-time political luminary and leader of the Democratic Party, Chuan Leekpai was pivotal during Thailand's democratic transition and rapid economic development. Born on July 28, 1938, in the southern Thai province of Trang, he is often described with reference to his "working class" background. While Thai political commentators and fan Web sites praise his moderate politics and reputation for personal integrity, Chuan's acerbic speaking style and straightforward approach have also earned him many detractors. As a focus for liberal causes and consensus building, Chuan Leekpai is an elder statesman of the Thai political establishment.

Chuan was the first Thai prime minister who came from neither an aristocratic nor military background. He was also the first civilian prime minister to have been educated entirely in Thailand. Educated at Trang Wittaya and Silpa Suksa (Silpakorn Demonstration) Schools and having two degrees from Thammasat University's Faculty of Law, he has demonstrated a lifelong commitment to strengthening the country's education system.

Chuan's early work experience was also unique in that he was not originally employed by the government. After a short period spent working as an attorney, Chuan was elected to Parliament in 1969. He became a leading southern Thai politician during the turbulent 1970s. At various times of political upheaval, he was accused of being a Communist and went into hiding after the bloodshed in Bangkok of October 1976.

Early in his career, Chuan experienced a relatively rapid rise through the ministerial ranks. His varied career as a government minister included leading the ministries of justice, commerce, education, agriculture and cooperatives, and public health. As minister of public health, Chuan was instrumental in Thailand's initial steps to combat HIV/AIDS in the late 1980s, a move supported by the World Health Organisation and facilitated by donated supplies of condoms.

Chuan's first term as prime minister, from September 23, 1992 to July 12, 1995, was marked by its departure from the ideology of the brief Suchinda regime. In contrast, Chuan's coalition government, where his Democratic Party held the most seats, was antimilitarist and prodemocracy. Although billed as a reformist administration with an ambitious decentralisation agenda, this coalition government was often criticised for its weakness and inexperience.

Defeated in the 1995 elections, Chuan's Democratic Party was in opposition for the tumultuous events of 1997. In that year, the country's financial crisis led to the downfall of the government of political stalwart General Chavalit Yongchaiyudh. As the Thai currency (the baht) was floated and rapidly devalued, the Thai economy contributed to a major fiscal crisis throughout the Asian region. Chuan subsequently returned as Prime Minister to face the International Monetary Fund and a barrage of international interest and criticism. During this difficult period, he gained much recognition and respect for his shrewd international maneuvering.

Thailand's new constitution, which was adopted in 1997, was the culmination of a long process of violence, activism, and reorganisation. It imposed a number of major reforms on the country's political system, particularly targeting corruption and human rights violations. Promoting a progressive social and environmental agenda, the constitution was the result of a political evolution in which Chuan played a major role. This constitution defined the decentralisation and administrative reforms of his second term as prime minister.

Chuan's second term as prime minister, from November 9, 1997 to November 17, 2000, was marked by a new level of confidence. Assuming concurrent appointment as prime minister and defence minister, Chuan directed attention to reinforcing the preeminent role of civilians in administering the country. During this period, the occurrence of sporadic military *coups d'état*, which were once a common part of Thailand's political tradition, lessened.

Although his government was relatively successful in managing the country's recovery from the economic crisis, some of Chuan's closest political allies were implicated in a series of highly publicised corruption scandals. While this damaged the Democratic Party's standing, Chuan's reputation as an honest politician emerged from these controversies relatively unscathed.

Chuan's influence on Thailand's broader political and economic transformation is significant. During his two terms as prime minister, he consistently struggled to displace the military from its previously unassailable position in Thai politics. He encouraged and pressured the military to professionalise and, crucially, undermined its ability to impose itself on the fledgling constitutional and democratic reforms.

He also emphasised the role that Thailand could play within Southeast Asia. By championing the nation's seaboard developments, particularly in eastern Thailand, Chuan intended to make Thailand a hub for wider economic development. He marketed the country as a "financial gateway" for the region.

Defeated in the January 2001 elections, Chuan Leekpai is widely regarded as being overwhelmed by the charisma of his CEO-style opponent, the former policeman turned media magnate, Thaksin Shinawatra. The Democratic Party, with only 128 seats, became the major opposition to the Thaksin government. Ironically, under the new constitution, this small number of seats was not enough to effectively obstruct government legislative programs that could depend on the Thaksin government's enormous majority.

During Chuan's political career, southern Thailand has been Chuan's stronghold; his influence over its development is considerable. Because of Chuan's solidarity with southern issues, he elicits special affection among southern Thais who generally regard him as one of their "favourite sons." Even when the Democratic Party, Thailand's oldest political party, polls poorly in other regions, it often dominates the southern Thai political landscape. Chuan's mother, Thuan Leekpai, who lives in the family home in Trang, has also assumed some importance as a regional "mother figure." Even after Chuan stepped down as leader

in 2003, the Democratic Party retained much of its support in southern Thailand.

Many Thais define Chuan's periods as prime minister according to his personal honesty and dependability. While some members of his Democratic Party governments experienced serious claims of corruption, Chuan remained largely unsullied. His consensus-driven approach to negotiation and capacity to build coalition governments mark an important stage in Thailand's late twentieth-century political and economic upheavals.

NICHOLAS FARRELLY

See also Southeast Asia: History and Economic Development; Thailand

References and Further Reading

Connors, Michael Kelly. *Democracy and National Identity in Thailand*. New York, London: RoutledgeCurzon, 2003.

Hewison, Kevin, ed. *Political Change in Thailand: Democracy and Participation*. London, New York: Routledge, 1997.

McCargo, Duncan, ed. *Reforming Thai Politics*. Copenhagen: NIAS, Richmond, VA: Curzon, 2002.

Ockey, James. "Thai Society and Patterns of Political Leadership." *Asian Survey* 36, no. 4 (1996): 345–360.

Phongpaichit, Pasuk, and Chris Baker. *Thailand, Economy and Politics*. Selangor Darul Ehsan, Malaysia; Oxford; New York: Oxford University Press, 2002.

Punyaratabandhu, Suchitra. "Thailand in 1998: A False Sense of Recovery." *Asian Survey* 39, no. 1 (1999): 80–88.

Suwannathat-Pian, Kobkua. *Kings, Country and Constitutions: Thailand's Political Development, 1932–2000*. Richmond, VA: Curzon, 2003.

CIVIC EDUCATION

Civic education, otherwise referred to as citizenship education, can be conceptualized along two dimensions. Viewed from a polity or societal perspective, it is the process through which public knowledge and public values, attitudes, and group identification norms, perceived to be germane to political stability, are transmitted from one generation to the other. Included in these attributes are the history and structure of political institutions, loyalty to the nation, positive attitudes toward political authority, belief in fundamental values (like the notion of equality and rule of law), interest in political participation, and dexterity in monitoring public policy. Civic education can also be viewed from an individual perspective, in which case it encapsulates the process of public knowledge as well as values and group identifications being accorded private meaning and internalized as guides for behavior (Torney-Judith *et al.* 1999: 15–16; 1992:158).

Civic education encompasses both explicit and implicit goals that may be articulated through an array of educational programs, activities, and statements. The most obvious of these include a statement of educational goals, curriculum guides, a context of instructional textbooks, and teacher-prepared lessons. Explicit routines and rituals, such as reciting the national anthem, using a community service, engaging in group cooperation, using discussion as a teaching tool, and learning strategies, further exemplify the variety of ways in which civic education is transmitted within the educational realm.

Nevertheless, civic education is controversial. There is a clear absence of consensus regarding the knowledge base and attitude orientation necessary to attain effective civic education (Hursh 1994:767). How much factual knowledge of history or government structures, for instance, is required for effective citizenship? Political problems are nebulous, and arriving at an appropriate consensus about resolving them is a vast territory riddled with numerous disagreements, both philosophically and epistemologically. Furthermore, disagreements abound regarding the extent to which schools should emphasize support for the prevailing political order if doing so sacrifices students' opportunity to develop a critical mind. One school of thought avers that successful instruction in civic education depends largely on a climate characterized by open debate in a range of political issues.

Regional and National Differentiation in Civic Education

The substance of civic education tends to differ by region and country, no doubt a consequence of the contextual reality prevailing in each area. Nations have been keen to align civic education programs to their sociopolitical interests against a backdrop of the need to foster national cohesion. Thus, nationalism and patriotism have been featured prominently in civic education programs of nations engulfed in ethnic divisions and rivalries. Civic education in this instance seeks to instill in students values that promote national consensus and formation of loyal citizens, leading to national political integration. Indeed, the emergence of the school as a formal institution is often regarded as a logical sequence in the process of national boundary-maintenance function (Fagerlind and Saha 1995:132). Through the founding president Julius Nyerere's educational philosophy of Education

for Self-Reliance, Tanzania managed to weave a political education program geared toward national unity with the Kiswahili language as the medium of communication and an emblem of cultural identity.

In other contexts, civic education has been conceptualized in spiritual and ethical terms. Many developing nations in Asia fall within this category. Countries espousing religious and moral principles in their civic education content tend to give prominence to interpersonal relationships and moral rectitude in contra-distinction to an emphasis on individualism and personal liberty, which is at the core of most civic education programs in the developed nations of the West.

Diversity in civic education extends beyond the concern for national integration and religio-moral fortitude. In some quarters, civic education is envisioned as a vehicle for inculcating in students an array of values that will inspire "and enable them to play their parts as informed, responsible, committed, and effective members of modern democratic system" (Butts 1980:1). Still, other scholars and practitioners situate civic education within the rubric of conflict in power relations. According to this view, civic education should focus on developing an educational climate and school structure that revitalizes civic culture; hence, students and teachers examine the nature of meaningful self-development in the context of the entire society, as well as the relationship between the individual and society and between the individual power and collective power (Hursh 1994:767).

Civic Education in Africa

Civic education in Africa has its genesis in the postcolonial era. The need to change the inherited colonial education system and to create national unity provided the dual impetus for citizenship education programs at the dawn of independence in the 1960s. Disciplines such as history, geography, and civics were attractive to national leaders and educators as entry points in the political socialization of students. The goals of civic education then were fourfold: (i) to enable students to understand people's interaction with their cultural, social, and physical environments; (ii) to help students appreciate their homes and heritages; (iii) to develop skills and attitudes expected of citizens; and (iv) to teach students to express their ideas in a variety of ways (Merryfield and Muyanda-Mutebi 1991:621). These goals still continue to underlie civic education in the African continent today.

The development and implementation of civic education programs in Africa has been documented by Merryfield and Muyanda-Mutebi (1991) and Clive Harber (1989) in their detailed research on social studies and political education, respectively. Central to civic education in Africa is the stress laid on national development as the ultimate objective of the program. Civic education for national development has been envisioned in a holistic fashion by incorporating the cultivation of a national consensus on sociopolitical issues, ethical behavior, addressing environmental challenges, and developing problem-solving skills. Under these conditions, civic education is expected not only to lead to national development but also to promote social harmony and self-sufficiency as a counter to political disintegration and as a catalyst for social solidarity. It is, in effect, an "important legitimating agency for establishing legal jurisdiction of state authority, and above all for defining the criteria for membership in the state, that is, the bestowal of citizenship" (Fagerlind and Saha 1995:132).

Even with a similar underlying philosophy of civic education, research is explicit that political messages transmitted tend to differ from one country to the next and even within the same country (Harber 1989:195). In each country, knowledge and skills are learned in a context in which high priority is given to certain unique values. In Tanzania (in *Siasa*), until recently, emphasis was placed on socialism, in Zambia it was humanism, while in Kenya it was capitalism (in the subjects of civics, as well as social education and ethics). Educational institutions have generally accepted that these goals are not open to criticism, but the process used or needed to attain them are open to discussion.

Civic education in the continent has not been without its challenges. The tension between the attempt to create basic national goals and the role of civic education in creating a critical awareness of political phenomena remains delicate. While this situation is not uniquely African, it does indicate the functional limits of civic education as a consensus builder in the continent. Another problem is the discrepancy that prevails between the conceptualization of civic education by educational officials and the practical realities of the classroom. Teachers have tended to view civic education as an amalgam of subjects unrelated to citizenship education; they do not associate civic education with the content, attitudes, or skills of citizenship education. Lack of clarity about the meaning of civic education and how it differs from individual subjects of civics, ethics, geography, and history, common among teachers and teacher educators, hampers the development and diffusion of the education (Merryfield and Muyanda Mutebi 1991:623). The preponderance of examinations in school curriculum is also a major drawback in the development of civic education.

Civic Education in Asia

Traditionally, civic education in Asia, especially in the eastern regions, has been characterized by a disproportionate influence of the Confucian tradition in providing legitimacy to schools as they take on the mantle in providing moral education. Schools in the region are at the hub in teaching a code of behavior for everyday life alongside political allegiance to the state. Thus, ethical behavior and loyalty to the state are not regarded as mutually exclusive attributes in civic life.

This philosophy of civic education and the pedagogical process have, however, undergone transformations depending on the political reality prevailing in each country in the region. As of today, hardly is the civic education *modus operandi* homogeneous across East Asia; distinctive features characterize each nation. South Korea, for instance, has used civic (values) education to instruct students in traditional Korean culture, nationalism, and anticommunism since the end of the Korean War in 1953. The aim has been to cultivate in the students a deep sense of cultural pride while at the same time build a strong fervor of nationalism as a counter to the threat posed by the next-door Communist North Korea (Hursh 1994:768; Suh 1988:93). The People's Republic of China stressed the importance of equality and redistribution up to 1979 when focus turned toward hierarchical values. Beginning in the later part of the 1980s, Chinese schools offered courses on Communist ideology and morality, extolling the virtues of "correct attitude towards labor" and "the ability to distinguish between right and wrong" (Meyer 1988:127).

Nowhere in Asia are the dynamics between realignment of civic education to the changing political equation more vivid than in Hong Kong. During the 1960s, 1970s, and the 1980s, when capitalist-oriented Hong Kong was ensured political-economic continuity as a colony of the British, civic education was less overtly political and was more concerned with instilling traits of good behavior "to enable pupils to be well-informed and to become civic-minded enough to act as good citizens in the larger community they belong" (Wing On 1999:315). The decision of the British government to transfer the administration of the colony to Communist China in 1997 gave impetus to a more overt form of civic education with emphasis on loyalty to Hong Kong political process and institutions as a distinct nation. The political stress became even more explicit in the 1996 Government and Public Affairs (GPA) syllabus, which placed stronger emphasis on understanding China and on Hong Kong's colonial transition (*ibid.* 1999:317). Observe the Curriculum Development Council's *Guidelines on Civic Education*:

> Politically speaking, one's civic identity is defined by ones national identity. The national community therefore constitutes the ultimate domestic context for one's civic learning. National spirit such as nationalism and patriotism is essential not only for one's national identity and sense of belonging, but also for the cohesion and strength of one's own nation. (*ibid.* 1999:321)

Research nevertheless demonstrates that civic education in the country is still encumbered by poor textbooks, inadequate attention paid to the issue of national cohesion, and a general apathy toward the subject.

Civic Education in Latin America

Latin America has had a long tradition of civic education. Indeed, one of the greatest advocates and practitioners of civic education, Paulo Freire, experimented his ideas and writings in Brazil. The country has had the most extensive civic education program, the MOBRAL, built around the Freire concept of "conscientization" of the masses, leading to sociopolitical and economic liberation. Cuba has also had a strong civic education program constructed around President Fidel Castro's Communist ideology with strong emphasis on loyalty to the state.

As in other regions of the developing world, goals of civic education in Latin America are as diverse as the multiplicity of political agendas. Those nations that have been under military rule have extensively used civic education programs to buttress their regimes. Argentina, Peru, and Uruguay, among others, have introduced political education in schools with the aim of securing support from the youth. Nations that were former colonies of European countries tend to share their goals in civic education. Finally, emergent democracies in the region are keen on using civic education to build a democratic culture (Hursh 1994:768; Cummings *et al.* 1988).

Colombia represents a recent example of a Latin American country trying to strengthen its fledging democracy. Via the 1994 Resolution 1600, the country added legitimacy to civics as education in and for democracy (Rueda 1999). The resolution stated

that civic education is "to live democracy" at school and that the student acquires a citizen's "way of being" basically from interpersonal relationship. The civic education initiative has realized a number of important developments, including (i) the increased sensitivity on the part of teachers and the wider community regarding the discourse on school education for democracy; (ii) the increased initiatives by government and nonprofit agencies toward the development of new approaches to education in democracy; (iii) reforms in the organization and administration of schools, resulting into more flexibility and less hierarchical structures; and (iv) advances in instructional content and teaching methodologies.

In spite of these achievements, the program suffers from a number of problems. Wide dissonance abounds between classroom discourse about democratic school climate and the daily reality in the school environment. There is also widespread discontinuity between the goals of education in democracy as articulated in the educational policies and how these goals are translated into legislation, interpreted, and implemented at the school level. Besides inadequate and inappropriate teaching and learning materials is the added problem of widespread violence and gang culture in the society, which runs counter to the goals of education in democracy.

Prospects and Problems of Civic Education

Undoubtedly, civic education continues to be featured prominently in the educational systems of many Third World countries. The education is either planned and systematic or simply the result of a lack of awareness of the political ramifications of school organization or the curriculum (the so-called hidden curriculum). The educational process takes place through textbooks, exposure to national symbols, the nature of classroom teaching, school structures, courses in political education, youth organizations, subject choice, access to schooling, and other such factors. The political messages transmitted differ from country to country and, sometimes, within the same country.

In evaluating the efficacy of the various approaches to civic education and how these have affected values held by students, it is imperative to underscore the research evidence. While the general intention of civic education curricula is to inculcate values consistent with national political aspirations, the realization of these objectives is influenced by the environment in which the classroom and school operate. In other words, students learn as much or more from what they experience and from the models that they see (hidden curriculum) than as from what they are told. Pedagogical techniques that center on student participation in class discussions and expressions produce students who are more politically knowledgeable and interested and less authoritarian (Torney *et al.* 1975:37). In contrast, those taught through a teacher-centered approach with stress on patriotic rituals and lectures tend to be more authoritarian and less knowledgeable about politics. Research has shown that African schools generally suffer from rigid bureaucratic structures, authoritarian leadership, lack of accountability amidst corruption, as well as shortages of resources and contemporary social pressures (Harber 1989:112–129). This hampers the effectiveness of civic education.

Issues surrounding the nature and form of civic education continue to cloud the programs. Developing countries are still caught in the debate over whether civic education should emphasize a narrow range of values, such as patriotism and nationalism, or a broader spectrum of values. These debates have intensified as agreements over what to emphasize have declined. In Kenya, for instance, the first and more explicit model of civic education in the 1970s was articulated through a school curriculum that was bland, descriptive, and rather conservative by avoiding or downplaying potentially controversial topics (Scott 1983:273). The curriculum displayed a complete absence of ideological orientation, and it did not mention the ruling party KANU or the national ideology of African Socialism. The syllabus in the current 8-4-4-education system has, however, been more radical in approach; through the twin subjects of history and government and social education and ethics, students have been instructed on the importance of subservience to the state, the president, and the ruling party KANU, notwithstanding that the country is an incipient multiparty democracy. Similar experiences abound in many Third World countries, and they indicate that civic education curricula are yet to move from standards implied in scientific-rational views of the state and instead create public discussions and seek to develop reasonable citizens who discharge their civic purposes.

The dichotomy surrounding civic education and national unity creates another obstacle. The basic premise of civic education is to serve as a catalyst for national consciousness and the formation of loyal citizens. Civic education in schools is viewed by some as an effective tool to break down local or regional identities and loyalties and replace them with national identities and loyalties. However, research in Ghana, Liberia, Kenya, and Nigeria shows that schooling has often been effective in increasing knowledge about the nation rather than enhancing national identity (Harber 1989:195). The case of Nigeria is significantly instructive in that it demonstrates the broader interface between ethnicity, religion, and role of religion in society in mitigating the role of the school in the forging national unity.

Rural schools in Nigeria have been less effective than their urban counterparts in teaching about the nation. Research is explicit that ethnic differences have been exaggerated and aggravated through the education system with the result that the impact of education has been disintegrative rather than integrative (Fagerlind and Saha 1995:133). Historically, from the colonial times to the present, Nigeria has been an ethnically and culturally divided country. The British colonial policy supported the development of Christian missionary-led Western education in the southern part of the country while the north was left intact under the influence of Muslim culture. At independence, the South provided the bulk of the political elite. This disparity was later to become a disintegrative factor in Nigerian society as corrective measures in employment had to be taken, which led to charges of discrimination expressed by the South. Indeed, the tendency for educational access and attainment to discriminate unequally along ethnic, racial, regional, and other distinctions create real obstacles to the effectiveness of civic education in political integration.

ISHMAEL IRUNGU MUNENE

References and Further Reading

Butts, R. F. *The Revival of Civic Learning: A Rationale for Citizenship Education in American Schools*. Bloomington, IN: Phi Delta Kappan Educational Foundation, 1980.

Fagerlind, Ingemar, and Lawrence Saha. *Education and National Development: A Comparative Perspective*. Oxford: Butterworth-Heinemann, 1995.

Harber, Clive. *Politics in African Education*. London and Basingstoke: Macmillan Publishers, 1989.

Hursh, D. "Civic Education." In *The International Encyclopedia of Education*, edited by Torsten Husen and Neville Postlethwaite. New York: Elsevier Sciences, 1994.

Merryfield, Merry, and Peter Muyanda-Mutebi. "Research on Social Studies in Africa." *Handbook of Research on Social Studies Teaching and Learning*. New York: Macmillan Publishing, 1991.

Meyer, J. "A Subtle and Silent Transformation: Moral Education in Taiwan and The People's Republic of China." In *The Revival of Values Education in Asia and the West*, edited by W. Cummings *et al.* Oxford: Pergamon Press, 1988.

Rueda, Alvaro Rodriquez. "Education for Democracy in Colombia." In *Civic Education Across Countries: Twenty-Four National Case Studies from the IEA Civic Education Project*, edited by Judith Torney-Purta *et al.* Amsterdam: International Association for Evaluation of Educational Achievement, 1999.

Scott, G. *Education for Political Development in Kenya and Tanzania: A Comparative Analysis of the Development Policies in Two Independent States.* Unpublished Ph.D. University of Liverpool, 1983.

Suh, S. "Ideologies in Korea's Morals and Social Studies Texts: A Content Analysis." In *The Revival of Values Education in Asia and the West*, edited by W. Cummings *et al.* Oxford: Pergamon Press, 1988.

Torney, Judith, *et al. Civic Education in Ten Countries: An Empirical Study.* New York: Wiley, 1975.

Torney-Purta, Judith. "Civic Education." In *Encyclopedia of Educational Research*, edited by Marvin Alkin. New York: Macmillan Publishing Company, 1992.

———, *et al.*, eds. *Civic Education Across Countries: Twenty-Four National Case Studies from the IEA Civic Education Project.* Amsterdam: International Association for Evaluation of Educational Achievement, 1999.

Wing On, Lee. "Controversies of Civic Education in Political Transition in Hong Kong." In *Civic Education Across Countries: Twenty-Four National Case Studies from the IEA Civic Education Project*, edited by Judith Torney-Purta *et al.* Amsterdam: International Association for Evaluation of Educational Achievement, 1999.

CIVIL DISOBEDIENCE

Civil disobedience is the deliberate defiance of a law or norm upheld by duly constituted governmental authority. The defiance is public and based on reasoned argument. It usually consists of a symbolic act and is carried out for a specific end. It is also referred to as passive resistance or "satyagraha."

Since the time of Socrates, civil disobedience was practiced by individuals and groups, such as the early Christians. St. Thomas Aquinas and later John Locke have also justified civil disobedience.

During the sixteenth century, an important thinker in France, la Boétie, attacked the basis of the theoretical foundations of royal absolutism. In linking power and popular consent, he emphasized that the former emerged only out of the latter.

Over time, a tradition of popular dissent developed in the West, and in the nineteenth and twentieth centuries, with the spread of democratic ideas worldwide, a corpus of political practices centering on the concept of civil disobedience developed. In this connection, the essay of the American thinker Henry David Thoreau, "On the Duty of Civil Disobedience" (1849), marks an important milestone.

It was, however, Mohandas Karamchand Gandhi who, in leading the Indian national struggle against British rule, refined mass civil disobedience as a tool of political action to bring about political change. His sources of inspiration were both Eastern and Western thought. He termed his method *satyagraha*, which means an insistence upon and holding on to truth.

After an initial movement in Transvaal against the government in South Africa in 1906, Gandhi led his most famous campaign, the Salt Satyagraha of 1930–1931. The campaign began with Gandhi symbolically breaking the unjust salt law of the British government in India. Gandhi believed most conflicts in society and between the citizens and government could be solved by resorting to satyagraha, which he called a science in the making. What made Gandhi's philosophy distinctive was his insistence on *ahimsa* (nonviolence) and love.

The civil disobedient acts in accordance with a higher law, which may be divine or natural law, or indeed a person's own conscience. The civil disobedient frequently chooses intentionally to break the law publicly and sometimes with dramatic effect. By doing so, the protestor brings the injustice they are protesting against into the public eye.

An important aspect of civil disobedience is that the protestor must be acting not to achieve some private gain but to bring an end to an unjust act or law, which the protestor believes must be abolished for the common good. In doing so, the civil disobedient does not want to do away with the entire established order but targets some specific law; and this person does it according to the dictates of his or her conscience, which is considered the highest moral authority.

It is clear that civil disobedience has a chance of being carried out only in a system with some democratic norms and morality. It would be impossible as a strategy in a dictatorship. When civil disobedients do perform an act of defiance, they know they are going against the law and are committing a crime. They, in effect, deliberately court punishment. At the same time, they make a reasoned defense of their actions: on no account can an act of disobedience of law be taken lightly.

The term *civil* in "civil disobedience" is not easily explained because it has meant different things to different people. But the following meanings can be construed. "Civil" may mean the reverse of "uncivil" or "uncivilized," and in carrying out acts of civil disobedience, the protestor holds up a model code of conduct, which will inspire citizens to conduct themselves according to a higher ideal of morality. "Civil" may mean that the protest recognizes the legitimacy of the political authority overall and the duties of citizenship.

"Civil" may further indicate opposition to violence of all kinds and include a determination to adhere to nonviolence. In addition, in this sense, it may mean an acceptance that the state alone has the monopoly of the legitimate use of violence. The insistence on nonviolence is found in most civil disobedience movements and is a function of the belief that they are based on a higher morality.

Civil disobedience has been criticized on the ground that it encourages disobedience of all laws, and its logical culmination would be anarchy. What needs to be understood is that the context and circumstances in which civil disobedience takes place would be different in each specific instance, but the nature of the action would essentially be the same. Since the achievement of independence by India in 1947, the technique of civil disobedience has been applied by national liberation struggles in other Asian and African countries.

In America, the greatest civil disobedient was Dr. Martin Luther King, Jr., who led the Black Civil Rights Movement and suffered eventually the same fate as Gandhi—death by an assassin's bullet. This type of fate also underscores the opposition such movements may face from within the community itself.

In Western Europe, civil disobedience has been resorted to by the suffragette campaign in England and by groups favoring disarmament, particularly nuclear disarmament. Eastern Europe, during Communist rule, witnessed civil disobedience acts, particularly in Poland, to wrest greater freedom from the government.

In more recent times, the popular movement in the Philippines against the Marcos government and the Movement for Democracy led by Aung San Suu Kyi of Myanmar have been inspired by Gandhi's example as well as by the Buddhist precepts prevalent in that country. Suu Kyi and her followers, through nonviolent acts of civil disobedience, have tried to gain more freedom for the people of Myanmar and eventually for the restoration of democracy.

AMRITA SINGH

See also Gandhi, Mohandas

References and Further Reading

Bleiker, Roland. *Popular Dissent, Human Agency and Global Politics*. Cambridge: Cambridge University Press, 2000.
Cohen, Carl. *Civil Disobedience: Conscience, Tactics and the Law*. New York: Columbia University, 1971.
Parekh, Bhikhu. *Gandhi*. New York: Oxford University Press, 1997.

CIVIL RIGHTS

The establishment and augmentation of civil rights has been a difficult process. The general recognition of popular sovereignty, a system of nation-states requiring legal order for recognition, and a global economic system requiring legal protections all militate in favor of the recognition of certain basic civil rights. But the institutionalization of civil rights, especially in a globalizing world, is problematic and nowhere more so than in developing countries. There the contradiction between the civil rights imperatives of protecting freedom and providing for equal citizenship is complicated by the "cruel choice" between accepting continued vulnerability and taking steps toward economic independence (Berlin 1958; Goulet 1975).

Rights can be described as set of human attributes that are necessary for adequate functioning and, consequently, should be protected for each individual (Freeden 1991). Civil rights—rights that particularly concern limits on and obligations of governments—are a subset of these. Two aspects of social activity are usually included. The first is economic rights. Here the acceptance of individual economic freedoms, such as the right to work and contract, the right to free movement, the right to own property, and the acceptance of the rule of law in economic relationships are paramount (Marshall 1965). Associated with these are political rights; recognition of equal citizenship status, including the right to vote and to hold office, the right to free expression and association, the right to legal processes to challenge government action individually and corporately, and the right to an affirmative defense of equal citizenship.

As can be seen, the concept of civil rights combines both limitations on governments ("civil liberties") and affirmative duties of governments to maintain the legal status of citizens ("civil rights"). Since complicated ideas usually result in complicated policies, it should come as no surprise that civil rights policy has been a difficulty for most governments. Governments in developing countries have several characteristics that make this difficulty even more intractable.

First, developing countries must contend with the legacy of their colonial past. Needless to say, in colonial times both aspects of civil rights received short shrift from metropolitan governments. Economic freedoms were denied because extensive legal discriminations deprived the native population of equal property rights, educational opportunities, and the freedom to work as and where they chose. This was combined with a subordinate legal status that destroyed the rule of law in colonial dominions (Mamdani 1978; Prado 1969). Second, political rights were severely limited. Not only were natives deprived of meaningful participation in government, but also the colonial governments made an active effort to facilitate political divisions and economic exploitation (Olorunsola 1972).

As independence was achieved, new governments faced a quandary. Their populations demanded equal citizenship status, but ethnic groups favored by colonial governments resented losing their position, while others insisted on reducing it. The sudden extension of political rights further activated these internal conflicts (Olorunsola 1972). Lurking in the background, there were the unfulfilled tasks of the preindependence period, particularly the need to accelerate growth in poverty-stricken economies.

While different regions faced this dilemma at different times, the response of the new states was remarkably similar. First, great progress was made in the legal extension of economic rights. The colonial economic and educational discriminations were removed from law as were restrictions on the right to work, though economic inequalities often negated the effect of legal changes. Political changes were made as well, with suffrage rights and basic civil liberties legally, though again not practically, guaranteed.

Second, the new governments also came to grips with the problems of promoting economic growth. This led to immediate conflicts with the new rights environment that had been created. Growth demands capital accumulation, and capital accumulation requires sacrifice. Different growth strategies demanded different sacrifices, but all required state capacities for meeting and ameliorating political demands unlikely to be found in newly institutionalized environments (Huntington 1968). The result was a sometimes striking diminution of civil rights as governments attempted to construct the necessary political consensus through authoritarian means. In the later part of the twentieth century, this often took a familiar course: the establishment of one-party regimes, harassment of political enemies, resulting political and economic turmoil, overthrow of civilian government by the military, establishment of dictatorial polities, and a spiral downward toward economic autarky and political repression.

As the twentieth century ended, new forces improved the civil rights picture worldwide. First, the collapse of the Soviet Union meant that authoritarian regimes allied to one side or the other in the Cold War and could no longer depend on support from the respective opponents. This was coupled with a new international concern with respect for human rights, a concern partially institutionalized by the end of the twentieth century. International and nongovernmental organizations joined the democratic developed nation-states in putting pressure for increased civil rights on regimes worldwide (Brysk 2002). Second, this pressure was reinforced by the demands of international financial organizations for governmental reforms aimed at loosening the already weakening regulatory grip of governments in the new states. Economic growth had slowed in lock step with dictatorial rule. As the global economy became more integrated and, coincidentally, more stressed, the IMF and World Bank began to demand changes in "governance," leading to greater accountability in return for exchange credits. Part of these new demands was an insistence on respect for political and, particularly, economic rights (World Bank 1992).

The results of this new emphasis on civil rights, accompanied by an international consensus in favor of democratic regimes, have had salutary effects in the developing countries. The number of democratic governments has increased, acceptance of *coups d'état* against elected governments has decreased, and the level of protection for civil rights at the national level is at historic levels. Despite this new acceptance, however, the cruel choice is still present. While a few developing countries have shown signs of developing self-sustaining growth, others have stumbled badly after initially favorable starts, and many have shown little progress of any kind. Indeed, decades of economic and political reform have done nothing, on average, to accelerate economic growth. At the same time, economic inequality has actually increased, both within and between countries. Making civil rights fit within development projects that could create independent economies and democratic polities in developing countries remains a problem for the future (Seidman 1978).

TRACY L. R. LIGHTCAP

See also Democratization; Human Rights as a Foreign Policy Issue; Human Rights: Definition and Violations; Legal Systems

References and Further Reading

Berlin, Sir Isiah. *Two Concepts of Liberty*. Oxford: Oxford University, 1958.
Brysk, Alison, ed. *Globalization and Human Rights*. Berkeley, CA: University of California, 2002.
Freeden, Michael. *Rights*. Minneapolis, MN: University of Minnesota, 1991.
Goulet, Denis. *The Cruel Choice: A New Concept in the Theory of Development*. New York: Atheneum, 1975.
Huntington, Samuel. *Political Order in Changing Societies*. New Haven, CT: Yale, 1968.
Mamdani, Mahmood. *Politics and Class Formation in Uganda*. New York: Monthly Review, 1978.
Marshall, T. H. *Class, Citizenship, and Social Development*. Garden City, KS: Anchor, 1965.
Olorunsola, Victor, ed. *The Politics of Cultural Sub-Nationalism in Africa*. Garden City, KS: Anchor, 1972.
Prado, Caio. *The Colonial Background of Modern Brazil*. Berkeley, CA: University of California, 1969.
Seidman, Robert. *The State, Law, and Development*. New York: St. Martin's, 1978.
World Bank. *Governance and Development*. Washington, DC: World Bank, 1992.

CIVIL SOCIETY

Twenty years ago, the notion of "civil society" hardly occurred outside circles of Hegel-students and Gramsci-specialists. In the twenty-first century, search machines come up with hundreds of titles. This booming civil society discourse, accompanying the development and promotion of civil society in Eastern Europe and the developing world, feeds on the philosophical notion and the historical development of civil society in Europe and North America. Both the factual and the discursive aspects of civil society must be taken into account because they do not coincide: Western society had not suddenly changed when the notion reappeared. This either means that Western society is not a civil society, which contradicts the fact that it is considered its main example, or that it is possible to *be* a civil society without being *named* civil society.

If *society* is the way in which the human species exists, *civil* society must be one of its specific forms. Since human beings organize their existence reflexively and consciously, the notion of "civil society" is part of the reflexive self-description of mankind. This implies that there is no external viewpoint, not even quasi-external, from which to describe civil society objectively. From a strictly empirical point of view, therefore, the concept has to be denied scientific status or to be instrumentalized in such a way as to leave out the normative aspects that account for its current popularity.

I propose a definition of "civil society" as a social sphere of free associational activity of individual citizens on and across the border between private and public and of the institutional effects of that activity. This definition presupposes an economic sphere—a market—from which it is distinct, a state that through legislation secures the space where free association can take place and contains individuals who are capable and willing to act as members of civil society. It also presupposes the reproduction of its conditions: resistance against state interference, protest against merger with market forces, courses in civic routines, reinforced association through meetings and mailings, and pluralistic theoretical civil society discourse, all of which constitute a complex reproductive process.

The organizing principle of civil society, namely voluntary or uncoerced association by individual citizens, is based on the more fundamental principle of free individuality, which equally lies at the basis of free market and liberal democracy. This, however, does not imply their necessary combination, nor does it exclude the formation of a community within civil society; what it does preclude is a community that is not ultimately based on the individual decision to associate.

One of the paradoxes of late modernity is that the type of society that was criticized by Hegelians, Marxists, Conservatives, and Communitarians for its atomizing and self-destructive individualism has reappeared as a major "vision of the good life" (Gellner 1994). Both in the liberal tradition, which identified civil and free society, and in the more critical Hegelian and Marxist traditions, civil society was thought to include the economic sphere as its substance. The crucial recent innovation is the distinction, and even opposition, of market and civil society. This innovation is an effect of the increased functional differentiation of late-modern society, but it also reflects an attempt to idealize civil society as a world of virtue, in contrast with a "demonic" market as the world of profit, exploitation, and self-interest. The same tendency is manifest in the opposition between civil society and the potentially oppressive state. In countries with a weak polity, this trend is even hazardous, especially when connected with foreign developmental programs that aim to strengthen civil society. Politics and market may be "dirty" and harsh, but that is not a reason to idealize civil society. Moreover, just as a liberal state presupposes a strong civil society, a flourishing civil society presupposes a strong polity to guarantee its legal basis.

Civil society discourse is an integral part of civil society itself, similar to the way in which phenomena like culture, nation, or philosophy are unimaginable without a discourse reproducing them through the double move of self-definition and self-delineation, meaning the exclusion of "others." What is excluded by civil society depends on how it defines itself. Here, two lines can be distinguished. Along the first line, civil society describes a type of society, distinguished from tribal or traditional society, believed to have preceded it and is contrasted with a totalitarian society, considered its major threat. In this broad sense, civil society is identical with the modern society that Ernest Gellner has labeled "Atlantic" (Gellner 1994).

Along the second line, civil society denotes a specific and central element of society in an increasingly large part of the world. This second, narrow sense of civil society excludes from itself, on the one hand, all other spheres of society, and, on the other hand, uncivil society. Concerning the first aspect, there is widespread consensus that civil society is distinct from the polity, that it is not identical with the strictly private sphere of family life and intimacy, and finally, that it is distinct from the market (Cohen 1997). The second aspect tends not to receive much attention but is crucial for a proper understanding: civil society is civilized society, the sphere of civility and organization as opposed to that of violence and disorder—civil war, crime, hooliganism, fanaticism, and terrorism (Keane 1998; Colas 1992, 1997). Civil society is, among other things, the transformation of potentially conflicting differences of interest, value, and opinion into a multitude of potentially competing associations. As such, it is closely related to a pluralistic democratic polity (Fine 1997).

Contrary to what civil society *discourse* often suggests, civil society is not a thing. It cannot be seen, measured, counted, made, or imported. It cannot, without arbitrary choices, be instrumentalized in social or political science. The number of non-governmental organizations (NGOs) or the size of their memberships are important indexes, but they do not exhaust the phenomenon. Factors such as commitment and self-description in terms of civil society have to be taken into account as well.

Civil society is unnecessary: freedom to associate presupposes freedom not to associate. Since individuals must breathe, eat, and live somewhere, but *must* not defend human rights, fight global capitalism, or collect stamps in uncoerced association with others, civil society is intrinsically fragile. From an economic perspective, civil society activity is one of *leisure,* however "profitable" its long-term results may be in terms of social cohesion and civility. Consequently, civil society is not makable. Necessary conditions for its existence and flourishing can be realized, but its sufficient condition, the repeated associative action, and commitment of individual human beings cannot. Therefore, programs to stimulate or protect it make sense wherever citizens are too much concerned with securing the means of their subsistence to engage in any kind of associative activity.

Until recently, civil society discourse has focused on a national civil society, territorially congruous with national states and national economies. However, the globalization of markets, the internationalization of politics, and the emergence of worldwide communication networks have facilitated rapidly growing "global civil society." While in principle covering the entire globe, this society is in practice limited to those who have access to the media in which it articulates and reproduces itself. Because large parts of the globe's population continue to be illiterate and have no access to telephones or the Internet, this civil society may well be global, but it certainly is not universal, and it generates new forms of exclusion and inequality.

The same global civil society, however, is yielding impulses in the direction of a political and social order that does match global capitalism and the withering away of the national state. The intrinsically conflicting nature of human society reappears at the global level, and transnational civil society is one of the ways of dealing with it (Walzer 1995). While civil society has always crossed national borders, transnational NGOs in the twenty-first century typically are not second-order associations of national associations, but they are institutionalized networks of individual human beings who by association with like-minded individuals transcend their national background from the outset and who are prepared to confront any global economic actor or national government.

In the foreword to the *Global Civil Society 2001* yearbook, Anthony Giddens writes:

> If civil society, rather than the state, supplies the 'grounding of citizenship' and is therefore crucial to sustaining an open public space, how can this be achieved outside the realm of the nation-state? If civil society is fundamental to constraining the power of both markets and government, and if neither a market economy nor a democratic state can function effectively without the civilising influence of civic association, how can this 'balancing act' be achieved at a global level? Can the concept of a global civil society provide an answer? (Anheier 2001)

In these few lines, Giddens indicates what are, to many concerned inhabitants of the planet Earth, burning questions and implicitly invokes the contemporary notion of civil society.

Historically, the concept of civil society reaches back to Aristotle's *koinonia politike,* translated into Latin as *societas civilis* and synonymous with political society as late as John Locke's *Second Treatise of Government* (1690). Scottish Enlightenment theorists were the first to draw the clear distinction between the polity (state) and civil society, which has since become classical (Seligman 1992). With Hegel and Marx, it obtained the negative connotation of a "bourgeois society" (*bürgerliche Gesellschaft*), which is why in contemporary German, a new concept of *Zivilgesellschaft* has been coined to distance the contemporary phenomenon from the older notion; similarly, in Russian post-Marxist vocabulary, *grazhdanskoye obshchestvo* replaces *burzhuaznoye obshchestvo*. All this shows that civil society cannot be a neutral category of the social sciences. Rather, it also performs an ideological function, legitimizing, for example, the attribution of research money in Western academia and the foreign aid industry in the developing world (van Rooy 1998).

Another important question is whether civil society, a product of European history, is not a trope for Western society: if so, civil society discourse appears as part of Western cultural imperialism and of economic globalization, and non-Western countries would have ample reason to be cautious to make it part of their own policies. The best answer to this problem is a deconstruction of the myth of Western society as an all-round success, a recognition of its contested and conflicting nature, and of the many forms of incivility covered by material wealth.

Civil society emerged in parts of the world with a predominantly Christian religious culture, and its emergence was connected with the Reformation, the Enlightenment, and secularization. But there is no pertinent reason why similar processes cannot occur in cultural realms dominated by such religions as Islam or Confucianism. Although some religious traditions may favor civil society more than others, it cannot be reasonably argued that any religion excludes its coming to be. Moreover, religiously motivated associations are important elements of civil society.

A substantial part of the recent discussion, finally, turns around the question whether civil society is a universal model that can be applied to any part of the world, irrespective of cultural and socioeconomic differences, or whether it needs to be adapted to local circumstances to such an extent that it becomes questionable if one is still talking about the same thing (Hann 1996; Kaviraj 2001). The least one can say is that in Western and non-Western contexts alike, civil society stands for the same things: limitation of state interference, control over market forces, and voluntary association of active and committed citizens. Whether this is the "good life" is a question only individual human beings can decide, but it definitely is a universal vision.

EVERT VAN DER ZWEERDE

See also Civil Rights; Constitutionalism, Definition; Democratization; Elections; Free Market Economy; Human Rights as a Foreign Policy Issue; Human Rights: Definition and Violations

References and Further Reading

Anheier, Helmut, Marlies Glasius, and Mary Kaldor, eds. *Global Civil Society 2001.* Oxford: Oxford University Press, 2001.

Cohen, Jean L., and Andrew Arato. *Civil Society and Political Theory.* Cambridge, London: MIT Press, 1997.

Colas, Dominique. *Le Glaive et le Fléau; Généalogie du Fanatisme et de la Société Civile.* Paris: Grasset, 1992. Translated as *Civil Society and Fanaticism.* Stanford, CA: Stanford University Press, 1997.

Fine, Robert, and Shirin Rai, eds. *Civil Society: Democratic Perspectives.* London, and Portland, OR: Frank Cass, 1997.

Gellner, Ernest. *Conditions of Liberty; Civil Society and Its Rivals.* London: Penguin, 1994.

Hall, John A., ed. *Civil Society: Theory, History, Comparison.* Cambridge: Polity Press, 1995.

Hann, Chris, and Elizabeth Dunn, eds. *Civil Society; Challenging Western Models.* London and New York: Routledge, 1996.

Kaviraj, Sudipta, and Sunil Khilnani, eds. *Civil Society; History and Possibilities.* Cambridge: Cambridge University Press, 2001.

Keane, John. *Civil Society; Old Images, New Visions.* Cambridge: Polity Press, 1998.

Seligman, Adam. *The Idea of Civil Society.* Princeton, NJ: Princeton University Press, 1992.

van Rooy, Alison, ed. *Civil Society and the Aid Industry.* London: Earthscan Publications, 1998.

Walzer, Michael, ed. *Toward a Global Civil Society.* Providence, RI, and Oxford: Berghahn Books, 1995.

COLLECTIVISM

Definition

Broadly speaking, the term "collectivism" denotes, along with "individualism," the extent to which an individual favors other people's interests by his or her behavior. Unlike the altruism/egoism dichotomy, however, the interests in question are not the ones of "the others" in general but those of a particular group or category of people to which the individual belongs.

Different cultures are obviously characterized by a different "relative weight" of individualism and collectivism. Both everyday observations and scientific research show that people in the so-called Western countries (such as in societies of Western Europe, North America, and Australia) place greater value on their individual autonomy: the freedom to choose their own purposes and goals and to take responsibility for their actions. By contrast, in the countries of Eastern Europe, Asia, Africa, or Latin America (the majority of which are seen as part of the so-called developing world), the emphasis is on harmony in relationships between members of a group, be it an extended family, a professional or religious community, a firm, or a neighborhood. The purposes of the individual members are subordinate to the common good. The members' attitudes to one another are quite different from their attitude to the people who do not belong to the community. Cultures, which are defined as "collectivist," are assumed to be characterized by mores and attitudes of this kind.

Of course, these are general tendencies only. It would be an inadmissible simplification and stereotype to expect every Chinese person, for example, to demonstrate traits of collectivism in his or her behavior. Even in very collectivist societies, there will be professional circles, such as in academia, that tend to be individualistic. Moreover, the collectivist social organization itself exists in different variants. H. Triandis and E. Suh, for example, make a distinction between vertical and horizontal collectivism, where the former is characterized by respect for in-group norms and for the directives of authorities, and the latter is characterized by empathy, sociability, and cooperation (Triandis and Suh 2002).

Besides the descriptive approaches to collectivism, interpretative ones can also be found in academic literature; for example, in collectivist cultures, the individual must have a sense of solidarity with the other members of the group. In addition, the individual identifies, to one extent or another, with them—that is, accepts their joys and sorrows as his or her own. The individual's self-understanding and self-esteem may also depend on his or her place in the group and on its achievements. Examples of such concepts in psychology are the social identity theory (Tajfel 1982) and the theory of self-categorization.

Theoretical Approaches

The relationship between collectivism and individualism is interpreted in different theoretical perspectives. In philosophy, it is at the root of the debate between liberal and communitarian thinkers. The liberal ideal is rational self-determination of the individual. Human behavior may be guided by universal standards of justice, insofar as it is distanced from the contingent circumstances in the individual's cultural environment (Rawls 1971). The communitarians, conversely, value precisely the cultural "embeddedness" of human behavior—the individual's unconditional identification with the communities to which he or she belongs by force of circumstance. These philosophers prefer values such as solidarity and identity to freedom and rationality (Walzer 1994).

These concepts of collectivism and individualism are essentially normative in character. The authors do not merely study the alternative patterns of behavior. They declare the one morally justified and the other morally unacceptable. This debate also has quite concrete dimensions that are politically relevant. One of them is the famous debate on human rights and Asian values. Representatives of some countries from Eastern and Southeast Asia argue that Western standards

of fundamental human rights, which claim to be universally valid, are, in fact, culturally specific or "tailored" to the notions of an individualistic culture. That is why they cannot be applied, or at least not directly, to collectivist societies (De Bary 1998).

A sociological perspective on patterns of collectivist and, respectively, individualistic behaviors is offered by F. Tönnies in his classical work *Community and Society* (*Gemeinschaft und Gesellschaft*). Admittedly, according to Tönnies, the selfsame individuals may behave in both ways depending on whether they are interacting within a community to which they belong or not. Yet, the distinctions that Tönnies makes—organic unity of wills in the community, on one hand, and interaction between free agents of their wills and abilities in society, on the other—are emblematic of the differences between collectivism and individualism in general (Tönnies 1988).

Another range of problems addressed by sociology—more specifically, by the theories of modernity—is also associated with the relationship between collectivism and individualism. A number of authors, such as Max Weber and Anthony Giddens, study the differences between modern and traditional societies, one of those differences being along the lines of the individualism/collectivism dichotomy. Modernity presupposes trust in an impersonal social order (Giddens 1991), which is more compatible with the values of individualism, whereas the personified social relationships in traditional societies rest on collectivist attitudes.

In psychology, the problem of collectivism is of immediate concern to the previously mentioned social identity theory and the theory of self-categorization. These conceptions assign an important role to the relationship between in-group and out-group, focusing on exclusive in-group solidarity at the expense of unequal treatment of the out-group. Collectivism and individualism, however, are key issues in cross-cultural psychology and intercultural communication theories (the latter also apply to anthropological methods). Quite representative in this respect are some studies by G. Hofstede (1994) and H. Triandis (1995).

Practical Implications for the "Developing World"

One of the key issues concerning modernization in the developing countries is whether their peoples ought to preserve their cultural identity. Collectivism is an emblematic feature of traditional societies. Is it possible to achieve technological and economic progress without "trading" collectivist for individualist mores? Generally, countries from the developing world, such as Singapore, Taiwan, and South Korea (which are making significant progress in modernization), demonstrate a tendency to preserve family-like relations within business organizations, which is in its turn a challenge when cooperating with the individualist-minded "Western" economic partners. Here again, the "Asian values" theme comes to the forefront (de Bary, Op. cit.).

Another dimension of the importance of collectivism for the developing countries is the political one. For the societies that have established a "Western-style" democratic social order, cultural collectivism is a source of problems when nourishing clients and, more generally, when trying to maintain clan and tribal solidarities against loyalty toward the nation and other civic values (Harrison and Huntington 2001). In the countries with Communist rule, collectivism as a cultural trait and collectivism as an ideological creed reinforce each other, which brings about in some cases extreme forms of oppression against the individual (such as in Cambodia under the Khmer Rouge regime) and also remarkable stability of collectivist forms of political organization in the face of transition to market economy (such as in China). Whatever the case, however, collectivism should not be approached in a simplistic way, although it is obviously a challenge to modernization.

PLAMEN MAKARIEV

References and Further Reading

De Bary, William Theodore. *Asian Values and Human Rights: A Confucian Communitarian Perspective*. Cambridge, MA: Harvard University Press, 1998.
Giddens, Anthony. *The Consequences of Modernity*, Cambridge: Polity Press, 1991.
Harrison, Lawrence, and Samuel P. Huntington. *Culture Matters: How Values Shape Human Progress*. New York: HarperCollins, 2001.
Hofstede, Geert. *Cultures and Organizations. Software of the Mind*. New York: HarperCollins, 1994.
Rawls, John. *A Theory of Justice*. Cambridge, MA: Belknap Press of Harvard University Press, 1971.
Tajfel, Henri, ed. *Social Identity and Intergroup Relations*. Cambridge: Cambridge University Press, 1982.
Tönnies, Ferdinand. *Community & Society*. New Brunswick, NJ: Transaction Books, 1988.
Triandis, Harry C. *Individualism & Collectivism*. Boulder, CO: Westview Press, 1995.
Triandis, Harry C., and Eunkook M. Suh. "Cultural Influences on Personality." *Annual Revue of Psychology*, 53, 133–160: (2002).
Walzer, Michael. *Thick and Thin: Moral Argument at Home and Abroad*. Notre Dame, IN: University of Notre Dame Press, 1994.

COLOMBIA

Colombia, the only country in South America that borders two oceans, is a country rich in natural resources, scenic beauty, and history. It also is one of the world's most violent places, with murder ranking as the number one killer of young adults. Despite the internal conflict, Colombia has managed to maintain a formally democratic political system since the late 1950s, and its economy has largely avoided the pitfalls of some of its neighbors. Despite a recent recession, its growth rate was a relatively robust 3.4% as of 2003. Colombia is known also as a major source of illegal drugs, though it is nearly impossible to estimate their impact on the economy, with best estimates ranging from 3–13% of gross domestic product (GDP). Colombia is the world's leading supplier of cocaine.

Geographically, Colombia is strategically located at the crossroads of the Americas. It lies at the top of the South American continent and is joined with North America via its border with Panama, a Colombian province until 1903. Its territory measures 1,038,700 square kilometers, excluding several islands in the Caribbean Sea and Pacific Ocean, making it the fourth largest country in South America. Colombia borders Venezuela, Brazil, Peru, Ecuador, and Panama. Its territory is divided politically into thirty-two departments and the federal capital of Bogotá. It is further divided physically by the three ranges of the Andes Mountains that run through it, north to south, and by its principal river, the Magdalena, which cuts through the center. Bogotá is located on a high mountain plateau in the eastern range, at some 2,590 meters above sea level. Colombia's climate varies widely from tropical rain forest to arid desert to temperate highlands. Consequently, it is among the most biodiverse countries in the world, claiming first place in the number of different bird species.

Despite the violence, Colombia has a relatively high population growth rate at 1.52%, and its population of 42.3 million places it second to Brazil in South America. The country is made up of mestizos (58%), whites (20%), mulattos (14%), blacks (4%), mixed black-indigenous (3%), and indigenous (1%). Some 90% of the population is at least nominally Roman Catholic, and literacy is high at 92.5%. Spanish is the official language, though English is an official language on the island of San Andrés in the Caribbean. The median age is 25.8 years.

The Colombian political system is a formal democracy, or republic, modeled on the presidential system of the United States. Under the 1991 constitution, the president is elected by popular vote every four years and may not seek reelection. The legislative branch consists of the lower House (*Cámara*) with 166 members and the Senate with 102 members, both elected by popular vote to four-year terms. Colombia uses a form of proportional representation, under which seats in the legislature are assigned according to the percentage of the vote received by each party. There are two traditional parties—the Liberals and Conservatives—and dozens of smaller parties that, in recent years, have been challenging the supremacy of the two-party system.

Coffee and the Economy

Historically, Colombia's economy has centered on coffee, and it was among the first producers in the world to actively market its own product, using the now familiar image of Juan Valdez, a fictitious coffee farmer. Colombian coffee production has focused on the Arabica bean, which grows at altitude and produces a rich yet mild coffee sought after for its high quality. And while coffee is grown and produced in much of the country, it is concentrated in what is known as the *Eje Cafetero*, a region that encompasses the small departments of Risaralda, Quindío, and Caldas and includes parts of Antioquia, Valle, and Tolima.

In recent years, oil has overtaken coffee as Colombia's primary export, although the economy in general is increasingly diversified. Major industries include textiles, food processing, clothing and footwear, beverages, chemicals, cement, and cut flowers. Its annual GDP is $255 billion, and its per capita income is $6,300. Aside from oil and coffee, exports include coal, apparel, bananas, cut flowers, gold, and emeralds. Colombia is the world's leading supplier of emeralds. The country's main trading partner is the United States, followed by Venezuela and Ecuador. It is a member of the Andean Community and the Group of Three. Its external debt totals some $39 billion.

A Violent History

Colombia first declared independence from Spain in 1810 but lapsed into six years of what has become known as *La Patria Boba*, an era of chaos. Real independence came in 1819 after the rebel forces under the command of Simón Bolívar defeated the Spanish at the Battle of Boyacá. Bolívar then became the first president of Gran Colombia, which included the modern-day states of Colombia, Venezuela, Ecuador, and Panama. The union did not last, however, and Venezuela and Ecuador declared their independence in what were largely peaceful events in 1830. Panama seceded in 1903 with the support of the United States, which had been unable to secure a favorable treaty with Colombia granting it a concession for a canal.

Between 1828 and 1902, Colombia experienced fourteen uprisings, *coups d'état*, which are attempted civil wars, most of which were unsuccessful. This frequent recourse to violence in the political realm is a constant in Colombian history. In the nineteenth century, following independence, some thirty-three thousand Colombians died as a result of "hostilities." In the three years of the War of a Thousand Days (1899–1902), three times that many perished out of a total population of 4 million. *La Violencia*, the internal conflict that began in 1948, claimed the lives of an estimated five hundred thousand Colombians.

There are various reasons cited for *La Violencia*, which on the surface appeared to be a civil war between the traditional parties—Liberals and Conservatives. As in other parts of Latin America, Colombia's political parties were not generous in victory, and each attempted to establish political hegemony to the exclusion of the other. The Conservatives had ruled from 1886 to 1930, when a split allowed moderate Liberal Enrique Olaya Herrera to become president, ushering in sixteen years of what has come to be called the Liberal Republic. During that time, the Liberals passed sweeping land reform laws and labor laws designed to co-opt the burgeoning peasant and unionist movements. The most acclaimed and visible leader of those movements was Jorge Eliécer Gaitán, whose National Leftist Revolutionary Union *(UNIR)* threatened to undermine the two-party arrangement and, more importantly, establish elite control over the political process. By 1935, though, Gaitán had been co-opted into the Liberal fold; by 1948, he was leading "silent marches" of tens of thousands through the streets of Bogotá and seemed poised to win back the presidency from the Conservatives, who had taken advantage of a Liberal split in 1946. But Gaitán was assassinated in downtown Bogotá on April 9, 1948, sparking several days of bloody rioting in the capital known as the *Bogotazo*, which was followed by ten years of violence in the countryside.

But while *La Violencia* may appear to have been just another civil war, many scholars argue it went further. For some, it represented a backlash by the elites against what they saw as a growing threat from the lower classes, championed by Gaitán. The fact that the Liberal Party was more often than not associated with the masses is more a coincidence than a reality. Others saw in *La Violencia* the culmination of decades of land colonization and the need for laborers in new agro-industries. Finally, some scholars point to the historically weak state of Colombia and its inability to make its presence felt throughout the national territory. Not coincidentally, much of *La Violencia* and the current conflict center on regions where new sources of wealth (legal and otherwise) have been discovered; these include oil and coca in the Llanos and emeralds in the Santanders.

La Violencia came to a formal end in 1958, when the feuding elites agreed on a power-sharing arrangement to replace the military dictatorship of General Gustavo Rojas Pinilla. Under the agreement, the Liberals and Conservatives would alternate the presidency every four years and divide evenly the other branches of government. Liberal Alberto Lleras Camargo was elected as the first president of the so-called National Front, which lasted until 1974. But while pacification appeared to be occurring, certain guerrilla groups associated mainly with the Liberals who resisted demobilization. One group in particular attempted to create an independent republic in a mountainous area south of Bogotá. Its efforts failed, but the survivors formed the nucleus of what became, in 1966, the Revolutionary Armed Forces of Colombia (FARC). Meanwhile, a group of radical students who had studied and trained in Cuba under Fidel Castro returned and in 1964 founded the National Liberation Army (ELN). Two other groups that appeared under the National Front were the Maoist-oriented Peoples Liberation Army (EPL) and the eclectic April 19 Movement (M-19). The National Front may have succeeded in mending the rift among Colombia's elites, but it excluded all other political voices, creating a democratic system that was rigid and closed.

Drug Trafficking and Violence

With the election of Liberal Alfonso López Michelsen in 1974, the National Front formally ended. Colombia's guerrilla groups clearly were on the wane by the end of the succeeding administration of Liberal Julio César Turbay in 1982. But it was about this time that a new factor entered the equation, breathing new life into the insurgency and spawning a counterinsurgency from the Right: drug trafficking. What began as a relatively small-time operation to grow and smuggle marijuana into the United States in the 1970s shifted to a more ambitious, well-organized cocaine trafficking effort in the 1980s. The ruthless Medellín Cartel quickly developed into a nonstate actor so powerful that its leader, Pablo Escobar, at one point offered to

pay off Colombia's national debt in return for amnesty. The Medellín Cartel was replaced in the early 1990s by the more business-like Cali Cartel, which in turn gave way to a number of smaller cartels by the turn of the twenty-first century.

Drug trafficking added a new dynamic, and logic, to the internal conflict, which by the mid-1990s had threatened to spill over into neighboring countries and had resulted in US decertification for Colombia in the "War on Drugs." In the areas where peasants grew coca and heroin poppy as a cash crop, the guerrillas protected them in return for a cut of the profits. The FARC grew to an estimated fifteen to twenty thousand fighters with a presence in much of the country. The ELN also saw its numbers swell to some five thousand, but their forces were concentrated mostly in the Middle Magdalena region. The guerrillas also continued to harass large landowners and engaged increasingly in kidnapping, a very lucrative activity. In turn, these actions adversely affected the drug traffickers, who used their newly acquired wealth to become landowners themselves. They helped finance what started as death squads in the late 1980s but that gelled into a fairly cohesive right-wing force, the United Self-Defense Forces of Colombia (AUC), under the leadership of Carlos Castaño. Negotiations between the government and the various actors continued throughout the 1990s, and at one point, President Andrés Pastrana had ceded to the FARC a large tract of land in the Llanos that later was rescinded and reoccupied by state-controlled forces. In 2002, independent candidate Alvaro Uribe was elected president, promising to gain the upper hand in the conflict.

Colombia experienced what some observers say was a partial collapse of the state in the late 1980s, at a time of renewed guerrilla and death squad activity and an all-out war declared by the Medellín Cartel, whose leaders vehemently rejected the government's plans to have them extradited to the United States. As a result, the 1990 elections were seen as a kind of watershed and led to momentous political and economic changes. A new constitution was promulgated in mid-1991, removing the last vestiges of the National Front and ushering in greater decentralization. At almost the same time, President César Gaviria introduced sweeping economic reforms known as the *Apertura* or opening. Colombia had emerged from the "Lost Decade" largely unscathed, but it nonetheless came under pressure to enact the same neo-Liberal reforms as its Latin American neighbors. Under Gaviria, the Colombian economy began to switch from import substitution industrialization to export-led growth, though the reforms meant that Colombian industries now would also be subject to competition from abroad. The latter began to adversely affect some of the country's more traditional industrial sectors—such as textiles and food processing—by the mid-1990s and, coupled with the sanctions imposed by the United States in 1996–1997, Colombia's economy sank into its worst recession in decades. At the same time, the demise of the international coffee agreement in 1989 kept prices for Colombian coffee low, causing that sector to also suffer.

LAWRENCE BOUDON

See also Drug Trade

Further Reading

Bergquist, Charles, Ricardo Peñaranda, and Gonzalo Sánchezeds. *Violence in Colombia 1990–2000*. Wilmington, NC: SR Books, 2001.

Bushnell, David. *The Making of Modern Colombia: A Nation in Spite of Itself*. Berkeley, CA: University of California Press, 1993.

"Colombia: The Forgotten War." *Latin American Perspectives* 28 (1) (January 2001).

Hartlyn, Jonathan. *The Politics of Coalition Rule in Colombia*. New York: Cambridge University Press, 1988.

Martz, John. *The Politics of Clientelism: Democracy and the State in Colombia*. New Brunswick, NJ: Transaction Publishers, 1997.

Randall, Stephen. *Colombia and the United States: Hegemony and Interdependence*. Athens, GA: University of Georgia Press, 1992.

Richani, Nazih. *Systems of Violence: The Political Economy of War and Peace in Colombia*. Albany, NY: The State University of New York Press, 2002.

Solimano, Andrés, ed. *Colombia: Essays on Conflict, Peace, and Development*. Washington, DC: The World Bank, 2001.

Stafford, Frank, and Marco Palacios. *Colombia: Fragmented Land, Divided Society*. New York: Oxford University Press, 2002.

COLOMBO PLAN

The Colombo Plan for Cooperative Economic Development in Asia and the Pacific was launched in 1950 to coordinate the disbursement of development aid to governments in the region. Emerging out of the spread of the Cold War to Asia by the late 1940s, the plan represented a significant foreign aid effort centered on the British Commonwealth and initiated by British Foreign Secretary Ernest Bevin. Following the establishment of the People's Republic of China in October 1949, the British government attempted to counter the threat thought to be posed by China and "international communism" by encouraging a regional program that focused on economic development. The British hoped that the promotion of the developmental and technical elements of the Colombo Plan would demonstrate to the peoples of South and Southeast Asia that there were viable alternatives to those provided by the Chinese Communist Party (CCP) and the Communist parties of the region. It was also hoped that the plan would provide a focus for the Indian and other Commonwealth governments and increase US involvement in British policy in the region. The Colombo Plan was formulated with the encouragement of the British government by an assembled group of Commonwealth delegates at the Colombo Conference (held in the capital of Ceylon, renamed Sri Lanka in 1972) in January 1950. It was formally launched in July 1951, following its ratification by all the governments of the Commonwealth except for South Africa.

At the conference in Colombo at the beginning of 1950, the British government sought to ensure that the emphasis was on economic development, technical assistance, and a regional approach, which it thought would distract attention from the different, and even opposing, political positions of the governments in attendance. At the Colombo Conference, Minister of Finance for Ceylon, J. R. Jayawardene, called for a program on the scale of the Marshall Plan to be directed at the recently established and emerging nation-states of Southern and Southeast Asia. However, it was clear that the British government, a recipient of Marshall Plan aid, was not prepared to provide technical and economic assistance on such a scale. At the initiative of Australian Minister for External Affairs Percy Spender (who played an important role at the conference), and following discussions between the Australian and Ceylonese delegations, the proposal that had been tabled by Jayawardene was withdrawn. The delegates to the conference eventually reached a unanimous agreement in support of a draft resolution written primarily by Spender and the Australian delegation. This resolution called on the Commonwealth governments to provide whatever technical and financial aid they could to the governments of Southern and Southeast Asia. This was to take place via existing organizations and newly established bilateral arrangements.

The Colombo Conference also called for setting up a Consultative Committee that would plan a range of long-term initiatives to coordinate the Colombo Plan and other Commonwealth initiatives with the activities of other governments and international organizations. The Consultative Committee is made up of representatives from all member states and it is supposed to meet every two years to evaluate the social and economic efforts of member governments as well as to discuss technical cooperation and the overall functioning of the Colombo Plan. Meanwhile, the

Colombo Plan Council has several meetings annually in Colombo, attended by diplomatic representatives from the member states, at which development questions are discussed and recommendations are passed on to the Consultative Committee. The actual implementation of various initiatives is the work of the Colombo Plan secretariat and the secretary-general of the Colombo Plan. At the outset, it was agreed that the member governments of the Commonwealth in Asia should produce development plans for the six-year period from July 1, 1950, to June 30, 1956, and that invitations to participate in the Colombo initiative should be extended to other governments in the region. After 1956, the plan was extended at five-year intervals until the Consultative Committee, meeting in Jakarta in November 1980, decided that the plan should continue to operate for an indefinite period into the future.

In the context of the outbreak of the Korean War, the United States joined the Colombo Plan in 1951 (as did Japan, somewhat later), dramatically increasing its resources. There were two overarching and interconnected components of the plan. The first was a program of technical cooperation that sought to provide expertise and equipment to the recipient nations and bring students to the donor countries for training. By 1957, 1,500 students had gone to Britain for training and education under the Colombo Plan, while 600 went to Canada, 375 to New Zealand, and 4,000 to Australia. The second part of the plan was a broad program of economic development directed at major public investment and infrastructure projects, including roads, railways, irrigation, electricity and communications, as well as various other services. By 1956, the United States had contributed at least $2 billion (US dollars, USD) worth of aid to the governments of Southern and Southeast Asia and was the single biggest donor government inside and outside the Colombo Plan. The corresponding figure for Canada was $168 million, $72 million for Austrialia, and $11 million for New Zealand (all in USD). By the second half of the 1950s, the Asian governments that were members of the Colombo Plan had expanded from Ceylon, Pakistan, and India to encompass Burma, Cambodia, Indonesia, Laos, Nepal, the Philippines, Thailand, and South Vietnam.

Given the scale and scope of the development problems in postcolonial Southern and Southeast Asia, the Colombo Plan represented an important but relatively modest effort to coordinate development initiatives. Against the backdrop of the Cold War, $72 billion USD was disbursed via the Colombo Plan between 1950 and 1983, and more than half of that amount ($41.2 billion USD) came from the United States. Funding has declined in the past two decades, but the Colombo Plan continues to operate. It held its thirty-seventh Consultative Committee Meeting in Manila in November 1998, at which the Consultative Committee endorsed the Manila Colombo Plan Agenda for Action in the Twenty-First Century (MACOPA 21). As of 2001, the member states of the Colombo Plan, which has now been in operation for fifty years, include Afghanistan, Australia, Bangladesh, Bhutan, Cambodia, Fiji, India, Indonesia, Iran, Japan, Korea, Laos, Malaysia, Maldives, Myanmar, Nepal, New Zealand, Pakistan, Papua New Guinea, the Philippines, Singapore, Sri Lanka, Thailand, and the United States. Mongolia is a provisional member.

MARK T. BERGER

See also Southeast Asia: History and Economic Development

References and Further Reading

Bullock, Alan. *Ernest Bevin: Foreign Secretary 1945–1951.* New York: W. W. Norton, 1983.
Colombo Plan. 2005. Home Page: www.colombo-plan.org/
Gifford, Peter. "The Cold War Across Asia." In *Facing North: A Century of Australian Engagement With Asia,* edited by David Goldsworthy. Melbourne, Australia: Melbourne University Press, 2001.
Lumsdaine, David Halloran. *Moral Vision in International Politics: The Foreign Aid Regime, 1949–1989.* Princeton, NJ: Princeton University Press, 1993.
Spender, Percy Claude. *Exercises in Diplomacy: The ANZUS Treaty and the Colombo Plan.* New York: New York University Press, 1969.
Singh, L. P. *The Colombo Plan: Some Political Aspects.* Canberra, Australia: Department of International Relations, Research School of Pacific Studies, Australian National University, 1963.
———. *The Politics of Economic Cooperation in Asia: A Study of Asian International Organizations.* Columbia, MO: University of Missouri Press, 1966.
Tarling, Nicholas. *Britain, Southeast Asia and the Onset of the Cold War 1945–1950.* Cambridge: Cambridge University Press, 1998.
Williams, J. E. "The Colombo Conference and Communist Insurgency in South and South East Asia." *International Relations* 4, no. 1 (1972): 94–107.

COLONIALISM: HISTORY

Definition of Terms

The terms "colonialism," "colonisation," and "imperialism" are often used in a confusing and interchangeable manner. Their explanation in this text will mainly follow Jürgen Osterhammel's definition of "colonialism" in his influential work *Colonialism: A Theoretical Overview*. Osterhammel defines "colonialism" as a relationship between two collectives in which all important decisions concerning the life of the "colonised" are made by a culturally different/alien minority of "colonisers" unwilling to adapt to local customs. External interests (be they economic, political, or ideological) are the main criteria in such decisions. Usually, ideological issues such as the alleged cultural superiority of the "colonisers" echo in the nature of the relationship. The German historian Wolfgang Reinhard employs a similar definition of colonialism and emphasises the importance of the colonisers' cultural alienness and the difference in the development of the two collectives/societies. He argues that a system of domination has to feature both these elements in order to be colonialist.

In historical periodisation, "colonialism" usually denominates the period of European overseas expansion beginning in the late fifteenth and early sixteenth centuries and ending with the process of decolonisation after World War II. Following its relatively narrow Marxist meaning, the term "imperialism" describes the last hundred years of this period starting in the middle of the nineteenth century, when colonial concepts gained new perspectives and thus new momentum. In Marxist Theory, imperialism emerged through the combination of capitalism and colonialism. Other historians allow for a wider definition of imperialism and subsume under the term any efforts and activities aiming at the creation and maintenance of a transcolonial empire. Following this political definition, "imperialism" means all collective efforts producing colonialism. However, in its economic sense, imperialism does not necessarily need colonialism and even has outlived the latter. Sometimes described as neo-colonialism or neo-imperialism, economic hegemony replaced the exertion of direct colonial rule after the process of decolonisation (for example, American imperialism).

This discussion provides a concise chronological description of the period of modern colonialism. The term "colonialism" in this text describes the primary form of relationship between the colonised and the colonisers during the period of European overseas expansion and domination starting around 1500 and ending more or less shortly after World War II. Accordingly, "imperialism" or "new imperialism" here refers to the last one hundred years of the period when colonialism gained a number of hitherto unknown qualities and when the established colonial powers together with the "latecomers" entered into a race for the domination of the last uncolonised territories. While preimperialist colonialism aimed at the formal or informal domination of diverse overseas territories for primarily economic reasons, imperialism intended to create a politically homogenous and centrally administered colonial empire.

Forms of Colonialism

Colonialism existed in various different forms and characteristics. In fact, it is important to consider the many different "colonialisms" characterized by the world region, the colonising country, the colonisers, and the role of the colony in the emerging world economic/political system. The most widespread and useable system of classification knows three types of colonies/colonialism:

1. **Colonies of domination**: A minority of colonisers exerts direct rule over an indigenous majority; most colonisers are civil administrators, soldiers, or merchants; there is only a small number of settlers; and colonies of domination are mostly the result of military conquest and are subject to economic exploitation. Typical examples include British India, French Indochina, British Egypt, or the American Philippines. The Spanish America is a less typical example because the European immigrants mixed with the indigenous people and a distinct Creole elite started to emerge.

2. **Settlement colonies**: A significant number of colonisers take up permanent residence in an (allegedly) empty or sparsely populated country; in most cases, the indigenous population has not yet developed sedentary agriculture and has either been pushed back by the newcomers or employed on their newly established holdings. In this situation, settlers usually came to stay and often quickly developed a taste for increased autonomy and/or self-government; such colonist societies frequently neglected the rights of the indigenous

population or completely displaced it. Typical examples include North America, Australia, Algeria, and South Africa. The plantation colonies of the Caribbean (and Brazil) are less typical examples because the colonisers imported vast numbers of African slaves as plantation labourers, and a new social structure emerged.

3. **Base colonies**: A merchant company or a country establishes a small (mostly coastal) foothold in a foreign country. Initially, these stations were merchant bases and served logistical purposes. Such colonies often had to rely on the goodwill of the "host" country; later, some of these holdings also served as centres of "informal control" over regions not formally under colonial domination. Base colonies primarily attracted merchants and service personnel from all around the world; typical examples include Malacca, Batavia, Singapore, Hong Kong, and Aden.

Early European Expansion

The word "colonialism" is generally associated with the period of European colonial expansion starting in the fifteenth century. The intra-European strife for a share in intercontinental trade between Europe and Asia urged the European powers to look for ways to circumvent the middlemen of the trade. The Portuguese conquered Ceuta in 1415 and explored the African coast southward to get direct access to the trans-Saharan trade routes, eliminating the Muslim middlemen. In the 1440s and 1450s, they reached the Senegal, Cape Verde, or Sierra Leone and entered the African slave trade. Spain tried to establish a foothold in the Atlantic by colonising the Canary Islands. Although the Pope had already acknowledged and sanctified the Portuguese monopoly in the Africa trade, Spain and Portugal needed the War of 1474–1479 to clarify their spheres of influence. Although Portugal lost the war, the Treaty of Alcáçovas in 1479 made African territory beyond twenty-six degrees latitude the country's exclusive sphere, whereas Spain obtained the Canary Islands. Portugal made excessive use of the monopoly and invested into the exploration of the African coast. Meanwhile, the Genuese seafarer Christoforo Colombo (Christopher Columbus) had developed a plan to reach India on a westward route to tap the eastern trade directly at its source. Both Portugal and Spain declined Colombo's ill-planed proposal. Only after Portugal's Bartholomeu Dias had circumnavigated the Cape of Good Hope and

thereby proved that Asia/India could be reached via Africa, the Spanish Crown—in an act of desperation—hired Colombo and equipped him with three ships. Colombo "discovered" the New World. He reached the Bahamas on October 12, 1492, and explored the northern coast of Cuba and Haiti before returning to Spain. Spain secured the newly discovered islands with the help of a Papal Bull, and Portugal acknowledged Spanish hegemony beyond a demarcation line 370 miles west of the Cape Verde Islands in the Treaty of Tordesillas in 1494. When Vasco da Gama circumnavigated Africa and finally reached India in 1498, the Treaty of Tordesillas separated the world into a Spanish sphere in the West and a Portuguese domain in the East.

The New World

Spurred by Portugal's success, Spain sent its ships farther to the West still hoping to find the westward passage to India at last. Spanish ships soon explored parts of the American continental coast. When a Portuguese fleet returning from India accidentally touched the Brazilian coast in 1500, it gradually became clear that Spain had "discovered" not just a few islands in the Caribbean but a seemingly endless new continent: the *Mundus Novus*. Colonising this New World, the Spanish Crown made use of a concept successfully employed in the *Reconquista*. The Crown authorised private *conquistadores* to explore and colonise the new land. They financed their enterprise privately and signed a *capitulación* that regulated their rights and duties and guaranteed them 20% of the profit. The rapid transition from exploration to conquest after 1500 can largely be attributed to the military background of these men and to their experiences during the *Reconquista*. They felt the urge to make quick and large enough profits in the New World to recover their considerable initial outlays. From Santo Domingo on Hispaniola, Spain started to expand its territory. Spanish conquerors took Puerto Rico in 1509, Cuba in 1511, and Jamaica in 1512. In Panama, they established an important centre on the mainland in 1519. From there, they conquered modern-day Nicaragua in 1526 and linked up with a northern group of *conquistadores* under Hernán Cortés, who had just pulverised the Aztec Empire. To the South, Francisco Pizarro started the conquest of the Inca Empire in 1531 to gain access to the legendary riches of Peru. By 1534, the Spanish controlled all important Inca centres and expanded their territory to northern Ecuador (1534), Colombia (1538–1539), and Chile (1540–1541). European technological superiority facilitated the American *conquista*. The conquerors took advantage of what might be called an early form of bacterial warfare. Unknowingly, they imported diseases common to the Old World but hitherto unknown in the Americas. The indigenous population lacked immunity against the imported germs, and millions succumbed to smallpox, bubonic plague, typhoid, influenza, yellow fever, or other diseases. Although estimates still vary considerably, recent studies believe that the indigenous population saw a decrease from about 40 million people in pre-Columbian times to 4 million in the middle of the seventeenth century.

The economically important highland centres of Peru, Chile, and—a little later—Mexico were the focal points of Spanish engagement in Latin America from the late sixteenth century onward. The productive silver mines in Zacatecas, Mexico, and Potosí, Peru, had become the pillars of Spanish America's economy. Spain exploited the mines with Indian labour and sent huge amounts of silver to the homeland. In 1565, the so-called Manila Galleon commenced its yearly service between Acapulco and Manila and started to feed American silver directly into the Asian market (in significant amounts from about 1600 onward). The galleon returned with Asian (predominantly Chinese) porcelain, silk, ivory, and spices.

North American Settlements

Apart from rich fishing grounds, natural resources were scarce in North America and did not attract the *conquistadores*. Only in the late sixteenth century did Europe develop a taste for North American furs, and the trade with beaver fur became economically profitable. France, the Netherlands, Sweden, and England established coastal settlements and entered into commercial alliances with the local Indian tribes. In 1608, Samuel de Champlain founded the first French settlement at the site of modern Quebec. During the 1620s, the Dutch established footholds on the East Coast. In 1626, they bought the island of Manhattan from an Indian tribe and founded New Amsterdam. Although both French and Dutch settlements attracted a certain number of European settlers, they were primarily fur trading stations, whereas the English very early aimed at the establishment of permanent settlement colonies. Jamestown in Virginia was founded in 1607. A little later, tobacco was introduced to the colony and soon proved to be a valuable export crop. In 1620, the Mayflower pilgrims established Cape Cod colony in Massachusetts.

England saw North American colonisation as a means to relieve rising population pressure in the homeland and furthered emigration. In the wake of the three Anglo-Dutch Wars ending with the Treaty of Westminster, the Dutch colonies in North America became English (and New Amsterdam became New York). Meanwhile, France had started to consolidate, reorganise, and expand its American holdings, such as to Louisiana. Although New France was now economically profitable and attracted more settlers, its vast territories were still sparsely populated. New England, however, concentrated its numerous settlers in smaller territories and was socially and economically self-sustaining. In 1760, the English colonies in America housed 1.6 million inhabitants, rising to 2.7 million only twenty years later. Massive immigration of Europeans and of African slaves, together with comparatively favourable living conditions, caused this increase. Toward the middle of the eighteenth century, tensions between New France and New England and its European motherlands grew and finally culminated in the global Seven Years' War (1756–1763), the European counterpart to the French and Indian War in North America (1754–1763). England won the war and took over the French possessions in America. Louisiana went to Spain as compensation for the English occupation of Florida.

The Plantations of the Caribbean and the Triangle Trade

The plantation economy of the Caribbean, Brazil, and some parts of coastal America constitutes another distinct form of colonial economy and social structure. White investors—most of whom only took up temporary residence in the colonies—developed the land to establish a (semi)industrial agricultural economy that profited from exporting produce to Europe. In America, suitable plantation land was abundant, but labour was scarce. Therefore, the economically profitable but labour-intensive cultivation of sugar cane demanded the import of cheap labour and gave great impulses to the African slave trade. A peculiar form of trade called the Triangle Trade thus developed between Europe, Africa, and the Americas. Ships from Europe brought manufactured goods to the African coast and traded these goods for slaves. The slave ships crossed the Atlantic and exchanged their load for agricultural export produce in the West Indian ports. Returning to Europe, the merchants had maximised profit and minimised time and cost involved in the trade.

The plantation model was first introduced in Brazil at the end of the sixteenth century. European investors had found the region around Bahia and Pernambuco extremely suitable for the cultivation of sugar cane. The plantation system proved a big success, and between 1580 and 1680, Brazil was the single most important producer of sugar. Labour demand soon could not be satisfied from local sources anymore, and the plantations started to rely on imported slaves. Only at the very start was the Triangle Trade with Brazil dominated by the Portuguese. Already in the 1620s, Dutch merchant companies entered the trade and quasi-monopolised it. Between 1630 and 1654, the Dutch even occupied important sugar planting regions in Brazil. The resulting conflicts between Portuguese and Dutch Brazil led to increased sugar prices on the world market and favoured the economic development of the Caribbean. During the 1620s and 1630s, England and France had secured themselves several islands in the Caribbean. In 1655, England expanded its territory to Jamaica. France took Haiti in 1697. After a brief interlude of tobacco planting, favourable world market prices induced many European planters to cultivate sugar in the Caribbean. Abundant land, suitable soil conditions, and the availability of imported slave labour led to the Sugar Revolution of 1630–1670, when large parts of the Caribbean were completely transformed to tropical export economies with huge slave-run and European-owned production units. The early years brought incredible profits and—although the profit margin had narrowed to about 5% by then—Caribbean sugar cultivation remained profitable until the 1820s.

The plantation system shaped the population and social structure of the West Indies, Brazil, some coastal regions of Spanish America, and the plantation regions of North America. Following reasonable estimates, the Triangle Trade brought between 9.5 and 11.5 million African slaves to the American plantations from the sixteenth century until the abolition of the slave trade in 1802 through 1833.

American Decolonisation

When England had taken over the French possessions in America after the Seven Years' War, London implemented an increasingly restrictive policy toward its colonies in North America. With the help of taxes and import duties, the motherland tried to recover the costs of the expensive war and started to alienate its overseas citizens. Tensions mounted when the East India Company was granted the right to import tea directly to the American colonies in 1773. At the so-called Boston Tea Party in 1775, American activists seized a load of tea and threw it into the sea. The conflict escalated and led to violent clashes between the Patriots and the Loyalists. When England refused to negotiate, the colonies declared independence in 1776. With the help of France, they were able to defeat a strong English force sent out to suppress the rebellion. With the Treaty of Paris in 1783, hostilities ended and the former colonies became independent. Although there had been attempts to conquer the former French-Canadian possessions, these colonies had chosen to stay a British colony and successfully resisted an American invasion.

The independence of the British colonies in North America is the first case of successful decolonisation. As such, it greatly influenced the Spanish-American independence movement(s). During the eighteenth century, many *criollos* had profited from the good economic performance of the Latin American colonies. They had developed a distinct self-consciousness as "Americans" and a desire for office. But absolutist Spain refused them access to the important offices and positions and filled these almost exclusively with *peninsulares*, those Spaniards born in Spain. When Napoleon installed his brother Joseph on the Spanish throne in 1808, the *criollos* reacted and formed regional *juntas* in the Latin American centres. At first, these local administrative bodies were loyal to the former Spanish Bourbon king, but from about 1810, they followed their own interests and advocated independence. Regional attempts to overthrow the Spanish regime in Venezuela, Mexico, and Chile all failed, however, due to the resistance of the local loyalist elites. After Napoleon's fall, the Spanish king was reinstalled and pursued his absolutist and restrictive policy against the American possession with new vigour. This fuelled the Creole desire for independence and unified large parts of the heterogeneous Creole elite. Simón Bolívar and José de San Martin successfully led their troops against the Spanish army. They "liberated" the South American continent between 1817 and 1825. Mexico declared independence in 1822. Central America first joined Mexico but soon split away again, thus illustrating the strong influence of regional interests in the decolonisation of Spanish America. Simón Bolívar had propagated the idea of a unified Latin America (following the North American example); instead, the diverse interests of the heterogeneous Creole elite and their pronounced regionalism (*caudillismo*) led to the emergence of a multitude of independent states.

Brazilian independence came as the consequence of a revolution in the home country as well. In 1821, a liberal *coup d'etat* overthrew the monarchy in Portugal. Accordingly, with the help of the Brazilian planting community, the heir to the throne declared Brazil an independent empire in 1822.

Europe and the Indian Ocean

Portugal had managed to enter the Indian Ocean trade by circumnavigating the Cape of Good Hope and reaching India by sea in 1498. Thereby the Portuguese had joined a millennia "Old World" system, connecting the eastern coast of Africa, the Red Sea region, the Middle East, the Indian subcontinent, Southeast Asia, China, and Japan. Although Portuguese Indian Ocean trade meant armed trade from the beginning, Portugal did not aim at territorial domination in Africa or Asia but at the interruption of the Muslim spice trade monopoly. From 1500 onward, Portugal sent an annual fleet to India to hinder Muslim trade and to return with pepper, cinnamon, nutmeg, and cloves. Five years later, the Portuguese started to establish bases and trade stations along the sea route to India. In 1510, they conquered the Indian port Goa, and a year later, they took Malacca. In 1515, they established themselves in Ormuz, and in 1518, they took over parts of the cinnamon island Ceylon. In 1544, Portugal began to trade with Japan, and in 1557, it was allowed to found Macao as a trading post with China. Although the Portuguese had established a tight network of bases between Mozambique and Japan, Portugal's territorial holdings did initially not extend beyond those trading posts. With the closing of the sixteenth century, rising Dutch engagement in the area, political instability, and the inflexibility of the Portuguese trading system led to a swift decline of the Portuguese enterprise in the Indian Ocean. When its holdings in the region began to run at a loss in the seventeenth century, Portugal refocused its attention almost exclusively on Brazil.

The seventeenth-century European trade with Asia was dominated by the Netherlands. Besides Bruges and Antwerp, Amsterdam had served as the main market centre for Portuguese-imported Asian goods. When Philip II of Spain became king of Portugal in 1580, the Dutch saw this lucrative business at stake. Hence, in 1594, Amsterdam merchants founded the first company for overseas trade and equipped a number of merchant ships. By 1602, there were eight merchant companies involved in the Asian trade. These were merged in the *Vereenigde Oost-Indische Compagnie* (VOC) that monopolised Dutch trade with Asia. Initially, the VOC was exclusively interested in the profitable spice trade, established trade links with the Moluccas, and founded a fort on Ambon

Island in 1605. Other bases in the region followed. In 1610, the Dutch established a factory in Hirado, Japan; a year later, they founded another one in Jakarta. To cement its foothold in the Asian trade, the VOC decided to make Java its regional headquarters, fortified its holdings in Jakarta, and made it its Asian capital in 1619 (calling it Batavia). However, the VOC did not aim at territorial domination, and if it did acquire territory it did so mainly for the sake of its trade interests. During the seventeenth century, the company had quasi-monopolised the spice trade. But its narrow focus on this trade segment also quickened its decline in the eighteenth century, when European demand for Asian products had long since diversified and more flexible English companies intruded the market. After several unprofitable business decades, the VOC was dissolved in 1799, and the Dutch government took over its territorial possessions.

Although founded two years earlier than its Dutch counterpart, the British East India Company (EIC) initially could not compete with the VOC. It commanded less capital and lacked the long-term perspectives and planning of the VOC. In its first years, the EIC had managed to establish a small network of bases and factories on the Indian coast, Malaya, Java, Sumatra, Sulawesi, and Japan, but was soon expelled from the spice regions and the East Asian trade by the Dutch. It was forced into contenting itself with a number of factories on the Indian subcontinent. The EIC had established a factory at the Indian port of Surat in 1613. In 1641, the English founded Fort St. George at Madras, and ten years later they established themselves at Calcutta. In 1668, the EIC acquired Bombay. With the turn of the century, the demand for cotton dramatically increased in Europe and in its American colonies, where huge numbers of African slaves needed cheap clothing. This favoured the EIC with its access to the Indian cotton and textile producers. The company's capital was increased in 1709, and the cotton trade flourished. While the VOC started to import Javanese coffee, the EIC became the prime importer of Chinese tea. By the middle of the eighteenth century, the Dutch had already lost their trade supremacy in Asia, and the EIC had become the single most important merchant company trading with Asia.

From Trade Stations to Colonies of Domination

Although the VOC had not aimed at the creation of a Dutch overseas empire, it had been the first European player in the Indian Ocean to bring larger territories under its direct domination. This practice had proved to be economically beneficial to the company, giving it direct and cheap access to the local markets and a certain security of investment; however, at the same time, administration costs skyrocketed. The EIC followed this example. When the local ruler (Nawab) of Bengal occupied Fort William at Calcutta in 1756 to end the EIC's trade privileges in Bengal, the company sent an army from Madras, defeated the Nawab's forces, and became direct ruler of Bengal. The EIC was granted full rights of jurisdiction and taxation by the Mughal emperor. In successive decades, the EIC expanded its territory in India using a similar "forward defence" strategy. Financed by local taxes, the EIC hired an Indian army, conquered practically the whole Indian subcontinent until 1818, and threw back French competitors in India. Being a private and profit-oriented company, the EIC ruthlessly exploited its territories after 1757. In 1773 (Regulating Act) and 1784 (India Act), the British government tried to stabilise and regulate company rule in India. However, after initial successes, the EIC's economic focus and its intercultural incompetence led to the so-called Indian Mutiny in 1857. Parts of the Indian *sepoy* troops revolted but were finally defeated by British forces. As a consequence, the British Crown took over the EIC's possessions in India in 1858. It reorganised the administrative structure and established a conservative administration based on the collaboration of the traditional local elites.

Ideas of "white superiority," "benevolent despotism," and "white man's burden" began to shape the relations between "colonisers" and "the colonised." British India had become the first large-scale classical colony of domination where a European minority governed a majority of indigenous people. Spanish and Portuguese colonialism in Latin America had already featured such attributes mixed with typical settlement elements. But British colonialism in India, Burma, Malaya, Ceylon, and Singapore lacked a significant participation of European settlers. Instead, these regions experienced an influx of European business agents and white planters. Following the Caribbean example, large-scale cash crop cultivation was introduced to parts of the region in the early nineteenth century. A dual economy evolved with a foreign-dominated, partially isolated plantation economy existing parallel to the traditional indigenous economy mostly based on subsistence agriculture. Yielding to the influence of the planting community and the European absentee investors, the colonial administration focused its attention almost exclusively on the welfare of the export economy and often neglected the indigenous sector. At the same time, European (and especially British) industrialisation had cheapened the production of textiles in Europe and flooded the Indian market with cheap cotton goods. This practice brought the swift ruin of the important Indian cotton sector. The process of "deindustrialisation" along with the high population pressure, especially in South India, led to the creation of a huge, landless wage-labour force. Following the abolition of slavery in the 1830s, South Indian excess labour was exported to the plantation regions of the world under the so-called indenture system.

New Imperialism and the Partition of Africa

Since the late eighteenth century, Britain had not experienced serious competition in its Asian empire building efforts. France had been occupied with the French Revolution and the Napoleonic Wars. The VOC had been dissolved, and the Dutch East Indies had been handed over to the government. This changed during the second half of the nineteenth century. France recovered from its internal problems and became engaged in Indochina and Africa. The German Unification of 1871 had created another global player that was hungry for colonial possessions. Italy developed colonial ambitions as well. The internal rivalry between these European powers made them overambitious colonisers and led to the period of "new imperialism." Most of the world had already been colonised (or even decolonised already)—only Africa and parts of the Pacific remained open for further empire building. Thus began what has been aptly named the "Scramble for Africa." Until the middle of the nineteenth century, the African continent had remained relatively spared from direct colonial domination. Although Africa had already been drawn into the world economy through the Triangle Trade, the Cape Colony and Algeria remained the only substantial European possession in the hinterland until the last quarter of the nineteenth century.

All major European powers started to occupy African territory for economic and strategic reasons. France moved into Tunis in 1881. A year later, Britain secured control over the Suez Canal by occupying Egypt. In addition, King Leopold II of Belgium and his International African Association privately acquired a huge territory in the Congo region in 1882; this territory was later known as the Congo Free State, and in 1908 it was transferred to Belgian rule. The Berlin Conference of 1884–1885 laid down the rules of engagement in the partition of Africa and quickened its pace. Britain occupied most of Southern Africa, modern Kenya, Uganda, and Sudan, as well as Nigeria and the Gold Coast in Western Africa. France subjugated modern Senegal, Niger, Mali, and Chad and held other colonies in western Sudan and Central Africa. Germany got Southwest Africa (modern Namibia) and German East Africa (now Tanzania). Portugal held Angola and Mozambique. During the "Scramble for Africa," European rivalry manifested itself in various crises. In 1898, clashing British and French interests in strategically important Sudan became known as the Fashoda Incident. German attempts to break the French hold over Morocco led to the Tangier Crisis of 1905 and the Agadir Crisis of 1911.

Outside Africa, the age of new imperialism saw the emergence of the United States of America and Japan as colonising countries. The former took over Hawaii and the Philippines, and the latter occupied Korea. Earlier, France had established a firm hold over French Indochina, and Britain had secured Burma. Germany colonised eastern New Guinea. China had become a target of European imperialism since its forced opening to European commerce in 1842. Although not formally colonised, China was subjected to continuous British, French, and American intervention.

The World Wars and Decolonisation

The European powers' aggressive colonial policy together with intra-European tensions eventually led to the outbreak of World War I (1914–1918). After four years of warfare in Europe and in the colonies, the victorious countries (particularly England and France) split up most of the colonial territories of the losers. Britain acquired most of the German colonies in Africa, as well as Palestine and Iraq from the crumbling Ottoman Empire. The British and French empires had thus reached their greatest extents. On the other hand, World War I had devastated Europe and ruined European economy. Even the victors found it hard to maintain control over their vast colonial empires. In addition, the colonies' exhaustive financial and military support of the home countries had spurred local independence movements that had already started to mobilise support for increased autonomy of the colonies. On that background, Egypt achieved quasi-independence in 1922 with British soldiers solely remaining at the Suez Canal. In India, the nationalist movement started to gain momentum and could not be satisfied by the halfhearted

British reforms of 1919 and 1935. But outside Egypt, effective decolonisation did not happen before the end of World War II, due to two different factors. First, most nationalist movements were carried by local elites and thus did not initially aim at the declaration of independence but at an increased political and economic autonomy within a colonial system. Second, the colonial powers—though seriously weakened by World War I—were not yet willing to release their overseas territories. In Asia, this changed rapidly after World War II. India had supported the British war effort with almost 2.5 million soldiers all around the world and had contributed heavily to the war expenses. In its post-World War II situation, Britain did not have the means to profit from the South Asian colonies anymore and swiftly granted India independence in 1947. Ceylon and Birma followed in 1948. South Asian decolonisation (much like the decolonisation of Africa in later years) was an unorganised process initiated by economic necessities and local nationalist ideas. In the case of India, decolonisation led to the partition of British India into a Muslim Pakistan and a Hindu India accompanied by a mass exodus on both sides and the death of more than 1 million people in the resulting atrocities. The United States granted independence to the Philippines in 1946. Since 1948, the United States also supported the Indonesian independence movement, leading to full independence from the Netherlands in 1956. France was less willing to leave Indochina. After alengthy and bloody war against the Vietnamese independence movement (Vietminh or the *Viet-Nam Ðoc-Lap Ðong-Minh* League for the Independence of Vietnam) and a devastating defeat at Dien Bien Phu in 1954, France had to accept the partition of Vietnam. After the French retreat, Vietnam became a prime stage for American neo-colonialism with tensions finally culminating in the (second) Vietnam War.

African decolonisation commenced only in the late 1950s. For France and Britain, the African colonies had been crucial for their economic recovery in the first ten years after World War II. But now Britain acknowledged rising national consciousness in the colonies and released Sudan (1956), Nigeria (1960), Sierra Leone (1961), Tanganyika (1961), Uganda (1962), Kenya (1963), Zambia (1964), Malawi (1964), the Gambia (1965), Botswana (1966), and Swaziland (1968). In most of these cases the transfer of power was comparatively smooth. In other cases, such as in Rhodesia or the French Maghreb (particularly in Algeria), the presence of substantial and influential white settler communities complicated issues of decolonisation and led to terrorism and guerrilla warfare in both countries. Algeria finally achieved independence in 1962. Rhodesia became modern Zimbabwe only in 1980.

Conclusion

Centuries of mainly European-dominated colonialism together with the often unorganised and rushed decolonisation of Africa and Asia have left long-lasting marks both on the colonised and on the colonisers. Unresolved territorial conflicts in Africa, the Near East, or in South Asia have their roots in colonial policies. Mass migrations of settlers, wage labourers, or religious communities during the age of colonialism have shaped the ethnic structures of large parts of the world and guarantee a constant potential of ethnic and/or religious conflict. Colonialism, imperialism, and later neo-colonialism have drawn regions into the world market that had hitherto remained almost untouched by global dynamics. Conquerors and colonisers, settlers, and missionaries with a pronounced Eurocentric ideology have spread European culture and values no matter whether it was welcome. Vast territories of land were claimed by the colonisers. Indigenous peoples have been disowned, pushed into wage labour, or even enslaved. European legal codes with legal concepts alien to the "colonised" were implemented in the overseas territories. European settlers and entrepreneurs installed agricultural and industrial forms of production hitherto unknown there. In colonies of domination without a significant percentage of permanent settlers, the greatest part of the financial profit was not reinvested but transferred to the mother country. In settler colonies, reinvestments primarily benefited the European economic sector.

However, oversimplifying interpretations of European colonialism that hold the colonisers responsible for exploiting and "underdeveloping" their dependencies does not fully correspond with reality either. It has been argued that the slave trade eased the effects of African food shortages or that European investments developed the colonies' infrastructure. The implementation of European legal codes helped to guarantee basic human rights. In many cases, health care and education were made affordable for the poor. The role of American gold and silver in the economic rise of Europe has also been questioned. Britain's economic backwardness against Germany in the early twentieth century has been attributed to its reliance on the resources of the Empire. More often than not, the real beneficiaries of colonialism have been private merchant companies, European entrepreneurs, and the members of the local collaborating elites.

ROLAND J. WENZLHUEMER

See also Colonialism: Legacies; Neocolonialism

References and Further Reading

Armitage, David. *The Ideological Origins of the British Empire*. Cambridge: Cambridge University Press, 2000.

Blaut, James M. *The Colonizers Model of the World. Geographical Diffusionism and Eurocentric History*. New York, London: Guilford Press, 1993.

Césaire, Aimé. *Discourse on Colonialism*. Translated by Joan Pinkham. New York: Monthly Review Press, 2000.

Chaudhuri, K. N. *Trade and Civilization in the Indian Ocean. An Economic History from the Rise of Islam to 1750*. Cambridge: Cambridge University Press, 1993.

Curtin, Philip D. The *Rise and Fall of the Plantation Complex: Essays in Atlantic History*. Cambridge: Cambridge University Press, 1994.

De Silva, S. B. D. *The Political Economy of Underdevelopment*. London, Boston, Henley: Routledge & Kegan Paul, 1982.

Fieldhouse, David K. *Colonialism 1870–1945: An Introduction*. London: Weidenfeld and Nicholson, 1981.

Frank, Andre Gunder. *ReORIENT. Global Economy in the Asian Age*. Berkeley, Los Angeles, London: University of California Press, 1998.

Loomba, Ania. *Colonialism/Postcolonialism*. London, New York: Routledge, 1998.

MacKenzie, John M. *The Partition of Africa 1880–1900 and European Imperialism in the Nineteenth Century*. London, New York: Methuen, 1983.

McAlister, Lyle N. *Spain and Portugal in the New World, 1492–1700*. Minneapolis: University of Minnesota Press, 1984.

Middleton, Richard. *Colonial America: A History, 1585–1776*. Oxford: Blackwell, 1996.

Osterhammel, Jürgen. *Colonialism: A Theoretical Overview*. Translated by Shelley L. Frisch. Princeton, NJ: Markus Wiener Publishers, 1997.

Reinhard, Wolfgang. *Kleine Geschichte des Kolonialismus*. Stuttgart, Germany: Alfred Kröner, 1996.

COLONIALISM: LEGACIES

Introduction

The continuities from the colonial to the postcolonial period are being increasingly acknowledged, but the real empirical relationship is not so easy to reconstruct. For instance, the links between colonialism and capitalism remain controversial. Mainstream historians regard the relationship as incidental and theoretically uninteresting, whereas radical Africanist historiography presumes that European colonialism in Africa and Asia was a product of European capitalism and was undertaken to serve its interests. Other historians underline that capital penetration was the basic process and that colonialism partly furthered and partly hindered capitalism.

The links between colonialism and economic processes are indirect and complex because of the fact that they were mediated by different historical agents at different historical moments and by different colonial states. As numerous studies underline, the main agent of colonialism was the state: primarily the metropolitan state, which was replaced later on by the colonial state. During the process of colonization, the role of the colonial state changed. At the beginning, most of the European colonial states envisaged no function for the state. Later on, the state had to keep law and order and to create possibilities for other colonial agents, mainly economic activities, such as agriculture and industry. The state had to create opportunities for economic agents and also for the missions who worked in colonies. Fields where economic gains could be expected were reserved for economic agents, while those that were needed for the maintenance of the colony and the colonial economy were left to the power of the state or other noneconomic agents.

Theoretically, the colonial process of letting go of a legacy remains rather poorly understood. This discussion suggests that colonial intervention initiated a process of change that was historically unprecedented and was rather different according to its historical periods and its geographic origins. A further presumption of this text is that colonialism had unintended and more or less dysfunctional consequences that consisted of including colonized regions in an ever-enlarging world system. This world system did not only include economic systems but also political, social, and cultural systems. Processes profoundly affecting the given economic, political, social, and cultural spheres of societies were started at the beginning of colonial rules, although most of them only became evident many decades afterward.

After the decision had been taken to establish a colonial system, new structural constraints were imposed and new actions were set in motion. Following these initial processes, further change was induced. Often, the outcome was something that was not intended and most of the time barely understood by political or economic agents themselves. The newly created system was dependent on colonized people and colonizers, even if they only had limited possibilities to introduce a planned process of transformation. Often, these processes were initiated by actors who were interested in a civilizing mission. The ideological impetus was *to bring light* to the alien groups or to develop their social, economic, and political institutions. The product after decades or

centuries of colonial rule was the integration in a world system of economies, politics, and cultures.

The legacies of colonialism thus include a process of development that was at the same time a goal and a means. To study these processes, it is important to ask whether these transformations can be understood as historical parallels produced by similar structural imperatives. This question will be discussed in the following paragraphs by differentiating between geographical areas that knew rather different colonial experiences due to given local cultures and to different historical moments. In this sense, the text will discuss the process of colonization in South America that took place some centuries before the European colonization in Africa. The Asian experience is the last discussion point. Surely, other forms of colonization could be tackled here, such as the Roman or Greek experiences. But these early forms of colonization are only marginal to this encyclopedia of the developing world. The interested reader may find information about these periods in historically oriented encyclopedias.

Colonialism: Legacies in Latin America

The hierarchy of races, which was introduced rather early in European history, meant that Europeans were at the top, followed in descending order by Asians, Amerindians, and Africans. Amerindian peoples enjoyed a more elevated status because they were regarded as fit to Christianization. The time frame of the colonizing efforts in Latin America was different from those time frames in Africa. Colonial development occurred here in slow motion and stretched out over three centuries, in comparison with Africa's colonial history of less than one century.

Another differentiating factor was that Iberian rule did not enrich the Portuguese and the Spanish as much as it did the English, French, or Dutch ruling groups. The two Iberian countries belonged to the less dynamic part of Europe. Nevertheless, they served as a transmission belt for the rising commercial *entrepôts* of England, France, and the Netherlands, as Tignor (1999) underlined. According to him, the Iberian conquerors were pushed by motivations that can be resumed as god, gold, and glory. The conquest of Spanish and Portuguese America was, as the early decades of European colonial rule in Africa, a period of pillage and plunder. Colonial debates and revelations about abuses led to a more rationalized colonial administrative system. Metropolitan authorities undertook a more rationalized utilization of colonial power. Ministries of colonies, recruitment, and training procedures for colonial officers were established. The Spanish recruited their colonial administrators from their leading universities, whereas France and Britain established specialized colonial schools for their colonial elites. In the Spanish, French, and British colonies, the local agents were often oppressive and venal officers. They carried out many formal administrative tasks, and they had numerous other duties essential to the success of their colony. They facilitated the implementation of institutions, such as wage labor, schools, and consumption patterns related to European consumer goods.

Research about the economic effects of colonialism is a field rather under-researched. Nevertheless, in the mining zones of Mexico, Peru, and southern Africa, European colonialists were faced with similar problems of finding labor supplies. The labor recruitment techniques were alike in these areas. The state supported labor recruitment and encouraged sometimes highly coercive labor-recruiting systems. In Spanish-America, mine workers were Amerindians who suffered, as did their African counterparts, from long journeys to the mines and dangerous working conditions. Similar mechanisms in front of this labor force, as well as high levels of mortality, could be found in the different geographic areas.

The culture of colonialism and such topics as education, urbanization, art and architecture, the role of women, law, and social rules have common aspects, resulting in syncretistic tendencies and hybrid processes. Nevertheless, this is a field in which local cultures were rather important and determined the sort of change that took place. Common factors in the two continents were religious conversions, which brought increasing literacy, and awareness of a Western-style of learning. The introduction of world religions led to a rapid social and economic change of given cultures and to population movements into urban areas. However, indigenous religious traditions did not disappear but were incorporated in newly introduced beliefs and practices.

Another common factor for Latin America and Africa is the artificial drawing of political boundaries that were established in imperial ages and continued after the independence of states. In Spanish-America, these boundaries evolved over a much longer period than in Africa and were thus more adapted to political and economic realities. A further similarity is related to the political instability that both continents experienced after independence. Spanish-American independence took two decades and was characterized by military conflicts. African postcolonial policies were overwhelmed with ethnic conflicts, which often originated in colonial divide-and-rule policies. Once the European colonial administrations had

disappeared, *coups d'état*, civil wars, and ethnic or religious conflicts could be found.

In many regions, the colonial heritage consisted of the creation of export economies that had a particular function within the world system of division of labor. The intertwining of export economies with indigenous structures of production left out an economic structure that has been interpreted to be a characteristic element of a situation of dependence. The former required the latter and adapted to it. The existing structure of production survived within the colonial system. Indigenous structures of production became a part of export economies. The effects of these practices were thus historically deep.

The middle of the eighteenth century constitutes the break between former and later colonial empires depending on the industrial revolution in Western Europe. Distinct characteristics of the Iberian colonization in Southern America are its long duration of three centuries and its profound impact on economic and social structures. White colonialists formed an urban upper class, living on the income of commercial exchanges and large landownerships cultivated by an indigenous subjugated peasantry. At this time, 80% of the colonized groups in the world lived in countries colonized by the Spanish and the Portuguese.

Colonialism: Legacies in Africa

For African countries, colonialism was the main constitutive factor. Hundreds of small societies existed in their later areas. The colonial power fixed these populations, breaking up their independence and integrating them into a colonial society. In Africa, south of the Sahara, colonialism existed about eighty years. Development processes, launched in this period, were carried over in more or less modified forms to the independent states. Sometimes, developments were overturned by later ones, proving and documenting continuities and discontinuities of African history. This discussion shows transformations in social, spatial, and ecological spheres brought about by colonialism. The no-less fundamental changes within African societies need another research approach that would begin with precolonial structures of these societies and analyze their gradual transformations during colonialism.

Perhaps the most important result of colonial development at the end of the nineteenth century was that it made Africa a continent with many small and some big countries. A geographical region, circumscribed by arbitrary borders, was appropriated by the colonial state and changed into a society. These countries were colonies with internal structures impregnated by colonialism. One of its most important characteristics was the separation between colonizers, on the one hand, and colonized people on the other. This social order was based on a racial and hierarchical division. Most of the Europeans were at the top of this hierarchy, and most of the Africans were at the bottom. The impact of this sort of colonial racism contributed to an enduring feeling of inferiority by Africans.

More and more, Africans became necessary for the colonial state and the economy. They were increasingly accommodated since the 1920s in intermediary positions in colonial bureaucracies, missions, plantations, and enterprises. These Africans received opportunities to improve their material and social standing and to acquire skills, which European colonialism appreciated and required. An increased number of literate Africans began to be employed by civilian or military bureaucracies of colonial states. In the interior of the countries, where more precolonial policies had been maintained than in coastal areas, local chiefs often were middlemen between their groups and the colonial administration. They were assisted by literate and paid personnel formed by missions or colonial schools. The armed forces, needed since the beginning of colonialism, could not have functioned without Africans.

Slave labor lost its economic significance since the abolition of the slave trade in the beginning of the nineteenth century. Slaves were replaced by free migrant laborers who were recruited by European employers. The situation was different in some eastern and southern African countries, where Asians replaced precolonial Arab competitors in merchant capitalism. Asian traders were active along the caravan routes and employed African itinerant traders. They supplied them with commodities and sent them to countryside. These Asians formed an ethnic minority occupying a middle level in the colonial society, even if they received the legal position of "natives."

Under modern European colonialism, very few Africans could gain the position of an employer. Colonial structures based on race obstructed this possibility. Economic advantages were strictly reserved for European employers, and only Africans with political resources, such as chiefs with access to the labor of their subjects, could compete with European employers. Other African farmers were disadvantaged because they lacked the necessary labor force. If they were Christians, who were required to be monogamous, only their wife could help them because all other laborers were needed for the colonial economy. Missions were one of the principal employers of paid and unpaid labor. They bought their lands from

Africans and helped to establish the idea of private land rights. Furthermore, missions introduced new crops, such as cotton and wheat, and they were the first to use the ox-plough. Most of their agricultural work was undertaken by Christians who frequented their schools and churches.

One of the central functions of missions was the spread of Christianity. Missions introduced the idea of personal responsibility before God, a notion that contributed to the collapse of former collectivist values and institutions in African societies. Missionaries were not ready to tolerate many African customs and values and, in effect, they undermined them. They focused on individual responsibility. The reading and writing they taught was a technique that favored individuality. Missions used the methods of Western medicine. All these measures contributed to underline the utilitarian value of Christianity and guaranteed the internal colonization of the African mind, which was necessary for the success of European colonialism. Christianity began to become a way of individual improvement. Furthermore, missions worked more and more with African clergymen, catechists, and teachers.

At the beginning of the twentieth century, economic change had to be imposed from outside the African societies, and African labor had to be found by force. As colonialism progressed in the following decades, an increasing number of Africans voluntarily joined the colonial economy by exchanging their labor force against returns they could use in the same economy, which changed their way of life and their welfare. Increased mobility and the possibility to gain money and to receive education gave young men a much more independent position in relation to elders. African cosmologies were transformed by new religions. Former loose ethnic identities were changed into more exclusive identifications. The introduction of a monetary economy implied the emergence and creation of new needs. The spread of money and the market mechanism sufficed for the creation of a stable workforce since the 1950s. The wider use of money meant the growing enrollment of Africans for work within the colonial system. Imported consumer goods were spread more and more in the interior of the countries and created new needs and wishes.

In the first decades of colonialism, the recruitment of migrant labor was backed by taxation. People were obliged to work or to deliver produce. Africans began to participate in the colonial economy, but most of them continued to work for some months on their farms. A paid occupation was not still an envisaged lifestyle until the 1940s. Africans could sell their labor by continuing to depend on their farmlands. This access to land prevented Africans from becoming poor city dwellers. Therefore, the state was obliged to intervene in the economy by pressure, force, and the creation of new needs. The colonial state had the task to keep law and order and to create possibilities for other colonial agents, especially private enterprises.

All these measures show that European colonialism laid the foundations of African countries as political, economic, social, and cultural entities. Processes that were set in motion by colonial measures changed political, social, cultural, and economic systems in the continent, forging them into entities that were taken over some decades later by African nationalist governments. What the twenty-first century calls "development" was really initiated by early colonizers. English, French, and German colonial governments conceptualized their actions in terms of development. Dual Mandate, *Mission civilisatrice*, and *Entwicklung* were notions used in strategies, measures, and ideologies. The development movement, diffused after World War II, can be seen as an essential part of the last years of colonialism in Africa and Asia. The European colonial nations wanted to change African societies. They invented strategies and discussed possibilities of progress and improvement. Development was seen as a qualitative social transformation for the better. It justified colonialism, which would otherwise have been a pure process of exploitation based on racism. In this sense, colonial development was a historically progressive process. Colonialists underlined the beneficialness of colonialism; radical and conservative scholars were sympathetic with this idea as well.

Even if colonial intentions and practices were partly exploitative, it can be claimed today that they brought Africans the means to live in the modern world. Colonialism acted as a powerful agent in a process that is called globalization. Its long-term consequences were much more important than its short-term goals. Colonialism had to serve European interests, but it became increasingly powerful in the local context of African societies. Global aims permitted local people to get access to benefits that they could accept as positive developments. Early colonialism introduced institutions, such as wage labor, furthered the monetization and commoditization of the economy, and led to a different class formation in African societies.

Colonialism: Legacies in Asia

In Asia, British, French, and Dutch colonialism was active for about 120 to 150 years. For a short period, Japan colonized Korea. In contrast to the parallel time frame of colonialism in Africa, the colonizing nations were opposed to highly developed cultures characterized by cosmologies and religions, such as Buddhism, Hinduism, or Islam. These religions were different from the often animist cosmologies of African territories, possessing institutions such as temples and monks, and being characterized by detailed ethical world views and religious duties. The European colonizing countries were confronted to these cosmologies. Due to their Christian background, Europeans did not try to adapt their politics to the different religions but used their colonial methods and practices as they did in other colonized regions. It seems that scholars only recently began to recognize the influence of these religious worldviews on the development of the different territories. The astonishing success of countries such as South Korea or Sri Lanka, characterized by the Buddhist religion that preaches an ethics that favors a healthy, industrious, and nonviolent way of life. In Buddhism, material well-being can be reached by work, and *Nirvana* is attained by an equilibrated spiritual life. In this sense, this cosmology resembles to the Protestant ethics, which Weber declared to be responsible for the success of modern Western economy. On the contrary, Hinduism and the caste system were already considered by Weber as obstacles to the development of a modern economy. Besides other factors in Asia, religious cosmologies seem thus to have had a rather different influence on the development of societies than in African countries South of the Sahara.

It is now important to review the legacies of colonialism in Asia. Here, colonialism took place as in Africa after the first industrial revolution in Western countries. Before 1880, the motivating forces of European expansion have to be looked for in the transformation of economic and social structures of Asia and Africa. In the long and rich history of Asian and African populations, the short period of European colonialism changed, on the one hand, perspectives and the timetable of their future. On the other hand, the colonizing nations were not able to change profoundly the economic and social structures of their overseas possessions. They lacked financial means even if the colonized people, having frequented the schools of the white man, required a rapid modernization and economic development.

Between 1760 and 1830, Great Britain and its empire were shaken up by profound upheavals. The metropolis was characterized by the outbreak of the industrial revolution that allowed the emergence of a different world. European economies were now interested in penetrating Asian countries to accrue the role of their private economic interests in front of a colonial state whose role it was to introduce a mode of administration. In Asia, populations who did not have any experience with European authority or who did not even know any centralized control were confronted with European colonialism. Therefore, colonial rule was obliged to intensify in a varying degree its influence: coastal regions were easier to administer than regions far from the coast. But everywhere, foreign norms related to bureaucracy and economy were imposed. Western concepts of administration did not any longer permit personal relations between upper and lower classes. Furthermore, the colonial state destroyed the autonomy of small local communities; it transformed the position of local elites and modified social actions at such a point that fundamental authority rules were obliged to change and to accept the alien model. By creating new political bodies, which laid the foundations of the development of nations in a modern sense, colonial rule induced a universal process for the creation of nation-states.

As already seen in Africa, the establishment of frontiers was poorly linked to economic, social, cultural, ethnic, or geographic realities. Former political centers were incorporated in newly created entities: the redistribution of the territory and the separation in several political and administrative unities were realized in the twentieth century by newly drawn frontiers. Direct administration was mixed with protectorates where an indigenous administration survived. But it was always the central colonial system, which controlled the territories, that decided each important question. The new political order was very different from the former one where power was exercised from the center to the periphery by successive circles of decreasing influence. The state could now reach villagers in their local life-worlds. Civil servants were charged to collect taxes, to apply law and order, and to administer the land and civil engineering according to uniform principles. Newly created administrative departments took charge of more activities: education, health, economics, and social politics. These transformations, introduced by colonial authority, signified a replacement of former traditional authorities.

Since the end of the nineteenth century until the 1940s, economic transformations were even more radical than political and administrative transformations. The European powers tried to provoke an economic development profitable to governments and metropolitan economic groups. Private investments of European businessmen and white male planters were favored. The transportation and communication network was extended, a fact that changed the economy and integrated the different regions in the world economy.

The legal change of land ownership was totally opposed to former land rights, which had given the peasant a right on the produce of the land but not its ownership. The indigenous nobility gained considerable remuneration by linking its interests to those of large enterprises. A disorientated proletariat was created that was removed from its original surroundings and its former social groups.

The new economy was based on rich cultures, the exploitation of mines, and large commerce that attracted the eradicated manpower and womanpower. Disequilibrium was created between a preponderant agriculture and a small industrial sector. During the whole colonial period, raw materials were exported from the colonized countries, and manufactured goods were imported from the metropolis.

The traditional economy was maintained in large sectors but rarely without any modifications. It became necessary to earn money, to pay taxes, and to exchange goods for money. The heavy load of taxes, usury, and the concentration of land led to a weakening of the peasant economy, to the loss of land by smaller and larger peasants. In the village community, social inequalities increased, and many peasants got to know impoverishment. Land became more valuable than labor force, and the cultural and intellectual ditch between administration and countryside increased.

Colonialism induced a more or less rapid weakening and disturbance of the former society. A new society was created that was characterized by a group of "developed" people and increasing numerous impoverished groups who were living in large cities. The village community had to accept the creation of social inequalities, a new organization based on the nuclear family with changing land rights and the weakening of the reciprocal rules between members of a community.

Reactions from the indigenous groups were diverse. Some notables whose interests were preserved or increased showed their gratitude. But most of the members of the ruling groups did not welcome the disappearance of their former customs and, in particular, of their personal status. Resistance was founded essentially on religion, such as Islam or Buddhism.

Nevertheless, the ruling groups were obliged to open their mind to Western culture. Asian modernity touched every field: Western science, new ways of thinking, medicine, and other such practices. To introduce new ideas and competencies, colonial authorities asked Christian churches to disperse modern education. In the countryside, there was a sort of closing in front of innovations brought by colonial powers. The overthrow of essential values and attitudes, linked to the weakening of former social structures, provoked disorder. People lost reference points and adopted an attitude of reaction against each innovation: they tried to defend traditional values. Colonialism did not erase existing hierarchies (such as princes), but it tried to integrate them in a new social stratification structure and in another functioning of Asian societies.

Economic changes, the creation of new social classes, class differentiation based on a way of life, existing cosmologies, and foreign influences were combined to bear new cultures and mentalities. In the twentieth century, situations, ideas, customs, and religious values introduced by colonization produced literary and musical expressions. They contributed to the creation of new behaviors without eliminating completely former ways of thinking and living. People were touched in different degrees according to groups, social classes, towns, and countryside. A sort of syncretistic encounter emerged, which has been studied more and more by scholars.

Most of these agrarian societies were weakly integrated in the Asian commercial space. The more or less uniformity of production systems and precolonial exchange systems was replaced by a high differentiation of economic and social spaces, unequally developed. The Asian continent became a historical reality with multiple and ineffaceable outlooks. The transfer of technical and scientific knowledge from industrialized societies, which was necessary for the functioning of the colonial economy, led to a changing relation of humans to nature. Nevertheless, at some places, the peasant economy subsisted without modern inputs beside a capitalized form of exportation of primary materials.

The success of Asian colonization was based on the goals of those who introduced plantations and mines, banks, and commercial enterprises. Profits and gains were destined to individuals, colonial enterprises, ruling groups, and middle classes in the metropolis. However, this historical break was not spread everywhere. In some regions of Vietnam, Cambodia, and Laos, there still exists precapitalist forms of community: large families, lineages, and village communities. They survive with elements of modern social classes and former familial structures.

Conclusion

To draw up historical balance sheets is most often a difficult endeavour. The complexity of problems and situations, as well as the different standards of comparisons and of making empirical investigations, contribute to a rather hazardous record of colonial achievements. The colonial legacy in South America, Africa, and Asia shows a history of a powerful diffusion of economic, political, cultural, and social standards that integrated these geographic areas in a world system, known since several decades as a "global village," and has been characterized by processes of globalization that are unique in human history. It is possible to say that the credit balance of colonialism, understood in this sense, outweighs its debit account even if our actual world is characterized by numerous problems that have to be resolved not only on a local scale but also on a global scale.

Because of the complexities of concrete situations, this discussion could only suggest some tentative legacies of colonialism without developing historical cases in length. The further reading proposes some concrete scholarly work. Many more historical studies exist that analyze particular phenomena. However, because of given theoretical conceptions, most scholars will not question the legacies of colonialism. Another problem is the rather short historical distance to African and Asian colonialism, which renders difficult the sort of endeavour presented in this discussion.

ULRIKE SCHUERKENS

See also Colonialism: History; Neocolonialism

References and Further Reading

Adelman, Jeremy, ed. *Colonial Legacies: The Problem of Persistence in Latin American History.* New York: Routledge, 1999.

Brocheux, Pierre, and Daniel Hémery. *Indochine, la Colonisation Ambiguë (1858–1954).* Paris: Éditions La Découverte, 1994.

Cesana, Andreas. *Geschichte als Entwicklung? Zur Kritik des Geschichtsphilosophischen Entwicklungsdenkens.* Berlin: W. de Gruyter, 1988.

Copans, Jean. "La 'Situation Coloniale' de Georges Balandier: Notion Conjoncturelle ou Modèle Sociologique et Historique?" *Cahiers Internationaux de Sociologie* CX (2001).

Etemad, Bouda. *La Possession du Monde. Poids et Mesures de la Colonisation (XVIIIe-XXe siècles).* Paris: Éditions Complexe, 2000.

Gann, L.H., and Peter Duignan. *Burden of Empire. An Appraisal of Western Colonialism in Africa South of the Sahara.* London: Pall Mall Press, 1968.

Koponen, Juhani. *Development for Exploitation. German Colonial Policies in Mainland Tanzania, 1884–1914.* Helsinki, Finland, and Hamburg, Germany: Finnish Historical Society and Lit-Verlag, 1994.

Lim, Timothy C. "The Origins of Societal Power in South Korea: Understanding the Physical and Human Legacies of Japanese Colonialism." *Modern Asian Studies* 33, no. 3 (1999).

McMichael, Philip. *Development and Social Change. A Global Perspective.* Thousand Oaks, CA, London, New Delhi: Pine Forge Press, 1996.

Piault, Marc, ed. *La colonisation, Rupture ou Parenthèse.* Paris: L'Harmattan, 1987.

Rotermund, Hartmut O. *L'Asie Orientale et Méridionale aux XIXᵉ et XXᵉ siècles. Chine, Corée, Japon, Asie du Sud-Est, Inde.* Paris: Presses Universitaires de France, 1999.

Schuerkens, Ulrike. *Du Togo Allemand aux Togo at Ghana Indépendants. Changement Social sous Régime Colonial.* Paris: L'Harmattan, 2001.

Sutton, Paul, ed. *Dual Legacies in the Contemporary Carribean: Continuing Aspects of British and French Dominion.* London: F. Cass, 1986.

Thomas, Nicholas. *Out of Time, History, and Evolution in Anthropological Discourse.* Michigan: The University of Michigan Press, 1989.

Tignor, Robert L. "Colonial Africa through the Lens of Colonial Latin America." In *Colonial Legacies: The Problem of Persistence in Latin American History*, Jeremy Adelman, ed. New York, London: Routledge, 1999.

COMMON MARKET FOR EASTERN AND SOUTHERN AFRICA (COMESA)

Headquartered in Lusaka, Zambia, the Common Market for Eastern and Southern Africa (COMESA) is the largest regional economic integration scheme in Africa in terms of spatial extent and the number of member countries. It was established by a treaty signed in 1993 in Kampala, Uganda, and was ratified in 1994 in Lilongwe, Malawi, as a strengthened successor to the erstwhile Preferential Trade Area (PTA) for Eastern and Southern Africa, which had existed since 1981. COMESA now has twenty-one members, including Angola, Burundi, Comoros, Democratic Republic of Congo, Djibouti, Egypt, Eritrea, Ethiopia, Kenya, Madagascar, Malawi, Mauritius, Namibia, Rwanda, Seychelles, Sudan, Swaziland, Tanzania, Uganda, Zambia, and Zimbabwe. The Republic of South Africa is not a member of COMESA, having instead opted for membership in the Southern African Development Community (SADC).

African countries have long favored regional economic integration of one form or another. In 1965, with the help of the Economic Commission for Africa (ECA), the newly independent nations of Eastern and Southern Africa convened a ministerial meeting in Lusaka to explore the possibility of forming a regional economic bloc. Following this meeting, an Interim Council of Ministers was set up to initiate programs for economic cooperation, pending the completion of negotiations on a formal treaty for regional economic integration. In 1978, a meeting of Ministers of Trade, Finance, and Planning in Lusaka adopted the "Lusaka Declaration," which called for the establishment of a regional economic community, beginning with a regional PTA. The PTA would be upgraded, over a period of a decade, to a common market until

an economic community had been established. The treaty establishing the PTA was signed on December 21, 1981, at a meeting of the Heads of States and Governments in Lusaka, but it came into force in September 30, 1982, following its ratification by more than seven nations, as required by Article 50 of the treaty. The transformation from the PTA into a Common Market, as envisaged by the PTA Treaty, came about in December 1994, in Lilongwe, when the Treaty of COMESA was finally ratified.

Objectives

Article 3 of COMESA's Treaty stipulates a sixfold objective for the organization: (i) to attain sustainable growth and development of the member states by promoting a more balanced and harmonious development of their production and marketing structures; (ii) to promote joint development in all fields of economic activity and encourage the joint adoption of macroeconomic policies and programs to raise the standard of living of the people; (iii) to cooperate in the creation of an enabling environment for foreign, cross-border, and domestic investment; (iv) to cooperate in the promotion of peace, security, and stability among the member states; (v) to cooperate in strengthening the relations between the common market and the rest of the world and to adopt common positions in international fora; and (vi) to contribute toward the establishment, progress, and the realization of the objectives of the African economic community.

COMESA has identified some priorities with which it expects to make the greatest possible impact in furthering its objectives. These include the creation of a full Free Trade Area that guarantees the free movement of goods and services; the free movement of people, capital, and investment through the adoption of common investment practices; the simplification and harmonization of trade documents and procedures; the elimination of production and manufacturing rigidities; and the adoption of common standards, measurement systems, and quality assurance practices. Others include the harmonization of macroeconomic policies and data collection procedures; the adoption of a common agricultural policy; the promotion of regional food sufficiency; and the enhancement of currency convertibility toward an eventual establishment of a monetary union among its members. As with most subregional blocs, COMESA has some fundamental principles to which it expects the entire membership to adhere. These, according to Article 6 of the COMESA Treaty, are the principles of equality and interdependence of member states; solidarity and collective self-reliance; nonaggression between member states; and the recognition, promotion, and protection of fundamental human rights. Other such principles are the commitment to liberty, fundamental freedoms and the rule of law, the assurance to peaceful settlement of disputes among member states, and the promotion of democracy.

Institutions

Article 7 of the COMESA Treaty identifies its main institutions as the following eight: the Authority of the Heads of State and Government (the Authority); the Council of Ministers (the Council); the Court of Justice; the Committee of Governors of Central Banks; the Intergovernmental Committee; the Technical Committees; the Consultative Committee of the Business Community and other Interest Groups; and the Secretariat.

The Authority, made up of all the heads of states or governments, is the supreme organ of COMESA. It is responsible for the general policy and direction of the organization. The authority meets once a year and may hold extraordinary meetings at the request of any member, provided such a request is backed by one-third of the members of the Authority. The Council of Ministers (the Council), the second highest organ, is composed of Ministers designated by the member states. It is responsible for monitoring COMESA's activities to ensure the proper functioning of the organization in accordance with its treaty. Among other things, the council makes regulations, issues directives, and monitors and reviews COMESA's financial and administrative management. The main judicial arm of the organization is the Court of Justice, which ensures the proper interpretation and application of the provision of the COMESA Treaty and adjudicates disputes that may arise between member states regarding the interpretation and the application of the treaty.

Made up of the governors of the monetary authorities of member states, the Committee of Governors of Central Banks is responsible for the development of COMESA programs in the field of finance and monetary cooperation, including the determination of the maximum debt and credit limits to the COMESA Clearing House and the setting of a daily interest rate for outstanding debt balances. The Intergovernmental Committee, which consists of principal secretaries from member states, is responsible for developing programs and action plans in all sectors for cooperation, except in the finance and monetary sector, and for overseeing the implementation of the provisions of the COMESA Treaty. COMESA has a total of twelve Technical Committees that are made up of designated representatives of the member states. They include committees on Administration and Budgetary Matters; Agriculture; Comprehensive Information Systems; Energy; Finance and Monetary Affairs; Industry; and Labour, Human Resources, and Social and Cultural Affairs. Others are committees on Legal Affairs; Natural Resources and Environment; Tourism and Wildlife; Trade and Customs; and Transport and Communications. These committees are responsible for the preparation, monitoring, and implementation of COMESA programs in their respective areas.

Made up of representatives of the business community and other interest groups from the member states, the Consultative Committee promotes dialogue between its constituency and the other organs of COMESA. It is responsible for ensuring that the interests of the business community and other interest groups are considered in COMESA programs. Finally, as with most such organizations, COMESA has a Secretariat, which is responsible for providing research-based technical support and advisory services to member states. The Secretariat is headed by a secretary-general who is appointed by the Authority to serve for a five-year term, with the eligibility for a second-term appointment.

Contribution to Development

With a population of about 400 million, the COMESA region obviously has a large reservoir of both skill and unskilled labour forces and a sizeable potential market. Eastern and Southern Africa also have an enormous natural resource endowment, which includes several extensive water bodies (the rivers of Nile, Congo, and Zambezi, as well as the lakes of Victoria, Malawi, Nyasa, and Tanganyika) that could be exploited for hydroelectric power, irrigation, fisheries, and water transportation. The region also produces a significant proportion of the world's diamond, gold, platinum, and manganese and is home to a large amount of the world's iron ore, phosphate, petroleum, and uranium. Despite this rich resource base, the COMESA region, like most parts of Sub-Saharan Africa, is still burdened with mass illiteracy, extreme poverty, heavy debt load, poor infrastructure, geopolitical conflicts, and a variety of devastating diseases, including the scourge of AIDS/HIV. Fifteen COMESA member states are now among the twenty-three least developed countries in Africa with most of them—Angola,

Burundi, Democratic Republic of Congo, Ethiopia, Madagascar, Malawi, Mauritius, Rwanda, Sudan, Tanzania, and Zambia—making the World Bank's list of "severely indebted" countries in 2000 (World Bank 2002). Manuel Castells estimates in his *End of Millennium* (2000) that by the mid-1990s, Sub-Saharan Africa accounted for about 60% of the nearly 17 million HIV-positive cases across the world, of which COMESA members such as Malawi, Democratic Republic of Congo, Zambia, Rwanda, and Uganda are among the worst hit. Indeed, AIDS is now the leading cause of death in Uganda. Making matters worse, geopolitical and ethnic conflicts have reduced to shambles much of the institutions and material bases of life in countries such as Angola, Sudan, and Rwanda.

It is against this background that COMESA seeks to use its integration initiatives to stimulate economic growth through cooperation and improved resource allocation. As a regional economic bloc, the removal of trade barriers has long been on COMESA's agenda. In pursuing removal, COMESA adopted a gradualist approach that called for the reduction of tariffs by 60% by October 1993, 70% by October 1994, 80% by October 1998, and 100% by October 2000, thus achieving a Free Trade Area by the latter date. However, only nine member states—Djibouti, Egypt, Kenya, Madagascar, Malawi, Mauritius, Sudan, Zambia, and Zimbabwe—were able to meet the 2000 deadline to form the COMESA Free Trade Area. This is hardly surprising because the acute lack of financial resources in the region makes it difficult for some members to eliminate custom duties on which they have come to depend for substantial portions of their government revenues. As part of its efforts to promote intrabloc trade, COMESA has initiated programs to harmonize trade statistics and the customs regulation and management system across the region. More specifically, the usability of COMESA's Customs Document (COMESA-CD), as well as its Automated System for Custom Data and Management (ASYCUDA), has been improved considerably.

COMESA expects to form a full custom union by the end of 2004 and a full-blown monetary union, with a common currencies and a common central bank, by 2025. To this end, the organization has again adopted a steady approach, entailing the consolidation of existing protocols on monetary cooperation and macroeconomic convergence by 1996; the introduction of a limited currency convertibility and information exchange rate union by 2000; and the creation of a formal exchange rate union by 2004, with an eye toward a full monetary union by 2025.

In addition, to enhance self-sufficiency in food production and to promote agro-based industrial development, COMESA has embarked on a number of noteworthy programs in agriculture, fishery, and irrigation. For instance, the organization has promoted free trade in agricultural products and fostered the dissemination of technical innovations and best practices in the production, processing, and marketing of agricultural products across the region. It has also embarked on land reforms and expanded training, as well as research and extension services aimed at empowering both small- and large-scale farmers in the region. In addition, plans are underway to establish the Common Marine Fisheries Investment and Management Policy for managing and protecting COMESA's marine fisheries against exploitation by nonmembers. Still involved the fishing industry, COMESA is promoting the processing and marketing of value-added fish and fishery product, based mostly on cultured tilapia, shrimp, tuna, and sardines. With private sector support, coupled with an increasing commitment to gender equity, COMESA has intensified its development initiatives in many other sectors, including manufacturing, tourism, energy, and forestry. Most of these development impetuses are backed by the Bretton Woods institutions through ongoing structural adjustment programs in the COMESA region.

The unparalleled growth in information and communication technologies provides unique opportunities for generating and accessing wealth, knowledge, and power. However, as with many parts of Africa, the COMESA region has only a meager telecommunication infrastructure and electronic network connectivity. This lack provides both a challenge and an opportunity to COMESA. For one thing, COMESA can leapfrog ahead in its economic development by taking advantage of the new satellite and wireless communication technology to circumvent the need to invest in expensive conventional telecommunication infrastructure. The possibility of creating a borderless and information-driven economy in the region, through the use of digital technologies and communication networks, is certainly greater now than ever before. The challenge for COMESA, however, is to work with the private sector to develop basic information technology infrastructure, in the likes of a reliable electricity supply, good telephone lines, and computerized network connectivity; COMESA also wishes to establish the necessary incentives and regulatory systems that could spur a sustainable economic growth in the region. Perhaps more important than the improvement of the region's information technology infrastructure is the need to resolve the duplication and conflicts of interest engendered by the existence of many overlapping integration schemes in that part of Africa. As it stands now,

COMESA members such as Seychelles and Mauritius belong to the Indian Ocean Commission; Burundi, Rwanda, and the Democratic Republic of Congo belong to the Economic Community of Central African States; Namibia and Swaziland are members of the Southern African Customs Union; and Mauritania, Seychelles, Malawi, Zambia, Zimbabwe, Angola, and the Democratic Republic of Congo are all members of the Southern African Development Community. The difficulties in sorting through the maze of agreements and commitments wrought by such multiple memberships can hardly be gainsaid.

JOSEPH MENSAH

See also East Africa: History and Economic Development; East Africa: International Relations; Economic Community of Central African States (ECCAS); Southern African Customs Union (SACU); Southern African Development Community (SADC); Southern Africa: History and Economic Development; Southern Africa: International Relations; Structural Adjustment Programs (SAPs)

References and Further Reading

Castells, Manuel. *End of Millennium*, 2d ed. Oxford: Blackwell Publishers, 2000.

COMESA. *Annual Report, 2002*. Lusaka, Zambia: COMESA, 2002.

Hansohm, Dirk, Willie Breytenbach, and Trudi Hartzenberg, eds. *Monitoring Regional Integration in Southern Africa*. Windhoek, Namibia: Gamsberg Macmillan, 2003.

Murinde, Victor, ed. *The Tree Trade Area of the Common Market for Eastern and Southern Africa*. Aldershot, Burlington, VT: Ashgate, 2001.

Schiff, Maurice, and L. A. Winters. *Regional Integration and Development* Washington, DC: The International Bank for Reconstruction and Development and the World Bank, 2003.

The World Bank. *World Development Indicators*. Washington, DC: The International Bank for Reconstruction and Development and the World Bank, 2002.

COMMONWEALTH (BRITISH)

The British Commonwealth of Nations, or the British Commonwealth, is now renamed as Commonwealth of Nations and is often referred as the Commonwealth. However, many prefer to use the old terms to avoid confusion between different commonwealths. The Commonwealth of Nations is a voluntary association of independent republic nations that recognize the British crown as the head of the free alliance, while some other member countries owe their common allegiance to the British Crown. All member nations have equality of status, and Britain does not retain hegemony in the association any longer. Though only independent states can be members, the political territories of individual nations within the Commonwealth can also be technically affiliated with the Commonwealth programs. Commonwealth is the heir to the British Empire. Membership has been traditionally based on prior association with the British Empire. It does not mean, however, that the Commonwealth membership includes all former parts of the British Empire. A few colonies or dominions of the British Empire, such as Burma, are not members of the Commonwealth. Mozambique was the first nation that was not a part of the former British Empire to join the Commonwealth (1995).

The number of members in the Commonwealth is not fixed. The members usually initiate admissions, readmissions, and suspensions. The membership list has changed often over the years based on new admissions, voluntary withdrawals, suspensions, and readmission of members. In addition, the formation of or withdrawal from federations of Commonwealth countries affects the number of members; for example, Malay and Singapore were separately admitted, they formed the federation of Malaysia, and then Singapore withdrew from the membership and recommenced with its original membership. South Africa left in 1961, reapplied for membership, and was readmitted in 1994. Similarly, Fiji left in 1987 and rejoined in 1997. The Commonwealth had fifty-four member countries in 2004, with more than a quarter of the world's population and about one-fifth of the planet's land surface. It is constituted of different religions, cultures, sizes of countries and populations, ethnicity, languages, and types of governments.

The meaning of the term "commonwealth" has changed over the years. The origin of the term can be traced back to "commonweal," and the term meant common welfare or public good. In archaic usage, it also meant body politic. The term commonwealth also has different historical connotations and precedents. Historically, England and Scotland were united into the Commonwealth of England under Cromwell in the seventeenth century. The term Commonwealth is also used to describe the federation of Poland and Lithuania formed in 1569. Commonwealth could also be interpreted to mean a nation, republic, state, or a union or federation of nations, republics, and states. Australia and the Bahamas, for example, are officially called commonwealths. In the United States, four states are called commonwealths, and the term is also used to describe the political association between Puerto Rico and the United States. Recently, twelve of the former states of the Soviet Union have formed the Commonwealth of Independent States.

The Commonwealth of Nations (the Commonwealth) originated and evolved from the British Empire. The loss of the American colonies very likely changed the British attitude, and later on, the British policies probably leaned more toward the granting of colonial self-government as a matter of practicality. For example, in response to the Canadian rebellion in 1837, demanding similar rights as the United States the Durham report recommended a responsible government along the British system of government and that a local assembly should be in charge of local affairs, leaving other affairs such as constitutional amendments, defense, foreign trade, and foreign affairs under the jurisdiction of Great Britain. Canada took the lead in extending the scope of Canadian self-government. The expansion of Canada, Australia, and South Africa gave further impetus to this trend. By the early twentieth century, the Commonwealth started to take shape. These partially self-governing colonies were later designated as dominions and were allowed to send delegations to the Colonial Conferences in London that were later called Imperial Conferences.

World Wars I and II were watershed periods in the development of the Commonwealth. The first period is the incorporation of dominions into a Commonwealth. The end of World War I resulted in major changes in the status of the dominions. This was the period when Britain tried moving away from colonial administration to self-governing dominions with the Parliament at Westminster maintaining overriding powers. During the Treaty of Versailles, dominions of the British Empire were allowed to participate independently as members of the League of Nations. As a result of the Imperial Conferences of 1921, 1923, 1926, and the consequent Balfour report and Statute of Westminster in 1931, autonomy of the dominions, free choice of membership, and equality of status of all members within the Commonwealth were recognized. The statute explained that legislation passed in United Kingdom that was applicable to the dominions had to be at the request or consent of the respective dominion governments. There were still other major issues, such as the Privy Council acting as the final civil and criminal appellate court of the dominions and the amendment of constitution of the dominions by the United Kingdom. The original members of this Commonwealth were Australia, Britain, Canada, Ireland, New Zealand, South Africa, and Newfoundland (which later became a province of Canada). Soon after in 1932, a trade agreement called the Commonwealth Preference was established, and tariffs for goods from these countries were eliminated; the agreement was followed by treaties among other Commonwealth countries.

The Commonwealth army played an even more crucial role in the survival and eventual victory of Britain in World War II. After the war, many countries in the British Empire gained independence. The development of the Commonwealth entered a new phase after the agreement of India to become a member while retaining its status as an independent republic. This new arrangement provided a new structural model for joining the Commonwealth without accepting the British monarch as the ruler. This was a period when the Commonwealth admitted a large number of countries ruled by people of color.

Another significant phase transpired in 1973 when Britain joined the European Union. Treaties between the Commonwealth countries and countries outside the Commonwealth were nothing new. However, the entry of Britain into the European Union is more inclusive than other trade agreements. For example, after it had joined the European Union, Britain had to discontinue, in 1977, the special trade agreements it had with the other Commonwealth nations.

The Commonwealth has neither a charter nor a constitution in written documentary form. This kind of an arrangement allows flexibility. Decisions are mostly made on the basis of common consent or near consensus, and the proceedings are marked by informality. Common law traditions and norms are shared by most of the group. Most of the Commonwealth nations have parliamentary forms of governments with the British system as the archetype but with many variations. The goal and emphasis of the Commonwealth have always been the rule of law and an honest and democratic form of government. The issue of human rights was also added in the first war.

The contributions of the Commonwealth have taken different forms. They include technical help, advice, negotiation, and the resolution of internal conflicts. The Commonwealth election observer groups have been sent to different countries to facilitate or monitor the democratic election process and suggest reforms in electoral laws. Many of the organizations also work in collaboration with other national and international agencies, such as the United Nations Development Program office in bringing about land reforms and improvements in transportation and communication.

The development of the Commonwealth has undergone changes from nomenclature to conceptualization. The Commonwealth has tried to address the changing needs and demands through announcements such as the Singapore (1971) and Harare (1991) Declarations. The Singapore Declaration issued the Commonwealth Principles, and the Harare Declaration, a significant event in the history of the Commonwealth, reaffirmed the earlier Singapore Declaration, emphasizing the protection and promotion of democratic processes and institutions, human rights, rule of law, honest government, and socioeconomic development of individual states. It was followed by the Edinburgh Economic Declaration in 1997.

There is no Commonwealth judicial tribunal to address disputes between two or more Commonwealth nations, and thus, disputes go before the International Court of Justice. Surprisingly, there have been only six cases that went before that court during the twentieth century to resolve national issues between two Commonwealth countries. The border dispute between Botswana and Namibia is a case in point. It was about a territorial dispute between two Commonwealth countries that was brought to the International Court of Justice for a judicial settlement. Both countries accepted the decision, and the issue was settled amicably without recourse to diatribe or borderline violence.

The Commonwealth consists of many agencies—governmental, quasi-governmental—that are sponsored or partially supported by the government and other nongovernmental organizations. The Commonwealth has offered a wide range of training programs and scholarships and facilitates communication among the universities, scientists, and athletes from different countries. The Commonwealth also provides economic aid, help with administration and governance, and technical assistance and consultation to the developing nations. The bureaucratic arm of the Commonwealth is the Secretariat with a multinational staff, and the secretary-general is appointed by the members of the Commonwealth on a rotational basis. The Human Rights Unit, for example, is one of the segments of the Secretariat. The Commonwealth Human Rights Initiative is a nongovernmental group supported by the Commonwealth Foundation. Numerous other organizations and activities exist: the Commonwealth Games (formerly known as The British Empire Games), Common Wealth Parliamentary Association and regional conferences, Commonwealth People's Festival, Commonwealth Parliamentary Association, Commonwealth Local Government Forum, Commonwealth Fund for Technical Cooperation, the Commonwealth Ministerial Action Group, the Commonwealth Heads of Government Meetings, and the Commonwealth Foundation.

The Commonwealth has been variously described as an elite club for heads of state or prime ministers, an ex-colonial power play in disguise, and a model international organization that has achieved many successes without much ado. Times of stress and tensions among the Commonwealth are common. India and Pakistan, both of which are members of the Commonwealth, have clashed a number of times. The issue of apartheid policy of South Africa created enough divisions in the Commonwealth that some observers wondered if the Commonwealth would survive the rifts. The readmission of Zimbabwe has been a hotly discussed issue during the twenty-first century. Britain is a member of the European Union in addition to the Commonwealth. The Commonwealth, however, has managed to survive these crises in the past.

The relevance of the Commonwealth in the age of globalization and changing political and economic or trade alliances is being seriously debated. Globalization has imposed new sets of demands on most of the Commonwealth countries. It has yet to be seen if Britain and the other technologically advanced countries can provide support to other countries in the Commonwealth and to what extent given the limited resources. It is too early to decide about those outcomes. However, it cannot be denied that smaller countries gain a higher status in international negotiations, participating as members of the Commonwealth. The Commonwealth is a unique institution different from other international organizations, including the United Nations. It is strictly based on the power of persuasion. The nature of the Commonwealth is bound to change even further with the membership of Britain in the European Union, and therefore, the significance and importance of the Commonwealth are likely to diminish. However, the assistance it has rendered is wide and varied in scope, and it has served a useful purpose for its members, especially for the smaller and poorer nations. Issues such as growing concern for human rights and establishment of democratic forms of government and globalization will most likely continue to be discussed in the Commonwealth forums. The Commonwealth has been slowly reinventing itself to keep up with the changing needs or demands of the member countries and the global situations from its very inception. The flexibility of the Commonwealth is likely to allow it to keep reinventing itself to focus on new problems as they arise. However, it is hard to foresee the precise directions, types of changes, and the resultant outcomes in the context of a fast-changing world. Regardless of scholarly opinions, the popularity of the Commonwealth cannot be denied because at least a couple more countries have expressed an interest in applying for membership in the Commonwealth in the twenty-first century.

SUBHASH R. SONNAD

See also Colonialism: History; Colonialism: Legacies

References and Further Reading

Burt, Alfred LeRoy. *The Evolution of the British Empire and Commonwealth*. Boston, MA: D.C. Heath and Company, 1956.

Chadwick, John. *The Unofficial Commonwealth: The Story of the Commonwealth Foundation 1965–1980*. London: George Allen and Unwin, 1982.

Cowen, Zelman. *The British Commonwealth of Nations in a Changing World: Law, Politics, and Prospects*. Evanston, IL: Northwestern University Press, 1965.

Griffiths, Percival. *Empire into Commonwealth*. London: Ernest Benn Limited, 1969.

Ingram, Derek, *Commonwealth For A Colour-Blind World*. London: George Allen and Unwin, 1965.

Lloyd, T. O. *The British Empire 1558–1995*, 2d ed. Oxford: Oxford University Press, 1996.

Mansergh, Nicholas. *The Commonwealth and the Nations: Studies in British Commonwealth Relations*. London: Royal Institute of International Affairs, 1948.

———. *The Commonwealth Experience*. Revised edition. 2 vols. Toronto, Canada: University of Toronto Press, 1982.

McIntyre, David W. *A Guide to the Contemporary Commonwealth*. New York: Palgrave, 2001.

McKenzie, Francine. *Redefining the Bonds of Commonwealth, 1939–1948: The Politics of Preference*. New York: Palgrave Macmillan, 2002.

Miller, J. D. B. *The Commonwealth in the World*. Cambridge, MA: Harvard University Press, 1965.

Wheare, K. C. *The Constitutional Structure of the Commonwealth*. Oxford: Clarendon Press, 1960.

COMMONWEALTH OF INDEPENDENT STATES: HISTORY AND ECONOMIC DEVELOPMENT

Origin

The Commonwealth of Independent States (CIS) is the successor of the Union of Soviet Socialist Republics (USSR). By the time of it dissolution, the USSR was in a deep political and economic crisis, and the USSR members were deeply dissatisfied by the excessively centralized nature of the Soviet Union that was established by the first Treaty of Union in 1922.

Between 1990 and 1991, the fifteen members of the USSR were negotiating a new (second) union treaty, but these negotiations were undermined by the steep economic recession caused by transition from the command-controlled economy to the market-oriented economy and by inconsistencies of the Soviet economic policy. Nonetheless, the negotiations over the new union treaty were not progressing, and the political situation continued to deteriorate. These circumstances were used by the hard-line members of the ruling Communist Party and the military, who organized a *coup d'état* in August 1991. The new military government could not, nonetheless, secure support among the political groups in the country and among the population or establish its control beyond Moscow. In a few days it surrendered; however, the far-reaching consequences of the *coup d'état* revealed themselves in a new development, the nation's dissolution, that was unexpected by many in the former Soviet Union.

The new round of the union treaty negations began immediately after the collapse of the *coup d'état* but in a very unfavorable environment. Three Baltic states—Estonia, Latvia and Lithuania—peacefully withdrew from the Soviet Union in September 1991, undermining the viability of the USSR. Meanwhile, the remaining twelve members of the USSR continued intensive negotiations over the future of the Soviet Union. However, on December 8, 1991, leaders of the three founding states of the USSR—President Yeltsin of Russia, Shushkevich of Belorussia (Belarus), and Kravchuk of the Ukraine—unilaterally signed an agreement on the dissolution of the USSR and expressed the desire to establish a new type of interstate cooperation. This was in spite of a national referendum when the Soviet citizens voted, confirming their desire to retain the Union of Soviet Socialist Republics as the institutional unity of the fifteen republics. Moreover, the agreement signed on December 8, 1991, was not drafted as a legally correct document. In the end, the dissolution of the USSR and establishment of the CIS was formally endorsed on December 21, 1991, in Alma-Ata, as leaders of Azerbaijan, Armenia, Belarus, Kazakhstan, Kyrgyzstan, Moldova, the Russian Federation, Tajikistan, Turkmenistan, Uzbekistan, and Ukraine signed the Protocol to the Agreement on the Establishment of the Commonwealth of the Independent States.

The eleven states also unanimously adopted the Alma-Ata Declaration that signified the beginning of independence of the former Soviet Union Republics and established the major principles of dealing with the problems of post-Soviet development.

Although Azerbaijan signed the Protocol in Alma-Ata, the republic's legislature voted against its ratification. However, Azerbaijan ratified the Protocol to the Agreement and joined the CIS in September 1993. Georgia—who initially was also reluctant to join the CIS—did so in December 1993, thus bringing the number of the CIS member states to twelve.

The CIS Charter, adopted by the Council of the Heads of State on January 22, 1993, states that the Commonwealth of Independent States is based on the equality of all its members. All the member states are independent and equal subjects of the international law. The Commonwealth serves to further development and strengthening of friendship, good neighborly relations, interethnic accord, trust, and mutual understanding and cooperation among its members.

Structure

The CIS is an amorphous union of the former Soviet Republics. Unlike the former Soviet Union, the Commonwealth does not have a rigid centralized structure, and there is little coordination in internal and external affairs among the member states. According to the CIS Charter, the Commonwealth "is not a state and does not have any supranational powers." All interaction among the member states of the CIS is conducted through its coordinating institutions. These bodies cover broad areas of common interests and cooperation in the fields of economic development, trade, banking and financing, foreign policy coordination, parliamentary cooperation, and defense and security policies.

- **Council of the Heads of State** is the supreme body of the Commonwealth of the Independent States. It mainly debates on the matters and solves the problems related to the common interests of the member states. Its decisions are adopted by consensus and are not binding. The council meets annually to discuss and decide on strategically important questions.

- **Council of the Heads of Government** coordinates cooperation between the executive powers of the member states in economic, social, and other spheres. Its decisions are adopted by consensus and are not binding.

- **Inter-Parliamentary Assembly** is a consultative institution of parliamentary cooperation created to coordinate constitutional reforms in all republics. The assembly is represented by parliamentary delegations of each member state.

- **Economic Court** of the CIS ensures implementation of economic commitments within the CIS. The court settles economic controversies and disputes among the member states.

- **Council of Foreign Ministers** is the main executive body of the CIS for cooperation in the foreign policy activities of the member states. Through this council, the member states attempt to formulate their common stand on such issues as a crisis in Bosnia and Herzegovina, a crisis on Kosovo, and wars in Afghanistan and Iraq. The

council was one of the main bodies in establishing the CIS peacekeeping forces.

- **Council of Defense Ministers** is a body under the Council of the Heads of State. It coordinates military cooperation of the CIS members.

- **Economic Council** is the main executive body responsible for implementation of the decisions adopted by the Council of the Heads of State and the Council of the Heads of Government concerning the Agreement on Creation of Free Trade Zone and its Protocol.

- **Executive Committee** is the executive, administrative, and coordinating body of the CIS. It organizes all activities of the Council of the Heads of State, Council of the Heads of Government, Council of Foreign Ministers, Economic Council, and other bodies of the CIS.

- **Council of Border Troops Commander** is a body of the Council of the Heads of State. It is responsible for maintaining stable conditions on the outer borders of the CIS and for coordination activities of the border guards of the CIS.

- **Council of Collective Security** is the supreme political body of CIS member signatories of the Agreement on Collective Security of May 15, 1992. It coordinates joint activities of the state signatories of the agreement.

- **Interstate Bank** is an organ for organization and implementation of multilateral interstate settlements of financial transactions between the central (national) banks as well as for coordination of monetary policies of the member states. This institution was working on the idea of establishing a common ruble zone though this idea did not materialize.

- **Interstate Statistical Committee** was established to coordinate activities of statistical organizations of member states, develop and implement a standardized statistical methodology, facilitate information exchange among the member states, provide assistance to national statistical services, and create and maintain the common statistical database. Presently, there are more than sixty organs of sectoral cooperation in the CIS, such as the Consulting Council for Labor, Transport Coordination Conference, Migration and Social Security of Population, and Interstate Ecological Council.

Activities

The Alma-Ata Declaration signed on December 21, 1991, officially announced that the USSR ceased to exist. All former Soviet states immediately began a period of political and economic transition. The CIS was formally established to coordinate political and economic cooperation. The Agreement on Armed Forces and Border Troops and the Agreement on Strategic Forces were reached on December 30, 1991, for peaceful transformation of former Soviet Armed Forces. Since the disintegration of the former USSR was unexpected, many issues were being resolved at an *ad hoc* basis, and many states were changing their positions and attitudes according to their internal and external environments.

In 1992, there were numerous items on the agenda list of the meetings of the CIS leaders. Among them were the questions of the legal succession of the Soviet Union, strategic forces, security, and economic cooperation. At these meetings it was decided that all long-range nuclear and strategic weapons would come under the joint control of the President of the Russian Federation and the Chief of the CIS Armed Forces. In January 1992, Commissions on the Black Sea Fleet and the Caspian Flotilla were established. In addition, an agreement was signed on legislative cooperation at the Inter-Parliamentary Conference. In February, the Council of the Heads of State reached an agreement on free movement of goods between republics. Also in February, the CIS Council of Heads of State decided to retain Russian ruble as a common currency within CIS economic space. Another agreement was signed in February on a unified command for general-purpose armed forces for a transitional period of two years. However, Azerbaijan, Moldova, and Ukraine decided to establish independent armed forces. In March, an agreement was adopted on repayment of foreign debt of the former USSR. At the meeting of the Council of Heads of Government, also in March, all states with exception of Turkmenistan reached an agreement on settling interstate conflicts. At the same meeting, an agreement on status of border troops was signed by five states. In April, an agreement was signed on establishment of the Inter-Parliamentary Assembly by Armenia, Belarus, Kazakhstan, Kyrgyzstan, the Russian Federation, Tajikistan, and Uzbekistan. In May, the meeting of the Council of the Heads of Government issued an accord on repayment of interstate debt, and statements on the issue of the balance-of-payments were adopted. On May 15, 1992, the Treaty on Collective Security was signed by six members of the CIS for a five-year term. It was also agreed to establish CIS joint peacemaking forces to intervene in the CIS disputes. In July, the Economic Court was established in Minsk. The leaders of the newly independent states agreed to honor all international agreements signed and ratified by the former

USSR. It was also agreed that the Russian Federation was the legal successor of the USSR in the United Nations Security Council. The CIS republics were admitted as members of the United Nations in 1992. The leaders were also discussing the economic legislation of the CIS, a common monetary system (ruble zone), and visa-free travel of CIS citizens within the Commonwealth.

In 1993, the focus of the meetings of the CIS leaders was on the strengthening of the CIS. On January 22, 1993, the CIS Charter was adopted at the meeting of the heads of state in Minsk (Belarus). It was signed by seven out of ten members, with exception of Moldova, Turkmenistan, and Ukraine. Question of a common finance system was still on their agenda; the documents on the establishment of the Interstate Bank were endorsed by all ten members of the CIS. In February, a foreign economic council was established. In April, a proposal by Presidents of the Russian Federation and Kazakhstan was discussed in an extraordinary meeting of the heads of state in Minsk. The presidents were interested in further strengthening of the role of the CIS in security system, in economic cooperation and creation of a common market, and in coordination of foreign policy and human rights protection. As a result, a month later—in May 1993 at the meeting of the Council of the Heads of State held in Moscow—the member states, with exception of Turkmenistan, adopted a decision on establishment of the Economic Union. In June, the CIS defense ministers decided to abolish CIS joint military command, which was to be replaced on a provisional basis by a joint staff for coordination of military activity. In September, the Council of the Heads of State reached an agreement on establishment of a Bureau of Organized Crime with headquarters in Moscow. The Treaty on Establishment of the Economic Union was signed on the September 24, 1993, by the member states with exception of Turkmenistan and Ukraine. The treaty provided a framework for the economic union within the CIS, which included creation of currency union and gradual removal of tariffs. Later in December 1993, Turkmenistan was admitted as a full member of the Economic Union and Ukraine as an associate member in April 1994.

On April 15, 1994, the most important outcome of the meetings of the CIS leaders was signature by all member states of the Agreement on Establishment of Free Trade Zone. A draft framework for customs legislation in CIS countries to facilitate the establishment of the free trade zone was approved by all member states with exception of Turkmenistan. In January, the issue of illegal migration was discussed at the meeting of the Council of Border

Troop Commanders. In March, a plenary session of the Inter-Parliamentary Assembly established a commission for the conflict resolution in Nagornyi Karabakh (Azerbaijan) and Abkhazia (Georgia) and endorsed the use of the CIS peacekeeping forces. In September, at the meeting of the Council of the Heads of Government, all member states, with exception of Turkmenistan, agreed to establish the Interstate Economic Committee to implement economic treaties adopted within the framework of the Economic Union. In October, the Convention on Rights of the Minorities was adopted at the meeting of the heads of state. At the first session of the Interstate Economic Committee in November, draft legislation on a customs union was approved. The Interstate Economic Committee was incorporated with other working bodies and sectional committees of the CIS into the CIS Executive Committee. In October, the Inter-Parliamentary Assembly adopted a resolution to send military observers to Nagornyi Karabakh (Azerbaijan) and Abkhazia (Georgia). Direct negotiations for peaceful settlement of the conflicts were proposed by the Inter-Parliamentary Commission on the conflict in Abkhazia and Georgia. In December, the mandate of the commander of the CIS collective peacekeeping forces in Tajikistan was enlarged by the Council of Defense Ministers. In 1994, the CIS was granted an observer status with the United Nations. A cooperation accord was signed between the CIS and UNCTAD in May 1994.

In 1995, the leaders discussed the issue of the collective security and extended the mandate of the CIS peacemaking forces in Tajikistan and Abkhazia (Georgia). In February, the heads of state adopted a memorandum on maintenance of peace and stability. The memorandum called for refraining from exerting military, political, or economic pressure on another member state. It also urged for peaceful resolution of border disputes. In November, the Council of Defense Ministers announced establishment of the Joint Air Defense System to be coordinated mainly by the Russian Federation.

In 1996, the Council of the Heads of State considered the draft of the long-term plan for the integrated development of the Commonwealth in 1996 and 1997. In January, a decision was approved on formation of the Council of Ministers of Internal Affairs. In January, the meeting of the Council of Heads of State approved Georgia's proposal to impose sanctions against Abkhazia. In April, a program to counter the organized crime within the CIS was approved by the heads of government. A cooperation accord was signed between the CIS and the United Nations Economic Commission for Europe in June 1996. In September, there was a first meeting of the interstate

commission for military economic cooperation, and a draft agreement on export of military services and projects to third countries was approved. In August, the Council of Defense Ministers, with exception of the Ukrainian minister, condemned the political, military, and economic threat posed by the expansion of NATO. In October, an emergency meeting of the Council of Heads of State discussed the situation in Afghanistan and possible security threats in the region. In November, the plenary session of the Interstate Parliament issued a statement urging the NATO countries to abandon the plans of the NATO expansion. However, Russian and Ukraine states began strategic cooperation with NATO from mid-1990s onward.

In 1997, at the meetings of the CIS leaders, the long-term plan for the integrated development of the CIS was adopted, and the mandate of the CIS peacemaking forces in Tajikistan was extended. In March, development of the Customs Union was discussed at the meeting of the Council of the Heads of Government, and the need for the free trade regulations was endorsed by all member states, with the exception of Georgia. Also in March, the principles of the program for greater military and technical cooperation were approved by the Council of Defense Ministers. During the 1997 meetings, the leaders admitted that the CIS failed to ameliorate economic conditions of some member states. Russia was criticized for failing to implement CIS agreements. Russia, for its part, urged the member states to be more active in defining and implementing the CIS agreements. Nevertheless, support for the CIS institutions was expressed. In December, the Inter-Parliamentary Assembly adopted fourteen laws relating to banking, education, ecology, and charity.

In 1998, the discussions were centered on improvement of the activities of the CIS, on its restructuring, and on development of military cooperation among the CIS members. Reform of the CIS was on the agenda list of the Inter-Parliamentary Assembly meeting in June. In March, Russia, Belarus, Kazakhstan, and Kyrgyzstan signed an agreement on establishing the Customs Union with the aim to remove trade restrictions; to standardize trade and customs regulations; and integrate economic, monetary, and trade policies. In April, the Council of Defense Ministers proposed to draft a program for military and technical cooperation among the CIS member states. In April, at the request of the Russian President, Armenia and Azerbaijan signed a statement expressing their support for a political settlement of the conflict in Nagornyi Karabakh. A document proposing the resolutions to Abkhazia conflict was prepared and adopted, but the resolutions were not accepted by Abkhazia. In June, a number of documents were signed by the Council of Border Troops Commanders and at the meeting of the CIS interior ministers. The first meeting of a special forum took place also in June. It discussed issues of restructuring the CIS. It was agreed that a new institution needed to be created. Working groups were established to coordinate proposals and documents on the CIS reform. However, in October, the proposals of the reform were unanimously rejected as inadequate by all twelve members of the CIS. The Inter-Parliamentary Assembly approved a decision to sign the European Social Charter in June 1998. At the same meeting, it adopted ten model laws relating to social issues. A declaration of cooperation between the Inter-Parliamentary Assembly and the OSCE Parliamentary Assembly was also signed. In December, the Council of Defense Ministers approved the draft proposal on military information security.

In February 1999, Tajikistan became the fifth member of the Customs Union that was established in 1998. In April, the Council of State of the Commonwealth of Independent States adopted the Protocol to the Agreement on Establishment of a Free Trade Zone. According to the agreement and its protocol, the existing bilateral free trade regime should be replaced by a multilateral regime to create a favorable environment for free movement of commodities and services within the CIS, thus creating the prospect of establishing the CIS common market. The Council of the Heads of Government met in April and adopted guidelines for restructuring of the CIS and discussing the future development of the Commonwealth. Armenia, Belarus, Kazakhstan, Kyrgyzstan, Russia, and Tajikistan signed a protocol in April 1999 to extend the Treaty on Collective Security for another five years. In October, the heads of the five member states of the Customs Union approved a program to harmonize their national legislation to create a single economic zone.

The year 2000 meetings were mostly dedicated to antiterrorism campaigns and fights with organized crime. During a June 20–21 meeting, the Council of the Heads of State adopted the program of the CIS members on the fight against terrorism and other types of extremism and decided to establish the Anti-Terrorism Center. It also adopted the Decision on Realization of the Decision by Council of State of the Commonwealth of Independent States of April 2, 1999, on establishment of a Free Trade Zone. By a request from Tajikistan, CIS decided to withdraw collective peacemaking forces from Tajikistan. The mandate of the CIS collective peacemaking forces in Abkhazia (Georgia) was extended. During the Minsk summit, held November through December 2000, a

final decision on launching the CIS Anti-Terrorism Center was adopted. A Joint Declaration on Closing of the Chernobyl Atomic Power Station was adopted. In May, the five members of the Customs Union signed a treaty establishing the Eurasian Economic Community. Russian Federation withdrew from the visa-free travel agreement reached in 1992. In June, five members of the Customs Union signed an agreement for visa-free travel within the Customs Union. The Eurasian Economic Community with headquarters in Astana (Kazakhstan) was officially inaugurated in October. In May 2000, the states signatories of the Treaty on Collective Security called for strengthened military cooperation in view of the threat from the Taliban regime in Afghanistan. In October, the parties to the treaty signed the Agreement on the Status of Forces and Means of Collective Security Systems.

In March 2001, the interior ministers of the CIS discussed the issue of increasing transnational crime and drug trafficking. The issues of the economic cooperation, health, education, crime and terrorism, and military and technical cooperation were discussed in the May meeting of the Council of the Heads of Government. In a May meeting of the Council of Defense Ministers, the ministers approved the plan for military cooperation until 2005. The tenth anniversary of the Commonwealth was the center of an informal "jubilee" meeting in November. The summit adopted a statement on cooperation in social and economic development and integration at a global level. In October 2001, with the view of September terrorist attacks against the United States, the parties to the Treaty on Collective Security adopted a new antiterrorism plan. Combating international terrorism became the main priority of the Treaty on Collective Security.

Topics of economic cooperation, perspectives for the free trade zone development, and security and improvement of the working methods of CIS organs were discussed in an October 2002 meeting of the CIS leaders in Chisinou (Moldova). In February, Kazakhstan, Kyrgyzstan, Tajikistan, and Uzbekistan announced formation of a new regional security union: the Central Asian Cooperation Pact. Establishment of a regional division of the Anti-Terrorism Center was discussed at October CIS summit.

In 2003, the joint meeting of the Council of the Heads of State, Council of the Heads of Government, and Council of Foreign Ministers took place in Yalta (Russian Federation) on September 18–19. The main concerns of the meeting were the issues of further development of economic cooperation, establishment of the free trade zone that would eventually lead to a single economic space, as well as the questions of social, humanitarian, and military cooperation. The meeting was addressed by the executive director of the United Nations Office on Drugs and Crime. Consequently, a decision on cooperation with the UN Office of Drugs and Crime was adopted.

In spite of numerous decisions adopted by the CIS supreme bodies and agreements signed by the member states, the goals of the CIS charter have not been fully implemented, and the agreements have not been ratified by the all of the member states. In 1993, for example, in spite of the decision on common currency zone (ruble zone), Kyrgyzstan decided to issue its own currency, called the som. This act spurred other CIS members to abandon the ruble zone and introduce their own currencies.

A trend also emerged that more and more CIS member states began to favor bilateral agreements and the formation of subregional groupings. In March 1996, Belarus, Kazakhstan, Kyrgyzstan, and the Russian Federation signed the Quadripartite Treaty for greater integration based on a common market and customs union. It was to be open for all CIS member states and the Baltic states. Consequently, these four states and Tajikistan founded the Eurasian Economic Community in October 2001. In April 1996, Belarus and the Russian Federation signed the Treaty on the Formation of the Community of Sovereign Republics that was aimed at extensive economic, political, and military cooperation. A year later, in April 1997, Belarus and Russia signed a further Treaty of Union and formulated the Charter of the Union, with an eventual goal of their voluntary unification. The charter was signed in May and ratified by Belarusian and Russian legislature in June. In December 2000, the presidents of Belarus and the Russian Federation signed an agreement for the Belarus adoption of Russian currency on January 1, 2005, and for the introduction of a new joint currency by January 1, 2008. The Central Asian states created their own economic community called the Central Asian Economic Union (CAEU) in 1994, which was later transformed into the Central Asian Forum. The GUAM (abbreviation of member states' names) Group united Georgia, Ukraine, Azerbaijan, and Moldova in the late 1990s in joint economic and transportation initiatives and in attempts to establish a subregional free trade zone. The group was later joined by Uzbekistan in April 1999, transforming GUAM into GUUAM. The heads of state of the group's members meet annually, and their ministers for foreign affairs meet twice a year. Another subregional grouping that unites the Russian Federation, Armenia, Azerbaijan, and Georgia meets regularly as the Caucasian Group of Four.

ALFIA ABAZOVA AND RAFIS ABAZOV

See also Armenia; Azerbaijan; Belarus; Georgia; Kazakhstan; Kyrgyzstan; Moldova; Russia; Tajikistan; Turkmenistan; Ukraine; Uzbekistan

References and Further Reading

Anders, Aslund. *Building Capitalism: The Transformation of the Former Soviet Bloc*. Cambridge: Cambridge University Press, 2001.

Brzezinski, Zbigniew, and Paige Bryan Sullivan. *Russia and the Commonwealth of Independent States: Documents, Data and Analysis*. Armonk, NY: M. E. Sharpe, 1997.

CIS Executive Committee. 2005. Home Page: www.cis.minsk.by

CIS STAT. 2005. Interstate Statistical Committee of the CIS www.cisstat.com

Olcott, Martha Brill, Anders Aslund, and Sherman W. Garnett, *Getting it Wrong: Regional Cooperation and the Commonwealth of the Independent States*. Washington, DC: The Brookings Institution, 2000.

Shevtsova, Lilia. *Putin's Russia*. Carnegie Endowment for International Peace, 2004: www.cis.solo.by

COMMONWEALTH OF INDEPENDENT STATES: INTERNATIONAL RELATIONS

The dissolution of the Soviet Union in 1991 led to the creation of fifteen new independent countries. After the Russian revolution of 1917, the new Union of Soviet Socialist Republics (USSR) inherited the multinational Russian Empire in which more than one hundred nationalities lived. Josef Stalin, a Georgian (not a Russian), as commissar of nationalities devised a system that created a hierarchy of nationalities. The major ones were assigned union republics; at the second level were those of autonomous republics found inside several of the union republics, chiefly the Russian federation. At the third and fourth level were national and autonomous districts also located within union republics. The hierarchal system, which placed the Russian federation above the republics, led to the split between Stalin and Vladimir Lenin just before the latter's death. Stalin's system held as the Soviet Union grew in power. During and after World War II, the number of union republics grew to fifteen.

When the Soviet Union dissolved, however, Moscow let the union republics go with relatively little bloodshed. The other national entities, autonomous republics and districts, were maintained, and those that wished to separate, such as Chechnya and Dagestan, led to bloody and pernicious civil wars. Under the Soviet system, Moscow represented the whole USSR in foreign affairs with a minor exception that the Ukrainian SSR and Belorussian SSR had seats in the United Nations but invariably backed Soviet votes. This resulted from a compromise that Moscow made with its former Western allies in establishing the United Nations in 1945. Instead of one ministry of foreign affairs, there were fifteen.

Out of the necessity of dealing with common problems, economic issues, and relations with the outside world, in 1992, twelve of the republics joined a new organization called the Commonwealth of Independent States (CIS). Three—Lithuania, Latvia, and Estonia—refused to join. These Baltic republics, which had been part of the Russian Empire since the eighteenth century and had a brief two-decade period of independence between the two world wars, were added to the Soviet Union through the infamous Hitler-Stalin pact of August 1938. Moldova, which also was added as a consequence of that treaty with some minor variation, also joined. The West designated the entire group of former union republics as the newly independent states (NIS). The CIS, thus, included Armenia, Azerbaijan, Belarus, Georgia, Moldova, Kazakhstan, Kyrgyzstan, the Russian Federation, Tajikistan, Turkmenistan, Ukraine, and Uzbekistan.

The Commonwealth began on December 8, 1991, even before the end of the USSR, with an agreement among the presidents of Russia, Belarus, and Ukraine. The CIS formally started two weeks later on December 21, with eleven republics. Georgia joined later. In January 1992, administration began at the designated center, Minsk, the capital of Belarus. The CIS administration coordinated issues and policies of economics, foreign relations, defense, environment, immigration, and legal matters. The Commonwealth Council, consisting of the presidents and prime ministers of the member states, led the Commonwealth. Pertinent cabinet members from the member republics in the areas of the Commonwealth's concerns also aided the council. However, in practice, the coordinated effort has proved difficult as it often runs counter to the varying policies of the individual states. One example was the initial proposal to maintain a unified military and nuclear arms command; however, some of the European republics wished closer relations with NATO and the European Union. Another area of difficulty was in the move toward market economies and privatization.

One immediate question regarded the relationship of the CIS and the Baltic republics to the United Nations. They agreed that Russia would take the Soviet Union's seat on the Security Council. The twelve other countries who were not already members applied and were admitted as members in 1992. Estonia, Latvia, and Lithuania, but not any of the CIS states, joined NATO and the European Union. All of the NIS states are in form parliamentary republics with an elected president, prime minister, and parliament.

Some of the states formed regional associations. Azerbaijan, Armenia, Georgia, Greece, Moldova, Russia, and Ukraine were members of the Black Sea Economic Organization. Estonia, Latvia, Lithuania, and Russia were on the Council of Baltic Sea States.

The CIS required independence of the states and respect for their borders. It promised joint cooperation on a unified nuclear policy. Russia claimed the Soviet property in Russia. Russia also took over the Soviet nuclear armament and held the greatest conventional military forces in the world. Soviet embassies and consulates, as well as the Soviet seat on the United Nations Security Council, fell to Russia. Russia, as the major power in the CIS, aroused the historic suspicions of Russian expansionist ambitions.

The republics argued over the division of Soviet assets, and within a few years, the CIS proved incapable of settling inter-republic disputes. The status of the Crimean peninsula inhabited by Russians but located in the Ukraine divided those republics. Kiev and Moscow also argued over the ownership of the Black Sea fleet. Moscow also leased Sebastopol and other Black Sea ports from Kiev. They settled the issue in 1995 with Russia getting 82% of the fleet, and two years later, Russia signed a ten-year friendship treaty. Ukraine and Belarus sent nuclear arms and missiles back to Russia. A collective security agreement introduced in 1992 did not include Moldova, Ukraine, or Turkmenistan, and in 1999, Azerbaijan, Georgia, and Uzbekistan refused to extend their participation. In 1999, Russia objected to the expansion of NATO into Eastern Europe and into the Yugoslav crisis. The Taliban in Afghanistan was also a concern of the confederation.

Trade began to recover after its decline from 1992 through 1994. The CIS established a customs union, although some republics, particularly the Ukraine and Turkmenistan, joined only reluctantly due to their fear of losing access to Western markets.

In 1999, Uzbekistan joined the GUAM group— Georgia, Ukraine, Azerbaijan, Moldova—formed in opposition to the CIS; the group then changed its acronym to GUUAM to include its new member state. However, CIS and Uzbekistan signed a bilateral agreement to fight Uzbeks Islamic rebels in Kyrgyzistan where CIS forces were helping them. The fighting spilled over into Tajikistan, and a treaty was created between Russia and Tajikistan to help end the civil war by stationing border guards.

Most of the CIS followed variations on a similar path to independence. In general, this occurred in two stages—a declaration of sovereignty within the USSR and then a declaration of independence. While some republics announced their intentions of separation from the Soviet Union, in the future independence occurred in all cases after the failed *coup d'état* against Mikhail Gorbachev on August 19–21, 1991. Another catalyst for the national movements was the Soviet parliamentary elections in March 1989, the first contested elections since 1918.

In the Caucasus, Armenia in the 1980s formed the Armenian National Movement, which won the 1990 republic parliamentary elections. On August 23, the parliament declared Armenian sovereignty, and thirteen months later (September 23, 1991) independence was also declared. Armenia had been engaged in a war with neighboring Azerbaijan since February 1988 over the Nagorno-Karabakh region, an autonomous Armenian national district, and Sumqayit, another Armenian area, both in what was then the Azerbaijan SSR. Azerbaijanis killed thousands of Armenians, and thousands more left the enclave for the republic. The Azerbaijani blockaded access to Armenia, strangling its economy. Moscow sent troops to support the Armenians in 1990, and the Armenians occupied Azerbaijan territory connecting Nagrono-Kabach to Armenia; they held on to the territory as political instability gripped Azerbaijan.

Although Azerbaijan declared its independence after the *coup d'état* against Mikhail Gorbachev, the Communist Party continued in power with its leader Ayaz Mutalibov elected president. In May 1992, the Azerbaijan Popular Front carried out a *coup* against Mutalibov and won new elections with Abulfez Elchibey on a platform of withdrawing from the CIS and defeating the Armenians in Nagorno-Karabach. However, the Communists carried out their own *coup d'état*, led by Heydar Aliyev in June 1993, and kept the republic in the confederation.

Georgia took advantage of Gorbachev's Glasnost policy to move toward independence even before the USSR collapsed. The nationalist opposition won the parliamentary elections of October 1990 and elected the political dissident Zviad Gamsakhurdia president after declaring the republic's independence in April 1991. Gamsakhurdia's opponents declared civil war, but the military deposed him in January 1992. They established a state council led by Eduard Shevardnadze, the former Soviet foreign minister and leader of the Georgian Communist Party. In new elections, the voters overwhelmingly elected Shevarnadze as the head of state of the republic. Opponents accused Shevarnadze of dictatorial methods, but because of his effectiveness, the public still supported him. Georgia joined the CIS in 1993 but also became an associate member of the European Union and a member of the Council of Europe and the World Trade Organization, as well as a partner of NATO. The republic faced secessionist movements by the Ossetians and the Abkhazians, former nationalist districts when they were part of the Soviet Republic. Abkhazia declared its independence in 1992 and put its old (1925) constitution in effect. Thousands of Georgians fled the area. Shevarnadze refused to recognize the state, and warfare began.

The Soviet Union finally agreed to the independence of the all the Baltic countries on September 6, 1991. The Baltic states refused to join the CIS. In Latvia, glasnost led to mass protests over environmental pollution. The Latvian Popular Front won the 1990 elections and announced the eventual independence of the republic. Moscow responded by sending in the army, leading to clashes in Riga in January 1991. After the failure of the August *coup d'état*, the legislature declared its independence immediately. Latvia held elections restricted to persons who were citizens before the incorporation of the country into the Soviet Union in 1940 or their descendants. The elected parliament restored the constitution of 1922. The government tried to expel those who were not citizens, especially the many Russians living there, and moved closer to the West. Relations with Moscow were strained; however, through the 1990s, Riga attempted to amend its relationship with Moscow.

Similarly, in Lithuania during glasnost period, the Sajudis reform movement appeared. The 1990 election produced a nationalist legislature that declared the republic's independence on March 11. Moscow established an economic boycott, which had little effect. In January 1991, during the Desert Storm crisis in Iraq, Gorbachev sent in troops to reclaim the state. Despite the bloodshed, the effort failed, and Moscow recognized Lithuania's independence after the *coup d'état* of August. In the election of 1992, the Communists, now called the Lithuanian Democratic Labor Party (LDLP), won a slight majority, but LDLP continued the nationalist policies, including moving closer to the West and liberalizing the economy. Because of corruption and recession, a coalition of the Christian Democrats and the Centre Party won the 1996 elections; in 1998, Valdas Adamkus, who had been an American citizen, was elected president. His policy was to liberalize the economy, stop corruption, and attract foreign investment. Up to this time Vilnius depended on Moscow as an economic partner. Now it linked more to the West, dramatically reducing inflation (from more than 1000% at the beginning of independence to less than 10% at the end of the century).

In addition, a Popular Front emerged in 1988 in Estonia, and this front won republican elections, declaring independence recognized by Moscow in September 1991. Like Lithuania, Estonia restricted the right of non-Estonians while recognizing as citizens those who had left after the Soviet Union and who had been incorporated the country. Estonia relied on Russia for trade but was able to ameliorate the strained relations over the citizen laws. Soviet forces left in 1994.

In Central Asia, native Kazakhs were a minority in the republic compared to the Russian inhabitants. The long time Communist leader Dinmukhamed Kunayev was a popular and imaginative leader who protected the interests of both groups. His dismissal in 1986 because of corruption caused riots of a magnitude not seen since the days before the dictatorship of Josef Stalin. Kazakhstan was also the site of many of the USSR's nuclear weapons. Kazakhstan announced sovereignty in October 1990 and independence on December 16, 1991. The republic elected Nursultan Nazarbayev as president, and he continued Kunayev's popular policies. Unlike in the Baltic states, relations between Russia and Kazakhstan remained good. Russia retained control over the nuclear facilities. Kazakhstan joined the United Nations and International Monetary Fund.

Kyrgyzstan of all the Central Asian Republics was the most anxious to break away from the USSR and declared its independence on August 31, 1991, right after the failed *coup d'état*. Askar Akayev was elected president; he was a reformer who instituted democratic institutions and looked more to the West than any of the five former Central Asian Republics. However, the emigration of Russian and German professionals brought about an economic recession. Turkmenistan has natural gas, which brought in foreign investors. It declared independence on October 27, 1991, but the dictatorial regime has done little to improve conditions in the republic.

In Tajikistan, independence came on September 9, 1991, but support for Russia and the Communist party was still strong. Anti-Communist and Islamic opposition led to civil war.

The opposition drove out the Communist President Rahman Nabiyev. Russian troops helped bring down the opposition and put in power Imomali Rahmonov, who won the 1994 presidential elections and ruled with an iron hand. Thousands of Muslims fled to Afghanistan from where they launched attacks on the republic. Tens of thousands were killed in the fighting, and hundreds of thousands were displaced.

In Uzbekistan, Communists maintained tight control. They supported the *coup d'état* against Gorbachev, but after its failure, they declared independence. Islam Karimov was elected president. Despite lip service to democracy, the still ruling Communist leadership imposed authoritarian politics. Opposition parties were stopped at the polls and their

leaders attacked, and international human rights groups criticized the government. The state remained close to Russia and Communist China, but ethnic minorities left the republic as the government leaders wedded their authoritarian regime to Uzbek nationalism.

In Russia itself, the failure of the attempt to remove Gorbachev in August 1991 brought the end of the Soviet Union on December 1991, and Boris Yeltsin came to power in Russia. Russia did not recognize minorities that declared their independence and frequently the state used violence to suppress uprisings, most notably the Muslim Chechens. Economic difficulties led to a breakdown of relations between Yeltsin and the Russian parliament, and a new constitution was drafted, giving the president more power. In 1998, because of corruption and economic difficulties, Vladimir Putin replaced Yeltsin, and the former won the presidential election of 2002. His regime, while committed to democracy and a market economy, nevertheless was not adverse to use of authoritarian measures.

Chaos reigned as Moscow attempted to transform from a Communist-controlled state with economic central planning to a multiparty democracy with a market economy. Longstanding ethnic conflicts reemerged, even though the major minorities were now separate countries in the CIS. The revived Orthodox Church and the Russian need for aid from the West were also political factors in the new Russia and the CIS. In 1997, Moscow signed a treaty that gave it observer status with NATO.

Belarus was less anxious to break away from the Soviet Union, although a nationalist spirit grew in the 1980s, especially since Belarius suffered greatly from the Chernobyl nuclear accident. Minsk declared sovereignty on July 27, 1990, and then full independence on August 25, 1991, but the Communists still dominated the government through the new elections. Belarius did not write a constitution until 1994. A complicated election system brought many independents and representatives from nonpolitical groups into the parliament. Aleksandr Lukashenko, who was elected president, supported Moscow. He then manipulated the government to rewrite the constitution and give him more power.

Moldova, the old Turkish and Romanian province of Bessarabia, was marked by its mixed ethnic character. The Moldovans themselves are closely identified with Romanians, but the Soviets tried to emphasize the differences, claiming that Moldovans were a distinct nationality. In the 1980s, however, the Moldovan national movement reappeared. The republic declared sovereignty in June 1990, and independence on August 27, 1991, right after the *coup d'état* in the Soviet Union. Moldovians debated whether they should move toward union with Romania, which was still ruled by former Communists, and the Gagauz and Russian minorities declared their own separatist republics. The government was militarily unable to contend with the Russian separatists, and the country remained in a state of inertia. The elections of 1994 brought the Agrarian Democratic Party to power in the parliament over both the pro-Romanian and pro-Russian parties. The legislature introduced a new constitution that gave autonomy to both the Gagauz and the Russian minorities, easing the civil tension and moving the country toward reform. In 1994, Moldova and Russia signed an agreement to remove the Red Army within three years.

In the Ukraine, a national movement arose in the late 1980s when concern over Russification moved the Ukrainian leadership to address issues of language and culture, including history and religion. In addition, the leadership raised the issue of the economy and environmental pollution. In 1989, the Ukrainian parliament passed a law making Ukrainian the official language of the republic. Historical Ukrainian figures, such as Ivan Mazepa, who allied with the Swedes in the eighteenth century against Peter the Great, and Mykhailo Hrushevsky, the noted Ukrainian president who served briefly as president of independent Ukraine in 1918, were now celebrated.

The Ukrainian Uniate Church revived, leading to conflicts with the Ukrainian Orthodox Church over property, churches, and politics. The environmental movement Green World, led by author Yuri Scherbak, arose in the wake of the Chernobyl nuclear disaster and became a force in Ukrainian politics. Strikes and opposition to Moscow arose among the Donbas miners as their conditions worsened. In the critical years at the end of the 1980s, they joined the Ukrainian nationalists even though most of them were linguistically closer to Russians. In independent Ukraine, they moved away as a split developed between pro-West Ukraine centered on Kiev and pro-Moscow Ukraine centered on the Donbas. There were also class and religious aspects involved in the split—Uniate versus Orthodox and Kievan intellectuals versus proletarian miners.

In the spring of 1988, the Ukrainian Helsinki Union of released political prisoners, an outgrowth of the 1970s Helsinki Watch, appeared as an opposition party. As elsewhere, the parliamentary elections of 1989 and 1990 brought antigovernment, nationalist, and anti-Communist representatives to the national and republic parliaments. The republic declared sovereignty on July 16, 1990. In response to the national movements, the Soviet Union tried to negotiate a new relationship with the republics, giving

more autonomy but keeping control over foreign policy, the military, and Soviet finances.

In Ukraine, the Communists pushed for the support of the Gorbachev plan, while the opposition group *Rukh* demanded independence. After the August 1991 *coup d'état* failed, Ukraine immediately declared independence (August 24), which was ratified by overwhelming support from all ethnic groups in a plebiscite on December 1. Ukraine immediately started relations with other countries, although it joined the CIS at its founding. Kiev joined NATO's partnership for Peace in 1994 and the Council of Europe in 1995. In 1998, it became associated with the European Union.

Leonid Kravchuk was elected president and Leonid Kuchma prime minister. Both promised to move toward a Western orientation and market economy, but Kravchuk refused to implement the promises, and the Communist-controlled Supreme Council of State backed him. Kuchma resigned, and Kravchuk reintroduced central state control over the economy. In the elections of 1994, Kuchma defeated Kravchuk, but the council was still in the hands of the Communists, which hindered development. Kuchma arranged for foreign loans to no avail. Meanwhile, the division between East and West Ukraine intensified.

A new constitution in 1996 gave the president increased authority, but the country was in perpetual economic crisis with inflation and strikes by the miners. At the end of the decade, the economy improved. Kuchma was reelected in a hostile election in 1999. Kuchma was accused of massive corruption and involvement in the murder of a journalist. In another disputed election in 2004, the pro-Russian eastern candidate Viktor Yanukovych narrowly defeated Viktor Yushchenko, the pro-Kiev candidate. Accusations of fraud and even attempts to murder Yushchenko led to a division of the country. The East threatened to separate. In November 2004, the Supreme Court ordered new elections.

FREDERICK B. CHARY

See also Armenia; Azerbaijan; Belarus; Georgia; Kazakhstan; Kyrgyzstan; Moldova; Russia; Tajikistan; Turkmenistan; Ukraine; Uzbekistan

References and Further Reading

Brzezinski, Zbigniew. *Russia and the Commonwealth of Independent States: Documents, Data, and Analysis.* Armonk, NY: M.E. Sharpe, 1997.

CIS and Eastern Europe on File. New York: Facts on File, 1993.

Heenan, Patrick, and Monique Lamontagne. *The Russia and Confederation of Independent States Handbook.* Chicago: Glenlake, 2000.

Jonson, Lena. *Peacekeeping and the Role of Russia in Eurasia*. Boulder, CO: Westview Press, 1996.

Khazanov, Anatoly M. *After the USSR: Ethnicity, Nationalism, and Politics in the Commonwealth of Independent States*. Madison, WI: The University of Wisconsin Press, 1995.

Morozov, Vladimir. *Who's Who in Russia and the CIS Republics*. New York: Henry Holt, 1995.

Mozaffari, Mehdi. *Security Politics in the Commonwealth of Independent States: The Southern Belt*. Houndmills, Basingstoke; New York: Macmillan Press; St. Martin's Press, 1997.

Olcott, Martha Brill. *Getting it Wrong: Regional Cooperation and the Commonwealth of Independent States*. Washington, DC: Carnegie Endowment for International Peace, 1999.

Shaw, Denis J. B. *The Post-Soviet Republics: A Systematic Geography*. Harlow, Essex, England: Longman Scientific & Technical; New York: John Wiley & Sons, 1995.

Shestakov, A. S. *Mapping of Risk Areas of Environmentally-Induced Migration in the Commonwealth of Independent States (CIS)*. Geneva, Switzerland: International Organization for Migration, 1998.

Shoemaker, Merle Wesley. *Russia and the Commonwealth of Independent States*. Harpers Ferry, WV: Stryker-Post Publications, 2001.

Streshneva, M. V. *Social Culture and Regional Governance: Comparison of the European Union and Post-Soviet Experiences*. Commack, New York: Nova Science Publishers, Inc. 1999.

Stroev, E. S. *Russia and Eurasia at the Crossroads: Experience and Problems of Economic Reforms in the Commonwealth of Independent States*. Berlin, New York: Springer, c1999.

United Nations Development Programme. Regional Bureau for Europe and the Commonwealth of Independent States. *The Shrinking State: Governance and Human Development in Eastern Europe and the Commonwealth of Independent States*. New York: UNDP, 1997.

United Nations. Division for Public Economics and Public Administration. *Decentralization–Conditions for Success: Lessons from Central and Eastern Europe and the Commonwealth of Independent States*. New York: United Nations, 2000.

COMMUNIST ECONOMIC MODEL

The Communist economic model, in the ideal sense of the term's theoretical conception, does not exist. In the idealist Communist society envisioned by Marx, the economy is operated on the principle of "from each according to one's ability and to each according to one's needs." In other words, workers contribute whatever they can to the society and get from the society whatever they need. In such an economic model, there will be no profit making, no value or commodity exchange, and no money.

To speak of the Communist economic model is to speak of an economic model that has been put into practice in the name of achieving this ideal. This usually refers to an economy in a country run by a Communist party. The historical role of a Communist party is supposed to facilitate, by means of violent revolution and economic reconstruction, usually in that order, the achievement of the goal of communism. However, this usually requires qualification, as in the case of China, a country run by the largest Communist party in the world, which since the 1980s has operated on an economic model that is very different from what it was during the era of Mao (Mao Zedong) from 1950s to the 1970s. Moreover, because of different historical and political–cultural traditions, the Communist economic model has been implemented very differently in different countries. Therefore, the Communist economic model is an abstraction.

Some Basic Features of Communist Economic System

The first, most salient and overriding feature of Communist economic model is that no private ownership of means of production (such as factories, lands, rivers, and natural resources) is allowed. The second most salient feature is that the most essential and majority of economic activities are carried out in accordance with top-to-bottom planning. This is called the "planned economy." Because economic plans are issued as governmental decrees, it is also called the "command economy." Thus, the central government may draw up a five-year plan for what to produce, including details on the priorities of production, raising revenue, and even on how much each citizen should spend. Both the former Soviet Union and China had five-year plans. Each five-year plan is further specified into a yearly plan. In such a planned economy, the prices of commodities do not fluctuate according to the supply and demand of the market but are fixed by the government. These plans are then issued to various administrative and bureaucratic levels for implementation. These administrator and bureaucrats may draw up their own plans to fulfill the targets, goal, or quotas of the central plans. The third feature of this system is that the bureaucrats and administrators who implement these plans are either ideologically committed or will obey the central government's command, willing or unwillingly. Bureaucrats and administrators in the system are usually members of the ruling Communist Party, and dissent is not allowed. The fourth feature of this system is that enterprise for public good may or may not be encouraged, but for private gains it is suppressed.

Ideological Origin

The Communist economic model originated from Communist critique of capitalism. Premised on the evidence of exploitation of the working class in terms of working conditions, child labour, and subsistence pay, as well as the increasing polarization between the rich and poor during the development stage of capitalism (as what is happening in China in the twenty-first century), Marxist critiques argued that capitalism encouraged greed and was orientated to profit making, therefore alienating human life. Overcoming this capitalist logic and creating a new society of production should aim at improving human conditions and human needs. The logic of this argument is that society should pool all resources together to produce what is best for the public good rather than private gains and what is best for human needs rather than profit.

A Case Study of China

Immediately after the Chinese Communist Party (CCP) took power in 1949, a revolutionary program of land reform was carried out. Land was confiscated from landlords and distributed equally to the rural residents on a per capita basis. However, to achieve better control and centralized planning and to avoid growth of private wealth and polarization, collectivization soon followed. In what was called the "commune system," land and means of production were pooled together, and everyone became a member of the commune in which one worked as one was able, and staple grain was distributed equally on a per capita basis irrespective of labour contribution. During the beginning of the commune experiment, when there was no household economy and everyone ate in a public canteen, the ideological zeal led to disastrous famine. Since the 1960s, however, households have been allowed to own private plots, and a point system that rewarded work was implemented.

During the era of Mao, capital was accumulated by exploiting rural surplus under the state plan for rapid industrial development. For the purpose of industrialization, state planning had kept consumption to the minimum by rationing food and daily necessities. Urban residents were compensated by social and economic security, such as lifetime employment, generous pension, free education, free health care, and virtually free housing.

The economy reform policies that went into effect in the late 1970s have meant a gradual transformation of China from a command economy to a largely market economy. China is now part of the world capitalist economy. Though China is still ruled by the CCP, its economy does not operate on the basis of a Communist economic model.

Industrialization and Economic Growth

Until the 1980s, both the former Soviet Union and China made tremendous progress in industrialization, and the economic growth was higher than that of the capitalist economy in many countries.

Because of this rapid growth, Soviet Russia became one of the two superpowers during the Cold War, and China has pulled a large amount of people out of absolute poverty in three decades. In terms of literacy, health care, and life expectancy for the poor, China has done better than India, which has often claimed to be the largest democracy in the world. Even in terms of industrialization, China under the Communist economic model performed better than India.

A Critique of Communist Economic Model

In countries where a version of the Communist economic model was run, shortages of food and daily necessities have been prevalent. Scarcity of commodities in the former Soviet Union, for instance, was legendary. Two basic problems with the command economic model led to this. First, though resources can be pooled together effectively and efficiently for a specific project, it is difficult to have an overall plan for an entire society. The second basic problem is related to the definition of human needs and who decides what is needed. Many Communist countries during the Cold War period concentrated on heavy industry and on military defense technology. As a result, daily necessities, such as socks and washing powder and even butter and bread, were considered secondary. The people in these countries were either implicitly or explicitly asked to sacrifice to compete with the capitalist system for the construction of a new society.

A final word of criticism concerning the Communist economic model is related to political oppression. Based on its very ideological orientation, the system not only demands individual sacrifices, but it also suppresses individual initiatives and creativity for private pursuits. For many, if not all, the lack of freedom of individual pursuit of "happiness" not only stampedes economic prosperity but is also intrinsically unacceptable.

MOBO C. F. GAO

See also Capitalist Economic Model; Collectivism; Development History and Theory; Free Market Economy; Socialist Economic Model

References and Further Reading

Engels, Frederick. *Principles of Communism.* Vol. 1. Moscow: Progress Publisher, 1969.

Mao Zedong. *On the Ten Major Relations. Selected Works.* Vol. 5. Peking: Foreign Languages Press, 1977.

Marx, Karl. *Value, Price and Profit* (http://ourworld.compuserve.com/homepages/PZarembka/Marx.htm) 2000.

Marx, Karl, and Frederick Engels. *Communist Manifesto.* London, 1948.

Meisner, Maurice. *Mao's China and After.* New York, London: The Free Press, 1987.

Mobo, C. F. Gao, *Gao Village: Rural Life in Modern China.* London: Hurst, 1999.

COMOROS

The Comoros are a group of islands of volcanic origin in the western Indian Ocean. The three westernmost islands form the independent Union of Comoros; the fourth island, Mayotte, remains a French territory. The population of 760,000 is Islamic and ethnically and culturally homogeneous. Economically, Mayotte is highly dependent on subsidies from France, while the independent islands rely on foreign aid and remittances; vanilla, cloves, and perfume essences are the only significant exports. Gross national income (GNI) per capita in the independent islands was $450 (US dollars) in 2003; real growth rates are generally positive but highly variable.

Relatively prosperous in the precolonial period due to their participation in regional trading networks, the islands' economies contracted following colonisation by France. The suppression of the slave trade and an almost complete lack of investment by the colonial power were accompanied by a severing of the islands from their natural socioeconomic environment—the East African coast—and orienting them toward Madagascar.

In 1975, the unilateral declaration of independence marked the end of six decades of colonial neglect. Independence prompted a French-backed revolution, but the lack of French support forced President Ali Soilihi to turn against his backers. Recognising the need for change, he embarked upon a radical Marxist-inspired program of social and economic reform. Soilihi's immediate objectives were achieving self-sufficiency in food production and educating the population; he dismantled colonial administrative structures and attacked the customary social order. Resistance to the latter, the tyranny of an increasingly unrestrained youth militia, a volcanic eruption, and a massive influx of refugees following anti-Comorian riots in Madagascar led to social discord and hastened economic collapse. A decline in public support reflected Soilihi's increasing lack of control and finally provoked the mercenary-led restoration of a pro-French government in 1978.

Since the end of the Soilihi regime, approaches to development have been both unimaginative and unsuccessful; the political life of the country has been marked by a succession of *coup* attempts, several that were successful; in 1997, the island of Ndzwani (Anjouan) seceded. Despite an appeal to free market forces and the encouragement of investors (many of dubious competence), there has been no coherent policy of economic or social development beyond mendicity: an ongoing quest for donors. Despite the reestablishment of national unity of the three independent islands in 2002, chronic political instability and economic mismanagement discourages investors. The country remains highly dependent on the colonial power, and the development process is constrained by the continued French role in shaping policy and the subsequent difficulty of independent political action or economic policy.

A number of development organisations, bilateral and multilateral, operate in the country, but many projects are marked by failure. A small handful do succeed in achieving social acceptance, but the majority of lasting infrastructure projects, particularly on the largest island of Ngazidja, are financed by the emigrant community and not by outsiders.

Ali Soilihi's presidency was brief, but his policies left a lasting impression, particularly in view of the lack of real progress since his fall, and a critical reevaluation of the period is currently benefiting from the perspective afforded by time. Although there is clearly an element of nostalgia in such retrospectives, there is also a recognition that the present political elite is not qualified to tackle the country's increasingly intractable economic woes. The country has no niche role—tourism suffers from a lack of air links, labour costs are high, and agricultural land is already overcrowded—and chronic corruption impedes all but the most persistent development initiatives.

IAIN WALKER

References and Further Reading

Ibrahim, Mahmoud. *Etat Français et Colons aux Comores (1912–1946).* Paris: L'Harmattan, 1997.

Msa, Abdallah. *Un Espoir Déçu. Bilan Économique et Social de Vingt-Cinq Années d'Indépendance aux Comores, 1975–2000.* Paris: L'Officine, 2001.

Mukonoweshuro, Eliphas. "The Politics of Squalor and Dependency: Chronic Political Instability and Economic

Collapse in the Comoro Islands." *African Affairs* 89, (357): 555–577 (1990).

Newitt, Malyn. "The Perils of Being a Microstate: São Tomé and the Comoro Islands Since Independence." *The Political Economy of Small Tropical Islands: The Importance of Being Small*, M. Newitt and H. Hintjens, eds. Exeter: University of Exeter Press, 1992.

———. *The Comoro Islands: Struggle Against Dependency in the Indian Ocean*. Boulder, CO: Westview Press, 1984.

Saïd Soilihi, Youssouf, and Elmamouni Mohamed Nassur. *Ali Soilihi: "L'Elan Brisé?"* Paris: L'Harmattan, 2000.

CONGO, DEMOCRATIC REPUBLIC OF THE

The Democratic Republic of the Congo, formerly known as Zaire, is located in Central and West Africa on both sides of the equator. The country has a small access to the Atlantic Ocean at its western border, but it is bounded on the west by Angola and the Republic of the Congo; to the north by the Central African Republic and Sudan; to the east by Uganda, Rwanda, Burundi, and Tanzania; and to the south by Zambia and Angola.

This region was first exploited by Europeans during the Portuguese exploration of Africa in the late 1400s. The taking of slaves from the region soon followed, with these being taken to the Americas. The slave trade continued into the nineteenth century, during which time King Leopold of Belgium established a colony of his own (not a colony of Belgium) in the region. This colony, the Congo Free State, had not been established in keeping with the other European colonies of the period, and the other European colonial powers objected to Leopold's personal rule. This resulted in the Belgian government taking control of the region in 1908, renaming it the Belgian Congo.

The purpose of European colonization was for economic gain, and the natural resources of the Belgian Congo (primarily copper, along with other minerals and natural products) were profitable. Profits dropped during the international depression of the 1930s, but resumed following World War II.

African movements for postwar independence met with mixed success in many areas, but in 1957, Belgium permitted limited home rule, and in 1960, full independence was achieved. The new government had a multiparty structure, like many European parliaments, with no group in clear control. Complicating the new independence was the fact that many Belgian military officers had held onto their positions of power. This led to local revolts and fragmentation of the country, and President Joseph Kasavubu had his prime minister, Patrice Lumumba, arrested.

Lumumba was assassinated, and civil unrest continued. At the invitation of the government, the United Nations sent in military forces to restore peace. Revolts continued for years until the Congolese army overthrew the civil government, and Colonel Joseph Mobutu declared himself president.

Five years of civil war had badly damaged the country's infrastructure, so Mobutu's first missions were to centralize power in the national government, end regional fighting and efforts at secession, and restore the economy. Unfortunately, just as production in the copper industry could resume, the world market price for copper dropped, and the price for oil increased.

From the time of independence in 1960, the economy and population of the Congo had changed dramatically. The people of the region had traditionally engaged in subsistence farming, with families providing essentially for themselves; with independence, however, a migration of the population to the cities began. This reduced overall food production, and Congo changed from being self-sufficient to a country requiring imports of essential materials. The potential mineral wealth (in addition to copper, some gold, silver, tin, manganese, and other minerals can be mined) made international credit easily available, and Congo became a major borrower. Only twenty years after independence, Congo (known as Zaire from 1971 to 1997) had a national debt of more than $4 billion.

The performance of the economy of Congo/Zaire was inconsistent, even after civil order was restored. While agricultural output expanded between 1967 and 1983, exports dropped, and gross domestic product (GDP) fluctuated, with an overall decline.

One of the country's largest creditors was the United States, which saw Congo/Zaire as a Cold War regional ally against the Soviet Union. This led to a continuation of international loans, with the result that by 1980 the World Bank and International Monetary Fund stepped in to attempt to bring order to Zaire's finances. The United States continued to stand by President Mobutu as an ally through the 1980s, after his earlier intervention against a Cuban-supported government in Angola and against Chad in 1983. Mobutu was able to sustain his rule easily through the 1980s, but regional conflict in the early 1990s brought about his downfall.

The 1994 genocide in Rwanda sent large numbers of refugees into Zaire, and in the eastern regions, an armed rebellion against Mobutu began. Forces led by Laurent Kabila's *l'Alliance des Forces Democratiques pour la Liberation du Congo-Zaire* (AFDL) steadily worked their way westward until Mobutu fled the country in 1997. Kabila's revolutionary government was quickly recognized by countries in the region, and he ruled the country (renamed the Democratic Republic of the Congo) until he was assassinated in January 2001. His son, Joseph Kabila, was named as his successor. The International Rescue Commission estimates that some 2.5 million people were killed in the civil war that led to Mobutu's overthrow.

Since the overthrow of President Mobutu, the Democratic Republic of the Congo has continued to import more than it exports, and its international debt in 2002 was more than $8 billion. Because much of this is believed to have been diverted by Mobutu for his personal use, the government is attempting to trace those funds and alleviate its international obligations.

As of 2005, the Democratic Republic of the Congo's future holds more promise than it has in decades. The new Kabila government is widely recognized as legitimate, regional fighting has subsided, and the first elections since 1960 have been scheduled. This relatively secure environment offers the opportunity for the nation's mineral resources to be developed and for agricultural exports to be increased.

THOMAS P. DOLAN

References and Further Reading

Glickman, Harvey ed. *The Crisis and Challenge of African Development.* New York: Greenwood Press, 1988.

Gould, David J. *Bureaucratic Corruption and Underdevelopment in the Third World.* New York: Pergamon Press, 1980.

Nzongala-Ntalaja ed. *The Crisis in Zaire: Myths and Realities.* Trenton, N.J.: Africa World Press, 1986.

Roberts, Les, *et al. Mortality in the Democratic Republic of the Congo: Results from a Nationwide Survey.* New York: International Rescue Committee, 2003.

Schatzberg, Michael G. *The Dialectics of Oppression in Zaire.* Bloomington, IN: Indiana University Press, 1988.

CONGO, REPUBLIC OF THE

The Republic of the Congo is located in western equatorial Africa on the northwestern banks of the Congo and Ubangui rivers. It has a short, 3-mile/150-kilometer Atlantic coastline and is bordered by the Central African Republic, the Democratic Republic of the Congo, Cameroon, Gabon, and Angolan Cabinda. The Mayombe escarpment extends into the coastal regions of Congo, reaching a height of about 875 yards/800 meters. The low (650–750 yards/600–700 meters) Bateke plateau dominates the country's center, while the swampy forests of the Congo River basin dominate the north. The Niari valley in the south contains the country's best agricultural land. Congo's climate is generally equatorial but varies somewhat depending on altitude and proximity to cold ocean currents off the coast. Pronounced rainy and dry seasons occur at different times of the year in the various regions.

From the sixteenth through the nineteenth centuries, three important African kingdoms occupied significant parts of the territory of contemporary Congo. These included the Loango kingdom along the Atlantic Coast, the Tio kingdom in the Plateau region of central Congo, and the Kongo kingdom extending into southeastern Congo. The belief in the supernatural powers of the kings served as an important ideological basis for power in all three. Their economies were based on agricultural production, with the slave trade becoming an important trading component in the sixteenth century. Pierre Savorgnan de Brazza was the first European to penetrate the Congo beyond the coastal region in 1875. In 1880, de Brazza gained the signature of the Makoko, King of Tio, on a treaty granting the French dominion in his territories, and a parallel signature from the King of Loango in 1883. These served as a legal pretext for French occupation of the territories over the coming two decades. In 1910, Congo became part of the federation of French Equatorial Africa (FEA), including the territories of Congo, Gabon, Chad, and Ubangui-Chari, with Brazzaville as the capital. From 1898 to 1930, Congo was under the dual administration of the French government and some forty "concessionary companies." These gained rights to exploit the natural and human resources of their individual concessions in return for rent and taxes, leading to horrible abuses but little lasting economic development. Between 1922 and 1934, the French constructed the Congo-Ocean railway connecting Brazzaville and Pointe Noire, at the cost of some fourteen thousand African lives. While per capita income in Congo has been bolstered since the 1970s by petroleum income, the economy remains largely unindustrialized and underdeveloped.

Following France's defeat in World War II, partisans of Free France and Vichy battled to control French Africa. After a Free French victory, thanks to the support of a key governor, Félix Éboué, Brazzaville became the headquarters of Free France in Africa during the war. In 1944, Charles de Gaulle chaired an important colonial conference in Brazzaville, at which time France promised political reform after the war. Congo's agricultural economy expanded during the war to meet increased allied demand for commodities. In 1946, France permitted the establishment of a territorial assembly and the election of two Africans to the French National Assembly. Felix Tchicaya, a Gabonese-born resident of Pointe Noire (Congo), was elected to represent the territory then known as "Moyen Congo." Until his political eclipse in 1957, Tchicaya had one chief rival in politics named Jacques Opangault, an Mbochi from northern Congo. In 1953, the French opened a dam on the Djoué River that provided electricity to Brazzaville, stimulating increasing migration into the colonial capital.

The politics of the late colonial period were dominated by personality and ethnoregional loyalties. No strong basis for national identity emerged. In 1956, Félix Youlou became a significant political figure when he rallied the Lari people to his cause and was elected mayor of Brazzaville. Congo became an autonomous state in the Franco-African Union in 1958 before its proclamation of independence in 1960. In 1959, the National Assembly elected Youlou as president. Although Youlou had charisma, he followed conservative, pro-French economic and foreign policies until his overthrow in 1963. Beginning in the late colonial period, Congo's main source of export revenue was timber harvested in its southern forests, with annual production varying between five hundred thousand to eight hundred thousand cubic meters. Congo also produced tobacco, sugar, cocoa, bananas, and peanuts on a small scale for export and local consumption.

After Youlou's fall, Congo's government created a new, single party for the state, the *Mouvement Nationale de la Révolution*, and followed a vaguely Socialist path to development. Alphonse Massamba-Debat, a former assembly president, became Congo's second president. He ruled, without fully consolidating power or fundamentally altering the economy, until being overthrown in 1968.

Congo's next three president were all northern Mbochi army officers. The first, Marien Ngouabi, renamed the country People's Republic of Congo, created a new state party (the *Parti Congolais du Travail*), and adopted Marxisim-Leninism as the state's official ideology. His regime coincided with large increases in oil production and prices in the early 1970s. The state took the leading role in the economy, nationalizing private enterprises (such as the Industrial and Agricultural Company of Niari, SIAN) and launching others (such as the Textile Printing Company of Congo, IMPRECO). After Ngouabi's assassination in 1977, Jacques Yhombi-Opango briefly served as president before being overthrown in a bloodless *coup d'état* in 1979. His successor, Denis Sassou-Nguesso, ruled Congo until the political transition of 1991. Oil revenues allowed substantial investments in Congo's state-dominated industrial sector, led by the Hydro-Congo petroleum product-marketing monopoly, during this period and caused massive urbanization of the country. Civil society was kept firmly under state control, however, following Marxist doctrine.

The revolution that overthrew Sassou was motivated by an economic crisis dating to the oil price collapse of 1985 and by the ideological shock of communism's collapse. Congo's leaders organized a "sovereign national conference" in 1991 and put in place a transitional government that drafted a new constitution. Multiparty elections in 1992 saw the election of Pascal Lissouba, a scientist and former prime minister from the 1960s, as president. Voting, again, exhibited an ethnoregional pattern. The revolution of 1991 led to the rebirth of a free press and of a nascent independent civil society. A political dispute at the end of 1992 led Lissouba to dissolve the assembly and organize new elections in 1993, which his party won by dubious means. Political protest, ethnic cleansing, and low-grade civil war between political militia groups ensued, leading to more than two thousand deaths.

The civil peace was restored during 1994, but political tension hung over Brazzaville and led up to the presidential elections scheduled for July 1997. The economy had performed poorly under Lissouba, with GDP *declining* by an average of 3.2% annually between 1993 and 1997. Annual inflation averaged more than 16% during the same years, owing mostly to the devaluation of the CFA franc in 1994. Civil society remained weak. Only weeks before the election, Lissouba attempted to arrest Sassou, who was to be a presidential candidate in the elections. This move precipitated another more deadly civil war between the political militia, ending with Sassou's victory in October. Some ten thousand Congolese died. Sassou owed his victory mostly to French support and Angolan intervention. As Sassou sought to consolidate his rule, yet another civil war broke out in December 1998, lasting a full year and killing fifty thousand. Relative peace returned to Congo by late 1999. Since then, some of the country's infrastructure has been rebuilt, but the economy remains utterly dependent on petroleum income and the civil society cowed by the threat of renewed war.

JOHN F. CLARK

Further Reading

Ballif, Noël. *Le Congo*. Paris: Karthala, 1993.

Bazenguissa-Ganga, Rémy. *Les Voies du Politique au Congo*. Paris: Karthala, 1997.

Bernault, Florence. *Démocraties Ambiguës en Afrique Centrale, Congo-Brazzaville, Gabon: 1940–1965*. Paris: Karthala, 1996.

Clark, John F. "Congo: Transition and the Struggle to Consolidate." In *Political Reform in Francophone Africa*, John F. Clark and David E. Gardinier, eds. Boulder, CO: Westview 1997, 62–85.

———. "The Neo-Colonial Context of the Democratic Experiment of Congo Brazzaville." *African Affairs* 101 (April 2002).

Coquery-Vidrovitch, Catherine. *Le Congo au Temps des Grandes Compagnies Concessionaaires, 1898–1930.* Paris: Mouton, 1972.

Decalo, Samuel, Virginia Thompson, and Richard Adloff. *Historical Dictionary of Congo*, 3d ed. Lanham, MD: Scarecrow Press, 1996.

Gauze, René. *The Politics of Congo-Brazzaville.* Translated, edited, and supplemented by Virginia Thompson and Richard Adloff. Stanford, CA: Hoover Institution Press, 1973.

Radu, Micahel, and Keith Somerville. "The Congo." In *Benin, the Congo, Burkina Faso: Politics, Economics, and Society*, Chris Allen *et al.*, eds. London: Pinter, 1989.

CONSTITUTIONALISM, DEFINITION

Determining how state power should be used and limited is probably the oldest and most intractable political problem. The sudden independence of the European empires after World War II and the more recent disintegration of the Soviet bloc in Eastern Europe made that problem inescapable and worldwide. One of its most vexing aspects involves the legal establishment of new sovereign powers. The general recognition of popular sovereignty, a system of nation-states requiring legal order for recognition, and a global economic system requiring legal protections all militated in favor of the promulgation of constitutions. But the uses of constitutions, especially in the developing world, are more problematic than might appear at first glance.

Constitutions are power maps; they are, at the same time, proclamations of sovereignty, institutional guidelines for the power and staffing of government offices, and listings of limitations on government power (Duchacek 1973). This combination of aims makes the definition of constitutionalism difficult. The more common definitions of the term view constitutionalism as long-term, self-imposed, and procedural; the term refers to substantive limitations on majority decisions (Elster and Slagstad 1988). Drawing on classical liberal political and economic theory, these definitions emphasize acceptance of limited government and the rule of law. For this perspective, the most important features of constitutional orders are the establishment of responsible governments, regular elections, an independent court system, public order, and protection of individual rights, especially to property and to secure contracts (de Smith 1962). Another, more functionalist view of constitutionalism focuses instead on the establishment of sovereignty and the need for constitutions to adapt to social and economic environments to secure legitimacy (Friedrich 1967; Loewenstein 1963). Constitutionalism, then, is not so much a matter of limitations on government as of establishing government in the first place. Constitutions that reinforce sovereignty through building national loyalties and adapting state power efficiently to other social and economic institutions are much more likely to succeed.

Both liberal and functionalist definitions of constitutionalism have some relevance to the problem of constitutionalism in developing countries, but both approaches have major weaknesses. Liberal definitions have pinpointed a major problem in developing countries. The new states have been characterized by authoritarian governments and accompanying depredations against individual rights. Obviously, legal limitations on state power might help alleviate these difficulties. Just as obviously, however, this approach assumes what is, in fact, problematical in much of the developing world. The concerns about limitations on government that motivate theorists in this school presuppose a level of state power and legitimacy to which most developing countries can only aspire. Calls for the rule of law when governments cannot consistently claim authority twenty kilometers from their capital cities are likely to prove unconvincing as well. Further, the main elements of this view are problematic. Obviously, the need to assert popular sovereignty runs directly into the establishment of governmental limitations (Poggi 1992). Further, the components of the rule of law, such as public order, security of contracts, and protection of property rights, beg several important questions: what institutions will establish public order; what types of contracts will be secured; and which property rights will be protected?

Functional definitions are similarly flawed. In a mirror image of the liberal view, its emphasis on establishing sovereignty spots the immediate problem for most governments in the developing world. What this approach fails to show is how stable, legitimate political orders can be established if constitutions are seen as adaptable instruments. Also, if governments are increased in power, what is to stop those who hold it from authoritarian excesses? Finally, the predominant role given to the formation of national loyalties, while certainly not trivial, avoids the hard task of establishing the institutional powers and limits that can help build them.

The difficulty of establishing a valid and useful constitutional theory for developing countries should not deter thinkers on the subject. It is evident, however, that present definitions of constitutionalism must be rethought. This task can be addressed, as Seidman (1978) shows, by looking at the task of development itself. Development is concerned with changing established patterns of social, political, and economic behaviors to different and more productive pursuits. Its main tools in achieving these goals are law and regulation. What both existing approaches to constitutionalism have avoided is how constitutions can be adapted to development purposes. The dominant liberal approach would achieve development goals by the rule of law and the institutions—an independent court system and strong security forces—to enforce it. The result would be an environment more conducive to capitalist development and, presumably, limited democracy. The functional approach would depend instead on increasing national integration to ensure that legal commands would be followed and development initiatives are achieved.

What both approaches avoid is that development involves a choice. Individuals in developing countries must take a sharp pencil to legal commands; their environment leaves little room for error. Only those laws and regulations that are clear and understandable in terms of that environment, which they have the opportunity and capacity to obey and which they perceive (at least) are in their interests, are likely to prove useful (Seidman 1978). One can assert the rule of law through nondemocratic institutions like independent court systems or call for loyalty to the new state and its ideologies to very little effect unless the legal order meets these criteria. And it is here that both definitions of constitutionalism fail. Both are based, de facto, on an elite controlled, top-down transmission of commands. Liberal constitutionalism seeks protection for urban, capitalist interests that cannot mobilize development initiatives through democratic institutions; functionalist constitutionalism seeks loyalty for national political leadership. The task, however, is to provide substantial communication concerning development laws and regulations between mass publics and legislatures and administrators. Hence "constitutionalism," to be relevant to the developing world, must be defined as a participatory exercise providing the power map for the development process. For this purpose, parts of both perspectives examined in this discussion will prove useful, but not unless they are recast with the aim of providing institutions that foster the necessary input functions to make development work. This problem awaits further thought.

TRACY L. R. LIGHTCAP

References and Further Reading

de Smith, S. A. "Constitutionalism in the Commonwealth Today." In *Constitutions and Constitutionalism*, William Andrews, ed. New York: Van Nostrand Reinhold, 1961.

Duchacek, Ivo. *Power Maps: Comparative Politics of Constitutions*. Santa Barbara, CA: ABC-Clio, 1973.

Elster, Jon, and Rune Slagstad, eds, *Constitutionalism and Democracy*. Cambridge: Cambridge University, 1988.

Friedrich, Carl. "Some Reflections on Constitutionalism in the Developing World." In *Patterns of Development:*
Five Comparisons, Herbert Spiro, ed. Englewood Cliffs, N.J.: Prentice Hall, 1967.

Loewenstein, Karl. "Reflections on the Value of Constitutions in Our Revolutionary Age." In *Comparative Politics: A Reader*, Harry Eckstein and David Apter, eds. New York: Free Press, 1963.

Neumann, Franz. *The Rule of Law: Political Theory and the Legal System in Modern Society*. Leamington Spa, Berg, 1986.

Poggi, Gianfranco. *The Development of the Modern State*. Stanford, CA: Stanford University.

Seidman, Robert. *The State, Law, and Development*. New York: St. Martin's, 1978.

CONTRAS

The Contras were a guerrilla army opposed to the Sandinista regime of Nicaragua during the 1980s and 1990s. Their attempt to defeat the Sandinista government badly damaged Nicaragua and helped to maintain the bitter divide between the Left and the Right, which has characterized much of that country's history. The secret funding of the Contras by the United States government, without Congressional approval, led to the Iran-Contra Scandal that tarnished the second term of the Reagan presidency.

Nicaragua

After becoming an independent nation in the nineteenth century, Nicaragua suffered under the rule of a succession of corrupt strongmen, often backed by the United States. These governments supported the interests of Nicaragua's wealthy elite and foreign, generally American, corporations, at the expense of the country's population of poor farmers.

In 1912, the US Marines intervened to protect American corporate interests and the presidency of Adolfo Diaz. The Marines stayed in Nicaragua until 1934, supporting a series of puppet presidents. They were opposed for much of their occupation by General Augusto Cesar Sandino, a political Liberal. Sandino was finally killed during a US-brokered peace negotiation, executed by order of General Anastasio Somoza Garcia, a US-trained leader of the Nicaraguan National Guard. After his death, Sandino became a folk hero among poor and left-wing Nicaraguans.

Somoza used his position as head of the National Guard—along with the support of the American government—to stage a *coup d'état* and seize power in 1937. He ruled until 1956, when he was replaced by his two sons, Luis and Anastasio Somoza, who ruled either directly, with one of them as president, or as the real power behind a series of puppet presidents. Their rule was characterized by rampant corruption.

In the 1960s, radical opponents of the Somoza regime established the *Frente Sandinista de Liberacion Nacional* (FSLN)—the National Sandinista Liberation Front—named after General Sandino. Brutally suppressed by the Somozas, the Sandinista's success was limited at first, but Anastasio Somoza's attempts to maintain his own one-man rule (Luis died in 1967) alienated more mainstream elements in the population who allied themselves to the Sandinistas. In 1979, Somoza was finally convinced he could no longer hold on to power, and he went into a US-facilitated exile. Tens of thousands died in the war to remove him from power.

The new government was led by Sandinista leader Daniel Ortega. It put into place numerous reforms, including confiscating the Somoza's land holdings and imposing agrarian reforms. Some of these measures were too extreme for Ortega's more moderate, non-Sandinista allies, including Violeta Chamorro. Chamorro's family owned the paper *La Prensa* and had opposed Somoza but also disagreed with the more radical Sandinista policies.

The US government began funding opponents to the Sandinstas, including *La Prensa*. However, the most controversial of the US actions involved the creation and support of the military army known collectively as the Contras.

The Contras

Immediately after Somoza's departure from Nicaragua, a number of his officers and men in the former Nicaraguan National Guard left the country and became involved in anti-Sandinista exile groups. Other Nicaraguans, including some ex-Sandinistas, opposed the regime because of specific policies, particularly its close ties with Cuba and its leader Fidel Castro. These anti-Sandinista forces were collectively called the "Contras," short for *contrarrevolucionarios* or counterrevolutionaries.

Generally, the Contras were right-wing in ideology but divided into several and not always friendly groups, and it therefore would be a mistake to lump them all together. For example, groups placed under the Contra label included Edén Pastora, a former Sandinista leader who, while not in agreement with more conservative Contras, opposed Sandinista leader Ortegas ties with Cuba. It was the more conservative Contra groups, however, particularly those whose roots lay in the dictator Somoza's

regime, which were the most prominent and the best funded.

In particular, the *Fuerza Democrática Nicragüense* (FDN)—Nicaraguan Democratic Force—became the group most identified with the label "Contra." The FDN was made up of ex-Somoza officers and led by former National Guard leader Enrique Bermúdez. The FDN was based in Honduras, Nicaragua's northern neighbor, and was supported by that country's conservative government. Very quickly, also, the FDN began receiving extensive financial and logistical support from the United States.

It is possible that some Contra elements received funding from the United States Central Intelligence Agency (CIA) during 1979 and 1980, although this was not the official policy of the US government under President Jimmy Carter. In 1981, however, Ronald Reagan was elected president of the United States, and American policy became strongly anti-Sandinista and pro-Contra. President Ronald Reagan opposed the Sandinista regime and was willing to use military force to remove them from power.

In late 1981, Reagan signed the National Security Decision Directive 17 (NSDD 17), which authorized secretly funneling millions of dollars in military aid to the Contras. Reagan made it clear that it was his administration's goal to remove Ortega and the Sandinistas from power. Reagan justified this attempt to overthrow the government of an independent nation on the grounds that the Sandinista's ties to Cuba made them part of the general Soviet alliance and therefore a threat to US interests. More specifically, Reagan and other conservatives in the United States also accused the Sandinistas, probably correctly, of supporting left-wing guerillas in El Salvador.

The CIA, under NSDD 17 authorization, spent millions arming and training the Contras, which eventually became an army of perhaps five or six thousand men. The Contras, and for the most part this meant the FDN, carried out bombing attacks against Nicaraguan civilian and military targets. In 1983, the Contras began large-scale raids across the border from their bases in Honduras (and with support from the Honduran army) but with only limited success. Nicaragua's economy was disrupted, but local pro-Sandinista militias were able to defeat the invaders. In 1984, US forces placed mines in Nicaraguan ports in an attempt to further destabilize the Sandinista government, a move that received widespread attention and international condemnation. The Contras also used terrorist techniques, including assassination, against the Nicaraguan government. By 1984, international hostility to the US's pro-Contra position convinced the United States Congress, then controlled by the Democratic Party, to temporarily end American funding of the Contras's military activities. The Boland Amendment, the amendment that ended the funding, was reluctantly signed into law by President Reagan on October 12, 1984.

Without US funding, the Contras, who lacked widespread popular support in Nicaragua, were unlikely to succeed in their efforts to overthrow the Sandinistas. Moreover, elections held in late 1984 gave the Sandinistas a strong majority in Nicaragua's National Assembly and elected Ortega president.

Iran-Contra Scandal

President Reagan was reluctant to allow the Contras, whom he likened to the US's founding fathers, to fail. With Reagan's encouragement, National Security Advisor Robert McFarlane authorized his subordinate Oliver North to organize further aid to the Contras. North, using the National Security Council (NSC) as his base of operations, raised funds from sympathetic countries around the world as well as from private donors (some of whom received the reward of a photo with President Reagan). The NSC was also aided in its activities by the CIA. All this was done against the Bolland Amendment and therefore was illegal under US law. It was also done entirely without congressional knowledge and kept secret because North and his superiors (McFarlane and later his replacement, Admiral John Poindexter) knew that it was illegal.

This illegal funding of the Contras gradually began to become public after 1985, when a CIA-operated plane piloted by Eugene Hasenfus was shot down over Nicaragua. Hasenfus was captured, and his confession, along with captured documents, revealed the tip of the illegal activities of the CIA. In 1986, after government officials, including President Reagan, denied US involvement, a congressional investigation was opened. Congressional committees gradually unraveled parts of the Contra funding story, particularly the central role of Oliver North and John Poindexter.

The investigation also revealed that the US government had authorized selling weapons to Iran, then an enemy of the United States, in return for helping to obtain the release of American hostages being held in Lebanon. Much of the money gained in these arms sales, which were themselves illegal, was funneled by Oliver North to support the Contras. It was the discovery of this unique funding method that exploded into the Iran-Contra Scandal.

An independent counsel, Lawrence Walsh, was appointed in December 1986 to investigate the Iran-Contra affair. In the end, both Poindexter and North were convicted of violating US law, but their convictions were overturned on appeal (largely because they had previously been granted limited immunity by congressional committees). It was never proven that President Reagan knew of the illegal nature of his subordinates' activities, although it is clear that he was in sympathy with the policies they were advancing—the destabilization of the Nicaraguan government. Later, President Bush, who had been vice president during Iran-Contra, pardoned many of the major participants in the scandal, including Robert McFarlane.

End of the Contras

The exposure of the Iran-Contra Scandal in the United States made further support of the Contras politically difficult. Furthermore, there was widespread hostility to the United States's pro-Contra policies in both Central America and in the larger international community. Well-documented reports of Contra atrocities reduced what limited popularity they once had, while the economic strain the conflict put on neighboring countries, such as El Salvador and Costa Rica, made ending the war seem a necessity.

Costa Rican President Oscar Arias put forward the Arias Peace Plan, which both demanded an end to outside intervention, as well as an agreement by the Sandinistas to hold new elections. President Ortega agreed but was rebuffed by the United States and the Contras, both still hoping for military success. In 1988, a Nicaraguan offense against Contra forces still in Nicaragua led to further Contra defeats and a recognition that the war was failing.

The Bush administration, which came to power in 1989, ended the Reagan policy of military action and supported the idea of Nicaraguan elections, pushing strongly for the defeat of Ortega by helping to fund his opponents. The 1990 presidential election led to Ortega's defeat and the victory of Violeta Chamorro, candidate of the moderate Right.

Some Contra forces, unhappy with the Chamorro government's decision to keep some Sandinista elements within the Nicaraguan government, fought on until 1994, when the last Contra bands made their peace with the government.

The Contras had some roots in a genuine reaction by anti-Leftist elements within Nicaragua, but they would have been impossible without extensive support and funding by the United States, funding obtained both within and outside the confines of US law. In the end, the elements must be viewed as an extension of US foreign policy, a policy that was opposed the Leftist pro-peasant policies of the Sandinista government.

Politically, the Contras achieved only limited success. They failed to oust the Sandinistas from power through military means. They did, however, put pressure on the Ortega government, and it may have been that pressure that eventually led to Ortega's defeat in 1990.

Economically and socially, the Contra War was a disaster for the people of Nicaragua. Nicaragua was forced to spend a large portion of its gross national product on troops and weapons, while much of Nicaragua's northern provinces were disrupted by Contra raids. The result was to make an already poor country poorer. The human cost of the Contra War is difficult to calculate but probably exceeds fifty thousand killed. To a country with a population of approximately 4 million, this was an immense loss.

CARL SKUTSCH

See also Central America: History and Economic Development; Central America: International Relations; Guerrilla Warfare; Nicaragua

References and Further Reading

Kagan, Robert. *Twilight Struggle: American Power and Nicaragua, 1977–1990.* New York: Free Press, 1996.

Meeks, Brian. *Caribbean Revolutions and Revolutionary Theory: An Assessment of Cuba, Nicaragua, and Grenada.* Kingston, Jamaica: University of the West Indies Press, 2001.

Parsa, Misagh. *States, Ideologies, and Social Revolutions: A Comparative Analysis of Iran, Nicaragua, and the Philippines.* Cambridge, New York: Cambridge University Press, 2000.

Walker, Thomas. *Nicaragua.* Boulder, CO: Westview Press, 2003.

Walsh, Lawrence. *Firewall: The Iran-Contra Conspiracy and Cover-Up.* New York: W. W. Norton & Company, 1998.

COPTIC CHURCH (COPTS)

The Coptic Orthodox Church is the indigenous church of Egypt, currently encompassing approximately 95% of the Christian population in that country. The Coptic Orthodox Church is the largest of the Oriental Orthodox Churches, distinct in its organization from the Eastern Orthodox and Roman Catholic Churches since the Ecumenical Council of Chalcedon in 451. Its independence from the rest of the world's churches is signified by its recognition as an "autocephalus" church. The head of the church is its patriarch, known locally as the pope of the Coptic Orthodox Church. Individual adherents are known as "Copts."

The term "Coptic" refers both to the church and to the Egyptian language in use in the first century when the church was founded, which has been retained as a liturgical language written in Greek characters. It is conjectured that the word is a derivative of a Greek term used for the nation of Egypt; thus, "Coptic" is synonymous with "Egyptian."

According to tradition, the Coptic Church was established by St. Mark in the first century CE. To this day, the Coptic Holy See of Alexandria is known as the Holy See of St. Mark. Over the course of the following four centuries, Christianity grew to become the most influential religion in Egypt, and several important early Christian leaders came from the Coptic Church, including Origen of Alexandria, Athanasius, and Dioscorus, who led the church out of the mainstream of Christian orthodoxy in 451. The division of the church led to widespread religious conflict in Egypt that came to an end with the Muslim conquest in 640. During the Islamic period, Copts were tolerated, but the internal weakness of the church and restrictions and taxation imposed upon non-Muslims contributed to the gradual erosion of the Christian population; by the end of the Ottoman period, they were a small minority.

During the late colonial period, Copts were gradually emancipated from feudal-era restrictions that controlled their public activity. They were freed from an obligation to pay a special poll-tax (*jizya*) in 1855, admitted as equals to the Egyptian armed forces, and began to achieve greater prominence in the early nationalist administrations. Copts became prominent in business and in the administration. One Copt, Boutros Ghali, became prime minister in 1908, only to be assassinated two years later. The event signaled an increase in hostility toward the Coptic Church, which was perceived as a fifth column for colonial authorities even as those authorities sought to mollify local Muslim religious sentiments. From the 1930s, restrictions on church construction were intensified under a ministerial rescript. Following the Free Officers' Revolt of 1952 and a subsequent republican administration, the Coptic Church was significantly weakened through the confiscation and nationalization of personal and institutional properties. Increasing levels of emigration further decreased the number of Copts resident in Egypt.

The decline of the Church came to a halt in 1959 with the appointment of a reformist patriarch,

Kyrillos VI. The patriarch saw to an intensification of Christian education and to the empowerment of lay and clerical leadership, encouraging the rise of several like-minded bishops. Among these was Nazir Gayed, a charismatic youth leader, who was instrumental in the growth of a rigorous new catechetical Sunday school movement. Upon the death of Kyrillos VI in 1971, Gayed succeeded him as Pope Shenouda III. The present patriarch has overseen the further institutional resurrection of the church. In the late 1970s, he led a more activist approach toward the regime in response to the growing threat of Islamist radicalism toward Christians and church properties, a radicalism tacitly courted by the government of President Anwar al-Sadat. His opposition to the regime amid the riots and violence of Sadat's final days caused the government to charge him with treasonous activities and to force him into internal exile in 1981. Following the assassination of Sadat later that year, Shenouda sought reconciliation with the government and was reinstated in 1985. During the past two decades, the Coptic Church has sought to consolidate the gains made under the reformers and to maintain a cordial relationship with the government and conservative Islamist elements. Through the 1990s, the church suffered as a target of the radical Islamist *Gama'a al-Islamiya* terror organization, but government repression of the radicals and international attention to the plight of the church have bolstered its position. The church has effectively modernized, providing significant local social services, such as relief, educational, health, and rehabilitative programs. In spite of the patriarch's traditional title as Bishop of the See of Alexandria, the administrative offices of the church are situated in Cairo.

In the twenty-first century, Copts are found throughout Egypt and in diaspora communities throughout Europe, North America, and Australia, where they have established indigenous dioceses appointed by the patriarch. While Copts are found throughout Egypt, they are especially concentrated in Cairo and in Upper Egypt, particularly in the governorates of Asyut, Minya, and Sohag. Their numbers are a matter of significant controversy: Copts are said to compose anywhere between 4% and 10% of the Egyptian population.

In the third century, a Coptic ascetic, St. Anthony the Great, became the founder of the Christian monastic movement when he retreated to a spot in the Eastern Desert of Egypt not far from the Red Sea coast. He was followed by many imitators, who established monasteries in the deserts of Egypt, most notably in the salt water depression known as Wadi Natrun, south of Alexandria. Monasticism became a key feature of the Coptic Orthodox Church, so much

so that the modern hierarchy is drawn entirely from the ranks of anchorite monks from the many monasteries that are scattered throughout Egypt. Thus, while the hierarchs are celibate, individual priests may marry. Despite a prolonged period of decline, the monastic movement has seen a resurgence under the past two patriarchs, and the largest monasteries have been refurbished and developed into major centers of spiritual retreat.

PAUL S. ROWE

See also Christianity

References and Further Reading

Bailey, Betty Jane, and J. Martin Bailey. *Who Are the Christians in the Middle East?* Grand Rapids, MI: William B. Eerdmans, 2003.
Carter, B. L. *The Copts in Egyptian Politics, 1918–1952.* London: Croom Helm, 1986.
Farah, Nadia Ramsis. *Religious Strife in Egypt.* New York: Gordon and Breach, 1986.
Ibrahim, Saad Eddin *et al. The Copts of Egypt.* London: Minority Rights Group, 1996.
Meinardus, Otto. *Two Thousand Years of Coptic Christianity.* Cairo: American University in Cairo Press, 1999.
Van Doorn-Harder, Pieternella. *Contemporary Coptic Nuns.* Columbia, SC: University of South Carolina Press, 1995.

CORRUPTION, GOVERNMENTAL

Corruption, in one form or another, remains an important development constraint in virtually all developing societies. Unfortunately, it is difficult to define and measure, making it very challenging for researchers to empirically test for it.

Defining Corruption

Traditionally, corruption is defined in terms of three basic models. First, corruption, as argued by Nye (1967:419), is "[b]ehavior which deviates from the normal duties of a public role" and hence is related to the performance of the duties of a public office. Second, it is related to the exchange concept, which is derived from the economic theory of the market. As argued by J. van Klaveren (1990:26), state custodians (civil servants and politicians) view their public offices as enterprises from which they can extract extralegal compensation. If a civil servant, for example, can generate for himself more resources from outside sources (such as through bribes) than from his regular employment, he may spend most of his time and effort meeting the needs of the entrepreneurs who bribe him than performing the public duties for which he was hired. Finally, corruption is related to the concept of the public interest. According to Carl Friedrich (1990:15), the "pattern of corruption may therefore be said to exist whenever a power holder who is charged with doing certain things, that is a responsible functionary or office holder, is by monetary or other rewards, such as the expectation of a job in the future, induced to take actions which favor whoever provides the reward and thereby damage the group or organization to which the functionary belongs, more specifically the government." Hence, the activities of opportunistic state custodians can severely damage public interest and must be considered important variables in the examination of corruption and its impact on society.

Classifying Corruption

The development literature identifies four categories of corruption: (i) cost-reducing corruption; (ii) cost-enhancing corruption; (iii) benefit-enhancing corruption; and (iv) benefit-reducing corruption (Alam 1989). The first category, cost-reducing corruption, involves situations in which civil servants reduce the costs imposed on an enterprise by government regulations. For example, the regulator can exempt an enterprise from complying with certain government regulations or eliminate the taxes owed by that business to the government. The civil servant and the business owner share (based on a prearranged sharing formula) the savings generated by the bureaucrat's actions.

In cost-enhancing corruption, the second category, civil servants who are placed in charge of public stocks of food and other public goods may extract rents by charging demanders a price that is higher than that allowed by law. In addition, bureaucrats whose job it is to grant licenses and permits, such as import licenses, for entrepreneurs to enter business sectors closed by government regulations can confiscate part of the monopoly profit associated with the licenses. Finally, the civil servant can illegally tax economic activity for his own benefit.

In the third category of benefit-enhancing corruption, civil servants transfer to citizens who are legally due public benefits more than the legal amount. In exchange, the recipient surrenders some of the benefits to the civil servant. Throughout developing countries, incumbent rulers use this mechanism to transfer resources to individuals and groups, such as military officers and labor unions, that have

developed enough violence potential to threaten regime security.

In the fourth and last type of corruption—benefit-reducing—civil servants illegally transfer to themselves benefits that belong to citizens. For example, the director of the country's public pension plan may delay the transfer of retirement benefits to retirees and, subsequently, appropriate the interest earned by the delayed funds. This type of corruption is quite pervasive in developing countries given the fact that civil servants have more information about public benefits programs than ordinary citizens.

Corruption and the Theory of Public Choice

Many economists, not satisfied with the explanations given for corruption in the development literature, have turned to the theory of public choice, which considers corruption as postconstitutional opportunism, designed to extract benefits for individuals or groups at the expense of the mass of the people. As argued by public choice theorists, the scope and extent of corruption in a society is determined by the society's institutional arrangements. After the constitution has been compacted and adopted, there is an incentive for individuals and groups in the society to subvert the laws or rules to generate additional income for themselves. The subversion of rules, if it can be undertaken successfully, can enhance the ability of individuals and groups to extract benefits above and beyond what they would have secured otherwise. Such behavior can take place in both democratic and nondemocratic societies (Ostrom, Schroeder, and Wynne 1993).

Civil servants and politicians may use their public positions to maximize their private objectives instead of carrying out the duties for which they were appointed or elected. The desire by civil servants and politicians to engage in opportunism, such as corruption and rent seeking, and the effort by special interest groups to subvert society's laws and generate benefits for themselves create opportunities for corrupt behavior. For example, a trader who wants to secure a lucrative import license may bribe a clerk at the trade ministry to easily secure the permit. The latter offers the trader opportunities to earn monopoly profit.

The regulatory activities of the government impose significant transaction costs on market participants and have a negative impact on firm profitability. To minimize these regulation-related costs and enhance firm profitability, some entrepreneurs may turn to the bureaucracy for help. The enterprise owner pays the regulator a bribe so that her business is treated favorably and she can minimize the burden of government regulation on her economic activities. For example, in exchange for the bribe, the regulator can exempt a business from meeting various government mandates, such as providing wheelchair access to the business or meeting certain safety and environmental standards. As argued by public choice theorists, bureaucratic corruption is related directly to the scope and extent of government intervention in the markets. Hence, an effective and sustainable corruption control program must involve the modification of existing rules so as to change the incentive structures faced by participants in markets (Mbaku 2000; Rose-Ackerman 1999).

The International Dimension of Corruption

Corruption is a universal problem. Although it affects both developed and developing countries, it does not have a uniform impact on each one of them. In recent years, many policy makers around the world have recognized corruption's global nature and have been attempting to coordinate their cleanup efforts. Corruption is no longer viewed as arising from the interaction of domestic entrepreneurs with their bureaucracies. Many politicians and civil servants, especially in Third World countries, are now arguing that the contributions of transnational corporations to the culture of corruption must be recognized to allow governments to more effectively deal with it.

Since the mid-1980s, many organizations have become interested in corruption cleanups. Some of the most important of these organizations include the United Nations (UN), the Organization of American States (OAS), the International Chamber of Commerce, Transparency International (TI), the World Economic Forum (WEF), the World Bank, Interpol, and the Organization for Economic Cooperation and Development (OECD).

Why is there renewed interest in corruption control? During the last two decades, there have been significant developments in the global political economy, which have changed the willingness of many people, especially in the developing countries, to tolerate venality and malfeasance in the public sector. In the late 1980s, many of these people took to the streets in demonstrations against incompetence, corruption, and inefficiency in the public sector and demanded institutional reforms to make their public sectors more efficient. Since then, the balance of power in many countries has been shifting in favor

of more open, transparent, and participatory forms of governance (Glynn, Kobrin, and Naím 1997).

Since the early 1990s, the world has become more economically interdependent. As a result, corruption in one country can easily spread to other parts of the world. Corruption distorts market incentives and makes it quite difficult for the market to serve as an effective and efficient tool for the allocation of resources. In many African countries, which have been engaged in privatization programs during the last several years, corruption has allowed many civil servants and politicians to mismanage the process and create windfalls for themselves. And, in Eastern Europe, corruption has so distorted the new capitalism that many of the poor are now actively calling for a return to the old system.

The new post-Cold War economic interdependence has helped internationalize corruption. According to Glynn, Kobrin, and Naím (1997), there are three changes that have contributed significantly to the globalization of corruption. First, increased levels of economic integration have made it much more likely that corruption in one region of the world will impact economic and political activities in another part of the world. For example, when the corrupt activities of the Bank of Credit and Commerce International (BCCI) forced it into insolvency in 1991, many of the world's economies, especially those in the Third World, were affected (Passas 1994).

Second, radical changes in information technology have had a tremendous impact on the international financial system and enhanced the ability of traders to behave opportunistically. For example, new, efficient, and fast systems of transferring funds electronically have made it quite difficult for national regulators to deal with corruption. Some anticorruption groups have argued that the ease with which funds can be moved from Africa to Europe or the Caribbean has meant that corrupt civil servants and politicians can easily and almost effortlessly hide their ill-gotten gains from the public, making it quite difficult for the government to recover these funds when and if the individuals are convicted of corruption. Law enforcement agencies in the West, however, continue to produce technological innovations that may actually make it possible to properly monitor these transnational transactions and gather the information needed to fight global corruption.

Third, since the Cold War ended, there has been a rise in the number of cooperative agreements between various economic units domestically and across borders. As argued by Glynn, Kobrin, and Naím (1997), although globalization exacerbates the problem of corruption, it also provides opportunities and instruments to fight against it.

Corruption is an important obstacle to the maintenance of a free, multilateral trading system. For a competitive international economy to function efficiently, participants must obey the rules and refrain from engaging in any form of opportunism. For example, countries that allow or encourage their businesses (for example, through favorite tax treatment) to pay bribes to foreign public officials place such firms at a competitive advantage over firms from countries where the paying of bribes to foreign civil servants and politicians has been criminalized. For many years, US multinational companies complained that they could not compete successfully with European firms for business contracts in developing countries because their counterparts were allowed and encouraged (until recently) by their national governments through favorable tax treatment to engage in corruption abroad.

Corruption Cleanups

All countries, at one time or another, have developed and implemented anticorruption programs. Many of these programs have been designed to change the behavior of public servants and improve efficiency and minimize venality in the public sector. The development literature identifies four main strategies that have been employed at various times in the past and in various countries to deal with corruption. These have met with various degrees of success, and they are societal, legal, market, and political strategies (Gillespie and Okruhlik 1991).

According to the societal strategy to "clean up corruption," the society is expected to define a common standard for judging morality and use it to determine if a given behavior qualifies as corrupt. Civil society must remain vigilant and seek out individuals who engage in corrupt behavior and report them to the police. Both the government and civil society organizations should educate the public about corruption and its negative impact on growth and development. Such an education program should enhance the ability of citizens to detect corrupt behavior and report it to the police for further action. The private media has an important role to play in this approach to corruption control. The media investigate and expose corruption, enhancing the ability of the police to further investigate and collect the evidence needed for the prosecution of offenders by the courts.

The legal approach works through the police, the judiciary, and the mass media. First, the law defines civil servants' jobs and their responsibilities and places the appropriate constraints on them. Second, the law defines corrupt behavior. Third, citizens are encouraged to watch out for and report incidents of corruption to the authorities. Fourth, the police are expected to investigate any reported incidents of corruption and gather the information needed for further action to be taken by the courts. Fifth, the judiciary system then uses the information provided by the police to prosecute and punish those found guilty of corruption. In cases where grand corruption is suspected or where high-ranking civil servants and politicians are involved, special prosecutors or commissions of enquiry may be convened to look into the situation.

While the police and the courts are very critical to the corruption cleanup process, one must note that unless these institutions are free of corruption, they cannot perform their jobs effectively. Hence, to perform their jobs well, the police and the judiciary must be effectively constrained by the law.

Throughout the developing world, low pay for public employees has been given as a factor contributing to high levels of venality and malfeasance in the public sector. Thus, as part of the effort to clean up corruption in these countries, it has been suggested that across-the-board wage increases should be granted to public workers to minimize the temptation to engage in opportunism. Higher pay, however, could simply force the civil servant to seek larger bribes to compensate for the probability of losing what is now a more lucrative public position. In fact, in most of Africa, a lot of the corruption that takes place in the public sector originates from high-ranking officials and not from low-level, poorly paid government workers, most of whom usually do not have any favors to sell to private-sector operators.

It has been suggested that any reforms in the public services must be accompanied by the provision of counteracting agencies, such as an independent judiciary or some type of independent review board, an ombudsman, or other investigative body (Rose-Ackerman 1978, 1997, 1999). It is important, however, to note that such institutions can become politicized (as is evident from many developing countries and used by the ruling coalition to punish the opposition and enhance its ability to continue to monopolize political power and the allocation of resources.

Those who subscribe to the market approach to corruption cleanups believe that there is a discernible relationship between the structure of the market and corruption. Government regulatory activities in the economy can distort market incentives and create opportunities for civil servants to extort bribes from entrepreneurs. Deregulation or decreased intervention is the solution usually recommended by scholars. This approach, however, has at least two problems.

First, it involves an effort to achieve certain outcomes within an existing incentive structure. Second, the problem is not with the market per se but with the existing incentive structures faced by traders. Of course, the incentive structure, as argued by Brennan and Buchanan (1985), determines the behavior of market participants and, hence, market outcomes. The most effective way to deal with corruption in this instance is to modify existing incentive structures (through rules reform). Reforming the rules, as indicated here, does not imply deregulation but reconstruction of the neocolonial state through a democratic constitution to provide institutional arrangements that adequately constrain state custodians.

Decentralization of state power is the heart of the political strategy to corruption cleanups. For many years, it has been argued that the concentration of power in the central government has made it possible for members of the ruling class to plunder the national economy and engage in corrupt behavior to enrich themselves. Thus, any reform that decentralizes power and brings the government closer to the people will improve accountability and civil service efficiency, as well as reduce corruption. It is also argued that part of the political strategy to deal with corruption should include increased transparency. These reforms, however, can easily be reversed through ordinary legislation by subsequent governments and power that is reconcentrated in the center.

Success of each anticorruption strategy enumerated in the previous paragraphs depends on the effectiveness and professionalism of the counteracting institutions (such as the judiciary, police, and mass media) that exist in a country. The assumption is that each one of these institutions is well constrained by the law and that those who serve in it are free of corruption. Unfortunately, this is not true. First, most developing countries do not have viable independent mass media that can investigate and expose corruption without the threat of censure or harm by the incumbent government. Second, many countries have judiciary systems that are not independent of the executive branch of government. In fact, throughout most of the Third World, the judiciary is under the complete control of the chief executive who has the power to appoint and dismiss judges. Third, public institutions are pervaded with corruption and, hence, cannot be expected to successfully carry out an anticorruption program. A viable, effective, and sustainable anticorruption program must begin with institutional reforms to select appropriate new rules, which (i) adequately constrain the state (and prevent its agents from engaging in corruption) and (ii) provide the foundation for the construction of new and

more effective counteracting agencies (an independent judiciary; a well-constrained police force; professional and neutral armed forces; a free press; an independent central bank; an efficient and representative parliament; and a professional civil service).

Constitutionalism and Corruption Cleanups

Public choice theory argues that corruption is a "rules-related" problem. Thus, dealing effectively with it requires a thorough examination of the rules that regulate sociopolitical interaction in the society in question. Because rules determine the incentives that market participants face, one cannot adequately understand the nature of corruption in an economy without a thorough examination of the country's laws and institutions.

In a study published in 1985, Brennan and Buchanan argued that rules (i) determine how individuals within a society interact with each other; (ii) arm the people with the means to peacefully resolve conflict; (iii) provide market participants with information, making it possible for them to anticipate the behavior of others in the market; and (iv) constrain the behavior of individuals as well as that of collectivities in the society. The police, for example, cannot function effectively as a check on corruption if it is not adequately constrained by the law.

Within each country, one can find both implicit (custom and tradition) and explicit (written constitution) rules. Corruption can be viewed as postconstitutional opportunism—that is, activities on the part of individuals designed to generate extralegal income for themselves, usually through subversion of existing laws. Hence, opportunism is defined as any behavior designed to improve the welfare of an individual or group at the expense of other members of society and includes such behaviors as shirking, corruption, adverse selection, moral hazard, and free riding (Ostrom, Schroeder, and Wynne 1993).

To design and execute an effective anticorruption program, then, requires that one begin by first thoroughly examining the country's existing laws and institutions. This review can then be followed by reforms through democratic constitution that enable the selection of institutional arrangements that adequately constrain the state but enhance entrepreneurial activities. This approach has many benefits. First, the institutional arrangements selected are most likely to reflect the values of the relevant stakeholder groups, enhancing the chance that the people will consider such laws and institutions as legitimate tools for the regulation of their sociopolitical interaction. When the people claim ownership of the rules that govern their interaction with each other and with the collectivity, compliance is significantly improved, thus minimizing the costs of policing. Second, this approach will allow the people to find ways to constitutionally constrain state custodians and prevent them from engaging in opportunistic behavior. Third, economic freedom can be entrenched constitutionally, enhancing entrepreneurship and maximizing wealth creation. Finally, the reforms can provide the economy with viable and effective structures for the management of ethnic diversity, resulting in significantly lower levels of intercommunal violence. Peaceful coexistence of groups should enhance wealth creation.

JOHN MUKUM MBAKU

References and Further Reading

Alam, M. S. "Anatomy of Corruption: An Approach to the Political Economy of Underdevelopment." *The American Journal of Economics and Sociology* 48, no. 4: 441–456, 1989.

Brennan, G., and J. M. Buchanan. *The Reason of Rules: Constitutional Political Economy.* Cambridge: Cambridge University Press, 1985.

Friedrich, C. J. "Corruption Concepts in Historical Perspective." In *Political Corruption: A Handbook*, A. J. Heidenheimer, M. Johnston, and V. T. LeVine, eds. New Brunswick, NJ: Transaction Publishers, 1990.

Gillespie, K., and G. Okruhlik. "The Political Dimensions of Corruption Cleanups: A Framework for Analysis." *Comparative Politics* 24, no. 1: 77–95, 1991.

Glynn, P., S. J. Kobrin, and M. Naím. "The Globalization of Corruption." *Corruption and the Global Economy*, K. Elliot, K., ed. Washington, DC: Institute for International Economics, 1997.

Mbaku, J. M. *Political and Bureaucratic Corruption in Africa: The Public Choice Perspective.* Malabar, FL: Krieger, 2000.

Nye, J. S. "Corruption and Political Development: A Cost-Benefit Analysis." *The American Political Science Review* 61, no. 2: 417–427, 1967.

Ostrom, E., L. Schroeder, and S. Wynne. *Institutional Incentives and Sustainable Development: Infrastructure Policies in Perspective.* Boulder, CO: Westview, 1993.

Passas, N. "I Cheat Therefore I Exist? The BCCI Scandal in Context." In *Emerging Global Business Ethics*, Hoffman *et al.*, eds. Westport, CT: Quorum Books, 1994.

Rose-Ackerman, S. *Corruption: A Study in Political Economy.* New York: Academic Press, 1978.

———. "The Political Economy of Corruption." *Corruption and the Global Economy*, K. A. Elliot. Washington, DC: Institute for International Economics, 1997.

———. *Corruption and Government: Causes, Consequences, and Reform.* Cambridge: Cambridge University Press, 1999.

van Klaveren, J. "The Concept of Corruption." *Political Corruption: A Handbook*, A. J. M. Johnston and V. T. LeVine, eds. New Brunswick, NJ: Transaction Publishers, 1990.

COSTA RICA

The Republic of Costa Rica is situated on the Central American isthmus between Panama to the west and Nicaragua to the north as well as the Caribbean Sea and the Pacific Ocean. While the country is small (a little larger than West Virginia at 31,689 square miles or 51,000 square kilometers), it has considerable geographical diversity and biodiversity and a relatively large population of 4 million. Most Costa Ricans (who refer to themselves as *Ticos*) are *mestizo* (a mix of European and Indian heritage). It is estimated that 1% of the population is indigenous and 1% is Chinese; West Indians make up 3% of the population. More than 76% of the population profess Catholicism, which is the state religion. Other religious faiths, though, are protected by a constitutional guarantee of freedom of religion. Protestant churches have grown rapidly in the last two decades and currently include more than 15% of the population.

Despite its small size, Costa Rica's geography varies from rain and cloud forests to arid regions. There are two basic seasons: a dry season (December to April) and a rainy season (May to November). It also enjoys some of the most intense biodiversity in the world, with hundreds of species of birds, animals, and insects residing in the region. The country is subject to periodic earthquakes, flooding, landslides, and volcanic eruptions.

Although Costa Rica was Spain's poorest colony in the region, it currently enjoys the highest per capita income in Central America. Much of Costa Rica's economic and political success was a result of the country's economic development model that was gradually implemented after a short, bloody civil war in 1948.

Costa Rica's postwar development has produced impressive results in both economic and political terms. In socioeconomic terms, the country stands out in contrast to its neighboring republics and in Latin America generally. For example, life expectancy at birth is 78 years for Costa Ricans compared with 69 years for neighboring Nicaraguans. The Human Poverty Index (percentage of the population living in poverty) is 4.4% for Costa Rica compared with almost 23% for Guatemala, 18% for Nicaragua, and 17% for Honduras. Similarly, Costa Rica's historical emphasis on education is reflected in its illiteracy rate of 4.2%; Guatemala has a 30% illiteracy rate, Nicaragua has 23%, and El Salvador has almost 20%. Finally, the stark contrast with the region's other countries is revealed through the United Nations Human Development Index, a composite measure of of human development, taking into account life expectancy, health, education, and standard of living. Costa Rica ranks 45th in the world (above some "developed" countries), while the next highest Central American country is El Salvador at 103rd (El Salvador). The region's other countries are ranked between 115th (Honduras) through 121st (Guatemala).

In terms of political development, Costa Rica again stands out from its neighbors. Costa Rica has one of the oldest and most respected democracies in the hemisphere. Elections regularly take place every four years and are completely transparent; the results have never been contested by any political party. With the end of the 1948 Civil War and the promulgation of the current constitution (1949), all aspects of the country's electoral life have been in the hands of a nonpartisan elections tribunal. The members of this tribunal cannot be members of any political party and are selected by a majority vote of the Supreme Court. This body, the Supreme Elections Tribunal (TSE), is responsible for maintenance of the electoral register and all other related issues. It supervises the conduct of the electoral campaigns and the elections themselves. The final results of elections have never been challenged since its creation. Until the late 1990s, general election turnout was consistently above 80%. In 1998, it declined to 70% and then slightly further in 2002.

The 1949 constitution prohibition on the existence of a standing army has allowed successive Costa Rican governments to divert that money for social and economic programs, while other countries in the region have spent a significant proportion of their gross national product (GNP) on defense.

The end of the civil war also marked a turn in the economic development of the country. While exports were still seen as the engine of the country's economy, successive governments (of both major parties) used the powers of the state to facilitate new industries and expand welfare provisions. This model, although introduced incrementally, was employed from 1949 through the early 1980s, when a major economic crisis and the rise of a neoliberal economic paradigm brought the gradual reform of the social democratic model. In 2002, the GDP per capita, taking into account purchasing power parity (PPP), stood at $8,840 (US dollars), which was almost twice the GDP of the second most prosperous country in the region, El Salvador at $4,890.

While the vast majority of the population still favors government intervention in the economy and the provision of social goods such as health care, insurance, and telecommunications, successive governments have reduced the role of the state in these areas.

In 1989, a constitutional amendment created a constitutional branch of the Supreme Court. This court, *Sala Constitucional* or *Sala IV*, immediately ended the almost two hundred years of court inaction. The new court instead took a direct and active role in the country's political life. Indeed, the number of cases reflects the increasing activity of the court. In 1990, the first full year of the court's existence, it received 2296 cases to more than 14,000 in 2003. The court has addressed claims that affect every article of the constitution, including the rights of former presidents to seek reelection, AIDS patients to receive antiretroviral medications, and labor unions to strike.

The major areas of the economy are services, industry, and agriculture. Within these areas, tourism dominates the service sector, and microprocessors the industrial sector. In agriculture, which employs more than 20% of the work force but only produces 9% of GDP, has not kept up with the growth areas of the economy. Low world coffee prices in the past few years and world overproduction of bananas (the country's two major agricultural products) have hurt this sector.

BRUCE M. WILSON

See also Central America: History and Economic Development; Central America: International Relations; Ethnic Conflicts: Central America

References and Further Reading

Biesanz, Mavis Hiltunen, Richard Biesanz, and Karen Zubris Biesanz. *The Ticos: Culture and Social Change in Costa Rica.* Boulder, CO: Lynne Rienner Publishers, 1998.

Daling, Tjabel. *Costa Rica in Focus: A Guide to the People, Politics, and Culture.* 2d ed. Interlink Publishing Group, 2001.

Hall, Carolyn, and Héctor Pérez Brignoli. *Historical Atlas of Central America.* Norman, OK: University of Oklahoma Press, 2003.

Palmer, Steven Paul, and Ivan Molina Jimenez. *The Costa Rica Reader: History, Culture, and Politics.* Durham, NC: Duke University Press, 2004.

Wilson, Bruce M. *Costa Rica: Politics, Economics, and Democracy.* Boulder, CO: Lynne Rienner Publishers, 1998.

United Nations Development Programme. *Human Development Report 2004* (http://hdr.undp.org/)

COTE D'IVOIRE (REPUBLIC OF THE IVORY COAST)

The Republic of the Ivory Coast, or the Cote D'Ivoire, lies on the Gulf of Guinea and borders on Liberia and Guinea (west), Mali and Burkina Faso (north), and Ghana (east). Most of its about 16 million inhabitants live in the southern regions, more fertile than the semi-arid interior plains and the mountainous northwest. The climate is hot, and dry seasons alternate with shorter wet ones.

Dense forests, heavy surf, and lack of natural deep harbors discouraged foreigners until after the Berlin Conference (1884–1885), when the French enforced their claim to the region. By 1895, the Ivory Coast was incorporated with neighboring colonies into the Federation of French West Africa (AOF). The French subjected Ivoirians to the *indigénat* and forced labor. The traditional elite disappeared, coerced into lower-level civil service or, if rebellious, eliminated. A small elite of cocoa and coffee planters arose. In the early 1940s, they organized opposition to French colonial policies by forming the African Agricultural Union (SAA) and later the Democratic Party of the Ivory Coast (PDCI), a local branch of the African Democratic Rally (RDA).

Under General Charles de Gaulle, members of the AOF gradually moved toward independence. The negotiations, which lasted from 1944 to 1960, brought to the forefront Félix Houphouët-Boigny, a founder and leader of the SAA, the PDCI, and the RDA; he was also a young doctor from a family of well-to-do Baule coffee planters. At independence, he was elected president of the new republic, and for thirty-three years he almost single-handedly determined its development; doing so, he acted as president, prime minister, head of the armed forces, and head of the PDCI. He remains a controversial figure: he is the founding father to some and to others a tyrant who sold out to French neo-colonialism and whose policies generated the country's current ills.

Houphouët-Boigny wished to make the nation prosperous and unify its sixty diverse ethnic groups. Under him, the Ivory Coast was technically a democracy. However, while the constitution allowed a multiparty system, the president successfully insisted on single-party rule, lest unity be threatened. He spent profusely on education to bring Ivoirians into the twentieth century. Results of his efforts were mixed; education remained essentially French and was never synchronized with local cultural perceptions and daily needs. He also attempted to introduce modern hygiene and medicine and succeeded in lowering infant mortality and bringing about an annual 4% population growth. But health services remained inadequate, and health education did not reach the masses.

Houphouët-Boigny based his plans for economic development on agriculture and on export of agricultural products. He concentrated on increasing production and improving the infrastructure to further expand exports. He attempted to diversify agricultural production to shield the country from the instability of world prices for its main exports of cocoa and coffee. He sponsored industrial development to

manufacture imported consumer goods locally. He encouraged Burkinabe and Malian immigration to enlarge the workforce. The government became the largest investor in the economy.

Growth and political stability attracted foreign investments. The Ivory Coast's cooperation with France became increasingly intimate. The South particularly prospered, not only because of the location of the capital, Abidjan, center of export activities, but also because the main cash crops required fertile land, rain, and shade provided by forest trees. Cash crops in turn caused growth of a service economy. The gross national product (GDP) of the Ivory Coast, alone among those of West African nations, rose almost steadily for twenty years. However, the policies that produced the "Ivoirian miracle" also contained the seeds of serious problems. Ivoirian prosperity was unevenly distributed. Uncontrolled migration of northern Muslims and urban growth created widespread unemployment and conflicts. Emphasis on cash crops for export caused food shortages.

The population protested and demanded "ivoirization" of jobs held by immigrants and by the French. Left-leaning students viewed the omnipresence of the French as neo-colonialism and demanded the end of one-party rule.

In the 1980s, the economy faltered, and payment on foreign debt was halted. The government was forced to trim expenditures and adopt structural adjustments mandated by the International Monetary Fund (IMF). Unrest mushroomed: corruption in the business community was blatant; unemployment, drug use, and violent crime accelerated; mandated economic austerity pitted ethnic groups against one another in competition for scarce resources; prisons were overcrowded; and security services were inadequate. Furthermore, protests arose against the president's self-glorification, which led him to extravagant expenditures to transform his birth place, Yamoussoukro, into a monument to himself. The president responded by liberalizing the political system and permitting open elections. Voters replaced three quarters of incumbents. Yet, because of his charisma, his conciliatory tone, and his apparent willingness to listen to all grievances, Houphouët-Boigny remained popular. By the late 1980s, however, his age and health were of concern. Party unity broke as its leaders competed to succeed him. Houphouët-Boigny died in December 1993, leaving the Ivory Coast in crisis.

In accordance with constitutional provisions, Henri Konan Bedié, president of the assembly, became president and had his appointment confirmed by elections (1995), questionable though they may have been. Bedié did little to resolve economic and social crises but concentrated instead on remaining in power. To eliminate his strongest opponent, Alassane Ouattara, he promoted the concept of *ivoirité* and engineered a constitutional amendment requiring both parents of political candidates to be Ivoirian-born. He thereby legitimized latent xenophobia and ethnic rivalries.

Bedié was overthrown in 1999 by the first ever military *coup d'état* in the country's history, led by General Robert Guei. Countrywide strikes and demonstrations occurred. The IMF expressed disapproval. Guei promised a return to civilian rule and held elections (October 2000). Unexpectedly, Laurent Gbagbo, the only other candidate who had qualified for the ballot under the exclusionary laws upheld by Guei, won. Guei contested election results. Mass demonstrations followed. The army refused to support him, and Guei fled.

From the point of view of the economy, Gbagbo, president of the Second Republic of the Ivory Coast, appears to be leading the country on the way to recovery. Anxious to lure back foreign donors, his government paid back debt arrears. The IMF ended its freeze. But creditors demand reestablishment of political stability. In response, Gbagbo created a Forum of National Reconciliation and met with his main political competitors: Bedié, Guei, and Ouattara. However, the laws disenfranchising Ouattara are still on the books. The Forum of National Reconciliation is at work. Its efficacy and Gbagbo's commitment to abide by its recommendations are still in question.

L. NATALIE SANDOMIRSKY

See also Houphouët-Boigny, Félix; West Africa: History and Economic Development; West Africa: International Relations

References and Further Reading

Attébi, Dadié. *Le Défi Africain: l'Urgence d'une Alternative Économique en Côte d'Ivoire.* Paris: L'Harmattan, 1995.
Fieldhouse, D. K. *Black Africa, Economic Decolonization and Arrested Development.* London: Allen & Unwin, 1986.
Gbago, Laurent. *Côte d'Ivoire: Agir pour les Libertés.* Paris: L'Harmattan, 1991.
———. *Fonder une Nation Africaine Démocratique et Socialiste en Côte d'Ivoire.* Paris: L'Harmattan, 1999.
Gora, Arsène Ouegui. *Côte d'Ivoire: Quelle Issue pour la Transition.* Paris: L'Harmattan, 2000.
Jackson, Robert, and Carl G. Rosenberg. *Personal Rule in Black Africa.* Berkeley, CA: University of California Press, 1982.
Loucou, Jean-Noël. *Le Multipartisme en Côte d'Ivoire.* Abidjan: Editions Neter, 1992.
N'Da, Paul. *Le Drame Démocratique Africain sur la Scène en Côte d'Ivoire.* Paris: L'Harmattan, 1999.

COUNTERINSURGENCY

Counterinsurgency and National Security

"Counterinsurgency" is defined as the measures and strategies, both military and political, that a government employs to defeat an armed resistance from within society. Armed conflicts between a government and a domestic opposition group are commonly known as asymmetric or low-intensity warfare because the combatants possess an unequal level of capabilities. In actual practice, armies have utilized the techniques related to counterinsurgency for centuries. Yet, the concept of counterinsurgency as a major feature of national security policy was first introduced in 1961, when President John F. Kennedy initiated an effort within the United States defense establishment to develop a new strategic doctrine that would present an effective response to the threat posed by unconventional forces or guerilla armies. This was deemed necessary to contain the various revolutionary or "national liberation" movements that endangered regimes in the developing world that were friendly to US interests.

The intellectual precedent for this doctrine was to be found in the strategies employed by the British forces in Malaya and the Philippines during the period 1948 through 1956. These operations emphasized the notion of "limited warfare," in which the application of military force played a minimal role, and political and economic reform programs were implemented to foster support for the government among the local population. In this manner, the British and local leaders were able to isolate the insurgents and occupy the "center of gravity," or the basis of political legitimacy that rebel groups must capture to succeed.

However, in many developing countries, counterinsurgency has often been associated with political repression and violations of human rights. Governments in Third World countries that have been faced with a lack of broad popular support have frequently resorted to the use of force to suppress dissent, in which large numbers of regime opponents and suspected collaborators are imprisoned or killed. Such actions became a central feature of the "national security state" in many Asian and Latin American countries that experienced mass social unrest or radical opposition movements. The prominent role assigned to the security forces in some cases has given them a position of influence that has brought them into conflict with civilian authorities.

The application of counterinsurgency doctrine became especially prominent during US involvement in the Vietnam War, in which civilian administrators were deployed to organize the rural population against guerilla activities. However, the success of this program was limited due to the emphasis of US strategy on overwhelming enemy forces with conventional firepower rather than building support for the government of South Vietnam. Counterinsurgency as a central feature of national security strategy enjoyed a resurgence during the Reagan presidency, as the administration promoted a foreign policy doctrine of covert or indirect intervention against alleged Soviet-supported movements in Central America, such as the Farabundo Marti National Liberation Front (FMLN) in El Salvador. This policy ended with the resolution of Salvadoran civil war in the early 1990s.

Counterinsurgency and Strategy

The circumstances for counterinsurgency arise as a result of problems that are frequently found in developing nations. These problems are often rooted in the gradual transition to modern social systems. In the initial stages of economic expansion, the process of industrialization and migration to urban centers replaces traditional forms of production such as subsistence agriculture. As certain segments of society benefit from economic growth before others, the resulting income inequality produces tensions between social classes. Many regimes in postcolonial nations have inherited weak institutions that are ill equipped to resolve disputes between competing interests. Therefore, discontent is often expressed outside of established political channels in the form of collective protests. More severe forms of internal uprisings take place where disenfranchised groups openly challenge the incumbent regime.

Insurgent movements in these countries are therefore fueled and motivated by political and economic conditions that seriously affect the quality of life of the average person in society. This assumes that a certain proportion of the population actively opposes the government and may be willing to take up arms to bring about a drastic change in the political system. Therefore, an effective counterinsurgency strategy must first attempt to determine the specific sources of popular discontent. The sole use of military force may reduce the immediate threat to stability but will not eliminate the primary causes of dissatisfaction that instigated the rebellion in the first place. Further,

an armed response may only reinforce resentment of the government's policies. Because the main goal of the insurgent group is to survive while garnering a social and material base of support, the regime is under increasing pressure to implement reform. On the other hand, if it pursues direct action against the insurgents without efforts toward improving the welfare of its citizens, it may only provoke a reaction that intensifies the conflict.

The Future of Counterinsurgency

The importance of counterinsurgency in national security policy has declined significantly in the post-Cold War era, as the ideological struggles that inspired many insurgencies have gradually subsided and as numerous civil wars in the developing world have come to an end. In addition, the interventions and peacekeeping operations that took place during the 1990s typically did not involve insurgent movements. Yet, some domains of recent internal conflict have seen the persistence of counterinsurgency exercises, such as exemplified by offensives against the Revolutionary Armed Forces in Colombia, the Kurdish Worker's Party in Turkey, and the Maoists in Nepal. At the same time, combatants in different types of conflicts may resort to guerilla tactics even if they do not pursue the objectives of classical guerilla warfare. This describes the conditions presently faced by the coalition forces in postwar Iraq, in which opposition is directed at terrorizing citizens and officials of the interim administration rather than establishing a new government. The adaptation of counterinsurgency strategy to new types of warfare must include the investment of resources in the reconstruction of civil services to convince the Iraqi population that the new government represents its interests.

JASON E. STRAKES

References and Further Reading

Galula, David. *Counterinsurgency Warfare: Theory and Practice*: Praeger, 1964.

Joes, Andrew James. *Resisting Rebellion: The History and Politics of Counterinsurgency*: The University Press of Kentucky, 2004.

Maechling Jr., Charles. "Counterinsurgency: The First Ordeal by Fire." In *Low Intensity Warfare: Counterinsurgency, Proinsurgency, and Antiterrorism in the Eighties*. Michael T. Klare and Peter Kornbluh, eds. New York: Pantheon Books, 1987.

Metz, Steven. *"Counterinsurgency: Strategy and the Phoenix of American Capability."* Carlisle Barracks,

PA: Strategic Studies Institute, US Army War College, 1995.

Snow, Donald M. *Distant Thunder: Patterns of Conflict in the Developing World*, 2d ed. Armonk, NY: M. E. Sharpe, 1997.

Tomes, Robert R. "Relearning Counterinsurgency Warfare." *Parameters* (Spring 2004): 16–2.

COUNTERTRADE

"Countertrade" is a term that covers a wide variety of commercial methods to engage in reciprocal trade. One partner may supply goods, services, and technology of economic value to the other partner for a return exchange of an agreed amount of goods and other things of value. Bartering is probably the oldest and best known example of countertrade. A formal definition of countertrade is given by Burnett (1999). This term also means a relationship between two trading partners that "counters" any imbalance in trade undertaken by them.

Countertrade is sometimes used as a form of currency exchange, to collect a debt or a means of finance. For example, as a form of currency exchange, a multinational corporation (MNC) may wish to sell breeding cattle stock to a local buyer with ¥ currency since the local buyer may not have US dollars (USD). The MNC can now buy sugar using ¥ currency and then sell the sugar to a food manufacturer for USD.

As a means of collecting a debt, the local buyer may have no USD to pay the MNC. The MNC, however, may accept payment in ¥ currency and then with the ¥ currency buy foreign goods and resell these goods in the MNC's own market for USD. As a means of finance, a local buyer may require the MNC to buy local goods as an offset to reduce or restrict the flow of scarce USD out of the local buyer's country. At the same time, the retained funds are used to finance the local industry's growth and development.

Forms of Countertrade

"Barter transactions" involve the direct exchange of goods or services between the MNC and local buyer, and normally no exchange of money or the use of third parties is involved. "Pure" or "true barter" is a simple exchange of goods, whereas "valued barter" refers to some value put on the exchanged goods because of the inequality of values of goods and services being exchanged. However, it is sometimes difficult to deal with two parties who may have similar "wants." Barter arrangements for which suppliers of homogeneous goods, such as oil, exchange those goods for mineral ores to save transport costs are called "swaps." Swaps are also used by countries in which both the government and the private sector face large debt burdens. In such cases, the arrangement involves the swapping of debt for something else, such as other debt, equity, products, nature preservation, and education.

"Counterpurchase" is the most common form of countertrade in which an MNC provides goods in one contract and undertakes to purchase goods for export from a local buyer in a second contract. These are two independent contracts. This reciprocal purchase or supply of goods and services is linked by a "universal" agreement. Two contracts are necessary because the delivery performance may depend on some future event, such as a crop harvest. Therefore, it is useful to have the timing of the performance of each of the contracts "unlinked." Since the goods are often not of equal value, some amount of cash is usually involved.

"Compensation" denotes partial exchange. An MNC receives payment either in full or in part from the local buyer in the form of goods to make up for the shortfall in value. Thus, a "buyback" or "reverse compensation" involves an MNC that provides industrial machinery to a partner in a foreign country with the commitment to purchase the goods produced by these machines. For example, the American clothing manufacturer Levi-Strauss sold equipment and know-how to a plant in Hungary and also agreed to buy a share of the production as payment. When the plant came into full production, Levi-Strauss took 60% of the plant's output. The terms "offtake" and "industrial cooperation" also describe such agreements. Another example could be the sale of a turnkey oil refinery that is paid for by the resultant refined oil. The word "turnkey" means literally the handing over of the keys to the refinery's local owners, who then begin production at the turn of the key. Most buyback terms often contain a most favoured customer (MFC) clause explaining that the local buyer will grant the MNC the most favoured price for the same goods when compared to another purchaser.

Arrangements called "offsets" are usually found in defense-related industries where the sales are frequently of high-priced items, such as aircraft and armaments. The arrangement is designed to "offset" the negative effects of the large purchases from abroad. It is also a feature of these arrangements to require that certain parts of the purchased product be produced or assembled in the purchasing country, called a "direct offset." The offset is "indirect" when the MNC invests in unrelated business, and a "mixed arrangement" refers to when there is a combination of direct and indirect offsets.

"Mixed agreements" include transactions known as "switch trading" or "clearing accounts." It is a two-country trade-and-payment agreement. The value of goods exported from country A to B is not actually paid for but is credited to A on a clearing account and vice versa as goods are shipped from B to A. An account is "cleared" when traders owe nothing to each other. Usually, outstanding balances and interest payments are cleared or settled at the end of each accounting year. Where the goods have a readily accessible commodity market, such as for oil, the exporter may engage a dealer to sell the goods on behalf of the exporter. However, where no commodity markets exist for the countertraded goods, the MNC may be unable to obtain payment from the local buyer. This is because the buying country may not permit the transfer of hard currency that it is lacking or because such funds are "blocked" by the government. However, the local buyer's country may have a trade surplus with a third country on a country-to-country clearing agreement. Hence, this credit surplus may be used as a way of paying the MNC for the goods.

"Switch" occurs after deliveries of the products begin. With commodities having no ready markets, discounts of up to 40% are given to trading houses or switch dealers. These trading companies maintain their own private networks that offer a market for discounted countertraded products. In general, switch trading and bartering have been used as legal methods to avoid currency controls and take advantage of bilateral trade arrangements between two countries.

Rationales and Experiences

The trend toward countertrade has been spurred on not only by the rise of high trade protection caused by a decline in confidence in the world trading system but also by a growing debt crisis among less developed countries (LDCs), contracting exports, a decline in foreign exchange earnings, and an inability to service foreign debt commitments. In addition, countries need to maintain existing market shares as well as penetrate new markets.

Among LDCs, while the objective of sustainable growth is a necessary one, that of earning "hard" stable currency seems to be a better way to foster growth as much as to reduce trade deficits. In this way, the economy will be able to maintain or even increase employment, reduce the technology gap, and stabilize prices of export commodities. For developed countries, however, condoning countertrade will mean the maintenance of sales volumes, market shares, and profit levels in international trade. To prevent LDCs from defaulting on their debts, developed countries may also assist LDCs to trade their way out of their financial problems by engaging in countertrade.

The experience of practitioners in Asia has suggested that countertrade may be a useful market development tactic rather than a problem to be avoided. Countertrade may be the answer to both cheaper imports and increased exports. It is unclear whether countertrade has led to an increase in business among developing countries. Rather, it seems that economic conditions may encourage growth in South–South trade through countertrade. This method of trade offers opportunities to enter new markets and to consolidate positions in old markets.

Commentators, however, are unsure of the long-term benefits of countertrading. Countertrade may put off the need by LDCs to correct poor export performance and may delay internal microeconomic and macroeconomic reforms. Countertrade also does not expand trade between developed and developing countries or make the economies more dynamic. Countertrade is backward in its return to bilateralism disguised as a modern system, in restricting choice, and compartmentalising markets. Countertrade is an inefficient form of trade. Many industrialized countries have condemned countertrade as a deviation from the true principles of the World Trade Organization (WTO). The restrictive clauses and conditions in countertrade contracts do not give LDCs any better control of their trade. When confronted with compensation agreements, MNCs may refuse rather than make offers to accept contract terms they are unable to fulfill.

Countertrade may work against attempts to modernize the economies of LDCs. It distorts the comparative advantage of countries that practice it, but at the same time it sustains and perpetuates inefficient and uncompetitive industries in countries that would otherwise perish. In enforcing a countertrade deal, a local buyer may quote unrealistically high prices for local goods, offer poor quality goods, or foist goods on the trade partner that are difficult to sell.

In prospect, countertrade is likely to be a longer term phenomenon than initially expected and will persist over the next few decades. Variations in defining countertrade and the scarcity of published data make it difficult to estimate the volume of countertrade. The International Monetary Fund (IMF) and WTO estimate that only 5% of world trade comes within countertrade arrangements, whereas the Organization for Economic Cooperation and Development (OECD) puts it at 8% of world trade.

Whatever its commercial value, the upsurge in countertrade has not resulted from commercial advantage but rather as a pragmatic response of world commerce to the financial crises of LDCs. Importing activities may be sustained only by guaranteeing the replacement of hard currency within a relatively short time. Moreover, most LDCs use countertrade as a temporary means of protectionism.

An Evaluation

Countertrade is a contradiction. Countertrade is in a state of evolution, and many governments are constantly reassessing their own programs. However, with the liquidity crisis in the world monetary system, the countertrade phenomenon may well continue into the twenty-first century given concerns over unemployment, poverty, and overpopulation. This form of trading seems to depend on the amount of natural resources that a country has at its disposal, its creditworthiness, nature of political system, and the policies of the government in using countertrade as a means of developing the country's economy.

It is recognised that countertrade may not be the most desirable form of international trade. Countertrade sits uneasily with the concept of an open, cash-based, and nondiscriminatory trading system that the WTO and OECD aim to promote. There are few laws in the United States that are specifically concerned with countertrade. The United Kingdom and Germany view countertrade as potentially distorting trade but have refrained from intervention in private sector decisions. On the other hand, France has actively intervened in countertrade.

The growth in international trade by way of barter and countertrade in the foreseeable future would depend on the price of major exports from LDCs and on the performance of the world economy. Where the price of LDCs major exports stabilize and there is growth in world trade, the consequent growth in foreign exchange reserves will enable many LDCs to return to their usual trading patterns. However, if the world economy were to be highly protected with continued recession and other adverse economic ills, then countertrade may expand. Whatever eventuates, countertrade will remain a permanent feature of international business transactions.

Countertrade is a deviation from the principles of the WTO system. This one-to-one trading is an antithesis to the multilateral (one-to-many) nondiscriminatory transaction of a free and liberalized trade regime. International trade based on most favoured nation (MFN) principles presumes a "level playing field" in which parties trade on an equal footing. However, this principle is unworkable in the light of inherent inequalities in resources and economic development. Managed trade may be more realistic than simply relying on MFN principles. While countertrade may distort trade, it is used by developed and developing countries because its short-term benefits are more attractive than its long-term detriments. Countertrade, however, is not a solution to the systemic problems of international trade.

GEORGE CHO

See also Free Market Economy; Trade Policies and Development; Trading Patterns, Global

References and Further Reading

Burnett, R. *Law of International Business Transactions*, 2 ed. Sydney, Australia: The Federation Press, 1999.

Islam, M. R. *International Trade Law*. Sydney, Australia: LBC Information Services, 1999.

Liesch, P. W. "International Countertrade." *International Transactions: Trade and Investment, Law, and Finance*, K. C. D. M. Wilde and M. R. Islam, eds. Sydney, Australia: Law Book Company, 1993.

London Countertrade Roundtable (LCR). 2004. Home Page: www.londoncountertrade.org

Pryles, M., J. Waincymer, and M. Davies. *International Trade Law. Comments and Materials*. Sydney, Australia: LBC Information Services, 1996.

Schmitthoff, C. M. *Schmitthoff's Export Trade: The Law and Practice of International Trade*, 9th ed. London: Stevens & Sons, 1990.

UNCITRAL. *Legal Guide on International Countertrade Transactions*. New York: United Nations, 1993.

COUP D'ÉTAT

The *Coup d'État* in Third World Politics

A "*coup d'état*" is a term that refers to the sudden and illegal transfer of political power from one individual or group to another. Specifically, it is brought about by the abrupt intervention of the armed forces in politics and the takeover of government conduct and national institutions by military elites. While most modern states employ a segment of their societies to defend their security against foreign or domestic threats, in certain political settings, armies have often abandoned their customary protective role. The interference of the military in politics has been a most frequent occurrence in developing nations of Third World countries and is an especially common characteristic of the political history of Africa and Latin

America. In some regions, *coups d'état* continue to represent the ongoing crisis of political development. Between the mid-1980s and the year 2001, there were a total of forty-one attempted and twenty-one successful coups in the countries of Sub-Saharan Africa alone. Scholars who study military *coups d'état* seek to determine which factors lead to the transfer of political authority by force and under what circumstances military regimes endure or eventually return the reigns of government to civilian hands.

Common Causes of the *Coup d'État*

Early studies that sought to identify the causes of *coups d'état* emphasized the characteristics of the military as an institution. This was based largely on the assumptions about Third World nations made by modernization theory. These authors argued that while the instruments of government in developing states were still in their primitive stages, militaries possessed a relatively high level of organization and efficiency that afforded greater degrees of influence and administrative capacity. Therefore, when formal political institutions were seen as weak or ineffectual in managing social and economic crises, military officers were provided with the necessary motivation to attempt to replace the civilian leadership. Some observers even suggested that *coups d'état* were a sign of progress, and they would take the place of traditional sources of authority and further the goals of development. However, subsequent analyses have demonstrated that the character or strength of the military alone does not adequately explain why *coups d'état* take place.

The causes of military coups have also been related to the overall political environments of countries. These theories have pointed to how the condition of a nation's political culture strongly influences the tendency of its military to challenge the existing order. This includes variables such as the degree of popular legitimacy enjoyed by the civilian regime, the size and scope of political parties, or the overall strength of civil society. Thus, the lower the level of stable representative government, the higher the likely incidence of successful *coups d'état*. Similarly, scholars have reasoned that political institutions in postcolonial societies are often unable to adequately channel or absorb the instability created by expanded participation and therefore require the resumption of strong centralized rule facilitated by the military.

More recent studies argue that despite their professional orientation, militaries possess corporate and pecuniary interests just as does any social organization. The amount of pay or benefits received by the armed services give them a direct stake in decisions regarding budget allotments for defense and national security. Once in power, military regimes have often sought to increase salaries and spending for facilities and weapons procurement to enhance their prestige. At the same time, armies may possess different levels of influence over elite policy making that conditions their propensity to intervene in politics. Therefore, when the actions of the existing government threaten or impinge upon their basic needs or values, officers may seek to maneuver the outcome of political contests or interfere directly in the process to restore their position or status.

Above all, the single greatest precipitating factor for military intervention in the developing world has been prolonged economic downturn accompanied by inflation, widespread unemployment, and social unrest. In Latin America, mass opposition and the presence of the radical Left often instigated *coup d'état* attempts on the part of officers who feared the leveling of traditional society. In these circumstances, problems such as official corruption within civilian institutions or intense agitation by organized labor and dissident groups have presented military leaders with a justification to respond to their alleged threat to elite values or the national welfare.

Political Development and Outcomes of *Coups d'État*

The primary concern in determining the impact of a *coup d'état* on a nation's political climate and economic welfare is whether militaries act as a moderating force in the service of traditional institutions or seek to entirely remake the social system. While some military regimes have successfully maintained their hold on power long after the conditions that inspired the coup have passed, other interventions have been short-lived, in which they simply facilitated a restoration of order through which civilian leaders quickly resumed control. The extent to which military regimes are able to govern effectively and the consequences for stability and economic development are dependent on both the goals and orientation of the military leaders. Officers who have led a *coup d'état* have often attempted to institutionalize their regimes over time by establishing an official political party and extending membership to the general population. These efforts at popular mobilization have also been accompanied by attempts at promoting an ideology that serves to legitimize their rule. Yet, the historical record indicates that military leaderships often have a limited ability to effectively manage the tasks of government, particularly in the area of economic policy. While a few military regimes, such as in Chile, Indonesia, and South Korea, have presided over steady growth, the majority of African and Latin American *juntas* have failed to correct the economic ailments that they alleged to remedy. This is due not only because of the absence of technical expertise among the military leadership but also because of a general lack of experience with accommodation and compromise that is a necessary aspect of civilian administration. It is this problem that commonly leads to the eventual decision of *coup* leaders to step down and return to the barracks.

JASON E. STRAKES

References and Further Reading

Clapham, Christopher, and George Philip. "The Political Dilemmas of Military Regimes." *The Political Dilemmas of Military Regimes*, Christopher Clapham and George Philip, eds. Barnes and Noble: 1985.

Finer, S. E. *The Man on Horseback*. London: Penguin Books, 1988.

Karsten, Peter. "The *Coup d'État* in Competitive Democracies: Its Appropriateness, Its Causes, and Its Avoidance." *Military and Society: Civil-Military Relations*, Peter Karsten, ed. New York: Garland Publishing, 1998.

Luttwak, Edward. *Coup d'État: A Practical Handbook*. Cambridge, MA: Harvard University Press, 1979.

Maniruzzaman, Talukder. *Military Withdrawal from Politics: A Comparative Study*. Cambridge, MA: Ballinger Publishing, 1987.

McGowan, Patrick J. "African Military *Coups d'État*, 1956–2001." *The Journal of Modern African Studies* 41, no. 3 (2003).

CROATIA

Location

The Republic of Croatia lies in southeastern Europe and stretches in a peculiar arc in the northwest corner of the Balkan Peninsula. Open to the Mediterranean Sea, Croatia serves as a gateway to Central Europe.

With a land area of 35,133 square miles (56,542 square kilometers), Croatia is bordered by Slovenia (north), Hungary (northeast), Serbia-Montenegro (east and south), and Bosnia-Herzegovina (south) and opens to the Adriatic Sea (west). The population of 4,496,869 (July 2004) consists of Croats (89.6%), Serbs (4.5%), Bosniaks (0.5%), and Hungarians (0.4%). Others minorities include those who are Slovene, Czech, Roma, Albanian, and Montenegrin (5%). The capital city of Zagreb has a population of 779,145 (2001).

Land and Climate

Croatia is a country of contrasts. In the northeast, the Pannonian plain is the main farming region. The Dinaric Alps, an area of densely wooded mountains and highlands, runs northwest-southeast through the center. Finally, Dalmatia, a rugged coastal region along the Adriatic shore, includes 1,185 islands. Approximately one-third of Croatia is forested; timber is a major export. Croatia's main rivers are the Sava, Drava, and Danube.

A continental climate prevails inland and around Zagreb, with hot summers and cold, snowy winters. A Mediterranean climate with mild winters characterizes the Adriatic coast.

History Until 1945

The Croats descend from Slavic tribes who settled in the Roman province of Pannonia during the seventh century. Early in the tenth century, the Croats developed a powerful *Triune Kingdom* that included Croatia, Slavonia, Dalmatia, parts of Istria and Bosnia, and Hungary later in the century.

The Croatian territories were coveted by their powerful neighbors. In 1526, following the Battle of Mohacs, most of Croatia became Ottoman, while the northwestern part became Austrian. Following the treaties of Karlowitz (1699) and Passrowitz (1718), the Habsburg established its sovereignty over the country. In 1868, one year after the establishment of the dual Austro-Hungarian monarchy, Croatia-Slavonia became an autonomous Hungarian crown land.

With the collapse of the Austrian-Hungarian Empire in 1918, the Croatian territories were united in the Kingdom of Serbs, Croats, and Slovenes, and that region became Yugoslavia (1929). Serbs ruled the state in a heavily centralized manner, ignoring the Croatian's request for federalism. In 1939, the Yugoslav government allowed the formation of an autonomous entity comprising Croatia, Dalmatia, and part of Bosnia-Herzegovina. In 1946, Croatia became one of the six republics that constituted the Federal People's Republic of Yugoslavia.

Croatia's Developments After 1945

After 1945, Croatia was granted the status of a federal republic, and the Croatian people were recognized as one of the five constitutive peoples of the Yugoslav federation. Under Josip Broz Tito's leadership, the Yugoslav Communist Party ruled the country.

During the 1960s, two contradictory tendencies emerged as the Communist Party retained complete authority over the institutions while the Constitution of 1963 granted decentralization and economical reforms (self-management). Croatian intellectuals denounced the federal system as a centralized one in the hands of a single party. They also resented Serbia's decisive influence in the ruling of the state. In 1971, students organized a series of mass protests called the Croatian Spring. Intellectuals demanded recognition of a separate Croatian language and more control over Croatian affairs. Tito reacted firmly and ordered a crackdown.

At that time Croatia enjoyed a relative prosperity due to tourism along the Adriatic coast, a popular destination for travelers from all over Europe. However, around one-third of the Croatian state income was taken away to subsidize the development of the southern regions, such as in Macedonia and Kosovo. Furthermore, although 80% of Yugoslavia's foreign trade went through Croatian ports, Croatia itself received only a small share of this income.

The conjunction of relative wealth and frustrated national aspirations partly explain Croatia's leading role in the disintegration of Yugoslavia. In January 1990, the Croatian delegates followed the Slovenes and walked away from the Congress of the Communist Party, one of the pillars of the Yugoslav system. On June 25, 1991, Croatia proclaimed its independence. In 1992, it was recognized as independent by the European Union (EU) and was admitted to the United Nations (UN) the same year.

The development of Croatia since 1991 has been challenged by two issues. First, the authoritarian regime of Franco Tudjman (1990–1991) isolated and compromised Croatia. As former general and leader of the Croatian Democratic Union (HDZ), Tudjman was elected president in 1990 following multiparty elections. Strongly nationalist, he exalted Croatia's past and enacted constitutional measures against the 12% Serbs minority who, with the military assistance from Belgrade, aggravated the already tense situation.

Second, the transition toward democracy was accomplished through two brutal wars (1991–1995). The Yugoslav National Army, following instructions of President Milošević, supported the Serbs of Croatia (region of Krainija). In 1992, the UN's intervention froze the front, but Croatia lost more than 30% of its territory to the Serbs. Then, as war erupted in neighboring Bosnia, Tudjman's regime encouraged Bosnian Croats. In 1995, Tudjman, along with Milošević and President Izetbegovic of Bosnia-Herzegovina, signed the Dayton Agreement under United States' supervision. In 1998, the last Serb-held lands were reunited with lands of Croatia.

Tudjman's death in 1999 and the election of a moderate government in 2000 gave Croatia the chance for a new start. First, under the leadership of President Stipe Mesic (reelected in 2005), structural reforms have been undertaken, the powers of the presidency have been curtailed, and the parliament assumes greater responsibility. Civil rights, freedom of speech, and independent media are respected.

Second, Croatian foreign policy is driven by a major objective: integration within the EU, which it joined in 2004. Croatia is also a NATO aspirant and member of the Adriatic Charter signed with Albania, Macedonia, and the United States in 2003. It has participated in UN activities, including contributing troops to UN operations in Sierra Leone, Ethiopia, and Kashmir. In 2001, it also sent a military police unit to Afghanistan, though Croatia refused to send troops to Iraq in 2003.

Croatia, however, has to undo the tragic legacy of the 1991–1995 wars. The key issue has been the implementation of the Dayton Agreement, which was stalled by Tudjman's regime. Since 2000, the questions of refugee's return, restitution of property, and negotiations with the war tribunal in La Hague have progressed although results remain inconclusive. Regional cooperation is growing as Bosnia-Herzegovina, Slovenia, and Serbia-Montenegro have reestablished close commercial ties, but borders issues remain unsolved.

Current Economy

Croatia has an economy based on services (46.2% in 2002), while industry represents 25.4% and agriculture 13.2%. The country's major products include chemicals, petroleum, ships, and textiles, as well as cement and steel. Zagreb is the largest manufacturing center. The natural resources comprise oil, coal, and bauxite.

Like most post-Communist states, Croatia suffers from a "substantial gray economy" and corruption. The transition has been difficult and damaged by the wars (1991–1995). From 1989 to 1993, the gross domestic product (GDP) plunged 40.5%. After 1995, tourism, a key industry, rebounded and the economy briefly recovered, only to fall into a recession in 1999. A year later, the economy again rallied, growing 2.9% in 2000 to reach 5.2% in 2002. Industrial production shows a healthy growth of 3.9% (2004 est.) as does the GDP at 4.3% (2004 est.). Croatia's major trading partners are Italy, Germany, Austria, France, and Russia.

Croatia is facing several issues that include structural unemployment (19.5% in 2004) and an insufficient amount of economic reforms aggravated by public resistance from people who fear a cut of social benefits. The inefficient judiciary system also seems unable to resolve long-standing property rights issues. The main concern remains the country's rising foreign debt. Global debt at $21.5 billion (US dollars) in November 2003 increased 40% from 2002 levels. The debt was expected to have further increased to $23 billion for the end of 2004, equivalent to 75% of GDP.

Uneven economic growth and uncertainty about the future can explain why the nationalist Croatian Democratic Union won the November 2003 parliamentary elections. However, new Prime Minister Ivo Sanader claims that his party is now moderate and will pursue a policy of democratization and reforms.

NADINE AKHUND

See also Bosnia and Herzegovina; Milošević, Slobodan; Montenegro; Serbia; Tito, Josip Broz (Marshall Tito); Tudjman, Franjo; Yugoslavia

References and Further Reading

Crampton, Richard J. *The Balkans since the Second World War*. New York: Longman, 2002.
Cuvalo, Ante. *The Croatian National Movement 1966–1972*. New York: Columbia University Press, 1990.
Djokic, Dejan. *Yugoslavism. Histories of a Failed Idea 1918–1992*. Madison, WI: University of Wisconsin Press, 2003.
Goldstein, Ivo. *Croatia. A History*. Montreal: McGill-Queen's University Press, 1999.
Jelavich, Barbara. *History of the Balkans*. Cambridge: Cambridge University Press, 1983.
Lampe, John, R. *Yugoslavia as History*. Cambridge: Cambridge University Press, 1996.
Magas, Branka, and Zanic, Ivo. *The War in Croatia and Bosnia-Herzegovina 1991–1995*. London and Portland, OR: 2001.
Ramet, Sabrina. *Nationalism and Federalism in Yugoslavia, 1962–1991*. Bloomington, IN: Indiana University Press, 1992.

CUBAN REVOLUTION

One of the most significant events during the Cold War occurred ninety miles from the shores of the United States on the island of Cuba. In 1959, the Cuban Revolution threatened the ideological, political, strategic, and economic hegemony of the United States in the Western Hemisphere by challenging the historical relationship existing between the island and the United States. This relationship primarily involved an economic nexus of dependent development that distorted the nation's internal political and social processes. The historical roots of this relationship for the twentieth century originated with the end of the Spanish–American War (1898).

After the war, US capital penetration of the lucrative sugar industry accelerated and intensified, continuing a process well underway by the end of the nineteenth century. Sugar became Cuba's primary export, with the US market its principal destination. Economic dependency on one export product not only contributed to the social dislocation experienced by Cuba's peasantry but also left the nation's political and social development exposed to the vagaries of the world market. Internal political, social, and economic development experienced frequent disruption coinciding with the boom/bust cycle of the dependent economy. The Platt Amendment, which was enacted in 1901 by the US Congress and subsequently incorporated into the first Cuban Constitution, allowed the United States to directly intervene militarily in the political life of the country to achieve stability and assure its citizens continued economic dominance.

While the Platt Amendment contributed to the development of Cuban nationalism, US capital penetration caused the Cuban elite to enter the political arena by frustrating their participation in the economy. Politics became a battleground for contending factions since the winners had access to government revenues. This situation contributed to instability, corruption, and repeated US interventions. The world depression of 1930 intensified the recurring internal political, social, and economic crises that the nation experienced since independence. While workers organized labor strikes that the government harshly repressed, the middle class and intellectuals also organized against the existing state of things. The government's inability to contain the increasing political instability and violence led to the loss of US support, which opened the door to the Revolution of 1933.

The revolutionary nationalist government quickly abrogated the Platt Amendment and instituted major political, social, and economic reforms for the benefit of the working class, peasants, women, and other previously neglected social groups. These measures not only alienated the entrenched conservative Cuban elite but, most importantly, its US political and economic allies. In 1934, the rapid unraveling of the revolutionary government created a power vacuum that the military, led by Fulgencio Batista y Zaldívar, filled. Batista ruled the destiny of the island through puppet presidents from 1934 to 1940 and directly as president from 1940 to 1944. The United States, secure in its hegemony over the island, abrogated the Platt Amendment in 1934. In 1940, the government promulgated a new constitution that contained progressive political, social, and economic clauses that became standards for judging the performance of politicians and governments. The island's socioeconomic development continued to depend on sugar exports as World War II stimulated demand for the product. There was an uneven distribution of the wealth generated by sugar production and export as some sectors of the society benefited while others languished in poverty.

In 1944, Batista allowed elections to be held, which brought Dr. Ramón Grau San Martín and his *Auténtico* party to power. The *Auténtico* period, which lasted from 1944 to 1952, ushered in an episode of unparalleled political corruption. In 1947, the *Ortodoxo* party, which represented a radical nationalism and espoused a program of social and economic reform, emerged as a response to this corruption. Batista launched a *coup d'état* in 1952 against the *Auténticos*, which brought him to power a second time. Lacking popular support, various opposition groups emerged against his rule as corruption continued and the economy remained open to the vagaries of the boom/bust cycles associated with monoculture. In 1953, a young *Ortodoxo*, Fidel Castro, organized a revolt against the government. Although the raid on the Moncada Barracks on July 26 failed, it gave a name to the movement and brought Castro to national attention. His defense during his trail condemned the trajectory of Cuban national history and presented a reform program. In prison, Castro continued to plot the overthrow of Batista's government. Released during a general amnesty for all political prisoners in 1955, Castro left Cuba for Mexico and formally organized the July 26th Movement, which issued a manifesto calling for a revolution against Batista, and the Cuban Revolution was born.

In Mexico, Castro met Ernesto (Che) Guevara, with whom he planned the guerrilla struggle against Batista. Purchasing the yacht *Granma* in 1956, Castro, along with eighty-one men, left Mexico on November 25 to invade the island. On December 2, they landed in Oriente Province and, a few days later, had a disastrous encounter with the Cuban army in which all but twelve men were killed or captured. The small band headed for the Sierra Maestra, where they regrouped and organized the guerrilla movement. The numerous victories against government forces bolstered the July 26th Movement's popularity as rural and urban opposition increased against Batista's rule. In February 1957, Castro had an important interview with Herbert Matthews, a *New York Times* reporter, which presented him to a US public while refuting the government's claim of his death. That same year, Batista had trouble maintaining power as junior naval officers revolted against him. He alienated the United States when he utilized US-supplied military equipment to crush the revolt.

In March 1958, the United States suspended arms shipments to the government. Batista lost the support of the middle class, and the Catholic Church called for a coalition government, but the general continued in his intransigence against the social forces engulfing the country. In April, a general strike called by the July 26th Movement failed, but the movement continued its success in the countryside. In May, Batista launched a general offensive against the guerrillas in the Sierra Maestra, which met with stiff opposition and successes by Castro's forces. The US government saw this situation with alarm as it feared a victory by the July 26th Movement, which would bring Castro to power. The US embassy negotiated with Batista in an attempt to stave off this outcome. By December, the rebels were on the outskirts of Havana, and on January 1, 1959, Batista and his allies abandoned the island, seeking refuge in Miami. Castro's entrance into the capital one week later ushered in a new page in Cuban history as the Cuban Revolution triumphed over the corrupt and discredited social, political, and economic elite that had ruled the country since independence.

The triumph of the revolution, with its radical nationalist ideology, soon alienated Cuba's historical patron, the United States, during a period of heightened Cold War fears of the spread of communism into the Western Hemisphere. The revolution's leadership sought to remedy the nation's underdevelopment by concentrating on a radical land reform policy, codified in the Agrarian Reform Law of 1959, which expropriated the large landed estates that belonged to the traditional elite, allies of US political and economic interests. In the Cold War environment, this policy appeared to be a step toward communism, a fear further heightened by the subsequent nationalization of the economy in 1960. Although this nationalization had popular support, as US economic penetration had angered many, it polarized the business elite and sectors of the middle class and came up against US economic interests. The one event that symbolized the growing radicalization of the revolution was when the Cuban government demanded that Russian oil should be processed by US-owned oil refineries. When they refused, the government confiscated the US-owned oil companies, creating a rift with the US government, which suspended the sugar quota. The Cuban government retaliated by seizing all US property and continuing its radical nationalization of numerous national and foreign industries. The Soviet Union stepped into the vacuum of deteriorating trade relationships between the United States and Cuba when it signed a trade agreement with Cuba, which not only provided credit to the nation but also ensured a market for the nation's sugar exports. Subsequently, the Soviet Union provided military and technical assistance as well as cultural missions to Cuba, further heightening tensions between the island nation and the United States, ultimately leading to a break in diplomatic relations in January 1961.

The Cuban revolutionary nationalists sought an alternative egalitarian society free from cultural, political, and economic dependence on the United States. To achieve their goals, the revolutionary government instituted a series of measures and reforms in education, health, housing, and labor relations. Mass mobilization of workers, peasants, students, and women contributed to the implementation of these measures and reforms. Perhaps the most successful campaign was the Literacy Campaign of 1961 that sought to eliminate illiteracy in the Cuban population. The radical direction of the revolution influenced the decision by many of the wealthy upper class and sectors of the middle class to flee to Miami, Florida. With the support and financial assistance of the Central Intelligence Agency (CIA), this group of expatriates soon coalesced into an opposition force that, in April 1961, invaded Cuba and met defeat at the Bay of Pigs. This invasion demonstrated that in the name of anti-communism, the United States intended to overthrow the Cuban Revolution, restore the traditional elite, and roll back its social, political, and economic gains. In the Cold War atmosphere, the Soviet Union stepped in to defend Cuban socialism by providing missiles to the government, leading to the Cuban Missile Crisis of October 1962. Averting nuclear disaster, Nikita Khrushchev, the Soviet Premier, agreed to withdraw the missiles on the condition that the United States would not invade Cuba. President John F. Kennedy secretly agreed to this condition, but covert attacks against the revolution continued through the use of the exiled Cubans sponsored by the CIA.

With the continuation of the US trade embargo instituted by President Dwight Eisenhower, the Cuban government sought to diversify its economy and lessen its dependence on the monoculture production of sugar exports. In the initial years of the revolution, it took land out of sugar production and turned it over to the production of previously imported agricultural commodities. The Cuban government also pursued a policy of industrialization during these early years. Both the attempts at agricultural diversification and industrialization ended in failure as a result of poor administration and the failure of central planning. Many skilled technocrats and workers had left Cuba during these years, and the revolutionaries had to improvise the transition to a socialist economy. In addition, for industrialization, the government needed foreign exchange earnings that only sugar exports could provide. By 1963, the government had abandoned its industrialization plans and shifted its focus on sugar production. It pledged a 10 million ton sugar harvest for 1970.

The Soviets had strongly advised the Cuban government to concentrate on its most lucrative export, sugar, and reverse its policy concerning industrialization. Although larger than the 1963 harvest of 3.8 million tons, the 1970 sugar harvest of 8.5 million tons proved to be disappointing for the nation and the government that had invested heavily in achieving this goal. Hoping to construct an alternative model to the competitive individualism that is the basis of capitalism, the revolution sought to create the "new socialist man," who was predicated on the creation of a new consciousness based on selfless dedication to the collective good. Although "Che" Guevara had resigned from his government position as a result of his failed economic and industrialization policy, his ideas continued to influence the direction of the Cuban Revolution during the 1960s.

In 1965, after resigning his Cuban citizenship, which was granted by the Cuban Council of Ministers after the revolution, "Che" traveled to Africa, Asia, and Latin America to promote revolution in these Third World countries, an idea supported by Castro and the revolutionary government. Hoping to foment revolution in Latin America, "Che" met his death in Bolivia on October 9, 1967, when he was captured by US-trained Bolivian Rangers. This event brought an end to the hope of exporting revolution abroad, a policy that the Soviet Union had never fully supported. Castro's support of the Soviet invasion of Czechoslovakia in 1968 signaled not only a rapprochement with the Soviet Union but also a return to revolutionary orthodoxy concerning the export of revolution to the Third World. Although Guevara's revolutionary internationalism was abandoned, the government continued proclaiming his revolutionary idealism and "Che's" selflessness in the name of revolution as a model for Cubans to follow in their construction of socialism and the "new socialist man."

The 1970s began with two major reversals for the Cuban Revolution, an abandonment of the policy of exporting revolution and the failure of reaching the 10 million ton sugar harvest, which contributed to a reassessment of revolutionary ideology and policy. After ten years, the revolution had not fulfilled many of the promises or satisfied the hopes of many Cubans. The immense emphasis on the 10 million ton target had drained other productive sectors of capital and labor, which caused a decline in consumer goods and basic agricultural products. There was also an increased economic dependence on the Soviet Union, which resembled the economic dependence that Cuba had with the United States in the past. Although the revolution demonstrated success in the areas of education, health, housing, nutrition, and literacy, even Castro had to admit that the revolution had failed the Cuban people.

On July 26, 1970, Castro admitted this failure and took full responsibility for it. His speech signaled a new direction for the Cuban Revolution. The initial revolutionary idealism gave way to revolutionary pragmatism as the government injected more orthodoxy into its economic policies. The increase in absenteeism during the 1960s caused the government to reevaluate its policy of preaching moral incentives to the workers to increase productivity. In a vast departure from the ideal of the "new socialist man," it reintroduced the profit motive and material incentives. In another reversal, it also abandoned the earlier policy of strict centralization in government planning. The 1970s was a period of new challenges as the Cuban Revolution reversed direction by attempting to follow the orthodox socialist model represented by the Soviet Union and Eastern Europe.

After the experimentation of the 1960s, the Cuban Revolution sought to institutionalize itself through the creation and reorganization of mass organizations. A trend toward personalism and autocracy had emerged after the Cuban Revolution as the Cuban Communist Party (PCC), as well as trade unions, had been severely weakened during the decade of experimentation. During Cuba's Revolutionary Offensive (1968–1969), Castro had invited numerous Marxist scholars to evaluate the direction of the revolution and make recommendations to remedy the ossification and bureaucratization of the revolution. They concluded that it was necessary to open the political process and institute a democratic and participatory type of socialism. The revolution's economic failure and its failed attempt to export revolution caused it to endorse these recommendations as evidenced by Castro's criticisms of the revolutionary process and proposals to correct the situation.

At the heart of the rectification of the revolutionary process were the continuation of the socialist path and the strengthening of the PCC. The PCC would be revitalized by allowing the politburo, secretariat, and central committee to meet regularly and increase the number of members that would represent more of a mass base. The PCC would be responsible for coordinating and supervising the administrative function. In a further move toward decentralization, the extreme diffusion that had characterized the relationship between the central administration, the party, and the army during the 1960s was rectified by prescribing a clear separation between these three important institutions. The number of military men in the party also decreased, while the number of workers increased. Although Castro had announced that a party congress was to be held in 1966 and 1969, this latter one was canceled on the grounds that all energies had to be focused on the 1970 sugar harvest; thus, the first party congress was held December 17–22, 1975, which demonstrated how far the Cuban Revolution had come to embrace Soviet orthodoxy by following the Soviet model to socialism.

The new direction of the Cuban Revolution in the 1970s also sought to champion the working class by revitalizing trade unions. During the 1960s, the trade union movement had declined as a result of the almost total identification of the unions and the government. In the late 1960s, a policy of concentrating on vanguard workers that embodied the self-sacrificing new socialist man diminished the number of workers in local unions. The unions had lost their ability to represent the workers' interests independently of government party policy. To rectify this situation, the Cuban Revolution pursued a policy of reconstituting the unions as mass organizations. With few members of the past reelected after elections based on a secret ballot (held November 9–December 9, 1970), the new membership represented the direction toward creating a mass base responsive to the defense of workers' rights. From 1970 to 1973, twenty-three new unions were also established in agriculture, industry, transportation, the military, and services. Although the government advocated a new direction for labor and Castro had announced in 1971 that the Thirteenth National Congress of the Central Organization of Cuban Trade Unions (CTC) would be held in 1972, the last Congress being held in 1966, the new trade union members caused some concern for the revolutionary leadership, so the government postponed the meeting until November 1973. The issues discussed revolved around the defense of workers' rights and how the unions could participate in the national decision-making process concerning productivity and labor discipline. With the abandonment of the late 1960s' vanguardism, the revitalized trade union movement embraced its role as a mass organization through the 1970s and early 1980s under the direction of the Communist Party.

Since taking power, the Cuban Revolution had benefited previously neglected social groups, peasants, workers, and, especially, women. Since its inception, it has sought to incorporate women into all aspects of the revolutionary process. Passing legislation favorable to women's rights, especially regarding labor, education, and health, it exhorted women to defend the revolution and their place within it. The July 26th Movement had a women's affiliate organization, the Revolutionary Feminine Unity, that organized this mobilization during the early years of the revolution by including women in the agrarian reform and exhorting them to participate in the labor force. Women not only increased their numbers in production, especially during the late 1960s, but they were also incorporated into all levels of the educational system by the 1970s. Women working outside of the household created the need for child care centers that the government provided. In 1975, the government instituted a Family Code that emphasized gender equality at home and at work. The government also instituted reproductive policies favoring contraception, as well as making abortion readily available on demand during the first twelve weeks of pregnancy. This shift in the role of women as active participants in the revolution created tensions within the patriarchal household, which was captured in two important films, *Lucía* (1969) and *Retrato de Teresa* (1979), from the creative revolutionary Cuban cinema. Even with the revolutionary government taking a conscious active posture in promoting and improving women's position in society, many inequalities continued, such as in hiring practices and being underrepresented in administrative positions in government and state enterprises. The Federation of Cuban Women (FMC), created in 1960 to promote women's participation in the revolution, was another mass organization that contributed to the institutionalization of the revolution in the 1970s.

The Cuban Revolution's foreign policy shifted from actively promoting guerrilla warfare in Latin America to searching to extend fraternal ties with other Latin American nations during the 1970s. A thaw occurred in the icy relations that Cuba had with the rest of Latin America when Salvador Allende was elected president of Chile in 1970. With this election, Castro found an ally in Allende, who invited him to visit the country in 1971. By 1975, Cuba had reestablished diplomatic relations with eight nations of Latin America and the Caribbean. Cuba continued its international relations with the Third World through the Nonaligned Movement, with Castro participating personally in the 1973 Fourth Nonaligned Movement Summit in Algeria. Cuba's socioeconomic and military commitments to liberation movements and nations in Africa and the Middle East increased throughout the 1970s. The most well-known episode of this internationalism is the sending of thirty-six thousand Cuban troops to support the Popular Movement for the Liberation of Angola (MPLA) in 1975 through 1976. In 1977, Cuba sent fifteen thousand troops to the aid of Ethiopia when Somalia invaded that country. Both of these African actions had the logistical support of the Soviet Union. Cuba also provided socioeconomic aid to other Third World nations in the form of doctors, technicians, agronomists, teachers, and construction workers. Foreign students from Latin America and Africa also came to the island to study in medical schools, universities, and technical schools. Cuba's relations with the United States were also improving by the mid-1970s; however, the sending of Cuban troops to Angola dampened these efforts at normalization. Although the United States looked askance at these efforts, especially the military ventures, the nations of the Nonaligned Movement approved of these actions as evidenced by the holding of the sixth summit in Havana in September 1979, with Castro serving as chair.

Cuba's position within the Nonaligned Movement soured with the Soviet invasion of Afghanistan, a member of the Nonaligned Movement, in December 1979. Beholden to the Soviet Union for its economic support, Cuba took a tepid response regarding the condemnation of the invasion in the United Nations. As Cuba's fortunes declined within the Nonaligned Movement, since it was perceived to be acting as an extension of Soviet policy, its regional influence increased at the beginning of the 1980s. The Sandinista victory in Nicaragua in 1979 and the emergence of Maurice Bishop's government in Grenada in 1980 created new allies for Cuba. It also cultivated ties to other Latin American countries by championing their aspirations, such as Cuba's support for Panamanian control of the canal and its backing Argentina in the Malvinas–Falklands War in 1982.

Cuban/US relations improved under the presidential administration of Jimmy Carter from 1976 to 1980 as interests section was opened in Havana and Washington in 1977, which facilitated dialogue between the two nations. In 1980, relations that were already strained from Cuba's intervention in the Ethiopian–Somalian War further deteriorated with the Mariel boatlift; a total of 125,000 Cubans left the island for the United States, which demonstrated a large level of discontent with the achievements of the Cuban Revolution. Ironically, the thawing relations between Cuba and the United States contributed to this discontent and frustration with the Cuban Revolution when Castro allowed 100 thousand US relatives laden with consumer goods to visit the island in 1979. Ronald Reagan's election as US president in 1980 progressively worsened US/Cuban relations. In 1983, the overthrow of Bishop in Grenada and the subsequent US invasion of the island eliminated that nation as an ally. The civil wars in Central America also stiffened US rhetoric against Cuba, which was blamed for fomenting the popular struggles in the region. The Cuban government mobilized against the threat of a possible US invasion of the island. The Reagan administration also prohibited travel to the island by US citizens and began radio transmission to Cuba via Radio Martí in 1985, which scuttled a 1984 immigration agreement between the two nations.

Internally, the Cuban economy grew during the first half of the 1980s as a result of a liberalization policy instituted by the government, which sought to improve economic performance through stimulating private initiative by allowing free peasants' markets. The introduction of the free peasants' markets in May 1980 helped to supplement the government rationing system, but they soon came under attack by consumers who charged that prices were too high, that there was illegal profiteering, and that there was an emergence of a black market. In 1987, the introduction of the Rectification Program signaled a government reversal regarding the free peasants' markets. Castro initiated the "rectification" period in April 1986 during the Third Party Congress of the Cuban Communist Party, and this period lasted from 1986 to 1990. The initiation of this period was a reaction toward the heightened individualism exhibited during the introduction of market mechanisms in the economy. The government reintroduced the ideas of an earlier period concerning *conciencia* (consciousness) based on moral incentives and social obligations rather than on economic motives.

A major internal incident exemplifying this shift toward the reaffirmation of *conciencia* occurred in 1989 with the trial of Division General Arnaldo Ochoa Sánchez, a hero of the Angolan campaign, and other high-ranking military and security officers. Charged with corruption and drug trafficking, Ochoa and two other top officers were executed and the others given lengthy jail sentences. During this period, the United States had leveled charges that Cuba was involved in drug trafficking, so the government could not afford a showdown with the United States over the drug issue. Although some have characterized this incident as resulting from an internal power struggle,

the trial also demonstrated how no one, no matter his or her position, was above the law and that the revolution would not tolerate individualism and personal wealth acquisition that would threaten its existence and ideals.

The world economic crisis of the 1980s also affected Cuba by the end of the decade because there was a hard currency shortage caused by depressed sugar prices on the world market. The "rectification" period stressed a need for austerity, which meant reducing consumption and diverting economic production to exports for the acquiring of hard currency for the payment of foreign loans. Although the Soviet Union provided billions of dollars of aid and subsidies, Cuba also had borrowed heavily from the West. In 1986, Cuba defaulted on these loans. Cuba's trade relationship with the Soviet Union and the Council for Mutual Economic Assistance (CMEA) began to disintegrate in the late 1980s with the adoption of the policy of *perestroika* and *glasnost*, a policy that Cuba did not follow. Castro denounced *perestroika* and *glasnost* as being inapplicable to Cuba's situation because it was so close to the United States and that its brand of socialism had emerged from a social revolution. In 1989, Cuba also began its withdrawal from Angola, which it completed in 1991.

The fall of the Berlin Wall in 1989 and the subsequent collapse of the Soviet Union found Cuba increasingly isolated as it continued on the path toward socialism in the 1990s. To confront the economic crisis that emerged as a result of these international circumstances, Castro announced a "Special Period in a Time of Peace" in 1990 directed toward redoubling the nation's efforts to achieve socialism. Emergency austerity measures were introduced to counteract the disastrous economic consequences of the loss of the heavy subsidies that the Soviet Union had provided to Cuba. Imports of foodstuffs and fuel were heavily curtailed and a strict rationing system instituted. The government encouraged foreign investment and tourism to acquire hard currency for purchases on the world market. Economic reforms with a market orientation were also instituted, such as a policy of self-employment, the ability of citizens to hold dollars, the opening of "dollar stores," and the reintroduction of farmer's markets.

The United States decided to put economic pressure on Cuba during this period with the passage of the Cuban Democracy Act of 1992 (Torricelli Bill), which toughened the US embargo by punishing US subsidiaries in foreign countries trading with Cuba, along with Third World countries that traded with Cuba. This increased the economic hardship on Cuban citizens, many who left the island in 1994 when Castro allowed those who wanted to leave to go, creating another migration problem for the United States. Subsequently, the United States and Cuba signed an immigration agreement to control the *balseros* (rafters or "boat people") by allowing a legal immigration of twenty thousand Cubans per year. Cuban exiles continued engaging in hostile actions to discredit the Cuban Revolution, which led to a violent confrontation when Brothers to the Rescue, an anti-Cuban Revolution exile group, entered Cuban airspace in February 1996. The organization had previously been entering Cuban airspace to drop propaganda leaflets. Castro had warned Washington that deadly force would be used if these actions continued. The downing of two unarmed aircraft manned by the group led to a confrontation with the United States as President William Jefferson Clinton considered an air strike or a cruise-missile attack against Cuba. Dissuaded by his national security advisors from this course of action, Clinton sent a strongly worded secret missive warning Castro about a military retaliation if any more planes were shot down. The US Congress responded by passing the Helms-Burton Bill, which increased the sanctions against Cuba in a more aggressive manner by imposing US law on foreign nationals and companies trading with the island nation.

Although there was international condemnation of the Helms-Burton Bill, Cuba felt increasingly isolated by the end of the 1990s. In 1996, Cuba extended an invitation to Pope John Paul II to visit the island with the hope of getting a papal condemnation of the US embargo. During his visit to Cuba in January 1998, the pope not only resolutely condemned the US embargo but also criticized Castro by appealing for more political freedom, religious toleration, and concern for political prisoners. After the papal visit, Cuba released more than two hundred prisoners as a gesture of goodwill. The following year, in 1999, tensions increased again between the United States and Cuba over Elián Gonzàles, a young Cuban boy who became a cause célèbre for the exile anti-Cuban Revolution community in Miami. After his mother drowned when fleeing Cuba, the boy was adopted by his relatives in Miami. Elían became a symbol for both the exiled community and the Cuban Revolution as a heated confrontation exposing many old wounds played out in the law courts and in the media. In June 2000, the boy was returned to his father and became a symbol for the Cuban Revolution and its resistance against US imperialism. All of these events bolstered Castro's support among the Cuban people for the revolution.

With the end of the Cold War, opinion began to change within the United States regarding the embargo among business and agricultural interests, as well as among those Cubans who immigrated to United States in the 1980s and 1990s. This shift in public opinion was also reflected among public officials who criticized the embargo on medicine and food. In 2000, the embargo on the sale of food and medicine was lifted, but the law passed prohibited US government or private financing of such sales. Since 1991 the United Nations has also repeatedly condemned the US embargo on Cuba and called for its end.

President George W. Bush's administration, starting in 2001, increased the pressure on the Cuban Revolution by declaring that it would continue the embargo regardless of growing calls for its relaxation or for ending it. Restrictions on US citizens traveling to Cuba were increased and those traveling through third countries would be especially targeted. Increased tensions between the United States and Cuba led to the arrest of Cuban dissidents in 2003. These dissidents were accused of working with US diplomats to undermine the Cuban Revolution. These arrests coincided with highly publicized hijackings of ships and aircrafts by Cubans attempting to leave the island for the United States. In 2003, President Bush announced the creation of a Commission for Assistance to a Free Cuba, which would outline the steps to help in the overthrow of the Cuban Revolution and contribute to the transition of a postrevolutionary Cuba. Presenting its five hundred-page report in May 2004, the commission's conclusions included a restriction on the number of visits that Cuban Americans could make to the island, restricted the amount of dollars that a Cuban American could spend while on the island, and also curbed educational travel to Cuba. Cuban dissidents condemned the report, and the government saw it as a first step to a subsequent US military intervention to overthrow the Cuban Revolution. The US government instituted its new policy on Cuban Americans traveling to Cuba almost immediately, which divided the Cuban exile community between those who supported it by arguing that it deprived the revolution of vital tourist dollars and those who condemned it by stating that it would only hurt their family members on the island.

Castro continues to lead Cuba into a Socialist future and proudly proclaims the slogan of the Cuban Revolution: "Socialism or Death!" In comparison to other Latin American nations, the revolution has brought a level of education and health achievements that is not rivaled in the region. The Cuban people have access to free health and education. Literacy rates are higher than in many industrialized nations. The island's medical schools and universities enroll students not only from Latin America but also from other developing countries. Cuba also cooperates with other nations by exporting teachers and doctors for developmental goals. The Cuban Revolution's fortunes on the regional level have also improved with the election of Left-leaning presidents in Argentina, Brazil, and Venezuela. Venezuela has helped Cuba meet some of its energy needs by providing oil under preferential terms. The Cuban Revolution has met many of its social goals even though its economy has been under assault from the US embargo and the subsequent demise of the Soviet Union. It continues working toward creating a socialist Cuba in which all of its citizens will have a future free of the want that created the conditions for the revolution in the first place.

CARLOS PÉREZ

See also 26th of July Movement; Batista y Zaldívar, Fulgencio; Castro, Fidel; Cuba; Guevara, Ernesto "Che"

References and Further Reading

Benjamin, Jules R. *The United States and the Origins of the Cuban Revolution*. Princeton, NJ: Princeton University Press, 1990.

Domínguez, Jorge I. *To Make the World Safe for Revolution: Cuban Foreign Policy*. Cambridge, MA: Harvard University Press, 1989.

Eckstein, Susan Eva. *Back from the Future: Cuba Under Castro*. Princeton, NJ: Princeton University Press, 1994.

Feinsilver, Julie M. *Healing the Masses: Cuban Health Politics at Home and Abroad*. Berkeley, CA: University of California Press, 1993.

García-Pérez, Gladys Marel. *Insurrection and Revolution: Armed Struggle in Cuba, 1952–1959*. Boulder, CO; London: Lynne Rienner Publishers, 1998.

Horowitz, Irving L., ed. *Cuban Communism 1959–2003*, 11th ed. New Brunswick, NJ: Transaction Publishers, 1995.

Ibarra, Jorge. *Prologue to Revolution: Cuba, 1898–1958*. Boulder, CO; London: Lynne Rienner Publishers, 1998.

Mesa-Lago, Carmelo. *Cuba in the 1970s: Pragmatism and Institutionalization*, 2d ed. Albuquerque, NM: University of New Mexico Press, 1978.

Pérez, Jr., Louis A. *Cuba: Between Reform and Revolution*, 2d ed. New York: Oxford University Press, 1995.

Pérez-Stable, Marifeli. *The Cuban Revolution*. New York: Oxford University Press, 1993.

Smith, Lois M., and Alfred Padula. *Sex and Revolution, Women in Socialist Cuba*. New York: Oxford University Press, 1996.

Smith, Wayne S. *The Closest of Enemies: A Personal and Diplomatic Account of US –Cuban Relations since 1957*. New York: W.W. Norton, 1987.

Welch, Jr., Richard E. *Response to Revolution: The United States and the Cuban Revolution, 1959–1961*. Chapel Hill, NC: University of North Carolina Press, 1985.

Zimbalist, Andrew S., and Claes Brundenius. *The Cuban Economy: Measurement and Analysis of Socialist Performance*. Baltimore, MD: John Hopkins University Press, 1989.

CULTURAL PERCEPTIONS

Culture and Development

There are three areas where the concept of culture is implicated in development. First, while predominantly associated with economic transition, the dominant development model and its associated policies and programs underpinned by modernization theory were specifically designed to induce change in every aspect of life. This includes the whole range of institutions, behaviors, and beliefs that constitute the culture of a community, including everyday practices, values, social organization and relationships, roles and rituals, knowledge and artistic production.

Second, theories of cultural imperialism argued that the development model itself was imbued with the cultural values and practices of the country from which it originated—mainly the United States or other Western powers. This led to claims that development was simply a continuation of colonialism. Last, local existing or surviving cultural practices and values are being used to underpin alternative discourses and projects in the development debate.

Processes of acculturation, that is, where elements of one culture are adopted, adapted, or assimilated into another, have occurred continuously throughout history as civilizations came into contact with one another through trade or conquest. Development, as a systematic process of inducing cultural change, is generally considered a post-World War II phenomenon, following the success of the US Marshall Plan in rebuilding Europe. Western states and international agencies embarked on a program to eradicate poverty worldwide, targeting Third World countries that had been designated as "underdeveloped," that is, lacking a certain level of materialism. The point of comparison was the living standards of Western countries. There were also political imperatives as Cold War antagonists sought as much international influence as possible. Development aid became a potent political tool.

Consequently, it is argued that development was envisaged and constructed around beliefs and institutions that are valued in the West (Harrison 1988). The theoretical base for development is derived from two Western schools of thought: Socialist (centrally planned) and Capitalist (free market). It should be noted that these are broad definitions, and many differences exist between countries, in patterns of ownership, government regulation, and the scale of industrialization, for example.

Development under these circumstances is not homogeneous. However, there are important similarities. Both were ideologically driven with the end goal a "modern" society, industrial and urban, achieved through technological, financial, and administrative assistance. Progress was to be measured by economic growth. The nation-state became the unit for development, and it was necessary to ensure not only economic and political integration but also cultural integration, that is, the development of a single national identity.

With the end of the Cold War, it has been argued that only the Western model of development remains, overarched by cultural logics of mass production and mass consumption, individualism, and competition, together with the ideal liberal democratic state. This model was constructed from diverse sources: economic and political ideologies and sociological theories such as structural functionalism and systems theory. The idea was that as the systems and structures of the West were diffused into a traditional, generally agrarian, society, its progress would imitate the path of the West.

The classic concept of the modernization process that development policies attempted to replicate was that Third World societies could follow a linear path of change (Lerner 1958). The required economic, technical, and demographic conditions and appropriate social organization and value systems were outlined for agrarian societies to reach an economic "take off" point from which they could mature and enter an age of mass consumption (Rostow 1962).

What were deemed as deficiencies of a precolonial past were cited as the reason for initial economic failures. Those societies or producers that were deemed incapable of generating a flow of innovations or sustained economic growth were labeled "traditional," which was now a pejorative, signaling stagnation. The traditional was viewed as inhibiting development. If Third World societies were to advance along the path taken by industrialized countries, attachments to these former cultural practices, values, and relationships had to be attenuated. The dichotomy of "developed and underdeveloped" was established during this period, growing out of a lack of recognition of what was positive in other cultures.

These theories have been critiqued since their dominance in the 1960s. It is doubtful that even economic change in the West occurred along the lines suggested. A major criticism of development, particularly from writers in the Third World, was that it established a cultural hegemony.

Establishing Cultural Hegemony

Development in the form it was originally conceived, a universal cure for poverty and as a bulwark against communism, required a cultural hegemony in host countries to support the changes it proposed. During Europe's period of rapid upheaval brought on by the industrial revolution, massive social dislocation occurred. Durkheim labeled the effect as *anomie*—the suspension of previously held beliefs or principles of certainty. The effect could also be put into a postmodern context with competing cultural values, with practices and relationships no longer providing a sense of security, certainty, or meaning.

A similar situation occurred with the implementation of development programs in the Third World. Critics argue that local cultures were often overwhelmed. Rather than a more evolutionary process, the frames of reference for everyday living were shifting in one generation with important stabilizing features, such as the system of governance, social organization, and religion completely removed or disregarded if these were seen as impeding the development process.

Societies had to integrate rapidly not only a new economic model but also an entirely new culture to sustain it, that is, a new set of values, practices, and social relationships. Crises instigated by increasing urbanization, bringing a population into a waged sector, rural migration and unemployment, the disruption of gender and family roles, and new forms of social differentiation, were exacerbated by a crisis of values as former cultural patterns were stigmatized as being of less value, even "backward."

"Hegemony" can be defined as a form of domination whose legitimacy is based on a valued pattern of shared meanings (Friedman 1992). But it involves more than just physical coercion. It can be established in many ways, including the incorporation of oppositional ideas, the saturation of an ideology, or the control of material production matched by control over the production and dissemination of cultural symbols.

In the translocation of development models to the Third World, Western forms of knowledge were assuming preeminence to manage the conditions of the living. State and international agencies, bureaucracies, media, and academia attempted to establish a nexus between power and knowledge to influence indigenous institutions and attitudes (Foucault 1980). A regime of "truth" was created; that is, Western development was the only true model to follow if a country was to progress.

Wealthier countries not only had the resources and technology to secure their brand of progress internationally but also to dominate the research agenda, information flows, and even the language of the development discourse. Terms such as the gross national product (GNP), because of their association with, and emphasis on, economics and empirical formulae, are basic to the discourse of international bodies such as the International Money Fund (IMF), World Bank, and donor countries.

This internationally recognized vocabulary links development's administrative actors. Transnational corporations, diplomats, trade agencies, and international non-governmental organizations (NGOs) all operate and understand these lexicons. The dominance of this language is critiqued for excluding other dialogues that speak of development as something that should be more mutually inclusive of all cultural aspects of people, not just the economic aspects (Escobar 1995).

Alternative Culture-Based Perspectives on Development

Analyses of development programs began to reveal that the aim of eradicating poverty by restructuring a society had failed to improve material living conditions for many in the countries that underwent these programs. In some regions, poverty had even been exacerbated. There was, and continues to be, resistance in host countries to programs that local populations consider detrimental (protests against the Narmada Dam in India is an example).

In hindsight, trying to establish a uniform pattern of change throughout all countries whose cultural systems differed greatly was unlikely to succeed. Governments and international agencies began to look at new ideas such as sustainable development. Basic needs approaches were developed, although this was still problematic regarding how to define what is a "need" as opposed to a "want." The United Nations Development Program produced a new tool for measurement, the Human Development Index, which looked at development not only in terms of economic growth but also in terms of literacy, mortality rates, gender equality, and other such factors.

However, some writers, particularly from the Third World, began to advocate more radical approaches using alternative models based on existing cultural relationships. This included the strategic use of traditions and local knowledge, whose validity did not depend on Western regimes of truth, and

integrating cultural, spiritual, social, and economic dimensions (Sivaraksa 1990). Rather than large-scale development projects, such as dams or paper mills, small grassroots, community-based projects were seen to be more effective in implementing changes desired by local populations.

Deconstructions of the meaning of key terms such as poverty, underdevelopment, and modernity have taken place. They have become regarded as contestable cultural constructs. The broad, general term of "development" is now being paired with the words "self-reliant," "human scale," or "endogenous." Local terms avoid the use of development altogether: in Sri Lanka, *Gam Pubuduwa* means "awakening of the village." Assumptions about the role of technology and the nation-state have been challenged and new ideas put forward about the use of cultural heritage in the restoration of subjugated peoples, guided by new objectives, in other words, seeking ways of balancing tradition and modernity.

In many ways, these ideas are also utopian, and it is argued that Western governments, academics, and international agencies continue to dominate the development debate (Crush 1994). While Western agencies made attempts to redress the balance in the United Nations Decade of Culture and Development, 1988–1998, the relationship between Western development and the Third World is still one of tension and resistance.

Using local culture as a basis for resistance can be problematic in that tradition is not a manifest or solidified frame of reference. It is mobile and evolving. Traditions change and provide an insubstantial or unreliable source for a new dialogue if they ignore aspects of modernity that are beneficial, such as education or health. Local cultures are also being increasingly reappropriated by transnational corporations. A global marketing strategy of localization prevails that wraps global products in local cultural icons and meanings to better establish their product in that particular overseas market.

In the current era of globalization, some oppositional movements have tapped into cultural networks to harness identity politics and garner support, relying on cultural connections to bind them (the *Hindutva* movement in India is an example). This opposition is still articulated in the language of cultural imperialism. The fear is that local cultures will once more be overwhelmed by a homogenous Westernization. But the relationship between culture and development has shifted. It is now not a simple imposition but a more complex interaction between local and regional cultures and the global cultures, assisted by increased transnational flows of goods, technology, finance, images, and people (Appadurai 1997).

MELISSA BUTCHER

See also Basic Human Needs; Colonialism: Legacies; Globalization: Impact on Development; Modernization

References and Further Reading

Appadurai, Arjun. *Modernity at Large: Cultural Dimensions of Globalization*. New Delhi, India: Oxford University Press, 1997.
Crush, Jonathan. *Power of Development*. London, New York: Routledge, 1994.
Escobar, Arturo. *Encountering Development: The Making and Unmaking of the Third World*. Princeton, NJ: Princeton University Press, 1995.
Foucault, Michel. *Power/Knowledge: Selected Interviews and Other Writings 1972–1977*. United Kingdom: Harvester Press, 1980.
Friedman, Jonathan. *Empowerment: The Politics of Alternative Development*. Blackwell Publishers, 1992.
Harrison, David. *The Sociology of Modernization and Development*. UK: Unwin Hyman, 1988.
Lerner, Daniel. *The Passing of Traditional Society: Modernizing the Middle East*. New York: Free Press, 1958.
Madan, T. N. *Culture and Development*. New Delhi: Oxford University Press, 1983.
Rostow, W.W. *The Stages of Economic Growth: A Non-Communist Manifesto*. London: Cambridge Press, 1960.
Sivaraksa, Sulak. *Siam in Crisis*. Bangkok: Thai Inter-religious Commission for Development, 1990.
Verhelst, Thierry. *No Life Without Roots: Culture and Development*.UK: Zed Books, 1990.
Worsley, Peter. *The Three Worlds: Culture and World Development*. London: Weidenfeld & Nicolson, 1984.

CURRENCY DEVALUATIONS

Definition

Currency devaluation (revaluation) is the deliberate decrease (increase) in the value of a country's currency in relation to currencies of its trading partners. For example, if one unit of country A's currency exchanges for one unit of country B's currency, and country A decides to alter that rate so that two units of its currency exchanges for one unit of B's, then A's currency has been devalued. By definition, currency devaluation takes place in a "fixed exchange rate" regime. This means that the government of the country would have set the rate at which its currency would exchange for another country's currency: hence, the exchange rate is official (official exchange rate); it is set by the government.

When a government fixes an exchange rate, it indicates to the world that it will take all necessary actions to ensure that its currency will not change value in relation to other countries' currencies. Actions that governments take to maintain the value of their currencies include the purchase and sale of their own currencies, and the imposition of exchange controls (selective access and outright bans to foreign money). When a government is unable or unwilling to maintain the fixed exchange rate it has set, and decides to lower the rate of exchange, a devaluation is said to have taken place. There is an important distinction to draw between "currency devaluation or revaluation" and a closely related concept: "currency depreciation or appreciation." When a country's exchange rate is determined in a competitive market, without any explicit commitment by the government to maintain any fixed rate, the country is said to have a flexible or floating exchange rate regime. The value of the country's currency depends on the forces of the market. If the supply of the domestic currency exceeds the demand for it, the domestic currency will have to exchange at a lower rate—it *depreciates* in value. Conversely, if the demand for the domestic currency exceeds the supply of it, its value *appreciates*. Currency depreciation or appreciation is therefore the result of the forces of supply and demand, whereas currency devaluation or revaluation is a deliberate policy action. It should be mentioned, though, that it is common for governments to try and influence the exchange rate even in a flexible exchange regime.

Currency devaluation takes place to correct what is termed a persistent external imbalance, usually trade deficits. When a country's currency is overvalued (its price is high), imports are relatively cheaper, and the country's exports are relatively more expensive. This leads to external deficits. In theory, when the currency is devalued, it reverses the situation. It makes imports more expensive and exports less expensive, thus encouraging exports, discouraging imports, and improving the external imbalance or trade deficit.

How Does Devaluation Work: The Marshall-Lerner Conditions

For devaluation to work in the manner described in the previous paragraphs, there are some conditions that must be fulfilled. Economists refer to these conditions as the Marshall-Lerner conditions. The fact that imports have become relatively more expensive (as a result of the devaluation) does not necessarily mean that citizens will reduce the volume of imports sufficiently enough to decrease expenditure on them. If the volume of imports decreases sufficiently enough to reduce expenditure on them, then, everything else remaining the same, there will be an improvement in the external imbalance (or trade deficit). The same devaluation makes the country's exports relatively cheaper to foreigners. Again, the fact that exports have become relatively cheaper does not necessarily mean that foreigners are going to increase their total expenditures. If, however, the volume of exports increases sufficiently enough to increase the revenue derived from them, then, everything else remaining the same, there will be an improvement in the external imbalance (or trade deficit). These two conditions jointly determine whether a devaluation would improve or not improve the imbalance a country faces. In the technical language of economists, *the sum of the price elasticities of demand for exports and imports must be greater than one.* It is not necessary for both conditions to be met at the same time. Expenditure on imports need not decrease; but if it does not, export proceeds must increase sufficiently to make up for it. Similarly, it is not necessary for exports proceeds to increase; but if they do not, expenditure on imports must decrease enough to make up for it. Several studies suggest that most countries meet this condition in the long run. For example, a study by Marquez (1990) suggests that the only country that did not meet the Marshall-Lerner conditions was the United Kingdom. This means that for most countries, devaluation would remove the trade deficit or least ameliorate it.

A possibility exists that in the immediate aftermath of devaluation, a country's external deficit deteriorates rather than improves. The reasons are as follows. With the price of imports now higher than before, if residents of the devaluing country are unable to reduce their imports and/or are unable to find less expensive substitutes, then they are forced to spend a lot more on imports after devaluation than before. If, at the same time, it takes a while for the county to increase its exports, then export revenues will fall because each unit of exports sells for less abroad. In the long run, however, as domestic residents find less expensive substitutes and domestic producers respond to the increased demand for their products, the external imbalance gets better.

The different responses of external imbalance to devaluation in the short run and long run trace a time path that looks like a *J*; thus, economists refer to it as The *J* Curve. The longer the time span, the more likely it is that devaluation will improve the external imbalance. A slightly more technical way of discussing this idea makes use of "currency-contract period" and the "pass-through period." The currency-contract period is the period immediately following devaluation when previously negotiated contracts come due at the prices in effect before the devaluation. What happens to the devaluing country's trade balance depends on the currency in which previous contracts were negotiated. Assume that a developing country such as Nigeria devalues its currency (called the naira) so that more nairas now have to be given to obtain a unit of foreign money, such as the dollar. If importers in Nigeria have already negotiated to purchase certain items from abroad and such purchase agreements were written in dollars (as is often the case), with no protection for currency fluctuations (such as hedging), then the import bill goes up as a result of the devaluation. This deterioration in the balance of trade is the "currency-contract period effect." It may go away when old contracts expire and new ones are written at the new exchange rates. Sometimes, as a result of the need to protect sales, importers and exporters may sacrifice profits by absorbing the effects of the devaluation: they do not pass the increase or decrease in prices to buyers or may delay passing them on. If importers and exporters do not pass the price changes to buyers, then the devaluation would not have the desired effect on the balance of trade. The time it takes for importers and exporters to pass the price changes on to buyers produces the "pass-through period effect." A study by Catherine Mann (1986), for example, suggests that between 1977 and 1980, when the dollar was depreciating, the prices of imported goods did not increase because exporters absorbed the effects by reducing their profit margins. Similarly, she concludes that between 1980 and 1985, when the dollar was appreciating in value, prices of imports did not fall; rather, profit margins for exporters to the United States went up.

Effects of Devaluation

Devaluation could worsen the well-being of a country's citizens. It has already been mentioned that in the short run, as a result of the inability to find less expensive substitutes, the citizens of the devaluing country may be forced to continue buying the now more expensive imports. Since at the same time the value of their exports would have gone down, the devaluing country will in essence be getting less for each unit of its exports. In the economics literature, this is referred to as a worsening in the "terms of trade." For example, whereas before devaluation, one bag of coffee may have been enough to acquire a sack of flour from abroad, once the currency is devalued, two bags of coffee may be needed to acquire the same bag of flour; "real purchasing power" has therefore been reduced. Much more output is required to attain the same level of income and to maintain the same level of well-being. This side effect of devaluation often leads to increased pressure on governments by workers and the alleviation of erosion in living standards by enacting policies such as increases in minimum wages and in subsidies, which can counteract the effects of devaluation. At least one *coup d'état* in Ghana (General Kutu Acheampong's in the 1970s) was attributed in part to the high cost of living that resulted from devaluation. Ironically, though, the subsequent military government was itself forced to devalue the currency.

Additional complications in developing countries often defeat the impact of devaluation. Where governments come between domestic producers and international markets, domestic producers are often insulated from the variation in prices, and, as a result, incentives are not passed on. For example, in Ghana, whose main exports are cocoa, The Cocoa Marketing Board insulated growers by being the sole buyer and exporter of the crop. Currency devaluation under such circumstances does not necessarily affect the output of the main export crop of cocoa because it requires a separate action by the government to increase the price paid to farmers. More often than not, the government kept a substantial portion of the increased revenue. The inability or unwillingness of governments to pass the effects of devaluation on to farmers in this case jeopardizes improvements in the balance of trade deficits that the devaluation was meant to rectify.

When a country devalues its currency, it is essentially trying to switch expenditures by its citizens and its trading partners. It does so by reducing the prices of its goods relative to its trading partners. If the trading partners do not respond by also reducing their prices (devaluing), then the devaluing country could see improvements in its trade deficit. If the country's trading partners, however, also respond by devaluing, then the country could lose whatever improvements it gained initially. What is worse, the volume of trade declines for both the country and its trading partners. This tit-for-tat or "beggar-my-neighbor policy" was evident during the 1997 currency crisis in East Asia. The devaluation of the Thai baht, Thailand's currency (Gerber 1999), put exports from competing neighboring countries, such as Malaysia, the Philippines, Indonesia, and South Korea, at a disadvantage, forcing them also to devalue; thus, the currency crisis spread to several other countries. Others date the crisis to the Chinese devaluation of 1994 that itself was a response to the depreciation in

the Japanese yen and that made Chinese exports less competitive. Regardless of where it started, the conclusion is quite clear: devaluation could produce a contagion that could affect the volume of trade and losses to all countries. Although the East Asian financial crisis is a perfect illustration of what could go wrong, some have argued that there were other problems that worsened the crisis.

If a government maintains a fixed exchange rate regime but pursues macroeconomic policies that lead speculators to believe that it cannot defend the currency, then the expectation of a devaluation could precipitate capital flight. The capital flight would make it even more difficult for the government to maintain the fixed exchange rate and would lead to the expected devaluation. Such were the cases in East Asia. For most of the small developing countries, a one-time devaluation to correct external imbalances is unlikely to produce such an impact.

SAMUEL K. ANDOH

References and Further Reading

Carbaugh, Robert J. *International Economics*, 8th ed. South-Western, 2002.

Gagnon, Joseph E., and Michael M. Knetter. "Markup Adjustment and Exchange Rate Fluctuations: Evidence from Panel Data on Data and Automobile Exports." *Journal of International Money and Finance* (April 1995).

Gerber, James. *International Economics*. Mass.: Addison-Wesley Longman, 1999.

Husted, Steve, and Michael Melvin. *International Economics*, 5th ed. New York: Addison Wesley Longman, 2000.

Magee, Stephen P. "Currency Contracts. Pass-Through and Devaluation." *Brookings Papers on Economic Activity* 1 (1973).

Mann, Catherine L. "Prices, Profit Margins, and Exchange Rates." *Federal Reserve Bulletin* (June 1986).

Marquez, Jaime. "Bilateral Trade Elasticities." *Review of Economics and Statistics* (February 1990).

Marquez, Jaime, and Caryl McNeilly. "Income and Price Elasticities for Exports of Developing Countries." *Review of Economics and Statistics* (May 1988).

Moreno, Ramon. "Lessons from Thailand." *Economic Letters*. Federal Reserve of San Francisco, 1997.

Rose, Andrews. "Are All Devaluations Alike?" *Weekly Letter*. Federal Reserve Bank of San Francisco, 1996.

CURRENCY REGIMES

Developing countries have usually big shares of state property, their government spending is a high percentage of their gross national product (GDP), and their financial markets are subject to heavy official control and are also limited in size. Their inflation rates are usually high because their Central Banks print money to finance their outlays and also to index public sector wages and pensions. The exchange rate is set by their government rather than the foreign capital market, and the government also limits currency outflow for certain purposes. These practices, the capital control, and the use of different exchange rates for different transactions make the country's currency regime extremely vulnerable, as the East Asian and the subsequent Russian and Latin American crises had shown.

The question of which currency regime may be the most suitable for a developing country is hard to answer. Most people advocate the fixed exchange rate regime, meaning that domestic currency is exchanged at a fixed rate with respect to other foreign currencies, most notably to convertible hard currencies. This is thought to be necessary to slow down inflation and achieve macroeconomic stabilization. The problem is that while exchange rates are kept fixed, the public is expecting devaluation in case of poor macroeconomic performance. Thus, people would be willing to sell domestic currency assets, which will lead in turn to a balance of payment crisis. As devaluation takes place, the normal step for a Central Bank would be to increase its domestic interest rates to hedge the loss of confidence in the home currency. Otherwise, the demand for foreign currency will increase leading to capital flight. To counteract this trend and keep exchange rates fixed, the Central Bank has to sell foreign currency from its reserves, thus shrinking domestic money supply as it withdraws home currency from circulation. In extreme cases, the introduction of a currency board may be necessary. In that case, the money supply has to be backed completely by foreign hard currency reserves and gold. The chosen currency is usually one with great trading and investment significance on the world market (US dollars or the euro) or on regional markets (like the former German mark in Europe, the French franc in former French colonial Africa, or the British pound in the British Commonwealth countries). Pegging the domestic currency exchange rate to a foreign one under a currency board arrangement includes the recent examples of Argentina to the US dollar, Senegal to the franc, and smaller Yugoslavia to the German mark (DM). The DM was the strongest currency in Europe due to its stability characterized also by the lowest inflation rate the German economy exhibited through long periods.

Pegging a currency's exchange rate to another could also be risky since this may import inflation and have a contagion effect on the importing country's economy. In other words, what is good for a big country's currency may not be the best for the developing country's currency, especially if the reference currency's exchange rate fluctuates.

To mitigate the risks of pegging one's currency to a single one, most developing nations peg theirs rather to a basket of hard currencies. This basket and their Central Bank portfolio of foreign reserves are created according to the relative weights of their international trade in the component currencies. Thus, many developing countries, having initially a predominantly US dollar–based basket, are shifting gradually to a predominantly euro-denominated basket as the euro appreciates strongly.

Countries that have very intensive mutual trade may hedge their trade-related exchange rate risks by forming optimum currency areas, ranging from exchange rate unions to monetary unions. Thus, countries linked together closely by their trade and factor mobility (labor or capital) will join a fixed exchange rate area if benefits of macroeconomic stabilisation and the microeconomic efficiency gain from joining it will outweigh the losses from loosing monetary policy flexibility. The Europe and the European exchange rate mechanism is a good example where the partner currencies fixed their exchange rates while allowing fluctuation with respect to non-member states' currencies. By joining less-developed countries, such as Greece and Portugal that were benefiting from the system, tempering high inflation rates were experienced at home and were caused by the lack of domestic fiscal and monetary discipline. By forming a currency or monetary union, the transaction costs of trade are reduced, but this also curtails the domestic governments' playing field with currency exchange rates and interest rates, forcing them to abandon independent monetary policies.

Although there are some possible advantages in forming a currency union, when it involves a very small country forming a "union" with a very large one, the previous one inevitably accepts the monetary policy of the latter one. This could be beneficial if the small country exhibits a poor inflation management, but it would be disadvantageous when domestic monetary policy has been reasonable. Handing the sovereignty over monetary policy to a different state inevitably entails the risk that the interest and exchange rates that are suitable for the large country will be quite inappropriate for the small one, as it happened when Ireland joined the European Monetary Union.

Fixing exchange rates can go as far as the total rejection of the home currency, if necessary. A complete "dollarisation" can be a long-term effect with much deeper impact than a domestic currency reform, like the introduction of a new domestic currency.

Besides its advantages, the fixed exchange rate regimes present considerable dangers, most notably that they are particularly susceptible to crises unless backed by very strong political and institutional rules, as it happens in the case of currency boards.

Free-Float Regime

An alternative to the fixed exchange rate would be the floating exchange rate system used by developed countries. The floating regime may be a "free-float," meaning financial market forces are forming the exchange rate without any direct government intervention. A free-float may turn into a "dirty-float" if the home government secretly intervenes.

In case of free-float, Central Banks would not need to intervene in the currency markets for fixing their exchange rates, and countries would not import inflation or deflation from abroad. The system would ensure symmetry for all the participants and eliminate foreseeable speculations; thus, exchange rates would act as automatic balance of payment and economic stabilizers. In spite of these advantages, free-float was and is considered to be very risky by most of the developed countries. Only a few countries dared to use it as New Zealand did during the mid-1980s.

Advocates of free-float argue that this regime is least vulnerable to crisis than the pegged regime. This is argued because the exchange rate can adjust more quickly and more smoothly to real shocks. During the 1997–1998 East Asian crisis, both South Pacific dollars (New Zealand and Australian) exchange rates had adjusted promptly to new market realities by depreciations; this occurred in response to falling demand for the countries' commodity exports due to the weakness of their target markets' (East-Asian) currencies.

A second reason why floating rate regimes are less susceptible to crises is that domestic banks tend to hedge the currency risk of the foreign borrowing they undertake. If this is overlooked, for example, an undiversified and only US dollar-denominated debt portfolio of a country may cause a sharp depreciation of the national currency. This depreciation was the case of Thailand's baht. Ironically, the debt had increased and its portfolio was maintained due to the expectations of keeping "the dollar peg."

In the case of adopting free-float, the sharp depreciation of the currency produces no damages because banks have hedged all of their foreign currency exposure because of the lack of compulsory prudential regulations. By this hedging, most of the exchange rate risk is being carried by retail investors from the developed world, those that have invested in that currency. Another benefit of the floating-rate regime is that domestic corporations, mainly the exporters, have been either hedged or net beneficiaries of the currency depreciation.

Third, free-float has a low susceptibility to crisis because of the Central Bank's commitment to refrain from intervening in the foreign exchange market; big speculative plays will be made more difficult. Any speculator betting for an increase of the exchange rate can also find others acting inversely. Such reliance on the conviction that the Central Bank would not let down the domestic currency is the guarantee for the provision of the necessary liquidity, which will enable it to get out of from a speculative position. Thus, the currency may exhibit lower volatility because the free-float allows markets to act freely, and short-term volatility is probably not a real danger.

Arguments against free-float also abound. One of them is the "serious misalignment" argument. Some argue that free-floating currency regimes are particularly susceptible to serious misalignment as countries adopting it do not experience growth, in comparison with those (like India) that manage their currency heavily and maintain strong capital controls.

Another argument states that speculation could lead to money market disturbances and destabilize the foreign exchange markets. Imprevisible floating would harm both traders and investors. Free-float opens up world currency markets to harmful practices, destroying the discipline imposed by the Bretton-Woods system and will lead to uncoordinated economic policies.

Other arguments add that free-floating exchange rates tend to appreciate strongly with capital inflow; thus, they will squeeze export sectors and lead to a large balance of payment deficits. On the contrary, this latter point is of no concern if that capital is absorbed by the private sector.

The last argument against free-float concerns it leaving only an illusion of independence or greater autonomy because Central Banks would be forced to intervene often, and such currency regime, instead of providing more economic policy freedom, will rather increase chaos.

International experience has shown that the regime is neither a panacea nor an evil toy in the hands of official and private speculators. To yield better results, policy coordination failures between restrictive/nonrestrictive home and foreign monetary policies have to be avoided.

The most common currency regime of the twenty-first century is that of "managed float," which allows the currency value to fluctuate within a band around the "pegged exchange rate." This can be seen as a combination of a free-float and a fixed exchange rate regime. Having a managed float, the Central Bank sells foreign reserves, thus supplying the increasing home demand for foreign currency, tempering the devaluation pressure on the home currency, and keeping exchange rates within the band. The bank buys back foreign currency when the domestic currency appreciates, replenishing its reserves and stopping future depreciation of the domestic currency.

In the case of managed float, if domestic and foreign bonds are imperfect substitutes, the Central Bank can control the money supply and also the exchange rates through sterilized intervention, which cancels in aggregate the effect of an earlier intervention. The reserve currency country's monetary policy maneuvers influences output at home as well as abroad. This asymmetry comes from the fact that the resource center has no obligations of financing its own balance of payments; asymmetry could be overcome only if all the countries fix their exchange rates, say, in terms of the gold reserves they have.

In developing countries, the fragile financial markets make the Central Bank the major player, which sets up the conditions for private transactions of the foreign currencies. These transactions are regulated and limited around a reference exchange rate declared by the state, leading to the emergence of a black market.

The Crawling Peg Regime

Developing countries usually suffer from high inflation, so they cannot maintain their exchange rates fixed for long periods, even when using currency board arrangements, as Argentina had shown in the 1980s. Thus, these countries make use of a combined regime that fixes the exchange rate initially but also allows domestic currency to depreciate continuously. Thus, the price of the foreign currency crawls upward over time as home currency is devaluated continuously at a constant devaluation rate.

The advocates of the "crawling peg regime" suggest that such a crawling band is the best option, but its opponents consider this heavily managed float as being inherently more susceptible to serious misalignment problems. Fixing a currency to a larger, but still floating, currency does not seem to be a way of safely avoiding serious misalignment, as the very strong 45% real appreciation of Hong Kong's dollar and the 109% appreciation of Argentina's peso illustrate, in spite of their peg to the US dollar. Such strong appreciation of the domestic currency exerts considerable pressure on the export sector and was and still is a major contributing factor to the balance of payments deficit.

Developed countries have had similar experiences but with less dramatic effects. Colombia's 49% and Ecuador's 65% real exchange rate appreciations show that these processes do not characterise a particular type of currency regime. This contradicts those who consider that the strong appreciation of the real exchange rate can be avoided by pegging to a major currency or by "dollarising." Some suggest that capital controls like Chile's attempt may have had a beneficial effect on slowing down capital inflow at times of appreciation (at a rate of 45% in the 1990s), but Chile had also experienced a similar current account deficit as a proportion of its gross domestic product, as a country without any capital control.

Finally, it is assumed that crawling-pegs, in contrast to free-float, can be used to maintain a competitive real exchange rate, to the benefit of the country's balance of payments and growth rate. In reality, choosing a proper currency regime has to take into account many macroeconomic as well as regime-linked factors, such as the regime's susceptibility to crisis, to volatility, and to serious misalignment.

LASZLO KOCSIS

See also Currency Devaluations

References and Further Reading

Baltensperger, E., ed. *Conference of European Economic Association: Exchange Rate Regimes and Currency Unions.* London: Macmillan, 1992.

Cukierman, Alex. *Choosing the Width of Exchange Rate Bands. Credibility Versus Flexibility.* London: London Centre for Economic Policy Research, 1994.

Dabrowski, M., ed. *Disinflation in Transition Economies.* New York: CEU Press Budapest, 2002.

Daviddi, R., and E. Espa. *Regional Trade and Foreign Currency Regimes Among the Former Soviet Republics.* Florence, Italy: European University Institute, 1993.

Emil-Maria, Claasen. *Exchange Rate Policies in Developing and Post-Socialist Countries.* San Francisco, ICS: Press, 1991.

Gaspar, Pal. *Exchange Rate Policies in Hungary after 1989.* Budapest: Institute for World Economics, 1995.

Kignel, M., and W. Liviatan. *Exchange Rate-Based Stabilization in Argentina and Chile.* Washington, DC: World Bank, 1994.

Korhonen, Iikke. *Currency Boards in the Baltic Countries. What Have We Learned.* Bulletin of the Finnish Institute for Economies in Transition, 1999.

Krugman, Miller P. *Exchange Rate Targets and Currency Boards.* Cambridge: Cambridge University Press, 1992.

Liviatan Nisan, ed. *Proceedings of the Conference on Currency Substitution and Currency Boards.* Washington, DC: World Bank, 1993.

Sweeney, R, and Willett, T. *Exchange Rate Policy for Emerging Market Economies.* Boulder, CO: Westview Press, 1999.

Ziya, Onis, and Barry Rubin. *The Turkish Economy in Crisis.* Portland, OR: Frank Cass, 2003.

CYPRUS

Cyprus is a small Mediterranean island, forty miles south of Turkey and some five hundred miles east of mainland Greece. Its population of 776,000 people is roughly 77% Greek and 18% Turkish, with Maronite Christians, Armenians, and other groups forming the remaining 5% .

Due to its strategic location, Cyprus was ruled by many successive empires throughout history. Most recent were the Venetians (up until 1571), the Ottomans (until 1878), and finally the British (until 1960). From 1930 onward, elements of the Greek Cypriot community began struggling against British rule and pushing for *enosis* (the union of Cyprus with Greece). The British responded with a colonial policy used effectively in most of their colonies: "divide and rule." They turned to the Turkish Cypriot minority, many of whom were already nervous about *enosis,* for help. The Turkish Cypriots favoured either continued British rule or *Taksim* (partition of the island, handing over the halves to Greece and Turkey). Britain also encouraged Turkey to renew its claims on Cyprus, which it had abrogated in the 1923 Treaty of Lausanne. This would function as a counterweight to Greek claims upon the island.

The predictable outcome of such a climate in Cyprus was increasing tension and conflict between Turkish and Greek Cypriots, in addition to continuing anti-British agitation. By the late 1950s, the situation had become untenable for the British, and together with Greece and Turkey, the British negotiated independence for Cyprus. Three treaties resulted from the negotiations: the Treaty of Guarantee, the Treaty of Alliance, and the Treaty of Establishment. Among other things, the three treaties guaranteed the independence and sovereignty of Cyprus; forbade any actions that might lead to political or economic union with other states; pledged Britain, Turkey, and Greece to uphold the state of affairs on the island and intervene jointly or individually if necessary to uphold them; allowed Greece and Turkey to station 950 and 650 soldiers on the island, respectively; and created a *consociational* political structure, which is a system with many complex power-sharing arrangements between the two main Cypriot communities. This structure guaranteed a specific number of seats in the legislature, military, civil service, and other institutions to ethnic Greek and Turkish Cypriots.

Unfortunately, the bi-communal constitution of the new republic was so complex and riddled with power-sharing arrangements that the government soon found itself deadlocked. Greek Cypriots complained that Turkish Cypriots had been allotted a proportion of government posts greater than their percentage of the population warranted and that they used their position to veto crucial government policies and programs. Turkish Cypriots in turn feared that the Greek majority still wanted to sideline them and either completely Hellenise or unite the island with Greece. In 1963, Greek Cypriot leaders attempted to change the constitutional power-sharing arrangement, at which time the Turkish Cypriots withdrew from the government and began establishing their own system in the mostly Turkish north of the island. This led to a period of inter-communal violence in which the more vulnerable Turkish minority fared much worse than the Greek majority. During this period, which lasted up until 1974, Greek and Turkish Cypriots who spoke out in favour of reconciliation between the two communities were often targeted by extremist groups from their own communities, the EOKA (Greek) and the TMT (Turkish).

In 1974, the situation came to a boiling point, when the military *junta* that ruled Greece engineered the overthrow of the Cypriot president, Archbishop Makarios III, and replaced him with Nicos Sampson, a virulently pro-*enosis* EOKA militant. Turkey invaded the island seven days later, invoking the Treaty of Guarantee to justify its action (the Treaty of Guarantee gave Turkey, Greece, and Britain the right to intervene in Cyprus under certain conditions). Turkish forces killed hundreds of Greek Cypriots, both armed and civilian. At the end of the campaign, the island was effectively partitioned—the Turks had the northern 37%, including a majority of the island's productive resources (farmland, water, and industry). Missing persons amounted to 1,619 Greek Cypriots and 503 Turkish Cypriots. The southern part of the island absorbed 160,000 Greek refugees from the north, and the northern Turkish-controlled area absorbed forty-five thousand Turkish refugees from the south. Roughly thirty-five thousand Turkish and three thousand Greek troops remain stationed on the island.

United Nations (UN) peacekeepers, present since the intercommunal strife of 1964, still in the twenty-first century maintain a tense buffer zone between the northern and southern Cypriot communities (Australia took over the Cyprus peacekeeping mission from Canada in 1994). The Turkish north declared itself the independent Turkish Republic of Northern Cyprus (TRNC) in 1983 but was recognized only by Turkey. The TRNC continues to face international boycotts and is denied all the benefits of a recognized state, in contrast to the Greek Cypriots to the south (who continue to officially represent the

Republic of Cyprus). The TRNC is heavily dependent on Turkey, receiving $100–$200 million dollars of aid annually, in addition to military protection. In addition, approximately 100,000 settlers from Turkey have moved to the TRNC, altering the demographics of the island and even creating some tensions with Turkish Cypriots.

Lack of recognition by the international community has isolated northern Cyprus, preventing it from signing trade treaties, joining international institutions, receiving development aid (from countries other than Turkey), or having its citizens travel freely. By contrast, southern (or Greek) Cyprus, which continues to represent the entire island abroad as the Republic of Cyprus, has enjoyed more economic growth and development, especially due to tourism. Gross domestic product (GDP) per capita in the Greek part of the Island was $19,200 in 2003, compared to just $5,600 in the Turkish north of Cyprus.

Negotiations between the two Cypriot communities aimed at reunifying the island have been frequent and universally unsuccessful. In April 2004, a UN-brokered plan to unite the island just before the ascension of the Republic of Cyprus to the European Union was presented to the population of both sides of island in a referendum. Although the referendum proposal passed in the Turkish north, it was rejected in the Greek south. A divided Cyprus then entered the European Union in May 2004, wherein all Cypriots are now considered European citizens, but only Greek Cyprus enjoys direct trade and other links to Europe.

The Greek Cypriot government continues to oppose the establishment of any international trade, cultural, or political dealings with northern Cyprus, in the hope that Turkish Cypriots continue to feel pressure to reunite the island and address problems stemming from the 1974 Turkish invasion of Cyprus. Lack of foreign investment and aid (apart from that provided by Turkey) will therefore continue to bedevil northern Cyprus, and its economy can be expected to remain dependent on Turkey and much less developed than that of southern Cyprus. Because its quasi-state status removes it from most international treaties, regulations, and conventions, Turkish Cyprus also attracts an unusual amount of illegal economic activity, especially smuggling and money laundering. Greek Cyprus likewise suffers from underground market activity, including even piracy on occasion. The Greek Cypriot economy, although much more advanced than that of the north, nonetheless suffers from its vulnerability to external shocks, a problem shared by many small states dependent on

tourism and international trade. Cyprus's proximity to the Middle East also means that when political conditions there deteriorate, the tourism industry on the island also suffers. Insufficient fresh water resources throughout the island constitutes the most pressing environmental problem for Cyprus. Relative to most of the developing world, however, both northern and southern Cyprus score very high on indicators for literacy (above 95%), unemployment (3.4% in south Cyprus, 5.6% in north Cyprus), infant mortality rates (7.36 deaths per one thousand live births), and life expectancy (77.46 years).

DAVID ROMANO

See also Turkey

References and Further Reading

Christou, George. *The European Union and Enlargement: The Case of Cyprus*. New York: Palgrave Macmillan, 2004.
Denktash, Rauf. *The Cyprus Triangle*. London: K. Rustem & Brother, 1988.
Dodd, C. H. *Disaccord on Cyprus: The UN Plan and After*. Huntingdon, United Kingdom: Eothen, 2003.
Ertekun, M., and Necati Munir. *The Cyprus Dispute and the Birth of the Turkish Republic of Northern Cyprus*, 2d ed. Nicosia, North Cyprus: K. Rustem & Brother, 1984.
Hitchens, Christopher. *Hostage to History*. New York: The Noonday Press, 1989.
Ioannides, Christos P. *In Turkey's Image*. New York: Aristide D. Caratzas, 1991.
Panteli, Stavros. *A History of Cyprus: From Foreign Domination to Troubled Independence*, 2d ed. London: East-West, 2000.
Richmond, Oliver P., and James Ker-Lindsay, eds. *The Work of the UN in Cyprus: Promoting Peace and Development*. New York: Palgrave, 2001.
Salem, Norma, ed. *Cyprus: A Regional Conflict and Its Resolution*. Ottawa: St. Martin's Press and CIIPS, 1992.
Stolsen, Eric, ed. *Cyprus: A Country Study*. Washington, DC: Federal Research Division, Library of Congress, 1991.

CZECH REPUBLIC

The Czech Republic is a land-locked country with a population of 10.4 million and consists of the Czech Lands of Bohemia and Moravia and part of Silesia. Located in the heart of Europe, the Czech Republic is bordered by Poland to the north, Germany to the west, Austria to the south, and Slovakia to the east. The Czech Republic's 18,933 square miles encompass both the mountain-rimmed Bohemian Plateau in the west and the Moravian Lowland in the east. There is little climatic variation across the country; summers are hot and humid, and winters are cold.

Political History

Czech historical development is best understood in terms of several phases from medieval to modern times. The initial phase, spanning the sixteenth through the early twentieth centuries, was its incorporation into the Austro-Hungarian Empire. The second phase was the founding of an independent Republic of Czechoslovakia after World War I that lasted until World War II. Occupation by Nazi Germany constituted phase three. Phase four began with the Communist takeover shortly after World War II and lasted until the Velvet Revolution of late 1989. The fifth phase lasted from the transition from a restored free Czechoslovakian republic until the "velvet divorce" from Slovakia in 1992. The sixth, current phase is its integration into the parliamentary and pro-West European democracies.

After the fall of the Austro-Hungarian Empire in World War I, Czech philosopher Thomas G. Masaryk (1850–1937), who was married to an American and who identified with and was heavily influenced by the leadership model of Abraham Lincoln, visited the United States to proclaim the Republic of Czechoslovakia based on support from President Woodrow Wilson and the Allies. The new nation became the most industrialized and prosperous economy in Eastern Europe, tempting the ambitious Adolf Hitler after his rise to power in 1933.

Agitation in the Sudetenland, the area in northern Bohemia inhabited by about 3 million German-speaking people, offered Hitler an excuse to pressure the major European prime ministers to cede Czech land to him. At that time, Bohemia was the industrial center of the Austro-Hungarian Empire, due to rich coal deposits and a developed railway network. The remainder of Czechoslovakia was invaded in 1939, and the Nazis established a protectorate in Bohemia and Moravia. Thomas Masaryk's son, Jan (1886–1948), served as the Czech government's foreign minister from exile in London. After Nazi Germany's defeat, the pre-1938 frontiers of Czechoslovakia were restored, and nearly all the German-speaking inhabitants were expelled.

Soon after World War II, the Communist Party gained control of Czechoslovakia, converting it into a rigid Stalinist state. After the death, in 1953, of Joseph Stalin, some political relaxation occurred, and in July 1960, it was renamed the Czechoslovak Socialist Republic. Post-Stalin moderation was evident by January 1968 when Alexander Dubcek (1921–1992) became secretary of the party. Soon after, however, the more independent and moderate policies adopted during the Prague Spring of 1968 were terminated after the invasion of Warsaw Pact military forces. Gustav Husak replaced Dubcek and was the last head of Czechoslovakia during the final twenty years of its demise as a Soviet satellite regime.

Only one Prague Spring reform was retained. In January 1969, the Czechoslovak unitary state was transformed into a federation, an arrangement that allowed the Czech and Slovak republics to have separate local governments. At the same time, a national federal government was instituted, and the legislature was restructured into a bicameral body. Implementation of this single Prague Spring reform may be explained, in part, by the fact that both Dubcek and Husak were Slovaks and were sensitive to the underlying, persistent tension between the urban, industrial Czechs and the rural, agricultural Slovaks.

Both the 1989 fall of the Communist regime and the 1992 "velvet divorce" between what became the Czech Republic and Slovakia were accomplished rapidly. Demonstrations against the Communist government, triggered by reforms in the Soviet Union, began in 1988. The Velvet Revolution took place from November 17 to November 28, 1989. It signaled a dramatic, but largely peaceful, political change. Within a month, Vaclav Havel replaced Husak as the president of Czechoslovakia. Dubcek, who had been expelled from the Communist Party in 1975, was elected chair of the national parliament; the Communist Party lost its majority.

Confrontation of Two Inexperienced Political Leaders

Almost as soon as the old Communist regime fell, fissures developed between the two emerging political leaders: Vaclav Klaus in Prague and Vladimir Meciar from Bratislava. Klaus represented the dominant Czech party called the Civic Democratic Party (ODS), which favored anti-communism and economic reform. Meciar represented his Movement for a Democratic Slolvakia (HZDS), which favored retention of much of the previous economic framework from the Communist regime and promoted nationalism. Due to the political inexperience of both leaders, the collision of these two forces led to a so-called "velvet divorce" even in the absence of general public support for the split.

Vaclav Klaus, a former minister of finance, was a 1963 graduate of Prague's School of Economics and did his graduate work in economics both in Italy and the United States, where he attended Cornell University in 1969. He admired the United States's Milton

Friedman and viewed himself as the Margaret Thatcher of the Danube. He had been elected head of the anti-Communist Civic Forum in 1990 after it had grown more conservative, and he became the architect of Czechoslovakia's neoliberal economic program. At the same time, Klaus quickly earned a reputation for arrogance and an inability to accept criticism. By 1991, he was chair of the Civic Democratic Party (ODS), a center-Right party advocating a free market economy and a limited role for the state.

If Klaus was the Margaret Thatcher of the Danube, then Meciar was its Huey Long. A former boxer, corporate lawyer, and an authoritarian populist, Meciar became the darling of the Slovak Nationalists and made it clear that he would not accept a federal state from Prague dictating political policies to Slovakia. Capitalizing on the persistent undercurrent of resentment and jealousy Slovakians felt for their more urban Czech rivals, Meciar escalated his populist demands to such a level that Klaus quickly decided to dissolve the Czechoslovakian state. In doing so, Klaus considered himself rid of what he saw as both a demagogue as well as the economic drain of the less well-off Slovaks.

Struggle Between the Prime Minister and the President

No sooner had the velvet divorce been finalized that another internal struggle reemerged between the two Vaclavs: Vaclav Klaus, the first prime minister of the new Czech Republic from 1992–1997, and Vaclav Havel, the moral leader of the 1989 Velvet Revolution that had first freed Czechoslovakia from the Soviet bloc. Klaus, leader of one of the nation's two largest political parties, the ODS, began espousing a rapid change to free market economics, though advocating that the change be softened by major subsidies. Opposing his stance was Havel, the internationally renowned avant-garde playwright who was jailed repeatedly by the Communists in the 1970s and 1980s. Havel, born October 5, 1936, into an upper-middle class family, was instrumental in the proclamation of "Charter 77" that demanded respect of human rights. He became the best-known Czechoslovakian dissident against Communist repression, and in late 1989, Havel was selected as the president of Czechoslovakia. He was reconfirmed for another term in 1990, but he chose to resign his post two years later in an unsuccessful move to forestall the breakup of the seventy-four-year-old nation. Subsequently, on January 26, 1993, the new Czech

Republic parliament elected Havel as president. The occupant of that office, however, is not a member of a political party because the presidency is viewed as a ceremonial and moral role for the state that is above partisan political struggles. It was a fitting position for the dissident playwright who is a particular hero in the West.

Despite his ceremonial position, Havel has used the presidency as a platform to critique the materialistic values of Klaus. At the same time, he has championed greater regional representation, the new bicameral legislature, and a role for culture and religion in the Czech Republic. All are issues that continue to divide Havel from Klaus, who has attempted to undermine the constitutional position of the president. Havel also continues to be concerned with issues of human rights and justice. Like Thomas Masaryk, Havel quotes Abraham Lincoln. Like Lincoln, Havel has been willing to use the executive pardoning power, often acting contrary to public opinion. On January 20, 1998, Havel was reelected president. His term expired in 2003, at which time Vaclav Klaus replaced him on March 8, 2003.

A Contemporary Stalemate

A campaign finance struggle within Vaclav Klaus's ODS in the late 1990s led to a minor party breach with dissidents splintering into new parties. Klaus was forced to resign as prime minister in late 1997 but continues as a dominant force in Czech politics. In 1998, he entered his party into a controversial "opposition agreement" with the other major party in the country, the Social Democratic Party (CSSD). The agreement allowed the CSSD to govern with support from the ODS in exchange for a key role in parliament along with policy concessions. This unusual but workable arrangement, intended to undermine the power of much smaller political parties, would be on the ballot in 2002.

While Klaus's power was being checked by campaign scandals, Havel suffered a decline in his health. Havel's popular wife, Ogla Havlova, died of cancer on January 27, 1996, and in December of that same year, Havel underwent surgery for removal of half of his right lung due to lung cancer. Havel had been a heavy smoker since his youth and statistically was at high risk for developing lung cancer since Czech males have the second highest rate for risk of death from lung cancer in the world. His eventual marriage to Dagmar Veskrnova, a Czech stage and screen actress seventeen years his junior, divided public opinion.

Despite these setbacks for Klaus and Havel, each continues in the early twenty-first century to exert leadership in the Czech Republic. A new generation of leaders has yet to emerge to challenge these dueling founders.

The new Czech government inherited a low level of external debt from the old Communist regime: a cushion of government subsidies facilitated the country's transition to a free economy. The economic slowdown since the 1990s notwithstanding, the Czech Republic enjoys one of the highest growth rates in the region, in part due to the high foreign and domestic investments that contributed to a 2.4% rise in the gross domestic product (GDP) in 2000. The combination of an educated workforce and its status as a regional high-tech zone contribute to the country's historic industrial and cultural tradition. It has a richer educational tradition than its neighbors. The first Czech Technical University, dating from the eighteenth century, is one of Europe's oldest. By the mid-nineteenth century, the Czechs had the highest literacy rate in Central Europe. In the twenty-first century, the republic has the second highest number of students enrolled in the sciences. A United Nations technology report ranks the Czech Republic as a "potential world leader" in applying technologic innovations. It enjoys one of the highest living standards in Europe.

The Czech Republic joined the European Union (EU) in 2004 while its GDP per capita was about 30% below the EU average. It is set to receive considerable funding from the EU from 2005 to 2013 (estimates range from $16 billion to $40 billion). Bilateral trade and foreign investment are expected to increase. Germany is its most important trading partner. Transparency International presently ranks the Czech Republic 54th out of 149 nations on its corruption index. Concerns about corruption should diminish as its laws are changed to EU standards.

The foreign affairs of the Czech Republic are similarly impressive. In 1999, it was among the first new Eastern European nations to become a full member of the North Atlantic Treaty Organization (NATO).

WILLIAM D. PEDERSON

See also Central and Eastern Europe: History and Economic Development; Central and Eastern Europe: International Relations

References and Further Reading

Batt, Judy. *Czecho-Slovakia in Transition: From Federation to Separation.* London: Royal Institute of International Affairs, 1993.

Bryant, Christopher G., and Edmund Mokrycki, eds. *The New Great Transformation? Changes and Continuity in East-Central Europe.* New York: Rutledge, 1994.

Cottey, Andrew. *East-Central Europe after the Cold War.* New York: St. Martin's Press, 1996.

Dubcek, Alexander. *Hope Dies Last. The Autobiography of Alexander Dubcek.* Edited and translated by Jiri Hochman. New York: Kodansa International, 1993.

Leff, Carol S. *The Czech and Slovak Republics. Nation versus State.* Boulder, CO: Westview Press, 1997.

Kostelecky, Tomas. *Political Parties After Communism: Developments in East-Central Europe.* Baltimore, MD: Johns Hopkins University Press, 2002.

Kriseova, Eda. *Vaclav Havel. The Authorized Biography.* Translated by Caleb Crain. New York: St. Martin's Press, 1993.

Pridham, Geoffrey, and Tatu Vanhanen. *Democratization in Eastern Europe. Domestic and International Perspectives.* New York: Rutledge, 1994.

Pynsent, Robert B. *Questions of Identity. Czech and Slovak Ideas of Nationality and Personality.* New York: Central European Press, 1994.

Saxonberg, Steven. *The Czech Republic Before the New Millennium.* New York: Columbia University Press, 2002.

Skilling, H. Gordon. *T. G. Masaryk. Against the Current, 1882 1914.* University Park, PA: Pennsylvania State University Press, 1994.

Weiner, Robert. *Change in Eastern Europe.* Westport, CT: Praeger, 1994.

D

DA SILVA, LUIZ INÁCIO "LULA"

See Silva, Luiz Inácio "Lula" da

DALITS

See Untouchables (Dalits)

DAWN (DEVELOPMENT ALTERNATIVES WITH WOMEN FOR A NEW ERA)

DAWN (Development Alternatives with Women for a New Era) is a network of women scholars and activists from the South who engage in feminist research and analysis and are committed to working for economic justice, gender justice, and democracy. DAWN works globally and regionally in Africa, Asia, the Caribbean, Latin America, and the Pacific on the following themes: the Political Economy of Globalization; Political Restructuring and Social Transformation; Sustainable Livelihoods; and Sexual and Reproductive Health and Rights. Its numerous partnerships with other global non-governmental organizations (NGOs) and networks have positioned DAWN as a central actor in feminist activism at the global level. In addition to women's organizations, DAWN also works in partnership with a number of development networks and organizations at both regional and global levels.

DAWN seeks to contribute to creating a world without inequality that is based on class, gender, and race, and where relationships among countries are founded on equal voice and respect. It considers basic needs to correspond to basic rights, and strives to find ways by which poverty and all forms of violence can be eliminated. To generate global change toward these goals, DAWN emphasizes the need to reorient the massive resources now used in the production of the "means of destruction" (arms and environmental pollution, among others) toward the areas where they can relieve oppression both inside and outside the home. This would mean, among other things, reforming institutions so that they become participatory democratic processes where women share in determining priorities and making decisions. This political environment would provide enabling social conditions that respect women's and men's physical integrity and the security of their persons in every dimension of their lives.

DAWN began in 1984, on the eve of the international conference marking the end of the UN Decade for Women launched in 1975. A group of feminists from the South with similar visions prepared a platform document for that event and held a number of workshops at the Forum of Non-Governmental Organizations, which took place in parallel to the United Nations' International Conference on Women, in Nairobi, Kenya. DAWN's platform document, entitled "Development, Crises and Alternative Visions: Third World Women's Perspectives" and written by Gita Sen and Caren Grown (1987), was a feminist critique of three decades of development. It high-lighted the impacts of four interlinked and systemic global crises—famine, debt, militarism, and fundamentalism—on poor women of the South, and offered alternative visions.

The document made a significant impact at Nairobi, and for the first time put macroeconomic issues firmly on the agenda of the global women's movement. Since then, DAWN has continued to influence global debates on development by offering holistic analyses from a feminist perspective that are both grounded in women's experience and inspired by women's collective strategies and visions. DAWN's work at the regional level connects with the priorities of women's and civil society organizations in each region, and helps strengthen capacity to deal with issues arising from the impacts of globalization. One of the ways by which DAWN influences feminist activism in the South is through its Training Institute on gender justice. The inaugural session of the Institute was held in Bangalore, India, in 2003 and graduated twenty-eight young feminists from the South.

Much of DAWN's global advocacy work involves calling for a reform of international institutions through significant critiques of current institutions and proposals for designing new ones; participating in United Nations international conferences and review processes; monitoring state actions, policies, and laws to ensure that they live up to the commitments made in international conferences; and developing guidelines to mainstream gender in nongovernmental organizations' advocacy initiatives. Some of DAWN's past advocacy work includes the campaign "Peoples' Health Before Patents"; a campaign for the implementation of the Tobin Tax as part of DAWN's monitoring of the Financing for Development Process at the United Nations; chairing the External Gender Consultative Group of the World Bank; and participating in the ICPD +10 (review process after ten years of the International Conference on Population and Development) and Beijing +10 (International Conference on Women, held in Beijing in 1995) processes.

DAWN's work is supported by the Ford Foundation, HIVOS (Humanist Institute for Cooperation with Developing Countries), John D. and Catherine T. MacArthur Foundation, Swedish International Development Cooperation Agency, and United Nations Development Programme. At the regional level, DAWN relies on the support of a number of established networks, organizations, and institutions, including REPEM (Red de Educación Popular Entre Mujeres de América Latina y el Caribe) and ABIA (Associacao Brasileira Interdisciplinar de AIDS) in Latin America, Girl Power Initiative in Anglophone Africa, WAGI (Women and Gender Institute of the University of the Philippines) in Southeast Asia, IIMB (Indian Institute of Management Bangalore) in South Asia, and CAFRA (Caribbean Association for Feminist Research and Action) in the Caribbean.

DAWN's governing council is its Steering Committee, which is made up of the present and immediate past general coordinators, regional coordinators, and research coordinators. The Steering Committee meets once a year. DAWN also has a number of research/advocacy focal points who are scholars and activists whose expertise and knowledge can be drawn upon to inform DAWN's work and assist its research and regional work agendas.

DAWN's Secretariat was first located at the Institute of Social Studies Trust (ISST) in Bangalore, India, with Devaki Jain as the first general coordinator. In 1986, the Secretariat relocated to the Instituto Universitario de Pesquisas do Rio de Janeiro (IUPERJ) in Brazil, when Neuma Aguiar became the general coordinator. In 1990, the Secretariat moved to the Women and Development Unit (WAND) at the University of the West Indies in Barbados when Peggy Antrobus assumed the general coordinator's position. In 1998, it shifted to Fiji at the University of the South Pacific, with Claire Slatter as general coordinator. Bene Magunagu, former regional coordinator for Anglophone Africa, was appointed general coordinator in 2004. As of this writing, the General Secretariat has moved to Calabar, Nigeria.

DAWN's founding members are from a diversity of countries such as Brazil (Carmen Barroso), Pakistan (Zubeida Ahmad), Norway (Tone Bleie), Morocco (Fatima Mernissi), Kenya (Achola Pala Okeyo), Malaysia (Noeleen Heyzer), and the US (Katharine McKee), among others.

STÉPHANIE ROUSSEAU

See also Women: Legal Status; Women: Role in Development

References and Further Reading

Côrrea, Sonia and Rebecca Reichmann, eds. *Population and Reproductive Rights: Feminist Voices from the South.* London: Zed Press, 1994.

Côrrea, Sonia, ed. *Weighing up Cairo: Evidence from Women of the South.* Suba, Fiji: DAWN, 2000.

DAWN. *Markers on the Way: The DAWN Debates on Alternative Development.* Author, 1995.

Moghadam, Valentine. "Transnational Feminist Networks. Collective Action in an Era of Globalization." *International Sociology* 15(1), pp. 57–85, March 2000.

Sen, Gita, and Caren Grown. *Development, Crises and Alternative Visions: Third World Women's Perspectives.* New York: Monthly Review Press, 1987.

Slatter, Claire. *Beyond the Theory-Practice-Activism Divide. Tensions in Activism: Navigating in Global Spaces at the Intersections of State/Civil Society & Gender/Economic Justice.* Workshop on Gender & Globalisation in Asia and the Pacific: Feminist Revisions of the International, Canberra, Australia, November 2001. www.dawn.org.fj/publications/listofpublications.html (2001).

DE KLERK, FREDERIK W.

To understand how the white minority population (approximately 13%) accommodated to the inevitable transition to South African majority rule with a one-person, one-vote government, headed by Nelson Mandela and his African National Congress (ANC) party in 1994, an explanation is required. One of the key considerations is the essence of political leadership within the Nationalist Party (NP), which formalized apartheid (separate development of races) when it came to power in 1948 and governed as the last minority party before transition to majority (black) rule. Two further explanations include the escalating stakes and risk of civil war in the country, and the perceived shifts in the international environment as significant influences on South African governmental actions.

F. W. de Klerk served as the last Afrikaner president of the Republic of South Africa. In most respects he was an unlikely figure to guide a process that most white South Africans knew would lead unmistakably to negotiating themselves out of power, position, and privilege.

White domination of what later became the South African state began when the Dutch East India Company established a refreshment station on the southern tip of Africa in 1652. This naval port of call proved useful for provision of fresh fruits and vegetables on the long voyage from Europe to Holland's premier source of raw materials in the East Indies. De Klerk's French Huguenot ancestors arrived in Capetown by ship in 1688, early forerunners of the white migration to this distant region. His family and political roots in the area are extensive. Three generations of Afrikaner family members were prominent in provincial and national politics. His great grandfather served five years in the Senate of the first Union of South Africa government in 1910. His namesake on his mother's side served on the Provincial Council of what was then known as the Orange Free State, one of two territories dominated by the Afrikaner people. His paternal grandfather twice ran for Parliament, unsuccessfully. An uncle served as prime minister. De Klerk's own father had been a veteran National Party organizer, served as general secretary of the National Party in Transvaal Province, had stints as cabinet minister under three successive prime ministers, and culminated his political career as president of the Senate.

De Klerk was born March 8, 1936, in Johannesburg, South Africa. His family was deeply religious, adherents to the most conservative wing of the Dutch Reformed Church. His father had been a teacher, principal, and church elder, while he carried on most of his National Party work at night and on weekends, so he was often absent from the household. The family was of modest means, practiced an ethic of community service, and valued highly the intensity and inwardness of Afrikaner culture. A key part of this identity was acceptance of racial exclusivity, a cardinal tenet of Afrikaner culture since arriving in the region.

De Klerk graduated from the Hoerskool Monument secondary school in Krugersdorp and went on to pursue a conventional path for Afrikaner professionals. He went to Potchefstroom University for Christian Higher Education, an Afrikans university known for its conservatism, and in 1958 graduated with a combined degree in arts and law. Poorly skilled in athletics and music, he found his talents in student government and in the Nationalist Party Student Youth League, a training ground for young party comers. His first trip outside the country was a six-week fellowship to England, which included a small group of both Afrikans and English-speaking university students.

He practiced law for a period from 1961–1972 in Vereeniging, and simultaneously served in various local government posts. He was first elected as a member of Parliament in 1972. Appointment to the national cabinet followed as minister of posts and telecommunications, and later he held successive cabinet posts in multiple governmental sectors. By 1982, he became Transvaal leader of the National Party, a significant national pedestal, and his arrival came at a critical time for the increasingly besieged government of South Africa.

F. W. de Klerk's roots in Transvaal province, the most Afrikans part of South Africa, gave him great credibility among both Nationalist Party leadership and the rank and file. Philosophically, politically, and religiously conservative, he was skilled at negotiating with the opposition parties.

The long-term, extended pattern of state violence against its own people had brought on world condemnation, political and economic sanctions, an arms embargo, and prohibition from participation in virtually any international sports competitions. South Africa had become a pariah state among the community of nations.

By the early 1980s, internally South Africa also had become a repressive police state. The successive white governments firmly and with brutal force regularly suppressed internal black opposition, including the ANC, the Pan African Congress (PAC), and the Inkatha Freedom Party. By the late 1980s, it was clear to the more pragmatic white political leadership that change would have to come. A quiet and secret dialogue began between governmental representatives and key black influentials. The four-decade-old apartheid state had begun to corrode from within, with absolutely no prospect of salvation without radical political change.

When the previous president, P.W. Botha, still recovering from a stroke, proved unwilling to continue the largely secretive dialogue with the ANC opposition, he defiantly resigned. De Klerk had been elected National Party leader in February 1989, and with Botha's surprise resignation, that same year and with no opposition candidates, the Parliament unanimously elected him president of the Republic of South Africa.

An emergent political pragmatist and a centrist in the Nationalist Party, de Klerk took little time to inaugurate change. In a surprising policy speech in February 1990, he rescinded the ban on the ANC, the PAC, and the South African Communist Party; released most political prisoners; repealed all apartheid laws; and announced the release of Mandela after twenty-seven years in jail. Despite a volatile atmosphere of multiracial distrust and frequent outbreaks of civil violence, de Klerk and Mandela together kept the moderate white and black coalition elements together and formally opened negotiations for a new constitution.

In December 1991, the NP government and opposition parties convened a Convention for a Democratic South Africa (CODESA), following two years of hard bargaining. The draft constitution secured universal adult suffrage, a bill of rights, an independent judiciary, and abolition of the segregated homeland governments. It was the widest cross-section of opposition groups ever to assemble. The far right Conservative party, the extremist right white opposition party, the PAC, and Chief Mangosuthu Gatsha Buthelezi of the Zulus chose not to participate. However, Buthelezi's party, the Inkatha Freedom Party, did participate. The middle of the white and black political spectrum stayed engaged.

De Klerk's subsequent decision to hold a whites-only national referendum in February 1992, to approve his continued negotiation with the ANC and Mandela, secured his reform initiative. The result, with 85% of the white electorate voting, was that 68% approved continued negotiations with Mandela's ANC and other opposition parties. Although one result of the referendum was that many Afrikaners in the NP viewed de Klerk as a traitor, he successfully isolated his right-wing party opposition.

By December 1993, all but two major political parties endorsed a power-sharing agreement and the Parliament ratified an interim constitution. With the pivotal election of Mandela in April 1994, in which he won nearly 63% of the vote, the political transition was complete. De Klerk drew the second-largest number of popular votes, but the gap between the number of votes he and Mandela received was expansive. Nevertheless, it was enough for de Klerk to be named second deputy president. After nearly fifty years, apartheid as official state policy had ended. Thereafter, Western governments removed economic sanctions and the British Commonwealth restored membership to South Africa. It would only be the beginning of a much longer process of racial reconciliation and governmental transformation, a work in progress.

In retrospect, external changes also played a decisive role. In the fall of 1989, every Eastern European communist government was removed from power. By December 1991, the USSR as a state and empire had ceased to exist. The NP posture of rigid anti-Communism and its role as protector against the spread of that ideology into southern Africa had lost its rationale. The once highly touted threat and fear of Communist penetration into the region, used by previous white South African governments for Western support, proved hollow. Moreover, successful black independence movements in the wider southern African region already had isolated the white minority government in Capetown. After a seven-year civil war, the last white regime in Rhodesia had collapsed in 1980. Both Mozambique and Angola had achieved formal independence in 1975 despite ongoing civil wars. Finally, South Africa surrendered its old League of Nations mandate over Southwest Africa, and subsequently, Namibia became independent in 1990.

The de Klerk government also halted the state's nuclear, biological, and chemical weapons programs, became a party to the Nuclear Non-Proliferation Treaty, and signed the Chemical Weapons Convention. By the close of his presidency, the state had reestablished itself as a credible participant in the wider international community.

De Klerk resigned from office in 1996, and retired from politics in 1997. He and Mandela were jointly awarded the Nobel Peace Prize in 1993 for their respective leading roles in bringing about the historic, and largely nonviolent, transition to universal suffrage. After his departure from politics, de Klerk established a foundation in his name to work for peace in fractured societies.

Arguably, de Klerk's leadership of the NP may have gotten the best political prospect possible—permanent minority party status and opportunity for the white population to contribute as "backbenchers" to a multiracial political future. He tried to secure "group rights" for the white minority, but Mandela would have none of that. Politically, the drift toward one-man, one-vote rule appeared virtually inevitable, short of violent internal upheaval, which many critics thought likely. There was no credible nor viable alternative political strategy. The white minority was ultimately African and would try to make the best of their new circumstances. One could argue that heritage proved more compelling than race. F. W. de Klerk gradually, grudgingly, and skillfully moved his reluctant constituency to accept majority rule and the refashioning of the South African state after more than three centuries of white control and privilege.

JAMES E. WINKATES

See also Apartheid; Mandela, Nelson; South Africa

References and Further Reading

De Klerk, Willem. *F. W. de Klerk: The Man in His Time.* Johannesburg, South Africa: Thorold's Africana Books, 1991.
Giliomee, Herman. *Surrender Without Defeat: Afrikaners and the South African 'Miracle.'* Braamfontein, South Africa: South African Institute of Race Relations, 1997.
Meredith, Martin. *Coming to Terms: South Africa's Search for Truth.* New York: Public Affairs, 1999.
Mungazi, Dickson A. *The Last Defenders of the Laager: Ian D. Smith and F. W. de Klerk.* Westport, CT: Praeger, 1998.
Sparks, Allister. *Tomorrow Is Another Country: The Inside Story of South Africa's Negotiated Revolution.* London: Heinemann, 1995.
Thompson, Leonard. *A History of South Africa,* rev. ed. New Haven, CT: Yale University Press, 2001.

DEBT: IMPACT ON DEVELOPMENT

A large national debt, whether internal or external, is considered a major obstacle in achieving economic and subsequent social development. Many critics place the responsibility for the negative impacts of debt on the international financial institutions (IFIs), such as the International Monetary Fund (IMF) and World Bank (IBRD), led by the wealthier developed countries. The IFIs design structural adjustment programs (SAPs) intended to adapt the country's economy to the challenges of the globalized market. These SAPs are designed for achieving macroeconomic stability and subsequent debt relief, but

critics believe that they often do not fit the specific needs of the countries where they are implemented, and thus contribute to poverty and inequality. Local program mismanagement, embezzlement, lack of experience in implementation, and political dependency of the central banks also cause problems with SAPs.

Some critics view globalization as an obstacle toward local development, as it increases cross-country financial linkages that amplify the effects of various economic shocks and transmit them more quickly across national borders. However, many feel that economies of scale, which spill over national boundaries, as well as the free flow of capital and resources, yield a better international allocation of these factors of production and thus a more efficient global economy. Globalization's critics draw attention to international geopolitical interests that lead to unequal exchange, thereby perverting the democratization processes in the developing countries.

Between 1972 and 1982, the overall debt of developing nations rose from $130 billion to $600 billion, resulting in the first major debt crisis in 1982. However, the net gain of lending countries between 1982 and 1990 is estimated at $418 billion.

Debt and Growth

Large debt slows down or stops economic growth. The savings rates of the Developing Countries (DCs) generally fall, as they are unable to secure sufficient investment capital. Frequently, this forces developing nations to abandon their development plans in favor of building social safety nets. The neglect of the domestic savings, as a source of development finance, increases the country's debt-to-gross domestic product (GDP) ratio, increasing the country's economic dependence on foreign loans. High levels of foreign debt compared to GDP makes domestic economy vulnerable to debt crisis. This induces sovereign default on loan reimbursement and subsequent capital flight.

The first major debt crisis was caused by the recession in the developed world. Therefore, it became more profitable to invest the petrodollars in the West, then recycle it though western banks by lending to DCs. Thus the DCs' source of financing their development programs was drying out, but their debt service costs increased dramatically due to interest rates pegged to the London Inter-Bank Offered Rate (LIBOR). The LIBOR, the rate at which London banks borrow money from each other, is the most commonly used reference point for short-term interest rates. Fluctuations in the LIBOR have triggered massive default on debt repayments, also with a boomerang effect, causing recession worldwide. This has caused a –4% to –11% annual decrease of GDP, from Mexico to Yugoslavia, fostered also by the transition processes of the former communist countries to market economies. High levels of short-term debt and debt-to-reserves ratio, like Mexico's 5.2, Korea's 2.073, and Indonesia's 1.724 in 1994, signal long-term economic insecurity; in the case of East Asia, these ratios led to the 1997 financial crisis. The foreign debt-to-GDP ratios rose to 28% in Thailand and 21% in the Philippines, while exports shrank. The debt crisis's contagion effects spilled over Russia and Eastern Europe in 1998 and Brazil a year later. These reflect the higher instability of the interlinked, once attractive emerging capital markets of the developing world.

Debt and Trade

Trade liberalization, mainly the abolition and reduction of import duties, was prescribed for debtors as a prerequisite for qualifying for new IFI loans. To increase export earnings, a country has to increase its currency's real exchange rate; however, at the beginning a substantial initial nominal devaluation is recommended in order to make export price competitive. This free trade opens the markets of the developing world, even though developed countries continue to protect their own agricultural and basic commodity markets—the exact markets in which DCs could be more competitive.

Another recommendation for the debtors is domestic price liberalization, but this leads to high inflation in order to balance their existing fiscal deficits. As developing nations rarely have funds for technological research, they must purchase technology from developed nations, which serves to widen the existing technological gap. Developing countries, as debtors, are constrained to cheap large-scale exports of raw materials, which leads to resource depletion, while the decreased level of domestic transactions causes a multiplier effect in their own economy. This is a partial reason for dependency and poverty, since basic commodity prices are subject to heavy competition on world markets, which causes them to fluctuate and remain mostly depressed. For instance, the price of cotton has dropped by half since 1995, affecting 1 billion people worldwide. In spite of increased outputs, it has lead to decreased revenues and severely declining terms of trade for the exporting country. More than fifty developing countries have undiversified export structure, depending on three or fewer commodities for more than half of their export earnings.

Twenty such "single-commodity" countries are dependent on one or few commodities export for more than 90% of their total foreign exchange earnings.

Early trade liberalization for socially and economically unstable DCs forces these economies into price wars, which may become, in fact, a spiralling race to the bottom. Often, much of the population is left poorer and at the mercy of obscure market forces, also causing debt overhang. Once a country has fallen into poverty, it becomes more difficult to obtain contracts from the mega-retailers dominating the world trade, without severely cutting costs. To cut costs, many manufacturers resort to illegal and unsafe business practices such as child labour, lack of overtime pay, quotas, and less expensive but unsafe manufacturing practices. These in turn expose them to further trade sanctions, which reduces their competitiveness even more.

Forcing exports and stopping imports, like Romania did in the 1980s, condemns the country to backward development. This method neglects domestic markets, leading to supply shortages and inflation and decreasing living standards. Forced exports often lead to dumping, or selling goods in foreign markets for either less than they cost in the country of manufacture or less than the cost of producing the goods. Dumping then attracts protectionist countermeasures by foreign markets, which squeeze out DC products. As a response, international financial institutions initiate rescue plans that impose market-based pricing. Unfortunately, these plans often lead to increases in food and utility costs within developing nations.

Debt and Domestic Industries

In order to decrease dependency on imports, most developing countries have created import substitution industries, which requires heavy investment and increases the demand for foreign exchange. This leads to an overvalued exchange rate, which in turn diminishes exports, while the restrictions on imports cause growth prospects to worsen. Existing large amounts or ratios of debt leave no place for industrial diversification, exporting industries must be heavily subsidized, and agriculture often remains neglected. After prescribed privatization, domestic plants are often closed down by the foreign purchasers. Privatization carried out for the sake of efficiency has in some cases increased dependency on imports in the basic commodity sectors, wiping out domestic production. This affects economic sovereignty in the long run, encouraging corruption as politicians consider these sell-offs a source of commissions.

Debt and Monetary Policy

To overcome default all countries have to achieve macroeconomic stability, and in order to stop financing government deficits with seignorage and inflation tax (for example, Bolivia, Argentina, Yugoslavia), governments are required to fix their exchange rates or peg to their greatest lenders' currencies. Keeping the exchange rates stable and in favor of the lenders is costly, due to the high interest rates and reduced spending on domestic consumption. Governments then need to increase exports just to keep their currencies stable, which may not be sustainable, or appreciate them, which worsens their export terms, leading to growing deficits. In order to stop capital flight, DCs must raise interest rates to high levels to convince investors to return; however, this also fuels inflation further and can even discourage investment.

As an example, Russia fixed the ruble's exchange rate to the US dollar, attracting speculative foreign capital through the high interest rates offered on US dollar loans. The debt accumulated, and when short-term debt reached maturity, its overall size caused the collapse of the ruble's exchange rate and suppressed domestic growth. This had a boomerang effect on lender countries, causing recession in Germany, which had tried to support the Russian economy in gratitude for its stance during the German reunification. The excessive international mobility of capital shook domestic currencies. The $90 billion capital flight in Mexico between 1979 and 1983 was greater than the entire Mexican debt at that time. Brazil, as another example, wanted to freeze prices and wages to stop inflation caused mainly by high debt ratios. It opted to introduce a new currency, which led to short-run results; however, inflation doubled later, because of the loose fiscal and wage indexation policy.

Debt Service

Debt service becomes a burden in itself, hampering the development of most of the developing countries. For some it would have been even more advantageous to default on payments, but this alternative would block further lending, triggering the seizure of the county's assets abroad and a reduction of gains from international trade. If foreign lending possibilities are exhausted, governments return to domestic borrowing to a point where interest service on domestic governmental debt, as in Mexico, reaches 15% of GNP. This has led to a 50% increase in money supply for internal debt service purposes. In reality, complete country default on reimbursement is not allowed, because that may cause the worldwide collapse of the banking systems. Debt can be repaid through massive expenditure cuts and/or tax increases, but these are often politically infeasible and can be hard on a country's population, particularly if the country was impoverished to begin with.

Debt and Food

Debt obligations have driven the reorientation of agricultural production from meeting local needs, to production for export in highly skewed regional and global markets. This focus on export has decreased the self sufficiency of these countries, and increased their dependency on other nations for their food supplies. As developing nations have undertaken forced industrialization, investment sources for agriculture have dried out. In the 1950s, half of a typical developing country's GNP came from agriculture and 70–80% of its population was employed in that sector. Due to increased industrial labor demand, the workforce has migrated into urban areas, leaving labor-intensive agriculture without proper human capital, and leaving developing nations unable to produce their own food.

In the long run, improper heavy industry development strategies will exhaust the foreign credit opportunities, while failing to become competitive. So debt has to be repaid with whatever is left—agricultural products and raw materials, since these primary products' quality does not depend so much on technology. As an example, Argentina, once a world-class food exporter, has become a troubled country due to failed industrialization and its accompanying debt service, which triggered inflation of 3,000% in 1991 and led to food riots. As another example, Romanian communist dictator Ceausescu exported food, badly needed at home, to repay the country's $21 billion in external debt. He introduced food rationing, which was often carried out inequitably.

Heavily indebted poor countries (HIPCs) have sometimes turned to illegal drug production and trade, or have cut back their food subsidies. Moving toward exportable cash crops, land is diverted away from meeting local and immediate needs, which also affects the survival of millions.

Less developed countries and HIPCs cannot achieve self sufficiency in food as the first prerequisite for a sound economic development, without the large-scale use of pesticides. Debt's chain reactions and related effects are enormous. The restructuring of agricultural policies has led to the overuse of land, soil erosion, pollution, and deforestation. Wide-scale deforestation for extensive agriculture- and timber-exporting purposes causes local climate changes, contributing to global warming, severe drought, crop failure, famine, and the impossibility of sustainable development.

Debt and Living Standards

When countries first start to borrow, living standards may also rise, like in Hungary, where foreign loans were used for consumption, aimed at stopping popular discontent with the suppression of the 1956 anti-Soviet revolution. After becoming indebted, living standards have often fallen, even to poverty level as real wages declined, such as during the 1980s in Mexico, Argentina, and Peru, where wages dropped 50–70%. The value of labor decreased as world market prices were faced with planned economy wages. Additionally, the need to meet debt-servicing requirements led to a decrease in social spending. By the 1990s, most African countries were spending more on foreign debt service than on national health-care or education. Half of Africa's population lacks basic health care. In 1997, it was estimated that sub-Saharan African governments spent four to five times more for debt service than for health care. Debt affects education also, as spending for schools is decreased in order to pay off debt. Even if schools are available, economic conditions often force young children to work.

Debt and Social Change

Large debt contributed substantially to the fall of communism, predominantly in Hungary, Romania, Bulgaria, and Poland. Austerity programs led to a wave of strikes in Poland and a bloody revolution in Romania. Draconian measures aiming at debt servicing were used to justify totalitarianism. With debt repayment of developing nations to developed countries at the current rate, many argue that the world's poor are subsidizing the rich.

See also Development History and Theory; Modernization

References and Further Reading

Campbell, Bonnie K., ed. *Political Dimensions of the International Debt Crisis*. London: Macmillan, 1989.

Corbridge, Stuart. *Debt and Development*. Oxford: Blackwell, 1993.
George, Susan. *The Debt Boomerang: How Third World Debt Harms Us*. Boulder, CO: Westview Press, 1992.
Hertz, Noreena. *The Debt Threat: How Debt Is Destroying the Third World*. New York: Harper Business, 2004.
McCarthy, Mary, and G. McCarthy. *Third World Debt: Towards an Equitable Solution*. Dublin: Gill & MacMillan, 1994.
McEwan, Arthur. *Debt and Disorder: International Economic Instability and US Imperial Decline*. New York: Monthly Review Press 1996.
Payer, Cheryl. *Lent and Lost: Foreign Credit and Third World Development*. London: Zed Books, 1991.
Schwartz, Hermann. *In the Dominions of Debt: Historical Perspectives on Dependent Development*. Ithaca, NY: Cornell University Press, 1989.

DEBT: RELIEF EFFORTS

Mounting debt problems and crises ask for immediate action and also for careful balancing in deciding what are the best policies for alleviating existing indebtedness and counteracting potential financial crises. In the case of private borrowers, as those benefiting from commercial credit, or in the case of a possible default on repayment, creditors might look first to achieving debt consolidation with the debtor company's government. Consolidation of such debt is disadvantageous for the indebted developing country as foreign lenders want these governments to absorb privately contracted external debt, conditioning them with publicly contracted loan rescheduling. Thus the conversion of a foreign currency-denominated loan into domestic-currency state loans at reduced exchange rates, would, in fact, be used to subsidize the private borrowers, instead of financing the needs of the poor.

One of the first steps in alleviating the foreign debt crisis is the common action of the large banks, the International Monetary Fund (IMF) and lender industrial country governments, called concerted lending. This provides for continuous lending, imposing the will of the major lenders on the smaller banks. The debtor county's government starts negotiating an agreement with an advisory committee of the largest banks that represent the cartel of lenders. The coordination of many instances of involuntary lending is necessary to force banks to contribute new funds in accordance with their loan exposure. This will be a framework that provides consistency and predictability to borrowing countries, as well as to those who invest in emerging-market debt. This has taken the forms of extension of credit or new loans to abridge the financing gap, or debt rescheduling, which means the transformation of short-term debt into a long-term one. This rescheduling postpones the amortization of the principal, but additional interest charges may add up. In order to be able to repay maturing debt, first the country's current account deficit should be balanced with additional loans, in order to make possible a positive balance large enough to finance both interest and principal payment.

When an emerging-market country is threatened with a financial crisis, it faces the prospect of being forced to devalue its currency and default either on its government debt or on loans to the country's banks. There are two main options for avoiding these events: an IMF loan (a "bailout"), which, in fact, is also a creditor bailout, or debt restructuring (a "bail-in"). Even for restructuring purposes, countries borrow from the IMF and agree to its stabilization packages. Although the IMF loans are usually of a small size, they have a positive signaling effect for the international banking community.

Among the other goals of the IMF, it seeks to facilitate currency exchange in order to reach equilibrium for the whole economy. For that reason it established mechanisms to stabilize exchange rates. This was achieved by pegging a country's currency to the dollar and by the United States maintaining the dollar's full convertibility to gold on a fixed rate of $35 per ounce. Countries joining the Fund have a quota of special drawing rights on the fund's resources, in accordance with their money contribution to the reserve pool. The IMF initially had a central role in coordinating bank lending, but starting from the Mexican crisis in 1982, the Fund conditioned the approval of its lending on the existence of a similar consensus among private lender banks, which in turn was seen as a solvency guaranty of the debtor.

Much of that vision, however, has never materialized. Instead the IMF took to offering loans based on strict conditions. These become known later as structural adjustment (SAP) or austerity measures, dictated largely by the most powerful member nations. The IMF loan conditions focus mostly on monetary and fiscal issues. They emphasize programs to tackle inflation and balance-of-payments problems, often requiring specific levels of cutbacks in total government spending levels. The IMF prescribes usually the same four-step programs aimed at the structural adjustment of the debtor's economy, namely monetary austerity, fiscal austerity, privatization, and domestic market liberalization.

The monetary austerity measure looks at tightening up the money supply, devaluation of the domestic currency, and increase of the internal interest rates to whatever heights are needed to stabilize the value of the currency. Devaluation, however, may decrease investor confidence and imposing capital controls may result in capital flight.

Fiscal austerity aims at increasing tax collections and reducing government spending dramatically. A decreasing fiscal deficit assumes that monetary contraction would follow, but this is also unfortunately procyclical in the case of a global slowdown in economic growth. Furthermore, this measure targets the reduction or elimination of subsidies, but this hampers foreign competitiveness, and trade imbalances occur in spite of the currency devaluation. Moreover, simultaneous devaluation by many competing countries will offset the benefits of a single action in one of them. Another goal is reducing spending targets by freezing public sector wages with the hope of causing the same effect in the private sector, although inflation rates remain high. Another consequence of this policy measure is that wage cuts would further decrease domestic demand, which would already be lowered in the foreign markets. Thus, falling domestic consumption accompanied by high inflation would accentuate the recession.

The privatization policy looks to increase state revenues through the sellout of public enterprises to the private sector. Accompanied by import restraints, a trade surplus may be achieved painfully as restructuring destroys much of the existing production capacity as well as social capital.

This forced export causes resource transfer, needed for debt servicing, which is equal to net inflows of capital minus interest payments. This has ranged from a +$49.6 billion globally positive balance (+$24.6 billion to Latin America) in 1981, to a globally negative one from 1983 onward with a negative peak of –$59.1 billion in 1990. In Latin America the pattern of financing reversed even earlier, reaching –$34.7 billion in 1985. Thus, capital formation at home ended with a debt crisis, and future growth prospects were decreased as investment funds were drained by the previous debt-dependent development strategy. Although debt-service ratio as a percentage of exports had fallen to 45% in 1987 with the outstanding interest-debt ratio falling from 72%, 6% of the continent's overall production was ceded to foreign creditors. Banks could have created reserves for dealing with debt defaults, but commercial banks instead had swapped debt into equity.

The fourth main issue is domestic liberalization, which imposes financial and price deregulations. Financial liberalization removes restrictions on the flow of international capital, as well as on the operations, purchasing, and ownership of foreign businesses including banks. Price liberalization introduces world-market prices and inevitably leads to high inflation. Experience shows that successful developing countries have relied more on economic and commercial planning than on chaotic domestic half-free markets. Only when governments sign a "structural adjustment program" (SAP) agreement does the IMF agree to lend enough to prevent default on mature and unsustainable international loans. In addition, the IMF arranges a restructuring and rescheduling of the country's debt among private international lenders that includes also a pledge of new loans.

In 1956, emerging debt problems in Argentina led to the establishment of the Paris Club as a forum for negotiations between debtor country officials and the country's creditors under the supervision of a French treasury official. Paris Club principles impose equal treatment of all creditors during rescheduling talks. Prior to reaching an agreement, debtor countries sign an SAP conditional IMF loan contract aimed at enhancing the debtor's balance of trade. Private lenders negotiate through the Club in order to reschedule the public debt of foreign countries.

Usually the IMF offers a "stand-by" agreement with a one-year upper limit for financing balance-of-payment deficits in the short run. In the 1970s, the IMF programs were criticized by leaders of developing nations and by dependency economists as causing recession and punishing debtor counties for trade shortages caused by external factors or those which were endemic to their development processes. Critics charged these policies with decimating social safety nets and worsening lax labor and environmental standards in developing countries.

In response, the Fund developed new special lending facilities dealing with the consequences of the external shocks (like the oil financing facility) and loosened its conditionality. In addition, it developed longer-term, Extended Fund facilities. In spite of these improvements, many developing nations still avoided the IMF, turning instead to private credit sources, thus avoiding adjustment as well as conditionality. Therefore, the fraction of Latin American countries operating under the IMF was two-thirds between 1966 and 1970, and at the turn of the decade, 1979–1981, it had dropped to one-third. As world liquidity rose due to petrodollar recycling, the role of the Fund declined, but this was reversed by the debt crisis of 1982. After the crisis, most of the Latin American countries fell under some IMF program, with increased conditionality, which imposed austerity, without concern for its political consequences.

Even before the debt crisis, private banks offered loans only after the approval of an IMF stabilization program, and even after such has been accepted they were reluctant to increase their debt exposure toward the developing countries. The IMF prevented the banks' collective action in order to avoid a chain-default of the debtors. Thus, in the coming years, the Fund organized a cartel of creditors to dictate macro-economic policy by conditioning its loan on other inflows of capital from international banks, becoming a "central planner" of the banking world. Unwittingly, the IMF crisis policy also enabled a class-oriented distribution toward local elites, because a high proportion (40% in Argentina and Mexico, 70% in Venezuela) of the interest payments to international financial institutions (IFIs) has returned to those elites as interest on earlier capital flight.

Another key international financial institution created for such scope is the World Bank (The International Bank for Reconstruction and Development, or IBRD), which was initially designed to fund the rebuilding of the infrastructure in nations ravaged by World War II. The bank turned away from Europe after the mid-1950s, and began funding massive industrialization in the developing world. Critics have accused the bank of aggressive dealings with debtor nations, exacerbating the debt crisis and devastating many local ecologies and indigenous communities in the developing world.

The adjustment programs of the World Bank have broader views and focus more on the long term. But similar to those of the IMF, they highlight market liberalization and public sector reforms, and consider the best way of achieving growth to be through the expansion of cash crop exports. Despite these differences, World Bank and IMF adjustment programs reinforce each other, meaning that a government's plans must first be approved by the IMF before qualifying for an adjustment loan from the World Bank—this decision process is called a "cross-conditionality."

At first, debt-relief strategies made use of concerted lending. The method was seen as a temporary measure at the end of which countries would return to voluntary lending and the debtors would pay back their debt in full. In spite of some recovery shown in the early 1980s, the indebted developing countries have not been able to pay off their debts. The rising protectionism in the developed world has been named as a cause. This caused fluctuations in their terms of trade and caused a growing inability to service their debts.

The debt fatigue of developing countries became more evident as some countries limited their repayments to a certain percentage of their export revenues (Peru) or announced default (Brazil in 1987). As the chances of being repaid became slim, a secondary market for developing country loans emerged, where the price discount to face value reached 50% in 1987 and almost 70% in 1989. This reduced banks' willingness to offer more loans almost to zero, and was accompanied by an increase in bad loan reserves and fall of profits. These made necessary the adopting of an international, intergovernmental plan for debt relief. The Brady Plan abandoned the assumption of full repayment and created commercial bank syndication agreements, in order to share the banks' claims and losses and try to settle them with the debtors by lowering interest rates or forgiving the principal. The IMF was asked to lend for debt service reduction by providing new loans following a cash buyback of the debt on the secondary market. The plan also asked the IMF to stop its loan conditionality on third-party lenders' lending commitments. The Brady Plan has had only limited effects, especially on larger debtors, where it has reduced the face value of debt by only 4.7% to 18.8%. The 12% reduction in the case of Mexico was achieved through debt conversion into long-term maturity (30-year) bonds, covering face value with lower than initial debt interest rate, or lower (65%) face value with the same rate.

Notable success was registered only in small economies such as 47.1% reduction in Costa Rica, reaching 100% in Niger, which made debt cancellation a desirable target for most African countries. The supporters assert that full cancellation would enable African countries to tackle their social development challenges properly, and additional resources provided by the IFIs to support health and education programs should be conceived as public investment, not as new loans. It has been stated that the IMF and World Bank have ample resources to cancel all of the nearly $18 billion of the Highly Indebted Poor Countries' (HIPCs') debt owed to them, without jeopardizing their normal operations or cutting further grants to HIPC countries. Cancellation of the multilateral debt would be financed through contributions by rich countries and the revaluation of the IMF gold stocks. As another example, Malawi, Mozambique, Tanzania, and Uganda, between the years 2000 and 2015, would require about $72 billion in financing, but they will only be able to raise $12 billion domestically and therefore will depend on external sources, requiring that they pay more than $3 billion in debt service. This amounts to 25% of the total domestic resources available to spend in order to meet the Millennium Development Goals (MDGs).

Total debt cancellation for HIPCs would release resources to fight poverty, hunger, and disease, but even combined with existing grant schemes will still not be enough to cover HIPCs' needs to meet contemporary goals. Therefore, additional grants will be needed, because new concession—or market—loans are not feasible options as they would lead to high debt-to-GDP ratios.

Debt cancellation poses the threat of existing debt revaluation and appreciation and therefore needs intergovernmental coordination. Otherwise the incentives or coercion of collective action taken by the lenders is jeopardized, as individually no bank would voluntarily take the initiative when the possibility of cashing in the remaining debt by less generous lenders increases.

Debt relief can also be attained by trading the debt in the secondary market, where if sold it would mean a market-based reduction. If the debtor or a third party buys back its debt at a lower market rate, it runs the risk that the remaining debt will be overvalued by the market and thus the gains from the buyout would be outweighed by the costs, as happened in the case of Bolivia in 1988. The country had received a $34 million rescue pack to pay back most of its $53 million in debt. As a consequence of this transaction, the remaining debt of $19 million was overvalued by the capital market to $43.4 million, amidst growing investor confidence, thus the proceeds ended up in a large-fund giveaway to creditors.

In order to increase reaction efficiency to debt crises, it is debated that sovereign debt restructuring should be made less disorderly and costly by ranking debt according to a precise system of priorities, like in the case of non-sovereign debtors. This requires legal reforms, reducing the economic disruption that accompanies sovereign debt restructuring without upsetting the balance between the rights of creditors and debtors, in order to enable the sovereign debt market to work.

As of 2004, the external financing environment of the developing countries has improved, due to the continuous global growth experienced in 2003. As a result, prices for key commodities rose in general, especially that of oil in 2004, and financial markets have recovered, while interest rates in the developed world have remained at historically low levels. As a consequence, private capital flows to developing countries increased to $200 billion—their highest level in the last five years, but much of the developing world still has difficulty accessing the international capital markets, many exhausting their bond-issuing capacities as well. International investment in developing-country infrastructure has declined dramatically since the financial crises of the late 1990s, and with the exception of trade finance, private capital flows remain heavily concentrated in specific emerging economies and regions. Former communist countries are still in a difficult position due to their great indebtedness and unfinished structural adjustment processes. Though the most developed have become EU members, many CIS countries struggle to achieve a functioning market economy status.

LASZLO KOCSIS

See also Debt: Impact on Development; International Bank for Reconstruction and Development (IBRD) (World Bank); International Monetary Fund (IMF); Structural Adjustment Programs (SAPs)

References and Further Reading

Dale, R. S., and R. P. Mattione. *Managing Global Debt: A Staff Paper*. Washington, DC: Brooking Institution Press, 1983.

Dornbusch, R. *The Road to Economic Recovery: Report of the Twentieth Century Fund Task Force on International Development*. New York: Priority Press, 1989.

Dornbusch, R., ed. *Alternative Solutions to Developing Countries Debt Problem*. Washington, DC: University Press of America, 1989.

Dornbusch, R., and Steve Marcus, eds. *International Money and Debt: Challenges for the World Economy*. San Francisco: ICS Press, 1991.

Krugman, P., and M. Obstfeld. *International Economics: Theory and Policy*. New York: Harpers Collins College Publishers, 1994.

Pastor, M., Jr. "Latin America, the Debt Crisis and the International Monetary Fund." *Latin American Perspectives*, 16 (60).

Pilger, John. *Hidden Agendas*. New York: The New Press, 1998.

Rocha, Bolivar Moura. *Development Financing and Changes in Circumstances: The Case for Adaptation Clauses*. London: Kegan Paul International, 1999.

Stiglitz, Joseph. *Globalization and Its Discontents*. London: Penguin Books, 2002.

Weeks, John F., ed. *Debt Disaster? Banks, Governments, and Multilaterals Confront the Debt Crisis*. New York: New York University Press, 1989.

Welch, Carol. "Structural Adjustment Programs & Poverty Reduction Strategy." *Foreign Policy in Focus, Vol. 5*, Number 14, April 2000.

DEFORESTATION

An ever-increasing demand for timber and land has led to a rapid and steady decline in the world's forest reserves. Almost half of the forests that once covered the Earth some 8,000 years ago have been lost. Deforestation, or the permanent loss of expansive areas of natural forest, occurs from the large-scale logging, burning, or damaging of trees. The world's remaining forested areas are evenly distributed between boreal and temperate-zone forests covering North America; Europe; the Commonwealth of Independent States and Central China; and tropical forests of South America, Africa, and Southeast Asia. This total area is estimated to be 3.6 billion hectares. However, the remaining total forest area does not fully convey the true nature of the world's forests. This measure includes plantations as well as fragmented, degraded, and restored forests of reduced ecological value. The destruction and degradation of natural forests have enormous impact on both the local and global environment.

Causes of Deforestation

Historically, forests have been cleared for agriculture, but with increasing world population the impact on forest reserves is no longer negligible. Forests are a renewable resource, but they are finite and rapidly diminishing under present conditions. Forests are cleared for farming and pastureland and logged, often illegally, for timber. Government policies have often worked to encourage the clearing of large areas of forest. Across the globe, agricultural subsidies have promoted land conversion and intensive farming. In South America, countries such as Brazil have rewarded city dwellers with negative interest rates in return for clearing Amazonian forests for farming and large-scale cattle ranching. In the United States, timber companies are compensated for road construction, reducing the cost of tree harvesting. In Asia, forests are cleared to establish large plantations of cash crops such as rubber and oil palm.

Timber is a highly valued commodity on both local and global markets. The substantial demand for wood and other forest products for construction material, paper, fuel, pulp, and other industrial uses drives commercial logging. This industry has the ability to rapidly clear large areas of forest using chainsaws and heavy machinery. Roads are cut into the forest for access, fragmenting adjacent forest and compacting and eroding the topsoil, making regeneration of the ecosystem difficult. After commercial logging has finished, patches of cleared land and abandoned access roads facilitate the migration of local farmers further into previously closed forest.

Subsistence shifting cultivation as traditionally practiced by indigenous forest dwellers in tropical forests was once sustainable. Small areas of trees are cut down and their trunks burnt, the released organic matter adding nutrients to the soil. This process is known as slash and burn. Crops are grown on this cleared land until the area is no longer viable, usually between three and five years. Soils in tropical forests are poor and the nutrients are rapidly depleted when used for intensive crop cultivation. The farmers then move on and the area is left fallow to regenerate naturally. However, increasing population and economic demands combined with the opening up of forests by logging, encourage new colonists into the forests. The fallow rotations are shortened and the forests have less time to recover. As a result, replacement, or secondary, forest ecosystems are of a degraded quality, usually with less species diversity.

Fire sparked by lightning or spread from plantations and farms can be a crucial agent of deforestation. Forests can become degraded when only commercially viable trees are removed by selective logging. Secondary forests, forests fragmented by logging operations, and areas affected by agricultural expansion are more susceptible to fires than virgin forests. Wide gaps in the forest canopy open these forests up and they become more susceptible to drought. Flammable leaf litter on the forest floor provides fuel for fires that easily spread out of control. One example of fire-related deforestation was seen in the forest fires of Indonesia in 1997, where it is estimated that up to three hundred thousand hectares of primarily secondary forest were lost.

Another factor contributing to global deforestation is the rapid expansion of urban areas, particularly in South America, Africa, and Asia. Forests are cleared for cities and highways and flooded by reservoirs to supply drinking water. In the developed world, much of the deforestation associated with urbanisation occurred in the nineteenth and early twentieth centuries. In temperate zones, there has been a net increase in forest cover in recent years as a result of reafforestation programs. Today, much of the forest degradation in North America and Europe is due to air pollution. Fossil fuels are burnt for energy and the process releases toxic chemicals such as sulphur dioxide and nitrogen oxides into the atmosphere. These chemicals combine with water moisture in the air to produce acid rain. Exposure to acid rain has seen the destruction of 50–75% of Europe's remaining forests as trees die back in response. Regeneration of native species is prevented by the subsequent acidification of the soils.

Environmental Effects of Deforestation

Forests perform a number of ecological functions that help keep Earth habitable. Forest ecosystems contain the richest diversity of plant and animal species on Earth. As well as wood, forests offer shelter, habitat for game, fruit, forage, dyes, barks for tanning, and ingredients for medicines. However, deforestation has caused the mass extinction of many forest plants and animals. Habitats are lost too rapidly for animals to migrate to other areas, even when suitable areas exist. Genetic diversity within species decreases as the breeding pool is reduced. Animals become more susceptible to disease and less able to adapt to ecosystem changes caused by fire or declining habitat quality.

Extinctions can also occur under extended pressure from reduced animal numbers. Plant species diversity is so rich in tropical rain forests that many species are being lost before being identified or studied by scientists. As plant diversity is reduced, the integrity of the internal forest structure becomes degraded. This may mean a great loss in potential medicines and cures. Ultimately, such a forest is unsustainable, as it is vulnerable to diseases, pests, and fire.

Forests protect the topsoil, sheltering it from the effects of sun, rain, and wind. When exposed to direct sunlight, tropical soils become sterile. Without the tree roots to bind the particles together into a solid soil structure, individual particles are easily eroded by wind and rain. Without the protection of the forest canopy, intense rainfall can cause flash flooding and landslides in large cleared areas. The topsoil consists of nutrients and organic matter, and in tropical soils this surface layer is shallow. Once removed, natural regeneration of vegetation and crop cultivation is almost impossible. Deterioration of tropical soils in particular is in many respects irreversible.

Forests cleared for modern agriculture or cattle ranching are often impossible to regenerate. Intensive farming rapidly depletes the soil of nutrients, leaving it infertile. Intensive grazing rapidly weakens the soil, particularly tropical soils ill-suited to pastureland. The hooves of livestock crush the unprotected soil, reducing it to a fine dust that is easily eroded. This process is called desertification. Without a fertile, solid soil structure, natural forests cannot regenerate.

Forests influence local and global climates through the regulation of water supplies. Trees collect, store, filter, and recirculate water from the land to the atmosphere through *evapotranspiration*. Water moisture is released from the leaves in the transpiration phase of this process, increasing the humidity in forest areas and influencing local rainfall. Different trees transpire at different rates, requiring varying amounts of water. Native Australian Eucalyptus trees depend on groundwater stored in the soil for their survival. As large areas of forest have been cleared, groundwater levels have risen because of the reduction in water demand. Minerals and salts naturally contained deep in Australian soils have dissolved in the groundwater as it has risen and salinity is now increasingly affecting agricultural land, rendering it infertile. Conversely, Eucalyptus trees were planted in areas of India as part of a reafforestation program. These areas have experienced a rapid draining of the groundwater due to the high water requirements of this species.

Globally, forests significantly reduce the Earth's temperature by reflecting incoming solar radiation. In addition, the burning of forests releases carbon dioxide into the atmosphere. It is estimated that deforestation contributes 20–30% of carbon dioxide released into the atmosphere each year. Trees absorb carbon dioxide from the air and are considered to be carbon sinks. With the reduction in global forest reserves, less carbon dioxide can be absorbed. Potentially, the net effect of these processes is a significant increase in global warming and climate change.

Movements to Counter Deforestation

Forests have aesthetic, recreational, spiritual, and intrinsic value and provide a home for many forest dwellers. The past several decades have seen many groups and organisations form, locally and globally, to oppose the ongoing destruction of forests. Nongovernmental organisations such as Greenpeace, the World Wildlife Fund, and the Wilderness Society campaign to halt deforestation. These groups lobby governments to change legislation to protect more virgin forests and increase the use of plantation wood. They work to educate the public about the environmental effects of deforestation. They work with scientists and government agencies to improve understanding of forest functions, implement reafforestation programs, and conserve old-growth and other endangered forests.

Other groups organise protests to physically halt the logging of trees. One example is the Chipko Movement. Created in 1973 in India to oppose deforestation of the Indian Himalayas and the devastating floods and landslides experienced as a result, local villagers protested by embracing trees to protect them from the saw. The word "Chipko" means "'to hug." A hunger strike in 1980 achieved a moratorium on the felling of green trees in the area. Importantly, this movement has had much success in their afforestation programs, achieving a sapling survival rate of up to 85% compared to the rate of 10–15% for government plantations.

Deforestation was formally recognised as an issue of international concern in 1992 at the United Nations Conference on Environment and Development in Brazil. The Convention on Biological Diversity and the Framework Convention on Climate Change were opened for signature at this conference. These two treaties recognise the importance of forests to the global environment. In 1990, the International Timber Organisation (ITTO) defined the criteria and indicators necessary to manage forests sustainably. Members are both timber-producing and -consuming countries. The ITTO set the goal that all forest products are to come from sustainably managed forests by the year 2000. Whilst not fully achieved by 2000, the organisation has made considerable progress toward it. The Forest Stewardship Council is one nonprofit organisation that uses an internationally recognisable trademark so consumers can identify these products.

The Economic and Political Debate

Collectively, countries in the developing world have amassed a foreign debt in excess of US$1.3 trillion. The five countries containing the largest rainforest areas in the world are also those most heavily in debt. In order to finance debt repayments, developing countries cut and clear large areas of forests. In many cases, the money was originally borrowed from developed countries to finance environmentally destructive projects that can then only be repaid through further resource exploitation. The most productive land is devoted to earning export income through cash crops. Local subsistence farmers are forced onto marginal lands and into a cycle of land degradation and poverty.

In addition to international programs encouraging the sustainable management and trade of forest, there has also been recognition of the economic pressure on developing countries to log their remaining forests. The Kyoto Protocol to the United Nations Convention on Climate Change, in 1997, established the concept of emissions trading. Carbon credits may be allocated to carbon sinks such as plantations, reforestation of cleared forests, and afforestation of areas where forests have never existed. This may allow developed countries to continue emitting carbon dioxide by purchasing carbon credits from countries with significant remaining forests. This will provide an economic incentive for developing countries to protect their forest resources. As yet, there is much debate as to the definition and measurement of carbon sinks and the details of a potential trading system are yet to be established.

Unless there is significant public demand for change, governments have no real incentive to implement long-term policies for forest preservation and protection. The short-term monetary benefits and job generation from the timber industry provide economic incentive for many governments to continue sanctioning forest clearing. Until the environmental impacts are factored into the cost of timber and other forest products or demand decreases, unsustainable forest clearing will continue.

ALISA KRASNOSTEIN

See also Acid Precipitation; Biodiversity Conservation; Desertification; Environment: Government Policies; Environmentalism; Erosion, Land; Global Climate Change; Green Revolution; Pollution, Agricultural; Rain Forest, Destruction of

References and Further Reading

Amelung, Torsten, and Markus Diehl. *Deforestation of Tropical Rain Forests: Economic Causes and Impact on Development*, Tubingen, Germany: J.C.B. Mohr, 1992.

Banuri, Tariq, and Frédérique Apfell Marglin, eds. *Who Will Save the Forests? Knowledge, Power and Environmental Destruction*. London and New Jersey: Zed Books, 1993.

Colchester, Marcus, and Larry Lohmann, eds. *The Struggle for Land and the Fate of the Forests*. London: Zed Books, 1993.

Hecht, Susanna, and Alexander Cockburn. *The Fate of the Forest: Developers, Destroyers, and Defenders of the Amazon*. London and New York: Verso, 1989.

Khan, Sudruddin Aga. *The Vanishing Forest: The Human Consequences of Deforestation*. A Report for the Independent Commission on International Humanitarian Issues. London: Zed Books, 1986

Painter, Michael, and William Durham, eds. *The Social Causes of Environmental Destruction in Latin America*. Ann Arbor, MI: University of Michigan Press, 1995.

Palo, Matti, and Gerardo Mery. *Sustainable Forestry Challenges for Developing Countries*. Dordrecht and Boston: Kluwer Academic, 1996.

Richards, John, and Richard Tucker, eds. *World Deforestation in the Twentieth Century*. Durham, NC: Duke University Press, 1988.

Salim, Emil, and Ola Ullsten. *Our Forests...Our Future*. Report of the World Commission on Forests and Sustainable Development. Cambridge: Cambridge University Press, 1999.

Sandler, Todd. *Global Challenges: An Approach to Environmental, Political, and Economic Problems*. Cambridge and New York: Cambridge University Press, 1997.

Wells, K. F., N. H. Wood, and P. Laut. *Loss of Forests and Woodlands in Australia: A Summary by State, Based on Rural Local Government Areas*. Canberra, Australia: CSIRO, Division of Water and Land Resources, 1984.

DEMOCRATIZATION

The spread of, or transition to, democracy, or democratization, has been a seemingly unstoppable phenomenon, especially in the post-Cold War era. Many less developed and most former communist nations have been moving away from either right-wing authoritarian or left-wing totalitarian political regimes and moving toward embracing some form or degree of democracy, albeit at different speeds and under varying conditions. For instance, military dictatorships in Latin America have been replaced by elected civilian officials. Communism continues to be in retreat throughout most of Eastern Europe and the former Soviet Union. Many Caribbean and Pacific Ocean nations have increased political freedom and civil liberties almost to the extent of the more developed nations. Some Arab and Islamic nations in North Africa, the Middle East, and Asia have begun to open and make more transparent their political systems. In addition, women have made some steps toward more political equality. Many African nations have moved away from military domination toward some semblance of civilian control over their polities. By and large, ethnic strife has diminished. Hence, democracy can be witnessed as the preferred form of government throughout most parts of the world regardless of national boundaries, levels of development, or cultures. The theoretical acceptance of democracy on a universal basis appears to be translated increasingly, although unevenly, into practice throughout the world.

Conceptual, theoretical, methodological, and practical issues surrounding democracy and democratization are ubiquitous throughout the social sciences. These issues are related to or intertwined with a litany of other concepts and practices: accountability, representativeness, legitimacy, independence, development, modernization, colonialism, imperialism, dependency, self-determination, civilization, civic and political culture, people empowerment, grassroots participation, localization, globalization, constitutional framework, individual rights, governmental restraints, regime type, party system, human rights, economic reform, ethnic conflict, militarism, terrorism, dictatorship, repression, statism, policy orientation, capitalism, liberalization, nationalism, regionalism, globalization, gender, race, and class, among others.

Definition and Dimensions

The complexities and controversies involving democracy and democratization reflect the lack of intellectual or academic agreement as to their specific meanings. There is a general consensus, though, that democratization is a relative process leading to either a conditional or permanent state of democracy, thereby implying some goal or leading to some end point within or across societies. As such, democratization usually entails the incremental aggregation, articulation, and dissemination of democratic norms, rules, regimes, values, interests, institutions, processes, practices, and expectations in a society, regardless of national or cultural boundaries in the world. Furthermore, the amount of democracy necessary for a nation to be considered democratic is open to differing standards. In addition, the preference for a particular type of democracy (for example, liberal, communitarian, social, popular, or majoritarian) varies according to divergent, even contending, value systems and ideological perspectives. Thus, there is no universally accepted ideal or typical model of democracy existing in the theoretical world of ideas. And, there is no unanimity as to the best empirical referents or examples that should be emulated by those societies wanting to democratize their polities within the perceptual world of the senses.

A liberal form or conception of democratization appears, however, to be the most widely accepted ideal throughout many parts of the world. At its core is the value of individual freedom and is the type of democracy preferred by more economically and politically developed nations, as well as by universities, organizations, and think-tanks based primarily within them. As such, liberal democratization is a process leading toward greater political freedom for more individuals in a society. A liberal political system might typically possess, at the minimum, an authoritative constitution, a legitimate state apparatus, limited governmental power, the promotion and protection of individual civil liberties and political rights, free and competitive elections with voting rights and multiple political parties, an open legislative process, and an independent judicial system. Although liberal democratization supports, in theory, a "one-person, one-vote" conception implying political equality, the latter is seldom a realistic goal in practice for any nation, regardless of the level of development. This is because an increase in political freedom does not always correspond with or generate an equal increase in political participation, especially among the majority of the masses who appear to be less informed, more apathetic, and very inconsistent when it comes even to voting in elections.

Democratization as a change-oriented process is related to other terms implying democratic movements: diffusions, transitions, consolidations, and, sometimes, revolutions. These movements can be reduced to two main empirical dimensions: (1) more extensive democratic growth or expansion across nations, and (2) more intensive democratic development or consolidation within nations. The first dimension has been more relevant for many developing and post-communist nations with little, if any, democratic experience. The second dimension has been more applicable to modern or more fully developed nations with some democratic tradition. The telescope versus microscope analogy might be a useful way in which to analyze these dimensions of democratization and democracy over time and space.

For certain, democratization has been an uneven developmental process, historically, implying waves of expansion and contraction. Empirical research has produced contradictory results in assessing the causes, concomitants, and consequences of democracy. "Democratic deficits," "low-intensity democracy," lack of consolidation, and democratic reversals, all suggest that democratization is essentially a rather ambiguous and unpredictable phenomenon in a world of many nation-states, subnational and transnational regional organizations, and international institutions with varying ideological orientations and policy agendas.

Causes and Preconditions

The causes of democratic transition, along with the necessary or sufficient preconditions to promote democratization, have been theorized and often supported by empirical research as being generic for all nations (that is, free-market capitalism, higher levels of economic development, growing wealth, a growing middle class with improved living standards, earlier date of independence, the existence of liberal cultural values, a Protestant religious orientation, and historical experiences including lessened political instability and violence, and civilian control over the military). Some studies have produced, however, evidence that indicates that the primary cause for democracy is specifically unique to each nation. And, that there is no guarantee that either national or global capitalism will, automatically or even eventually, produce a liberal society with an open, tolerant, and democratic political system in each and every nation, especially in the Third World.

Problems of Democratization

Although the triumph of liberal capitalism over communism has apparently spurred democratization within and across these nations, evidence suggests that certain weaknesses in, and dilemmas confronting, contemporary democracy exist for many nations. That is, most of these democratizing nations possess relatively weak democratic institutions with very little democratic experience and stability. No doubt, democratic consolidation is a very complex and arduous task unless economic prosperity continues, ethnic conflict remains tempered, and interstate war is diverted. In addition, further democratization in the more developed nations does not appear to be forthcoming. In most instances, both the extension and the intensity of democracy in these nations have come to a virtual standstill, if not eroded to some degree due to internal security problems, the failure of earlier political reforms, and, possibly, because the limits of liberal or procedural democracy may have been reached with what appears to be growing apathy and decreasing activism by citizens.

Political Development

Political development is sometimes implied by democratization, a process of political change and, more explicitly, as the final part of the change process, namely democracy. Barrington Moore described and explained how a mode of production, when combined with unique historical experiences, could conceivably produce different modes of societal development, thereby determining social structure, political organization, and some forms of political behavior across societies. Therefore, economic and social development determines, in large measure, the degree and type of political development existing within societies. Seymour Martin Lipset suggested that economic wealth and political legitimacy would lead to democracy as a form of political development. Kenneth Bollen's quantitative analyses confirmed the hypothesis linking higher levels of economic development to democracy. O'Donnell found evidence to the contrary, such that higher levels of modernization, identified with liberalization and capitalism, tended to coincide with different types of authoritarianism in Latin America. He labeled this as "delayed dependent-development." Overall, contention revolves around defining which and at what levels nations should be considered politically developed, regardless of context.

Concomitants and Consequences

Democratization as a form of political development is typically thought to bring forth a number of beneficial aspects to the citizens of a society. Democratization points to increased political participation, eventually leading to greater popular control, sovereignty, and self-determination. Democratization is also thought to possess important materialistic or utilitarian advantages via government social policies covering a larger number of citizens. Government benefits as well when it is legitimized by popular voting. Then, too, there are psychological benefits for the average citizen who feels more politically empowered through increased opportunities to participate in election and legislative processes. It has also been suggested that democratization reduces class struggle and ethnic conflict, and may have a dampening effect on political violence and war. It may reflect the power of a larger and growing middle class exhibiting a higher quality of life. All in all, democratization is thought to lead to more personal freedom, psychological and material well-being, and peaceful relations.

Democratization and Globalization

Over the course of centuries, democratic theory and theorists have taken the nation-state apparatus as an essential or generic given, assuming that democracies can only be understood within a heuristic framework of societal actors and forces that are defined, objectified, and restrained by land-based territorial boundaries. This assumption has been questioned by both proponents and opponents of liberal economic development, historically, and of capitalist globalization, currently. Today, any discussion on issues associated with democracy and democratization involves global economic concerns. More specifically, the nature of the relationship between democracy or democratization and economic liberalization or capitalism is open to discourse and research. The major research question confronting scholars here is: How and why do some societies make the transition away from autocracy, authoritarianism, or totalitarianism to democracy, or become more democratic through some democratization process? Underlying this question is an ideological contention among first those theorists who assert that both domestic and global capitalism produce greater democratization and second those theorists who postulate the opposite effect including authoritarianism, and third those theorists to be found somewhere in the middle, emphasizing low-level democracy or even reversing the direction of the causal relationship, from democratization to globalization.

Clash of Civilizations

With the reunification of Germany, the freeing of Eastern Europe, and the dismantling of the Soviet Union, Samuel Huntington describes the "third wave" (that is, 1970–1990 and beyond) of democratization in the world during the late twentieth century. He defines a democratization wave as a group of highly diverse and ultra-complex transitions from nondemocratic to democratic polities and regimes occurring within certain temporal and spatial parameters.

This wave is thought to be more dominant, both quantitatively and qualitatively, than transitions to non-democratic regimes and polities during the same time frame. His argument is that, although the first two waves (that is, 1828–1926 and 1943–1962) produced some reverse waves in which some regimes and polities digressed back to non-democratic practices, the third wave of democratization is likely to be different because of the intellectual influence of neoliberal ideas and the dynamic power of global capitalism. Such a bold prediction can be made due to the fact that these liberal capitalist causes or concomitants of democratization currently have very few, if any, challengers since fascism and communism have been defeated and are no longer viable threats to liberal democracy in the twenty-first century. In a later work, Huntington (1993) speculates about the increased probability for a "clash of civilization," with world politics entering into a new phase where cultural differences will be the primary sources of international conflict, as was the case during the Crusades. According to Huntington, civilizations are differentiated from each other on the basis of culture including history, religion, language, and tradition. He posits that the new cleavages for conflict will be in the Middle East, the Balkans, and Central Asia because modern Western or Northern ideas and forces (for example, rationalism, secularism, materialism, capitalism, liberalism, and democracy) and traditional cultures or religions (for example, Islam and Confucianism) pointedly and rigidly intersect without much understanding and compromise, thus leading to competition and conflict.

End of History

Francis Fukuyama posits the thesis that history and its internal spirit, represented by the long evolution of human endeavor with all its impediments, end with the creation of democracy as the final resting place for humankind. Modernization and modernity have reached their climatic zenith or finish with democracy as the essential part of the new human condition. Fukuyama goes on to establish a view that the triumph of liberal-capitalist democracy on a global level fulfills the human struggle or striving for a universal rational order. The end of the quest changes, once and for all, a substantial part of the human condition, possibly reducing many human afflictions, removing humans from the scourge of history and transmitting them to their future destiny within a single world, guided by a singular logic—global liberal capitalism.

STEVEN S. SALLIE

See also Authoritarianism; Bureaucratic Authoritarianism; Constitutionalism, Definition; Dictatorships

References and Further Reading

Beetham, David. "Conditions for Democratic Consolidation." *Review of African Political Economy*, 21, no. 60, 1994.

Bollen, Kenneth A., "Liberal Democracy: Validity and Source Biases in Cross-National Measures. *American Journal of Political Science*, 37, 1993.

"Democratisation in the Third World." Special issue, *Third World Quarterly: Journal of Developing Areas*, 14, no. 3, 1993.

Diamond, Larry. "Democratization and the Third World." In *Global Transformation and the Third World*, edited by Robert E. Slater, Barry M. Schutz, and Steven R. Dorr. Boulder, CO: Lynne Rienner, 1993.

Diamond, Larry, Marc F. Plattner, Yun-han Chu, and Hung-mao Tien, eds. *Consolidating Third Wave Democracies*, Vol. 1. Baltimore, MD: Johns Hopkins University, 1997.

Dryzek, John S. *Democracy in Capitalist Times: Ideals, Limits, and Struggles*. New York: Oxford University, 1996.

Falk, Richard. "Democratising, Internationalising, and Globalising: A Collage of Blurred Images," *Third World Quarterly: Journal of Developing Areas*, 13, no. 4, 1992.

Fukuyama, Francis. *The End of History and the Last Man*. New York: Free Press, 1992.

Gill, Stephen. "Globalization, Democratization, and the Politics of Indifference." In *Globalization: Critical Reflections*, edited by James H. Mittelman. Boulder, CO: Lynne Rienner, 1996.

Gills, Barry. "Low Intensity Democracy." *Third World Quarterly: Journal of Emerging Areas*, 13, no. 3, 1992.

Huntington, Samuel P. *The Third Wave: Democratizing in the Late Twentieth Century*, Norman, OK: University of Oklahoma, 1991.

Huntington, Samuel P. "The Clash of Civilizations." *Foreign Affairs*, 72, no. 3, 1993.

Lipset, Seymour M. "Some Social Requisites of Democracy." *American Political Science Review*, 53, 1959.

Moore, Barrington, Jr. *Social Origins of Dictatorship and Democracy: Lord and Peasant in the Making of the Modern World*. Boston, Beacon Press, 1966.

O'Donnell, Philippe, C. Schmitter, and Laurence Whitehead, eds. *Transitions in Authoritarian Rule: Latin America*. Baltimore, MD: Johns Hopkins University, 1986.

DENG XIAOPING

Deng Xiaoping (1904–1997) assumed leadership of the People's Republic of China following the momentous Third Plenum of the Eleventh Central Committee of the Chinese Communist Party (CCP) in December 1978. He was the chief proponent of the policy of openness and reform (*gaige kaifang*) that stimulated rapid economic growth and social development in China throughout the 1980s and early

1990s. Until his death in 1997, Deng continued successfully to promote Chinese economic development, while at the same time preserving the political predominance of the CCP in the face of major challenges to its authority.

Born in the village of Paifang, Guang'an County, Sichuan Province, China, on August 22, 1904, Deng rose through the ranks of the CCP during the course of a lengthy career of dedicated service to the Communist cause. His involvement in revolutionary politics began in the early 1920s when he became a leading member of the Communist Youth League while studying in France under a work-study program sponsored by the French government. In 1926, he relocated to Moscow where he studied for a year at Eastern University, newly established by the Third Communist International (Comintern).

Following his return to China in 1927, Deng served in the upper ranks of the CCP in the aftermath of the "April Massacre," when the Party's united front with the Guomindang (Nationalist Party) led by Chiang Kai-shek was brought to an abrupt and violent end following the reunification of China in the Northern Expedition. In July 1931, Deng was dispatched to the Jiangxi Province where Mao Zedong and other members of the Communist leadership had established a rural soviet. During the Party's narrow escape from Guomindang forces in the "Long March" of 1934–1935, he became one of Mao's most competent and trusted advisors, serving in the top leadership of the CCP as it built a new base of power in the remote village of Yenan in Shaanxi Province.

During most of World War II, Deng served as political commissar for the 129th division of the Eighth Route Army during its heroic struggle against the Japanese occupation of northern China. In the CCP–Guomindang civil war that followed (1946–1949), he continued as a top political commissar in the People's Liberation Army and achieved great renown for his outstanding successes in defeating Chiang Kai-shek's Nationalist forces in northern China. In the years immediately following the establishment of the People's Republic of China in 1949, Deng led the Southwest China Bureau that consolidated Communist control over Sichuan and surrounding regions.

Transferred to the central government at Beijing in 1952, Deng assumed a number of official titles before rising to the eminent rank of general secretary of the Politburo in 1956. Following the disastrous Great Leap Forward (1958–1960) and Mao Zedong's subsequent retirement from the frontline leadership, Deng and Liu Shaoqi emerged as China's top officials. Throughout the early 1960s, these two men strove with considerable success to restore the country's agricultural and industrial economies.

Mao's great displeasure with the "right opportunist line" of the CCP under the leadership of Deng and Liu prompted him to initiate the Great Proletarian Cultural Revolution in 1966. Banished from the capital by Mao's radical supporters in October 1969, Deng resided in Jiangxi Province until February 1973, when a series of bizarre shifts in Cultural Revolution politics led Mao to recommend his political rehabilitation. His return to the central leadership did not last long, however, and in April 1976, he once again ran afoul of the radicals and was forced from his position. But following the death of Mao in September 1976, and the subsequent arrest of Mao's wife, Jiang Qing, and the other extreme leftists that comprised the notorious "Gang of Four," he was welcomed once more into the ranks of the central leadership.

Following the Third Plenum of the Eleventh Central Committee of the CCP in December 1978, Deng emerged as the most powerful leader in the Communist hierarchy and moved quickly to bring reform-minded supporters such as Hu Yaobang and Zhao Ziyang into the ruling Politburo. Adopting the slogan "practice is the sole criterion of truth," Deng condemned the leftist radicalism of the Cultural Revolution and vigorously promoted the "Four Modernizations" in the areas of agriculture, industry, national defense, and science and technology.

Among the earliest innovations associated with the Four Modernizations was the establishment of "key universities" to train a new generation of scientists and technicians. In the countryside, peasants were permitted to engage in formerly forbidden "side-occupations," which included a wide range of private initiatives in growing, processing, and marketing agricultural commodities. The managers of state industries were allowed greater flexibility in rewarding individual productivity among their workers and in determining output on the basis of market considerations. In general, throughout China private incentives and market forces were allowed to function more freely as a stimulus to social and economic development.

Attention was also directed toward political reform, and major efforts were undertaken to combine "centralism" with "people's democracy," thus broadening the base of decision making within the ranks of the CCP. Measures were also taken to ensure judicial organizations greater independence and to reinforce the principle of equality of all people before the law. These political reforms and new legal protections did not, however, extend as far as many had hoped. Deng's harsh suppression of the Democracy Wall movement in early 1979 following publicly posted appeals for a "fifth modernization," or democracy, clearly demonstrated the limits of political change. While new freedoms would be allowed in the sphere of economic development, the Party led by Deng would tolerate no challenge to its political supremacy.

Throughout the 1980s, Deng's policy of *gaige kaifang*, or "reform and openness," was progressively expanded as new programs were implemented to stimulate growth in agriculture and industry. To promote foreign investment and develop China's export industries, four "special economic zones" were created near major coastal cities. These zones served as the incubation quarters for a variety of new joint enterprises with foreign corporations. Improved political relations with Japan and the United States at this time opened the markets of these countries to Chinese goods, creating a favorable balance of trade and encouraging a greater flow of capital into China.

Unfortunately, the phenomenal economic growth of China in the 1980s also generated some negative consequences, such as high inflation, unemployment, and increased corruption among government officials. The hardships and uncertainty of the new economy, combined with a lack of democratic reform by the Communist government, led university students to take to the streets in protest, culminating in the tragic Tiananmen Square incident in the summer of 1989. Deng's ruthless suppression of the mass demonstrations at Tiananmen effectively squashed political dissent and reasserted the authority of the CCP at a time when the Communist governments of the Soviet Union and Eastern Europe were rapidly collapsing.

Until his death in Beijing on February 19, 1997, Deng continued to promote modernization and economic expansion in China while handing the reins of political power over to a new generation of technocratic leadership represented by such men as Jiang Zemin (President, 1993–2004) and Zhu Rongji (Premier, 1998–2004). And while the CCP struggles to redefine its evolving ideology with slogans such as "socialism with Chinese characteristics," the rapid emergence of China as an economic superpower in the 1990s provides abundant testimony to the effectiveness of Deng Xiaoping's pragmatic, albeit authoritarian, political leadership.

MICHAEL C. LAZICH

See also China, People's Republic of; Chinese Communist Party; Communist Economic Model; Mao Zedong

References and Further Reading

Baum, Richard. *Burying Mao: Chinese Politics in the Age of Deng Xiaoping*. Princeton, NJ: Princeton University Press, 1994.

Deng Xiaoping. *Selected Works of Deng Xiaoping (1975–1982)*. San Francisco: China Books and Periodicals, 1984.

Evans, Richard. *Deng Xiaoping and the Making of Modern China*. New York: Viking, 1994.

Goodman, David. *Deng Xiaoping and the Chinese Revolution*. London and New York: Routledge, 1994.

Salisbury, Harrison. *The New Emperors: China in the Eras of Mao and Deng*. Boston: Little, Brown & Co., 1992.

Shambaugh, David, ed. *Deng Xiaoping: Portrait of a Chinese Statesman*. London: Clarendon Press, 1995.

Shirk, Susan. *The Political Logic of Economic Reform in China*. Berkeley, CA: University of California Press, 1993.

Teiwes, Frederick. *Politics and Purges in China*. Armonk, NY: ME Sharpe, 1993.

Yang, Benjamin. *Deng: A Political Biography*. Armonk, NY: ME Sharpe, 1998.

DESERTIFICATION

Desertification is the spread of desert-like conditions into previously nondesert areas. The process invariably impoverishes the terrestrial ecosystem and degrades the biological productivity of the soil, limiting its ability to support crops and livestock. Since the early 1970s, when the phenomenon gained attention in academic and public discourse, several other terms, including desertization, aridification, aridization, sahelization, and desert encroachment, have been proposed as substitutes for desertification. However, the latter has been much more utilized than any of its contenders over the years (Grainger 1990). Desertification is a broad concept, characterized by the degradation of soil and vegetation. It is neither drought nor soil erosion nor vegetation degradation, per se; it involves some combination of all these and much more (Verstraete 1986).

Deserts are situated in subtropical zones, mainly between latitudes 15° and 30° north and south of the equator, where the global wind circulation system limits rain-producing convection. While the places that are mostly affected are the desert margins, it is important to stress that, contrary to popular belief, the process can occur in any dryland area. Furthermore, desertification is not the desert expansion of popular imagination, for it does not proceed with a smooth, broad frontline; rather it develops like a subtle, insidious, patchy "rash," and usually occurs far away from the desert fringes. However, as the random collection of desertified land grows and links up, it can eventually join with deserts, with the final result looking as though the desert itself had expanded.

Desertification is a primordial problem, but was brought into sharp public focus by the severe drought and famine that afflicted the Sahel region of Africa between 1968 and 1972. The Sahel is the semiarid region lying just south of the Sahara. The drought resulted in about 250,000 human deaths, loss of millions of livestock, and the exodus of millions of people. This tragedy prompted the United Nations to organize a "Conference on the Human Environment" in Stockholm in 1972, culminating in the formation of the Committee for Drought Control in the Sahel; the Sahel Club; and the United Nations Saharo-Sahelian Office to coordinate combating strategies and aid to the drought-stricken countries. When the Sahelian drought reoccurred in 1975, the UN Conference on Desertification (UNCOD) was organized in Nairobi, Kenya, to explore ways to alleviate desertification. The United Nations Environment Programme (UNEP) was founded in Nairobi to implement UNCOD's Programme of Activities to Combat Desertification (PACD).

Against this backdrop the available literature asserts that desertification is routinely associated with drought, famine, and underdevelopment. While the impact of desertification is far more dramatic in developing countries, the phenomenon is not limited to them; the infamous Dust Bowl that swept across the Great Plains of the United States during the 1930s attests to this. Today, the regions facing intense desertification are those along the fringes of existing deserts, especially countries bordering the southern margins of the Sahara Desert, where the rate of encroachment is estimated at seven kilometers per annum. Other prime regions flank the Gobi in China, Thar in India and Pakistan, and the Atacama Desert in the South American countries of Chile and Peru. Other specific countries that are affected by desertification include Mali, Niger, Sudan, Ethiopia, Somalia, Mauritania, Algeria, Iraq, Jordan, Lebanon, India, Pakistan, Afghanistan, China, Australia, and the United States. Estimates of the global landmass impacted by desertification range from 20 million to 32 million square kilometers; some seventy thousand square kilometers of land (an area the size of Ireland) is desertified each year.

Causes and Consequences

The causes of desertification are still in dispute. The relative importance of human activities vis-à-vis drought or climate change to the spread of desert-like conditions is still a matter of debate, mainly because of the acute lack of reliable scientific data on the phenomenon. Whereas some attribute desertification to short-term periods of intense drought, others believe it is caused by long-term climate change toward aridity. Some trace the phenomenon solely to human activities, while others see it as a result of an intricate combination of poor land use and climate change. Presently, the favoured explanation among many scientists accords the causal primacy to human activities, with drought (or climate change) acting as a catalyst; thus, desertification can occur with or without drought, but it proceeds faster in the presence of drought (Grainger 1990).

Desertification is epitomized by the degradation of vegetation and soil, both of which are attributable to poor land use through processes such as overgrazing, overcultivation, deforestation, and poor irrigation. Even under the best of circumstances, cropping puts intense pressure on the land, as it normally requires the clearance of vegetation and the tilling of soil. With extensive fallow periods and innovative agricultural practices (such as, the use of mulches, manures, and fertilizers), soil capability is sustained over a protracted period. However, where overcropping is somehow necessitated by severe population pressure and a dire struggle for survival on marginal lands, soil degradation becomes inevitable.

Overgrazing is yet another practice that reduces the productive capacity of soil, as it exposes the land to climatic elements and ruins soil through intense stumping and trampling by livestock. As grazing animals pack the earth down with their hooves, it creates soil compaction, which, in turn, blocks the natural seepage of air and water through the soil. Under such circumstances, grass and other vegetation may be too disrupted to even reseed themselves. The eventual loss of vegetative cover renders the soil susceptible to erosion.

Trees play a crucial protective role in the dryland ecosystem, and their removal for timber and fuel supply increases the soil's vulnerability. However, the vast majority of people across the developing world still depend on wood as their main source of household fuel. In African countries such as Mali, Burkina Faso, and Chad, fuelwood accounts for more than 75% of the total national energy consumption. Traditionally, fuelwood has been gathered from dead wood, but due to population pressure, many people are resorting to the wholesale cutting of trees for fuelwood. In places such as India, Pakistan, and Bangladesh, the shortage of fuelwood has forced many to rely on animal dung for fuel. But this is also robbing the farmlands of nutrients and organic matter.

Undoubtedly, one of the most resourceful mechanisms for cropping in drylands is irrigation. Not surprisingly, many governments and development organizations have supported irrigation schemes over the years. However, soil salinization resulting from the poor management of irrigation projects has led to waterlogging and the formation of salt crust on dryland surfaces in many countries in Southwest Asia, the Middle East, and North Africa. Recently, human activities such as industrial mining; uncontrolled tourism; and military actions, including troop manoeuvres, testing of nuclear and strategic weaponry, and the use of biological and chemical weapons, have all been implicated in desertification (Babaev 1999).

While poor land practices such as overgrazing, overcultivation, and deforestation are the main culprits for desertification in the developing world, it is important to stress that these variables are intricately interwoven with the quintessential problems of mass poverty, economic deprivation, illiteracy, population pressure, and misguided government policies. To increase the production of cash crops in the face of severe population pressure, marginal lands are routinely brought under cultivation in many developing countries, with little regard to their carrying capacity. Several governments in the developing world are also supporting agricultural practices that replace sustainable traditional farming systems with cash-crop production under ill-conceived plantation and mechanization schemes.

A crucial factor in the dynamics of desertification in the developing world is population pressure. High population densities have put enormous stress on farmlands, and extended cropping into unsustainable arid and semi-arid environments in places such as Pakistan, Bangladesh, Somalia, and Ethiopia. Yet, from the standpoint of many people in these countries, large families make splendid economic sense, as children are usually the prime source of farm labour and sometimes the only social security against old age and sickness. Indeed, high population, like desertification, is not only a result of underdevelopment, but also a potent explanatory variable of underdevelopment.

Desertification is a serious ecological hazard. Large parts of the dry areas of the world are being degraded, with serious consequences for the well-being of millions of people. While desertification anywhere has global repercussions, the human impact is by far the most damaging in and around drylands. Desertification is essentially a human problem, in the sense that both the main causes and effects are linked to humans. The most dramatic consequences of desertification are manifested in the economic hardships, land abandonment, famines, diseases, refugee crises, and premature deaths that are so common in the developing world. Apart from the physical hardships engendered by desertification, the process puts mammoth emotional stress on its victims. Those who are hard hit experience a deep sense of hopelessness, uncertainty, and apathy, stemming from the customary loss of control and social status associated with the phenomenon.

Combating Desertification

Over the years, several countries have embarked on programs to control desertification. In the Negev Desert of Israel, for instance, a desert reclamation program of tree planting and "drip or trickle irrigation," involving the use of perforated plastic pipes to drip water into the soil directly, have been in place for years now. Similarly, in the United States an expensive system of subsurface irrigation, using perforated plastic, has been deployed extensively in California's Imperial Valley. In both cases, the plastic acts as mulch to reduce evaporation, while the perforated holes drip precise amounts of water and fertilizer directly on plants to economise water and to alleviate salinization. Also, in the Australian arid outback, windbreaks of drought-resistant trees have been planted to slow the spread of desert. While some of these reclamation programs have been successful, others, especially in the developing world, have failed. For instance, China's attempt to plant grasses and trees along the fringes of the Takla Makan and Gobi deserts proved a fiasco; so did efforts by African countries such Algeria, Mauritania, and Mali to develop greenbelts along the Sahara. Libya's attempt to halt the spread of sand dunes by spraying oil on them failed as well.

Limited financial resources and the lack of expertise and reliable data on desertification are among the key problems militating against desert reclamation programs worldwide. Remote sensing techniques such as satellite imagery and aerial photography are well-positioned to assist in this area. With the appropriate expertise and logistics, such tools can help monitor drylands to provide early warnings on the spread of desert-like conditions. The poor land practices that foster desertification are mediated by several socioeconomic factors, such as poverty and population pressure. Consequently, measures to combat desertification must not focus solely on technical, agricultural, environmental, and engineering approaches alone, but must also address the socioeconomic and cultural dimensions of the phenomenon. Moreover, because most of the farmers who till marginal lands tend to be poor, they usually have little or no choice but to make their living from such lands. Therefore, in addition to improving the agricultural practices of these farmers, combating policies should also include measures that favour low-income farmers.

More specifically, programs should be initiated to encourage the development and eventual substitution of other energy sources such as natural gas, electricity, and solar energy for fuelwood. Moreover, effort must be made to increase the productivity of rain-fed cropping on good land so as to limit the infiltration of farms into marginal lands. Tree planting and environmentally sound irrigation methods should be encouraged to restore the vegetative cover and to alleviate salinization, respectively. There is also the need to develop indigenous science and technology to monitor the spread of desert-like conditions in drylands. Finally, authorities need to expand local awareness of desertification and the skill with which to combat the phenomenon through mass educational campaigns. All the combating measures need to be contextual and flexible enough to encompass a wide range of local situations, as the affected areas vary in their environmental and socioeconomic settings. Desertification may be reversible, but the possibility and the speed of recovery will ultimately depend on the stage of deterioration reached, the regenerative power of the ecosystem, and the support of the local people.

JOSEPH MENSAH

See also Deforestation; Salinization; Sahel; United Nations Development Program (UNDP)

References and Further Reading

Babaev, Agajan G., ed. *Desert Problems and Desertification in Central Asia*. Berlin, New York, Tokyo, London: Springer, 1999.

Caldwell, J. C. *Desertification, Demographic Evidence 1973–1983*. Occasional Paper No. 37. Canberra: Development Studies Centre, Australian National University, 1984.

Glantz, Michael H., ed. *Desertification: Environmental Degradation in and around Arid Lands*. Boulder, Colo.: Westview Press, 1977.

Grainger, Alan. *The Threatening Desert: Controlling Desertification*. London: Earthscan Publication Ltd (in association with United Nations Environment Program, Nariobi), 1990.

Heathcoat, R. L., ed. *Perception of Desertification*. Tokyo: United Nations University, 1980.

Heathcoat, R. L. *The Arid Lands: Their Use and Abuse*. London and New York: Longman, 1983.

Mabbutt, J. A., and Andrew W. Wilson, eds. *Social and Environmental Aspects of Desertification*. Tokyo: The United Nations University, 1980.

Mainguet, Monique. *Aridity: Drought and Human Development*. Berlin, New York, Tokyo, London: Springer, 1999.

Mechelein, Wolfgang, ed. *Desertification in Extremely Arid Environments*. Stuttgart, Germany: International Geographical Union, 1980.

Turk, Jonathan, and Amos Turk. *Environmental Studies*, 4th ed. Philadelphia, New York, and Toronto: Saunders College Publishing, 1988.

United Nations. *Desertification: Its Causes and Consequences.*, Oxford, England; Elmsford, NY; Toronto, Canada; Rushcutters Bay, NSW, Australia; Pferdstrasse, Germany: Pergamon Press Ltd, 1977a.

United Nations Draft Plan of Action to Combat Desertification. UN Conference on Desertification, Nairobi, August–September 1977, Document A/CONF.74/L.36, 29. Nairobi, Kenya: United Nations Environmental Program, 1977b.

Verstraete, Michel, M. "Defining Desertification: A Review," *Climatic Change* 9, pp. 5–18.

Walls, James. *Combating Desertification in China*. Nairobi, Kenya: United Nations Environment Programme, 1982.

Well, Stephen G. and Donald R. Haragan, eds. *Origin and Evolution of Deserts*. Albuquerque, NM: University of New Mexico Press, 1983.

DE-STALINIZATION (1953–1956)

De-Stalinization is the term commonly applied to the hesitant efforts by J. V. Stalin's successors in the Soviet Union, and their counterparts in some other Communist states, to dissociate themselves from the tyrannical aspects of Stalin's rule after his death on March 5, 1953. They began by de-emphasizing Stalin's much-acclaimed achievements and silently abandoning the previous practice of citing his writings as authoritative in virtually every context. What was called the "cult of the individual" (sometimes translated as "cult of personality") was repudiated in favour of "collective leadership" by members of the party Presidium. Paradoxically, the widely feared security chief, Lavrentii Beria, led the way in introducing reforms. These included an amnesty for criminal offenders and an exoneration of the eminent physicians who, in January 1953, had been charged with conspiring to kill party and government leaders ("doctors' plot"). A cautious start was made on releasing and rehabilitating prominent political prisoners, among them the wife of Foreign Affairs Minister Viacheslav M. Molotov. In foreign policy a "new course" was proclaimed that involved removing minor irritants to diplomatic relations with the Western powers and furthering an armistice to end the Korean War. In a symbolic gesture the Kremlin was opened to tourists. In affairs, Beria signaled a readiness to appoint non-Russians to leading posts, while Georgii M. Malenkov, as chairman of the Council of Ministers, hinted at greater solicitude toward consumers' needs.

These "liberal"-looking policies were unwelcome to Nikita Khrushchev, who had taken control of the party machinery. In June 1953, he staged a dramatic confrontation with Beria, who was arrested at a party Presidium meeting and subsequently (December 1953) shot, along with six other senior

455

security officials, after Stalinist-style pseudo-judicial proceedings. The party leader then consolidated his power by charging Malenkov with "errors" in agricultural policy (February 1955) and forcing him to yield his post as head of government to a Khrushchev associate, Nikolai A. Bulganin. Some months later Molotov was publicly humiliated by being made to acknowledge an ideological transgression.

In foreign and defense policy Khrushchev took a "hawkish" line that appealed to the military lobby. This implied priority for heavy industry, especially armaments, at the expense of consumer goods. But, simultaneously, Khrushchev pushed forward major reforms in agriculture. Collective farmers were paid higher prices for the produce they delivered and had their obligatory quotas reduced. However, restrictions on household plots were maintained, since they were seen as reprehensible islands of "bourgeois" individualism in a collectivist society. Rural residents gained less than workers or state employees from introduction of a minimum wage (1956) and improved pensions. Urban dwellers, whose share of the population was rising fast, earned higher incomes and benefited from a more balanced diet and better social services (education, health), as well as a boom in housing construction. Even so, Soviet living standards still lagged behind those in Eastern, let alone Western, Europe and the lot of working women with families was particularly harsh.

By 1956, a secret investigation had disclosed the massive scale of repression under Stalin. The information may have genuinely shocked Khrushchev; in any case he realized that a limited publicizing of the record would discredit those of his associates more deeply implicated in these crimes than he had been. On Feburary 24–25, 1956, at a restricted session of the twentieth party congress, he revealed selective evidence of Stalin's misdeeds: the torture and murder of countless innocent citizens, his failings as war leader, and his fraudulent claims to ideological correctness and scientific expertise. Khrushchev's report made a tremendous impact on his listeners, many of whom were privately glad that the guilt was conveniently placed on the deceased leader, leaving them free to function much as before; Khrushchev explicitly denied that Leninist single-party rule was at fault and called on the faithful, not to examine their consciences, but to work even harder at "building communism."

This was to overestimate people's gullibility. The disclosures shattered the party's moral authority and exposed it to challenges at home and abroad. Within the USSR expressions of discontent could be quelled easily, but in some satellite countries, where

Communist power was shakier, the ruling parties faced open resistance. In October 1956, when Polish Communists installed a new leadership under the moderate Wladyslaw Gomulka, who had been persecuted under Stalin, Moscow reluctantly concurred with the change. In Hungary, revolution broke out. Soviet forces were withdrawn only to return in force a few days later: the reformist leader Imre Nagy was seized and later killed; there were twenty-one thousand casualties and ten times as many Hungarians fled to freedom. Westerners who had deemed communism "progressive" were disillusioned. De-Stalinization also widened the breach between the USSR and the Chinese People's Republic, where Mao Zedong—a dictator cast in a Stalinist mold—objected to what he saw as Khrushchev's naiveté and treachery.

The Soviet leader was temporarily forced on the defensive but rebounded in early 1957, having secured support for his reformist course among party cadres. This proved decisive in defeating a plot by his colleagues to depose him (June). The members of this so-called anti-party group were demoted but not physically liquidated in Stalinist style, for the political climate had become more civilized. This was Khrushchev's achievement. He reformed the judicial system and largely dismantled the vast network of forced-labor camps and settlements (gulags): by January 1959, the number of inmates stood at less than 1 million, as against more than 5 million six years earlier. Those released received minimal compensation for their sufferings and could not mention them publicly; yet in human terms this was the most significant result of de-Stalinization.

JOHN KEEP

See also Central and Eastern Europe: History and Economic Development; Central and Eastern Europe: International Relations; Russia

References and Further Reading

Burlatskii, Fedor M. *Khrushchev and the First Russian Spring: The Era of Khrushchev Through the Eyes of His Advisor*. Translated by Daphne Skillen. New York: Scribners; Maxwell Macmillan International, 1991.

Conquest, Robert. *Power and Policy in the USSR: The Study of Soviet Dynastics*. London: Macmillan, 1960; New York: St. Martin's, 1961.

Filtzer, Donald A. *The Khrushchev Era: De-Stalinization and the Limits of Reform in the USSR, 1953–1964*. Basingstoke and London: Macmillan, 1993.

Rigby, T. H. *Political Elites in the USSR: Central Leaders and Local Cadres from Lenin to Gorbachev*. Aldershot and Brookfield, VT: Edward Elgar, 1990.

Zubkova, Elena Yu. *Russia After the War: Hopes, Illusions and Disappointments*, translated by Hugh Ragsdale. Armonk, NY, and London: ME Sharpe, 1998.

DEVELOPMENT HISTORY AND THEORY

The Idea of Development

From prior to the time of recorded history to well into the Common Era (CE), ideas of development and progress did not play a salient role in peoples' lives. For the many generations of humans who lived as hunter-gathers, for instance, the rhythms of the earth and the pattern of life suggested recurrent cycles and constancy. Each generation expected to live much the same as their parents and grandparents. Even with the advent of agriculture some twelve thousand years ago and the rise of recorded history, this basic view of life was manifested in philosophical and religious thought. Agriculture certainly reinforced the notion that cycles were the norm, and religious ideas and rituals emphasized such natural patterns. The classical historians duly recorded that entire peoples and empires would rise and fall in time, with no hope of escaping life's ineluctable pattern.

Around the seventeenth century, however, certain modes of thought began to draw attention to the potential of the human intellect and the power of knowledge. Francis Bacon, Rene Descartes, Baruch Spinoza, and Isaac Newton, for example, fostered faith in the potential of science to unlock the mysteries of God's universe and a consequent pride in the achievements of human reason. As the world was explored and different, non-European peoples and cultures were encountered, there developed a greater openness to new ideas about the patterns of life.

By the eighteenth century, a host of powerful thinkers such as Locke, Montesquieu, Hume, Voltaire, Rousseau, and Kant had initiated a revolution in thought that would be labeled the Enlightenment. Increasingly, people began to believe that through the acquisition of knowledge and the application of Reason, an individual could expect improvement. Indeed, whole nations might progress in this manner. Ideas of progress and development began to take root and to flourish.

Among the first to apply these insights to the subject of development were economists Adam Smith, David Ricardo, Thomas Malthus, and Jean-Baptiste Say. In his seminal work, *The Wealth of Nations* (1776), Smith advocated a negative liberty for the individual ("freedom from" arbitrary government) and a minimum of restraints on the operations of the market. He viewed these as the keys to development as defined in economic terms. The state would provide only for national defense, for protection of

individual rights against invasion by other citizens, and for collective (public) goods, which could not be supplied through the autonomous workings of the market. The market would assign rewards and burdens according to the rules of supply and demand. This necessarily entailed inequality in the distribution of wealth, which was justified on the grounds that it reflected individual merit. That is, those were rewarded who displayed initiative and worked hard to efficiently satisfy consumer wants and demands.

An early emphasis on specifically material development was thus evident in the ideas of progress as elaborated by the classical political economists: production would contribute to the progress of society by generating abundance and wealth. This classical formulation gave rise to the doctrine of laissez faire economics while the emphasis on economic, or material, expansion would characterize much subsequent development thought. Economic historian Karl Polanyi's influential study, *The Great Transformation: The Political and Economic Origins of Our Time* (1944), detailed the process of industrialization followed by the European countries, and provided a model of economic growth for many subsequent economists. Though he offered a radical dissenting view, Karl Marx also assumed that development meant primarily industrialization and the accumulation of material wealth. Between Smith and Marx, a central dichotomy had been established in development theorizing: individual freedom defined in negative terms and reliance on the operations of the market to provide incentives for productivity and efficiency versus an active state embodying the collective will to promote equality and satisfy basic social needs.

Economists would not have a monopoly on development theory, however, in large part because the realities of development did not match the predictions. Soon voices representing various disciplines weighed in with their insights. Franz Boas, Margaret Mead, Ruth Benedict, and other anthropologists began to stress the cultural differences between countries, which they argued made each case distinct and different. The clear implication was that one model of development would not fit every country. Sociologists, including Max Weber, Talcott Parsons, and Seymour Martin Lipset, elaborated on the subtleties of different stages of development, factoring in modes of social operation previously overlooked by the economists. Parsons, for example, offered explanations for the ways in which religion, authority, leadership selection, organization of production, and community bonds functioned in traditional (underdeveloped) societies, as opposed to modern (industrialized) societies. Lipset and Karl Deutsch illuminated the phenomenon of social mobilization. In sum, these thinkers suggested that sociocultural factors, rather than economic, drive development.

Political scientists would also challenge the assumption that economic development reflexively led to political development, usually meaning democratization. Samuel Huntington, Gabriel Almond, and others noted the failure of many states to develop politically in the wake of economic growth. They shifted their focus to political parties, interest groups, political socialization, public opinion, and the like. These, they reasoned, are the means through which policies of development are formulated and implemented. Between the economists, anthropologists, sociologists, and political scientists, the concept of development was enriched if not made more consistent. Theorists and practitioners would have to operate with more subtle notions about the relevant factors and relations of development: simplicity would yield to growing complexity.

The Post-Colonial Context of Development

It is perhaps an historical irony that at mid-twentieth century the industrialized countries of Europe and the United States, having just waged two horrific wars unprecedented in their scope over access to resources and markets, still viewed themselves as the models for world development. Paternalistically, they turned attention to the development of nations in Asia, Africa, the Middle East, Latin America, and the Caribbean, which formerly they had colonized. Excepting the United States, their physical capital was largely exhausted after years of struggle. The former colonial powers (including Great Britain, France, Germany, Spain, Portugal, The Netherlands, Belgium, Italy, and Japan) therefore necessarily, if gradually, relinquished direct control over their colonies as a wave of independence movements swept across the globe after World War II.

South America had been colonized earlier than other areas; most of its countries emerged from colonial rule by the 1830s. Nevertheless, they continued to operate under the close scrutiny and extensive influence of the United States in what some have characterized as a neo-colonial relationship. For about one hundred years, they were suppliers of raw materials and cheap labor to European countries and the United States. The Great Depression drastically impacted these countries so that they began to consider alternatives to their export-oriented economies. In the 1930s, many South American countries began to pursue a strategy of development called Import

Substitution Industrialization (ISI). An active state would either establish industrial firms of its own or provide incentives to private firms to produce goods for the domestic market in order to obviate the need for imports. Industrialization was still seen as the goal of development, but state protectionism ideally would allow nations to create the means to satisfy their own demands and insulate themselves from the vagaries of the world market, freeing them from dependence on first-world markets.

In the 1950s, the theoretical rationale for this strategy was fashioned retrospectively by Raul Prebisch, an Argentine economist who headed the UN Economic Commission for Latin America, and others (like Hans Singer) who argued that the developing countries had been consigned to an inferior position in the scheme of world trade and development. As suppliers of primary materials for the industrialized countries, they could expect to see the terms of trade steadily deteriorate. Over time, capital tends to concentrate and larger firms in the developed nations assert growing control over their markets, reducing competition and securing larger profit margins. Meanwhile, the primary suppliers remain in competitive environments, subject to lower profits. Under such conditions, the gap between rich and poor countries would increase. Accordingly, they concluded that the obstacles to development faced by the countries of Latin America were sown into the structure of world trade. Prebisch and like-minded social scientists, labeled structuralists, determined that it would take state-sponsored industrialization to correct the situation.

For a while, the nations of Latin America experienced some progress toward industrialization pursuing ISI policies. Over the long term, however, the strategy proved deficient: The gap between those employed in state-protected industries and the urban and rural underemployed or unemployed grew dramatically. Millions of people were marginalized. Government policies frequently resulted in favoritism and inefficiencies and led to heavy debts. The critical agricultural sector was neglected, or even compelled to subsidize industrialization in the cities, leading to depressed conditions, rural flight, and a growing urban underclass. Social tensions often led to military interventions and even dominance, thwarting healthy political development. Nor did dependency cease, especially as technology and other inputs used in production often had to be imported; so foreign capital and its influence significantly increased. By 1970, the Organization for Economic Cooperation and Development (OECD) reported that ISI had negatively impacted those countries that adopted the strategy. The structuralist approach did not, however, disappear, but would soon be reworked by dependency theorists.

After World War II, the sheer proliferation of states was bewildering. As a result primarily of decolonization over the several decades following the war, the total number of independent countries soared from about fifty to almost two hundred. Most countries in Asia, Africa, the Middle East, and the Caribbean were at some time colonized, with the exceptions of China, Iran, and Thailand. (Ethiopia avoided colonization until late in the process when it fell prey to Italy's Mussolini.) These newly independent states faced serious problems, many stemming from their colonial legacies. As the former colonial powers retreated, they left behind national boundaries that often disregarded the natural divisions between peoples: racial, ethnic, tribal, linguistic, religious, cultural, historical, geographic, and other. Additionally, in every case the colonial relationship had rested on a centralized, authoritarian system of politics, more or less harsh, and on the economic and psychological subordination of indigenous groups. That is, the subjects in these colonies had generally been inured to patterns of hierarchy and dominance.

Sociopolitical systems of these countries therefore tended to reflect their colonial experiences: Western legal and political ideals were awkwardly cobbled together with traditional, indigenous modes and customs. By the standards of the industrialized West, these newly formed states were deemed to be underdeveloped in numerous respects. They were often independent in name only, continuing, in fact, to be dependent economically, politically, and militarily. They remained internally fragmented due largely to their arbitrary boundaries. The level of development of domestic industries and markets was generally very low. Moreover, the social indicators of development were correspondingly poor: per capita incomes; literacy rates; infant mortality and death rates; access to food, potable water, sanitation, and health care; and the like. In many of these former colonies, women especially had suffered a decline in their social status and their control over the resources that traditionally had sustained families.

Developmentalism, or Modernization Theory

Scholars and policy makers subsequently transferred their focus from development in Western Europe and North America to development in the newly created, post-colonial states. Several factors help to account for this shift. The many problems associated with emergent countries naturally drew the attention of development theorists, especially since the industrialized Western nations continued to rely heavily on raw materials and resources from these countries. This fact necessitated a degree of stability and infrastructure that was absent or fragile in most developing countries. Additionally, the proliferation of post-colonial countries coincided with the rise of tensions between the Western capitalist nations, or First World (especially the United States), and the so-called Communist countries, or Second World (particularly the Soviet Union). The Cold War therefore placed these post-colonial states at the center of a struggle for world dominance. Consequently, development theorists labeled as Third World the countries of Asia, Africa, and Latin America, which were in the field of contest.

The urgency of development problems was therefore recognized immediately in the wake of the Second World War. The United States and its allies acted quickly to shore up the developed countries of Western Europe and Japan through such programs as the Marshall Plan and the Bretton Woods System, under the auspices of which were created the International Monetary Fund (IMF) and the International Bank for Reconstruction and Development (better known today as the World Bank). Authorized in 1944, these institutions aimed at stabilizing financial markets and exchange rates and at rebuilding infrastructures. In 1948, the General Agreement on Trade and Tariffs (GATT) was founded to augment them, with its goal of promoting trade. The World Trade Organization (WTO) supplanted GATT in 1995. Their institutional missions soon encompassed the post-colonial world. Additional programs to address social problems and to win hearts and minds in the developing countries were enacted in the 1960s, including the Peace Corps and the Agency for International Development (AID). The growing Western focus on the problems of this large group of developing countries, representing almost three-quarters of the world's people, was also manifested in an increase of programs in higher education and of funding for scholarly research including the Fulbright Program; Ford, Rockefeller, and McArthur foundations; and Asian, African, and Latin American studies associations.

W. W. Rostow proffered, in 1960, a capitalist alternative to Marx's version of economic development in *The Stages of Economic Growth: A Non-Communist Manifesto.* Yet his views shared with Marx some optimistic, basic assumptions: the fundamental equation of development with industrialization; a belief in the primacy of economic growth, which would then result in sociocultural development and political democratization; the belief that the European and US experiences could serve as satisfactory models of development for all other countries; and the conviction that development flowed in a natural and rather orderly fashion from the accepted economic model. Dubbed modernization theory, Rostow and others, like Seymour Martin Lipset and Gabriel Almond, assumed that every underdeveloped country should emulate the Western-style industrial model. Given the organizational and other imperatives of industrialization, he thought this path would eventuate in a convergence of countries, economically, socially, culturally, politically, and ideologically. Increased trade and contact with the industrialized, Western nations would facilitate development in the poor, "backward" countries.

Modernization theory essentially defined the developing countries in terms of the elements they lacked, from the perspective of industrialized countries of the West. The peoples of Asia, African, and Latin America were generically classified as traditional, as opposed to modern: rural and agrarian rather than urban and industrial; clan-based, preliterate, fatalistic, and religious as opposed to universalistic, literate, scientific, and secular in their outlooks. Modernization entailed overcoming these negative traits. Obviously, the poor countries faced a shortage of savings and capital, which an interventionist state in Keynesian-like fashion would correct. Worse, however, these countries were missing the cultural requisites of modern (Western) societies, like an achievement-oriented and entrepreneurial spirit. All these deficiencies would in time be remedied. Clearly, modernization theory equated development and modernization with industrialization and Westernization. Rostow posited five stages through which these societies would travel on their way to development, including the initial traditional stage. With the advance of science and technology, economic growth would become normal and social and political institutions would mature as measured by Western standards and values. Ultimately, these countries would become modern societies with mass consumption economies, as in the affluent West. Policy makers in the United States especially found Rostow's vision very appealing.

Scholars were less enamored. Harvard professor Samuel Huntington faulted modernization theorists for drawing upon a flawed, overly optimistic evolutionary tradition from sociology. Other critics claimed that Rostow's notion of traditional society was impoverished: It ignored elements of universalism, individualism, and orientation to achieve, which were indeed present in these countries. It thereby established a set of false dichotomies. In fact, the modernization development scenario failed to unfold as predicted. The rich and poor countries did not converge over time, but rather the gap grew markedly. It became increasingly clear that development would entail neither an automatic nor a smooth process of transition. Subsequent global history has raised even more serious questions about the modernization thesis: Is there really any reason to believe that the advance of modernization goals (industrialization, literacy, secularization, and the like) results in democratization? Do such developments actually reduce conflicts based on religious or ethnic differences? Is there reason to think that they are linked to progress in social justice? That is, the facile linkage of development defined as modernization with democracy, social justice, and peace can no longer be assumed.

Dependency Theory and Marxism

Largely in response to modernization theory as propounded mostly by Western and especially US scholars, theorists in the developing countries began to offer an alternative development analysis that would be labeled dependency theory. Many dependency theorists hailed from Latin America and had been influenced by the structuralist thought of Prebisch and Singer, and by strains of Marxist thought, sometimes commingled with Catholicism in the form of liberation theology, which focused on the needs of the poor and oppressed. Included in this group are (exceptional, neo-Marxist Westerners) Paul Baran and Paul Sweezy, Andre Gunder Frank, Fernando Cardoso, Theotonio Dos Santos, and Immanuel Wallerstein. Dependency theorists claimed that modernization theory was ethnocentric and insensitive to the variety of cultures and social arrangements manifested throughout the developing world and to their unique historical experiences. The critics charged that modernization theory was indeed ahistorical in that it failed even to consider the ways in which colonial experiences had affected these countries. It was the colonial experience, they asserted, that had instituted the fundamental, highly unfavorable conditions faced by developing countries. They observed that the global environment had changed since the Western countries underwent their process of development, so what worked before might not work under contemporary conditions. Rostow's stages thus displayed an inappropriate "one size fits all" assumption. In the opinion of some, such gross simplifications and misconceptions had led directly to the disastrous US policies culminating in the Vietnam War.

Dependency theorists vociferously denounced the growing gap in wealth, income, and power between rich and poor nations and chided modernization theorists for overlooking conditions of obvious exploitation inherent in the economic relations between the developed and underdeveloped countries—in trade, investment, and finance. Drawing on Marxist ideas of imperialism, class analysis, and economic surplus, Baran, Frank, and others distinguished between the *core*, rich and powerful capitalist countries of the West, and the *periphery*, so-called less developed countries (LDCs) from which resources, cheap labor, and wealth in general were being extracted by the core. Oligopoly control of markets by the multinational corporations (MNCs) of the core countries made this dominance possible, with the aid of compliant and corrupted local elites whose interests were married to those of the MNCs. These powerful corporations would bring in industry that crushed local businesses and reduced employment by replacing workers with technology, imposing highly unfavorable terms of trade (raw materials for manufactured goods) and repatriating their profits to the core. Baran viewed the world capitalist economy as a web entangling the countries of Asia, Africa, the Middle East, and Latin America in a relationship that systematically distorted their development. In his analysis it would take an interventionist, socialist state to implement policies in the interests of the masses and to correct this situation.

With Sweezy, Baran analyzed the irrational waste of economic surpluses in developing countries, which they maintained reflected an attempt by the capitalist system to deal with its principle, recurrent problem: stagnation. Extensive spending on the military was one strategy that was easy to justify without provoking many questions about the use of resources or social justice. Elites squandered resources on luxuries rather than permitting these resources to be invested in ways that were genuinely, socially productive. Frank likewise counted underdevelopment as the product of a long-term process of exploitation: The capitalist powers of the metropolitan core continuously took economic surpluses from the world's vast majority for the enrichment of a small minority. Underdevelopment was, in effect, the byproduct of so-called development in the core. The result was a polarization of countries between core and periphery. In West Africa, scholar Samir Amin arrived at similar conclusions. These theorists described what has been called neo-colonialism (or neo-imperialism), an exploitative, colonial-like relationship but without formal governance by a colonizer. Though indirectly, the peripheral states were being dominated economically, politically, culturally, and (when deemed necessary) militarily.

For this reason, suggested Wallerstein, theorists of development must focus on the global system rather than on individual nations. Higher-level economic activities like manufacturing and finance were jealously preserved by the core countries; left to the periphery were the less profitable activities such as supplying raw materials. Wallerstein distinguished a middle group of countries, which he designated the semi-periphery, that engaged in somewhat more profitable trade and manufacturing. One unfortunate consequence was that this fragmentation of the peripheral countries helped the core to maintain its control. Correspondingly, the core countries had developed strong states, but in the periphery, states were weak, which limited their ability to deal with outside forces or to develop internally. So as long as a peripheral country remained linked with the core, meaningful, national development and political independence were precluded.

Many dependency theorists called for the general implementation of ISS policies by the LDCs; and in this spirit a *Group of 77* (G-77) developing nations enunciated, in 1974, a set of twenty principles designed to promote development. The New International Economic Order (NIEO) called for extensive reforms of world trade, aid, and financial arrangements to secure for the world's poor a greater share of resources. However, like those for whom they attempted to speak, dependency theorists remained largely marginalized. Policy makers seldom openly adopted political agendas in their name, Chile under Allende and Jamaica under Manley being two very brief exceptions. NIEO demands withered in the face of resistance from the Western countries, themselves facing economic problems. The theory met with a scornful barrage of criticism from Western and especially US ideologues on the political right. Even in the 1980s as the debt crisis became acute and very unpalatable structural adjustment programs (SAPs) were being imposed on LDCs by Western governments and international institutions, dependency theory nevertheless came under increasing attack and declined in influence.

Neo-Classical Liberalism, or the Washington Consensus

With the oil shocks, stagflation, and the demise of the Bretton Woods System, as the financial costs of the Vietnam War caught up with the United States in the 1970s, development theory was thrown into disarray, any social-democratic consensus evaporated, and faith in state-led development waned.

Into this vacuum strode an emboldened New Right, with their faith in a free-market panacea. Offering a neo-classical version of laissez faire economics, and with the help of the wave of conservatism that swept into office both Ronald Reagan in the United States and Margaret Thatcher in the United Kingdom, they seized the high ground of policy making in the 1980s. They rejected both the dominant Keynesianism of the modernization theorists and the more active, state-sponsored developmentalism espoused by dependency theorists. Their ideology, in fact, informed and guided the policies of the World Bank, the IMF, and the US State Department for at least a decade, which is why their policies have been labeled the Washington Consensus. With the end of the Cold War their confidence grew, and they expressed the view that liberalism and free-market capitalism had been established so securely that it amounted to the effective end of ideological debates.

Neo-classical liberals argued that LDCs were not being exploited by developed Western countries, but rather were victims of their own failings, including corrupt and inefficient governments and an inadequate commitment to market values and principles. In their estimation, economic development had been stunted in the LDCs due to an overextension of state authority: Disregarding comparative advantage and competitiveness, government subsidies, regulations, and controls had distorted markets, which led to an inefficient allocation of resources. State-sponsored developmentalism had permitted too much discretion, contributing to rampant corruption. Neo-classical liberals could also point to the 1970 report from the OECD, which concluded that ISI policies had overall negative economic consequences for the countries adopting them. As opposed to ISI, they advocated an export-oriented approach to development.

By reducing the role of government, claimed neo-classical liberals, LDCs could limit opportunities for corruption and mismanagement, and realize a more rational allocation of resources based on market forces. The mounting level of debt in the developing countries was used as leverage by Western policy makers to oblige these countries to adopt the elements of a neo-classical liberal agenda. Enforced through the World Bank, the IMF, and US State Department policies, SAPs usually entailed the following requirements: trade liberalization (reduction or elimination of tariffs, quotas, subsidies, and other barriers); privatization of government-run enterprises; a general deregulation of the economy, including labor and finance; devaluation of the currency (tight monetary policies to control inflation); opening domestic markets to entrepreneurs and investors and providing them incentives to stimulate an entrepreneurial flourishing; and fiscal austerity with respect to social programs including education, subsidies for food and housing, and health care, which were deemed a drain on investments needed for private enterprise. Even falling wages due to labor deregulation, according to this view, would benefit society by attracting more investments and increasing the level of employment.

Again, the optimistic predictions of the theory proved to be overblown. Neo-classical liberals did not think in terms of the global conditions affecting development. Rather, as with modernization theory, they assumed that national economic growth and development would flow naturally from a proper application of the theory, in this case a free-market mantra. As well, they assumed that a fixed set of policies would fit all countries, whatever their situation. Not surprisingly, failure to consider the specific characteristics of each country undermined their goals. The posited rise of a dynamic entrepreneurial class did not materialize, as the theorists had underestimated the difficulty of cultivating such individuals. Corruption did not diminish, but took on new forms involving patronage and cronyism. Rather than improving, unemployment worsened; labor deregulation depressed wages and consumption, so domestic markets contracted. The gap between rich (those few who could take advantage of some of the policies) and poor (those who did not benefit) yawned dramatically. Cuts in social programs acutely affected the majority, and even future development was threatened by the withdrawal of investments in human capital. Nor had the theorists considered the possibility that some types of public spending might generate more economic activity than much of the private investment.

As the impacts of SAPs became more broadly recognized, they frequently met with widespread resistance or outright violence. Increasingly, many countries had to resort to military repression to implement the neo-classical liberal agenda. In many countries, years of development efforts were rolled back to the serious detriment of the general welfare. The harshest critics of neo-classical liberal theory have charged that it was little more than a veneer for the global aggrandizement of the MNCs and the elite minority that controls and benefits from them, and that it both undermined democratic institutions and sapped the strength and legitimacy of developing states. Whatever our assessment of the neo-classical liberal program, it indisputably recast the global development environment. Though it purported to remove government from the realm of economic planning, in fact, it selectively culled government programs and policies, leaving those that supported corporate enterprise while deleting mostly the social commitments of states. Simultaneously, it removed from the sphere of public discourse many of the basic questions about the allocation of resources and transferred these to the private sphere (the marketplace where MNCs dominate) or to international organizations dominated by Western corporate capital, like the WTO.

Globalization and Trends in Development Theory

Development theory has always been embedded contextually and simultaneously challenged by ongoing, complex changes. By its nature, then, it must be a dynamic theory. The vast intricacies of globalization, though, have presented theorists with perhaps more daunting challenges than ever before. With the demise of the Cold War, the Western sense of urgency about development in the LDCs has waned. In place of the previous bipolar dichotomy, we see a world system that is, depending on one's perspective, either unipolar (with a single superpower, the United States) or tripolar (with spheres of influence centered in the United States, Europe, and Pacific Asia). The last of these would include Japan, China and Hong Kong, the Asian Tigers (Taiwan, South Korea, and Singapore), Australia, and New Zealand.

The putative success of the Asian Tigers, originally including Hong Kong (which has been reabsorbed into China), drew much attention and raised hopes of development theorists. Neo-classical liberals sought to claim these newly industrialized countries (NICs) as examples of the success of market-oriented development policies; but in truth these countries had active, interventionist governments and supportive cultures, and they invested heavily in human capital. Moreover, they developed at a particularly favorable time in history, and may not therefore serve as suitable models for future development. Chalmers Johnson and others at the Institute of Development Studies (University of Sussex) have drawn lessons from the experiences of these NICs to create a model they call developmental state theory. An interventionist state would set development as its chief goal, and would encourage national savings while directing the flow of investments and spending heavily on human capital. The state would carefully regulate the economy and, though remaining committed to private property and markets, it would redistribute land, if expedient.

Clearly, altered global conditions demand new strategies. Diffuse strains of thought, not among the more or less distinct schools identified so far and often dissenting from the mainstream views, have nevertheless enriched development theory and may be able to help us meet the challenges of the future. One unmistakable and hopeful trend in the theories has been a growing sensitivity to the definition of goals of development, and the use of measures more carefully tailored to those goals. Early economic thought, as previously noted, had fostered an emphasis on material measures. Critics complained that Gross National Product (GNP) and Gross Domestic Product (GDP), both measures of national outputs of goods and services, were too crude to really capture meaningful development. In response, and to get at issues of equity, the Gini index was developed. Then, in 1990, the United Nations (UN) adopted a more comprehensive gauge of development, the Human Development Index (HDI), which is a composite of measurements including life expectancy, real GDP per capita, literacy rates, access to education, and average years of schooling. Theorists had become aware that development is really about *human* development, and that beyond the basic needs, human flourishing requires access to things like education, employment, and participation in the life of a political community.

Equity and quality-of-life concerns have also been reflected in the growing body of literature focused on the plight and rights of women; and on the environment and sustainability. Half of the world's people, women, had been largely neglected in the mainstream theories of development. Without considering the place of women in society, it was increasingly obvious that the most critical global issues could not be effectively addressed: hunger and food production, health issues, pollution and the environment, population control, literacy and education, distribution of property, and human rights, among others. It had been widely assumed that the progress of industry would automatically entail an improvement in the situation of women. However, as with democracy, social justice, or peace and security, no such progressive evolution transpired. To improve the lot of women and, in turn, those who depend upon them—in effect, everyone else—women would have to be fully incorporated into any scheme of development. Such views have gained attention from the international community; for example, the 1995 *Beijing Declaration and Platform for Action* addressed women's issues and offered an action plan. Real progress, however, has so far been elusive.

Because women play the key role in developing countries in terms of providing for family health and nutrition, the plight of women is often intertwined in development thought with environmental issues, for example, in ideas promulgated by physicist-turned-social-activist Vandana Shiva. Women in LDCs account for the majority of food production to meet family needs; the figure for Africa is about 70% of agricultural production. The condition of water, air, and soil therefore critically impacts women as chief stewards for the health and nutrition of their families and communities. In many cases, development defined as industrialization has eroded the quality of these essential life factors and made things harder for women while jeopardizing entire communities. Out of such concerns grew a focus on environmentalism and sustainability. Significantly, the UN-sponsored *Brundtland Report* (1987) posited a nexus between democratic participation and sustainable development. Some have been led to question both the feasibility and the moral-ethical desirability of global industrialization and development toward mass consumption-oriented societies (for example, E. F. Schumacher and Herman Daly). It is also noteworthy that one of the poorest states of India, Kerala, has achieved levels of human development surpassing those of many LDCs and some developed countries, but without a commensurate increase in GDP, industrialization, or consumption.

Sadly, despite the broad range of development thought and years of efforts, many LDCs are no better off today than they were at independence; and in some cases, most notably in the countries of Sub-Saharan Africa, the quality of life has actually deteriorated due to depletion of resources, increasing pollution, declining life expectancy and health (due especially to AIDS), growing economic and social disparities, and violence and strife. There is an urgent need to rethink development theory to address the grave problems affecting the peoples of the developing world and all humankind in our interwoven, global environment. Past experience suggests that no generally applicable development model is feasible. So there will be no shortage of challenges for development theorists in the years ahead.

WM. GARY KLINE

References and Further Reading

Almond, Gabriel A., and James S. Coleman, eds. *The Politics of Developing Areas*. Princeton, NJ: Princeton University Press, 1960.

Baran, Paul. *The Political Economy of Growth*. Harmondsworth, Middlesex, UK: Penguin Books, 1973.

Calvert, Peter, and Susan Calvert. *Politics and Society in the Third World*, 2nd ed. Essex, England: Pearson Education, 2001.

Frank, Andre Gunder. *Capitalism and Underdevelopment in Latin America*. Harmondsworth, Middlesex, UK: Penguin Books, 1967.

Handelman, Howard. *The Challenge of Third World Development*, 3rd ed. Upper Saddle River, NJ: Prentice Hall, 2003.

Huntington, Samuel P. *The Clash of Civilizations and the Remaking of World Order*. New York: Simon & Schuster, 1997.

Political Order in Changing Societies. New Haven, CT: Yale University Press, 1968.

Preston, P. W. *Development Theory: An Introduction*. Oxford, UK: Blackwell, 1996.

Rapley, John. *Understanding Development: Theory and Practice in the Third World*. Boulder, CO: Lynne Rienner, 1996.

Rostow, Walt Whitman. *The Stages of Economic Growth*. Cambridge: Cambridge University Press, 1960.

Seligson, Mitchell A., and John T. Passe-Smith, eds. *Development and Underdevelopment: The Political Economy of Global Inequality*, 3rd ed. Boulder, CO: Lynne Rienner, 2003.

United Nations Development Programme. "Publications." http://www.undp.org/dpa/publications/

Wallerstein, Immanuel. *The Modern World System*. New York: Academic Press, 1974.

Weatherby, Joseph N., Emmit B. Evans, Jr., Reginald Gooden, Dianne Long, and Ira Reed. *The Other World: Issues and Politics of the Developing World*, 5th ed. New York: Addison Wesley Longman, 2003.

Wiarda, Howard J. *Political Development in Emerging Nations*. Belmont, CA: Thompson Wadsworth, 2004.

DEVELOPMENT, MEASURES OF

Development is both a complex, multidimensional process and a term laden with emotional connotations. Any attempt to define and measure development is likely to be both arbitrary and inadequate, if not outright ethnocentric and ideologically biased.

First-world or Global North views emphasizing modernization and developmental theories can be said to form the "mainstream" perspective on development. It advocates both free-market capitalism and liberal democracy as the ideals that third-world and former second-world nations should attempt to reach. Such values or objectives as individual freedom in both the marketplace and the polity, limited government, economic openness, political transparency, entrepreneurialism, efficiency, legitimacy, and the protection of private property rights, among others, best reflect the mainstream conception of development in the political economy within and across nations. The economic strategies emphasized to accomplish development have varied over time: from import-substitution industrialization in the 1950s and 1960s to export-led industrialization in the 1970s and 1980s as practiced by some Latin American and South Asian nations, to neo-liberal policies and practices related to capitalist globalization in the 1990s, to the present encouraging of all nations to find their niches in the global economy. Throughout the last fifty years or so, these economic strategies have tended to coincide with certain political objectives: initially promoting modern state-building and legitimate political stability by ending civil strife, later replacing state repression with political openness and accountability through reforms, and now increasing individual political freedom and civil liberties in the process of liberal democratization. This overarching view is likely to support social scientific research employing cross-national designs, quantitative data, and measures from capitalist international institutions and think-tanks in order to assess the progress made toward modernization or development. In sum, empirical measures of development are dependent on the type and definition of development employed by varying ideological perspectives.

Some third-world or Global South dependency and neo-Marxist imperialist and world-system theories can be said to form much of the "critical" perspective on development and underdevelopment. This view highlights the negative effects on third-world nations of colonialism, imperialism, dependency, and neo-colonial globalization emanating from first-world practices and processes. Third-world integration into and conditioning by the capitalist world-system produce consequences such as: "economic stagnation" (that is, some economic growth experienced but no real or meaningful economic development attained, especially in Africa), or "distorted development" (that is, establishing artificial, not natural, processes of development throughout most less-developed nations), or "uneven development" (that is, much greater development in a foreign enclave sector than in the rest of the native economy as with, for example, India, China, Egypt, and many Caribbean nations), or "associated-dependent development" (that is, economic development but with loss of national political and economic freedom such as in Argentina, Brazil, and Chile), or "delayed development" (that is, preventing the earlier fulfillment of political self-determination or national independence as with most non-Latin American third-world nations), "the development of underdevelopment" (that is, the simultaneous development of first-world nations at the expense of third-world underdevelopment as posited for most third-world nations, especially in Latin America), or "techno-bureaucratic authoritarianism" (that is, promoting institutionalized government that is politically repressive through high-technology means, particularly in South America), or "special relationship development" (that is, nations that have special relationships with the United States and are getting certain economic advantages, including Taiwan, South Korea, and Israel), or "special resource development" (that is, the oil-producing and -exporting nations or members of OPEC, especially in the Middle East).

Foreign trade, direct foreign investment, foreign aid, and foreign debt measures, among others, are used, through interpretation, as causal factors producing many third-world afflictions including underdevelopment, dependency, inequality, and repression. For example, a mainstream measure thought to promote development, such as direct foreign investment per capita by multinational corporations, is deemed by the critical view to be a measure of foreign capital penetration, a violative act reflecting a relationship of dominance and dependency. Assessments of these causal linkages including conditions, attributes, and contexts often require the use of more qualitative methodologies such as either for case-study analysis (that is, a relationship between a first-world nation or an international institution and a third-world colony or nation) or for broad relations of production within the capitalist world-system (that is, core–semiperiphery–periphery relations).

Placed more neutrally within an historical context, any sizeable movement away from being poor, backward, or underdeveloped, toward developing, appears to be a meaningful change, thereby reducing abject or absolute poverty within a society. To move from being less or least developed to being more or most developed would be considered a major developmental improvement, as a form of convergence, thus reducing relative inequality among societies. Probably the most neutral and widely used, albeit an imperfect, aggregate indicator to detect an improvement in the human condition over time, space, and ideology continues to be per capita income. This empirical measure requires dividing the national income by the population for each year. Its use facilitates the detection of any long-term trends or patterns. Another indicator often used in empirical studies is energy consumption per capita or its natural log, involving either electricity or coal usage. The interpretation is that the greater the amount used, the higher the level of economic development. Other indicators that can be used and interpreted in the same direction include those related to the value added to goods and services during the production or servicing stages, or to the number of personal computers or Internet linkages per capita, among others.

There are at least four major kinds of development deemed to be desirable within a society: economic, political, social/human, and sustained. Although these types of development are widely thought to be highly interrelated, the empirical indicators used for their measurement tend to be different. For certain, the meanings and measures of each of these forms of development vary depending on the type of historical analysis employed, or ideological perspective taken, across research agendas. Quantitative cross-national analysis requires the collection of data for empirical indicators in order to make comparative national and regional assessments, thereby permitting the creation of broad generalization. Qualitative case-study analysis attempts to identify specialized attributes or factors in order to detect developmental trends within a society, thus allowing for a comparison of key forces and factors over time for a single society in the detection of developmental trends. Whereas quantitative analysis often employs economic, political, and social-empirical indicators, qualitative analysis emphasizes cultural, religious, and historical aspects.

Economic Development

Economic development implies a structural, presumably progressive and preferred, change in the economy, emphasizing economic growth and increased consumption. Two dimensions of economic development that can be measured are rates of change and levels attained. For example, economic development can often be observed when nations have relatively higher economic growth rates over a sustained time, as well as with the creation of leading economic sectors and the decline of noncompetitive ones, and/or the more efficient flow of factors of production from one sector to another sector in the economy. Economic development is also a particular level that has been attained consisting of both quantitative and qualitative attributes. These rates of economic growth and levels of economic development are, in turn, quite dependent on greater access to natural resources, higher capital formation, improved technical expertise, instilled entrepreneurialism, and the removal of structural rigidities and impediments in the economy.

Basic empirical indicators or quantifiable measures of economic development usually include: gross national product (GNP) as the total value of goods and services produced plus or minus the foreign trade sector during a year, or GNP per capita as the total yearly production value divided by the population, or the gross domestic product (GDP) as the value of goods and services produced in a society without including the foreign trade sector, or GDP per capita where the total value of domestic production and services is divided by the population. These measures can be used either for single-year points or in creating estimates of average annual growth rates of GNP or GDP per capita covering different periods, anywhere from five to twenty years. The World Bank's annual *World Development Report* provides useful data and information covering both the process and the conditional state of economic development on primarily a comparative national basis. It also aggregates nations on the basis of region and level of economic development. Or, nations can be stratified and then ranked on the basis of the level of economic developed attained at a specific point in time. Although economic growth rates for a single national economy generally vary over time, most relative rankings of national economies with respect to the level of economic development attained have remained largely consistent and stable.

Other measures used to gauge economic development include the percentages of either production value or workers employed within certain economic sectors such as agriculture, manufacturing, industry, services, trade, and technology. It is commonly thought that if an economy moves its factors of production from one economic sector to the next, roughly in the order given above, thereby reflecting a different economic specialization over time, then it is likely reaching a qualitatively higher level of economic development. Still, an economy specializing predominately in neither industry nor high technology, with a relatively closed foreign trade sector, might be progressing toward greater economic development. For instance, if an economy is well-diversified and its sectors are highly integrated, then it might well represent a more desirable and secure balance across economic sectors, leaving a nation less vulnerable to the vicissitudes of domestic and world-market forces compared to one that is highly open and interdependent.

Economic development can also be witnessed when a smaller amount of the population or work force is involved in agriculture and, concomitantly, more people are involved in manufacturing, industry, services, trade, and high technology. Savings and investments are higher, stronger credit and marketing facilities and institutions exist, the infrastructure of the economy supports improved transportation and communication systems, and the satisfaction of basic human needs is almost assured.

Political Development

Political development is both a process and an attained level presumed to be desirable and beneficial for individual nations or societies. One conception of political development is democratization leading to democracy. Empirical or quantifiable measures of (liberal) democracy often include the existence of a constitution with individual political rights and some curb on governmental power; the continuous use of voting in competitive elections; maintenance of multiple parties; and the separation of powers in the form of the legislative, executive, and judicial branches of government, among other measures.

A liberal conception of political development, as the dominant paradigm of political economy in the post-Cold War era, includes the process of democratization leading eventually to some end state, democracy. From 1972 to the present, Freedom House has done an annual comparative survey rating the degree of freedom for nations in the international system. The status of freedom within nations is determined by two sets of indicators: political rights and civil liberties. Political rights include whether or not the chief executive and legislature are elected by meaningful popular processes; free and fair elections exist; the distribution of political power reflects voter preferences, multiple parties meaningfully compete, a transference of power takes place after a change-oriented election, opposition votes are significant, military or foreign influences interfere with civilian-controlled political processes, self-determination of peoples proceeds, societal and governmental powers are decentralized, and consensual and opposition powers are fairly balanced. Civil liberties are determined by having: media protection from political censorship, open and free public discourse on salient political issues, freedom of assembly and demonstrations, freedom to organize politically, nondiscriminate application of the rule of law, freedom from political terror and repression, free trade unions and business associations, free professional organizations and religious institutions, and the right to personal and social privacy.

Institutionalization is another conception of political development that recognizes state-building and infrastructure formation as functional institutional processes. Societal institutions including the political structures of the state become formally established and functional. Those legitimate institutions of the state are expected to possess elements of authority and sovereignty. Those institutions in the broader society become political vehicles with rights, obligations, and powers. When these institutions combine, they perform functions including political socialization and recruitment, interest aggregation and articulation, political organization and communication, law-making, law-enforcing, and law-adjudicating. Modern political systems are more able and willing than their counterparts to use power capabilities to produce policies that are distributive, regulatory, redistributive, or extractive, in order to function and respond well to societal demands. A higher level of political development will be demonstrated by political systems that are more differentiated, autonomous, secular, and decentralized in nature.

The date of institutionalization can be used to determine the nature and duration of political development or maturity. The assumption is that the earlier the date, the greater the likelihood of higher forms of political development, including national autonomy or independence, self-determination, and higher forms of political development. Hence, longevity can be translated more easily into stable, workable government. Measures of longevity can include the date of effective institutionalized government, the date of declared independence, the date of formal independence, the date of entrance into the United Nations or other universal organization, the date of the last major constitutional change, the date of the last political regime change, the date of either unification or reunification, or the date of the last revolution.

Human Development

Human development is a broader term than either economic or political development. It is a people-centered concept that emphasizes human choices intended to promote a higher quality of life for as many people as possible. Human development is more observable when there have been improvements in the following areas: reducing fertility and infant mortality rates; promoting nutrition, health, sanitation, and education; as well as other factors that enhance the quality of life for more people, especially for the poor, minorities, women, and children. The main objectives are to reduce abject poverty and gross inequalities.

The United Nations Development Programme's annual *Human Development Report* has the following concepts and indices for understanding and measuring human development: life expectancy at birth, adult literacy rate, combined gross first-through-third levels of educational enrollment, real GDP per capita, adjusted real GDP per capita, a life expectancy index, an educational index, a human development index (HDI), and the real GDP per capita rank minus the HDI rank.

Two closely related aspects of human development are gender empowerment and human poverty, both containing multiple indicators to form separate indexes. Gender empowerment consists of the overall rank on a gender empowerment (GEM) index, the percentage of seats in parliament held by women, the percentage of female administrators and managers, the percentage of female professional and technical workers, the percentage of women's share of earned income, and the raw score of GEM values. Human poverty is measured by: the overall human poverty index (HPI), percentage of people not expected to survive to age forty, adult literacy, population without access to safe water, population without access to health services, population without access to sanitation, percentage of underweight children under age five, children not reaching grade five, refugees by country of asylum, population below income poverty line of $1 per day, population below income poverty line making up national poverty, as well as the raw scores for both real GDP per capita for the poorest 20% and real GDP per capita for the richest 20% of the population. The computing methods to form these indices are outlined in each report.

Other indicators, in the form of either percentages or ratios, have also been used to assess a wider domain of human development: women's access to education, child survival, health profiles, food security, government expenditures on education, labor conditions and benefits, access to information and communications as indicators of quality of life, political life, and military expenditures and resource imbalances, urbanization and population trends, social stress and change, and acceptance of human rights instruments and laws.

Sustainable Development

Sustainable development, the broadest term related to development, requires balancing the fulfilling of basic human needs; promoting economic growth; and protecting the environment from excessive population growth, natural resource depletion, and environmental degradation in order to protect current and future generations. Within either a World Bank or United Nations agenda, sustainable development is concerned with "intergenerational equity," whereby all future generations have the same chances as the present one of succeeding in their developmental efforts. It also supports more equitable development in terms of resource distribution and use between wealthier and poorer nations. One way to assess sustainable development is to measure the stock of all capital assets for a nation. The overall stock should increase in size over time. The types of capital assets include manufactured (such as, computers, tractors, roads, and airports), human (such as, knowledge, skills, work ethic, and entrepreneurialism), social (such as, individual, group, class, and institutional relationships), and environmental (such as, forests, mountains, rivers, waterways, and coral reefs).

As a holistic concept, sustainable development recognizes that the broader environment contains interdependencies among the physical, biological, and socio-pyschological worlds. By impacting upon one of these, you affect the others over time and space. Resource use and consumption should be efficient, equitable, intelligent, and compatible with protecting the environment. The World Bank's measures of sustainable (environmental) development relate to land and water uses, agricultural use, deforestation, protected areas, energy use, and emissions: percentage of land under permanent crops, percentage of irrigated cropland, arable land as hectares per capita, agricultural machinery as tractors-per-thousand agricultural workers, agricultural productivity as value added per agricultural worker, a food production index with a base year, freshwater resources as cubic meters per capita, annual freshwater withdrawals as percentage breakdowns in agricultural and industrial uses, annual deforestation in terms of square kilometers and average annual percentage change, nationally protected areas in terms of thousands of square kilometers and percentage of total land areas, commercial energy use as kilograms of oil equivalent and average annual percentage growth, GDP per unit of energy use as dollar per kilogram, and carbon dioxide emissions as a total in terms of metric tons and per capita in metric tons. Exact calculations for each measure are described in detail. Hence, sustainable development is concerned with capturing as many factors as possible in order to assess and promote the quality of life for both present and future generations of people, specifically outlining men, women, and children, as well as other species, across the planet.

STEVEN S. SALLIE

See also Development History and Theory

References and Further Reading

Banks, Arthur S. *Cross-National Time-Series Data Archive.* Binghamton, NY: Center for Social Analysis, 1994.
Bollen, Kenneth A. "Political Democracy and the Timing of Development." *American Sociological Review,* 44, 572–87, 1979.
Burkhart, Ross E. and Michael Lewis-Beck. "Comparative Democracy: The Economic Development Thesis." *American Political Science Review,* 88, 4, 903–10, 1994.
Chilcote, Ronald H. *Theories of Development and Underdevelopment.* Boulder, CO: Westview Press, 1984.
Evans, Peter and James Rauch. "Bureaucracy and Growth: A Cross-National Analysis of the Effects of 'Weberian' State Structures on Economic Growth." *American Sociological Review,* 64, 5, 748–765, 1999.
Freedom House. *Freedom in the World: The Annual Survey of Political Rights and Civil Liberties 1999–2000.* New York: Freedom House, 2000.
Ingelhart, Ronald. *Modernization and Postmodernization: Cultural, Economic, and Political Change in 43 Societies.* Princeton, NJ: Princeton University Press, 1997.

International Monetary Fund, Organization for Economic Cooperation and Development, United Nations, and World Bank. *2000: A Better World for All—Progress Towards the International Development Goals.* Washington, DC: Author, 2000.

Jackman, Robert W. "Cross-National Statistical Research and the Study of Comparative Politics." *American Journal of Political Science*, 29, 161–82, 1985.

Lane, Jan-Erik and Svante Ersson. *Comparative Political Economy: A Developmental Approach*, 2nd ed. London and Washington, DC: Pinter, 1997.

United Nations. *Critical Trends: Global Change and Sustainable Development.* New York: Department for Policy Coordination and Sustainable Development, 1997.

Weide, Erich. "The Impact of Democracy or Repressiveness on the Quality of Life, Income Distribution, and Economic Growth Rates." *International Sociology*, 8, 177–95, 1993.

World Bank. *World Development Report 2000/2001: Attacking Poverty.* Oxford, UK: Oxford University Press, 2001.

DICTATORSHIPS

Dictatorship is government without the consent of the governed. Dictatorships are established through military force or political manipulation. They dissolve or disempower elected assemblies, suspend elections, abolish political parties, or supplant independent legal systems. Dictatorships score low on the political freedom index (PFI) as calculated in 1994, based on the implementation of human rights and the likelihood of regular legitimate contests of ruling power. The developing nations of Cuba, Haiti, China, North Korea, Sudan, Zaire, Saudi Arabia, Syria, and Iraq were among the countries with the lowest PFI in 1994 (Haynes 1996). Dictatorships are often justified as short-term emergency governments, but many survive for a long time. Kim Il Sung (North Korea, 1948–1994) holds the modern record of forty-six years, but more than twenty twentieth-century dictatorships have lasted twenty-five years or more.

Models have been developed to analyse dictatorship, but although they apply to some instances, none seems to hold true for all (Smith 1996). This is because nations' varying histories; institutions; resources; combinations of bureaucratic, capitalist, and military power; and international relationships all affect the emergence, style and longevity of their dictatorships.

Dictatorships can be political, military, religious, or pragmatic (interested only in power). Ideals that have motivated dictatorships include the communism of Fidel Castro (Cuba, 1959–) and Mao Zedong (China, 1949–1976), the anti-communism of Ernesto Geisel (Brazil, 1974–1979) and Augusto Pinochet (Chile, 1973–1989), and the Islamic fundamentalism of Ruhollah Khomeni (Iran, 1979–1989) and Mohammad Omar (Afghanistan, 1996–2001). Pragmatic

seekers after power have included Rafael Trujillo (Dominica, 1930–1938, 1943–1961); Papa Doc Duvalier (Haiti, 1957–1971); Alfredo Stroessner (Paraguay, 1954–1989); Sese Seko Mobuto (Zaire, 1965–1997); Idi Amin (Uganda, 1971–1979); and the notorious Jean-Bedel Bokassa (Central Africa, 1965–1979), who participated in the murder of his opponents, indulged in ritual cannibalism, and declared himself emperor in 1977.

Different people judge dictatorships in different ways. Liberals and democrats view them as temporary and undesirable systems to be replaced by representative and responsible government as soon as possible. Zealots view them as evil if they impose someone else's ideology and benevolent if they impose their own. Marxists view them as an instrument of class domination if they have capitalist leanings, or as a way of regulating the struggle between the classes if they are communist or socialist.

International situations can modify ideological positions. The Cold War led to US support for favoured dictatorships including Fulgencio Batista (Cuba, 1940–1944, 1952–1958), Chiang Kai-shek (Taiwan 1949–1975), Carlos Armas (Guatemala, 1954–1963), Alfredo Stroessner (Paraguay, 1954–1989), Ngo Dinh Diem (South Vietnam, 1955–1963), Ferdinand Marcos (The Philippines, 1965–1986), and Augusto Pinochet (Chile, 1973–1989). The United States has supported other dictatorships because they maintained order and supported modernisation. These include Reza Pahlavi (Iran, 1941–1979), Haile Selassie (Ethiopia 1930–1935, 1940–1974), and Sese Soko Mobutu (Zaire, 1960, 1965–1997). Ex-colonial powers have felt licensed to intervene in their ex-colonies to support. The British supported the conservative Hastings Banda (Malawi, 1966–1994) and France supported pro-French capitalist, Félix Houphouët-Boigny (Ivory Coast, 1960–1993), and even Jean-Bedel Bokassa (Central Africa, 1965–1979) until he became an embarrassment; then they contributed to his overthrow.

The Making of Dictatorships

The support of the army is an essential ingredient in the making of dictatorships. Sometimes the military themselves form the government; sometimes they install or support a civilian government. In The Philippines and Thailand, the military have played decisive roles in changing governments. In Argentina, the army paved the way for the nationalist and populist regime of Juan Perón (1943–1955). In Zaire, Sese Soko Mobutu (1960, 1965–1997) returned power to civilian politicians after his first coup, but his second coup made him president. In Indonesia, the military installed and supported Suharto (1967–1998), who gave them a formal political as well as military role. In Iran, Reza Pahlavi (1941–1979) used the military to suppress opposition in 1963 and in 1977–1979.

The military often claim to have the national interest at heart, but this is not always so. In Nigeria, the coup leaders of 1966 claimed to be motivated by a desire to end tribalism, but, in fact, the coup was led by and favoured the Ibos, and subsequent divisions along tribal lines deteriorated into civil war. In Uganda, Idi Amin (1971–1979) exploited tribal divisions to remain in power. In Syria, division within the military forced President Hafiz Al-Assad (1971–) to depend on support from his own clan and village (Randall and Theobald 1998).

The political route from democracy to dictatorship usually involves banning opposition parties. One-party states merge leader, party, and state so that disloyalty to any one is disloyalty to the others; party credentials become essential for state positions and the party bureaucracy helps the state bureaucracy to maintain power. Communist countries operate this way, but there have also been non-communist one-party dictatorships including those of Kwame Nkrumah (Ghana, 1960–1966), Habib Bourguiba (Tunisia, 1963–1981), Julius Nyerere (Tanzania, 1962–1985), and Daniel Moi (Kenya, 1978–).

Many dictatorships are consolidated in response to "emergencies." Ferdinand Marcos (The Philippines, 1965–1986) imposed martial law in 1972 when faced with Communist insurgents, Muslim separatists, and an economic crisis. Habib Bourguiba (Tunisia, 1957–1987) responded to left-wing protests with increased repression in 1976, 1977, and 1980. Failed coups led to the outlawing of opposition by Daniel Moi (Kenya, 1978–) in 1982 and by Geydar Aliyev (Azerbaijan, 1968–1989, 1993–) in 1995.

Once dictatorships are established, new dictators may take over an existing position. Reza Pahlavi (Iran, 1941–1979) succeeded to a throne that had been seized in 1924; Saddam Hussein (Iraq, 1979–2003) succeeded President al-Bakr, who had taken power after a 1968 coup; and Jean-Claude "Baby Doc" Duvalier (Haiti, 1971–1986) inherited his dictatorship from his father.

Factors Predisposing Developing Countries to Dictatorship

No single overriding factor predicts the emergence of a dictatorship. Poverty, absence of democratic experience, and political instability all play a role.

Of these, the absence of democratic experience may be the most significant. Stable parliamentary democracies, such as Botswana and Mauritius, have been built on sound economies, but also had experienced the working of Westminster-style constitutions. Botswana was a protectorate rather than a colony and had the advantage of British tutelage from 1885. Mauritius had eleven years of internal self-government before achieving full independence in 1968. It is also notable that India, which significantly engaged its indigenous people in political processes before independence, has not succumbed to post-colonial dictatorship. By contrast, in Madagascar and Ghana, the absence of established political institutions contributed to a series of emergency dictatorships.

In many ex-colonies, the years of colonial rule denied indigenous peoples access to legislatures, political parties, local councils, and other processes of accountable responsibility. Ingrained authoritarian habits resurfaced as many apparently democratic African ex-colonies transformed after only one election into personal or party dictatorships (Andreski 1992). In Tanzania the one-party state was seen as necessary for continued economic development, and in Kenya the people were said to be not yet ready for democracy (Smith 1996). In South America the absence of democratic tradition led to a series of dictatorships, briefly interrupted by democratic experiments. After initial post-colonial attempts to introduce constitutional government were thwarted by wealthy oligarchies, industrialisation created new industrial capitalist elites, who used established authoritarian patterns to curb post-war democratic and welfare experiments (Smith 1996; Andreski 1992). As a typical example, Guatemala, accustomed to brutal repression under Spanish colonisation, experienced only brief periods of liberalisation from 1944–1954 and from 1966–1970. Between 1964 and 1976, military dictatorships supplanted civilian governments in Brazil (Castelo Branco, 1964–1967), Uruguay (Juan Maria Bordaberry Arocena, 1972–1976; Apariccio Méndez Manfredini, 1976–1981), Chile (Augusto Pinochet, 1973–1989), and Argentina (Jorge Videla, 1976–1978; Roberto Viola, 1978–1981; Leopoldo Galtieri, 1981–1982).

People become accustomed to living under dictatorships and may even derive an odd sense of security from an authoritarian state. Revolutions often end up replacing one dictatorship with another, as was the case in Cuba where Fulgencio Batista (1940–1944, 1952–1958) was replaced by Fidel Castro (1959–) and in Iran, where Reza Pahlavi (1941–1979) was replaced by Ruhollah Khomeni (1979–1989).

Instability, disunity, and poverty provide fertile ground for dictatorship. Because the boundaries of developing countries were usually imposed by colonising powers, often disregarding ethnic and cultural distribution, they are prone to instability and fragmentation. Ethnic and religious fragmentation has had serious effects in Angola, Benin, Cameroon, Chad, Ivory Coast, Indonesia, Iran, Kenya, Liberia, Malawi, Mozambique, Nigeria, Sierra Leone, Tanzania, The Philippines, Uganda, and Zaire (Haynes 1996).

Disunity leads to the formation of rival armies, and poverty encourages young people to fight for very small rewards. Thus, power is arbitrated through military victories (Andreski 1992). Between 1960 and 1980, three-quarters of Latin America, half of Asia, and more than half of Africa experienced coups. Through the 1980s there was at least one coup or attempted coup in a developing country each year. In the first half of the 1990s there were coups or attempted coups in Chad, Togo, Peru, Sierra Leone, Haiti, Guatemala, Nigeria, and Gambia (Smith 1996). Dictatorship is a way of counteracting this, an attempt by post-colonial states to maintain territorial integrity and unify populations, either by force or by apportioning ethnic representation through the dominant party (Andreski 1992; Smith 1996). Tribal conflict contributed to the coup of Idi Amin (Uganda, 1971–1979); Robert Mugabe (Zimbabwe, 1980–) justified bullying his opposition as preventing tribal fragmentation; Achmed Sukarno (Indonesia, 1945–1968) responded to fragmentation with an authoritarian constitution in 1957 and then in 1960 by establishing himself as dictator.

Mistrust of alternative groups that might gain power leads to widespread popular support for some military governments (Smith 1996). Sometimes "veto" coups (Randall and Theobald 1998) occur to prevent an unwanted government from even coming into power. In Pakistan an emerging middle class, threatened by the instability that followed partition, supported the coup that brought Ayub Khan to power in 1958. In Algeria the army established a military junta in 1992 to prevent the Islamic Salvation Front from winning an election.

One-party systems make countries less prone to military coups and often represent an attempt to provide stability and impose unity (Randall and Theobald 1998; Smith 1996). The strongest one-party governments occur where the party has a strong grass roots presence, as well as a national organisation. The resulting binding effect can be seen in the ideologically disparate examples of Kenya, Tanzania, and Cuba.

Pre-colonial political traditions also play a role in establishing dictatorships. Sukarno (Indonesia, 1945–1968) drew on the Javanese notion of consensus.

Leopold Senghor (Senegal, 1960–1980), and Julius Nyerere (Tanzania, 1962–1985) based one-party approaches on African traditions of consensus, unity, and egalitarianism. In China the regime rests its legitimacy on a strong tradition of centralised power and the Confucian doctrine of putting the national good above the interests of the individual (Sorensen 1991). In many nations, pre-colonial "clientelism," meaning mutual obligation between the powerful and their dependents, contributes to the way dictatorships are sustained by rewarding loyal supporters through distribution of tasks and power (patrimonial bureaucracy). Armed forces that support and are supported by regimes rely upon patronage. Military dictatorships tend to arise when the absence of an influential and educated indigenous middle class makes the military the main source of organisational status and personal power, attracting politically ambitious people to military careers. One such person was Muammar Quaddafi (Libya, 1969–), who led a bloodless coup against King Idris in 1969 and became virtual president of a one-party state.

In many developing countries, the impetus built up by fighting for independence gave individuals or organisations the momentum to carry them into dictatorial power. Marxist-Leninists took over after leading the independence movements of Indo-China, Angola, and Mozambique. Freedom fighters who became dictators include Kim Il Sung (North Korea, 1948–1994), Houari Boumédiènne (Algeria, 1965–1978), Robert Mugabe (Zimbabwe, 1980–), Félix Houphouët-Boigny (Ivory Coast, 1960–1993), and Achmed Sukarno (Indonesia, 1945–1968).

Although military dictatorships usually emerge in countries at peace (Andreski 1992), they can follow wars when military defeats are blamed on governments' failure to modernise. Military action established the modernising dictatorships of Kemal Ataturk (Turkey, 1923–1938) and Gamal Abdel Nasser (Egypt, 1954–1970). Military dictatorships do not, however, always lead to modernisation in developing countries (Randall and Theobald 1998). The 1971 coup in Uganda resulted from the army opposing modernisation because it felt diminished by the power of the Westernised elite (Smith 1996).

Development and Dictatorship

It is argued that strong dictatorship is good for economic development because it provides planning and political continuity, controls the strategic direction of investment, and suppresses opposition to foreign investment and the modernisation process (Andreski

1992; Sandschneider 1991; Smith 1996). These very qualities, however, mean that economic development under dictatorships often involves significant social and human cost (Sorensen 1991).

Socialist and Communist dictatorships manage the economy directly to encourage economic development. Public management also fills the vacuum in developing countries that lack significant privately owned capital, such as Tanzania (Smith 1996). Public management can be very effective. China's rate of post-war industrial growth, particularly since the 1970s, is among the highest in the developing world (Sorensen 1991).

Socialist and Communist dictatorships tend to combine economic with social goals, using authoritarian power to undermine existing elites and redistribute wealth (Sorensen 1991). In China social goals after the revolution extended to eliminating opium addiction, prostitution, and gambling, and taking steps toward the equality of women (Sorensen 1991). Deng Xiaoping (China, 1978–1997) even used his power to enforce environmental considerations. Subsequently, population control has been an area of concern and some success, although the one-child policy has affected the survival rate of female babies (Andreski 1992; Sorensen 1991).

The problem with centralist planned economies is that those in charge have no material incentive to promote efficiency or quality control, or to pursue innovation (Sorensen 1991). There is also a tendency to promote heavy rather than consumer industry, as there is no need to woo consumers. Furthermore, dictators' lack of accountability can mean economic devastation when a dictator gets a dysfunctional idea. In China two periods of economic improvement (1949–1956 and 1977–) were interrupted by Mao's push for huge agro-industrial communes, which produced a famine that killed 20 million people. A similar catastrophe was perpetrated by Pol Pot (Cambodia, 1976–1978) when at least 15% of the population was wiped out in an attempt to achieve total collectivisation.

Capitalist dictatorships direct and control private-sector development. Through such initiatives, Chung Hee Park (South Korea, 1963–1979) achieved greater economic development than that achieved by the ideological dictatorship in China. Investors' greed is the incentive, but this also brings disadvantages. It is notable that the recent move toward capitalism in China has been accompanied by increasing corruption (Sorensen 1991). Capitalism without democracy has no incentive to pass on economic benefits to the people (Smith 1996). An exception is Taiwan. Perhaps because it has been dependent on, and shaped by, the support of the United States, it has accompanied rapid capitalist industrial growth under dictatorship (Chiang Kai-shek, 1949–1975) with successful economic redistribution and improved welfare (Sorensen 1991).

Ultimately, dictatorships only enhance economic and social development if they want to do so. Some are ideologically opposed to development, others are too focused on personal aggrandisement. Islamic dictatorships, such as those of Ruhollah Khomeni (1979–1989) and Mohammad Omar and the Taliban (Afghanistan, 1996–2001), have reversed the process of modernisation and secularisation (Randall and Theobald 1998). "Predatory" dictatorships (Randall and Theobald 1998) damage rather than enhance national economic development through depleting resources to sustain their political position and to amass private wealth. Dictators such as Fulgencio Batista (Cuba, 1940–1944, 1952–1958) and Syngman Rhee (South Korea, 1948–1960) retard development through corruption and favouritism. Vast personal fortunes were amassed by Félix Houphouët-Boigny (Ivory Coast, 1960–1993), Hastings Banda (Malawi, 1966–1994), and Sese Soko Mobutu (Zaire, 1960, 1965–1997).

Development is also retarded when foreign aid is lost through dictatorships' policies. In the 1990s, both Britain and France made aid conditional on good records of democracy and human rights. Global aid agencies such as the World Bank have similarly tied aid to "good government." Dictatorships whose policies have stopped international aid include Saddam Hussein (Iraq, 1979–2003) and Mohammad Omar and the Taliban (Afghanistan, 1996–2001).

In the end, a dictatorship's success in promoting economic development depends upon intention, competence, resources, minimising internal disruption, and maintaining international support.

Maintaining Dictatorships

Dictatorships depend on arbitrary use of power. When people do not know where the wrath or benevolence of the dictator will next descend, they become compliant through a mixture of fear and hope. Fear is generated through combinations of denial of human rights, suppression of women, environmental destruction, and ethnic and religious persecution. The same can also generate hope that one might be spared. In addition, corrupt practices can generate hopes of rewards for loyal supporters.

Maximum repression occurs where opposition is too weak or too oppressed to challenge the regime. Maintenance of dictatorship thus requires continual suppression of opposition through outlawing political parties; repressing or co-opting trade unions; and purging, arresting, and/or executing leading citizens likely to oppose the regime. Kim Il Sung (North Korea, 1948–1994) established his power base by eliminating rival political factions. The 1993–1994 military regime in Nigeria purged the Provisional Ruling Council; imprisoned the president-elect (Abiola) for treason; arrested leading trade unionists, civil rights workers, and newspaper editors; and banned the courts from hearing cases that challenged its authority. Reza Pahlavi (Iran, 1941–1979) imprisoned opponents and abolished or suppressed hostile political parties. Hafez Al-Assad (Syria, 1971–) ruthlessly repressed opposition, particularly religious extremism. Omar Hassan Ahmad al-Bashir (Sudan, 1989–1999) based his regime on disappearances, torture, and arbitrary executions. Thojib Suharto (Indonesia, 1967–1998) purged his supporters, detained thousands of political prisoners, and ruthlessly put down regional unrest. After the 1965 coup in Indonesia, at least half a million "communists" were exterminated by the military. Public demonstrations of opposition are brutally put down, as in Mexico in 1968, at Kwangju in South Korea in 1979, and on Tiananmen Square in China in 1989.

Dictatorships often justify repression of opposition by vilifying it as a "subversive" threat to the national good as defined by the dictatorship (revolution in China, Vietnam, and North Korea; modernisation in Mali, Ghana, and South Vietnam; religious tradition in Iran, Pakistan, and Afghanistan).

Institutions where debate thrives are controlled or closed down. In Chile, Augusto Pinochet (1973–1989) starved education of funds and curbed freedom of thought. In Kenya, Daniel Moi (1978–) recognising the danger of a politicised educated class, censored the media, and closed the universities temporarily whenever opposition was voiced. Programs of mass education can also be used to shore up a regime, for example, as in the government-sponsored literacy program in Brazil in the 1970s.

Dictatorships either colonise or undermine constitutions. Haile Selassie (Ethiopia, 1930–1935, 1940–1974), Reza Pahlavi (Iran, 1941–1979), and Ruhollah Khomeni (Iran, 1979–1989) implemented constitutions that ensured continuity of their personal power. Daniel Moi (Kenya, 1978–) ruled through control of parliament, the judiciary, and many social organisations. When under international pressure to hold an election in 1992, he made constitutional changes to ensure his reelection. Robert Mugabe (Zimbabwe, 1980–) controlled a multi-party system until 1987 through bullying the opposition; he then became president and established one-party rule.

Alfredo Stroessner (Paraguay, 1954–1989) manipulated a parliament, political parties, and elections. Ferdinand Marcos (The Philippines, 1965–1986) and Thojib Suharto (Indonesia, 1967–1998) regularly won elections through fraud and intimidation.

Dictatorships often resort to state terror, in which the primary role of the police and the military is to coerce the civilian populations. Secret police, such as the "National Information Service" in Brazil or the "Security of the Revolution" in Sudan, with vast powers of interrogation and the right to torture, are put in place, loyal only to the regime, to which they owe their existence. Augusto Pinochet (Chile, 1973–1989) has been accused of two hundred thousand arrests and up to fifty thousand killings in his regime's first ten years (Randall and Theobald 1998). Daniel Moi (Kenya, 1978–) used security forces to enforce political detention without trial and implement systematic torture.

Personal dictatorships often build personality cults, which generate support through the symbolism of the father figure and rhetoric that claims unique wisdom and commitment to the nation's welfare. Achmed Sukarno (Indonesia 1945–1967) expounded his "five principles" (*Pantjasila*) of nationalism, tolerance, democracy, social justice, and religious belief. Kim Il Sung (North Korea, 1948–1994) claimed that his genius was behind Korea's economic miracle. Alfredo Stroessner (Paraguay, 1954–1989) took credit for "peace and progress." Sese Soko Mobutu (Zaire, 1960, 1965–1997) launched a campaign of "African Authenticity," even changing his country's name from Congo to Zaire.

The attraction of a paternal protector is enhanced if he can claim to be protecting his people from an identifiable enemy. Kim Il Sung (North Korea, 1948–1994) had the US-backed South Korea as a permanent enemy. Saddam Hussein (Iraq, 1979–2003) has had a series of enemies from Iran in his early years to the United States and the West after the first Gulf War. Leopoldo Galtieri (Argentina, 1981–1982) attacked the Falklands in 1982 as a distraction from the deteriorating economy. Enemies are most effective if they are not actually engaged in battle. When military dictatorships fight wars, they tend to lose (Andreski 1992). Furthermore, the need to deploy troops at home against the civilian population means even sabre-rattling dictators prefer pacific foreign policies.

Ending Dictatorships

When dictators cease to effectively contain, divert, or oppress opposition, they fall (Sandschneider 1991), and personal dictators often come to violent ends on account of their lack of legitimacy (Colburn 1994). Some few such as Kim Il Sung (North Korea, 1948–1994) and Haiti's Francois "Papa Doc" Duvalier (1957–1971) survive to die of natural causes. Some lose their effectiveness due to health reasons. Hastings Banda (Malawi, 1966–1994) lost power when he became senile and international pressure coupled with internal dissent forced multi-party elections. Most, however, come to violent ends.

Some dictators lose power through military overthrow or popular uprisings resulting from economic problems, social tension, or revelations of intolerable abuses of power, particularly squandering or misappropriating resources. Dictators displaced by military action include Stroessner (Paraguay, 1954–1989), Idi Amin (Uganda, 1971–1979), and Sese Soko Mobutu (Zaire, 1960, 1965–1997). Cases of civil rejection include Augusto Pinochet (Chile, 1973–1989), Ferdinand Marcos (The Philippines, 1965–1986), and Suharto (Indonesia, 1967–1998). Popular revolutions removed Fulgencio Batista (Cuba, 1940–1944, 1952–1958), Anastasio Somoza (Nicaragua, 1937–1947, 1950–1956), and Reza Pahlavi (Iran, 1941–1979). Assassination was the fate of Carlos Armas (Guatemala, 1954–1963), Ngo Dinh Diem (South Vietnam, 1955–1963), Haile Selassie (Ethiopia, 1930–1935, 1940–1974), Rafael Trujillo (Dominica, 1930–198, 1943–1961), and Chung Hee Park (South Korea, 1963–1979). Occasionally, legal processes bring dictators to justice. Jean-Bedel Bokassa (Central Africa, 1965–1979) was placed on trial and sentenced to death, but the sentence was commuted to life imprisonment.

Dictatorships may be modified through international pressure, as happened in Angola, Ghana, the Ivory Coast, Nepal, and Zambia, and some dictators themselves move toward constitutional rule. In Guatemala, General Mejia Victores' 1983 coup led to liberalisation, a constitution, and elections. In the Ivory Coast, Félix Houphouët-Boigny (1960–1993) called multi-party elections when democratisation hit Africa in 1989.

A dictatorship can end in civil war because it legitimizes illegitimate access to power and frustrates those who would like power but have no access to it. Paradoxically, civil strife then weakens civil society, making recurrence of dictatorships likely, as can be seen in Afghanistan, Algeria, Angola, Burundi, Liberia, Mozambique, Somalia, and Zaire (Smith 1996).

Globalisation undermines dictatorships with the political intervention of powerful states or of international organisations such as the UN, NATO, or the European Union. Economically, major decisions are now made by transnational corporations.

Developments in communications technology make restriction of information and ideology increasingly difficult. Yet, even as dictatorships are undermined at the level of nation-states, there are growing possibilities for international dictatorships by powerful countries, international alliances, transnational corporations, or maverick groups and individuals.

LEONORA RITTER

See also Authoritarianism; Bureaucratic-Authoritarianism; Democratization

References and Further Reading

Andreski, Stanislav. *Wars, Revolutions, Dictatorships.* London: Frank Cass, 1992.

Colburn, Forrest D. *The Vogue of Revolution in Poor Countries.* Princeton, NJ: Princeton University, 1994.

Haynes, Jeffrey. *Third World Politics: A Concise Introduction.* Oxford, UK: Blackwell, 1996.

Kavanagh, Denis. *A Dictionary of Political Biography.* Oxford, UK: Oxford University Press, 1998.

Meller, Patricio. *The Unidad Popular and the Pinochet Dictatorship.* Basingstoke: Macmillan, 2000.

Randall, Vicky and Robin Theobald. *Political Change and Underdevelopment.* Basingstoke: Macmillan, 1998.

Sandschneider, Eberhard. "Successful Economic Development and Political Change in Taiwan and South Korea." In *Rethinking Third World Politics*, edited by James Manor. London: Longman, 1991.

Smith, B. C. *Understanding Third World Politics.* Basingstoke: Macmillan, 1996.

Sorensen, Georg. *Democracy, Dictatorship and Development.* Basingstoke: Macmillan, 1991.

DISASTER RELIEF

One measure of a country's level of development is its ability to cope with the effects of disasters. Highly developed countries are as likely to experience natural disasters as less-developed ones, but they are much more likely to be able to cope with the effects of disasters. Droughts in North America and Europe do not lead to disastrous famines. They may lead to severe local or regional dislocations, but not to widespread starvation. Earthquakes, hurricanes, and floods strike in all parts of the world, but in wealthier countries property is widely insured and logistical capacities are much better developed. Rarely do wealthy countries need large amounts of outside help to cope with damage from such natural disasters. Of the approximately sixty disasters that took more than a thousand lives in various parts of the world in the last three decades of the twentieth century, fewer than a half dozen involved developed countries. The most deadly disasters occur in Latin America, Africa, and Asia. Disasters are often also associated with man-made phenomena, such as civil wars that disrupt food production in developing countries. Political instability in the developing world thus exacerbates natural disasters when they do occur. International disaster assistance programs tend to be focused on disasters that occur in the developing world, while disasters that strike developed countries are normally addressed through their own national disaster response mechanisms.

Disaster and Poverty

The association of disasters with poverty-stricken countries is significant. A distinction can be made between countries that are disaster-prone and those that are vulnerable to large loss of life. Disaster-prone countries, wealthy and poor alike, are situated in geographic or climatic zones where disasters such as earthquakes, various kinds of storms, or drought conditions are frequent occurrences. Poor countries are almost always more vulnerable to the effects of disasters than similarly situated wealthy countries. Poverty is closely related to loss of life in disasters for a number of reasons. First, in poor countries large percentages of the population settle in areas more prone to disasters, including low-land areas susceptible to floods and along mountainsides where poorly constructed housing is more susceptible to damage from earthquakes and mudslides. Second, food supplies in poor countries are often barely sufficient to meet domestic needs, even in normal times, and such countries subject to periodic drought are also highly vulnerable to famine. Third, poor countries generally lack the logistical and infrastructural capacity to respond effectively to disasters. Poor people generally cannot afford to locate and build residences that are safe, nor are they wealthy enough to ensure their property. These factors also contribute to the vulnerability of poor countries to disasters. Wealthier countries have sufficient resources to hedge against the most serious effects of disaster, and they are better able to weather them. By contrast, less-developed countries must often turn to the international community for assistance during times of natural disaster and national emergency. Fortunately, there are a number of governmental, intergovernmental, and non-governmental agencies that provide disaster aid.

The International Disaster Assistance Network

When a country lacks the ability to provide for the medical, housing, and food needs of populations adversely affected by disasters, it may turn to the wider international community for assistance and support. Many developed countries have governmental agencies tasked to respond to foreign disaster situations. Within the United States Agency for International Development (USAID), for instance, the Office of Foreign Disaster Assistance (OFDA) is charged with assessing and responding to the emergency needs of countries struck by disaster. Many donor countries have similar agencies charged with provision of emergency and humanitarian assistance. These bodies may respond with bilateral assistance or cooperate with international agencies in a multilateral response to an emergency. For many years, the United Nations Disaster Relief Organization (UNDRO) served as the focal point of international responses to disaster situations. In 1992, the UN reorganized its disaster aid structure, forming a Department of Humanitarian Affairs (DHA), which was charged with coordinating the wide variety of UN agencies that performed disaster assistance functions, including the UN High Commissioner for Refugees (UNHCR), which takes primary responsibility for provision of emergency assistance in refugee situations; the UN Development Program (UNDP), which coordinates emergency aid programs with the long-term development programming of host states; the UN Children's Fund (UNICEF), which supplies emergency aid for the benefit of children; and the World Food Program (WFP), which supplies emergency food aid, among others. The DHA was later succeeded by a new body called the UN Office for the Coordination of Humanitarian Affairs (UNOCHA), which now serves as the major coordinating body for international responses to disaster situations. UNOCHA is headed by the Emergency Relief Coordinator who also serves as the Under-Secretary-General for Humanitarian Affairs. The Inter-Agency Standing Committee (IASC) of UNOCHA coordinates emergency responses of UN agencies to emerging disasters, performs needs assessments, encourages the consolidation of agency financial appeals during disasters, and attempts to coordinate disaster assistance activities in affected countries.

In addition to governments and to a variety of UN agencies that supply emergency relief, there are large numbers of non-governmental organizations (NGOs) that are actively engaged in disaster-related assistance activities. The International Committee of the Red Cross (ICRC), which is the oldest disaster response organization in existence, coupled with its cousin, the International Federation of Red Cross and Red Crescent Societies (IFRC), has served the needs of populations caught in the cross-fire of international and civil wars, which are often complicated by natural disasters, droughts, and famine. The ICRC is today charged with assistance and protection functions for civilian populations adversely affected by civil conflict. The IFRC is a coordinating body of various national chapters of the Red Cross, which routinely offer disaster assistance within their respective countries.

Dozens of additional NGOs that have consultative status with the United Nations are also actively involved in the provision of disaster or emergency assistance activities on behalf of displaced persons and refugees. Agencies such as Africare, Catholic Relief Services, CARE, Church World Service, Food for the Hungry, Doctors Without Borders, Lutheran World Federation, Oxfam, Salvation Army, Save the Children, and World Vision, to name but a few, are regular participants in the provision of disaster and emergency relief assistance throughout the world. In the United States, many NGOs are members of Interaction, an umbrella organization through which they maintain contact, communication, and collaboration in the assistance activities. The International Council of Voluntary Agencies (ICVA) provides another focal point for international NGO communication with the host of UN agencies headquartered in Geneva. In Europe, the European Union (EU) maintains ties with European NGOs through the European Community Humanitarian Office (ECHO) and a liaison office for NGOs. These bodies in turn deal with a consortium of European NGOs known as the Voluntary Organizations in Cooperation in Emergencies (VOICE).

The International Disaster Assistance network consists of a wide range of agencies and organizations. Efforts to coordinate this wide array of governmental, non-governmental, and intergovernmental agencies are complicated by the sheer number of bodies that take an interest in the provision of disaster aid, and by the often differing political and ideological motives such groups hold dear. Disaster aid is both about logistical efficiency and about politics. Coherence and efficiency are not easily achieved, but given the rather recent rise of such humanitarian bodies, largely in the latter half of the twentieth century, the system does offer hope and consolation and material assistance to people adversely affected by disasters throughout the world.

Early Warning

Relief during disasters is essential. Food supplies, medicine, and shelter are often needed in large amounts over short periods. Depending on the type of disaster, logistical support, search teams, and technical assistance may be needed in the aftermath of floods, hurricanes, and earthquakes. For creeping disasters, such as drought and famine, agricultural assistance, water supply, reforestation programs, and the like may be necessary. Whatever the circumstances of the disaster, there is a growing awareness that early warning of disasters is critical to minimizing the loss of life. Weather-related disasters can be mitigated through sharing of meteorological data. The World Meteorological Organization (WMO) tracks dangerous storms and disseminates weather information to governments so that preparations for evacuation of vulnerable coastal areas can be effected. The WMO's computer-based information network, or CLICOM, is linked into the UNOCHA's early warning system, which attempts to identify emerging disaster situations. UNOCHA maintains a Humanitarian Early Warning System, which is an extensive database that tracks a variety of factors likely to precipitate disasters in various countries. In addition to threats from disease and natural disasters, assessments are made pertaining to potential violent uprisings and conflict. Considered are such factors as genocide, human rights violations, regime failure, refugees, environmental crises, and food shortages. UNOCHA has also established a variety of regional bodies, including the Integrated Regional Information Network in Nairobi, Kenya, which tracks the Great Lakes region of Africa, and a similar program in Abidjan to monitor humanitarian emergencies in West Africa.

Good advance information and warning is critical to avoiding massive loss of life in disaster situations. However, ultimately, governments and agencies must be willing to act on the information received, by prepositioning logistical support and assistance or readying emergency relief mechanisms for swift action. This requires that governments be willing to risk stimulating flows of refugees and displaced persons by the very acts of prepositioning assistance. Countries are not always ready to risk precipitating population movements that might otherwise be avoided.

Disasters are mitigated not only by good data predicting potential disaster occurences, but also by long-term policy responses by governments to enforce building codes in earthquake-prone areas, build up food storage capacities, improve basic transportation infrastructure, and develop a capacity within the government to manage disaster-relief activities. By developing disaster-planning abilities and taking steps to improve early warning, governments contribute to the development of their nations.

Disasters and Development

The connection between disaster and development is a two-way street. Disasters hamper development and development mitigates disaster. Because of this reality, disaster-relief organizations and development agencies both need to take an interest in the work of their counterparts, so that disaster-relief agencies supply forms of disaster aid in ways that will foster rather than inhibit development. Similarly, development agencies must consider how a country's long-term development strategy can help to insulate a country's economy, its infrastructure, and its population from the most egregious and harmful effects of disasters. Good disaster-relief policy should enhance the ability of a country to recuperate and good development policy should help countries develop disaster prevention and mitigation strategies, so that future disasters can be weathered with fewer negative consequences for the country's long-term development situation.

Disaster-relief agencies need to consider how their emergency assistance activities can potentially harm long-term development policy in a country. This is especially true of droughts and famines, the "creeping disasters" that develop over time, often producing substantial population movements as starving populations stream into neighboring regions or even cross international boundaries. Clearly, it is necessary under such circumstances for food and medical assistance to be provided on a priority basis, just to preserve life. But the way the food is acquired and delivered makes a difference. If external food aid is dumped into a developing country's economy, local grain prices will drop with the sudden surge of supply in free grains. This gives local farmers in the affected country no incentive to increase production. If less grain is planted, domestic food production and supplies could be permanently depressed as the country comes to rely on external food aid, leading to an unhealthy dependency. However, if disaster-relief agencies first purchase local supplies of grain, reducing local stocks and only supplementing them with external assistance when local stocks are exhausted, incentives for further local food production can be sustained to the benefit of local peasant populations, and to the overall benefit of food self-reliance in the aid-receiving country, allowing it to spend precious foreign currency reserves on other national needs.

Disaster-relief agencies must also be careful about putting disaster victims, displaced persons, and refugees in situations of personal dependency on external charity. In all cases, the object should be to restore disaster victims to a condition of self-reliance. This means paying attention that aid be delivered to disaster victims in such a way as to promote their attainment of work, of new skills, and of opportunities for settlement where their skills can be put to productive use. Foreign disaster-relief agencies also need to work with their domestic counterparts in such a way as to ensure that the latter, together with the larger beneficiary population, are involved in the emergency-assistance planning and implementation. The development of the local managerial capacity is a central feature to the healthy and long-term restoration of a society.

Development agencies have a part to play in this process, even though their outlook emphasizes long-term planning horizons, rather than the emergency aid approach that must by necessity focus on immediate needs. But just as disaster agencies need to be aware of how immediate needs can be addressed without compromising long-term development, so development agencies need to think about how the long-term development strategy addresses the ability of the beneficiary country to cope with disasters. For example, in countries prone to earthquakes or floods, is there a comprehensive national strategy regulating the placement and construction of buildings and neighborhoods? In countries prone to drought, is agricultural policy adequately focused on the establishment of self-sufficiency in the production of cereal grains and other foods for domestic consumption? Has the country developed adequate programs to minimize post-harvest loss of grain and to ensure adequate food storage facilities? Have the national transportation networks, especially the road networks in rural areas, been adequately maintained and developed to ensure better integration and supply from farm to market? Have drought mitigation strategies been adequately explored? Do adequate livestock and agricultural extension facilities exist in the country to promote a healthier rural economy? These are but a few examples of the many ways in which national development policy can be made to strengthen a country's capacity to cope with disasters and mount more effective domestic mechanisms for disaster response.

Interdependence, Globalization, and Cooperation

Disasters in one part of the world inevitably have effects not only in the country immediately affected, but in neighboring countries and regions. Natural disasters cannot be eliminated. But governments can take steps to minimize the adverse effects of natural disasters. Disasters that are the result of civil war, human interactions with the environment, and short-sighted national policies could, in a perfect world, be eliminated. Since it is unlikely that perfection will be attained by human political and social institutions, we can probably expect man-made disasters to continue, often alongside of their natural counterparts. Still, whether disasters take the form of natural or human-caused events, there is much that can be done to anticipate them, respond to them, and minimize their adverse effects.

This is first and foremost a matter of national and local policy making. But where countries lack the resources and capacities to develop strong disaster prevention, mitigation, and response programs, the international community is in a position to assist. A wide array of agencies and organizations, many of them already mentioned, have been established by governments to encourage swift and effective disaster responses throughout the world. Governments needing international assistance need only seek it. Developed countries have both humanitarian and economic motives for assisting countries in need. The increased economic interdependence and globalization that has marked the progress of the international economic relations in the latter half of the twentieth century, coupled with the speed of international communication and transportation, have made rapid disaster responses throughout the globe possible for the first time in human history. The effectiveness of international coordination to this end is not always perfect and is often fraught with difficulty, but the very existence of a global response capability must be accounted a major advance in a world where adverse effects of national disasters and instabilities are felt in neighboring countries and regions, attracting the concern of the wider international community. This increased global awareness guarantees that future attention to disasters and disaster-relief coordination will continue to be a matter of great and ongoing international concern.

ROBERT F. GORMAN

See also CARE; Doctors Without Borders/Médecins sans Frontières; Humanitarian Relief Projects; International Committee of the Red Cross; Natural Disasters; OXFAM; Salvation Army; United Nations Children's Fund (UNICEF); United Nations Development Program (UNDP)

References and Further Reading

Awotona, Adenrele, ed. *Reconstruction After Disaster: Issues and Practices.* Aldershot, UK: Ashgate, 1997.
Benthall, Jonathan. *Disasters, Relief, and the Media.* London: IB Tauris, 1993.
Blaikie, Piers, et al. *At Risk: Natural Hazards, People's Vulnerability and Disasters.* London: Routledge, 1994.
Cahill, Thomas, ed. *A Framework for Survival: Health, Human Rights, and Humanitarian Assistance in Conflicts and Disasters.* New York: Basic Books, 1993.
Cuny, Frederick. *Disasters and Development.* New York: Oxford University Press, 1983.
Dacy, D. C. and H. Kunreuther. *The Economics of Natural Disaster.* New York: Free Press, 1969.
Gorman, Robert F. *Historical Dictionary of Refugee and Disaster Relief Organizations.* Lanham, MD: Scarecrow Press, 2000.
Green, Stephen. *International Disaster Relief: Toward a Responsive System.* New York: McGraw-Hill, 1977.
International Federation of Red Cross and Red Crescent Societies. *World Disasters Report.* Oxford, UK: Oxford University Press, 1996.
Kent, Randolph. *Anatomy of Disaster Relief: The International Network in Action.* London: Pinter Publishers, 1987.
Natsios, Andrew S. *US Foreign Policy and the Four Horsemen of the Apocalypse: Humanitarian Relief in Complex Emergencies.* Westport, CT: Praeger, 1997.
Wijkman, Anders and Lloyd Timberlake. *Natural Disasters: Acts of God or Acts of Man?* London: Earthscan, 1984.

DJIBOUTI

The Republic of Djibouti (*Jumhouriyya Djibouti*) is a small East African country located on the Horn of Africa at the western end of the Gulf of Aden. The country is bordered to the west by Ethiopia, by Eritrea in the north, and by Somalia to the southeast. The northeast part of the country is the western boundary of the Bab al Mendeb waterway, which leads to the Red Sea; across from this is the country of Yemen, the southern tip of the Arabian Peninsula. The capital of Djibouti, also called Djibouti, is located on the mouth of the Bay of Tadjoura, approximately twenty kilometers from the border with Somalia.

Because of its lack of natural resources, the region had no independent identity until the partitioning of Africa by the Europeans. The city of Djibouti was built by the French to consolidate trading, and was identified as the region's capital in 1891. Prior to that time the regional capital had been the city of Obock (*Obok*).

Prior to adopting its present name, this region was known as French Somaliland until 1967, when it became the French Territory of the Afars and Issas until 1977. The Afar tribe is indigenous to modern-day Eritrea, Ethiopia, and Djibouti, while the Issa (*Esa*) clan exists primarily in northern Somalia. The Afars still make up more than half the population of Djibouti, while the Issa and other Somali clans make up about a third of the population. French and Arabic are recognized as the official languages of

Djibouti, with the traditional Afar and Somali languages used to a lesser extent.

France actually led the other European powers in its colonization of the Horn of Africa, before Great Britain and Italy established British Somaliland and Italian Somaliland, respectively. In 1862, a relative of the Sultan of Tadjoura ceded the city of Obock and surrounding coastal regions to France. This foothold in the region became substantially more important when the opening of the Suez Canal in 1869 brought shipping traffic from the Mediterranean into the region. In particular, the availability of a port in Djibouti enabled France to tend to its colonies in Southeast Asia.

While the late nineteenth century was marked by French and British competition in the region, the early years of the twentieth century brought competition between the colonial holdings of France and Italy in the Horn. A railroad from the city of Djibouti to Addis Ababa in Italian Ethiopia had been completed during World War I, expediting shipment of materials formerly carried by caravan, but Italy also established a railroad from Addis Ababa to the port of Assab in Eritrea, which would compete with the trade from Djibouti. The Italian government began pressuring France for concessions in its territories, and this competition for territory (along with the interruption of commerce it was causing) led French interests to reinforce the military garrisons in French Somaliland. This set the stage for the realignment of the European powers seen in World War II: France and Great Britain, the former competitors, were allied against the Axis powers, which included Italy.

The French capitulation to Germany in June 1940 put French Somaliland in the difficult position of formally being under the control of the Vichy government but not actually under Axis control, while many French in Djibouti still resented the idea of cooperation with the British. While the British were able to defeat the Italians to the north, Djibouti itself was blockaded until the governor surrendered to the British in December 1942, and French Somaliland came under control of the Free French.

Following World War II, the government of French Somaliland was changed, creating a council with two representative bodies, one made up of French citizens and the other chosen from the native population. Some degree of home rule (in minor matters) was permitted, and this council provided representation to the French Republican Assembly and the *Conseil de la République*. Local procedures differed from France's other African colonies, and in particular Muslim courts (*sha'ria* courts) were permitted.

Also following World War II, most of the French military presence was removed from the colony. By the 1960s the French Foreign Legion was brought in to keep the public order if necessary.

In 1967, the people of French Somaliland voted to remain a part of France, but on different terms. The government was reorganized to expand local rule, with five regional districts, or *cercles*, being established, of which Djibouti was the largest. However, the new government faced challenges including a terrorist kidnapping of a busload of school children by members of *le Front de la Libération de la Côte des Somalis* (FLCS) in February 1976. This precipitated a new view of the territory in the French government, and in May 1977, a vote on independence was permitted. The voters of the territory overwhelmingly chose independence and France lost its last colony in Africa.

The recent history of Djibouti is the result of decisions made decades ago. As was the case with many European colonies in Africa, the artificial boundaries established by the Europeans resulted in the groupings (and division) of tribes in the colonies. The result of such groupings and divisions leads to ethnic unrest, as evidenced by the division of Ethiopia (creating Eritrea) in the year 2000. In particular, the Afars and Issas were at odds because the Issas had been accused by their neighbors of intruding into regions used by the Afars for grazing their animals. The new leader of Djibouti chosen in 1977 was Hassan Gouled, an Issa, and he favored his own ethnic group over the Afars. This led to conflict between the groups in the 1990s, and a subsequent agreement on government gives the post of president to a member of the Issa clan while the prime minister is an Afar.

Djibouti's economy is based primarily on its location, its port facilities, and its status as a free trade zone. Other than commercial trade, very little local industry exists.

THOMAS P. DOLAN

See also East Africa: History and Economic Development; East Africa: International Relations; Ethnic Conflicts: East Africa

References and Further Reading

Lewis, I. M. *Peoples of the Horn of Africa*. London: International African Institute, 1955.
Tholomier, Robert. *Djibouti: Pawn of the Horn of Africa*. Metuchen, NJ: Scarecrow Press, 1981.
Thompson, Virginia, and Richard Adloff. *Djibouti and the Horn of Africa*. Stanford, CA: Stanford University Press, 1968.
United States Government, US Department of State. *1996 Post Report, Djibouti*. Washington, DC: Author, 1996.

DOCTORS WITHOUT BORDERS/ MÉDECINS SANS FRONTIÈRES

Médecins Sans Frontières (MSF) is a private, non-profit international humanitarian aid organisation that provides emergency medical assistance to populations in danger in the field, most of the time following a humanitarian crisis. MSF was born out of the exasperation of a group of French doctors working in desperate conditions in the Biafra War in Africa in the early seventies. One of the founders was Bernard Kouchner (who later had a political career in France and was health minister in 1993, and special representative of the secretary general of the United Nations/head of the United Nations mission in Kosovo in 1999–2001). This group of doctors believed that all people have the right to medical care regardless of race, religion, creed, or political affiliation and that the needs of these people supersede respect for national borders. They were determined to create a movement to deliver independent humanitarian aid wherever it was needed, particularly one that would speak out about the plight of the victims it helped. MSF was created in 1971, and started the movement of "French Doctors"—nongovernmental organisations that provide humanitarian assistance on the ground in an impartial and independent manner. "French Doctors" refers to organisations such as *Médecins du Monde* (Doctors of the World), Handicap International, and *Action Contre la Faim* (Action Against Hunger). MSF was the first non-governmental organization to both provide emergency medical assistance and publicly bear witness to the plight of the populations they served. It remains the world's largest independent international medical relief agency.

MSF has developed to its current position as an international humanitarian movement with offices in eighteen countries and ongoing activities in Africa, the Americas, Asia, Australia, and Europe. The success of MSF in France captured the imagination of other doctors across Europe. Operational "sections" of MSF sprang up in Belgium, Switzerland, the Netherlands, Luxembourg, and Spain. This expansion continued with the creation of support sections in Australia, Austria, Canada, Denmark, Hong Kong, Italy, Japan, Norway, Sweden, Germany, United Arab Emirates, the United States, and the UK. Each year, more than 2,500 volunteer doctors, nurses, other medical professionals, logistics experts, water/sanitation engineers, and administrators join fifteen thousand locally hired staff to provide medical aid in more than eighty countries.

To be able to speak and act freely, MSF remains independent of any political, religious, or economic powers. The majority of all MSF activities are paid for with private donations. Other sources of funding are provided by the European Union (Office of Humanitarian Affairs), national governments, and international organisations such as the United Nations Office of the High Commissioner for Refugees. In 2002, the total income of *Médecins Sans Frontières*, for all its national sections, was estimated at 366 million Euros (approximately $450 million USD), of which more than 80% was from private income.

The organisation intervenes in a variety of humanitarian crises such as armed conflicts, epidemics, and natural and man-made disasters. Interventions are also undertaken with populations that are particularly marginalised and vulnerable due to social or geographical isolation (such as inmates, women in prostitution, street children, ethnic minorities, and the elderly). The organisation brings health care to remote, isolated areas where resources and training are limited. The type of programmes run by MSF include assistance to people affected by armed conflicts, assistance for refugees and displaced population, medical assistance to victims of violence, and food and nutrition assistance. MSF works in the rehabilitation of hospitals and dispensaries, vaccination programmes, and water and sanitation projects. MSF is also active in remote health care centres and slum areas, and provides training of local personnel. In countries where health structures are insufficient or even nonexistent, MSF cooperates with authorities such as the Ministry of Health to provide assistance. MSF provides primary health care, performs surgery, rehabilitates hospitals and clinics, runs nutrition and sanitation programs, trains local medical personnel, and provides mental health care. Through longer-term programs, MSF treats chronic diseases such as tuberculosis, malaria, sleeping sickness, and AIDS. In 1999 *Médecins Sans Frontières* received the Nobel Peace Prize for its actions.

In carrying out humanitarian assistance, MSF seeks also to raise awareness of crisis situations; MSF acts as a witness and will speak out, either in private or in public, about the plight of populations in danger for whom MSF works.

MSF offices worldwide facilitate the organisation of gatherings for individuals and groups who want to speak in their home communities. MSF also mounts exhibitions and, from time to time, releases publications with the aim of raising awareness. In some instances MSF has decided to denounce abuses and misuse of humanitarian relief in the field, and has even withdrawn from countries when it considered that it could not provide assistance in situations that were satisfactory. In June 2004, following the murder of five of its staff, *Médecins Sans Frontières* became the first major aid agency to quit Afghanistan since the fall of the Taliban. The reason for this withdrawal was that the Afghan government failed to act on evidence that local warlords were behind the murders and MSF considered that the framework for independent humanitarian action in Afghanistan had ceased to exist.

It is part of MSF's work to address any violations of basic human rights encountered by field teams, whether perpetrated or sustained by political actors. It does so by confronting the responsible actors themselves, by putting pressure on them through the mobilisation of the international community, and by issuing information publicly. In order to prevent compromise or manipulation of MSF's relief activities, MSF maintains neutrality and independence from individual governments.

CLÉMENTINE OLIVIER

See also Health Care; Humanitarian Relief Projects; Non-Governmental Organizations (NGOs); World Health Organization (WHO)

References and Further Reading

Anderson, K. "Humanitarian Inviolability in Crisis: The Meaning of Impartiality and Neutrality for UN and NGO Agencies Following the 2004–2004 Afghanistan and Iraq Conflicts," *Harvard Human Rights Journal* 17, pp. 41–74, 2004.

Carey, H. F. "States, NGO's and Humanitarian Intervention." In J. Carey, W. V. Dunlap, and R. J. Pritchard (eds.), International Humanitarian Law: Challenges, Vol. 2 (pp. 123–174). Ardsley, NY: Transnational Publishers, 2004.

Danieli Y., ed. *Sharing the Front Line and the Back Hills: International Protectors and Providers: Peacekeepers, Humanitarian Aid Workers and the Media in the Midst of Crisis.* New York: Baywood, 2002.

Humanitarian Studies Unit. *Reflections on Humanitarian Action: Principles, Ethics, and Contradictions*, London: Pluto Press, 2001.

Médecins sans frontiers. *In the Shadow of "Just Wars": Violence, Politics and Humanitarian Action.* Edited by Fabrice Weissmann. Ithaca, NY: Cornell University Press, 2004.

Weber, Olivier. *French Doctors.* Paris: Robert Laffont, 1999.

DOI MOI

During the late l980s, the government of the Socialist Republic of Vietnam began to pursue *doi moi,* a development strategy that moved the country's economy away from a Soviet-style, centralized system toward one featuring decentralized markets. Three fundamental factors compelled Vietnam's leadership, including high-ranking officials in the Communist Party of Vietnam, to choose a capitalist-oriented course of action even though many thought that it was ideologically distasteful to do so and that the approach was fraught with risks. First, during the 1980s, Vietnam's economic partners (the former Soviet Union, the former German Democratic Republic, the former Yugoslavia, and the former Czechoslovakia) were experiencing persistent economic failures and were facing national disintegration. With them Vietnam held membership in the progressively more dysfunctional Council for Mutual Economic Assistance (CMEA), and this meant isolating their economy from the broader global economy contacts. The Vietnamese dong remained convertible only into the *globally non-convertible* Soviet ruble and this further isolated the country's economy.

Second, Vietnam's Southeast Asian neighbors were experiencing widespread and rapid economic growth accompanied by political stability, and their collective response to Vietnam was to create the Association of Southeast Asian Nations (ASEAN) and bar the Vietnamese from participating in it. Third, Vietnam's economy was failing as per capita income was declining annually, incidences of poverty and deprivation were growing, the infrastructure was deteriorating, prices were soaring annually (including for rice and other agricultural output), and needed goods and services were in short supply. Capital stocks were eroding as annual private and public investments fell sharply, causing both production and employment levels to decline.

These factors convinced Vietnam's socialist planners, who were also members of the Communist Party, that clinging to the status quo was intolerable. They began to examine both Vietnam's economic failures and those of its CMEA partners, as well as the successes of its organized regional neighbors. The examination convinced both the National Assembly and the Office of the Prime Minister to escape ideological boundaries and seek practical ways of moving toward an economic structure that would be guided by socialist principles while the market system was introduced. The Sixth Party Congress of the Communist Party voted to accept the principles of *doi moi* at its 1987 meeting, thereby ending decades of isolation and beginning the road toward economic reform.

Doi moi not only introduced the market mechanism but it also legitimized private property, privatized state-owned enterprises (SOEs), and struggled to put into place a supportive legal system. Macroeconomic management was improved on both the monetary and fiscal fronts; reforms opened Vietnam to the outside world; and all of this spurred the development of basic legal, tax, and regulatory infrastructure changes. The reforms presented the country's leadership with enormous administrative tasks and, consequently, *doi moi* proceeded slowly but without reversal. Externally, the dong was made convertible with the Singapore dollar, the Thai baht, the Japanese yen, and both the Australian and United States dollars. Internally, reforms began to relax legal and administrative impediments to trade, and then government took steps to welcome foreign investment and financial capital transfers.

The government's reform agenda was ambitious and unambiguous, and one of its key foci was on integration with the world economy by maintaining relationships to "big countries and neighboring countries" while giving special attention to "traditional ties and the non-aligned movement." Past associations would remain important, but the ultimate direction of the reform agenda would be Vietnam's integration with the global economic system. The government was determined to continue implementing open-door trading policies and has mapped out the road to honor its commitments to global and regional trading initiatives. The fact that this has meant making economic sectors more competitive is proving a major challenge as the country integrates into the global economy. Making economic sectors more competitive requires finding ways to blend the attributes of Vietnam's workforce and physical environment with physical and financial capital and industrial technology obtained from global markets and allocate them to the production of exports, import substitutes, and non-traded goods. This process could lead to a problem if gaining competitive edges creates economic enclaves that give rise to dysfunctional relations among Vietnamese who are separated by culture, ethnicity, and economic class. Exacerbating cleavages and inequalities among Vietnamese is a serious matter, and it's one that foreign economic interests may be neither willing nor able to understand and confront.

Externally, *doi moi* included membership in both ASEAN and the Asia-Pacific Economic Cooperation (APEC) because of four factors. First, external integration facilitates the development of comparative advantage, promotes the international division of labor, and enables participating countries to benefit from reasonable international resource allocations that harness the capacity of productive resources. Second, liberalization of trade in goods and services and investment, lower tariff barriers, simplification of procedures, and reduction of administrative controls combine to promote investment, raise output, reduce unemployment, and serve consumer interests. Third, global linkages create new investment opportunities, accelerate the flow of capital and industrial technology, and enhance efficiency that improves investment climates by reducing the risk of commercial failure. Fourth, global integration, beyond promoting investment, leads to the transfer of management and other skills, as well as making available critically important knowledge and information about production and distribution processes.

Vietnam also assumed risks, and one was inherent in the persistent instability in world financial markets wherein unstable financial capital flows can adversely affect a country such as Vietnam. The reason centers on the main difference between direct foreign investment and financial capital. Direct foreign investors, once they have disbursed their funds to build factories and purchase equipment, cannot undo their investment quickly. But portfolio investors have more flexibility due to the high degree of transferability of security purchases and the short-term nature of bank loans. Financial capital is unequally distributed globally and centers in large industrial and financial countries. In good times, capital flows from these centers to developing countries such as Vietnam, but when signs of instability begin to emerge, that is, when the flow of financial capital begins to reverse, it quickly begins to be repatriated by capital centers domiciled in developed countries.

Doi moi has remained the intellectual cornerstone to post-war Vietnam's pursuit of economic growth and development. Despite the risks, government and party leaders remain convinced that the benefits derived from reform and reformation clearly outweigh them.

ROBERT L. CURRY, JR.

References and Further Reading

Boothright, Peter and Pham Xuan Nam. *Socioeconomic Renovation in Vietnam: The Origin, Evolution and Impact of Doi Moi.* Singapore: Institute of Southeast Asian Studies, 2000.

Fford, Adam. *Doi Moi: Vietnam's Renovation Policy and Performance.* Canberra: Australian National University Press, 1991.

Fford, Adam. *Doi Moi: Ten Years After the 1986 Party Congress.* Canberra: Australian National University Press, 1997.

Gates, Carolyn L. and David Truong. *Reform of a Centrally Managed Developing Country: Vietnam in Perspective.* Stockholm: Nordic Institute of Asian Studies, 1992.

Jamieson, N. L., et al. *The Challenges of Vietnam's Reconstruction.* Fairfax, Va.: Indochina Institute, George Mason University, 1993.

Marr, David and Christine White. *Post War Vietnam: Dilemmas in Socialist Development.* Stockholm: Swedish International Development Agency, 1991.

Nghiep, L. T. *The Vietnamese Economy: Past Developments, Present Situation and Current Problems.* Tokyo: Sasakawa Peace Foundation, 1991.

Ronas, P. and O. Sjorberg. *A Socio-Economic Strategy for Vietnam.* Stockholm: Swedish International Development Agency, 1991.

DOMINICA

Dominica, an island of 750 square kilometers (290 sq. miles), is approximately the size of St. Louis, Missouri. Its population of more than seventy thousand people approximates that of Cheyenne, Wyoming. Its economy relies chiefly on the export of bananas and emerging tourism.

Dominica lies midway in an arc of islands known as the Lesser Antilles, facing eastward to the Atlantic Ocean and westward to the Caribbean Sea. It was under French control until the mid-eighteenth century, when it passed by treaty to the British. Therefore, three-fourths of the population is Roman Catholic, the remainder adhering to several Protestant sects. While English is the dominant language, much of the population also speaks a local patois or Creole version of French.

Dominica is a tropical island with a singularly rugged terrain marked by steep mountains reaching heights of well over a thousand meters (nearly four thousand feet). The island is riven with narrow valleys, gorges, and cliffs, and wrapped in thick tropical forest and hazy mists. Of volcanic origin, the island has sizable thermal lakes lying in dormant craters. Its features are more formidable than other islands in the Caribbean because it is of relatively more recent volcanic origin (some 25 million years ago); Dominica has not been as worn and smoothed down by time as the others.

The challenging physical dimensions of the island have directly affected its economic, social, and cultural character. Discovered by Christopher Columbus in 1493, the island was named "Dominica" since he set foot on it on a Sunday. The Carib Indians on the island successfully resisted Spanish occupation. They had reacted against the Spanish elsewhere among the islands but had been defeated. On Dominica, however, they had the advantage of a uniquely mountainous and forested terrain that provided abundant favorable locations for attack and defense. The profusion of tropical vegetation, rising and falling over Dominica's rich volcanic soil, has earned it the title, "Nature Island of the Caribbean."

For nearly two centuries no European power controlled Dominica, and it remained a surviving remnant of the original Carib inhabitants of the Caribbean. By the seventeenth century, however, due to repeated foreign incursions and diseases that devastated the indigenous population, the French began to settle on Dominica. The island did not have extensive flat land for large-scale agriculture. Where such a terrain did appear, however, the French laid out sugar plantations. For labor, they imported African slaves, establishing the large black and mixed-blood population of the island today. Such a pattern of land occupation and labor employment recalled the French development of Haiti.

The broken, uneven terrain discouraged a dominant pattern of plantations controlled by large landowners. Therefore a small, anomalous pattern of peasant farmers emerged who cultivated fragments of land for subsistence and market farming. Although Dominica was not exceptional economically, the absence of an overwhelmingly dominant planter class was unusual. Unusual, too, was the survival of a portion of the native Carib population, which otherwise had disappeared throughout the rest of the Caribbean. Much of this population survived based on subsistence farming.

Together with the white planter group, there was a small, mixed white and black peasant class. The mass of inhabitants was the enslaved black population. The island had sufficient commercial activity to allow some slaves to acquire income from small-scale agricultural marketing. Accumulating sufficient funds to buy their freedom, some of these freedmen acquired plantations and slaves themselves.

By the end of the eighteenth century, the French ceded Dominica to the British. The most lasting consequence of French influence was the Roman Catholic religion to which most Dominicans adhere. The entry of the British continued the plantation agricultural focus of the Dominican economy. However, slavery was abolished at the beginning of the nineteenth century. A population of liberated slaves without property or education determined a pattern of low-wage labor, social unrest, and political disenfranchisement that long characterized the island.

Acquiring independence from Britain in 1978, the island only achieved a measure of political stability with the much-admired government of Prime Minister Maria Eugenia Charles. The first woman to govern a Caribbean nation, she was in office from 1980 to 1995. Although the island's primary source of export income is bananas, both the conditions and the market for this product are unstable. While agriculture is still the main area of employment, Dominica is steadily developing its services sector, which now produces most of its income. The gross domestic product (GDP) is slightly more than a third of a billion dollars. The per capita GDP amounts to approximately $5,000 per year and the annual per capita income is just under $3,000. A third of the population lives in poverty. Population growth is negative due to the rate of emigration. The median age of the population is just under thirty.

Tourism is the principal service activity, but it is not the typical Caribbean tourism. The island does not possess areas of wide beaches for luxury resorts.

Its special terrain and vegetation, however, allow it to offer ecotourism. For the ecologically conscious tourist it presents a breathtaking tropical environment. Dominica's Morne Trois Pitons National Park is a UNESCO World Heritage site.

Another objective for economic development is to establish Dominica as a center for offshore banking and financial operations. This, however, requires appropriate social capital. Dominicans have a high rate of literacy, more than 90%, but limited access to technical or higher education. Moreover, for foreign financial interests, the country does not have a long record of stable political and administrative continuity. An oil refinery base has also been considered, possibly on the model of the Dutch Caribbean island of Curaçao. However, this project must be carefully weighed in relation to the priorities for ecological and environmental balance.

EDWARD A. RIEDINGER

See also Association of Caribbean States (ACS); Caribbean: History and Economic Development; Caribbean: International Relations

References and Further Reading

Craig, Susan. *Contemporary Caribbean: A Sociological Reader*, 2 vols. Port of Spain, Trinidad: College Press, 1981–1982.
English, Lydia L. *Behind God's Back: The Everyday Lives of Women and Men in Dominica, West Indies*. Doctoral dissertation, Yale University, 1991.
Honychurch, Lennox. *The Dominica Story: A History of the Island*. London: Macmillan, 1995.
Meditz, Sandra W. and Dennis M. Hanratty, eds. "Dominica." In *Islands of the Commonwealth Caribbean: A Regional Study. Area Handbook Series.* Washington, DC: Federal Research Division, Library of Congress, 1989.
Myers, Robert A. "Dominica." *World Bibliographical Series*, 82. Oxford, UK: ABC-Clio Press, 1987.
Pezeron, Simone Maguy. *The Carib Indians of Dominica Island in the West Indies: Five Hundred Years after Columbus*. New York: Vantage Press, 1993.
Trouillot, Michel-Rolph. *Peasants and Capital: Dominica in the World Economy*. (Johns Hopkins Studies in Atlantic History and Culture.) Baltimore, MD: Johns Hopkins University Press, 1988.

DOMINICAN REPUBLIC

The Dominican Republic occupies the eastern two-thirds of the island of Hispaniola. In 1821, Spanish-speaking colonists declared themselves independent, but they were conquered by neighboring Haiti in the following year and did not regain independence until 1844. From 1844 until 1930, the Dominican Republic experienced internal war, foreign intervention, and incompetent and corrupt governments.

In 1930, Rafael Leonidis Trujillo Molina, the leader of the US-created National Guard, overthrew the government and established an authoritarian dictatorship that lasted for over three decades. Ruthlessly suppressing all opposition to his regime, during the Great Depression Trujillo was faced with governing a poverty-stricken nation with an empty treasury, a huge foreign debt, and a capital city destroyed by a hurricane. Within two decades, Trujillo had paid off the nation's foreign debts, developed a national infrastructure, and laid the groundwork for economic development by promoting industrialization. Sugar exports accounted for the majority of government revenue. In the process, he accumulated a personal fortune worth almost $1 billion (USD).

The cost of fiscal solvency during the Era of Trujillo was the complete loss of personal freedom of the Dominican people. Trujillo's seven intelligence agencies enabled the dictator to establish one of Latin America's most brutal authoritarian dictatorships. One of Trujillo's most notorious acts was the massacre of twelve thousand Haitians in the northern border region in 1937. To deflect criticism of his regime, Trujillo offered sanctuary to one hundred thousand Jewish refugees from Europe. By the end of the 1950s, Trujillo had managed to lose the support of the nation's elites, the Roman Catholic Church, and the US government. Trujillo's failed attempt to assassinate Venezuelan President Rómulo Betancourt in 1960 convinced the United States that continued support of the Trujillo dictatorship could damage US hegemony in the Caribbean region. The murder of three elite sisters—Minerva, Patria, and Maria Teresa Mirabal—on November 25, 1960, motivated the Dominican population to increase anti-Trujillo activities. On the evening of May 30, 1961, Trujillo was assassinated by a group of conspirators who had been both accomplices to and victims of the dictatorship. The conspirators, armed with weapons provided by the United States, assassinated Trujillo as he was preparing to visit one of his numerous mistresses. Attempts by Trujillo's son Ramfis to continue the dictatorship were futile and the entire Trujillo family fled the island by the end of 1961.

In December 1962, the Dominican people began their first experience with democratic government. In US-supervised elections, Juan Bosch, a chain-smoking poet who had lived in exile for most of the Era of Trujillo, was elected president with 60% of the vote. Initially hailed by the Kennedy administration as a potential showcase for democracy, the Bosch administration soon lost the support of the nation's military and the United States. When Bosch attempted to limit the power of the Dominican military, he was ousted from office in September 1963.

A new regime, dominated by Donald Reid Cabral, a former car salesman, lasted until April 1965 when pro-Bosch military officers, led by Francisco Caamaño Deñó, staged a revolt to return the exiled Bosch to power. As the death toll in the civil war mounted, and it became increasingly apparent that Caamaño Deñó's Constitutionalists were taking control of the capital city of Santo Domingo, US President Lyndon Johnson ordered twenty-three thousand Marines to invade the Dominican Republic. Although the Organization of American States (OAS) eventually sanctioned the intervention by agreeing to send in additional troops, this was the first overt use of US military forces in Latin America since the Marines were withdrawn from Haiti in 1934. Ostensibly sent to protect lives and prevent the establishment of a pro-Castro government, the OAS forces supervised democratic elections in 1966, which were won by Joaquín Balaguer, who had been the titular president at the time of Trujillo's assassination. During Balaguer's tenure in office from 1966 to 1978, the Dominican Republic experienced the most spectacular growth of any Latin American nation during the 1970s. The nation's economic boom was made possible by political stability and a revitalized sugar industry.

High inflation and unemployment undermined Balaguer's hold on power during his third term. In 1978, Balaguer lost the presidential elections to the Partido Revolucionario Dominicano (PRD). Although Antonio Guzmán's administration implemented numerous health and education projects, by 1980, the economy had fallen into a recession. Plagued by the rising cost of oil imports, a sharp decline in the profits from sugar exports, and accusations that his daughter Sonia was involved in corrupt activities, Guzmán, a wealthy cattle rancher, decided not to run for reelection in 1982. The 1982 elections were won by PRD candidate Salvador Jorge Blanco. The day before he would have left office, President Guzmán committed suicide. Jorge Blanco's administration experienced a tremendous loss of popularity and legitimacy when it implemented International Monetary Fund (IMF) austerity measures in May of 1984. A series of violent riots broke out, which led to the death of dozens of Dominican citizens. Jorge Blanco was found guilty in a court of law of massive corruption and misappropriation of government funds and sentenced to twenty years in prison. Given the poor performance of the PRD governments, Balaguer returned to office in 1986. Balaguer won subsequent elections in 1990 and 1994. Acknowledging that there were voting irregularities in the 1994 election, Balaguer agreed to step down from the presidency in 1996 and hold new presidential elections.

The 1996 elections pitted José Francisco Peña Gómez (PRD) against Bosch protégé Leonel Fernández, who represented the Partido de Liberacion Dominicano (PLD). Fernández, a young lawyer who had grown up in New York City, initiated a series of reforms designed to modernize the political economy and infrastructure. Sugar exports no longer represented a substantial component of Dominican revenue. Instead, tourism, mining (especially nickel), and remittances from Dominicans living abroad, primarily in the United States, accounted for the majority of Dominican revenue. Attempts were made to convert the sugar-growing lands to the production of other agricultural crops, such as pineapples, for export. Fernández was barred by the Constitution from running for reelection in 2000. PRD candidate Hipólito Mejía won the 2000 presidential elections. Mejía's administration has been characterized by excessive corruption, rising inflation, and a greatly devaluated national currency. The 2004 presidential elections were won by Fernández, who promised to reinvigorate the Dominican economy.

MICHAEL R. HALL

See also Haiti; Trujillo, Rafael Leonidas

References and Further Reading

Atkins, G. Pope and Larman C. Wilson. *The Dominican Republic and the United States: From Imperialism to Transnationalism.* Athens, GA: University of Georgia Press, 1998.

Hall, Michael R. *Sugar and Power in the Dominican Republic: Eisenhower, Kennedy, and the Trujillos.* Westport, CT: Greenwood, 2000.

Moya Pons, Frank. *The Dominican Republic: A National History.* Princeton, NJ: Marcus Wiener Publishers, 1998.

Roorda, Eric Paul. *The Dictator Next Door: The Good Neighbor Policy and the Trujillo Regime in the Dominican Republic, 1930–1945.* Durham, NC: Duke University Press, 1998.

Vargas Llosa, Mario. *The Feast of the Goat: A Novel.* New York: Farrar, Straus, and Giroux, 2000.

DOMINO THEORY

The domino theory, or domino effect, was made famous by US President Dwight D. Eisenhower (1953–1961), who, in order to justify US commitment to South Vietnam in 1954, compared the nations of Southeast Asia to a row of dominoes: if the Communist guerrillas were victorious in Vietnam, the rest of Indochina, and then the rest of Asia, would also eventually fall to Communism. The rapid advent of Communist regimes in Hungary, Poland, Czechoslovakia, Romania, Bulgaria, Albania, and

Yugoslavia following the end of World War II was used as evidence to support this premise.

By the same token, the demise of Communism in the Soviet Union would affect all Eastern European countries one after another, much like a chain reaction. It was hence popularly assumed to be a case of domino effect. This view overlooked that the Soviet bloc and its satellites represented a highly centralized system held together by an overarching ideology. Once the center and ideology could not hold, the periphery had no other choice but to loosen. Socialist countries were not so much independent entities prone to one another's influence, as parts of a single unified framework.

The metaphor evoked by the falling dominoes is used in both social and exact sciences, where several competing permutations can be found with slightly different meanings: chain reaction, forest fire models, avalanche dynamics, branching process, and so on. Moreover, the theoretical setup is based on medical-biological assumptions of "contagion," "disease," "viruses," and similar epidemiological jargon.

The concept reached its peak of influence during the Cold War, but continued to be applied to various international events in the aftermath of epochal changes. Even before the official end of the Cold War (marked by the fall of the Berlin Wall, in 1989), the concept was used to describe the possible spread of nationalism. The theory was adopted by both liberals and conservatives in the United States.

The concept's heuristic validity is complicated by its partisan political use. Indeed, the ghost of a domino effect has been used by various regimes in order to hamper broader democratic reform, while curtailing ethnic dissent. This was particularly the case among several developing countries during and after the Cold War. In the early 1990s, a long series of human rights violations by Asian states was dictated by fear of a hypothetical nationalist domino effect caused by the disintegration of the Soviet Union and Yugoslavia, including: China's stepping up of repression in Tibet and Sinkiang; Burma's refusal to allow democratic reforms in fear of civil war; Indonesia's uneasiness about revelations of mass slaughter in East Timor, Acheh, and West Papua; India's stranglehold on Assam, Punjab, Kashmir, and other restless areas; Pakistan's repression of the Sindhi minority; Sri Lanka's offensive against Tamil separatism; Georgia's move to autocratic rule; Turkey's confrontation with the Kurdish insurgence; and Iran's resort to radicalism in the face of occasional tensions in border areas. In Africa, the fear of a domino effect was amplified by Eritrea's independence and the separation of northern Somaliland. In Zaire (now Democratic Republic of Congo), Mali, and Nigeria,

thousands died in ethnic clashes, often linked to the central governments' refusal to come to terms with ethnic demands. Finally, Iraq's decision to invade Kuwait in 1990 can be seen as a classic case of "externalization" of internal tensions resulting from a fear of contagion of both political Islam and ethno-national tensions.

All these cases were related to a worldwide concern about the inevitable dissolution of multinational states. The ghost of "balkanization" was raised as a tangible threat. Although threats from political opposition were sometimes tangible, they often became only a pretext to eliminate internal dissidence. Indeed, the same illiberal trend has pervaded the domestic and foreign policy of most multinational states, with the possible exceptions of federations like Canada and the European Union—the latter through the elasticity of Brussels' accommodating politics.

Although the theory had initially some strategic validity, the fear of a domino effect was, and will remain, at the roots of catastrophic choices in foreign policy. It was this fear that impelled Western elites to support Saddam Hussein's totalitarian regime in his war against Iran (1980–1988). The consequences of this decision, causing over a million deaths, will probably carry through for decades. The tragic blunder stemmed from the conviction that, following Iran's Islamic revolution, the fall of the Shah (1979) would be the first domino to tip other autocratic states in the Middle East toward Islamic rule. A panic-struck Western world reacted by supporting Iraq's Ba'athist regime with massive input of weapons and cash.

The danger of expanding Communism was certainly vivid in the aftermath of the Korean War (1950–1953). However, the theory's more recent adaptations rely mostly on a paranoid vision of the world and are rather characteristic of nationalist or imperial *geopolitics* (*Geopolitik* in German). The latter discipline was associated with the German geographer Friedrich Ratzel (1844–1904) and his theory of the organic nature of the State. Geopolitics was easily appropriated by the Nazi expansionist state, with its idea of *Lebensraum* ("Living space") as "essential" for the survival of the German race.

The domino theory has been particularly influential among US foreign policy and security experts, as an exemplification of what Richard Hofstadter called *"The Paranoid Style in American Politics"*: "The exponents [of the] ... paranoid style ... regard a 'vast' or 'gigantic' conspiracy as the motive force in historical events... The paranoid spokesman sees the fate of this conspiracy in apocalyptic terms—he traffics in the birth and death of whole worlds, whole political orders, whole systems of human values. He is always manning the barricades of civilization" (1996, p. 29).

A more "assertive," less defensive, version of the theory was adopted by the interventionist hawks in President George W. Bush's administration: They argued that Saddam Hussein's fall would be followed by the quasi-automatic embrace of democracy by other Arab states in the region.

There is often some confusion between the factual image of falling dominoes and the ideological influence the theory may exert in action. The phrase "domino effect" refers to a movement of possible structural and international changes brought about by the emulation of successful political movements. It can be considered the subcategory of a more general demonstration effect: the latter refers to the reshaping of ideological orientation within political movements across frontiers as stimulated by international events. The domino effect is a more restricted concept, insofar as it is only a particular kind of demonstration effect with immediate implications in real political alignments: "domino" is about supposed or feared political change at the regime level, whereas "demonstration" is about ideologies and putative models at the grassroots level. Various assumptions underlie this approach, often defined as "ideological diffusionism," mostly that ideologies spread in a parallel outward and top-down process. That is, ideas are disseminated horizontally from an ideological centre to the periphery, and vertically from the elites to the masses, both in a non-reciprocal way.

Given the domino theory's incapacity to adequately explain, let alone predict, changes at the regime level, it remains at best an illusion, especially when accounting for non-institutionalized political movements. In particular, non-state nationalism and political Islam are often too vague, pervasive, malleable, and unpredictable a force to be prognosticated on the grounds of the diffusion of immanent forces.

DANIELE CONVERSI

References and Further Reading

Chomsky, Noam. *What Uncle Sam Really Wants.* Tucson, AZ, and Berkeley, CA: Odonian Press, 1993

Conversi, Daniele. "Domino effect or internal developments? The influences of international events and political ideologies on Catalan and Basque nationalism." *West European Politics,* vol. 16, no. 3, July 1993, pp. 245–270.

Hofstadter, Richard. *The Paranoid Style in American Politics and Other Essays.* Cambridge, MA: Harvard University Press, 1996.

Ninkovich, Frank. *Modernity and Power: History of the Domino Theory in the Twentieth Century.* Chicago: University of Chicago Press, 1994.

DRAFT DECLARATION ON THE RIGHTS OF INDIGENOUS PEOPLES

In an effort to specify and ensure greater respect for the rights of indigenous people to lands traditionally utilized by them, as well as to ensure their access to resources and the protection of their languages and cultures, the formation of a United Nations Declaration on the Rights of Indigenous Peoples was first proposed in 1985 by a series of resolutions submitted by the UN Sub-Commission on Prevention of Discrimination and Protection of Minorities. A Working Group on Indigenous Populations was formed to prepare the Draft Declaration, taking into account the comments and suggestions of participants in sessions composed of representatives of both indigenous peoples and governments. In July 1993, the Working Group agreed on a final text for the draft Declaration on the Rights of Indigenous Peoples and submitted it to the Sub-Commission. The Draft has been under review by the Inter-Sessional Working Group of the Commission on Human Rights, who hoped to have it approved by 2004, the close of the United Nations' International Decade of the World's Indigenous Populations.

Although the Working Group within the Commission on Human Rights held annual meetings with participation from government representatives and indigenous organizations each year between 1995 and 2004, no consensus was reached. Significant polarization between indigenous and state positions characterized the Working Group from the start, particularly surrounding the issues of self-determination, collective rights, and territorial rights. As the year 2004 came to a close, several drafts had been proposed but none had been agreed upon. Hunger strikes (called spiritual fasting) by indigenous peoples delegates and an Appeal of Indigenous Peoples at the United Nations Palais des Nations in Geneva, expressed the concern that the mandate of the Working Group would not be extended or that critical principles would be weakened in negotiations. The strike was ended when the Office of the Commission on Human Rights agreed to recommend to the General Assembly a second International Decade of the World's Indigenous Peoples, to follow the conclusion of the present International Decade in December 2004.

Although disagreements remain between indigenous representatives and governments, and the amount of power to be accorded each in the process is still contested, the process of debate can be seen as contributing to awareness about indigenous rights within communities, among government representatives, and within supranational decision-making bodies. It has created a space for indigenous participation within the United Nations and altered some of the fundamental regulations for participation in UN discourse by non-governmental parties. The ongoing initiatives of the Permanent Forum on Indigenous Peoples, the International Decade of Indigenous Peoples, and the deliberations within the Working Group to arrive at a Declaration on the Rights of Indigenous Peoples, have established cooperation between indigenous peoples and the United Nations. A Declaration on the Rights of Indigenous Peoples would be a substantial advance. The Declaration would be the first international instrument on human rights and fundamental freedoms to promote and protect the rights of indigenous peoples.

JANET M. CHERNELA

DRUG TRADE

The term "drug trade" has two commonly understood meanings. The first is the focus of this article, but both will be briefly described.

The first concerns the illegal or illicit production, distribution, and trafficking (sale and profit-making) of drugs that are banned as narcotics internationally or nationally. It also describes the distribution and sale of drugs such as tobacco or alcohol, on which local taxes have not been paid (not really a significant problem in developing countries). The second meaning relates to the national and international production, distribution, sale, and prescription of medical drugs and pharmaceuticals. In both instances, the developing countries of the world are variously involved at all points in the cycle of supply and demand. The fact that both meanings exist in the English language often leads to confusion and misinterpretation. There is also an overlap between the two categories, when pharmaceutical, synthetic drugs such as amphetamines are sold for non-medical use.

In both instances, there have been significant economic and social effects from the existence of the drug trade, and the legislative, political, and even military efforts to eradicate or control supply in entire countries and sometimes continents. The related problems affect both developed and developing nations, but the impact of the drug trade itself and strategies to control it are not simple to assess. Indeed, they are at the heart of much controversy and global disagreement among governments, politicians, and professional and lay commentators.

The War on Drugs

This concept of the world being engaged in a war against drugs in the last quarter of the twentieth century and into the new millennium is a direct successor to the USA's attempt at the internal prohibition of alcohol from 1920 to 1933. The contrary claims for and against strategies that are aimed at cutting off the supply of drugs and criminalizing the production, use, or trade in drugs, are now quite well-known and irreconcilable. The zero-tolerance prohibitionist stance is aimed at all elements in the drug trade: primary producers, traffickers and distributors, and drug users.

Prohibitionists argue that the drug trade causes:

- Potentially chronic health problems for users, and social and economic problems for themselves, their families, friends, and relatives;
- The escalation of violence, crime, and corruption linked to production and trade in illegal drugs;
- The deterioration of law and order and social functioning of communities, particularly in inner-urban areas, with resultant degeneracy and social decay;
- Many rural developing nations to become dependent upon drug crop income as primary producers;
- Other developing countries to become centres of drug-trafficking on the principal drug trade routes into the United States and Western Europe; and
- The creation of a criminal economy, with international money laundering based on the illicit income of violent gangs and drug traffickers.

Opponents of this view argue that ever-more stringent drugs-control strategies have already been shown to be a failure. There is a growing divide between drug experts in much of Europe and in the United States, with the Europeans stressing the need for a reevaluation of strategic policy on illegal drugs and to refocus resources on harm-reduction measures and demand reduction through education and treatment.

Opponents of the war on drugs argue that it has:

- Failed to decrease supply or production, while demand has if anything increased;
- Created an illegal international market worth US$400 billion, and local illegal economies, which in turn have nurtured much of the associated violence and criminality;
- Criminalized producers and users; and
- Been a waste of money and resources as illegal drugs have tended to become cheaper and qualitatively purer.

The United Nations had traditionally occupied something of a middle ground between these points of view. The UN's "balanced approach" to drugs control shifted in 1998 following the appointment of Pino Arlacci, who had previously worked against organized crime in Italy, to the Executive Directorship of the United Nations International Drug Control Programme (UNDCP). Arlacci's uncompromising approach to target the countries where drugs are grown has proved popular with prohibitionists, but has led to abuses of human rights, such as the $250 million the UNDCP pledged in 1997 to the Taliban regime in Afghanistan to stop opium production. The UNDCP has also attempted to change the types of crops grown by farmers in countries such as Bolivia and Colombia, where peasant farmers often cultivate the coca bush and opium poppies. However, in many instances the alternative crops do not produce the same revenue returns and often the farmers operate with the protection of rebel groups, such as FARC in Colombia, to continue growing illegal crops while accepting government handouts for the "new" crops. This is sometimes called "parallel development" rather than "alternative development."

For the farmers in developing countries to forgo the production of illegal cash crops requires that socioeconomic standards improve enough to guarantee economic stability for all, independently of drugs-control policies. This has occurred in Turkey and Thailand, but many commentators have argued that the drug trade in these countries moved to trafficking rather than production, which simply moved it to their neighbours, Iran and Burma.

Legislation

As the total market value of illegal drugs matches oil or arms at about 8% of the entire world economy, international action against the drug trade has also become an increasingly global affair. The legislative base for these actions is primarily the United Nations. In 1961, the UN passed its first agreement among UN countries to work together to control illicit drugs. By 1988, psychotropic substances were added to the UN Convention Against Illicit Traffic in Narcotic Substances and Psychotropic Substances. This convention is still the bedrock of more recent UN-led actions such as the 1998 drug summit, with its ten-year plan proposed by Pino Arlacchi to "create a drug-free twenty-first century," with targets for all 150 member countries. The declaration adopted by the summit targeted money-laundering operations and illicit crop cultivation.

However, despite this legislative base, it is often pragmatism—the "carrots" (aid) and "sticks" (sanctions) of international cooperation—that determine the actual operation of local policies on enforcement. Economic sanctions and international aid are two determinants of the degree to which countries work against the drug trade. Developing countries, with fragile agricultural economies and often unstable governance, are often insufficiently consulted regarding implementation of these international actions. For example, the use of aerial crop spraying of coca and opium with virulent herbicides such as tebuthiuron has had a negative impact on the land. In addition to the environmental impact, this does not inhibit production as crop growers in countries such as Colombia just move on from the denuded, sprayed land and grow crops somewhere else.

Production

The figures and trends indicated in the *World Drug Report 2000* (UNDCP 2000) are treated optimistically by their authors, who suggest that significant progress has been made in controlling the production and trafficking of cocaine and heroin.

However, cannabis, which has been effectively de-criminalized in countries like the Netherlands, is grown in at least 112 countries, both developed and developing, and the UNDCP estimates that cannabis production adds up to about thirty thousand tonnes per year—perhaps ten times the total of coca and opium crop production taken together. Developing countries have also pointed to the fact that the eighteen main anti-drug trade operations of the 1990s have targeted the urban poor in the United States and the economically disadvantaged producers and traffickers, rather than the wealthy and well-armed networks and kingpins in the developing worlds. Comparatively, there has been little action taken against the producers and traffickers of drugs such as ecstasy (MDMA), amphetamines, and cannabis, which are spread much more widely across the world, with production and distribution centres in European countries such as the Netherlands, Belgium, and the UK. There are also moves toward legal cannabis production centers, such as the underground Sunless City of Flin Flon in Manitoba, Canada. There, three thousand plants are being cultivated under strict security, to be prescribed for Canadian citizens suffering from acute pain.

Trafficking

The UNDCP defines trafficking as the distribution process for illicit drugs; therefore figures reflect the rates for the apprehension of drugs. UNDCP perceives the success rate for the seizure/production of opiates to be 15% and 39% for cocaine, but others have estimated that interceptions may be as low or lower than 10% of the drugs actually being distributed. The UNDCP (2001) offers the following observations:

- Combined global heroin and morphine seizures amounted to 61 tonnes in 1999. Trafficking in those two substances continues to be concentrated in Asia (71% of all seizures in 1999);
- Trafficking increased in southwest Asia and declined in the southeast; and
- The seizures of synthetic drugs more than doubled in 1999 from a year earlier; seizures of cannabis herb rose by a third and opiates by 14%; cocaine seizures fell by 6%.

Medicinal Drugs

Developing countries have often found it difficult to obtain affordable medicines for the treatment of disease and illness. One problem relates to patent laws that prevent cheap drugs being traded to these countries. These patent laws have been established World Trade Organization agreements, specifically the 1995 TRIPS (Trade-Related Aspects of Intellectual Property Rights) Agreement, which preserve the industrial patents for twenty years. There has been a recent movement, initiated with the Doha Declaration at the 2001 WTO ministerial conference, to relax or abandon altogether patent laws on drugs for diseases such as HIV/AIDS, which has reached epidemic proportions in Africa. Several countries, such as Zambia, South Africa, Guatemala, and Brazil, have repealed or defied their domestic patent laws, as well as international trade agreements, in order to produce generic versions of drugs necessary to combat major threats to public health; other countries with production capability, such as Canada, have amended their own laws in order to facilitate export of low-cost drugs to developing nations. Additionally, some organizations, such as Médecins Sans Frontières/Doctors Without Borders, have engaged in civil disobedience and illegally imported generic drugs to countries suffering from epidemics but whose patent laws prohibit the distribution of drugs by anyone except the company, usually the manufacturer, which holds the patent.

The World Health Organization (WHO) has identified that, "irrational prescribing, dispensing and consumption of medicines remains widespread" in the developing countries. Since the 1985 WHO Conference on the Rational Use of Drugs, held in Nairobi, WHO has run annual courses in Asia and Africa for health professionals to try and deal with the problem. Meanwhile, poverty makes the purchasing of appropriate medicines acutely difficult, accentuated by improper prescribing based too often on drug promotion by pharmaceutical companies.

Two further problems are the dumping of medical drugs that are not licensed in the USA or Europe on the market in developing countries, and the growing resistance to common antibiotics such as penicillin in many developing countries, which makes diseases like meningitis, tuberculosis, and gonorrhoea far more serious and harder to treat effectively.

As the history of the drug trade, with its various facets, unfolds into the twenty-first century, it is uncertain whether international policy will continue to back the prohibitionist stance. Since much of the criminality surrounding drugs use is related to the trading of illicit drugs, many feel that freeing that market would be part of the solution. However, the international "jury" of policy makers and experts is still far from certain as to whether a gradual de-criminalizing or legalisation of drugs would be part of the answer.

ALAN DEARLING

See also Drug Use

References and Further Reading

Blickman, T. *Caught in the Cross-Fire: Developing Countries, the UNDCP, and the War on Drugs*. London: Transnational Institute and the Catholic Institute for International Relations, 1998.
Rational Drug Use Strategy and Monitoring. http://www.who.int/medicines/strategy/rational_use/strudmon.shtml
South, N., ed. *Drugs: Cultures, Controls & Everyday Life*. London: Sage, 1999.
United Nations Drug Control Program. *Global Illicit Drug Trends 2001*. Vienna: UNDCP.
Williamson, K. *Drugs and the Party Line*. Edinburgh: Rebel Inc, 1997.

DRUG USE

The meaning of "drug" can be very different depending upon the cultural, social, and geographical context in which the term is being used. In reality there are many thousands of drugs available in the world. The taxonomy (classification) of a drug is problematic, so any list of drugs, description, or the use of the term may have an ideological and interpretive element. Similarly, the use of drugs and their effects is highly dependent upon *set* (the mood of the user) and the *setting* (where and with whom they are used).

Traditionally, the source of most drugs has been the plants, shrubs, and trees growing wild in the fields and forests of the world. However, with scientific and pharmaceutical preparation, many drugs are now synthesised—produced in some sort of laboratory—manufactured into medicines and treatments for illness, or for illegal use. Finally, there are a variety of drugs such as tobacco, alcohol, and caffeine-based drinks that are prepared for consumption by humans for relaxation or recreation. The legality or otherwise of specific drugs is a societally determined issue.

According to the United Nations International Drugs Control Program (2001), 180 million people worldwide—4.2% of people aged fifteen years and older—were consuming drugs in the late 1990s, including cannabis (144m), amphetamine-type stimulants (29m), cocaine (14m) and opiates (13.5m including 9m addicted to heroin). However, figures at a worldwide level are approximates, as many countries, especially in the developing world, do not collect drug use data. Also, much of what is known is based on the perceptions of authorities in the various countries and international organizations and will reflect such sources as police statistics, drug seizures, reports from social welfare organizations, and even media reportage.

The problems associated with drug use (or abuse) are given different prominence according to particular commentators' personal, political, or organisational convictions. These problems fall into a number of categories. Principally these are identified as:

- Health and social problems caused by use, especially when the user is a habitual or addicted user;
- Problems of criminality associated with the use of drugs, for instance, violent behaviour to others, self abuse, or theft and robbery; and
- Secondary problems such as those experienced in developing countries where intravenous use of drugs without an available needle exchange has abetted the spread of the number of people who have AIDs, hepatitis C, or who are HIV-positive.

There are also problems of corruption, intimidation, and extreme violence connected with the drug trade, particularly in predominantly peasant, agricultural economies where illegal drugs constitute the major cash crops and source of overseas income, such as Colombia and Bolivia (coca and opium) and Afghanistan and Iran (opium). This problem has also spread over into countries on the supply routes such as Jamaica, Nigeria, Cote d'Ivoire, and Turkey. In the past fifteen years, the specific countries involved in production and trafficking have continued to change, usually in response to interventions by outside countries and international organisations.

Today, the world's politicians, criminologists, and drug and health experts are divided on how to respond to these problems and what policies regarding supply and demand are effective. These range from prohibition and zero tolerance to legalisation and harm minimisation.

An Historical Perspective

During the evolution of mankind through the second millennium CE, most of the world's inhabitants lived close to nature. With an existence based on hunting and gathering, the indigenous inhabitants' knowledge and understanding of plants and natural preparations was far greater than currently exists. Indeed, many scientists and pharmacologists are only now beginning to collect and examine the properties of plants in the remaining rainforests of the world.

Historically, drug use has played a major part in everyday life, providing natural sources of food, a means of relaxation, mind-altering experiences, and medication. Ginseng is an Asian plant, which has an ancient history in Chinese medicine, but which has recently been rediscovered by the West as a drug made from ginseng roots for alleviating headaches, exhaustion, and possibly kidney disorders. Cannabis Sativa, now banned in many countries, was the main analgesic used in the United States in the nineteenth century and until 1937 was recommended in the American Pharmacopoeia as being useful in curing more than one hundred illnesses. Sigmund Freud called cocaine, extracted from coca leaves, a "wonder drug." It was used as an anti-depressant before amphetamines became widely available in the 1930s. Opium-based medicines were freely available even to children in nineteenth-century Europe and the United States, and laudanum—opium in an alcohol solution—was commonly prescribed as medication.

However, it must be noted that it is hard to generalise from any analysis of drugs made from fresh or dried plants, since each one has unique properties and potency, affected by soil conditions, propagation, location, sunlight, and many other variable factors. Similarly, it has been found in analysis that the active ingredient of a drug, usually an alkaloid, may weaken quickly or may not have much efficacy when separated from the rest of the plant's constituents. Synthetic drugs, on the other hand, can be standardized through manufacturing techniques.

Herbal drugs, which reached their height of popularity during the seventeenth century, were the precursors of modern pharmacology, but their association with astrology, magic, and the arcane left their legacy largely discredited until recently. It is possible to trace drug use in different cultures and at different times through a pattern of use in magical rites, religion, science, hedonism, and recreation. These patterns of use are called "socially situated" or "socially created" realities, which must be seen in the context of specific societies, their ethnicity, beliefs, cultural lives, and often the age and gender of the users.

Many tribes throughout the world have used plant extracts as a means of intoxication. One of the most common is the chewing of betel nuts, which are actually the seeds of the areca palm. This habit is practised by up to a tenth of the world's population, in a broad range of countries stretching from Tanzania across the Indian subcontinent to the western Pacific islands. Despite its common usage, the exact effects of the nine alkaloids present in the betel/lime mix are not precisely known, but they include creating a sense of well-being and euphoria, suppression of hunger, and in heavy users, some hallucinations. Arecoline is believed to be the most active alkaloid.

Other common drugs have a much stronger connection with ritual and initiation rights. Peyote and kava are two well-documented psychotropics. Ritual kava use was particularly widespread across Melanesia in the western Pacific, and especially in New Guinea. Kava is a species of pepper plant that grows up to four metres tall. Women and children traditionally chewed the roots and lower stems and spat the residue into a large bowl into which water was added. The resulting infusion was then drunk by elite men, the elders or initiates of the tribe, as part of their rites, usually in conjunction with a ritual regime of fasting, dancing, and chanting. It is still available by mail order in many parts of the developed world as a "legal high." Peyote and the closely related mescal derived from cactus plants (lophophora williamsii) in Mexico and South America are, along with magic mushrooms (including amanita muscaria/fly agaric), probably the best known of the ritual hallucinogens used in the celebration of shamanistic religion and more recently as a route to mind-altering states in urban areas. The use of peyote in religious ritual amongst the Huichol Indians of Mexico, who believe that the plant has a soul, pre-dates the Spanish Inquisition's arrival in Mexico in 1571. Members of the Native American Church can still legally use peyote in rituals in many American states. In the Andean region of South America, chewing coca leaves, again coated with a lime paste to release the active alkaloids, is used as a stimulant, and the average daily intake by the Indian population is estimated to be two ounces of dried leaves (about 0.5 grams). The use of coca is seen as an essential part of the Andean cultural heritage, for social and medicinal purposes, not to be confused with the patterns of use of cocaine in Western nations.

The perception of different drugs and their uses continues to change with each century, especially in the new age of globalisation.

The Legality and Use of Drugs

The earliest recorded prohibition of drugs was probably made by the prophet Mohammed in the seventh century CE, who forbade his followers to use alcohol, because of its centrality in Christianity, where wine represents the blood of Christ in the sacrament. This prohibition still exists in many Islamic states. In more recent times, Christian missionaries brought alcohol, along with a new religion, to many indigenous cultures including the Native Americans, the Aborigines of Australia, and the Maoris of New Zealand. Some indigenous religions did survive, such as the Bwiti cult around the Gabon in West Africa. They make ritual use of the iboga plant, whose active element is ibogaine, from the dogabne family. Iboga is an hallucinogenic that many doctors and others in the West believe possesses extraordinary medicinal properties.

The world's developing nations are both consumers of a variety of drugs and the major producers/primary supply sources of many drugs—both those deemed illegal and legal. Industrialised nations have frequently looked to apportion the blame for the problem of drugs on producers, traffickers, and users. Inevitably this has meant that much of the "war" on drugs has been focused on the developing nations. It has also caused huge disparities of opinion over whether prohibition and regulation of drug use actually have a positive effect on the people of the world, either in terms of whole countries that may produce banned drugs as primary crops, or individuals who can be criminalized as well as potentially suffering from ill health through their use of drugs.

Drug Use in Developing Countries

Developing countries that are involved in the production and trafficking of drugs are the most affected with the problems associated with illegal drug use. The World Bank (1997) has compiled a great deal of information about the prevalence of drug use in developing countries. There are some caveats to this data, as it comes from many sources over a period of approximately ten years. It is likely that much of the data consists of estimates, as some countries have not undertaken research on issues such as the prevalence of injecting drug use. However, the World Bank data remains one of the best indicators for ascertaining the patterns of use in developing countries.

According to this source, injecting drug use has been spreading globally and is especially prevalent in Thailand, Argentina, Puerto Rica, Hong Kong, Malaysia, and some parts of India. Heroin is the main drug injected in Asia, and cocaine is the main drug in South America. The availability of cheap, relatively pure, refined heroin or cocaine in areas of primary production and along trafficking routes appears to coincide with centers of drug use. The move from smoking unrefined brown sugar heroin in India and China to injecting refined heroin again mirrors the changes in the production, though smoking is still more common in areas close to the poppy fields such as in Myanmar. It is also thought that because injection is a more efficient form of administration, this may have led poorer users to utilise the most economic means of use.

Law enforcement programs against drugs around the world have caused considerable displacements of both primary suppliers and traffic routes. Thailand began an aggressive law enforcement program against opium and heroin production, and initiated crop-replacement programs for farmers who relied on these as cash crops. Production took a corresponding downturn; trafficking, however, did not.

Drug users in the developing countries are typified as being more than 75% male and relatively young, mostly from twenty to forty years old. Information has mostly come from drug clinics in urban areas, therefore it may not reflect rural drug use. As might be expected, the social and economic characteristics of injecting drug users varies from country to country. In Manipur, India, more than 70% are employed, whereas users in Brazil are mostly classified as "deprived" and unemployed. In relation to the potential spread of AIDs through infected needles, there is evidence that 72% of the users in both Rio de Janeiro and Bangkok have shared needles.

The Future

The European Monitoring Centre for Drugs and Drug Addiction, based in Lisbon, Portugal, has noted an increase in the use of more synthetic drugs such as ecstasy, LSD, ketamine, and amphetamines in the West. Meanwhile, cannabis is still the most used drug in developed countries. The popularity of synthetic drugs in part reflects the rave culture of the 1990s and the subsequent move of many of its aspects, from music to dress to drugs, to the mainstream. But it has also probably resulted from shifts in production, since it is easier for laboratories to be set up close to demand centres. Most synthetic drugs are simple to produce, which has resulted in cheap supplies of such drugs, particularly in the Netherlands, Belgium, and the UK. Whether these drugs will also become the focus of production and use in the developing countries, it is too early to speculate.

ALAN DEARLING

References and Further Reading

Abel, E. *Marijuana, the First 12,000 Years*. New York: Plenum Press, 1980.
Blickman, T. *Caught in the Cross-Fire: Developing Countries, the UNDCP, and the War on Drugs*. London: Transnational Institute and the Catholic Institute for International Relations, 1998.
Burrows, J. *Coca: An Andean Tradition*. New York: Center for World Indigenous Studies, 2001.
Emboden, W. *Narcotic Plants: Hallucinogens, Stimulants, Inebriants and Hypnotics, Their Origins and Uses*. London: Studio Vista, 1979.
European Monitoring Centre for Drugs and Drug Addiction (EMCDDA) www.emcdda.org
Neal, R. "Africa Backs UN Anti-Drugs Fight." *Africa Recovery*, vol. 12, No 1, 1998.
Richardson, M. *Flowering Plants, part of the Encyclopedia of Psychoactive Drugs*. New York: Chelsea House, 1986.
Riehman, Kara S. "Patterns of Drug Use in Developing Countries." *Injecting Drug Use and AIDS in Developing Countries: Determinants and Issues for Policy Consideration*. 1997. At http://www.worldbank.org/aids-econ/confront/backgrnd/riehman/indexp4.htm
Rudgely, R. *The Alchemy of Culture: Intoxicants in Society*. London: British Museum Press, 1993.
South, N., ed. *Drugs: Cultures, Controls & Everyday Life*. London: Sage, 1999.
Williamson, K. *Drugs and the Party Line*. Edinburgh: Rebel Inc, 1997.

DRUZE

The term *Druze* refers to both an Islam-based sectarian belief system and its adherents. Within the global Islamic community, the Druze are not generally regarded as true Muslims. This attitude toward the Druze is directed at the faith's divergence from the main body of Islam and many of its core beliefs.

Druze Origins

The Druze faith was established during the eleventh century CE in Cairo under the reign of the Fatimid

Caliphate. It began as an Islamic reform movement. Among the reforms advocated were the abolition of both slavery and polygamy, as well as the introduction of a form of secularism in terms of religious and governmental separation. Other sectarian Islamic groups also adopted and instituted these ideas, while mainstream Islam did not.

The early history of the Druze faith centers around three figures in particular, the first of which is Hakim, the sixth caliph in the Fatimid succession and the individual regarded as the founder of the Druze faith. The second important figure is Hamza, a religious writer, teacher, and leader appointed by Caliph Hakim. Many of the Druze manuscripts and records of the teachings of Hakim are attributed to Hamza. The third figure is that of Darazi, from whom the faith takes its popular name, though most Druze prefer to be collectively known as *Muwahedin,* or monotheists. Darazi was an underling of Hamza who sought to rise through the ranks to surpass his master. Darazi began twisting the faith to help meet his ends and became branded as a heretic. He was most likely ordered put to death by Hakim and Hamza in 1019.

Druze Beliefs

The belief system of the Druze is Islam-based, and also respects the traditions of Judaism and Christianity. The Druze find both metaphorical and literal messages in the Qur'an, the Bible, and the Torah. While the Druze regard the texts of the three Abrahamic faiths as messages from God, they have their own scriptures, in the form of various manuscripts, most of which were written between 1017 and 1043 CE.

The Druze believe that God is beyond the comprehension of the human mind. While the Druze faith is an offshoot of Islam, its beliefs deviate from Islam considerably. One such belief is that of reincarnation, which is not contained in any of the three Abrahamic faiths. The motivation behind this belief is that humans are imperfect; therefore, they cannot attain the level of equality to be united with God. Hence, humans are forced to repeat the cycle of life until reaching either Heaven or Hell. Reaching either destination, humans no longer endure the reincarnation process. According to Druze doctrine, God's presence is not limited to the caliph. Elements of God can also be found in a hierarchical system of leadership ranging from clerics down to community leaders. Another difference between the Druze faith and that of the Sunni and Shi'a is the place of religious observance. The Druze do have mosques, but they also have the *khalwa*, which serves a purpose similar to that of a monastery. The *khalwa* is usually located on top of a hill outside a city, and serves as a place of seclusion for the learned of the Druze faith.

Druze Society

The basic structure of Druze society is a division between the *uqqal*, or wise, and the *juhhal*, or ignorant. Both men and women may be initiated as *uqqal*. The *uqqal* are those members of the faith understanding its specifics and adhering to its doctrine and demonstrating piety, while the *juhhal* are the majority of the population and understand only the basics of the faith. A member of the *juhhal* is able to become *uqqal*. A further division exists within the *uqqal*. The best of the best are known as *ajawid*, and they are the decision makers and leaders within Druze society. Despite the divisions, a sense of communalism and unity prevails among the Druze. Family is also an important aspect of Druze society, with individuals often remaining close to their family members.

The Druze in History

Upon the conquering of the Levant by the Ottoman Turks in 1516, the Druze were able to maintain their air of independence and resistance in their mountain strongholds, while the neighboring Arabs were forced to submit and become part of the Muslim empire.

Druze communities exist in Lebanon, Syria, Israel, and Jordan. The Druze have often been in conflict with their host governments, especially when control over Druze communities by the host governments has been strong. On the other hand, because the Druze have been excluded from the power structure in some countries, the Druze have enjoyed some autonomy in their isolation. The Druze have made their presence known to the outside world at various times in history. Conflict between the Druze and the Maronite Christians in Lebanon led to European intervention, on the part of France and England, during the 1800s. The Europeans helped the Ottomans restore order, but the Ottomans engaged in playing the Druze and Maronites against each other, which led to a major civil war in 1860. Over the course of four weeks, the Druze killed around twelve thousand Maronites, and the Maronites forced around one hundred thousand Druze from their villages. With an interest in protecting their fellow Christians, France and England landed troops at Beirut and invaded Damascus.

The two European powers then forced the Ottomans to establish the autonomous province of Mount Lebanon with Christian leadership.

At the end of the First World War, the Sykes-Picot Agreement between the British and the French, reinforced by the Treaty of Versailles and the League of Nations, allowed for the establishment of semi-independent Arab states in the Ottoman territories under French and British mandates. In effect, this was colonialism, and was not viewed with favor by the Druze communities falling under the new French administration. By 1925, the French had a Druze revolt on their hands in Syria, which took some effort to quell. The leaders of the revolt were arrested and exiled to Palmyra, in the northwestern part of Syria. The European mandates in the Near East lasted relatively briefly, with Iraq gaining its independence in 1932, Lebanon in 1943, Syria and Transjordan in 1946, and Palestine in 1948. At the end of the British Mandate in Palestine was the war for Israeli independence, which began immediately. When France relinquished Lebanon, they left it with a hierarchical power structure with the Christians at the top, then the Sunni, then Shi'a, with the other minority groups including the Druze in exclusion. Problems emerged in the power balance in 1958, and a civil war ensued only to be silenced months later. This was an attempt at wresting power from the hands of the Lebanese Christians to unite the country with the newly formed United Arab Republic, composed of Egypt and Syria.

Some of the Druze in Israel serve in the Israeli Defense Force (IDF), which has led to further resentment from much of the Islamic world. More Druze communities were added to Israeli jurisdiction in 1967, when Israel was able to seize the Golan Heights from Syria. Though these Druze were offered Israeli citizenship when Israel annexed the Golan Heights in 1981, many chose to resist. Some of these communities have rebelled against Israeli authority, but not to an extreme. Despite all the effects of warfare and changes in political geography, the Druze have been able to maintain their beliefs and sense of independence for more than one thousand years. The Druze of Lebanon experienced some difficulties in displacement and stability from the 1975–1990 civil war in that country.

Today, the Druze number more than six hundred thousand worldwide. The Druze communities remain somewhat isolated, although many within the various communities have abandoned subsistence agriculture in favor of capitalist ventures. The Druze are one of the least studied and most misunderstood groups in the Levant and the Near East.

WHITNEY D. DURHAM

DUBCEK, ALEXANDER

Alexander Dubcek (1921–1992) was born in Uhrovec, Czechoslovakia (existed 1919–1992; now part of the Slovak Republic), on November 27, 1921. Both of his parents were dedicated communists. He grew up in Slovakia but moved to Kirghizia (today Kyrgystan) when his father answered the call of the Soviet Communist Party to "build socialism in one nation [Soviet Union]." The Dubcek family returned to Slovakia in the spring of 1938, and that summer Alexander formally joined the Slovak Communist Party (SCP), which was illegal at the time.

In September 1938, following the Munich Conference, Nazi German forces occupied the Sudetenland (western Czechoslovakia) and, the next spring, all of Czechoslovakia. Over the next six years, Dubcek fought German occupation forces both as a partisan soldier and as an underground political activist for the Slovak National Uprising.

Since the communists played a leading role in the resistance, they were in a strong political position within Czechoslovakia after the war. In 1948, they took power with Soviet support. Dubcek rose rapidly through the Party ranks, gaining membership on the Central Committee of the SCP in 1951. In 1955, SCP leaders sent him to the Moscow Political College, from where he graduated with honors in 1958. Upon his return he joined the Czechoslovak Communist Party (CCP) and by 1962, he had become a full member of the SCP and CCP Central Committees.

During the 1950s and early 1960s, the Czech economy, suffering from the ravages of World War II and

CCP mismanagement, languished. They lacked capital to rebuild the nation's business and industrial base as well as its infrastructure. In addition, Slovakians began to chafe at their second-class status in a nation run by Czechs from the old Bohemian capital of Prague. Perhaps most unsettling was the apparent easing of Soviet controls brought on by the de-Stalinization process begun by Soviet Communist Party First Secretary Nikita Khrushchev (1956–1964) in 1956. In spite of the Soviet repression of Hungarian and Polish reform movements, by the early 1960s, many Czech and Slovak Party intellectuals believed the time was ripe for liberal reforms in their parties and nation.

During a Central Committee meeting in October 1967, Party reformers, led by Dubcek, openly challenged the policies of First Party Secretary Antonin Novotny (1957–1967). Opposition to Soviet-style communism and the rise of an anti-Novotny coalition within the CCP led to the confrontation. In December 1967, the failure of the Soviet Party's First Secretary Leonid Brezhnev to support Novotny helped lead to the latter's fall from power. The resulting Party shakeup made Dubcek First Party Secretary of the CCP on January 5, 1968. The whole world waited to see what Dubcek would do and how the Warsaw Pact would react.

From March to August 1968 (known as the "Prague Spring") Dubcek attempted to "liberalize" and "democratize" both the Party and the state. Providing what he called "socialism with a human face," his political reforms made Czechs and Slovaks, communists and noncommunists, politically and legally equal. Economic reforms attempted to open the nation to Western trade and investment.

However, the Prague Spring caused great consternation among the Eastern Bloc states (mostly Poland and East Germany) and the Soviet Union. Throughout, Dubcek sought to reassure his communist brethren that his nation was still communist and loyal to Moscow. He argued that the reforms were an internal matter that should not affect Soviet–Czech relations. As tensions mounted, a series of meetings ensued, which Dubcek hoped would placate the Soviets. They did not!

On August 21, 1968, Soviet and Warsaw Pact tanks rolled into Prague. Dubcek and other reformers were seized and taken to Moscow where they were forced to rescind all their reforms and accede to Soviet demands to "fall into line." The citizenry resisted with large public nonviolent protests. They even renamed towns and villages names such as Dubcekovo ("belonging to Dubcek") to confuse the occupiers and demonstrate support for their leader. Their efforts failed. On August 27, with tears streaming down his face, Dubcek told the nation that all their efforts at reform had been thwarted.

While Dubcek was temporarily allowed to stay in the government and the Party, slowly but surely his authority was eroded, at the behest of the Soviets. By April 1969, he had been expelled from all Central Committee posts. He served as ambassador to Turkey from 1969 to 1970, but was soon expelled from the CCP and sent into internal exile as a "forestry official." He was not permitted to speak to anyone outside of his family without government consent.

Dubcek survived, and when the Soviet Union began to fall apart and its grip on Eastern Europe relaxed, he returned to abet the so-called Velvet Revolution of November 1989. He made a stirring speech to a deliriously happy throng of Slovaks in Bratislava. Later, standing on the balcony of the Presidential Palace overlooking Wenceslas Square with newly elected President Vaclav Havel, he received cheers and accolades as a national hero from thousands of Czechs and Slovaks. On December 28, he was elected Chair of the National Assembly and was reelected a year later.

Dubcek also found time to write about his and his nation's struggle for independence and democracy. In November 1992, he published his memoirs, *Hope Dies Last*. Sadly, only one month later he died, on December 7, from massive injuries suffered in an automobile accident.

Dubcek's legacy is one of a national political, social, and economic reformer. In many ways, in 1968, his vision of his nation's future formed the foundation of relative prosperity, democracy, and freedom that both the Czech Republic and Slovak Republic enjoy today. In the 1990s, not only did both peoples prosper but they also demonstrated that even major disagreements can be peacefully settled. The best example of this was the dissolution of Czechoslovakia into the Czech Republic and Slovak Republic on December 31, 1992. Indeed, the two neighbors continue to enjoy good commercial relations and open political interaction. As such, one can reasonably say that Alexander Dubcek is the modern father of both nations.

WILLIAM P. HEAD

See also Central and Eastern Europe: History and Economic Development; Central and Eastern Europe: International Relations; Czech Republic; Slovakia

References and Further Reading

Dawisha, Karen. *The Kremlin and the Prague Spring.* Berkeley, CA: University of California Press, 1984.
Dubcek, Alexander, with Jiri Hochman and Paul DeAngelis. *Hope Dies Last: The Autobiography of Alexander Dubcek.* Prague: Kodansha International Press, 1993.

Navazelskis, Ina L. "Alexander Dubcek." In Arthur M. Schlesinger, Jr., gen. ed., *World Leaders, Past and Present*. New York: Chelsea House, 1991.

Shawcross, William. "Dubcek." *International Crisis and Behavior*, Vol. 4. New York: Simon & Schuster, 1990.

Tracey, Patrick Austin. *Political Reform Leaders in Eastern Europe and the Former Soviet Union*. New York: Facts on File Press, 1997.

Valenta, Jiri, forward by Alexander Dubcek. *Soviet Intervention in Czechoslovakia, 1968: Anatomy of a Decision*. Baltimore, MD: Johns Hopkins University Press, 1991.

DUVALIER, FRANÇOIS

President of Haiti from 1957 to 1971 and sometimes known as Papa Doc, François Duvalier was born in the capital city of Port-au-Prince. One of his early teachers was Dumarsais Estimé, known as a champion of the underprivileged Black majority and later was to become president of Haiti. Another of his teachers was Jean Price-Mars, whose writings romanticized voodoo and the Haitian peasantry. Duvalier went on to medical school in Haiti, and later became involved in a successful campaign against malaria and yaws. He practiced medicine in a village just south of Port-au-Prince and would later claim to have gained an intimate knowledge of rural Haiti from his work there.

He developed the traditional color model of Haitian politics into the notion that all the progressive heroes, notably Estimé, were Black, and that the mulatto elite had always blocked reform.

In 1946, Estimé became president, and his government introduced many progressive reforms, leading to what some have called the Social Revolution of 1946. Duvalier saw himself as the intellectual and political heir to this revolution.

Four years later the army ousted Estimé, and a former colonel, Paul E. Magloire, became president. Enjoying the support of the mulatto elite, as well as the USA, Magloire tried to reverse the reforms of Estimé. Duvalier, who had risen through various government posts to become the secretary of Labor and Public Health, left public life to help organize the opposition to Magloire. In 1956, Magloire fled into exile, the army once again took over, and after several provisional governments, Duvalier emerged as the primary proponent of the Estimé social revolution and won the presidency.

Inaugurated on October 22, 1957, Duvalier promised to continue the social revolution by raising the standard of living primarily through stabilizing the economy and increasing the literacy rate. After facing several invasions and insurrections early in his presidency, however, he became obsessed with the perpetuation of his rule. His ruthless suppression of all opposition became legend. After an attempt on the life of his children in April 1963, he became increasingly isolated, never traveling outside Haiti and rarely leaving the National Palace. The Haitian treasury was treated as the family budget, and aid monies were funneled to the first family and Duvalier cronies. Meanwhile, political opponents were tortured and executed, professionals left the country in large numbers, the economy deteriorated, the Duvaliers invested their stolen monies abroad, and foreign investment evaporated. In 1963, US President John F. Kennedy canceled most of the aid from the United States. Over the years the government of Duvalier provided very few services to the general public, and agricultural development in what is essentially an agricultural country was almost totally ignored.

During the last years of Duvalier's life the economy was somewhat bolstered by the establishment of some small industries attracted by the cheap labor, but the living standard for most of the population remained immeasurably low.

During the night of April 21, 1971, Papa Doc Duvalier died, and his nineteen-year-old son Jean-Claude was proclaimed president-for-life the next day.

ROBERT LAWLESS

See also Caribbean: History and Economic Development; Caribbean: International Relations

References and Further Reading

Abbott, Elizabeth. *Haiti: The Duvaliers and Their Legacy*. New York: McGraw-Hill, 1988.

Bellegarde-Smith, Patrick. *Haiti: The Breached Citadel*. Boulder, CO: Westview Press, 1990.

Ferguson, James. *Papa Doc, Baby Doc: Haiti and the Duvaliers*. Oxford: Blackwell, 1987.

Prince, Rod. *Haiti: Family Business*. London: Latin American Bureau, 1985.

Trouillot, Michael-Rolph. *Haiti, State Against Nation: The Origins and Legacy of Duvalierism*. New York: Monthly Review Press, 1990.

E

EAST AFRICA: HISTORY AND ECONOMIC DEVELOPMENT

Conceivably one of the most diverse in Africa, the nucleus of this region is best viewed as consisting of the *East African Plateau* and the *Ethiopian Highlands*, which are both intersected by the *Great Rift Valley*. This spectacular geological fault that began forming approximately 20 million years ago was named by the nineteenth century Scottish explorer John Walter Gregory. Stretching approximately four thousand miles, it actually begins in Jordan and follows the course of the Jordan River into the Dead Sea. From there it passes through the Gulf of Aqabah and follows along the Red Sea entering Eritrea at the Dana-kil Depression. From there the valley slices through Ethiopia and splits near the Kenya border. The eastern branch enters Kenya at Lake Turkana and then proceeds southward into Tanzania at Lake Natron. The western branch of the valley follows the border between Uganda, Rwanda, Burundi, Tanzania, and Zaire and includes lakes Albert, Edward, Kivu, and Tanganyika. The two branches of the Rift Valley reunite at Lake Rukwa in Tanzania, where it continues through Malawi to the Indian Ocean coast near Beira in Mozambique.

Although most of the countries of this region are geographically heterogeneous, extensive portions of Ethiopia, Eritrea, Kenya, Rwanda, Burundi, Uganda, and Tanzania are comprised of highlands, whereas most of Somalia, Djibouti, and the Sudan tend to be relatively low. When the land on both sides of the Rift Valley erupted, a series of volcanic peaks were created. These include Africa's highest mountain, Mt. Kilimanjaro in Tanzania (19,321 feet), as well as Mt. Kenya (17,007 feet), Mt. Meru in Tanzania (14,955 feet), Mt. Elgon in Kenya (14,152 feet), and the Virunga Volcanoes, comprised of eight mountains ranging from ten thousand to over fourteen thousand feet elevation on the border of Uganda, Rwanda, and Democratic Republic of Congo. The valley floor gradually sank into a low and flat plain which varies in width from thirty to forty miles and in elevation from 1,300 feet below sea level in the Dead Sea to about 6,000 feet above sea level in parts of Kenya.

East Africa's active geological processes have also generated a series of lakes. Though not technically in either branch of the Rift Valley, nonetheless *Lake Victoria*, which borders Kenya, Uganda, and Tanzania, is Africa's largest lake (26,830 square miles) and the world's second largest freshwater body. Its fisheries provide sustenance for millions of people in the three countries it borders. The ultimate source of the world's longest river, the Nile, is located in Jinja, Uganda, near Lake Victoria. The Rift Valley's western sector contains smaller lakes, such as Albert, Edward, and Kivu. It also holds *Lake Tanganyika*, on the borders of Tanzania, Democratic Republic of Congo, Zambia, and Burundi, which is Africa's second largest lake (12,471 square miles) and the world's second deepest (4,700 feet). *Lake Malawi*, which borders Malawi, Mozambique, and Tanzania, is Africa's third largest lake (2,471 square miles) and essentially lies at the end of the Rift Valley. *Lake Turkana* (2,703 square miles), on Kenya's northern border with

Ethiopia, has no outlet; hence water is lost mainly through evaporation and is therefore highly alkaline. It does manage to sustain ample stocks of both fish (especially Nile Perch and Tilapia) and crocodiles. In fact a number of smaller Rift Valley lakes tend to be shallow and have a high mineral content, specifically sodium carbonate, as the evaporation of water leaves these salts behind. This creates an ideal scenario for breeding blue-green algae, and these so-called "soda lakes"—Nakuru, Elementaita, Magadi, and Bogoria in Kenya, Natron, and Eyasi in Tanzania, and Ziway, Langano, Abiyatta, and Shalla in Ethiopia—are famous for attracting a huge number of flamingoes.

If the African continent is the birthplace of humanity, then East Africa is surely the cradle of the human species, and a majority of paleoanthropologists believe that the Rift Valley holds most of the clues to our past. The earliest known hominid[1] fossils date from between four to five million years ago (MYA) and come from parts of the Rift Valley situated in what is now Ethiopia. These include specimens that presumably represent species such as *Ardipithecus ramidus* (4.4 MYA), *Australopithecus anamensis* (4 MYA), and *Australopithecus afarensis* (3.5 MYA). Certainly the most famous hominid fossil is *Lucy*, a 3.2-million-year-old example of *A. afarensis* found by Donald Johanson and Tim White in Hadar, Ethiopia, in 1974. This was where our ancestors took their first great strides—especially bipedal locomotion. The 3.4-million-year-old footprints found in Laetoli, Tanzania, by Mary Leakey and Tim White provided corroborating evidence of bipedalism around the same time period. Sometime between two and two and a half million years ago hominids named *Homo habilis* began making and using stone tools. In addition to their use as digging implements, these stone tools might have enabled *H. habilis* to scrape meat off scavenged carcasses and extract protein-rich marrow from animal bones. Ample evidence of tool manufacture was first uncovered by Louis and Mary Leakey at sites such as Olduvai Gorge in Tanzania. Tool making and fire use would later enable members of several subsequent species—*Homo erectus* and *Homo sapiens*—to emanate outward to other parts of Africa, as well as the Middle East, Asia, Europe, Australia, and eventually the New World. Every year ongoing discoveries by paleoanthropologists either push back the date for the earliest hominid or refine the proposed evolutionary sequence, but none alter the certainty that East Africa holds the ultimate key to understanding our species' past.

Historically, two cultural factors—the Swahili language and the Islamic religion—have acted to partially integrate segments of this vast region. *Kiswahili,* the Swahili language, is spoken over a large part of East Africa, principally in Kenya and Tanzania, but also in portions of Uganda, Rwanda, and Burundi, although to lesser degrees. Kiswahili *is* an indigenous African language of the Bantu sub-family of the Niger-Congo language family, but it is also heavily infused with words borrowed from Arabic and Persian. It arose along the coastal portion of East Africa in a specific social niche where Arab traders mixed with Africans to create the *Swahili people*, language, and culture. In the eighth century, the Swahili and neighboring peoples adopted Islam along the coast. Many scholars think because it contributed to the atmosphere of trust and security that was necessary to sustain such a far-flung trading network with links not only to the Arabian peninsula but also the Indian sub-continent, Malaysia, Indonesia, and China. A Greek mariner's account from the first century AD, known as the *Periplus of the Erythraean Sea,* refers to the well-established East African trading routes and export of commodities such as ivory, tortoise shell, coconut oil, and rhinoceros horn. For centuries a wide range of goods, including gold from the southern African kingdom of Great Zimbabwe as well as slaves taken from the interior, were exported and imported by the Swahili merchants, who acted as middlemen between the Arab traders who sailed *dhows* (sailing vessels with unique triangular sails) down from the Arabian peninsula and then back according to the prevailing monsoon winds. The arrival of the Portuguese on the East African coast in the fifteenth century interrupted the hegemony of the independent Swahili city-states, of which there were perhaps as many as forty. In the late eighteenth and early nineteenth centuries, the Portuguese influence waned and the Swahili city-states came under the control of the Sultans of Oman. In 1840, Sayyid Said relocated his court from Muscat to Zanzibar island, off the coast of what is now Tanzania. His influence continued until the European intrusion in the late nineteenth century.

Most of the countries which constitute this region today, and indeed most of Africa, derive from the workings of European minds rather than from any types of indigenous political boundaries. This recognition is absolutely critical for understanding the roots of East Africa's contemporary problems. Initial European contacts with Africa were chiefly commercial in nature and usually conducted by trading companies. For example, the German East Africa

---

[1] Modern humans and our immediate ancestral species.

Company and Imperial British East Africa Company were licensed by their home governments and, hence, were more or less given free reign. As Europeans began to discern the African continent's substantial economic potential, what came to be known as *the scramble for Africa* ensued. Economic competition was fueled by the inter-European political rivalries, particularly between the British and the French. In a conference sponsored by Chancellor Bismarck of Germany and held in Berlin from December 1884 to April 1885, European powers began the act of formally partitioning the African continent. In the process, East Africa was divided between Germany, France, Belgium, Italy, and Britain, although by far the latter exerted the strongest influence over the region. The mood of the time is embodied in the much quoted remark of King Leopold of Belgium, who declared at the Berlin Conference, "I am determined to get my share of this magnificent African cake."

The boundaries laid down over the ensuing decades have, by and large, remained untouched into the twenty-first century. By the end of World War I, when Germany's colonies were assumed by Britain, the political map of Africa was largely completed. When these nations, as well as all the other African states, gained their independence from their European colonial overlords, they consciously made decisions to retain the political borders drawn by outsiders. The ramifications have been enormous—members of some ethnic groups were divided artificially by political borders, while in other cases members of groups which have long been mutually hostile were forced into close proximity and association. Then there was the famous colonial strategy of divide and rule to consider, whereby Europeans deliberately accentuated "tribal" differences among Africans in order to play one group off against another. Many East African tribal amalgamations are in fact not primordial, but are rather the result of twentieth century colonial rule.

Ethiopia (471,776 square miles) was exceptional for being one of only two African countries—the other being Liberia—to escape colonization by European powers in the late nineteenth and early twentieth centuries. Both the Ethiopian monarchy and Orthodox Christianity have long and rich histories. Although it did manage to avoid initial colonization, Italian forces, from 1935 to 1941, occupied Ethiopia, along with part of Somalia. Many Pan-Africanists considered Italy's act of aggression to be highly inflammatory, and the Italian occupation of Ethiopia is widely considered to have been the major catalyst for the incipient nationalist movements around the continent. After returning to power Emperor Haile Selassie ruled until 1974 when he was ousted in a Marxist

coup d'etat. **Eritrea** (46,718 square miles) was established as an Italian colony in 1890 and subsequently transferred to British control in 1941. It was henceforth incorporated into Ethiopia in 1962 and later attained independence in 1993 after a prolonged armed struggle between the Eritrean Peoples' Liberation Movement and the Ethiopian government. **Djibouti** (8,494 square miles), the smallest country in this region, evolved in 1977 out of the colony known as French Somaliland which itself was established out of France's desire to control the entrance to the Red Sea. **Somalia** (246,201 square miles) was declared a British Protectorate in 1886. Around the same time Italy had established a colony in southern regions, but this was relinquished to the British in 1941. From 1950 to 1960, Italian Somaliland was a United Nations Trust Territory. British Somaliland became independent in June 1960 and in July of the same year it united with Italian Somaliland to became the Somali Republic.

Most Americans are probably unaware that the *Cold War* was not fought just in Europe and Asia—it was also played out on African soil. Although the best-known examples come from southern Africa, for example Angola and Mozambique, of particular relevance for East Africa were Ethiopia and Somalia—both lying in the strategic Horn of Africa and the sea route between the Red Sea and the Gulf of Aden. The United States and the Soviet Union each sought an active presence in the region. Until 1974, the US backed Emperor Haile Selassie's government in Ethiopia, while the Soviets had provided military equipment and training to Somalia. After the Marxist coup in Ethiopia, the superpowers exchanged spheres of influence as the Soviet Union proceeded to back the regime of Major Mengistu Hailie Mariam, while the US supported the Somali strongman, Mohamed Siad Barre. With the demise of the Soviet Union in 1991, assistance to both countries dried up. This quickly led to major political changes: in the case of Somalia the government disintegrated as Mohamed Siad Barre fled while rival warlords fought for supremacy; in Ethiopia it meant another coup, this time with Mengistu being removed by the Ethiopian People's Revolutionary Democratic Front and EPRDF chairman Meles Zanawi.

Sudan (967,493 square miles) is Africa's largest country at over one quarter the size of the continental United States. It was once the Anglo-Egyptian Sudan, created by the Anglo-Egyptian Condominium of 1899. Prior to that date and for most of the nineteenth century, Egypt had actually exerted control over most of Sudan. In reality neither Egyptian nor British rule sought to do what was best for the Sudanese people nor heal the tremendous cultural and religious rifts between the peoples of the northern and southern parts of this enormous country. In 1953, Britain and Egypt signed an agreement to grant independence to the Sudan, which came in 1956. Since then the country continues to be divided along cultural and religious lines, as the government has been dominated by the Muslim peoples of the north, who treat the Africans living in the south as second-class citizens. Forming the *Sudanese People's Liberation Army* (SPLA), these southerners, led by Colonel John Garang until his death in 2005, are mostly adherents of Christianity and animist religions. They have been waging a civil war against the northern-dominated government since 1972. Several rival rebel groups formed in the early 1990s. The *Intergovernmental Authority on Drought and Development* (IGAAD) was organized in 1993 under the chairmanship of President Daniel arap Moi of Kenya, comprising heads of state and ministers from other neighboring countries—Eritrea, Ethiopia, and Uganda. Under the assumption that the Sudanese civil war was a *regional* rather than national conflict, IGAAD began mediation efforts to try and find a framework for peace in Sudan. The civil war has most definitely impeded the Sudan's economic development and fostered political instability, thereby perpetuating a cycle of fragile military and civilian governments. Large oil fields that have recently been discovered in southern Sudan now complicate things even further.

In the early part of the twentieth century, **Kenya** (224,959 square miles) became a white settler colony largely as an afterthought. When it was declared a Protectorate in 1895 Britain's first priority was to build a railway to **Uganda**, which was coveted primarily to ensure control over the headwaters of the Nile. Only after completion of the railway did the British realize the agricultural potential of the central and western highlands of Kenya, thereby leading Lord Delamere, in 1905, to declare it "white man's country." White settlers came to these fertile highlands and displaced tens of thousands of Africans, mainly Kikuyu, for large coffee plantations. Of course this would later come back to haunt them as it was primarily Kikuyu, Kenya's largest ethnic group, who comprised the so-called *Mau Mau* (who actually called themselves the *Land and Freedom Movement*). Although the settlers and the colonial government assumed him to be the mastermind behind Mau Mau, Jomo Kenyatta was hardly involved in this violent guerilla resistance organization, which itself was widely misunderstood by whites. Nonetheless, Kenyatta was arrested and subsequently convicted of treason. After serving eight years in prison he was released and in 1963 went on to become independent Kenya's first prime minister, and then president. For

much of the 1960s and into the 1970s, Kenya was regarded as a miracle of free market capitalist development (Bates 1989). Moreover, the successive governments of Jomo Kenyatta (1963–1978) followed by Daniel arap Moi (1978–present), have been exceptionally stable for Africa as a whole and East Africa in particular. However, this political stability may have come at a high price, as both the Kenyatta and Moi governments were accused of massive human rights violations. Additionally, the economic growth has all but halted and corruption has become rampant in all levels of government. As with other African governments, the IMF has taken a firm stance with Kenya and withheld loans for much of the 1990s. In December 1991, Moi's government finally succumbed to pressure for the introduction of multiparty politics. Open elections were held in 1992 and 1997. The *Kenya African National Union* (KANU), the ruling party, won both times amid allegations of massive irregularities. Additionally, both times the process was preceded by ethnic clashes, which many observers claimed were government sponsored.

What was originally designated **Tanganyika**, and taken by Chancellor Bismarck at the Conference of Berlin, was later ceded to Britain after Germany's defeat in World War I. Unlike her northern neighbor, Kenya, Tanganyika never became as popular a destination for white settlers. Consequently, independence came much easier and without the bloody struggle of Mau Mau in Kenya. It attained independence in 1961 and in 1964 was united with the newly independent island of Zanzibar to become **Tanzania** (364,899 square miles). Under its first President, **Julius Nyerere**—affectionately referred to as *Mwalimu*, Kiswahili for "teacher"—Tanzania embarked on a very different course from her capitalist neighbor, Kenya. Nyerere's socialist policies aimed at wedding the best of traditional African values with the teachings of Marx. A major thrust of development was the creation of centralized villages, ostensibly to better facilitate provision of basic needs, such as health care and education. He collectivized village farmlands, carried out mass literacy campaigns and instituted free and universal education. He referred to these forced settlements as *ujamaa* ("familyhood") villages. Although later criticized for his overreliance on socialism, thereby leading to the failure of the Tanzanian economy, nevertheless Nyerere's *ujamaa* policy and his promotion of *Kiswahili* as a cultural and linguistic unifying force helped Tanzania avoid many of tribal/ethnic problems of her neighbors. Throughout the 1980s, it became clear that socialist economics was not working. In 1985, Nyerere succumbed to pressure and stepped down, paving the way for his two successors—first Ali Hassan Mwinyi and then the current President,

Benjamin Mkapa. Nyerere remained head of the ruling party until 1990. Over the course of the 1990s Tanzania's economic fortunes have moderately improved, and the country has held several multi-party elections, although *Chama Cha Mapinduzi*, the ruling party, won both.

Uganda (91,135 square miles), dubbed "the pearl of Africa" by Winston Churchill, comprises a number of indigenous states, such as Buganda, from which the country's name is derived. Others include Bunyoro, Basogo, Banyankore, Batoro, and Bagisu. The British declared Buganda a protectorate in 1894 and gradually extended control over the other areas by 1914. Unlike Kenya, however, Uganda never became popular with white settlers. Since independence in 1962, Uganda has been racked by political instability. Considerable strain emerged out of the federation of four autonomous regions—Buganda, Ankole, Bunyoro, and Toro—under Buganda King Mutesa II acting as non-executive president. In February 1966, Milton Obote staged a coup by suspending the constitution and deposing the president. Soon thereafter, in April 1966, Obote withdrew regional autonomy and introduced an executive presidency, filled by himself. The new constitution, adopted in September 1967, abolished traditional leadership and established a unitary republic. In 1971, Field Marshall Idi Amin Dada seized power while Obote was out of the country. The following year, 1972, Amin expelled all noncitizen Asians and seized British companies. Untold thousands of Ugandan civilians lost their lives under Amin's brutal regime in the 1970s. Amin's tyranny continued until 1979 when the Tanzanian army, aided by the *Ugandan National Liberation Army*, invaded and took Kampala in April. Troubles were far from over for the people of Uganda since in the 1980 elections the Uganda People's Congress won and thus Milton Obote was selected to serve a second term. Instability again took over as various guerilla factions sought to oust Obote, who spent the first half of the 1980s trying to subdue the rebels. In 1985, he was overthrown in a military coup, led by Brigadier General Okello. Rebel activity continued until January 1986 when the *National Resistance Movement* took Kampala. Yoweri Museveni became president and formed a *National Resistance Council* made up of both military and civilians. In spite of attempts at reconciliation, Museveni's government continues to be plagued by rebel activity in the north and west. On the other hand, as a result of agreeing to comply with the structural adjustment policies mandated by the IMF and World Bank, Museveni became a favorite of the IMF, much like former President Jerry Rawlings of Ghana. Both implemented many of the tough austerity policies required as conditions for continued loans, and as a result, the economies of both nations grew substantially more than their neighbors in the 1990s. Additionally, Uganda under Museveni has made substantial progress in dealing with the AIDS epidemic, and the openness with which the Ugandan government has faced this challenge is unparalleled in Africa.

Rwanda (10,170 square miles) and **Burundi** (10,745 square miles) are nearly identical in physical size, ethnic composition of their populations, and tragic experiences. In many ways their situations illustrate the impact of the brief yet potent European colonial period, from the late nineteenth to mid twentieth centuries. They are two of the most densely populated countries in Africa, both about the size of Maryland and both are composed of about 85% Hutu, 14% Tutsi, and 1% Twa. Traditionally these people are said to have been farmers, pastoralists, and hunters, respectively. The Tutsi herders, supposedly of Hamitic origin, are said to have entered the region in the fifteenth century, establishing a monarchy headed by a king and a feudal hierarchy of Tutsi nobles and gentry, who dominated the serf-like Hutu farmers. These farmers were said to have made a contract to pledge their services and those of their descendants to a Tutsi lord in return for cattle loans and use of land for grazing and farming. Rene Lemarchand has seriously questioned this simplistic view. While certainly not denying the clientage that historically existed between Tutsi and Hutu, he asserts that the seeds of twentieth century conflicts between the Hutu and Tutsi were really sown by the Germans during their occupation and then the Belgians during their colonial tenure. Germany added Burundi and Rwanda to German East Africa in 1899, but both were turned over to Belgium under the League of Nations Mandate of 1916. Belgium continued the German approach of using indirect rule, favoring the Tutsi "elite" and thereby solidifying the ethnic cleavage between Hutu and Tutsi. Since independence was achieved in 1962 there have been a series of genocidal massacres, with Hutu and Tutsi exchanging roles as victims and perpetrators. Perhaps the most prominent was in Rwanda in 1994 when perhaps eight hundred thousand people were killed, primarily Tutsi by Hutu. The ensuing exodus of refugees into neighboring countries has contributed to their further destabilization, for example the rebels, based in the eastern provinces of the Democratic Republic of Congo. Today both Rwanda and Burundi remain in a tense state of existence as both governments battle rebels, while the United Nations tribunal in Arusha, Tanzania, tries to sort out responsibility for the genocidal attacks of the 1990s.

Thus, in the post-independence era, East Africa has clearly experienced some of the continent's worst calamities. Partial regional interaction has always been present to some degree, and in the past several years the *East African Community* (EAC), comprising Kenya, Tanzania, and Uganda, has been resurrected. It will be interesting to see if the EAC will be able to follow the lead of the European Union (EU) in terms of regional economic integration. The numerous political and military setbacks have substantially delayed the course of economic development and the growth of civil society in East Africa. It is important to acknowledge that these have been primarily man-made disasters: the Ethiopian famine of 1984–1985; the recurring Hutu-Tutsi rivalry and genocidal outbursts in Rwanda and Burundi; the ongoing twenty-five-year-old civil war in Sudan; the war between Ethiopia and Eritrea; the dictatorial regimes of Idi Amin and Milton Obote in Uganda during the 1970s and early 1980s; and the steady disintegration of civil society in Somalia under Mohammed Siad Barre, culminating in the chaos of the 1990s. Once again, in order to fully comprehend the frequency and magnitude of these misfortunes, it is absolutely vital to situate these problems in the larger historical context of European colonial rule and its aftermath. Of course this does not absolve post independence African leadership of culpability but that, in fact, could be the subject of another entire essay.

BRUCE D. ROBERTS

See also Amin, Idi; East Africa: International Relations; Ethnic Conflicts: East Africa; Kenyatta, Jomo; Mau Mau; Nyerere, Julius; Obote, Milton; Okello, John; Selassie, Emperor Haile; Structural Adjustment Programs (SAPs).

References and Further Reading

Bates, Robert H. *Beyond the Miracle of the Market: The Political Economy of Agrarian Development in Kenya.* New York: Cambridge University Press, 1989.

Collins, Robert O. *Eastern African History.* New York: Markus Wiener Publications, 1990.

Edgerton, Robert B. *Mau Mau: An African Crucible.* New York: Ballantine Books, 1989.

Kesby, John D. *The Cultural Regions of East Africa.* New York: Academic Press, 1977.

Leakey, Richard. *The Origin of Humankind.* New York: Basic Books, 1994.

Lemarchand, Rene. "Burundi : The Politics of Ethnic Amnesia." In *Genocide Watch,* edited by Helen Fein. New Haven, CT: Yale University Press, 1992.

Middleton, John. *The Swahili: An African Mercantile Civilization.* New Haven, CT: Yale University Press, 1992.

Museveni, Yoweri K. *Sowing the Mustard Seed: The Struggle for Freedom and Democracy in Uganda.* London: MacMillan, 1997.

Nyerere, Julius K. *Freedom and Development/Uhuru na Maendeleo. A Selection From Writings and Speeches 1968–1973.* London: Oxford University Press, 1973.

Ogot, Bethwell A. *Zamani: A Survey of East African History.* Nairobi: East Africa Publishing House, 1968.

Shorter, Alyward. *East African Societies.* London: Routledge and Kegan Paul, 1974.

Were, Gideon S. and Derek A. Wilson. *East Africa Through a Thousand Years.* London: Evans Brothers, 1968.

EAST AFRICA: INTERNATIONAL RELATIONS

Defining East Africa

The area of East Africa or Eastern Africa is located in the eastern part of the African continent and comprises the *East Africa Zone, the Northeast Zone,* and a country, *Sudan.* The East Africa Zone includes the following countries: Burundi, Kenya, Uganda, Rwanda, and Tanzania and occupies a surface of 727,176 square miles with a population of about 97.3 million, of which 29% is urban. The Northeast Zone comprises Djibouti, Eritrea, Ethiopia, and Somalia, with a surface of 801,201 square miles and 75.2 million inhabitants, of which 21% are urban. The tenth state member of the area, Sudan, is the most extensive country, with a surface of 1,002,325 square miles and is often included within the Northern Africa or Central Africa countries. Sudan will be included among the Eastern Africa countries due to the strong and steady relations this country maintains with the rest of the eastern countries.

The East Africa area is mainly rural, as the East African countries' economies are all based on agriculture. Unlike Southern and Western Africa, the Eastern countries don't have great amounts of mineral resources. As for natural resources such as petroleum, chromium, zinc, and iron, Sudan is the wealthiest country. Tanzania has gold and platinum and Ethiopia also has gold. Kenya and Uganda have some zones rich in wood. Within this area is situated the Nile Basin, which is shared by several countries in arid or semi-arid areas.

This area presents very low living standards. All countries previously named, with the exception of Kenya, are listed among the poorest countries in the world, according to the Human Development Index established by the United Nations (UN).

Food shortages have reached alarming levels throughout the region. In Somalia, Uganda, Ethiopia, and Eritrea this situation is of extreme urgency. The climate conditions, the lack of means to develop agriculture, the displacements, refugees, and acquired immunity deficiency syndrome (AIDS) are factors that contribute to worsen this situation.

The spread of human immunodeficiency virus (HIV) in the region is quite high. In addition to this, public health conditions are inadequate. Hospitals are lacking or non-existent and the public expenditure on health (percent of the GDP) is low.

Another of the problems that faces the region is the constant loss of biodiversity and the threat to the ecosystem and the environment. International organizations consider environmental conservation in East Africa as a high priority because of the outstanding richness in wildlife and the variety of ecosystems. Recently, the East African countries have begun to work together to maintain cooperation policies on environmental issues.

The distribution of East African territory among the colonial powers occurred during the twentieth century. As a consequence, during the 1960s, several new States emerged whose main characteristic, besides having little experience in the exercise of their sovereignty, was clear political instability. This has resulted in large numbers of refugees; displaced, deprived, and marginalized people; economic crises; famines; and disease.

The borders of many African states weren't originally established as borders between independent states, but as territorial dividing lines belonging to the great powers in the years of imperialism. Like in Central Asia, the borders of the countries were established in an artificial and arbitrary way, without regard for the demographics of ethnic or religious groups. The division of these groups into arbitrarily delineated territories and nations has given rise to territorial, ethnic, tribal, and religious disputes. Often ethnic identity and religious fanaticism are encouraged and exploited by political and military elites who want to monopolize the access to power and resources by excluding the members of other ethnicities or religions.

There are also several areas with potential conflicts due to natural-resource reserves. These disputes are usually described as ethnic wars or political rivalries, though the real interest is focused on the natural resources.

Two other factors tend to increase the internal climate of constant conflicts. The socioeconomic crisis, which is also a consequence of the wars, and the sale of weapons, which helps to maintain the existing conflicts or to create new ones in other countries, both lead to further conflicts. Additionally, these conflicts are not only the result of internal causes but also a consequence of the interaction between internal dynamics and external influences, which often worsen the internal factors.

International Conflicts and Development

Ethiopia–Eritrea Conflict: Ethiopia is one of Africa's oldest countries. On the contrary, Eritrea is quite new, emerging from Italy's occupation. In 1952, an agreement was signed and both countries formed a federation. However, ten years later Ethiopia annexed Eritrea as one of her provinces, causing the beginning of a series of guerrilla wars. In 1991, a provisional government was established in Eritrea, accepted by the United States, with the condition of conducting a referendum on its independence in 1993. That same year Eritrea obtained regional and international recognition.

Somalia–Eritrea Conflict: Somalia used to claim the Ogaden region, inhabited in most parts by Somali ethnic groups. During the conflict with Eritrea, Ethiopia had controlled almost the whole of the Ogaden region. In 1988, after eleven years of constant confrontation, Ethiopia retired the troops of the border with Somalia, reestablished diplomatic relations and signed a peace treaty. Ethiopia and Somalia have always had aspirations over the territory of Djibouti, Ethiopia desiring access to the sea and Somalia the reunification of its territory.

The Nile Basin: the Nile River runs through nine states: Egypt, Burundi, Tanzania, Uganda, Sudan, Kenya, Rwanda, Ethiopia, and Congo. In spite of that, Egypt is the country that makes the most profit of its water flow. Recently, the countries through which the river flows have not been able to divert the water flow because of the constant conflicts. The shortage of and demand for fresh water in addition to the population increase in the region have become serious problems.

During the Cold War, many African political leaders resorted to American or Soviet aid. The Soviet Union helped Ethiopia during her conflict with Eritrea; Kenya became allied with the United States. In Somalia, Gen. Mohammed Siad Barre proclaimed his adhesion to the Soviet Union, but soon after breaking relations with this country, the United States began supporting Barre's government. But then, as Barre intended to normalize his relations with the Soviet Union, his government was frozen.

By the end of the Cold War era, the United States had a strong influence over the different countries, directly or through its several organizations and allied countries such as Uganda, Ethiopia, Eritrea, Rwanda, Burundi, and some factions in Sudan. The United States, together with Great Britain, France, and Belgium, exerted influence in African conflicts, providing the allied group's political, financing, and military support to defend their economic, political, and strategic interests in the area. In East Africa several disputes arose, many of which still exist. The constant corruption and climate of insecurity and instability have been a major setback for investments and foreign capital flow. The short-term governments have been more concerned with maintaining power than improving people's living standards.

Economic Bloc Formation, Trade, and Development

During the 1990s, the African countries abandoned their exclusive bilateral policy with the superpowers or former colonialist countries. However, this has also caused them to be more vulnerable. Despite their opposition to neo-colonialism and efforts to work as a bloc in the global market, these countries still depend economically on their relations with the Western world. They have opened their economies, and also agreements have been made to form regional organizations. Often these organizations have faced financial difficulties along with other conflicts derived from the region itself.

Kenya, Tanzania, and Uganda have formed the East African Community (EAC); Burundi and Rwanda are associated with the states of Central Africa in the Economic Community of Central African States (ECCAS) and also with the Southern African Development Coordination Conference (SADCC). Somalia, Djibouti, Eritrea, and Sudan are members of the Community of Sahel-Saharan States (CEN-SAD), established in 1998. Somalia, Sudan, and Djibouti belong to the Arab League.

Except Tanzania and Somalia, the rest of the states of East Africa belong to the Common Market for Eastern and Southern Africa (COMESA). All countries in this study belong to the African-Caribbean and Pacific (ACP) group, a trade agreement between African members and European Union countries, to the African Development Bank and also to the African Union. In spite of these efforts to improve their economies by forming blocs, the participation of these countries in the world economy remains marginal and dependent.

Most countries located in East Africa do not have commercial relations with each other or even with other African countries but with extra-continental countries instead. Uganda and Kenya constitute an exception, as these two countries maintain regular exchange trade relations. However, countries like Eritrea, Ethiopia, and Tanzania have trade relations

with countries like China, Saudi Arabia, the United States, Malaysia, and Italy, among others, but not with other African countries. Other nations such as Somalia, Rwanda, or Djibouti are more commercially connected with East Africa countries, although they also have trade with extra-continental nations.

This general trend of East Africa countries to be so dependent on trade with extra-African partners has not been helpful for the area's development, as most countries do not work together towards a shared objective but work alone. Therefore, in spite of the bloc they have formed, their economies still are very fragmented.

Lack of monetary resources has delayed development throughout East Africa. International financing organizations have demanded adjustment and budget-cut policies in the region. Kenya, for instance, has carried out a liberalization policy based on the decrease of public expenditure and the privatization of state companies, along with the disappearance of exchange control, with the purpose of attracting investors. These policies were rewarded with loans given by the World Bank and the International Monetary Fund (IMF).

Other countries followed these trends. Sudan and Tanzania adapted their government policies to the aims set by these international organizations. Although the IMF praised Tanzania, the country's social development hasn't improved. In Uganda, the government established similar measures. Though the number of foreign investments increased, the cuts in the budget worsened the situation of most people, who live in an alarming situation of poverty.

International Conflicts After the End of the Cold War

The fall of the bipolar system destroyed the east-west alignments. The retirement of the Soviet Bloc began in December 1988 with the withdrawal of Cuban troops in Angola and later with the withdrawal of American troops from Somalia.

Although the continent seemed to lose strategic interest for the central superpowers, some conflicts remained and new ones arose. The countries found neighbouring countries who acted like partners, but also as rivals.

In 1991, relations between Uganda and Kenya, which had been tense since 1987, worsened. Kenya's and Sudan's governments accused each other of protecting rebel groups that operated in each neighbour's territory.

In Somalia, in 1991, Ali Mahdi Mohammed deposed the government, while the capital city, Mogadishu, was in the hands of Mohamed Farad Aidid, both belonging to different clans. The National Somali Movement formed its own government in the ancient territory of British Somalia, establishing the Republic of Somaliland. In 1992, the UN sent a group of observers, and soon the United States began a military operation in Somalia. However the arrival of a foreign army provoked further conflicts, and in response the UN Security Council approved the dispatch of UN forces to support American troops. It was the first time the UN used military intervention in the internal affairs of another state without that state's consent. Despite the interventions, hostilities continued, and in 1994 the United States announced the withdrawal of the troops, without any foreseen solution to the conflict. Somalia still lacked a central government, and a large part of its territory was subject to civil conflicts.

The fall of the Somali state caused a serious situation of regional and international insecurity together with a flow of refugees and internal displaced persons. In 1998, a new government was created in northeastern Somalia, Puntland.

In February 1999, tensions between Somalia and Ethiopia increased, and Ethiopia's troops invaded Somalia's frontier. This conflict ended in October 1999 when Ethiopia withdrew the troops from Somalia. However, in January 2001 relations between them got tense again.

In 1994, the governments of Sudan and Uganda accused each other of supporting rival guerrilla groups and in 1995 Uganda broke off diplomatic relations with its neighbour. Although negotiations to solve their differences began in 2001, Uganda deployed its troops in the north of the country.

In 1997, the relations between Ethiopia and Eritrea worsened after the latter adopted a new currency, which meant an economic downturn in both countries. In May 1998, war broke out between these two countries after each accused the other of encroaching on the country's territory. After several failures on behalf of international organizations and the Organization of African Unity (OAU) in June 2000, a peace treaty was signed, committing both countries to cease-fire and to accept a future demarcation of a security zone in the frontier of both countries established by the United Nations.

Relations between Eritrea and Sudan deteriorated in 1994 and diplomatic relations were broken off. In 1997, Sudan accused Eritrea of launching attacks against its troops in the frontiers.

In 1993 the United Nations sent a mission to Rwanda (MINUAR) with the purpose of decreasing the violence, but did not engage in combat. Since the first interethnic violence outbreak, Rwanda has suffered continuous bursts of varying intensity.

The conflict in Sudan seems to be improving, as in January 2005 a peace treaty was signed. In Tanzania, in spite of internal instability, a peace agreement was celebrated in October 2001 between the two most influential political parties of Tanzania and Zanzibar.

East Africa: A New Strategic Location and Future Development Opportunities

At the end of the Cold War, a new strategic geography arose. In the old formulation, conflicts had an ideological-political bias; now, however, control of resources was more important than ideologies. Therefore some countries that had not historically been attractive for the superpowers began to occupy a prominent place in the political and strategic planning of the United States and other European powers.

From 1997 on, in the G7 and Russia meeting in Denver, Colorado, the necessity of encouraging the integration of African countries in the world economy as well as the need to facilitate their social and political development was discussed. Several multinational companies have been permitted to interfere with reserves of African natural resources, in many cases taking advantage of the conflicts in the region. In East Africa these corporations have allied countries, some of which have benefited economically from the conflict in other countries. Rwanda and Uganda are countries important to the interests of companies settled in Africa. A 2002 United Nations Report charges both of these governments with obtaining profits from the war in the Democratic Republic of Congo. Both countries export diamonds and coltan—minerals that are imported from the Congo. Neither Rwanda nor Uganda have such minerals. Often the economic exploitation of these resources does not foster the countries and people's development, but instead only provides companies with large profits.

However, the strategic interest of the region is not only *economic* but also *military*. When the United States became the most important power in the global arena, the enemy was no longer communism but terrorism and the groups who support it.

The instability in East Africa has been to the advantage of terrorist organizations. Al Qaeda has concentrated its operations in East Africa. In 1998 Tanzania and Kenya suffered terrorist attacks, Sudan was accused of promoting international terrorism, and the United States bombed installations in Sudan's capital.

The United States has created a special fund of about $100 million to fight terrorism, intended to form security personnel in Djibouti, Kenya, Tanzania, and Uganda. After the attacks of September 11, 2001, the American concept of security changed completely and so did its strategy in foreign policy. Africa was designated as a confluence point for terrorist organizations, and the United States considers East Africa as the most dangerous region of the African continent.

Somalia has been described as the next US military target, after the Afghanistan operation, as it is believed to be a possible shelter for al Qaeda members. American troops have settled in Djibouti.

All this information suggests that in the forthcoming years East Africa will remain a conflict-ridden area and a source of profit for Western companies. The threats of terrorism, ethnic tensions, and other sources of conflict are likely to continue, furthering violence in the region. Until these conflicts are resolved, development will be made impossible.

DIEGO I. MURGUÍA AND VERÓNICA M. ZILIOTTO

See also Amin, Idi; Burundi; Common Market for Eastern and Southern Africa (COMESA); Djibouti; East Africa: East African Community; East African Development Bank (EADB); History and Economic Development; Eritrea; Ethiopia; Ethnic Conflicts: Kenya; Organization of African Unity (OAU); Refugees; Rwanda; Siad Barre, Mohammed; Somalia; Sudan; Tanzania; Uganda; War and Development.

References and Further Reading

Harlow, Vincent, and E.M. Chilver, eds. *History of East Africa*. London: Oxford University Press, 1965.

Johnson, John W. *The strange blood of East Africa*. Minnesota Collector's Books Ltd, 1995.

Kennedy, Paul. *The Rise and Fall of the Great Powers*. New York: Random House, 1988.

Kennedy, Paul M. *Preparing for the Twenty-first Century*. New York: Random House, 1993.

Klare, Michael T. *Resource Wars: The New Landscape of Global Conflict*. New York: Henry Holt, 2001.

———. "The new geography of conflict" *Foreign Affairs*, May/June 2001.

Markakis, John, and Fukui, Katsuyoshi, eds. *Ethnicity and Conflict in the Horn of Africa*. Athens, OH: Ohio University Press, 1994.

Maxon, Robert M. *East Africa: An Introductory History*. Morgantown, WV: West Virginia University Press, 1994.

Nabudere, Dani Wadada. *Imperialism in East Africa*. London: Zed Press, 1981.

Ogot, Bethwell A., and Kieran, J. A. eds. *Zamani: A Survey of East African History*. New York: Humanities Press, 1968.

Reusch, Richard. *East Africa*. New York: F. Ungar Publisher Co, 1961.

United Nations Development Program. *Human Development Report 2004*. New York: Oxford University Press, 2002. (http://hdr.undp.org)

EAST AFRICAN COMMUNITY

In East Africa, the very first steps of sub-regional cooperation spread over a period of nearly fifty years, that is, from 1900 to 1947. In Uganda, Kenya, and Tanganyika (after 1914), the colonizing power was Britain. In order to effectively exploit the resources of these territories, in their interest, the British introduced services that accelerated the rate of this exploitation. These services included customs, civil aviation, income tax, posts, and telegraphy, etc. These services were under the umbrella of the East African Common Service Organisation.

After Tanzania, Uganda, and Kenya achieved their independence, their leaders, Julius Nyerere of Tanganyika (now Tanzania), Apolo milton Obote of Uganda, and Jomo Kenyatta of Kenya signed the Treaty for East African Cooperation on June 6, 1967. The mission and goals of the East African Community (EAC) were the fostering and promotion of economic cooperation in the sub-region.

Because the EAC ushered a common market in East Africa with the goals of ensuring economic development in the sub-region, the numerous trade restrictions that had existed previously were lessened. In trade circles, two vital principles were cultivated, namely, maximum limits on tariffs and non-discrimination. The headquarters of the EAC organs were distributed, with Kenya retaining East African Airways and East African Railways. Uganda acquired East African Posts and Telecommunications and the East African Development Bank, while Tanzania took the EAC Headquarters and Harbours Corporation. In addition, Uganda and Tanzania were allowed to apply a predetermined transfer tax on certain Kenyan goods to foster location of new industries there. This is because Kenya was clearly more developed than both Uganda and Tanzania as the result of British colonial policies. Thus, one of the goals of the EAC was to foster even development in East Africa.

Despite the new effort by the post-colonial East African states to create an economic community, this effort lasted ten years only. By 1977, the common services had disintegrated. A multiplicity of factors contributed to the demise of the EAC. They are summarized under five headings. First, there was the polarization and perception of unequal gains among the three states. Kenya, the most favoured by British colonialism, continued to gain more from the EAC arrangement. Uganda and Tanzania, the ready market for Kenyan products, had fewer and less efficient industries, and thus, could hardly compete with Kenya. Indeed, foreign companies continued to establish more and more industries in Kenya rather than in either Uganda or Tanzania. Such companies preferred Kenya because it already had a broad manufacturing base and a better infrastructure.

Both Tanzania and Uganda, but especially the latter, ran into serious trade deficits between 1967 and 1976; the share of manufactured goods in both countries' exports declined, while that of Kenya rose. The demise of the EAC was partly due to perceived and objective inequitable distribution of small benefits.

The second factor in the collapse of the EAC had to do with lack of effective compensatory and corrective measures. There were no measures for collecting and sharing of customs revenue in accordance with a pre-negotiated formula which favoured the disadvantaged; neither was there effective transfer tax which provided revenue and protected infant industries in both Uganda and Tanzania. Moreover, the principle of the free movement of goods within East Africa failed and the aim of discouraging duplication of inefficient industries in order to realize economies of scale was also lost partially.

Relocating the headquarters of common services, decentralizing some of its operations, and subsidizing different parts of the services and different areas—none of these worked effectively. Indeed, some services, such as the airways corporation, the railways corporation, and the road networks, became Kenyan-dominated.

The third factor was the problem of personalizing the decision-making process due to inadequate governmental institutions. The EAC lacked a relatively autonomous and a democratically established decision-making body. This increased the danger of instability and of transforming personal rivalries into national and intra-sub-regional conflicts. Personalization of power and the decision-making process enabled each head of state to determine the fate of the EAC. Nyerere's refusal to convene a meeting of the Authority due to his dislike of Idi Amin of Uganda can only be explained in such terms.

The fourth factor had to do with ideological differences and economic nationalism. By the time of the collapse of the EAC, there was an intense ideological rift among the partner-states. While the Kenyan leadership (the ruling and dominant class) became increasingly dominated by foreign monopoly capital, the Tanzanian leadership became increasingly radical and the Ugandan leadership (before the Amin coup in 1971) became increasingly opposed to foreign domination. Whereas Kenya's stronger economic base and stable capitalist system enabled it to attract external investment and to exploit the opportunities which the EAC offered, Tanzania's weaker economic base and socialist system had the opposite effect.

The economic gap widened and domestic stresses were explained in ideological terms. As Tanzania ridiculed Kenya's growth as based on a "man-eat-man" philosophy, Kenya retaliated by labeling Tanzanian socialism as founded on the principle of "man-eat-nothing". Tanzania then took steps that were meant to prevent the intrusion of what it saw as Kenya's bourgeois capitalist values and decadence. It also sought to eliminate Kenyan exploitation of the Tanzania market. It took measures to protect its people from the affluence of the Kenyan bourgeoisie, which was already causing large-scale smuggling of currency, coffee, and other consumer items and thus jeopardizing its socialist programmes. In brief, the increasing degree of mutual hostility culminated in the border closure—a move that precipitated a series of reactions which were punctuated by the collapse of the EAC.

The final factor was external: A multiplicity of multinational corporations and their subsidiaries extracted generous concessions and further foreign investment and then made efforts to service the sub-regional market from plants in Kenya. There emerged close links with such foreign partners as Britain, the US, and West Germany. These relationships were far more lucrative than the EAC arrangements. Tanzania developed a relationship with the then Eastern bloc, especially with China, while simultaneously maintaining links with the Western bloc. Thus, competition developed for foreign partners and markets. This impeded the coordination and harmonization of national development plans vis-à-vis external resource procurement, which was vital for pan-African and sub-regional economic integration.

In 1977, the EAC disintegrated.

However, a new EAC was launched on January 15, 2001. In the new EAC, the three member-states are pursuing the same socio-economic policies. They are all market-led and emphasize private sector development, and all are working within the structural adjustment programmes negotiated within the framework of the Bretton Woods institutions. The goal is regional over national cooperation, and thus the new EAC depends on the three member-states' proven ability to coordinate security, taxation, foreign policies and diplomacy, conflict management, etc.

The old EAC collapsed without resistance from the public. The contemporary EAC, however, has seen positive public reaction to integration.

P. GODFREY OKOTH

See also East Africa: History and Economic Development; East Africa: International Relations

References and Further Reading

East African Community: A Handbook 1972. Nairobi: East African Community Printer, 1972.

Nyer, Joseph. *Pan Africanism and East Africa, Integration.* Cambridge, MA: Harvard University Press, 1965.

Nyerere, Julius. "A United States of Africa". *Journal of Modern African Studies.* Vol. 1, March 1963.

Okoth, Godfrey P. "The OAU and the Uganda–Tanzania War, 1978/79". *Journal of African Studies.* Vol. 14, No. 3, Fall, 1987.

Proctor, Haas J. "The Efforts to Federate East Africa". *Political Quarterly.* Vol. 7, No.1, January–March, 1966.

Rothchild, Donald. *Politics of Integration: An East African Documentary.* Nairobi: East African Publishing House, 1968.

Sesay, Ray I. *The Future of Regionalism in Africa.* London: Macmillan, 1985.

The Treaty for the Establishment of the East African Community. Arusha: East African Cooperation, November 30, 1999.

EAST ASIA: HISTORY AND ECONOMIC DEVELOPMENT

For the purposes of this essay, East Asia comprises Hong Kong, Taiwan, South Korea, China, and North Korea. The post-war development of the region has generally been very successful, especially in the economic realm. With the exception of North Korea after the 1950s, the region has generated remarkable levels of economic growth, reductions in poverty and improvements in education, health, life expectancy, infant mortality, and most other indices of social development. Political development has been uneven. Democratization has taken remarkable strides in South Korea and Taiwan since the 1970s but North Korea and China remain one-party communist states. Hong Kong was a British colony until 1997, when it became a Special Administrative Region (SAR) within China; but as a SAR it retains substantial autonomy in many areas—the notable exceptions are foreign affairs and defence.

In terms of geography and population China has always been the giant of East Asia. Along with the other four countries of the region, it lies between 53° and 18° N and 73° and 134° E. China's landmass is over 3.7 million square miles and the population is approaching 1.3 billion (of whom approximately 80% still live in rural areas and are engaged primarily in agricultural production). In China the climate of the populous south and southeast is generally temperate but the north is extremely cold in the winter. In the west and northwest, desert conditions inhibit development. The other four countries of the region are located along China's east coast. The Korean peninsula lies between the Yellow Sea and the Sea of Japan. The Yalu River marks North Korea's northern border with China. The island of Taiwan lies off the coast of China's Fujian province and Hong Kong is further south adjacent to Guangdong province. In terms of both landmass and population, all four are very small compared to China. East Asians other than the Chinese and to a lesser extent the North Koreans are now substantially urbanised, and only a minority engage in agriculture and fishing; in Hong Kong, this is a tiny minority. Hong Kong and Taiwan are densely populated with a small landmass and mountainous terrain; the mountains also make much of the land unsuitable for industrial or agricultural use. The harsh climate on the Korean peninsula, especially in the north, combined with a lack of arable land, means that large quantities of food have to be imported. Geographical proximity has long enhanced economic and other contacts between the countries of East Asia and also, most importantly, with Japan. However, political differences have at certain times severely curtailed these relations, especially those that arose out of the Cold War. Other factors that also contribute somewhat to the definition of the region are ethnicity and culture.

The ethnic composition of China and Hong Kong is predominantly Chinese, as were the anti-communists who fled the mainland for Taiwan after the 1949 Communist victory. This group came to dominate the politics and economy of the island, and it is only recently that native Taiwanese have started to take prominent political positions. In both North and South Korea over 99% of the people are ethnically Korean; there are tiny minorities of Chinese, Japanese, and other foreigners. Chinese characters are used and understood throughout most of the region, but in Korea governments have actively promoted the use of the Native Korean alphabet, *hangul*.

Of more significance than ethnicity *per se* have been the Confucian values and ideals that some scholars argue have functioned throughout the region as a fundamental spur to economic development in a way similar to the Protestant ethic in Western Europe after the Reformation.

Features of Development

The East Asian region, with the exception of North Korea, has generally experienced remarkable levels of economic growth since 1945. The 1950s was essentially a decade of recovery from the ravages of war and preparation for modernization. However, even during the 1950s Taiwan and Hong Kong began to show tangible signs of economic vitality. The process was somewhat delayed in South Korea by the effects of the Korean War (1950–1953), but from the 1960s to the first half of the 1990s all three countries achieved annual gross domestic product (GDP) growth rates approaching 10%. For the region as a whole GDP growth during the four decades from 1960 averaged over 7%. The mid-1980s witnessed extraordinary growth rates. In 1986, for example, Taiwan's GDP grew by 18%, South Korea's by 13%, and Hong Kong's by 12%. However, there were marked disparities within the region. This can be illustrated most vividly by comparing North and South Korea.

The North Korean economy grew strongly during the 1950s due to vigorous industrial development, but its economy has generally stagnated since then, and especially since the early 1990s. South Korea depended heavily on American aid and technical assistance to recover from the devastation of the Pacific and Korean Wars. By 1960 the GDP of both North and South was less than $5 billion. From the 1960s onwards, however, the North Korean performance faltered due to its inward-looking policies and excessive defence expenditure. Its problems were aggravated further by several severe floods and droughts in the mid-1990s that curtailed agricultural production and even resulted in large-scale famines. The end of the Soviet Union in the early 1990s was followed by reduced aid and trade. North Korea remains a poor country with low growth and a generally isolationist communist party which has taken only tentative steps in the direction of China's comprehensive economic reforms. In stark contrast, South Korea embarked on an ambitious export drive in the 1960s. High levels of American aid initially supported this, but in the following decades investment and technology from the USA and Japan and easy access to foreign markets, especially that of the United States, have accounted substantially for the rapid growth of the South Korean economy. In 1999, North Korea's GDP was $22 billion, compared with $625 billion in the South.

China's sustained economic boom began after the post-Mao reforms started to take effect in the late 1970s and early 1980s. The enormous potential of China was highlighted in 1984–1985 when GDP growth rates approached 25%; they have averaged 10% over the last twenty-five years.

The pattern of regional post-war growth has broadly followed that set by Japan. The first stage involved the use of cheap labor in textile and simple manufactures, most of which were exported to the West, with the US being the major export market. This was followed by the development of heavy industries such as ship building and petrochemicals. Thirdly was the venture into more sophisticated manufacturing such as automobiles and complex machinery. Finally, there have most recently been moves into advanced areas like biotechnology, computers, and information technology. Of the East Asians, South Korea and Taiwan followed this model about a decade behind Japan and did so quite closely; Hong Kong has not been able to pursue the more ambitious industrial visions due to economies of scale; North Korea's abiding insularity has meant that its progress has been minimal and slow; and finally, China's opening up since the demise of Mao has been so profound and aggressive that all of these steps have been hastened and condensed such that there have been many achievements on all these fronts at the same time.

Hong Kong, Taiwan, and South Korea are the three capitalist countries in the region. In general, their economic, political, and social development began before China's and North Korea's and has generally been more consistently sustained. Nevertheless, within the capitalist and communist 'blocs' there are significant differences. Hong Kong remained a British colony until 1997 when sovereignty reverted to China but under a 'one country, two systems' formula according to which Hong Kong will retain a *laissez-faire* economy until 2047. The belated democratic reforms of the British in the early 1990s were reversed by Peking after July 1997, but the importance of Hong Kong as a financial center and entrepot suggest that the CCP will be reluctant to interfere with the island's economy. Taiwan and South Korea gained independence from Japanese colonialism shortly after the war and have remained pro-Western and capitalist since then. However, both had authoritarian right-wing governments until the 1980s; their strong economic growth from the 1960s onwards was accompanied by frequent abuses of human rights and the repression of political dissidents. China and North Korea became one-party communist states shortly after the Pacific War and remain so to this day. Challenges to the status quo such as the Hundred Flowers Campaign in 1956 and the mass protests in Tiananmen Square in 1989 were harshly suppressed.

With the exception of South Korea, the region was largely insulated from the effects of the 1997 Asian financial crisis. Nevertheless, it brought the regional average growth rate for the 1990s down to 5%. The currency crisis that started in Thailand in July 1997 affected South Korea profoundly due to the combination of the following: exposure to high levels of very nervous short-term foreign debt, productive overcapacity, an overvalued currency that reduced the competitiveness of its exports, and a financial system that lacked transparency. This combination of factors existed in no other country in the region. China maintained controls on the outward movement of foreign capital and had not linked the *yuan* to the appreciating US dollar. China has continued with very strong growth, broadening and deepening its relations with the rest of the world especially in the areas of trade, investment, finance, technology, and education, and there has also been a modest degree of social liberalization. Capitalist East Asia has recently had good but not outstanding growth, substantial democratisation, and far-reaching regional and global integration. Along with the growth of the middle class and the end of cheap labor, these factors suggest that South Korea, Taiwan, and Hong Kong have become mature economies where sustained high growth can no longer be expected.

There has been significant social development throughout the region. Despite substantial population growth over the last fifty years, there have been large reductions in poverty levels. This has been especially notable in Hong Kong, Taiwan, and South Korea, and over the last two decades, in the vibrant coastal regions of southern China. The whole region has seen remarkable improvements in educational opportunities and attainments, including literacy and numeracy. Access to and success in higher education has also improved; these have enhanced the quality of life of individuals as well as contributing to overall economic development. Progress has also been made with population control. More educational and occupational opportunities for females have resulted in later marriage and lower fertility. The rights of women have been widely promoted although laws protecting these rights are often not adequately enforced.

The speed of the region's transformation has had negative side-effects. Modernisation, and especially industrialisation, required rapid urbanisation to bring workers from rural areas to the cities to work in factories and offices. This has been accompanied by many different forms of pollution, the breakdown of traditional support structures, and the *anomie* and stress characteristic of modern city life. Death from overwork has long been noted in Japan along with very severe psychological problems in increasing numbers of school children due to the competitive pressures to succeed. Some argue that these are the inevitable costs of progress. Such problems have also started to appear throughout East Asia. For example, fifty-five hour working weeks are not at all unusual in South Korea. Although the burgeoning middle class has been important in demanding political reforms from the region's authoritarian governments, this class's high levels of consumption have aggravated problems of urban congestion and environmental pollution. This vignette illustrates the more general point that the great achievements of East Asian development have been accompanied by problems and dangers whose severity and incidence have been exacerbated by the very fast pace of economic development.

Explaining East Asian Development

Understanding and explaining the successes and failures of East Asia has not been easy. Different scholars highlight different aspects of the East Asian experience and this leads to a host of divergent explanatory models. Some but by no means all of these aspects are the high quality of the political leadership, cooperation between government and business, commitment to free market economics and cultural features such as Confucianism, and the values and attitudes it has promoted. As each model has at least some merit, consideration will be given to all of these factors. Scholars will continue to dispute the relative weight of these factors.

The following discussion highlights the major factors but also the fact that their importance varied in different parts of the region. Moreover, there are often close connections between different kinds of factors. For example, the propensity to save, (arguably a Confucian value) rather than consume, was reinforced by government policies to encourage high levels of domestic saving. These funds were often made available at very low interest rates to firms—usually very large firms—that governments had decided to support. This example suggests how economics, politics, and culture have been closely interwoven in East Asian development.

The whole region suffered from the effects of colonialism and imperialism. The British colonised Hong Kong during the nineteenth century and Japan did the same in Taiwan (1895) and Korea (1910). From the demise of the Qing dynasty in 1911 until the end of the Pacific War, China was wracked by civil conflict and foreign intervention. After victory in the 1895 Sino-Japanese war, Japan increasingly exploited the Chinese. With the substantial exception of mainland China, the colonial legacy was mixed. In Hong

Kong the British promoted educational opportunities and trade and established systems of law and public administration that encouraged the emergence of a flourishing entrepot. The industrialization of Taiwan and the Korean peninsula began when they were colonies of the Japanese. For example, essential infrastructure including roads, railways, electricity, and irrigation systems were built and educational and work opportunities expanded. Japanese rule also destroyed the aura of both Western invincibility and of the indigenous, landed elites, and this paved the way for multi-faceted post-colonial changes. Although the British and Japanese rulers were the main beneficiaries of colonialism their contribution to the framework of postcolonial development was significant. The Pacific War itself (1941–1945) caused enormous damage and suffering, yet it also propitiously hastened the end of colonialism in East Asia.

North Korea inherited the vast bulk of the modern infrastructure built up during Japanese rule as well as most of the peninsula's mineral and energy resources. These benefits provided a solid foundation for its strong growth performance during the 1950s but they could not compensate in the long term for the institutional weaknesses and policy mistakes that increasingly afflicted the country from the 1970s onward.

In China, both Koreas, and Taiwan, radical land reform programs were implemented in the early post-war years. Broadly speaking this resulted in either expropriation of land or its purchase at low prices from the wealthy, traditional landlords. This broke the power of the backward-looking traditional elites, whose role was taken over by new rulers who aspired to achieve development through modernisation. These new governments were therefore much freer to pursue modernising programs. These reforms also led to more equitable distributions of wealth and income and this in turn contributed to the defusion of rural discontent and the legitimacy of the post-war authoritarian governments. The introduction of modern machinery and farming techniques reduced the demand for rural labor. This surplus labor could at least partly alleviate the labor shortages that soon arose with the incipient industrial boom in the large cities and urban centers.

Under the 1950 Agrarian Reform Law in China, land owned by the gentry and rich landlords was expropriated and distributed amongst poor peasants. Gains in productivity were marginal however as the average size of holdings of the 300 million peasants was one-third of an acre. The next step involved the collectivisation of agriculture; this proved to be a disaster. As there were no incentives for individuals to work hard, people chose to do the bare minimum required and productivity plummeted as a result. In the early 1960s, collectivisation also resulted in terrible famines. Collectivisation was only reversed as a part of the post-Mao reforms, so that farmers can now grow produce and sell it on open markets after providing a certain amount to the state as taxation.

Land reform was associated with endeavours to increase the productivity of agricultural labor, through mechanisation for example. The drop in demand for rural labor meant that many peasants moved to the cities to work in the newly burgeoning factories where incomes were often higher and more reliable.

In the early post-war years low-cost labor gave East Asia a strong competitive advantage over many other countries. Cheap labor drew in investment capital from the US, Europe, and, later, Japan. However, not only was labor cheap, it was also highly disciplined, flexible, enthusiastic, and well-trained. It was really the combination of all of these factors and not just the low cost of labor that made East Asia successful in both industrial and post-industrial development but also made the region so attractive to foreign investors. This also meant that in the early stages priority was given to labor- rather than capital-intensive industries. As both government and private savings and capital increased, so did the capacity to purchase sophisticated technologies and machinery from abroad. These gradually came to contribute increasingly to the economic power of the region, a process that was encouraged by the energy and drive to succeed of workers, management, government, and investors. However, the development process resulted in wage rises—in both absolute and relative terms—so that now China alone clearly remains a low-wage country. The fact that regional productivity and competitiveness has been so strong has nevertheless substantially offset the effects of higher wages.

The Cold War was the overarching international conflict that provided the broad framework within which East Asian development occurred up to the 1970s, and in a more diluted sense, up to the end of the 1980s. The West, and most importantly the US, regarded Japan, South Korea, Taiwan, and Hong Kong as bulwarks in Asia against communist expansion. The colonial British government retained control of and responsibility for Hong Kong until 1997. On the other hand, the Soviet Union saw China and North Korea as bastions of communism in Asia.

The Americans tried to ensure that their allies in the region would not succumb to communist influence or force and various steps were taken to this end. Troops were stationed in South Korea and Taiwan to protect these countries from attack by communist aggressors; substantial amounts of foreign aid were provided to South Korea and Taiwan during the 1950s; land reform was encouraged to defuse rural discontent and promote a fairer distribution of income and wealth; American markets were opened up to exports from the region; and American investment, technologies, and management skills were also readily made available. These measures collectively provided an enormous boost to capitalist East Asia, especially in the early post-war years. Most South Koreans, Taiwanese, and Hong Kong people were anti-communist, so they willingly accepted assistance from the West in the effort to contain communism. The Vietnam War provided a significant boost to East Asian industries as they provided many of the goods, materials, and services needed by the American military during that decade-long conflict.

Both China and North Korea were supported in different ways by the Soviet Union in the early post-war years. Soviet technicians and scientists were sent to China to help with heavy industrial projects and Chinese efforts to develop nuclear weapons. This support was substantially reduced due to the Sino-Soviet dispute of the early 1960s. Support from China and the USSR contributed to North Korea's good growth performance during the 1950s. However, the warming of relations between the US and China in the early 1970s, the reforms of the post-Mao era from the late 1970s, and especially the demise of the Soviet Union ten years later eroded the military, financial, and technical support provided to North Korea by the two communist giants.

Although North Korea and China have substantial natural resources that have contributed to their development, the opposite is true of the rest of the region. For this reason South Korea, Taiwan, and Hong Kong had to rely upon the skills, knowledge, initiative, and nous of their people as the keys to survival and growth. Huge sums of money were invested in education and training programs so that a skilled labor force was created that could supply goods and services to overseas markets to earn the money necessary to buy the food, raw materials, and energy that could not be produced domestically.

Strong political leadership and effective, intelligent bureaucrats have made important contributions to economic growth. This leadership has taken different forms. Until the 1980s, all of the East Asian governments were authoritarian at best and dictatorial at worst. In Hong Kong until 1997, the British colonial government ruled with little internal opposition and few demands for democratic reform from the commercially oriented population. Pro-Western military rulers dominated in South Korea until the 1980s and the right-wing Kuomintang dominated Taiwan's political scene for most of the post-war period. China's

communist party has retained a solid hold on political power since 1949 but it has presided over pro-Western and pro-market reforms since the late 1970s.

Development depends upon the existence of a reasonable level of political stability. In capitalist East Asia up to the late 1970s, this has been provided by authoritarian governments (or the British colonial government in the case of Hong Kong). Some scholars have argued that before these countries could aspire to achieve democracy and vibrant civil societies, a reasonably high level of economic development and welfare was essential. The apparent acquiescence of most of the public in these countries in the first three post-war decades supports this notion. East Asian authoritarian governments were not just strong. Unlike authoritarian governments in most of the developing world, the governments in East Asia were effective and remarkably free of corruption. The ever-present if usually latent threats from China and North Korea have also contributed to the apparent acceptance of authoritarian rule in capitalist East Asia.

A high level of co-operation between government and big business was apparent in most of East Asia; the partial exception to this was Hong Kong. South Korea, following the model set by Japan, created institutions in which planning and consultation for economic development were pursued jointly by government and business. This meant that time and effort were not wasted in the resolution of disputes between the two and that each was committed to a broad common vision as long as this did not conflict with the basic interests of each side. Consultation and discussion generally ensured that this common vision and co-incidence of interests was achieved. However, even though governments had the stronger hand in these institutions and often gently directed policy through 'administrative guidance' measures, politicians knew that taking a confrontational position in dealing with business could ultimately be to their own detriment as well as adversely affecting development generally. There were two distinguishing features of the East Asian situation. First, businesses were generally not protected from market forces, and in particular, they could not ignore international price signals. Second, in general governments did not allow or encourage the creation of monopolies. The main exception to this was if a vital national interest was seen to override the economic benefits of competition. Both of these features ensured that competitive pressures and market forces ensured the maintenance of efficiency, profitability, and productivity.

South Korea came to build up and rely on a small number of very large industrial conglomerates known as *chaebols*. Political and business leaders realised that in many lucrative activities large size was essential to achieve economies of scale. As a result there was a high level of consultation and cooperation between government, the bureaucracy, and business in setting and achieving the goals involved in industrial development.

East Asian governments created meritocratic bureaucracies that were very effective in implementing government policies and plans. These bureaucracies had the considerable advantage of being largely insulated from public scrutiny and criticism and the demands of narrowly based interest groups. Unlike the situation in many Western countries, the civil service was highly respected and many of the top university graduates moved into its most powerful and important parts. Not only were these graduates socially respected and quite highly paid, they also saw themselves as important players in their countries' nation-building projects. For all of these reasons the selfless pursuit of the public interest was very common in East Asia, unlike much of the rest of the developing world, where corruption was rampant. Meritocracy also was the main principle in the education system.

However, the growth of the middle class and increasingly well-educated populations that had travelled abroad and witnessed the achievements of Europe and the US meant that the depoliticisation of the public could not be sustained in the long term. This is certainly the case in South Korea and Taiwan; the ruling communist parties in North Korea and China look very strong at present but the Tiananmen Square protests of 1989 show that challenges are possible.

Macroeconomic stability has been a significant factor in East Asian economic growth. The maintenance of low inflation and sustainable levels of debt, and especially foreign debt, have distinguished East Asia from most of the developing world. Taiwan, China, and Hong Kong have been the most successful in this; their large foreign exchange reserves helped to protect them from the worst effects of the 1997 Asian financial crisis. In contrast, South Korea had to be rescued by the IMF due to its inability to pay its foreign creditors when very large short-term loans were called in as the 'contagion' of the crisis began to spread. North Korea has been in states of stagnation or crisis over the last two decades partly because it has not been able to achieve the kind of macroeconomic stability that has characterised most of the region.

In the early post-war period, policies of import replacement and protection of local industry were implemented to nurture economies that were recovering from war and civil turmoil and that were struggling to establish economic and political stability. South and North Korea and China relied heavily on such policies. The greater success of more open and less restricted countries such as Hong Kong and Taiwan led eventually to the phasing out of import replacement along with tariffs and quotas to protect local industry. The worst effect of the latter policies was that protection made improvements in competitiveness and productivity very hard to achieve, so that consumers often paid high prices by international standards for goods produced in protected sectors.

Export-led growth from the early 1960s followed the short period of import replacement after the war. South Korea, Taiwan, and Hong Kong took advantage of open foreign markets, especially that of the US. All had relatively small domestic markets and a paucity of natural resources—in order to buy essential imports a successful export strategy was vital. China also gave increasing attention to the importance of exports from the late 1970s, and its continuing commitment to open trade was indicated by its recent admission to the WTO.

Traditionally civil society and the protection of individual human rights have been weak compared with the power of the state in East Asia. This weakness was reflected in the priority given to social and group interests over those of individuals and the ready acceptance of and respect for social hierarchy and the structures of rule and subordination that these embodied. The emergence of a docile and obedient labor force during the post-war years was made much easier by strength of these values and mores. From the 1950s to the 1970s, the workforce was usually willing to endure comparatively low wages, poor work conditions, and long hours to ensure the success of businesses, the competitiveness of their products on world markets, and the promotion of the national interest. Thrift and financial prudence are also often regarded as Confucian values that have promoted the high domestic savings rates that characterise East Asian societies.

Scholars such as Peter Berger argue that Confucian values, including respect for authority, collective solidarity, diligence, thrift, respect for education and learning, and meritocracy, contributed to the remarkable successes of East Asian development. Berger argues that the region provides a *sui generis* developmental model that is quite distinct from the Western pattern. A contrasting argument is that institutional structures and good policymaking and implementation are far more significant than cultural values and norms. Furthermore, China's development was retarded by its adherence to collectivism and state control until the late 1970s, and this remains the case in North Korea. Max Weber argued that Confucianism was backward looking and too contemptuous of trade and commerce to spur economic activity in a way similar to the Protestant ethic in the West. However, the significance of all cultural phenomena including bodies of thought like Confucianism changes over time. It is very likely that there was a substantial consonance between Confucian values and the institutions and policies that help to account for East Asia's successes. These values provided the motivation on both individual and social levels for many of the economic, social, and political achievements of East Asia. This remains the case even if the religious foundation for the values disintegrates or is combined with other sources. For example, Christianity became very influential in South Korea after the war but its people remained extremely hard-working and conscientious.

East Asia faces enormous challenges. Economic growth must be maintained to achieve reasonable living standards but it is also essential to protect the natural and human environment. Over the last fifty years the extent of environmental degradation of the air, rivers, seas, and land and the loss of biodiversity in the region indicates a lack of balance, planning, and comprehensive vision in the development process. The welfare of future generations within the region and beyond it depends upon the prompt and substantial rectification of these shortcomings.

CHRIS CONEY

See also China, People's Republic of; East Asia: International Relations; Hong Kong; Korea, North; Korea, South; Taiwan

References and Further Reading

Berger, Peter and Hsiao, Hsin-Huang, editors. *In Search of an East Asian Development Model.* New Brunswick and New Jersey: Transaction Publishers, 1988.

Borthwick, Mark, with contributions by selected scholars. *Pacific Century: The Emergence of Modern Pacific Asia.* Boulder, CO: Westview Press, 1998.

Chowdury, A. and Islam, I. *The Newly Industrialising Economies of East Asia.* London and New York: Routledge, 1993.

Leipziger, Danny and Vinod, Thomas. *Lessons of East Asia: An Overview of Country Experience.* Washington, DC: The World Bank, 1993.

Lingle, Christopher. *The Rise and Decline of the Asian Century: False Starts on the Path to the Global Millennium.* Hong Kong: Asia 2000, 1997.

Mackerras, Colin, editor. *Eastern Asia: An Introductory History.* 3rd edition. Frenchs Forest, Sydney: Pearson Education Australia, 2000.

McLeod, Ross and Garnaut, Ross, editors. *East Asia in Crisis: From Being a Miracle to Needing One?* London and New York: Routledge, 1998.

Sung-Joo, Han, editor. *Changing Values in Asia: Their Impact on Governance and Development.* Singapore: Institute of Southeast Asian Studies, 1999.

The East Asian Miracle: Economic Growth and Public Policy, A World Bank Policy Research Report. Oxford and New York: Oxford University Press, 1993.

Tipton, Frank. *The Rise of Asia: Economics, Society and Politics in Contemporary Asia.* Melbourne: Macmillan Education Australia, 1998.

Vogel, Ezra. *The Four Little Dragons: The Spread of Industrialization in East Asia.* Cambridge, MA: Harvard University Press, 1991.

EAST ASIA: INTERNATIONAL RELATIONS

While economic interdependence can serve as a catalyst for reshaping international relations in East Asia, unresolved border disputes, confrontations on the Korean peninsula, fears of an arms race, national self-interests, lingering historical animosities, sharp inequalities, and a difference in economic systems are rendered obstacles to regional cooperation. At the same time the region increasingly grapples with such issues as environmental pollution, human rights abuses, and repression of ethnic minorities.

Regional Order

In the Northeast Asian security complex comprising the United States, China, Russia, Japan, and a divided Korea and Taiwan, the interests of major powers have long been interwoven. The pendulum has swayed between good and poor relationships in the bilateral and multilateral interactions with elements of rivalry and cooperation. As cyclical patterns of amity and enmity forge new alliances within the region, relative power balances have been changing in the evolving international environment.

Whereas international relations in East Asia during the Cold War period were heavily influenced by the US-Soviet dynamic, the post–Cold War transformation has shifted towards intra-regional relations with reduction in the layering of conflict involving outside powers. Intra-regional tension has been focused on the Korean peninsula and China-Taiwan. Political complexity presented by two divided states affects political and strategic calculations of major powers.

Once the weight of US-Soviet rivalry was lifted, a more diversified set of cooperative and competitive relations shaped multidirectional patterns of Northeast Asian geopolitics. The Sino-Russian border demarcation process created a new environment for regional cooperation in 1991–1992 (following a series of high-level contacts, starting with the Sino-Russian summit). On the other hand, disputes over the Kuril Islands and adjacent territories still linger over Russo-Japanese relations, although they are mostly symbolic and historical, without much strategic and economic significance. Political relations in the sub-region are still viewed as volatile and unbalanced. Increasing Chinese military posture and force projection capabilities are seen as threats by other regional powers. The nationalist views of Japanese politicians and their military build-up provoke historic fears of Japanese militarism in East Asia.

In the absence of international peace agreements in the Korean peninsula, North Korea has been left out of diplomatic relations in Northeast Asia following the demise of the Soviet Union and Chinese recognition of South Korea without the reciprocal recognition of Pyongyang by the United States and Japan. Differences remain between North Korea and the United States on the issues of long-range missiles and nuclear weapons. North Korea's long-range missile development programs have become part of the Asia Pacific security equation since the August 1998 launching test of a three-stage Taepodong missile over Japan generated discussion about missile proliferation. The US/North Korean tension was somewhat eased with North Korea's agreement to dismantle its existing nuclear programs, but the agreement has to be implemented through the establishment of a formalized mechanism such as the Korean Peninsula Energy Development Organization.

The trans-Pacific axis has been complementing multidirectional intra-Asian relationships. American preparedness is affected by the shift in the balance of power in Northeast Asia brought about by a series of Chinese initiatives to modernize its military forces. A United States balancing role would be required because of the fear of dominant powers such as China and Russia along with high levels of conflict in the Korean peninsula and the Taiwan Strait.

With the presence of American military bases in Far East Asia, Japan maintains a strategic relationship with the United States while recasting priorities in exerting its influence in Asia. In the absence of any collective defense mechanism like the North Atlantic Treaty Organization, Japan and the Republic of Korea have maintained their respective bilateral alliances with the United States for the past five decades without developing trilateral alliance among the three. The dominance of the United States in the region obviated the need for multilateral military cooperation.

As the United States continues to remain involved in the region, Sino-American political relations can be complicated by various factors. A variety of outstanding political and economic disputes would not be solved in the year ahead despite the United States agreement with China's World Trade Organization (WTO) entry in November 1999. The question of human rights casts a dark cloud over the prospects for improved relations.

US/China relations can also be thought of in terms of their triangular relationships with Japan. The United States and Japan are cooperating for missile defense technology research and development despite being opposed by China. The debates in the United States to offer Taiwan more defense commitment increase tension in the China/US relationship. The emergence of a hegemonic alliance in Northeast Asia can generate Chinese fear of being isolated.

The Strategic Environment

In uncertain alliance relationships, a strategic environment is beset by suspicion and distrust. The military build-up has been driven by uncertainty instead of concrete threats. Any increase in the military capabilities of one country is viewed as a potential threat by its neighbors and rivals, often prompting them to build up their own forces as well. The strategic environment in East Asia is complicated by a lack of regional arms control or disarmament pacts. We are witnessing the emergence of significant arms races in the Asia-Pacific region.

Despite the general relaxation of military tensions in many areas of the world with the end of the Cold War, military spending by East Asian countries has significantly increased across the board. Global military spending was falling from a peak of $1.3 trillion in 1987 to $840 billion in 1994; contrary to this trend, across the region of East Asia, military expenditures went up from an average of $126 billion per year in the 1984–1988 period to $142 billion annually in 1992–1994. These increased military allocations were devoted to strengthening and modernizing the existing armed forces and to acquiring new capabilities for power projection as well as building up domestic capabilities to manufacture modern weapons.

The rise in military spending in East Asia (made possible by increased wealth with success of their exports) is, in part, related to the persistence of regional disputes. These arms races could pose a substantial threat to both regional and international security. Promoting mutual security requires transparency measures such as provision of conventional arms data, regular meetings of defense officials, and exchange of visits of military personnel.

East Asia lacks the deeply rooted security institutions (for example, the Organization for Security and Cooperation in Europe) which provide a multilateral framework to resolve regional disputes. Regional security can be undermined by disagreements over the control of offshore territories in the East and South China Seas. China and South Korea both claim a continental shelf with unresolved boundaries involving basins with good petroleum potential. There is a new need for rules, codes of conduct, and harmonization of domestic practices to deal with the sovereignty disputes over Exclusive Economic Zones (EEZs).

Northeast Asian countries have started a bilateral security dialogue at the fringes of the Asia-Pacific Economic Forum and other multilateral meetings. Despite the stress on broader regional dialogues at private levels, a complex web of bilateral alliances and diplomatic arrangements has not been aggregated into multilateral structures. China has been traditionally skeptical of multilateral approaches to security, preferring bilateral interaction with its neighbors which allows them to take an advantage of one-on-one negotiation. On the other hand, Russia is more enthusiastic with Northeast Asia multilateral security dialogues, being concerned about its exclusion from the Asia-Pacific security discourse.

Main impediments to sub-regional cooperation include nationalist jockeying for geopolitical advantage. Other forces involved in the division of the region encompass different political systems and levels of economic development as well as inadequate efforts to overcome the past legacy. A regional identity, shared senses of the past and future destiny, and transnational civil society have not yet emerged.

Economic Cooperation

The region has exhibited an economic dynamism even with the experience of slow growth rates of recent years resulting from the Asian financial crisis of 1997–1999. National income has risen in recent decades as a result of their success in promoting economic growth through export-oriented industrialization. Economic interdependence has been a major trend in the post–Cold War Asia-Pacific region, with a dramatic increase in trade between China and Japan, and between Korea and Taiwan. While the United States serves as the biggest market for consumer goods manufactured in Asia, Japan has provided loans, technology, and investment. The region's economy has been dominated by Japan's trade surplus with other countries in the region, far exceeding that with other countries.

Russia has been cultivating relations with China and South Korea, since Western aid has not been enough to draw Russia out of its economic slump. Hopes of fruitful integration of the periphery economies of the Far East region with the Pacific Rim arise from the opening of the Sino-Russian border to trade and investment. Russia retains control over natural resources and Soviet-era industries while depending on the East Asian Pacific Rim for food and consumer goods. Economic cooperation in the border areas of North Korea, Russia, and China was discussed through the Tumen River Area Development Plan (1992–1994) and its successor, the Tumen River Economic Development Area (1994).

Significance in the economic realm has an impact on the political dimensions of major power relations. Most Northeast Asian governments now accord a higher priority to maximizing wealth, and their increasing economic interdependence makes outright conflict too costly. Economic considerations (e.g., the operation of East Asian capitalist markets) can result in a more predictable and less antagonistic foreign policy behavior.

The sub-region has discussed numerous ideas for multilateral measures, including a regional development bank, an economic development zone, energy and environmental cooperation. While most people agree that the flourishing commerce in the region provides a further potential of growing into more formal cooperation in the future, Northeast Asia has not yet espoused economic and political integration comparable to the magnitude of the European Union and the creation of regional institutions and interactions along the Southeast Asia lines. Shared interests in regional cooperation have not been translated into reality due to political differences and a lack of infrastructure. Regionalism most strongly manifests in the economic realm with the decline of ideology offset by diverging values and perceptions along with the emerging nationalism.

China's Economic Rise

The size of China's market and the rate of economic expansion put the country in a strong position to change the regional economic dynamics. China's development strategy combines market forces and an oppressive authoritarian government with the promise of private wealth. China has gone through transition from a socialist, planned economy to development of private economic sectors and markets.

High growth has been made possible by cheap docile labor and a high level of foreign investment. In competition for investments, China received the lion's share of the total investments poured into East Asia.

China has great advantages in labor-intensive exports through cheap labor with the repression of any attempts for organizing trade unions. China's low-cost production exerted a tremendous pressure on export industries of neighboring countries in an international market. Southeast Asian countries engaged in the garment-exporting industry and other light industries have steadily lost out in the competition. The competitive economic threat from China is expected to have an impact on more industrially advanced countries, in particular, Japan, South Korea, and Taiwan, as China plans to move beyond the exports of toys, clothes, and other low-tech products. Such products as electronics, cars, ships, chemicals, and steel can erode manufacturing bases of the neighboring countries. Countries which do not have technical prowess are, in particular, vulnerable to China, which is a much lower-cost producer. While China is regarded as a major competitor, it is also seen as a source of joint ventures and as a partner in regional growth. In a show of tripartite economic cooperation, Korea, China, and Japan developed formal forums for trade and finance ministers as well as a business forum to be attended by key business organizations and industrialists from the three countries. It deals with such issues as trade promotion and monetary and other macroeconomic policy coordination. China plans to expand its influence in Southeast Asia through creating a regional free trade area within the decade. As one of the largest trading countries, China entered the World Trade Organization (WTO) following fifteen years of participating in free trade negotiations. The difficult negotiations reflect concerns with its poor treatment of labor, including unpaid prison labor and forbidding organization of unions.

Since low wages and poor labor protection have driven China's surge as an export power, many countries regard poor treatment of Chinese labor as unfair advantage. Undertaking all the obligations to comply with WTO rules and disciplines means opening up China's market to international competition, lowering its industrial and agricultural tariffs, limiting subsidies, and liberalizing foreign investment norms in telecommunications, insurance, and banking services. There is a general hope that the labor standard would improve with the system of international regulations governing free trade. In addition, some argue that the onset of a domestic free market could release the momentum for the democratization of Chinese society as well as free economic entrepreneurship.

Human Rights Conditions

The worst human rights conditions are reported in China and North Korea, which were accused of arbitrary detention, torture, and executions. The authorities in those countries have carried out a serious crackdown on peaceful dissent. According to various international human rights reports, arbitrary detention and torture of criminal suspects and convicted prisoners are common and widespread across the country. Most executions take place after sentencing rallies in front of massive crowds in sports stadiums and public squares. Prisoners are also paraded through the streets past thousands of people on the way to execution by firing squad in nearby fields or courtyards.

In the case of China, economic reform in China moved ahead without concurrent liberalization of a political process. Profound social and economic changes in the past twenty years have not made any impact on civil and political freedoms. Social divisions and alienation caused by continuing restrictions on basic rights stunt economic progress. Beijing signed two key international human rights conventions on political, civic, social, and economic rights in 1997 and 1998, but a broad range of people who seek their rights to freedom of expression or association were sentenced to long prison terms for subversion under sweeping national security provisions introduced in 1997.

Only a handful of tiny NGOs are allowed to exist, but they are kept on a tight rein. Ordinary citizens are not organized to provide any credible challenges to the government. The Chinese government routinely blocks websites of Western media outlets, human rights groups, Tibetan exiles, and other sources of information it deems politically sensitive or harmful. While promoting the Internet for commercial purposes, the government tries to control its political content.

There is no sign of any relaxation of the crackdown on fundamental freedoms nor a promise for improvement in the human rights situation, which has seriously deteriorated. Years have passed since the brutal killing of hundreds of unarmed citizens in Beijing who participated in the 1989 Tiananmen Square pro-democracy protests. The Chinese government still refers to the crackdown as a 'political incident' and argues (faced with the campaigns of the relatives of those killed for justice) that a 'counter-revolutionary riot' had to be crushed.

According to Amnesty International, the authorities have turned the clock backwards and created a new generation of prisoners of conscience, including those who raised a new range of issues, such as labor, the environment, and religious freedom. Many individuals are currently imprisoned solely for organizing free trade unions or strikes and simply for speaking out for livelihood issues. Some have been sent for re-education through labor camps or forcibly detained in psychiatric hospitals. Officials must approve religious practice; otherwise it is considered counter-revolutionary. More people are executed every year in China than in the rest of the world put together. For those sentenced during the 'Strike Hard' campaign, punishment was swift and ruthless. It was justified to tackle the serious economic crime situation before entry to WTO and the challenge of globalization.

Minority Issues in China

China includes fifty-five minority groups, amounting to 120 million inhabitants (almost ten percent of the population). Ethnic minorities, in particular, were subject to brutal suppression, with the common practice of torture and summary trials of political suspects. In particular, China's Islamic minorities have been almost invisible behind centuries of repression. Many political prisoners in the Xinjiang Uighur Autonomous Region have been executed, accused of separatism, religious activities, and a range of alleged violent crimes.

In Xinjiang, the Turkic-speaking Muslim Uighurs, identified strongly with their neighbors across the steppe, seek autonomy from Beijing. Since the region was annexed to China in 1950, it experienced ethnic brawling. Owing to its rich minerals, with one-third of China's oil resources, the government wanted to have a tight control over the region. Nuclear testing at Lop Nor, in 1964, by the Chinese government resulted in hundreds of thousands of deaths. For the recent years, the repression has been more severe, with the outlawing of Koranic schools since 1998.

The Beijing government has established a state of virtual apartheid; the industrial, bureaucratic, or top-level employment is overwhelmingly held by Han Chinese, while the Uighurs are concentrated in the agrarian sector. In addition, the state-sponsored policy for the relocation of Han Chinese into Xinjiang has dramatically changed the population mix, with the Uighur population shrinking from approximately 70% in 1950 to just 49% today. The situation is even bleaker with the planned migration of displaced Han Chinese after the Three Gorges Dam Project.

The international community has been silent about the crushing of Uighur independence aspirations due to Islamic association. The annual Shanghai Five summit organized in 1996 by China, Russia, and three secular Central Asian states (Tajikistan, Kazakhstan, and Kyrgystan) supported Beijing's position on national separatism and religious movements in Xinjiang. Due to repression, the prospect of peace in Xinjiang looks less likely than ever. The international 'war on terrorism' provided some justification for Beijing's eight-year crackdown on separatist Muslim movements.

The Status of Tibet and Mongolia

Chinese occupation of self-governing Tibet traces back to October 1950 with the dispatch of units of the Chinese army, but a complete control of Tibet by Beijing accompanied crushing the 1957 peaceful Tibetan revolt and flight of the Dalai Lama to India. Prior to the exile of the Tibetan leadership in Lhasa under the Dalai Lama, Beijing signed a seventeen-point agreement in May 1951. In the document, the Chinese leadership originally promised the preservation of the Buddhist religion, Tibetan lifestyles and traditional polity as well as its authorities, headed by the Dalai Lama and his Cabinet of Ministers. The past four decades observed the increasing integration of the territory and its people into Chinese political, economic, military, and demographic control with the influx of bureaucratic cadres, technical personnel, and troops along with Han Chinese settlers. In addition, Beijing closely regulates and monitors monastic activities and religious worship in Tibet. There is the real fear that Tibetan culture and religion will be obliterated by Chinese immigration.

In order to keep alive their hopes of returning to a freed homeland, Tibetans in exile, together with their Western supporters, have promoted the internationalization of the Chinese occupation of Tibet. These activities include lobbying, fund-raising events, concerts, and publication of books on Tibet and Tibetan Buddhism. Other activities involve the organization of meetings between the Dalai Lama and Western parliamentarians, as well as US presidents and congressional leaders.

While encouraging civil disobedience in response to oppression, the Tibetan government-in-exile has pursued political discussions with representatives of the Chinese government. The Dalai Lama already signaled his willingness to accept Chinese control over the defense and foreign relations of Tibet in exchange for a guarantee of basic human rights and genuine autonomy for the territory's people. The Chinese leadership did not respond to the proposal for limited authority, insisting that it is not genuine but a strategy for seeking independence.

Mongolia was fortunate to avoid Chinese annexation since the end of World War II, and has been successful in its struggle to keep its independence. In order to attract Western recognition and support, Mongolia adopted a conscious strategy of promoting democracy and human welfare in the post–Cold War international order. The Mongolian government carried out the country's first free elections in April 1990 replacing the unraveling of the old communist system. Mongolia began to attend regional forums on political and confidence building measures as part of efforts to circumvent Beijing's growing diplomatic influence and represent its security interests.

Mongolia is also seeking extended relations with Japan and South Korea through trade, investment, and aid while strengthening cultural, educational, and economic ties with Taiwan. At the same time, it has cultivated military ties with the United States, while being careful to manage nonalignment and balanced relations with its two immediate neighbors, Russia and China. In addition, the encroachment of mainstream Chinese culture and its increasing materialism is counteracted by actively enhancing local, native consciousness through a revival of its traditional Tibetan Lamaist faith and reverence for Genghis Khan.

Taiwanese Sovereignty

China-Taiwan remains a recurrent source of tension, international as well as domestic. Whereas most Taiwanese want to keep the statehood, China wants to pursue the path of the island's forcible integration into the mainland. Taiwan became a genuinely democratic country, surviving despite its diplomatic isolation. China regards Taiwan as an internal affair, but its attempts for coercive integration will provoke international legal, political, and moral opposition.

Although Taiwan's status in the international state system is ambiguous, it has been maintaining de facto statehood. Its international legal status was undermined with the successful diplomatic campaign of Beijing. Taiwan's diplomatic relations are limited to about thirty countries, mostly small states, although its cultural and economic relations are extensive. Taiwan began to lose its international status following Kissinger's grand strategic bargain to counterbalance the Soviet Union with mainland China in the early 1970s. During the Carter administration (more specifically, the end of 1978), the United States severed all formal diplomatic ties, "derecognizing" the

Taiwan-based government and accepting Beijing in its place as "the sole legal government of China."

Since then, Taiwan has embarked on the path of democratization to ameliorate political discontent in the middle class and help Taiwan break out of its increasing isolation after its exit from the United Nations (UN). In order to win international support needed to stand up to mainland China, Taiwan consolidated democratization through constitutional changes. Political liberalization not only enhanced the protection of human rights, but also guaranteed freedom of speech and press in Taiwan. Ethnic Taiwanese were actively recruited into the government and the Kuomintang Party, which used to be controlled mainly by those who fled from mainland Communist China in the late 1940s.

The cross-strait dialogue between Beijing and Taipei has not been easy, since the Taiwanese are not interested in unification with China in accordance with the One Country, Two Systems model insisted on by Beijing. The Chinese leadership has even threatened to invade Taiwan if the Taiwanese authorities continue to refuse to be reintegrated with the mainland and seek for the recognition of statehood. Beijing's determination has been supported by rising Chinese nationalism. The mainland grew increasingly aggressive in its efforts to force Taiwan to submit to its rule. In response to a visit by high-level politicians to the United States (such as the attendance of President Lee Teng-Hui at his graduate-school class reunion at Cornell University in 1995), Beijing reacted with furious denunciations followed by firing missiles into Taiwan's coastal waters. The same menacing gesture was also exhibited as the island's voters were preparing to go to the polls for the presidential election in the spring of 1996.

In response to the latter event, Washington was compelled to send two carrier battle groups as a token of United States disapproval and a warning against even more forceful Chinese action. The United States has helped the Taiwanese government develop a well-equipped military to reduce the gap with the mainland's largest standing army in the world. However, Taiwan's efforts to improve its relations with the United States were hampered by the Clinton administration's policy for a strategic partnership with Beijing.

In the foreseeable future, the isolation of Taiwan is likely to continue, and it would be difficult to regain de jure independence status. There are not enough votes in the UN to push for Taiwan's readmission in the world body. In spite of its occasional tiffs with China, the United States maintains a one-China policy by recognizing Beijing as the only government representing China and does not acknowledge Taiwan as a separate political entity. On the other hand, it has expressed a desire to see the issue of Taiwan resolved peacefully.

Taiwan may search for various ways to coexist with the mainland government. Taiwanese might be open to the idea of a federal China comprising the mainland, Taiwan, Tibet, and Hong Kong in a democratic structure with some common foreign and defense policies, but with complete internal autonomy and separately elected governments. However, the Chinese government has not accepted diversity and considers itself an integrated state entity.

The political identity of the Taiwanese people has moved away from that of China's mainland populace with the election of President Chen Shui-Bian in March 2000. The election ended the fifty-year rule of the Kuomintang Party (KMT), whose principal identity has been associated with a unified China. While the new president made relatively conciliatory gestures toward the mainland in order to avert an immediate crisis, his Democratic Progressive Party charter contains a commitment to Taiwanese independence.

A campaign for independent identity is represented by the reconceptualization of Taiwanese culture as having its own "pluralist, indigenous, and international" characteristics. Teaching Chinese history as a foreign subject is advocated along with the increase in teaching local Taiwanese languages in elementary school. It is in total contrast with the suppression of Taiwanese consciousness with the prohibition of local and aboriginal languages in schools and the showing of movies in any language other than the official Mandarin Chinese during KMT rule following the 1947 massacre of Taiwanese demonstrators.

The mobilization of Taiwanese consciousness is reflected in such concept as the "New Taiwanese." Taiwan is searching for a common identity transcending the traditional divide between native Taiwanese and mainlanders by encouraging people to identify with Taiwan. More importantly, the "New Taiwanese" concept underlines the emergence of a Taiwan identity separate from that of China and closely associated with Taiwan's homegrown democratic system. The democratic system in Taiwan is not negotiable, as it is a fundamental part of Taiwan's identity.

Japan's Legacy

Japan has not given serious thought to what can be done toward reconciliation with its neighbors while the resentment of Japan's past occupation lies deep below the surface in formal relations. Japan has not fully apologized for mistreating the neighboring populations under their occupation prior to the end of World War II. Occasional diplomatic tension was created by Japanese justification of destruction of neighboring countries. Relations between Japan and South Korea (most seriously affected by Japanese war campaigns) are at the lowest ebb, with the Japanese government's approval of history textbooks that omitted any mention of war crimes committed against the Korean population as well as Prime Minister Junichiro Koizumi's visit to Yasukuni Shrine in Tokyo (a symbol of Japan's imperial past).

In particular, it remains an international issue to compensate and make an apology to the "comfort women" who were victims of the Japanese military's highly organized system of sexual slavery throughout its occupied territories in the 1930s and 1940s. Of the two hundred thousand so-called comfort women, only a quarter survived their ordeal; many died of injuries, disease, madness, and suicide soon after they were forced into sex with Japanese troops. For years the ones who survived stayed silent with their marginal lives. Beginning in 1991, however, hundreds of elderly women from Korea, China, Taiwan, and the Philippines came forward demanding the Japanese government's acknowledgment of its responsibility, an apology, and reparations.

Despite a vigorous campaign of international protest following mass demonstrations in Korea and Taiwan, Japan has not officially accepted the responsibility, though the Japanese prime minister offered unofficial apologies in 1995. A small fund to be financed on a voluntary basis by business was set up to help the women, but the Hiroshima high court overturned a modest award to three Korean women later. In addition, a popular comic-book history of Japan alleges that the comfort women were volunteers. Any mention of the government's role in the comfort-woman program has been widely ignored by the Japanese public.

The Inter-Korean Talks

The relations between North and South Korea have been affected by the legacy of the Korean War. The country was originally divided by American and Russian troops occupying the peninsula following World War II. The situation on the Korean peninsula has been affected by the nature of bilateral relationships with neighboring powers. Currently, thirty-seven thousand United States military troops are stationed in South Korea to help thwart any possible military action from the North. South Korea, Japan, and the United States have coordinated their policies toward North Korea.

The *Sunshine Policy* of reconciliation promoted by South Korean President Kim Dae-Jung represents efforts for a gradual easing of tensions with Pyongyang. South/North Korea relations have been improving following a historic visit of the South Korean President to the North in June 2000. Based on the Inter-Korean Joint Declaration, limited family visits were allowed, and there have been indications of more restrained military behavior from Pyongyang. In addition to further discussions about the reunion of divided families, meetings of the inter-Korean economic cooperation committee along with inter-Korean ministerial talks were held to search for closer economic ties.

The North-South Korean peace process produced a joint pledge to resume building a railway to join the two halves of the divided peninsula through the direct route across the 38th parallel, closed for fifty years. Work financed by the South will also start on an industrial zone in Kaesong near the South Korean border. Hyundai's tourism project involving ship cruises to the North's scenic Kumgang Mountains was encouraged by the government. The North also recently made a request for electricity needed to revive its crippled economy.

Such events as the inter-Korean summit of June 2000 clearly stimulated joint efforts for forward movement in the stalled inter-Korean relations. The younger generation of North Korean leadership following the death of Kim Il Sung has pursued more pragmatic approaches. However, Pyongyang is reluctant to quickly implement an early reunion for separated families at a certain permanent facility and free exchange of letters owing to concerns for their political implications. Inter-Korean talks for reconciliation and exchanges have not resulted in a dramatic breakthrough in the security arenas, and concrete actions have not been taken to replace the current armistice system on the Korean peninsula. Given lingering suspicion, North-South Korea talks have been slow, and a reciprocal visit to South Korea by the North Korean President has not been yet scheduled.

The conditions for reconciliation have further deteriorated due to the reluctance of the United States administration to be engaged in a dialogue with North Korea, reversing a high-level contact between the United States and North Korea during the Clinton administration. While a peaceful reunification is desirable, a sudden collapse of North Korea would place new financial and social strains on the country just when it has to concentrate on overcoming the global economic challenge.

Future Challenges

East Asia is a part of the globe destined to shape the twenty-first century economically, politically, and strategically. In this coming decade, dramatic changes are expected with the re-establishment of the international order in East Asia. National economies have been integrated into international production networks and widely exposed to market trends abroad. While old borders come down with economic integration, social fragmentation creates new ones.

The Chinese leadership is not open yet to political reform which allows a peaceful transfer of power. In addition, Chinese leaders have to pursue structural reform, which has to be accompanied by its entry into WTO. The Chinese leadership will continue to confront the status of Taiwan, demands for autonomy by Muslims, Tibetans, and other minorities, and face criticisms against human rights abuses and environmental pollution.

Environmental problems have become acute recently. The phenomenal expansion over the past several years of the national economy has made China the largest producer of carbon dioxide among newly industrializing countries. Whereas the country is now responsible for about ten percent of all the greenhouse gas emissions directly contributing to heat waves and floods on the planet, China is expected to emit more carbon dioxide, at its current pace of development, by 2025 than the present total of North America and Japan combined.

Following its miraculous economic growth, Japan has been in deep recession since the early 1990s. The ruling Liberal Democrat Party failed to reverse years of economic stagnation despite spending tens of billions of dollars on public infrastructure. There is pressure on Japan to tackle structural weaknesses in the financial system, in particular, attributed to Japan's fragile banking system burdened by massive debts. The efforts to revive the economy have not yet produced any visible outcome.

The United States' role in East Asia will be determined by interpretations of the degree of preparedness by the American government to meet with the shift in balance of power in East Asia. In the short term, the terrorist attacks on the World Trade Center and Pentagon on September 11, 2001, have resulted in support for a United States–run international campaign. While South Korea and Japan provide logistical support for humanitarian operations in Afghanistan, North Korea joined treaties on anti-terrorism as a gesture to improve relations with the US government.

HO-WON JEONG

See also China, People's Republic of; East Asia: History and Economic Development; Hong Kong; Korea, North; Korea, South; Taiwan

References and Further Reading

Christensen, Thomas J. "China, the US-Japan Alliance, and the Security Dilemma in East Asia," *International Security*. Volume 23, Number 4, Spring 1999.

Jones, Clive and Caroline Kennedy-Pipe, editors. *International Security in a Global Age: Securing the Twenty-First Century*. New York: Frank Cass Publishers, 2000.

Lampton, David M. *Major Power Relations in Northeast Asia: Win-Win or Zero-Sum Game*. New York: Japan Center for International Exchange, 2001.

Self, Benjami L. and Yuki Tatsumi, editors. *Confidence-Building Measures and Security Issues in Northeast Asia*. Report No. 33, Washington, DC: The Henry L. Stimson Center, February 2000.

Teo, Eric. "The Emerging East Asian Regionalism," *Internationale Politik und Gesellschaft/International Politics and Society*. Number 1, 2001.

EAST TIMOR

East Timor is the eastern half of the island of Timor, including the enclave of Oecussi surrounded by Indonesian West Timor. Similar to nearby Indonesian islands, its climate is dry, with a rainy season roughly from November to February. It is mountainous, although there are some plains and littoral regions. There are at least a dozen distinct languages native to East Timor, with dozens more dialects, although Tetum is a lingua franca, as is Indonesian, and some speak Portuguese and English. The population is predominantly Malay with sizable Austronesian and Melanesian populations, as well as ethnic Chinese and Arab populations, and a large mestiço population due to the Portuguese colonial period.

Portuguese traders and missionaries arrived in the early sixteenth century. The colonial period was marked by the "benign neglect" experienced by other Portuguese colonies; the Portuguese were interested mainly in the region's sandalwood. When the vast stands of sandalwood had been depleted by the early twentieth century, the Portuguese turned to coffee and copra production.

As it did most of Southeast Asia, Japan took over East Timor during World War II, and approximately sixty thousand East Timorese perished during the course of the war, representing over one-tenth of the population. As nationalist movements agitated for independence throughout Southeast Asia following the war, East Timor reverted back to colonial rule due to the lack of a strong, united nationalist front because of the low level of education in the region

(although sporadic small-scale rebellions against the Portuguese flared, usually easily and brutally repressed). A Catholic seminary was built in the 1950s in Dare in order to train an indigenous clergy and provide secondary education for elites. Nationalist leaders such as José Ramos Horta and Mari Alkatiri were educated there, and nationalists were often influenced during periods of exile in other Portuguese colonies with more developed movements, such as Mozambique.

Following the 1974 "Revolution of the Carnations" in Lisbon, Portuguese decolonization began throughout the Lusophone empire. Three main political parties emerged in East Timor, the Timorese Democratic Union, Revolutionary Front for Independent East Timor (FRETILIN), and the People's Democratic Association of East Timor. FRETILIN commanded the largest support by far. After months of Indonesian subterfuge in East Timor, including cross-border excursions, FRETILIN unilaterally declared independence on November 28, 1975, hoping for international recognition in order to prevent an invasion.

On December 7, 1975, Indonesia invaded, with approval from the West. Within a few months sixty thousand East Timorese had perished, and within five years that number had increased to approximately two hundred thousand, representing around one-third of the population. The Indonesian occupation was marked by widespread campaigns of terror, rape, forced sterilization, torture, and disappearances. The armed wing of FRETILIN, FALANTIL, maintained a guerrilla war, bolstered by popular support.

By the mid-1980s, after securing most of the territory, the Indonesian administration began development projects in East Timor, such as roads, telecommunications, electricity, and other infrastructure projects. Although this work aided the East Timorese economy, it also helped facilitate Indonesian consolidation of control. In 1986, the University of East Timor opened, with a focus on agriculture and vocational training. Much of the profit of development in East Timor went to the Indonesian military elite and bureaucrats stationed in East Timor; many industries, such as road construction and coffee, were monopolies owned by Indonesian generals. Throughout the occupation, East Timor remained one of the least developed regions in Indonesia, although the vast reserves of oil in the Timor Sea made it potentially one of its richest. During the occupation the conversion rate to Catholicism skyrocketed, as a reaction to the invaders' belief in Islam, and East Timor is around 95% nominally Catholic today.

The integration of East Timor was viewed by most as a *fait accompli,* yet following the Santa Cruz Massacre of November 11, 1991, caught on film and broadcast globally, solidarity movements emerged worldwide calling for self-determination. The movement was heartened in 1996 when Bishop Carlos Ximenes Belo shared the Nobel Peace Prize with resistance leader Ramos Horta.

Following the 1998–1999 economic and political crisis that engulfed Indonesia, President Suharto's successor, B.J. Habibie, agreed to a referendum in the long-suffering territory. Despite widespread intimidation by militia groups supported by the Indonesian military, 98% of those registered voted, and 78.5% chose independence. After the results were announced on September 4, 1998, East Timor erupted in a militia-led spasm of violence. Within two weeks the unarmed UN force had evacuated, contrary to their guarantees, allowing the militias and Indonesian military to carry out their scorched earth campaign. When UN peacekeepers arrived on September 20, East Timor lay in ruins. Over seventy percent of all buildings were destroyed, water, electricity, and telephone services were dismantled, systematic killing and rape had occurred, and nearly half the population had been displaced, many sent at gunpoint to West Timor or other areas in Indonesia. The Indonesian military and militias retreated, and the task of rebuilding fell to the United Nations Transitional Authority for East Timor (UNTAET).

UNTAET faced a myriad of problems. Education under Indonesia was poor, and in the period before the referendum, almost all of the teachers, who were Indonesian, left. Schools and the university were destroyed. To stave off famine and disease, UNTAET and NGOs organized food relief, temporary housing, and medical facilities, and UNTAET engineers began rebuilding the shattered infrastructure. Few UNTAET jobs were filled by East Timorese, however, justified by a lack of English skills or training, and unemployment remained around eighty percent since the referendum, causing resentment. The UNTAET presence led to a clearly bifurcated economy, with UNTAET and most aid workers occupying the top tier, and most East Timorese stagnating in poverty. There has been surprisingly little violence, however, including toward returning former militia members, who are being reintegrated into society.

On May 20, 2002, East Timor was granted full independence, recognized by the United Nations, with former FALANTIL commander and Indonesian prisoner José Alexandre "Xanana" Gusmão becoming the country's first elected president. Ramos Horta became the country's Minister of State and Minister of Foreign Affairs, and Alkatiri Prime Minister. East Timor has begun establishing economic and diplomatic relations with its neighbors, including Indonesia. Per capita income is around $450 US dollars, unemployment remains high, and the country relies on foreign aid and profits from coffee exports. East Timor has not experienced economic growth; its growth rate was estimated at −3% in 2003. A windfall is expected as soon as the oil in the Timor Sea can be exploited; however, maritime boundaries and the rights to the oil remain in dispute between Australia and East Timor. Challenges that remain in East Timor include establishing a modern education system, rebuilding the shattered infrastructure, and establishing a viable economy that can alleviate the high rates of unemployment. Non-governmental organizations have spread and continue to add to a lively civil society, including continuing their calls for justice in the form of an international tribunal for those responsible for the tragedy of the Indonesian occupation. The East Timorese leadership, however, including Gusmão and Ramos Horta, have taken a more politically pragmatic approach, denying the need for a tribunal and citing the importance of strong political and economic ties to Indonesia, its major trading partner. An Indonesian tribunal with very limited scope exonerated most of those brought before the court, but was widely viewed as illegitimate by outside observers.

CHRISTOPHER LUNDRY

See also Indonesia

References and Further Reading

Aditjondro, George J. *In the Shadow of Mount Ramelau: The Impact of the Occupation of East Timor.* Leiden: Indonesian Documentation and Information Centre, 1994.

Anderson, Benedict. "Gravel in Jakarta's Shoes," *London Review of Books.* 17, no. 21 (1995).

Franks, Emma. "Women and Resistance in East Timor: The Centre, They Say, knows Itself by the Margins," *Women's Studies International Forum.* 19, nos. 1-2 (1996).

Gunn, Geoffrey C. *A Critical View of Western Journalism and Scholarship on East Timor.* Manila: Journal of Contemporary Asia Publishers, 1994.

Jardine, Matthew. *East Timor: Genocide in Paradise.* Tucson: Odonian Press, 1995; 2nd edition, 1999.

Kohen, Arnold S. *From the Place of the Dead: The Epic Struggles of Bishop Belo of East Timor.* New York: St. Martin's Press, 1999.

Pinto, Constancio and Matthew Jardine. *East Timor's Unfinished Struggle: Inside the Timorese Reistance.* Boston: South End Press, 1987.

Ramos Horta, José. *Funu: The Unfinished Saga of East Timor.* Trenton, NJ: Red Sea Press, 1987.

Saldanha, Joao Mario Sousa. *The Political Economy of East Timor Development.* Jakarta: Pustaka Sinar Harapan, 1994.

Taylor, John G. *Indonesia's Forgotten War.* London: Zed Books, 1991.

ECONOMIC AND CUSTOMS UNION OF CENTRAL AFRICA (ECUCA)

Popularly identified by its French acronym, UDEAC (the Union Douanière et Economique de l'Afrique Centrale), ECUCA is a regional grouping that was meant to promote cooperation and integration among the Central African states with a view to fostering sub-regional development. This was to be done through the harmonization of its fiscal policy and customs duties, the coordination of its industrialization programs, and the free circulation of the factors of production as well as produce. It was created on December 8, 1964, and in 1974 the Treaty was revised, with the members pledging to work to form an economic union. Initially, it had five members: Cameroon, the Central African Republic (CAR), Chad, the Republic of the Congo, and Gabon. Chad and CAR withdrew in 1968, though CAR later rejoined that same year. Chad did not renew its membership until 1985, when Equatorial Guinea also became a member. Commonalities among them such as the French language (except for Equatorial Guinea, where the official language is Spanish) and a common currency, the CFA (Communautaire financière africaine, or the African Financial Community), as well as cultural affinities were expected to have a synergistic effect on the Union. Cumulatively, it covers a geographical area of 3,020,561 square kilometers, that is, about one and a half times the size of the European Community in 1990. The combined population of its six members was 22 million, that is, a tenth of the inhabitants of Europe (Mouafo 1991). As such the grouping began to provide an answer to the economies-of-scale problem that had dogged its individual members, who were considered micro-states. Other factors, however, could still decrease its attractiveness value to potential investors. In 1987, their total GDP was about $18 million US dollars, that is, about a tenth that of Holland (Kitchen 1992). And this has fallen over time, causing most of the states to sign Structural Adjustment Programs with the World Bank. *Prima facie*, this can be seen as evidence of ECUCA's failure to provide a new impetus to development in the sub-region. The requisite political will was also in short supply among the contracting parties.

Though it was endowed with several instruments, the Common External Tariff (CET) stood out because it was trade driven, as well as its *Droit de Douane* (single custom duty), a Single Tax, and a *taxe complémentaire* (complementary tax [CT]). The CET applicable to non-member states comprises a common external customs duty, a *taxe d'entrée* (entry tax), and a *taxe sur le chiffre d'affaires à l'importation* (turnover tax). The CT, designed to compensate the states' revenue losses suffered as a result of the application of the CET, is determined by the various member-states. Initially conceived to cover a transitional period of twenty-five years, it has become permanent because of its revenue generating capacity. The *Single Tax*, which seeks to promote *intra-UDEAC* trade in the manufacturing sector, is a preferential tax granted to companies upon application. Beneficiaries have a lighter tax burden than the CET plus the CT. However, its tendency to vary from state to state undermines both the CET and the principle of fair competition. The members shared a common central bank, the Banque des Etats de l'Afrique Centrale (BEAC), as well as a common development bank, the Banque de Développement des Etats de l'Afrique Centrale (BDEAC). Noteworthy, however, is the fact that powers of decision-making were vested in the Council of the Heads of State and Ministers that met once a year; its Secretary General had only administrative functions.

Despite the incentives, trade creation was negligible, as demonstrated by the sluggish growth in intra-UDEAC trade as a percentage of the overall volume of trade. It oscillated between 1.6% in 1960 and 2.0% in 1983 (the year in which the secretariat stopped collecting data) after hitting a high of 4.1% in 1980 (Kitchen, 1992). Most of its inter-African trade is carried out with the members of the Economic Community of West African States (ECOWAS). Historical trade patterns have continued, as France remains the principal trading partner of these countries. Granted, these figures were skewed by the high levels of contraband and unofficial trade in UDEAC. Two groups of products dominate official intra-UDEAC trade: energy products and manufactures. Trade in the latter is hindered because most of these economies have identical industries.

Trade in Single Tax products was largely to the benefit of the more developed states where most of these industries are located. To redress any prejudice that this may cause the poorer states, the redistribution of the proceeds of this tax was based on the level of a state's consumption of the Single Tax products. Because of this, the amounts varied, a trend that was exacerbated by the fact that variable rates were applied during a six-year transition period, and the 1974 treaty simply stipulated that the rates for the same products should be reduced progressively.

Confidence-building measures, such as the creation of regional industries with a view to fostering the deepening process, were aborted. Plans for creating the "Société Equatoriale de Raffinage" (Equatorial Refining Company) to refine crude oil suffered when states such as Gabon reneged on their initial commitment to participate and withdrew their investments. This produced a domino effect. In the textile sector, for instance, a decision to locate a communal textile factory in Congo aborted as states simply built their own factories. It is noteworthy that the creation of forward and backward linkages was not a factor in the decision allocating these regional industries. Even BDEAC failed to devote up to 50% of its credit to the creation of regional industries as stipulated in the 1974 treaty. Rather, it was more exposed to the more developed states in the Union (Jua 1986). Against this backdrop, lesser developed UDEAC members saw payments from the Solidarity Fund as only budgetary compensations, which could not help to reduce the asymmetry in levels of development.

Though factors such as investment shortfalls and a historical bias to reinforce the umbilical cord between France and its member states account for UDEAC's mitigated results, a deficit, if not lack of political will among the various states, was also crucial. Its secretariat, tasked with implementing the agenda, was hobbled by a lack of funds as member states failed to pay their dues. Because leadership in the various states privileged national over a sub-regional focus, rhetoric diverged from reality. For example, despite the commitment to benefiting from the economies of scale as showcased in the regional agenda, constraints to free movement of people became stronger and nationals of other states were even expelled. Contradictions seem to abound for expulsions are being carried out simultaneously with the creation of instruments meant to foster integration. To this end, it has signed a protocol of understanding for transport, *Transport Inter-Etat des Pays d'Afrique Centrale* (TIPAC). To tear down barriers in other sectors, it created the Commission Bancaire d'Afrique Centrale (COBAC) in January 1993 that would adopt a common code for banking in the region and the Conférence Interafricaine des Marchés d'Assurance (CIMA) for insurance in July 1992 as well as the integration of their business laws under the auspices of l'Organization pour l'harmonization en Afrique du Droits des Affaires of the Organization for Commercial Code Harmonization (OHADA) entered into by Francophone African countries, notably West African Economic and Monetary Union (the l'Union Economique et Monétarie Ouest Africaine (UEMOA)) in 1995.

Following this phase of "integration of regulations," the states committed themselves to adopting coherent macro-economic policies and common sectoral policies. This was achieved with the signing in 1994 of the treaty for the Central African Economic and Monetary Union (CEMAC), ratified in 1999. Replacing UDEAC, its objective was to promote economic integration among its members. To this end, intra-regional trade would be regulated by the value added tax. Significantly, this reform brings about the end of most of the quantitative restrictions and simplifies most customs procedures. CEMAC also provided for the setting up of a Court of Justice which includes a judicial chamber (chambre judicaire) and an auditing court (chambre des comptes) for the settlement of disputes arising as a result of these provisions. Cooperation from donors is also important in realizing integration. The World Bank and other developed countries assuaged the fears of the lesser developed states by pledging financial aid to compensate them for any financial prejudice they may suffer consequent to this reform. Under the Lomé IV Convention, the EU set aside ECU 84 million for Regional Indicative Programs. Some of this money has been given to the TIPAC project and is being used to develop a number of regional transit routes such as the Bertoua-Garoua-Boulai-Bangui road to link Cameroon and the CAR, and Garoua Boulai-Ngoundere with a view to facilitating transport between Cameroon and Chad. Similarly the World Bank, which identified the easing of transport regulations as one of the key objectives of its Regional Program, pledged financial aid of $340,000 to help strengthen the Institutional Development facility. Disbursement of this fund was contingent on, *inter alia*, participants becoming more responsible for the maintenance of their road transport patrimony. Notable also is its contribution to other projects that have a federating impact such as the Chad-Cameroon pipeline, one of the biggest private investments undertaken in sub-Saharan Africa, which was inaugurated in October 2003. Consciousness raising in the World Bank vis-à-vis sub-regional projects was prompted by the UDEAC secretariat, which on the heels of its adoption of its "New Economic and Social Integration Strategy" noted the failure of SAPs to promote regional projects.

NANTANG JUA

See also Central Africa: History and Economic Development; Central Africa: International Relations

References and Further Reading

Bakoup, F. and D. Tarr. "The Effects of Economic Integration in the Central African Customs and Monetary Community" in *Africa Development*. Vol. 12, No. 2, pp. 161–190, (2000).

Jua, N. "UDEAC: Dream, Reality or the making of Sub-Imperial states," *Afrika Spectrum*. Vol. 21, No. 2, pp. 211–223, (1986).

Kitchen, R. "Problems of Regional Integration in Africa: The Union Douanière et Economique de l'Afrique

Centrale" in *Policy Adjustment in Africa*. Edited by Chris Milner and A. J. Rayner. London: MacMillan, 1992.

Mbaku, J. M. and D. R. Kamerschen. "Integration and Economic Development in sub-Saharan Africa: the case of the Customs and Economic Union of Central African States," *Journal of Contemporary African Studies*. Vol. 7, No. 1/2, pp. 3–21, (1988).

Mytelka, L. K. "Competition, Conflict and Decline in Uion Douniére et Economique de l'Afrique Centrale" in *African Regional Organizations*. Edited by Domenico Mazzeo. Cambridge: Cambridge University Press, 1984.

Mouafo, D. "Les difficultés de l'integration économique inter-regionale en Afrique noire: UDEAC," *Les Cahiers d'Outre Mer*. Année 44, no. 174, pp. 167–185, (1991).

Schulder, G. "Economic Growth and Structural Adjustment in Central Africa," http://alpha.moncalir.edu/~lebelp/CERAFRM015Schulder1990.pdf.

Tamba, I. "Integration Régionale en Afrique: Zone Franc: Le Cas de L ÚDEAC," *Etudes et Statistiques/BEAC*. No. 196, pp. 289–299, 1992.

ECONOMIC COMMISSION FOR AFRICA (ECA)

The Economic Commission for Africa (ECA) is the regional arm of the United Nations (UN) in Africa. It was established in 1958 with the mandate of fostering economic and social development of its fifty-three member states. Headquartered in Addis Ababa, Ethiopia, under the leadership of its Executive Secretary, the ECA is one of five such regional economic commissions created by the United Nations to serve different parts of the world. It reports to the UN Economic and Social Council (ECONOC) through the Joint Conference of African Finance, Planning, and Economic Development Ministers.

For administrative and operational purposes, ECA has divided Africa into five sub-regions, with each having its own head office, which caters to the needs of the countries under its jurisdiction and also provides vital links between the ECA headquarters, the various regional economic blocs, and the individual member states. These sub-regions include (a) Central Africa (head office in Yaoundé, Cameroon), with seven members: Cameroon, Chad, Congo, Equatorial Guinea, Central African Republic, Sao Tome, and Principe; (b) East Africa (head office in Kigali, Rwanda), with thirteen members: Burundi, Comoros, Democratic Republic of Congo, Djibouti, Ethiopia, Eritrea, Kenya, Madagascar, Rwanda, Seychelles, Somalia, Tanzania, and Uganda; (c) North Africa, (head office in Tangier, Morocco), with seven members: Algeria; Egypt, Libya, Mauritania, Morocco, Sudan, and Tunisia; (d) Southern Africa (head office in Lusaka, Zambia), with eleven members: Angola, Botswana, Lesotho, Malawi, Mauritius, Mozambique, Namibia, South Africa, Swaziland, Zambia, and Zimbabwe; and (e) West Africa (head office in Niamey, Niger), with fifteen members: Burkina Faso, Benin, Cape-Verde, Côte d'Ivoire, Gambia, Ghana, Guinea, Guinea-Bissau, Liberia, Mali, Niger, Nigeria, Senegal, Sierra Leone, and Togo.

Informed by, and cognizant of, the limitations wrought by the acute lack of technical know-how on Africa's development, the ECA for the most part pursues its mandate through the development and dissemination of culturally sensitive, research-based knowledge and best practices on such matters as good governance, poverty reduction, the empowerment of women, conflict prevention and resolution, and regional cooperation among African countries. Thus, research projects and publications, workshops and conferences, and the provision of library and technical information services—through CD-ROMs, audiovisual materials, printed media, and databases—constitute the bedrock of ECA's development endeavors. Some of the noteworthy ECA publications are the *Economic Report on Africa* (an annual publication), which reviews the continent's economic performance and short-term prospects; the *Africa Governance Report,* an annual publication first released in 2004, to identify the best practice in governance for peer learning, to identify gaps in theory and practices, and to make recommendations for improvement; and the *Cartographic and Remote Sensing Bulletin*, which provides valuable information on research, advocacy, and policy analysis on remote sensing technologies and spatial and mapping information pertaining to Africa. Other important publications of the ECA are the *Africa Statistical Yearbook; Compendium of Environmental Statistics; Compendium of Intra-African and Related Foreign Trade Statistics;* and *African Index.*

Program Divisions

The ECA is organized around six main program divisions. First—not in any particular order, though—there is the Development and Policy Management Division (DPMD), whose goal is to enhance institutional capacity of African governments by establishing baseline measures on the nature and quality of institutions, by advising African governments on best practices, and by strengthening civil society organizations on the continent. This division is premised on the conviction that no meaningful social and economic development can be accomplished without effective, transparent, and accountable institutions. Secondly, the ECA has an Economic and Social

Policy Division (ESPD) which provides pertinent research on economic and social policies to African governments and non-governmental institutions. Its operations are generally focused on such themes as social and economic policy, trade and finance, and poverty reduction. The third major division is the Development Information Services Division (DISD), which publishes and disseminates ECA's research outputs to all of its members.

Another important ECA program division is the Gender and Development Division, which works in conjunction with the African Center for Gender and Development (ACGD), to promote gender equity, which invariably connotes the advancement or empowerment of women, given the high level of patriarchy across Africa. The ECA also has a Sustainable Development Division, with which it seeks to enhance African governments' capabilities in the use of scientific and technological innovations in achieving environmentally sustainable development; to improve their stewardship of the natural environment; and to strengthen their ability to design and implement development policies that reflect and reinforce the intricate, dialectical nexus between food security, population, and environment sustainability. Finally, the ECA has a Trade and Regional Integration Division (TRID), which promotes regional cooperation and economic integration across Africa, focusing mainly on policy issues and infrastructure development. This division also works to strengthen the capacity of African countries to engage in substantive trade negotiations in the global arena, especially within the context of the World Trade Organization (WTO) agreements and initiatives. In addition to the preceding six divisions, the ECA has a number of subsidiary organs or committees—e.g., Committees of Regional Integration; on Development Information; on Sustainable Development; on Women and Development; on Human Development and Civil Society; on Industry and Private Sector Development— which provide expertise in their respective areas in pursuance of the ECA's mandate.

Accomplishments

The ECA has made remarkable, and, indeed, commendable, contribution to Africa's social and economic development over the nearly fifty years of its existence. Among other things, it has been instrumental in the establishment of several national, sub-regional, and regional development-related technical institutions, encompassing such fields as technology, remote sensing, finance and banking, and planning and management. The African Development Bank, headquartered in Abidjan, Côte d'Ivoire; the Eastern and Southern African Management Institute (ESAMI), headquartered in Arusha, Tanzania; and the African Institute for Economic Development and Planning (IDEP) located in Dakar, Senegal, are just a handful of African institutions which owe much of their foundation to the efforts of the ECA.

Likewise, over the years, the ECA has facilitated the creation and sustenance of a number of subregional economic blocs in Africa. For instance, in 1965, it was the ECA that initiated the Lusaka meeting of the newly independent Eastern and Southern African states, which culminated in the formation of the Preferential Trade Area (PTA) in the subregion, and ultimately led to the establishment of the Common Market for Eastern and Southern Africa (COMESA) in 1994. Similarly, the first major effort to bring Francophone and Anglophone West African nations toward the formation of the Economic Community of West African States (ECOWAS) was made by the ECA, through resolutions passed at its Seventh Session in Nairobi in February 1965. With its Trade and Regional Integration Division (TRID), the ECA continues to be instrumental in the operations of sub-regional blocs in Africa, providing them with technical support in such areas as multilateral trade promotion and negotiations and infrastructure development. The ECA sees sub-regional economic integration bodies as the building blocks for the eventual integration and self-sufficiency of Africa as a whole.

The ECA has been a major player in the negotiations and articulations of nearly all the major Pan-African development strategies, initiatives, and declarations, including the Monrovia Declaration of Commitment of the Heads of States and Governments of the Organization of African Unity (OAU), signed in 1979; the Lagos Plan of Action for the Economic Development of Africa and the Final Act of Lagos, signed in the second Extraordinary Session of the OAU in 1980; the African Charter for Popular Participation for Development, signed in 1990; the New Partnership for Africa's Development (NEPAD) formally adopted by the OAU in July 2001; and the recent negotiations that led to the transformation of the OAU into the African Union (AU) in July 2002.

As the African arm of the United Nations, ECA plays a significant role in advocating for Africa's development interest within the UN system, mostly by coordinating various national, sub-regional, and regional UN programs across Africa in furtherance of the continent's social and economic development goals. Of special importance here is the ECA's role in the implementation of the UN System-wide Special Initiative on Africa, which was launched in March 1996 to help accomplish the UN's New Agenda for the Development of Africa, launched in 1991. Indeed, ECA routinely discusses strategies with, and advocates for, African governments in various global forums and trade, finance, and debt relief negotiations, especially those involving such multilateral organizations as the WTO and the Bretton Woods institutions. Also, ECA participates in, and follows up on, global initiatives and Conferences such as the UN International Conference on Population and Development in Cairo (1994); the 1995 Beijing Women's Conference; and the Washington DC–based Global Development Network's annual Global Development Conferences.

Given the acute dearth of reliable development-related data across Africa, it is hardly surprising that the ECA has put considerable energy into strengthening the capacity of African nations to collect, process, and analyze data in support of their respective development policies and programs. Through a number of workshops, conferences, and expert group meetings over the years, the ECA has identified and disseminated best practices in the development of macroeconomic-, poverty-, and gender-related indicators across Africa. The ECA's African Gender and Development Index (AGDI), launched in 2002, deserves a special mention in this regard. With this index, the ECA was able to compile (in 2003) gender profiles for all of its fifty-three member states, based on the following six indicators: women in decision-making positions; educational enrollment ratios; health and HIV/AIDS; women's access to credit; women's participation in the labour market; and human rights of women and girls. Plans are also under way at the ECA secretariat to develop similar indicators for measuring the extent of food sufficiency and security among African countries.

Working with a number of UN agencies and the African Development Bank, the ECA is also striving to improve access to safe drinking water and basic sanitation across Africa; a Pan-African Implementation and Partnership Conference on Water (PANAFCO) was held in Addis Ababa, Ethiopia, in 2003, under the auspices of the ECA and the African Ministerial Council on Water (AMCOW) to facilitate this process. The extent to which the lack of good sanitation and safe drinking water impacts the human condition in Africa arguably demands no further elucidation, not even to the most cursory observer of the continent's development imperatives.

To help bridge the infamous digital divide between Africa and the rest of the world, the ECA, with the support of the government of Canada, has recently set up the African regional node of the Global Electronic Policy Resource Network (ePol-NET) to coordinate the demands of African institutions and governments seeking guidance and support on such matters as electronic commerce, Internet policies, and telecommunication regulations.

As the regional arm of the UN, the ECA, unlike many other regional development organizations in Africa, is not financially incapacitated. Additionally, the ECA has for the most part benefited from a very insightful and dedicated leadership, in the likes of the renowned Nigerian economist Adebayo Adedeji (who led the organization from 1975 to 1991) and the influential Ghanaian-born development economist K.Y. Amoako (the current executive secretary of ECA). Still, the organization faces a number of daunting problems, having to deal with African governments, many of whom lack the necessary technical personnel, political will, and, to some extent, insight and foresight to support many of the development initiatives of ECA, not to mention having to work on a continent gripped by perennial geopolitical conflicts and ethnic violence, extreme poverty, and the scourge of AIDS and many other devastating diseases.

JOSEPH MENSAH

See also African Development Bank (ADB); Common Market for Eastern and Southern Africa (COMESA); Economic Community of Central African States (ECCAS); Economic Community of West African States (ECOWAS); International Bank for Reconstruction and Development (IBRD) (World Bank); Organization of African Unity (OAU); Southern African Development Community (SADC); United Nations Economic and Social Council; World Trade Organization (WTO)

References and Further Reading

Economic Commission for Africa. *Annual Report, 2004.* Addis Ababa, Ethiopia: ECA, 2004.

Economic Commission for Africa. *Proposed Programme of Work for the Biennium, 2004–2005.* Addis Ababa, Ethiopia: ECA, 2003.

Economic Commission for Africa. *Economic Report on Africa, 2004: Unlocking Africa's Trade Potential.* Addis Ababa, Ethiopia: ECA, 2004.

Economic Commission for Africa. *Economic Report on Africa, 2002: Tracking Performance and Progress.* Addis Ababa, Ethiopia: ECA, 2002.

Economic Commission for Africa. *Assessing Regional Integration in Africa.* AddisAbaba, Ethiopia: ECA, 2004.

ECA website: http://www.uneca.org [Accessed on December 6, 2004].

Gruhn, Isebill V, ed. *Regionalism Reconsidered: The Economic Commission for Africa.* Boulder, CO: Westview Press, 1979.

ECONOMIC COMMUNITY OF CENTRAL AFRICAN STATES (ECCAS)

The treaty instituting the Economic Community of Central African States (ECCAS) was signed on October 18, 1983, and came into force on January 1, 1985. It consists of eleven member states and was a fusion of Union Douanière des Etats de l'Afrique Centrale (UDEAC) (Cameroon, Central Africa, Chad, Congo, Equatorial Guinea and Gabon) and the Economic Community of the Great Lakes (CEPGL) (Burundi, Rwanda, and the then Zaire) as well as Sao Tome and Principe. Angola remained an observer until 1999, when it became a full member. Initially, it sought to "promote and strengthen harmonious cooperation and a balanced and self-sustained development in the industrial, transport and communications, energy, agricultural, and natural resource sectors." Though constituting one of the smaller sub-regions of the continent from the point of view of demographics, with only 68 million inhabitants, occupying circa 6.7 million square kilometers that spreads from the equatorial forests to the Sahel, it is endowed with many and varied natural resources. It has one of the remaining rain forests of the world while some of its members are world leaders in diamond production and almost all of them have large oil deposits. Seen from a regional level, ECCAS was to constitute one of the building blocks of the African Common Market envisaged in the 1980 Lagos Plan of Action. However, there was no formal contact between ECCAS and the African Economic Community until October 1999, when they signed the Protocol on Relations.

To contribute to the realization of this project, the Treaty created the following structures: the Conference of Heads of State and Government as its supreme organ, the Council of Ministers, the Secretariat General (one secretary-general elected for four years and three assistant secretaries-general), a Court of Justice, and a Consultative Commission. Conferring all decision-making powers in the juridical division of powers on heads of state and government who cling to their political sovereignty in a regional integration scheme was counterintuitive and perforce had to be counterproductive. Unlike the Economic Community of West African States (ECOWAS) and the Southern African Development Community (SADC), it was not endowed with formal structures. Meetings at the technical and ministerial levels have been infrequent. The effect of this lacuna was exacerbated by what the secretary-general of ECCAS described in a June 1999 report as "the double language" of the officials who speak in favor of integration but avoid implementing the Community's regulations. Palpable proof of this lack of political will was their failure to pay membership fees between 1992 and 1998, a situation that paralyzed and provoked the dormancy of ECCAS. Because of this, the timelines prescribed in the Treaty could not be met.

Its Article Six, for instance, provides that the Customs Union would be achieved after a twelve-year period or not more than twenty years from the date of the entry into force of the Treaty and would be preceded by two stages. The first stage, a study to determine the timetable for the progressive removal of tariffs and non-tariff barriers to intra-Community trade as well as for the increases or decreases in the customs tariffs of member states with a view to adopting a common external tariff. Stage two consists of the establishment of a free trade area by applying the timetable for the progressive elimination of tariff and non-tariff barriers to intra-Community trade. However, the likelihood of meeting these timelines were problematic because of the safeguard clauses and escape windows provided for in Article 34, which allows states to impose quantitative restrictions or non-tariff barriers per Article Two of Annex II on goods originating from other member states for the purpose of redressing their balance of payments and protecting strategic infant industries. Arguably, these derogations have stifled intra-Community trade, as shown by the fact that it ranks ninth out of thirteen groups studied by the Economic Commission for Africa.

Measures to reverse this trend, such as the freedom of movement of the factors of production contained in the Treaty, have not been respected. Article Two of Annex VII of the Treaty provided for the free movement of nationals of the member states four years after the Treaty entered into force, and workers could accept employment in any state and continue to reside there even after the end of the employment. The reality has been different. The Cameroonian Ministry of Foreign Affairs lists Gabon (and France) as the countries where the social integration of their nationals is most problematic, even after they have paid for the visas and acquired the residential permits, which cost circa $450 US dollars each and are renewable after two years at $200 US dollars. Chadians have similarly complained against "unfriendly treatment and the violation of diplomatic rules by Cameroonian forces." Expulsions, engendered by reciprocity considerations, are commonplace, and in some cases even workers are affected by these measures with "the confiscation of their property." Structural hurdles such as the lack of good roads already hamper social communication among ordinary citizens in the region.

The Community's Court of Justice is given the competence to settle questions of interpretation of the Treaty per Article 16. Though its decisions are binding on member states and institutions of the Community, it is hobbled by the fact that this is just an advisory opinion. Furthermore, only the Conference of the Heads of State and Government as the Council of Ministers can bring matters before this Court. The secretary-general, the Consultative Commission, the Technical Committees, and all above individuals who may suffer a prejudice or whose rights may be violated are not so empowered.

Despite these structural/textual deficiencies, the heads of state and government identify the lack of confidence engendered by tensions and conflicts as the main cause of the stagnation and paralysis of integration. Ideological competition in the sub-region early into the postcolonial era, exemplified by the Congo crisis served to promote local proxy wars. Apartheid South Africa exacerbated this situation as it recruited client states in the region in a bid to build its constellation of states with a view to protecting and promoting the white redoubt. Of course, prebendalism and other exclusionary practices and the tendency of intra-state conflict mutating into inter-state conflict also led to the normalization of war. Because of this, the region served as the theater for what has been dubbed Africa's First World War, and most of the states for variable periods of time have virtually failed. The end of conflicts has not ushered in peace as the region is awash with light weapons and small arms that have a long shelf life because of that require little maintenance. They are now used for social wars that blight these states.

To overcome this, they turned to the United Nations (UN), and on their initiative Resolution 46/37 B was adopted in December 1991, in implementation of which the secretary-general of the United Nations established the United Nations Standing Advisory Committee on Security Questions in Central Africa in May 1992. It seeks to assist the states to develop confidence-building measures, and in disarmament with a view to benefiting from the peace dividend. Thus, the Standing Advisory Committee has engaged in the development of preventive diplomacy, peace-making, and peace-building. To this end, it has been involved in training the personnel of its member states in peacekeeping activities. Above all, the Standing Committee prepared a non-aggression pact that was signed at the heads of state summit in July 1996 at Yaounde, Cameroon, by nine states. Significantly, Angola and Rwanda were not signatories. And at the February 1999 summit of the United Nations Standing Advisory Committee that was held in Yaounde, the member states decided to create an organization for the promotion, maintenance, and consolidation of peace and security in Central Africa, which would be called Council for Peace and Security in Central Africa (COPAX). Coming on its heels, Gabon hosted a regional peacekeeping exercise, "Gabon 2000," whose goal was to increase the capacity of ECCAS states in the fields of peace keeping, conflict prevention, and management. This direction represented a direct application of the French RECAMP concept (reinforcement of African peacekeeping capacities).

Because of the premium that the heads of state and government placed on confidence building measures, COPAX was established at the June 1999 summit in Malabo, Equatorial Guinea, Cameroon. It was supposed to foster sub-regional cooperation in the realms of defense and security. Another pact for mutual assistance between the eleven member states was also signed. To enable the realization of these goals, the Summit provided for the creation of a Central African Multinational Force, a Central African early-warning mechanism, and the Defense and Security Commission. This skewed focus on peace and security has caused some to posit that the sole aim of COPAX is to "save heads of state in distress." Sustaining this assertion is regime instability that inheres from their status, in the words of the State Failure Task Force, as "partial democracies."

However, other measures that seek to empower the population of the sub-region have also been undertaken. Notable among them is the establishment of the Sub-regional Center for Human Rights and Democracy as well as the creation of a network of Central African parliamentarians, as a prelude to the establishment of a Community Parliament. Arguably, this should provide an opportunity for the conversion of the peoples of the sub-region into federators.

Measures were also taken with a view to giving a new impulse to integration. Notable among them was the establishment of an autonomous financing mechanism for ECCAS and integration activities. To enable this, a tax of 0.7% of custom duty on all goods imported from third parties was introduced. A Council of Ministers meeting also decided that all outstanding arrears in contributions from member states would be paid on a trimester basis over a two-year period by an automatic debit, and pledged in the future to guarantee all contributions are secured to ECCAS, even if this be by an automatic debiting of the accounts of member states in their respective central banks. A fund for development and sub-regional solidarity was also created. At the heads of state and government conference at Brazzaville, Congo, in January 2004, it was decided that all member states would levy a special tax for this purpose.

ECCAS failed to spur trade creation. Failure of macroeconomic harmonization was arguably due to the fact that the economies of its members are competitive rather than complementary. With a view to jump-starting this, a scheme for the liberalization of intra-Community trade and the free movement of persons and goods was to be launched per Decision No. 03/CCEG/VI/90. A recommendation for the studies on harmonization of customs and tax legislation was tabled only at the January 2003 meeting of Council of Ministers of Economy and Finance and is proof that ECCAS had failed dismally to meet the timelines prescribed in 1983 for sectoral integration in the realm of trade. It was only at the Brazzaville summit that it was finally conceded that a free trade zone would become operational in June 2004. A new consciousness also seemed to emerge on the need for partnership in this endeavor. Political will that was in short supply is now becoming more manifest, as demonstrated by a decision at the Brazzaville summit to grant the right of free circulation to businessmen, students, religious, tourists, researchers, and university professors. Several missing links mitigate the growth of intra-ECCAS trade. Notable among them is the lack of a viable road network. The only significant road link is between Kigali and Bujumbura. Inadequate infrastructure and physical integration helps to increase overhead costs, thereby adding to the high costs of doing business at the intra-ECCAS level. To begin to reverse this situation, ECCAS has adopted a realistic policy, as in accepting external actors such as the European Union to aid in the building of road infrastructure.

Whereas cooperation in sectors that are normally given priority in regional integration schemes has been slow, ECCAS has taken new initiatives in cooperating in new areas such as combating poverty and the anti-drug campaign. Though this may contribute to alleviate the quality of life of its population, it would not necessarily move the integration process forward. It is evidence of a lack of political will. Seemingly, this is more manifest in the Central African Economic and Monetary Community (CEMAC) that replaced UDEAC in 1994. Though the AEC confirmed the importance of ECCAS as the major community in Central Africa because of its comprehensive nature at the third preparatory meeting of its Economic and Social Council (ECOSOC) in June 1999, CEMAC still seems to be privileged in the sub-region. This may be attributable to the cultural affinity of its member states, which are all Francophone, use of a common currency, the franc CFA, and fear of the viral effect of conflict from the CEPGL zone. Admittedly, Equatorial Guinea, Sao Tome, and Principe (after the 2004 Brazzaville summit) have acceded to this organization. Plausibly, because of lack of confidence

ECCAS has caused the leaders to focus their attention in integration in CEMAC. Thus, despite COPAX, they signed a mutual non-aggression and solidarity pact at the January 2004 Brazzaville summit.

On the whole, even the functionalist approach to integration adopted by the ECCAS member states has had a limited payoff. Essentially, due to a lack of political will, this situation has not been challenged because integration was conceived by the leaders and has not been people-centered so far. Its failure to impact on the everyday life of the common man, for whom space remains bounded, preempts it from serving as a catalyst for integration. On the whole ECCAS remains a work in progress.

NANTANG JUA

See also Central Africa: History and Economic Development

References and Further Reading

Africa News Service. "Africa: Sub-regional Integration runs Out of Inspiration." 02/26/2001 and 02/27/2001.
Berman, E. G. and Sams, K. E. "Le maintain de la paix en Afrique" in *Forum du désarmament*. Trios, pp. 23–34, 2000.
Economic Commission for Africa. *Annual Report on Integration in Africa 2002: Overview*. Addis Ababa, March 2002.
Makoundzi-Wolo, N. "Le Droit International African de l'intégration économique est-il porteur d'autonomie (souveraineté) collective?: L'exemple de la Communauté des Etats de l'Afrique Centrale (C.E.E.A.C)" in *Revue Congolaise de Droit*. Janvier-Juin 1987, No, 1, pp. 15–35.
———. "Le Droit International Africain de l'intégration économique est-il porteur d'autonomie(souveraineté) collective?: L'exemple de la Communauté des Etats de l'Afrique Centrale (C.E.E.A.C)" (suite) in *Revue Congolaise de Droit*. Juillet-Decembre 1987, pp. 9–24.
Organization of African Unity, Department of Foreign Affairs. *Profile: Economic Community of Central African States (CEEAC)*. ECCAS/CEEAC Profile, 07-05-2000.
South Africa Economic Committee. "Regional Integration in Sub-Saharan Africa, Toward rationalization and greater effectiveness" GCA/EC/04/02/2001.
The Economic Community of Central African States. *Treaty Establishing the Economic Community of Central African States*. Libreville, Gabon, 1983.

ECONOMIC COMMUNITY OF WEST AFRICAN STATES (ECOWAS)

Origin

The idea of regional integration has a long-standing history in West Africa. Indeed, many of the African leaders who opposed Kwame Nkrumah's ambitious attempt to create a union of African states during the peak of the Pan-African movement in the late 1950s opted for various forms of integration at the sub-regional level. President William V. S. Tubman of Liberia, for instance, forged a free trade agreement between Liberia, Cote d'Ivoire, Guinea, and Sierra Leone in 1965. However, the scheme, like many others in West Africa at the time, failed primarily because of hesitations and power struggles among its members. Further, with the support of France, many francophone nations in West Africa established a variety of economic unions in the early post-independence period. Notable examples include the West African Custom Union or Union Douaniere de l'Afrique de l'Ouest (UDAO)—which was formed in 1959 and replaced in 1966 by the West African Economic Union or Union Douaniere et Economique de l'Africa de l'Ouest (UDEAO)—and the West African Economic Community or Communaute Economique de l'Afrique de l'Ouest (CEAO) formed in 1973.

Unlike their francophone counterparts, anglophone West African countries did not pursue much economic integration in the immediate post-independence era, as the British administrative structure accorded little sense of economic unity among its colonies. While most of the exclusively francophone unions were successful, the few attempts made to integrate francophone and anglophone nations, including the Burkina Faso–Ghana union and the Ghana-Guinea-Mali experiment failed, mainly because of the inability of most West African nations to break their colonial ties during the immediate post-independence period (Asante 1986).

The first major attempt towards the formation of an economic union embracing all West African nations was made by the Economic Commission for Africa (ECA) through two main resolutions, 142 (VIII) and 145 (VII), passed at its seventh session in Nairobi in February 1965 (Ezenwe 1983). Notwithstanding the enormous institutional and financial support given by the ECA, it took a decade for West African nations to finally come together to form ECOWAS in 1975. . The indecisiveness that thwarted the ECA efforts stemmed from several factors, not the least of which were attempts by France, Britain, and Portugal to preserve their economic ties with their respective former colonies, through various incentives and preferential arrangements; the existence of several competing economic unions in the sub-region; and the uncertainties created by the 1967–1970 Biafra war in Nigeria.

A 1972 meeting in Lomé between General Yakubu Gowon of Nigeria and President Gnassingbé Eyadéma of Togo culminated in a communiqué which many analysts (e.g., Asante 1986; Ezenwe

1982; Onyemelukwe and Filani 1983) consider as the "embryo" of ECOWAS. A series of bilateral and multilateral meetings on the viability of an economic union, spearheaded by these two leaders, led to the signing of the ECOWAS treaty on May 28, 1975, in Lagos. The original signatories were fifteen West African nations: Benin, Burkina Faso, Code d'Ivoire, Gambia, Ghana, Guinea, Guinea-Bissau, Liberia, Mali, Mauritania, Niger, Nigeria, Senegal, Sierra Leone, and Togo. Cape Verde joined in 1977, bringing the membership to the current total of sixteen. A revised ECOWAS treaty, designed to accelerate economic integration and to increase political cooperation, was signed in July 1993.

Objectives

The ECOWAS treaty has as its prime objective to:

> [P]romote co-operation and integration, leading to the establishment of an economic union in West Africa in order to raise the living standards of its people, and to maintain and enhance economic stability, foster relations among Members States and contribute to the progress and development of the African Continent (Article 3).

To accomplish this broad objective, ECOWAS, *inter alia*, seeks to eliminate custom duties among member states; adopt a common external tariff and trade policies towards non-members; remove barrier to the movement of goods, services, and people; and harmonize trade, agricultural, energy, and environmental policies of its members. The treaty also makes provisions for the synchronization of investment codes and standards, and the establishment of a special fund for sub-regional cooperation and development, paying attention to the special needs of the 'poor,' landlocked, and small member states. The underlying values of ECOWAS, according to Article Four of the treaty, include adherence to the principles of equality, solidarity, accountability, non-aggression, maintenance of peace, and the promotion of democratic system of government in each member state. The Treaty permits ECOWAS members to join other regional and sub-regional associations, as long as such concurrent memberships do not conflict with the spirit and purpose of ECOWAS.

Institutions

The official duties of ECOWAS are undertaken through its institutions, the most powerful of which is the Authority of Heads of States and Governments. This supreme body, made up of all the leaders of the member states, meets at least once a year under a rotated chairpersonship. Next in importance is the Council of Ministers, which is responsible for monitoring the activities of ECOWAS, and for making recommendations to the Authority of Heads of States and Governments for the attainment of ECOWAS goals. This council comprises two ministers from each member state; it meets at least twice in a year. Another important institution is the Executive Secretariat, headed by the Executive Secretary, who performs the main administrative and executive duties of ECOWAS and coordinates the activities of all other institutions. The Executive Secretary is appointed by the Authority of Heads of States and Governments for a four-year term, renewable only once for another four years. Other notable ECOWAS institutions are the Community Parliament; the Economic and Social Council; the Community Court of Justice; and the Fund for Co-operation, Compensation and Development. ECOWAS has five main Specialized and Technical Commissions, including those of Trade, Customs, Immigration, Monetary and Payments; Transport, Telecommunication, and Energy; Agriculture and Natural Resources; Administration and Finance; and Social and Cultural Affairs. ECOWAS is headquartered in Abuja, Nigeria, where it has its own buildings and administrative staff.

Contributions to Development

The main goal of ECOWAS is to enhance the collective self-sufficiency of West African nations, through economic integration and cooperation. The organization was founded on the premise that the domestic markets of the individual members were too small to be competitive in a global economy characterized by large trading blocks such as the European Union (EU) and the North American Free Trade Agreement (NAFTA). With a potential single market of about 210 million people, ECOWAS expects to promote specialization and large-scale industrialization; enhance job opportunities and wealth creation; and limit the sub-region's dependence on foreign market.

It bears stressing from the outset that the concrete achievements of ECOWAS to date are modest. Yet, given the wide ethno-cultural diversity in West Africa, the mere fact that these nations were able to come together is an epic feat; at the very least, ECOWAS has fostered intra-regional understanding and cooperation and alleviated the tensions and suspicions that characterized intergovernmental relations in

West Africa. More substantively, ECOWAS has facilitated the free movement of people within the region; improved transportation and telecommunication links between member states; and helped maintain peace and security in West Africa. It has also made remarkable advances in the agriculture and energy sectors, and forged reputable coalitions with international organizations such as the Organization of African Unity (OAU), the Economic Commission on Africa (ECA), and the World Bank. ECOWAS citizens can now enter and reside in any member state for ninety days without visas or entry permits, as long as they have valid passports or travel certificates and international vaccination certificates. ECOWAS has introduced its own travel certificate, which is currently in circulation in such countries as Burkina Faso, Ghana, Gambia, Guinea, Niger, Nigeria, and Sierra Leone. With this document, ECOWAS travelers are, in theory, exempted from filling out any immigration papers in member states; however, it is worth noting that, in practice, many countries still require ECOWAS travelers to fill immigration forms, and nearly all member states have road checkpoints at which police and immigration agents routinely subject travelers to harassment and extortion.

Through its Trade Liberalization Scheme, ECOWAS seeks to establish a custom union and to eliminate tariffs among its members; the original timeframe was to remove tariffs on unprocessed goods by 1990, and on industrial goods by 2000. While many members (e.g., Cote I'dviore, Burkina Faso, Gambia, Ghana, Niger, Nigeria, and Benin) have eliminated their tariffs on unprocessed goods, only Benin has so far lifted tariffs on industrial goods. The persistence of tariffs and other trade restrictions among members continue to undermine intra-ECOWAS trade, which now account for a mere 11% of members' total trade, valued at some $3.6 billion US dollars.

Economic integration invariably entails easy access to each member's market, which, in turn, requires the development of adequate transportation and telecommunication systems. However, such systems are scanty, patchy, and poorly developed across West Africa. Further, while the bulk of the goods traded among ECOWAS members is transported by sea, most of the shipping companies in the sub-region are non-African. Likewise, most of the sub-regional air travel and telecommunication transactions are done through non-African companies. ECOWAS is currently building inter-state highways from Lagos to Nouakchott, Mauritania; and from Dakar, Senegal, to N'djamena, Chad, to improve spatial interaction among its members. ECOWAS also has proposals under way to establish an airline company, ECOAIR; to strengthen the railway networks in the sub-region; and to improve the telecommunication facilities in the sub-region, through its INTELCOM I and INTELCOM II projects, initiated in 1979 and 1992, respectively.

In the energy front, ECOWAS has a master plan to develop hydroelectric power in several countries, including Ghana, Guinea, Sierra Leone, Mali, and Togo. Plans are also under way to develop about 5,600 kilometers of electricity lines connecting various segments of national grids; establish a "power pool" to facilitate the exchange of electrical energy between members; and diversify the energy capabilities of members into biomass, solar, and other renewable energy sources. Similarly, the organization has programs to improve the sub-region's agriculture: In 1982, an Agricultural Development Strategy, which included plans for selecting seeds and cattle species and called for solidarity among members during international commodity negotiations, was adopted.

Concerns for peace and security have long been on ECOWAS' radar screen: In 1978 ECOWAS adopted a non-aggression protocol. This was followed with a defence assistance protocol in 1981; the creation of an ECOWAS Cease-Fire Monitoring Group (ECOMOG) in 1990; and a declaration of democratic political principles in 1991—the latter condemns the seizure of power by force of arms in any member state. Perhaps, the most important accomplishment of ECOWAS regarding regional peace is the decisive role played by ECOMOG in ending the Liberian war.

Despite these achievements, ECOWAS continues to struggle with its primary objective of trade liberalization and market integration, mainly because of the limited potential that exist for trade between its members: Since they are all primary producers, with agriculture accounting for the bulk of their respective GDPs, the demand for their exports and the supply of their imports invariably emanate from advanced nations outside the sub-region. The existence of other rival integration schemes—e.g., the West African Economic Community (or the Communaute Economique de l'Afrique de l'Ouest (CEAO)) and the West African Economic and Monetary Union (the l'Union Economique et Monétarie Ouest Africaine (UEMOA))—also creates unhealthy competition, duplication, and conflicts of interest among some ECOWAS members. The limited financial resources of member states is yet another daunting drawback that undermines ECOWAS' effectiveness. Indeed, several members are incapable of meeting their financial commitments to ECOWAS, forcing it to depend more and more on the financial support of foreign governments and organizations. Notwithstanding

these difficulties, recent trends in the sub-region point to a promising future for ECOWAS: Among these are the increasing prevalence of democratic governance; the move towards privatization and liberalization of national markets; and the increasing cooperation between ECOWAS and other international organizations such as the Organization of African Unity (OAU), the African Development Bank (ADB), and the European Union (EU). Still, for ECOWAS to thrive, the need for the unflinching support of political leaders and citizens of West Africa for its programs cannot be gainsaid.

JOSEPH MENSAH

See also Economic Commission for Africa (ECA); West African Monetary Union (WAMU)

References and Further Reading

Akinyemi, A. B, S.B. Falegan, and I.A. Aluko, editors. *Readings and Documents on ECOWAS: Selected Papers and Discussions from the 1976 Economic Community of West African States Conference.*, Lagos, Nigeria: Nigerian Institute of International Affairs, and Lagos and Ibadan, Nigeria: Macmillan Nigeria Publishers Ltd., 1984.

Asante, S. K. B. *The Political Economy of Regionalism in Africa: A Decade of the Economic Community of West African States (ECOWAS)*. New York: Praeger Publishers, 1986.

ECOWAS. *Silver Jubilee Anniversary (1975–2000): Achievements and Prospects*. Abuja, Nigeria: ECOWAS, 2000.

ECOWAS. *An ECOWAS Compendium on Free Movement, Right of Residence and Establishment*. Abuja, Nigeria: ECOWAS, 1999.

Ezenwe, Uka. *ECOWAS and the Economic Integration of West Africa*. London: C. Hurst & Company, 1983.

Gambari, Ibrahim A. *Political and Comparative Dimensions of Regional Integration: The Case of ECOWAS*. New Jersey and London: Humanities Press International, Inc., 1991.

Lavergne, Réal, editor. *Regional Integration and Cooperation in West Africa*. Ottawa, Canada: International Development Research Council (IDRC) and Trenton, NJ and Asmara, Eritirea: African World Press, Inc., 1997.

Masson, Paul and Catherine Pattillo. *Monetary Union in West Africa (ECOWAS): Is it Desirable and How could it be Achieved?* Washington, DC: International Monetary Union, Occasional Paper #204, 2001.

McLenaghan, John B., Saleh M. Nsouli, and Klaus-Walter Riechel. *Currency Convertibility in the Economic Community of West African States*. Washington, DC: International Monetary Fund, 1982.

Obiozo, G. A., A.O. Olukoshi, and C.I. Obi, editors. *West African Regional Economic Integration: Nigerian Perspectives for the 1990s*. Lagos, Nigeria: Nigerian Institute of International Affairs, 1994.

Okolo, Julius Emeka and Stephen Wright, editors. *West African Regional Cooperation and Development*. Boulder, CO, San Francisco, and Oxford: Westview Press, 1990.

Onyemelukwe, J. O. C. and M. O. Filani. *Economic Geography of West Africa*. London, Lagos, New York: Longman, 1983.

Robson, Peter. *Integration, Development and Equity: Economic Integration in West Africa*. London, Boston, and Sydney: George Allen & Unwin, 1983.

Shaw, Timothy M. and Julius Emeka Okolo, editors. *The Political Economy of Foreign Policy in ECOWAS*. Houndmills, Basingstoke, Hampshire and London: The Macmillan Pres Ltd. and New York: St Martin's Press Ltd., 1994.

ECONOMIC COOPERATION ORGANIZATION (ECO)

Original roots of this group can be traced to 1964, when it was established as a regional political entity to promote greater political and military consultations and cooperation among its members. The Economic Cooperation Organization was established in its current form in 1985 with its headquarters in Tehran. Initially it included Iran, Pakistan, and Turkey.

In the new environment the ECO intended to promote regional economic cooperation especially in such fields as regional trade and development of regional transportation and communication infrastructure. In 1992, the newly independent Azerbaijan, Kazakhstan, Kyrgyzstan, Tajikistan, Turkmenistan, and Uzbekistan were invited to join the organization. After expansion the member countries sought to promote intraregional trade and to gradually establish a common market or trade economic zone similar to the European Union (EU). They also planned to develop new transportation routes for Central Asian gas and oil and for their other natural resources to international markets. The Central Asian governments also hoped that trade with ECO partners would reduce their dependency on the Russian and Commonwealth of Independent States (CIS) markets. Almost immediately after the ECO membership grew to ten, the organization declared that it was "directed against no country or group of countries," since there were concerns expressed by India, Russia, and some other international players about the nature of the grouping.

At present the total population of the ECO members is about 340 million and their territories cover over six million square kilometers (twice the size of India). Its members control about 15% of the world's proven reserves of oil and about 10% of the world's proven reserves of natural gas as well as significant resources of the hydroelectric power. The ECO members also produce a significant proportion of cotton for exports to international market. The principle working bodies of the ECO are as follows: the Council of Ministers, the Regional Planning Council, the Council of Permanent Representatives, and the Secretariat.

The Council of Ministers is the highest policy-making organ of the ECO and it consists of the Ministers of Foreign Affairs of the Member States. The Council meets at least once a year in different locations each year on a rotating basis. The Regional Planning Council consists of the Heads of the Planning Organization or the equivalent ministry of the Member States. Its members meet at least once a year prior to the annual meeting of the Council of Ministers. The Council of Permanent Representatives is composed of Ambassadors from the Member states and its members meet as often as needed.

The Secretariat of the ECO's permanent working institution initiates, coordinates, and monitors the implementation of ECO activities.

In addition the ECO created several other agencies that coordinate works in specific fields. The Directorate of Energy, Minerals, and Environment monitors and coordinates efficient utilization of regional natural resources and facilitates cooperation in environmental protection. The Directorate of Trade and Investment promotes intra-regional and supra-regional trade, trade liberalization. The Directorate of Agriculture, Industry, and Health promotes cooperation in the agricultural sector, including such issues as food safety, new technologies, and desertification. The Directorate of Transport and Communications promotes development of a regional road and railway networks in the region. The Directorate of Economic Research and Statistics assesses development projects, studies perspectives for the regional economic cooperation, and facilitates information and statistical exchange. The Directorate of Project Research focuses on inter-sectoral coordination among various departments of the ECO Secretariat, organizes meetings, and prepares reports and documents. The Coordination and International Relations plays a key role in facilitating relationships with major regional and international organizations including those within the United Nations (UN) system.

Since the 1990s, the ECO has organized regular meetings at ministerial level and discussed simplification of the cross-border transit of goods and investments, simplification, and unification of the taxation code and some other measures. The ECO adopted the Quetta Plan of Action (February 1993), the Istanbul Declaration (ECO Long Term Perspectives) (July 1993), the Almaty Outline Plan for the Development of the Transport Sector in the ECO Region (October 1993), the Ashgabat Declaration of 1997, the Program of Action for the ECO Decade of Transport and Communications (March 1998), and the Transit Transport Framework Agreement.

Among the major projects sponsored or supported by the ECO was the Tejen-Mashhad-Serakhs railway line (1996), which opened up railway traffic on the northern line of the Trans-Asian Railway of the "East-West" Transport Corridor, and on the "North-South" Transport Corridor linking Central Asian Republics with the ports of the Persian Gulf; and the development of an infrastructure for the "East-West" (including "Europe-Caucasus-Asia") and "North-South" Transport Corridors. According to ECO statistics, in 1998 there were a total of 52,882.2 kilometers of railways in the region compared with 48,496.6 kilometers in 1994. In 2002, the ECO members announced completion of several projects, including the opening of a container route Kazakhstan-Turkmenistan-Turkey (Istanbul) through the Trans-Asian Railway route, international passenger route Almaty-Tashkent-Tehran-Istanbul, and Almaty-Tashkent-Turkmenabat-Istanbul. In March 2004, the ECO Council of Heads of Customs Administrations (CHCA) discussed the establishment of a Data Bank on Smuggling and Customs Offenses; and the Transit Trade Committee discussed the Transit Trade Agreement. The experts discussed measures to simplify and harmonize customs procedures for the development of trade among ECO member states.

Memoranda of Understanding were signed between the ECO and following agencies: UNDP, UNODC, UNESCAP, UNIDO, UNFPA, FAO, UNESCO, UNICEF, UNECE, UNCTAD, UIC, ITC, OIC, IDB, OSJD, ICARDA, WCO, and Colombo Plan.

RAFIS ABAZOV

See also Afghanistan; Azerbaijan; Iran; Kazakhstan; Kyrgyzstan; Pakistan; Tajikistan; Turkey; Turkmenistan; Uzbekistan

References and Further Reading

Economic Cooperation Organization. *ECO Bulletin*. Tehran: ECO, 2002.
Economic Cooperation Organization. *The ECO Guide Book*. Tehran: The ECO Secretariat, 1999.
Economic Cooperation Organization. *MOUs and Agreements with International and Regional Organizations and Agencies*. Tehran: ECO, 2000.
Economic Cooperation Organization. *Summit Communiqués and Declarations, 1992–1999*. Tehran: The ECO Secretariat, 2000.
Economic Cooperation Organization: http://www.ecosecretariat.org/.
Handbook of Economic Integration and Cooperation Groupings of Developing Countries. Volume 1, Regional and Subregional Economic Integration Groupings. New York: UN, 1996.
International Business Publications. *Economic Cooperation Organization Business Law Handbook (World Offshore Investment and Business Library)*. New York: International Business Publications, 2001.
Jдgerhorn, Marita. *The Economic Cooperation Organization (ECO): Potentials and Prospects of Economic Cooperation in Central and West Asia*. Helsinki, Finland: Ministry of Trade and Industry, Industry Dept., 1993.

ECOTOURISM

Ecotourism is tourism which: uses the natural environment as the primary attraction; is actively managed to minimise impacts on the natural environment; actively teaches tourists about the natural environment; and contributes to conservation of the natural environment. Cultural aspects, particularly indigenous cultures, may also be included. The term is sometimes misused to refer to nature-based tourism more broadly, irrespective of impacts, but this is a misnomer. Such misuse has caused extensive conflicts between tourism developers and operators, community and environmental groups, and government agencies in many countries. From a tourism market perspective, ecotourism is one component of the broader nature, eco, and adventure tourism (NEAT) sector. Ecotourism can be significant for developing countries because it can bring hard currencies from relatively wealthy tourists, both foreign and domestic, directly to relatively impoverished regions, communities, and national parks agencies; creating an industry sector which uses the plant, animal, scenic, and sometimes cultural wealth of developing nations with far less impact than primary industries such as logging, farming, or mining.

Ecotourism ventures can be either small- or medium-scale, and there are successful examples of each, though the former are currently more common. There do not as yet appear to be any examples of ecotourism at the scale of mega-resorts or holiday towns, but there are individual ecotourism enterprises which operate dozens of individual facilities across several developing countries, employ over one thousand people, and turn over many millions of dollars per year. Internationally, there are ecotourism companies which offer only a single product but generate annual revenue of over $10 million US. Many of these rely on capital-intensive infrastructure, such as large ocean-going vessels. In most developing countries, however, the focus of ecotourism development is on large numbers of small developments. There has also been a strong emphasis on involving local communities, either as owner-operator of an ecotourism venture, or as partner and beneficiary. Whoever owns the company, local involvement avoids local antagonism. Equally, however, for financial viability, any ecotourism venture needs skills in tourism management and marketing; and for an upmarket international clientele, an upmarket international standard of hospitality.

The economic and social significance of ecotourism can be considerable. For most developing nations, it is nature, culture, and adventure which are the primary tourism attractions: that is, the bulk of the country's tourism industry lies at least within the broader NEAT sector. For example, Kenya and Botswana each received over 1 million international visitors in 1997, and Zimbabwe over 1.5 million. Ecuador and Peru each received over half a million international visitors. For comparison the global total for that year was over 600 million, and over 50% were within Europe. Whilst globally, tourism accounts for a little over 10% of worldwide economic activity, in some smaller countries it can contribute a far higher proportion—up to 83% in the Maldives, for example. Much of this money, however, is used immediately to buy imports, in a pattern known as economic leakage (q.v.). In some countries, a significant proportion of tourism revenue is retained by central governments, either through direct taxes, through differential pricing for foreigners, or through foreign exchange conversion requirements and systems. At a national scale, very little of the tourist income generated by natural assets is reinvested in conserving those assets. In Costa Rica, a country which advertises itself internationally as a leader in ecotourism, the proportion is still only around 1%. The proportion is similar, incidentally, in developed nations such as Australia. Even where national parks and other public land management agencies collect fees from visitors or tour operators, the agency may not be allowed to keep the funds collected. Private ecotourism ventures in developing countries, therefore, often emphasise direct local reinvestment.

These social and economic issues are critical to the success of ecotourism in developing countries. If the ecotourism sector is small, it may have little significance, and may be swamped by mainstream tourism and other industry sectors. As it gets larger, its environmental and social impacts increase, and it may also lose market appeal. Unless it yields benefits to local communities it faces local antagonism which may lead to loss of land access; but unless it also provides gains to people with national political power, it may lose its natural assets to other industry sectors such as logging or agriculture.

Developing nations may have both advantages and disadvantages as ecotourism destinations. For all forms of tourism, their main advantages are that they are simply different, and therefore interesting; and that their currencies are often weaker than those of the countries where most international tourists originate. The price advantage does not necessarily apply for the NEAT sector, especially for the low-volume high-yield product which many developed countries now aim for, and especially since many prices are now set in US dollars. Where developing countries have their principal competitive advantage is in the diversity of plants and animals, and the opportunity to watch them; i.e., specifically in the ecotourism sector. Comparable wildlife viewing opportunities in the developed world, for example, are generally available only in sparsely populated areas such as parts of Alaska, the Arctic, sub-Arctic and sub-Antarctic, and protected areas in North America, Australia, and Russia. Many developing nations also attract tourists through their scenery, climates, and cultures. These appeal to a broader market, but the comparative advantage is less than for animals and plants.

One of the principal distinguishing features of ecotourism is the deliberate attempt to minimise impacts on the natural and cultural environment, but even with such precautions, ecotourism can produce substantial impacts. Since many ecotourism destinations are in areas of high conservation significance, such as national parks or other pristine or protected areas where there is little human impact other than tourism, the ecological impacts of ecotourism are disproportionately significant. Some of these impacts are immediately apparent but usually quite localised, such as soil erosion and vegetation trampling along tracks, trails, and campsites. Others are less obvious but potentially much more significant ecologically, such as the introduction of weeds into national parks, contamination of water with pathogens, and disturbance to rare or endangered wildlife. Different activities produce different impacts in different ecosystems, and different management tools can be used to control them. Promoting tourism as a tool to protect the biological wealth of developing nations from other forms of exploitation always carries the risk of impacts from tourism itself, and ecotourism attempts to maximise the environmental benefits and minimise the environmental costs.

Similar considerations apply for cultural impacts. Where any indigenous or ethnic group uses traditional culture as part of a tourism product, then the more successful their tourism business, the more their culture will be changed. If the host culture changes too much, however, it will no longer be a tourist attraction. The usual outcome is so-called staged authenticity, where hosts carry out traditional activities using traditional artifacts solely for tourists, and no longer as part of their own day-to-day life. Strictly, this commoditisation of culture is associated with cultural tourism rather than ecotourism but in practice many holiday packages combine both.

Similarly, other commonplace social impacts, such as widening inequities between those members of a host community who benefit from tourism and those who do not, apply to all types of tourism. The same applies to the argument, sometimes made by politicians and social commentators, that tourism to developing countries is a form of cultural neo-imperialism. These issues are significant for ecotourism businesses in developing countries because they influence community attitudes, which in turn affect both land access and customer satisfaction. Ecotourism ventures worldwide have therefore tried a variety of community participation models. Different models are appropriate in different countries, depending on land tenure arrangements, social traditions of mutual assistance or individual entrepreneurship, and established structures for community leadership or group action.

Ecotourism has developed along different pathways in different continents and regions, reflecting their different environments, societies, infrastructures, and tourism development histories. Private game reserves, lodges, and safaris in southern and eastern Africa, for example, have made significant contributions to the conservation of endangered wildlife species and to local community development, as well as the tourism economies of the countries concerned. In central and south America, the mountain scenery of the Andes and the national parks of the far south have for many decades attracted trekkers and mountaineers, supporting a wide range of small-scale tourist accommodation, guides, and tour operators. Some of this is based in national parks and some at small privately owned lodges. In some areas there is also a cultural tourism industry based largely on ancient buildings; and an adventure tourism sector which includes, e.g., diving in the Caribbean, whitewater rafting and kayaking, and mountaineering on the high peaks of the Andes.

In the Himalayas, longstanding mountaineering and trekking tourism has been expanded in recent decades by a large whitewater industry, wildlife tours in limited areas, and most recently a high-altitude heliski operation. Throughout the larger developing nations of southern and eastern Asia, the emphasis historically has been primarily on cultural attractions, but tourists also visit nature-based attractions such as the deserts of the southwest and centre and the mountains and forests of the southeast and far north. Some of these areas have attracted travelers for many millennia, and the majority of their modern visitors are still domestic tourists. Similar growth in the NEAT sector has occurred in southeast Asia, with forests, wildlife, and adventure now increasingly important attractions for Western visitors. For tourists

from developed eastern nations, shopping and golf probably still remain paramount, but this may be changing with new generations. Finally, the small-island developing states (SIDS) of the Indo-Pacific region deserve particular mention as destinations for a growing marine ecotourism market.

In all these regions, ecotourism is at risk from other land uses and industry sectors, both legal and illegal. The whalewatching and marine mammal industry is threatened by commercial fishing practices, and the dive tourism sector by dynamite fishing. Ecotourism opportunities in developing countries worldwide are threatened by industrial logging and by clearance for industrial agricultural plantations. In many areas this is happening on a very large scale and at a very high rate, e. g., in Cameroon and Gabon in West Africa, Sumatra and the Solomon Islands in the Indo-Pacific, and in the Amazon basin in South America. In many of these areas there is also extensive clearance for small subsistence agriculture. Many of the larger animals which provide the mainstay for wildlife tourism are also subject to poaching, both for the illegal wildlife trade and for subsistence bush meat, or are killed when they move into agricultural areas. Well-known examples include elephant, rhino, and mountain gorilla in Africa; tiger, snowleopard, sunbear, and orangutan in Asia; and jaguar and many forest species in South America.

In some countries, ecotourism opportunities have been lost through water pollution from mining, manufacturing, pulp mills, processing, and power plants. Lake Baikal is a famous example, but there are many more throughout developing and indeed developed nations worldwide. Additionally, in developing countries, many large-scale industrial projects are financed by bilateral or multilateral aid funds. These same agencies or their subsidiaries may also finance small-scale ecotourism projects but rarely consider how these will be affected by other industries.

The potential advantages of ecotourism for economy, community, and environment in developing nations have been widely promoted, and there are indeed some outstanding examples of success. Equally, however, there are many examples where developing-country governments have given lip service to ecotourism whilst simultaneously promoting conflicting industry sectors or high-impact mass tourism developments. There are also many examples where despite hard work and the best of intentions, new ecotourism ventures have never grown large enough to have much effect.

To overcome these difficulties, ecotourism practitioners and proponents in many developing nations have now established local ecotourism associations.

Some developing-country governments have also prepared national ecotourism strategies, often with assistance from international non-government organisations such as the World Conservation Union (IUCN), the Worldwide Fund for Nature (WWF), and intergovernmental agencies such as the United Nations Environment Program and the World Tourism Organisation. The International Year of Ecotourism and World Ecotourism Summit in 2002 provided an opportunity to improve international cooperation between all these organisations.

RALF BUCKLEY

See also Environment: Government Policies

References and Further Reading

Buckley, Ralf. *Environmental Impacts of Ecotourism.* Oxford: CABI 2004.
———. *Case Studies in Ecotourism.* Oxford: CABI, 2003.
———. "Tourism and Biodiversity in North and South," *Tourism & Recreation Research,* 27. No. 1, 2001.
———. "NEAT Trends: Current Issues in Nature, Eco and Adventure Tourism," *International Journal of Tourism Research,* 2. No. 6, 2000.
Fennell, David. *Ecotourism: an Introduction.* London: Routledge, 1999.
Harrison, David. *Tourism in the Developing World: Issues and Case Studies.* Oxford: CABI, 2001.
Honey, Martha. *Ecotourism and Sustainable Development: Who Owns Paradise?* Washington DC: Island Press, 1999.
IUCN. *Guidelines for Tourism and Biodiversity in Developing Countries.* Gland: IUCN, 2001.
Liddle, Michael. *Recreation Ecology.* London: Chapman & Hall, 1998.
Weaver, David. *Encyclopaedia of Ecotourism.* Oxford, CABI, 2001.

ECUADOR

Ecuador is a South American republic located on the west coast between Colombia on the north and Peru on the south and east; encompassing an area of 109,000 square miles with a population of approximately twelve million in 2001. Ecuador's ethnic makeup consists of indigenous 25%, mestizo 55%, caucasian 10%, and African 10%. A white elite dominated the political life of the country until the latter half of the twentieth century, when the mestizo population became more assertive. Recently the indigenous populations have formed coalitions and are participating more and more in the political life of the country. Although small in area, Ecuador has varied geographical features including lush tropical coastal lowlands, temperate highland valleys, rain forests, arid deserts, and numerous active volcanoes. The famous Galápagos Islands are also part of Ecuador. Ecuador's exotic and rugged geographical features have inhibited its development throughout history. Until recently transportation has been difficult and many Ecuadorians seldom ventured beyond the immediate milieu of their villages and hamlets. The Andes separate the political and economic life of the nation into two competing zones: the Costa, centered at Guayaquil; the bustling, tropical, Pacific port; and the Sierra, dominated by Quito, the sedate colonial capital. Natural resources include petroleum, fish, shrimp, timber, and gold while the agricultural sector produces bananas, seafood, flowers, coffee, cacao, sugar, corn, rice, and livestock. The gross domestic product (GDP) in 2002 was $24.3 billion. Ecuador's largest export market (41%) is the United States. Ecuador has made great strides in social development (literacy rate 90%, life expectancy 70.8 years, infant mortality 19 per 1,000) but still lags behind much of Latin America.

In the last three decades of the twentieth century Ecuador's most vexing international problem was a territorial dispute with Peru. In 1941, Ecuador was involved in a short but disastrous war with Peru that resulted in the temporary relinquishment of its claim to a vast territory in the Amazon. This "loss" of territory would also hinder Ecuador's development, as populists would use the issue to inflame public opinion, and the armed forces would demand a larger share of the budget in the name of national security. In January 1995, war again erupted in the disputed upper Cenapa Valley. A cease-fire brokered by Argentina, Brazil, Chile, and the United States led to serious negotiations. On October 16, 1998, a comprehensive agreement was reached, ending the dispute that began in 1830.

New petroleum fields were discovered in Ecuador's Oriente region in 1967. A surge in petroleum exports resulted in favorable foreign exchange earnings that climbed from $43 million in 1971 to over $350 million by 1974. The GDP increased at an annual rate of 9% in the period 1970–1977, raising Ecuador to the status of a lower-middle-income country. However, the oil boom proved to be a mixed blessing, as a period of inflation eroded many of the gains. Moreover, governments used oil earnings as collateral for international loans and the external debt soared from $324 million in 1974 to $4.5 billion by 1979. Inflation continued to plague the economy throughout the remaining decades of the twentieth century. In March 2000, Ecuador adopted the US dollar as its national currency in the hopes of curbing inflation.

During much of the oil boom, several military governments that attempted structural reforms ruled Ecuador. The first junta, headed by General

Guillermo Rodríguez Lara, took power in a bloodless coup on February 15, 1972, promising to boost development. This, and a subsequent military regime, did make infrastructure improvements, including highways, hydroelectric projects, oil refineries, and the establishment of the Ecuadorian State Petroleum Company (CEPE). In 1973, Ecuador joined the Organization of Petroleum Exporting Nations. However, oil exports did not keep pace with imports and inflation soon eroded many of the gains. Disillusioned with the difficulties of governing, the military returned the country to civilian rule in 1979.

For fifteen years Ecuador experienced relative political stability, alternating between moderate leftist-oriented governments (Jamie Roldós and Osvaldo Hurtado 1979–1984, Rodrigo Borja 1988–1992), and conservative neo-liberal administrations (León Febres Cordero 1984–1988, Sixto Durán Ballén 1992–1996). Despite constitutional rule, internal wrangling, corruption, and a 1995 war stalled Ecuador's development with Peru over the long-standing border dispute. In 1996, Abdalá Bucaram, a charismatic populist, won the presidency and promised economic and social policies that would end the power of the elite and redistribute the wealth of the nation to the masses. But Bucaram's administration was marred by corruption, and Congress removed him in February 1997. In 1998, Jamil Mahuad, the competent mayor of Quito, was elected president. Mahuad resolved Ecuador's vexing international problem by negotiating a peace agreement with Peru that was accepted by the Ecuadorian public as a just settlement. Unfortunately, Mahuad did not reap the reward of this peace dividend. His plan to replace Ecuador's currency, the sucre, with the US dollar met with opposition. Mahuad was forced to leave office after popular demonstrations against his economic proposals led to the military announcing plans to take over the country and establish a junta. In the end, Ecuador's vice president Gustavo Noboa assumed the presidency. Noboa was able to implement dollarization and obtained private funding for a much needed second oil pipeline. Noboa returned Ecuador to a measure of stability and in January 2003 turned over the government to the newly elected president, Lucio Gutiérrez, a former army colonel who had played a key role in Mahuad's ouster.

Gutiérrez's policies have proven to be surprisingly moderate, and he has negotiated with international lending and development agencies to restructure Ecuador's debt. As a result, foreign investment reached a record high, inflation was held to 6%, and the GDP grew by 2.7% in 2003. Ecuador's future development hinges on the resolution of the nation's historic problems of class and regional cleavages, corruption, overreliance on one commodity, and episodes of political chaos, problems that are not easily remedied in the best of circumstances.

GEORGE M. LAUDERBAUGH

References and Further Reading

Gerlach, Allen. *Indians, Oil, and Politics: A Recent History of Ecuador*. Wilmington, DE: Scholarly Resources, 2003.

Hurtado Larrea, Osvaldo. *Political Power in Ecuador*. Albuquerque, NM: University of New Mexico Press, 1985.

Pallares, Amalia. *From Peasant Struggles to Indian Resistance: The Ecuadorian Andes in the Late Twentieth Century*. Norman, OK: University of Oklahoma Press, 2002.

Schodt, David. *Ecuador: An Andean Enigma*. Boulder, CO: Westview Press, 1987.

EDUCATION

The provision of education in developing countries is essentially a political issue. It can serve the ruling classes or overthrow governments; build or undermine democracy; contribute to modernisation, conservation, or reactionary outcomes; serve the whole community or a dominant elite. Many questions must be addressed. Should the priority be political empowerment, economic development, or social improvement? Is it most effectively driven by international aid, government action, or community initiatives? Is the most effective elementary education achieved through schooling children or adult literacy campaigns? Are traditional Western schools the most appropriate institutions for third world needs? How should limited resources be distributed between elementary education and higher education? How can sufficient teaching resources be provided? Is technology a way of increasing access to teaching resources, or does it only increase the gap between rich and poor?

The West values the potential of education to contribute to the growth of democracy in developing countries. This led the United Nations (UN) to promulgate the right to an education "directed to the full development of the human personality and to the strengthening of respect for human rights and fundamental freedoms" (Declaration of Human Rights article 26) and literacy to promote peace and security as the goal of the United Nations Educational Scientific and Cultural Organisation (UNESCO) founded in 1946. UNESCO launched the World Experimental Literacy Program in eight countries in 1963. This idea of education, however, runs counter to many nations' ideological positions. Education cannot promote human rights if the accompanying social and political climate is unfavourable. Where education systems are affected by economic rationalism and/or right-wing politics, they are limited to providing utilitarian instruction, training, and/or indoctrination. The lower socio-economic groups get poorer schools and less qualified teachers; girls are much less likely than boys to receive formal education, particularly secondary and above; and discrimination rises at each level of the educational ladder.

Under the impact of economic rationalism, the West's vision of education as a contribution to modernisation becomes narrowly focused on the economic aspect of modernisation. International support for education increasingly focuses on 'development' as defined by international capital, the World Bank, and the International Monetary Fund (IMF), concerned with developing human resources for profit. Since the 1980s, the impact of economic rationalism, demanding reduced public sector spending, has harmed poor nations; both school attendance and adult literacy have fallen and have been predicted to fall further over the next decades (Welch 2000). In Jamaica IMF-induced economic restructuring meant spending on health and education declined by over a third (Hickling-Hudson 2000).

Conversely, when the social and political climate is favourable, education becomes a tool for social improvement. In Granada the socialist revolution of 1979 attempted to equalise access to education, including experiments in non-formal adult education, and in Chile the 1989 return of democracy led to the Program for the Improvement of Equity and Quality of Education. India, Malaysia, Indonesia, Korea, and the Philippines all use education programs to tackle their desperate need for fertility control, described as "among the most significant curriculum innovations of our time" (Bishop 1986).

Where education is provided and controlled by the state, its priority can become the political goal of promoting national unity. This idea is strong in ex-colonies which have inherited it from their erstwhile masters. In Malaysia, with at least ten different indigenous peoples, education is used to counteract cultural, religious, and linguistic diversity; a centrally administered system imposes the official language, Bahasia Malaysia, and behavioural conformity is encouraged through Muslim study of Islam and non-Muslim study of 'Moral Education'. In many countries, including Azerbaijan, China, Cuba, Georgia, Iran, Nicaragua, and Tajikistan, state education enforces the dominant ideology. To counter the dominance of ruling elites, non-government agencies such as trade unions, churches, or community groups run non-formal education programs for disadvantaged adults such as the 'popular education' movements in Latin America.

In addition to politics, a nation's wealth is an important factor in determining its levels of education; there is a strong correlation between the gross national product per head (GNP) and the adult literacy rate of a nation. Wealth is, however, also modified by politics; there has to be a strong national commitment to education. The GNPs of Djibouti, Liberia, Mauritania, Morocco, and Senegal are higher than in many developing countries, but adult literacy is below 50%. By way of contrast, Azerbaijan, Georgia, Tajikistan, and Vietnam have literacy rates above 90% in spite of a low GNP. In South Asia, primary school enrollment is much higher than it is in sub-Saharan Africa in spite of a lower GNP. In Malaysia, because schooling has been considered important, the adult literacy rates are better than in wealthier, similarly Islamic, countries of the Middle East and North Africa (UNICEF 1988).

Political stability is also an important element. In countries with stronger economies, political instability can jeopardise education. In Chile a right-wing coup in 1973 reduced the education budget from 4.3% of national income to 2.6% and education was increasingly privatised, including selling off state schools (Quinteros 1999); in Nicaragua the revolution in 1978 led to a drop in education and health expenditure from 50% of the national budget to 25%, and privatisation of education removed it further from the grasp of the poor (Arnove 2000; Hickling-Hudson 2000); in Bolivia expenditure on education declined by 42% over five years following the military coup of 1980 (Arnove 2000).

International aid is seen as a good way to encourage countries to invest in education, but external aid is not always tailored to the specific needs of a situation. The internationally recognised value of education has led international aid agencies to take a significant role in education programs in developing countries, but they may lack understanding of the needs of communities and can offer simplistic and technocratic solutions. Externally funded projects can fail through lack of maintenance and/or because they are placed in areas of great need, but with insufficient resources to maintain them (Bishop 1986). Programs can turn out to be one-off funded showcases without long-term benefits, such as the doomed instructional television station that UNESCO helped to build in Senegal, or the Niger instructional television project.

Government-sponsored programs are also seen to be effective, but they can also fail if they do not maintain momentum. In 1970, the Brazilian Government combined the federal administrative network and municipal involvement to set up the Movimento Brasileiro de Alfabetização (MOBRAL) literacy foundation aimed at the fifteen to thirty-five age group (Bishop 1986). Although every municipality in the country was engaged, within a few years the enthusiasm disappeared. Ninety percent of the people who participated in the courses remained functionally illiterate in the long term (Luis 2001). MOBRAL ended in 1985, and subsequent projects to teach adults basic literacy have had little success, so resources have reverted to basic schooling of children.

Government-initiated programs are most likely to succeed where the stakeholders are involved in their creation and at least some authority is devolved to the communities and the schools involved (Ahlawat and Billeh 1997; Reimers 1997). An example is Project Impact, launched in the Philippines and Indonesia in 1974, which engaged the parents, community, and teachers. It added programmed self-instruction to traditional formal schooling and invited community members into the school to share their skills with the students. It was augmented by adult-oriented learning centres in the villages (Bishop 1986). Sometimes bottom-up action is effective. Also in the Philippines, communities themselves initiated action under the Barrio Village Education Movement, setting up local high schools by using available resources and facilities and enabling students to meet their school expenses through paid work in the community-centred and rurally oriented vocational school curriculum (Bishop 1986).

The strong correlation between literacy, GNP, and life expectancy suggests that mass literacy is both a means and a symbol of economic and social development. Mass education includes both traditional elementary schooling for children and literacy campaigns targeted at adults. Adult literacy campaigns have been favoured as cheaper than, but at least as effective as, school education for enhancing mass literacy and as promoting equality by reaching those who missed adequate schooling. In China and Cuba resources have been released for non-formal education, particularly of the rural poor, by allowing only those destined for professional careers to access more than ten years schooling.

Both measures of mass education are included in the Human Development Index devised by the United Nations Development Program in 1990: adult literacy (two-thirds weighting) and average years of schooling (one-third weighting). These are not, however, as simple as they seem. In the case of literacy, claims may not match realities. In Nicaragua a national literacy campaign in the 1980s was claimed to have reduced illiteracy from 50% to 13%, but a 1992 study by the University of Nicaragua found that one-third of five hundred women who claimed to be literate could not read or write a basic sentence (Arnove 2000). School attendance is also an inadequate indicator, as quantity of schooling does not equate with quality. In Jamaica up to 50% of children who completed primary school were still functionally illiterate (Hickling-Hudson 2000). Jordan achieved rapid expansion of mass education between 1959 and 1993, but at the expense of quality (Ahlawat and Billeh 1997).

While spending more time at school does not necessarily increase learning, spending less time at school does not necessarily decrease learning. UNESCO has found that four years is sufficient for long term effectiveness, and that extending the number of school hours per day beyond a minimum (five hours a day three times a week) does not enhance student achievement. Indeed, smaller classes for shorter periods can be more effective than larger classes for longer periods (Bishop 1986).

National governments may legislate and provide for education, but they cannot ensure that appropriate institutions will be developed, that children will attend, or children will learn. Brazilian law provides for at least eight years basic education, but there are not enough programs for street children, and only 33% of students who enter first grade stay in school until the end of eighth grade (Welch 2000; Luis 2001). In Latin America and Africa more than 50% of students leave before they finish primary school (Bishop 1986). Child labour, which can contribute up to 30% of family income, interferes with schooling in countries as diverse as Brazil and Iran (Welch 2000).

Furthermore, Western-style schools may not be the most appropriate instruments for educating children in developing countries. The value of Western-style institutional schooling has been questioned from both right- and left-wing perspectives. From the right, with its focus on economic development, the World Bank reported in 1974 that Western-style education systems had been "irrelevant to the needs of developing countries for the past two decades" (cited in Bishop 1986). From the left, with a focus on social justice, Hickling-Hudson (2000) predicted that under such education systems "poverty and dependence are likely to increase rather than decrease."

Because of the problems inherent in the traditional Western model of schooling, some developing nations have extended or adapted it, often combining generalist with vocational education. The Basic Education and Life Skills (BELS) program, begun in 1993 by UNESCO and transferred to the University of the South Pacific in 1995, combined in-service of teachers, community involvement, planning, management, and agricultural curriculum development (Townsend and Vakaotia 1999). A number of African countries have experimented to make education more relevant to indigenous needs, including vocational training and community involvement. Such experiments have included continuation schools in Ghana, the Brigade Movement in Botswana, rural primary schools in the Cameroons, the Bunumbu project in Sierra Leone, and the village polytechnic movement in Kenya (Bishop 1986).

The Western model is also unsuitable where families do not remain for long in the same place. Nomadic communities in places as diverse as Iran and Northern Kenya have a particular problem because education is offered in a fixed location. There are also increasing numbers of people affected by forced migration and asylum seeking. Attempts to establish mobile schools have been frustrated by the reluctance of trained teachers to take on a nomadic lifestyle. This was tackled in Iran in 1957 by the establishment of a Tribal Teacher Training School offering twelve months training to tribal youths, who would then return to their tribes. In 1976, this was augmented with a boarding school for tribal children who wanted to go on to secondary education (Bishop 1986).

Adequate provision of education requires not only mass elementary education, but also increased access to higher education produces indigenous technicians and professionals, who, unlike contracted foreign experts, bring cultural awareness, continuity, and commitment.

Politics determines how education budgets are distributed between elementary education and higher education, to what extent the provision of higher education comes at the expense of elementary education. The South East Asian Centre for Educational Innovation and Technology has suggested spreading resources by reducing the basic curriculum to an essential minimum (Bishop 1986). In South America and Africa, some countries, including Nicaragua, Nigeria, Zimbabwe, and Zaire have moved towards skilling the elite by reducing resourcing of mass education of the poor (Bacchus 1987; Arnove 2000). Others attempt an integrated balance. In the Cameroons, rural primary schools have offered the foundations for secondary education for an elite, while preparing the majority for rural and agricultural work. It is important to get the balance right for a nation's stage of development. In Sri Lanka increased access to higher education resulted in a highly educated unemployed and inflated qualifications for even basic jobs (Little 2000).

All attempts to extend education are dependent on adequate teaching resources. The cost and supply of teachers are major problems for developing nations. For governments on restricted budgets, reduction of teaching becomes a goal as teachers' salaries comprise up to 90% of recurrent education budgets. Thus class sizes have been increased, with studies in Brazil, Chile, Puerto Rico, and Venezuela suggesting that variations between twenty and forty make little difference to outcomes (Bishop 1986). Multi-grade teaching has been tried in the Philippines (Miguel 1997). Programmed instruction, albeit often handicapped by lack of good instructional materials, has reduced demands on teachers in Korea, the Philippines, Singapore, Indonesia, India, Pakistan, and Sri Lanka (Bishop 1986; Lee 1997).

Teacher competence is as much of a problem as teacher costs. In developing countries, as few as half of the teachers are properly trained (Townsend and Vakaotia 1999). A variety of programs have addressed this. A Chilean Program for the Improvement of Equity and Quality of Education focused on new teaching methods and improving the training and status of teachers (Quinteros 1999). In Papua New Guinea teacher training was enhanced in the 1990s through government initiatives that engaged the Association for Teacher Education, the teachers' colleges, the Queensland University of Technology and the University of Papua New Guinea (Avalos 1997). Some countries, including India, Sri Lanka, and Botswana, have turned to correspondence education for teacher education. This overcomes problems of distance and allows teachers to be trained without removing them from their schools (Bishop 1986).

Correspondence programs are also more generally used to overcome the problems of higher education for dispersed populations. The University of the South Pacific and the University of the West Indies cater to archipelago nations through extensive correspondence education. Other developing countries draw on the resources of universities in the developed world through correspondence courses. These are often augmented by short periods of intensive face to face teaching by visiting lecturers.

Recently, technology has provided alternative teaching resources and been seen as an economic way to increase access to education. Radio programs for schools have been broadcast in countries as diverse as Thailand, Pakistan, Kenya, and Botswana. The Mauritius College of the Air has gone further, offering in-service to teachers, who then support children in correspondence and radio based education (Bishop 1986). Radio broadcasts have also offered community education for over half a century. Colombia began broadcasts offering basic education, life, and vocational skills in 1947. Radio Togo and Radio Sanata Maria in the Dominican Republic began radio literacy projects in 1964. In 1970, Tanzania instituted radio broadcasts for community development. In Guatemala the Basic Village Education project has been offering agricultural education to farmers by radio since 1978. In Brazil regionally broadcast evening courses have reached over fifteen thousand village radio schools. Combinations of techniques include All-India Radio combining broadcasts with print and study groups, the Dominican Republic combining radio with work sheets and locally recruited mentors, and the Republic of Niger combining radio with visual stimuli.

Since 1970, UNESCO has also been promoting television as an educational tool. In the Ivory Coast television has been helping to reorient primary education towards rural development; in Niger it has been offering beginner instruction in a range of subjects; in Mexico and El Salvador it has been extending access to secondary education (Bishop 1986). Access to television is, however, more limited than access to radio in developing countries, because, while transistor radios are relatively widespread, television requires electricity and many developing countries do not have a stable power supply. Television also requires new attitudes to incorporate it in education. In Brazil equipment provided through a TV-school plan ended up unused due to lack of interest and training (Luis 2001).

More recently, computers have also been increasingly used to augment teaching resources. In 1984, Brazil began a national program to computerise education. Subsequently, the Education Ministry has invested $480 million to put one hundred thousand computers into six thousand secondary schools and to train teachers to use the equipment (Luis 2001).

Connecting computers to the Internet is the latest technological aid to education. Since the 1990s, it has had an impact in many parts of the developing world, including the initiatives of the Chinese academic network (CERNET); the Red Hemisférica Inter-Universitaria de Información Científica y Tecnológica sponsored by the United States in Latin America; the Caribbean Academic Scientific and Technologic Network; the World Bank initiated African Virtual University; and the Association of African Universities.

The Internet, however, requires not only computers and electricity, but also a telephone connection. Eighty percent of the world's population has no telephone line; 70% of Africans live in remote, rural areas that need satellites for Internet services. Of the countries with full Internet connectivity, only six have local dial-up facilities outside the major cities and some capital cities do not have full connectivity. Even where the Internet is available, connection costs rule out access for the majority of people. Besides the issues of connection, computers and modems cost more of an average weekly wage in the

developing than in the industrialised world (World News 2001).

Another Internet issue is content. The Internet remains largely an English-language medium, dominated by the commercial interests of large Western service providers, with the information flow running from industrialised countries to developing countries. There is a need for more local, relevant content, such as produced through the InfoDev program creating secondary school material in South Africa, and for more initiatives that harness existing relevant resources, such as UNESCO's project of transferring printed material in African libraries onto the Net.

Information technology may turn out to be as much of a problem as it is a solution, because it increases the gap between rich and poor. In the developing world, mostly only private universities serving the rich minority can afford the necessary infrastructure. At the other end of the scale, Internet access is not an option for people who are not yet literate, too hungry or sick to learn, or in schools too poor to even afford books.

LEONORA RITTER

References and Further Reading

Ahlawat, Kapur and Victor Billeh. "Decentralizing national education data to support local use: the Jordanian experience" in *From planning to action: government initiatives for improving school level practice*. Edited by D. W. Chapman. Oxford: Pergamon, 1997.

Arnove, Robert F. "The Tension Between Quantity and Quality in Nicaraguan Education" in *Third World Education*. edited by Anthony R. Welch. New York: Garland Publishing Inc, 2000.

Avalos, Beatrice and Paul Koro. "Information and the reform of initial teacher education in Papua New Guinea: strategies, challenges and results" in *From planning to action: government initiatives for improving school level practice*. edited by D. W. Chapman, Oxford: Pergamon, 1997.

Bishop, G. *Innovation in Education*. London: Macmillan, 1986.

Hickling-Hudson, Anne. "'Post Marxist' Discourse and the Rethinking of Third World education Reform" in *Third World Education*. edited by Anthony R. Welch. New York: Garland Publishing Inc, 2000.

Lee, Yongsook. "Bottom-up and top-down strategies for improving classroom instruction, case studies from Korea" in *From planning to action: government initiatives for improving school level practice*. Edited by D. W. Chapman. Oxford: Pergamon, 1997.

Little, Angela. "Qualifications, Quality and Equality; A Political Economy of Sri Lankan Education 1971–1993" in *Third World Education*. Edited by Anthony R. Welch. New York: Garland Publishing Inc, 2000.

Luis, Emerson. *Learning Disabilities*. <www.brazzil.com/cvrapr97.htm>

Miguel, Marcelina M. and Eligio B. Barsaga. "Multi-grade schooling in the Philippines, a strategy for improving access to and quality of primary education" in *From planning to action: government initiatives for improving school level practice*. Edited by D. W. Chapman. Oxford: Pergamon, 1997.

Quinteros, Haroldo. "Chilean educational reform; an opportunity to extend high achievement to all schools" in *Third Millenium Schools*. Edited by Tony Townsend, Paul Clarke, and Mel Ainscow. Lisse: Swets and Zeitlinger, 1999.

Reimers, Fernando. "Changing schools through participatory knowledge management in El Salvador: can education systems learn?" in *From planning to action: government initiatives for improving school level practice*. Edited by D. W. Chapman. Oxford; Pergamon, 1997.

Townsend, Tony and Asenaca Vakaotia. "Improving the effectiveness of schools in Pacific Island countries: a regional approach to teacher development" in *Third Millenium Schools*. Edited by Tony Townsend, Paul Clarke, and Mel Ainscow. Lisse: Swets and Zeitlinger, 1999.

UNICEF. *The State of The World's Children 2005*. http://www.unicef.org/sowc05/english/index.html.

Welch, Anthony. "Quality and Equality in Third World Education" in *Third World Education*. Edited by Anthony R. Welch. New York: Garland Publishing Inc, 2000.

EGYPT

Egypt is located in the northeast region of the African continent with a size of approximately one million square kilometers (or the landmass of the states of Arizona, New Mexico, Utah, and Colorado combined). The country is broken up into four major regions to include the Nile Valley and Delta, where about 99% of Egypt's 76 million population resides; the Western Desert; the Eastern Desert; and the Sinai Peninsula.

The three most important aspects about Egypt are water, location, and history. Regarding water, Egypt is the northernmost country along the Nile River, the longest river in the world at 6,500 kilometers. Evidence of civilization along the Nile dates back over six thousand years. The river provides over 90% of Egypt's water. Hence, Egypt has often been called "the gift of the Nile." Because of the importance of the Nile to its very existence, Egypt has officially warned the states to the south not to affect the flow of the river in any way. Historically, summer monsoons in central Africa caused the Nile to flood every year bringing rich, dark soil to the valleys of Egypt and to the delta at the Mediterranean Sea. It was this soil and water from the Nile that allowed early civilizations to flourish. In the late 1950s, Egyptian President Gamal Abdul Nasser envisioned a dam near Aswan to control the annual flooding and provide a reservoir of water for national emergencies such as droughts. With the financial and technical assistance of the Soviet Union, the Aswan High Dam ten-year national project was completed in 1970 and dedicated by President Anwar as Sadat.

The other water aspect of note for Egypt is the Suez Canal, which connects the Mediterranean Sea to the Red Sea, and subsequently to the Indian Ocean. The idea of a canal linking the Mediterranean Sea to the Indian Ocean dated back to ancient times. The first attempt at digging such a canal was in the sixth century BCE. After a period of time, the rudimentary canal fell into disrepair. It was neglected until Roman Emperor Trajan had it re-dug to promote Roman trade. It was once again abandoned with the discovery of the trade route around Africa. Finally, the French Emperor Napoleon revived the idea of a shorter trade route to India using the canal. After ten years of Egyptian labor and French expertise and financing, the 160-kilometer Suez Canal was again open to navigation in 1869. The Suez Canal is Egypt's third major source of foreign exchange, bringing in well over $1 billion US dollars every year from passage tolls (assessed at around 6.5% of a ship's tonnage).

Egypt occupies a geographic focal point bridging Africa with the Middle East on land, and with Europe by sea. Unfortunately, this strategic location also made Egypt susceptible to numerous conquests, including those of the Romans, Greeks, Arabs, Ottomans, French, and British. The British granted Egypt partial independence in 1922, but only withdrew completely in 1954 as a result of an Egyptian military uprising led by Nassar. Of these foreign rules, the Arab Muslim rule had the greatest impact on Egyptian life and culture, to where today Egypt is considered both an Arab and an Islamic country (the vast majority of Egyptians are Sunni Muslim). Hence, Egypt is simultaneously an African, an Arab, and a Muslim nation. While it has the second most number of people on the African continent (see Nigeria) and the most in the Arab world, with around 75 million, it does not have the most Muslims living in it (see Indonesia).

With civilization along the Nile River dating back over six millennia and with so many foreign conquests of the area, Egypt has a very rich history to fashion its unique identity and culture. Egyptian ancient history is hard to date because the only accurate records kept consisted of tracking the rule of Egypt's pharaohs. Unfortunately, some pharaohs fell into disrepute and were excised from history. As well, many of the existing pharaonic lists are in disrepair, hence, are missing names and dates. Finally, many of the pharaohs took several different names causing more uncertainty among Egyptian historians.

One of the most important historical events in Egyptian history was the unification of Upper and

Lower Egypt by King Menes sometime in the third millennium BCE. As a result, King Menes became the first Egyptian pharaoh ruling over the planet's first organized society. The Arab conquest by Amr ibn al-As in 641 CE was another important historical event as it spread Islam throughout the land as well as Arab language and culture (which endure to this day). It was during Arab rule that Cairo was established as the permanent capital of Egypt. Another significant historical event occurred in 1260 when the Egyptian ruler, Qutuz, and his forces stopped the Mogul advance across the Arab world in Palestine. In 1517, Egypt was conquered by Sultan Selim I and absorbed into the Ottoman Empire until 1882 when the British began its occupation of Egypt.

Egypt's pharaonic history, to include its numerous pyramids, temples, and tombs, draws in tourists from all over the world. They come primarily to see the three great pyramids at Giza (a suburb of Cairo) built over four thousand years ago. The Great Pyramid of Khufu is considered one of mankind's greatest structures, consisting of approximately two million blocks of stones, each weighing more than two tons. The Khufu Pyramid ranked as the tallest structure on Earth for more than forty-three centuries at 137 meters high. About 350 meters from this pyramid rests the Great Sphinx. It is seventy-three meters long and represents a lion with a human head to stand guard over the pyramids. Its worn appearance today reflects the effects of thousands of years of severe blowing sand and gravity.

Other significant tourist sites from Egypt's pharaonic past include the Karnak Temple at Luxor, the largest temple supported by columns and among the largest temples in size in the world. Luxor itself was known in the past as Thebes, the capital of the Egyptian Kingdom during the Memphis era. In the mountains near Luxor, there are many small valleys of which the Valley of the Kings is most famous. Many pharaohs, beginning with Tutmose I, decided to be buried there, secluded from possible poachers. However, the history of this valley is one long story of pillaging and plundering. Less than two kilometers away is the Valley of the Queens. Eighty tombs have been discovered there to date, all badly damaged. One queen not buried there was Queen Hatshepsut, daughter of Pharaoh Tutmose I. She had a funerary monument built for herself near Luxor. Unfortunately, it was the site of a mass terrorist attack in which sixty-eight tourists were gunned down on November 17, 1997. In Cairo, tourists often visit the Mohammad Ali Mosque and the National Museum, built by the French. The museum was opened in 1902 and consists of one hundred exhibition rooms occupying two floors. It contains the impressive relics of King Tutankhamon's burial tomb, which was discovered in 1922. (In September 1997, nine tourists were killed by terrorists in front of this museum.) Finally, tourists often visit the large temple of Abu Simbel, 320 kilometers from Aswan in Nubia. This temple, consisting of four twenty-meter-high statues, was the source of one of the greatest monumental movements in history beginning in 1965, as the Aswan Dam when completed was projected to permanently flood the area where it stood.

Egypt receives most of its revenue not from tourism, which accounts for over $3 billion US dollars each year, but from remittances sent back by Egyptians working in foreign countries. Before the US-led military operations against Iraq in 1991 and 2003, Egypt had over three million of its citizens working abroad and sending as much as $18 billion US dollars back to Egypt every year. (It is difficult to estimate the exact amount of remittances because workers often remit earnings directly to their families and not through official banking channels.)

Petroleum and gas are the second highest source of income for the Egyptian economy. Crude oil production in 2001 was over eight hundred thousand barrels per day, with proven reserves estimated at over 3 billion barrels.

Because survival in this region required strict management of the Nile river water, Egypt has always had a strong ruler, beginning with the pharaohs and ending with the constitutional dictatorship in place today. The primary reason for a strong central authority in recent times is to overcome and counter foreign threats to Egypt's independence. As a result, all of Egypt's presidents since the 1952 Revolution have been military officers. Lieutenant Colonel Nassar led the nationalist-reform movement to finally overthrow British rule, and promptly instituted land reform, social welfare, and a nationalist foreign policy. He destroyed the political and economic power of the old feudal, landowning class. Women were encouraged to get an education and were given the right to vote. Nassar's government fixed the exchange rate of the Egyptian pound, began development planning, controlled foreign trade, and nationalized numerous foreign businesses, to include the Suez Canal. This property grab led to the Suez Canal Crisis of 1956 where British, French, and Israeli military forces moved on Egypt to secure the canal. The military operation failed due to lack of international political support led by the United States.

The 1956 and 1971 Egyptian constitutions largely reinforced authoritarian traditions, with the president at the center of power. Nassar was a charismatic leader who was able to balance off the elites against each other while using his popular support to curb them as needed. Sadat did not have the charisma that Nassar had nor the support of the masses. He gained support from the elite through a tacit social contract in which he curbed the traditional presidential arbitrary use of power. Finally, President Hosni Mubarak has maintained the authoritarian presidency, although he is even less of a dominant figure than either Nassar or Sadat. Mubarak lacked the military comrades of Nassar and the upper-class patronage of Sadat. He never sought to reshape Egypt, only to maintain stability while making incremental changes. The Egyptian constitution calls for a vice president to become president following the death of the president, which occurred following the deaths of both Nassar and Sadat. To date, Mubarak has decided not to appoint a vice president due to concerns about a possible rival once a person was identified. As such, Egypt faces a succession crisis if something were to happen to President Mubarak.

Egypt was the leading Arab country in the numerous conflicts with Israel beginning in 1948 with its declaration of independence. In each of the four major conflicts fought involving Israel (1948, 1956, 1967, and 1973), Egypt ended up losing. Wanting to regain the Sinai Peninsula lost in the 1973 war and to quell domestic disturbances, Sadat decided to accept an invitation by Israel Prime Minister Menachem Begin to begin a road to peace. On November 19, 1977, Sadat flew to Jerusalem to address the Israeli Knesset. Once peace talks stalled in September 1978, US President Jimmy Carter invited both delegations to Camp David to work out the problems. The result was the Camp David Accords and the signing of the Egyptian–Israeli peace treaty on March 26, 1979. Israel then withdrew from the Sinai, while diplomatic and economic relations were established between the two countries, and Israeli ships were authorized to use the Suez Canal. Unfortunately, while Sadat was a hero in the West, he was vilified in the Arab world. The Camp David Accords brought peace to Egypt, but not prosperity, though the US has given over $1 billion US dollars every year to Egypt since 1979 for signing the Accords. Eventually, Sadat paid for this brave and bold move with his life, when religious conspirators in the army assassinated him in 1981. However, without Egypt's military power and strategic location, no Arab state or combination of states could effectively confront Israel.

Finally, Egypt's Armed Forces consist of 448,000 personnel, most being draftees serving for three years, and four services—the army, navy, air force, and air defense force. The defense budget runs around 10% of Egypt's GNP. Egypt is one of the major military powers in the Middle East, and its senior officers play an influential role in the nation's affairs.

STEPHEN R. SCHWALBE

References and Further Reading

Hasou, Tawfig Y. *Struggle for the Arab World: Egypt's Nassar and the Arab League.* Kegan Paul International Limited, 1985.
Jankowski, James P. *Egypt: A Short History.* Oneworld Publications, 2000.
Loti, Pierre, and WB Baines. *Egypt.* Kegan Paul International Limited, 2003.

807 INDUSTRIES

As used today, the term "807 industries" is an informal reference to a provision in the US tariff code that allows US goods, produced by certain industries, to be shipped to another country and returned with import taxes placed only on the value that has been added to the goods while out of the country. For the US firm, a major advantage of this process is access to lower labor rates for unskilled work in other countries.

Since the early 1980s, this provision has been used in combination with other US government programs, such as the Caribbean Basin Initiative, which are designed to promote economic growth in developing countries. Long-run strategic benefits include increased employment, political stability, and the development of markets for US products.

Technically, the term "807" refers to a classification found in the Tariff Schedule of the United States (TSUS), which was implemented in 1963 and replaced in January of 1989 by classification "9802" of the Harmonized Tariff Schedule of the United States (HTS). The HTS is administered by the US International Trade Commission (formerly the US Tariff Commission). The founding legislation for this provision is the Tariff Act of 1930 (Hawley–Smoot), which is currently included as Chapter 4 of Title 19 (Customs Duties) of the Code of the United States of America.

Regional Impacts of the 807 (9802) Provision

Latin America and Asia are the most heavily affected by this trade provision, combining for approximately 68% of the dollar amounts of all imports under the 9802 HTS category in 2001. Mexico alone accounted for 23%, and Japan accounted for 29%.

Four other Latin American nations (Dominican Republic, Honduras, El Salvador, and Costa Rica) accounted for 8%, and four other Asian nations (Philippines, Malaysia, China, and Korea) also accounted for 8%. Sixty-two other nations accounted for the remaining 32% of all imports under the 9802 HTS classification. A second and more revealing statistic is the percent of US content contained in the imported goods. US imports from Mexico under HTS 9802 contained 50% US content, whereas US imports from Japan under HTS 9802 contained only 4% US content. Goods imported by four other Latin American nations (Dominican Republic, Honduras, El Salvador, and Costa Rica) contained 70% US content and imports from four other Asian nations (Philippines, Malaysia, China, and Korea) contained 25% US content. US imports from each of sixty-two other nations contained an average of 8% US content.

These statistics make clear that, in 2001, the amount of US imports from Latin America under HTS 9802 was disproportionately large in that, even though they accounted for 31% of the total amount of such imported goods, the content of those goods originated primarily from the US. This was not the case for other regions of the world. Since tariffs rates under HTS 9802 are based on the percentage of foreign content, the major beneficiaries of the 9802 provision have been the economies of Latin America and those US manufacturers of goods that are shipped to Latin America for assembly under the 9802 provision. Further, among Latin American nations, Mexico and the Dominican Republic were the largest exporters to the United States under the provision. The top twenty items imported under 9802 from Mexico in 2003 consisted of various types of clothing, electronic equipment, and medical equipment. Specifically, $6.8 billion in customs value was imported under 9802 from Mexico: $1.5 billion (men's and womens' trousers, short stockings, t-shirts, and sweaters; $1.5 billion (electronic connectors, motors, switches, wires, televisions, and other cathode-ray tube machines), and $0.3 billion (medical instruments and appliances). The top twenty items imported under 9802 from the Dominican Republic in 2003 consisted of various types clothing, electronic equipment, medical equipment, plastics, and articles made from precious metals. Specifically, $1.4 billion in customs value was imported under 9802 from the Dominican Republic: $0.75 billion (men's and womens' trousers, shorts stockings, t-shirts, underwear, coats and sweaters), $0.15 billion (electronic circuit breakers, switches and connectors), $0.07 billion (medical instruments and appliances), $0.07 billion (plastics), and $0.02 billion (articles made from precious metals).

The Caribbean Basin Initiative and the 807 (9802) Provision

The 807 (9802) tariff code provision is one of three major duty-free or duty-reduction programs available for US imports from the Caribbean (Schoepfle 2002). The other two programs are the Generalized System of Preferences (GSP) and the Caribbean Basin Initiative (CBI). During a speech to congress on February 24, 1982, President Reagan described his vision for trade relations between the United States and the Caribbean that would provide for free or reduced tariffs on a wide range of goods. This general vision became known as the Caribbean Basin Initiative and has been implemented through time in the form of three federal statutes: The Caribbean Basin Economic Recovery Act of 1983 (CBERA), The Caribbean Basin Economic Recovery Expansion Act of 1990 (CBERA Expansion Act), and The US–Caribbean Basin Trade Partnership Act of 2000 (CBTPA).

The original political purpose of the CBI was to enable economic development of the Caribbean region, which, in turn, was to provide greater political stability and closer relationships with the United States. At the time, the region had recently witnessed a successful revolution in Nicaragua, active insurgencies in El Salvador and Guatemala, and coups in Grenada and Suriname. These events had resulted in the establishment of leftist regimes that were perceived as being opposed to the interests of the United States. These dramatic political changes, coupled with an international economic crisis characterized by high oil prices, unprecedented interest rates, and declining commodity prices, rekindled the interest of the United States policymakers in the region (Haggerty 1991). The hope was that economic assistance and closer business relationships with certain nations of the region would help to balance increased political antagonism of others.

In 1987, in an attempt to expand economic growth and US influence through "free trade and free markets" in the Caribbean region, President Reagan implemented a CBI companion program called the Special Access Program (SAP). The SAP had been drafted earlier by the American Caribbean Trade Association and focused on expanding Caribbean clothing assembly and exporting activity under TSUS 807. Specifically, the SAP resulted in the establishment of opportunities for Caribbean nations to enter into bilateral agreements with the United States for Guaranteed Access Levels (GALs). These GALs essentially consisted of unlimited quotas for textile products and were incorporated into the tariff code under the special provision classification "807A." This 807A provision, which was informally referred to as the "Super 807," incorporated very specific rules of origin, that required that textile material used in manufacturing clothing in Caribbean factories had to have been "formed and cut" in the United States (Rosen 2002). Through the SAP, the 807 provision became closely aligned with the Caribbean Basin Initiative.

Controversial Aspects of the 807 (9802) Provision

Surrounding the 807 (9802) provision and related programs are several controversial issues. These issues relate to consequences which critics argue are outside of the stated objectives of the provision and which have damaging effects on the Caribbean, the United States, and Asia. Three such issues have been hotly debated:

1. The development of undesirable "sweatshop" working conditions in the Caribbean;
2. Restriction on free trade with Japan and other Asian nations; and
3. The "exporting" of jobs held by US workers to other nations.

At the center of the criticisms stemming from these issues are the related beliefs that US firms have used the 807 provision to benefit their own profitability at the expense of Caribbean workers, US workers, and US consumers, and that the original objectives of fostering economic development of other nations and providing markets for US goods have not been met.

Concerning the first issue, a "sweatshop" is typically defined as working conditions that do not meet US standards such as those prescribed by the US Fair Labor Standards Act (FLSA) of 1938, as amended, and the US Occupational Health and Safety Act of 1970, as amended. These statutes cover such items as minimum wages, overtime pay, child labor restrictions, and safety and health standards. The general criticism aimed toward foreign firms that participate in the 807 program with US firms is that they do not meet these standards, and thus, US business and the policy itself are encouraging the violation of generally held ethical and moral workplace values. Concerning the second issue, while it was the intention to foster economic development in the Caribbean, especially through the 807A special access program, one clear consequence has been the reduction of US imports from Asia. As a response, Asian firms moved

operations to Latin America and gradually became the beneficiaries of the 807 trade program through the establishment of manufacturing firms that employed Caribbean workers, which in turn reduced employment opportunities for Asian workers. Concerning the third issue, a clear trend in the United States has been the growing gap between wages paid to skilled versus unskilled workers. One source of this gap has been the outsourcing of unskilled work to other nations, with the resulting painful unemployment and underemployment experienced by displaced workers.

Countering these positions are the following views:

1. While working conditions in Caribbean 807 firms are below those of the United States, they are generally higher than typical for Caribbean nations hence a net benefit to the foreign workers.
2. US and Japanese workers who have been displaced through the 807 and related programs are being retrained for more sophisticated jobs that provide higher wages (Feenstra, Hanson, and Swenson 2002).
3. US consumers enjoy a wide range of alternative products from Japan and other non-Caribbean nations, such as electronics and automobiles as well as products produced in the Caribbean by US and Japanese firms through the 807 (9802) provision.

STEVEN PAULSON

See also Caribbean Basin Initiative; Caribbean: History and Economic Development

References and Further Reading

"Caribbean Basin Economic Recovery Act of 1983" Title 19, Chapter 15 of the United States Code, Washington, DC: US House of Representatives, Office of the Law Revision Counsel, 2000.

Dypski, Michael Cornell. "The Caribbean Basin Initiative: An Examination of Structural Dependency, Good Neighbor Relations, and American Investment," *Journal of Transnational Law and Policy*, Vol. 12, No. 1, Fall, 2002, pp. 95–136.

Feenstra, Robert C., Gordon H. Hanson, and Deborah L. Swenson. "Offshore Assembly from the United States: Production Characteristics of the 9802 Program," pp. 85–122 in Robert C. Feenstra (ed.) *The Impact of International Trade on Wages*, Chicago: University of Chicago Press, 2002.

Haggerty, Richard A. (ed.). *Dominican Republic and Haiti Country Studies*, Washington, DC: US Library of Congress, Federal Research Division, Area Handbook Series, Appendix B Caribbean Basin Initiative, 1991.

Irwin, Douglas A. "From Smoot–Hawley to Reciprocal Trade Agreements: Changing the Course of US Trade policy in the 1930s," pp. 325–352 in *The Defining*

Moment, Michael D. Bordo, Claudia Goldin and Eugene N. White (eds.) Chicago: University of Chicago Press, 1998.

Rosen, Ellen Israel. *Making Sweatshops: The Globalization of the US Apparel Industry,* Berkeley, CA: University of California Press, 2002.

Schoepfle, Gregory K. "US–Caribbean Trade Relations: The First Fifteen Years of the Caribbean Basin Initiative," pp. 118–149 in *Caribbean Economies in the Twenty-First Century,* Irma T. Alonso (ed.), Gainesville, FL: University Press of Florida, 2002, pp. 118–149.

EL SALVADOR

El Salvador is located on the Pacific coast of Central America, nestled between Guatemala to the northwest, Honduras to the northeast, and the Gulf of Fonseca to the southeast. Lying on top of the infamous Ring of Fire of seismic and volcanic activity, the country has experienced disastrous earthquakes (four significant ones in 2001 alone), leading to thousands of deaths and billions of dollars in damage. The northeastern region of the country was devastated by Hurricane Mitch in 1998, as was most of Central America. Despite a number of beautiful lakes, volcanoes, and beaches, uncontrolled deforestation in the last two decades has led to a near collapse of the country's riverbeds, droughts, and overall water scarcity. Along with Haiti and Paraguay, El Salvador is one of three Latin American countries with no remaining large tracts of undisturbed, biologically-intact forests. The country's generally comfortable tropical climate ranges between 70°F and 80°F, its beaches becoming a regular destination for regional tourists. The smallest and most densely populated Central American nation, El Salvador's geography and topography have brought significant challenges for the country's development. More than any other natural resource, land has historically been at the center of struggles over development, growth, private profit, and the well-being of the majority. The official population estimate for 2001 was 6.3 million.

Following independence from Spain in 1821, El Salvador became part of the United Provinces of Central America from 1823 to 1839, thereafter becoming a fully independent political state. From the beginning export agriculture dominated economic life, with communally held indigenous lands also dotting large regions of the country. These communal holdings prioritized subsistence agriculture. When the world demand for indigo collapsed in the 1860s, coffee became the new dominant export cash crop, displacing traditional systems of food production. In 1882, three quarters of all land passed into the private ownership of a small elite class when the government abolished all common lands. This single decree concentrated the country's most abundant natural resource in the hands of an estimated 2% of the population, and set in motion an historical and still ongoing battle over access to land. This tiny elite class, popularly known as the "Fourteen Families," held all control over the state, the land, and national capital. The country became an oligarchy despite formally proclaiming a constitutional republican government. With land, economy, and political life serving the private interests of these few, large segments of El Salvador's impoverished laboring class organized themselves into protest. Labor unrest and protest included the growth of the Communist Party in the 1920s, largely repressed through the infamous Hernández Martínez government massacre of roughly thirty thousand indigenous and mestizo peasants of 1932, known as *la matanza.*

El Salvador's economy did not develop significantly until after World War II, and especially with the creation of the Central American Common Market (CACM). Entrepreneurial capitalists, some national but mostly foreign, benefited from a growing industrialization in this period. The creation and expansion of a regional Central American internal market, the first of its kind in the hemisphere, was the single most important factor in the relative modernization of the country's industries. The construction of the country's first dam in 1950 on River Lempa increased geothermal and hydroelectric power, potentially lessening its dependence on imported petroleum. Along with coffee and cotton, sugar became another important export cash crop in the twentieth century. The commercial fishing industry too expanded following the war, and especially in the 1960s, along with manufacturing and the production of tobacco, textiles, and beverages. Despite relative economic growth, gross inequalities were evident throughout. The extreme polarity between a wealthy elite class and a poor, largely rural but increasingly urban majority grew further in the postwar period.

Those benefiting the most from the growth of Salvadoran manufacturing and industrialization after 1960 were foreigners, and those affiliated with them. Of the fifty-five foreign investments established in El Salvador after 1960, forty-one were joint ventures between foreigners and nationals. The CACM favored transnational corporations' interests in the region rather than the development of Central American productive forces. The profits from growth, thus, did not translate into overall national development. That which remained in the country went to the few elite, while the largest portion actually left the country. Those suffering the most from growing industrialization and economic activity were the laboring class. Between 1970 and 1980, the change in real wages for workers in the manufacturing industry was a −7%; for those in agriculture it was a −15%.

These labor and social conditions in the postwar period were at the root of growing 1970s protest and organizing among peasants, students, teachers, and workers. With increased political repression of this civil unrest, organized political and armed protest eventually took the form of a coalition of five guerrilla forces under the name of the FMLN (Farabundo Martí Front for National Liberation). With a 1979 military coup, an armed twelve-year-long civil war began, eventually claiming the lives of over eighty thousand civilians and combatants. An additional one-third of the country's population was displaced internally or forced into economic or political exile, having additional negative effects on the national economy. Despite population growth, the production of basic foodstuffs decreased between 1980 and 1993, a year after the signing of peace accords that brought the war to an end. More recently in the 1990s, the growth of *maquiladoras*, or large sweatshop garment industry plants, has led to creation of thousands of jobs, though offering economic wages insufficient for procuring a basic standard of living. Unfair wage practices and reports of abuse have also brought international attention to these mostly foreign-owned *maquiladoras*. Today, it is the transnational Salvadoran community that is most responsible for keeping the national economy from collapsing. There are critical economic ties between hundreds of thousands of Salvadorans in the United States and those remaining in El Salvador. It is estimated that in 2000, Salvadorans abroad sent over $1.6 billion in remittances to their friends and families. Less a form of national development, this economic reality makes of El Salvador a truly transnational experiment dependent on the global traffic of workers and goods. That the US dollar became legal tender alongside the national *colón* effective January 1, 2001, marks further this tie to globalization.

HORACIO N. ROQUE RAMÍREZ

See also Central America: History and Economic Development; Central America: International Relations; Export-Oriented Economies; Mexico: History and Economic Development; Mexico: International Relations

References and Further Reading

Asociación Equipo Maíz, eds. *El Salvador: Imágenes para No Olvidar*; as *El Salvador: Images We Must Not Forget*. San Salvador: Equipo Maíz, 1999.
Berry, Tom. *El Salvador: A Country Guide*. Albuquerque: Inter-Hemispheric Education Resource Center, 1991.
Dalton, Roque. *Miguel Mármol: los Sucesos de 1932 en El Salvador*. San José, Costa Rica: EDUCA, 1972; as *Miguel Mármol*, translated by Kathleen Ross and Richard Schaaf. Willimantic, CT: Curbstone Press, 1987.
Dalton, Roque. *El Salvador (Monografía)*. San Salvador: UCA Editores, 1989.
Gorkin, Michael. *From Grandmother to Granddaughter: Salvadoran Women's Stories*. Berkeley, CA: University of California Press, 2000.
Martínez, Ana Guadalupe. *Las Cárceles Clandestinas de El Salvador: Libertad por el Secuestro de un Oligarca*. San Salvador: UCA Editores, 1996.
McClintock, Cynthia. *Revolutionary Movements in Latin America: El Salvador's FMLN & Peru's Shining Path*. Washington, DC: United States Institute of Peace Press, 1998.
United Nations. *Informe sobre Desarrollo Humano: El Salvador, 2001*. San Salvador: Programa de las Naciones Unidas para el Desarrollo, 2001.

ELECTIONS

Elections are a procedure for selecting officials to fill decision-making positions in the political system, or to settle issues concerning policy. Elections are an important component of the overall process of decision making within the democratic political system.

History of Elections

The earliest historical data about elections come from the ancient Greek polities in the fifth and sixth centuries BC. Local general assemblies that included free male citizens were widely used to approve appointments for public offices.

During the Middle Ages, the church preserved the tradition of elections. Passing through a complicated and controversial process of institutional development, national assemblies, or parliaments, gradually began to acquire more jurisdictions. Part of this process was extending the active participation in the process of decision making. A significant political advancement during the bourgeois revolutions of the seventeenth through nineteenth centuries was enforcement of the assumed powers of the parliaments, as well as putting their members up for elections. Initially, a very limited share of the population was eligible to vote and to be elected. The right of citizens to participate in elections was limited by a wide variety of prerequisites—property qualifications, and religious, sex, or age requirements. Equality of influence of the vote was additionally limited by diversity in the ratio of population to elect representatives in different constituencies. Other inequities resulted from some traditional patterns of representation—e.g., granting some persons more than one vote. Countries dominated by estate interests kept traditional oral voting well into the twentieth century—Denmark until 1901, Prussia until 1918, and Hungary until the 1930s. The tendency since the nineteenth century has been toward broadening the suffrage, suspension of multiple voting, adjusting constituency representation ratios, and lowering the voting age. During the nineteenth and twentieth centuries, the evolution of electoral systems throughout most of the world was marked by three important trends: (1) expansion of the right to vote to nearly all mature population; (2) approximation of the foundations of representative government; and (3) adoption of standard electoral procedures.

This steady expansion of the electorate invoked some organizations to bring substantial numbers of voters at the constituency level to permit winning the elections. Most of the European countries as well as the overseas territories of France, Great Britain, Belgium, and the Netherlands had by the end of World War I more or less full males suffrage. Extension of the vote to women was delayed. The United States adopted universal female suffrage in 1920, and the Scandinavian countries between 1906 and 1921. British women were given limited voting rights in 1918, and completely in 1928; women in Russia could vote by the Revolution in 1917. Democratic countries that achieved independence after World War II generally provided for universal male and female suffrage.

Voter equality was also enhanced by the advancement toward greater uniformity in population–representation ratios. Equal districting in the United States was not enforced until after the 1962 Supreme Court decision of *Baker* v. *Carr*. Extensive redistricting thereafter brought the basis of electoral representation much closer to the principle of "one person, one vote."

Increasing standardization of administrative procedures in all phases of the electoral process was the third major trend having great impact for shaping modern electoral systems. This includes registration, balloting, tabulation of votes, and corroboration of winners. Most of these measures became essential with the involvement in the elections of earlier-excluded social, economic, ethnic, racial, confessional, and gender groups. Among the crucial innovations was the secret ballot. By 1946, most countries had voting rights extended to all capable citizens beyond the age of twenty-one, and a trend toward lowering the voting age continued. Today most of the countries comply with eighteen years as the age of voting rights. The United States established this voting age for all elections by passage of the 1970 Voting Rights Act extension and the 26th Amendment (1971).

Functions of Elections

Elections serve a variety of functions within the political system. This is the formal procedure to fill public offices or specific policy actions to be adopted. Elections decide the contest in the countries, where two or more candidates compete for the same office. As much as competing candidates may advocate substantial discrepancies in the policy options, elections may deeply affect the governmental public policy choices.

In many countries elections have also symbolic function. Participation in the selection of their governmental leaders involves citizens in the democratic governmental process. On the other hand, choosing of leaders through established and sanctioned election procedures definitely grants the government a base of support and legitimacy among the mass public.

The fundamental challenge for elections is whether there exists a working competition between opposing candidates. This is most often the case with the democratic countries, while under oppressive regimes such competition is absent. In countries with autocratic, totalitarian, and dictatorial regimes, elections are only a prevaricated pageant. Typically, 99%–100% of the votes are cast for the official party candidates. By contrast, in democratic countries, the allotment of the winning vote is normally less than 55% of the total.

Formally, elections in non-democratic countries comply with some of the above mentioned functions. They provide for the regular filling of public offices, and, through vast participation in voting (often obligatory or pending chastisement in case of abstention), they may serve as a proof for the regime popular support. Actually, in these countries elections never allow a genuine contest, or choice, between competing groups of office seekers. As a rule, in the communist, quasi-Marxist, and fascist-type regimes, the leader exercises power until his death, or until he is deposed in a *coup d'état*. Most other personal changes are decided in a narrow circle of senior cadre of the ruling party, while certain positions may be voted at party plenary sessions, congresses, or conventions.

The British pattern of parliamentary government is followed in the most countries of Western Europe and the Commonwealth of Nations. Some of the post-communist countries also adopted such a system. There, voters elect members of the legislative body, who, in turn, elect a prime minister—usually the leader of the majority in the legislature. The prime minister chooses his team to serve as ministers, and they all constitute the executive branch.

Under the congressional system of government in the United States, where terms are fixed, elections for the president and members of Congress are held in even-numbered years: every two years for all members of the House of Representatives and for one third of the Senate, and every four years for president (and vice president). In countries having a parliamentary system there is usually a requirement that legislative elections be held within a set period of time. A government may also be forced to call a general election if it loses a vote in parliament on a major issue.

Types of Elections

There exist several different types of elections, depending on the office or policy issue that is to be settled.

General Elections

Most often, a general election is actually the last stage of a number of elections, held simultaneously throughout a country, to make the final choice among candidates for all public offices that are pending for filling. In some cases, nominating procedures may require primary elections as a prerequisite to the general election. In some countries voters may also vote directly on policy issues or constitutional amendments at the time of the general election. However, in some countries a national general election may also be held to fill only the office of the chief executive.

Primary Elections

Typical mainly in the United States, these are held prior to the general election in order to permit voters to directly select party candidates, who will then run for public office. Generally, the turnout in the primary is much lower than in the general election.

Run-off Elections

Where no candidate in the general election secures a clear majority, a run-off election may be held between the two candidates (rarely three) who have received the most votes. Run-off elections are held in many countries both for legislative and presidential elections, while in the United States there is no provision for a run-off for president. If the electoral college fails to produce a majority, the House of Representatives may arrange a vote for president.

Special Elections

Where a public office is vacated by the incumbent before the term has expired through death or retirement, a special election may be held. In the United States this refers to the seats in the House of Representatives and state legislatures. In Britain, elections to fill vacated seats in Commons are called by-elections. Often in this case the turnout of voters in one and the same constituency is lower than when general elections are held.

Local Elections

On the local level, elections are used for filling a wide variety of offices—mayors, governors (where they are elected and not appointed), members of local or municipal legislatures (councils), etc. Elections are held also to decide issues of local policy. Local elections may coincide with statewide or national elections or be called separately.

Direct and Indirect Elections

In a direct election each member of the electorate votes directly for the candidate of his or her choice, and, depending on the appropriate rules, the candidate with a plurality or a majority of the popular vote is certified as the winner. Indirect elections are decided by vote of a special electoral body. In the Fifth French Republic an electoral college composed of members of the National Assembly, the members of the departmental assemblies, and representatives of the municipal councils elects members of the Senate. In the United States people vote for a special electoral college that in due time elects the president. The electoral college's power of independent judgment is, however, promptly restricted, after the political parties erect slates of electors bound explicitly to one or another presidential nominee.

Election Procedures

The *initiative* is a procedure by which a legally designated number of eligible voters may induce a popular vote to be summoned on a draft legislation, amendment, enforcement, or other public policy question, or to force the legislators to ponder a certain action. The *referendum*, used most often in Switzerland, but also in many other countries, is a kind of election where an issue is submitted directly to a popular vote. In some countries—especially when majority vote is implemented—a number (designated by law) of eligible voters may initiate a removal of a public official, or a *recall* election, usually by petition and collection of signatures. In such cases, special, or partial, elections are held to replace the removed official.

The Electoral Process

All procedures and rules for the conduct of elections are specified by law.

Apportionment and Districting

Apportionment is the way in which representation (i.e., the seats in the legislative body) is distributed among established territorial or other units vested with representation in a political jurisdiction. Districting is the process by which are established exact geographical boundaries of territorial constituencies. Some parties may enjoy the convenience of having their representatives elected by fewer votes than others.

Single-Member and Multiple-Member Districts and Proportional Representation

Additional factors that affect the nature of a country's electoral system are the type of district—single- or multiple-member—in which representatives are elected, and whether the system requires proportional representation or the plurality method of establishing the winning candidates. The United Kingdom and many of the countries in the Commonwealth use single-member constituencies, where the winner is the candidate who redeems the greatest number of votes. In the United States, both types of districts apply in the state legislatures' elections. In most of the world's democracies, including France, Germany, Italy, Sweden, Israel, and Japan, multiple-member constituencies with proportional representation are mostly the case. Under the common version of proportional representation, the list system, voters cast their ballots for a party rather than for specific candidates. Seats are assigned to the parties according to their proportion of the total vote. This system is criticized as strengthening the party leaders' dominance. Many experts argue that the single-member

constituency–plurality election system, where a minor party may get many popular votes but not enough to elect a candidate, tends to maintain the two-party system. However, miscellaneous other factors also contribute for the prevalence of two major parties. Further, proportional representation appears to foster certain minor parties by warranting their representation in the legislative body. In order to qualify for proportional representation, the party must transcend the required percentage of the total popular vote. Some countries combine both systems.

Nominations

A vital element in the total electoral process is the procedure by which candidates are nominated by political parties. In Britain and continental Europe this nominating function is frequently performed by a relatively small group of activists in individual constituencies, party conventions, or conferences, or by national political leaders. In the United States, nominating procedures have evolved to the party convention, which in turn gave way to the direct primary in many states by the early twentieth century. The convention system is still used to nominate presidential candidates, but states increasingly are selecting delegates by primary elections.

Election Campaigns

Political campaigns are ubiquitously conducted differently from country to country. In the totalitarian states, election campaigns are used as a propaganda venture to advertise ruling party's "monumental" successes. Some countries with competitive elections strive to promptly restrain campaign costs and media involvement. In the United States, campaign expenditures grow dramatically with each new election. Typical sources for funding of political parties, such as party dues and profits from party publications, have proved to be insufficient to meet these rising costs. Quite generous public subsidies are available in Germany, while public financing in the United States is restricted. Traditional techniques for campaigning—newspaper coverage, circulation of leaflets, rallies and social gatherings, lectures to civic groups, door-to-door solicitation—are still in use in developing countries with large uneducated and illiterate constituencies.

Campaigns differ also when an incumbent or a challenger is involved or the candidate is from the majority or minority party. Public opinion polls have an important role in political campaigning. Relying on commissioned polls, candidates and their parties devise their strategy, checking categories of the electorate that support them, are against them, or hesitate in their attitudes. Media publicize opinion polls, and often the likely winner is known well in advance. This may induce some voters to refrain from going to the polling stations, considering their individual vote as making no difference. Observers differ in their surmise about the educative or manipulative significance of the polls, and some countries impose restrictions on conducting polls and publishing their results. Clearly, ratings of various parties and candidates attract or thwart financial support.

Administration and formal setting of elections relate to the requirements for registering and voting, the time of the year and day of the week when elections are assigned, the hours polling stations are open, the opportunities for absentee voting, and others. The administration of elections can be of significant impact on the turnout and even the outcomes.

In many countries elections are administered by a particularly designated body, an election commission; in others they are administered by a central or local government official.

Registration

The procedure of registration verifies that given person qualifies to vote. The list of eligible voters is displayed in advance of any election. In most cases this procedure does not demand any action from the prospective voter. In most states of the United States, however, the individual citizen usually must take the initiative. US Blacks as well as minority groups in other countries often need additional incentives to register.

Casting Votes

Most commonly, voting is exercised by paper ballot listing only candidates' names. In some countries ballots are different for each candidate —white or colored. In Turkey, India, and most of Africa parties use specific logos, for example, in the form of animals, to facilitate identification by illiterate or undereducated voters. A more sophisticated method is use of mechanical or digital voting machines, computer punch cards, or insertion of a marked ballot into an optical scanning device. Recent expansion of computer technology increases pressure for introducing distant voting, but especially in the underdeveloped countries this is curbed by the low availability of access to computers.

Absentee Voting

Provisions for absentee voting by mail have spread during the last decades, and the United States has the most advanced system. Most other countries provide voting places for their nationals abroad in the diplomatic missions.

Observation and Monitoring of Elections

In order to prevent abuses and forgery, political parties and independent organizations may provide observers in the polling stations to monitor the whole process, and especially tabulation of votes. In the new democracies opposition often invites foreign observers, including respected political figures, to further ensure fairness of the elections.

Calculating, Reporting, and Verifying Outcomes

Election officials at the precinct polling places, often in the presence of authorized party workers, usually count votes. In some countries ballot boxes are taken to a central place in each constituency for counting. In most of the cases local election officials report their official election figures to the regional or central designated officials. This process may take days or even weeks, especially in countries with poor infrastructure. Major election competitions attract extensive television and newspaper coverage, and they report unofficial vote totals early after closure of poll stations. By analyzing the results in sample constituencies, or through the exit-poll technique, expert pollsters forecast the probable distribution of seats.

Authorized public officials, or a special election board, certify election outcomes and winners. A recount may be demanded if the initial vote count is very close.

Voter Turnout

In Europe, Denmark and Germany demonstrate an especially high voter turnout, while the percentage of voter participation is lower in the United States than in Britain, the Commonwealth, and much of Europe (where the average is closer to 60%). On average, only half of all Americans eligible to vote are registered, and less than half of the registered participate in a given election.

STEPHAN E. NIKOLOV

See also Authoritarianism; Bureaucratic Authoritarianism; Civic Education; Civil Society; Constitutionalism; Democratization; Dictatorships; Legal Systems; Marxism; Monarchic Government; Political Culture; Single-Party States; Totalitarianism

References and Further Reading

Asmal, Kader. *Electoral Systems: A Critical Survey*. Bellville: Centre for Development Studies, University of the Western Cape, 1990.

Butler, David, and Martin Westlake. *British Politics and European Elections*. New York: St. Martin's, 2000.

Farrell, David M. *Electoral Systems: A Comparative Introduction*. Palgrave, 2001.

Katz, Richard S. *Democracy and Elections*. Oxford, 1997.

Lijphart, Arend. *Electoral Systems and Party Systems: A Study of Twenty-Seven Democracies, 1945–1990*, New York: Oxford University Press, 1994.

————. « Electoral Systems », pp. 412–422 in Lipset, A. ed. *The Encyclopedia of Democracy*, Washington, DC: Congressional Quarterly Press, 1995a.

————. « Proportional Representation », pp. 1010–1015 in Lipset, A. ed. *The Encyclopaedia of Democracy*, Washington, DC: Congressional Quarterly Press, 1995b.

Mueller, Dennis C. *Public Choice III*. Cambridge, 2003.

O'Donnell, Guillermo and Phillippe C. Schmitter. *Transitions from Authoritarian Rule: Tentative Conclusions about Uncertain Transitions*. Baltimore, MD: The Johns Hopkins University Press, 1986.

Reeve, Andrew and Alan Ware. *Electoral Systems: A Comparative and Theoretical Introduction*. London and New York: Routledge, 1992.

Reynolds, Andrew and Ben Reilly. *The International IDEA Handbook of Electoral System Design*. Stockholm: International Institute for Democracy and Electoral Assistance, 1997.

Rose, Richard, ed. *International Encyclopedia of Elections*. CQ Press, 2000.

Shade, William G., et al., eds. *American Presidential Campaigns and Elections*, 3 vols. Sharpe, M. E. 2003.

Taagepera, Rein, and Matthew S. Shugart. *Seats and Votes: The Effects and Determinants of Electoral Systems*. New Haven, CT: Yale University Press, 1989.

Thompson, Dennis F. *Just Elections: Creating a Fair Electoral Process in the United States*. University of Chicago Press, 2001.

ENERGY: ALTERNATIVE DEVELOPMENT

The Importance of Renewable Energy

Human society cannot survive without continuous use, and hence supply, of energy. Modern economies are energy dependent, and one of the major problems for their existence and further development is the sufficient energy supply. The world's increasing energy demands and rapidly diminishing reserves of oil, natural gas, and coal have led to developing strategies and plans for using alternative energy sources. Dependence on fossil-fueled power plants to produce electricity has an adverse impact on public health and environment. Burning of coal or natural gas emits substantial amounts of sulfur dioxide and nitrogen oxides into the atmosphere. Sulfuric acids and metric acids are formed when these gases combine with atmospheric water vapor. These acids form acidic precipitation which has an adverse effect on public health, flora and fauna, and building constructions. The combustion of fossil fuels also releases carbon dioxide. The content of this gas in the atmosphere has risen in the last century because of the high consumption of coal, oil, and natural gas. The Intergovernmental Panel on Climate Change (IPCC) identified emissions of carbon dioxide as the chief contributor to global warming. World scientists identify the threats of global warming as the greatest challenge to the future generations. It presents unprecedented hazards of rising oceans, flooding and inundation of coastal zones, agricultural disruption, loss of biodiversity, and climate changes. Global warming can be effectively addressed if significant steps are taken that reduce adverse environmental impacts and hazards. Overreliance on fossil-fuel electricity generation has also other negative impacts on consumers and economy. As fossil fuel reserves are increasingly depleted in the future, the price of fossil-fuel electricity will continue to grow up.

Alternative development of energy resources and efforts to find clean energy options are among the key issues not only in global warming discussions but also when suggesting sustainable development paths. Against the environmental and economic backdrop faced when there is reliance on fossil fuels, there are many compelling reasons for countries to seek to increase their use of renewable energy. Nowadays there are a lot of programs promoting renewable energy technologies with the objective to reduce fossil-fuel consumption. One of the most advanced technologies is based on fusion processes. In this reaction deuterium and tritium (hydrogen isotopes) are used as fuels. Deuterium is obtained from water, while tritium results in the processes run into the fusion reactor. It is considered that one gram of fusion fuel can produce as much energy as nine thousand liters of oil. Unlike fossil fuels, fusion does not cause environmental pollution. Herewith fusion will not be discussed further because of its complex character and way of operation. Rather it should be considered as an advanced means for energy development and an alternative to nuclear energy and fossil fuels.

Renewable energy resources hold great promise for meeting the energy and development needs of countries throughout the world. Renewables include a considerable number of proven and emerging technologies, which permit the execution of needed tasks presently performed by use of fossil fuels. Renewable resources vary widely in technical and economic characteristics. They play a crucial role for developing countries. Some renewable resources, such as solar energy, wind, geothermal, biomass, and small hydroelectric energy are widely spread and accessible throughout the world. They offer both environmental and economic advantages. The present article will discuss the previously mentioned renewable resources, but it will exclude nuclear energy, large hydroelectric dams, and waste to energy power plants as alternatives to energy production. Nuclear energy is excluded because of the problems related to proliferation and nuclear waste disposal. Moreover, it requires high capital and operating costs. Large hydroelectric dams are not presently considered because of the environmental damages they can cause and expenses for their construction and maintenance. Waste to energy power plants is also excluded because it is highly polluting.

Solar Energy

Solar energy presents great development opportunities. It is an attractive energy resource because of its nonpolluting character and inexhaustible supply opportunities. Solar energy is the radiation from the sun capable of producing heat, causing chemical reactions, or generating electricity. The sunlight that reaches the Earth consists of nearly 50% visible light, 45% infrared radiation, and the rest forms of ultraviolet light and other forms of electromagnetic radiation. Solar radiation can be converted to heat and mechanical or electrical power. The former conversion is easier to accomplish.

Solar energy is captured and converted by two main types of collectors: flat-plate collectors and concentrating collectors. Both types of collectors should have large area because of the low intensity of solar radiation reaching the Earth's surface. Flat-plate collectors are commonly used for hot-water heating and house heating. This system can supply a household with hot water drawn from an insulated storage tank, or it can provide space heating when warm water runs through tubes inserted in floors and/or ceilings. The temperatures that can be reached when flat-plate

collectors are used vary between 66°C and 93°C (150°F and 200°F). When higher temperatures are needed, then a concentrating collector is used.

Solar radiation can be converted into electricity by photovoltaic cells. Electrical voltage is generated when light strikes the junction between a metal and a semiconductor (for instance silicon) or a junction between two different semiconductors. Solar technologies provide environmentally clean options for energy production. Although based on an inexhaustible primary energy resource, the costs for solar energy production, collection, conservation, and storage limit its exploitation.

Wind Energy

Wind energy is a pollution-free technology. It derives from wind turbines that can be situated either onshore or off-shore. Wind electric systems have siting problems such as wind exposure, aesthetic impacts, danger to birds that fly into the blades, and noise. On-shore wind energy is extensively deployed and commercially developed technology. Off-shore wind is a less developed source, but potentially has a better future. It usually provides better exposure to wind resources and allows bigger turbines than those sited on shore. However, off-shore turbines are poorly accessible and require higher maintenance costs (e.g., linking to the power grid).

The utilization of wind energy systems grew in the last decade. In Europe, Denmark started the use of wind energy for electricity generation. The country is a leader in turbine technologies. Extensive wind applications are applied also in Germany and Spain. The successful experiences, combined with proper siting of wind turbines, can be a model for alternative energy resource for developing countries as well.

Biomass

Biomass resources are used for deriving ethanol (ethyl alcohol, grain alcohol) and methanol, which are the two alcohols commonly considered for fuel use. Ethanol is produced by yeast fermentation of hexose sugars (such as those derived from cereal grains, sugar cane, or sugar bean) and subsequent separation from the aqueous solution by distillation. Methanol can be produced from cellulose products such as wood or crop residues by gasification.

Alcohol fuels can be used in different ways. The best-known fuel use for alcohol is as a substitute for gasoline. They can also be used in heating and lighting, in simple wick lamps or heaters, or in pressure stoves and lanterns. They are clean and comparatively safe fuels, which unlike petroleum are miscible with water. The growth and conversion of various plant species to fuels can be an alternative to petroleum use in many countries worldwide, and especially those with favorable climate conditions. Brazil has pioneered the growth of biomass for producing alcohol fuels. In 1979, the country imported more than 80% of its petroleum. A combination of factors—availability of land and labor, favorable climate, a need for liquid fuels—has resulted in ambitious alcohol fuel programs. This led to halving country's oil imports. Argentina, Costa Rica, and the Philippines are among the countries where biomass is used on a large scale as an alternative energy resource.

A widely feared social consequence of large-scale alcohol fuel production is that it will limit food staples. This will have a negative impact especially in poor regions where the need for liquid fuels will be satisfied at the expense of food production. Another argument against large-scale alcohol fuel production is that it will lead to soil erosion and depletion, or that widespread monocultural crop production will make large areas vulnerable to pests or diseases. All of these limitations must be considered before applying large-scale activities for alcohol fuel production.

Geothermal Energy

Geothermal energy is the energy generated and stored in the core, mantle, and crust of the Earth. However, this energy source can be tapped in relatively restricted zones, where heat can be extracted in the form of hot water or steam. It can be used for electricity generation, heating, drying, or freezing. Locating proper geothermal sources depends on finding a suitable heat source and the presence of a suitable medium for transferring the heat. Geothermal exploration is a complicated activity as it involves methods from geology, geophysics and geochemistry.

The geothermal fields used to produce electricity are associated with young igneous intrusions. The latter are situated on three types of plate boundaries: constructive, destructive, and transform faults. Constructive boundaries are those which occur where two plates move apart and a new plate is formed on the ocean floor. These types of boundaries are located in Iceland, the Gulf of California, and the Red Sea. Destructive boundaries are where two plates collide and one remains under the other (Japan, Indonesia,

New Zealand, and the Phillipines). Transform faults occur where two plates slide past each other (for instance, California and Hawaii).

Geothermal energy has been known for centuries, but not until the beginning of the twentieth century was geothermal water used to heat houses in Iceland. In 1904 at Lardello, Italy first used it to produce electric power. Water and steam hotter than 356°F (180°C) are generally required for electric-power generation. Among the world's largest users of this alternative energy source are Japan, Iceland, Italy, the United States, Italy, and New Zealand. Other countries that are generating 10%–20% of their electricity through geothermal are Costa Rica, El Salvador, Kenya, and Nicaragua.

The development of geothermal resources has become increasingly attractive owing to the rising cost of petroleum and the nonpolluting character of geothermal energy production. However, it is arguable if geothermal energy constitutes a renewable energy resource. Generally, over time, the pressure in the fields where hot water or steam is found declines. The lifetime of a field can vary. One of the applied measures that ensure longer operations at the site is reinjection with geothermal fluid that can help to maintain the pressure.

Tidal Power

Tidal power can be used also for electricity generation. This is achieved through turbines that are run by tidal flows. One of the plants that produce electricity using tidal power is the Rance power plant in the Gulf of Saint-Malo, Brittany, France. Another tidal plant was also constructed in 1969 in the ex-Soviet Union on the White Sea. Despite the large amounts of power available from the tides in favorable locations, this power is intermittent and varies with the seasons.

Hydroelectricity Generation

One of the possible means of electricity generation is through generators driven by water turbines that convert the potential energy of falling water or fast-flowing water to mechanical energy. Hydroelectric power plants are usually placed in dams that impound rivers, thereby raising the water level behind the dam. Nowadays it is believed that large dams create environmental problems, as well as displacing people and agriculture. Because of this, small dams are considered an environmentally harmful form of hydroelectric power production.

Falling water is one of the three principal sources of energy used to generate electric power; the other two being fossil fuels and nuclear fuels. It has advantages over the other two. It is constantly renewable owing to the recurring nature of the hydrologic cycle; and it does not produce either thermal or particulate pollution. Some countries, such as Sweden, Canada, and Norway, rely heavily on hydroelectricity.

Hydrogen

Hydrogen is the most promising alternative fuel for the future. It currently is produced from photovoltaic or wind-powered electrolysis, from separating hydrogen from water, from some seawater algae, and from natural gas. Hydrogen is considered to be an alternative fuel that can power vehicles. Its combustion is pollution free (resulting in water). The challenges to wide use of hydrogen are to reduce the cost of hydrogen production and construct the proper infrastructure to transport the hydrogen.

Conclusion

Despite the many advantages of renewable energy use, the renewable energy to produce electricity is extremely low, especially of renewable resources other than non-large hydro. There are a number of economic, regulatory, and political barriers to increase the percentage of applied renewable energy resources. These obstacles are tackled with various policy tools. The European Union has set a target of achieving 22% of renewables as part of Europe's electricity by 2010. India has proposed that 10% of annual additions to electric capacity come from renewables by 2012. The promising future of renewables is revealed by scenarios that point to 20%–50% of renewable energy supplies in the second half of the twenty-first century.

All of these policy measures are possible because renewable energy sources hold enormous potential. They enhance diversity in energy supply markets, sustain energy supplies, and reduce environmental pollution. They provide attractive options to meet specific needs for energy services, and this is particularly important for developing countries and rural areas. Most renewable technologies are still at an early stage of their development and implementation. This requires further research, development, and public awareness for the benefits of the renewable resources.

MILENA NOVAKOVA

See also Energy: Impact on Development; Sustainable Development

References and Further Reading

Ingvar Birgir Fridleifsson. *Geothermal energy exploration and utilization*, In Energy Research in Developing Countries. Volume 7: Nonconventional Energy. Ottawa: International Development Center, 1994.

McNelis, Bernard and Peter L. Fraenke. *Solar and Wind Energy Technology*. In Energy Research in Developing Countries. Volume 7: Nonconventional Energy. Ottawa: International Development Center, 1994.

Ottinger, Richard L. and Mindy Jayne. *Global Climate Change – Kyoto Protocol Implementation: Legal Frameworks For Implementing Clean Energy Solutions*. New York: Pace University School of Law, 2000.

Prager, Stewart. *Fusion Reactor*. In Encyclopaedia Britannica Deluxe Edition 2004 CD-ROM.

Russell, Charles R. *Energy Convertion*. In Encyclopaedia Britannica Deluxe Edition 2004 CD-ROM.

Subramanian, D. K. and T. V. Ramachadra. *Ecologically Sound Energy Planning Strategies for Sustainable Development*. Bangalore: Indian Institute of Sciences.

Turkenburg, Wim. *Renewable Energy Technologies* In World Energy Assessment, http://www.undp.org/seed/eap/activities/wea/drafts-frame.html [last consulted on February 18, 2004].

ENERGY: IMPACT ON DEVELOPMENT

Energy is arguably one of the most important aspects of developing a modern society. By nature, energy resources are unevenly distributed across the globe. Control of energy resources is therefore one of the most important strategic issues in international relations. Energy resources are at the heart of much of the conflict in the Middle East, a hotbed for conflict after World War II. The importance of the region for outside interests is directly tied to the preponderance of petroleum supplies there. For that reason, US, Japanese, and European foreign policy have historically been willing to overlook their democratic and human rights values in dealing with despotic regimes in the region. While most international trade and investment occur in the developed world, with the exception of China, the dependency on external supplies of fuel is the Achilles' heel of Western economies. This vulnerability has, in recent years, raised questions as to whether the heightened strength of oil exporters can change the dynamic of relations between the developed and developing world. Within countries, such as Nigeria, regions with energy endowments have become the source of conflict, including issues such as levels of autonomy and fair and efficient distribution of the revenues from the resources.

Energy has also had profound effects upon the trajectories of developing countries. The key to energy is not only the existence or lack thereof of natural resources, but also the types and quality of resources that are available. For example, petroleum, as perhaps the most valuable energy commodity, is concentrated in some areas of the globe, leading to a situation of differing levels of development. While countries with such resources enjoy high standards of living, in some cases well above the average of Northern countries, other developing countries without such resources have been at a severe disadvantage in terms of their energy costs and vulnerability to outside economic shocks (sudden changes in energy prices). Moreover, because of the strategic importance of energy, developing country governments steadily increased control through expropriations, nationalizations, and the formation of state-owned enterprises through most of the latter part of the twentieth century.

Last but not least, energy has been at the center of discussions of "sustainable development." Sustainable development is a broad concept often used to convey the idea that the development process should not create long-lasting or permanent damage to the natural environment. Since energy used as a fuel for transportation and manufacturing is one of the primary sources of pollution, finding ways to create sustainable energy sources and consumption systems has become a focal point for research and policy discussion. This conversation has also translated into North–South dimensions, in terms of the levels and types of responsibility polluters have at different levels of output and different stages of development.

Profile of Energy in Development: Energy Sources and Uses

There are a few primary sources of energy, based on historical (technological) development and on the costs for producing energy. Historically, the modern machines of industry, transport, and household comforts grew hand-in-hand with the development of fossil fuel sources. Fossil fuels include coal, petroleum and its derivatives, and natural gas. More recently, hydroelectricity has become an important source of energy in countries endowed with fast moving and high volume water flows. We should note that having some resources is considerably different from having abundant resources that can be extracted at a reasonable price.

The most primary fuel used may be wood. Burning wood is an obvious choice for ease of use and the low level of technology needed to use it for cooking or heating. While not all areas of the globe have forested areas, they tend to be relatively common. However, wood tends to burn energy fast, and creates high levels of pollutants. In addition, wood can not easily be stored, as it is heavy to transport and can rot over time if it becomes moist. Because of the ease of use, wood is still used in many poor rural areas in the developing world as a primary source of fuel. This has led to strong concerns about deforestation and soil erosion as rapid population growth have led to an "overuse" of forests. A related fuel source is biomass, which is essentially the burning of organic matter, such as animal waste. While the cost is relatively low, the fuel output of biomass is also relatively inefficient, and transportation and storage difficult. The growing use of biomass in the developing world and the health and environmental problems thereby created are growing concerns.

Coal is one of the most abundant energy sources naturally available and has a long history of use. Coal, in its various forms, is found naturally in often large mineral deposits in a wide variety of locations globally. Coal has long been used as a source of heating, and at the turn of the century, was an important fuel for transportation (fueling steam engines) and industrial uses as well. Because of its heavy weight, coal is often transported upon railway cars. In recent decades, coal has become less important as a fuel source because of growing awareness of the high levels of air pollution emissions. The consequences of coal-created emissions upon human and natural health, including "acid rain," have led to policies designed to reduce its use.

Petroleum is also a fossil fuel that is naturally found, but abundant and easily accessible sources tend to be more concentrated geographically. Technology for finding, developing, and refining petroleum is capital-intensive and highly sophisticated. Petroleum exploration and drilling now occur offshore as well as in remote areas where it can be found. Unlike coal, petroleum can be transported through pipelines and so transportation costs tend to be considerably lower. Petroleum is also a fast burning fuel, ignitable at a low temperature, that delivers a very high energy output. In other words, petroleum is a very efficient energy source considering the costs of supply versus the energy output. Petroleum has a very wide variety of uses besides energy, including the creation of synthetic fibers and plastics as well as lubricants and medicinal purposes, that reinforce its strategic importance. While diesel fuel derived from petroleum is sometimes used to make electricity, the most important use is as the source for almost all global vehicles' fuel, gasoline. However, in recent years, natural gas, a related fuel that is usually found along with petroleum, has become the fastest growing fuel of choice for both heating and electricity generation, because of its clean burning properties. For all these reasons, petroleum will remain an important part of developed and developing societies.

The other major energy source internationally is hydroelectricity, which is created by the natural movement of water from a higher place to a lower one. Some of the largest man-made projects are dams designed to capture this natural source of energy through turbines. While hydroelectricity is the most clean-burning fuel (as nothing is burned), it is not without its disadvantages. Hydroelectric fuel sources depend on the presence of strong and consistent volumes of strong water flow. These sources are not always close to population centers, and exist only in limited quantities globally. In addition, dams must be designed and located strategically both so that energy production is maximized and to ensure safe water supplies. Concerns about the flooding created by dams and the effects of dams on local fauna and flora have created strong resistance globally to large new projects. One of the few to have recently been created is the Three Gorges dam project in China, which sparked international controversy.

Finally, nuclear energy, based upon the energy released when radioactive atoms are split under pressure, remains an option for developing countries without abundant fossil fuels. Great concern surrounds the nuclear energy industry, however, for a number of reasons. The most obvious is that the nuclear energy industry can be used to develop nuclear weapons as well, which may increase its attractiveness for states interested in increasing their strategic power. Secondly, while nuclear energy is relatively efficient and clean burning, the high levels of radioactivity from spent fuel, which can persist for thousands of years, in combination with the complex technical aspects of its operation, creates a major public health hazard. The question remains open as to where spent nuclear fuel can be safely stored. The near disaster of the Three Mile Island plant in the United States and the continuing health effects of the Chernobyl meltdown in Russia continue to haunt the industry. Activists in the North have been successful in slowing the spread of new nuclear reactors, and, in some cases, in shutting others down. Therefore, nuclear energy remains a small and stagnant portion of most developing countries' energy portfolio.

As previously discussed, there are several basic categories of energy use: heating, cooking, transportation, industrial, and electricity generation. Electricity, while it relies upon the fuel sources previously discussed, has all of the other uses of fuel sources. If we define development as the creation of an advanced industrial economy with standards of living comparable to those in Northern society today, we can see that the use of energy will continue to increase over time. In addition, the development of a Western lifestyle means the continual development of new technology and modes of consumption, so that even in the North, energy use is continuing to accelerate. This also suggests that the types of use for energy will change over time, with more fuel being used proportionally for services, including transportation and household appliances, as incomes rise.

As can be seen from Table 1, the North consumes the lion's share of total and relative amounts of energy consumed in the world. We also see some striking differences by region in terms of the types of energy used. In part, the differences reflect natural resource endowments, such as high oil usage in the Middle East, the fact that high quality coal in Latin America is scarce and abundant in Asia, and that Latin America has, by contrast, an abundance of hydroelectric sources. However, usage by fuel sources also reflects

Table 1: Energy usage by region and fuel type, 2001 (percent of world total)

Region	Energy usage	Crude oil production	Coal	Hydroelectricity	Nuclear
OECD	53.2	28.4	37.1	48.9	86.3
China	11.5	4.8	34.6	10.5	<0.1
Asia	11.5	4.9	12.5	6.6	2.2
Former USSR	9.3	13.1	8.3	9.1	8.5
Middle East	3.9	28.5	<0.1	0.6	<0.1
Latin America	3.7	9.5	1.5	19.5	<0.1
Africa	3.5	10.6	5.9	3	<0.1
non-OECD Europe	1.0	0.2	0.1	1.8	1.1

Source: International Energy Agency, *Key World Energy Statistics, 2003.*

Table 2: Top CO_2 polluting countries (in cubic feet)

Country	1999
United States	1,519.89
China	668.73
Russia	400.09
Japan	306.65
India	243.28
Germany	229.93
United Kingdom	152.39
Canada	150.90
Italy	121.28
France	108.59
Korea, South	107.49
Ukraine	104.30
Mexico	100.56
South Africa	99.45
Australia	93.90
Brazil	88.90

Source: US Energy Information Agency.

levels of internal conflict and state and technological capacity. Africa is much poorer in both relative and absolute levels of consumption in part for the inability to develop large local energy projects. Hydro projects, in particular, by their geographic nature, often require high levels of international cooperation. What is not highlighted in the table is the fact that developing countries have been rapidly increasing their relative share and absolute levels of energy consumption. However, the levels of increase tend to be quite unevenly distributed, with larger and more rapidly developing nations such as China and Mexico increasing their share while smaller nations have not, as reflected in Table 2.

Table 1 does not adequately demonstrate the huge levels of inequity in terms of access to modern energy sources. According to the International Energy Agency (IEA), about one fourth of the world's population does not have access to electricity. The majority of these are in Africa, and South and Southeast Asia. Moreover, even where available, basic energy tariffs remain well beyond the reach of large numbers of the poor.

The Rise of OPEC

In the early 1970s, petroleum supply nations acted upon long-standing dreams and created an oil cartel for the first time. The Organization of Petroleum Exporting Countries, or OPEC (see entry for further details), created an important change in the international history of energy. With OPEC, for the first time, the developing countries were able to act in concerted fashion to attempt to reshape the relations of international exchange between the North and the South. OPEC gave rise to a lively debate in the 1970s about these terms, leading the South to request a number of changes, capped by discussions of a New International Economic Order (NIEO) (see entry).

OPEC created a sense of optimism that other developing countries attempted to follow through the creation of cartels based on other commodities, such as coffee, nickel, and tin. However, the general optimism that OPEC marked created a turning point in North–South relations for the benefit of the latter, and the idea that a number of commodity cartels could be created to turn the North's supposed dependency on the South against it proved short-lived. There are a number of reasons for this, but our previous discussion suggests a few. The first is the strategic value and dependency on petroleum is much greater than for any other commodity. While demand continues to increase internationally for oil, supplies are both limited and concentrated. This brings us to the second point, which is that a commodity like rubber or coffee, as a plant-based product, can have an "elastic supply" function, meaning that if the price goes up, farmers can simply plant more. Given the costs and difficulties as well as the finite nature of petroleum, it is much harder for suppliers to respond to price increases in the short to medium term. Third, some of the largest concentrations of petroleum exporters are in the Middle East. Key producing states such as Saudi Arabia and Kuwait have had fairly low population bases, making it easier for them to lead cutbacks on supply in order to bolster prices. More importantly, developing countries that have a large population and seek development are also dependent upon fuel supplies. Thus, when OPEC raised oil prices, they directly slowed down the development of large importers, such as India and Egypt. In many cases, developing countries who were energy *importers* borrowed money in order to pay for this increase in prices, leading to the debt-recession spiral of the 1980s throughout the developing world.

For better or worse, 1979 appears to be the last year when OPEC was able to act in a concerted fashion to create a major oil price shock. While OPEC continues to work in a concerted fashion, its relative level of influence has dropped considerably from the heyday of the 1970s. The key reasons for this include the unexpected elasticity of supply, and political turmoil internationally. While there were major shortages in the North in the 1970s due to the oil price increases, by the early 1980s, the price increases had actually spurred on the development of new petroleum suppliers, some of whom are not OPEC members, such as Mexico, the North Sea finds off the United Kingdom's coast, and Norway. In addition, major importing countries such as Brazil have been motivated to develop their own sources of petroleum and other fuels. Meanwhile the Iran–Iraq war of the 1980s in particular led to the breakdown of internal cohesion within OPEC. Later in the 1980s, the breakup of the Soviet Union led to Russia entering the international market as a major new supplier, along with its former colonies in the Caucusus and Central Asia. The re-taking of Kuwait in the 1990s Gulf War and the more recent invasion of Iraq by the United States are all related to the desire to ensure an abundant supply of petroleum. At the same time, the growing population base and needs of oil exporters such as Iran, Mexico, and Saudi Arabia have made supply cutbacks by key exporters difficult. In sum, while the demand side of the world energy has not really adjusted to reduce OPEC's power, a number of supply side factors have.

Even among the developing countries that have become active exporters, the results have often been less than hoped for. Terry Karl points out in her book *The Paradox of Plenty* that much of the development of Venezuela's vast oil wealth has been accompanied by the inability to diversify the economy and particularly exports; a growing consumptive lifestyle, including dependence on previously produced goods, such as food; and huge concentrations of wealth and corruption that do not raise the standards of large portions of the population. While there are some partial exceptions in the cases of Indonesia, which for a time was able to diversify its exports, and Libya, which has some basic social welfare services, many petro-states, such as Nigeria and Equatorial Guinea do seem to fall into the trap described by Karl. Karl points out that it is not just the concentration of revenue flows from the industry, but the fact that states that lack well-developed institutions, political cohesion, and long-term visions for their development will naturally have difficulty in handling a sudden gush of new revenues. As institutions and politics develop around the control of these resources, it becomes difficult to move back to a more egalitarian and merit-based form political and economic decision-making.

Energy Markets

Given the strategic importance of fuels for the economy and national security, there has long been a high level of state intervention in the energy sector. National and government-supported energy companies, such as Petro-Canada and British Petroleum were the norm for many years. While many of these companies have been privatized and energy sectors deregulated, energy remains an area where governments remain active. The reason goes beyond the overall importance of energy to the nature of the energy sector itself. Coal mining, like other types of mining enterprises, requires heavy doses of skilled labor. As a result, large coal mining states, such as Britain until recent decades, experienced important political influence from labor unions of miners. In some developing countries, such as Bolivia and Chile, miners have become key political actors in development decision-making. Petroleum and natural gas as well as large hydroelectric dams, meanwhile, require vast amounts of capital investment, and high levels of risk in developing potential new deposits and the flooding of areas respectively. In turn, they require a large number of readily available and technologically up-to-date engineers. Therefore, the state has an important role in terms of providing financial human capital and/or managing deals with foreign companies and governments who provide these resources in exchange for supplies and financial returns. As a result of these market characteristics, energy markets tend towards natural monopolies or oligopolies (markets in which there is only one or a few main suppliers). Moreover, since state defensive capabilities rely upon a stable source of fuel, governments see energy as a key sector that must be nurtured and protected.

For all these reasons, the recent turn towards deregulated and privatized energy markets has been accompanied by strong pressures towards state guidance, if not direct intervention. The move towards deregulation and privatization in the electricity sector the developing world began in the early 1980s, with Chile being one of the first to experiment internationally with creating a free market. From the 1980s until the present, the pace of privatization and deregulation has continued to spread across the developing world. The timing of this movement can be directly linked with the debt crisis of the 1980s and the rise of neoliberal thinking on economic development. Because of the debt crisis, developing country governments could no longer afford to hold on to state-owned enterprises, which in many cases were losing money due to large numbers of employees and corruption related to the company being run for political as well as economic and financial reasons. Even in the cases where state-owned enterprises were making money, the demographic explosion and rising incomes (at least in some segments of the population), have led to increasing demands for energy consumption. These demands require heavy investments of capital at a time when local capital markets are generally weak, governments broke, and the local private sector lacks the financial and technological capability to undertake major new investments. Therefore, privatization and deregulation of the energy sector have been accompanied by a growing relationship and renewed dependence upon foreign multinational companies for new investment. In addition to the risks inherent in developing new sources of fuel, energy tends to be a "network" industry in terms of getting supplies to the consumer, whether that is through gas pipelines or electricity transmission lines. Therefore, deregulation designers have struggled with this "public good" aspect of the need for private producers to share the main transmission lines or pipelines while maintaining a healthy and fair competitive market. Secondarily, designers have struggled in terms of finding funds and/or incentives to entice private companies to invest in remote, rural, and low income areas. The deregulatory and privatization process is being questioned internationally after recent fiascos such as the complete gridlock of the California power system and a major blackout in Eastern North America. In both cases, the lack of incentives for new investment figured prominently. In the developing world, these design problems have been accompanied both in energy and other basic services, such as water, with a more nationalistic reaction to maintain local control. While scandals of major international energy companies such as Enron in 2002 reflect a volatile market and some reasons for state intervention, critics have yet to propose an alternative method to procure the growing energy investment needs of developing countries.

Energy and the Environment: Alternatives?

As seen in Table 2 on CO_2 emissions, the North also produces the lion's share of world pollution, with the US economy certainly the largest producer. However, the table also demonstrates that large developing countries, such as India and China, have been rapidly increasing their pollution levels.

Public policy and activist groups have been concerned with the pollution created by energy development and consumption since at least the 1970s. Their efforts have led to important policy changes in the North, such as the requirements for the use of unleaded gasoline, coal emission limits, and the virtual stagnation of the nuclear energy industry, as discussed previously. Energy conservation programs

and incentives for alternative sources and ways to use fuel have also become an important part of policy experiments internationally. Of particular concern is the exponential increase in automobile usage internationally, particularly in rapidly developing countries. Given the devastating effects of the oil crisis upon importing countries as described previously, many countries began to look for alternative sources of fuel.

A number of alternative energy sources are parts of important experiments. These include the development of solar energy, windmills, tidal-based, and geo-thermal sources. In addition, major efforts have been made to develop non-gasoline-based cars to reduce emissions and dependency on foreign oil imports. Brazil has had some success in producing a sugar-cane-fired gasohol (mixture of sugar cane and gasoline) vehicle, for instance, and the attempt to develop natural gas-based and hydrogen-based (fuel cell) cars continues. However, so far none of these sources has proven either economically viable on a large-scale, which relates in part to the fact that our technology was developed with fossil fuels, or available in a form that would be acceptable for the modern middle- or upper-class consumer. Though there are significant variations by area, in general the modern consumer expects energy on demand at any time of day or night, without delay, and in a form that allows for individual consumption (i.e., such as a car as opposed to shared transportation). The most important technological hurdle has therefore been the lack of an adequate and economical technology for storing electricity. Because electricity cannot be economically stored, due to the present state of battery technology, even if economically viable, solar, tidal, and windmill energy would not be consistently available. Moreover, there is a cost in lost energy as well as expense to transport energy from one location to another. All of this has led a number of observers to wonder if the problem is not so much one of inadequate technology, but rather of unsustainable consumption choices.

ANIL HIRA

References and Further Reading

Gilbert, Richard J. and Edward P. Kahn, eds. *International Comparisons of Electricity Regulation*. New York: Cambridge University Press, 1996.

Hira, Anil. *Political Economy of Energy in the Southern Cone*. Westport, CT: Praeger, 2003.

International Energy Agency. *Key World Energy Statistics*, Paris: OECD. *World Energy Outlook: Energy and Poverty*. 2002.

Karl, Terry. *The Paradox of Plenty: Oil Booms and Petro-States*. Berkeley, CA: University of California Press, 1997.

The Journal of Energy and Development.

United Nations 2002. *Energy and Sustainable Development: Case Studies.* New York: 2002.

US Energy Information Agency, www.eia.doe.gov

Yergin, Daniel. *Prize: The Epic Quest for Oil, Money, and Power.* New York: Free Press, 1993.

ENTREPRENEURSHIP

Entrepreneurship is the act of establishing a new business to take advantage of an opportunity identified for the first time. Although it is often thought to require an important innovation or invention, entrepreneurship can flourish even with very small changes or improvements to existing businesses. For example, opening a new food stall very similar to those already present in an area but located close to a new office block to meet new demand is an example of entrepreneurship, as too would be providing a bundle of goods or services together rather than individually (e.g., hamburgers and noodles in one shop). In economic thought, the role of the entrepreneur (or businessperson) was considered by the influential writer Joseph Schumpeter to be central to the growth of capital and hence economic development. He observed that the entrepreneur was often also directly responsible for the addition of technology to capital forming activities and that this was another critical activity determining overall growth. This has been hotly contested, and it is difficult to identify specifically in history exactly where and when entrepreneurial ability has represented a significant aspect of the wealth creation process. When something is difficult to measure, it is difficult to find the conditions necessary to replicate it. Certainly those organising the university courses that try to foster entrepreneurship in students have generally accepted that while some knowledge and skills can be taught, there is a fundamental aspect that seems to be either innately present or not within people. However, focusing on specifics such as innovation management can have practically applicable results.

Implications of Entrepreneurship

Entrepreneurship may originally have developed from the practice of organising stage and theatre shows but it is now very closely linked with small and medium sized enterprises (SMEs), which generally have fewer significant investments in plant or machinery and so can more easily switch production or marketing methods. SMEs are considered crucial to an economy's health because they are the firms that tend to adapt to new technology or opportunities first. SMEs are generally defined as being business enterprises with between 20 and 250 employees. However, many smaller businesses—known as micro-businesses—can also be crucial for the entrepreneurial ability of an economy. As the tendency for firms to have fewer core employees and more contracted freelancers and part-time or portfolio workers increases, then the more importance micro-businesses will have.

Entrepreneurship has a negative side in that it can also lead people into undesirable or ultimately unproductive activities, which nevertheless offer short-term profit. Selling individual cigarettes outside schools or illegal narcotics are examples of profitable but undesirable entrepreneurship. It is also true that most entrepreneurs fail far more often than they succeed: it is a frequently quoted statistic that 80% of all businesses fail within two years but it is essentially a true one and it means that even the world's most successful entrepreneurs (e.g., Bill Gates, Richard Branson, and Thaksin Shinawatra) can have a series of bankruptcies or other failures behind them. More successful entrepreneurs emerge from countries such as the United States, therefore, where the implications of bankruptcy are very minor, compared with those of the United Kingdom, where implications remain punitive. Failure can often result not from the inability of the entrepreneur or the business idea but rather poor timing, poor location, or just bad luck. It is reported that Colonel Sanders knocked on more than one hundred restaurant doors before he could find someone willing to try his fried chicken recipe and profit-sharing concept.

Entrepreneurship in the Developing World

As a result of their general inability to gain maximum value from their existing assets, developing world entrepreneurs suffer particularly from the problems that beset SMEs and micro-businesses around the world: inability to obtain capital funding for investment, lack of managerial skills and knowledge, lack of time to develop human capital, and general lack of access to resources.

To overcome some of these difficulties, micro-finance schemes have been successfully established in some locations. Following the example of Bangladesh's Grameen Bank scheme, micro-finance schemes offer very small loans at preferential interest rates primarily to rural villagers but also to urban residents. The potential recipient is generally expected to demonstrate a potential entrepreneurial opportunity that is currently impossible to exploit because of lack of capital. Eligible schemes include such ideas as buying a cow to provide milk and ultimately meat, purchase of a bicycle to make a food hawker stall become mobile, or paying an outside worker to enable a child to attend school. Experience suggests that these schemes are often of particular use to and benefit of women, who are considered more apt at identifying very small scale opportunities without becoming too ambitious and also more disciplined in using the funds for the purpose for which they are intended. However, like all stereotypes, this is a simplification of reality. Nevertheless, the model has spread with some success to countries in Africa, Latin America, and other parts of Asia.

However, important as empowering local people can be, a more powerful force for entrepreneurship in the modern world is the impact of globalisation—that is, the increased ability of individuals and firms to organise business activities around the world, taking if necessary only temporary advantage of cheaper inputs or other locational benefits. As a result, factories utilizing low-cost, low-skilled labour have been established in countries such as Indonesia, Vietnam, and China, exporting some manufacturing jobs from the developed world and creating some in the developing world. It is of great importance for hosting governments to ensure that any capital, skills, or competencies gained by the national labour market by means of such activities are retained and harnessed in the effort to establish home-owned businesses.

Stimulating Entrepreneurship

Government attempts to stimulate entrepreneurial activity have generally received only mixed success. This is not just because of the opportunity for rent-seeking activities (i.e., cheating the system) but because not everyone has the desire or ability to become a successful entrepreneur and, just as importantly, often very small differences in circumstances can make the difference between success and failure. In a business with tiny profit margins, a short illness or a minor accident can represent a disaster. Similarly, many entrepreneurs profit from short-term trends and fashions which are almost impossible to predict or influence.

Nevertheless, it appears that some cultures or ethnic groups tend to display greater levels of entrepreneurial desire and ability than others. For example, immigrants from South Asia to the United Kingdom have demonstrated entrepreneurism in such fields as retailing and distribution, which have in turn led to large internationalised businesses. Entrepreneurial ability can be stimulated by historical or cultural factors—for example, in much of pre-modern Europe Jewish people were forbidden to own land and so had to turn to finance to make a living. In other countries, such as China and some parts of Britain, entrepreneurial ability, just like all forms of commercial ability, was looked down upon and considered a lower-class act. While merchants might therefore obtain great wealth and popular prestige, they were generally precluded from participating in the highest levels of government, although they might from time to time be called upon to finance it. This situation changed to some extent during the twentieth century and, especially, its second half and in the developed world. While the United States had historically welcomed new blood into the ranks of decision-makers, this was not the case in more traditionally feudal-based societies such as many in Europe and also in Japan. There, the exhausting rigors of constant warfare and social change led to the often involuntary acceptance that entrepreneurs were representatives of a new social order in which possession of capital was deemed a social good no matter how it was obtained.

Conclusion

Entrepreneurs offer great benefits to society insofar as their ability to recognise and exploit new business opportunities provides not just wealth for those individuals but also employment opportunities and the adoption and adaptation of valuable skills and knowledge. States can best stimulate this activity by providing a stable economic environment with good property rights, while also providing the highest possible quality of education and access to required capital and other inputs. They also need to provide a suitable information technology infrastructure to try to ensure that new skills and knowledge are available to everyone in the country.

JOHN WALSH

See also Capitalist Economic Model; Marxism; Socialist Economic Model; State-Directed Economy

References and Further Reading

Bornstein, David. *The Price of a Dream: The Story of the Grameen Bank*. Chicago: University of Chicago Press, 1997.

Crow, Ben. *Markets, Class and Social Change: Trading Networks and Poverty in Rural South Asia*. Basingstoke, Hampshire, and New York: Palgrave, 2001.

Drucker, Peter F. *Innovation and Entrepreneurship*. Harper-Business, 1993.

Landes, David. *The Wealth and Poverty of Nations: Why Some Are so Rich and Some Are so Poor*. W.W. Norton and Company, 1999.

Schlosser, Eric. *Fast Food Nation*. London: Allen Lane, The Penguin Press, 2001.

Schumpeter, Joseph A. *Essays: On Entrepreneurs, Innovations, Business Cycles, and the Evolution of Capitalism*. Transaction Publishers, 1989.

ENVIRONMENT: GOVERNMENT POLICIES

The Environmental Division: Developed Versus Developing Countries

When considering environmental policies and the environmental degradation in developing countries, a series of variables and factors play an important role. Concern for the environment first appeared as a dichotomy between environment and development. After World War II, the term *development* was often used to refer to the process of growth and to the introduction of technological innovations as a whole. In the 1950s, the debate began on consumption patterns and the lifestyle of industrialized countries' inhabitants.

During the 1970s, the idea of development held two decades before was severely criticized, especially by many of the "third world" authors, that is, by authors whose nationality was not European, North American, or Russian. These social scientists of the "third world," with many Latin Americans among them like Fernando H. Cardoso, said that developing countries were not just going through a phase that would later lead to development but that, instead, that their situation as non-developed countries was structural and would remain so. This structural dependency situation was characterized like the Dependence Theory, disseminated by authors like Cardoso, André Gunder Frank, or more recently Brazilian Teodonio Dos Santos. During the 1970s, the idea was also put forth that low levels of development contributed to the degradation of the environment, an idea that has since been criticized from a number of angles.

In 1972, the Club of Rome, a Germany-based nongovernmental organization (NGO) focused on global issues, released a report entitled *The Limits to Growth*. Known as the Meadows Report after its lead authors, it put forth the idea that the growth as a whole, but especially in a demographic sense, shouldn't be unlimited. The report claimed that by the year 2000, if the growth rhythms weren't changed, the Earth would suffer a collapse. Although this report criticized the lavishing economies and the consumption culture of the western countries, the solution it proposed to avoid the collapse was the *zero growth*, that meant the annulment of any kind of growth, be it of population or economies. This conclusion was criticized by the *Bariloche Foundation*, an Argentina-based NGO focusing on climate change, which pointed out that the major troubles of the modern world were not physical, meaning about resources, but socio-political instead and based on the asymmetrical distribution of the power both in an international as well as in a national level. This perspective provoked a debate between developed and developing nations.

More recently, in 1987 the concept of sustainable development appeared linked with the satisfaction of present needs without compromising the capacity of future generations to satisfy their own. This concept first came into existence in 1987 by a report by the World Commission on Human Medium and Development titled "Our Common Future," also known as the Brundtland Report after the Commission's chair, Norwegian Prime Minister Gro Harlem Brundtland. The Brundtland Report constituted a groundbreaking contribution to the debate. It suggested a new kind of development, including a reorientation of the industrial nations and also an international reorganization of the north–south relations.

Environmental Problems in Developing Countries

In the so-called third world countries, there are socio-economic pressures that affect the environment, namely the poverty, the income differences, the non-sustainable development of activities like agriculture, industry and tourism, and the population growth. The environmental degradation problems that face the whole world are similar but the social degradation problems are different between developed countries, where most of inhabitants satisfy their basic needs, and developing countries, where basic human needs are often not met.

One major difference between northern and southern countries is that, in spite of the fact that developing countries possess most of the natural resources reserves, they are not the ones who use and consume them most. It is most often the developed nations who consume such resources, often in non-sustainable ways. Latin America, the Caribbean area, Pacific Asia, and Africa possess most of the natural resources reserves of the whole world. In the case of petroleum, Saudi Arabia and the Persian Gulf countries are also important. But despite their many natural resources and reserves, these countries continue to face severe environmental problems.

On the one hand, in most developing countries the utilization of natural resources is still characterized by a non-sustainable and overexploitation that leads in the long run to exhaustion of them. For instance, the vast areas of cultivable land that these countries possess are constantly threatened by desertification provoked by deforestation and the degradation of soil.

On the other hand, the intensification of agricultural activities has caused a noticeable increase in the toxicity levels of the environment due to the use of agrochemicals. The overexploitation of forests, mining, and fishing resources propels an increasing loss of species, vegetal cover and the deteriorations of marine and terrestrial ecosystems.

In spite of the fact that some developing countries have a great hydraulic potential, the water reserves in many African and Middle East countries have been reduced. Moreover, there are regions that have already exceeded their environmental limits and are consuming their underground aquifers.

Another of the major problems for developing countries is the fresh water shortage. The United Nations estimates that around fifty percent of the fresh water supply systems in developing countries is being lost due to an inadequate maintenance and the lack of investments.

At the same time, these countries are the ones that use less resources, while developed countries consume resources in excess. For instance, in Canada the average use of water for a typical family is of 91 gallons a day, in Europe the average is of around 42.9 gallons a day while in Africa is of around 5.2 gallons a day.

Another of the great environmental issues of developing countries is related to the urban environment. Especially in Latin America, most people live in huge cities where the air and the water are usually contaminated which becomes a permanent threat to their health. Developing countries have also historically lacked demographic planning that helps them distribute their populations in a more balanced way. This concentration of millions of persons in a large metropolis causes a great pressure on the environment and often the deterioration of metropolitan coastal areas (such as in Rio de Janeiro and New York City), together with a lowering of the water quality. Also, the lack of urban planning has permitted massive urban sprawl in the major cities of developing nations. The creation of these suburbs often lacks the provision of basic infrastructure such as water supply,

sewage, electricity, and exerts even more pressure on the environment. Another potential impact that affects these countries are the consequences of the climate change around the world.

International Environmental Institutions and Policies

During the last decades, the concerns over environmental issues have caused the outburst of pressures to fight the environmental degradation process in the international and local levels. The cornerstones of these processes were the 1972 Stockholm Declaration over the Human Environment, the 1982 World Nature Letter, and the 1992 Rio Declaration on the Environment and the Development. In 1972, environmental problems were linked to underdevelopment, a fact that encouraged underdeveloped countries to develop themselves but taking into account the environment. Also environmental problems were associated with the industrialized countries, the industrialization and the technological development. In this same Declaration there was a general claim to obtain the so-called "shared responsibility" and the cooperation between nations.

In the 1992 Rio Convention, there was a strong advancement towards an international and national commitment to achieve a sustainable and balanced development. To accomplish that, the Declaration generated an Action Plan, the so-called Agenda XXI signed by a hundred and seventy countries, which then gave birth to the local Agenda XXI.

These forums and conventions encouraged the establishment of a series of global environmental institutions and multilateral agreements and also provided a new approach to the north–south relations. They have also contributed to the creation or modification of national laws related to environmental issues, to the creation of new institutions, and regional policies adopting in all cases the new sustainable development concept. Their role was also important in the generation of a new set of preventive regulations and rules as well as in the creation of territorial planning disposals, environmental impact evaluations, and diverse sanctions that have helped the strengthening of environmental policies. Important regional meetings play a fundamental role in the development of environmental regional policies and in the maintenance of common positions of the regions facing environmental issues in the international Agenda. National, regional, and local policies and programs have been carried out to protect the biodiversity in areas like the Amazonas, Asian, or African regions, which possess the biggest biodiversity in the whole planet, and also to protect endangered species.

Governments and international organizations have also established policies against desertification and the misuse of soil, to improve the living standards of the population in relation with their sanitation conditions, their accessibility to fresh and potable water. Conservation and reforestation programs have been fulfilled in order to work as coal drains while the certification, environmental audits, and eco-labeling processes peak.

Regional and international organizations that collaborate with the national states perform most of these actions. The development of reports, evaluations, and studies over the state of the environment provide assistance to different organizations in the elaboration of politics, programs, and projects at all levels (international, regional, or local).

The establishment of such policies and programs have been performed with a series of instruments like the international technical cooperation through specific programs and funds destined exclusively for environmental issues. Technical cooperation includes the design and the strengthening of those institutions that are in charge of the formulation and execution of environmental policies. Bilateral cooperation relationships are common, among which we find the following agencies: the German GTZ (Deutsche Gesellschaft für Technische Zusammenarbeit or German Society for the Technical Cooperation) or the Japan International Cooperation Agency (JICA). Besides, there are multilateral organizations like the United Nations, the Organization of American States (OAE), the United Nations Environment Programme (UNEP), the Inter-American Development Bank (IADB), among others. At its beginning the technological cooperation occurred in a vertical way, meaning that there was one steady direction: from rich countries to poor countries or from international organizations to developing countries. However, the new way combines the vertical way with a horizontal one in which local technologies and cultures are valued.

International cooperation is financed in several ways. In general, international finance institutions, such as the World Bank or the IADB, have the funds to do so. But as for environmental issues, we find the Global Environment Facility (GEF), the Multilateral Fund for the Implementation of the Montreal Protocol or the Fund of the Americas, financed by the United States.

Although many African countries are working to put into action new national and multilateral environmental policies, their effectiveness is often low due to lack of adequate staff, expertise, funds, and equipment for implementation and enforcement. The same happens in many Latin American countries and Caribbean ones. In Africa environmental policies are mainly based on regulatory instruments but some countries have begun to consider a broader range, including economic incentives implemented through different tax systems. There is a growing recognition that national environmental policies are more likely to be effectively implemented if an informed and involved public supports them.

In most Asian countries the high densities of population are becoming a problem in the same way as the fresh water supply. In this sense domestic investment in environmental issues is increasing. Environment funds have also been established in many countries and have contributed to the prominent role that non-governmental organizations now play in environmental action. Many countries are in favor of public participation, and in some this is now required by law. However, education and awareness levels amongst the public are often low, and the environmental information base in the region is weak, the same as it happens in Latin America and mostly in the Caribbean region.

Present Environmental Situation as a Result of Environmental Policies

In spite of the previously mentioned actions, policies, and the established changes, there still have not been considerable improvements in the environmental management of most developing countries. The policies and institutions created and performed in developing countries have encountered serious difficulties. By one or another reason they have always been left as a secondary mission instead of becoming a priority. The reasons are:

1. The lack of adequate financing to fulfil their projects and programs. It is estimated that developing countries would need US$70 million in addition to the help they are receiving, to be able to afford new efficient environmental programs.
2. The absence of adequate technology, training, and personnel.
3. The lack of specific institutional structures.
4. The existence of inconsistent and/or inconclusive legal framework for environmental issues.
5. Difficulties in the transference of "clean" technologies from developed countries to developing ones.

6. The growth of the exporting sector and the entry of foreign capital are still a fundamental axis in the economic agenda of developing countries and go beyond the consequences for the environment. Therefore these economic policies do not take into account the environmental costs.

7. Although in the last decades new democratic governments have appeared in the international scene, militarism is still very much present in Latin America, Central America, Middle East, Africa, and Asia. This situation has catastrophic consequences for the society and the environment since a large part of the national budget goes to defense rather than social and environmental programs.

8. In most developing countries environmental problems are treated sectorially and not as a whole. Environmental policies lack strategic planning that enables governments to develop these policies as integrated ones. Besides, due to the large scale privatization and deregulation that occurred in the 1990s as a result of the transition to capitalism or conditionality of foreign aid, state environmental policies have lost some of their strength.

9. During the 1980s and 1990s, developing countries have become more and more dependant on international organizations due to their huge external debts. Many developing nations must use their economic resources to pay off debt rather than promote strategies of sustainable development.

Recommendations to Overcome the Environmental Crisis

The environmental crisis the developing countries face is an eco-political one since it is connected with the institutional and power-related systems that control and regulate the property, distribution, and use of the resources. The environment is no longer just an "environmental problem" and becomes a problem concerned with the use and distribution of natural resources, with the way in which decisions are made, who take them and to the benefit of whom, who wins and who loses with political decisions. The possible solutions for this problem can only be found within the own social system since the development models are linked with the social organization ones. The governments of developing countries also face the challenge of guaranteeing the existence of a transparent and participative process in decision-making.

DIEGO I. MURGUÍA

See also Biodiversity Conservation; Cardoso, Fernando Henrique; Deforestation; Desertification; Ecotourism; Environmentalism; Erosion, Land; Non-Governmental Organizations (NGOs); Pollution, Agricultural; Pollution, Industrial; Rain Forest, Destruction of; Sustainable Development; Third World; Underdevelopment

References and Further Reading

Brown, L., Flavin, C., & French, H. *State of the World: A WorldWatch Institute Report on Progress Toward as Sustainable Society.* New York: W. W. Norton & Company, 1998.

Caldwell, L.K. *International Environmental Policy. Emergence and Dimensions.* Durham, NC: Duke University Press, 1984.

Jones, L. and John Baldwin. *Corporate Environmental Policy and Government Regulation.* Greenwich, CT: JAI Press, 1994.

Kennedy, Paul M. *Preparing for the Twenty-first Century.* New York: Random House, 1993.

Klare, Michael T. *Resource Wars: The New Landscape of Global Conflict.* New York: Henry Holt, 2001.

Meadows, D., Meadows, D., Randers, J., and Behrens, III, W. *The Limits to Growth: A Report for the Club of Rome's Project on the Predicament of Mankind.* New York: Universe Books, 1972.

Rosenbaum, Walter A. *Environmental Politics and Policy.* Washington, DC: CQ Press, 2002.

Rothenberg, Lawrence S. *Environmental Choices: Policy Responses to Green Demands.* Washington, DC: CQ Press, 2002.

United Nations Environment Programme (UNEP). *GEO-2000. Global Environment Outlook.* 2000. (http://www.grida.no/geo)

World Commission on Environment and Development. *Our Common Future.* New York: Oxford University Press, 1987.

ENVIRONMENTALISM

In the period since the World War II, "environmentalism" has become the umbrella term used to describe the growing movement of green consciousness. However, environmentalism covers an almost unlimited range of meanings and nuances, particularly since it is used to describe the activities and lifestyle options taken by individuals: the actions and campaigns of non-governmental organisations such as Greenpeace, Friends of the Earth, and Earth First! to combat both localised and global environmental problems, and international and governmental initiatives that have attempted to take a lead in the conservation of the world's environment.

The environment and environmentalism also have very different meanings for people in the Northern and the Southern hemispheres. In the largely industrialised North, large-scale environmental problems are frequently perceived as being located in Eastern Europe and the developing countries in the South: problems such as deforestation and desertification. More localized problems of the North are focused on issues such as genetically modified crops and traffic pollution. Combating environmental problems has therefore often become part of a new form of neocolonialism, with the developed countries setting environmental policy targets for the developing nations without addressing the results of past industrialization and economic development. For people in the more rural South, such as India, environmental problems are perceived as global pollution and waste caused by the rich, developed countries. In developing countries, overcoming poverty and attaining a faster rate of economic development are the major objectives and their attainment can be contradictory to environmental protection.

What Is the Environment?

In what he termed the "Gaia theory," James Lovelock argued that we live on a complex 'living planet' and all our actions cause reactions. Environmentalism at its most holistic seeks to preserve and nurture these biosystems (also referred to as ecosystems) and to preserve the rich biodiversity of life forms on the planet. Gaia theory also presupposes that these biosystems are self-regulating, and will if necessary deal with the *problem of humans* by making us extinct.

Before looking at ways in which environmentalism is being actioned locally and globally, it is important to grasp the fact that environmentalism is not just concerned with the protection of the natural world. It is equally concerned with people's cultural, economic, and social activities, and in developing an understanding of the nation, world, and universe which they inhabit. The environment also includes 'us'—the way we live, issues such as commuting, the built environment, poverty and illiteracy, as well as global problems in the larger world, which can often be too abstract for many people to comprehend.

One model for seeing individual people and communities as part of the global environment was developed by the artist and eco-dwellings designer Friedensreich Hundertwasser. Hundertwasser developed a pictorial metaphor to describe every person's power over, and relationship with, the other essential elements in the environment. He called these our five skins, and maintained that people have a responsibility to show ecological commitment in the way that they 'wear' them. This picture of people as individuals actively choosing their identity through their body, their clothes, their dwelling, their friends or people with whom they interrelate, and their interaction with the global environment, provides us with a model depicting the 'five skins' of environmentalism.

The Confusing State of Environmental Debate

Governments of developing nations are aware of the increase of global environmental problems, but they are often not prepared to delay or retard economic development to support what they see as interference by the energy guzzling, polluting developed countries of the world. The developing nations have their own forum at conferences held under the banner of the Group of 77 (G77), where there are now 133 countries represented. Together they are the largest coalition of what are often referred to as the "Third World" nation states.

In Delhi in 1989, the G77 concluded that they supported careful management of the atmosphere in principle, but that for their countries, development should have priority over environmental concerns. The Group of 8 (G8, which includes Canada, United States, Britain, France, Germany, Italy, Russia, and Japan), however, at their Genoa conference in 2001, concluded that they would continue progress towards providing debt relief for the poorest nations of the world, while cutting greenhouse emissions (largely carbon dioxide, methane, and nitrous oxide) in order to curb global warming. Historically, fossil fuels have been a major component of the economic development of the industrial countries. Private transport and waste are also major sources of pollution, particularly in Australia, the United States, and Canada. However, scientific speculation is intense and variable about the effects, location, and rate of change to temperature (perhaps a 1°C–3.5°C rise over the next one hundred years); drought and desertification; melting of the polar ice caps; and increased rainfall in some areas.

The Recent History of World Environmentalism

In 1987, the first World Commission on the Environment and Development, chaired by the then

Norwegian prime minister, Mrs. Gro Harlem Brundt-land, produced the influential Brundtland Report. This built on the work of the earlier environmentalists, including Rachel Carson (*Silent Spring*) and E.F. Schumacher whose book *Small is Beautiful* became one of the most important in raising people's consciousness about the environment and consumption. The Brundtland Report, published as *Our Common Future,* proclaimed sustainable development as the route away from global environmental catastrophe. It stated that sustainability offers "development that meets the needs of the future without compromising ability of future generations to meet their own needs." The United Nations (UN) Framework Convention on Climate Change was drawn up during the Earth Summit meeting that took place in Rio de Janeiro in 1992. That meeting has acted as a launch pad for much of the subsequent environmental activity, including the wide range of sustainable development activities for local and global action called Agenda 21 and Rio plus 10 in Johannesburg 2002.

It also led directly to the 1997 Kyoto Protocol which aimed to reduce the average emissions of greenhouse gases across the planet by 5% by the years 2008–2012. It attempted to get different countries to agree to differential targets, so while Portugal was allowed a 27% increase, Luxembourg was expected to reduce emissions by 28%. The developing nations of the world were expected to observe limits in the growth of their emissions, while the European Union as a whole was given a target of an 8% cut. However, the United States, one of the major producers of greenhouse gases, has refused to ratify the Kyoto Protocol, claiming that it would impede the nation's economic development. Additionally, many developing countries do not wish to use more expensive fuel technologies when fossil fuels, which may exist as native natural resources, are abundant and cheaper than alternatives. They see this as interference by the developed nations in their chances to industrialise and gain economic development. The protestors against globalization also see these mandates by the rich developed countries as the cornerstones of a form of new corporate colonialism. On the other side of the opposition, a number of scientists, particularly from industry, see environmentalism as a threat to future economic growth.

Possible Action

Effective sustainable environmental action depends, among other things, upon the current world leaders of the developed countries to take appropriate action on:

- Reducing emissions and other forms of pollution and waste;
- Giving developing countries appropriate financial and technological aid to assist their sustainable economic development;
- The development of sustainable agricultural policies and practices in developing countries;
- The development of alternative technologies and supporting their use in all countries;
- Proactive actions, such as supporting the planting of more trees, the reduction of deforestation and the protection of vulnerable habitats such as the wetlands and the oceans;
- Stabilising global population growth; and
- Reduction of the indebtedness of the developing countries.

Among the actions individuals may take to help preserve the environment are:

- Reducing consumption, especially of goods not sourced locally;
- Using public transport and car pools to reducing car use;
- Recycling waste materials and re-using materials;
- Energy efficiency in the home and consumption of less water and electricity;
- Living in homes which have a lower impact on and are more harmonious with the natural environment;
- Using sustainable energy sources such as wind, water, and solar power;
- Producing more of their own food, especially using organic principles; and
- Voting for policies and officials who support corporate accountability for environmental impact.

The Problems Remain

Many developing nations feel that the industrialized countries became wealthy by doing precisely what the developing nations wish to do now—only now the industrialized nations are attempting to hold back other countries from taking these same steps towards development. Many in the developing world feel that it should be the responsibility of industrialized nations to provide the means for sustainable development, as it was the industrialized nations that contributed to the present environmental damage.

For many environmentalists, especially those of 'deep green' persuasion—those who use only plants indigenous to the region—even this is not at the heart of the matter. They point to what the Dalai Lama called the ethical responsibility of mankind to examine what we have inherited, what we are responsible for, and what we will pass on (Porritt 1991).

ALAN DEARLING

See also Biodiversity Conservation; Environment: Government Policies; Global Climate Change

References and Further Reading

Carson, Rachel. *Silent Spring*. Boston: Houghton Mifflin, 1962.
Chapman, Graham; Kumar, Keval; Fraser, Caroline, and Gaber, Ivor. *Environmentalism and the Mass Media*. London: Routledge, 1997.
Hinrichsen, Don. *Our Common Future: A Reader's Guide: The Brundtland Report Explained*. London: Earthscan, 1987.
Lovelock, James. *Gaia, a New Look at life on Earth*. Oxford: Oxford University Press, 1979.
Myers, Norman, editor. *The Gaia Atlas of Planet Management*. London and Sydney: Pan Books, 1985.
Porritt, Jonathon. *Where on Earth are We Going?* London: BBC Books, 1990.
———. *Save the Earth*. London: Dorling Kindersley, 1991.
Quarrie, Joyce, editor. *Earth Summit 1992*. London: The Regency Press, 1992.
Restany, Pierre. *Hundertwasser: the painter-king with the five skins*. Glarus, Switzerland: Gruener Janura AG, 1998; Cologne, Germany: Taschen, 2001.
Schumacher, E.F. *Small is Beautiful*. London: Abacus Books, 1973.
Seymour, John and Giradot, Herbert. *Blueprint for a Green Planet*. London: Dorling Kindersley, 1987.
Ward, Barbara and Dubois, René. *Only One Earth, the Care and Maintenance of a Small Planet*. London: André Deutsch, 1972.

EQUATORIAL GUINEA

At the end of the eighteenth century, Portugal ceded to Spain two islands in the Bay of Biafra in West Africa, and in the late nineteenth century Spain was able to acquire a small piece of the African mainland known as Rio Muni, between German Cameroon to the north and French Gabon to the south and east. The three areas then constituted Spanish Guinea, which was ruled from Santa Isabel (today Malabo) on the main island, Fernando Po. Lying close to the equator, both Fernando Po, which the local Bubi people knew as Bioko, and Rio Muni were extremely hot and malaria-plagued. Fang people from the mainland were used to help suppress Bubi resistance to Spanish rule, which was brutal and exploitative.

Cocoa was the main export; attempts to find commercially viable oil deposits were unsuccessful. After the nearby countries had become independent by the early 1960s, the Franco regime in Madrid decided to cut its losses and grant its colony first self-government and then independence. At independence on October 12, 1968, the country had no tertiary educational institution and social services were extremely rudimentary.

In elections held before independence the Fang leader, Francisco Macias Nguema, also known as El Glalo Rojo (the Read Rooster), won an overwhelming victory, but few Bubi participated and they remained alienated from the new government. Most Spaniards left soon after independence, and Macias Nguema then ruled the country in an extremely brutal and despotic manner. When his deputy president seemed to pose a challenge, he was murdered, as were tens of thousands of others. In this reign of terror, professional people and intellectuals were targeted, and those who were not killed fled the country. Cocoa production collapsed and Equatorial Guinea sank ever deeper into poverty, as such businesses were owned by the ruling clique.

In August 1979, Macias Nguema was overthrown in a palace revolution led by his nephew Teodoro Obiang Nguema Mbasongo, the commander-in-chief of the armed forces. After Macias Nguema was executed, Obiang Nguema was sworn in as president and de facto dictator. Using Moroccan guards for his personal security, he foiled a number of attempted coups in the decades that followed, and consolidated his grip on power. The international community largely forgot the country, though in 1985 the French African franc became its official currency and some Spanish investors returned to rehabilitate cocoa production. In 1989, Obiang Nguema was elected president unopposed, and from the early 1990s, in the new international climate after the Cold War, some pretence at competitive democracy was permitted, but Obiang Nguema so regulated the process in his favour that his political opponents rejected the elections that were held as neither free nor fair. In the 1996 presidential election, he received 99.2% of the vote; in December 2002, he received 97%. In the face of his brutal rule, many of his political opponents fled into exile, mainly to Spain. The most prominent of these was Severo Moto, who styled himself president-in-exile. In 2004, he denied being involved in an attempt to topple Nguema, but those who devised the plot intended to put him into power. They hoped to do this by using a detachment of mercenaries from South Africa, but news of the planned coup spread and the South African authorities warned their Equatorial Guinean counterparts. The mercenaries were then arrested, some in Malabo and others when their plane landed in Harare, Zimbabwe, to pick up arms, before the coup attempt could be launched.

The fortunes of Equatorial Guinea had changed dramatically and fundamentally in 1996, when oil production began in the waters off Bioko Island. Until then, the country had been a decaying backwater: the production of cocoa, the main crop of Bioko, fell very sharply after independence and then stagnated, as did production of coffee, the country's third most important agricultural export. The most important was timber from the mainland province of Rio Muni, and by the mid-1990s the only new road to have been built since independence was from the interior to the port of Bata, though which the timber was exported. In the 1990s, the over-exploitation of the forest, especially close to easily accessible areas, gave rise to doubts about the sustainability of the industry, as the country began losing an ever-larger amount of forest. By then timber was no longer so important as an export earner, for thanks to oil the country had the potential to become the Kuwait of Africa. By the beginning of the twenty-first century, it had become Africa's fastest growing economy and the continent's third-largest oil producer after Nigeria and Libya. Production soared to four hundred thousand barrels a day and was expected to increase further when the vast oil reserves under the sea off the islands were tapped. United States companies led the way in exploiting the oil, and the United States, which re-opened its embassy in Malabo in December 2001, saw Equatorial Guinea as a major new supplier. But the country's human rights record, which included routine extra-judicial punishments such as torture and summary executions, continued to be denounced by organisations such as Amnesty International. While most of the country's half million inhabitants continued to live in poverty, the president and his family arranged that most of the massive new revenues from oil revenues were paid into overseas bank accounts. In mid-2004 it was revealed that $300 million of oil money had gone into a New York bank account controlled by Obiang Nguema. Yet it was then that the South African government announced that it was to open an embassy in Malabo, and Obiang Nguema paid a number of visits to South Africa before and after the mercenaries were arrested in Malabo and Harare, suggesting that a deal was being put together to allow South Africa to obtain a share of the oil. Meanwhile, the mercenaries arrested in Malabo were put on trial. Though the state asked for the death sentence for their leader, Nick du Toit, who was a former member of South Africa's Special Forces, was given a thirty-four-year prison sentence instead. It emerged that funding for the attempted coup had come from a number of wealthy Britons, including Sir Mark Thatcher, son of the former British Prime Minister, but the Equatorial Guinea authorities were unable to secure the extradition of Thatcher from South Africa, where he had been arrested, or any of the others alleged to have been involved. There was some hope, however, that the international exposure brought by the attempted coup might help ameliorate some of the worst features of the Nguema regime.

CHRISTOPHER SAUNDERS

See also Ethnic Conflicts: West Africa; West Africa: History and Economic Development; West Africa: International Relations

References and Further Reading

Castro, M. 'Equatorial Guinea: Recent History', *Africa South of the Sahara 2004*. London, Europa Publications, 2003.

Cronje, S. *Equatorial Guinea: the Forgotten Dictatorship*. London: Anti-Slavery Society, 1976.

Lininger-Goumaz, Max. *Historical Dictionary of Equatorial Guinea*. Metuchen, NJ: Scarecrow Pres, 1979 (2nd ed., 1988).

———. *Colonisation-neocolonisation-democratisation-corruption: a l'aune de la Guinee Euatoriale*. Geneva: Les Editions du Temps, 2003.

ERITREA

Eritrea, the newest independent country in Africa in 2004, lies along the western shores of the Red Sea in Northeast Africa. It is one of the five countries (the others are Djibouti, Ethiopia, Somalia, and Sudan) that constitute the region known as the Horn of Africa and has an area of approximately 121,000 square kilometers, slightly larger than the state of Pennsylvania. It borders Sudan on the west, Ethiopia on the south, Djibouti on the southeast, and the Red Sea on the East, with a coastline almost one thousand kilometers long. Like Ethiopia, its neighbor to the south, Eritrea is a land of extreme contrasts, both in terms of its topography and climate. Its mountains and highlands extend from north to south, with the lowlands on the western and eastern flanks. The lowlands in the west extend to Sudan and those in the east to the Red Sea. The highlands have a moderate climate with temperatures ranging from near freezing to as much as 30°C, while the temperature in the lowlands varies from 30°C to 50°C, occasionally reaching 60°C in the Danakil Depression.

The rainy season in the highlands extends from June to August, while the lowlands in western Eritrea are semi-arid with much less rainfall. There is almost no rainfall in the eastern lowlands bordering the Red Sea, especially in Dankalia. The population of Eritrea was estimated at 4.14 million in 2000, almost half of which are Christians and the other half Muslims. The Christians live mostly in the highlands and are sedentary farmers, while the Muslims live mostly in the lowlands and are agro-pastoralists. Because of their common experience and struggle against outside powers, the cohesion of the various ethnic and religious groups has been remarkably strong.

Eritrea is the only country in Africa to successfully break away from another African country. It was part of Ethiopia for almost forty years and only became independent in 1993. Like Ethiopia, Eritrea has a long history and was part of the ancient Kingdom of Axum. In fact, located in Eritrea and now in ruins, Adulis served as the main seaport of the Kingdom. The Eritrean people, therefore, had established contacts with much of the Near East and the Greeks in the distant past. After the advent of Islam, parts of Eritrea, and especially the lowlands bordering the Red Sea and Sudan, had been occupied by the Turks and Egyptians, and towards the end of the nineteenth century, by the Italians. Present-day Eritrea, as a political unit, however, came with the advent of Italian colonialism in 1890. The Italians were defeated in 1941 and the British provisionally administered Eritrea until 1952, when, despite the wishes of the majority of its peoples, it was federated with Ethiopia. The status of Eritrea as a federal unit ended in 1962 after Ethiopia dissolved the federal system and absorbed Eritrea as one of its administrative units.

Appeals to the United Nations (UN) by various Eritrean groups to reverse the absorption did not succeed, and the Eritreans started a thirty-year-long armed struggle for self-determination in 1960. The independence movement, first started by the Eritrean Liberation Front (ELF), continued earnestly with Eritrean People's Liberation Front (EPLF), which became dominant in the latter half of the 1970s and the 1980s. The EPLF had split from the ELF around 1970 apparently because of the sectarian tendencies of the latter. Although both movements unquestionably stood for Eritrean independence, the ELF was seen as Muslim-dominated, Arab-influenced, and more sectarian compared with the EPLF, which was seen as uncompromisingly independent and autonomous, more secular and, in its early days, more Marxist-oriented. The war of independence waged by both groups against Ethiopia progressively became more intense, especially after Emperor Haile Selassie of Ethiopia was overthrown in 1974.

Consequently, much of the infrastructure laid during Italian colonization had been destroyed. Indeed, the Italians had invested heavily in Eritrea in the early 1900s to help in their 1935 war against a much larger Ethiopia. However, Ethiopia, itself economically underdeveloped and politically under an absolute monarchist rule, was not in a position to undertake both economic and political development in Eritrea. On the contrary, with the conflict between Ethiopia and the two Eritrean nationalist movements escalating, the hitherto existing infrastructure had been destroyed, including the railway system that once ran from the seaport of Massawa to Akordat in western Eritrea. Massawa itself declined because most of Ethiopia's import-export trade passed through Assab on the southern tip of Eritrea. Thus, Eritrea regressed in the fifty years that preceded independence in 1993.

With relative peace since then, however, Eritrea has been able to register significant progress in terms of infrastructure development. Most of the roads, either neglected or destroyed during the thirty-year-long war, including the asphalted road linking Asmara, the capital city, and the port city of Massawa, have been rehabilitated; a new road between Asmara and Assab on the southern tip of the Red Sea has been constructed; a new medical school has been established, various bridges deliberately destroyed by the conflicting parties to disrupt the supply lines of the opponent have been rebuilt, and new water diversion schemes in western Eritrea have become operational. Despite these, Eritrea remains one of the least developed nations, with gross domestic product (GDP)—calculated in terms of the value of all final goods and services produced within Eritrea, and computed on the basis of purchasing power parity (PPP)—estimated at $2.5 billion in 1998, and GDP per capita estimated at $660.

In the political realm, Eritrea is a unitary state currently ruled by the victorious EPLF, now renamed People's Front for Democracy and Justice (PFDJ). Other political organizations remain illegal. However, the constitution, ratified in 1997, includes provisions for multi-party democracy. Despite this, the government has remained reluctant to implement the constitution and continues to insist that the time is not right for competitive party elections. Thus, although the PFDJ may still have significant popular support among the population, Eritrea remains as one of a few countries without an elected government and no legal political party except, of course, the PFDJ. Recently, however, there were calls from within the leadership of the PFDJ to open the political system and allow the opposition to compete.

Similarly, there are no independent civic organizations and the few that exist, such as women, youth, and labor organizations, are all government-affiliated. The few independent newspapers founded in the early 1990s have closed, and there remain only government-owned and/or controlled news outlets. Recently, however, the government has come under enormous pressure to open the political system. Also, there are calls for the establishment of independent civic organizations in Eritrea, especially from the Diaspora, who have recently established various independent Eritrean civic organizations in their countries of residence. The government has so far resisted such demands on the grounds that the conflict with Ethiopia has to be comprehensively resolved first.

The recent Eritrean-Ethiopian conflict (1998–2000) has had a deep and negative impact on the remarkable unity of its people. With the end of the conflict and the impending demarcation of the border in 2004, hopes for a more open and transparent political system are running high.

ASSEFAW BARIAGABER

References and Further Reading

Bariagaber, Assefaw. "The Politics of Cultural Pluralism in Ethiopia and Eritrea: Trajectories of Ethnicity and Constitutional Experiments," *Ethnic and Racial Studies*, 21, no. 6 (1998).

Cliffe, Lionel, and Basil Davidson, editors. *The Long Struggle of Eritrea for Independence and Constructive Peace.* Trenton, NJ: Red Sea Press, 1974.

Habte Selassie, Bereket. *Conflict and Intervention in the Horn of Africa.* New York: Monthly Review Press, 1980.

Iyob, Ruth. *The Eritrean Struggle for Independence: Domination, Resistance, Nationalism, 1941–1993.* New York: Cambridge University Press, 1995.

Longrigg, Stephen H. *A Short History of Eritrea.* Westport, CT: Greenwood Press, 1974.

Markakis, John. "The Nationalist Revolution in Eritrea," *Journal of Modern Africa Studies*, 25, no. 4 (1987).

Negash, Tekeste. *Eritrea and Ethiopia: The Federal Experience.* Uppsala, Sweden: Nordiska Afrikainstitutet, 1997.

Ofcansky, Thomas P., and LaVerle Berry, editors. *Ethiopia: A Country Study*, 4th edition. Washington, DC: Library of Congress, 1993.

Tesfai, Alemseged, and Martin Doornbos. *Post-Conflict Eritrea: Prospects for Reconstruction and Development.* Lawrenceville, NJ: Red Sea Press, 1999.

Yohannes, Okbazghi. *Eritrea: A Pawn in World Politics.* Gainesville, FL: University of Florida Press, 1991.

ERITREAN LIBERATION FRONT (ELF)

The Eritrean Liberation Front (ELF) is the smaller faction in the Eritrean struggle for independence from Ethiopia, overshadowed by the Eritrean People's Liberation Front (EPLF).

After the Second World War, the former Italian colony of Eritrea was under British occupation. Britain pressed for a partition of Eritrea between Ethiopia and Sudan, the so-called Bevin-Sforza Plan. The United States threw its support behind Emperor Haile Selassie's ambitions to secure the whole of Eritrea and Ethiopian access to the Red Sea. For the United States, Christian Ethiopia represented a strategic ally on the edge of the oil-rich Muslim Middle East. The Eritreans were divided; many Christian Eritreans supported closed union with Ethiopia, while many Muslim Eritreans and the small western-educated elite favoured independence.

A United Nations (UN) commission of inquiry was divided. The United States opposed a referendum and used its influence in the UN to pass General Assembly Resolution 390-A(V) in 1950, federating Eritrea with Ethiopia. The Resolution called for 'full autonomy for the Eritrean government in all domestic affairs,' and 'a democratic regime in Eritrea with all its requisites and safeguards: respect for human rights and fundamental liberties, and government of the people by the people.' Emperor Haile Selassie opposed Eritrean autonomy as a threat to his autocracy and set out to undermine the elected Eritrean Assembly.

The ELF was founded in Cairo in 1960 by a loose confederation of Muslim Eritreans opposed to federation with Ethiopia. It was not the first Eritrean nationalist group: the clandestine Eritrean Liberation Movement (ELM) had been established some years earlier, hoping to undermine Ethiopian rule by plotting a police coup. The Islamic ELF viewed the secular, socialist ELM with suspicion. The ELM was unable to effectively counter ELF accusations of being both a communist front and unwilling to use 'armed struggle'. ELF denunciation exposed the ELM to the Ethiopian authorities, who repressed the ELM, banned trade union, and suppressed independent newspapers. Meanwhile the ELF successfully recruited former ELM sympathizers, including a number of key figures who had escaped the Ethiopian dragnet. In 1962, under Ethiopian armed coercion, the autonomous Eritrean Assembly voted itself out of existence and Eritrea was annexed as a province of Ethiopia.

The ELF built a network within Eritrea through the Islamic brotherhoods, and diplomatic contacts with Islamic states in the Middle East and Somalia, who supplied arms and training for the Eritrean Liberation Army (ELA). The major weaknesses of the ELF were its lack of organization, divisive personality politics, and sectarian and ethnic rivalries.

ELF president and former president of the Eritrean Assembly, Idris Adem, secretary Idris Galadewos and Osman Saleh Sabbe constituted a supreme council in Cairo, directing diplomatic activities but with loose control over the military operations in the field. The ELA was divided into regional, essentially ethnic and religious, 'zones,' with little coordination of command. There were tensions between the illiterate Muslim peasant soldiers and, following the demise of the ELM, better-educated Christian recruits. The religiosity of Eritrean Orthodox Christians and their allegiance to Emperor Haile Selassie also led to attacks on Christian villagers by Muslim factions within the ELA. When the Christian Wolde Kahasi defected, Muslim soldiers murdered a number of Christian recruits.

When, in 1967, the so-called ESLAH reformed movement of younger officers tried to lessen ethnic and religious tensions in the ELA and introduce wider discussion within the ELF, they were blocked by Islamic hardliners and the supreme council, who saw such moves as a threat to their personal power.

A further attempt at reconciliation and reorganisation by ESLAH officers floundered in 1969, and was followed by renewed attacks on Christian recruits and the assassination of several prominent Christian ELF personalities, including Wolfe Ghiday and Kidane Kinfu. The ELF began to break up with numerous Christians defecting to an emergent radical sub-group linked to Osman Saleh Sabbe and led by Mohamed Nur and Isaias Afwerki. The majority of Muslim recruits remained loyal to Idris Adem.

In 1970, the Adem faction established urban guerrilla units and adopted hit-and-run tactics. They blew up bridges and trains in Eritrea, as well as attacks on Ethiopian Airline planes. While raising the ELF's international profile, such acts facilitated Emperor Haile Selassie declaring a state of emergency, abrogating the few remaining civil rights. Ethiopia also obtained increased military assistance from America and Israel, while Haile Silassie's personal diplomacy increasingly isolated the ELF from Middle Eastern leaders and even China's Mao Tse-tung. Thousands of Eritreans fled as refugees into the Sudan.

In 1971, the ELF held its first National Congress, ostensibly to restructure the political and military organisation, but it was a fragile coalition. Meanwhile the faction allied to Osman Saleh Sabbe joined with remnants of the ELM and former soldiers of the ELA Zone Three command to form the People's Liberation Front (PLF). From 1972, the liberation forces were locked in a civil war, as much as the struggle against Ethiopia. The ELF-PLF was formed in 1972 as a result of a merger of Sabbe's followers with several radical secular factions led the Mohammed Nur and Isaias Afwerki, in opposition to the old ELF. Gradually the radical reformers took over the ELF-PLF, sidelining Sabbe. The civil war, which erupted between the ELF and EPLF in 1972, ostensibly ended with a 1974 accord.

The Second ELF National Congress in 1975 saw the removal of Idris Adem and many older Muslim traditionalist, but Christians were barred from full membership. The new leadership struck a deal with Sabbe, a conservative Muslim anti-communist, to bring the ELF-PLF back into the fold, but Sabbe was denounced by the field commanders who went on to form the EPLF.

At the time, the ELF was the larger force, but lacked discipline, organisation, and a clear set of policies, in contrast to the EPLF. Further purges of Christians within the ranks of the ELF in the late 1970s only led to increasing numbers joining the EPLF. The ELF also suffered the brunt of the Ethiopian offensive in 1978–1979.

The ELF leadership under Ahmed Nasser then tried to broker a deal with the Ethiopian Revolutionary Derg, through Arab and Soviet intermediaries, at the same time order ELF troops to withdraw into the Sudan. It was a military, political, and diplomatic disaster.

Whereas the ELF maintained a significant profile in the Islamic world, it was soon overshadowed on the domestic front and in the Western media by the propaganda of the EPLF. On the battlefield, the ELF was also eclipsed by the EPLF as a fighting force.

DAVID DORWARD

See also East Africa: International Relations; Eritrea; Ethiopia

References and Further Reading

Cliffe, Lionel, and Basil Davidson, editors. *The Long Struggle of Eritrea for Independence and Constructive Peace.* Nottingham: Spokesman, 1988.

Erlikh, Hagai. *The Struggle over Eritrea, 1962–1978: War and Revolution in the Horn of Africa.* Stanford, CA: Hoover Institution Press, 1983.

Gebre-Mahdin, Jordan. *Peasants and Nationalism in Eritrea: A Critique of Ethiopian Studies.* Trenton, NJ: Red Sea Press, 1989.

Holland, Stuart. *Never Kneel Down: Drought, Development and Liberation in Eritrea.* Nottingham: Spokesman, 1984.

Iyob, Ruth. *The Eritrean Struggle for Independence: Domination, Resistance, Nationalism, 1941–1993.* Cambridge: Cambridge University Press, 1995.

Markakis, John. "The Nationalist revolution in Eritrea", in *Journal of Modern African Studies* (1988) 26 (1) 51–70.

Pateman, Roy. *Eritrea: Even the Stones are Burning.* Trenton, NJ: Red Sea Press, 1990.

Woodward, Peter, and Murray Forsyth, editors. *Conflict and Peace in the Horn of Africa.* Brookfield: Dartmouth Pub, 1994.

EROSION, LAND

Land erosion is the natural process by which the Earth's surface is gradually worn away. Over millions of years, the weathering effects of wind and flowing water break down the Earth's rock surface and carry away the resulting rock fragments and soil. Today's landscapes were created through the combination of these processes. Along the coast, the impact of ocean waves constantly hitting the shore slowly wears away the rock and collects loose particles. The slow but abrasive movement of glaciers detaches loose rocks in their path. Wind transports the sand of deserts and beaches to other areas.

Land, or more specifically soil erosion, has become an environmental concern because human manipulation of the environment has accelerated these processes. Current global loss of productive land due to soil erosion is estimated by the Food and Agriculture Organisation of the United Nations to be between 5 and 7 million hectares per year.

Soil Composition and Erosion

Soils are formed from the broken down mineral material of rocks and the decomposition of organic matter. Their composition can vary greatly: from deep and fertile to shallow and unproductive. The mineral, or parent, material forms the skeleton structure of the soil and provides much of the nutrients required by plants for growth.

Nutrients are also provided by the decay of organic matter, such as leaf litter, in the topsoil. Humus, a by-product of this breakdown of plant tissue, can help protect the soil from erosion as it is cohesive and binds individual soil particles together. Clay particles, weathered from the parent material, can also group together to form larger particles. These strengthen the general soil structure and improve its resistance to erosion.

Material is continually lost from the soil profile and because the organic-rich topsoil layer is exposed, it is eroded first. Wind, or aeolian, erosion blows the smaller particles off the surface. Soil particles are scattered by the impact of raindrops, or rainsplash, falling onto the exposed soil surface. Soil particle displacement increases with the force of the rain. Water, or fluvial, erosion occurs through the movement of surface runoff, generated when the amount of rain falling on an area exceeds the total amount of water evaporated, intercepted by vegetation and infiltrated into the soil. Fluvial erosion occurs on a larger scale than rainsplash. Runoff tends to subdivide into rills, which are networks of shallow channels. Gullies are formed when these channels are deepened by further water erosion and a permanent drainage network is established. These three mechanisms funnel surface runoff, increasing the speed of water flow and thus increasing its ability to erode and transport soil particles.

Factors Influencing Erosion

Increases in wind or water speed and slope increase the potential for soil erosion. However, the amount of soil eroded depends on the nature of particles present on the surface. Vegetation protects the soil by reducing the impacts of wind and rain. Complex vegetation stands of diverse plant species create a multi-story canopy and slow down the flow of wind and surface runoff. As the runoff is slowed, a greater proportion of it can infiltrate the soil surface, decreasing fluvial erosion. The canopy intercepts rainfall, reducing the force of individual raindrops. Plants also provide further structure to the soil because soil particles bind to their root systems. When vegetation is cleared, there is no longer a continuous supply of organic matter to the soil. The humus layer is no longer replenished, and eventually the mineral particles are exposed and are far more easily eroded. Vegetation around wetlands and along riverbanks acts as a buffer. Plants in these areas, such as reeds, have dense foliage and are low to the ground. Soil particles transported from eroded areas in surface runoff are therefore trapped before reaching the lake, stream, or river.

Soil erosion has been accelerated across the globe mainly through the large-scale clearing of trees and vegetation. Globally, it is estimated that 500 million hectares or more of land have been degraded since 1950. Protective vegetation cover has been lost through deforestation, agricultural clearing, mining, fire, and urbanisation. In addition, agricultural practices such as ploughing, tilling, irrigation, and grazing have caused the soil to lose its structure and cohesion. Other factors such as the planting of monoculture crops and the ploughing and farming of marginal lands unsuitable for crop cultivation allow the topsoil to be washed and blown away. As agricultural land becomes increasingly degraded, and less productive, farmers apply fertilisers to the soil to replace the nutrients lost to erosion. Subsequent intensive agriculture only causes further soil degradation. The dust storms experienced in the 1930s in the midwest of the United States, which then became known as the 'Dust Bowl,' are one of the most famous examples of the devastating impact of land erosion.

Overgrazing on fragile soils is a significant issue for one third of the world, which is now threatened by desertification. Erosion has affected 413 million hectares of land in Africa due to increases in livestock on productive land. This includes 65% of the sub-Sahara, which has been degraded by both wind and water erosion. In Asia, 663 million hectares of land have experienced erosion. One-third of the land in Latin America has been degraded, largely due to water erosion. In South and Central America, the figures are 165 million hectares and 51 hectares of land degraded through erosion, respectively. Once the soil structure has been destroyed and the topsoil removed, agricultural land can no longer sustain crops or vegetation. Desertification is very difficult, often impossible, to reverse.

Effects of Erosion

Erosion is a form of soil degradation. It changes and weakens soil structure, quality, and texture, in turn reducing its fertility and water-holding capacity. Drier soils are more susceptible to droughts and wind erosion. Wind erosion is the dominant form of erosion in arid zones of the world, causing 60% of land degradation. Particles picked up by the wind can remain suspended in the air and add to the atmospheric dust load. If severe enough, this dust pollution can decrease visibility and become a health hazard, particularly affecting people with respiratory diseases.

Water erosion is the dominant form of erosion in semi-arid and dry sub-humid regions of the world, contributing up to 51% of the land degradation. Soil lost to erosion can destabilise riverbanks and increase the potential for flash flooding and landslides. The disposal of the eroded material is also a serious issue. It may be dumped downslope, burying seeds and seedlings and lowering their survival rate. More likely, sediment deposits will be washed or blown into rivers and streams, reducing the water quality downstream, degrading aquatic wildlife habitats and fish spawning areas. In still waters, like reservoirs, silt can drop out of the water column and settle on the floor. In sufficient amounts, this sedimentation reduces the water storage capacity and life of the impoundment and eventually may lead to increased water treatment costs for drinking water. When sedimentation occurs in channels, expensive dredging may be required to keep the waterway deep enough for water and barge traffic. Suspended material in rivers and streams flows downstream and is eventually transported out to the ocean and lost.

Agricultural areas affected by topsoil erosion become less productive and more vulnerable to weeds. The loss of soil nutrients results in poor crop growth and a reduction in crop yield. Fertilisers are usually added to the soil to replace missing nutrients while poisons and pesticides are sprayed to combat weed infestation. These pesticides and fertilisers will be transported with any subsequent soil erosion and are often washed into waterways. Pesticides can be poisonous to aquatic life and pose a health hazard for downstream drinking water sources. Excess nutrients in water bodies can exacerbate algal blooms.

Combating Soil Erosion

Loss of topsoil and reduction in crop productivity has increased global awareness and concern for soil erosion. The impacts of erosion reach further than environmental degradation. Soil erosion can have grave effects on the economy, impacting sectors such as energy and water supply. Commercially, many developing countries rely heavily on the export income provided by cash crops. Ongoing land degradation translates to a significant economic loss of agricultural income. Perhaps more importantly, reduced crop productivity threatens the global food supply and security. Africa, for example, has become very reliant on food imports and aid. With an ever-increasing global population, there is a real incentive not only to conserve current fertile lands but also to increase crop yields.

Declining food per capita and increases in poverty have led to impacts on health in the developing world. For example, the number of undernourished people in Africa has doubled from the 1960s to 200 million in the late 1990s. In many developing countries the combined pressures of poverty, landlessness, and increasing population force local farmers to continue environmentally destructive farming practices. Population pressures force subsistence farmers to use illegally cleared forests and marginal lands to survive. Once an area is depleted of nutrients, they move on. Soil conservation techniques require time and energy. Many farmers in developing countries struggle with severe poverty and cannot afford the resources required to implement these measures. Often, there is no incentive for these farmers to conserve the topsoil because they do not own the land that they cultivate. Mismanagement of these areas leads to further degradation.

The problem of erosion is being tackled, to varying degrees, around the world. Progress is hampered by the lack of training, basic information, and funding for rehabilitation and land reclamation projects. However, an increasing number of countries in the developing world are making progress. Agricultural methods aimed specifically at soil conservation are increasingly being implemented. Techniques such as horizontal ploughing and hillside ditches slow and redirect surface runoff while planting hedgerows reduce the impact of wind. Planting cover crops provides a more complex system and protects the cash crops below from the effects of wind and rain. Tilling crop residues into the soil replenishes nutrients through the addition of organic matter. Degraded land is being rehabilitated through the natural regeneration of trees and the planting of a rich diversity of other vegetation. In the Upper Niger River Valley Zone, farmers have begun to use fertilizer and improved seed varieties that have been engineered to grow in harsh conditions on fields that have been built up organic matter. In Niger's Majjia Valley, farmers are planting windbreaks of tall trees to combat the effects of wind on the soil. In Burkina Faso, farmers are using rocks and other debris as barriers along contours to reduce the intensity of surface runoff. In Thailand and the Philippines, farmers are planting tall, deep-rooted perennial grasses for the same effect. No-till farming, where the previous crop is left in the ground and seeds for the new crop are planted via holes in the ground made without ploughing, is gaining popularity across South America and Africa.

Forests are being replanted in Argentina and Mozambique, stimulating the economy by both employing jobless young people and generating income from forest products from previous degraded lands. Agroforestry is also being promoted in the developing world as another method of combating erosion. Plant and tree species are encouraged to be left or planted in fields as resources in their own right. In the Sahel region, selected trees are being grown amongst the crops and pastures. The trees lessen the effects of the wind and torrential rains on sandy soils as well as improving soil fertility and offer additional resources such as timber, firewood, leaf litter, seeds, oils, fruits, and gums. In China and Vietnam, land tenure reform has seen land reallocated to individuals and families. This has had a positive impact on land management, with production increases and more trees being planted than cut down.

The importance of soil conservation and the need to encourage and assist developing countries with this issue was internationally recognised at the Earth Summit, formally known as the United Nations Conference on Environment and Development, held in Rio de Janeiro in 1992. A plan of action concerning the planning and management of land resources, combating deforestation, and sustainable agriculture and rural development was agreed upon. Responsibility for the development and implementation of this plan was given to the Food and Agriculture Organisation. This organisation assists governments with advice for incentives to encourage and reward sustainable land use and continues to develop indicators and guidelines for sustainable agricultural practices.

Although topsoil is still being lost at an alarming rate, soil erosion is now accepted as a significant issue worldwide. Its potential to impact on food supply and export income in particular has caused many countries to implement specific environmental policies to regulate agriculture and land practices. However, while such policies are valuable, the real change in practice must occur at a grassroots level. The work of agencies, such as the Peacecorps and the Initiative for the Social Action and Renewal in Eurasia, with communities and local non-government organisations to educate and to improve land use practice may ultimately determine whether soil erosion can be managed effectively.

ALISA KRASNOSTEIN

See also Deforestation; Desertification; Pollution, Agricultural

References and Further Reading

Anderson, Jock R., and Jesuthason Thampapillai. *Soil Conservation in Developing Countries: Project and Policy Intervention.* Washington, DC: World Bank, 1990.

Bennett, Hugh H. *Elements of Soil Conservation.* New York: McGraw-Hill, 1955.

de Graaff, J. *The Price of Soil Erosion: An Economic Evaluation of Soil Conservation and Watershed Development.* Wageningen: Agricultural University, 1996.

Gabler, Robert E., Robert E. Sager, Shieler Brazier, and Jacqueline Pourciau. *Essentials of Physical Geography.* United States: Holt, Rinehart and Winston, 1977.

Knapp, Brian, Simon Ross, and Duncan McCrae. *Challenge of the Natural Environment.* Harlow, Essex: Longman, 1991.

Lal, Rattan, editor. *Soil Quality and Soil Erosion.* Boca Raton, FL: CRC Press, 1999.

"Land and Food." UNEP Global Environment Outlook 2000. http://www1.unep.org/geo-text/0043.htm. United Nations Environment Programme, 1999.

McIntosh, Phyllis. "Land Management." *Desertification: Earth's Silent Scourge.* http://usinfo.state.gov/products/pubs/desertific/land.htm.

Morgan, Royston P. C. *Soil Erosion and Conservation.* Harlow, Essex, England: Longman, 1995; New York: Wiley, 1995.

National Research Council (US). *Sustainable Agriculture and the Environment in the Humid Tropics.* Washington, DC: National Academy Press, 1993.

Pimentel, David, editor. *World Soil Erosion and Conservation.* Cambridge and NewYork: Cambridge University Press, 1993.

Sanders, John H., Douglas D. Southgate, and John G. Lee. *The Economics of Soil Degradation: Technological Change and Policy Alternatives.* West Lafayette, IN: Purdue University, Dept. of Agricultural Economics for USAID, 1995.

Seymour, John, and Herbert Girardet. *Far From Paradise: The Story of Human Impact on the Environment.* London: Green Print, 1990.

Sfeir-Younis, Alfredo, and Andrew K. Dragun. *Land and Soil Management: Technology, Economics, and Institutions.* Boulder, CO: Westview Press, 1993.

Thapa, Gopal B., and Karl E. Weber. *Soil Erosion in Developing Countries: Causes, Policies and Programs.* Bangkok, Thailand: Division of Human Settlements Development, Asian Institute of Technology, 1991.

ESTONIA

The Republic of Estonia is one of the Baltic Republics and a part of the former Soviet Union. Estonia borders Russia, Finland, Latvia, and the Baltic Sea. The total area of the country is 45,266 square kilometers and with its population of about 1.4 million Estonia is among the smallest European countries.

Estonia first gained its independence in 1918, but in 1940 was incorporated into the Soviet Union. The country gained its independence again in 1991 at the collapse of the Soviet Union. Estonia is a highly urbanized country and about three quarters of the population lives in towns and cities. Its capital is Tallinn, an old medieval city. The second largest city is Tartu, a significant academic center in Eastern Europe. Other cities are Narva and Pärnu. The native people of Estonia are Finno-Ugric. All ethnic groups include Estonian 65.3%, Russian 28.1%, Ukrainian 2.5%, Belarusian 1.5%, Finn 1%, and other 1.6%. The official language is Estonian (family of Baltic languages).

Generally, the terrain of the country is flat in the north and hilly in the south. There are about 1,500 small islands on the Baltic that remain Estonian territory. The region is boggy, and it contains swamps, rivers, wetlands, and more than one thousand lakes. Forests cover most of the country's area. The elevation is above sea level with the highest point Suur Munamägi reaching 317 meters above sea level. Because of the proximity of the sea, the climate of Estonia is milder than on the rest of the continent. The maritime climate provides wet moderate winters and cold summers. Because of the geographic location summer days are long and winter days last for only several hours. Nights are not very dark from May until July. The temperature in Estonia is unpredictable and might change within a day by about 20°C. Average summer temperature is 15°C–18°C, while average winter temperature is −4–5°C. Winters are usually snowy. Days are often cloudy and frequently rainy (annual precipitation is 750 millimeters).

The Estonian ecosystem also consists of several species of animals, among which the most numerous are large mammals like deer, elk, and boar, but also beaver, lynx, wolf, brown bear, and. gray and ringed seals in coastal waters. There are about 333 species of birds; among them are the black stork and eagle. About 10% of the country area is under environmental protection, namely seashore wetlands and some woodland areas. The Estonian ecosystem is not destroyed like in most of Europe.

Culturally, Estonia is divided into lowlands and highlands, and such division relates to the economic activities and accumulation of wealth. Highland people were predominantly agricultural while the lowland populations subsisted on fishing. Estonian prehistory is not well known, but the archaeological record confirms that the first inhabitants were foragers and fishermen of the Mesolithic period. The first farmers inhabited the region about four thousand years ago. Although some remarks on the region can be found in the Roman sources, or Scandinavian sagas, Estonian history starts in the twelfth century with the introduction of Christianity and feudalism. Several powers occupied the present-day Estonia in the past, among them Denmark, Sweden, Poland, and Russia. About 1170, the Holy See tried to establish its province there. The earliest historic source on the land is the Chronicle of Henry of Livonia which describes thirteenth century Estonia. In the beginning of the thirteenth century, German and Danish military expeditions entered the regions of present-day Estonia. First parishes were established in the beginning of the fourteenth century. Three significant periods in Estonian history shaped its culture: the introduction of Christianity, class society, and urbanization throughout the thirteenth century led by German and Danish rulers; the Reformation period when the Estonian language was introduced to liturgy, schooling, and administration; and modernization of the society after 1860 linked to the industrialization of the Baltic region. Estonia gained independence in 1918, but lost it in 1940 when it was incorporated into the Soviet Union. It regained independence on August 20, 1991, at the time of the collapse of the Soviet Union and that date was proclaimed as a national holiday. On March 29, 2004, Estonia joined North Atlantic Treaty Organization (NATO) and a month later, on May 1, 2004, it became a member of the European Union. Despite a long period of colonization, Estonian culture prevailed and the Estonian language is still spoken. It contains many words borrowed from other languages, namely German, Swedish, Russian, Finnish, but also French and English.

Estonia has limited natural resources, mostly oil, shale, peat, clay, limestone, and timber. Because of the lack of economically significant natural resources, the Estonian economy is based on services, like tourism, which attracts about 2–3 million people a year, trade, and banking. Various service-based industries provide about 65% of Estonian gross domestic product (GDP). The rest is provided by light industries, like fishing, timber, paper, and textiles. Other branches of industry include: mechanical engineering, electronics, wood and wood products, textile industry, information technology, and telecommunications. The labor force by occupation includes: agriculture 11%, industry 20%, and services 69%. Forests are among the most significant natural resources providing timber for the paper industries. Electronics and engineering industries are developing. The chemical industry after difficult times during the 1990s is presently recuperating and developing. Tourism is one of the most significant economic sectors. Every year 2–3 million tourists visit Estonia (this includes shopping tourism from neighboring countries, especially Finland).

Estonian arable land covers 16.04% of the area. Agriculture employs only about five percent of the workforce and consists mostly of small farms and corporations. The main agricultural products are dairy products, poultry, meat (beef and pork), potatoes, and cereals. Many foodstuffs are organic. Agriculture also includes fisheries, cattle breeding, and honey bee keeping.

The Estonian economy is one of the best among countries that joined the European Union recently. The economy attracts many foreign investors with its fast and stable growth. Most significant trade partners are Finland and Sweden. Its export commodities include: machinery and equipment 33%, wood and paper 15%, textiles 14%, food products 8%, furniture 7%, metals, and chemical products. Its export partners include: Finland 21.9%, Sweden 12.5%, Russia 11.4%, Germany 8.4%, Latvia 7.4%, Lithuania 4% (2003). Its import commodities include: machinery and equipment 33.5%, chemical products 11.6%, textiles 10.3%, foodstuffs 9.4%, transportation equipment 8.9% (2001). Its import partners include: Finland 15.9%, Germany 11.1%, Russia 10.2%, Sweden 7.7%, Ukraine 4.3%, China 4.2%, Japan 4.1%.

The official Estonian currency is the kroon. Estonia, as a new member of the World Trade Organization, is steadily moving toward a modern market economy with increasing ties to the West, including the pegging of its currency to the euro. The economy benefits from strong electronics and telecommunications sectors. Estonia joined the European Union in May 2004. The economy is greatly influenced by developments in Finland, Sweden, Russia, and Germany, four major trading partners. The high current account deficit remains a concern. However, the state budget enjoyed a surplus of $130 million in 2003.

Estonia is a parliamentary republic with a 101-seat parliament. The parliament selects a president for a five-year term. The president can serve only two terms. The president is the head of state, and leader of the government. There are several political parties which have 5% votes, a condition to be represented in the Parliament. A party that collects the most votes has the right to form the government.

LUDOMIR LOZNY

See also Central and Eastern Europe: History and Economic Development; Central and Eastern Europe: International Relations

References and Further Reading

Laar, M. and Tiina Ets. *War in the Woods: Estonia's Struggle for Survival 1944–1956*. Compass Press, 1992.
Raun, Toivo U., *Estonia and the Estonians: Studies of Nationalities*, 2nd edition. Hoover Institution Press, 2002.
Smith, David J., Artis Pabriks, Aldis Purs, and Thomas Lane. *The Baltic States: Estonia, Latvia, and Lithuenia (Postcommunist States and Nations)*. Routledge, 2001.

ETHIOPIA

Situated in the region known as the Horn of Africa, Ethiopia has an area of approximately 1.27 million square kilometers, slightly smaller than twice the area of Texas. It borders Eritrea on the north and northeast, Djibouti on the east, Somalia on the east and southeast, Kenya on the south, and Sudan on the west. It occupies a significant portion of the Horn of Africa landmass and extends almost 1,640 kilometers from east to west and 1,580 kilometers from north to south. Ethiopia is a land of extreme contrasts, both in terms of its topography and climate. It is mountainous in the northern and central regions, some with elevations as high as 4,617 meters above sea level, and has vast stretches of lowlands in the eastern and southeastern regions, some of which lay as much as 116 meters below sea level. An important feature of the Ethiopian landscape is the Great Rift Valley, running roughly from north to south, essentially dividing the country into two.

The temperature in the highland areas runs from near freezing to as much as 30°C, and in the lowlands from 30°C–50°C, occasionally reaching 60°C. The rainy season in the highlands extends from June to August, while there is not much rain in the eastern lowland regions of the country. Most of the population, estimated in 2000 at 61 million, professes Christianity or Islam. In general, Christians, who constitute about 43% of the population, live in the highland areas and are sedentary farmers; the Moslems, who comprise nearly 48% of the population, live in the lowlands and are generally agro-pastoralists. Although Ethiopia is associated more with the Tigray and Amhara national groups of the north and north-central parts of the country, the largest group, about 40% of the population, is the Oromo national group. This population group lives in the western, southern, and south-central parts of Ethiopia.

Ethiopia is one of the two countries in Africa (the other is Liberia) that was never colonized, or briefly colonized (1936–1941), by a European power. Ethiopians, or more appropriately Abyssinians, extend their history as a nation to pre-Christian times when the powerful Kingdom of Axum flourished in northern Ethiopia, circa 300 BC. The kings of Axum adopted Christianity as their official religion in the fourth century and this made the people one of the earliest to practice Christianity officially. The Kingdom of Axum, however, declined around the seventh century, and highland Ethiopians, unable to maintain trade and cultural links with the outside world, were cut off for about a millennium until the middle of the nineteenth century. With minimal outside contact, the economic, social, and cultural system had remained frozen in time. This is particularly true of the Ethiopian Tewahdo Orthodox Church, which still continues to practice elements of ancient Judaic traditions.

Ethiopia came out of its isolation around 1855, when Emperor Tewodros established a relatively unified but a much smaller Ethiopia as compared with the present. The emperors who followed him, including Yohannes IV, Menelik II, and Haile Selassie I, successively enlarged and established a more centralized Ethiopia. Thus, traditional Ethiopia, by incorporating the areas in the periphery, became a multi-cultural state whose peoples differed in religion, ethnicity, and psychological outlook. Although apparently successful in pacifying the peoples of the newly incorporated regions initially, the "question of nationalities" became an important variable in the political, economic, and social development of contemporary Ethiopia. This and issues related to poor governance and limits on the powers of the emperor are taken as causal factors for the attempted coup d'etat in 1960.

As a result of its history, the nature and foundation of the Ethiopian state became a hotly contested issue from the 1960s onward. Emperor Haile Selassie, the last of the Ethiopian monarchs, was unable to resolve the ethnic disputes and other issues of development, and was overthrown in 1974 by the military. The military government, which assumed power with the promise to resolve the problem of ethnicity, also failed in its endeavor. Consequently, various ethnic-based armed opposition movements in various parts of the country emerged to press their demands for more communal rights. Unable to address communal grievances, both political and economic, the military government was likewise overthrown in 1991. For almost thirty years (1962–1991), therefore, Ethiopia had a disproportionate share of political violence, first in Eritrea and later in other parts of the country. Partly because of these issues and partly because of its long isolation, Ethiopia remained under-developed both politically and economically.

Politically, Ethiopia remained an absolute monarchy until 1974, and under a military dictatorship until 1991. Hence, Ethiopia had no tradition of a government accountable to the people, no peaceful competition for power by political parties, and no civil society to speak of. Since 1991, however, Ethiopia has been a federal republic of ethnic-based territories ruled by the Ethiopian Peoples' Revolutionary Democratic Front (EPRDF). Similarly, EPRDF-allied parties control regional governments. There are also many opposition parties, some of which are legal. However, they have not been able to break the monopoly of the EPRDF, as the results of the elections held in 1995 and 2000 show. EPRDF handily won because many opposition parties had boycotted these elections. Among the illegal political movements are the Oromo Liberation Front and Ogaden National Liberation Front, both of which have resorted to arms to force the government to agree to a full measure of self-determination for Oromia and the Ogaden, respectively.

Although there is debate as to whether or not the present government is democratic, the political environment now is far more open compared with the pre-1991 period. Indeed, the present constitution gives ethnic groups the right to decide their future, and this theoretically includes the right to secession. The Ethiopian constitution is the only one in the world today that explicitly includes constitutional provisions for secession. Also, since 1991, independent civic organizations have flourished. They include, among others, the Ethiopian Teachers' Association, the Ethiopian Women's Lawyers Association, the Ethiopian Free Press Journalists Association and the Ethiopian Human Rights Council. Many independent civic organizations in the Diaspora are also actively involved in the political, social, and human rights issues affecting Ethiopia.

In the realm of economics, Ethiopia remains one of the least developed countries. The gross domestic product (GDP)—calculated in terms of the value of all final goods and services produced within Ethiopia, and computed on the basis of purchasing power parity (PPP)—is about $33 billion, with GDP per capita of about $560. Coffee accounts for about 60% of export earnings. With such an overwhelming dependence on a single commodity and the inevitable fluctuations and ever-decreasing price of coffee, Ethiopia has a long way to go before experiencing sustained growth, especially because its economy is based on small-holder and rain-fed agriculture susceptible to the periodic drought the country faces. There were, however, positive signs in the last ten years. The economy grew by an average of 6% for most of the 1990s and early 2000s because of a combination of many factors. These include the adoption of market-oriented economy, the implementation of International Monetary Fund's Structural Adjustments Programs, and relative political stability. There are renewed hopes of a more accelerated economic growth.

ASSEFAW BARIAGABER

References and Further Reading

Araia, Ghelawdewos. *Ethiopia: The Political Economy of Transition*. Lanham, MD: University Press of America, 1995.

Bariagaber, Assefaw. "The Politics of Cultural Pluralism in Ethiopia and Eritrea: Trajectories of Ethnicity and Constitutional Experiments." *Ethnic and Racial Studies*, 21, no. 6 (1998).

Clapham, Christopher. *Transformation and Continuity in Revolutionary Ethiopia*. Cambridge: Cambridge University Press, 1998.

Jalata, Asafa. *Oromia and Ethiopia: State Formation and Ethnonational Conflict, 1968–1992*. Boulder, CO: Lynne Rienner, 1993.

Kebbede Girma. *The State and Development in Ethiopia*. Atlantic Highland, New Jersey and London: Humanities Press, 1992.

Marcus, Harold G. *History of Ethiopia*. Berkeley, CA: University of California Press, 1994.

Ofcansky, Thomas P., and LaVerle Berry, editors. *Ethiopia: A Country Study*, 4th edition. Washington, DC: Library of Congress, 1993.

Punkhurst, Richard. *The Ethiopians*. Malden, MA: Blackwell Publishers, 1998.

Tiruneh, Andargachew. *The Ethiopian Revolution, 1974–1987: A Transformation from an Autocratic to a Totalitarian Autocracy*. New York: Cambridge University Press, 1993.

Zewde, Bahru. *A History of Modern Ethiopia, 1855–1974*. London: James Curry; Athens, OH: Ohio University Press; and Addis Ababa, Ethiopia: Addis Ababa University Press, 1991.

ETHNIC CONFLICTS: CARIBBEAN

The scenario of ethnic relations and conflicts in the Caribbean reflects the staggering complexity of the regional panorama of nationalities, languages, and religions. In addition to English, Spanish, and French, other major languages are spoken in the numerous islands that comprise the Greater and Lesser Antilles, including Chinese, Hindi, and Arabic. There are also communities of worship for all major world religions as well as uniquely Caribbean religious traditions, like Santería in Cuba and Voodoo in Haiti.

The Antilles, to which the expeditions of Columbus and others arrived from Europe at the end of the fifteenth century, found an ethnically diversified native population, with various groups of Ciboney, Arawak, and Carib stock. The greatest part of this indigenous population disappeared after the ravages of war, disease, and forced labor and was soon being replaced by black Africans brought as slaves over the Atlantic.

Resting on the bedrock of the three institutions of the plantation, slavery system, and colonialism, the modern Caribbean is a scenario where ethnicity, that is the identification of a certain group with real or imagined cultural links to an ancestral past, with language and religion (Baronov and Yelvington 2003) is a crucial element. The historical background is important not only as a tool for a better understanding but also as a main element in the very constitution of this ethnicity. The distinctiveness of the Carib as an ethnic group, for instance, has much to do with the circumstances of early colonial rule, when resistance to Spanish hegemonism stimulated their militarism. Soon after, the Caribs found it convenient to make alliances and agreements with colonial powers of later arrival. In that manner, they obtained trade privileges, confirmation of authority, merchandise, and ceremonial staves from the Dutch, English, and French. Thus, trade and ethnic soldiering was an important factor in the establishment of solidarities, oppositions and adversarial identities. This insight corrects an earlier interpretation of the conflicts between Caribs and Arawaks that have been seen as the continuation of pre-Columbian rivalries (Whitehead 1990).

Today, there are some three thousand Caribs living in villages of what is called the Carib Territory on the East coast of Dominica. There are also descendants of Arawak and Carib Indians in the island of Aruba, where the population also includes groups of Dutch, Spanish, and African provenance.

The predominance of inhabitants with black ancestry reflects the massive proportions of the slave trade. Between 1662 and 1867, almost 10 million Africans were exported as slaves to America; Jamaica only received 662,400 (Mintz 1985).

This population brought along much of its culture, its religion, its means of expression. Orality had here a central significance and from the crucible of Afro-American orality, in the forced submission and pain of the plantation, rebellion transformed oral tradition into a folklore of fugitive rebels. Creole languages that developed as a basic part of runaway slave culture facilitated communication. Escaped slaves coming together to form small communities had a need to create a common language that would overcome cultural diversity and resist isolation. Creole was a synthesis of West African languages, fused together with loaned words from English and Spanish. In the island of Aruba, the official language is Dutch but the common language used is Papiamento, a Creole that evolved mainly from Portuguese, Spanish, and Dutch.

Later, with the end of slavery, indentured laborers were taken to the Caribbean in great quantities. More than 125,000 Chinese came to Cuba, Guyana, Jamaica, and Trinidad. More than 100,000 East Indians arrived to Jamaica, Guyana, and Trinidad. The end of slavery resulted then in the formation of one of the most ethnically diversified regions of the world (Baronov and Yelvington 2003).

Traditionally, ethnicity was anchored in the indigenous *bohio*, a hut with thatched roof. Today, ethnic identity can be said to be rooted in the private space of the urban tenement yard, and by the tenants themselves, the yardies. These ghettoes, for instance in Kingston, Jamaica, are enclaves whose ethnicity is simply their poverty (Chevannes 2001). This intimacy of the household was translated into a carefully managed system of racial discrimination in the public sphere. In the late eighteenth century there were in the French colony of St. Domingue, today's Haiti, nine possible racial categories between a pure white and a pure black. Today, those harsh and clear-cut tokens of discrimination have been replaced, at least in more public arenas, by a code tinted with what Isar Godreau, for the case of Puerto Rico, calls a slippery semantics, *semántica fugitiva*, by which one refers to racial types by mentioning various degrees of rainfall (Baronov and Yelvington 2003).

This aspect of indeterminacy in the negotiation of notions of ethnic and racial identity stands in clear contrast to at least two ways of asserting an identity, one silent and exclusive, the other vociferous and inclusive. The first one can be seen in the sense of exclusiveness present in elite groups like the white Creole elite of Martinique. There, 150 patronymic names could in the 1970s trace their ancestry in such ways that race, class, and a sense of great historical role in the island formed the pillars of their ethnocentrism. The sacred duty of this group is then to maintain the purity of the stock by following the norms of endogamy (Maingot 1996). The second, and opposite, manner of assertiveness is the deeply felt sense of ethnic identification and urge of revindication that is characteristically expressed in popular music and lyrics throughout the region. In Cuba, the sacred drummers of Lucumí ancestry are the collective

sound of an African presence that refuses to disappear (Benkomo 2000). To the east, the songs of bitterness of the *bachata* are also known as the Dominican blues. Derived from the classic *bolero*, the bachata has become a form of protest Latin rock, combining Dominican folk motifs, Jamaican reggae, and layers of Zairian guitar. Also, the soul of Trinidad and Tobago can be summarised in the steel drum or pan, paraded in defiant street festivals. Originally, African skin drums were used until banned in the 1880s by the British authorities who feared that the drummers transmitted coded messages that could possibly lead to rebellion (Meschino 2002). Panorama, the annual steel band competition with its uproarious atmosphere, is one of the most anticipated events of Carnival.

The two constants of Caribbean Africanness, words and drums, and their common core, rhythm, are elements that remain essential in the emergence of a literature of cultural revindication. This can be seen in the poetry of Martinican Aimé Césaire (b. 1913) and of the Puerto Rican Luis Palés Matos (1898–1959), himself a white. In the poem Black Majesty by Palés Matos, the sense of defiant urgency expressed by the rows of Congo blacks dancing rumba and macumba to the rhythms of their bongo drums, while they follow their glorious queen Temblandumba de la Quimbamba, is expressed in the sound of the words themselves. In the poem *Ñañigo Al Cielo*, The Ñañigo Comes to Heaven, also by Palés Matos, a member of the Ñañiga, the Cuban secret society also known as Abakuá, confers to the celestial court his own brand of bandit blessing when he and God embrace in a smelly cloud of intoxicating Antillean rum.

Considering then that not even the most exalted realms seem to be beyond the scope of this sense of defiance it is perhaps not surprising that fear and suspicion is ever present throughout the region. It was this terror that in Jamaica led to the ruthless repression of the Morant Bay rebellion of 1867. Not only were five hundred blacks executed, self-government was also suspended and direct Crown Colony rule was implemented (Maingot 1996).

The basic premise seems to be "not another Haiti." St. Domingue was by the time of the French Revolution the most prosperous colony in the Antilles, where a mere 32,000 whites owned 550,000 black slaves. The revolution in what was to become Haiti, a milestone in the history of the region, was in many ways precipitated by the agitation caused by the group of some thirty thousand black freedmen, *affranchis*, many of them slave owners themselves. Their demands were for a larger share in the benefits of plantation slavery and better access to the benefits of French culture

(Mintz 1974). The armed conflict began in August 1791 and ten years later the military leader Toussaint-Loverture, a former slave, became governor only to be imprisoned after coming to terms with a French expeditionary force sent by Napoleon to restore the old colonial regime. Finally, the forces of Jean-Jacques Dessalines and Henry Christophe defeated the French in November 3, 1803.

Haiti was far from unique. Slave revolts were numerous, and escaped slaves, known as maroons, were the living testimony that resistance to slavery was always a latent factor (Randall 2003). Thus, the specter of a new Haiti, known in Cuba as *El Gran Susto, the Great Fear,* has been an ever present menace. This was experienced most critically in 1844, when the serious rebellion of *La Escalera* occurred (Maingot 1996).

A precise assessment of many regional conflicts is often not an easy task. There is a long struggle, extending back to 1830, of the peasantry in Cuba fighting against the evictions and usurpations of expanding sugar-cane corporations. In the following generations, then are the Mambises, peasants fighting in the wars against Spain in 1868 and 1891. By 1905, after American intervention had increased noticeably, there were thirteen thousand American properties in Cuba, covering 10% of the total surface of the country. Many peasants had been evicted in the process, and as a result of this, massive mobilizations took place, like in Caujeri and Camagüey in 1923 (Huizer 1977). The question is, to what extent is this long story of peasant struggle in Cuba to be understood in terms of class or ethnic struggle? This and other cases are a reminder of the provisional character of our analytical constructs.

The ethnic African referent rooted in the past has its modern counterpart in the contemporary process of the Caribbean diaspora. By the last decade of the twentieth century, for instance, 43% of Puerto Ricans were living in the United States, 23% of the population of the Dutch Antilles in the Netherlands, and about 50% of Jamaicans in the United Kingdom and United States. Forging new identities in their adopted countries, these vast communities abroad often take on a heightened meaning of nationalism and ethnicity, while maintaining linkages with their homelands (Baronov and Yelvington 2003).

Also the original inhabitants of the Caribbean have been increasingly reasserting their presence, demanding recognition of their political and territorial rights. After being declared extinct centuries ago, it is now well known that thousands of Taino-Arawak descendants are alive and well, not only in Cuba but in the Dominican Republic and Haiti. Many are also living in Florida, in other parts of the United States, and even Spain. Since 1997, Taino Indians have been reunited annually with their relatives of the diaspora at a conference held in Baracoa, eastern Cuba. The meetings have opened up to the world the reality of the continued existence of this group and although the Cuban government has not formally recognised them as an indigenous people, it has pledged support and protection. Other Taino living in the diaspora now visit their ancestral lands in Boriken, Puerto Rico.

It seems that in the multicultural societies of the Caribbean there is an integrative Creole model that in spite of all tensions and rivalries, allows for the relative absence of ethnic and racial violence in modern times (Hillman and Serbin 2003). When attempting a comprehensive understanding of this ever-changing scenario where, in a perennial combination of assertiveness and indeterminacy, notions of identity, class, and nationality are constantly being negotiated and contested, terms like "ethnic" and "racial," even when confusing and misleading, seem still useful.

JUAN-CARLOS GUMUCIO CASTELLON

See also Caribbean: History and Economic Development; Caribbean: International Relations

References and Further Reading

Baronov, David, and K. A. Yelvington. Ethnicity, Race, Class and Nationality. In *Understanding the Contemporary Caribbean*, edited by R. S. Hillman and T. J. D'Agostino. London: Lynne Rienner Publishers, pp. 209–238, 2003.

Benkomo, Juan. Crafting the Sacred Batá Drums. In *Afro-Cuban Voices. On Race and Identity in Contemporary Cuba.* edited by P. P. Sarduy and J. Stubbs. Gainesville, FL: University Press of Florida, pp. 140–146, 2000.

Chevannes, Barry. Jamaican Diasporic Identity. In *Nation Dance. Religion, Identity, and Cultural Difference in the Caribbean*, edited by P. Taylor. Bloomington, IN: Indiana University Press, pp. 129–137, 2001.

Hillman, Richard S., and A. Serbin. Trends and Prospects. In *Understanding the Contemporary Caribbean*, edited by R. S. Hillman and T. J. D'Agostino. London: Lynne Rienner Publishers, pp. 355–367, 2003.

Huizer, Gerrit. The Role of Peasant Organizations in the Struggle Against Multinational Corporations: The Cuban Case. In *Western Expansion and Indigenous Peoples*, edited by E. Sevilla-Casas. The Hague: Mouton Publishers, pp. 255–262, 1977.

Maingot, Anthony P. Haiti and the terrified consciousness of the Caribbean. In *Ethnicity in the Caribbean*, edited by G. Oostindie. London: MacMillan, pp. 53–80, 1996.

Martinez Montiel, and Luz Maria. African Orality in the Literary Culture of the Caribbean. In *Literary Cultures of Latin America*, edited by M. J. Valdés and D. Kadir. Oxford University Press, vol. 1, pp. 460–470, 2004.

Meschino, Patricia. Pan's People. *Songlines. The World Music Magazine.* Sept/Oct 2002, pp. 68–73.

Mintz, Sidney. *Caribbean Transformations.* Chicago: Aldine Publishing Co, 1974.

Sweetness and Power. The Place of Sugar in Modern History. New York: Penguin Books, 1985.

Whitehead, Neil Lancelot. Carib Ethnic Soldiering in Venezuela, the Guianas, and the Antilles, 1492–1820. *Ethnohistory*, vol. 37, nr. 4, pp. 357–385, 1990.

ETHNIC CONFLICTS: CENTRAL AFRICA

Cameroon

Although Cameroon has strong ethnic rivalries, particularly between the Muslim north and the Christian south, it has not faced the ethnic violence common to many of its neighbors. There are also political tensions between the French speaking and English speaking portions of the population. (Cameroon is a merger of two former colonies, one English and one French.)

Central African Republic

Although divided into more than eighty ethnic groups, ethnic violence is not a major problem in the Central African Republic. The two largest ethnic groups, making up about 50% of the country's population, are the Baya and Banda.

Chad

Chad, like its neighbor Sudan, has a north-south ethnic divide. Northern Chad identifies with the Arab Islamic world which it borders, even though intermarriage has led to a population not dissimilar in appearance to that of the south. Many northerners consider themselves Arab and speak Arabic as either a first or second language. Southern Chad is Christian and animist and is dominated by the ethnic groups Sara, Toubouri, and Masa.

In the early years after its independence, granted by the French in 1960, Chad was dominated by southerners, not surprising given the south's larger population. In 1965, however, a northern revolt backed by Libya attempted to change this. After seventeen years of fighting, a northerner, Hissène Habré, finally took power. Habré, despite his Muslim background, supported a fairly broadly based coalition. His main opposition, moreover, came from Libya, which had formerly supported him but which now had ambitions to annex part of northern Chad. Despite

his attempts to maintain alliances with southerners, Habré faced widespread resistance in the south and used violence against southerners to maintain himself in power. In late 1990, Idriss Deby, another northerner, replaced Habré.

Deby also targeted southerners who were perceived as resisting his regime with violence, and southerners have responded in kind. Nevertheless, compared with neighboring Sudan, a country with a similar north-south division, Chad is relatively peaceful. The numbers killed in ethnic conflicts remain in the thousands rather than in the tens or hundreds of thousands.

Republic of Congo

The Republic of Congo is the Democratic Republic of Congo's far smaller neighbor, with a population of about 3 million. Congo is divided between three major ethnic groups, the Bakongo, who make up almost half the population, the Batéké, who make up 20%, and the M'Boshi, who constitute 15%.

Although the Batéké are the largest group, the M'Boshi have had a disproportionate influence on politics, dominated the countries post-independence leadership as well as its military. Ethnic tensions are fanned by the fact that all three major ethnic groups maintain their own militias in the country's capital.

The Democratic Republic of Congo

With a population approaching 50 million, the Democratic Republic of Congo (formerly called Zaire) is the largest state in Central Africa and the one with the bloodiest history of conflict. Congo's modern history of ethnic conflicts begins with the Belgian conquest in the 1870s. Belgium's rule over Congo was one of the bloodiest in Africa's colonial history, leaving the country with a legacy of bitterness and misrule. (Some of the horror of this period is depicted in Joseph Conrad's fictional masterpiece, *Heart of Darkness*.) Belgian troops and administrators killed millions.

Independence was granted in 1960, but the situation in Congo did not improve. Belgium had trained almost no local administrators and upon independence essentially abandoned the country to its internal ethnic conflicts, which were many.

There are hundreds of ethnic groups in Congo and nothing had been done during Belgian's period of misrule to meld them into a single nation. Congo's first post-colonial ruler, Patrice Lumumba, fought a series of conflicts with regional strong-men who based their power on local ethnic groups. The most powerful of these was Moise Tshombe based in Katanga province (since renamed Shaba).

Led by Tshombe, the Katangese fought for three years to maintain their independence. They were eventually defeated when a new strong-man, Joseph Mobutu, came to power. A United Nations (UN) force that intervened in his defense helped Mobuto. The UN supported a unified Congo and so opposed the desires of the Katangese. The Katangese were defeated and Mobutu ruled Congo (which he renamed Zaire) until 1996. However, he was only partially able to suppress ethnic unrest. Insurrections occurred in Shaba on a regular basis. Mobutu also faced ethnic in other parts of the country, particularly Upper Zaire. He responded by packing his administration with members of his own ethnic group, the Ngande.

The 1994 genocide in next-door Rwanda was the occasion for further ethnic conflict, as well as the partial cause of Mobutu's downfall. Ethnic Hutu in Rwanda had created a dictatorship that attempted to wipe out the ethnic Tutsi, Rwanda's main minority. When a Rwanda army based in Uganda was able to overthrow the Hutu regime, hundreds of thousands of Hutu fled from Rwanda into Zaire in the summer of 1994. Hutu refugee camps became bases from which Hutu extremists hoped to retake Rwanda. Hutu extremists also attacked ethnic Banyarwanda, who were ethnic cousins to the Tutsi.

To defend their borders, as well as aid the Banyarwanda of Zaire, Rwanda supported local Banyarwanda militias against the Hutu and the local Zairian military, which had supported the anti-Banyarwandan attacks. Mobutu responded by expelling some Banyarwanda from Kinhasa, the capital. Despite these efforts, or perhaps accelerated by them, Mobutu's corrupt regime quickly began to collapse and the local war became a general revolution. An alliance of anti-Mobutu groups was created, and, led by Laurent Kabila, was able to force Mobutu from the country and take power in 1997. Upon capturing Kinhasa, Kabila renamed the country Congo.

Kabila's accession to power did not end ethnic violence in Congo. Unable to maintain control over much of the country, and often using ethnic rivalries to his own advantage, Kabila was unable or unwilling to stop the fighting. Various ethnic groups continued to be supported by outside military intervention by Rwanda, Uganda, Burundi, Angola, and Zimbabwe. The widespread fighting has led to the deaths of millions as well as widespread rape, the use of child soldiers, and the creation of a refugee problem numbering in the millions. Kabila himself was assassinated in 2001 and replaced by his son, Joseph Kabila, who was equally unable to solve Congo's ethnic violence.

Although the original Rwandan intervention was in the name of self defense as well as defense of the Banyarwandan minority, most of the interventions, including Rwanda's, have since taken on the appearance of a power grab, with all parties intent on looting as much as they can of Congo's extensive natural resources. There have been widespread reports of massacres committed by all sides in Congo's many-sided conflict. Among those massacred are many Hutu refugees, and among those supporting their killing are the Tutsi who had been victims of massacres in neighboring Rwanda.

The result of this ongoing violence, some of the worst in Africa, is to leave most of the country impoverished. This despite the fact that Congo is extremely rich in natural resources ranging from diamonds to rubber. The total death toll of the conflict cannot be accurately stated but certainly numbers at least 3 million.

Gabon

Gabon, a small country with a population of under 2 million, has more than fifty ethnic groups. The largest of these is the Fang, who make up some thirty percent of the population. Despite this plurality, the Fang have long been kept from power by coalitions of rival ethnic factions. President Omar Bongo, who has ruled the country since 1967, comes from the Batéké ethnic group and has favored this group in government jobs and patronage.

CARL SKUTSCH

See also Cameroon; Central Africa: History and Economic Development; Central Africa: International Relations; Central African Republic; Chad; Congo, Democratic Republic of; Congo, Republic of; Gabon

References and Further Reading

Berkley, Bill. *The Graves Are Not Yet Full: Race, Tribe, and Power in the Heart of Africa.* New York: Basic Books, 2003.
Edgerton, Robert. *The Troubled Heart of Africa: A History of the Congo.* New York: St. Martin's Press, 2002.
French, Howard. *A Continent for the Taking: The Tragedy and Hope of Africa.* New York: Knopf. 2004.

ETHNIC CONFLICTS: CENTRAL AND EASTERN EUROPE

Ethnic conflict is an international experience. The elimination of colonial powers, the dissolution of strong central governments, and a multiplicity of other factors have all contributed to tensions and outright conflicts between ethnic groups. Gurr and Harff, in their book *Ethnic Conflict in World Politics*, describe a typology of ethnic conflict that includes ethnonationalists who desire to establish or reestablish their own state, indigenous peoples who wish to preserve their traditional culture and environment, communal contenders interested in sharing political power among competing ethnic groups, and ethnoclasses who want equal rights and opportunities to make up for past discrimination. In and around these five groups are religious minorities who define themselves in terms of their religious beliefs.

There are many reasons for the initiation or increase of ethnic conflict in a region. These involve actions and behaviors that include persisting cleavages between ethnic groups, the uneven treatment by elites of different ethnic groups within society, a history of elite reliance on suppression as a means of maintaining power, sudden political upheaval, and the targeting of a minority group as expendable or as the cause of recent upheaval or economic problems. In Central Europe the primary reasons for the current ethnic conflict are the historical persistence of ethnic cleavages and sudden political and economic upheaval.

Most of the ethnic groups within Central Europe fall in the communal contenders category, with some in the ethnonationalist category. The sudden collapse of the Soviet Union and its satellite communist systems overturned what were relatively stable social and political hierarchies. The dissolution of the imposed stability of the Soviet system provided an opening for various groups to begin asserting their rights as political and economic constituencies. Different ethnic groups found themselves in competition with each other for scarce economic and political resources. All of these groups are competing for a share of political power within their respective states. Most do not want to secede and form separate states but would rather share power with the current majority group. The multiplicity of ethnic groups in Central Europe includes Russians in the Baltics, Hungarians in Romania, Romanians in Hungary, Germans in the Czech Republic, Muslims in Bosnia, Roma (gypsies) in Hungary, Romania, and the Czech Republic, Poles in Lithuania, Germans in Poland, Turks in Bulgaria, and Jews in all states.

Ethnic conflict in Central Europe is not a new phenomenon. Central European history is replete with attempts by different groups to assert their control over other groups through language suppression, religious suppression, and/or legal discrimination against various ethnic and religious groups in society. European history in general is rife with wars started and fought on the grounds of ethnic superiority. The

post-1989 period of transition and democratic consolidation in Central Europe has often been compared to the post–World War I era. At the end of World War I, many states seized the opportunity to declare their independence from previous empires and dominant states. Free from the forced integration of the Austro-Hungarian empire, the Hohenzollern empire, and Russian domination, the political parties in the newly independent states emphasized the uniqueness of their language, culture, and nation. The concurrent rise in nationalism has been credited with the subsequent downfall of those independent states as they were unable to come together to resist Nazi and Russian aggression. At the end of the Cold War, these same states experienced a similar rise in nationalism and a similar birth of political parties with the same message of nationalism, and in some cases outright xenophobia.

1945–1989

Ethnicity was a dominant force in the rise of communism in Central Europe. It has been suggested that numerically weak groups with traditional or ethnic ties to Russia found a great deal of appeal in the communist ideology, while those groups with no ties to Russia, despite their numerical weakness, were less attracted to communism. Despite the egregious example of nationalism run amok found in Nazism, other groups had taken advantage of the chaos of war to attempt to create states based on single nationalities or ethnicities. Eastern European communists pointed to the Soviet claim that the USSR had successfully overcome ethnic divisions with the imposition of a communist political system. The implication was clear; Eastern Europe could solve its ethnic dilemmas if communism was embraced.

At the end of World War II, international borders were recreated according to the occupation zones of the Allied forces. This resulted in eastern parts of Germany being handed back to Poland, while western areas of Poland were given to the Soviet Union; these actions stranded many people in what was considered a foreign country. Cultural Germans found themselves in Poland and Poles found themselves now considered to be Russian in citizenship if not in culture. In addition, a large German minority became a part of Czechoslovakia, and parts of Romania became Hungarian. Over all of this were the difficulties faced by the small remaining Jewish population and the Roma (gypsy) population.

It is true that during the communist period, there was very little overt ethnic conflict in Central Europe.

This was less because all groups had embraced the ideology, and more because the communist governments moved to stamp out all forms of independent expression and non–state sponsored institutions. This resulted in the atomization of society to such a degree it appeared that all ethnic conflict in the region had finally been eliminated. The imposition of Soviet control over the Baltics resulted in a Russian suppression of Baltic cultures and languages. The official language in all three Baltic States was Russian; Estonian, Latvian, and Lithuanian were not taught in schools and were not utilized outside of private life. In the Balkans, Tito managed to suppress ages-old ethnic conflict by the simple expedient of using the Yugoslav army to crack down on any overt ethnic conflicts.

Soviet takeover of the Baltics led to the forced migration of thousands of Russians into the Baltics and the beginning of a program of Russification of the Baltic nationalities. As sovereign states within the Soviet sphere of influence, the other Central European states were not subject to this type of forced cultural assimilation, although many forms of cultural expression were illegal under communist control. Communism operated on the premise that national aspirations were to be secondary to the international interests of the proletarian state. Ethnic and national disputes within the Soviet bloc were not resolved but rather suppressed.

Jews Under Communism

The imposition of communism and its ideology of atheism caused a great deal of trouble for what remained of the region's Jewish population. From over 5.5 million people, the Jewish population of Central Europe had been reduced to about 150,000. Those that did not emigrate to Israel or other western states found themselves caught between official party pressure to renounce Judaism and local anti-Semitism that blocked efforts to assimilate into the new communist society. Unlike the Soviet Union, the governments of the satellite states did not implement the practice of registering Jews as a separate nationality. Jews were free to define themselves as Czechs, Poles, etc.; however, any attempts to train children in language or culture immediately denied them entry to schools or party organizations. All of these state actions were compounded by the trauma of surviving the Holocaust and attempts to rebuild their lives.

Until 1950–1951, hundreds of thousands of Jews were allowed to leave the region, and did so, moving to Israel and the United States, but many preferred to remain. Romania was left with a large Jewish population that did not wish to emigrate, nor did it wish to assimilate. In Hungary, many Jews embraced communist ideology or were deeply attached to the country and the culture. Those few Jews that remained in Poland were deeply committed to renouncing their heritage or were bent on establishing what Charles Hoffman terms a "Jewish Communist" culture based on Yiddish. In Bulgaria, a majority of Jews who survived the war departed en masse for Israel leaving behind only those who were committed to creating a "Jewish Communist" culture in that country.

1989–present

The communist system had ignored ethnic differences in its quest to create the socialist citizen. The disintegration of the communist political system in 1989 left a political and ideological vacuum in Central Europe. The increased economic and political uncertainty led people to come together over what they did have in common, their ethnic identity. The sudden ability of nationalist ethnic groups (i.e., Lithuanians, Latvians, or Estonians) to define for themselves their state and its legal framework led to the Baltic opposite of the old Soviet Russification program. Ethnic Russians were denied citizenship in the newly independent states; language requirements were implemented for some jobs, etc. In Central Europe, minority ethnic groups began agitating for collective rights for their particular groups. Hungarians in Romania looked to the Hungarian government to press their case with the Romanian government while Romanians in Hungary pursued the same path with respect to their position.

It was expected that with the transition from communism to democracy, the old problems of nationalism and ethnicity could be controlled or avoided through rapid transitional political and economic reform programs. Once the lid of communist control was lifted, however, a rash of apparently long-simmering ethnic conflicts surfaced. Perhaps the most obvious conflict arose in Yugoslavia, with Serbian aggression into Bosnia-Herzegovina and the accompanying campaign of "ethnic cleansing" carried out in the name of regional stability. A large proportion of the population of Bosnia-Herzegovina is Muslim, a legacy of the domination of the Ottoman Empire, and the Yugoslav conflict had both ethnic and religious overtones.

By 1992 Czechoslovakia had undergone the "velvet divorce," which was partly justified by the ethnic and national differences between Czechs and Slovaks. In Poland, a resurgence of anti-Semitism has been particularly troubling, and there have been incidences of violence against the Roma, or gypsies, in all of the Central European countries. In addition, the Yugoslav conflicts have contributed to a rising number of refugees from the Balkans adding to the difficulties of controlling ethnic tensions. Finally, there have been tensions between Hungary and many of its neighbors over Hungarian minorities in Slovakia, Transylvania (Romania), Ukraine, and Vojvodina (Serbia).

The issue of Hungarian communities outside of Hungary has been one of the more problematic challenges facing Central Europe. The largest concentrations of Hungarians outside of Hungary reside in Transylvania, southern Slovakia, and Vojvodina. These clusters of Hungarians are a legacy of the collapse of the Austro-Hungarian Empire at the end of World War I. The 1920 Trianon Peace Treaty, by redrawing international boundaries, made one-third of the Hungarian population citizens of other countries. Almost immediately these minority groups became engaged in what would turn out to be a decades-long struggle to achieve educational and cultural rights in their new countries. With the end of the Cold War the Hungarian government began drawing the world's attention to these communities and began campaigns to formalize their rights within the CSCE and through bilateral agreements with the respective countries.

Throughout Central Europe tensions between majority groups and the Roma minority only recently became an item on the states' agendas. As a condition of their admission in 2004 to the European Union, the Central European states created and implemented policies designed to protect the rights of Roma citizens. The Roma have long been the target of ethnic violence and often legalized discrimination in jobs and housing.

The Holocaust and the questions of remaining anti-Semitism have troubled Central Europe for a long time. Increased anti-Semitism in the wake of the collapse of communism has raised the specter of a renewal of increased tensions in the region. Some states, like Poland, are experiencing very little public anti-Semitism primarily because the Polish Jewish population was among the hardest hit by the Holocaust.

Membership in the European Union, achieved in 2004, sped up the passage and implementation of anti-discrimination legislation in the Central European states. The argument has been made that the stability of the new democracies is jeopardized by continued ethnic conflict. However, despite gloomy predictions of a return to the extreme nationalism and ethnic conflicts that characterized the period between World Wars I and II, Central Europe appears to be finding solutions to old and new sources of ethnic conflict.

REBECCA R. JONES

See also Central and Eastern Europe: History and Economic Development; Central and Eastern Europe: International Relations

References and Further Reading

Bugajski, Janusz. *Nations in Turmoil: Conflict and Cooperation in Eastern Europe.* Boulder, CO: Westview Press, 1993.
Cordell, Karl, ed. *Ethnicity and Democratisation in the New Europe.* London; New York: Routledge, 1999.
East European Politics and Societies, various issues.
Griffiths, Stephen Iwan. *Nationalism and Ethnic conflict: Threats to European Security.* Oxford: Oxford University Press, 1993.
Gurr, Ted Robert, and Barbara Harff. *Ethnic Conflict in World Politics.* Boulder, CO: Westview Press, 1994.
Hoffman, Charles. *Gray Dawn: The Jews of Eastern Europe in the Post-Communist Era.* New York: HarperCollins Publishers, 1992.
Horowitz, Donald L. *Ethnic Groups in Conflict.* Berkeley, CA: University of California Press, 1985.
Mandelbaum, Michael, ed. *The New European Diasporas: National Minorities and Conflicts in East Europe.* New York: Council on Foreign Relations Press, 2000.
Ramet, Sabrina P. *Whose democracy? Nationalism, Religion, and the Doctrine of Collective Rights in Post-1989 Eastern Europe.* New York: Rowman & Littlefield Publishers, Inc, 1997.

ETHNIC CONFLICTS: CENTRAL ASIA

Central Asia has long been a kaleidoscope of many religions, ethnicities, and national groups. As a result, national identification and ethnic boundaries among the people of Central Asia have always been fluid and manipulated by the state. In fact, one of the most salient features of contemporary Central Asia has been the expansion of the role of the state as an independent variable in shaping the balance of societal forces, including managing competing political, social, and economic claims of ethnic and nationality groups. Many Central Asian countries, which until recently had exercised at best spasmodic control over their own people, have now expanded the reach of the state in order to impose, *inter alia*, a rigid definition of their own "pure" national identities. At the same time, the range of governmental interference has expanded beyond the concern with raising revenues and maintaining order.

Furthermore, the challenge of globalization has accelerated the need to incorporate an ever-increasing number of citizenry, irrespective of one's ethnicity, into the labor pool. One unintended consequence of globalization in Central Asia has been the rise of socioeconomic demands for ethnic equality and fairness. This, in part, has led to ethnic conflicts among sub-national groups and between the state and various nationalities in almost every country in Central Asia. However, we need to be cautious about overgeneralizing the dangers of ethnic conflicts and chaos in the post–Cold War Central Asia. Complicating the matter is the issue of overlapping identities which, for the most part, reflects the Soviet influence in the region. The Soviet Union traditionally promoted ethnic rivalries and even fostered primordial identities among Central Asia's diverse ethnic groups to advance Moscow's domestic and foreign policy objectives.

We can appreciate the complexities of the current inter- and intra-ethnic conflicts in Central Asia by analyzing some concrete examples. Today, almost 45% of the population of Tajikistan is under the age of fifteen and over 75% of the country's total population lives in rural areas. Since most European-descended residents of Tajikistan live in urban areas, buttressed by large numbers of Uzbek and Kyrgyz urban dwellers, the proportion of native Tajiks residing in rural areas exceeds 80%. According to the 1989 census, some 918,000 Tajiks lived in neighboring Uzbekistan and 72,000 resided in neighboring Kyrgyzstan. This fact alone has created a fluid cultural boundary between Tajiks, Uzbeks, and Kyrgyzs.

Furthermore, Tajikistan may be divided into five distinct regions in terms of socioeconomic development, topography, and to some extent, culture, religion, language, and ethnicity. The regional differences and loyalties have played a decisive role in political strife and regional turmoil in which the country has been involved. The most distinct region, the Gorno-Badakhshan Autonomous Oblast located in southeast Tajikistan in the Pamir mountain range, is, in many ways, the least developed area. Its inhabitants regard themselves as Pamirs, not Tajiks. They speak six languages or dialects belonging to the eastern Iranian linguistic family as distinct from the western Iranian variety spoken by most Tajiks. Unlike the Sunni Tajiks, the Pamirs generally belong to the Ismaili branch of Shia Islam.

The second region, the Leninabad or Khojand district, is the most developed area of Tajikistan and contains a significant Uzbek community. The Dushanbe region and its western Hissar area, the third geographic subdivision, are relatively developed and also contain some Uzbek people. The fourth part, the Garm valley northeast of Dushanbe, is mountainous and agricultural. Religiously, it is the most traditional part of Tajikistan and one of the most conservative areas in Central Asia. The southern oblasts of Kulab and Kurgan-Teppe, now joined in the Khalton Oblast (the fifth region), are also traditionalists.

Given their configuration, Tajik ethnicity is not well defined. In recent years, some Western and Russian scholars have sought to construct a Tajik identity based on a combination of language and religion. According to this concept, a Tajik is any Sunni Muslim Persian speaker. This definition helps to distinguish Iran's predominantly Shia inhabitants from their Persian-speaking counterparts in Tajikistan, but it fails to pose a clear and cohesive definition of Tajik ethnic identity. Some 8 million people in Afghanistan fit this definition of Tajik identity but have shown little inclination to identify with their brethren to the north politically. Generally, the difficulty of establishing a Tajik identity is the principal obstacle to developing a strong sense of Tajik nationalism among Tajikistan's population. In many respects, this also explains the persistence of a strong regional loyalty that has bedeviled the nation-building process in post-Soviet Tajikistan and elsewhere in Central Asia.

In some respects, many groups in today's Central Asia are victims of Stalin's nationality policy that sought to create distinct ethnic groups based on a presumed common history, language, and territory. Stalin's nationality policy was designed to restructure age-old complex identities that had been formed in Central Asia in order to allow the state to manage conflict between Russian and non-Russian nationalities. Stalin ignored the fact that Central Asia was a multiethnic region with shared overlapping ethnic identities and common Turkic and Persian cultures, especially in literary, academic, and administrative domains. The vast majority of Central Asian people lacked a territorially-based national or ethnic identity. Stalin's policy of artificially creating this type of attachment failed in Tajikistan, partly because he deliberately excluded important parts of Persian-speaking and Tajik-inhabited areas from the Tajik Soviet Socialist Republic. Two important centers of Persian culture, the cities of Samarkand and Bukara, emerged as parts of Uzbekistan. The isolated capital city of Dushanbe, once the site of a small market, had little attraction for Tajik intellectuals whose absence severely hampered the subsequent development of Tajikistan and contributed to the Tajik-Uzbek tension for years to come.

On the other hand, Uzbeks constitute over 23% of Tajikistan's total population. Owing to a long history of miscegenation, many families have Tajik and Uzbek identities. It is common for some members of a nuclear family to identify themselves as Tajiks and others as Uzbeks. This partly explains the sensitivities of Uzbekistan to political developments in Tajikistan, and why the Uzbek government has sought to create a friendly protectorate in Tajikistan. We see the same pattern of shifting identities in other places in Central Asia. In Kazakhstan, for example, the large Russian minority has intermingled with the local Kazakhs for decades leading to the creation of a dual Russian-Kazakh ethnicity. Of all the Central Asian countries, Uzbekistan has been the most active practitioner of using its ethnic brethrens to advance its influence in other parts of the region. In the case of Kyrgyzstan, the government has provided incentives to its Russian-origin population to reverse their out-migration in order to balance the influence of Uzbek's population in the country.

Islam, especially political Islam, has also been a major source of ethnic conflict in Central Asia. Most Central Asians are Sunni Muslims with varying degrees of religiosity. Prior to the Bolshevik Revolution of 1917, more than twenty-five thousand mosques functioned in Central Asia. Beginning in 1928, the Soviet government destroyed the overwhelming majority of these mosques. World War II temporarily halted the Soviet destruction of mosques and other houses of worship. In fact, during the War, some mosques were allowed to reopen as Stalin sought to appease the Muslims of Central Asia. From 1959 to 1964, Stalin's successor, Nikita Khrushchev, launched the second major concerted assault against Islam in Soviet Central Asia. Despite its brief duration, this period left more devastation than the earlier attacks, as nearly all village mosques throughout the Soviet Union were eliminated. Beginning in 1978, a new rapprochement between the Soviet government and Islam resulted in new mosques being built and a certain revival of Islam permitted in Central Asia. Mikhail Gorbachev's accession meant the onset of glasnost, and religious revival as a form of the reassertion of cultural and ethnic identity received a new boost. Throughout these periods, Islam and Islamic identity remained vivid in Central Asia, especially in rural areas.

The vitality of Islam and its persistence as a part of people's identity in Central Asia was partly traceable to the existence of a "parallel" or "nonofficial Islam" in the region. In 1941, the Soviet Union installed an "official clergy" to control the religious activities of its Muslims and to formally recognize their spiritual needs. The disintegration of the Soviet Union led to the demise of the official religious hierarchy and institutions, and many of the Soviet era Muslim religious officials lost their authority. However, some members of the official clergy were able to reassert their authority and reinvent themselves as champions of their national or ethnic communities. For example,

Haji Akbar Turojonzade, the young *Qazi Kalan*, or Grand Qazi, in Dushanbe at the time of Gorbachev's *glasnost*, revived his source of authority independent of the state apparatus, and became one of the influential religious personages in Tajikistan. Turojonzade later emerged as an important member of the political opposition and led the United Tajik Opposition delegation in its negotiations with the government of Tajikistan from 1994 to 1997. Shortly after returning to Dushanbe in February 1998, Turojonzade joined the government as first vice prime minister in charge of Tajikistan's cooperation with the Commonwealth of Independent States, the loosely organized entity that binds the former union republics of the Soviet Union. Tajikistan represents a good example of how political Islam has served as a vehicle for ethnic conflict management by providing the country's diverse groups an inclusive umbrella to resolve their differences. Uzbekistan, on the contrary, has instituted an iron fist policy against the country's religious elements and has suppressed dissent. Thus, political Islam in Uzbekistan has been forced to operate underground and has become radicalized to the detriment of inter-ethnic harmony in the region.

Perhaps the unintended consequence of combating political Islam in Central Asia has been the revival of seemingly nonpolitical Islam in the region. A good example of this development is the popularity of the various Sufi mystical brotherhoods throughout contemporary Central Asia. Two Sufi *tariqa* (brotherhoods)—the Naqshbandi and Qadiri orders—dominated Soviet Islam in Central Asia and the Caucasus. The former was founded in Bukhara in the fourteenth century, while the latter was a twelfth century Baghdad-based order but became important in the Caucasus after the nineteenth century. The Naqshbandi *tariqa* had a long tradition of opposition to Soviet control, and the Sufi masters, or *murshids*, were highly revered by their followers and the general populace. Although these "parallel" Islamic movements are now generally apolitical and socially conservative, they nevertheless have a potential of developing into opponents of Central Asian governments, especially the most repressive ones. Also, since the base of support of these movements is regional, rather than being focused in one country, they can serve as a lightning rod for ethnically based political movements throughout Central Asia.

In general, Central Asia has fared better than many other parts of the so-called Soviet bloc in managing its ethnic conflicts. Notwithstanding its ethnic diversity, its regional rivalries, and its relative underdevelopment, various nationalities, and ethnic communities in the region have coexisted peacefully for the most part. This is largely due to the region's common history, its tradition of accepting outsiders and outside influences, and accommodating them to their own unique circumstances.

NADER ENTESSAR

See also Afghanistan; Bangladesh; Bhutan; Central Asia: History and Economic Development; Central Asia: International Relations; Ethnic Conflicts: Commonwealth of Independent States; India; Iran; Kashmir Dispute; Maldives; Nepal; Pakistan; Sri Lanka; Sufism

References and Further Reading

Ahmed, Akbar S. *Pakistan Society: Islam, Ethnicity and Leadership in South Asia.* Oxford; New York: Oxford University Press, 1986.

Ali Banuazizi and Myron Weiner, eds. *The State, Religion, and Ethnic Politics: Afghanistan, Iran, and Pakistan.* Syracuse, NY: Syracuse University Press, 1986.

Beeman, William O. *Language, Status, and Power in Iran.* Bloomington, IN: Indiana University Press, 1986.

Cartlidge, Cherese. *The Central Asian States.* San Diego, CA: Lucent Books, 2001.

Daniel, Elton L. *The History of Iran.* Westport, CT: Greenwood Press, 2001.

Ewans, Martin, Sir. *Afghanistan: A Short History of its People and Politics.* New York: HarperCollins, 2002.

Goodson, Larry P. *Afghanistan's Endless War: State Failure, Regional Politics, and the Rise of the Taliban.* Seattle: University of Washington Press, 2001.

Jaffrelot, Christophe, ed.; translated by Gillian Beaumont. *A History of Pakistan and its Origins.* London, Anthem: 2004.

Manz, Beatrice, editor. *Central Asia in Historical Perspective.* Boulder, CO: Westview Press, 1994.

McGowan, William. *Only Man is Vile: the Tragedy of Sri Lanka.* New York: Farrar Strauss Giroux, 1992.

Pfaff-Czarnecka, Joanna, et al. *Ethnic Futures: the State and Identity Politics in Asia.* New Delhi; Thousand Oaks, CA: Sage Publications, 1999.

Soucek, Svat, *A History of Inner Asia.* Cambridge, England: Cambridge University Press, 2000.

Talbot, Ian, and Gurharpal Singh. *Region and Partition: Bengal, Punjab and the Partition of the Subcontinent.* Oxford; New York: Oxford University Press, 1999.

Vanaik, Achin. *The Furies of Indian Communalism: Religion, Modernity, and Secularization.* New York: Verso, 1997.

ETHNIC CONFLICTS: COMMONWEALTH OF INDEPENDENT STATES

Stalin's celebrated formula—nationalist in form, socialist in content—seemed to many of his followers (as well as to some who were not) a brilliantly successful solution to the problems posed by nationalities in conflict. In the USSR, Soviet identity came to take precedence over any other. This seemed true to such a seamless degree that when Mikhail Gorbachev (1985–1991) initiated Perestroika he was genuinely taken aback by the irruption of nationalism which took place on home ground as well as in Eastern Europe. The evolution of socialist society had made such manifestations redundant, or so it was thought. Even more unexpected was the emergence of interethnic hatred, a phenomenon last witnessed during the Second World War.

To Gorbachev's astonishment it reappeared in February 1988. This is when the Armenians in High Karabakh (a mountainous enclave of less than two hundred thousand people inside Azerbaijan) declared its borders (drawn up artificially under Stalin) as invalid. Their intent to make the territory a part of Armenia was greeted by a fury of killings by both Azeris and Armenians, which began in the industrial town of Sumgait near the Caspian Sea. In the next two years, the bloodshed turned into something between an insurgency and war. Azerbaijan refused to surrender High Karabakh, and turned against Moscow too when Soviet troops fired on nationalist crowds in Baku early in 1990. Moscow was thought to favor the Armenians because they were fellow-Christians: Armenians for their part tended to believe that Moscow surreptitiously supported the Azeris because of their oil.

Georgians, although Orthodox Christian too, were also tempted to remember ancient wrongs, particularly the way in which the Red Army at Stalin's urging stamped out their independence at the end of the Civil War in 1921. In April 1989, strikes and demonstrations in Tbilisi, the Georgian capital, called for a return to the country's independent status and were promptly broken up with shovels wielded lethally by the security forces. More than a dozen Georgians were killed, their bodies being laid out on the capital's main street and covered solemnly with flowers.

In the same year, there were riots in Central Asia, when Uzbek gangs assaulted and killed Meshketian Turks of Georgia, who had been deported to Uzbekistan in 1944, the year in which Stalin had several nationalities in the Caucasus rounded up by Beria and Abakumov. In 1990, a massacre of Uzbeks by Kirgiz occurred in and near Osh, the second city of Kirgizia; but the Russia Federation's most serious locus of ethnic strife turned out to be Chechnya.

The First Chechen War

The tiny Autonomous Republic of Chechnya-Ingushetia was formed in 1934, and by the 1990s had a population of about nine hundred thousand indigenous people as well as about three hundred thousand Slavs, most of them Russians. Chechens could not forget or forgive the treatment they received at the hands of the NKVD (Soviet Secret Police) at the end of the Second World War. Accused of collaborating with the German occupying forces, male Chechens were dispatched in freight wagons to eastern islets of the Gulag Archipelago, where their courageous conduct in standing up to the brutality and indignities of the camp guards was praised by Alexander Solzhenitsyn in his famous book.

The moment for revenge dawned under the charismatic leadership of General Jokhar Dudaev (1949–1991), a Chechen who served in the Soviet strategic Air Command. While stationed in Estonia, Dudaev came to admire the Estonian struggle for independence, and in 1991–1992 he declared separation from the new Russia of Boris Yeltsin (1991–1999) as well as from Ingushetia. Dudaev's nationalism did not take the Baltic form. The street names in downtown Grozny, the Chechen capital, retained their Cyrillic nomenclature, but Dudaev did assert his new-found Islamic identity. So did most of his comrades who had previously been considered Soviet and therefore free of religious contagion.

Yeltsin for his part (when he ousted Gorbachev from power at the end of December 1991) had allowed the union republics to fall away from the USSR, inviting them in a generous moment, to help themselves to sovereignty. The Commonwealth of Independent States that replaced the Soviet Union was seen as a free association of ex-Soviet republics with few spelled out commitments; but Yeltsin's view of the Russian Federation over which he presided was very different. The 1992 Federation Treaty (which Chechnya and Tatarstan did not sign) bound together eighty-nine territorial units. Of these fifty-seven were largely Russian provinces and other units and thirty-two autonomous republics and regions.

Given this complex patchwork, Yeltsin feared an unraveling effect on the so-called autonomous republics within the Federation if he allowed Chechnya to secede. He sent in airborne units to quell separatism; and when this did not work, he tried negotiation and other tactics. In December 1994, the distrust and mutual provocations turned into the First Chechen War.

Forty thousand troops entered Chechnya through Ingushetia, and the bombing and battering received by the towns and villages reminded television viewers of the horrors of the Second World War. Although the capital was captured in January 1995, the "uprising" could not be crushed. Chechens fought a guerrilla war they believed in on familiar terrain. Russian troops, on the other hand, were largely conscripts whose conventional tactics and poor pay and training resulted in the loss of some eighty thousand to one hundred thousand lives. This is four times the number of losses the USSR sustained in the Afghan war. What made the Chechen war even more bitter was the fact that the massacres and atrocities were not confined to Chechnya itself. In 1995 Chechens kidnapped about one hundred hostages in the south Russian town of Budennovsk. A Chechen raid on Russian-held Kizlyar followed this in 1996.

In light of all these reverses and casualties it is not surprising that the Duma passed a no-confidence motion on Yeltsin, and even officers who had earlier supported the war joined the anti-war chorus. On the Chechen side the greatest loss was the death of General Dudaev in April 1996, when a Russian missile homed in on his cell phone. In August General Alexander Lebed (who had supported Yeltsin during the attempted Communist coup three years earlier) was dramatically sent off to Chechnya to work out a peace treaty with Dudaev's feuding successors. It was finally agreed to postpone the insoluble issue of Chechen independence for another five years. But the legacy of hatred and suspicion failed to fade away, being kept alive in Moscow by the presence of Chechen crime gangs. In 1999, the war broke out anew, this time under the aegis of a young president in whose favor Boris Yeltsin had resigned at the end of that year.

The Second Chechen War

The second Chechen war began in September, and it seemed at first to boost President Vladimir Putin's popularity. After an eight-week siege, Russian Federation forces were able to occupy the Chechen capital again, but in the process Grozny was largely destroyed. Among the casualties were the city's remaining Russian-speaking inhabitants who, unlike the Chechens, were unable to escape to the hills. Their timely evacuation was not—or could not be—considered. Putin's prosecution of the war (which he was told by his advisers would quickly end) had substantial backing. At the beginning of the year 2000, close to a quarter of the public supported it. But in the following year this slipped to 7%.

What seemed like a victorious war, won by impressive conventional onslaughts with artillery, tanks, and air power, soon came to remind the public of Afghanistan. There too a conventional Soviet war had turned into an insurgency which the Red Army was not trained to fight. President Putin's refusal to abandon Chechnya, however, is not difficult to explain since it reflected Yeltsin's earlier fear of the "Yugoslavization" of Russia. With the flame of Moslem fundamentalism ignited in the Caucasus, it could catch fire on the Volga and pass on to Tatarstan, the worst-case scenario being the fragmentation of the Russian Federation into independent and belligerent republics of which Chechnya would be the first.

Chechnya and September 11, 2001

Putin was convinced that the bombing of Moscow apartment houses in 1999 was carried out by Chechen terrorists (and not, as some Muscovites believed, by Russian security forces, doing their utmost to justify a new war). These convictions of Putin's were instrumental in shaping his attitude to the events of September 11, 2001. The Russian president was the first foreign leader to call President George W. Bush to express his sympathy and condolences. On September 22, he went further still by meeting the leaders of his armed forces on the Black Sea, where he won their support for America's war on terrorism. At Putin's behest Russian air space was opened to US airplanes in prosecuting that war, and he used Russian influence in the Central Asian republics to permit American use of the Russian Federation's facilities in pursuit of American anti-terrorist aims in Afghanistan.

As a result of all this, the Chechen war came to be seen in a different light in the United States. Putin had all along claimed that the Chechen conflict was inspired not by a quasi-legitimate national movement for independence (as most Europeans believed) but by traditional banditry and barbarism, sustained by Islamic fundamentalism and terrorism.

The US government, given its own experiences in the second war with Saddam Hussein's Iraq, came to be far more sympathetic to this view, as a result of which American media coverage of the conflict in the Caucasus (for the most part unfavorable to Moscow) changed. In fact, atrocities continued to be committed on both sides.

Nor did international organizations cease their criticism of Russian military and security forces for their human rights violations. Hostage taking, abductions, torture, executions of both civilians and military or quasi-military personnel as well as of journalists, and looting became regular features of the conflict, marked too by the daily disappearance of Chechens suspected by Russian officers of working with the terrorists. The election in October 2003 of Ahmed Kadyrov as Chechen president, who enjoyed Putin's backing and formed his own militia to protect his supporters, did little to put a stop to this violence. Indeed, half a year later Kadyrov was assassinated in a bomb attack which demonstrated again that despite the detention camps and massive Russian outlays in munitions and armaments, not only was Chechnya ungovernable, but the insurgency had developed ties with Islamic terrorism which could not be controlled.

Some such realization first dawned on Muscovites in 2000 and 2001 when bombs were set off in a subway station and then in a pedestrian tunnel, killing eight people and injuring twenty. Then, in October 2002, at a Moscow theater staging a popular musical, a large group of Chechen men was joined by "black widows"—a female contingent who had come to avenge their missing relatives. The entire audience was taken hostage.

The Chechens promised to start killing their hostages at the end of three days. To prevent this, special forces surprised both the Chechens and the hostages by pumping a gas into the auditorium. This certainly disabled the Chechens, some of whom were finished off by commandos in gas masks who stormed the theatre. But due to the effects of the gas—the name of which was kept secret from the medical personnel called in to help—many more hostages died than Chechens, i.e., more than a hundred.

The horrors continued. In July 2003, also in Moscow, two "black widows" blew up seventeen young people at a rock concert (as well as themselves). At the end of the year, another "black widow" blew herself up in front of the National Hotel, which faces the Kremlin. Five other people were killed. In February 2004, there was a suicide bombing inside a crowded subway car. Some forty people were killed and more than a hundred injured.

The most savage killing occurred not far from Chechnya's borders in September 2004, at an Ossetian school in Beslan. With the help of an Ingush carpenter who had helped hide explosives inside the school during the summer, Chechen terrorists blew up the school gymnasium in response (so it was claimed) to an emotional incursion by fathers trying to save their sons and daughters. Of the more than three hundred and fifty people who died, more than half were children. Millions witnessed this particular horror. Television cameramen were at the scene from almost the beginning of the gruesome crisis.

Yet despite the atrocities of the Chechen conflict, the breakup of the Soviet Union, which resulted in the appearance of fifteen independent states, was surprisingly peaceful. The inter-republic wars many had predicted did not occur. Nor is it likely that Ukraine's Orange Revolution of January 2005 will bring that prospect closer. The Chechen wars, the roots of which can be traced to tsarist colonial expansion in the nineteenth century, represent a struggle within the Russian Federation itself rather than one between the Federation and another newly created republic. It is also worth noting that Russian troops—except in the case of Chechnya—have not played a major role in any of the ethnic conflicts previously described. In the fighting between Armenia and Azerbaijan over Nagorno-Karabakh Gorbachev tried to be fair to both sides. Nor is the more recent (and successful) rebellion of the Abhazians against Georgia one in which the presence of Russian troops decided the outcome. Russian interventions have been marginal and are in the future more likely to be economic in nature, rather than military (as in the Chechen case).

VALENTIN BOSS

See also Armenia; Azerbaijan; Belarus; Commonwealth of Independent States: History and Economic Development; Commonwealth of Independent States: International Relations; Georgia; Kazakhstan; Kyrgyzstan; Moldova; Russia; Tajikistan; Turkmenistan; Ukraine; Uzbekistan

References and Further Reading

Dallin, Alexander. *German Rule in Russia, 1941–1945: A Study of Occupation Policies.* Boulder, CO, 1981.
Herspring, D.R., ed. *Putin's Russia: Past Imperfect, Future Uncertain.* New York, 2003.
Khazanov, A.M. *After the USSR: Ethnicity, Nationalism, and Politics in the Commonwealth of Independent States.* Madison, WI, 1995.
Lieven, A. *Chechnya: Tombstone of Russian Power.* New Haven, CT, 1998.
Pilkington, Hilary. *Migration, Displacement, and Identity in Post-Soviet Russia.* London, 1998.
Shaw, Denis. *Russia in the Modern World: A New Geography.* Oxford, U.K., 1999.
Shevtsova, L. *Putin's Russia.* Washington, D.C., 1999.
Shlapentokh, Vladimir; Munir Sendich; and Emil Payin, eds. *The New Russian Diaspora: Russian Minorities in the Former Soviet Republics.* Armonk, NY, 1994.
Suny, Ronald. *The Revenge of the Past: Nationalism, Revolution, and the Collapse of the Soviet Union.* Stanford, 1993.
Yeltsin, Boris. *Midnight Diaries.* New York, 2000.

ETHNIC CONFLICTS: EAST AFRICA

East Africa is usually considered the area between the Indian ocean and Central Africa, bordering with Somalia, Ethiopia, and Sudan on the north, Great Lakes in the west, and Mozambique, Malawi, and Zambia on the south. There we see a variety of languages, cultures, and historical experiences. Probably the only reliable criterion to detach the region is the spread of the Swahili (or Kiswahili—a form mixed with the Arab language) group of languages. Included within the linguistic rubric of Swahili is an entire diverse and heterogeneous region. Swahili is both the native tongue of a specific people—"the Swahili"—and a lingua franca spoken by more than 50 million people throughout the region. This language is one the few lingua francas among the more than one thousand languages spoken on the African continent, and therefore one of the most widely used. Countries that primarily make up the Swahili-speaking region are Kenya, Tanzania, Uganda, Rwanda, and Burundi. The Swahili-speaking area also extends into southern Somalia, eastern Democratic Republic of Congo, and parts of northern Mozambique as well as the Comoros Islands. Geographically, the region is prominent with its magnificent physical features—the two highest mountains in Africa, Mount Kilimanjaro and Mount Kenya, the biggest lake in Africa, Nyanza—also known as Lake Victoria—the source of the longest river in Africa—Nile. The region is also famous for its wildlife reserves, located at the Serengeti and Ngorongoro crater in Tanzania and Masai Mara in Kenya. Instability and clashes, however, not only reduces prospects for international tourism, but seriously endangers these natural treasures. Many anthropologists locate here one of the primary sources of the human civilization over 2 million years ago.

Pre-colonial East Africa has been politically important with the several large kingdoms dominating regional affairs. Two of them—the Kingdoms of Uganda, and of Rwanda—now constitute the core of the modern nation-states, respectively, of Uganda and Rwanda. The coastal regions' powerful city-states brokered trade between the interior and the Indian Ocean. Extensive trade networks penetrated the region and linked together various people, reaching deeply inside of Central Africa and eastward across ocean as far as India. At various times the esteemed trade items were gold, ivory, gems, slaves, salt, and foodstuffs, especially spices grown in Zanzibar. Swahili and Arabic-speaking merchants were interacting for at least one thousand years, and thus Islam was brought to the shores of East Africa. Politically, the region is known for its arrangements that generally prevented well known elsewhere in Africa military coups d'état and military regimes. Kenya and Tanzania created relatively stable polities that survived shakings following the departure of historical leaders such as Jomo Kenyatta and J. K. Nyerere. African socialism Ujamaa system created by Mwalimu Nyerere, the first president of Tanzania, avoided extremities and rigidity of the Soviet- and Maoist-based quasi communist regimes.

This region also became known for its hospitality to refugees and other politically deprived. It was known for its involvement in the fight against apartheid in South Africa and for providing refugee facilities for freedom fighters from Zimbabwe, South Africa, Mozambique, and Angola. More recently it has appreciated refugees from Rwanda, the Sudan, and Somalia.

In the same time East Africa was the stage of the one of largest-scale wars in the post-colonial Sub-Saharan Africa, that between Tanzania and Uganda. It was not spared of sparkling ethnic conflicts. Scarce and unequal access to natural resources and power, inadequate state structures, ethnic mistrust and ethnocentrism, border tensions and proliferation of illicit arms into the hands of tribal chiefs, warlords, and fellow tribesmen are among the causes of many other inter-ethnic conflicts in the region. Among the other, East Africa endured within less than a century change of several colonial powers—Belgian, British, German, as well as the Portuguese and Italian. As elsewhere in Africa, these colonial powers have settled borders between colonies—inherited later by the independent states there—without reference to the distribution of territory among local tribes and ethnicities. This left a potential for territorial disputes and clashes.

Cattle rustling and land clashes are the main, often underestimated, manifestation of conflicts in Kenya, Tanzania, and other countries in the region. In response to the cattle rustling menace that has ravaged the vast and rugged region, indigenous communities have elaborated and institutionalized mechanisms of resolving intra- and inter-community conflicts whether. The elders in the involved communities form a dominant component of these traditional mechanisms of conflict management. They command authority that makes them effective in maintaining peaceful relationships and community way of life. They control resources, marital relations, and networks that go beyond the clan boundaries, ethnic identity, and generations. The elders are believed to hold and control supernatural powers reinforced by belief in superstitions and witchcraft. This shapes basis of the legitimacy of traditional conflict resolution mechanisms amongst the pastoralists.

Such traditional structures are, however, considered as archaic, barbarian, and thus they lack a place in the modernity. As a result, governments fail to appreciate, collaborate, and complement the traditional methods of resolving conflicts. Instead, there should be enhanced collaboration and networking between the government and customary institutions of governance. Official authorities should recognize and support how customary courts enforce their

rulings. The elders should be trained in modern methods of arbitration and at minimum, traditional mechanisms of conflict management should be more sensitive to the universally accepted principles of human rights.

The regional problem of illicit arms that has scaled up the severity and frequency of cattle raids should be addressed by the governments in the region. These arms have also sneaked in the veiled aspect of commercialization of cattle raids in the region. Pastoralists are no longer raiding to replenish their stocks especially after periods of severe drought and animal diseases, but are increasingly raiding to enrich themselves by engaging in trade of stolen livestock. This aspect has overwhelmed traditional conflict resolution mechanisms and should be addressed.

This region already knows a relatively brief, but devastating war between Uganda and Tanzania in 1978–1979. During the eight years of his rule, Ugandan dictatorial president-for-life, Idi Amin, expelled all Asians, killed thousands of tribespeople and Christians, and excessively built up his army. As a result of defections and executions, by 1978 Amin's circle of close associates narrowed significantly. Hoping to divert attention from his internal troubles, in October 1978, Amin sent troops still loyal to him to invade Tanzanian territory. He accused his perennial enemy, Tanzanian President Julius K. Nyerere, of waging war against Uganda. President Nyerere reacted with sending an army, reinforced by Ugandan exiles who had fled their homeland to escape Amin's tyrannical rule, and united as the Uganda National Liberation Army (UNLA), across the border into Uganda. The Ugandan Army retreated steadily, expending much of its energy by looting along the way. Tanzania and the UNLA surrounded the Ugandan capital of Kampala, but were halted briefly by a three thousand-strong Libyan force that had come to fellow Muslim Amin's aid. Kampala was captured in April 1979, and Amin fled by air, first to Libya and later to a permanent exile at Jiddah, Saudi Arabia, leaving behind an impoverished Uganda and a brutalized people. The war cost Tanzania an estimated $1 million US dollars per day.

The bloodiest among ethnic conflicts in the region is the one between the Tutsi (known also as Batutsi or Vatutsi) and Hutu. Ethnic tension between the Hutu and Tutsi tribal groups has centuries old record. A pre-colonial feud between the Hutu and Tutsi was based principally on a basic contradiction between the agriculture and cattle-breeding, and social interchanges between the two groups remained uncongealed. The Hutu are generally shorter than the Tutsi, have darker skin and tend to be farmers, while the Tutsi are generally herdsmen. Both the German and Belgian colonial rulers favored the

Tutsis for positions of local power. This severely prompted processes of increasing ethnic distrust, anxiety, and hatred. The Hutu "revolt" of 1959 led to Rwandan independence in 1962, which, however, led to further divisions, ethnic segregation, and discrimination. Existing ethnic rifts were then exacerbated by such significant factors as the scarcity of land, the civil war, structural alignments, decline of the coffee prices at world markets, Rwanda's position as a landlocked country with limited prospects for economic diversification, and an implicated and hostile governmental regime. Ethnic rivalries in the mountains of East Africa have claimed the lives of millions of Africans. When Rwanda's and Burundi's Presidents Juvenal Habyarimana and Cyprien Ntaryamira died in a plane crash in the skies above Kigali on April 6, 1994, this triggered violence that had clutched the country for the past more than three years. Many experts in the region now believe a Hutu extremist shot down the plane. A French investigation points at the current President of Rwanda, Paul Kagame, as directly involved in the plot. Between April and August of 1994, this accumulated tension turned into one of the most terrible acts of genocide of the twentieth century. More than 1 million people, primarily Tutsi, were killed, and 2 million forced into exile. The roots of this tragedy are exceptionally complicated, involving environmental scarcity, overpopulation, poverty, victimization, and ineffective, corrupt governmental policies. However, the inherited burden of severe ethnic cleavage and animosity certainly played a meaningful role. Ethnic tensions in the region continue, though most Hutu and Tutsis had returned to their homes by 1997.

One of the most important questions that has been asked frequently since the resultant genocide is, "Could this tragedy have been prevented?" Most atrocities seem impossible to imagine until they actually happen. Nevertheless, there might be warning signals that should be acknowledged and acted upon in the interests of preventing the eruption of similar conflicts and tragedies in the future.

Renewed fighting in 2004–2005 among various groups in eastern Democratic Republic of Congo in areas close to the border with Uganda, has triggered new influx of refugees. Fighting in eastern Democratic Republic of Congo is cleaving open a bloody front in a long-standing ethnic conflict in Africa's Great Lakes region. The battle for Bukavu implicate politicised disputes over a national Congolese army formed under a peace deal to end one of Africa's worst ever wars. The renewed fighting is essentially an extension of the ethnic struggle between Hutus and Tutsis. This conflict covers already four neighbor states—Congo, Rwanda, Burundi, and Uganda. The bitterest

national enmity is between Congo and Rwanda's Tutsi-led government, which twice invaded its massive neighbor, in 1996 and 1998, accusing Congo of not doing enough to control Hutu militia known as Interahamwe who fled to eastern Congo's mountains and jungles after leading the 1994 genocide. Years of warfare polarized the two governments on opposite sides of the Great Lakes ethnic fault line, with both supporting proxy fighting forces in the conflict in eastern Congo, where local ethnic Tutsis are known as Banyamulenge.

Rwanda backed Congo's main rebel movement in a five-year war, leaving 3 million people dead, mainly from hunger and disease. Congolese President Joseph Kabila accused Rwanda of helping the renegades. Rwanda denied the accusation, but warned that it would "play its role in opposing genocide." This recent fighting in North Kivu between former rebels-turned-government soldiers and former Mayi-Mayi militias, integrated into the Congolese national army, proved once again that tension in the region continues. Analysts say mineral riches, which include gold and diamonds, are a major draw for containing forces in the war, complicating any conflict in the area.

An additional aspect that proves to be a menace for the region are crucial aspects of political change, ethnic conflict, and conflict regulation in the larger region around the Horn of Africa, with the interplay of ethno-regionalism, religious identity, and elite power politics in the context of growing international or global pressures (political, economic, and cultural) furnishes such concomitant factor. It comes with another source of refugees from war-torn areas in southern Sudan, Ethiopia, Somalia, arms smuggling, and armed gangs' proliferation. This complicates situation in Eastern Africa and puts under severe ordeal otherwise resource-poor capacity of the region to cope with challenges.

STEPHAN E. NIKOLOV

See also African Development Bank; African Monetary Fund (AfMF); Amin, Idi; Burundi; Congo, Democratic Republic of; Congo, Republic of the; East African Community; East Africa: History and Economic Development; East Africa: International Relations; Ethiopia; Ethnicity: Impact on Politics and Society; Kenya; Organization of African Unity (OAU); Rwanda; Sudan; Tanzania; Uganda

References and Further Reading

Cook, D., ed. *Origins of East Africa: A Makerere Anthology.* Heinemann, 1965.
Davidson, Basil. *A History of East and Central Africa: To the Late Nineteenth Century.* Doubleday, 1969.

Gulliver, Philip H., ed. *Tradition and Transition in East Africa: Studies of the Tribal Elements in the Modern Era.* Berkeley, CA: University of California Press, 1969.

Mair, Lucy P. *Primitive Government: A Study of Traditional Political Systems in Eastern Africa.* Bloomington, IN: Indiana University Press, 1978.

Middleton, John. *The World of the Swahili: An African Mercantile Civilization.* New Haven, CT: Yale University Press, 1992.

Mpangala, Gaudens P. *Ethnic Conflicts in the Region of the Great Lakes: Origins and Prospecta.* Tanzania, Institute of Kiswahili Research, 2000.

Obama, Barack, *Dreams from my Father: A Story of Race and Inheritance.* New York: Random House, 1995.

Ogot, B.A., ed. *Zamami: A Survey of East African History.* EAPH/Longman, 1974.

Pouwels, R. *Horn & Crescent, Cultural Change & Traditional Islam on the East African Coast.* Cambridge Univ. Pr., 1987.

Salih, M. A. Mohamed and Mohamed, ed. *Ethnicity and the State in Eastern Africa.* Nordic African Institute, 1998.

Spear, Thomas and Richard Waller, eds. *Being Maasai: Ethnicity and Identity in East Africa.* London: James Currey, 1993.

Trimingham, John S. *Islam in East Africa.* Claredon Press, 1964.

ETHNIC CONFLICTS: EAST ASIA

Historical Background

In terms of geopolitics, one of the most important developments in continental eastern Asia in recent centuries was the expansion of China at the expense of several other countries. During the last ethnically Chinese dynasty (the Ming, 1368–1644), China was confined to what we might call "China Proper," that is the ethnic Han (Chinese) areas. When the Manchus swept down from their homeland north of Korea and overran China Proper in 1644, they then kept marching until several other countries were incorporated into their empire. The Republic of China (founded in 1912) laid claim to most of the old Manchu-controlled territories. However, it was able to directly control few of the non-Han lands, and was forced to give up its claim to Mongolia Proper ("Outer Mongolia"), retaining only Inner Mongolia.

China Under Communism

The People's Republic of China (PRC, established in 1949) was able to realize control over virtually all of the territory that the old Republic had claimed, except Taiwan (where the Republic was perpetuated). The non-Han areas have been administered according to a variant version of Leninist ethnic principles. That is, the state is structured in such a way as to give these territories nominal autonomy, but the Chinese Communist Party (in which the real power usually resides) has been strictly centralized and dominated by Hans.

Altogether, on Mainland China there are fifty-four officially recognized minorities, with a population of over one hundred million people, occupying about 60% of the PRC. Sometimes, ethnic designations were created precisely to permit the Chinese to handle ethnic issues their way. Thus, China's largest ethnic minority, the Zhuang, is essentially an artificial construct. Some minorities have never been officially recognized. In a few cases, the Chinese have practiced divide-and-rule. Thus, for example, more than half of ethnographic Tibet was carved off and assigned to various Chinese provinces. Although the Chinese have been able to hold all of this together, the system they created has given rise to tremendous tensions.

Depending on the political winds, ethnic groups are usually granted some *cultural* autonomy. (There is no meaningful *political* autonomy, and self-determination is out of the question.) But even cultural autonomy has its limits. Many of the ethnic groups are deeply religious, which sets up an immediate contradiction with the atheistic Communist rulers. Although certain "patriotic" religious groups are officially permitted, members of the Communist Party are required to eschew religion. In the case of devoutly Buddhist Tibet, during the Cultural Revolution (1966–1976) Red Guards and others ran roughshod, destroying the vast majority of temples, and killing many people. Today the Tibetans comprise an occupied nation, with virtually everyone longing for the return of their exiled leader, the Dalai Lama.

Ten of China's ethnic groups adhere to Islam: Hui, Uyghur, Kazakh, Donxiang, Salar, Bonan, Kyrguz, Tajik, Uzbek, and Tatar. Aside from the issue of religion, the Hui are closest to the Chinese in language and culture. Most speak Chinese and are scattered around the PRC; they often live in harmony with the Hans. However, the Hui comprise a complex mosaic, and ethnic conflicts are not uncommon. For example, in 2004, in Henan Province fighting, sparked by a motor vehicle accident, broke out between Hans and Hui, the latter soon aided by brethren from other parts of the country. Unofficial reports of the number killed ranged from a dozen to 150. Ten thousand anti-riot and military police were required to restore an uneasy peace. The event was widely reported abroad, but there was no mention of it in the Chinese media, which is tightly controlled, especially when it comes to sensitive ethnic issues.

Uyghur-Han relations are even more problematic. The Turkic Uyghurs occupy a discrete territory, the Xinjiang Uyghur Autonomous Region, which some would prefer to call Eastern Turkestan. Since 1949, there have been at least ten serious clashes, and more than a hundred minor ones. Those who would be rid of Han domination are deemed criminally subversive. In 1994, the authorities variously identified sixty counterrevolutionary Uyghur organizations, and in 1999, there were said to be sixty-eight underground organizations. When caught, such dissidents are subject to long prison terms and sometimes are executed. Some independence advocates have sought asylum abroad (especially in Turkey, Germany, North America, and the countries of the former Soviet Union), where they continue to press their cause. The "cause," for moderates, means achieving genuine autonomy within, and for radicals it means to emulate the world's other seven Turkic countries as a sovereign state, theirs to be based on Muslim law and traditions.

Even though birth control policies are somewhat more relaxed for ethnic minorities like the Uyghurs compared to Hans, demographics do not favor ethnic minorities such as the Uyghurs. Pursuant to China's "Go West" campaign, there is a continuing influx of Hans into Xinjiang from other parts of the PRC. Uyghurs now comprise only 47% of Xinjiang's population, down from about 90% in the 1940s. This is a trend that breeds considerable resentment. However, the international "war on terror" has provided China some cover in waging its own struggle against China's Uyghurs and other Moslem militants.

The half of greater Mongolia that is not part of the Republic of Mongolia (the designation dates from 1992) is comprised of a truncated version of Inner Mongolia, known officially as the "Inner Mongolia Autonomous Region" of China. Although the area now appears relatively stable, during China's Cultural Revolution it saw worse interracial carnage than any place else in the PRC. Inner Mongols were caught up in the conflict between China and the then pro-Soviet Mongol People's Republic. Their loyalty was often doubted, and people were subject to systematic screening. By official reckoning, sixteen thousand Inner Mongols lost their lives. Following the Cultural Revolution, Han-Mongol conflict continued, and 1981 saw large-scale protests over such issues as Han immigration. Following the democratization of Outer Mongolia in 1990, several nationalist-democratic movements sprang up in Inner Mongolia, only to be repressed by the Chinese. With the recent conversion of "leagues" to "municipalities," many Inner Mongols appear to be losing even nominal autonomy.

In the various ethnic regions, Hans, though usually a minority of the local population, occupies key positions. Party secretaries have almost always been Han, though the government is sprinkled with token ethnics. Hans also tend to obtain the best jobs. For example, in the television station in Xinjiang's capital, more than 90% of the employees have been Hans. Furthermore, upward mobility for indigenous peoples is generally dependent upon their proficiency in Mandarin. Local cultures tend to atrophy under such circumstances.

Most non-Hans do not receive a Chinese education, and those who do not tend to end up in poverty. Twenty of China's twenty-five poorest counties are in Xinjiang. Much of Tibet is also impoverished, and child malnutrition is a serious problem. Often, these areas are rich in natural resources, but the locals derive little benefit from their exploitation. Furthermore, China's notorious corruption is especially prevalent in non-Han areas; Hans appear to be the beneficiaries. All of these factors breed consternation and fuel inter-ethnic hostility.

The quality of life and people's incomes have been adversely affected by environmental degradation. This is not entirely the fault of the Han, though they are the ones in a position to institute better stewardship of the land. In Inner Mongolia, grassland degradation has caused serious sandstorms and fodder shortages. The Chinese response has been to close numerous pastures so that they can recover ecologically. Hundreds of thousands of Mongol herders have been resettled in suburban areas, much to their resentment. In Xinjiang, Qinghai, and western Inner Mongolia, atomic weapons programs appear to have negatively impacted the health of the locals. The same may be true of China's Xinjiang-based experiments in bacteriological weapons. Ethnic minorities resent these harmful activities, which they believe the Hans would never carry out in their own areas.

The history of these regions is usually written by Hans, who adhere closely to ethnocentric Chinese interpretations. According to this view, these were all backward peoples who were liberated by the Chinese around 1949, and any progress since is due to the Communist Party. Non-Han scholars and journalists suggest other interpretations at their peril. Many Uyghur books have been banned and destroyed. In Tibet, entry to the Tibetan Department of the main university was suspended for two years in 1995 so that all textbooks could be reissued with less emphasis on religion and especially on the Dalai Lama. Since 2002, several books, including a major encyclopedia of Tibetan history and culture, have been banned for such reasons as having failed to properly convey the Party's policy on religion and nationalities, and overstating Tibet's cultural distinctiveness.

Resistance In Xinjiang tends to be violent. An incident typically begins with a shooting or bombing, attributed to a Uyghur. Then there is a crackdown by the Chinese, with many arrests and some executions. For example, after one incident in 2004, fifty people were sentenced to death for "separatist" and "terrorist" activities. Sometimes retribution is even more swift, with indiscriminate shootings of demonstrators and bystanders, and extra-judicial executions.

By comparison, since the mid-1970s, resistance in Tibet has generally been non-violent. The Chinese reaction has been more targeted, with the arrest and long-term imprisonment of dissidents (usually monks and nuns). Resistance has often taken the form of political ritual (the "circle of protest" around the main temple in Lhasa), that earns it considerable legitimacy in the eyes of the international community, where the Tibetan diaspora calls attention to the Tibetans' cause.

Still, it should be said that not all ethnic minorities are dissatisfied with their situation. The ethnic Koreans in the Northeast, for example, have a higher standard of living and education level than the Hans, and are hardly sorry that fate did not render them citizens of the Democratic People's Republic of Korea (DPRK). To be sure, during the Cultural Revolution they often faced persecution (and some even fled to the DPRK). But today, the main Korean victims of Chinese repression are the undocumented refugees from North Korea.

Taiwan, Korea, and Mongolia

Taiwan has an aboriginal minority (about 2% of the population) comprising twelve different tribes, all of Austronesian origin. They often live in the mountainous area of eastern Taiwan. The Hans themselves, depending on one's interpretation of the situation, may be deemed to be comprised of different ethnic groups. The "native Taiwanese" (who came from China centuries ago but speak the language of southern Fujian province) are in the majority; they were once discriminated against, and sometimes brutally repressed, by the Mainlanders, who ruled the island after 1945. There has been a debate about whether the Taiwanese are the same ethnic group as the Hans, or whether cultural factors and the fact that many have some aboriginal blood make a difference. With the advent of democracy in the early 1990s, relations among the various groups have improved, but the Taiwanese and Mainlanders tend to vote for different parties. Among the indisputable Hans, there is a Hakka minority, who have had considerable success

in gaining recognition and legitimacy for their distinct culture. Virtually all islanders speak Mandarin in addition to any native tongues. Thus, Taiwan today enjoys reasonably harmonious inter-ethnic relations, except, of course, when it comes to the cross-straits relationship.

Korea is mono-ethnic. The tensions on the peninsula are between north and south, with ethnicity not a fundamental problem. Still, the thousands of North Korean refugees who have managed to immigrate to South Korea find themselves in an alien culture, and few are able to make the adjustment to life in the South. The even larger (but unknown) number of Korean Chinese there, though sometimes targets of discrimination, are somewhat more able to adjust. They are often in the country illegally, though there has been pressure from them and from many South Koreans to grant them citizenship. Unlike Korean Chinese, Koreans who left South Korea after 1948 (usually to go to the United States) have virtually the same rights as Korean citizens. The courts have ruled that this form of discrimination is unconstitutional. However, discrimination against Korean Chinese continues, and the legal distinction between older and newer migrants has yet to be resolved.

The Republic of Mongolia comprises only about half of Greater Mongolia. Greater Mongolia actually has numerous ethnic Mongol subgroups, mainly the Halh (who predominate in the Republic), Buryats and Kalmyks (in Russia), groups falling under the rubric of Övör Mongol (Inner Mongolia), and various other Oirat groups elsewhere in China (Xinjiang and Qinghai). To some extent these designations have long cultural roots, but to an even larger extent they have been defined by great-nation geopolitics and socialist experimentation. Although today these sub-ethnic distinctions have strong emotive force (centering on the issue of Mongolian authenticity), they give rise to little outright intra-Mongol conflict, as most Mongols are more concerned with protecting their identity as Mongols vis à vis the Russians or Chinese.

JAMES D. SEYMOUR

See also Buddhism; East Asia: History and Economic Development; East Asia: International Relations; Hong Kong; Islam; Macao; Mao Zedong; Minorities/Discrimination; Mongolia; Self-Determination; Taiwan; Terrorism; Tibet

References and Further Reading

Barnett, Robert, ed. *Resistance and Reform in Tibet.* Bloomington, IN: Indiana University Press, 1994.
Becquelin, Nicholas. "Criminalizing Ethnicity: Political Repression in Xinjiang," *China Rights Forum*, 2004 (1),

pp. 39-46. http://www.hrichina.org/fs/view/downloadables/pdf/downloadable-resources/b1_Criminalizing1.2004 pdf

Benson, Linda, and Ingvar Svanbert. *China's Last Nomads: The History and Culture of China's Kazaks*. Armonk, NY: M. E. Sharpe, 1998.

Bulag, Uradyn E. *Nationalism and Hybridity in Mongolia*. Oxford: Clarendon Press, 1998.

Gladney, Dru C. *Muslim Chinese: Ethnic Nationalism in the People's Republic*. Cambridge, MA: Harvard University Press, 1991.

Kaup, Katherine Palmer. *Creating the Zhuang: Ethnic Politics in China*. Boulder, CO: Lynne Rienner, 2000.

MacKerras, Colin. *China's Ethnic Minorities and Globalisation*. London: Routledge/Curzon, 2003.

Schwartz, Ronald D. *Circle of Protest: Political Ritual in the Tibetan Uprising*. New York: Columbia University Press, 1994.

ETHNIC CONFLICTS: MEXICO AND CENTRAL AMERICA

As a result of the Spanish Conquest in the sixteenth century, the Indian population of the Americas was greatly diminished: from 80 million in 1492 to 3.5 million in 1750. Genocide against Indians is continued today, e.g., in Paraguay, Guatemala, and Brazil. Indians were also subjected to slavery and forced submission.

Some Mexican Indian groups, mainly in the South, were able to maintain pre-conquest self-government. In Central America, where the subjugation was concentrated on the more accessible lands along the western coast, indigenous groups on the Caribbean side either remained out of reach for the Spanish colonizers or resisted them.

Amerindian Struggles for Autonomy, Recognition, and Social Justice

There were several cases of armed ethnic conflict in Mexico and Central America: The Kuna in Panama in 1927, the Miskitu and Sumu in Nicaragua 1981–1987, the indigenous peoples of Chiapas beginning in 1994, the Popular Revolutionary Army EPR-EZLN in Guerrero and Oaxaca since June 1996, and the URNG (1960–1996). All of these groups attained some degree of autonomy, recognition, or political reforms.

The organic mixture of ethno-nationalist and Indian issues with left-wing politics is characteristic for most of these movements. The ethnic conflict of the Indian vs. Hispanic oligarchy and state is also a class conflict: the Indian population is synonymous with the most impoverished and suppressed section of the population. The main aim of the EZLN, URNG, and EPR was to do away with the absolute power of the small class of (land) owners. The low level of support for the political and institutional system among the Indians reflects the humiliation and general neglect they continue to suffer.

Root Causes of Conflict, Hybrid Identity, and Racism

The root cause of conflict is the (neo-) colonial mission of spreading *Hispanidad*, a hybrid European-type of civilization. It included the idea of centralizing power and aimed at erecting homogenous nation states, based on assimilation of non-Hispanic groups. But in reality there is no single homogenous nation-state existing in Central America. Recognizing multiplicity would consequently lead to a relationship of mutual respect between Ladinos, Indians, and Blacks in Latin America. But instead the endless search for a so-called "national identity" became the permanent project of the ruling classes in Latin America.

Structural and institutionalized racism in Central American states and in Mexico is based on a doctrine of Ladino superiority and "Indio" inferiority. The militarization of state and society was a strategic objective which was defined, planned, and executed institutionally by the security forces (in Guatemala) or jointly with paramilitary gangs (Mexico). In Guatemala indigenous populations suffered genocidal politics exercised by the small ruling oligarchy through the armed forces, regardless of the form of governance (military or civilian).

Guatemalan Genocide Against the Mayans 1962–1996

Counter-insurgency against leftist guerrilla forces (EGP, Rebel Armed Forces [FAR], Revolutionary Organization of the People in Arms [ORPA], URNG) imposed "total war" on the Indian peoples. Mayan Indians made up a large part of the guerrilla force. In 1996, after internal armed conflict for thirty-six years, the guerrillas signed a peace accord after a long negotiation process. But the accomplishments of the accords remained very limited. Despite the documentation in the 1999 report of the Guatemalan Truth Commission of atrocities committed by the armed forces 1962–1996, the gravity of the abuses suffered by Indian people has yet to become part of the national consciousness. Massacres eliminated entire Mayan rural communities as well as the urban political opposition; Ladinos were also oppressed, though to a lesser extent. During the final period, 1986–1996, repressive action affected the Mayan and Ladino population to a similar extent. One of the chief organizers of the Guatemalan genocide, general Rios Montt, became president of parliament and so far enjoys impunity.

Minority and Majority Indian Populations at the Edge

Population numbers for non-Mestizos depend on who is counting them and based on what criteria. Governments tend to minimize numbers while some indigenous organizations inflate them. Mexico has by far the largest Amerindian population in the Americas, with forty-eight indigenous groups numbering 30 million of its total population of over 100 million.

Within the seven Central American states of Guatemala, Belize, El Salvador, Honduras, Nicaragua, Costa Rica, and Panama are over fifty indigenous nations and nationalities with a population of 9 million people. In Guatemala, native nations (Maya-Quiché peoples) constitute a 50% majority of the 14-million population. The other five countries have a combined population of 25 million people of which 2 million are Amerindians and 1.5 million are Afro-Americans.

The majority of the Indian peoples of Mesoamerica are **Mayan**, who are mostly small-scale peasants. Their epicentre is Southern Mexico and the *altiplano* of Guatemala, but Mayan peoples live throughout Mexico and Guatemala as well as Belize, El Salvador, and Honduras. The single largest Indian group in Mexico is the Aztec in central and Southern Mexico, numbering 1.2 million people. Other major peoples include the Zapotec, Otomi, Mixtec, Totonac, and Mazatec, all numbering between two hundred thousand and five hundred thousand.

Pipil and **Lenca** (probably 20% of El Salvador's population) have suffered very high casualties in the war between Farabundo Martí National Liberation Front (FMLN) guerrilla and the US-supported regime. State security and death squads systematically caused "Peasant disappearances." Pipil lands were expropriated by "land reforms."

Garifuna (Black Caribs) were relocated by the British to the island of Roatán some three hundred years ago. They now live along the Caribbean in Creole-ruled Belize (40,000), Honduras (150,000), and Nicaragua (5,000). They have suffered racial discrimination and were used as cheap labour force. In Honduras, the Garifuna, Tawahka Sumu, Miskitu, Petch (Payas), Sikakes (Stolopán), and Lenca recently formed the *Confederación de los Pueblos Autóctonos de Honduras* (CONPAH).

Arbitrary boundaries of today's American states often cut across the homelands of Indian peoples. The **Ngobe** or Guaymíes (120,000) live in western Panama (2,500 in Coast Rica). The delimitations of the proposed autonomous area (*comarca*) are still under negotiation (since the 1980s); Latin settlers have invaded a part of their lands. Some Ngobe (Guaymí) work on banana plantations of United Brands, a US-based transnational corporation. The **Kuna** (70,000) live along the Caribbean of southeastern Panama. An armed uprising in 1925 forced the new state of Panama to recognize the first autonomous Indian area (*Comarca* San Blas) in Latin America. The state of Panama has developed a reasonably successful nationality policy for its indigenous peoples (15% of Panamá's population) since the 1960s and several more autonomous areas (*comarcas*) have been created.

Afro-Americans Look to the Caribbean

Afro-Americans (Blacks and Creoles) live along the Caribbean from Belize to Columbia, with the largest numbers in Panama and Honduras. With a total population of 120 million (which includes 35 million in the United States), Afro-Americans are third largest ethnic group in the Americas, next to 360 million Ladinos, and 230 million white Europeans.

Afro-Americans dominate demographically and/or rule in twelve smaller states of the Caribbean region. Black rule exists mainly on the islands (Haiti, Jamaica, most Caribbean micro-states) rather that the continent (Belize, one of three Guayanas). Blacks have large numbers in a several Ladino-dominated states such as Brazil (over 40 million), Colombia, and Ecuador.

White Rule in All but One Country—Indians Nowhere

Even though indigenous Americans are the majority of the citizens in four of twenty Latin American states, they rule nowhere. **European descendants** continue to exert almost total hegemony on the Americas; although Whites are only a majority in one Central American country (Costa Rica) they rule in all but tiny Belize.

Regionally, there has been some progress towards indigenous control: in May 1990, the very first Indian government took an oath in Bilwi, capital of Yapti Tasba, Eastern Nicaragua.

Autonomy and Self-Rule as Conflict Resolution

Many Indian territories are rich in natural resources, and the states that contain them are reluctant to give them up. Issues of (collective) ownership of land by indigenous peoples and access to natural resources, were the subject of political debate in Nicaragua and also externally, within the framework of the international Indian movement. In the case of Mosquitia, the land issue was one of the factors that directly contributed to the outbreak of war. In the autonomy law issued in 1987, it has been agreed that revenues from natural resources will be distributed 'in just proportion.'

Nicaragua: Autonomy for the Caribbean Regions

Nicaragua's scheme of regional autonomy for its two Caribbean areas (Región Autónoma Atlántico Norte: RAAN, and Región Autónoma Atlántico Sur: RAAS) embraces almost 50% of the national territory but only 9.5% of the population. The division into two regions precludes dominance by one ethnic group (the *Mestizos*). The two regions are multicultural in composition, comprising four indigenous communities, an African diaspora (mainly in RAAS), and a number of *Mestizos*. Autonomy in the two Caribbean regions has existed on paper since September 1987 and in concrete shape in a few pilot projects. The provisions delineate the indigenous settlement-areas but afford them no further legal protection against *Mestizo* immigrants. In practice, the agricultural border is being constantly shifted eastwards as a result of immigration by impoverished *campesinos*.

The rights and guarantees set out in Nicaragua are the confirmation of the multi-ethnic, pluricultural, and multilingual character of the *costeños* (coastal inhabitants) and stipulation of non-discrimination against them, with cultural rights (bilingualism in education and administration); the recognition of the communal property of the indigenous communities, including the land, waters, and forests; the establishment of two autonomous regions independently administered by elected regional parliaments with elements of a presidential system, since not only a *junta executiva* but also a *coordinador* is elected; and the right to self-identification. The system is based on a balancing and combination of demographic representation and the formal principle of equality. The aim was to reduce inter-ethnic tensions and protect the rights of the small ethnic groups (Sumu, Rama, and Garifuna) against the disproportionate influence of the Hispanic *Mestizos* in the West and the Afro-American Creoles in the South and the Miskitu Indians in the North.

The full implementation of the autonomy law was hampered by political conflicts from 1990 onwards. The political struggles between Sandinistas and the right parties in Managua are continuing in eastern Nicaragua. Conservatives in central government regard the autonomy arrangement as too drastic. The Indian movement has also suffered from internal conflicts.

The Nicaraguan autonomy law is undoubtedly imperfect, but qualitatively speaking it is the best so far produced in Latin America; how much influence it will have, however, depends on whether and to what extent it is ignored or dismantled by Managua. The weak-point lies in the area of regional council control over territory and resources: neither the respective competencies nor the share of revenues between regional and central government is clearly laid down.

Panama: the *Comarca* System

Panama is regarded as progressive when it comes to recognition of certain Indian rights and the granting of cultural autonomy (though not bilingual education). Territorial self-governance existed for years for the Kuna and Emberá Choco, but not for the more numerous Ngobe (Guaymí) Indians, whose area—due to be designated a *comarca*—has been overrun by *Mestizo* settlers and banana companies.

The best-known area is Kuna Yala, the 'land of the Kuna' (official name Comarca San Blas), a territory extending from El Porvenir up to the Colombian border and including some four hundred Caribbean coral islands. In Kuna Yala, too, penetration by *Mestizo* settlers, loggers, and drug dealers (from Colombia) is difficult to halt. The Kuna largely manage their own affairs. However, the school system is currently run in Spanish. Thanks to their being relatively sealed off from the outside world, their sociocultural community has survived. However, the economy is partly dependent on external factors, and unequal bartering goes on.

Native inhabitants have guaranteed representation in the Panamanian parliament; this applies to the Kuna and Ngobe (Guaymí). However, the *caciques/ congreso* system of internal Indian organization has its shortcomings. Where necessary, it can be manipulated more easily by the authorities than can an elected representative body (such as those in Mosquitia in Nicaragua); on the other hand, it keeps traditions alive.

In the case of the Ngobe (Guaymí) Indians, the authorities have dragged their feet over autonomy negotiations in a series of protracted conflicts over land and administrative rights and roles. Contributing factors have included the size of the territory claimed, which extends over several provinces as well as the disunity, poor organization, and lack of militancy among the Ngobe. However, to combat the government's 'divide and rule' policy, the various Indian congresses in Panama formed a union.

Mexico: Response to the 1994 Indian Revolt

In the Mexican state of Chiapas, cattle ranchers use an estimated 45% of the territory as pastureland. In contrast, a large number of campesinos work on small plots of generally unfertile land. The constitution of 1917 promised *ejidos*, pieces of the communal farming land, to the peasants, but in Chiapas much less land was redistributed than in the rest of the country. In the 1960s, the struggle for land became violent.

In 1994, the primarily indigenous Zapatista Army of National Liberation (EZLN) staged an armed uprising in Chiapas. Six municipalities around San Cristóbal de las Casas were taken by the rebels. After two weeks of heavy fighting with high casualties a cease-fire was declared. Direct talks between the EZLN and the federal government in January 1995, moderated by San Cristóbal's bishop, reached an agreements to twenty-four demands of the EZLN but excluded political issues on a national level. However, the following month, arrest warrants were issued for EZLN leaders, and the Mexican government launched a large military operation against the EZLN, which fled, along with some twenty thousand indigenous supporters, into the mountains. The Mexican government was never able to find the EZLN leaders, and in March 1995, the Mexican Congress approved dialogue with EZLN. From fall 1995, talks started in San Andrés Sacamch'en de los Pobres (Larrainzar), a Tzotzil Zapatista community in the highlands north of San Cristóbal, but were suspended in August 1996. Militarization

once again replaced dialogue. About 30% of the national army (sixty thousand soldiers) is based in Chiapas.

After winning the 2000 presidential election, Vicente Fox admitted international observers and ordered the withdrawal of Mexican Army. The EZLN accepted to resume negotiations for peace and indigenous rights. They reached some agreement on the rights of indigenous communities and in April 2001 the Mexican Congress approved a constitutional reform on indigenous rights and culture. However, the EZLN rejected the reform, saying it went behind the agreement reached in San Andres and does not answer the demands of the Indian peoples.

EZLN raised the awareness of indigenous rights and culture throughout the country and internationally. It is noteworthy that the Zapatistas do not want independence from Mexico, but rather to be equal citizens without giving up their indigenous identity.

JÜRGEN BUCHENAU

See also Belize; Central America: History and Economic Development; Central America: International Relations; Costa Rica; El Salvador; Farabundo Martí National Liberation Front (FMLN); Guatemala; Honduras; Menchú Túm, Rigoberta; Mexico: History and Economic Development; Mexico: International Relations; Nicaragua; Panama; Zapatista National Revolutionary Army (EZLN)

References and Further Reading

Assies, Willem, and André Hoekema, eds. *Indigenous Peoples' Experiences with Self-Government*. Amsterdam/Copenhagen: IWGIA, 1994.

Centro de Investigaciones y Documentacion de la Costa Atlantiba (CIDCA) / Development Study Unit: Univ. of Stockholm / Kranz, Lasse (ed.). *Ethnic groups and the nation state. The case of the Atlantic Coast in Nicaragua*. Stockholm: DSU, 1987.

Diaz-Polanco, Hector. *La cuestion étnico-nacional*. Mexico (Ed. Linea), 1985.

Escobar, Arturo, and Sonia E. Alvarez, eds. *The Making of Social Movements in Latin America*. Boulder, CO: Westview Press, 1992.

Ethnic Conflict Research Project, ECOR. *Struggle for survival in the decade for the world's indigenous peoples*. Moers: IFEK-IRECOR, 1998.

Horowitz, Donald L. *Ethnic Groups in Conflict*. Berkeley, Los Angeles: University of California Press, 1985.

Martínez, Miguel Alfonso / UNHCHR. *Study on treaties, agreements and other constructive arrangements between states and indigenous peoples*. Final Report. E/CN.4/Sub.2/1999/20. Geneva, 22 June, 1999.

Minority Rights Group. *No Longer Invisible: Afro-Latin Americans Today*. London: Minority Rights Group, 1995.

República de Nicaragua. Constitución Política, *La Gaceta, Diario Oficial*, Año XCI, No. 5, Managua 9 Jan., 1987.

Scherrer, Christian. *Structural Prevention of Ethnic Violence*. Houndmills / New York: Palgrave, 2002.

UNCHR (United Nations Commission on Human Rights)/ ECOSOC.var. years. *Reports of the Working Group on Indigenous Populations.* Annual sessions, July/Aug.

———. *Establishment of a Permanent Forum on Indigenous Issues.* Decision of UNCHR. E/2000/87. Geneva 27 April, 2000.

———. (Chávez, Luis-Enrique). *Indigenous Issues.* Report of the working group established in accordance with CHR resolution 1995/32. E/CN.4/2000/84. Geneva, 6 December, 1999.

———. (Daes, Erica-Irene). *Indigenous people and their relationship to land.* Second progress report. E/CN.4/ 1999/20. Geneva, 22 June, 1999.

ETHNIC CONFLICTS: MIDDLE EAST

According to J. Milton Yinger in *Ethnicity*, an ethnic group can be defined as one whose members share a common origin, whether real or perceived, and share a common culture, including, but not limited to, characteristics such as language, religion, race, and ancestral homeland. An ethnic group may be defined by the larger society around it, or by its own self-perception. All of these characteristics define ethnic, religious, and nationalist groups in the Middle East.

There are competing views of the importance of ethnic identity in creating conflict in the Middle East. Some view conflict to be driven by the deeply-entrenched, hereditary nature of ethnic, sectarian, and religious identities of communities. Others view political conditions to be a stronger factor in manipulating identity-based kinship networks. Identity only becomes politicized when access to resources or power is unevenly distributed between various groups, and membership in a particular group becomes a driving factor in determining that access to political power. Thus, while the Middle East is diverse and multiethnic, ethnic conflict is not inherently caused by this diversity.

Ethnic conflict in the Middle East encompasses ethnic, religious, and political groups engaged in nationalist struggles in the post-WWII era. For example, since the creation of the state of Israel in 1948, the ongoing Israeli-Palestinian conflict centers around competing claims for a separate national homeland for the Palestinian and Jewish peoples. Another case is that of Kurdish nationalists who are seeking political autonomy in the form of an independent Kurdistan in the area encompassing parts of Turkey, Iraq, Iran, and Syria. In Lebanon, competition for political power among Christian Maronites, Sunni, Shia, and Druze led to a breakdown of the political system and to civil war in 1975.

There are several different factors which have led to ethnic conflict in the Middle East. Primary among these is the impact of British and French colonialism in the region. Colonial policies favored particular minority groups over others in an attempt to create ethnic or religious divisions within the local population and to weaken potential resistance to colonial power. The historical legacy of this divide and rule policy was political instability which erupted into outright conflict once the colonial power withdrew. Lebanon, Syria, and present-day Israel are examples of countries where colonial legacy has exacerbated political tensions between different ethnic groups.

The following subsections highlight the main conflicts in the region, demonstrating the interplay between colonial legacy, nationalist struggle, and ineffective political systems which resulted in competition for political power among the different ethnic religious groups.

Israeli–Palestinian Conflict

The Israeli-Palestinian conflict has been ongoing for most of the twentieth century. The historical roots of the conflict can be traced back to the British Mandate over Palestine. Both the Arabs living in Palestine and Jewish Zionists seeking a national homeland wanted national independence and self-determination granted to them by the British colonial power. In 1948, the British withdrew from Palestine without resolving the ongoing civil conflict between the two groups. After the state of Israel was created in 1948, Israel annexed more surrounding territory in two subsequent Arab–Israeli wars in 1967 and 1973.

While religious identity is important in defining the foundation of the Jewish state, it is not the only factor in the current Israeli–Palestinian conflict. Primarily the issue is over ownership of territory, and the competing rights to national self-determination between the Palestinians and the Israelis.

One of the outcomes of this conflict is the massive displacement of the Palestinian population into refugee camps in surrounding Lebanon and Jordan, as well as the Israeli-occupied territories. Palestinians in Jordan and Lebanon have caused political tensions in those countries. In the Lebanese case, Palestinian presence exacerbated the Lebanese civil war in the early 1970s. After the second intifada of 2000, the relationship of Palestinians living in the West Bank and Gaza with Israel remains tense and violence-ridden.

Alawis in Syria

In Syria, the French colonialists divided the country into separate administrative units, stressing the status of two minority groups, the Alawi and the Druze, as distinct from the rest of the Sunni Muslim population by placing them each in their own administrative unit in opposite ends of Syria. In the meantime, the urban Sunni Muslim population in Damascus, Aleppo, Hama, and Homs became the class that forged nationalist policies and shaped the eventual political future of Syria.

When Syria became independent in 1946, the new political state had to contend with the outcome of these colonial policies. The Alawi made up about ten percent of the population. Post-independence, they inherited a marginalized status in Syrian society, which was dominated by Sunni Muslims. Many Alawi families sent their sons into the military for the opportunities it afforded them. One of these was the Syrian dictator, Hafez al-Assad, who ruled the country from 1963 to 1999. After he took power in 1963, he consolidated his regime by creating an inner circle of Baath party loyalists who shared the same Alawi background. A regime composed of a religious minority ruling over a majority Sunni population created tensions. The result of this was a stronger, authoritarian style of government which effectively suppressed any and all opposition.

Sectarian Politics in Lebanon

French colonial policies of divide and rule in Lebanon are the roots of political conflict between ethnic and religious minorities after independence. French colonialists deliberately emphasized these differences within the local population in order to prevent them from banding together and effectively challenging French power. France favored the Christian (Catholic) Maronites of Mount Lebanon, on the grounds that it was part of France's religious and moral duty to protect Christian communities of the region. This preference alienated the Muslim majority, an alienation that intensified over time due to other political factors.

Confessional politics became a mainstay of the Lebanese political system after its independence in 1946. The 1932 census, in which Christian Maronites outnumbered Muslims six to five, became the basis of the National Pact of 1943. The pact set up a power-sharing arrangement between the four main communities, based on proportional representation on the basis of demographics. Since the Maronites were the majority in 1932, they took the presidency, a position elected by the Chamber of Deputies. The position of prime minister went to the Sunnis. The Shia community was underrepresented in the power structure, due

to their low numbers. In theory, the system prevented any single group from gaining a monopoly on power. In practice, the executive held more power than the parliament. Since the system was based on sectarian identity, this exacerbated any tensions within the government and the population.

Though the demographics of the population changed over the next few decades, the political system did not adapt in line with these realities. In particular, the Shia population outstripped the Christian Maronites in numbers, and yet the Shia remained the most underrepresented in the political structure. This grievance placed a strain on the confessional political structure, which was already beginning to feel pressure from other factors.

The rise of armed militias based on sectarian identity was a contributing factor to the Lebanese civil war. Among these militias were the Christian Maronite Phalange and the Lebanese National Movement, led by the Druze political leader Kamal Jumblatt. Militant Shia organizations, Amal and Hizballah, also joined the conflict.

The conflict lasted for fifteen years, from 1975 to 1990. In 1989, the Taif Accord succeeded in resolving this conflict by negotiating a more equitable system of representation in the political system, based on current population demographics instead of an outdated census.

Kurdish Nationalist Struggle

The Kurds are the fourth largest ethnic group in the Middle East, after the Arabs, Turks, and Persians. They have their own cultural and linguistic identities. The Kurds reside in an area that encompasses portions of present-day Turkey, Iran, Iraq, and Syria. Although the Kurds are the largest stateless minority in the Middle East, their numbers are not concentrated in any single country among these four. Thus, their status as a minority remains precarious and subject to government policies of each country.

The Kurdish struggle for self-determination dates from the end of World War I. The Kurds were granted partial autonomy according to the Treaty of Sevres, but without the military or financial assistance of the Allies, Kurdistan never became a reality.

Since then, the Kurdish nationalist movement, represented by the Kurdistan Workers' Party (PKK), has called for the creation of an independent Kurdistan carved out of present-day Turkey, Iran, Iraq, and Syria. The PKK is known for engaging in guerilla tactics to further its goals. However, the Kurdish struggle for self-determination has been challenged and suppressed by state power in each country.

Iraq and Turkey have seen the greatest violence and confrontation between the state and Kurdish nationalist groups. Turkey has historically refused to recognize Kurds as a distinct ethnic group and has actively suppressed them. In 1984, the PKK launched an attack on the Turkish military, and throughout much of the 1990s, there was active violence and conflict between the Turkish military and Kurdish nationalists. Turkey has since given limited recognition of their cultural and linguistic rights to the Kurds.

Kurds enjoyed limited autonomy in northern Iraq under Saddam Hussain's regime. However, they were also subject to military action by the government. In 1988, after the end of the Iran-Iraq war, the regime gassed the Kurdish village of Halabja, killing the entire population. A Kurdish revolt at the end of the Gulf War in 1991 also met with a similar violent reaction from the government. It was brutally repressed, and many Kurds fled as refugees to neighboring Turkey and Iran. After the war, a UN-protected zone was created for them in northern Iraq. After the fall of Saddam Hussain's regime in 2003, the future of the Kurdish communities in the north remains undecided.

The Kurds have also been used as pawns in regional conflicts. For example, during the Iran–Iraq war, which lasted from 1980 to 1988, the Kurds were used as pawns by both sides. Kurdish villages on both sides of the border were destroyed, and many killed. Kurdish resistance groups in each country were given clandestine support by the opposing side at various points during the war.

The current Kurdish drive for national self-determination needs to be viewed as a result of a historical demarcation of borders by European colonial powers. The division of land left the Kurds marginalized as a distinct ethnic community. While they have a historic connection to a particular territory, they remain stateless. Their minority status in each country has been exploited by regional governments, and continues to affect their struggle for political autonomy and self-determination today.

Conclusion

The changing configurations of political power between various communities inevitably results in power imbalances between dominant and minority groups. Whether these groups are defined by ethnicity or religion, or combination of factors, it does not matter as much as the fact that access to political power, or the lack thereof, is a contributing factor to political ethnic conflicts in the Middle East. In some cases, as previously demonstrated, British and French colonial policies exacerbated these identity-based differences and shaped the power structures that countries such as Lebanon and Syria inherited.

UZMA JAMIL

See also Arab-Israeli Wars (1948, 1956, 1967, 1973); Arab Nationalism; Druze; Iran; Iraq; Iran-Iraq War, 1980–1988; Kurds; Lebanon; Palestine Liberation Organization (PLO); Palestinian Diaspora; Syria; Turkey

References and Further Reading

Cleveland, William L. *A History of the Modern Middle East.* 2nd ed. Boulder, CO: Westview Press, 2000.
Gurr, Ted Robert. *Minorities at Risk: A Global View of Ethnopolitical Conflicts.* Washington, DC: US Institute of Peace, 1993.
Kedourie, Elie. *Nationalism.* 4th ed. Oxford, UK: Blackwell Publishers, 1993.
Shehadi, Nadim and Dana Haffer Mills, eds. *Lebanon: A History of Conflict and Consensus.* London: Center for Lebanese Studies and I.B. Taurus, 1988.
Yinger, J. Milton. *Ethnicity.* Albany, NY: SUNY Press, 1994.

ETHNIC CONFLICTS: NORTH AFRICA

Ethnic Conflict in its North African Regional Context

North Africa is a geographic region comprising five independent states: Egypt, Libya, Tunisia, Algeria, and Morocco. The region may be viewed as having a predominantly Arabo-Islamic identity, but it is by no means homogeneous. Distinctions in spoken Arabic exist and while the population is overwhelmingly Sunni Muslim, religious diversity is manifested in the many religious brotherhoods and more recently, the resurgence of a militant fundamentalist Islamism reacting to the region's recent modernization and secularization.

Within the region, vestiges of ethnic groups exist that pre-date the Arab-Islamic dominance. These include the Christian Copts in Egypt, the Berbers in the Maghrib states, and Jewish communities in each of the states. Most of the Jewish population has emigrated to Israel or Europe. In contrast, significant Coptic and Berber populations are part of North

Africa today. While some cultural differences persist between Arabs and Berbers, centuries of acculturation, intermarriage, and socialization have blurred sharp distinctions.

The region has experienced two patterns of ethnic conflict since 1945. The first involved nationalist movements moving against European imperial domination and the second, ethnic tensions within the newly independent states. During the nineteenth and early part of the twentieth centuries, each of these countries was under some form of colonization. The year 1945 saw the end of World War II, the founding of the United Nations (UN), and the growth of indigenous nationalist stirrings on the Asian and African continents. In less than two decades, each of the North African states succeeded in emerging from foreign domination. Running through the process of independence is a basic ethnic clash between the indigenous Arabo-Muslim way of life and the modernizing force of Christian European culture.

The Anti-Imperialist Phase of Ethnic Conflict

Egypt was nominally an independent constitutional monarchy since 1922, but through military treaty arrangements the country was under British hegemony. Anti-British nationalist agitation led to the formation of the Liberation Movement under the leadership of a small Free Officers Group. In 1952, it engineered a bloodless coup and dethroned the "puppet" King Farouk. Egypt emerged fully from under British domination in 1956 when President Gamal Abdul Nasser expelled the British from the Suez Canal. The ensuing Suez War of 1956 in which Egypt withstood the Anglo-French attack on its territory represents a distinct form of ethnic conflict—the resistance of an indigenous population to imperialist domination. Accentuating the ethnic character of the revolution was the declaration in the new constitution that Egypt was an Islamic Arab Republic, in contrast to the constitutional monarchy which followed the British monarchical structure.

Libya, an Italian colony, came under British administration during World War II following the defeat of the Axis in the Libyan Desert. The seeds of nationalist opposition to Italian rule and for independence were planted in the 1920s but it did not grow into a nationalist movement while the country was under military occupation. Independence came to Libya, not as a result of nationalist pressure within the country but by a United Nations resolution that came about because of pressure from the then small number of independent Muslim states in the General Assembly. Their persistence and bargaining power constituted an exercise of *diplomatic ethnicity*.

The nationalist ethnic conflicts in the three states of French North Africa were more intense and bloodier. The conflicts between the nationalist movements to French rule in the Maghrib contain an important ethnic dimension, i.e., religion and culture—but as classic colonial situations they also contain class, economic, and political aspects. Most leaders of the nationalist movements were Westernized intellectual elites. They spoke and wrote in French. They were conversant with international ideological trends such as democracy, capitalism, socialism, and communism. At the same time, Islamic reformers emerged who deplored the French *mission civilisatrice*, which they associated with Christianity and the presence of French settlers, *colons*. Together, these two strands of nationalism built nationalist movements that challenged French policy over favoritism towards the *colons* and discriminatory practices towards the indigenous Maghrib populations. Islam became one of the most potent factors in the spread of nationalism in the Maghrib.

The post–World War II ethnic nationalist conflict in the Maghrib can be traced back to the beginnings of colonization, particularly in Algeria and Morocco where France met with armed resistance that took decades to overcome. Although the Algerian, Moroccan, and Tunisian nationalist movements share much in common, not the least of which were a common adversary, separate nationalist movements developed due to basic differences in historical background and political status. Algeria was juridicially "an integral part of France" where the French *colons*, about a twelfth of the population, occupied a privileged position. Tunisia and Morocco, by contrast, were nominally sovereign states but were French protectorates. In the protectorates, the percentage of *colons* was smaller than in Algeria but they all but ran the country.

Nationalist pressure was first felt in the protectorates, Tunisia and Morocco. As the nationalists put forward demands for reform, aiming at eventual independence, they were met by counteractions by the *colon* element. French policy in both protectorates promoted a policy that would establish a permanent status for the *colons*, which was rejected by the nationalists. The *colons* were French citizens and as nationalist agitation mounted, the French authorities pushed hard to introduce co-sovereignty which would undermine the nationalists demands. Encouraged by the United Nations role in Libya, the nationalists appealed to the world body for support. The French staved off this effort but tension was mounting, marked by native boycotts of French products and the outbreaks of mass demonstrations and violence. As part of their strategy, the French played a "Berber Card" in Morocco—a "divide and rule" tactic designed to undermine the nationalist movement. The Berber Dahir of 1931, whereby Berbers were to be governed by their traditional law rather than by Islamic law, the *Sharia,* represented the boldest effort of this policy. This policy proved to be a wake-up call for the Arabo-Islamic religious community. In 1951, the French artificially created a "Berber Revolt" against Sultan Mohammed V who was balking at the demand of the French government to denounce the *Istiqlal* (independence) Party, the leading nationalist party. Thousands of Berber tribesmen suddenly appeared in Rabat and surrounded the palace. Although the Sultan capitulated after two hours to an ultimatum, the tactic proved a fiasco and only further encouraged the nationalists. It drew attention to the *Istiqlal* and helped catapult the Sultan to the forefront of the struggle against French rule. The French embarked on a program to force the Sultan to share his sovereignty with them. Mohammed V refused to acquiesce to this demand and he was exiled to Madagascar in 1952 and a more amenable settler-controlled Sultan installed. This touched off a period of unrest. On the second anniversary of Mohammed V's deposition, a chain of violence blazed across Morocco. Nearly two thousand persons lost their lives and scores of villages and towns were razed. Berber tribesmen were leading participants in the disturbances. The situation was finally resolved in 1957, when Mohammed V was restored to his throne and Morocco achieved independence the following year. A variation of this scenario was played out in Tunisia, where the local sovereign, Moncef Bey, also was deposed when he resisted French demands that he disavow the leading nationalist party, the *Neo-Destour* (Constitution). Intricate negotiations on reform and the creation of an elected legislature broke down over the issue of "co-sovereignty." Tunisia also experienced provocative street demonstrations and intermittent low-level violence. The situation was diffused in July 1954, when French Premier Pierre Mendès-France granted Tunisia "internal autonomy." Within two years, Tunisia was granted full independence.

Algeria's war of national independence, 1954–1962, was the longest and most fiercely fought struggle in the era of post-war decolonization. The French invasion of Algeria in 1830 was met with dogged resistance, which lasted for several decades. This early rejection of French colonial rule provided a historical precursor for the ultimate emergence of Algerian nationalism. French colonial policy effectively undermined the traditional Algerian social structure but a strong attachment to Islam persisted. At the same time strong assimilationist tendencies and flirtations with Marxism appeared and were reflected in the several Algerian nationalist parties that emerged between the end of World War I and 1954. On November 1, 1954, a group of younger dissidents calling themselves the *Front de Libération Nationale* (FLN) issued a proclamation calling Algerians to rebel, and launched an attack on French positions in five provinces. These initial steps of the Algerian revolution were hardly auspicious, as the guerrillas were small in number and poorly armed. Their most successful operation was in the Aurès mountains, a Kabyle (Algerian Berber) region. Within two years the insurrection gathered momentum, fueled in part by the repressive measures, including torture, taken by the French army and police. Ultimately, France committed some five hundred thousand troops, many of them conscripts, to the war. As the war dragged on, the fighting, which had been waged primarily in the hinterland and the mountain regions took on a new course when the FLN, in 1956, launched a clandestine network of terror in the Battle of Algiers. While the French military, resorting to torture, was succeeding in containing the urban terrorists, repercussions of these tactics created a groundswell in France for an end to the war, even if it meant granting independence to Algeria. This did not sit well with the *colons* or with certain elements of the French army. *Colon* extremists organized, with some disaffected French generals, the *Organizasion armée secrète* (OAS) to carry out a putsch against the French government, headed by General Charles de Gaulle. Their failure was the last gasp of the ethnic conflict waged by the settlers. De Gaulle had signaled the end of the old regime in Algeria, gradually accommodating to the idea of Algerian independence by coming out in favor of an *Algérie algérien,* and an eventual Algerian Republic.

Ethnic Conflicts After Independence

In the nationalist conflict with European imperialism, a broadly perceived Arabo-Islamic culture emerged, the product of Islamisation and Arabisation. The two are intimately interconnected but by no means identical. Thus, Egypt has been totally Arabicized, but not Islamicized, while the Maghrib states have been totally Islamicized but not Arabicized. Under the overarching North African Arabo-Islamic tent, there exists significant religious, linguistic, and cultural diversity. The constitution of each independent modern national North Africa state establishes Islam as its official religion and Arabic, its official language.

Despite this uniformity, local customs and traditions persisted and in many instances were reinvigorated. Relations between centralized authority and various ethnic groups were marked by fluidity and diversity. However, the states of North Africa are free of disintegrative tendencies, prevalent elsewhere among groups of ethnic minorities. Neither the Copts in Egypt nor the Berbers in Algeria and Morocco have pressed for political separateness or autonomy. Each in their own way seeks recognition and acceptance within their respective states. But the existence of these ethnic minorities constitutes a source of ever-present tensions which have the potential of local outbreaks of violence.

The Christian Copts, representing about 6% of the population, call themselves the "Original Egyptians." They are the vestiges of the Egyptian population that was not Islamicized following the Arab conquest of the seventh century. Though they do not tend to intermarry with Muslims, they are linguistically Arabicized. The Copts have always identified themselves with Egyptian nationalism, particularly its Arab dimension, but an ingrained religious antipathy exists between Muslims and Copts. Intermittent clashes between the two groups, sometimes leading to communal riots are part of the Egyptian political scene. The resurgence of Islamic militancy has exacerbated the situation. Anti-Coptic sentiments were spread by Muslim fundamentalists who were implicated in the bombing of Coptic Churches in Alexandria and anti-Coptic marches by thousands of Muslim militants in downtown Cairo. In 1981, President Anwar el-Sadat, under severe attack by the Islamic fundamentalists for his peace treaty with Israel, retaliated by conducting a purge to stifle religious dissent. In a strange twist, Sadat's crackdown also included deposing the Coptic patriarch, Pope Shenuda III. Some 1,500 Muslim clergyman, Coptic priests, journalists and academicians were arrested and charged with "sectarian sedition." The Copts have been caught in the power struggle over Islamic fundamentalism within the majority Egyptian community. Provocation by Islamic fundamentalists has usually evoked responses from Copts, fueling the tension been them.

The other manifestation of ethnic tension in independent North Africa concerns the Berbers in the Maghrib. Unlike the Copts in Egypt, they cannot be referred to as an ethnic minority, since the entire population of the Maghrib is of mixed Arab and Berber stock, yet the concept of "Berber ethnicity" exists, as does intra-ethnic tension between Berberism and Arabism. The tension is primarily over language and traditions. A Berber language is the mother tongue of many inhabitants of the Atlas mountains of Morocco and the Algerian Aurès and Kabyle mountains. With the intent to displace French as the dominant language of education and literacy, the newly independent states of the Maghrib proclaimed Arabic as their official language. An unintended consequence was to undercut the use of Berber tongues, particularly in local assemblies, rural schools, and the mass media. This did not sit well with Berbers, whose resentment has led to demand changes that would help preserve Berber identity. The direction of ethnic conflict over Berberism is still unfolding. Berbers participated in the nationalist struggle against French colonialism and continue to participate in the contemporary body politic. There is no thought of secession or of "Berber Nationalism." There is no single Berber language, but a group of closely related spoken languages. The notion of "Berberland" is a most unlikely thought, since the Berber population does not live in a contiguous area. Berber enclaves exist in rural and mountainous regions, but a good portion is integrated urban dwellers. But, the potential for ethnic conflict exists, since an activist Berber segment of Moroccan and Algerian society is dedicated to the preservation of Berber uniqueness, and believes in countering "Arab colonialism" by pressing for the recognition of Tamazight, the main Berber language, as an official state language, its more prevalent use in media and communities, and the removal of discriminatory treatment of Berbers. The seeds for inter-ethnic conflict over Berberism exist but it must be considered within the context of broader challenges of Islamist fundamentalism and the chronic problems of economic and development facing the Maghrib states.

BENJAMIN RIVLIN

See also Algeria; Berbers; Coptic Church (Copts); Egypt; Ethnicity: Impact on Politics and Society; Libya; Maghrib Peoples; Morocco; Nasser, Gamal Abdel; North Africa: History and Economic Development; North Africa: International Relations

References and Further Reading

Abun-Nasr, Jamil M. *A History of the Maghrib*, Cambridge: Cambridge University Press, 1971.

Bernard, Stéphane. *The Franco-Moroccan Conflict, 1943–1956*, New Haven, CT: Yale University Press, 1968.

Entelis, John P. *Culture and Counterculture in Moroccan Politics*. Boulder, CO: Westview Press, 1989.

Gordon, David C. *The Passing of French Algeria*. London: Oxford University Press, 1966.

Gurr, Ted Robert and Harff, Barbara. *Ethnic Conflict in World Politics*. Boulder, CO: Westview Press, 1994.

Hermassi, Elbaki. *Leadership and National Development in North Africa*. Berkeley and Los Angeles: University of California Press, 1972.

Khadduri, Majid *Modern Libya: A Study un Political Development*. Baltimore, MD: The Johns Hopkins Press, 1963.

Lam, Maivan Clech. *At the Edge of the State: Indigenous Peoples and Self-Determination*. Ardsley, NY: Transnational Publishers, 2000.

Leeder, S. H. *Modern Sons of the Pharaohs: A Study of the Manners and Customs of the Copts of Egypt*. New York: Arno Press, 1973.

Rivlin, Benjamin. *The Italian Colonies: United Nations Action Series No.1*. New York: Carnegie Endowment for International Peace, 1950.

Ruedy, John. *Modern Algeria: The Origins and Development of a Nation*. Bloomington, IN: Indiana University Press, 1992.

Stavenhagen, Rodolfo. *The Ethnic Question: Conclicts, Development, and Human Rights*. Tokyo: The United Nations University Press, 1990.

Wakin, Edward. *A Lonely Minority: The Modern Story of Egypt's Copts*. New York: William Morrow & Company, 1963.

Wright, John L. *Libya: A Modern History*. Baltimore, MD: The John Hopkins University Press, 1982.

Zghal, Abdelkader. "Nation-building in the Maghrib", *International Social Science Journal*, Vol. XXIII, No. 3, 1971, pp. 435–451.

ETHNIC CONFLICT IN OCEANIA

Oceania is a huge region that consists of the islands of Polynesia, Melanesia, and Micronesia, as well as New Zealand, Australia, and Hawaii. As a geographical entity, Oceania contains metropolitan states, colonial territories (e.g., New Caledonia and French Polynesia) and independent developing nations. Ethnic conflict takes place in all these social formations. This article focuses on major ethnic strife in the developing nations of Oceania, the island countries of the South Pacific. The viability of three Pacific Island states, Papua New Guinea, the Solomon Islands, and Fiji, has been seriously undermined by ethnic violence. Each country was a colonial creation, a cobbling together of disparate peoples, cultures, and traditional societies. The difficulties of building nations out of such colonies are always great. This is especially so when issues having to do with development reinforce ethnic differences as they have in these three cases.

The longest and most bloody fighting in contemporary Oceania occurred on the island of Bougainville, a province of Papua New Guinea. It is estimated that approximately ten thousand people died because of the conflict.

Bougainville

Far from the rest of Papua New Guinea—about one thousand kilometres from the capital, Port Moresby—the island of Bougainville is a short launch ride to the Solomon Islands. The island has an area of about 5,400 square miles and a population of 170,000. Like the rest of Melanesia, it is inhabited by a diverse group of people who live in small autonomous villages. Colonization and incorporation into Papua New Guinea sewed the seeds of a wider Bougainvillean identity. Bougainvilleans came to see themselves, and be seen by other Papua New Guineans to be more like their near neighbors than like people from the mainland. Known in the local vernacular as "Buka" (crows) because of their dark skin, they call other Papua New Guineans "Redskins".

The development of a mining project at Panguna both accentuated this sense of difference and transformed it into one of grievance. Exploration in the 1960s uncovered large deposits of copper and gold. Open cast mining operations began in the early 1970s. The resultant alienation of land and damage to the environment greatly disrupted the lives of local people. The pit alone covered four hundred hectares and generated a billion metric tons of waste. People were generally unhappy with the amount of compensation they received. The uneven distribution of the costs and benefits from the project also led to disputes and divisions on the local level.

Revenue from the mine provided the central government with almost half its foreign exchange earnings. However, little of this came back to large parts of an island lacking economic and educational opportunities for its people. The need for labour at the mine site stimulated an influx of workers who migrated from other parts of Papua New Guinea. This influx of "foreign natives" brought with it problems of urbanization and attendant troubles with law and order that Bougainville had not seen before.

In 1988, young men from local groups attacked the mine, demanding its closure and adequate compensation for damage caused to local lands. The central government deployed forces to control the situation but their heavy-handedness caused the violence to escalate into a full-scale uprising. The mine ceased operations in 1989. Although the central government withdrew its troops as part of a cease-fire arrangement, the Bougainville Revolutionary Army declared independence in 1990. The Papua New Guinea government responded by imposing a blockade that had severe consequences. The embargo of medical supplies in particular caused a significant number of the overall casualties of the conflict. The control of tropical diseases broke down and other facilities, like schools and roads, deteriorated.

The situation inside Bougainville became increasingly violent and chaotic. The Bougainville Revolutionary Army was, in reality, a loose coalition of groups of young men from heterogeneous societies who had a variety of agendas. With the mine shut down and the remaining non-Bougainvilleans brutalised, local elements began fighting amongst themselves. Leaders on small outlying islands requested government intervention. After establishing themselves on Buka, Papua New Guinean troops began to push onto the main island. After years of continued fighting, and failed cease-fires, the government hired mercenaries to assist its own troops in a final effort to defeat the rebels and occupy the mine. However, the commander of the Papua New Guinea Defence Force refused to work with the mercenaries, the mission was aborted and the Prime Minister resigned his post in 1997.

The situation today is much improved. Tired of war and unable to achieve their aims by violence the opposing forces began signaling a willingness to negotiate. New Zealand took on an essential role in facilitating a truce. Meetings near Christchurch in 1997 established a procedure for negotiations and the deployment of an unarmed Truce Monitoring Force. Questions of Bougainville's future status were subordinated to establishing a cease-fire and the withdrawal of Papua New Guinean forces. A peace agreement was signed in 2001 that promises Bougainville autonomy, development aid, and an eventual referendum on independence.

The Solomon Islands

The Solomon Islands are a Melanesian Island chain—with a population of four hundred thousand—that lies just south of Bougainville. The main island, Guadalcanal, site of the capital city Honiara (population forty-nine thousand), has attracted a steady stream of migrants from other parts of the country, especially Malaita. As was the case in Bougainville, this influx created resentment amongst the indigenous population. The migrants were perceived as a threat to the people and culture of Guadalcanal, taking land and jobs in a declining economy. In late 1998, groups of men seized weapons from a police armoury. They attacked Malaitans living in rural areas. About one hundred people were killed and twenty thousand fled to Honiara or back to their home island. People from Guadalcanal began to leave Honiara for their home villages and the capital became a Malaitan stronghold cut off from the rest of the island.

In June 2000, Malaitan militants also stole weapons from a police post and successfully counter attacked Guadalcanal fighters. They staged a coup, seized the Prime Minister, and forced him to resign.

The formation of a new government and the arrival of naval vessels from Australia and New Zealand led to the signing of a peace treaty in Townsville, Australia, in October 2000. Unfortunately, the accord did not rectify the situation. Roving gangs continued to operate unopposed on Guadalcanal because the Solomon Islands had no national army that could deal effectively with them.

Sponsored by the United Nations, a group of people with extensive knowledge of the Solomons met in Brisbane Australia to suggest ways to effectively implement the peace treaty. Dr. John Roughan, of the Solomon Island Development Trust, noted that an economic downturn, urban-based development, and a large population of disaffected youth sparked the conflict. Undoubtedly, the Guadalcanal militants were also influenced by events in Bougainville, which had sent thousands of migrants to Guadalcanal. The similarities in culture and situation between the Bouganvilleans and people of Guadalcanal, and the fact that Bouganvilleans succeeded in driving out the foreigners, helped spark local actions.

The Brisbane meeting noted that restoring normalcy to the Solomons requires a series of fundamental changes. Development should be de-centralized and based on the rural activities that occupy most of the population. Benefits must be shared more equally, with a special emphasis on opportunities for young people and women. The country's economy and infrastructure needed rebuilding. Solomon Islanders also need to value their country's cultural diversity.

In July 2003, a force of over two thousand police and military personnel from Australia, New Zealand, Fiji, Tonga, Kiribati, and the Cook Islands arrived in the Solomons at the invitation of the government to restore order in the country. RAMSI, Regional Assistance Mission Solomon Islands, has been well received by the local population. It has arrested 2,800 individuals, disarmed militants, and re-established a large measure of security. Although these accomplishments are important milestones, stabilizing the Solomon Islands will require a great deal more work. The necessary improvements in communications, infrastructure, economic development, and political reform may prove more difficult to implement than peace and security. RAMSI has, however, established the conditions necessary to begin the task of constructing a viable Solomon Islands state.

Fiji

Like Papua New Guinea and the Solomon Islands, Fiji (population 180,000) consists of many islands scattered over a wide area. The country is also a former British colony. When the Colonial Sugar Refining Company originally set up operations it imported indentured laborers from India rather than local people to work the plantations. Fiji developed into a classic plural society with different cultural groups dominating separate spheres of the economy and having few social ties to each other.

Prior to independence in 1970, the British attempted to preserve what they saw as the traditional chiefly nature of Fijian society. In Fiji's constitution were clauses protecting native land and granting chiefs' special powers in regard to indigenous affairs. When their indenture period ended, Indian agricultural workers were prohibited from buying land, and could only lease it from Fijians. More Indians migrated to Fiji from Gujarat, settling in the cities where they dominate retail trade. Big businesses like banks and resorts tend to be controlled by Europeans.

When Fiji became independent, the indigenous population retained control of the political system and Indo-Fijian leaseholders were granted security of tenure. Public service jobs were shared between the two groups, but indigenous Fijians controlled the armed forces. This system of accommodation broke down by the 1980s. Native Fijians migrated to Suva and class differences developed among them. Tensions emerged between chiefs in the eastern and western parts of the country, and the Indo-Fijians came to outnumber indigenous people.

When a bipartisan labor coalition defeated the chiefly dominated Alliance Party, the military launched a coup to preserve indigenous political domination. New constitutional clauses guaranteed that an indigenous Prime Minister would head a government that controlled thirty-seven of the sixty-four seats in Parliament. Mobile Indo-Fijians left the country, taking their skills, businesses, and jobs with them.

Expulsion from the Commonwealth and other sanctions led to the adoption of a new non-racist constitution in 1997. The party of the coup leader, Sitiveni Rabuka, lost the next election to a coalition led by Mehendra Chaudhry, who became Fiji's first Prime Minister of Indian descent. In May 2000, his government was toppled by another coup led by a group of armed civilians. Although the Army generally controlled the ensuing civil unrest, nevertheless it proved very disruptive. Indo-Fijians were often intimidated by unruly elements. Another 4,500 people, mostly skilled, left the country. Tourism suffered, sugar production dropped by 30%, and thousands of jobs were lost in the textile industry.

The most recent election, held in August 2001, was characterised by voting along racial lines. Although the results were accepted as democratic, the British Commonwealth and the New Zealand government will not yet remove their sanctions against Fiji because the new Prime Minister is violating the constitution by refusing to give cabinet posts to members of Chaudhry's Labour party. Indo-Fijians, who now make up 44% of the population, still face sporadic intimidation and an uncertain future.

Conclusion

These three conflicts in Oceania provide examples of how ethnic differences become foci of violence when ethnicity becomes attached to issues such as land and economic inequality. In all three cases, armed indigenous groups acted to defend what they perceived to be their rights. Weak central governments were unable to respond to social change in a positive way and lacked effective institutions to control the violence. In Fiji, the site of the Pacific's only military coup, the Army was at least able to prevent the levels of bloodshed and disruption that emerged in the more anarchic situations on Bougainville and the Solomon Islands.

Relatively quiet at present, Papua New Guinea, the Solomon Islands, and Fiji have not solved the underlying problems that led to violent ethnic conflict. Each country faces several daunting tasks. They need to build stronger governments that can maintain order and promote national unity. They also require economies that can advance the legitimate aspirations of their heterogeneous, mobile, youthful populations. No doubt, they will require politicians of exceptional integrity and considerable external assistance to achieve these goals.

HAL LEVINE

See also Oceania: History and Economic Development; Oceania: International Relations

References and Further Reading

Adams, Rebecca. *Peace On Bougainville: Truce Monitoring Group = Gudpela Nius Bilong Peace.* Wellington, NZ: Victoria University Press In Association with the Centre for Strategic Studies, New Zealand, 2001.

Amnesty International. *Solomon Islands: A Forgotten Conflict.* London: International Secretariat, 2000.

Denoon, Donald. *Getting Under The Skin: The Bougainville Copper Agreement And The Creation Of Panguna Mine.* Melbourne: Melbourne University Press, 2000.

Dusevic, Tom. *After the Storm – An Australian Led Resuce Mission Has Stopped The Bloodshed – But The Job Of Rebuilding The Solomon Islands Has Only Just Begun.* Time Magazine, Nov. 30 2004.

Experts Group. *Meeting On the Post Conflict Situation in Solomon Islands*. Brisbane: Customs House, 2000.

Henderson, John. "Fiji: Coups And Conflict In Melanesia", *New Zealand International Review* V 25 (2000).

Lal, Victor. *Fiji: Coups in Paradise*. London: Zed Books, 1989.

May, R. J., and Matthew Spriggs, editors. *The Bougainville Crisis*. Bathurst: Crawford House Press, 1990.

Mclean, Denis, editor. *Solomon Islands: Report of A Study Group*. Wellington: New Zealand Institute Of International Affairs, 2001.

Oliver, Douglas. *Black Islanders: A Personal Perspective Of Bougainville, 1937–1991*. Honolulu: University Of Hawaii Press, 1991.

Premdas, Ralph. *Ethnicity and Development: The Case of Fiji*. New York: United Nations Research Institute for Social Development Report No 46, 1993.

Robertson, Robert. *Multiculturalism and Reconciliation in an Indulgent Republic*. Suva: Fiji Institute Of Applied Studies, 1998.

ETHNIC CONFLICTS: SOUTHEAST ASIA

One of the legacies of European and American colonialism in Southeast Asia, as in other parts of the world such as Africa, Latin America, the Middle East, is the creation of borders, generally made through agreements between the colonizers, which often bisected ethnic groups (although Thailand was never formally colonized, its borders were as much a direct result of this as were those that were colonized). Prior to colonialism, Southeast Asia was for the most part ruled by local kings, rajas, sultans, etc., with the occasional empire emerging (such as Majapahit, Sri Vijaya, Angkor, Pagan, etc.) which controlled and consolidated large areas of land. Distinct borders, however, were non-existent, in part because they were viscous and constantly shifting in relation to the exercise of power, but also because the nation–state, and its requirement of sovereign territoriality, was still foreign to Southeast Asia. Furthermore, most minorities were little affected by the earlier indigenous rulers; power generally circulated outward from the center, and the farther one was from the center the less one felt the influence of a ruler. A distinction must be made among ethnic groups in Southeast Asia to clarify this point: most majority populations (Tai, Burman, Khmer, Lao, etc.) are lowland dwellers, occupying coastal lands and concentrated around river deltas or occupying fertile river valleys and plains in which rice cultivation allowed for the creation of surplus (and later capital), which in turn allowed for these communities to thrive and multiply. Most ethnic minorities, however, are upland dwellers; in Southeast Asia the vast majority of ethnic diversity is found in the hills and hinterlands. Because of their location they remained, for the most part, outside the reach of the lowland kingdoms. Furthermore, their cultivation methods were (and are) generally swidden (slash and burn) agriculture, which meant that these minorities did not produce much surplus, and were much more spread out, as swidden agriculture requires large parcels of land in order to rotate areas of cultivation.

As colonialism advanced and firm borders were drawn up, little thought was given to these minority populations. Yet once these borders were established, all of those who fell within the boundaries became subjects first of the colony, and later citizens of the nation-state following independence, and the problem arose of how to consolidate the colony (and later nation-state) through the inclusion of these minorities. In the colonial period, colonizers were also interested in exploiting the resources of these upland or peripheral areas, including forest products, mineral, gems, and metals. They were also interested in proselytizing, which often served the functions of bringing minorities to the support of the colonizers, and allowing for the colonizers to use minorities in colonial armies (and in other capacities), often pitting ethnic groups against each other. Throughout the colonial period, however, many minorities were relatively untouched by these processes, as they required too much effort and expense. As the wave of decolonization following World War II spread throughout Southeast Asia, and colonies became nation-states, the inclusion, or consolidation, of these minorities became part of the nation-state building process.

Due to the histories of these minorities, and the attempts to include them, many ethnic minorities are suffering persecution or discrimination, and some are fighting the nation-state in which they have been subsumed. Similar to other regions in the world, ethnic conflict in Southeast Asia is inseparable from conflicts concerning religion, resources, and rights. One would be hard-pressed to find a purely ethnic conflict without one or more of the other elements.

The most explosive ethnic conflicts, which also have strong bases in religion, are Aceh and the Moluccas in Indonesia, the Karen of Burma, the Malays of southern Thailand, and the Moros of southern Philippines. Aceh, at the northern tip of Sumatra and an entrance to the Strait of Malacca, has a long history of independence and prominence dating back to the sixteenth century. Aceh has historically been a deeply Muslim area, and was known as the doorway to Mecca for pilgrims making the Haj from other parts of Southeast Asia. In the early nineteenth century, the Acehnese forged a trading alliance with the British, but as the Acehnese expanded their rule southward and the Dutch moved northward, the two finally clashed. Britain ceded its claim to any part of Sumatra in the Anglo-Dutch Treaty of 1871, and the Acehnese perceived this a declaration of war. The Aceh War (1871–1913) was history's longest colonial war, and perhaps most bloody, and although the Dutch gained control of the larger urban areas, resistance continued throughout the colonial period. Since Indonesian independence, Aceh has been considered a special autonomous region (except from 1950–1957) but there has always been conflict between the Acehnese and the central government, over religious issues (the Acehnese support Shariah Law, and were finally allowed to implement it in 2002), and over resources. Although Aceh is the site of some of the richest oil and natural gas fields in Indonesia, it is also among the poorest and least developed regions. Aceh supported the Darul Islam rebellion (1953–1957) against the central government, but widespread overt resistance to the central government ceased until the founding of the Free Aceh Movement (*Gerekan Aceh Merdeka*, or *GAM*) in the early 1970s. Since then, GAM has been fighting the central government as a separatist movement. Since 1999, Indonesia has granted some measure of autonomy, but development remains low, and the conflict has been escalating. In the Maluccas (or Maluku), conflict has raged between Christians and Muslims since 1999. The central government's policy of transmigration, moving people from more populated islands such as Java, Bali, and Madura, to less populated ones has exacerbated tension by diluting the majority Christian population. There is much speculation as to how the violence was sparked and why, as the region had been relatively peaceful up until 1999, but following the outbreak of violence, both sides have recruited members from other regions, with the central government, and some sectors in the military, supporting the Muslims. The Southern Moluccas (Ambon) has a history of separatism that dates back to the founding of Indonesia, and is related to its colonial history. There, the Dutch converted much of the population to Christianity, and used Christian Ambonese in the colonial army to suppress rebellion elsewhere in the Indies. The Republic of the South Moluccas has had a government in exile, located in Holland, since 1949.

The Karen of Burma (Myanmar) are fighting a conflict in which a hill tribe minority, many of whom have been converted to Christianity, are fighting a Buddhist central government over rights and autonomy. Similar to the Moluccans, the Karen were drafted into the colonial army and fought the majority Burmans, most notably choosing the British side over the Japanese-allied Burmans during World War II. Promises of greater autonomy, such as those promised in the Panglong Agreement of 1947, have never materialized. More recently, the Hmong of Laos have been facing persecution at the hands of the Lao central government for their role in aiding the United States against the communist Pathet Lao during the Vietnam conflict. In southern Thailand, Malays (who are Muslim) are fighting the Thai central government, with various goals that range from greater autonomy and development to full-fledged separatism. The four southernmost provinces, Songkhla, Pattani, Yala, and Narathiwat are, despite being large rice producers, comparatively underdeveloped and persecuted by the ethnic Tai and Buddhist majority. In southern Philippines, Muslims (Moros) have been fighting the Christian majority since Spanish colonialism and the mass conversion of the north. Southern Philippines is also home to vast natural resources, but is among the least developed regions of the Philippines.

Resources and rights are two other exacerbating factors in ethnic conflict in Southeast Asia. West Papua (formerly Irian Jaya), Indonesia, is an egregious example. West Papua was formally integrated into Indonesia in 1969 after eight years of occupation (and the ousting of the Dutch, who did not cede control of West Papua with the rest of the Indies in 1949) through the "act of Free Choice," a United Nations referendum that was viewed at the time as a sham, a mere formality to give Indonesia's seizure of the territory *de jure* recognition. Some eight hundred West Papuans, most of them hand-picked by the Indonesian government and under coercion, out of a population of around 1 million, voted unanimously to integrate with Indonesia. Cold War considerations must be taken into account (this was just four years after the Indonesian purge of communists began, President Suharto had firmly allied with the West, and the Vietnam conflict was raging). It was also known that West Papua held vast mineral deposits, as well as virgin tropical forest, oil, and natural gas. President Suharto had reopened Indonesia to foreign investment (after Soekarno had banned it) and one of the first to take advantage of the opening was Freeport McMoran, an American mining multinational corporation. West Papua is home to the largest gold reserve, and the mine is the second largest open pit copper mine in the world. Moving inhabitants off of their traditional land has facilitated mining operations, and the operation is responsible for tremendous environmental degradation. Since Indonesia's annexation of the territory, the Free Papua Movement (*Organisasi Papua Merdeka*, or *OPM*) has been waging a low-level guerrilla war against the central government, with a goal of separation. West Papua is among the least developed regions in Indonesia, but among the richest in resources, and despite promises of autonomy, little has been done to alleviate the terrible poverty and lack of rights of the West Papuans.

Another major area of ethnic conflict is ethnic Chinese (or overseas Chinese) in Southeast Asia. Every nation-state in Southeast Asia has an ethnic Chinese minority (except for Singapore, in which the majority of the population is ethnic Chinese), although their treatment varies widely from country to country. Most ethnic Chinese came to Southeast Asia in the twentieth century, generally as coolies for the European overseers and in an attempt to save money in order to return to China, but Chinese trade and settlement in Southeast Asia predates European colonialism. In some societies, ethnic Chinese have been incorporated without significant problems, including in Vietnam (long influenced by China), Laos, and Thailand. Ethnic Chinese are relatively well integrated into Philippine culture as well, but some resentment remains due to their disproportionate wealth. This resentment has led to a recent rash of kidnappings of ethnic Chinese, with the kidnappers often in league with Filipino police or military. In Malaysia, ethnic Chinese are not clearly integrated, retaining much of their Chinese culture. After serious ethnic conflict in the 1950s and 1960s, however, and perhaps due to the strong-handed influence of the central government in combination with affirmative action programs for ethnic Malays, there have been few incidents of serious violence against ethnic Chinese. In Indonesia, however, ethnic Chinese have been used as a scapegoat since independence. Similar to other countries in Southeast Asia, ethnic Chinese control a disproportionate amount of wealth, which fuels resentment. Ethnic Chinese are often scapegoated in order to draw attention away from other problems, the most recent manifestation of this being the anti-Chinese riots of May 1998, in the aftermath of widespread student demonstrations and the shooting of several student activists in Jakarta. Ethnic Chinese businesses in Jakarta were targeted for burning and looting, rape was committed against ethnic Chinese women, and acts of violence including murder were perpetrated against the ethnic Chinese community in general in Jakarta, and few perpetrators were prosecuted. Exacerbating the conflict is the fact that most ethnic Chinese are Christian or Buddhist, adding a religious element, and included in the turmoil of 1998–1999 was a rash of church burnings throughout Java.

CHRISTOPHER LUNDRY

See also Brunei; Cambodia; Indonesia; Laos; Malaysia; Myanmar; Philippines; Singapore; Southeast Asia: History and Economic Development; Southeast Asia: International Relations; Thailand; Vietnam

References and Further Reading

Anderson, Benedict R. O'G. *Imagined Communities: Reflections on the Origins and Spread of Nationalism.* New York: Verso Press, 1983.

Canoy, Reuben Rabe. *The Quest for Mindanao Independence.* Cagayan de Oro City, Philippines: The Mindanao Post Publishing Company, 1987.

Christie, Clive J. *A Modern History of Southeast Asia: Decolonization, Nationalism, and Separatism.* New York: I.B. Tauris Publishers, 1996.

Chua, Amy. *World on Fire: How Exporting Free Market Democracy Breeds Ethnic Hatred and Global Instability.* New York: Doubleday, 2003.

Garnaut, Ross, and Chris Manning. *Irian Jaya: The Transformation of a Melanesian Economy.* Canberra: Australian National University Press, 1974.

Gurr, Ted Robert. *Minorities at Risk: A Global View of Ethnopolitical Conflicts.* Washington DC: United States Institute of Peace Press, 1993.

Gurr, Ted Robert. *Ethnic Conflict in World Politics.* Boulder, CO: Westview Press, 1994.

McVey, Ruth. "Separatism and the Paradoxes of the Nation-State in Perspective." In *Armed Separatism in Southeast Asia.* Lim Joo-Jock and Vani S., eds. Singapore: Institute of Southeast Asian Studies, 1984.

Yegar, Moshe. *Between Integration and Secession: The Muslim Communities of the Southern Philippines, Southern Thailand, and Western Burma/Myanmar.* Boulder, CO: Lexington Books, 2002.

ETHNIC CONFLICTS: SOUTHERN AFRICA

Because ethnicity and race are pivotal within Southern Africa's social and economic framework, racial and ethnic struggles tend to be central drivers of the region's politics. The region's core racial markers originally evolved in the Cape Colony and Natal but were spread regionally by the British Empire's expansion. In Southern Africa skin colour tends to be a marker of 'race,' while home language is a marker of 'ethnicity.' Although both race and ethnicity have been the sources of conflict, inter-ethnic conflicts have been more common.

Sources of Ethnic Conflict

Five key sources of ethnic conflict can be identified in Southern Africa.

Political boundaries are a colonial legacy. Colonial boundary-makers generally ignored existing ethnic boundaries. Hence, most Southern African states incorporate a number of different ethnic groups, often speaking mutually unintelligible languages. (South African's eleven languages, ranked from the most to least spoken, are: Zulu, Xhosa, Afrikaans, Pedi, English, Tswana, Sotho, Tsonga, Swazi, Venda, and Ndebele). Often the groups placed into the same state were historically antagonistic towards one another. Only two Southern African states (Lesotho and Swaziland) are ethnically homogeneous. However, over 50% of Swazis and Sothos live outside Lesotho and Swaziland because of how the colonial boundaries were drawn.

New racial and ethnic groups were planted into the region during the colonial era. Dutch, Anglo, and Portuguese colonials settled in the region. In South Africa and Namibia, this European settlement has apparently created permanent white populations who have substantively indigenized themselves. This is especially true of the Afrikaner group. The colonial settlements (especially the Cape Colony) also produced mixed race populations called coloureds. South African and Namibian coloureds are a mix of Khoi (Hottentot), San (Bushmen), Dutch, Indonesian, and some black. In South Africa and Namibia most coloureds speak Afrikaans and share many cultural practices with white Afrikaners. The Angolan colonial period produced a *mesticos* population of mixed Portuguese/black ancestry and *assimilados* (Portuguesized-blacks). Further, the colonial period saw Indians brought to Natal as indentured labourers. Many Indians subsequently migrated to Johannesburg, Pretoria, and Zimbabwe. In a number of Southern African states, tension (and even conflict) has often characterized the relationships between the 'new' and indigenous groups.

Within Southern Africa the following definitions of 'race' have been normalized —'black' means someone of 'pure' (Bantu) African ancestry; 'white' someone of 'pure' European ancestry; 'coloured' someone of mixed ancestry. 'Indian' means someone of Indian or Pakistani ancestry. These four racial categories continue to be very powerful markers of status, life chances, identity, and conflict within Southern Africa.

A racial-ranking system was introduced into the region by the British. Donald Horowitz has called this race-ranking system 'positional psychology.' This colonial race/class system created an Empire-wide social hierarchy (to 'justify' English-rule over an Empire of lesser human-types). In Southern Africa the ranking from top/'advanced' to bottom/'backward' was: British-born Anglos, colonial-born Anglos, Afrikaners Indians, coloureds, Westernized-blacks, and traditional-blacks. Some black groups (e.g., Zulu) were ranked higher than others (e.g., Shona) because the British ascribed higher status to 'warrior groups' that fought back. Within this colonial race/class system, individual worth was ascribed according to the ethnic group one was born into. This

affected one's economic life chances, and one's perceived worth. Exclusion from the 'advanced' group produced feelings of envy, insecurity and deprivation, which were to have profound effects on subsequent socio-political developments in South Africa because it produced 'catch-up nationalism'—for example, Afrikaner nationalism and black nationalism were born of groups trying to re-rank themselves upwards.

The use of majoritarianism against minority groups has ensued. Post-colonial Southern African states have political systems based upon the principle of majoritarianism. This has generally meant larger ethnic groups secure a permanent (and unchallengeable?) position of dominance, e.g., Shona in Zimbabwe; Bemba in Zambia; and Ovambo in Namibia. For a number of Southern African minority groups majoritarianism has bred resentment because they believe themselves to be disadvantaged and disempowered, e.g., Matabele in Zimbabwe; whites, coloureds, and Indians in South Africa; Nama, Basters and San in Namibia; Shona in Mozambique; and San in Botswana.

Historical animosities born of past conflicts have often been carried into the present where they negatively impact on inter-group relations. Many Southern African ethnic groups have been involved in armed conflict, which has necessarily left legacies of animosity, mistrust, and resentment of 'old enemies.'

South African Conflicts: Historical Legacies

The nineteenth century was an especially violent period in South Africa which left residues of inter-ethnic animosity that have subsequently negatively impacted upon inter-group relationships. Four sets of conflicts were especially important in this regard.

The Mfecane ("the great upheaval") in the early nineteenth century was a period of intense instability and conflict born of Shaka's violent expansion of his Zulu kingdom. This produced a chain reaction of conflict, conquest, and economic devastation across southeast Africa, with the Sotho tribes being especially badly affected. Most Sotho fled into the mountains of Lesotho (forming a new state); the mountains of the northern Transvaal; and to western Zambia. This emptied large areas of the Highveld and Natal of people. Waves of refugees also destabilized neighbouring areas. Regional instability worsened when some of Shaka's generals broke away and launched conquests of their own—Mzilikazi's conquered the Tswana and built a Matabele state on the Highveld. Soshangane conquered the Tsonga in Mozambique and built the Gaza state. Other Ngoni breakaway groups spread the *Mfecane* to Malawi and Tanzania.

The *Mfecane* left much bitterness towards the Zulu especially amongst the Sotho, Tswana, Pedi, and Xhosa. This bitterness was exacerbated by an ongoing Zulu's attitude of superiority born of their belief that their conquests under Shaka made them the natural rulers of the region.

The Great Trek of the 1830s saw Afrikaners migrate inland to escape British rule. (The British annexed the Cape Colony in 1806). Afrikaner *voortrekker*s moved to areas of the Highveld and Natal depopulated by the *Mfecane,* which created conflict with the Matabele and Zulus. When the Matabele were defeated most migrated northwards. This transferred hegemony over the Tswana, Pedi, and Sotho from the Matabele to Afrikaners. A series of wars established a border between the Boer republics and Moshoeshoe's Lesotho kingdom. Afrikaners enforced their Highveld hegemony through an alliance with Swazis. The Matabele eventually settled in western Zimbabwe, violently imposing their hegemony over the Shona. Defeating the Zulus transferred hegemony of much of southeast Africa from the Zulus to Afrikaners. However, the British, concerned at this expanding Afrikaner hegemony, annexed Natal.

The Great Trek saw an Afrikaner hegemony violently imposed over South Africa's Highveld interior. Subjugated black tribes became labourers within a neo-feudal agricultural economy (pastoralism and grain) geared to serve Afrikaner needs. This produced a legacy of black resentment towards Afrikaners (born of conquest and subjugation).

British subjugation of black tribes took place throughout the nineteenth century. The 1870s saw the British army defeat the Zulu, Pedi, and Xhosa, which effectively secured white hegemony over South Africa for the next century. As a result black people lost large swathes of their land and lost their traditional way of life/economy. Defeat saw black people forced into a labor market governed by the practices of racial-capitalism (wherein blacks were at the bottom of the race-ranking system). This necessarily produced resentments born of defeat, subjugation, and economic exploitation.

The Boer War

The end of the nineteenth century saw the British launch a war against Afrikaner Highveld states in order to seize the newly discovered Johannesburg goldfields. To defeat Afrikaner guerrillas, the British burned all Afrikaner farming-homesteads and crops and placed women and children into concentration camps. By 1902, the Afrikaners were defeated and British hegemony was extended over the whole of South Africa. Defeat generated an Afrikaner lumpenproleteriate underclass of ex-farmers disposed after the war. A program of enforced Anglicization of Afrikaners was also attempted. Post-war poverty and the Anglicization program produced Afrikaner nationalism.

The Boer War generated a legacy of Afrikaner resentment towards Anglos, born of defeat, concentration camp memories, fear of Anglicization, and Afrikaner impoverishment within Anglo-run capitalism. For their part, Anglos generally stereotyped Afrikaners in ways reminiscent of Anglo attitudes towards the Irish. Hence, twentieth-century Anglo-Afrikaner relationships have often been characterized by a mutual antipathy.

Apartheid and Its Legacies

Afrikaner nationalism (which grew out of the Boer War defeat) had two main objectives: to rank Afrikaners upwards (and overcome Afrikaner poverty); and create an "autonomous space" for Afrikaners where they would be culturally protected from both Anglicization and from being swamped by a black majority. Apartheid (called "separate development" by Afrikaner nationalists) aimed to create "separate spaces" for all ethnic groups along the lines of the Dutch *verzuiling* principle. In the process of implementing this policy, Afrikaners used violence to resettle blacks into separate ethnic territories and violence to maintain exploitative economic relations (which promoted Afrikaner welfare at the expense of black and coloured workers). This gave rise to a 1980s civil war between anti- and pro-apartheid forces. Both sides in this civil war drew supporters from every ethnic group in the country. However, the anti-apartheid side drew most support from urban blacks, coloureds, and Indians, while the pro-apartheid side attracted most support from Afrikaners and Anglos. However, anti-apartheid forces also found themselves opposed by Zulus led by Buthelezi.

Apartheid left a legacy of black resentments and the civil war a legacy of bitterness. As a consequence, the black nationalist-led post-apartheid government actively promotes "black empowerment" policies (aimed at re-ranking the old racial hierarchies), and insists on a strong unitary state that eschews the promotion of cultural distinctness (because granting too much latitude for ethnic groups to exercise 'cultural autonomy' is now equated with apartheid). This has produced a post-apartheid anti-government alliance of minorities (whites, coloureds, and Indians) based upon a fear of 'black domination' and growing pressures towards cultural and economic 'Africanisation.' In Cape Town, Muslim coloureds launched a terror-war against the post-apartheid government.

Zimbabwe: Ethnic Conflicts

Zimbabwe has experienced two sets of ethnic animosities. Tension between Shona and Matabele date back to the mid-nineteenth century when the Matabele fled South Africa. The Matabele settled in western Zimbabwe on land seized from the Shona and violently extended their hegemony over wide swathes of the Shona lands. The Shona were treated with contempt ("Shona" is derived from the Matabele word for 'dog'). When Zimbabwe became independent in 1980 the new Shona-rulers launched a genocidal campaign of state-terror against the Matabele and, until the present, the Matabele are regarded as foes of Zimbabwe's Shona-led government.

The second ethnic animosity is between blacks and whites. White (mostly Anglo) settlers violently subjugated the Shona and Matabele at the end of the nineteenth century. As a result black people lost large swathes of their land and were forced into an exploitative labor market wherein blacks were at the bottom of the race-ranking system. A 1970s civil war brought a Shona-dominated government to power. Black-white tensions reemerged at the start of the twenty-first century when the Zimbabwe-government encouraged its supporters to violently drive white settlers off their farms.

Namibia: Ethnic Conflicts

Animosity between blacks and whites began with nineteenth century German colonial repression of black resistance (when the Herero were subjected to genocidal treatment). Afrikaner settlers arrived in the twentieth century, and black people lost large swathes of their land and were forced into an exploitative labor market wherein blacks were at the bottom of the race-ranking system. A 1970–1980s guerrilla war necessarily heightened black-white tensions. Namibian independence brought to power an Ovambo-dominated government. Since independence, ethnic groups—e.g., the San, Nama, and Basters— who were seen to have supported the white forces against the guerrillas, have faced government policies unsympathetic to their interests.

Mozambique: Ethnic Conflicts

With the end of Portuguese rule, nearly all white settlers fled, removing the conditions for continued white-black ethnic tension inside Mozambique. At independence Mozambique was peopled by three main ethnic groups, namely the Makua-Lomwe (the largest ethnic group), Shona, and Tsonga. During the 1970–1980s, a guerrilla group drawing its support from the Shona (a minority group feeling excluded from power) launched a destructive war against the Mozambiquean government. They received support from Portuguese settlers who had migrated to Rhodesia and South Africa, as well as white Rhodesians and South Africans.

Angola: Ethnic Conflicts

The end of Portuguese rule saw most white-settlers flee Angola. However, a large population of *mesticos* and *assimilados* remained in urban areas like Luanda. An on-going civil war has raged since the Portuguese left. On one side is the Luanda-based government dominated by *assimilados* and *mesticos* in alliance with the Mbundu, an ethnic group with a long history of contact with the Portuguese. On the other side is a guerrilla group operating in southeast and central Angola, which draws support from Angola's largest ethnic group, the Ovimbundu. The Ovimbundu are more rural and less Westernized, and regard their war as an 'African heroic' struggle against the 'less African' nature of their *assimilados/mesticos* opposition.

ERIC LOUW

See also Angola; Apartheid; FRELIMO (Front for the Liberation of Mozambique); Mozambique; Popular Movement for the Liberation of Angola (MPLA); South Africa; Zimbabwe

References and Further Reading

Adam, Heribert, and Hermann Giliomee. *The Rise and Crisis of Afrikaner Power*. Cape Town: David Philip, 1979.
——— and Kogila Moodley. *South Africa without Apartheid*. Berkeley, CA: University of California Press, 1986.
Hamond-Tooke, W. O. *The Bantu-Speaking Peoples of Southern Africa*. London: Routledge & Kegan Paul, 1974.
Horowitz, Donald. *Ethnic Groups in Conflict*. Berkeley, CA: University of California Press, 1985.
Louw, P. Eric, "South Africa's second post-apartheid elections: A reaffirmation of racial politics but a loosening of ethnic bonds", *Australian Journal of International Affairs*, Vol. 54, No. 2, 2000.

O'Meara, Dan. *Volkskapitalism. Class, capital and ideology in the development of Afrikaner Nationalism.* Johannesburg: Ravan, 1983.

Price, Robert. *The Apartheid State in Crisis.* Oxford University Press, 1991.

Somerville, Keith. *Angola: Politics, Economics and Society.* Boulder, CO: Francis Pinter-Lynne Rienner, 1986.

ETHNIC CONFLICTS: SOUTHERN CONE (LATIN AMERICA)

Ethnic conflicts throughout South America are in part related to an increased level of ethnic awareness and in part the consequence of worsened living conditions among many indigenous groups. In other words, at the same time that these groups see themselves increasingly threatened by global processes they do not control, they are increasingly refusing to be "Victims of Progress" to use Bodley's expression (1990), and assuming an expanded role in market economies as well as the active management of their own political agendas.

The various theoretical perspectives of the concept of ethnicity notwithstanding and focusing on the Southern region of the continent, it seems useful to start with a definition of indigenous groups such as the one formulated by the Asociación Indígena de la República Argentina:

> Indigenous is the original population of a certain place, that sharing a common past, present and future, are aware of being indigenous and speak or have spoken the language of their forebears. They preserve their values, norms and cultural heritage, and are recognised as such by other members of the group and by outsiders. (AIRA 1986)

In Brazil, the expansion of settlers, prospectors, loggers as well as missionary and government agents into the most remote regions of the Amazon has caused considerable disruption to tribal societies. The Amazonian basin has been the scene of major population displacements since early colonial times. Many of the so-called "primitive" tribes are descendants of groups that were forced to migrate as far away as possible from forced labor or outright persecution. While FUNAI, Brazil's National Indian Foundation, has on paper designated millions of hectares as Indigenous Areas, such as Jaú, Vale do Javari, Mundurucú and others, no serious effort has been made to prevent the invasion of these areas by local or multinational development interests. In 1952, for example, eighty-five thousand square kilometers in the state of Matto Grosso were designated off limits to colonisation. However, before the area had been properly delimited, the local government ceded 75% of it to land speculators. In Rio Grande do Sul, tribal lands that in 1913 amounted to eighty-one thousand hectares, had by 1967 diminished to thirty-two thousand (Bodley 1990).

The protracted conflicts in the Yanomami area in the border with Venezuela, which contain the familiar elements such as loss of territory, epidemics, and a general loss of integrity, have received much international attention. Developments in the Kayapó Indigenous Area, in central Amazon, represent on the other hand a case in which a tribal group, in this case the Kayapó, has retained territorial and social integrity by using revenues obtained from timber and gold mining to employ modern equipment such as radios and airplanes. With these means, foreign encroachment has been largely avoided. In 1989, the Kayapó were also able to successfully oppose the projected building by the government of a series of hydroelectric dams along the Xingú River.

Contrary to popular belief, the indigenous population of Brazil, of about three hundred thousand, represent a mere 0.03% of the total population in the country. However, the Brazilian Amazon has been a testing ground for processes by which local and tribal groups have become connected to a greater world, establishing a significant political presence (Conklin 2002).

At the same time, ethnic conflicts are closely related to conflicts of race and social class. In Brazil, for many of the upper- and middle-classes, Indians, Blacks, and poor people are just different varieties of "problematic others" who bring about a variety of social evils. The envisaged solution to these perceived evils is assimilation or extinction, and not seldom, expressed in a jocular vein that veils deep-felt emotions, outright extermination (Scheper-Hughes 1992).

A striking feature in Argentina, a country with a predominantly white and mestizo population, is the growing movement of ethnic revivification present among an indigenous population that represents about 1.4% of a total population of 38 million inhabitants. There are approximately sixteen different ethnic groups in the country, from the Guaraní groups in the Chaco lowlands of the north to the Ona (Selknam) of Tierra del Fuego. In the face of nationally inspired projects of integration and assimilation, many of these small groups have to fight for the very recognition of their condition of indigenous peoples. Thus is particularly true for those who claim descent from seemingly assimilated groups, like the Kolla in the north, or supposedly extinct groups such as the Huarpe in Mendoza and the Ranquel in La Pampa (Gordillo and Hirsch 2003). There is often widespread dissension within these groups, reflecting the fact that in this ongoing process nobody has a final answer to the complex issues of policy, identity, and belonging.

In the northwest, Salta and Jujuy, the Guaraní people, along with other indigenous groups such as Toba and Wichí that also inhabit the region, are actively promoting the strengthening of communities and development of various economic projects. Through their uses of confrontational discourse in the political arena, they have established new relationships with the traditional centers of power, abandoning clientelism, and demanding the right to self-determination. A basic tenet for Guaraní leaders is that borders do not exist for them: they are one people from Brazil, Paraguay, Bolivia, and Argentina, who share in common a struggle against oppression and discrimination (Hirsch 2003).

About one quarter of the almost 1 million Mapuche of southern Chile and Argentina, live in rural settlements that cover no more than 7%–8% of the territory they possessed until the end of the nineteenth century. These Mapuche, in Rio Negro and Chubut provinces in Argentina, and in the Bio-Bio, Araucania, and Los Lagos regions in Chile, now feel the pressure from the increasing exploitation of minerals, water, oil, as well as tourism, forestry, and agroindustry.

This expansion has reduced to utter marginality the subsistence economies of most rural communities. All surveys made in Mapuche communities on both sides of the Andes show levels of income, health, and education that are below the national averages. This critical situation has led to the mobilisation of many Mapuche groups in Argentina and to an increased level of conflict in southern Chile, where some 250,000 Mapuche live in rural communities, cities, and towns. In many of these communities, forest plantations have drastically diminished water levels, leaving the local population destitute.

In response, many communities have retaliated with land occupation, attacks on employees of forest companies, and the burning of buildings, trucks, and other machinery. Many consider these violent incidents as the prelude to an explosive situation like Chiapas in Mexico. The state has treated these eruptions as a serious challenge to the established legal order and, under the influence of vested economic interests, has reacted with measures such as the Law of State Security, inherited from the period of military dictatorship (1973–1990). Special Forces of Carabineros, the semi-military Chilean police, conduct regular raids into Mapuche communities, breaking into homes with or without search warrants in search of individuals wanted by the courts. The courts have sentenced many Mapuche activists to long jail periods, but have not taken the same initiative to investigate and prosecute the documented excessive use of violence by police forces or the illegal covert actions undertaken by forest companies and landowners. As a result, many Mapuche refuse to acknowledge a legal situation that involved the forceful appropriation of more than 90% of their territory and now operates with a manifest lack of equanimity.

The Andine Pewenche have been at the center of a protracted conflict related to the construction of several hydroelectric dams in their lands along Upper Bio-Bio river for years. Despite legal actions and protest, the second of these dams, at Ralco, was completed in 2004, after the relocation of dozens of Pewenche families. In another much publicised case in the early 1990s, the Pewenche community of Quinquen was on the verge of being evicted from their holdings after losing an appeal to the Supreme Court regarding land that had been inhabited by the same family for the past century but which was now being claimed by a forest company. The state finally resolved the case by purchasing the land in dispute.

In Chile, as in Argentina, the state has implemented a series of social, economic, and educational programmes in order to ameliorate the living conditions of ethnic minorities. However, these measures are only directed at individuals, families, or communities rather than on tribes or groups as a whole. While many organizations of ethnic groups have demanded various degrees of autonomy, these claims have often been ignored or denied. In Chile, indigenous groups are not constitutionally recognised as *pueblos*, peoples, because of the possible separatist connotations carried by the term.

While the national media in the Southern Cone countries has often called the ethnic unrest the action of militant factions, ethnic revindications like these in southern Chile are rather the result of increasingly self conscious peoples or nations that, as emergent societies in their own right, reject the colonialist policies of the past and the worsening living conditions. For instance, some 95% of the Aymara population of northern Chile have abandoned their Andine villages and moved to cities due to a water shortage caused by the diversion of local water resources to the mines of the region. Traditionally a pastoralist and horticultural society, the Aymara were no longer able to practice agriculture or animal husbandry.

The regional ethnic struggles have much in common, in that they reach beyond demands for land and political rights. They also involve the reconstruction of extensive nets of collaboration across national borders and the recognition of the contribution of native societies to process of development. At the same time, these conflicts demonstrate the numerous factors that ethnic identity and conflicts include. In Brazil, many of the conflicts are a reaction against the expansion of modern society into lands hitherto inhabited by tribal societies. In Argentina we witness a process of ethnification that includes small and even invisible groups. In Chile and Argentina, many conflicts result from a determined resistance against the consequences of economic processes that threaten the viability of indigenous communities.

This variety shows that ethnic groups are not backward-looking social groups, and neither can they be regarded as totally homogenous. While individuals or factions belonging to a certain ethnic group might be involved in a struggle as members of that precise group, others might feel uncomfortable with the ethnic label and choose to pursue their aims as private citizens of the dominant society.

As elsewhere, ethnic conflicts in the Southern Cone are the product of present discourse, experience, and interest enacted by collectives with a common past. They reflect the interests of groups that employ culture and history as both their claim and their weapon in the pursuit of political, economic, and social gains (Eller 1999). Ultimately, they are struggles for a renewed sense of belonging.

JUAN-CARLOS GUMUCIO-CASTELLON

See also Ethnicity: Impact on Politics and Society; Southern Cone (Latin America): History and Economic Development

References and Further Reading

Aylwin, José. Indigenous Peoples Rights in Chile. Progresses and Contradictions in a Context of Economic Globalization. Paper presented at the Canadian Association for Latin American and Caribbean Studies (CALACS) XXVIII Congress, Simon Fraser University, Vancouver, B.C., March 19–21, 1998. (http://www.xs4all.nl/~rehue/art/ayl2.html)

Bodley, John H. Victims of Progress. Mountain View, CA: Mayfield Publishing Co. (3rd. ed.), 1990.

Conklin, Beth A. Shamans versus Pirates in the Amazonian Treasure Chest. American Anthopologist, 104(4), 1050–1061, 2002.

Gordillo, Gastón, and Silvia Hirsch. Indigenous Struggles and Contested Identities in Argentina. The Journal of Latin American Anthropology 8(3): 4–30, 2003.

Hirsch, Silvia Maria. Bilingualism, Pan-Indianism and Politics in Northern Argentina. The Journal of Latin American Anthropology 8(3): 84–103, 2003.

Schefer-Hughes, Nancy. Death Without Weeping. Berkeley, CA: University of California Press, 1992.

ETHNIC CONFLICTS: WEST AFRICA

West Africa is composed of sixteen countries, most of them situated along the Atlantic coast on the western bulge of Africa: Benin, Cote d'Ivoire, The Gambia, Ghana, Guinea, Guinea-Bissau, Liberia, Mauritania, Nigeria, Togo, Senegal and Sierra Leone. Burkina Faso, Mali, and Niger are landlocked, while Cape Verde is a group of small islands off the coast of Senegal. With a population larger than any other sub-region of the continent, West Africa is also the most ethnically diverse. Among its hundreds of ethnic groups are the Akan (Ashante and Fante), Fulani, Hausa, Malinke, Wolof, and Yoruba. Because some of these groups, such as the Fulani, Hausa, and Malinke, have a long history of cross-border migration, they are scattered in more than one West African country. The languages of these dispersed peoples however unify them culturally.

West Africa's ethnic plurality varies from country to country and has some bearing on interethnic relations and conflicts in each country. Among the 250 or so ethnic groups in Nigeria, the largest—Hausa, Fulani, Yoruba, and Ibo—have dominated national politics since independence in 1960. In Ghana, the Ashante, Fante, Ga-Adangme, and Ewe are the main contenders for political power among thirty or more other groups with similar aspirations. In Liberia, by contrast, the minority Americo-Liberians (descendants of freed slaves repatriated from the United States) monopolized national leadership for more than a century until 1980, when a military coup toppled the government of President William Tolbert. One of the coup leaders, Master-Sergeant Samuel Kanyon Doe, a Krahn, became the first full-blooded indigenous Liberian president since independence in 1847. The Liberian civil war (1989–1996) was the climax of a fierce struggle to oust Doe from power as Americo-Liberians, Bassa, Kru, Mandingo, Mano, and Vai, among nine other groups, resisted a decade-long dictatorship.

In West Africa, as in other parts of the world, ethnic conflicts pose a major threat to regional security and stability. Scholars seeking an historical explanation for such conflicts in the sub-region often cite the balkanization of Africa sanctioned by the Berlin Conference (1884–1885) as a defining moment. At the conference, European colonial powers outlined the rules for partitioning Africa to avoid mutual conflict. Yet by grouping together different ethnic groups and splitting some haphazardly in demarcating colonial boundaries, critics argue, the colonial powers sowed the seeds of future ethnic rivalries and violent confrontations throughout Africa. Although European colonial practices in West Africa exacerbated ethnic divisions in numerous instances, however, it is historically inaccurate to suggest that such conflicts originated with European colonization. Pre-colonial West Africa experienced its fair share of ethnic conflicts, which on occasion resulted in warfare between rival groups. The disputes for the most part revolved around control of territory, trade routes, scarce resources, and religious differences, especially with the spread of Islam across West Africa from about the tenth century CE on.

After gaining independence in the 1960s, most West African nation-states had to grapple with ethnic rivalries, some of which were manifest while others remained latent. Competition for political power at times turned violent when power-sharing arrangements between opposing ethnic groups proved intractable. The Nigerian civil war (1967–1970), for example, broke out because Ibo leaders of Biafra in southeastern Nigeria felt marginalized in a federal system of government dominated by Hausa and Fulani political leaders of northern Nigeria. Led by Lieutenant-colonel Emeka Ojukwu, Biafra decided to secede, a decision the Hausa-led government rejected by going to war in defense of the federation's integrity. Biafra only capitulated after four years of intense fighting.

By contrast, the secessionist movement spearheaded by the Movement of Democratic Forces of Senegal (MFDC) in the southern Casamance region of Senegal has sustained its insurgency intermittently since 1983. Although Casamance, like the rest of Senegal, has a predominantly Muslim population, its main city, Ziguinchoir, has a sizeable Diola Christian community, which was exposed to Portuguese and Roman Catholic influences during the colonial period. By contrast, the country's largely islamized Wolof, Fulbe, Tukolor, Serer, and Malinke populace experienced strong French influence. The MFDC seeks autonomy, contending that Casamance is relatively undeveloped because the Senegalese government considers it peripheral in both its centralized administration and developmental schemes. Until its expulsion from Guinea-Bissau in 1997, the MFDC launched its attacks from the former Portuguese colony south of Senegal. The Economic Community of West African States (ECOWAS) has been mediating between the Senegalese government and the MFDC to end hostilities. A peace accord signed in March 2001 has been violated now and again, while the sporadic fighting has displaced an estimated thirty thousand refugees, a large number of them living in The Gambia and Guinea-Bissau.

Not all ethnic conflicts in West Africa arise from a yearning for secession or separatism, however. In some countries, because ethnic affiliation was a dominant factor in the formation of political parties in the early post-colonial phase, the potential for interethnic violence was particularly high. During the 1960s in Sierra Leone, for instance, the Mende (one of two major groups) dominated the ruling Sierra Leone's Peoples Party (SLPP) led by the country's first prime minister, Dr Milton Margai. In contrast, the opposition party, the All Peoples Congress (APC), received support mainly from the Temne (the other main group). In subsequent years the polarization of national politics along ethnic lines would deepen, which compounded by other problems including corruption, mismanagement, and nepotism, set the stage for civil war in Sierra Leone (1991–2000). Led by an ex-corporal, Foday Sankoh, a Temne, the Revolutionary United Front (RUF), which took up arms against the then government of President Joseph Saidu Momoh, boosted its size by recruiting fighters, sometimes by forcible abduction, without consideration for ethnic background. The bulk of the fighters were unemployed youths in Freetown (capital), provincial towns, and villages, assisted by mercenaries from Liberia and Burkina Faso, for whom control over the diamond mines in eastern Sierra Leone was a major attraction.

North of Sierra Leone, in the Republic of Guinea, which gained independence from France in 1958, ethnic conflict would play out differently. The country's first president, Ahmed Sékou Touré, a union leader and head of the Democratic Party of Guinea (PDG), surrounded himself mostly with members of his Susu ethnic group, while he persecuted, jailed, and forced into exile his Malinke and Fula political opponents. Touré sustained his autocratic rule by ethnicizing politics, bankrolling the Guinean army, and severely punishing anyone opposed to his heavy-handed measures. Guinean prisons became torture chambers for those who dared to voice criticism against Touré's regime. Most of his exiled opponents returned to Guinea only after Touré died in March 1984 during a heart surgery in Cleveland, Ohio. While the country's future leadership was still in doubt following Toure's demise, Colonel Lansana Conté, also a Susu, usurped power in a military coup. Conté won successive presidential elections held in 1993 and 1998, which aroused a lot of criticism for their lack of transparency. Although large-scale ethnic clashes have been rare in Guinea, the continued hold on power by Conté's Susu-dominated government has not gone down well with other ethnic groups.

Ethnic conflicts in West Africa, as elsewhere worldwide, vary in their causes, potential for exacerbation, and prospects for long-term resolution. In northeastern Ghana, ethnic clashes between the Konkomba and the Dagomba, Nanumba, and Gonja, which broke out in February 1994, claimed about one thousand lives and displaced several thousands others. The clashes arose from lingering discontent over land ownership and the privileges of traditional chiefs. Although a military contingent restored peace a few months after the fighting erupted, the government did not rescind its state of emergency declared in the region until August. Despite the tolerance characteristic of interethnic relations in Ghana, this violent episode signaled the existence of ethnic tension in the country. In a bid to curb ethnocentric politics, the Ghanaian government thereafter declared as unconstitutional the formation of political parties based mainly on ethnic affiliation.

To Ghana's north, in the Republic of Niger, before the signing of a peace accord in 1995, the nomadic Tuareg in the northern part of the country engaged in a five-year insurgency the government found difficult to suppress. The Tuareg insurgents accused the government of marginalizing them and attempting to change their nomadic lifestyle forcibly. Even though most Tuareg continue to live their traditional lifestyle, many others have moved into cities like Niamey (the capital), Maradi, and Zinder where they participate in mainstream politics and commercial activities.

Although some scholars and the Western media often oversimplify the wars in Liberia, Sierra Leone, and Cote d'Ivoire, like those elsewhere in Africa, as "tribal" or "ethnic" conflicts, the underlying causes of these hostilities are far more complex and scarcely parochial in most cases. In varying degrees, the politicization of ethnicity, poor governance, corruption, exploitation by multinational companies, dwindling resources, poverty, foreign interference, the proliferation of small firearms, and religious differences aggravate ethnic rivalries and fuel most wars in West Africa as well as the rest of the continent.

Impact of Ethnic Conflicts on Development

In its extreme form, ethnic conflict provokes civil war, which in turn produces a debilitating effect on a country's economic development. As in Nigeria's case in the late 1960s, the protracted fighting in Liberia and Sierra Leone stifled economic activities in both countries, especially as most multinational and other investment companies found it difficult to operate productively and were obliged to pull out. During the Liberian war, the country's main export industries, iron ore and timber, registered losses not yet recovered to date. Similarly, the economy of Sierra Leone took a downturn during the 1990s, because multinational companies interested in diamonds, the country's major export, were reluctant to do business in the prevailing atmosphere of instability. In the absence of foreign investors, the pace of business activities in both the private and public sectors slowed down considerably. Moreover, the loss of foreign exchange earnings made it difficult for the governments of both countries to repay loans from the

International Monetary Fund (IMF) and World Bank, stimulate economic growth, and implement development plans.

The strain on national economies caused by recurrent armed conflicts in West Africa is evident in the declining standard of living, dwindling cross-border trade, increasing unemployment, and widespread poverty and disease (notably HIV/AIDS), especially in the "axis of conflict" encompassing Liberia, Sierra Leone, Cote d'Ivoire, and, to a lesser degree, Guinea. Furthermore, the majority of those killed in Liberia and Sierra Leone were young people, the core of the workforce in both countries. In Liberia, about 150,000 people were killed, roughly 5% of an estimated 3.3 million population. Likewise, in Sierra Leone, around seventy-five thousand people died out of an estimated 5 million inhabitants, while hundreds of thousands were injured, mutilated, and displaced. Consequently, the 2004 UNDP Human Development Report based on its human development index (HDI), which measures life expectancy, education, and gross domestic product per capita, ranks Sierra Leone the poorest country in the world.

Indeed developing economies like those in West Africa are particularly prone to the disruptive effects of violent confrontations. Nigeria, potentially one of the richest countries on Africa, is a case in point. During the last couple of decades, the proliferation of small firearms in the sub-region either has re-ignited or intensified conflict, especially in countries where ethnic tensions run high. Because the Nigerian government has been unable to control cross-border smuggling so far, small firearms are easily available from clandestine firearm dealers. In 2004 alone, the government announced the seizure of 112,000 illegal firearms. During various interethnic and religious clashes, between 1999 and 2004, notably in Ogun state, the central Plateau state, and the northern state of Kano, rival groups used sophisticated semi-automatic and automatic rifles in the indiscriminate shooting and killing of several hundred people. The communal violence involving Fulani, Hausa, Ibo, and Yoruba, among others, has forced many businesses in the states concerned to either relocate or shut down.

Even more disruptive for the Nigerian economy, since 1997, violence has escalated in the southern oil-rich Delta State, where armed Ijaw and Urhorbo ethnic militias dealing in stolen crude oil use modern firearms and traditional spears and machetes in a standoff with their Itsekiri ethnic rivals, the government, and its multinational oil partners. The Ijaw have attacked Itsekiri villages and oil facilities in the Niger Delta repeatedly and disrupted oil production on several occasions. Not even military intervention by the government in 1999 could stop the violence and pillage. Besides claiming the lives of hundreds of people, the ongoing violence has caused the displacement of thousands more and the destruction of properties worth millions of dollars. The damage to infrastructure has had a draining effect on Nigeria's oil production. Overall, ethnic conflicts and violence in West Africa weaken its fragile economy and undermine its prospects for economic development.

TAMBA E. M'BAYO

See also West Africa: History and Economic Development; West Africa: International Relations

References and Further Reading

Adebajo, Adekeye, and Ismail Rashid, eds. *West Africa's Security Challenges: Building Peace in a Troubled Region*. Boulder, CO: Lynne Rienner Publishers, 2004.

Daddieh, Cyril K., and Jo Ellen Fair, eds. *Ethnicity and Recent Democratic Experiments in Africa*. New Brunswick, NJ: African Studies Association, 2001.

Ferme, Mariane C. *The Underneath of Things: Violence, History, and the Everyday in Sierra Leone*. Berkeley, CA: University of California Press, 2001.

Le Vine, Victor T. *Politics in Francophone Africa*. Boulder, CO: Lynne Rienner Publishers, 2004.

Nnoli, Okwudiba, ed. *Ethnic Conflicts in Africa*. Dakar: CODESRIA, 1998.

Olowu, Dele. *Governance and Democraticisation in West Africa*. Dakar: CODESRIA, 1999.

Otite, Onigu. *Ethnic Pluralism and Ethnicity in Nigeria*. Ibadan: Shaneson C.I. Ltd., 1990.

O'Toole, Thomas E. *Historical Dictionary of Guinea*. 3rd ed. Lanham, NJ: Scarecrow Press, 1995.

Schwab, Peter. *Designing West Africa: Prelude to 21st-Century Calamity*. New York: Palgrave Macmillan, 2004.

ETHNICITY: IMPACT ON POLITICS AND SOCIETY

The post–World War II era, and in particular the post–Cold War era, has witnessed a dramatic increase in the number of "ethnic conflicts" around the world. There exists a widespread sentiment that ethnicity, as a socially and politically relevant variable, is experiencing a dramatic upsurge. This trend belies the predictions of many scholars, who argued within the liberal tradition that with the advent of modernization, ethnic, religious, and other prescriptive traditional values would give way to the ascriptive values of individualism, materialism, and "rationality." Modernization theorists of the 1950s, 1960s, and 1970s in particular argued that as developing countries modernize, they would become more like Western industrial countries, and a civic, national

identity would come to supersede older, ethnic identities. Scholars of the Marxist school of thought likewise argued that ethnic based identities would recede as people recognized their true class interests.

Definitions of Ethnicity

Understanding the nature and source of ethnic identity is central to examining ethnicity's social and political role. There exists no consensus on the meaning of the term, however, and entire books have been devoted to the subject. In the past, most scholars treated ethnicity as a given, typically consisting of deeply rooted historical experiences, a shared historical past, common language, a collective perception of being part of the same group of people, and in some cases biological and genetic traits held in common. Milton Esman describes this *primordialist* view: "Individuals are bonded early in life to their ethnic community and these bonds tend to be perpetuated intergenerationally as distinctive peoples, tribes, or nations" (Esman 1994:10). Anthropologists such as Clifford Gertz typified work coming out of this tradition of viewing ethnicity.

There are simply too many modern day examples of newly emergent identities and older identities that have declined to the point of insignificance, however, for the *primordialist* view to remain unchallenged. For example, Crawford Young notes that "In the Nigerian instance, we find at the vortex of conflict the crystallization of Ibohood, an identity pattern which became salient only in the twentieth century" (*The Politics of Cultural Pluralism* 1976:6). New ways of viewing ethnicity therefore argued that "ethnicity is not a historical given at all, but in fact a highly adaptive and malleable phenomenon. In response to changing conditions, the boundaries of an ethnic collectivity can expand or contract, individuals move in and out and even share membership in more than one community. The very content, symbols, and meaning of a particular collective identity can and do evolve. In effect, ethnicity is a dynamic, not fixed and immutable element of social and political relationships" (Esman 1994).

Ethnicity is not infinitely malleable, however. Historical, territorial, and social "realities" do exist, and depending on the context these serve to limit the range of possibilities for the expansion, contraction, and relevance of ethnic identities. Hence, although a Kurd may adopt the Turkish language and culture and become an "ethnic Turk" (or vice versa), a Chinese person cannot generally become an "ethnic

Malay" (or Kurd, for that matter). Some individuals of mixed parentage may enjoy more flexibility in choosing their ethnic identity, however. Context also plays a role in determining the meaning of ethnicity. Religion, for instance, may or may not be an important part of ethnic identity depending on the situation. In the Balkans, religion forms a central component of ethnicity—Catholic Croats share virtually the same language and are physically indistinguishable from Orthodox Serbs. Jews, especially since the founding of Israel, often see themselves as a people (i.e., an ethnic group with a shared language, history, and culture) as much as a religious denomination. Within the Jewish polity, however, people claiming ethnic identities ranging from Russian to Ethiopian exist. Likewise, an Arab may be Christian or Muslim (and until modern political conflicts between Israel and the Arab world made the identities somewhat mutually exclusive, Jewish as well). In short, the term 'ethnicity' contains within it many contradictions, overlapping aspects and irregular usages, most of which remain unresolved in literature and practice.

Depending on the context, ethnic identification may remain in the private realm of the individual and family, such as an Argentinian of German background (their German "roots" are a personal matter to them, rather than a factor that impacts strongly on their social or political role in society). Ethnicity may also, however, serve as the justification for political demands, such as Berbers demanding language and cultural rights in Algeria. Ethnic nationalism (a fairly recent ideological phenomena coming out of Europe) refers to cases wherein ethnicity forms the basis of demands for a state controlled by the group in question, such as Kurdish aspirations for a state of "Kurdistan," or the Thai state of Thailand. The vast majority of states today, however, contain a plethora of ethnic groups (Thailand, for example, includes many non-Thai ethnic groups, while India includes hundreds of different cultural-linguistic ethnic groups). Many ethnic groups are likewise divided across several states.

The Impact of Colonialism

In the developing world, European colonialism played a central role in both exporting the idea of ethnic nationalism and creating state borders that bear little or no relevance to ethnic boundaries and population distributions. Especially in Africa, but also in the Middle East, Latin America, and parts of Asia, state borders were drawn up according to colonial interests—often in neat, straight lines that divided communities belonging to the same ethnic group and put very different, often competing ethnic groups within the same state boundaries. After the First World War ethnic Kurds, for instance, became a minority in the new Arab dominated and colonially created states of Iraq and Syria, as well as Turkey and Iran (states which were formed from the remnants of the Ottoman and Safavid empires rather than by colonial powers). Numbering around 25 million people or more today, Kurds are sometimes referred to as the "largest nation without a state." In other colonial states such as South Africa, European "white" populations settled, creating various ethnic distinctions ("whites" in South Africa were predominantly Boer or English, while "blacks" included various groups such as the Zulu, Xosa, and "Bushmen," and "coloured" functioned as a residual category that included various groups from the Indian subcontinent and others). Different categories became relevant depending on the context—while "Bushmen" might differentiate between themselves according to additional ethnic divisions ("San" or "Basarwa," for instance), a Zulu would likely see them as "Bushmen" and a Boer would relate to them as "blacks." Until the 1990s, *apartheid* state policy in South Africa relied heavily on ethnic divisions that were exacerbated precisely because of the focus and definition given to them. Ethnicity is always relative in some sense: ethnic groups are defined in relation to other groups, what they are *not* being at least as important as what they are. Post *apartheid* South Africa is now trying to move away from such ethnic distinctions, promoting an equal "South African" civic identity for all citizens irrespective of their ethnic backgrounds.

Colonial "divide and rule" policies also had the effect of fomenting ethnic conflict and sometimes even creating ethnic distinctions that did not previously exist. Belgium, for instance, distinguished between "ethnic Hutus" and "ethnic Tutsis" in the regions that became Rwanda and Burundi. These were largely fictional categories based primarily on physical appearance (Hutus being shorter and stockier, Tutsis taller and thinner—the groups speak the same language and share the same culture). They became very real categories of ethnic identification when the colonial rulers issued identity cards that specified ethnic identity (generally Hutu or Tutsi). Animosity arose between the new ethnic groups as Hutus observed Belgian colonial policies that favoured Tutsis. In general, colonial powers throughout the world usually recruited public servants and military levies disproportionately from one ethnic group over another.

Ethnic Conflict and Development

Scholars such as Donald Horowitz (1985) have argued that just by virtue of living in proximity and differentiating between one another, ethnic groups risk falling into conflict. Many theories also posit that societal and political competition in multi-ethnic contexts breeds heightened conflict along ethnic lines. Modernization, with all its attendant changes, insecurities and dislocations, in turn exacerbated such competition. Finally, the colonial legacies previously described likewise exacerbated the risk of ethnic conflict, as different ethnic groups struggled for power in fragile, newly-independent states, or pursued secessionist and/or irredentist ambitions to forge new states that coincided more neatly with ethnic population distributions.

The logic of such accounts can typically be described as follows: During colonial rule, members of some ethnic groups felt disadvantaged as members of another group received a disproportionate number of privileges (jobs, commercial opportunities, government posts) from the colonial power. In a movement (or war) of national liberation, many ethnic groups united to oppose their colonial masters (although in some cases, some groups supported the colonial rulers until the end). Once the colonial power conceded independence to its former subjects and left, however, various ethnic groups (as well as economic classes) then began competing amongst themselves to control the newly independent state. Ethnic groups that had been favoured under colonialism were often better placed to win this internal struggle, or more at risk of vengeful actions by other groups seeking to redress the favouritism that had previously disadvantaged them. Especially in poor, weak states, the resulting political struggle sometimes became an "all or nothing" game—those who took the reigns of government power would use it to enrich and further empower themselves and their ethnic kin, at the expense of those who lost the political contest. In new "artificial" colonially created states, ethnicity thus often became a handy tool to mobilize and act collectively to secure one's interests. This occurred to the detriment of an alternate civic identity encompassing all citizens of the new state, and the resulting civil wars (such as the extremely bloody one that led to the separation of Pakistan from India, or long enduring internal conflicts in states like Angola, Mozambique, the Congo, and Iraq) led to unimaginable levels of death and destruction. Just as it took European citizenries decades or centuries to develop a state-level national identity, many developing states still have populations who attach much more importance to their ethnic identity than to the national entity listed on their passports (if they have a passport).

Even long after independence, however, modernization (and especially its attendant increasing levels of rural-urban migration) sometimes exacerbated ethnic conflict. In the previous example, as individuals of ethnic group 'X' lost their land and migrated to the city, they discovered a bewildering new world full of modern complexity and insecurity. Lost in the "urban jungle" and in search of employment and housing, they turned to any available support groups. In most cases, these turned out to be religious organizations, kin networks, and ethnic (or tribal) associations of group 'X.' Members of ethnic groups 'Y' and 'Z' would do likewise, and in a short time society and politics would become more divided along ethnic lines. If resources in the new modernizing state turned out to be particularly scarce, then the resulting intense competition to secure them would contain even more seeds of conflict.

Some notable cases of ethnic conflict in the developing world (often ascribed to the processes previously discussed) include: the 1994 genocide in Rwanda (Hutu militias used the colonial-issued identity cards to identify Tutsis at roadblocks and other locations), the Congo (where up to 3.8 million people have been killed), Nigeria from 1967–1970 (the so-called Biafran war of secession mainly pitting ethnic Ibo against Hausa-Fulari), Cyprus (the Greek and Turkish dominated parts of the island have been separated by UN Peace Keepers since 1974), Sudan (whether this conflict is primarily driven by rivalry amongst Sudan's many ethnic groups, disagreement over Islam's role in a country with a significant Christian minority, or simply competition over oil-wealth and power, more than twenty years of civil war in the country have led to more than a million deaths, between 2 million and 4 million refugees, and some 4 million people internally displaced persons), Ethiopia between 1974 and 1991 (the Eritrean federal region succeeded in breaking off to form an independent Eritrea in 1993), India (various conflicts including the secession of Pakistan, the war over Bangladesh, conflicts in the Punjab and Kashmir), and a plethora of Kurdish uprisings (against Turkish, Persian, and Arab dominated central governments).

Even if one accepts the contention of some observers that ethnicity merely served as a cover for contests over money and power in many or all of these conflicts, ethnic divisions nonetheless played a crucial role in the conflicts. Inter-state conflict also sometimes occurs when an ethnic group in one state acts to support their kin in a neighbouring one (the

Turkish invasion of Cyprus, Arab-Israeli wars, or the interventions of various states in the Congo, for instance). Diaspora communities may likewise provide important funding and other resources to rebel ethnic movements in their home countries, or ethnic conflicts may spread to the immigrants' new host countries in the form of terrorism or 'race riots.'

Additionally, ethnicity played a central role in many instances of discrimination and inter-communal violence in the developing world. In 1972, Ugandan dictator Idi Amin expelled all "Asian Ugandans" from the country and confiscated their property. A large proportion of the roughly seventy thousand deportees were Indians and Pakistanis who were born in Uganda, their family having immigrated there generations earlier. In Zimbabwe, Robert Mugabe's government in 2000 began violently confiscating 'white'-owned land as a strategy to shore up its flagging popularity amongst some of its 'black' supporters. In Latin America, many governments have persecuted indigenous populations. The Guatemalan government, for instance, identified the country's Mayan population as disproportionately supportive of leftist guerrillas and opposed to government attempts to propagate a Spanish Guatemalan identity. As recently as during the 1980s, the Guatemalan state conducted widespread massacres of Mayan communities. One of these, the Rio Negro massacre of 1982, occurred in order to help clear the way for the construction of a World Bank funded hydroelectric dam project (the Chixoy dam).

Different ethnic groups also often end up occupying different niches in politics, society, and the economy. In Syria, the Alawiis have controlled the levers of state power since the late 1960s. In Malaysia, the Chinese community play a disproportionately strong role in the economy, similar to that of Indians in parts of Africa (often, such a focus on economic activity occurs in part because of various obstacles preventing these groups from taking up government positions). Such ethnic segmentation can promote the emergence of stereotypes, and at times even "scapegoating," as in Uganda when Idi Amin deflected criticism of him onto the relatively wealthy Indian merchant class of the country, eventually expelling them and confiscating their property. The result of the Indian expulsions in Uganda, as well as Robert Mugabe's more recent seizures of white farmers' property in Zimbabwe, was a precipitous economic collapse, as these countries lost many of their most experienced, active, and productive businesspeople. Societal and governmental discrimination often emerges certain ethnic identities as prioritized or valued over others.

Mitigating Potential Ethnic Tension

Various democratic strategies for power-sharing in multi-ethnic societies have been devised to mitigate ethnic strife, however. Different forms of *federalism* are perhaps the most well known of these. Most frequently adopted in states where ethnic groups are geographically concentrated in "home" regions, federalism attempts to remove the "all or nothing" element of political struggle or the risk of "dictatorship of the majority" by devolving significant powers of self-government to various regions. A well-known example of federalism in the developing world is India, the world's largest democracy. Critics of federalism most often point to the system's tendency to make it easier for some federal regions to secede. *Consociationalism* is another form of government that aims to guarantee power sharing, and hence peace, between different ethnic groups in a country. Consociationalism explicitly reserves a specified number of positions in government and the public services for members of each ethnic community, depending on their proportion of the overall population. Important government decisions are also typically subject to veto by the various ethnic groups. Examples of consociational political systems include pre-1974 Cyprus and Lebanon. The biggest liabilities of consociationalism are its difficulty in adjusting to changing population balances, the risk of gridlock when it comes to contentious government decisions, and its tendency to reify ethnicity. Finally, various electoral systems, such as requiring all political parties to field candidates throughout the country (rather than just within their ethnic strongholds), a minimum threshold of votes to elect representatives (which discourages small single-issue parties), and multiple vote systems (which require voters to choose more than one party at election time), exist to encourage ethnic harmony rather than strife.

In authoritarian systems, discouraging ethnic strife can involve something as simple as including important ethnic groups within the power system and sharing the fruits of power with them. Authoritarian governments also commonly seek to propagate an ideology that appeals to all citizens regardless of ethnic identity—in the multi-ethnic former Soviet Union, *communism* sought to unite all groups on the basis of class, whether they were ethnic Russians, Latvians, Georgians, Chechens, Uzbeks, or Tajiks. In the Islamic Republic of Iran, the theocratic government attempts to unite Persians, Azeris, Kurds, Baluchis, and Arabs under the banner of Islam. In some cases, however, attempts are made to assimilate minority ethnic groups to a dominant national ethnic identity.

Such attempts could range from mandatory education in the dominant group's language, history, and culture, to banning minority groups' language, changing place names that reflect the minority group's history, and even denying the existence of ethnic minorities. For instance, as late as 1991 Turkish state policy was to deny the existence of Kurds (some 20% of the population) in the country, or for that matter, any Muslim minorities (non-Muslims were recognized as a minority, but all Muslims were considered Turks). Turkish state policy advanced the principal that all citizens were equally Turkish, and on this basis free to advance to the highest sociopolitical levels. If any group made demands based on their ethnicity, however (such as language or education rights), these would until quite recently be severely suppressed.

In actuality, most states are indeed dominated by one ethnic group. The dominant group typically has its language made the official language of the state (and/or its religion). Ethnic conflict also often erupts over not only a struggle for power and wealth, but also over important symbols and demarcations of respect for an ethnic group. According to scholars such as Azar and Burton (1986), individuals often attach their own sense of value and worth to the status of groups they belong to, especially ethnic groups. Hence they are sometimes willing to fight ferociously for the relative status of a group, which is partly reflected in state policy recognizing and assigning importance to symbols of the group such as language, culture, historical figures, and other public references ("respect"). Because such symbols are not as negotiable as money or seats in the government, contests over them can become polarized and difficult to address. Some developing states also contain so many different ethnic groups with their own language or dialect that a colonial language (generally English, French, Spanish, or Portuguese) becomes one of the official languages (India, for example) or the only official language (the Congo).

Positive Aspects of Multi-Ethnic Societies

Ethnic identification and differentiation need not only produce negative effects, however. Many people view ethnic differences as something to be celebrated—ethnic identity functions as a repository of culture, history, tradition, religion, and language. Modern liberal ideology in particular now celebrates a rich diversity in these things as an important part of humanity's heritage, a value in its own right. Postmodern thinkers, for instance, place great importance on understanding the social world around us from a variety of perspectives, and a variety of different identities facilitate such an endeavour.

In some cases, multi-ethnic societies have also derived material advantages from the diversity of their populations. Mauritius, for example, is a small African island nation with a mixed population of Indian (67%), Creole (27%), Chinese (3%), and French (2%) ancestry. Hinduism, Christianity, and Islam are practiced by 53%, 28%, and 17% of the population, respectively. Instead of descending into sectarian conflict and authoritarianism, however, Mauritius has enjoyed a democratically elected consociational style government since the 1960s. Mauritius also used its ethnic diversity to increase diplomatic and economic linkages throughout the world: in addition to its membership in the Organization for African Unity, the country also became a member of both the British Commonwealth and La Francophonie. Indo-Mauritians, Sino-Mauritians, and Franco-Mauritians all excelled at attracting investments from and finding markets in South Asia, East Asia, and Europe, respectively. Hence, Mauritius has grown into a middle-income, diversified economy with a stable democratic society and government—in short, a 'success story' of ethnic diversity. South Africa likewise seems poised to become another example of success from ethnic diversity, as the country puts its past of ethnic discrimination behind it and adopts pluralistic, inclusive policies, reconciliation, and increasing international engagement.

International migration and globalization have also increased inter-cultural communication, as more and more ethnic groups come into contact with each other. Diaspora communities may maintain very important political, cultural, and economic links with their home country populations. In some cases, these links can foster democratization and development, as diaspora groups in Western industrial nations transfer ideas, investments, and skills back home. The reverse process can also occur, as immigrant groups bring these same things to their new host countries and energize their societies, economies, and political systems. Continuing movement back and forth between countries accelerates this process.

Development, International Aid, and Ethnicity

With the correct combination of good governance and astute economic policies, many other multi-ethnic states may be able to follow such a model of development. International donors must be careful to design aid and development projects that do not encourage ethnic strife, do not appear to favour one group over another, or play into state policies to crush dissident communities. Especially because ethnic groups appear extremely sensitive to their socio-economic status vis-à-vis neighbouring groups, any policy that disproportionately benefits one group over others contains within it the seeds for conflict. Especially projects that involve displacing local communities carry the danger of supporting government policies of repression, such as when the World Bank financed Chixoy dam project allowed the Guatemalan government to displace a Mayan population it suspected of rebel sympathies.

Private investors must likewise be made to consider the impact of their policies in host countries. In Latin America, corporations such as the United Fruit Company became implicated in states' repression of many indigenous and poor communities, as well as the overthrow of democratically elected governments. In countries such as Nigeria and Sudan, Western oil companies also invested in projects that displaced hundreds of thousands of people and fueled the military budgets of governments engaged in systematic repression of dissident ethnic communities. Because oil reserves are often found in the homeland regions of specific ethnic or religious communities (Ogoniland in Nigeria, non-Arab regions of the Sudan, Kurdish regions of Syria, Turkey and Iraq, Shiite areas of Eastern Saudi Arabia, and the coast of Moroccan-occupied Western Sahara, for instance), their exploitation includes a marked tendency to foster government repression and conflict, especially as local communities clamor for a share of the income derived from their region.

Finally, no policy can remain truly neutral in situations of ethnic conflict. Everything comes to be interpreted in terms of which group benefits from what. Hence, trade and development assistance to a state combating a domestic insurgency automatically benefits the state and harms the insurgents. For example, some Iraqi Kurdish groups have even discussed legal action against corporations and states that continued to do business with Saddam Hussein's Iraq after his regime's use of chemical weapons against Kurdish civilian communities in 1988.

Aid provided to insurgents, especially secessionist ethnic groups, also violates international legal norms that require states to respect each other's sovereignty. In such a context, even humanitarian aid provided to regions affected by the insurgency can become suspect, such as when the Sudanese government accused various NGOs of aiding the Sudanese People's Liberation Army in the south of the country. In the wake of the 2004 Asian Tsunami disaster, international aid also had difficulty reaching many parts of Sri Lanka, as Tamil rebel groups and the Sinhalese government projected their conflict onto questions of humanitarian assistance. In short, everything becomes politicized in protracted conflicts, highly polarized societies, and ethnic strife.

DAVID ROMANO

See also Cultural Perceptions

References and Further Reading

Anderson, Benedict. *Imagined Communities*. London: Verso, 1983.
Azar, E., and J. Burton, eds. *International Conflict Resolution: Theory and Practice*. Boulder, CO: Lynne Rienner Publishers, Inc., 1986.
Brass, Paul. *Ethnicity and Nationalism*. London: Sage Publications, 1991.
Enloe, Cynthia. *Ethnic Conflict and Political Development*. Boston: Little, Brown and Company, 1973.
Esman, Milton J. *Ethnic Politics*. Ithaca, NY: Cornell University Press, 1994.
Geertz, Clifford. *The Interpretation of Cultures*. New York: Basic Books, 1973.
Gellner, Ernest. *Nationalism*. London: Weidenfeld & Nicolson, 1997.
Gurr, Ted Robert, and Barbara Harff. *Ethnic Conflict in World Politics*. Boulder, CO: Westview Press, 1994.
Hechter, Michael. *Principles of Group Solidarity*. Berkeley, CA: University of California Press, 1987.
Horowitz, Donald. *Ethnic Groups in Conflict*. Berkeley, CA: University of California Press, 1985.
Hutchinson, John, and Anthony D. Smith, eds. *Ethnicity*. New York: Oxford University Press, 1996.
Ignatief, Michael. *The Warrior's Honor: Ethnic War and the Modern Conscience*. Viking Press, 1998.
Kedourie, Elie. *Nationalism*. London: Hutchinson & CO LTD, 1966.
Kingston, Paul, and Ian Spears, eds. *De Facto States*. Palgrave Macmillan Ltd., 2004.
McCready, William, ed. *Culture, Ethnicity, and Identity*. New York: Academic Press, 1983.

EUROCENTRISM

Definition

The term "Eurocentrism" refers to views that present European cultural standards as universally valid. It is a pejorative term (hardly any author would declare himself/herself a Eurocentrist). Here "European" is used in the broad sense of the word—as a synonym of

"Western," i.e., applying also to the countries and cultures of North America and Australia.

Eurocentrism signifies both a tendency to conceptualize ideas and events in terms of categories that are based on European cultural experience and to assume that this understanding is objectively valid rather than a subjective point of view. European cultural norms are regarded as a frame of reference for evaluation of all cultural achievements.

These views obviously imply that European civilization is of unique worth. Seen from the Eurocentrist perspective, it is superior not only due to its technological and economic dominance, but also because of its role in human progress. Its superiority is not merely registered as a fact. It is also justified in moral categories: European civilization does not dominate by force of circumstance but deserves its leading position because of its advanced level of cultural development. Conceptually, Eurocentrism is premised on cultural evolutionism.

Origins

Eurocentrism is evolutionism in the broadest sense— a conception of historical processes in terms of development. Its roots may be traced back to the eschatological character of Christianity. Evolutionary concepts are involved also in the formation of the self-understanding of Modernity. Some prominent representatives of the Enlightenment, for instance, regarded history as development. Both Voltaire and Montesquieu wrote about a transition from savagery through barbarism to civilization. In the nineteenth century the idea of progress was associated with the names of thinkers such as Charles Darwin and Herbert Spencer. Formed against such a conceptual background, the science that is now most immediately concerned with the problems of cultural development, i.e., cultural anthropology, has been characterized by evolutionist dispositions since its very inception.

These are not simply notions that nature and society tend to evolve from a lower to a higher level of perfection. The "founding fathers" of cultural anthropology as, for example, L. H. Morgan and E. B. Tylor, adhere to the concept of the psychic unity of humankind (cf. Morgan 1976; Tylor 1993). In philosophical terms, this means to assume that there is a universal human nature. Hence it follows that evolution follows the same course throughout the world, but that in the different places it is at a different level. Precisely this last circumstance accounts for cultural differences.

In worldview terms, this concept is at the root of an unfounded self-esteem of the representatives of "more advanced" cultures, combined with a patronizing attitude to the "more backward" peoples. In social terms, cultural evolutionism offers arguments in favor of the so-called "cultural imperialism." A detailed critique of these ideas is provided by anthropologists from the school of cultural relativism (cf. Boas 1948; Kroeber 1944). They recognize cultural development but argue that it does not occur as a global process. Every culture follows its own path of development, according to its priorities and values. The meaning of cultural traits can be properly understood only if they are seen in their genuine cultural context. In this sense, all cultures are of equal value.

In sociology and philosophy, Eurocentric views are consciously or unconsciously affirmed foremost by the interpretation of the relationship between modern and traditional cultures. It is assumed in an evolutionist spirit that sooner or later every traditional society will undergo modernization, and that the sooner this happens the better for everybody. Consequently, modern social order should serve as an example to traditional societies. And since the main distinctive feature of the West is precisely modernity, European civilization should be a guiding light in the development of all others.

Philosophical liberalism plays an impressive role in this respect. Leading liberal philosophers argue that establishing liberty, rationality, and justice as principles of the organization of modern society requires, so to speak, emancipation of reason from culture. People can rationally choose fair norms of social life only if they dissociate themselves from their own cultural environment (cf. Rawls 1971). However, the opposition between reason and body, between subject and object is widely regarded to be precisely a Western cultural trait.

Criticism

The so-called "Western" values are approached from two opposite perspectives. Individualism, rationalism, liberty, equality, human rights, the rule of law, the separation of church and state, and the free market play an important role in the self-understanding of European-type cultures. Viewed from outside, however, the distinctive features of this value system appear to be different. Representatives of other cultures place more emphasis on the inclination of Western thinking to perceive the world in dichotomies, e.g., subject/object, reason/body, and culture/nature. This, in its turn, entails desubjectification of knowledge, and hence pretensions to objectivity of science, as well as a relationship of exteriority to "nature" which clears the way for reckless treatment of the latter (cf. Alatas 2002).

The acceptance of European cultural standards as universal has far-reaching effects that may also be traced in two dimensions. On one hand, this is the Western "well-intended" aspiration to dominate "the developing world." The formula "the white man's burden" from Rudyard Kipling's eponymous poem is emblematic in this respect (cf. Kipling 1899). On the other hand, the "interiorization" of those standards in non-Western cultures hinders the latter's progress. The discrepancy between "imported" cultural norms and local cultural traditions generates tensions at both the social and intra-personal levels. Trying to achieve a self-understanding in terms that are foreign to your life-world is neither easy nor productive.

Eurocentrism has been criticized from many standpoints. Here we will mention only a few examples. In the struggle for racial equality in the USA, the idea of the so-called Afrocentrism has been advanced as an antithesis of Eurocentrism (cf. Asante 1999). The discourse through which the attitude to the East has been formed and perpetuated in Western societies is exposed as Eurocentric by Edward Said in his seminal book *Orientalism* (cf. Said 1978). Scholars from East and Southeast Asia have initiated a debate on the so-called Asian values. Contrary to the Eurocentric notions, they insist that there may also be a non-individualistic modernity in which there is a balance between individual rights and common good as well as between tradition and modernity (cf. Brems 2001).

Eurocentrism is debated on two levels. Some of the criticisms against it reveal its logical inconsistency. Indeed, Eurocentrism is premised on a pretension to universal validity of specific cultural norms. This cannot be justified by invoking the idea of total cultural evolution because that idea itself lacks empirical corroboration. Furthermore, mere technological and economic dominance cannot substantiate the claims of the West for a leading role as a civilization. The possibility of comparing different cultures by civilizational value is itself very problematic. Ultimately, the said pretension seems unjustifiable in principle.

Another type of criticism focuses on the fundamental issue of the relationship between cultural universalism and cultural relativism. If we presume that universalism cannot be based on an absolute validity of the European cultural norms, does this mean that it is impossible in principle? Should we accept that the only alternative to Eurocentrism is cultural relativism? Wouldn't that pose obstacles to the progress of countries from the so-called developing world? (cf. Harrison and Huntington 2000). Thus it seems that

against all odds Eurocentrism may somehow be valuable—as a challenge for the development of social theory and practice.

PLAMEN MAKARIEV

See also Colonialism: History; Colonialism: Legacies

References and Further Reading

Abdo, Nahla *Sociological Thought: Beyond Eurocentric Theory*. Toronto: Canadian Scholars' Press, 1996.

Alatas, Syed Farid *Eurocentrism and the Role of the Human Sciences in the Dialogue among Civilizations*. The European Legacy, 7, No. 6: (2002): 759–770.

Amin, Samir. *Eurocentrism*. New York: Monthly Review Press, 1989.

Asante, Molefi Kete. *The Painful Demise of Eurocentrism: An Afrocentric Response to Critics*. Trenton, NJ: Africa World, 1999.

Boas, Franz. *Race, Language and Culture*. New York: Macmillan, 1948.

Kipling, R. *The White Man's Burden*. McClure's Magazine 12 (1899).

Kroeber, Alfred. *Configurations of Culture Growth*. Berkeley, CA: University of California Press, 1944.

Lambropoulos, Vassilis. *The Rise of Eurocentrism: Anatomy of Interpretation*. Princeton, NJ: Princeton University Press, 1993.

Morgan, Lewis H. *Ancient Society: Or, Researches in the Lines of Human Progress from Savagery through Barbarism to Civilization*. New York: Gordon Press, 1976.

Said, Edward. *Orientalism*. New York: Pantheon Books, 1978.

EUROPEAN BANK FOR RECONSTRUCTION AND DEVELOPMENT

The European Bank for Reconstruction and Development (EBRD) is a multilateral development bank (MDB) that began operations in 1991 with the goal of assisting the countries of Central and Eastern Europe (CEE) and the Commonwealth of Independent States (CIS) with the transition to democratic institutions and market-based economies, through promotion of private and entrepreneurial initiatives. The Bank is based in London.

The mandate of the European Bank for Reconstruction and Development (EBRD) is to promote development in twenty-seven countries in Central and Eastern Europe and the Former Soviet Union. The Bank extends a comprehensive range of financial instruments to advance restructuring, privatization, and liberalization in this region.

Though it is oriented toward the private sector, the EBRD is unique among regional development banks in that it is specifically engaged in promoting a political agenda: the advancement of democratic values in former Communist countries. The EBRD expressly affirms the conjunction of economic and political reform. Political issues are significant when making loan decisions. The Bank's charter charges it with utilization of standards of multi-party democracy, pluralism, the rule of law, market economy, and human rights. It provides investments, loans, equity, and guarantees for private and public sector projects in areas of finance, infrastructure, industry and energy, and technical assistance and encourages co-financing and foreign direct investment from the public and private sectors. It has invested more than 21.6 billion EUR in the region since its establishment. The Bank is made up of shareholders from sixty countries and two intergovernmental institutions: the European Union (EU) and the European Investment Bank (EIB).

Transition Policy in Eastern Europe

Economic and political transition in the East was not initiated to accentuate negotiating power in deliberations with the EU about adapting to varying economic resources. The aim instead was internal reform in order to allow world prices and foreign investors to ascertain the value of Eastern European capital. There was thus the trauma of sudden deregulation in the international division of labor. One of the original roles of the EBRD was to mitigate this trauma.

South East Europe (SEE)

Part of the Bank's current focus is on the regional dimension. SEE is a diverse area with a population of 60 million, and an average per capita income extending from $460 to $4,640 US dollars. During the last decade, the countries of the region were plagued with military, political, and economic conflicts and crises. The SEE was left with a heritage of declining living standards. These traumas affected neighboring countries through disturbances in trade and transportation, the flow of refugees, and loss of investor confidence. But since the end of the Kosovo conflict in 1999, there has been significant improvement. A great deal of civil disturbance was mastered and a political balance achieved that facilitated economic recovery and more regional cooperation.

After the Kosovo crisis, the international community fortified the attempt to aid in rebuilding the war-torn countries of SEE and to assist them in striving for economic development and political stability.

More than 6 billion EUR was made accessible in annual commitments of official aid to the region, amounting to a per capita level of 100 EUR. The rebuilding efforts in Kosovo, Macedonia, Serbia, and Montenegro demanded special donor conferences with funds pledged and distributed against identified needs. A wide range of donor governments arranged these funds. In addition, high levels of aid were given by Multilateral and International Financial Institutions such as the EBRD, ordinarily arranged in the form of preferential loans.

The countries of the region are counted on to develop and execute reform programs rooted in national strategies that facilitate regional cooperation. The goal is to form regional outlooks on energy, trade, water resource management, and environment, which can provide political advantages and substantial welfare increases for all countries of the region. Moreover, a regional approach facilitates adequate prioritization of area infrastructure investments in SEE. The regional orientation and the necessity to improve regional cooperation is a foundation of the Stabilization and Association Process (SAP), as it is an essential element in the preparation for integration of the countries of SEE into European structures. The SAP is the EU policy context for relations with Albania, Bosnia and Herzegovina, Croatia, the Former Yugoslav Republic of Macedonia and Serbia and Montenegro. It is devised to assist domestic reform procedures which these countries initiated.

Commonwealth of Independent States (Central Asia)

The geopolitics of the struggle against terrorists alerted the world to the prominence of successor states of the Soviet Union, Kazakhstan, Tajikistan, Turkmenistan, Uzbekistan, and the Kyrgyz Republic. These countries have attained strategic significance being nearby Afghanistan. Security and political risk could ensue from neglecting to extend improvements in living conditions to the inhabitants of Central Asia. For the maintenance of regional and even global stability, the EBRD maintains that Central Asia needs to expedite transition to democracy and market economies. The Bank has worked closely with the Central Asian republics in order to assist them in achieving their economic goals.

Each of the five countries of the region possesses a specific economic climate and faces formidable tasks. But there are shared factors that can supply a foundation for deliberating on the way in which Central Asia can best advance. These countries have been independent in a post-communist atmosphere. They have dedicated themselves to the tenets of democracy, pluralism, and market economy, as exemplified by becoming part of EBRD. Yet success in accomplishing these goals has been inconsistent. The EBRD, nonetheless, persists in attempts to facilitate creation of micro- and small-enterprises in Central Asia. This effort acknowledges the connection between the furtherance of entrepreneurial enterprise at the community level and the subsequent appearance of civil society, which might buttress advancement toward effective economic and political reform.

Environmental Policy

The EBRD is the first MDB to incorporate a definitive environmental mandate in its charter. The charter asserts that the Bank is to "promote in the full range of its activities environmentally sound and sustainable development." Yet some of the Bank's most severe critics are environmentalists. They maintain that the EBRD is in some ways even less progressive in its environmental procedures and policies than other international lending institutions. The Center for International Environmental Law (CIEL), an organization that assists NGOs in CEE in monitoring the EBRD, carried out an evaluation of particular projects. It documented deficiencies in the EBRD's environmental policies and practices and maintains that the Bank was unsuccessful in fulfilling its mandate to promote environmentally sustainable development.

One project of concern to environmentalists is the Baku-Tbilisi-Ceyhan (BTC) pipeline Project, Azerbaijan/Georgia/Turkey. The pipeline will transport up to 1 million barrels of oil per day from an enlarged terminal at Sangachal on the Caspian Sea in Azerbaijan, through Georgia to the Mediterranean port city of Ceyhan, Turkey. But civil society concerns exist. Various local and international NGOs maintain that public financing should not be rendered to the project until the entire economic, environmental, social, and legal impacts are adequately evaluated, and until project sponsors make evident the actual development gains for the people of Azerbaijan, Georgia, and Turkey.

Accession to the European Union

Accession to the EU is a significant element motivating political and economic reform enterprises in Central Europe. The Czech Republic, Estonia, Hungary, Latvia, Lithuania, Poland, the Slovak Republic, and Slovenia became full members of the EU in May 2004. A roadmap has also been drawn up for the accession of Romania and Bulgaria, expected in 2007.

The EBRD, European Commission, and World Bank have signed a memorandum of understanding, which articulates fundamental standards for collaboration in assisting projects that will aid accession countries in fulfilling the requirements of the EU. Specifically, the accession countries confront particular obligations for investment in infrastructure to fulfill the conditions of the EU's *acquis communautaire*, or register of EU standards and laws. The EBRD assists projects where its mandate and EU accession obligations overlap. The accession of the first group of candidate countries brought up significant issues regarding the operationalization of the interagency memorandum and its connection with the graduation policies of the EBRD and World Bank.

The countries which won accession to the EU in 2004 will have more access to EU financial assistance and consequently become less dependent on EBRD funds for their economic development. There still exists the predicament, though, of countries that may not become EU members in the immediate future, if ever, in the instance of the former republics of the Soviet Union, and some of the more eastern countries of the region. Consequently, a number of countries will lag behind and need even more capital from the EBRD in order to reach a transitional condition equivalent to that of the recently acceded countries. Yet, on account of the self-imposed conditions under which the EBRD Board of Governors functions, the profit requisite that merchant banks demand, and the requirements of other crisis and disadvantaged areas of the world sited on the IMF and World Bank, the EBRD may no longer have a function in sectors of Eastern Europe in which it is needed most.

Transition to market-based economies goes on in the majority of the EBRD's countries of operation. The countries of CEE and CIS proceed toward these economies, though the incidence of reforms is currently mixed. Most transition economies are experiencing economic growth, demonstrating suppleness in situations of often demanding circumstances. Nearly all countries in the region persist in functioning competently in comparison with other emerging economies. The exception continues to be the more indigent countries in the CIS, where the reform process is delayed and unstable environments obstruct foreign and domestic investment.

After over fifteen years experience investing in the countries of Eastern Europe and the former Soviet Union, the EBRD has accumulated evidence of factors that can accelerate political and economic transition in post-Soviet states. Economic and political reforms operate in tandem in building the security and stability that characterize stable societies. The most advanced countries are the Baltic states (CEB) and in Central Europe, where the political landmark of being invited to join the EU is an indication that the underlying transition has made strong, if not yet complete, progress.

At its annual meeting in 2004, the EBRD issued a positive evaluation of the economic prospects for the accession countries in CEE and the Baltic states. It maintained that growth in the region would average 4.3% for the year with the upturn drawing strength from the recovery of the Czech Republic from floods in 2002 and a cyclical recovery in Poland. The subject of *Transition Report 2004* is infrastructure, covering telecommunications, energy, transportation, and water supply.

The Future of Concessional Development Aid

The EBRD, like other multinational institutions, fluctuates between the desire to manage and the necessity of cooperation. Political clashes take place between the EBRD's principal shareholders, the EU and the United States. This conflict over status and economic doctrine will persist in affecting CEE and its continuing capacity for transition. Any number of arguments employed by one set of states or the other are about wider ideological disagreements vis-à-vis the future economic and political nature of CEE. This is a struggle of a wider nature between Europe and the United States contested through the mechanisms of the EBRD. The construal of the role of the United States in the EBRD ($20 billion US of capital) is important since the Bank plays an increasingly significant role in America's relationship with the developing world and since it is a seasoned institution called upon to adapt its role and manner of operating to a new political and financial climate.

Regional cooperation and international integration transformed the global economy over the last fifty years. These two processes have been more pronounced in their rapidity and extent in the transition countries more than anywhere else. These countries have come out of protracted periods of communism and autonomy within the Council for Mutual Economic Assistance (Comecon) CMEA. Their transition has entailed in most instances a dedication to liberalization of trade and a disposition toward foreign investment. The subsequent modifications in the direction and structure of trade and inflow of capital have been substantive.

Yet some economists argue that transition to a market economy needs to be more than economically proficient. The outcome should also be satisfactory to the community, if the reforms are to remain in place. Development consequently demands not only privatization but at the same time, programs to guarantee that civil society participates in the benefits. MDBs such as the EBRD, it is objected, neglect to follow their own recommendations for political and social stability. By stipulating that governments privatize rapidly, they disregard detrimental effects on the allocation of capital. By asking for austerity while requiring liberalization, they neglect fundamental social needs.

Pervasive worldwide tendencies require a reevaluation of the system of MDB aid such as that employed by the EBRD. A central question is the future role of concessional aid, extended in the form of loans at lower than market rates. A sound rationale still exists for its continuance. That rationale, though, only has credibility if a new orientation develops which adjusts the nature of assistance to what has been learned about the character of development in the recent past and to a rapidly changing global environment. Some of this knowledge has to do with greater accountability, distinct objectives, local proprietorship of programs, and measurable outcomes. Lacking these conditions, ongoing donor country relief should not be anticipated. It will be necessary to develop a new context for future decision-making of MDB funding, founded on an increase of MDB investments in regional and global problem solving; resolution of operational conditions obstructing increased efficiency in allocation of financial assistance; and reorganization in the governance structure of individual MDBs. Multilateral institutions such as the EBRD are necessary in the global economy, but they do not have to be money-lending institutions. There is some sentiment for transforming them into principally negotiating forums that permit countries to collaborate in order to reduce obstructions to investment and trade.

KENNETH KEULMAN

See also Central and Eastern Europe: History and Economic Development; Commonwealth of Independent States: History and Economic Development; International Bank for Reconstruction and Development (IBRD) (World Bank)

References and Further Reading

Bronstone, Adam. *The European Bank for Reconstruction and Development*. Manchester: Manchester University Press, 1999.

EBRD Quarterly Economic Review: Current Economic Issues/European Bank for Reconstruction and Development. London: The Bank.

Eccles, Stephen and Catherine Gwin. *Supporting Effective Aid: A Framework for Future Concessional Funding of Multilateral Development Banks* (Policy Essay, No. 23). Washington, DC: Overseas Development Council, 1999.

Keulman, Kenneth. "The European Bank for Reconstruction and Development," in *Europe Since 1945: An Encyclopedia*, vol. 1, edited by Bernard Cook, 346–347, New York: Garland Publishing, 2001.

Lemierre, John. "Central Asian Economic Development and the Implications for Social and Political Stability – the Role of the EBRD." *Helsinki Monitor* no. 3 (2003): 233–241.

Shihata, Ibrahim F. I. *The European Bank for Reconstruction and Development: A Comparative Analysis of the Constituent Agreement.* London: Graham and Trotman, 1990.

Stiglitz, Joseph. *Globalization and Its Discontents.* New York: W.W. Norton, 2002.

Strand, Jonathan R. "Power Relations in an Embedded Institution: The European Bank for Reconstruction and Development." *European Integration* 25, no. 2 (2003): 115–129.

The Economics of Transition. Published on behalf of the European Bank for Reconstruction and Development 12, no. 3 (2004).

The European Bank for Reconstruction and Development: An Environmental Progress Report. Washington, DC: Center for International Environmental Law, 1995.

Transition Report 2004: European Bank for Reconstruction and Development. London: The Publications Desk, European Bank for Reconstruction and Development.

Weber, Steve. "Origins of the European Bank for Reconstruction and Development." *International Organization* 48, no. 1 (1994): 1–38.

EVANGELICAL PROTESTANTISM

Euangelion, the Greek word for evangel, means good tidings and is used by Christians to refer to redemption or salvation through the sacrificial death of Jesus. Early followers of Jesus adopted the word to mean the good news of his incarnation (birth), life and teachings, atoning death, and resurrection and ascent into heaven as described in the gospels and earlier precepts of Paul of Tarsus in the New Testament scriptures. The church, as it evolved before the sixteenth century, translated this evangel (gospel) into many languages and cultures of Africa, Asia, Europe, and the Americas, as missionary apostles made Christianity a more universal (catholic) religion under the direction of bishops of Rome and Constantinople.

But as is common with words, over time the meaning of "evangelical" changed as elements of the Christian community claimed it as their own. In Europe, after the Protestant Reformation in the early sixteenth century, evangelical began to mean Protestant as opposed to Roman Catholic or Eastern Orthodox Christianity. This distinction continued in Germany and Switzerland to distinguish Lutheran and Calvinist and Reformed church traditions. In particular it referred to Christians who emphasized justification by faith in the atoning death of Christ as opposed to salvation by works, including the church's demand for financial gifts. This salvation was found in scripture rather than in church tradition or the dictates of a priest. It meant a priesthood of believers, lay people as much as ministers, and direct access to grace through prayer, without benefit of priestly intervention.

In England, the Evangelical Party of the Church of England, known as a "low church" element, followed such evangelists as John Wesley and George Whitefield. In the eighteenth and nineteenth centuries, evangelicals in England and America preached the need for a revival in the church. Such awakenings would come through confession of sin and experience of conversion (turning to Christ). The evangelicals' "high church" (Anglo-Catholic) adversaries emphasized the sacraments as a means of grace and on the priesthood that administered them. Evangelicals emphasized more emotional preaching and hymn singing to common tunes.

In the mid-nineteenth century, Evangelical Alliances formed in Britain and North America to counter what evangelicals termed the corruptions of "popery," desecration of the Lord's Day (Sabbatarianism), excess drinking, and a weakening of Protestantism in a great migration to cities. This movement produced a number of voluntary societies such as Boy Scouts, the YMCA and YWCA, and the Salvation Army, and new evangelists such as Dwight L. Moody.

It was mainly these evangelicals that propelled the missionary movement that carried a Protestant message to Latin America, Asia, Africa, and the expanding British Empire in the nineteenth to twentieth centuries, often by the ministries of lay persons as opposed to ordained clergy.

In the post-World War II era, most Christian denominations, evangelical and catholic, had not turned over control of their missions in Africa, Asia, and Latin America to indigenous church leaders. This in spite of the fact that colonies had declared their independence from the rule of the Western states. Most evangelical churches had entered the colonies of European nations in the wake of nineteenth century military conquests. On the heels of governmental or company armies came Christian missionaries, most often of the evangelical branches in Europe and North America. Enthusiastic over the opportunity to bring the "pagan" world to Christ and thus produce the millennial rule of Christ on earth, missionaries flooded the colonies.

Accepting land grants and monetary stipends for their work, missionaries began to introduce what became known as "Western Christian Civilization" in the colonies. Thus, by labeling European and North American civilization as Christian, they termed Asian, and particularly African civilizations as "pagan." Thus the culture of language, as taught in mission schools, and the cultures of dance and dress, were rebaptized into Christian, Euro-American culture. Missions also rechristened native place names for cities and sacred landscapes with "Christian" Western names.

As the meaning of political liberation gradually dawned on Africans, Asians, and Latin Americans, so did the need for a religious liberation. As fervent as evangelicals were about their faith, it was hard for them to distinguish between faith and culture. In the 1950s, mission leaders began to hear a cry for "liberation" from their native co-religionists. As local leaders began to take charge of their churches, many missionaries took on roles as consultants and gave up their leadership posts to their former students.

Indigenous ministers, bishops, and lay people took their leadership roles seriously, although some were ill-prepared for the fast transition. With local church independence came a demand for financial self-support from denominational leaders in America and Europe. Native leaders began to look at western traditions that had wiped out local customs. Local custom demanded more use of vernacular scriptures, wedding ceremonies, dress, food, and music.

Perhaps most striking was the growth of Christianity in developing nations in the last three decades of the twentieth century into the twenty-first. As the number of evangelical Protestants in Europe and North America declined, those in Africa, Asia, and Latin America grew. Some growth was in mission churches, but much was in independent churches founded by indigenous leaders as strictly local ventures. Variety of theological distinctions may have been greater than that in western evangelicalism, with emphasis on gifts of the spirit (healing, speaking in tongues) and freedom of expression in worship with native songs and instruments. New denominations began in homes and kept their home-centered base.

The latest step for Christians of the developing world has been their muscle-flexing in international symposia. In world forums they appear to be showing a traditional theological stance in matters of homosexuality (single-gender marriage and homosexual clergy). Parent churches are being scolded by their children. And evangelicals in developing nations are sending missionaries to the West to develop churches that evangelize emigrants from their homelands as well as Euro-Americans whom they see as in need of revival.

NORMAN H. MURDOCH

See also Christianity

References and Further Reading

Bebbington, David, and Mark Noll. *Evangelicalism: Comparative Studies of Popular Protestantism in North America, the British Isles, and Beyond.* New York: Oxford University Press, 1994.
McGrath, Alister. *Evangelicalism and the Future of Christianity.* Downers Grove, IL: Intervarsity Press, 1995.

EXPORT-ORIENTED ECONOMIES

No economy solely counts on its own resources and lives in complete autarky. International trade plays an important role for every country. This obvious statement already highlights an important factor: since all countries rely on international trade, what defines an "export-oriented economy," and is there a level of exports that automatically qualifies a given economy as an export-oriented one?

This question, which is seldom raised by specialists, has yet to be addressed. However, a first definition can be drawn up: an export-oriented economy is an economy that relies, for its development, on exports of manufactured goods. But beyond this statement, the question remains, due to the large diversity of countries generally classified as export-oriented: from Hong Kong and Singapore, which export more than 100% of their gross domestic product (GDP) per year, to South Korea (its exports totaled about 40% of its GDP), Mexico (around 30%), and Brazil (less than 10%). These countries also differ in terms of economic organization, size, and even trade policies.

A related issue is nearly as old as economics itself: the advantages for countries to engage in trade have been discussed at length since Ricardo and Mills, but it is patent that with similar comparative advantages, some economies resort more readily to exports than others. This discussion found new life in the 1950s, when a long debate began between the proponents of an export-oriented policy and those who favored an import substitution. The debate has not been settled, and policies have constantly shifted from one strategy to one another.

Since the 1980s, with the impulse of the IMF and the World Bank, the pendulum has leaned toward export-oriented strategies, but nevertheless, the discussion is far from finished. For supporters of this policy, such as Anne Krueger or Bela Belassa, the two strategies differ in terms of government intervention. (The advocates of import substitution, such as Raúl Prebish, would easily agree with this statement.) Krueger noted that "economies that adopted import-substitution policies tend to rely on government controls ... and to suppress and regulate markets" (Krueger 1995: 27). Supporters of an export-oriented strategy generally impute the failure of this policy to a high level of government intervention, and the success of those economies practicing their strategy to a non-governmental and pro-market attitude.

Nevertheless, policies are seldom as clear cut as theories suggest. In other words, they need to be assessed in practice if export-oriented economies are not to rely on specific policies unrelated to laissez-faire ideology. The examination of the situation of the "Four Dragons" (Hong Kong, Singapore, Taiwan, and South Korea) will then be helpful in this respect. The "Four Dragons," as the first economies to enact the policy, had not only assumed for years the leading position of manufactured exports from developing economies (more than 80% in 1990), but they have also had an important role in promoting the "model."

Finally, two further points need to be made. First, while the economies of the first generation (the "Four Dragons") were small, with few natural resources and small populations, the second wave of countries are middle-sized (Mexico, Thailand, etc.) or even big and endowed with large mineral resources (Brazil, China, etc.). Second, while manufacturing is still the dominant component in these countries' economies, exports of services are also increasing rapidly.

The Birth of the Model and the Hong Kong Experience

In the 1950s, most newly independent countries that were classified as developing were commodities producers. These countries, for historical and practical concerns, as well as for ideological reasons, engaged in exporting these commodities—mainly to their former colonial rulers, where they benefited from networks and markets established during the colonization era.

On the other hand, other economies set up very different policies. The model started in Hong Kong and spread to other East Asian economies. Hong Kong's basic conditions were different from most developing countries: the then-British colony had almost no natural resources, nor an agricultural base, nor a population large enough to allow its policy-makers to resort to import substitution. But Hong

Kong benefited from a vast network of overseas business relations, due to the location and quality of its port, and its historical importance as a trading centre. Its weak industrial base was transformed from the late 1940s onwards by the arrival of Shanghainese industrialists. With limited government intervention, but with the help of an ambitious public housing program, wages were kept low, which gave a comparative advantage to the newborn industries in the first phase of Hong Kong's development (Schiffer 1985).

The Experience of Three Other "Dragons" and the Difficulty of Definition

The three other "dragons" shared somewhat similar characteristics with Hong Kong. As Little described, "The 'four' (...) are poor in minerals. (...) [They] are heavily dependent on imported energy. (...) Apart from a few city states (including Hong Kong and Singapore), Taiwan and Korea have also, together with Japan, the highest population density in relation to cultivated land" (1985: 25).

But the Four Dragons' pattern of development also showed some distinctive features, as they engaged actively in export-oriented policies later than Hong Kong. South Korea—one of the poorest countries in the world in the 1950s—started its takeoff with an import-substitution policy before progressively moving to export promotion. The South Korean experience is also interesting because its commitment to increasing its exports of manufactured goods did not stop its government from protecting its infant industries and practicing a certain form of import-substitution—even as late as the 1960s and 1970s. In Taiwan, also, the experience was not straightforward: the phase of export promotion only began after a first period of import-substitution, which lasted from 1953 to 1957 (World Bank 1993).

Historical experiences, rather than strict definitions from professional economists, have brought to light the success of export-oriented economies, which was difficult to predict in the 1950s. Since historical experiences are diverse, it is difficult to build up a set of criteria in order to define precisely what an export-oriented economy is, and the discussions aimed at providing an explanation for the growth of these economies—growth described at times as a "miracle" (World Bank 1993)—are endless.

Miracle or not, none of the "Four Dragons" had a significant industrial base prior to the 1950s. How these economies were able to become powerful manufactured goods exporters, their success as models for other countries, and the main issues related to their emergence as NICs (South Korea joined the OECD in 1996) are further examined.

Market Forces and Government Intervention

Grilli and Riedel, in *Sustaining Export-Oriented Development: Ideas from Asia*, suggest that three policies are required for export-oriented growth: the national government must ensure economic stability, maintain the country's infrastructures, both economic and social, and keep export traffic flowing smoothly via a stable exchange rate and lack of import barriers. These policies have been widely used. Some have even argued that they have, at times, been overused: the pressure exerted by the American Government over the depreciation of the Japanese Yen or the Chinese Renminbi is a clear illustration of this phenomenon.

Nevertheless, these policies have been supplemented by even more interventionist ones (Amsden 2001; Wade 1990). Hong Kong, quite possibly the most liberal economy in the world, has practiced urban planning and provided indirect subsidies (in housing, food, and transportation), as well as an industrial land policy, to its people and companies. For other economies, policies have varied greatly from one economy to another. The most popular approaches have been a pro-active attitude to attract foreign direct investments (FDIs)—by offering tax exemptions, for example, export credits, import quotas on selected items (in Taiwan and South Korea), the creation of state-owned enterprises (in Singapore), the implementation of Export Economic Zones (in Taiwan first, but in most export-oriented economies afterwards), and support to infant industries that are exporting, even if at a loss (like in South Korea).

Even though the success or failure of these policies is subject to debate, there is no doubt that governments have interfered widely in order to promote export-oriented strategies—it is nonetheless true that, with the influence of the World Bank and the IMF, the second generation governments have become less interventionist.

The Thesis of Dependency...

Some critics have observed that the "miracle" was boosted by a large inflow of foreign capital. But if foreign capital plays a leading role in the development of export-oriented economies, then two questions arise. The first one is linked to the reproducibility of the model. The second is the degree of dependency of these economies on developed countries and/or to international capital, and their place in the international division of labor.

It is generally accepted that the "Four Dragons" have all benefited, to a certain extent, from favorable historical circumstances and an inflow of foreign capital. These economies started their development during the Cold War, and all had an important geographical, political, and strategic importance for the United States. Even though precise data is difficult to provide, South Korea and Taiwan received the largest direct inflow of capital from the United States. Some companies from these economies have also benefited from doing business with the US Military (whether in the form of contracts or retail purchases made by military personnel), so this factor has to be taken into account. This is especially true for South Korea, but also, to a certain extent, for the three other dragons.

More importantly, these economies have set up specific policies to attract foreign capital. South Korea heavily relied on external loans, but also on Japanese capital. "In 1974 Japanese conglomerates still controlled 40% of South Korea's foreign trade, and 56% of Taiwan's" (Lipietz 1987: 77). Singapore also set policies in order to attract multinational corporations. The role of foreign capital for Hong Kong is less obvious, since it relies on a number of small and medium enterprises. Nevertheless, numerous foreign companies, especially from the electronics industry, set up subsidiaries in territory during the 1960s and 1970s.

Therefore, "an explanation which stressed the primacy of external factors would argue that the growth that has occurred in these four countries [sic] has deepened their dependency status and contributed little to their capacity for autonomous and balanced growth in the future" (Lee 1985: 7). A more extreme explanation would go further and stresses that the export growth, far from provoking development, has reinforced the dependency pattern. According to this view, the production of manufactured goods, generally with limited technology and a large cheap labor force, corresponds only with a deconcentration of production in the periphery: instead of importing cheap labor from developing areas, multinational corporations now decentralize to these peripheral locations, employing the same dependency pattern that has not fundamentally changed since the 1960s.

In defense of this view, supporters have emphasized that Export Processing Zones, in which most of the production is exported and most inputs are imported, "labor costs constitute the only element of domestic value-added" (Lee 1985: 8).

While the financial importance of Hong Kong, the development of a technological base in Singapore, and technological improvements in Taiwan and South Korea have defied these pessimistic forecasts, the pessimists have found new ground with the emergence of a second wave of export-oriented economies.

In "Sustainable Industrial Development? The Performance of Mexico's FDI-led Integration Strategy," Gallagher and Zarsky argue that if an export sector is not interwoven with the other sectors of the nation's economy (creating jobs, training a work force, making technological advancements whose effects can be spread around), the country's economy will receive any long-term benefits from the exports. They framed their argument using Mexico as an example; however, the same arguments were also put forward for big countries like China, defined as the "Sweatshop of the World." The fact that China is now the second largest recipient of FDIs in the world behind the United States boosts the argumentation one step further—especially since the goods manufactured there are mainly labor-intensive.

On the other side, the growing share of Chinese textile in the world's market (in the context of the diminishing importance of the Multifiber Agreement) has raised concerns in developed, as well as developing, economies. For instance, in 2004, China's share of quota-free apparel exported to the USA was 70%, up from 10% in 2001. In contrast, Thailand's share decreased from 10% to 3%, and Mexico's from 8% to 2% during the same period.

... Or the Validity as a Model?

The success of the "Four Dragons" makes it difficult to uphold the dependency theory. Some of them have caught up technologically, even though most enterprises (like Taiwan's Acer) are still heavily dependent on subcontracts granted by multinational corporations (Hobday 1996). Companies from the "Four Dragons" have even been delocalizing their industries in China and Southeast Asia. Foreign capital is only one factor for this phenomenon.

The question of the reproducibility of an export-oriented policy for other economies can therefore be raised—and it has been addressed numerous times—while the first wave of "exported-oriented economies" was followed by a second since the 1970s. If neoclassical economists have emphasized criteria, such a "uniform realistic exchange rate," low government expenditures, and so on, it is necessary to go further and pinpoint two main differences between the first and the second wave.

First of all, the historical context is very different: the Cold War effectively ended in 1989, and newcomers could no longer count on American generosity. On the contrary, US companies now see countries like China as potential threats. Second, the first wave numbered only a few economies, which were generally small. The newcomers range from middle-sized to giants, and are much more numerous. Such differences have profound consequences.

Even an efficient export policy may be not enough to provoke a country's development. The practice today is to concentrate production for export in designated economic zones, and then to build up backward linkages with the remainder of one's economy. The examples of Mexico and China show that this strategy has only been partly efficient (China's difficulty in stimulating development in its western provinces is a case in point). In addition, new "export-oriented" economies face competition from each other, especially in the labor-intensive segment, where their main comparative advantages lie—as demonstrated by changes in some countries' market share in the quota-free apparel market in the United States.

These circumstances do not mean that the success of the first wave of "export-oriented economies" cannot be reproduced, but that the validity of the policy as a general model appears more limited (for example, if currency depreciation occurs in each economy that follows an export policy, then the effectiveness of the depreciation tends to be reduced). Among the newcomers, there will be winners and losers, as well as new analyses. Newcomers are conscious of the difficulties of being latecomers, and of the risk of market congestion for their lower-end products. In response, they have adopted several countermeasures.

First, they have relied on the expertise of developed countries and NIEs. At the beginning of the 1980s, China established Special Economic Zones at its border with Hong Kong and Macau in order to attract Hong Kong investment. In Mexico, *maquiladoras*, bordering the United States, also followed the same logic. In their most ideal form, such cooperation would lead to "borderless economies" or "growth triangles," in which the comparative advantages of each economy complement and enhance the competitiveness of the other areas. The Johore/Riau/Singapore area is an institutional form of "growth triangle," formalized by international agreements between Singapore, Indonesia, and Malaysia. The aim is not only to attract FDIs, but also to promote technology transfers. The results of the policy are mixed, with technology transfers slow, but not insignificant.

An important intended effect of these international arrangements is to boost the importance of the NICs, not only as manufacturing and export areas, but also as service-oriented economies. Hong Kong and Singapore are now major international service centers, as demonstrated by their transport infrastructure (their ports are, respectively, the first and second in the world for containers) and their financial markets. This way, the appearance of new export-oriented economies has accelerated the transformation of the first wave economies, from industry to service providers and exporters.

Second, some export-oriented economies are trying to figure out how to complement, rather than compete with, their neighbors. In its most extreme form, this policy has manifested itself in the form of trade agreements (ASEAN, NAFTA, etc.). For example, in order to respond to concerns by Southeast Asian countries after it joined the WTO in 2001, China has promoted ASEAN-China cooperation.

A third strategy is to diversify production and escape from a too strong dependency on labor-intensive manufacturing, where competition is stiff. Some countries are now exporting services, and this trend will further develop in the future. American companies are now subcontracting to India some computer service jobs; the maintenance of Germany's Lufthansa fleet is now carried out in Shanghai. Examples are plentiful. Even though statistics are lacking, these services constitute a significant part of the newer export-oriented economies.

Therefore, export-oriented economies have become more diversified. The "Four Dragons" of the first generation, which have devoted resources to enhance their education and transportation systems, have become more balanced economies and societies with a larger part of their economies devoted to services. Their comparatively small economies helped accelerate this process, since labor shortages and increases in wages have led to the outsourcing of their labor-intensive jobs to places with cheaper labor. Thus, the pattern has been set for a second wave to eventually become export-oriented economies themselves. But competition has also pushed the original "dragons" to try to develop newer and more inventive solutions, while remaining, to a certain extent, dependent on labor-intensive activities.

LOUIS AUGUSTIN-JEAN

See also Development History and Theory; Foreign Direct Investments (FDI); Import Substitution Industrialization; International Monetary Fund (IMF); World Trade Organization (WTO)

References and Further Reading:

Amsden, Alice H. *The Rise of "the Rest": Challenges to the West from Late Industrialization Economies.* Hong Kong: Oxford University Press, 2001.

Cardoso, Eliana, and Ann Helwege. *Latin America's Economy: Diversity, Trends, and Conflicts.* Cambridge: MIT Press, c1992.

Gallagher, Kevin P., and Lyuba Zarsky. "*Sustainable Industrial Development? The Performance of Mexico's FDI-led Integration Strategy*", Medford, MA., Tufts University, Fletcher School of Law and Diplomacy, 2004.

Grilli, Enzo, and James Riedel. "East Asian Growth Model: How General is it?," In *Sustaining Export-Oriented Development. Ideas from Asia.* Ross Garnaut, Enzo Grilli, and James Riedel (Ed.) Cambridge: Cambridge University Press, 1995, pp. 31–61.

Hobday, Michael. *Innovation in East Asia: the Challenge to Japan.* Aldershot, Hants, England: Edward Elgar, c1995.

Kodama, Yoshi. *Asia Pacific Economic Integration and the GATT-WTO Regime.* London: Kluwer Law International, 1999.

Krueger, Anne O. "The Role of Trade in Growth and Development: Theories and Lessons from Experience," In *Sustaining Export-Oriented Development. Ideas from Asia.* Ross Garnaut, Enzo Grilli, and James Riedel (Ed.) Cambridge: Cambridge University Press, 1995, pp. 1–30.

Lee, Eddy. "Export-led Industrialization in Asia: An overview," In *Export-led Industrialization and Development.* Eddy Lee (Ed.) Geneva. ILO, 1985, pp. 1–22.

Lipietz, Alain. *Mirages and Miracles, The Crisis of Global Fordism.* London: Verso, 1987.

Schiffer, Jonathan R. "Anatomy of a laissez-faire government: the HK growth model reconsidered", In *State Policy and the Development Process. Proceedings of a Symposium on Social and Environmental Development,* Peter Hills (Ed.) Hong Kong: Centre of Urban Studies and Urban Planning, University of Hong Kong, 1985, pp. 1–29.

Wade, Robert. *Governing the Market: Economic Theory and the Role of Government in East Asian Industrialization.* Princeton, NJ: Princeton University Press, 1990.

World Bank. *East Asian Miracle. Economic Growth and Public Policy.* New York: Oxford University Press, c1993.

EXTRACTIVE INDUSTRIES

Since its early stages the human kind has been exploiting the natural resources that the Earth provides such as fish, minerals, water, soil, or oil. But it was after the first Industrial Revolution and mainly during the nineteenth and twentieth centuries that the global demand for such resources increased at high speed and exploitations at large scale began.

Above all, the international demand for coal and later for oil increased at exponential rates as the industries multiplied. Altogether the demand for extractive industries (EI), which include the oil, gas, and mining sectors, increased rapidly to keep up with the growth primarily of the western economies. The coming of the World Wars accelerated the demand for these products in order to produce weapons and all the necessary equipments and machinery for the wars.

After the end of World War II in 1945, the development of the industrial sector was even faster and the expansion of industries based on the extractive industries was astonishing. Therefore the living standards of most western societies improved accordingly. As a consequence, during the 1940s, 1950s, and 1960s, it was believed that resource-rich states that were financially poor could change their economic and social situation with foreign capital investments, in the same way that Western developed countries had. Most economists believed that the extractive industries exports would bring about high growth rates with development for the inhabitants.

However, the analysis of many extractive industries cases during the last fifty years has proved that mineral and oil dependent states have low average living standards and haven't had much advance in their development. Recent studies performed by Oxfam America, an affiliate of Oxfam International, have shown that countries dependent on extractive industries, especially the African nations, still have high poverty rates, low overall living standards, high rates of infant mortality and malnutrition, income inequality, corruption, authoritarian governments, and civil wars (Ross 2001). This means that the exploitation of extractive industries do not necessarily engender the development of a society. Most of the richness generated by this sector is not well distributed among the country's inhabitants but instead is accumulated by small groups of local or international elites.

Oil Extraction and Development

During the nineteenth and twentieth centuries, oil replaced coal and became the most important and necessary energy source to make our social and industrial organization function. Oil, or *petroleum,* also called *crude oil,* is a bituminous liquid composed of various organic chemicals. It is found in large quantities below the surface of Earth. Refined oil and its derivates are used to produce hundreds of products in the chemical industry, to move the engines of most transport means, to produce electricity and heating, to make industry machines work, to manufacture medicines, weapons, fertilizers, plastics, foodstuffs, building materials, paints, cloth, make up, among other uses.

The oil market has been on the increase for the last centuries, promoting the exploration and discovery of new wells around the world. At the beginning of the twentieth century, the scientific discovery of underground petroleum reserves in many countries around the world was a crucial moment in the world economy.

Under the production model named *fordism* after Henry Ford, cheap oil was the fuel that pushed most of the industries in the developed countries. The motorcar industry and the transport industries as a whole played a leading role at demanding regularly large amounts of gasoline, fuel derived from oil. Every manufacture based its price on the regular supply of cheap oil, which accounted for the low prices of the products during the *golden age* between the end of the World War II and the middle 1970s crisis. Most developed countries were extracting and refining their own oil but as the demand grew, imports from non-developed countries became necessary.

Therefore exploration activities and the latter extraction of crude oil provoked the installment of many crude-oil extracting facilities in non-developed countries such as Saudi Arabia, Venezuela, Iraq, Iran, Kuwait, Libya, Nigeria, and Mexico among others, which by that time were considered to be poor countries. The discovery of underground petroleum reserves and the consequent exports of the oil caused a break in the economic history of these countries: the GDP largely increased and the newly incomes favoured the social and economic development of the society.

In that age, the previously mentioned exporting countries obtained large revenues from oil and based most of their economies on these exports. By means of such incomes public schools, hospitals, houses, roads, dams, telephone lines, gas pipelines, harbours, and more public infrastructure was built. Employment rates were high.

The 1973 (Yom Kippur War) and 1979 petroleum crisis and the rising of international petroleum prices affected these oil-dependent economies. However, they recovered, especially during the 1990s when the oil prices went up again.

However, although the common people's social conditions improved, poverty, unemployment, poor health, and education conditions still remain a problem in some oil dependent countries like Nigeria, Saudi Arabia, Angola, Kuwait, Yemen, Bahrain, or the United Arab Emirates, some of the highest oil dependent states worldwide (Ross 2001). This all means that, for the past decades, the exports of oil and a consequent high oil dependency rate hasn't caused these countries to develop or to improve the living standards of the common citizens as it could have with such high profits that the oil business generates. Wealthier and more powerful countries like the United States, the United Kingdom, and Canada were largely economically benefited from the extraction of oil.

The major oil extraction areas worldwide are the Middle East, the former Soviet Union, and the United

States. Saudi Arabia is the major export partner and world producer (with an estimate of around 8.7 million barrels per day in 2001), has the largest petroleum reserves and plays a leading role in the Organization of Petroleum Exporting Countries (OPEC) at forming international oil prices. Sixty percent of the world petroleum reserves are located in the countries of Middle East. Saudi Arabia had 25% of oil proved reserves worldwide in 2002, Iraq was second with 11%, then Kuwait and Iran with 9% each, and the United Arab Emirates with 7%.

The international trade patterns show that the major consumers import most of the refined oil: United States with imports of around 9.3 million barrels per day in 2001, Western Europe (Germany, France, Italy), China and then Asia and Oceania and Africa. On the other side, the major oil producers (supply) are not the same. The list is ordered as follows: OPEC as the major producer with around 30 million barrels per day in 2000, then the former Soviet Union, Saudi Arabia, United States, Iran, Norway, China, and Venezuela among others. Some countries base almost their entire economy on petroleum. Saudi Arabia's petroleum sector, for instance, accounts for roughly 75% of budget revenues, 45% of GDP, and 90% of export earnings.

The Gas Industry and Development

Natural gas has become the second most important energy source worldwide. Natural gas is used for heating, cooling, as fuel for cars, for domestic and industrial purposes as well as for electricity production.

In the last twenty years the natural gas world reserves have doubled, having growth mostly in the former Union of Socialist Soviet Republics (USSR) and in the Middle East, Central and South America emerging countries. In 1999, important discoveries were made in Algeria and Egypt.

The United States and Saudi Arabia are the world major suppliers of natural gas, followed by the countries of the OPEC, Canada, Russia and Mexico. On the other side, the major consumers of natural gas are the United States in first place, then Russia, the countries of Western Europe, Canada, Ukraine, Iran and Japan among others. In 2002, the Russian Federation (33%) and Iran (15%) had around 48% of the world proved reserves of natural gas. Qatar possessed 10%, Saudi Arabia, the United Arab Emirate and the US only 3%.

The extraction and exports of natural gas have caused the development of infrastructure such as harbours, roads, and gas pipelines from the inner part of the countries towards the shore where gas is shipped and transported by ship. It has also generated increases in the GDP, which have benefited the countries' economies and richest people. However, many times the exploitation of such resources hasn't benefited most of the population itself as the incomes have not been used to develop social infrastructure as hospitals, schools, decent salaries for teachers, doctors, or public employees. Besides, many times the exploitation of these resources are at the stake of private actors and the gas is not available for the population of the country as it is exported. This type of situation has provoked many rebellions, the latest being the Bolivian Crisis in October 2003 when the government was overthrown by a popular uplifting demanding that the Bolivian gas wasn't exported but instead used to provide the Bolivians with affordable gas.

The Mining Industry and Development

Humankind has been extracting different minerals from soil since the early appearance of man on earth. Mining, in its broadest sense, is the process of obtaining useful minerals from the earth's crust. An ore is a mineral or combination of minerals from which a useful substance can be extracted and later marketed at a price that will recover the costs of mining. The naturally occurring substances are usually divided into metalliferous ones, such as the ores of gold, iron, copper, lead, and manganese, and the nonmetalliferous minerals, such as coal, quartz, bauxite, borax, asbestos, talc, feldspar, and phosphate rock. Building and ornamental stones usually are considered to form a separate group and they include slate, marble, limestone, travertine, and granite.

During the early times of mankind extracted minerals were used to produce simple weapons or tools, then inventing more complex devices to produce swords, coins, hammers, or chains. During the different early stages of mankind (Copper Age, Bronze Age, Iron Age, Petroleum Age, Information Age) and even today, mining resources are crucial for all industrial and daily activities.

However, technology has significantly advanced and today the mining process includes excavations in underground mines and surface excavations in open-pit, or open-cut (strip) mines. In addition, recent technological developments may soon make the mining of metallic ores from the sea floor economically feasible.

Globally the industrial countries consume more than two thirds of the global and annual production of the most important minerals. The United States, Canada, Australia, Japan, and Western Europe, with around 15% of the world population, altogether consume most of the metals produced every year: approximately 61% of all the aluminium, 60% of the plumber, 59% of the copper, and 49% of the steel.

Although the mining sector is a very profitable one, it has not always encouraged the development of the countries where the ore deposits are mined. According to a recent Oxfam America report, the most mineral dependent states, Botswana, Sierra Leone, Zambia, United Arab Emirates, Mauritania, Papua New Guinea among others, rank among the worst ranked countries in the Human Development Index provided by the United Nations Development Program (UNDP) (Ross 2001; UNDP 2004). This is the result of a long-lasting tradition of using ore deposits as if they were territories separated from their surroundings—to consider ore deposits as treasures that can be found and exploited without generating beneficial effects for the people who live in the near zones and for the citizens of the country where the deposit is located. Often the minerals are extracted by companies that generate low positive impacts on the society and obtain large profits without reinvesting them in the development of the country. This tendency explains the existence of many resource-rich states that are extremely poor, with high external debts and low development index. These examples can be found presently in most mineral dependent African countries like the Democratic Republic of Congo (rich in diamonds and coltan) or South Africa, in South American countries like Brazil, Peru, or Bolivia as well as Asian countries.

Environmental Effects of Extractive Industries

Extractive industries as previously depicted are highly risky and so far have caused several serious damages to the environment. One of the most recurrent and dangerous activities is the maritime transport of petroleum in oil tankers. In the last forty years, numerous accidents have occurred provoking disastrous ecological consequences on several ecosystems and in the fishing activities of the people who live upon that activity. The first accident occurred in 1967 with the *Torrey Canyon*, an oil tanker that crashed against a reef in southwest England and spilled more than 120,000 tons of petrol into the sea. As a result more than 200,000 birds died and the fishing industry was ruined for many months. Other major accidents were the *Polycommander* incident (1970), the *Metula* spill (1970), the *Amoco Cadiz* spill (1978), the *Exxon Valdez* spill in Alaska (1989), the intended spill of petroleum in the Persian Gulf by Iraq during the 1991 war, the *Nassia* incident (1994), the *Erica* oil tanker incident (1999), among others. All of them provoked irreparable and incalculable damages to the environment.

The mining sector is also another source contamination and several damages to the environment and human health, many times disregarding government regulations. The toxic smoke and powder released into the atmosphere in refinery facilities is very usual and can cause respiratory disorders to the people, plants, and animals. Another source of contamination are the toxic chemical wastes thrown to the rivers without any kind of treatment, which contaminate the precious resources of underground and superficial fresh water. Also in open-cast mines it is usual to have the emanations of toxic gases and steam, like sulphur dioxide, carbon dioxide and methane, gases that also contribute to the greenhouse effect worldwide. Mainly open cast mines are the most harmful because engineers use some heavy chemicals, like arsenic, mercury, and plumber, to separate minerals from the ore. These heavy chemicals contaminate underground water reserves and can easily reach the population, provoking high risk of serious diseases. Besides, most times these chemicals are drained to the near land and ruin it. These all means that the environmental and social costs are higher than the benefits for the population.

As for the gas industry, this one is the most environmental-friendly and safe of the three. Natural gas is considered one of the cleanest energies worldwide.

Sustainable Development and Extractive Industries

The concept of sustainable development first appeared in 1987 when the World Commission on Environment and Development (the Brundtland Commission), agreed on a definition of sustainable development that is now generally recognised as the standard: "Sustainable development is development that meets the needs of the present without compromising the ability of future generations to meet their own needs." Therefore this concept implies economic, social, and environmental processes to be interlinked. Public and private agents alike cannot be permitted to act one-dimensionally and in isolation. Instead, their actions must take into account the interplay between the three dimensions of environment, economy, and society. Also, sustainable development calls for long-term structural change in our economic and social systems, with the aim of reducing the consumption of the environment and resources to a permanently affordable level, while maintaining economic output potential and social cohesion. Sustainable development aims to bring about a long-term improvement in the quality of life of the majority of the human race, which lives in bitter poverty and inhuman conditions. This means that sustainable development has to ensure economic growth, social benefits for the population combined with a respectful and conscious treatment of the environment. To accomplish such a goal, different social actors with different and opposed interests must discuss and reach an agreement; otherwise it does not seem possible to develop the economy of a country in a sustainable manner.

Although these aims have been clearly stated and are widely accepted, it seems more like a theoretical statement than a guidance-line for most companies. Some firms have strived to change their exploitation measures but many others still work only after benefits without regarding the damages on the environment and the future generations. And the extractive industries are a field were these principles are not always respected.

Mining is an activity that has received extensive criticism and legal denunciations for polluting water resources. On the other hand, mining activities and transnational mining companies many times have a great deal of responsibility in civil wars, dictatorships, foreign armed interventions, human rights violations, deforestation, pollution, and other unfavourable effects on human beings and the environment in developing countries, especially in African ones. Mining companies many times do not respect protected areas either.

Nowadays there are several examples of unsustainable development in African countries as well as in Latin American ones. For instance, in the Democratic Republic of Congo there are permanent civil wars to settle which group is going to exploit the tantalum and diamond reserves. The tantalum is used in the industry of cellular phones and also to build Pentium computers. Owing to the sudden increase in the international prices of this mineral, there are constant fights among Africans to determine which group will be able to mine the ores.

Another example is provided by the "coltan wars." The name coltan is an abbreviation used only in parts of Africa for 'columbo-tantalite,' two minerals that combined form the coltan. Mineral concentrates containing tantalum are usually referred to as 'tantalite.' Columbite contains the element columbium, another name for niobium; tantalite contains tantalum. The coltan is used to produce mobile phones and game consoles. Many recognized international enterprises illegally finance these wars and extract loads of minerals by airplane from Congo or Rwanda to Europe or the United States.

In Argentina, a Latin American country, for instance, there are several conflicts with mining companies in the areas of Rio Negro and Esquel. These firms intend to use the cyanide method to separate valuable minerals from the ore in open cast mines, which would provoke serious ecological and health damages to the inhabitants. Therefore there have been popular movements who have rejected and temporarily stopped the beginning of the works.

Regarding the oil industry, there are also many examples that show how distant is this industry from achieving a sustainable development. An example is provided in Africa with conflict starring international petrol companies, the government, and other rebel groups in south Sudan. Since 1999, oil is exploited and civil wars are permanent. Some petrol companies support the military government that leads a war against the southern inhabitants of the country with weapons bought with petrodollars. Something similar takes place in Angola, where a civil war faces two groups: the rebels and the government. The first group obtains its financing from the control over the diamond mines and the latter obtains its incomes to finance the war from petroleum exports.

One final example of the African resources conflicts is the long-lasting dispute between the Royal Dutch Shell Company, the Nigerian military governments, and the Movement for the Survival of the Ogony People (MOSOP) in Nigeria, an oil-rich country in Western Africa. Shell has been accused of cooperating and collaborating with the different military dictatorships that ruled Nigeria from 1966 until 1999 and that killed hundreds of citizens who opposed them. Besides, the petroleum extractions have grown steadily over the years placing Nigeria as the major oil exporter in Africa while the poverty levels have doubled in the same period. Shell has also been accused of murdering a leader of the MOSOP, Ken Saro Wiwa, and also of causing a great destruction to the environment with the permanent oil spills of the pipelines due to lack of maintenance. Similar examples that show strong collaborative relations between petrol companies and governments are provided in the history of Latin American countries like Bolivia and Nicaragua.

The gas industry has proved to be less troublesome but there are also some examples showing that it is not always sustainable, like the Bolivian example previously mentioned.

As all these examples prove, at least in many countries the extractive industries have not helped development but on the contrary have pushed development backward, causing damages to the environment, non-pacific atmospheres, destruction, insecurity, poverty, corruption, and instability in the country. Likewise oil producing and exporting countries like Nigeria and Sudan still have high rates of poverty and unemployment. Mineral exporting countries like the Democratic Republic of Congo or Rwanda suffer from the same civil wars, which have not encouraged development in any dimension in the country. These countries are often entitled as "poor" because of the impoverished social conditions in which most of the population live. However they are rich in terms of natural resources. Therefore the problem lies within the distribution of the incomes generated with those resources, which are often concentrated in few people. These incomes have often been used to build infrastructure to exploit them but very little to promote the development of the social conditions of the inhabitants.

These examples are extreme and there are others where the extractive industries have promoted development in a fairly sustainable way. For instance, ecotourism is a fairly extended option that has helped many natural reserves survive, obtain incomes, and protect the wild life and flora. Many reserves like these are located in Africa, but also in south Asia and South America, protect wild species like Tigers, Pandas, Rhinos, or Lions with their ecosystems in a sustainable manner.

Regarding International Financing Organizations, lots of controversy has lately appeared towards the role of the World Bank (WB) and its financing programs. The WB had been accused of awarding loans to firms who didn't regard the environment or the inhabitant's development and only used the funds to exploit the natural resources, many times in illegal ways. For instance, the WB has been accused of supporting the use of a controversial technique in Papua, New Guinea, through which the mining wastes were thrown into the water without any treatment.

To defend itself the WB has conducted some research projects and in its 2003 report the World Bank clearly stated its commitment to keep on financing extractive industries projects but with some conditions. The report states that extractive industries can contribute to sustainable development *only* if the projects are carried out in the proper way, taking into account human rights, fighting against poverty, maintaining biodiversity, supporting mining activities on a small scale, encouraging the use of renewable energies, and the efficient use of energies to fight global climate change.

It also stated that the WB was committed to promote the sustainable development under a *selective approach*, regarding that the companies that had been awarded a credit should be transparent, establish projects that benefit the local inhabitants and have the support of the local community, protect the human rights, and mitigate the social and environmental risks (World Bank 2003).

In the near future extractive industries will probably keep on being more profitable for some companies than encouraging the development of the countries where the resources lay. However, the approach change mentioned on behalf of the World Bank should be an example of how extractive industries should function. The old approach should be forgotten and the different social actors should demand the implementation of an extractive industries sector that fights against poverty, respects the ecosystems and biodiversity, and supports the popular participation. Otherwise the firms and governments that operate the extractive industries will keep on with their business irrespective of development and improvement for all.

DIEGO I. MURGUÍA

See also Arabian American Oil Company (ARAMCO); Anglo-Iranian Oil Company (AIOC); Angola; Biodiversity Conservation; Bolivia; Congo, Democratic Republic of the; Congo, Republic of the; Environmentalism; Industrialization; Nigeria; Organization of Arab Petroleum Exporting Countries (OAPEC); Organization of Petroleum Exporting Countries (OPEC); OXFAM; Petrodollars; Sustainable Development; War and Development; Wildlife Preservation

References and Further Reading

Kassler, Peter. *Environmental Issues for the Gulf: oil, water and sustainable development*. London: Royal Institute of International Affairs, Middle East Programme in Association with Division of Research and Studies, Crown Prince Court of Abu Dhabi, 1999.

Ross, Michael. *Extractive Sectors and the Poor. An Oxfam America Report*. Boston: Oxfam America, October 2001.

Sachs, Jeffrey D., and Andrew M. Warner. "Natural Resource Abundance and Economic Growth" *Development Discussion Paper no 51*. Cambridge: Harvard Institute for International Development, 1995.

Terry Linn, Karl. *The Paradox of Plenty: Oil Booms and Petrol States.* Berkeley, CA: University of California Press, 1997.

Thoburn, John T. *Multinationals, Mining and Development: A Study of the Tin Industry.* Farnborough, Hampshire: Gower, 1981.

Tussing, Arlon R. and Connie C. Barlow. *The Natural Gas Industry: Evolution, Structure and Economics.* Cambridge, MA: Ballinger Pub. Co., 1984.

United Nations Development Program. *Human Development Report 2004. Cultural liberty in today's diverse world.* New York: Hoechstetter Printing Co. 2004. (http://hdr.undp.org)

World Bank. *Extractive Industries and Sustainable Development. An Evaluation of World Bank Group Experience.* Washington, DC: World Bank, 2003.

———. *Striking a Better Balance. The World Bank Group and Extractive Industries: the Final Report of the Extractive Industries Review.* September 2004.

———. *World Development Report 2000/2001: Attacking Poverty.* New York: World Bank and Oxford University Press, 2001.

INDEX

INDEX

INDEX

INDEX

U

INDEX